MOBILE SUIT

GUNDAM

THE ORIGIN

III

—RAMBA RAL—

YOSHIKAZU YASUHIKO

ORIGINAL STORY BY:
YOSHIYUKI TOMINO • HAJIME YATATE

MECHANICAL DESIGN BY:
KUNIO OKAWARA

Collector's Edition

Mobile Suit Gundam
THE ORIGIN

III

—RAMBA RAL—

CONTENTS

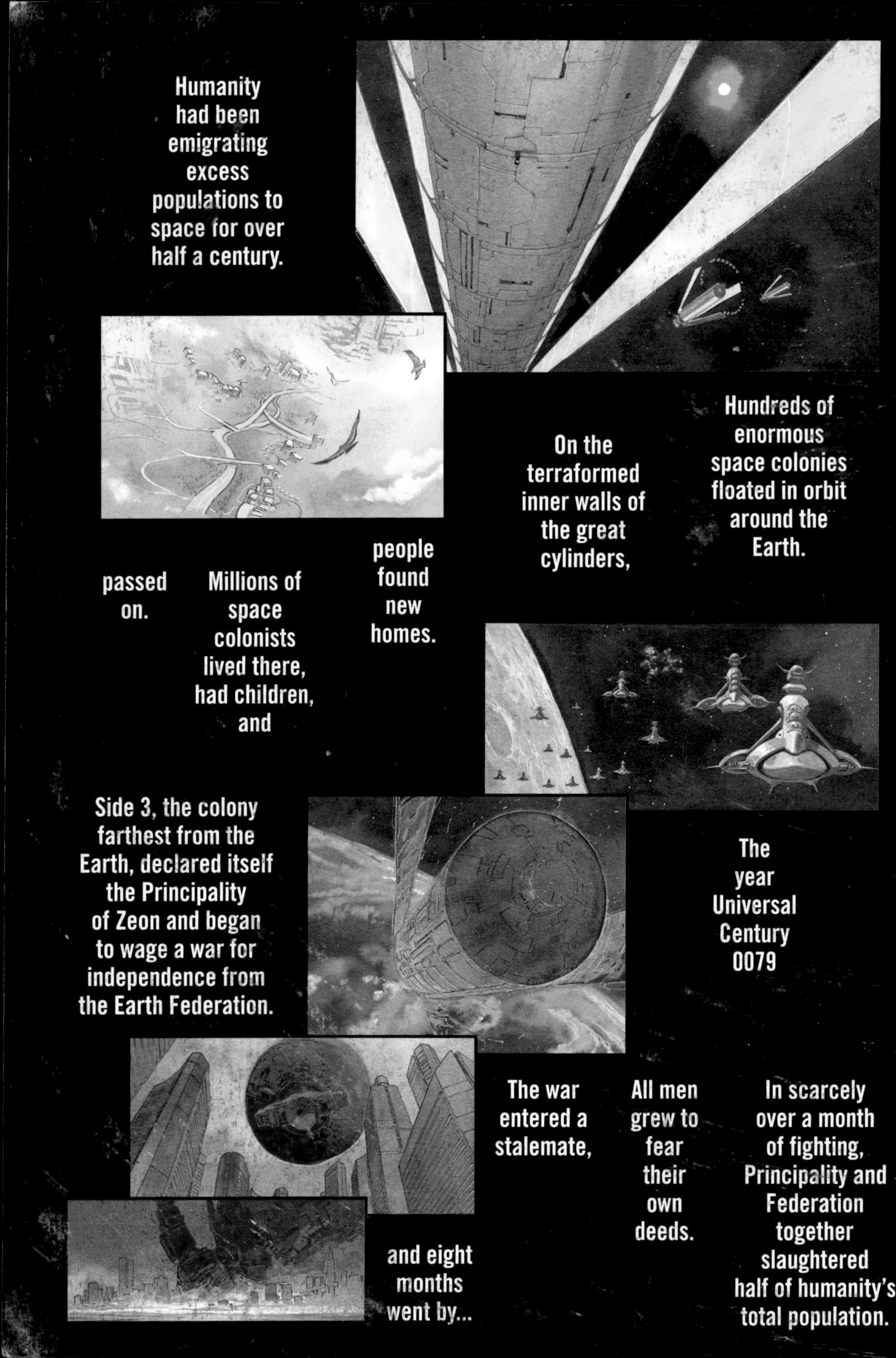

Humanity had been emigrating excess populations to space for over half a century.
Hundreds of enormous space colonies floated in orbit around the Earth.
On the terraformed inner walls of the great cylinders,
people found new homes.
Millions of space colonists lived there, had children, and
passed on.
The year Universal Century 0079
Side 3, the colony farthest from the Earth, declared itself the Principality of Zeon and began to wage a war for independence from the Earth Federation.
In scarcely over a month of fighting, Principality and Federation together slaughtered half of humanity's total population.
All men grew to fear their own deeds.
The war entered a stalemate,
and eight months went by...

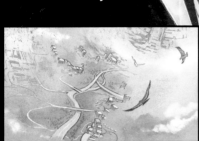

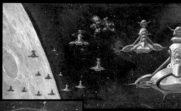

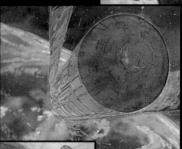

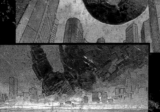

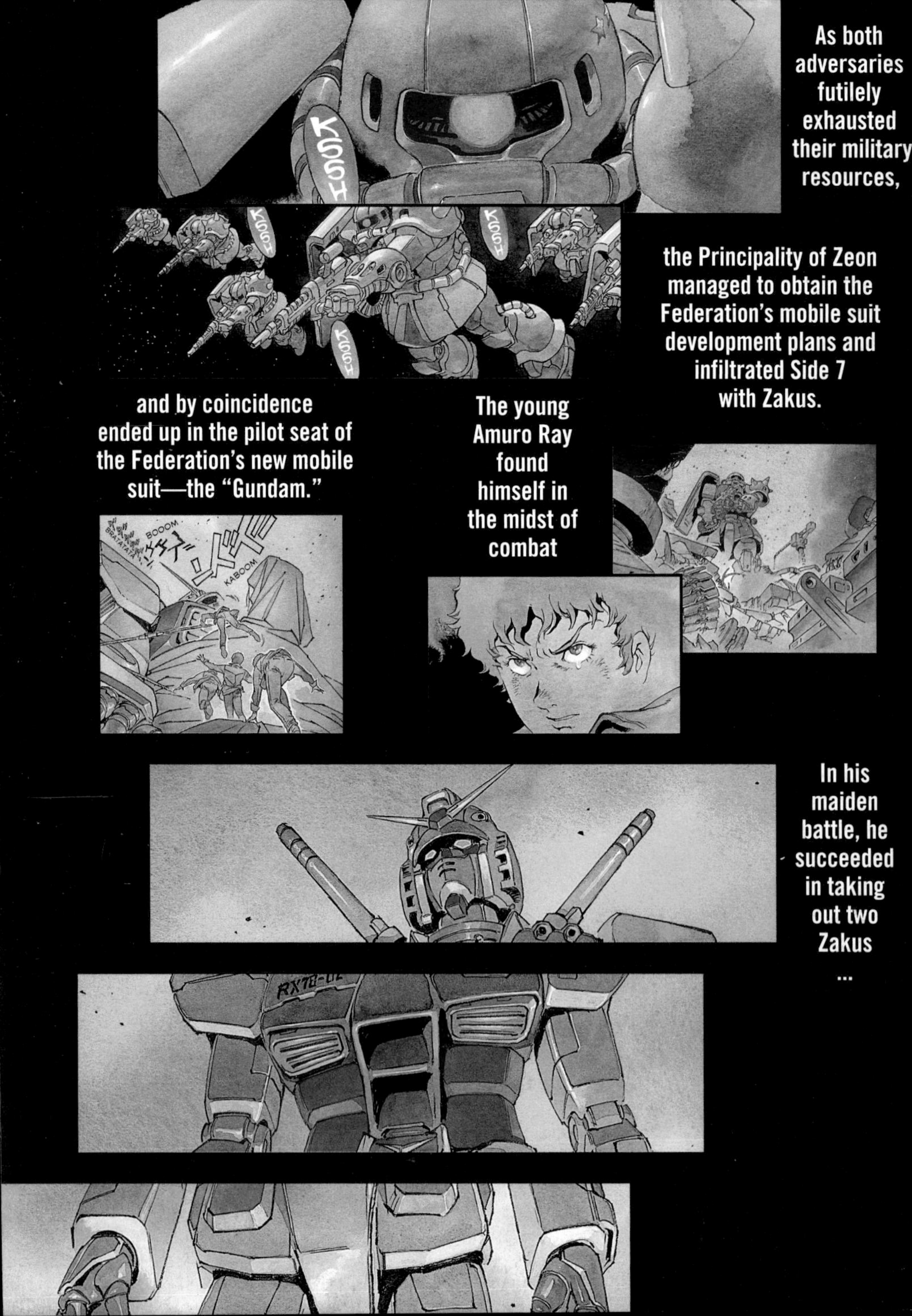
As both adversaries futilely exhausted their military resources,
KSSH
KSSH
KSSH
KSSH
the Principality of Zeon managed to obtain the Federation's mobile suit development plans and infiltrated Side 7 with Zakus.
The young Amuro Ray found himself in the midst of combat
and by coincidence ended up in the pilot seat of the Federation's new mobile suit—the "Gundam."
BOOOM
BRATATATA
KABOOM
In his maiden battle, he succeeded in taking out two Zakus
...
RX78-02

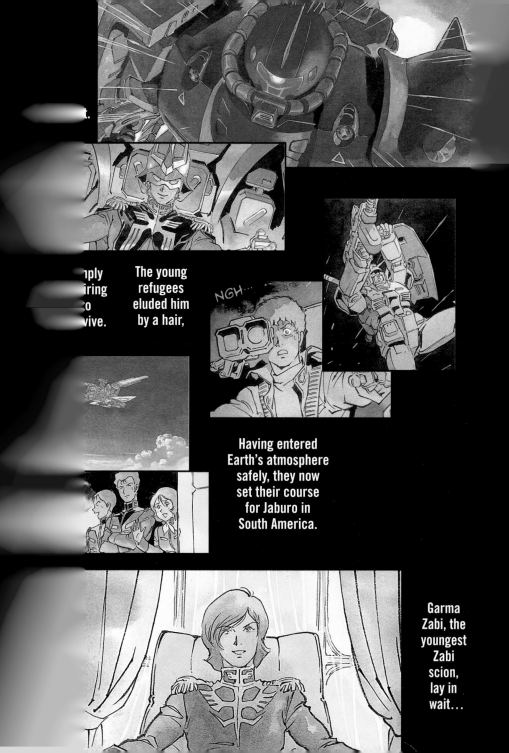

ply
iring
o
vive.

The young
refugees
eluded him
by a hair,

NGH...

Having entered
Earth's atmosphere
safely, they now
set their course
for Jaburo in
South America.

Garma
Zabi, the
youngest
Zabi
scion,
lay in
wait…

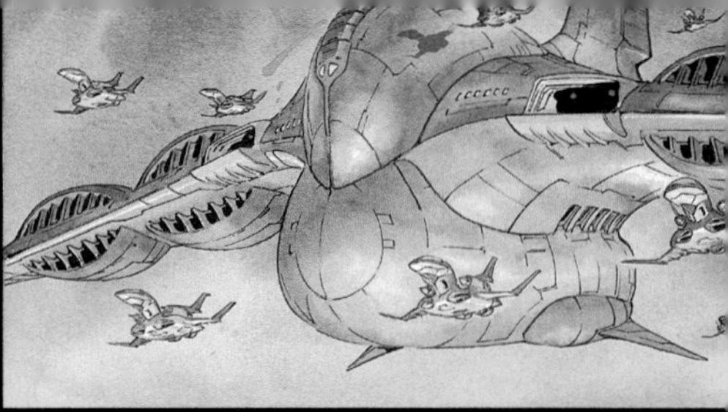

As Garma led the Zeon North American Forces in relentless pursuit of *White Base*

Char began to put his own ambitions in motion.

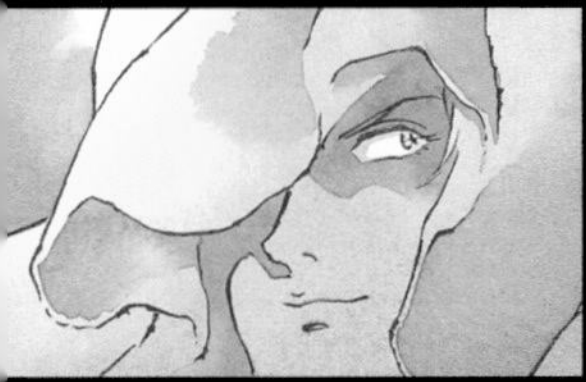

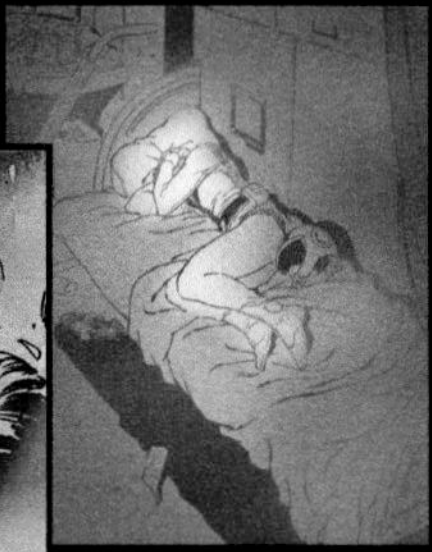

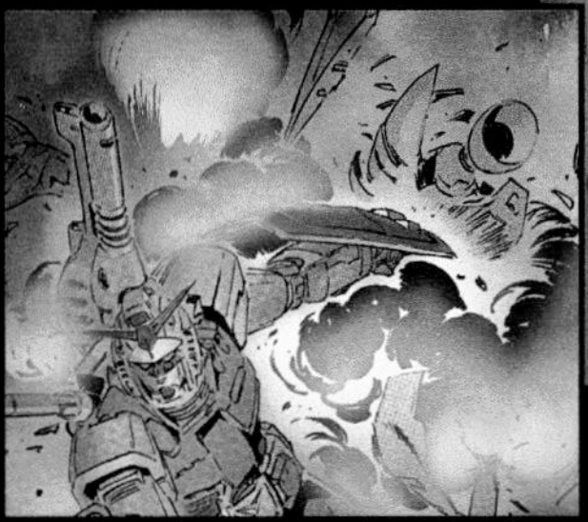

Meanwhile, Amuro had withdrawn into himself, overcome with terror from so much fighting,

but his determination to protect his friends finally brought him back into the Gundam's cockpit and into battle.

What awaited him, however, was a

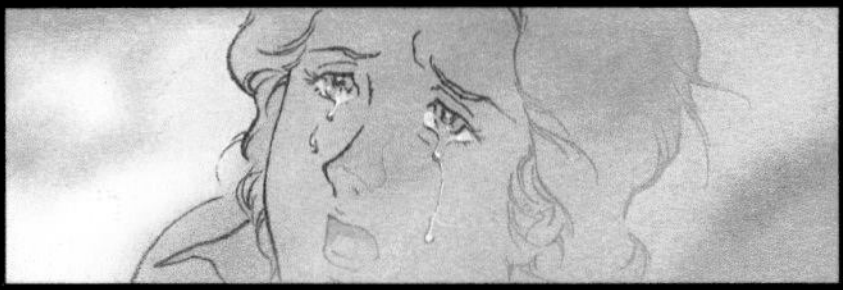

poignant parting with his dearly missed mother...

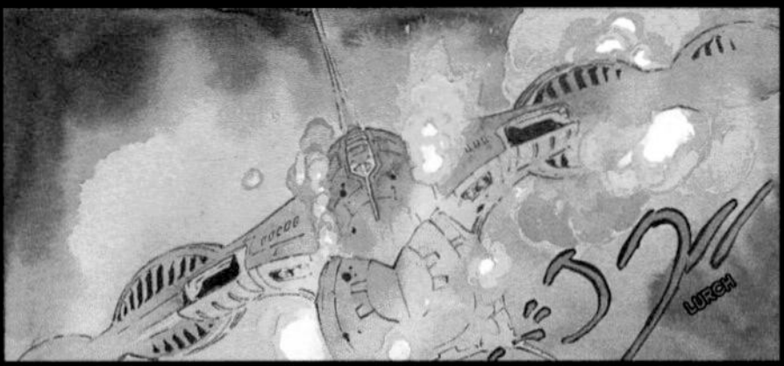
LURCH

In his zeal to destroy *White Base*, Garma fell into Char's trap and met a fiery end.

White Base and her crew made a narrow escape,

but ahead of them, a new enemy lies in wait...

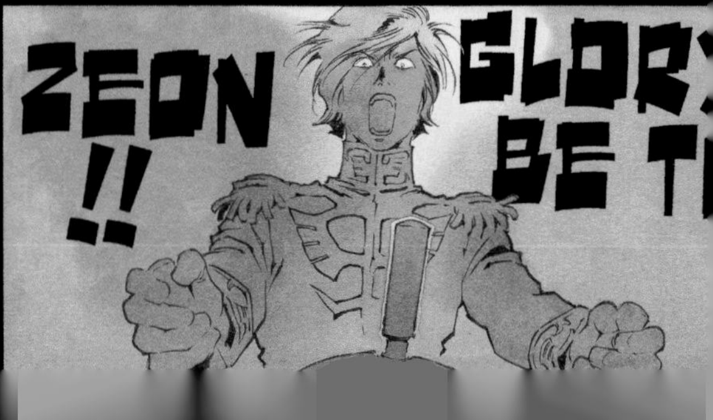
GLOR
BE T
ZEON
!!

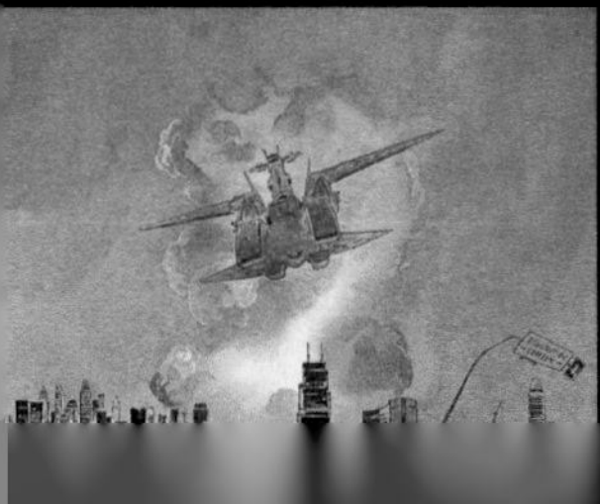

SECTION
I

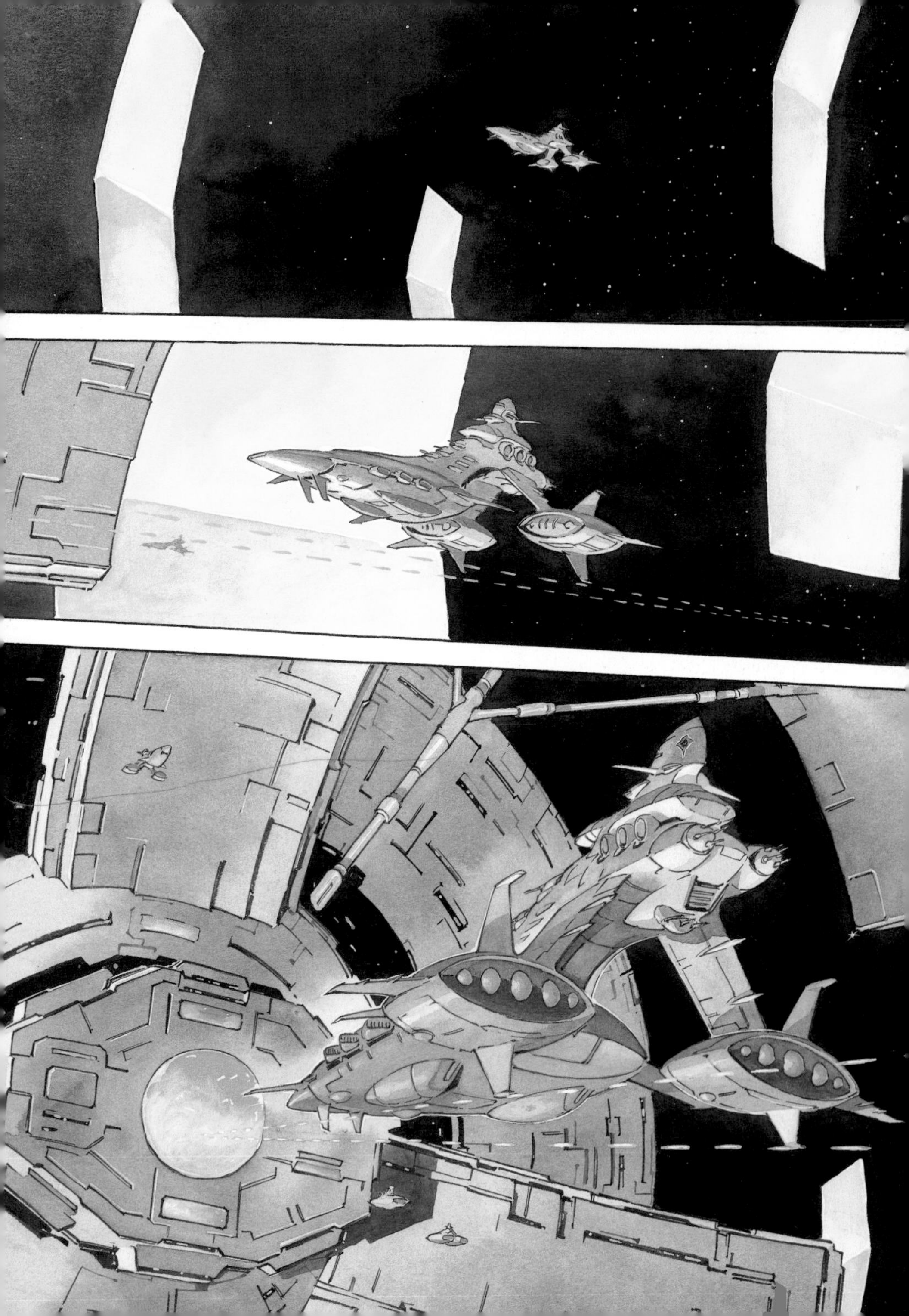

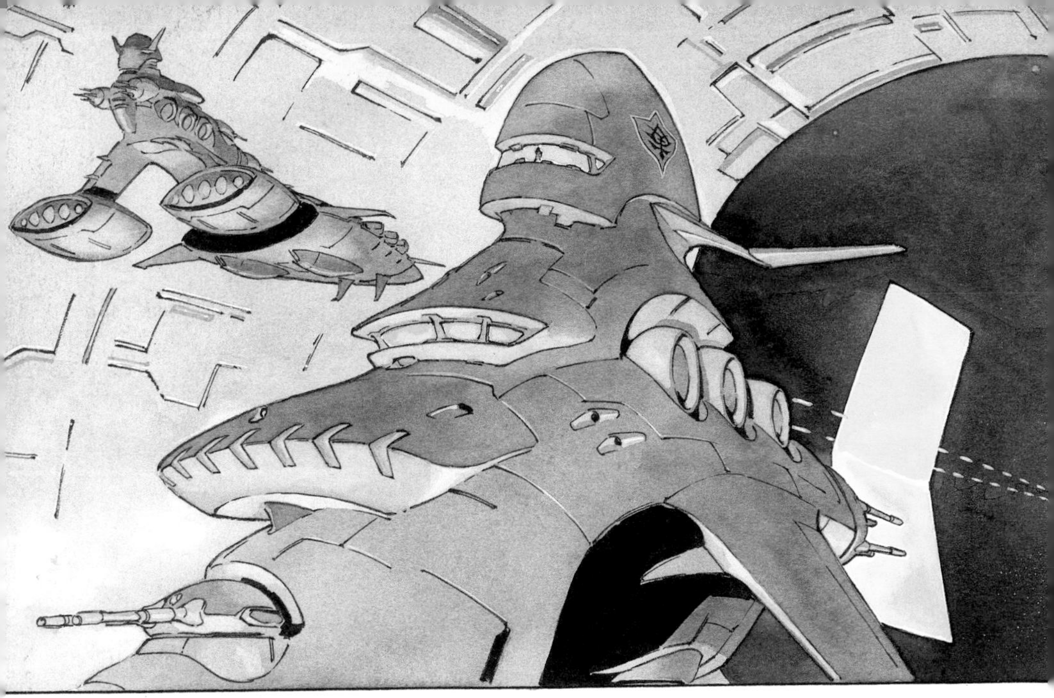

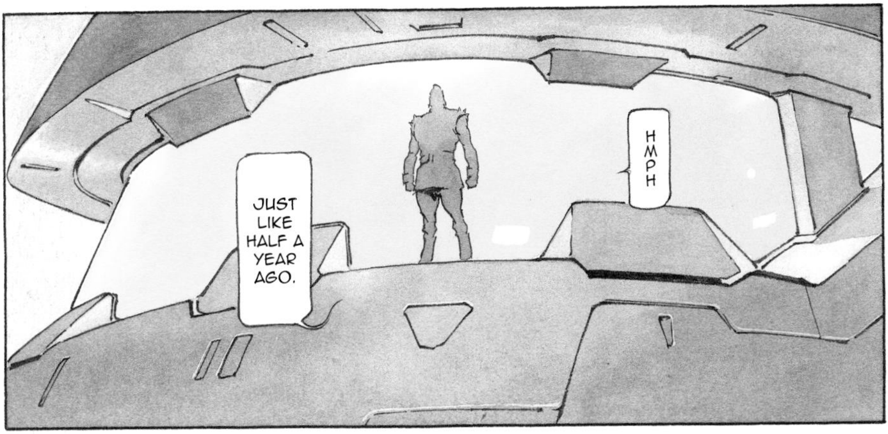
HMPH
JUST LIKE HALF A YEAR AGO.

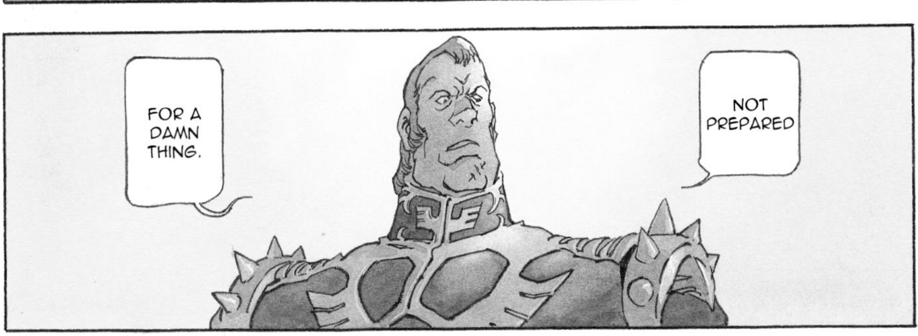
NOT PREPARED
FOR A DAMN THING.

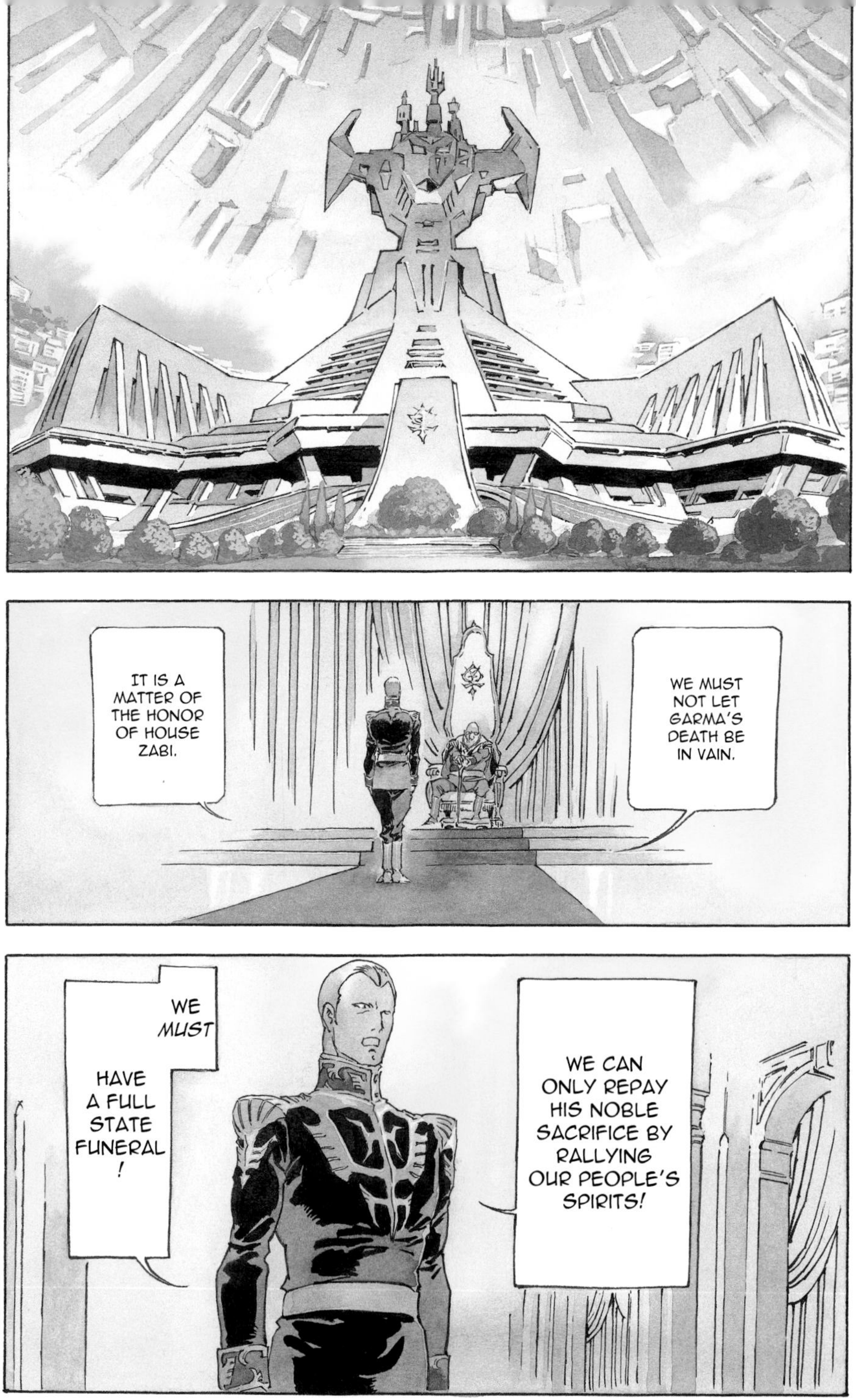
WE MUST NOT LET GARMA'S DEATH BE IN VAIN.
IT IS A MATTER OF THE HONOR OF HOUSE ZABI.
WE CAN ONLY REPAY HIS NOBLE SACRIFICE BY RALLYING OUR PEOPLE'S SPIRITS!
WE *MUST* HAVE A FULL STATE FUNERAL!

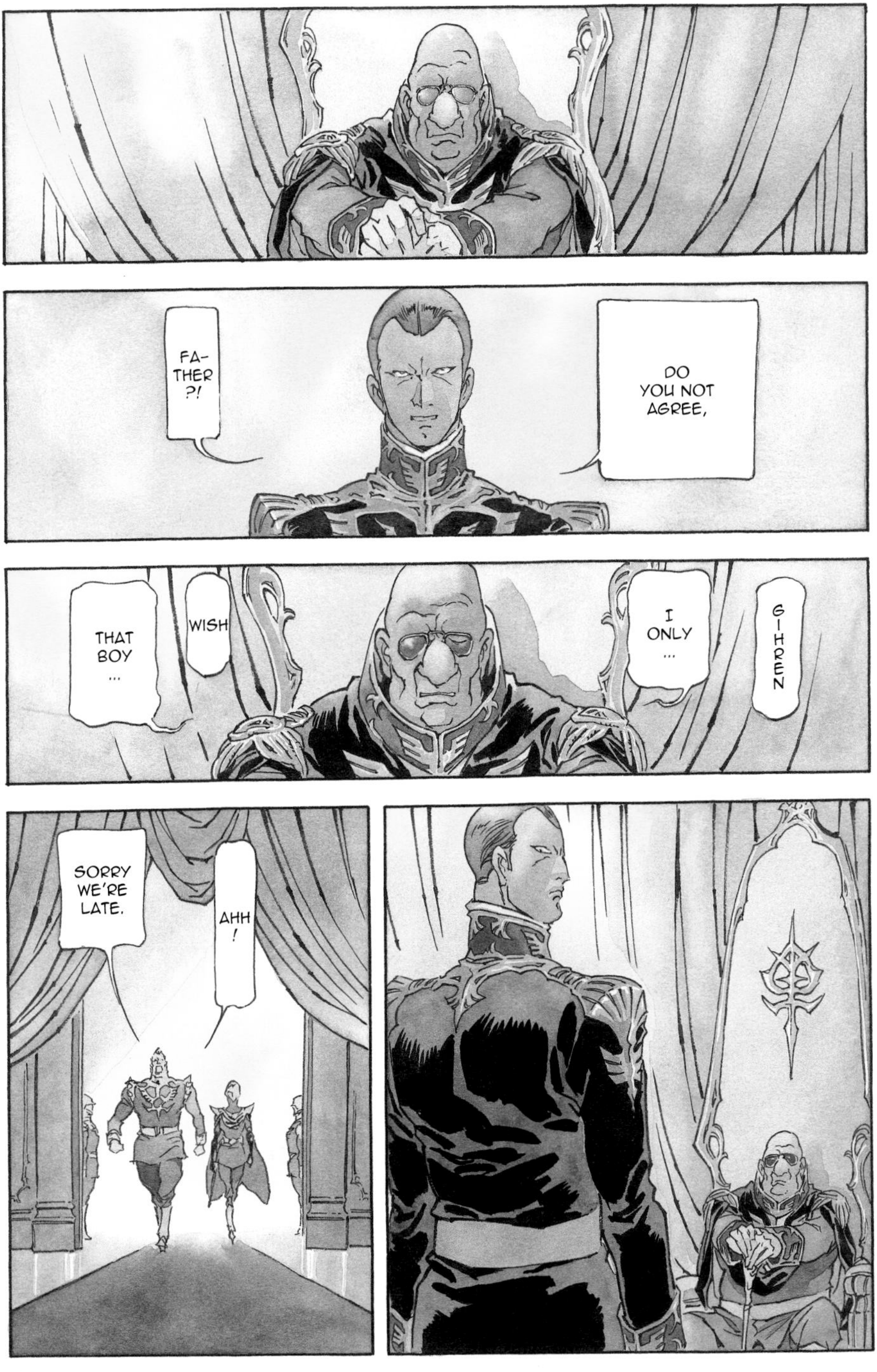
DO YOU NOT AGREE,
FA-THER?!
GIHREN
I ONLY ...
WISH
THAT BOY ...
AHH!
SORRY WE'RE LATE.

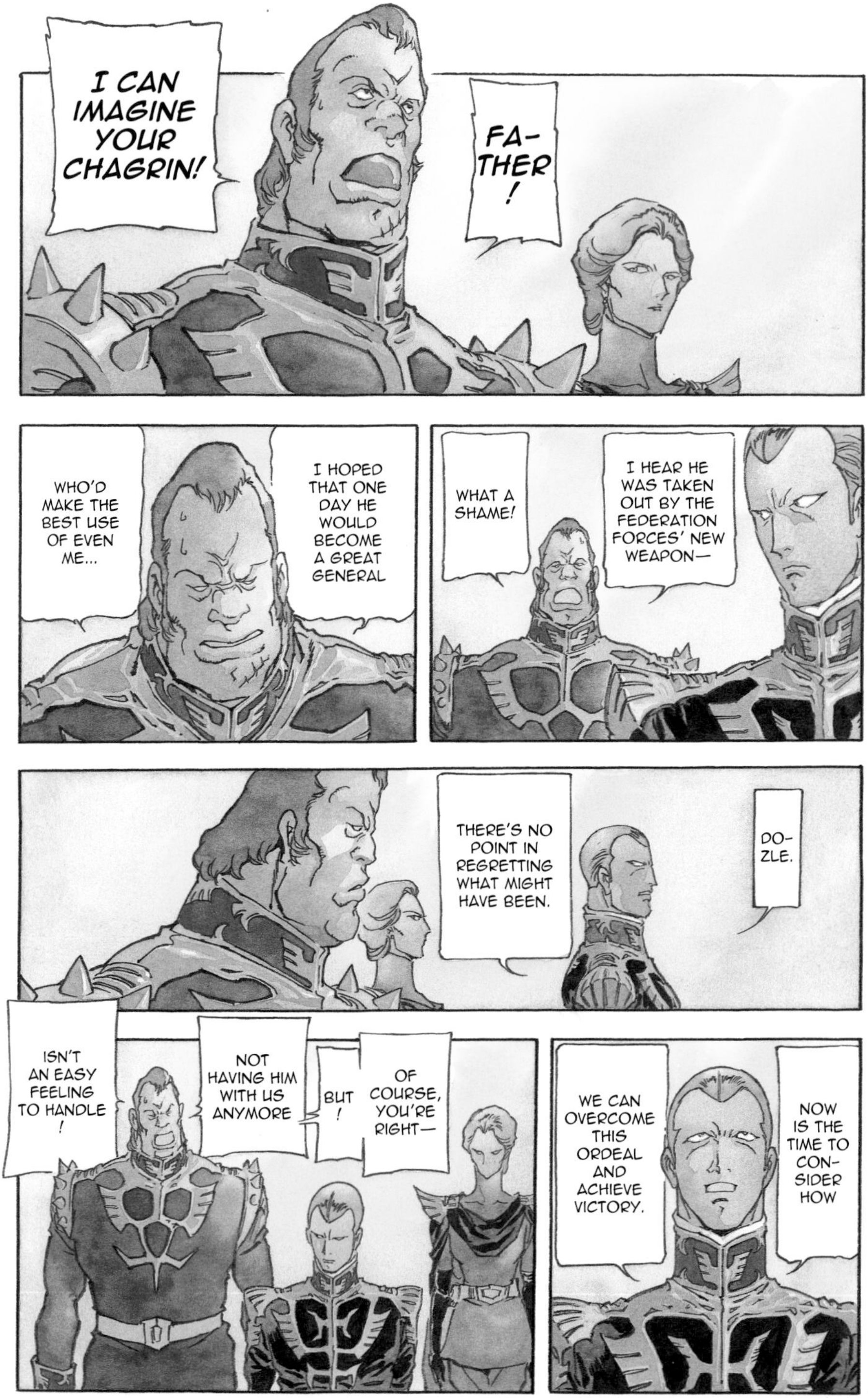
FA-THER!
I CAN IMAGINE YOUR CHAGRIN!
I HEAR HE WAS TAKEN OUT BY THE FEDERATION FORCES' NEW WEAPON—
WHAT A SHAME!
I HOPED THAT ONE DAY HE WOULD BECOME A GREAT GENERAL
WHO'D MAKE THE BEST USE OF EVEN ME...
DO-ZLE.
THERE'S NO POINT IN REGRETTING WHAT MIGHT HAVE BEEN.
NOW IS THE TIME TO CON-SIDER HOW
WE CAN OVERCOME THIS ORDEAL AND ACHIEVE VICTORY.
OF COURSE, YOU'RE RIGHT—
BUT!
NOT HAVING HIM WITH US ANYMORE
ISN'T AN EASY FEELING TO HANDLE!

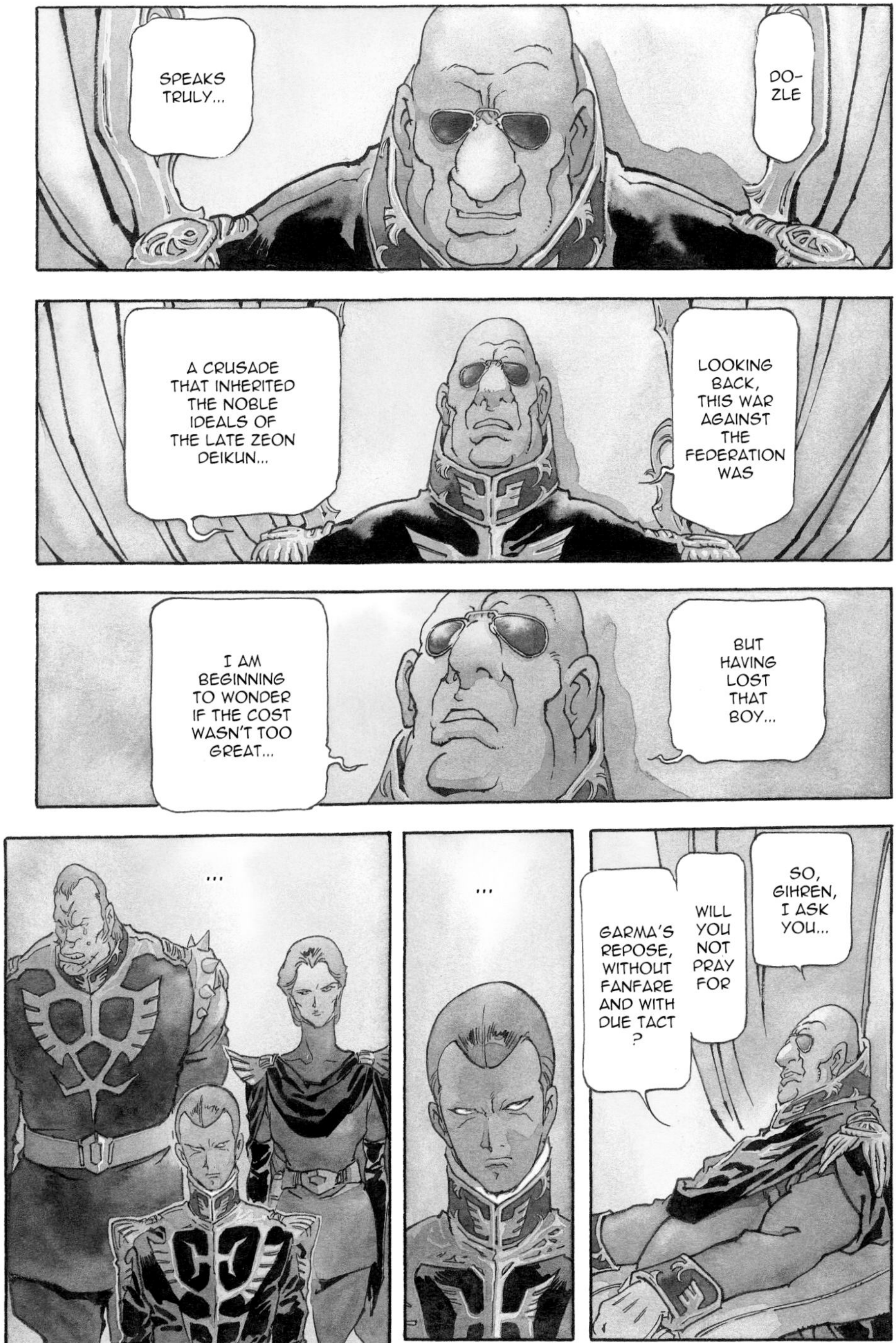
DO-ZLE
SPEAKS TRULY...
LOOKING BACK, THIS WAR AGAINST THE FEDERATION WAS
A CRUSADE THAT INHERITED THE NOBLE IDEALS OF THE LATE ZEON DEIKUN...
BUT HAVING LOST THAT BOY...
I AM BEGINNING TO WONDER IF THE COST WASN'T TOO GREAT...
SO, GIHREN, I ASK YOU...
WILL YOU NOT PRAY FOR
GARMA'S REPOSE, WITHOUT FANFARE AND WITH DUE TACT ?
...
...

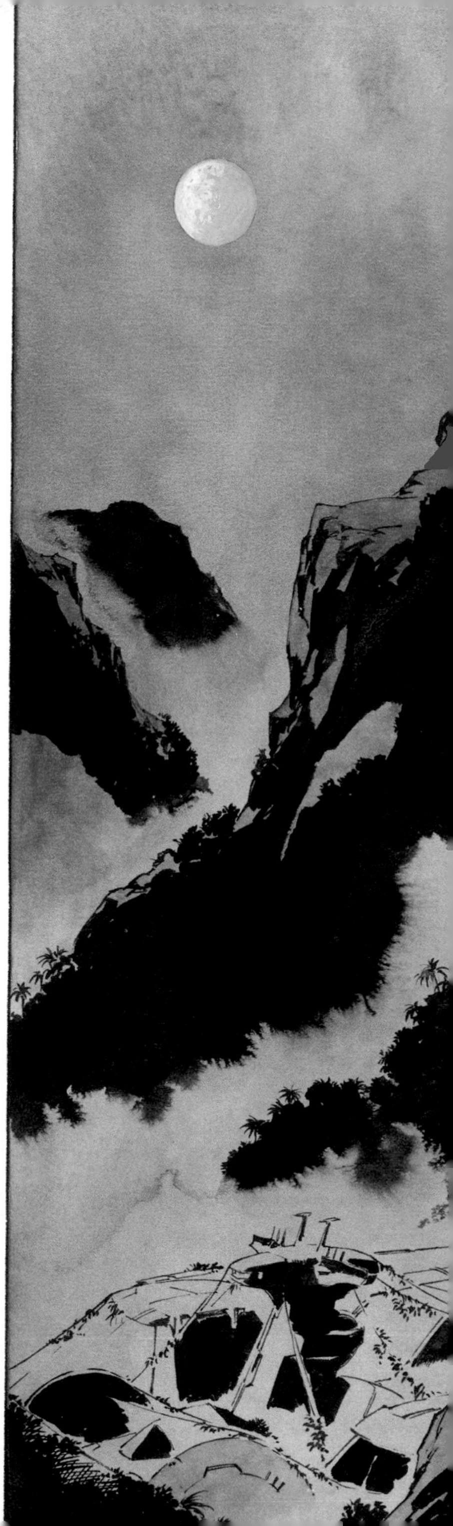

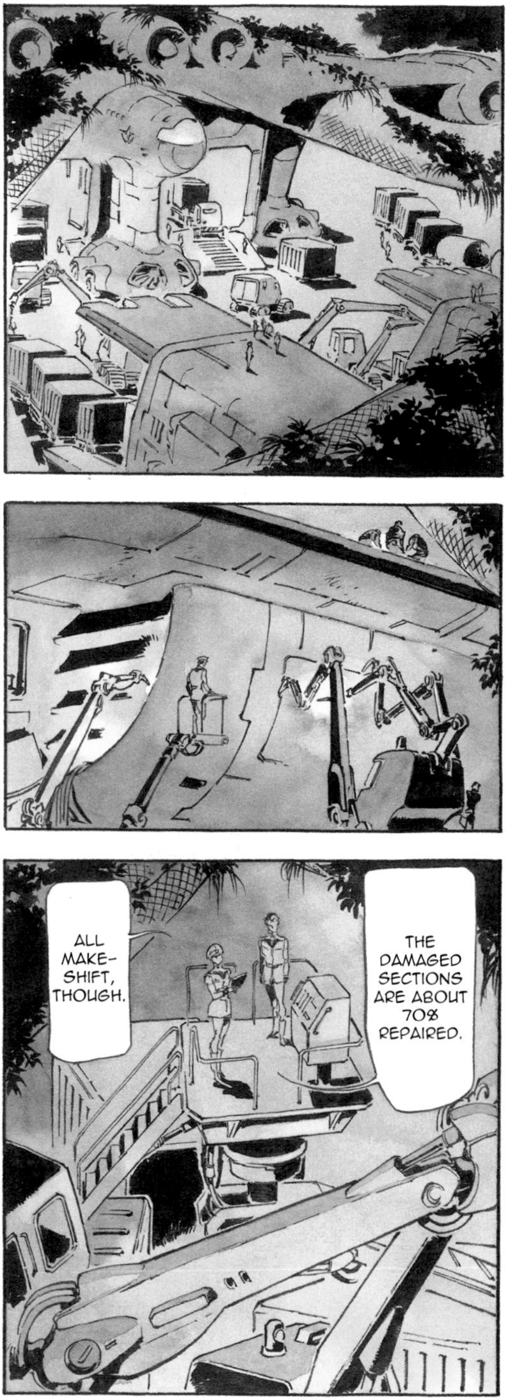
THE DAMAGED SECTIONS ARE ABOUT 70% REPAIRED.
ALL MAKE-SHIFT, THOUGH.

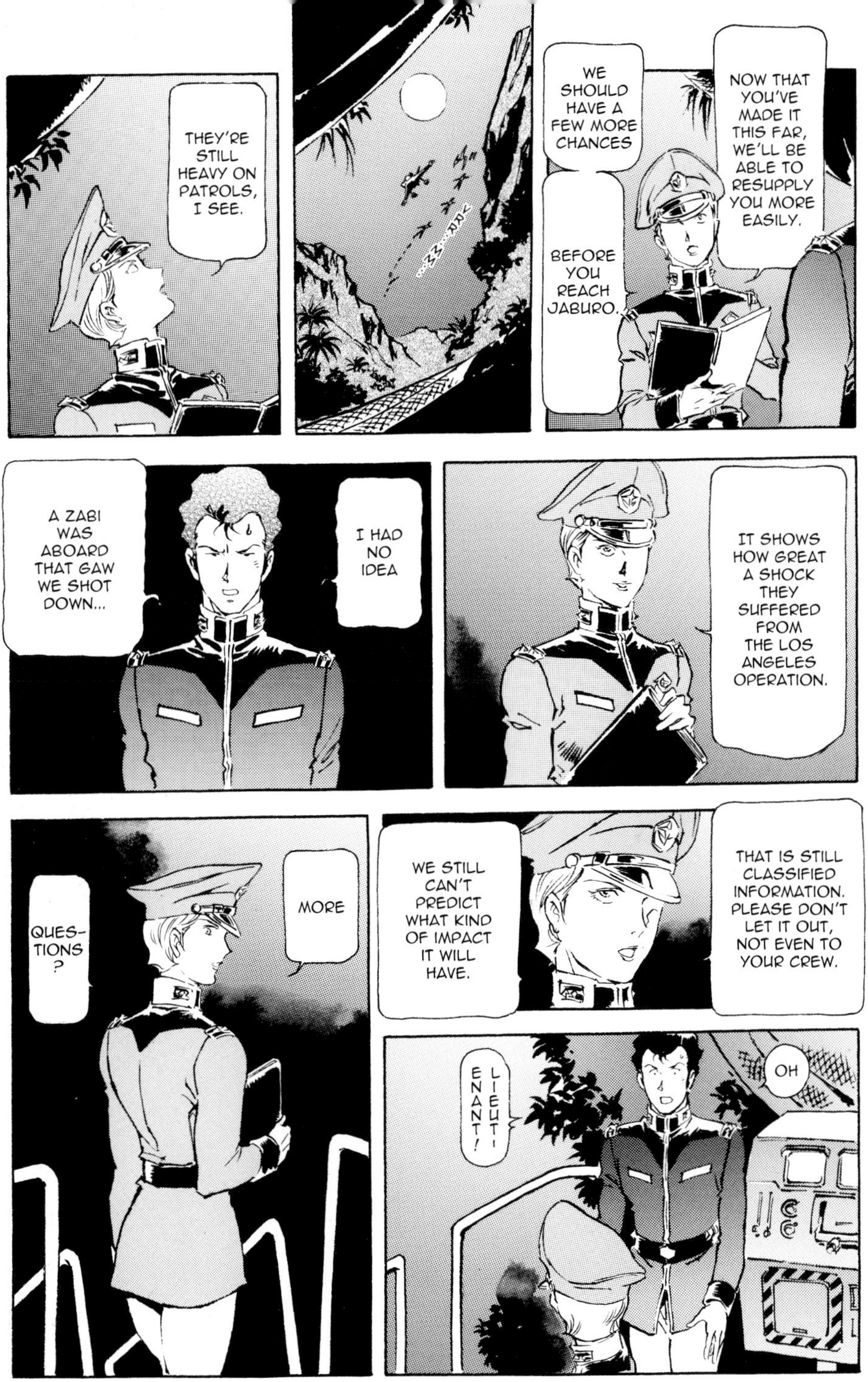
NOW THAT YOU'VE MADE IT THIS FAR, WE'LL BE ABLE TO RESUPPLY YOU MORE EASILY.
WE SHOULD HAVE A FEW MORE CHANCES
BEFORE YOU REACH JABURO.
THEY'RE STILL HEAVY ON PATROLS, I SEE.
IT SHOWS HOW GREAT A SHOCK THEY SUFFERED FROM THE LOS ANGELES OPERATION.
I HAD NO IDEA
A ZABI WAS ABOARD THAT GAW WE SHOT DOWN...
THAT IS STILL CLASSIFIED INFORMATION. PLEASE DON'T LET IT OUT, NOT EVEN TO YOUR CREW.
WE STILL CAN'T PREDICT WHAT KIND OF IMPACT IT WILL HAVE.
OH
LIEUTENANT!
MORE
QUESTIONS?

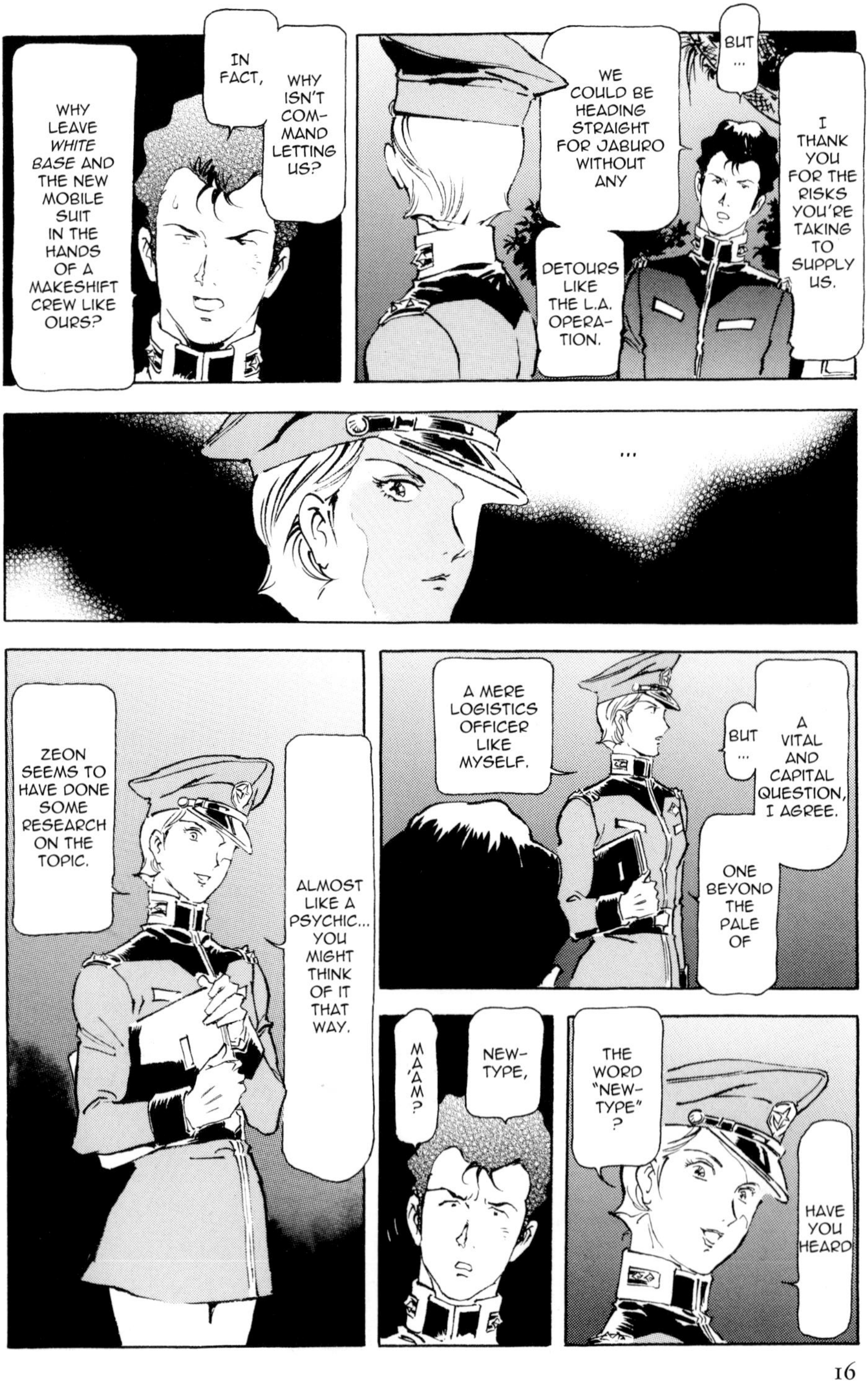
I THANK YOU FOR THE RISKS YOU'RE TAKING TO SUPPLY US.
BUT ...
WE COULD BE HEADING STRAIGHT FOR JABURO WITHOUT ANY
DETOURS LIKE THE L.A. OPERATION.
IN FACT,
WHY ISN'T COM-MAND LETTING US?
WHY LEAVE *WHITE BASE* AND THE NEW MOBILE SUIT IN THE HANDS OF A MAKESHIFT CREW LIKE OURS?
...
A VITAL AND CAPITAL QUESTION, I AGREE.
BUT ...
ONE BEYOND THE PALE OF
A MERE LOGISTICS OFFICER LIKE MYSELF.
HAVE YOU HEARD
THE WORD "NEW-TYPE"?
NEW-TYPE,
MA'AM?
ALMOST LIKE A PSYCHIC... YOU MIGHT THINK OF IT THAT WAY.
ZEON SEEMS TO HAVE DONE SOME RESEARCH ON THE TOPIC.

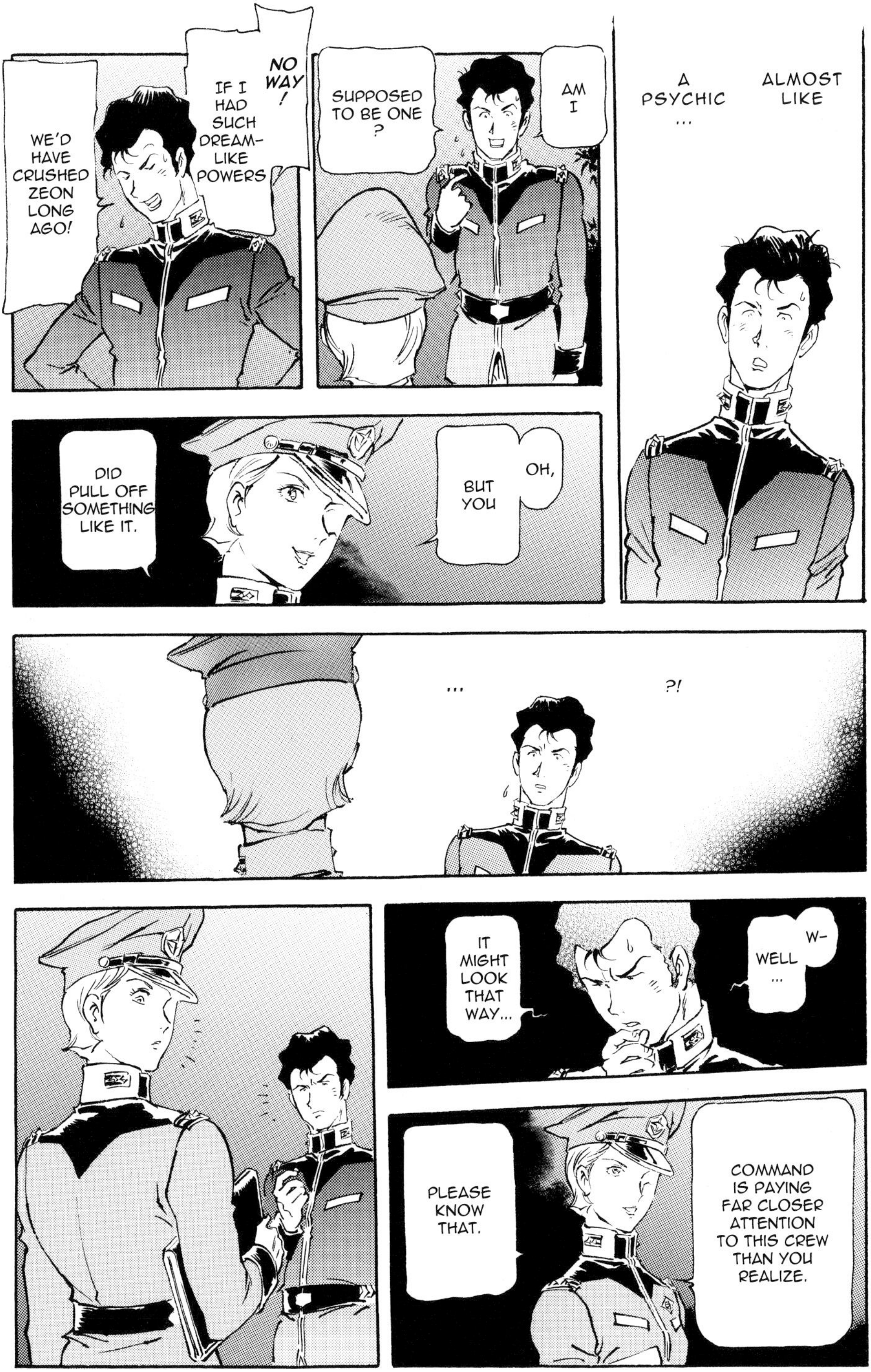
ALMOST LIKE A PSYCHIC ...
AM I SUPPOSED TO BE ONE ?
NO WAY!
IF I HAD SUCH DREAM-LIKE POWERS
WE'D HAVE CRUSHED ZEON LONG AGO!
OH, BUT YOU
DID PULL OFF SOMETHING LIKE IT.
?!
...
W-WELL ...
IT MIGHT LOOK THAT WAY...
COMMAND IS PAYING FAR CLOSER ATTENTION TO THIS CREW THAN YOU REALIZE.
PLEASE KNOW THAT.

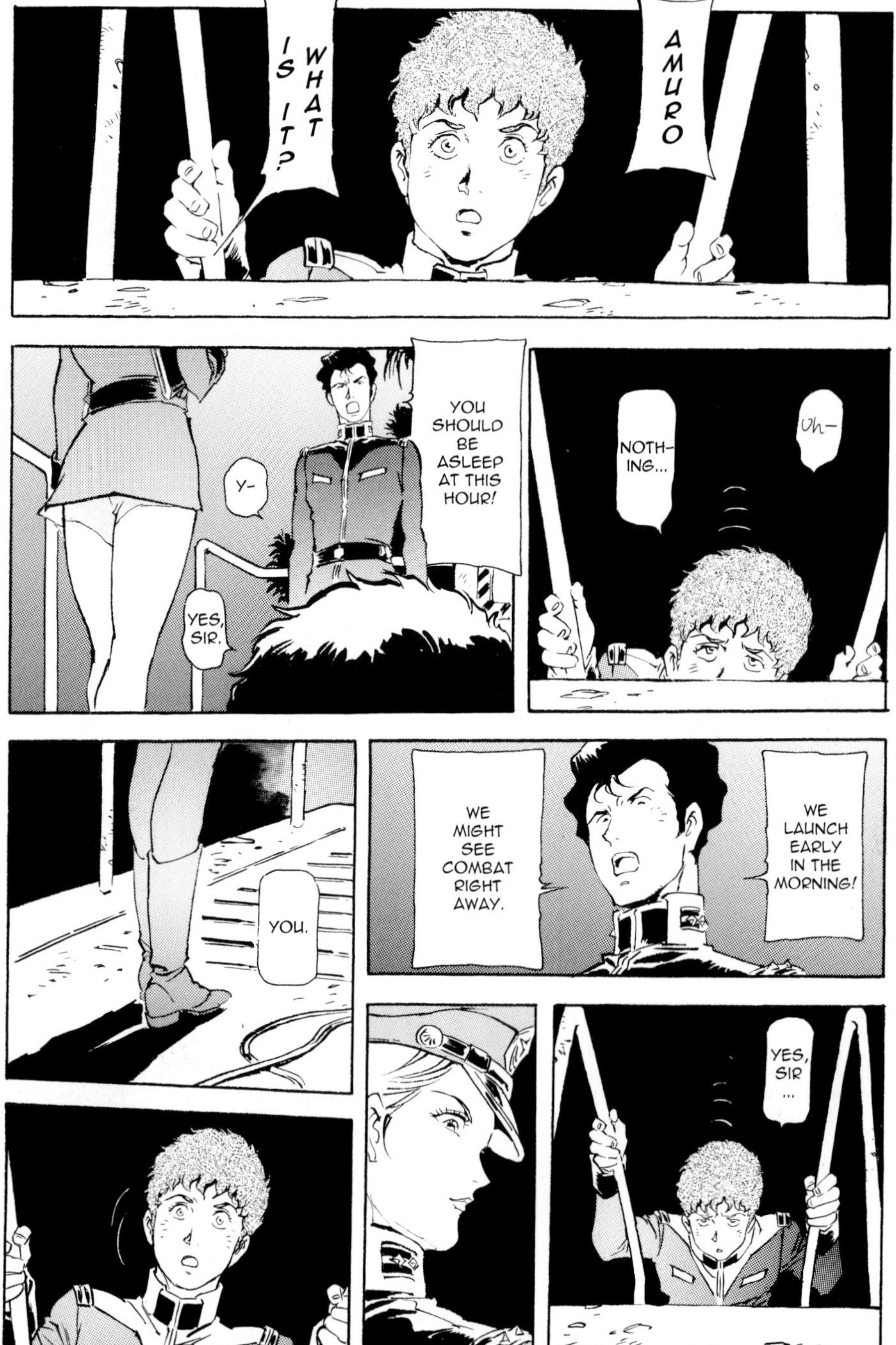
AMURO
WHAT IS IT?
Uh-
NOTHING...
YOU SHOULD BE ASLEEP AT THIS HOUR!
Y-
YES, SIR.
WE LAUNCH EARLY IN THE MORNING!
WE MIGHT SEE COMBAT RIGHT AWAY.
YOU.
YES, SIR ...

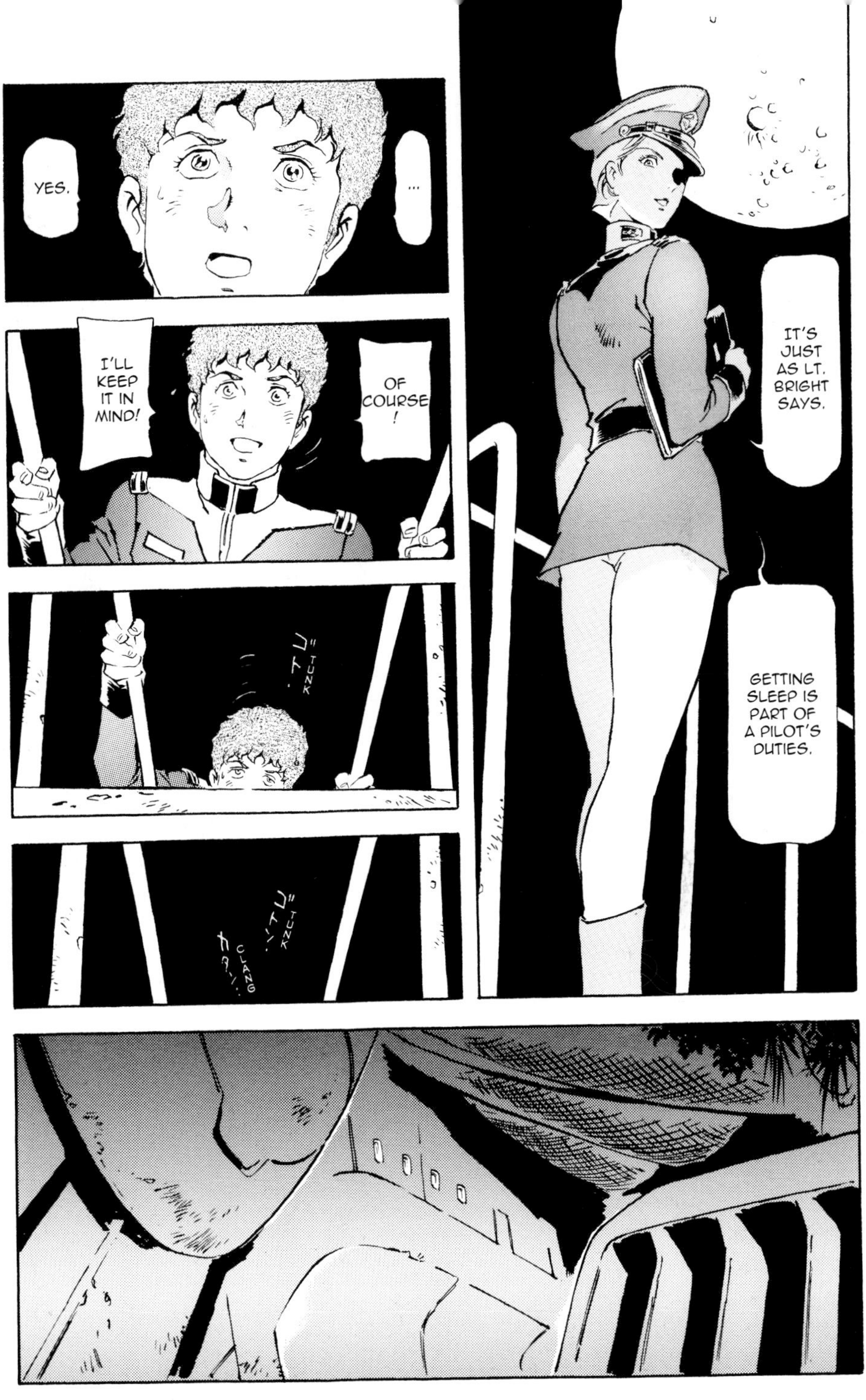
IT'S JUST AS LT. BRIGHT SAYS.
GETTING SLEEP IS PART OF A PILOT'S DUTIES.
...
YES.
OF COURSE!
I'LL KEEP IT IN MIND!
TUNK
TUNK
CLANG

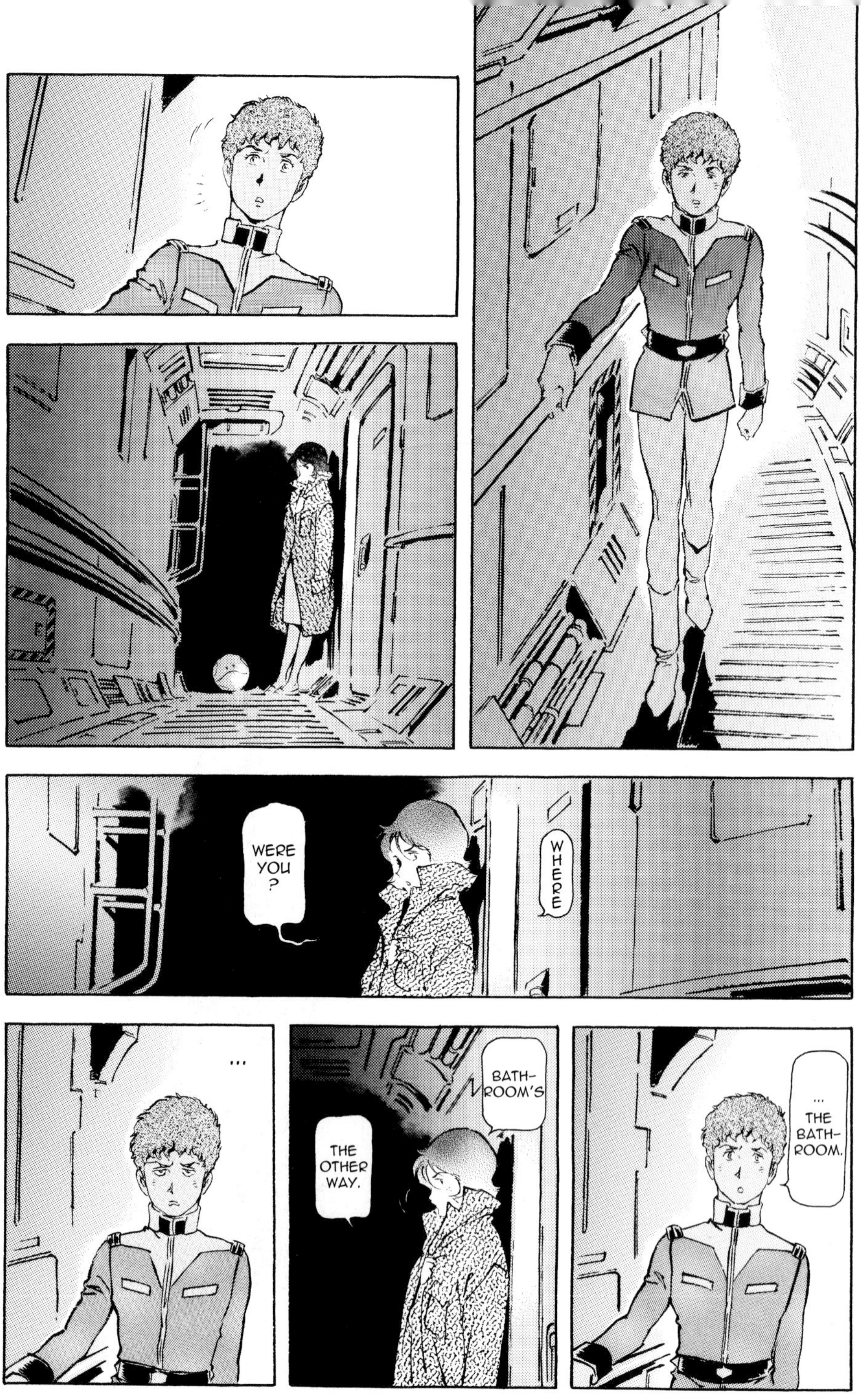
WHERE
WERE YOU?
... THE BATH-ROOM.
BATH-ROOM'S
THE OTHER WAY.
...

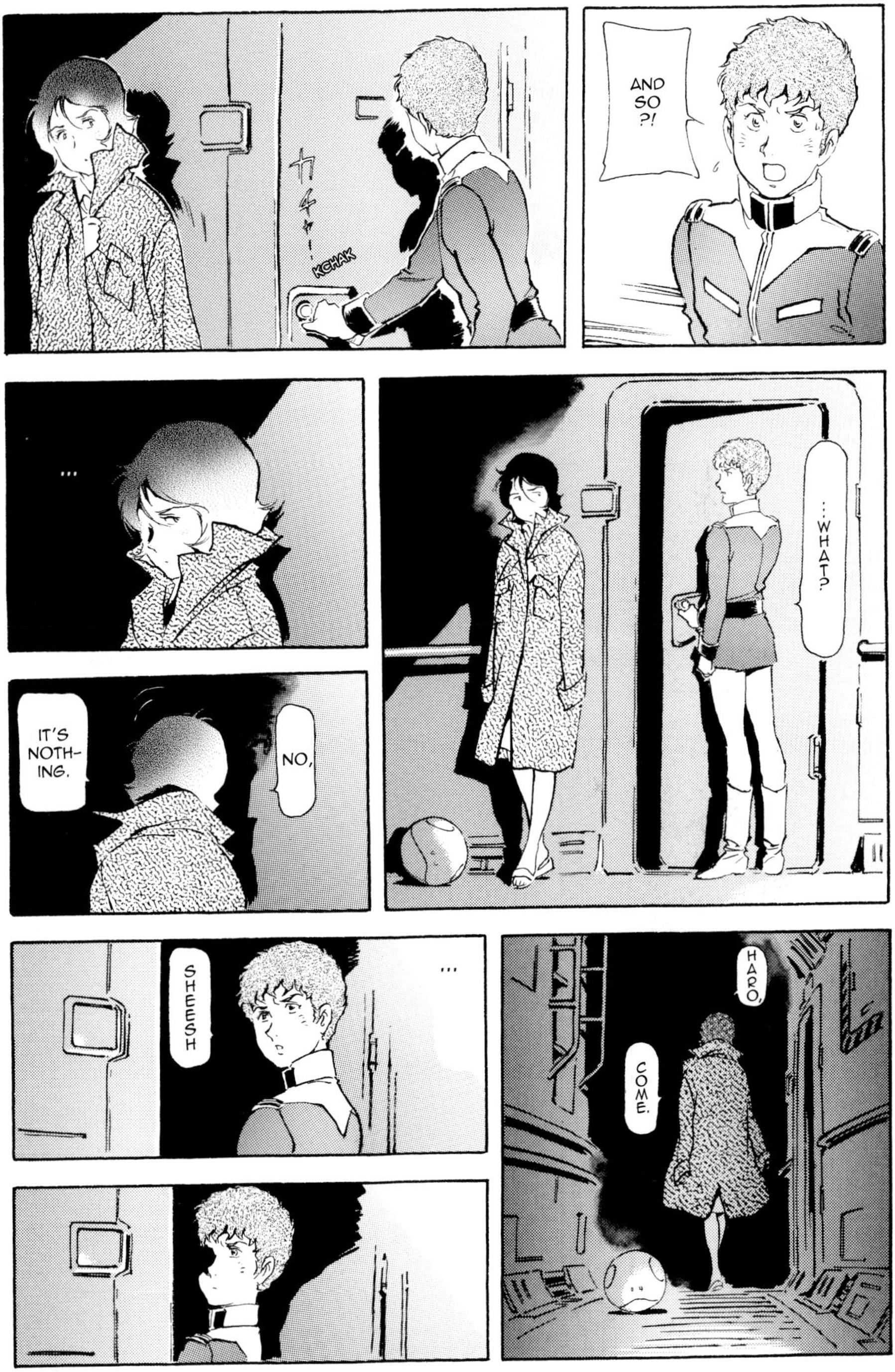
AND SO ?!
カチャ
KCHAK
...WHAT?
...
NO,
IT'S NOTHING.
HARO,
COME.
SHEESH
...

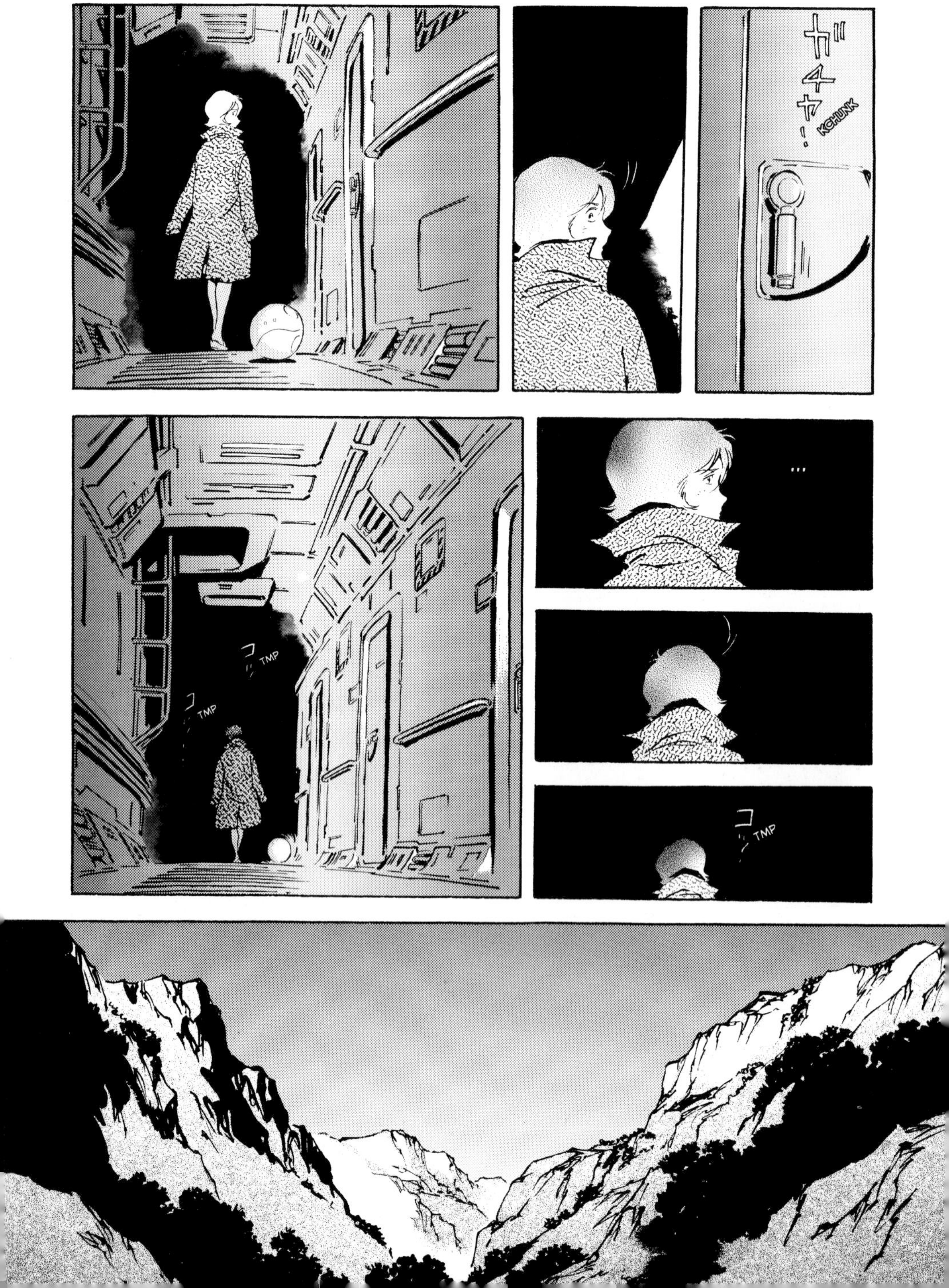
ガチャ!
KCHUNK
...
コッ
TMP
コッ
TMP
コッ
TMP

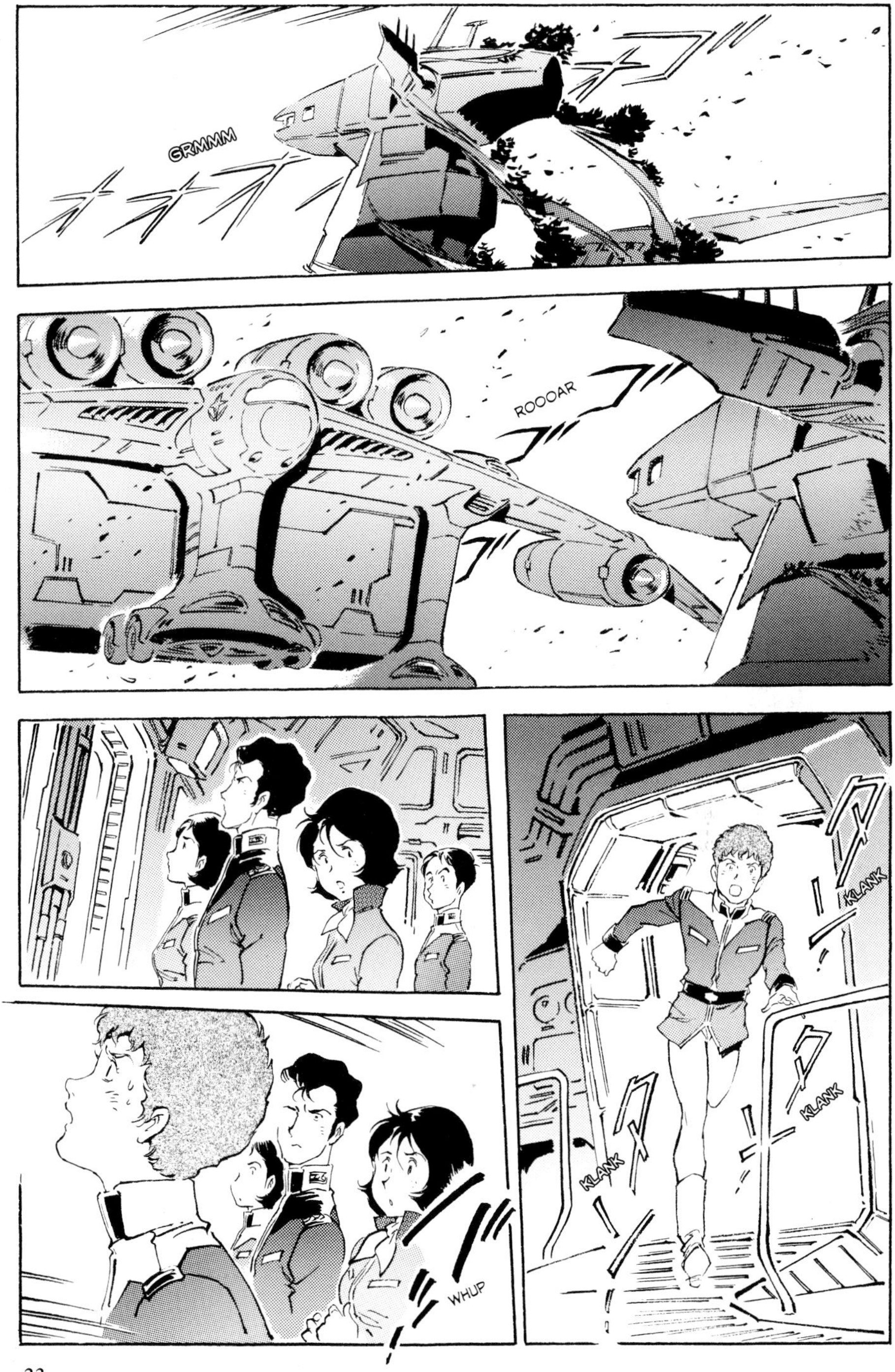
GRMMM
ROOOAR
KLANK
KLANK
KLANK
WHUP

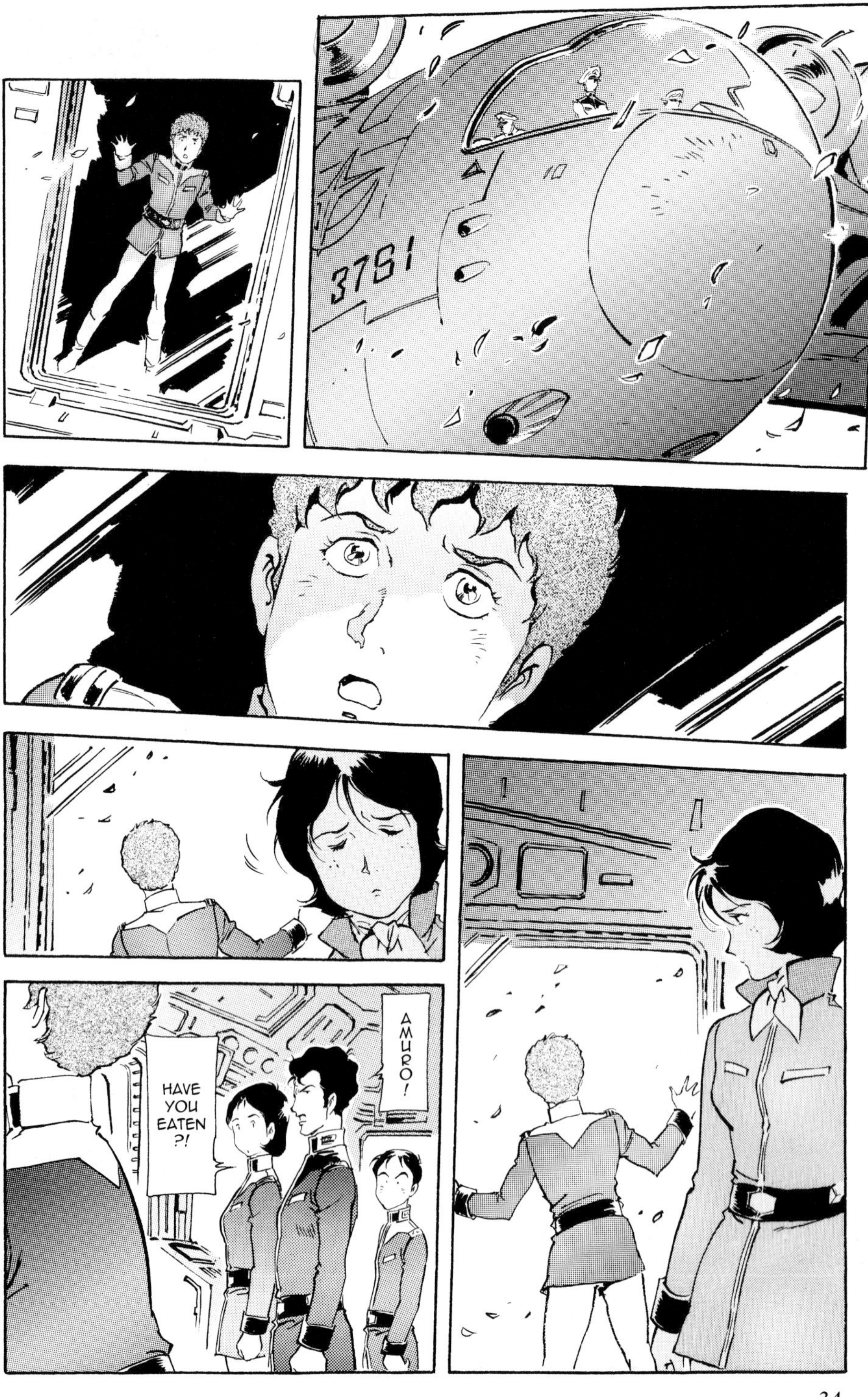
AMURO!
HAVE YOU EATEN?!

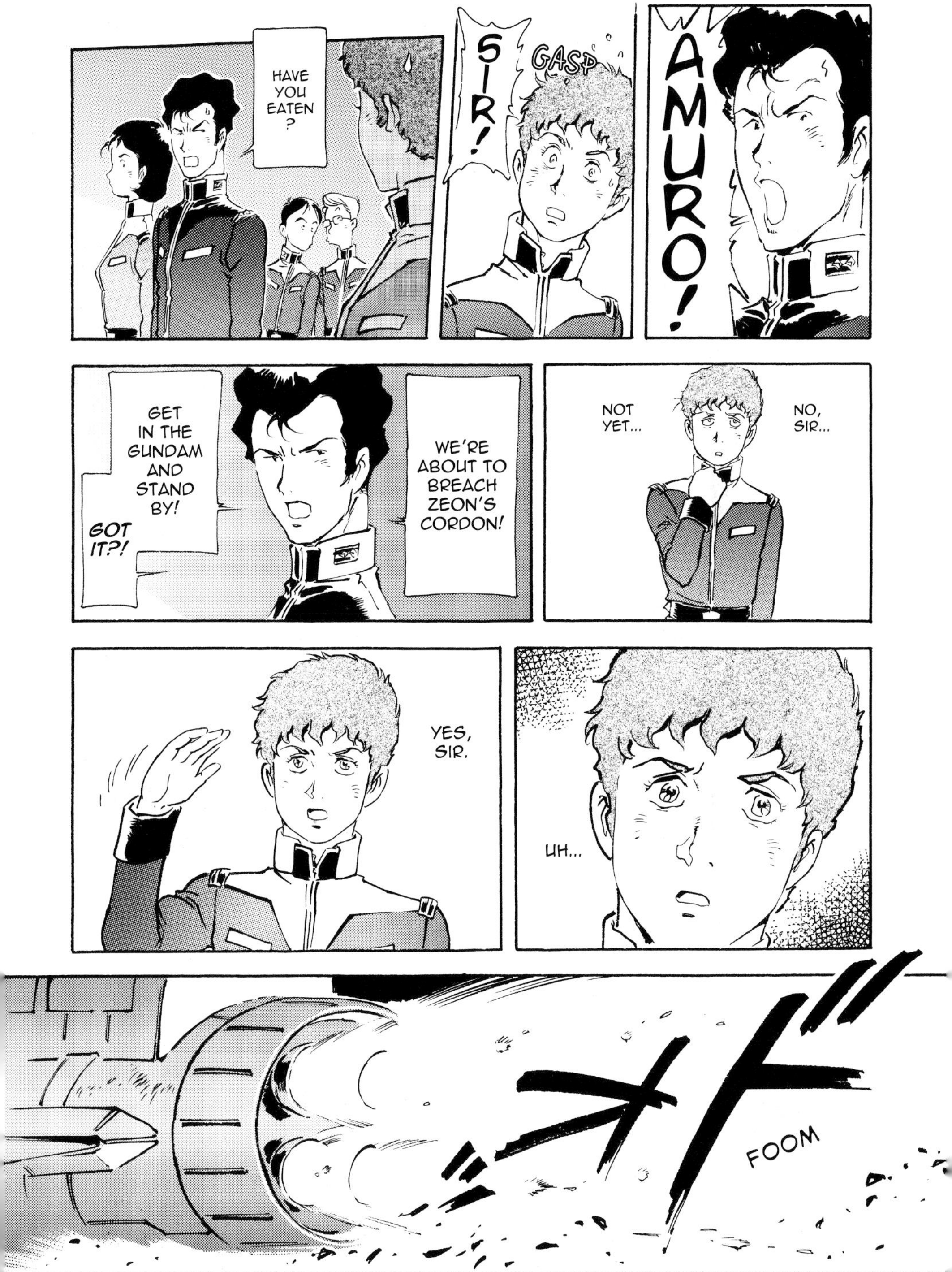
AMURO!
SIR!
GASP
HAVE YOU EATEN?
NO, SIR...
NOT YET...
WE'RE ABOUT TO BREACH ZEON'S CORDON!
GET IN THE GUNDAM AND STAND BY!
GOT IT?!
UH...
YES, SIR.
FOOM

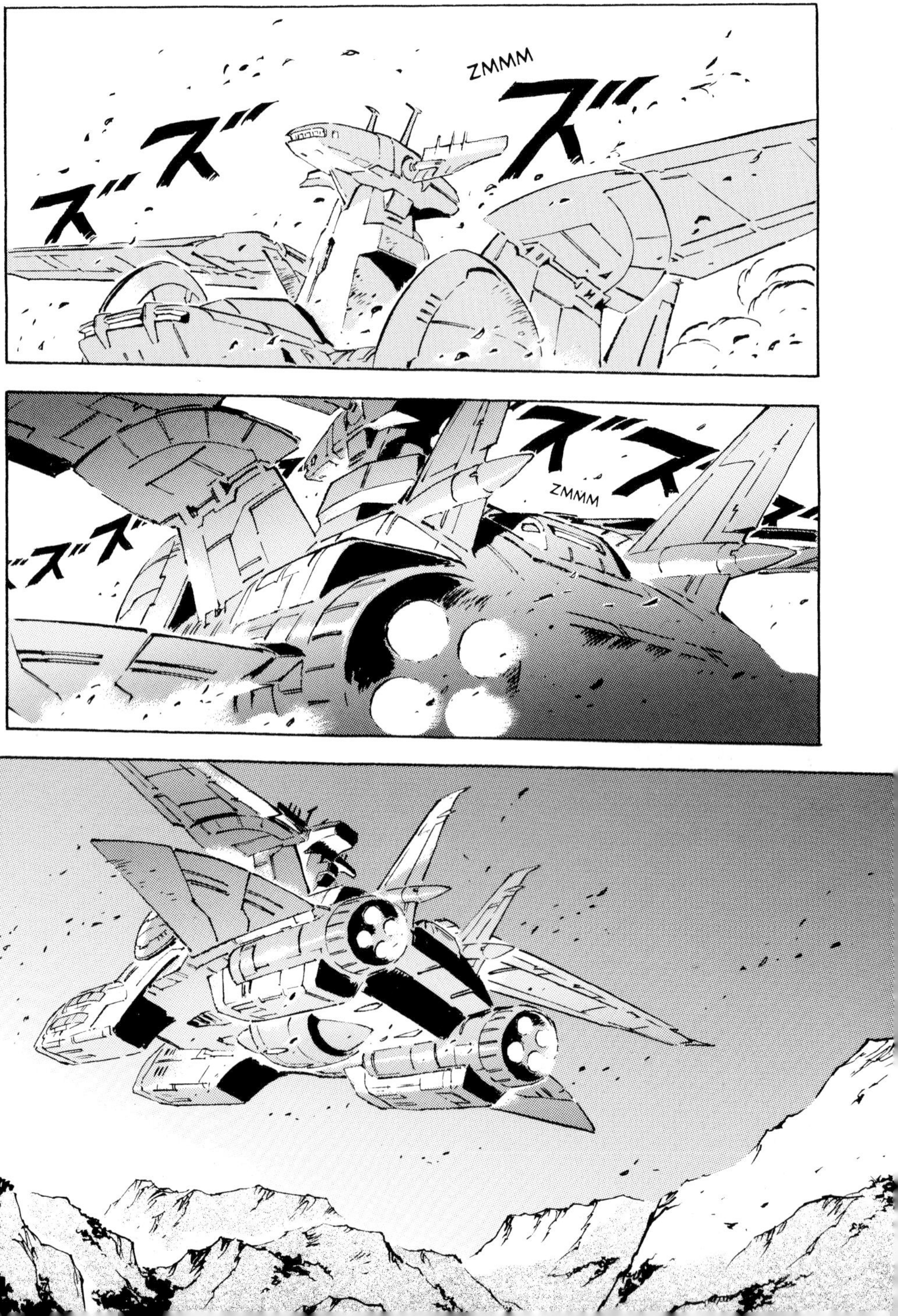
ZMMM
ズ
ズズ
ズズ
ZMMM
ズズズ

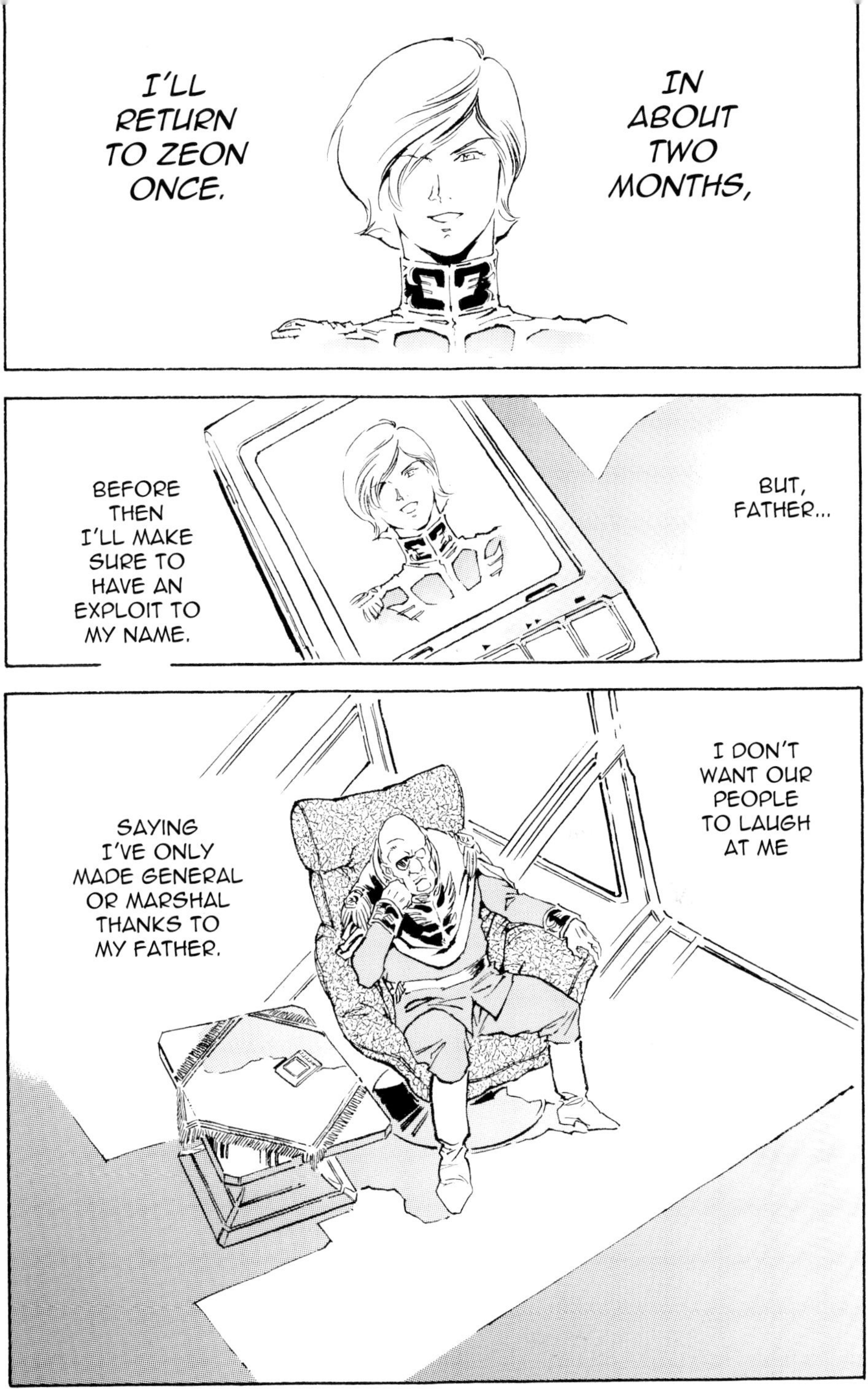
IN ABOUT TWO MONTHS,
I'LL RETURN TO ZEON ONCE.
BUT, FATHER...
BEFORE THEN I'LL MAKE SURE TO HAVE AN EXPLOIT TO MY NAME.
I DON'T WANT OUR PEOPLE TO LAUGH AT ME
SAYING I'VE ONLY MADE GENERAL OR MARSHAL THANKS TO MY FATHER.

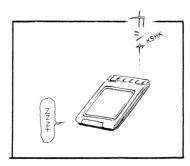

I LOOK FORWARD TO SEEING YOU.

...

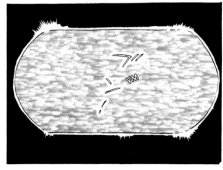

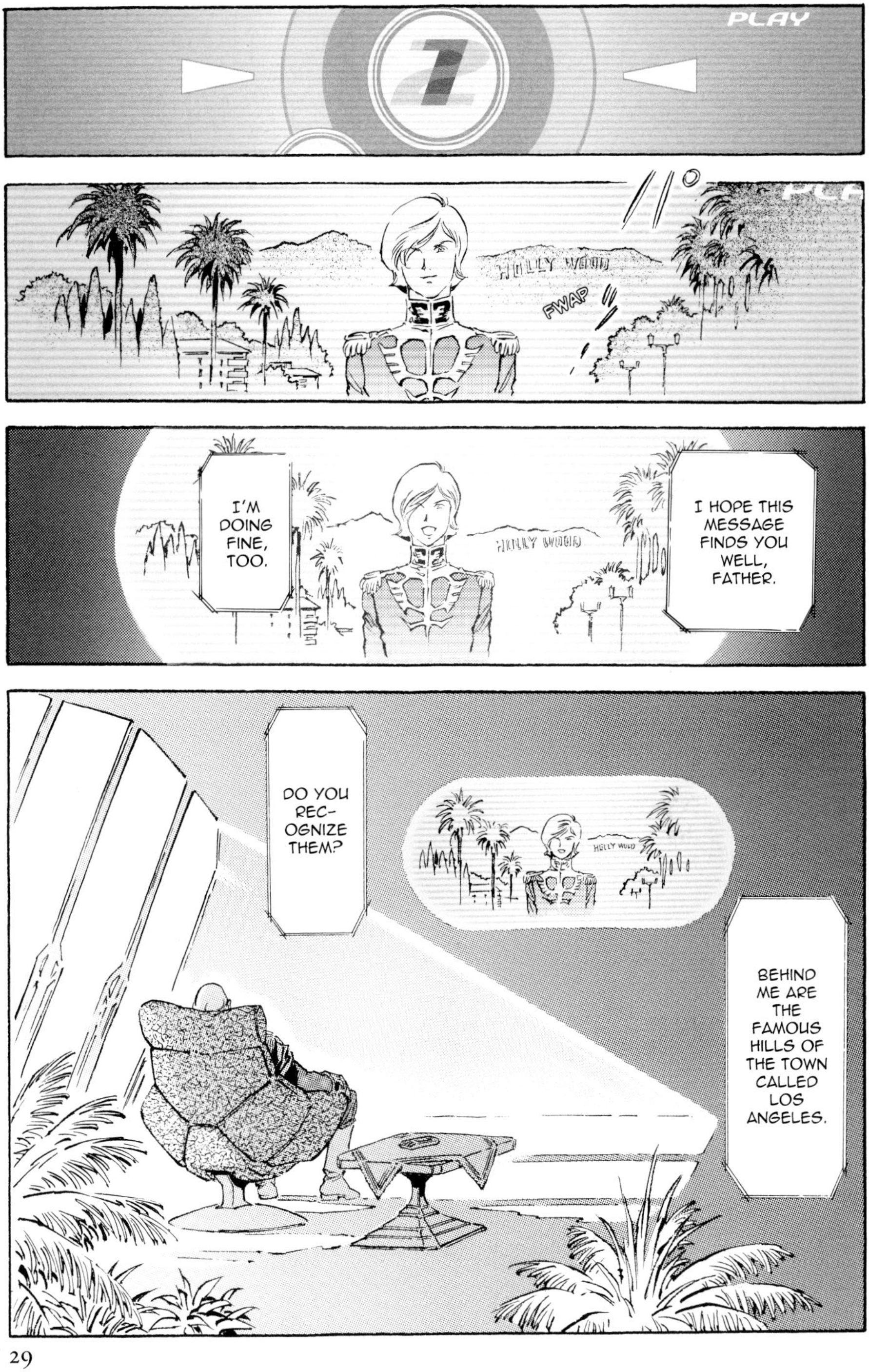
PLAY
HOLLY WOOD
FWAP
I HOPE THIS MESSAGE FINDS YOU WELL, FATHER.
I'M DOING FINE, TOO.
BEHIND ME ARE THE FAMOUS HILLS OF THE TOWN CALLED LOS ANGELES.
DO YOU RECOGNIZE THEM?

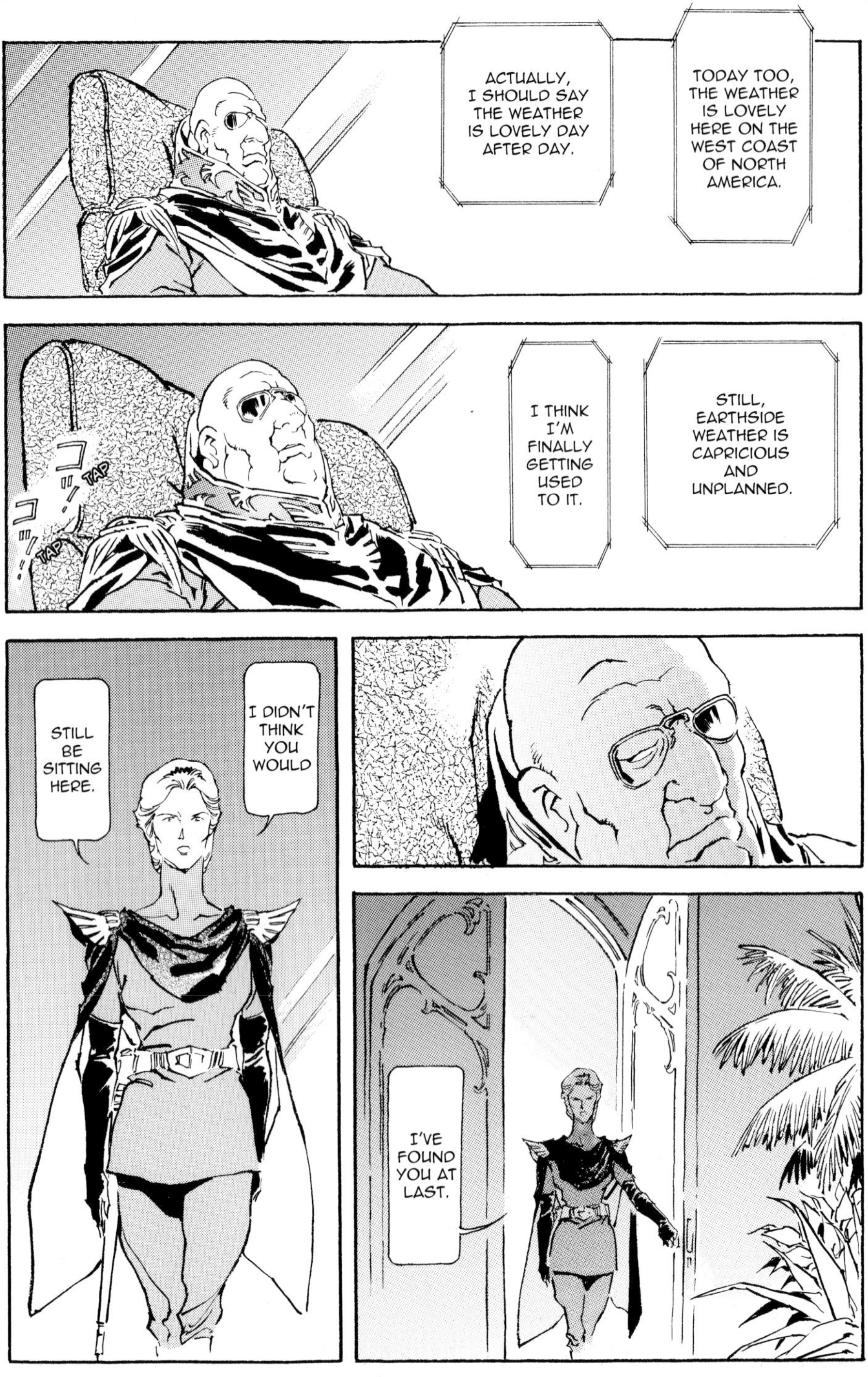
TODAY TOO, THE WEATHER IS LOVELY HERE ON THE WEST COAST OF NORTH AMERICA.
ACTUALLY, I SHOULD SAY THE WEATHER IS LOVELY DAY AFTER DAY.
STILL, EARTHSIDE WEATHER IS CAPRICIOUS AND UNPLANNED.
I THINK I'M FINALLY GETTING USED TO IT.
TAP
TAP
I'VE FOUND YOU AT LAST.
I DIDN'T THINK YOU WOULD
STILL BE SITTING HERE.

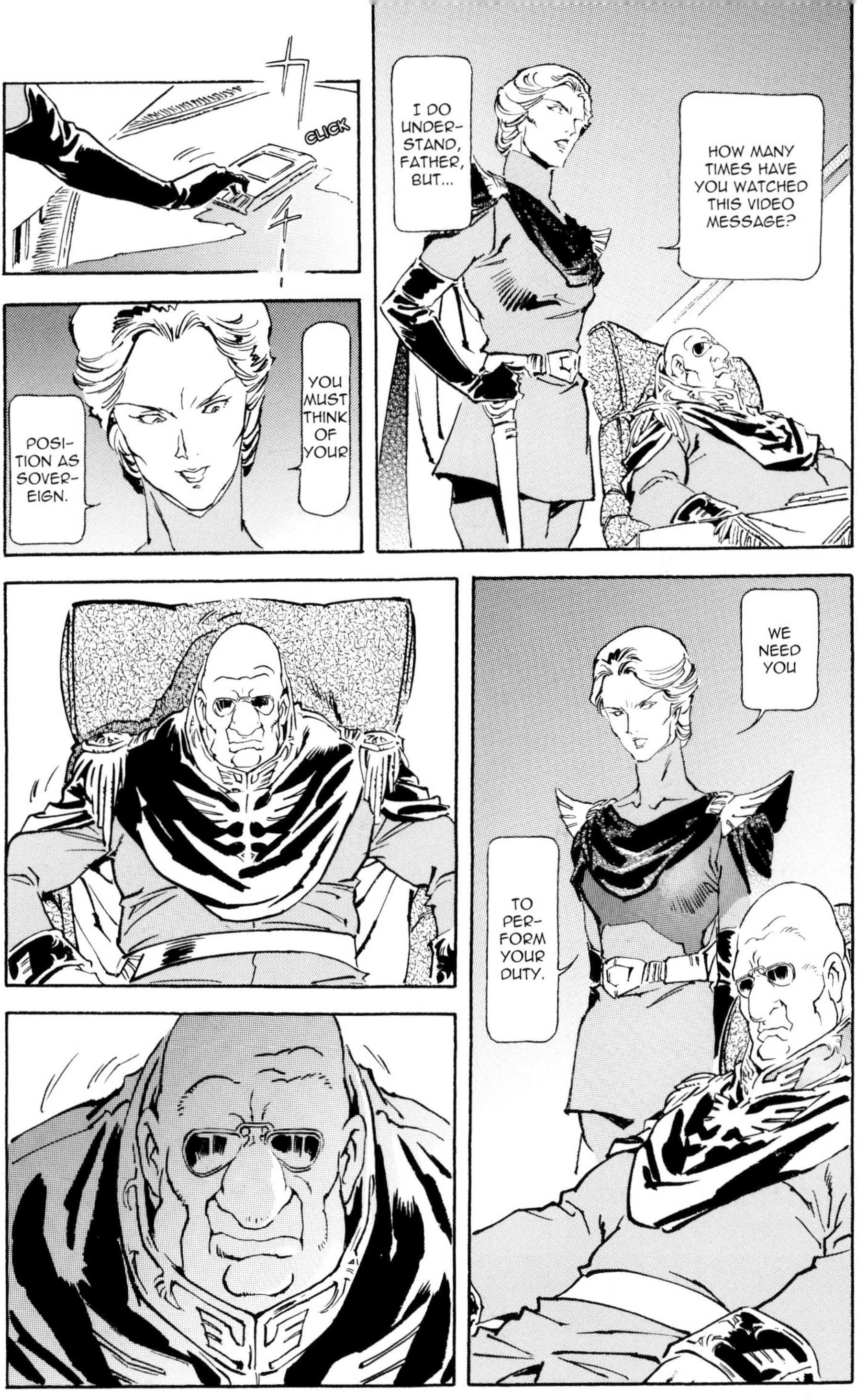
HOW MANY TIMES HAVE YOU WATCHED THIS VIDEO MESSAGE?
I DO UNDER-STAND, FATHER, BUT...
CLICK
YOU MUST THINK OF YOUR
POSI-TION AS SOVER-EIGN.
WE NEED YOU
TO PER-FORM YOUR DUTY.

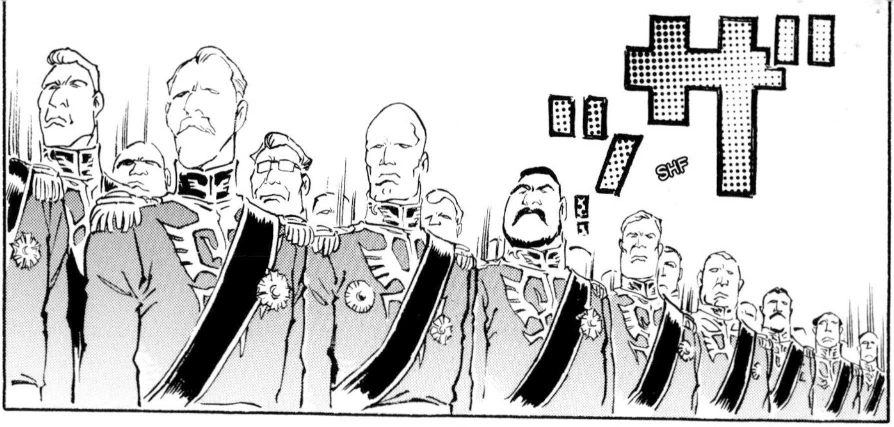
ザッ
SHF
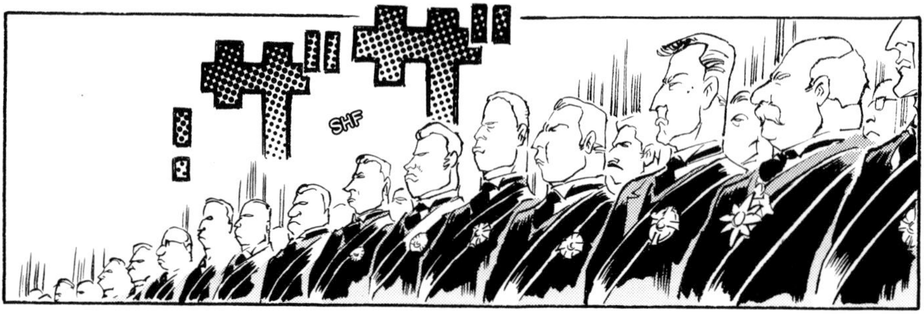
ザザッ
SHF
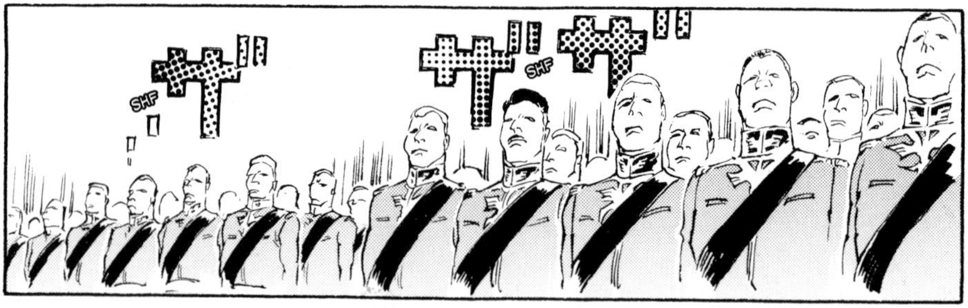
ザッ
SHF
ザッ
SHF
ザッ
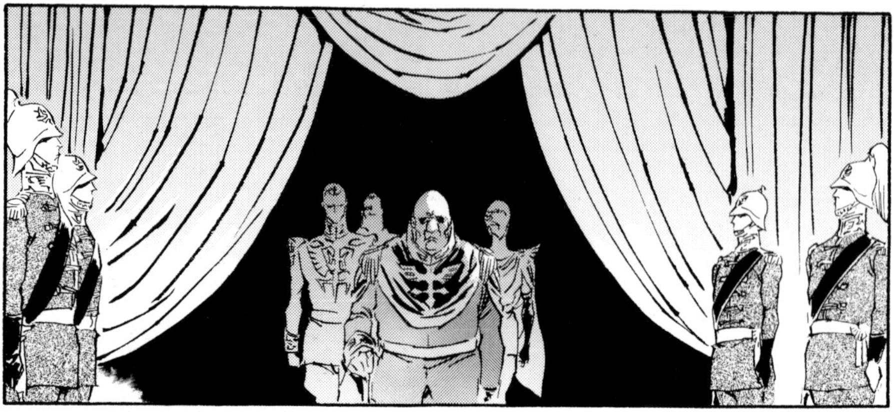

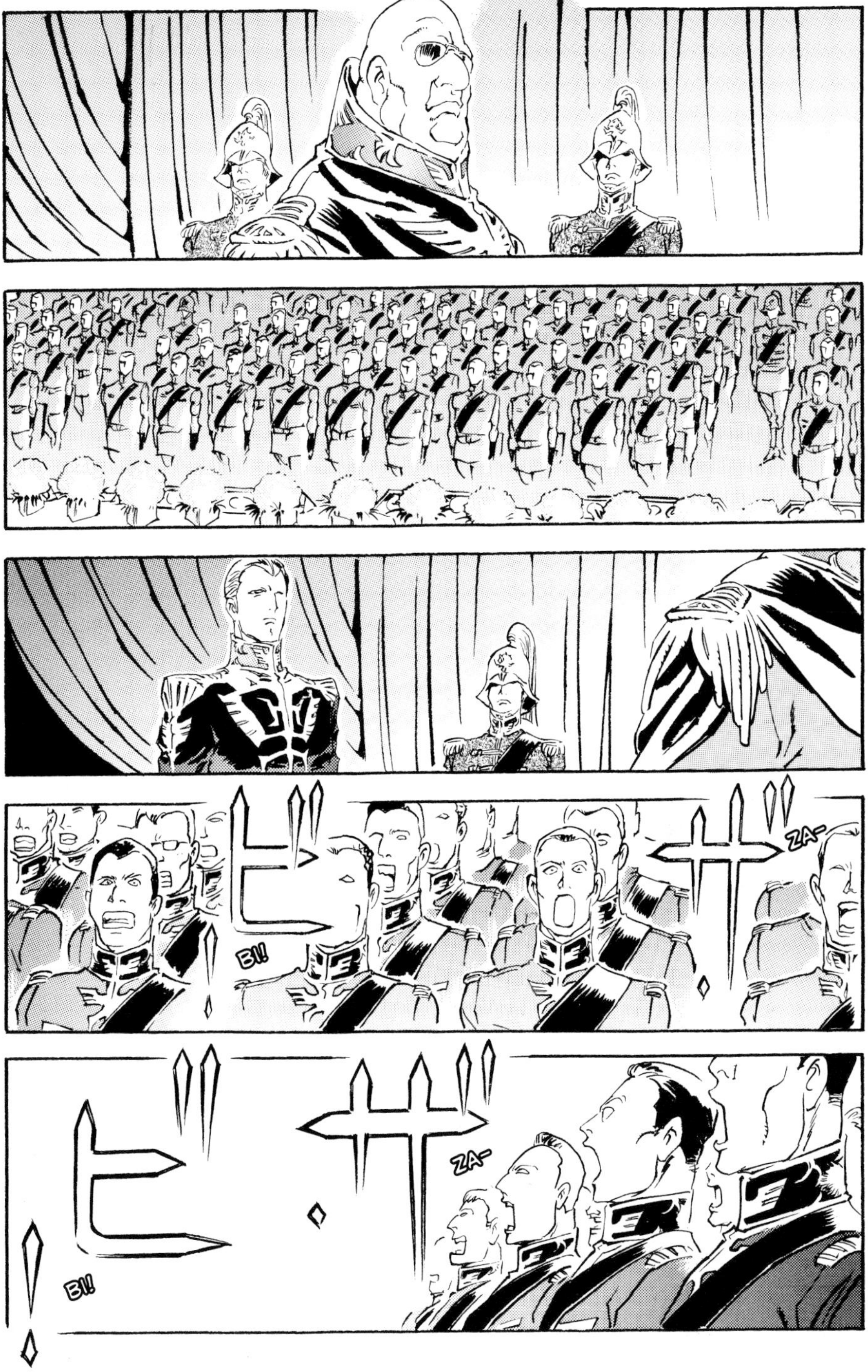
ザッ
ZA-
ビッ!
BI!
ザッ
ZA-
ビッ!
BI!

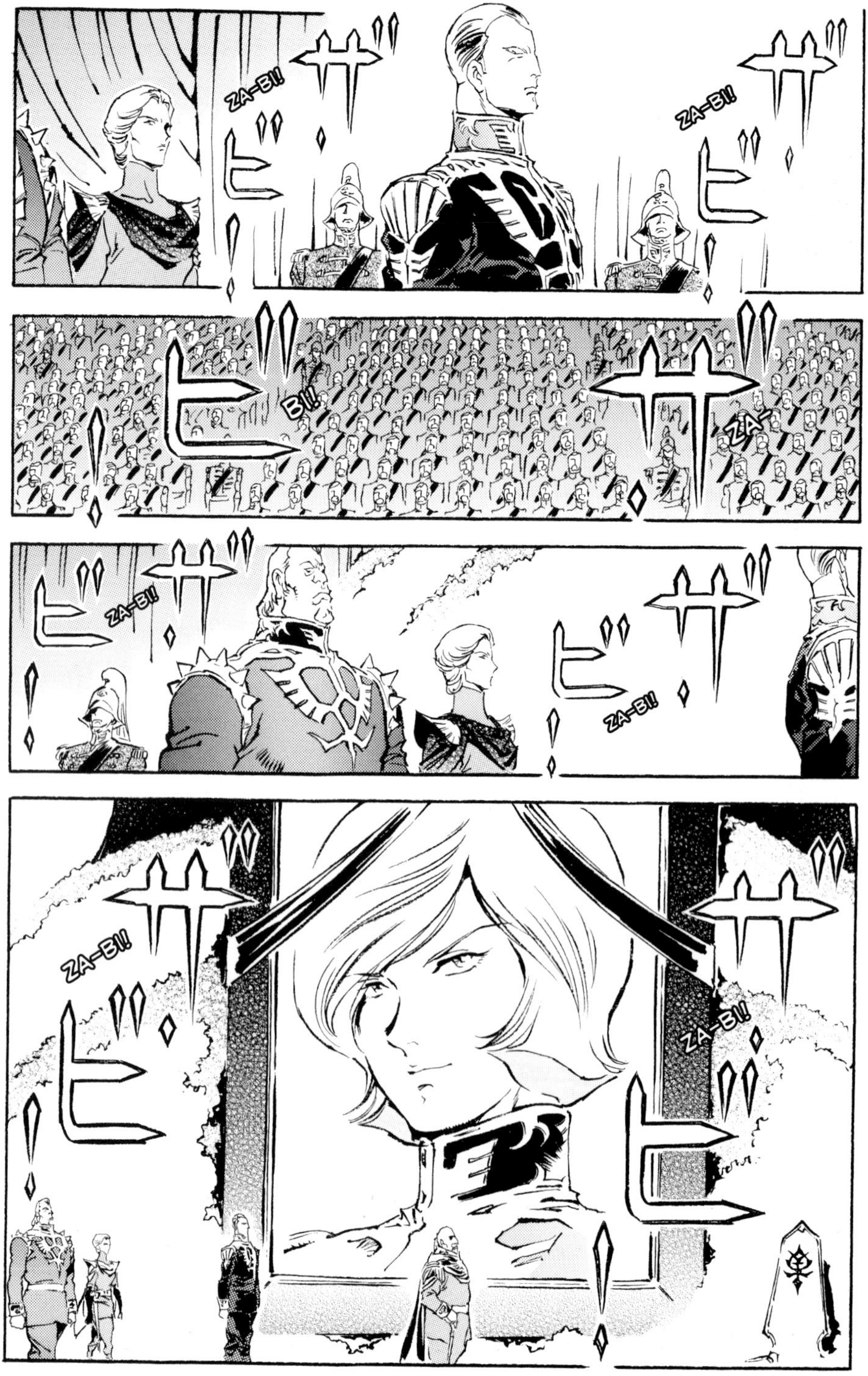
ザビ!
ZA-BI!
ザビ!
ZA-BI!
ザ
ZA-
ビ!!
BI!!
ザビ!
ZA-BI!
ビザ!
ZA-BI!
ザビ!
ZA-BI!
ザビ!
ZA-BI!

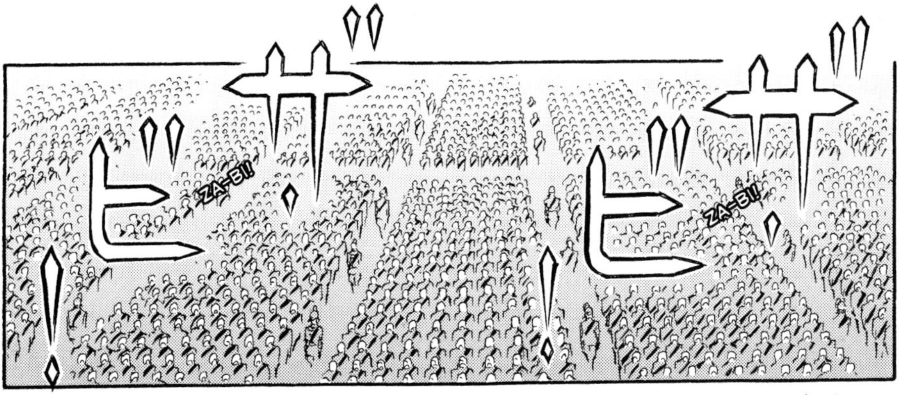
ザビ!
ZA-BI!!
ザビ!
ZA-BI!!

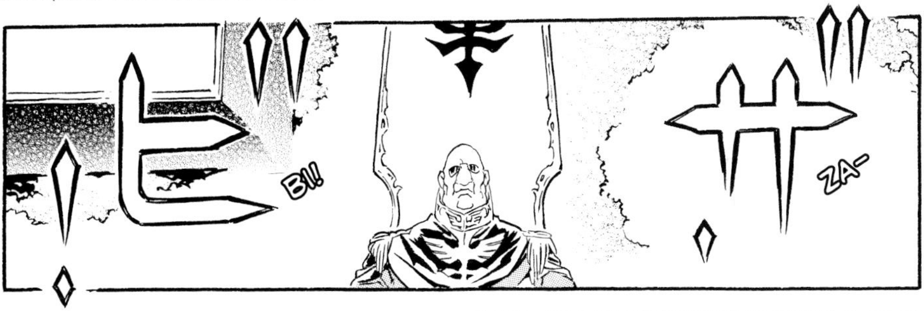
ザ
ZA-
ビ!
BI!!

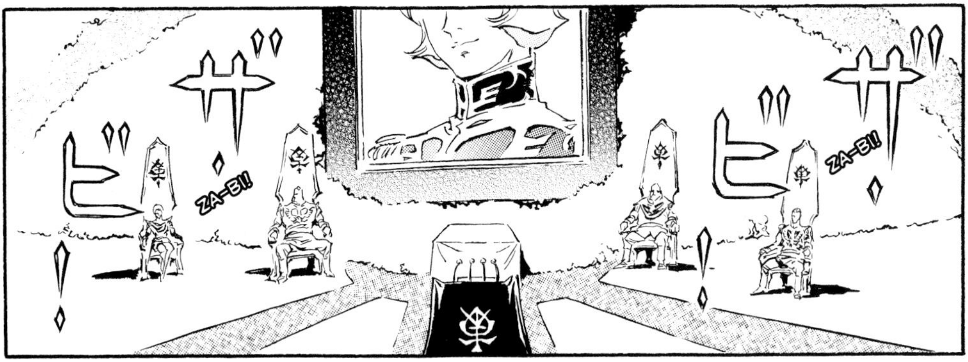
ザビ!
ZA-BI!!
ザビ!
ZA-BI!!

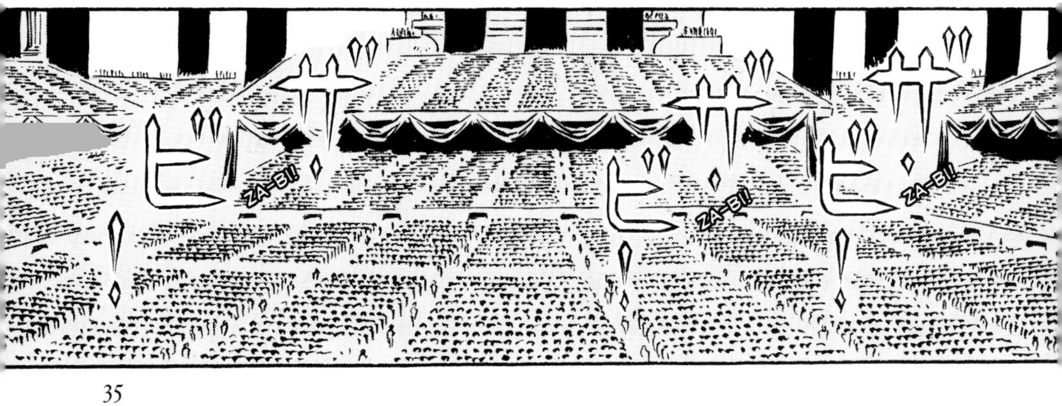
ザビ!
ZA-BI!!
ザビ!
ZA-BI!!
ザビ!
ZA-BI!!

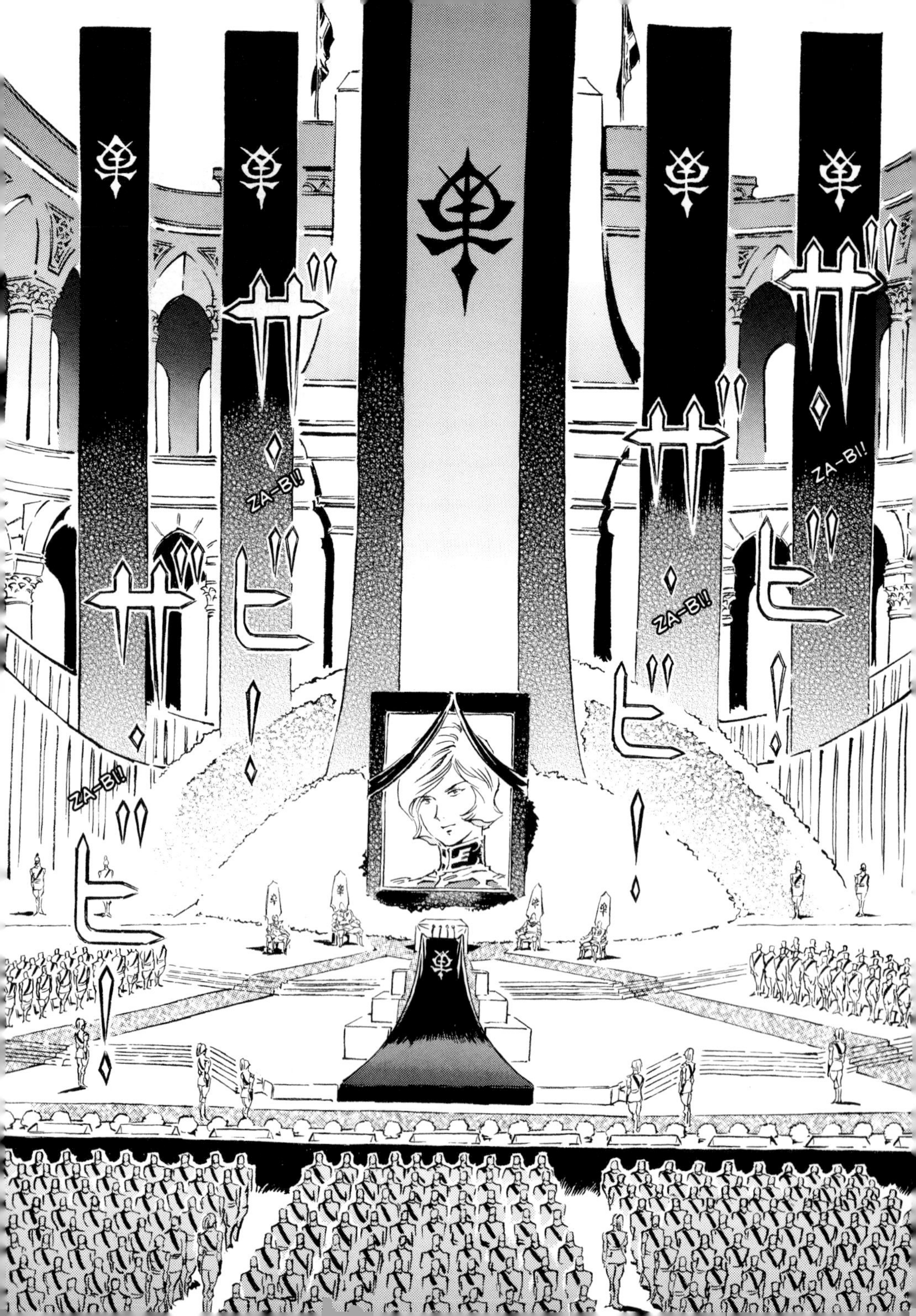
ザビ!
ZA-BI!!
ザビ!
ZA-BI!!
ザビ!
ZA-BI!!
ザビ!
ZA-BI!!

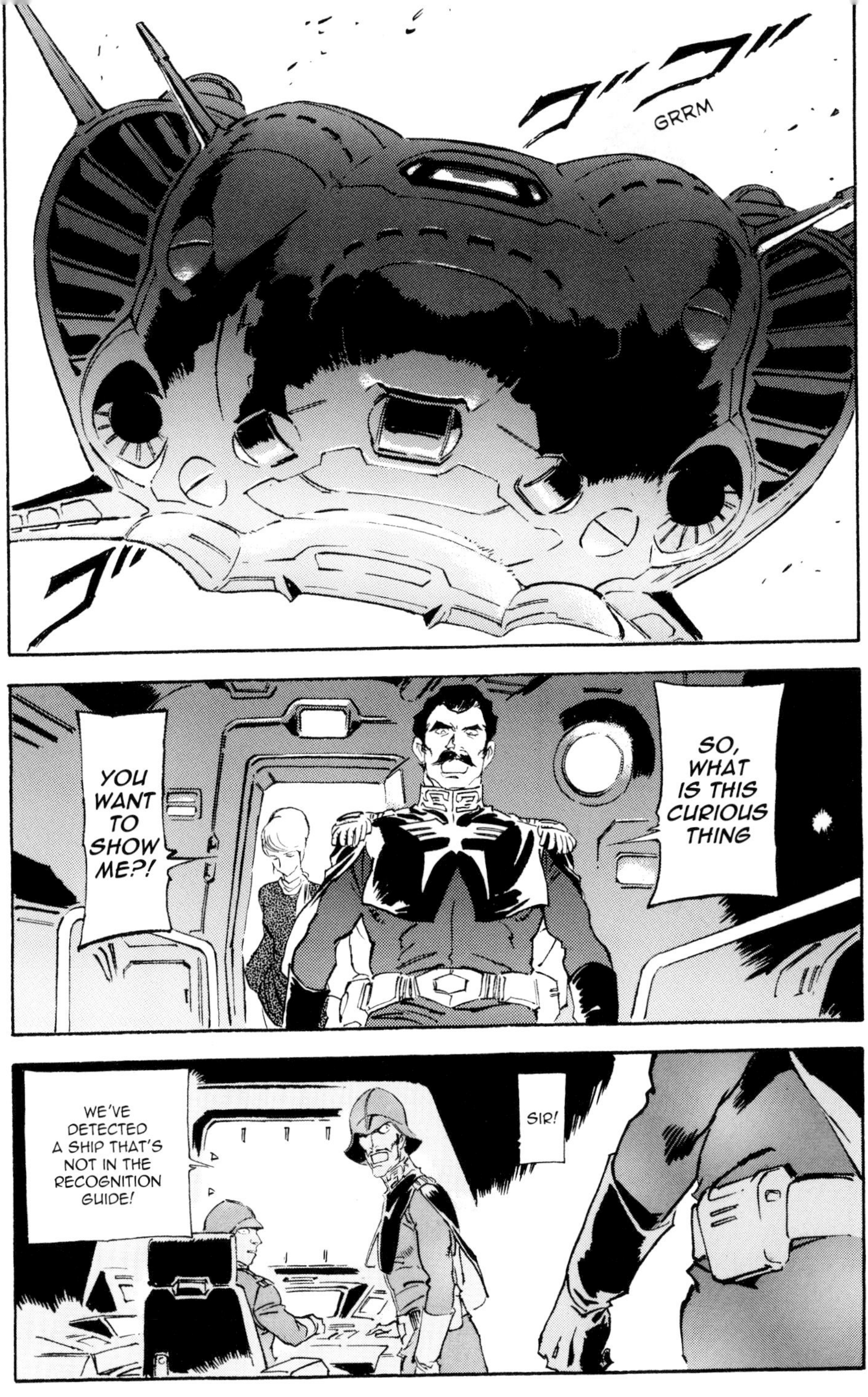
GRRM
SO, WHAT IS THIS CURIOUS THING
YOU WANT TO SHOW ME?!
SIR!
WE'VE DETECTED A SHIP THAT'S NOT IN THE RECOGNITION GUIDE!

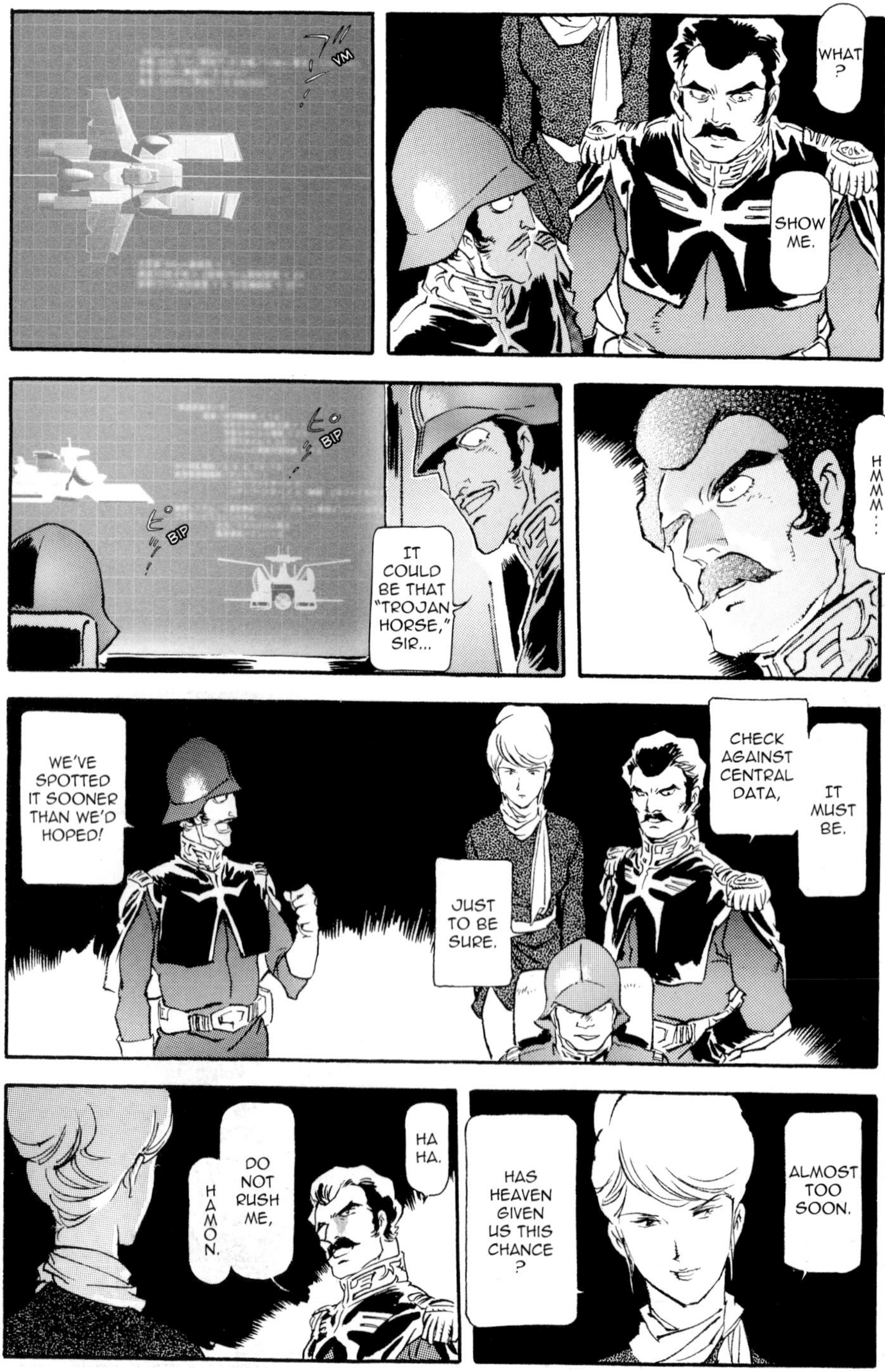
WHAT ?
SHOW ME.
VM
HMMM...
IT COULD BE THAT "TROJAN HORSE," SIR...
BIP
BIP
IT MUST BE.
CHECK AGAINST CENTRAL DATA,
JUST TO BE SURE.
WE'VE SPOTTED IT SOONER THAN WE'D HOPED!
ALMOST TOO SOON.
HAS HEAVEN GIVEN US THIS CHANCE ?
HA HA.
DO NOT RUSH ME,
HAMON.

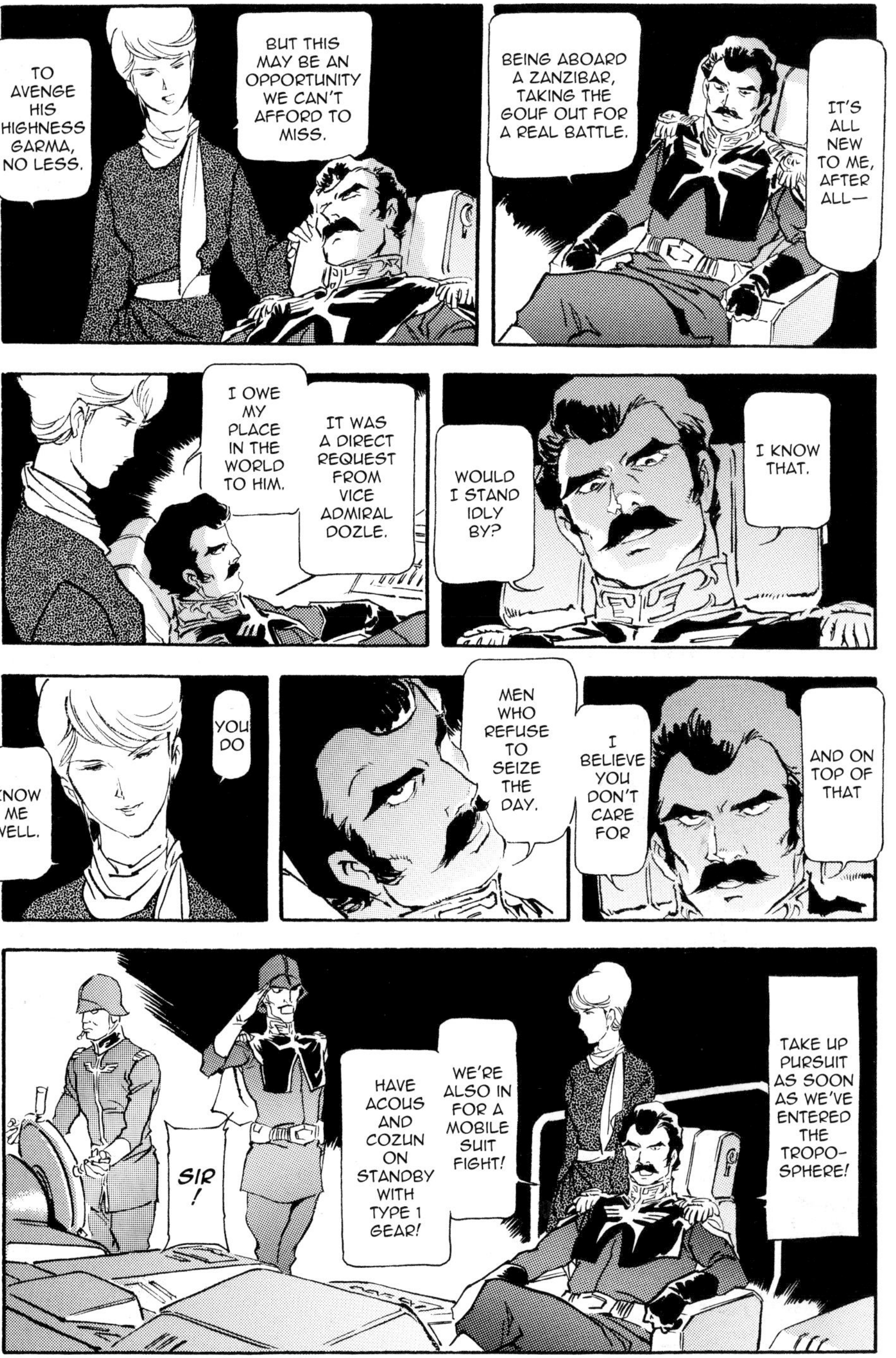
IT'S ALL NEW TO ME, AFTER ALL—
BEING ABOARD A ZANZIBAR, TAKING THE GOUF OUT FOR A REAL BATTLE.
BUT THIS MAY BE AN OPPORTUNITY WE CAN'T AFFORD TO MISS.
TO AVENGE HIS HIGHNESS GARMA, NO LESS.
I KNOW THAT.
WOULD I STAND IDLY BY?
IT WAS A DIRECT REQUEST FROM VICE ADMIRAL DOZLE.
I OWE MY PLACE IN THE WORLD TO HIM.
AND ON TOP OF THAT
I BELIEVE YOU DON'T CARE FOR
MEN WHO REFUSE TO SEIZE THE DAY.
YOU DO
KNOW ME WELL.
TAKE UP PURSUIT AS SOON AS WE'VE ENTERED THE TROPOSPHERE!
WE'RE ALSO IN FOR A MOBILE SUIT FIGHT!
HAVE ACOUS AND COZUN ON STANDBY WITH TYPE 1 GEAR!
SIR!

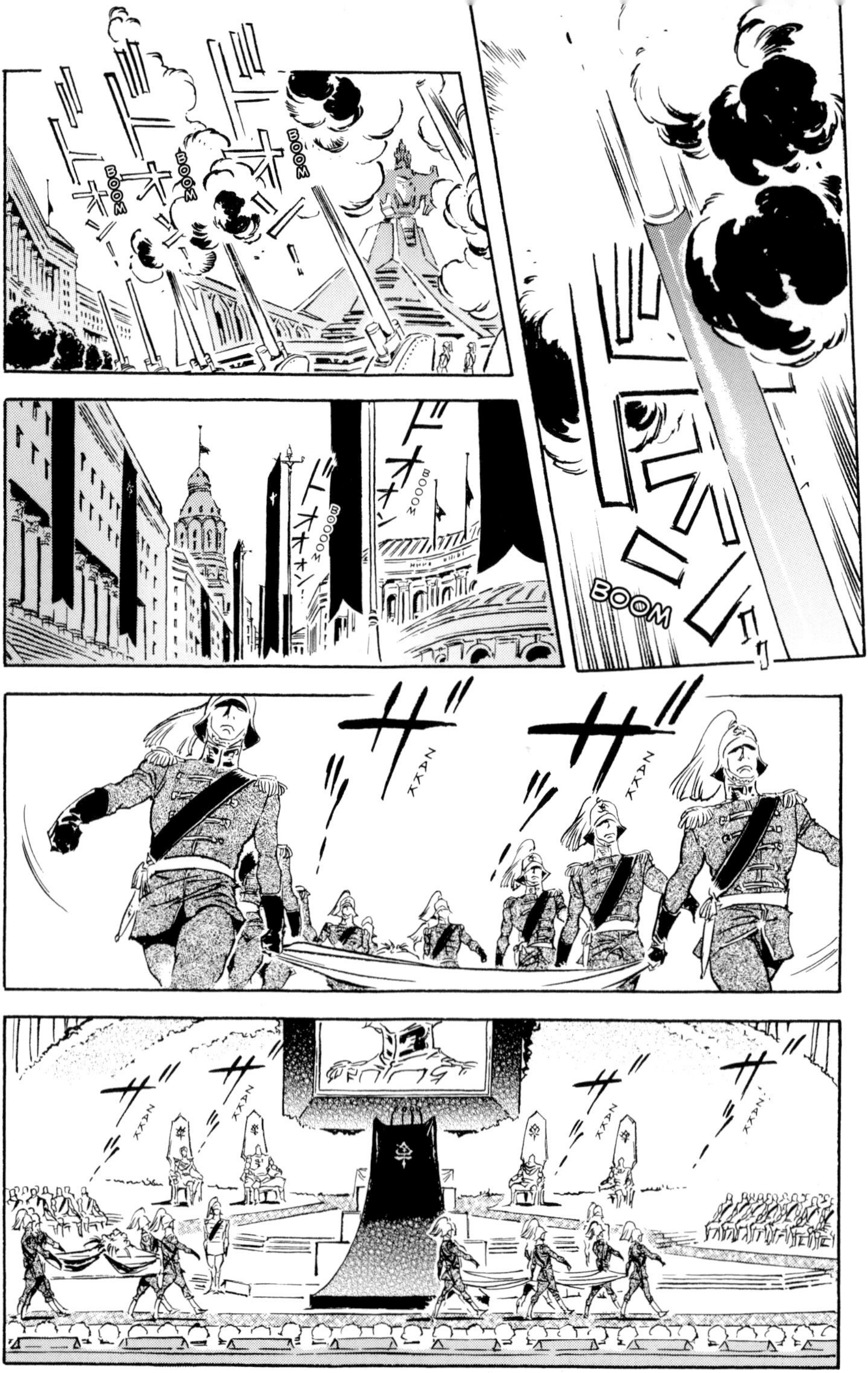
BOOM
BOOM
BOOM
BOOM
ドオン
BOOOOM
ドドオオオン!!
BOOOOOM
ザ
ザ
ザ
ザ
ザ
ザ

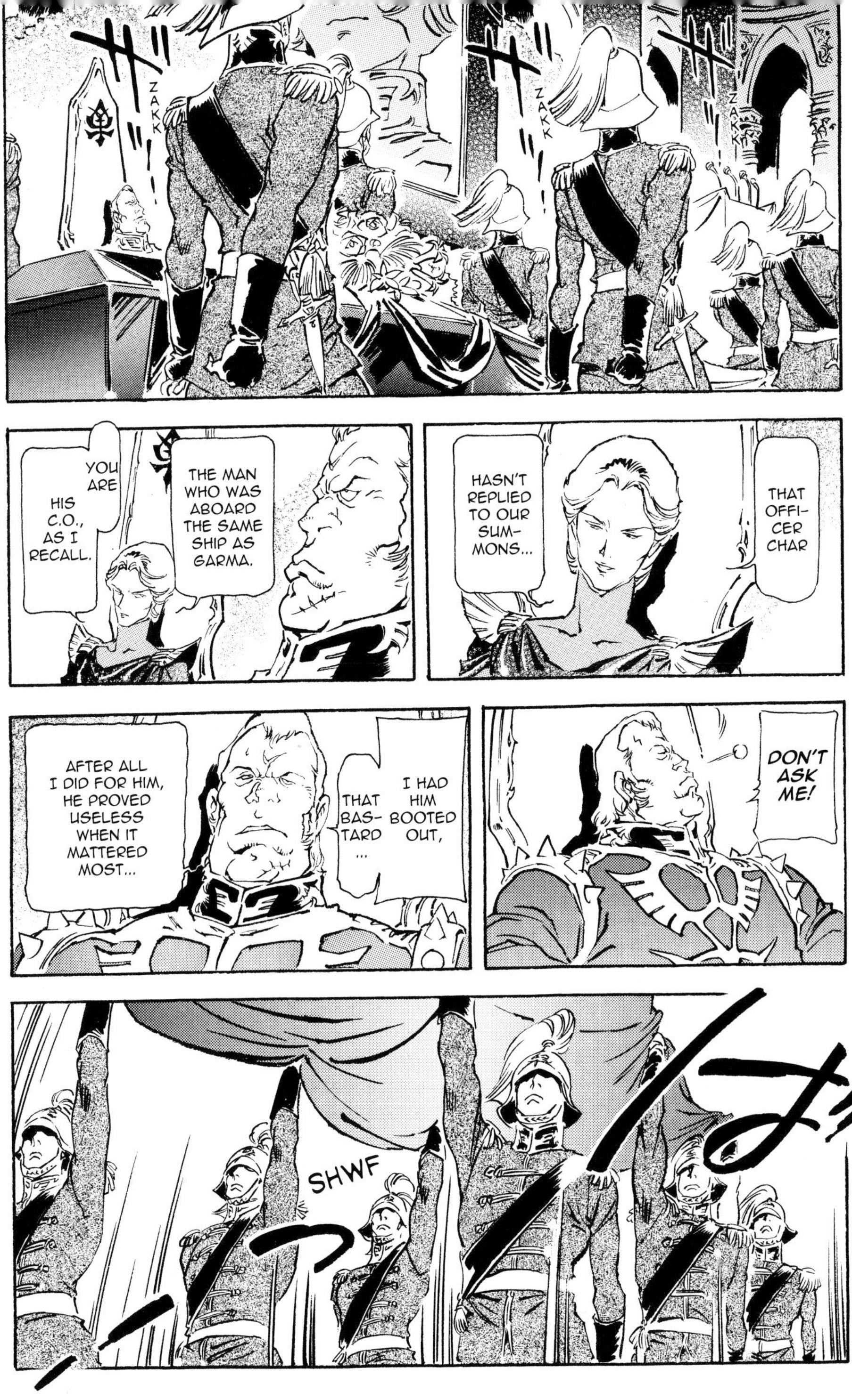
ZAKK
ZAKK
ZAKK
THAT OFFICER CHAR
HASN'T REPLIED TO OUR SUMMONS...
THE MAN WHO WAS ABOARD THE SAME SHIP AS GARMA.
YOU ARE HIS C.O., AS I RECALL.
DON'T ASK ME!
I HAD HIM BOOTED OUT,
THAT BASTARD...
AFTER ALL I DID FOR HIM, HE PROVED USELESS WHEN IT MATTERED MOST...
SHWF

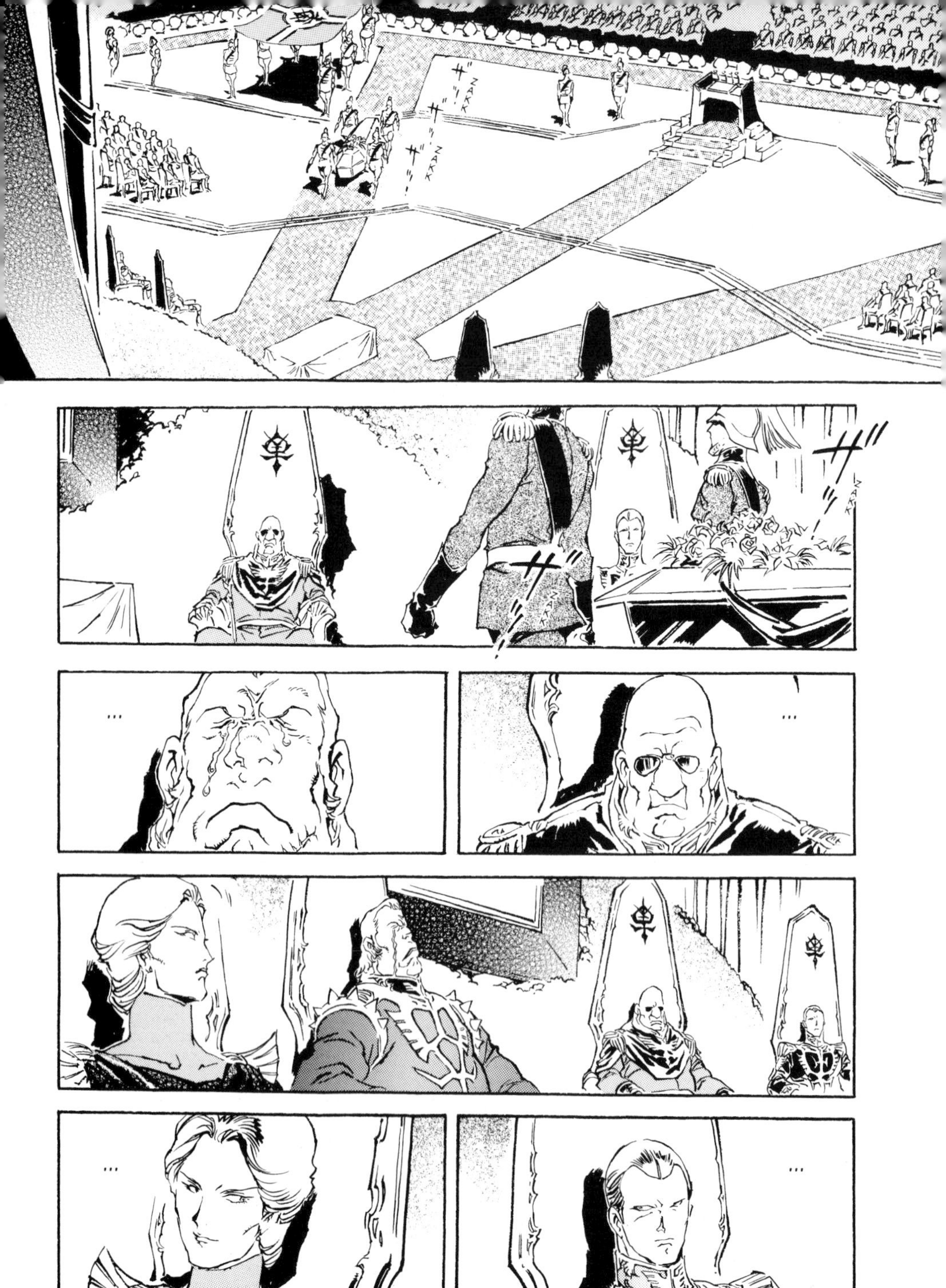

ZAKK
ZAKK
ZAKK
ZAKK
...
...
...
...

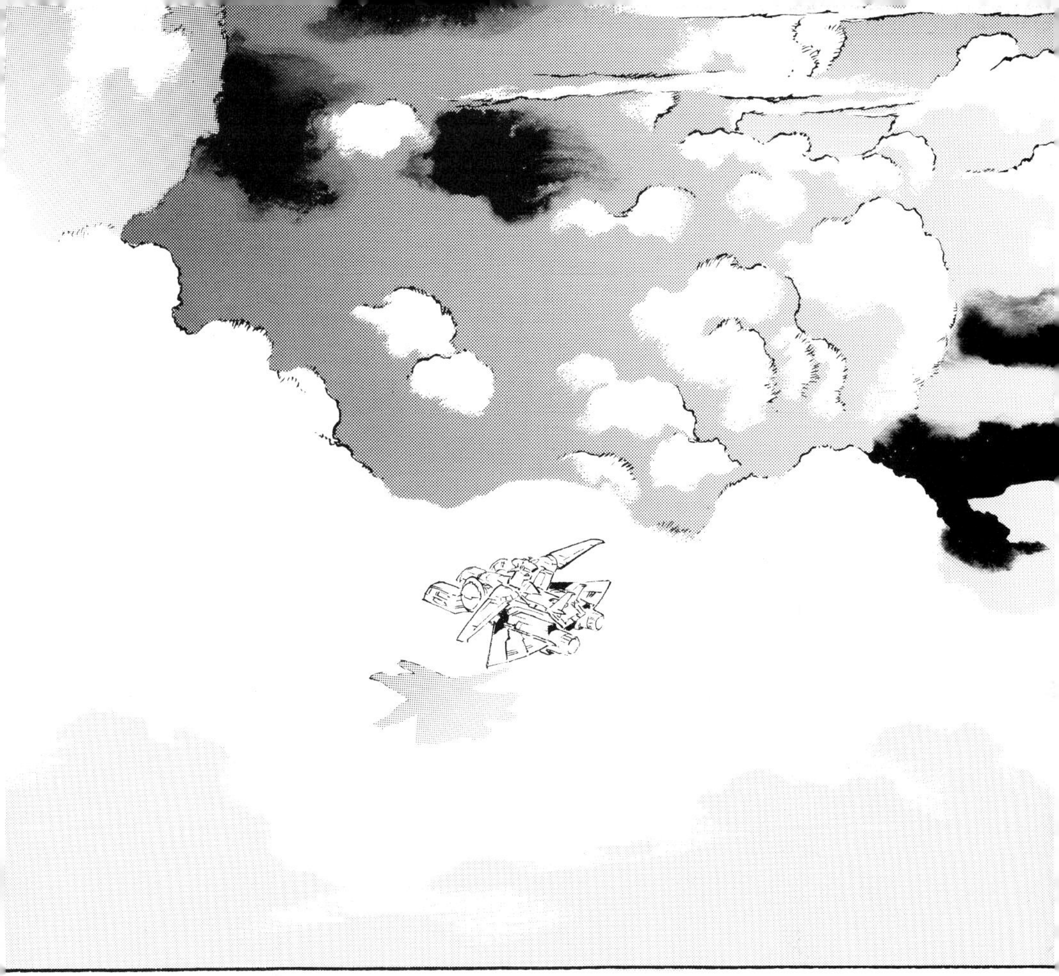

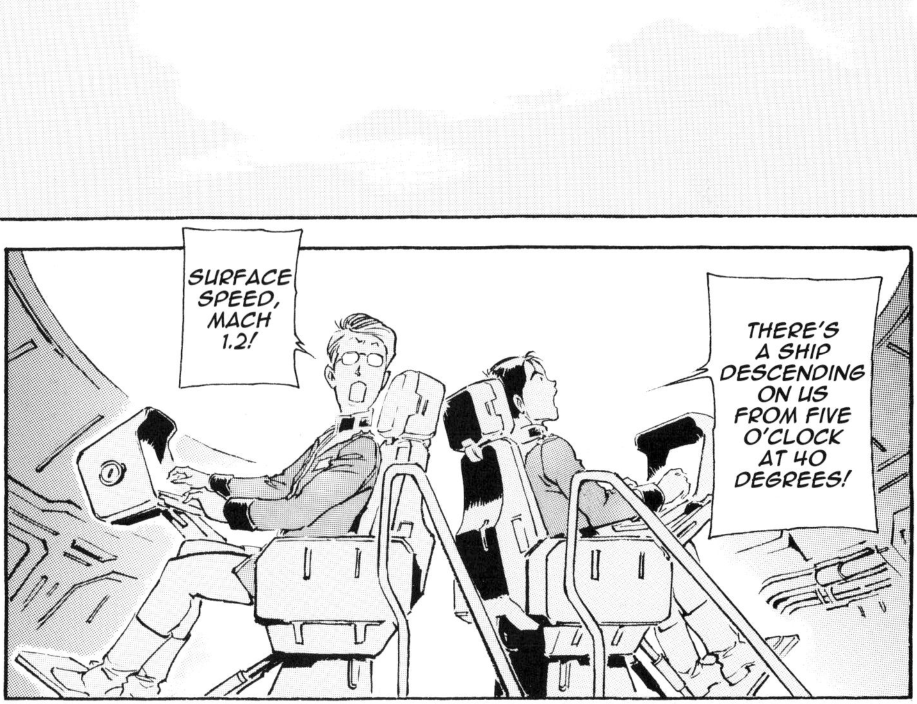
THERE'S A SHIP DESCENDING ON US FROM FIVE O'CLOCK AT 40 DEGREES!
SURFACE SPEED, MACH 1.2!

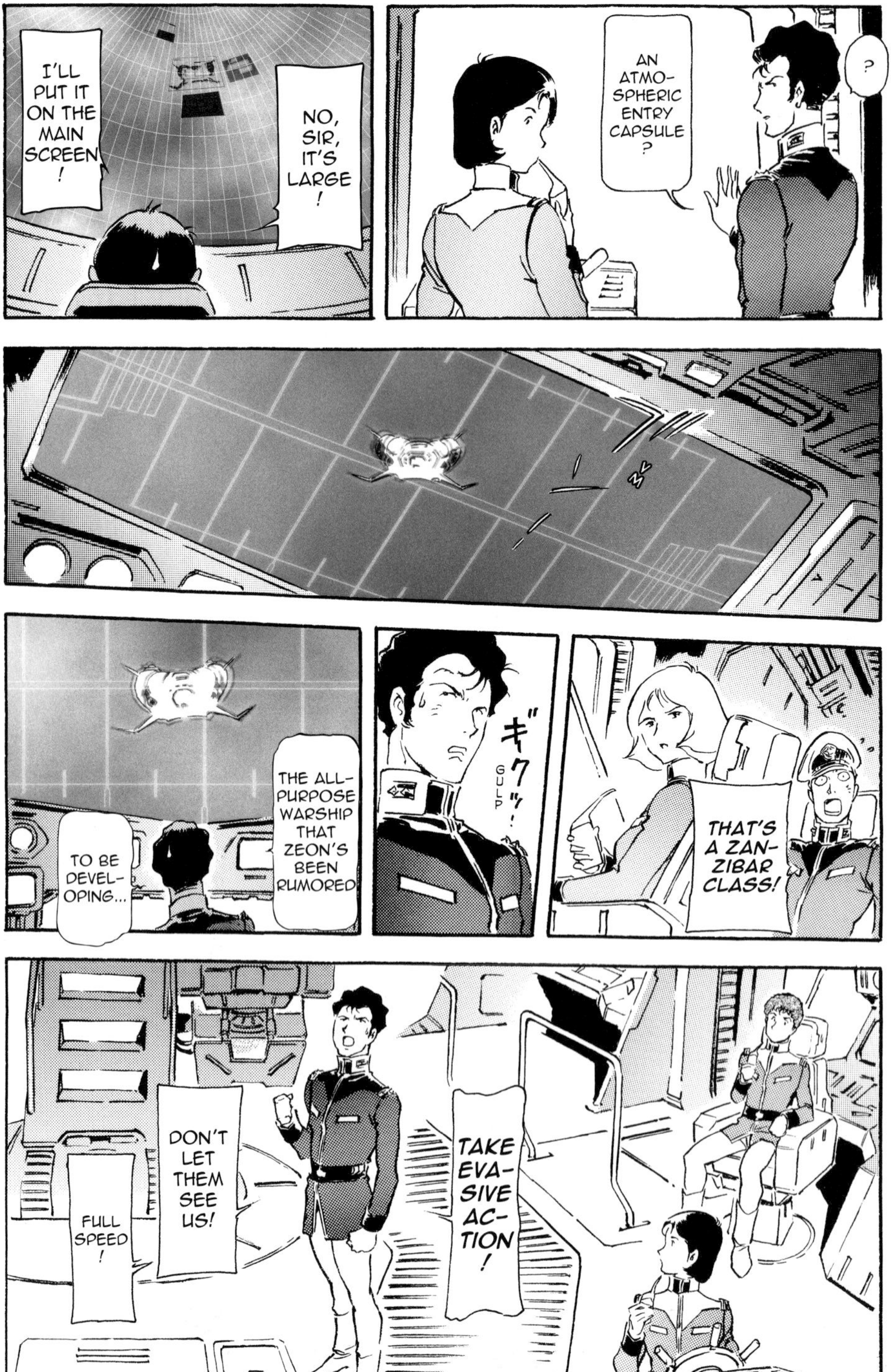
?
AN ATMOSPHERIC ENTRY CAPSULE?
NO, SIR, IT'S LARGE!
I'LL PUT IT ON THE MAIN SCREEN!
THAT'S A ZANZIBAR CLASS!
ギクッ!
GULP
THE ALL-PURPOSE WARSHIP THAT ZEON'S BEEN RUMORED
TO BE DEVELOPING...
TAKE EVASIVE ACTION!
DON'T LET THEM SEE US!
FULL SPEED!

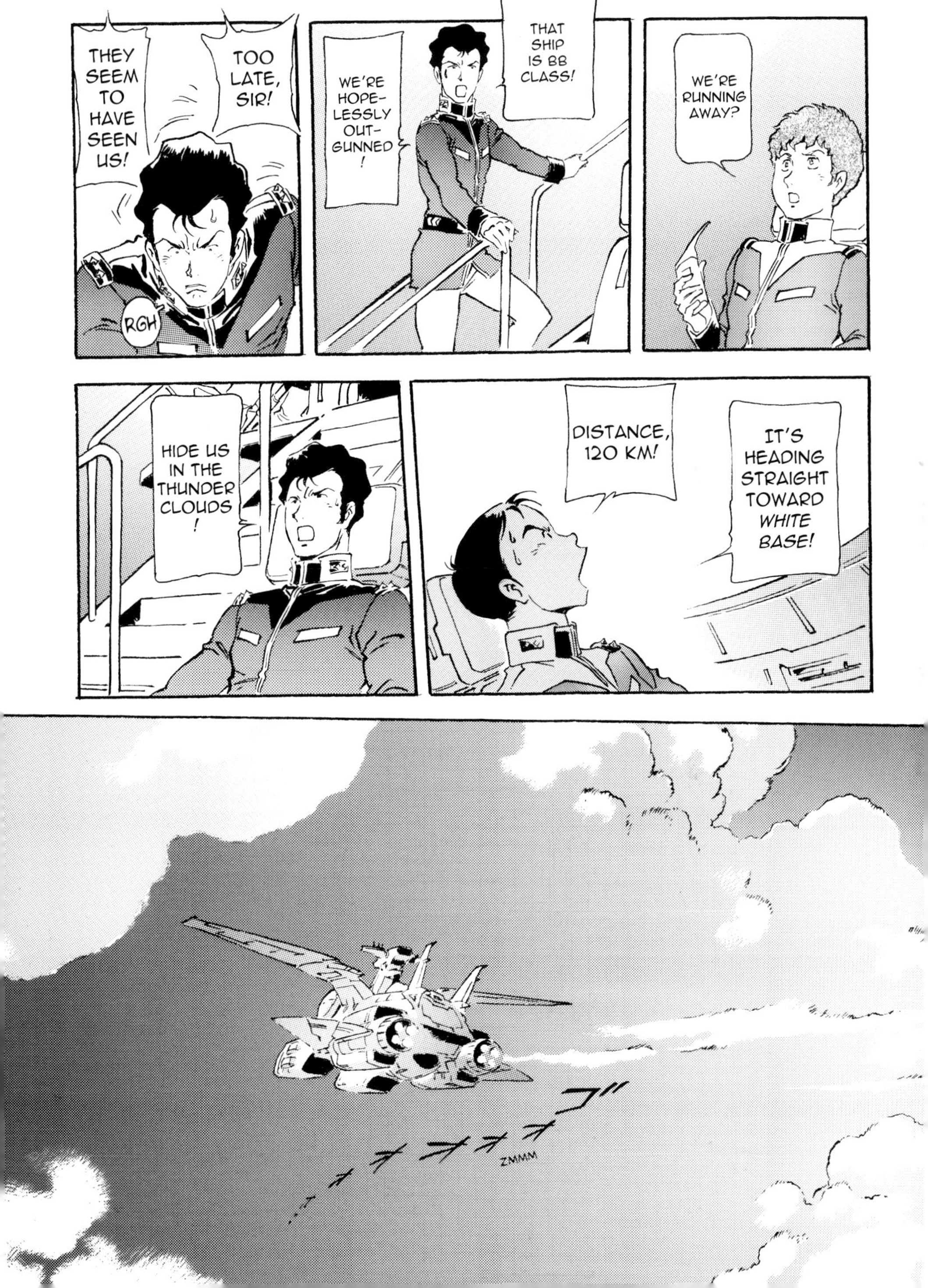
WE'RE RUNNING AWAY?
THAT SHIP IS BB CLASS!
WE'RE HOPELESSLY OUTGUNNED!
TOO LATE, SIR!
THEY SEEM TO HAVE SEEN US!
RGH
IT'S HEADING STRAIGHT TOWARD WHITE BASE!
DISTANCE, 120 KM!
HIDE US IN THE THUNDER CLOUDS!
ZMMM

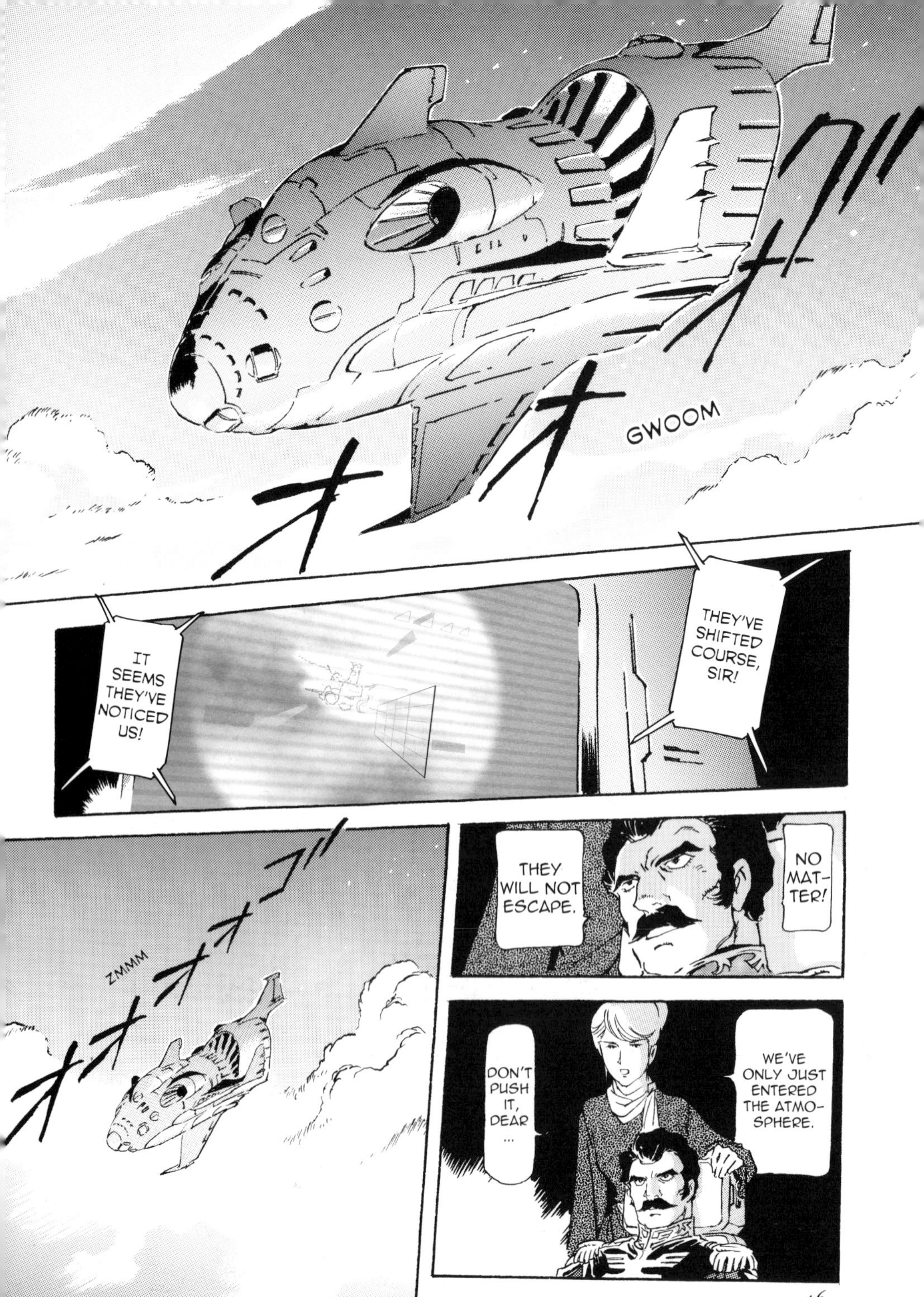
GWOOM
THEY'VE SHIFTED COURSE, SIR!
IT SEEMS THEY'VE NOTICED US!
NO MAT-TER!
THEY WILL NOT ESCAPE.
WE'VE ONLY JUST ENTERED THE ATMO-SPHERE.
DON'T PUSH IT, DEAR ...
ZMMM

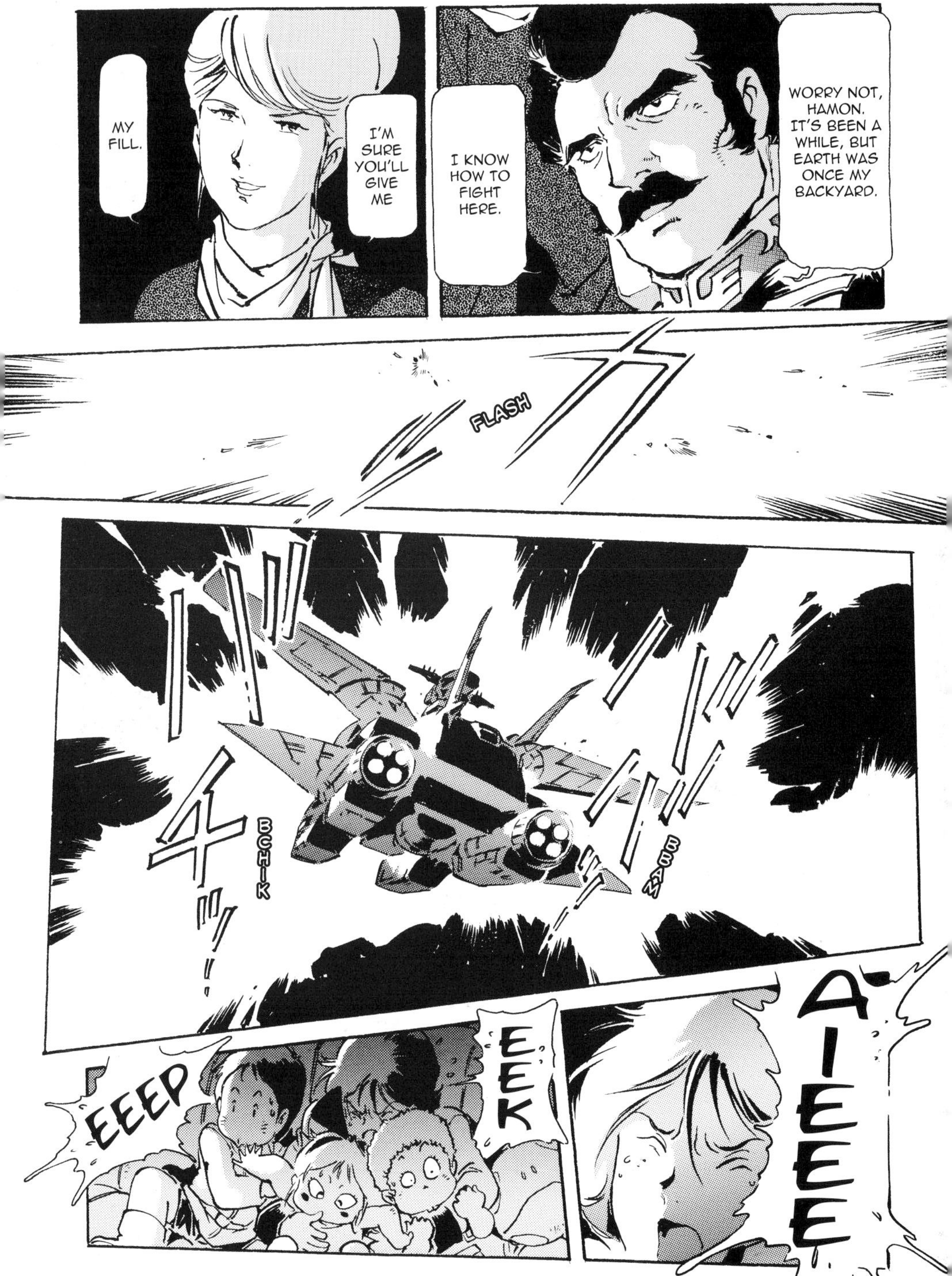
WORRY NOT, HAMON. IT'S BEEN A WHILE, BUT EARTH WAS ONCE MY BACKYARD.
I KNOW HOW TO FIGHT HERE.
I'M SURE YOU'LL GIVE ME
MY FILL.
FLASH
BEAM
BCHIK
AIEEE
EEK
EEEP

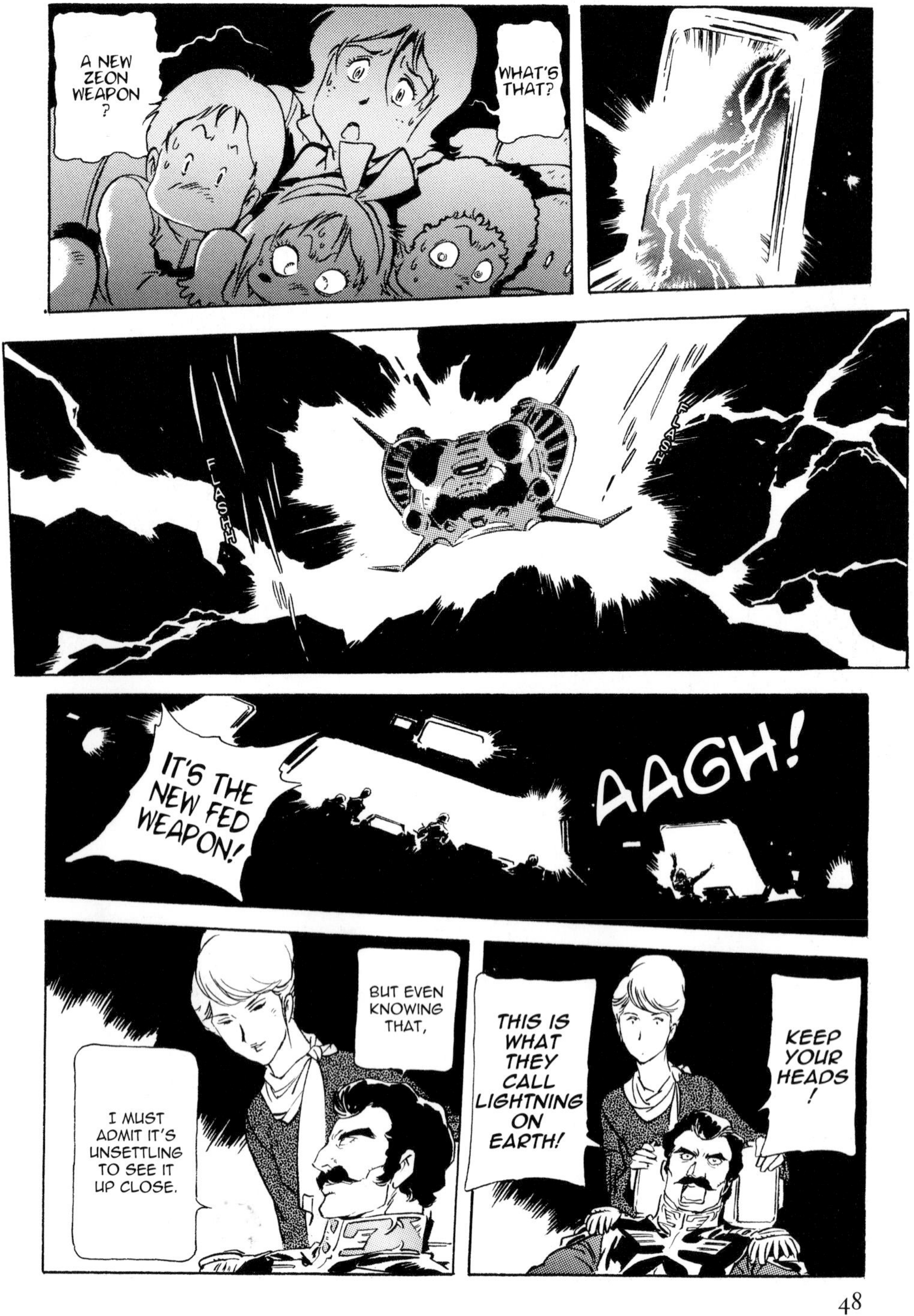
WHAT'S THAT?
A NEW ZEON WEAPON?
FLASH
FLASHH
AAGH!
IT'S THE NEW FED WEAPON!
KEEP YOUR HEADS!
THIS IS WHAT THEY CALL LIGHTNING ON EARTH!
BUT EVEN KNOWING THAT,
I MUST ADMIT IT'S UNSETTLING TO SEE IT UP CLOSE.

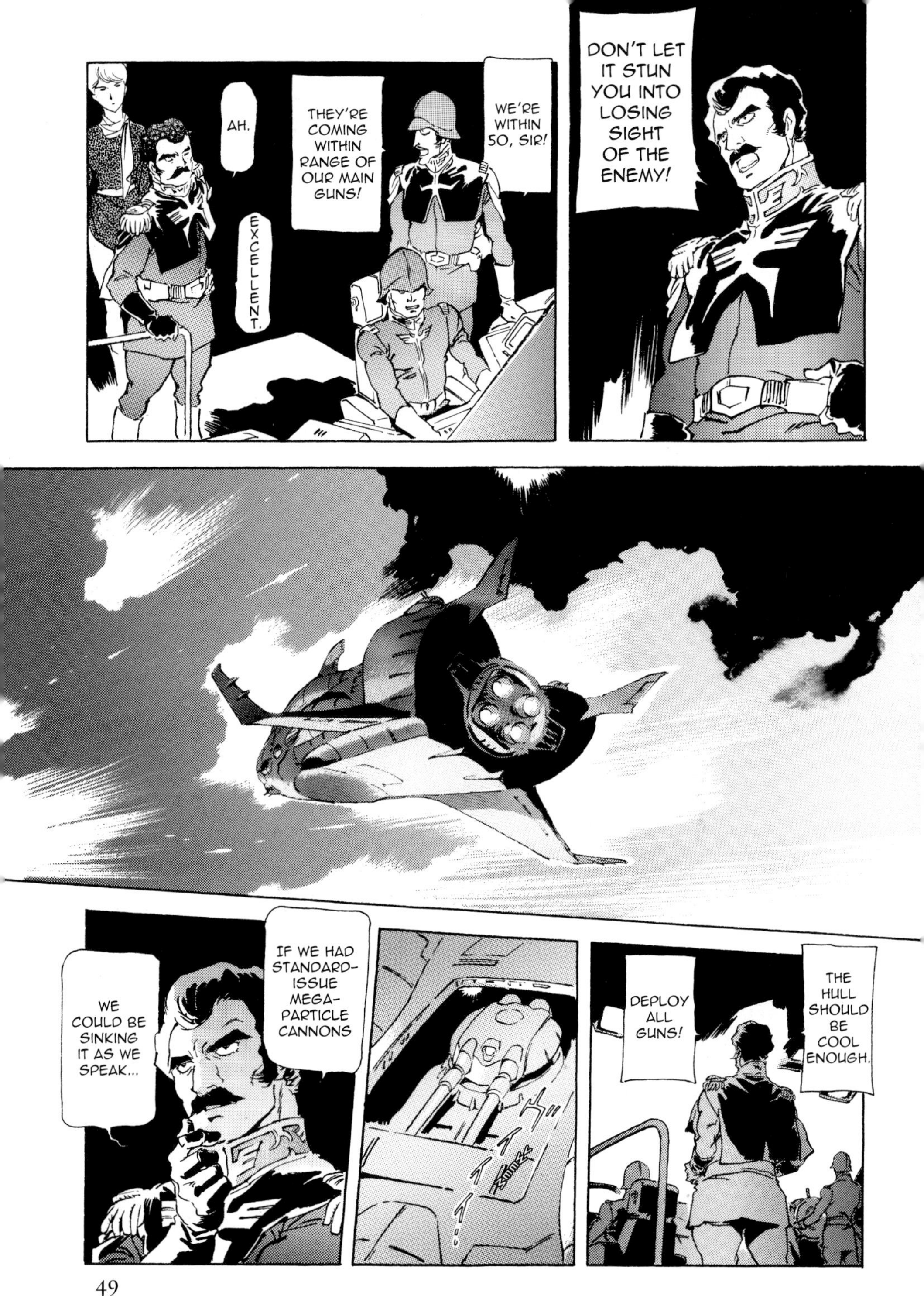
DON'T LET IT STUN YOU INTO LOSING SIGHT OF THE ENEMY!
WE'RE WITHIN 50, SIR!
THEY'RE COMING WITHIN RANGE OF OUR MAIN GUNS!
AH.
EXCELLENT.
THE HULL SHOULD BE COOL ENOUGH.
DEPLOY ALL GUNS!
IF WE HAD STANDARD-ISSUE MEGA-PARTICLE CANNONS
WE COULD BE SINKING IT AS WE SPEAK...

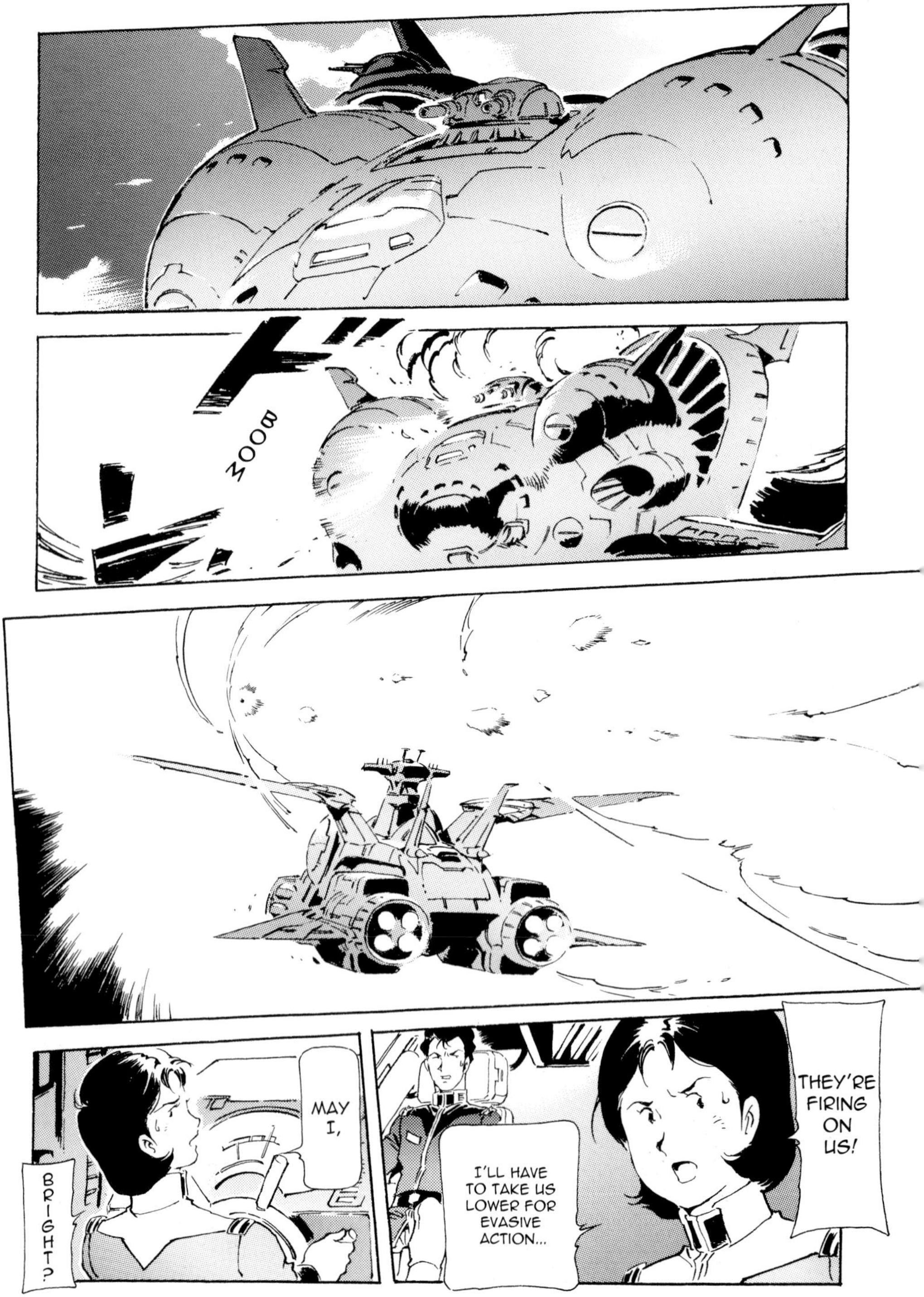
BOOM
THEY'RE FIRING ON US!
I'LL HAVE TO TAKE US LOWER FOR EVASIVE ACTION...
MAY I,
BRIGHT?

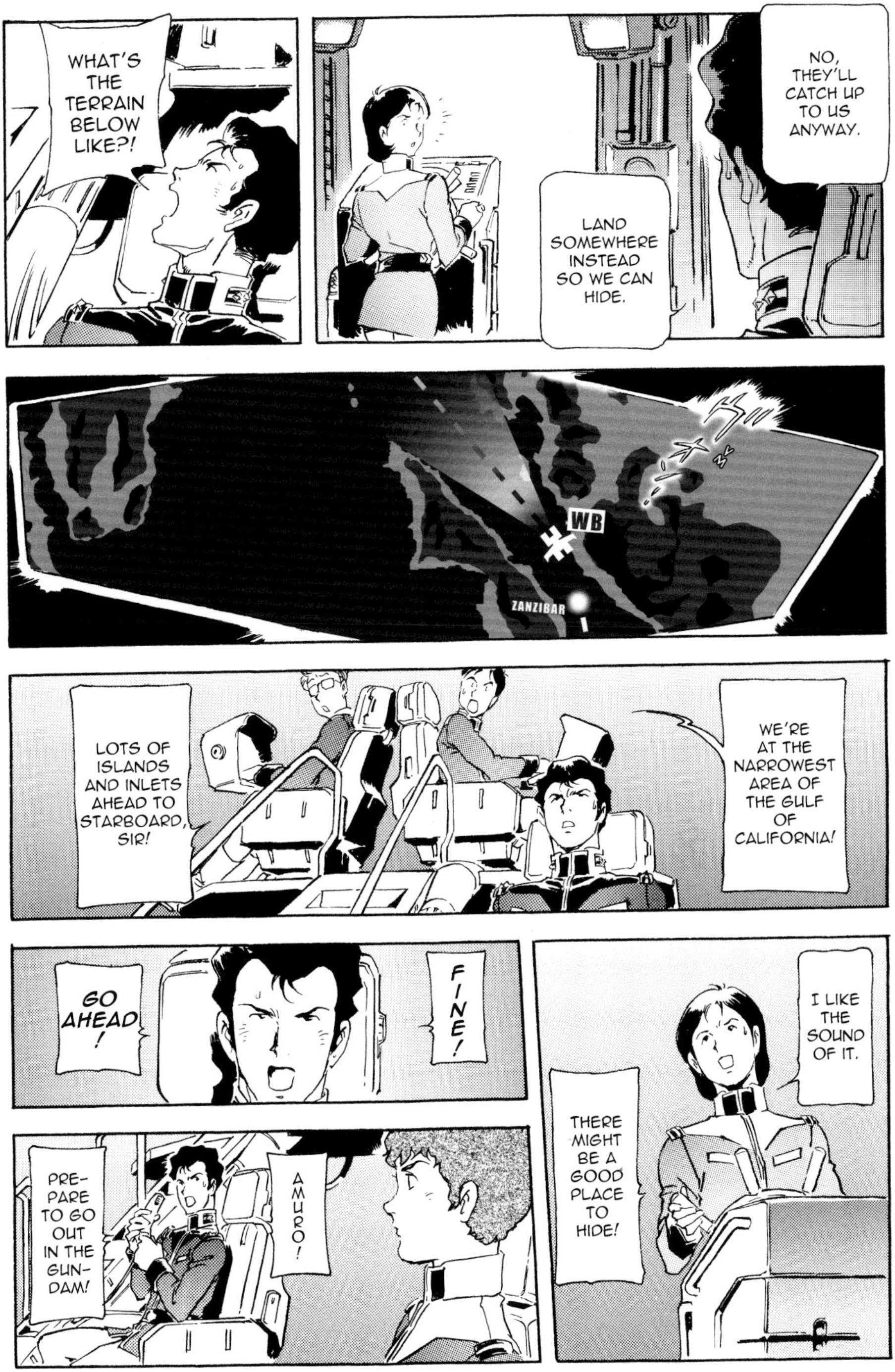
NO, THEY'LL CATCH UP TO US ANYWAY.
LAND SOMEWHERE INSTEAD SO WE CAN HIDE.
WHAT'S THE TERRAIN BELOW LIKE?!
WB
ZANZIBAR
WE'RE AT THE NARROWEST AREA OF THE GULF OF CALIFORNIA!
LOTS OF ISLANDS AND INLETS AHEAD TO STARBOARD, SIR!
I LIKE THE SOUND OF IT.
THERE MIGHT BE A GOOD PLACE TO HIDE!
FINE!
GO AHEAD!
AMURO!
PRE-PARE TO GO OUT IN THE GUN-DAM!

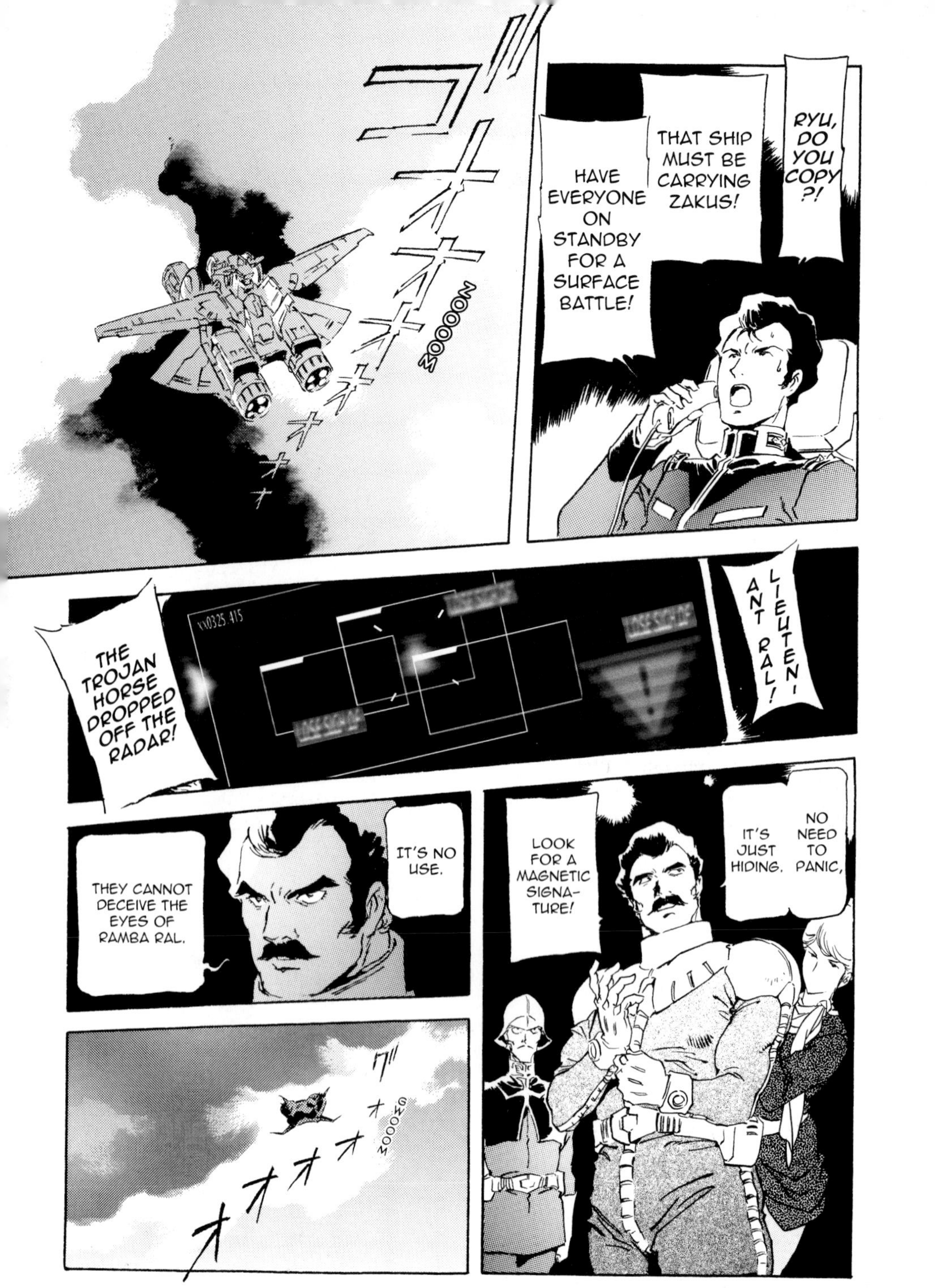
RYU, DO YOU COPY?!
THAT SHIP MUST BE CARRYING ZAKUS!
HAVE EVERYONE ON STANDBY FOR A SURFACE BATTLE!
LIEUTENANT RAL!
THE TROJAN HORSE DROPPED OFF THE RADAR!
xx0325.415
NO NEED TO PANIC,
IT'S JUST HIDING.
LOOK FOR A MAGNETIC SIGNATURE!
IT'S NO USE.
THEY CANNOT DECEIVE THE EYES OF RAMBA RAL.

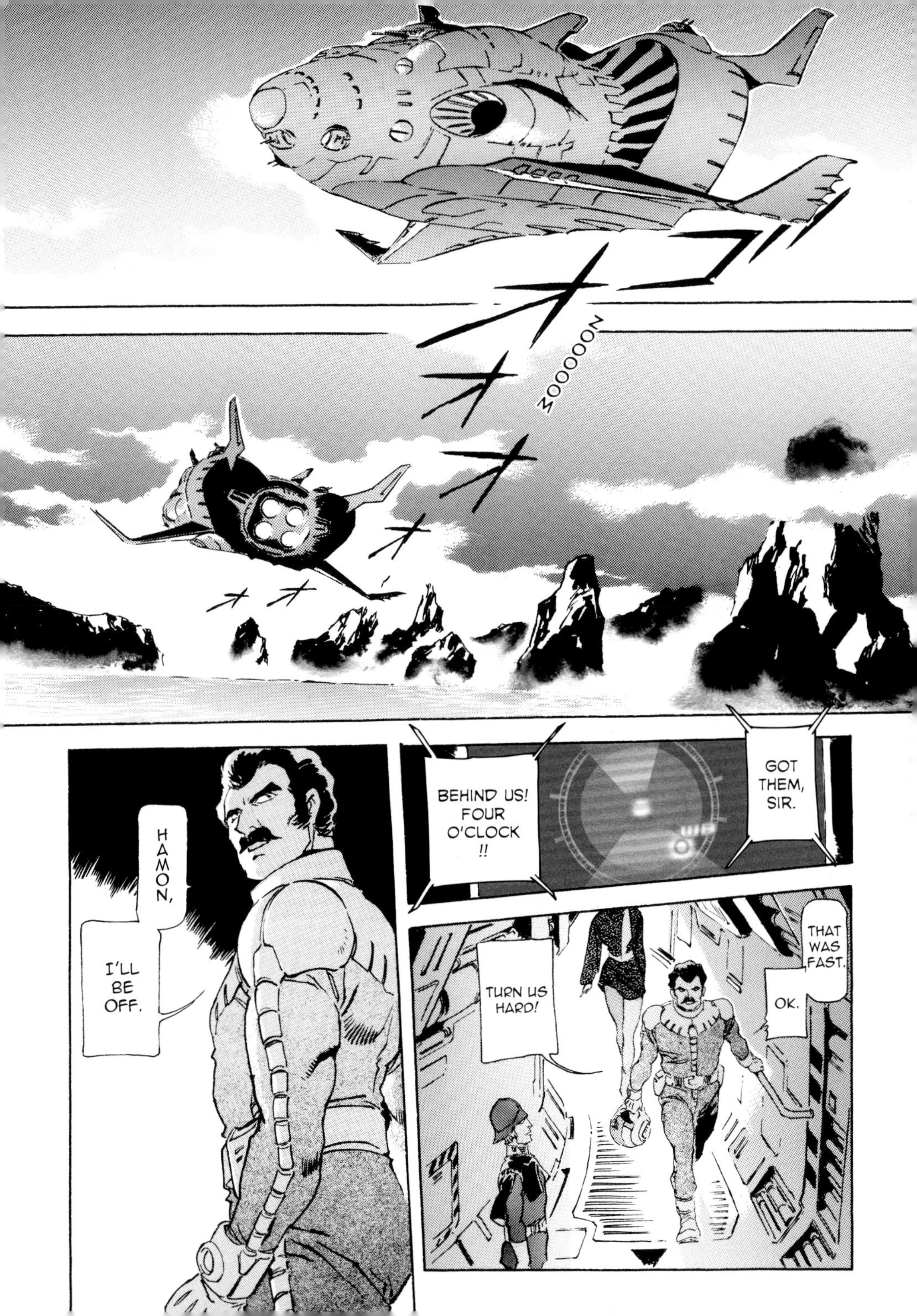
ZOOOOOM
GOT THEM, SIR.
BEHIND US! FOUR O'CLOCK !!
THAT WAS FAST.
OK.
TURN US HARD!
HAMON,
I'LL BE OFF.

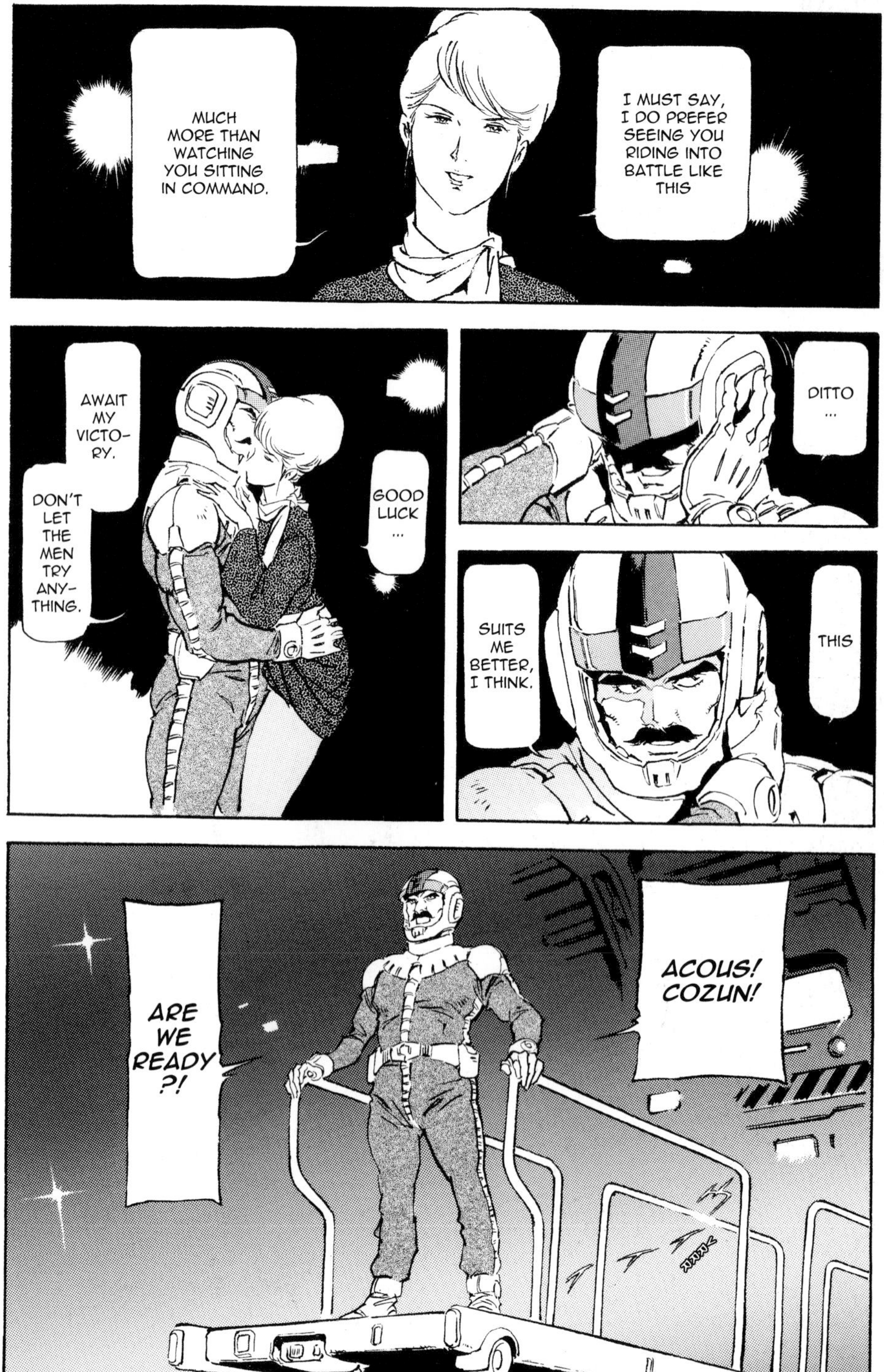

I MUST SAY, I DO PREFER SEEING YOU RIDING INTO BATTLE LIKE THIS
MUCH MORE THAN WATCHING YOU SITTING IN COMMAND.
DITTO ...
THIS
SUITS ME BETTER, I THINK.
GOOD LUCK ...
AWAIT MY VICTO-RY.
DON'T LET THE MEN TRY ANY-THING.
ACOUS! COZUN!
ARE WE READY?!

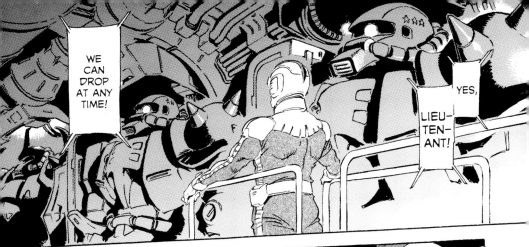

YES, LIEUTENANT!
WE CAN DROP AT ANY TIME!
VRR
HM.
OK.
CLAMP!
RECORD THE BATTLE DATA!

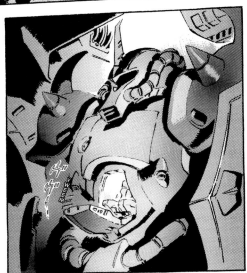

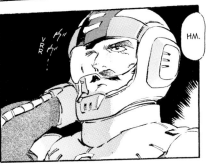

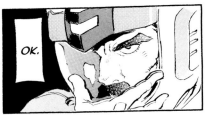

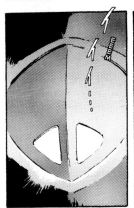

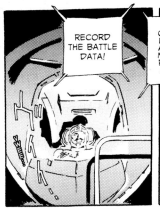

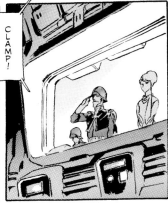

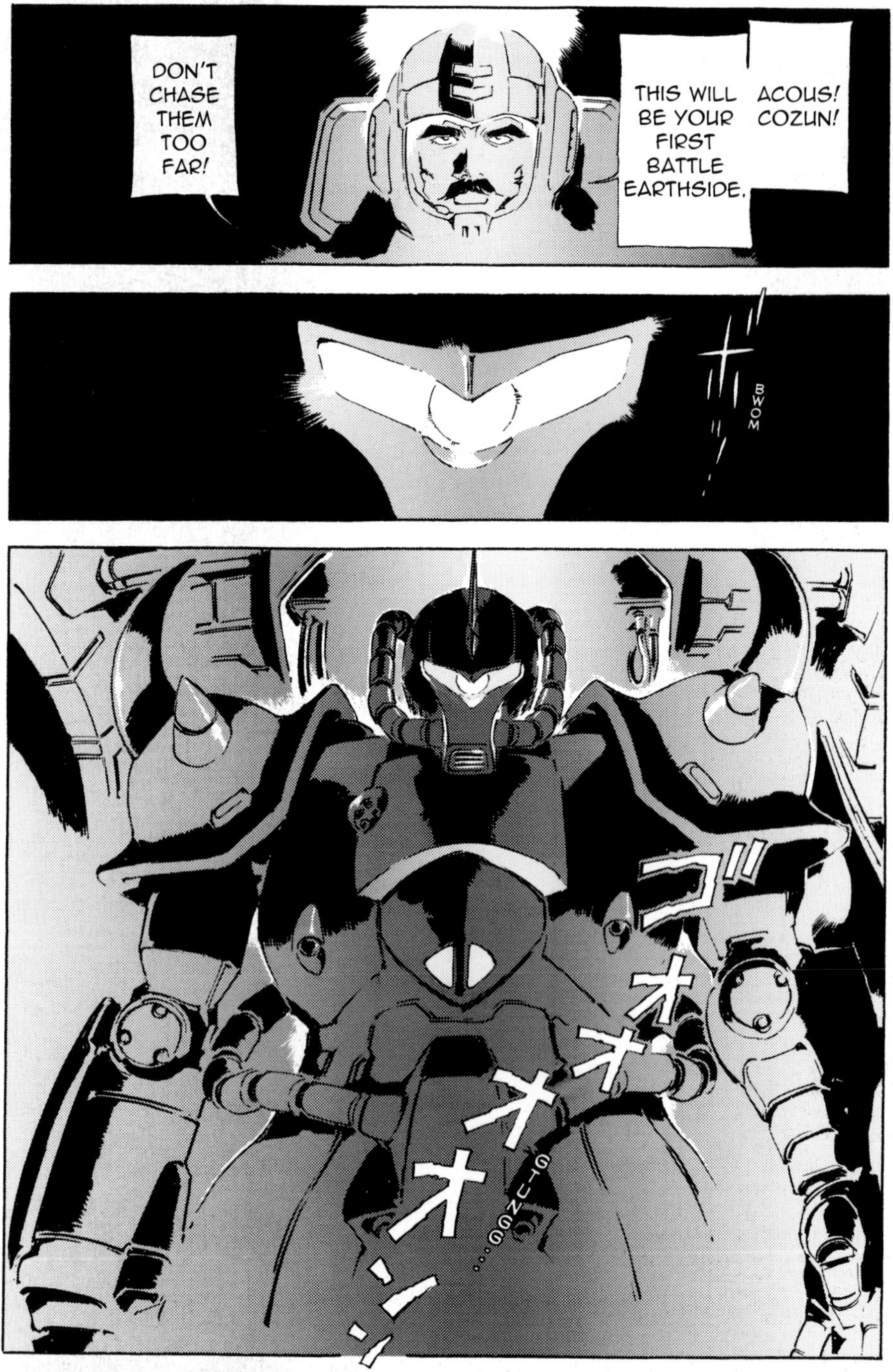
ACOUS! COZUN!
THIS WILL BE YOUR FIRST BATTLE EARTHSIDE.
DON'T CHASE THEM TOO FAR!
BWOM
ゴオオオオン
GTUNGG...

SECTION
II

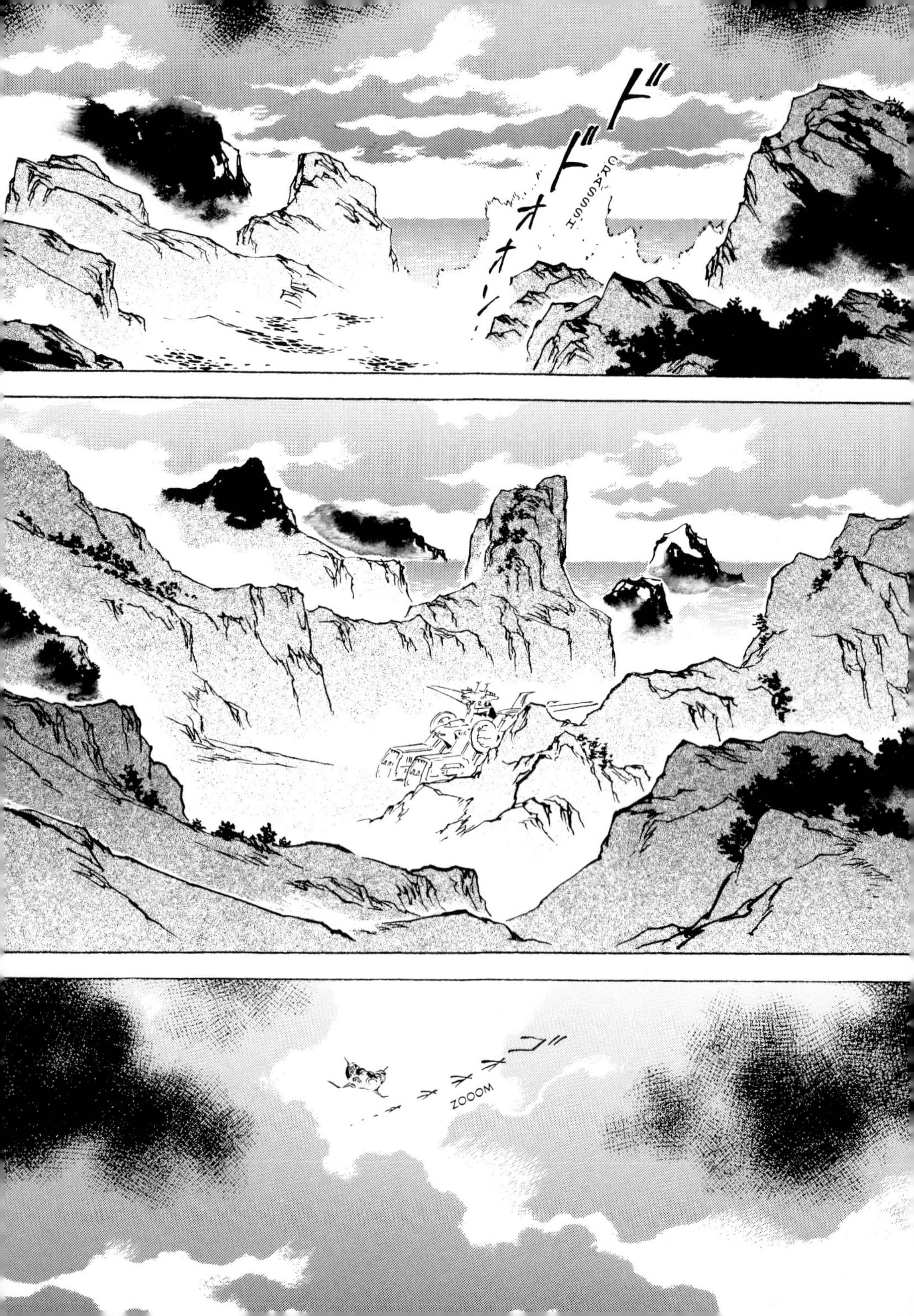
ドドオオン
CRASSSH
ゴオオオオ
ZOOOM

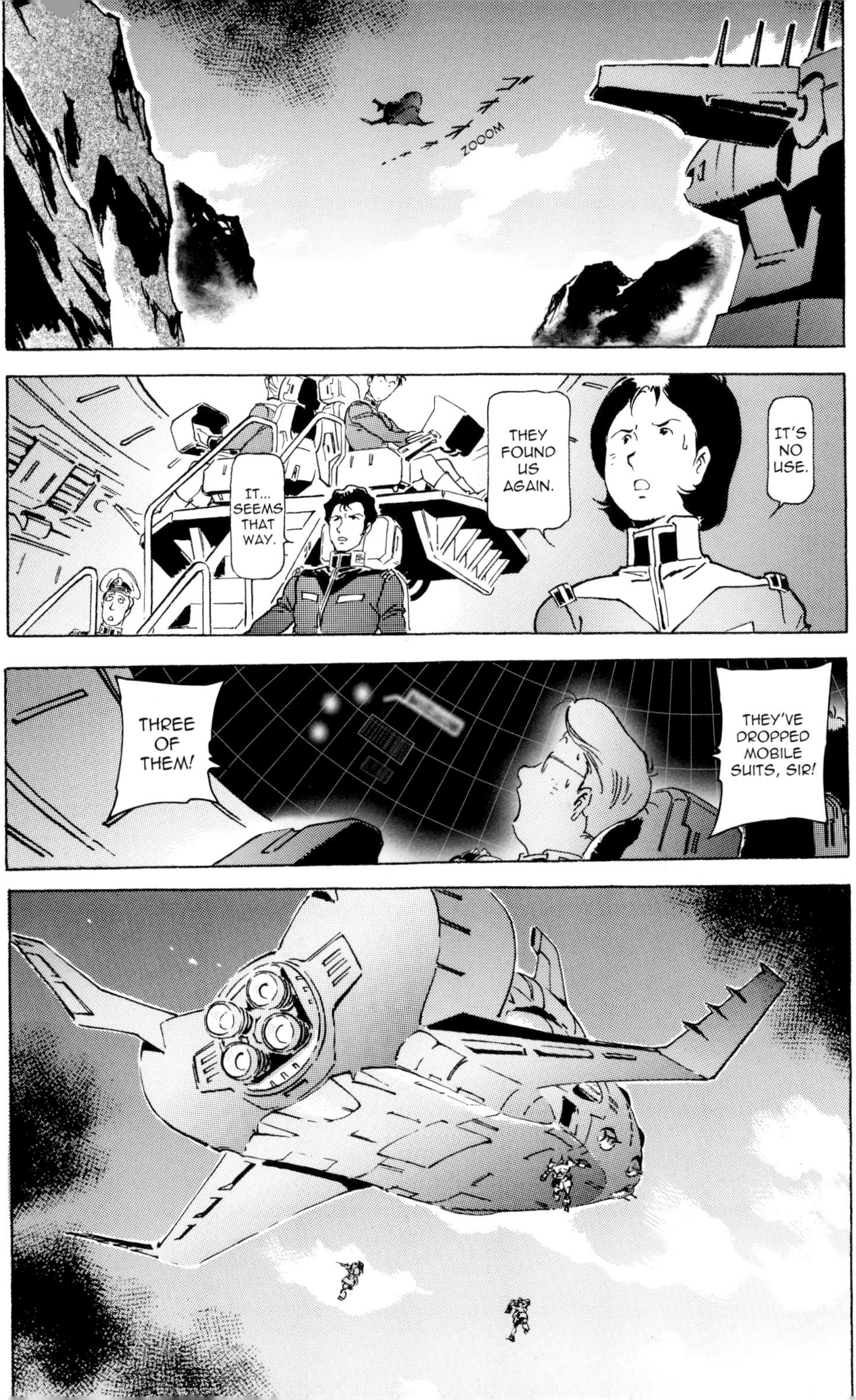
ZOOOM
IT'S NO USE.
THEY FOUND US AGAIN.
IT... SEEMS THAT WAY.
THEY'VE DROPPED MOBILE SUITS, SIR!
THREE OF THEM!

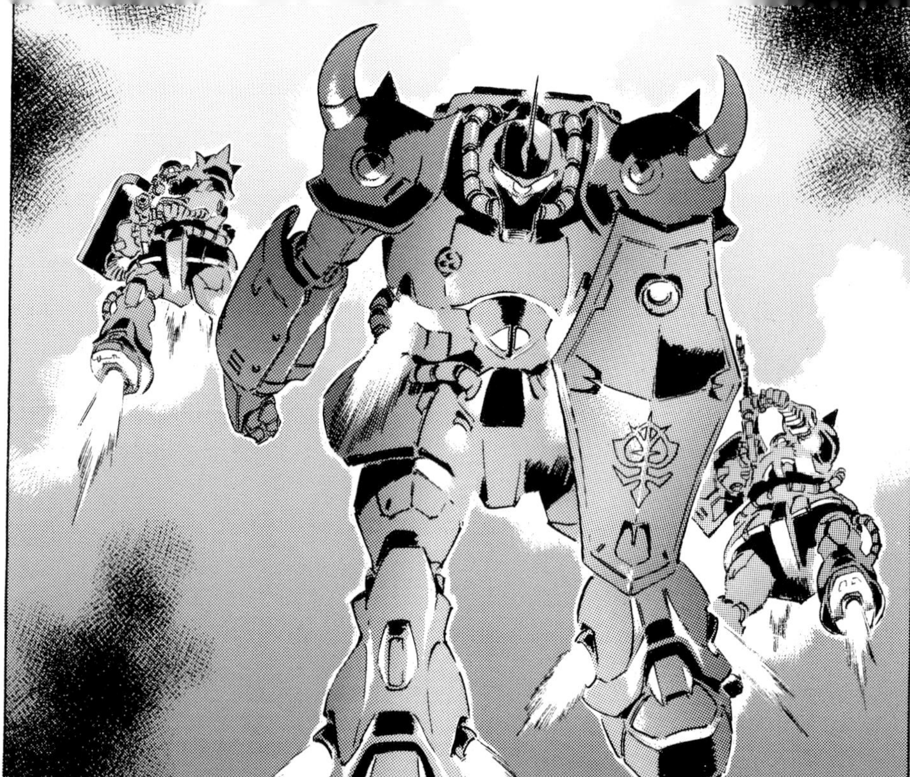
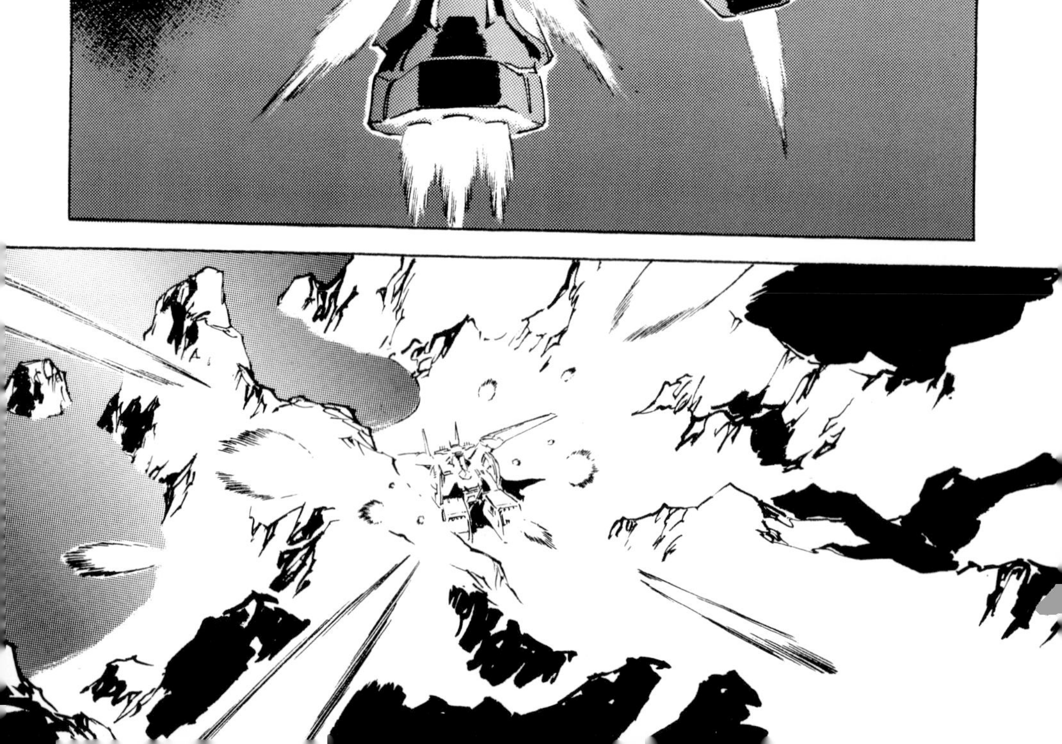

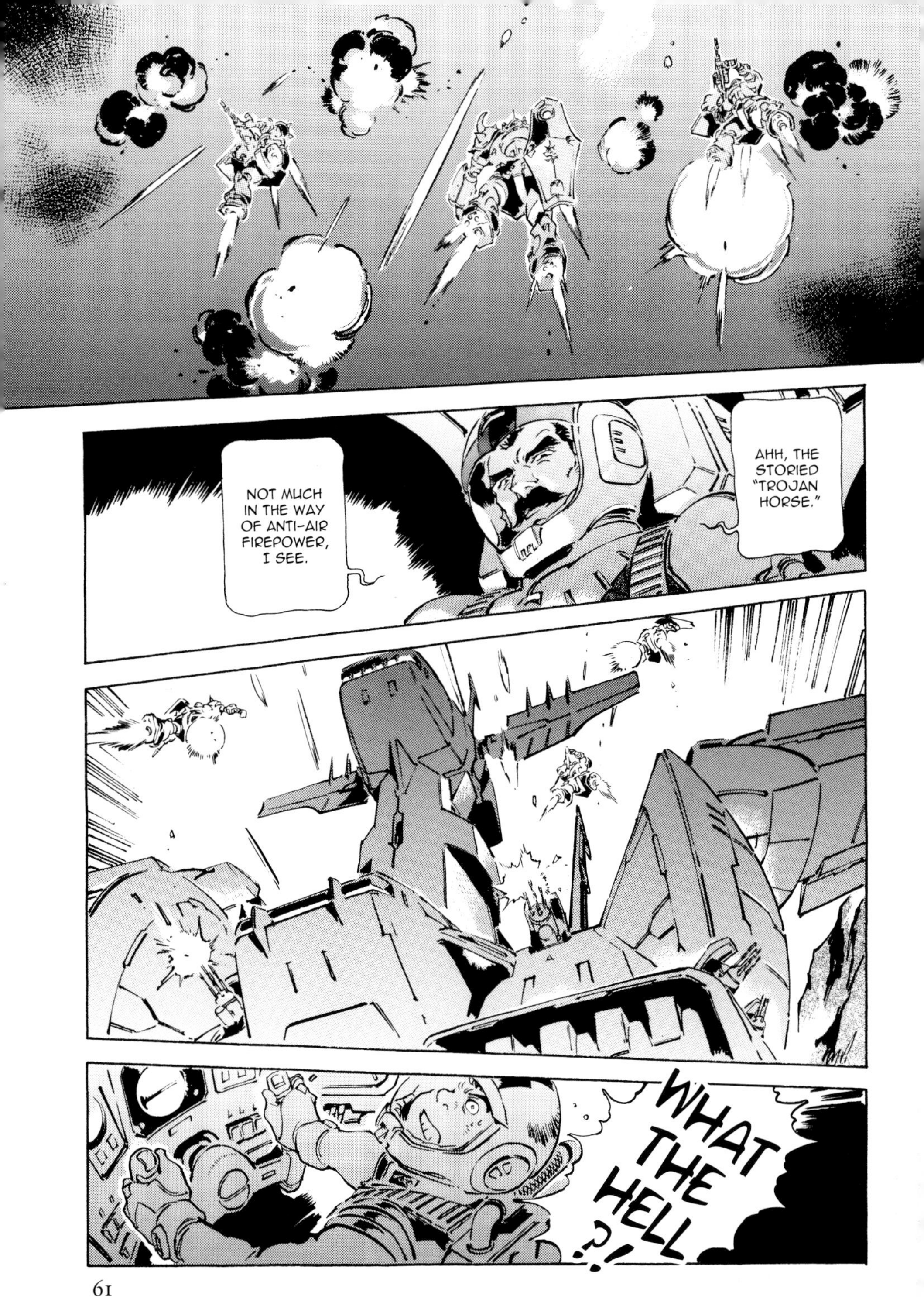
AHH, THE STORIED "TROJAN HORSE."
NOT MUCH IN THE WAY OF ANTI-AIR FIREPOWER, I SEE.
WHAT THE HELL?!

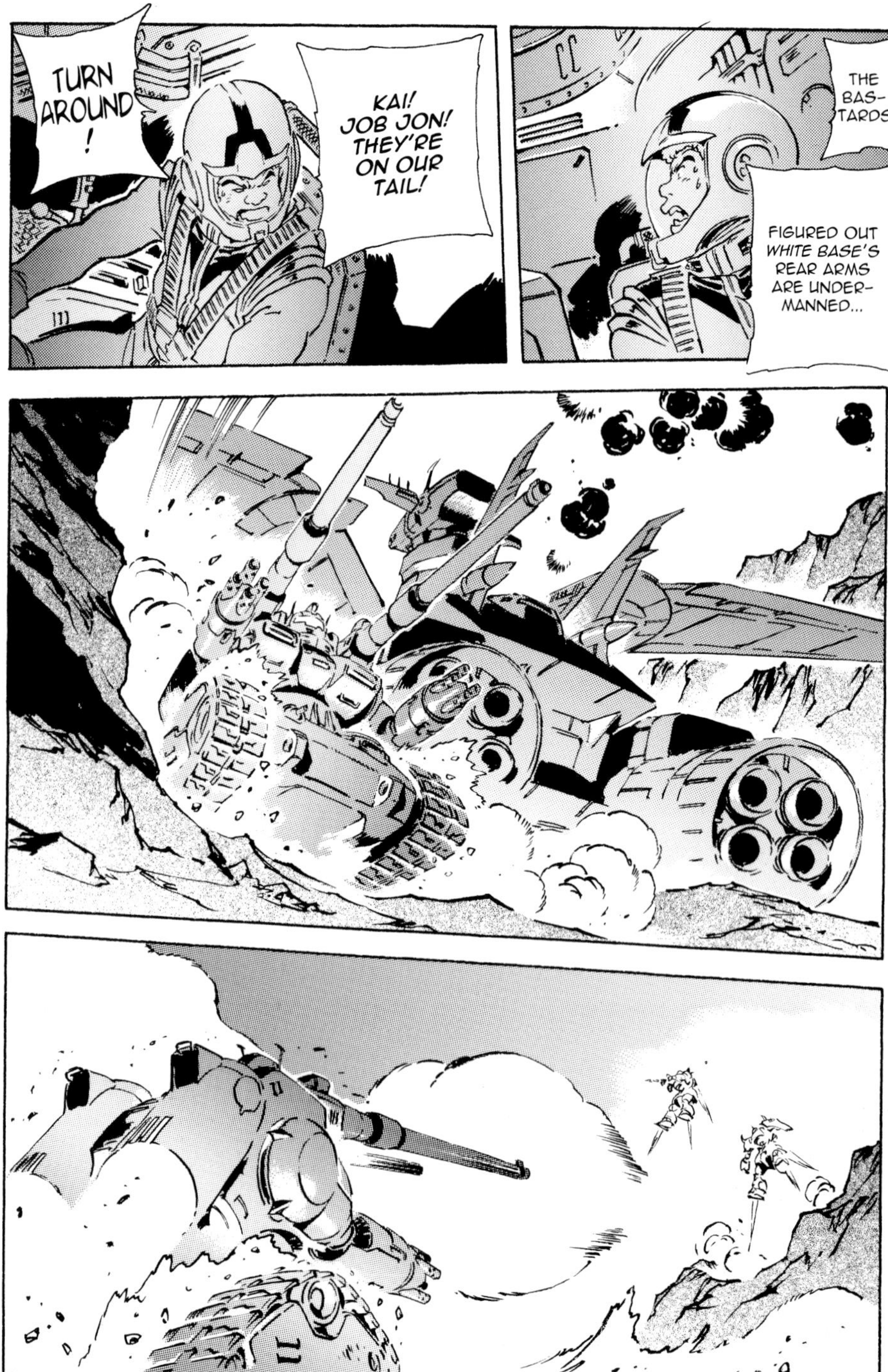
THE BAS-TARDS
FIGURED OUT WHITE BASE'S REAR ARMS ARE UNDER-MANNED...
KAI! JOB JON! THEY'RE ON OUR TAIL!
TURN AROUND!

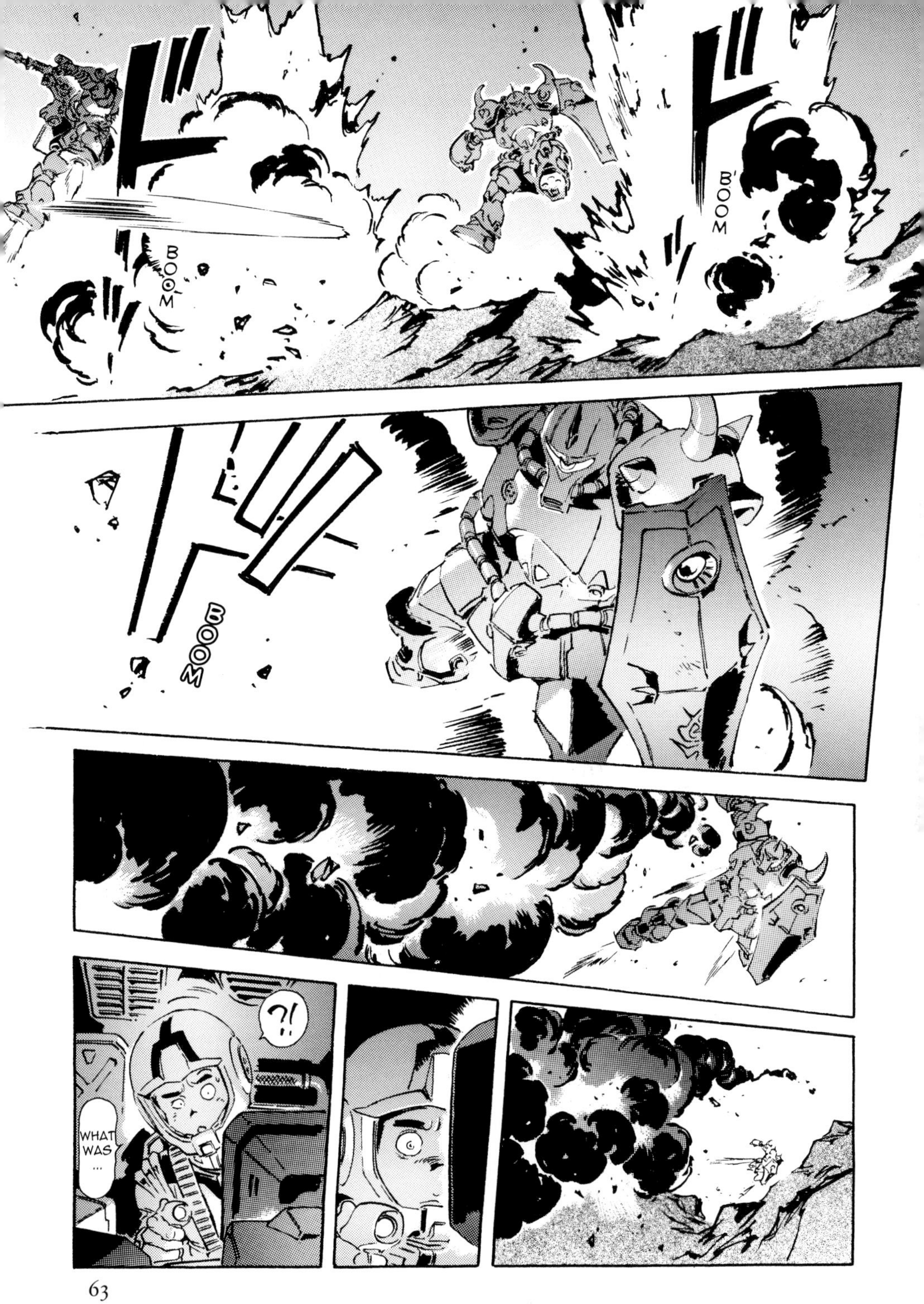

ドド
BOOM
ドド
BOOM
ド
BOOM
?!
WHAT WAS ...

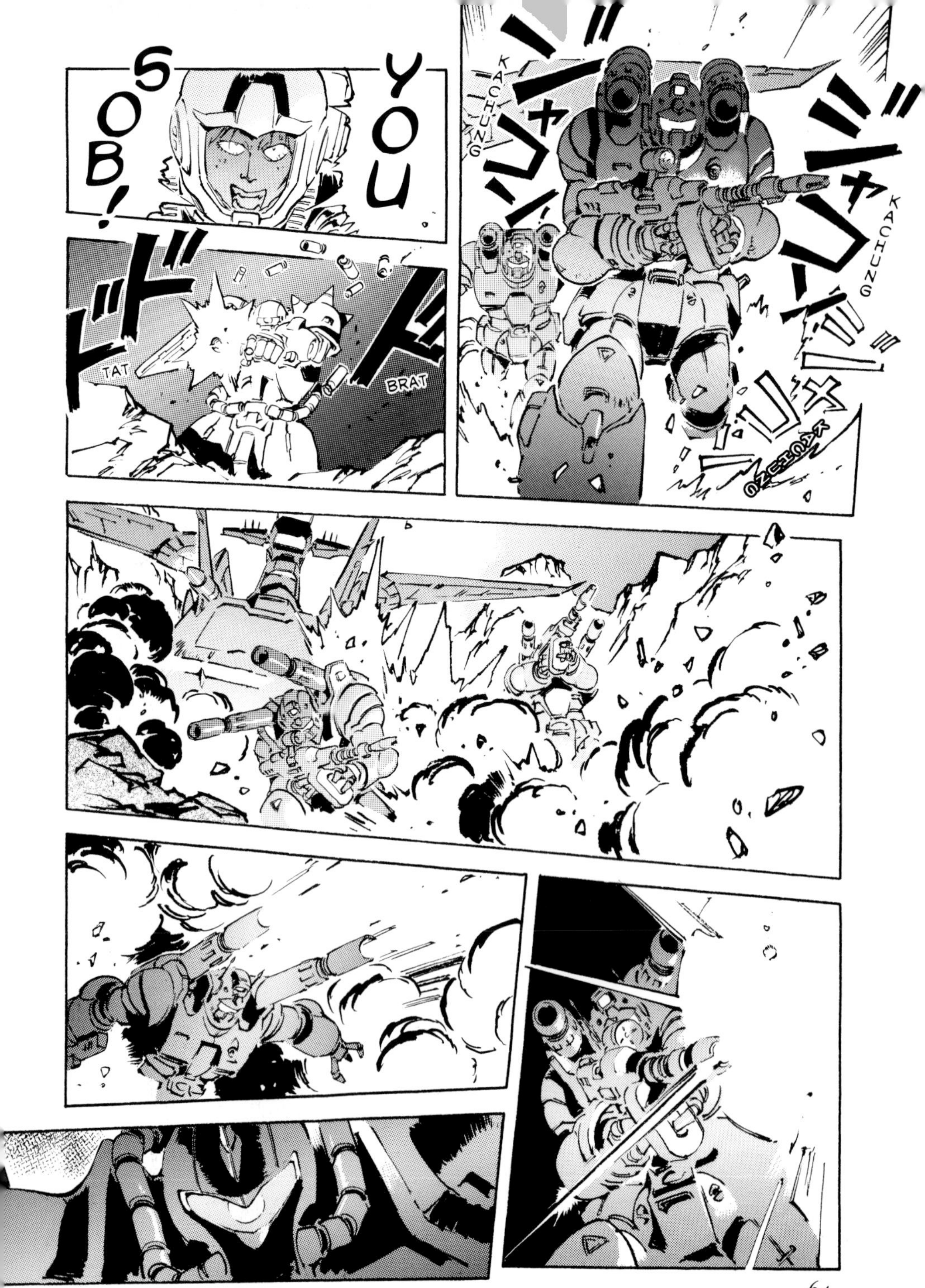
KACHUNG
KACHUNG
YOU SOB!
TAT
BRAT

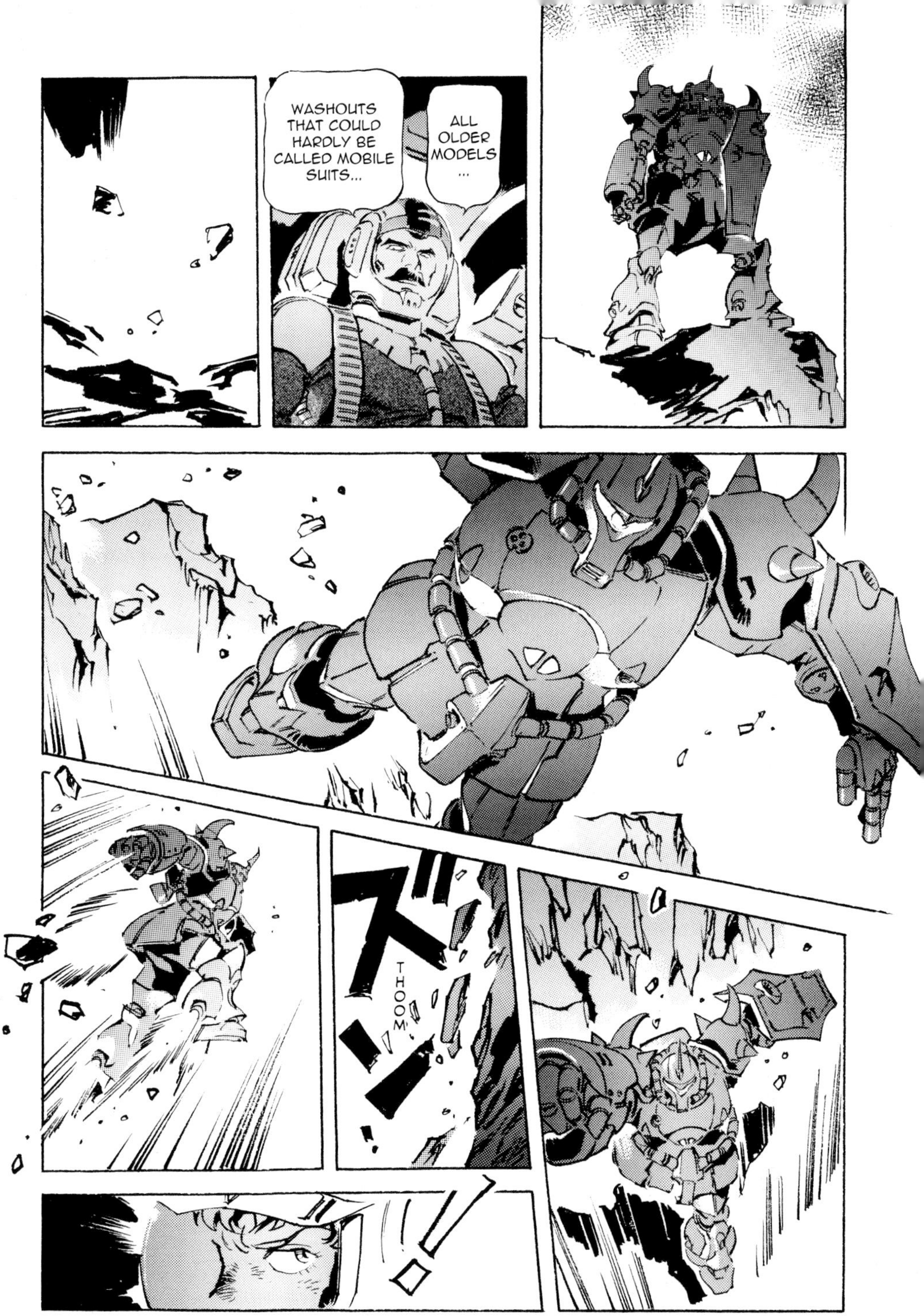
ALL OLDER MODELS ...
WASHOUTS THAT COULD HARDLY BE CALLED MOBILE SUITS...
THOOM

THOOM!!

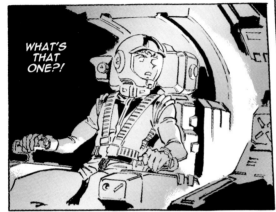

WHAT'S THAT ONE?!

X75-02

ZAKU?

A HIGH-MOBILITY...

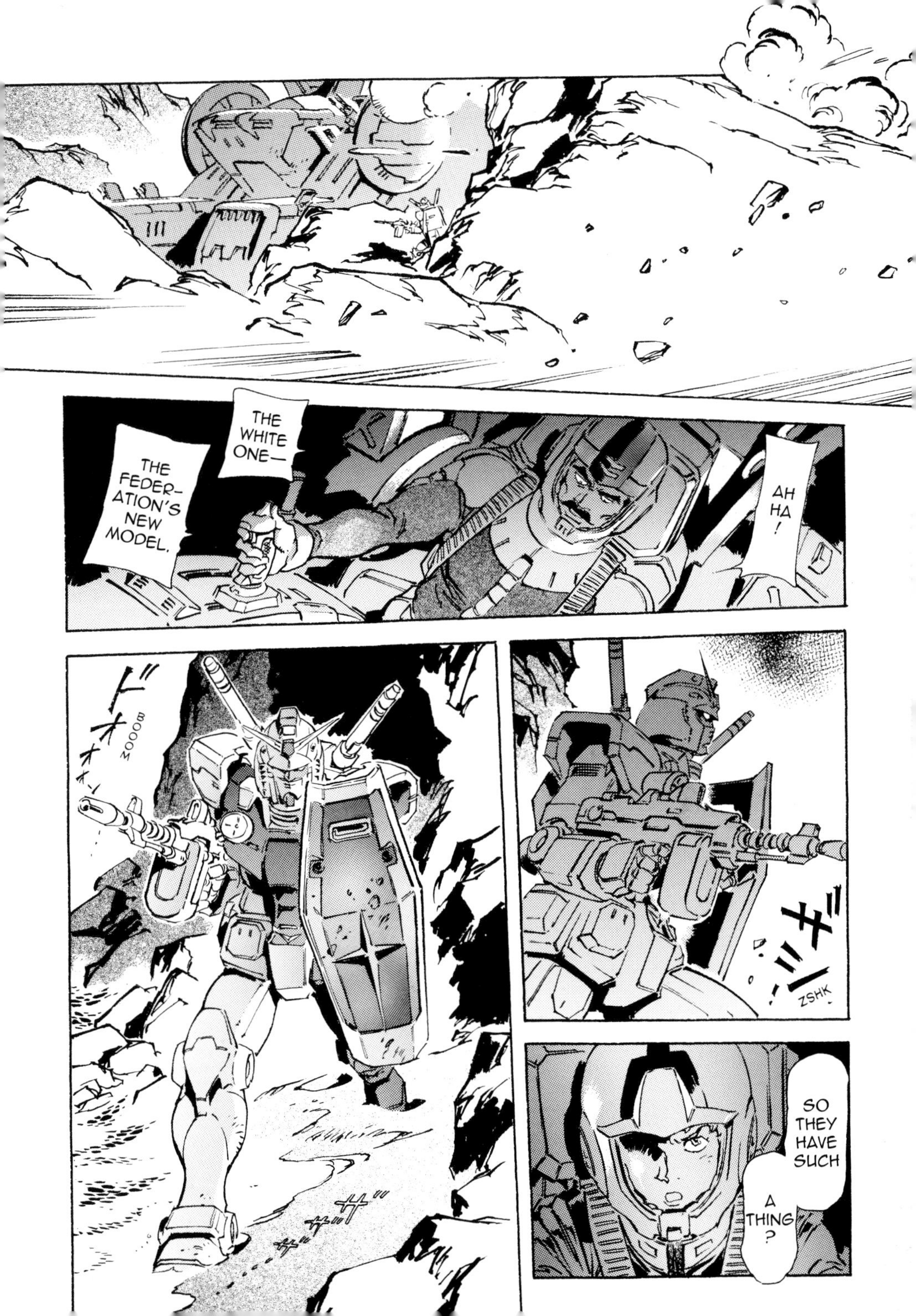

AH HA!
THE WHITE ONE—
THE FEDERATION'S NEW MODEL.
ZSHK
SO THEY HAVE SUCH A THING?
BOOOM

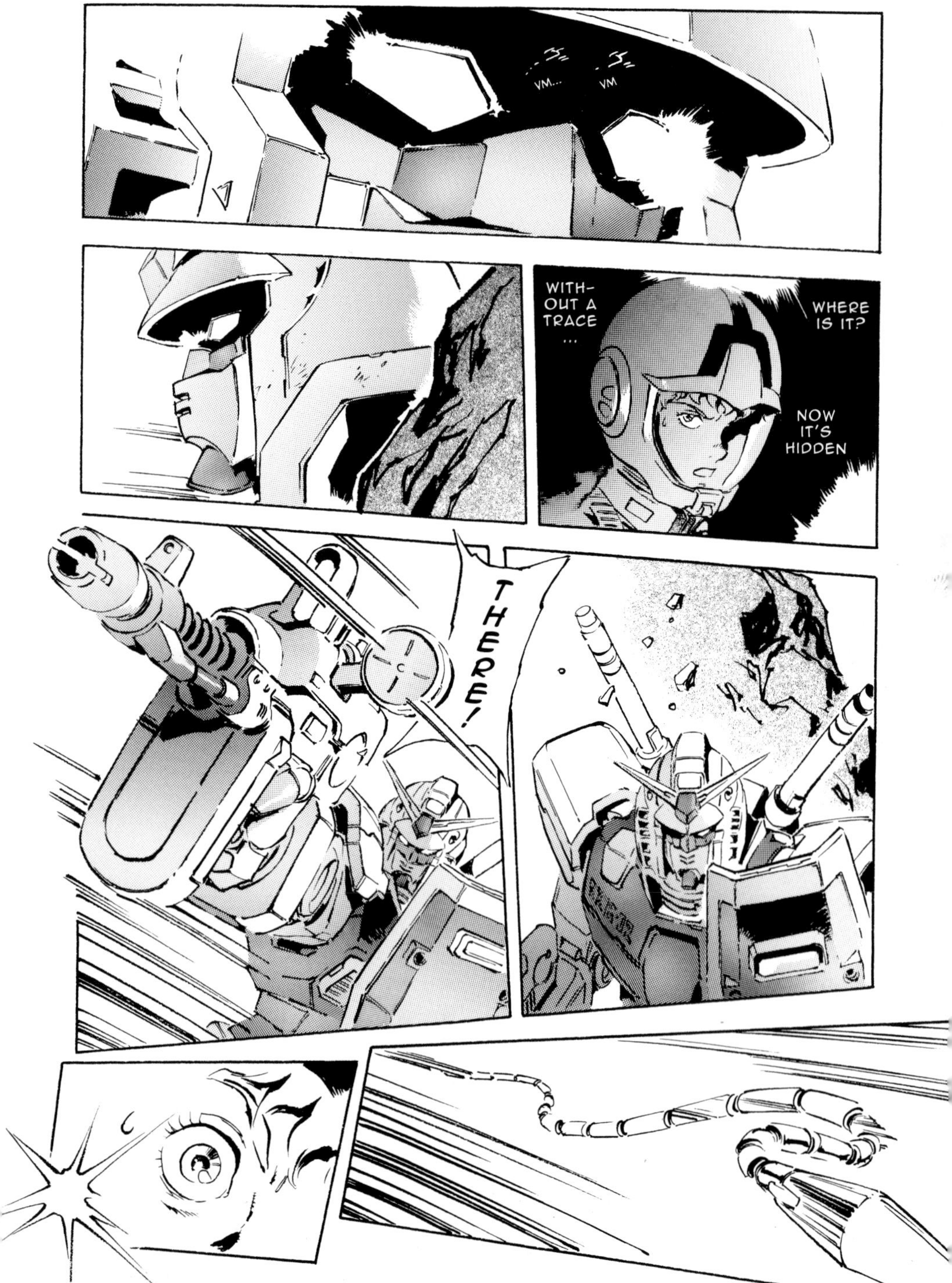
VM... VM
WHERE IS IT?
NOW IT'S HIDDEN
WITH-OUT A TRACE ...
THERE!

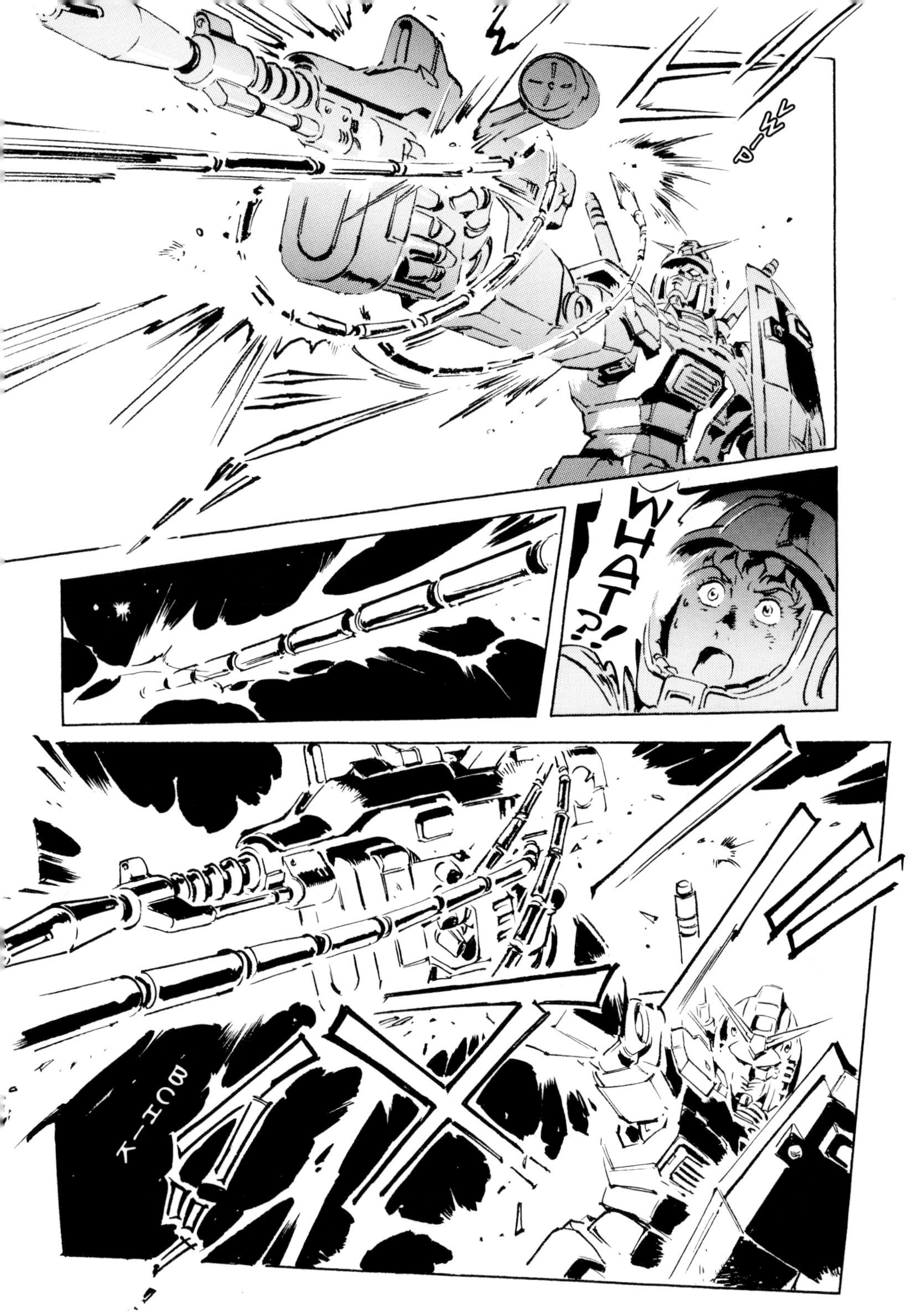
WHAT?!

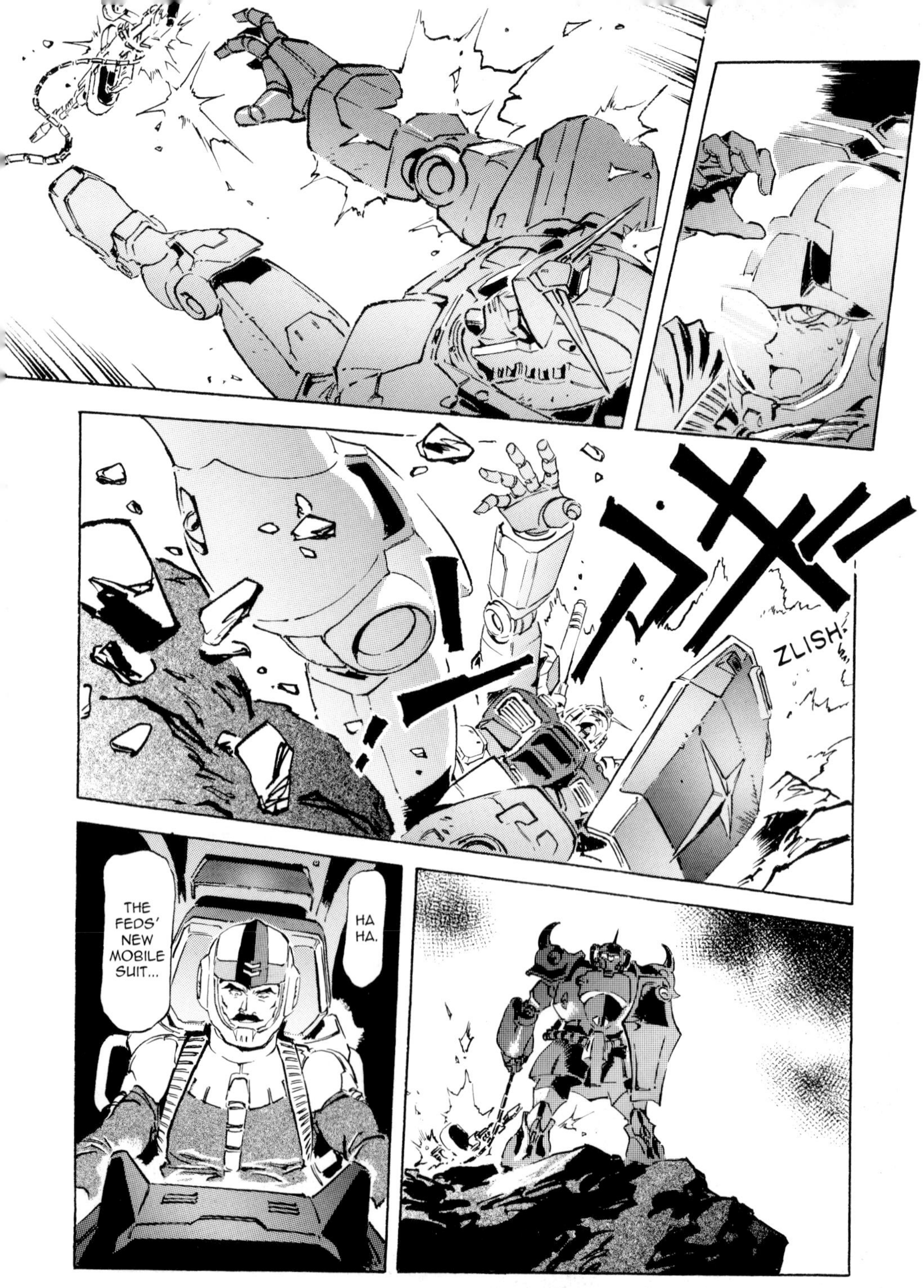
ZLISH
HA HA.
THE FEDS' NEW MOBILE SUIT...

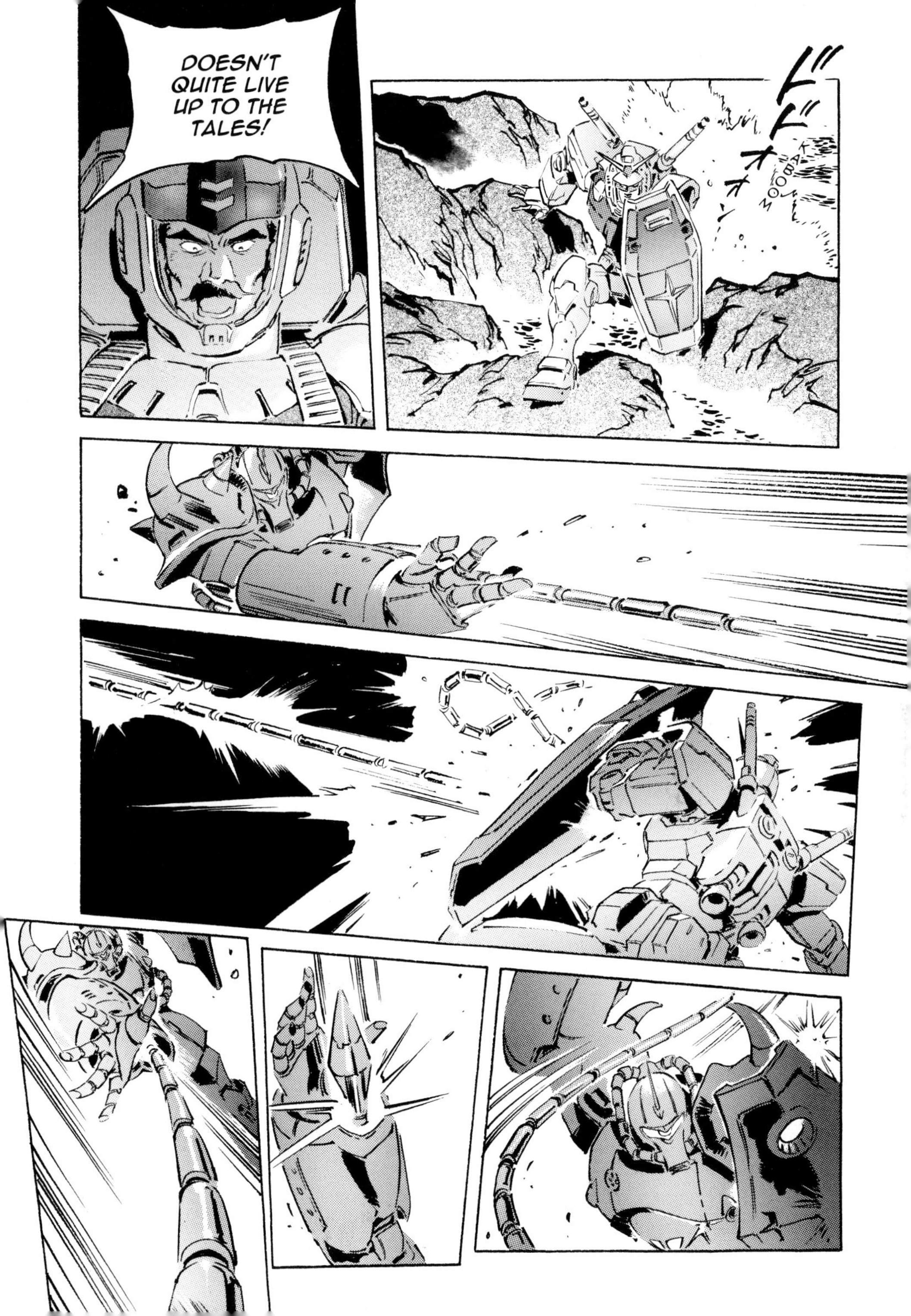
KABOOM
DOESN'T QUITE LIVE UP TO THE TALES!

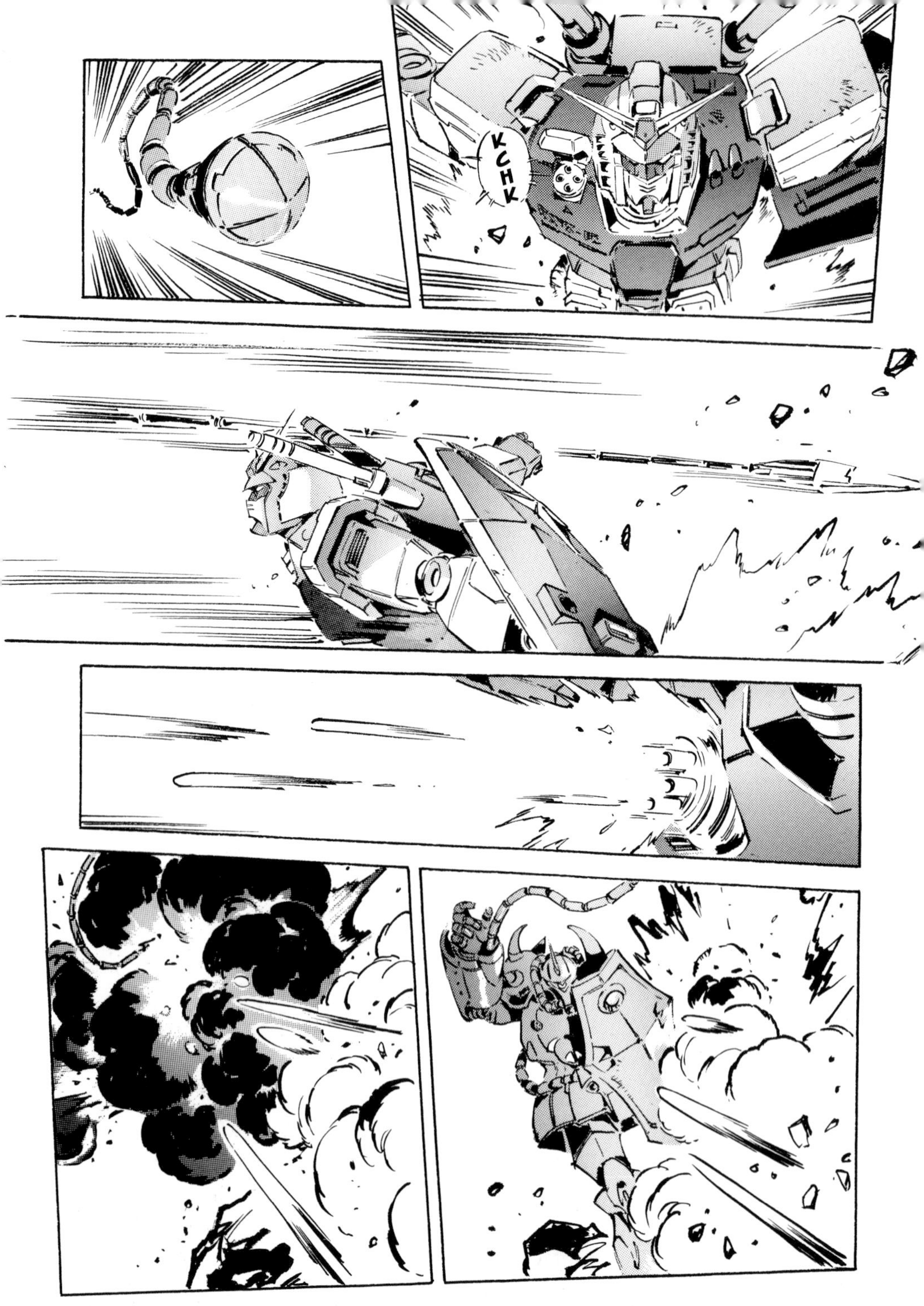
KCHK

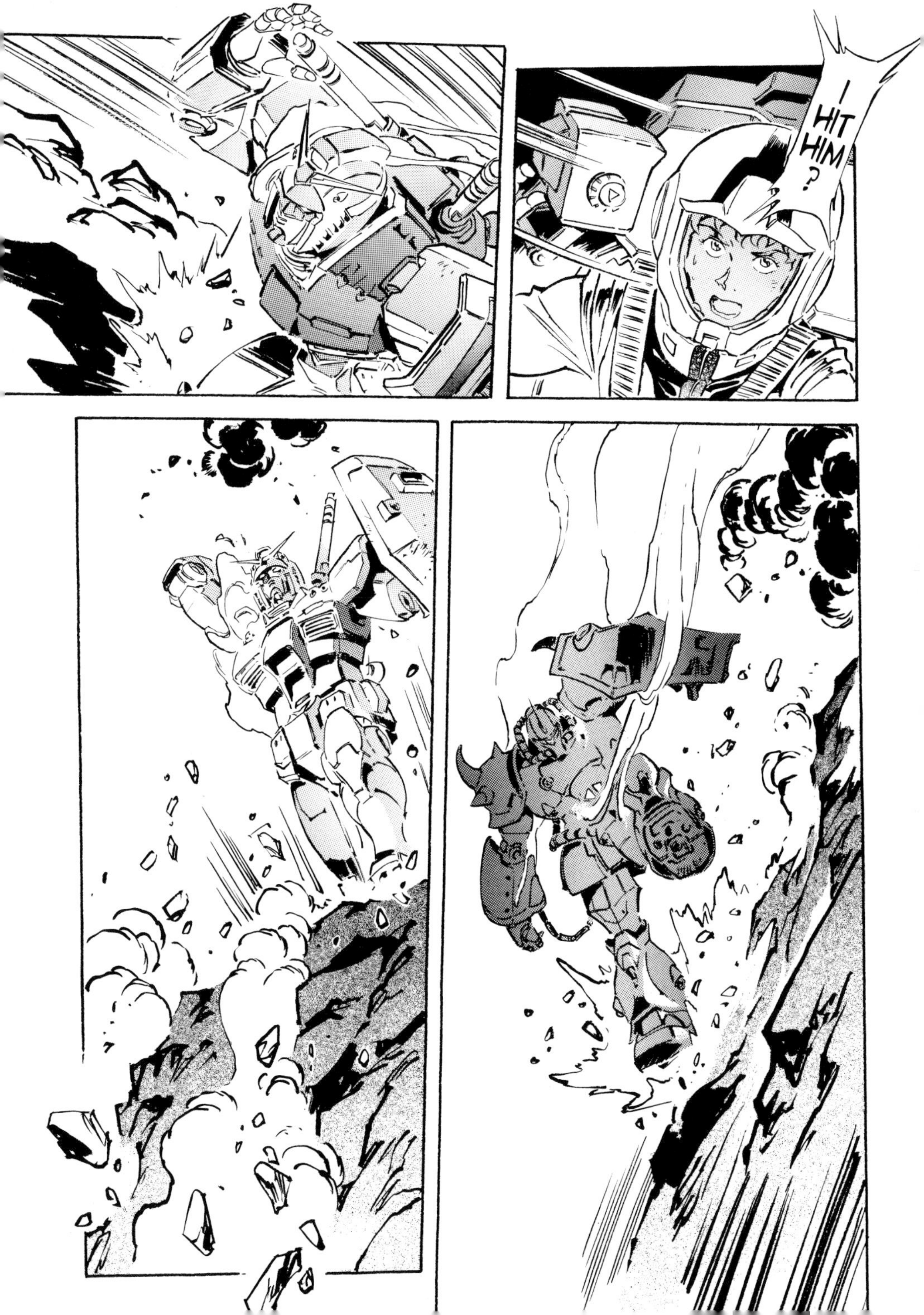
I HIT HIM?

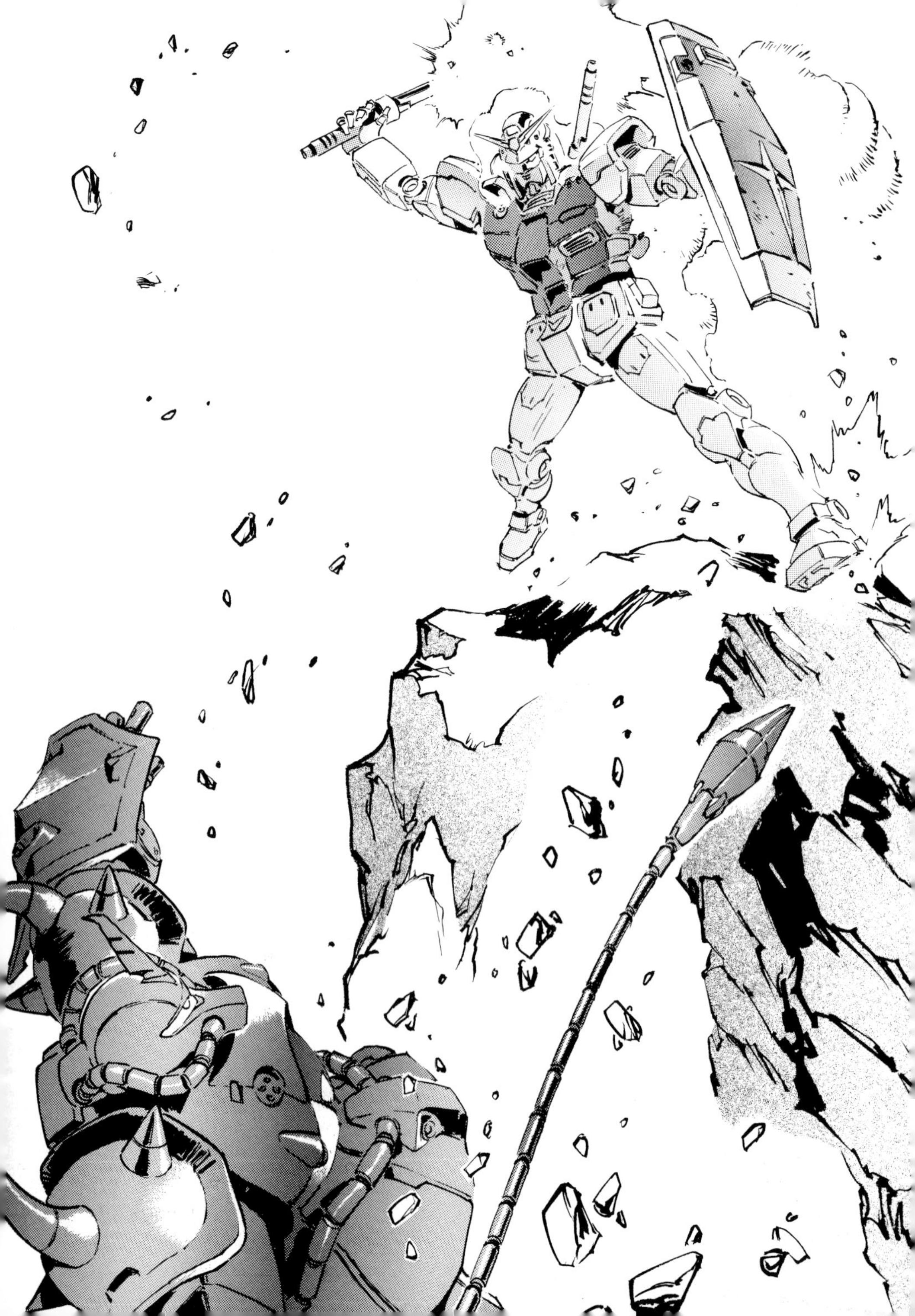

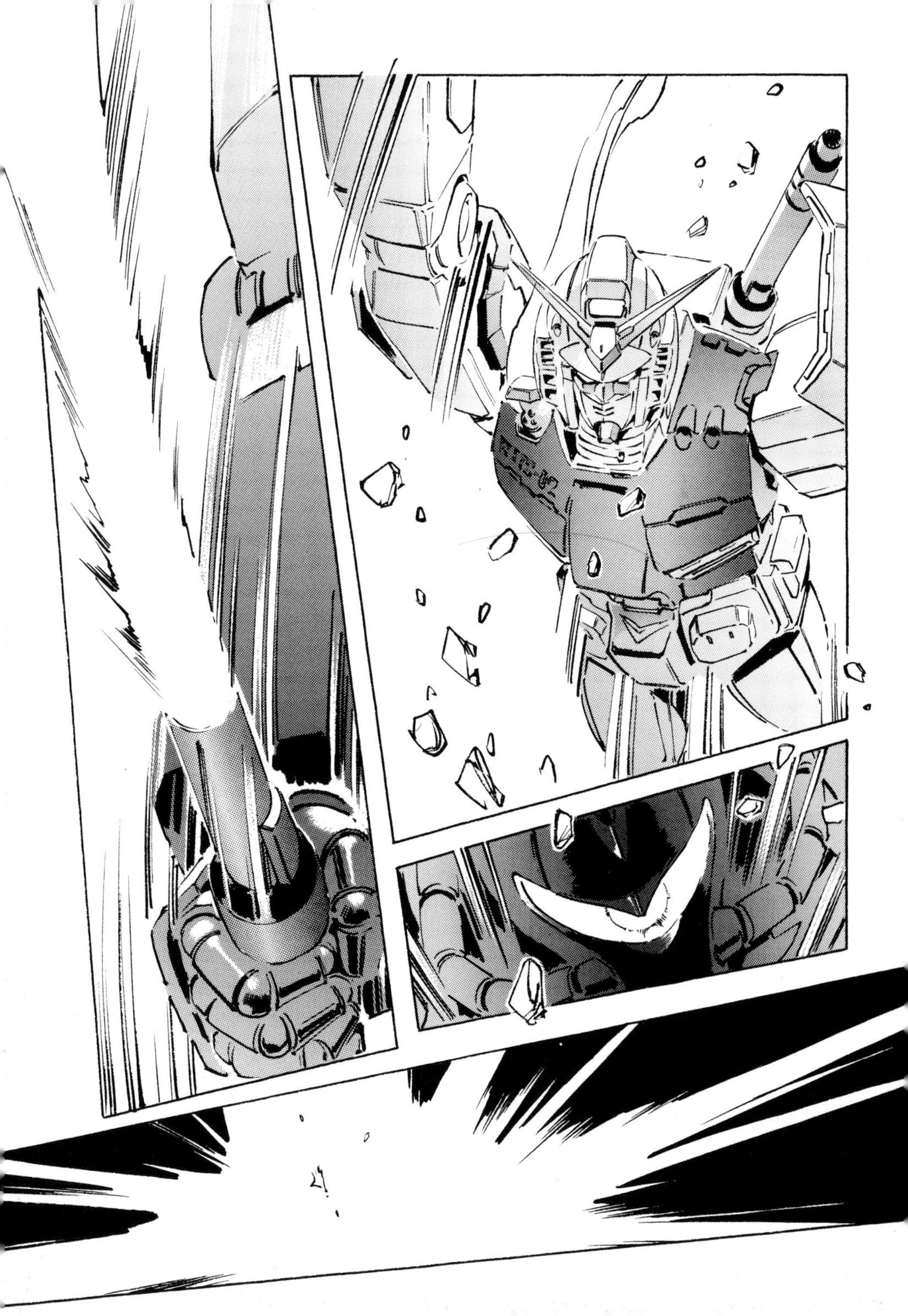

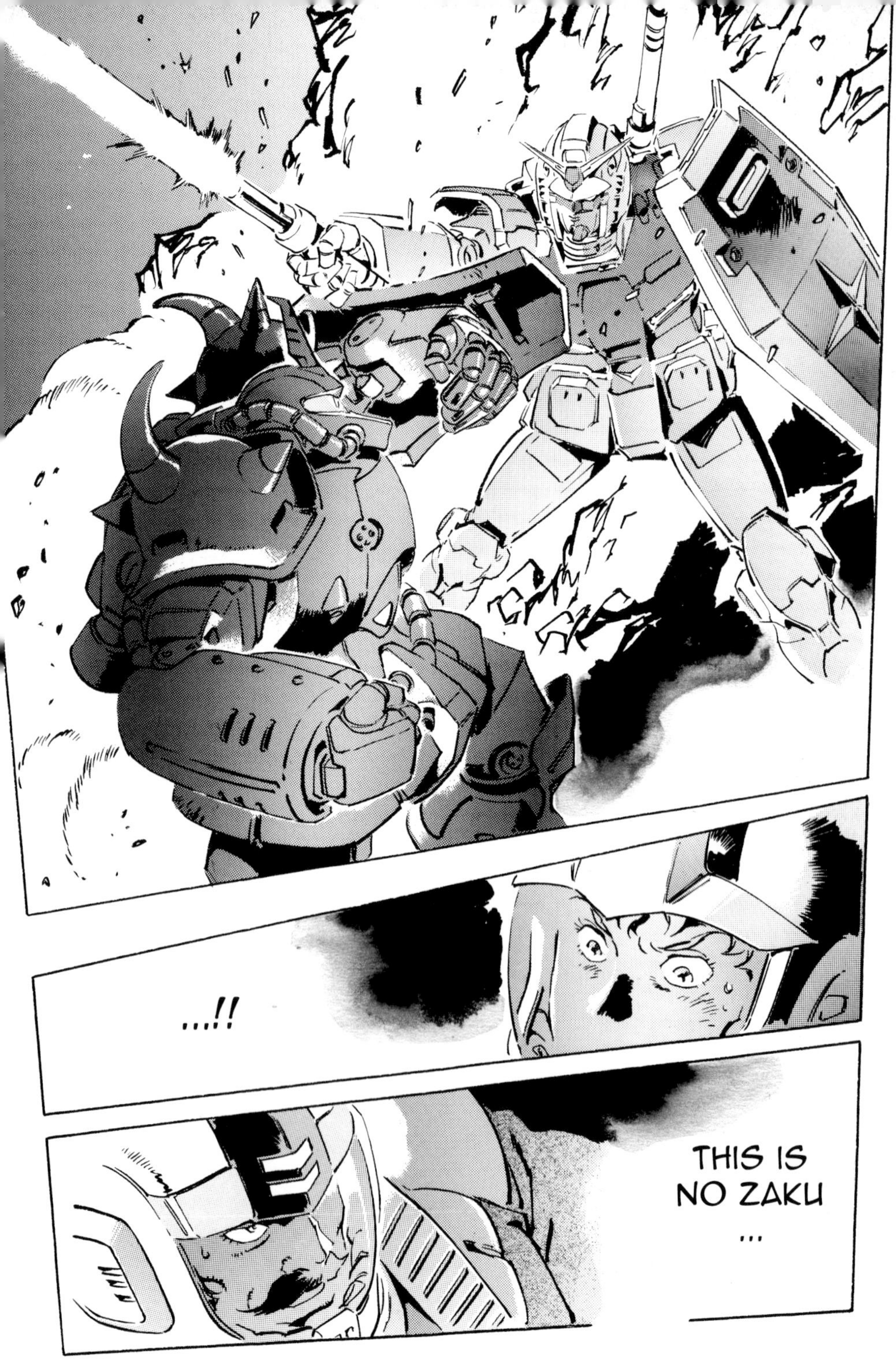
...!!
THIS IS NO ZAKU ...

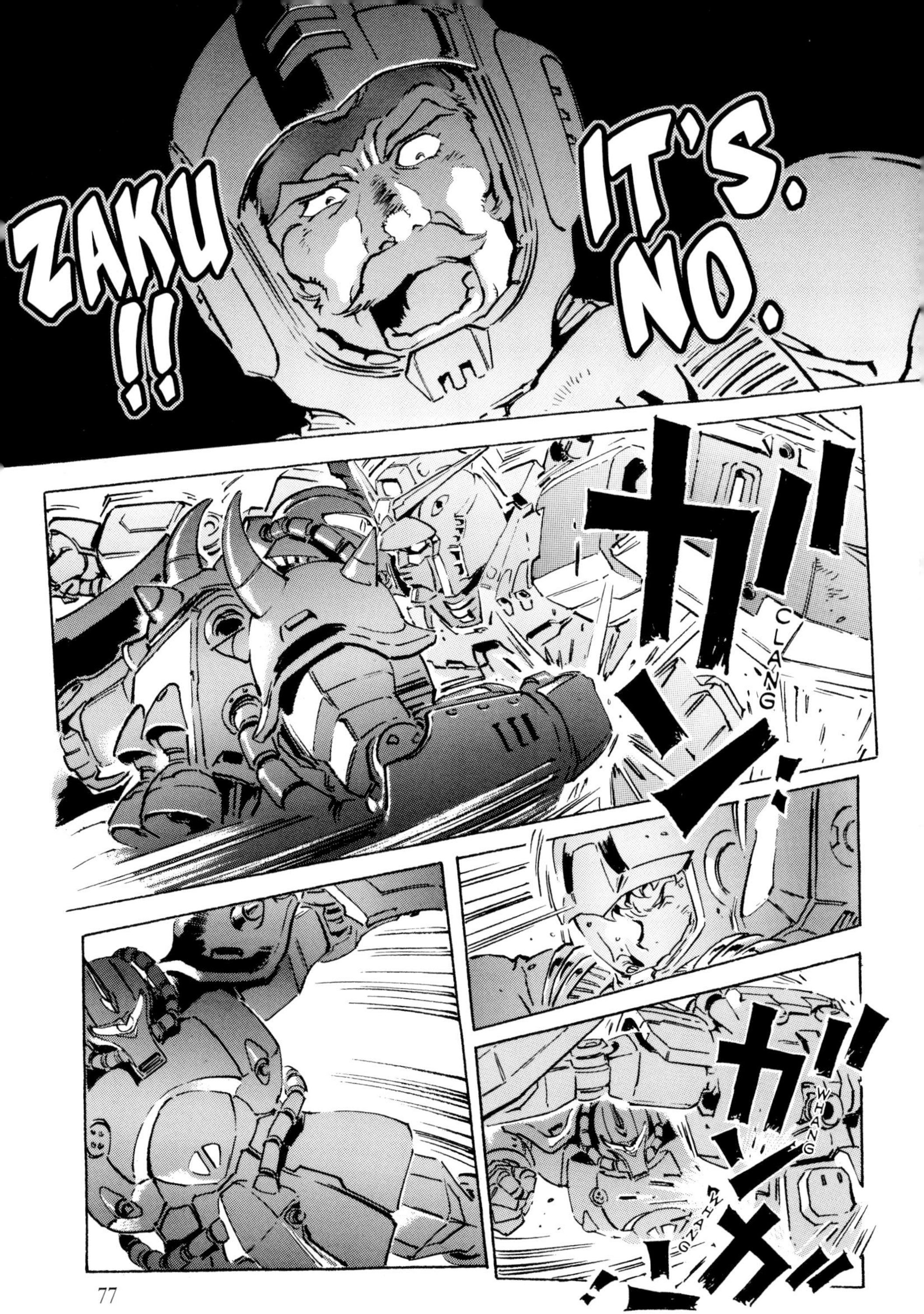
IT'S. NO.
ZAKU!!
CLANG
WHANG
WHANG

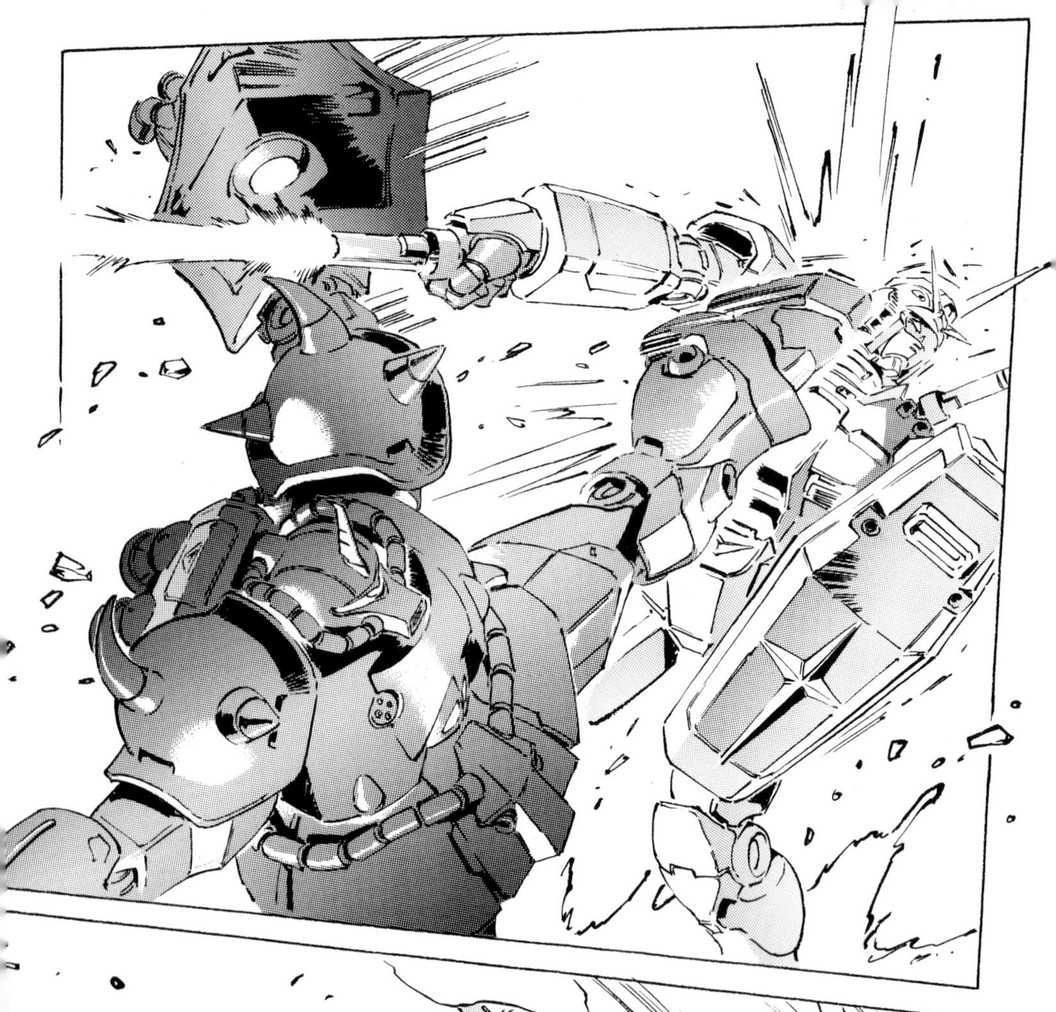
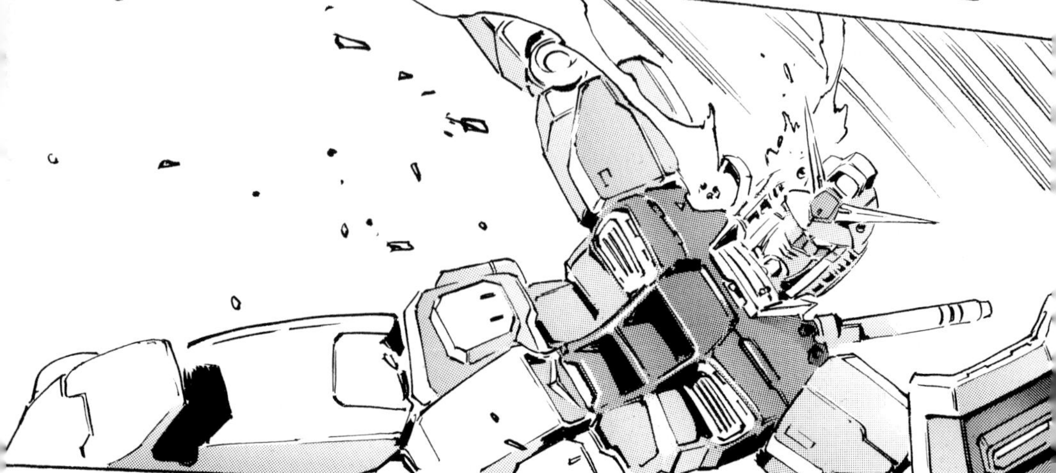

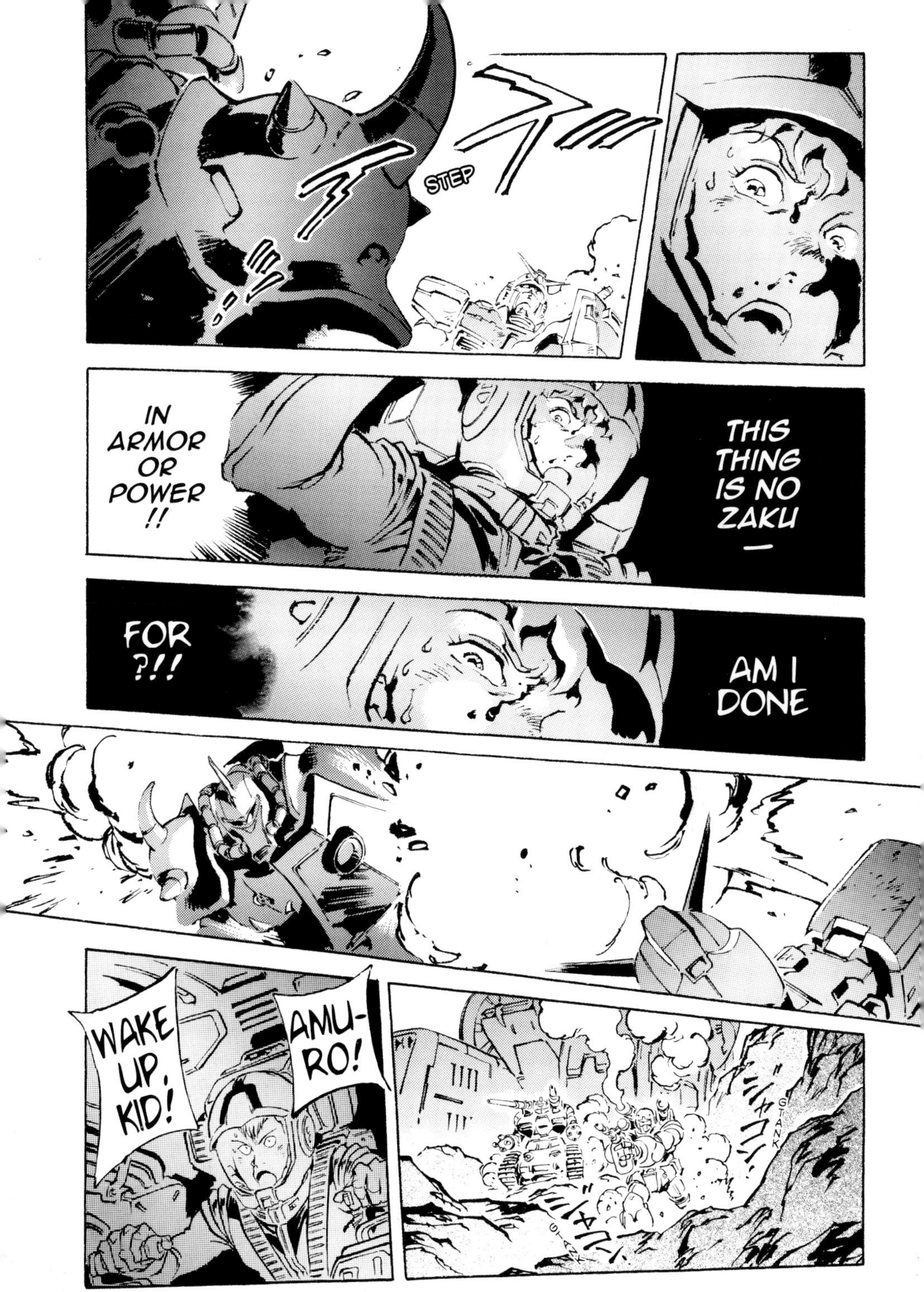
STEP
THIS THING IS NO ZAKU —
IN ARMOR OR POWER !!
AM I DONE
FOR ?!!
GTANK
GTANK
AMU-RO!
WAKE UP, KID!

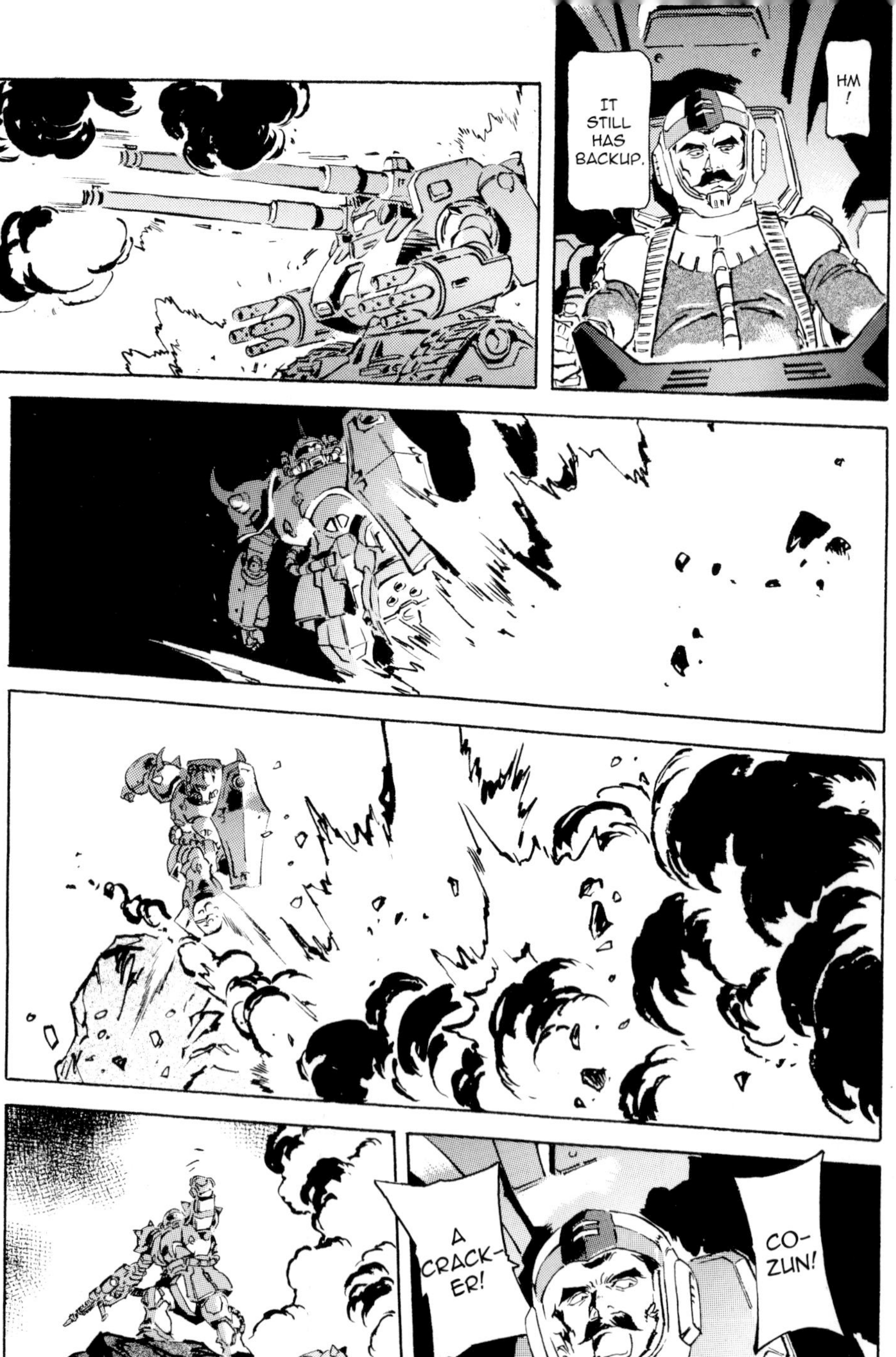
HM!
IT STILL HAS BACKUP.
CO-ZUN!
A CRACKER!

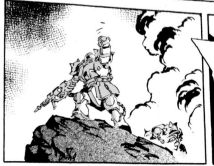

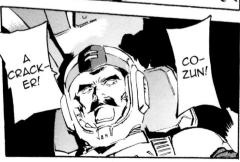

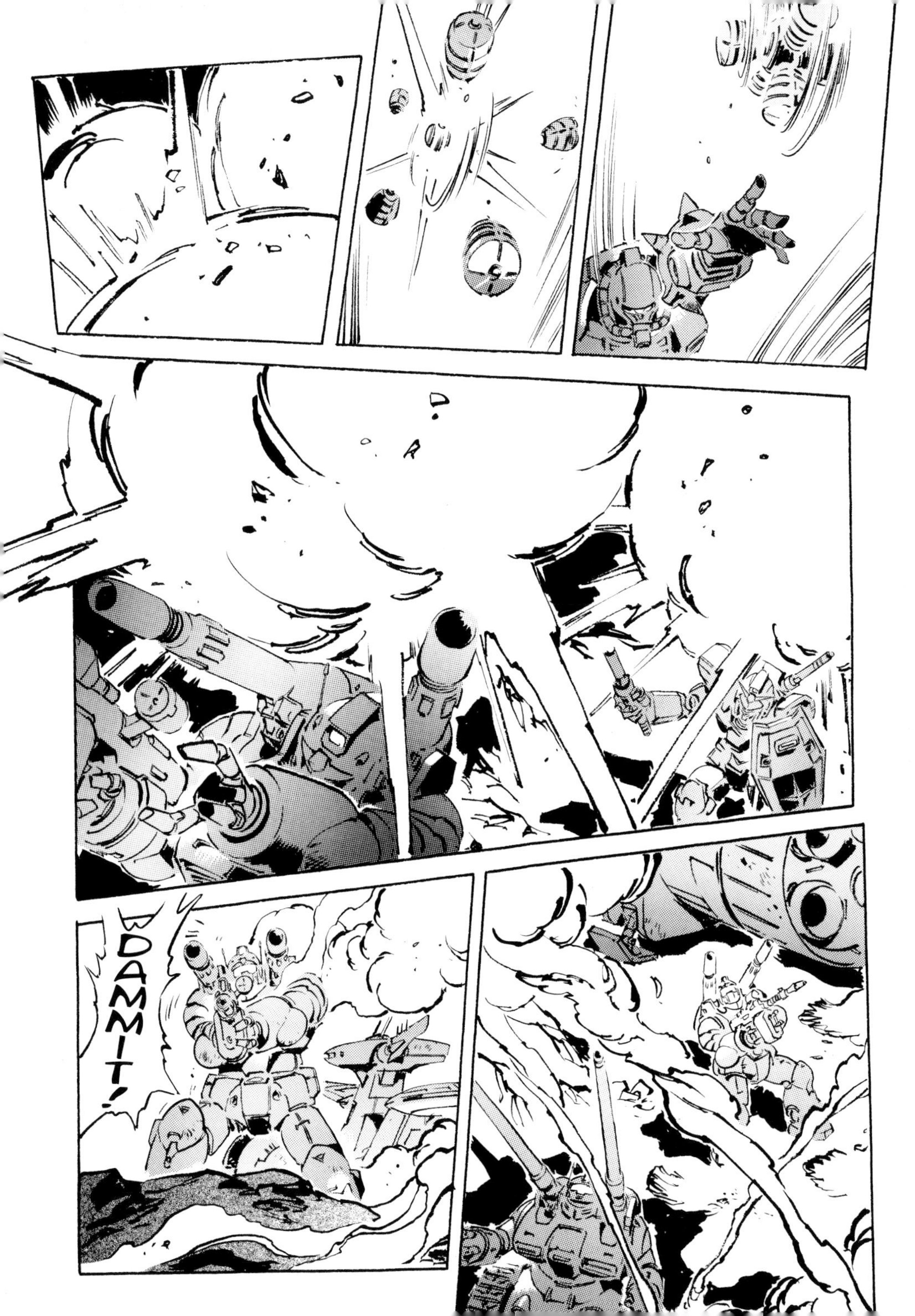
DAMMIT!

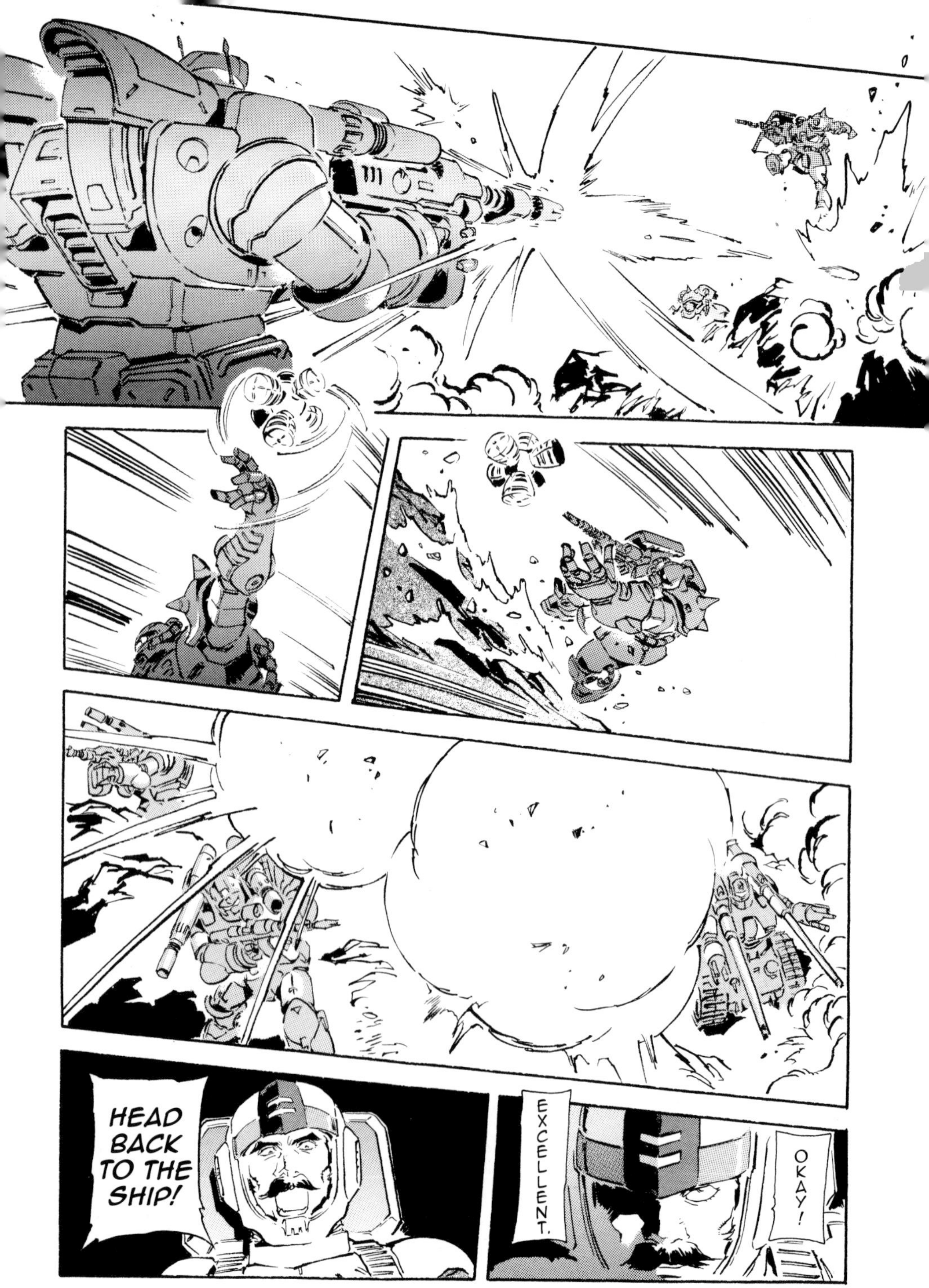
OKAY!
EXCELLENT.
HEAD BACK TO THE SHIP!

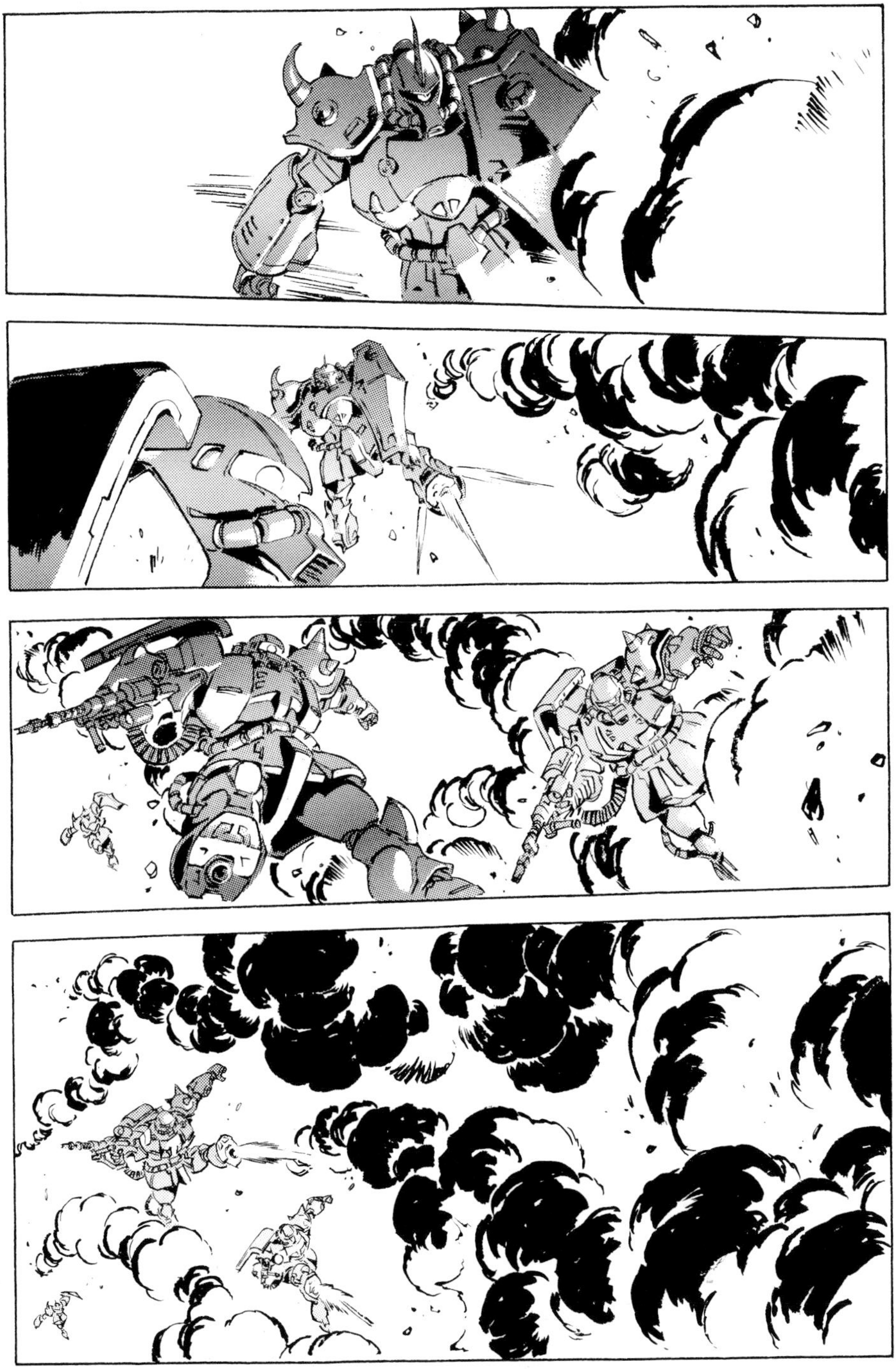

ブ
オ
ン
3000メの

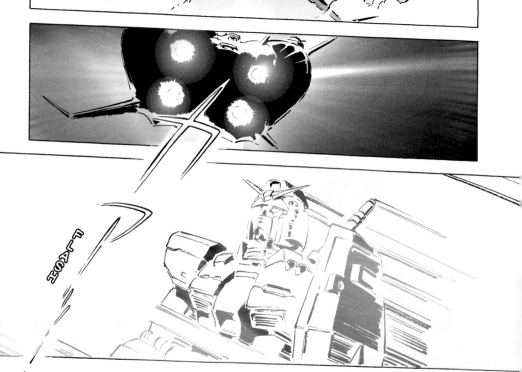

ヒュオオオー

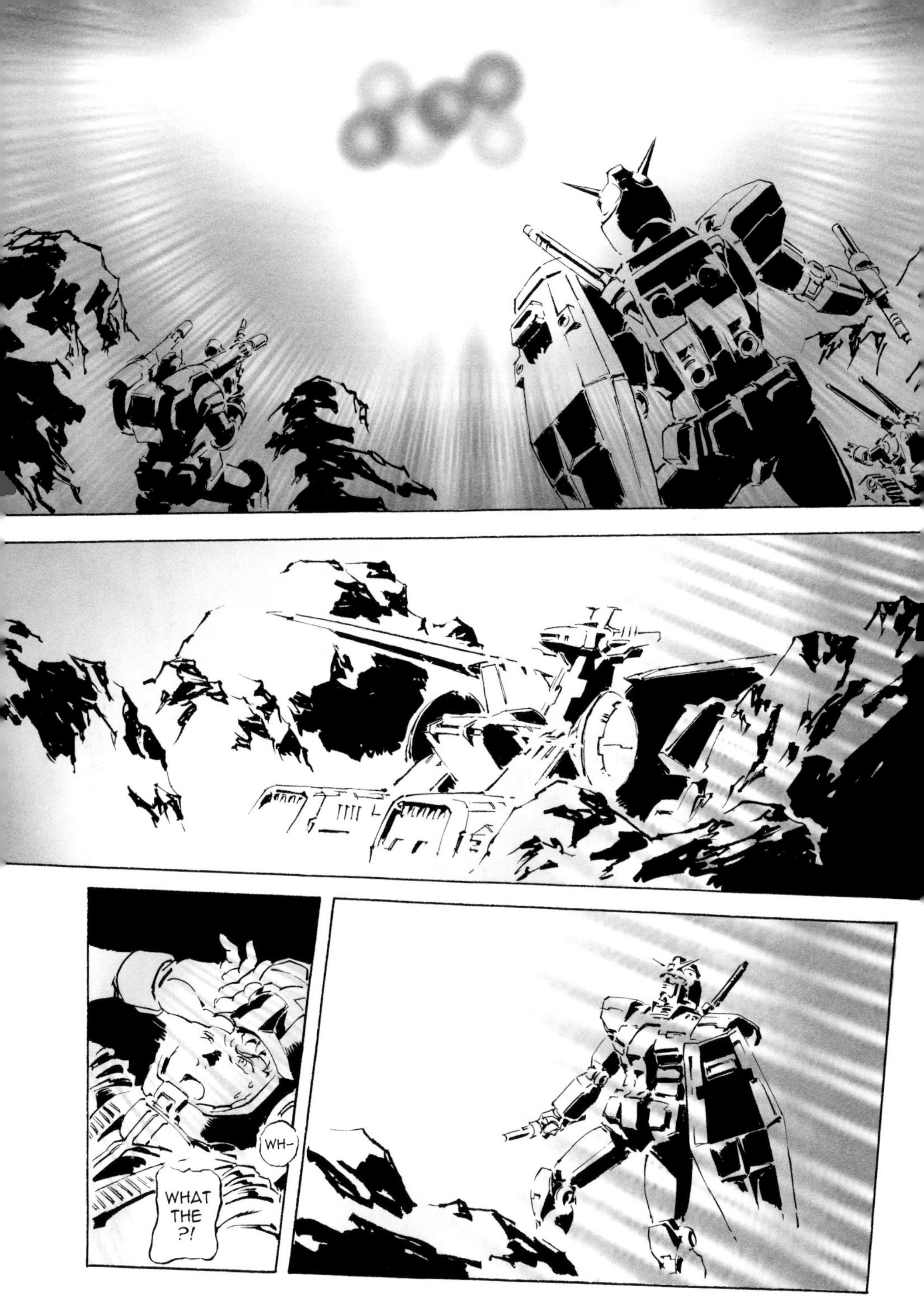
WH-
WHAT THE ?!

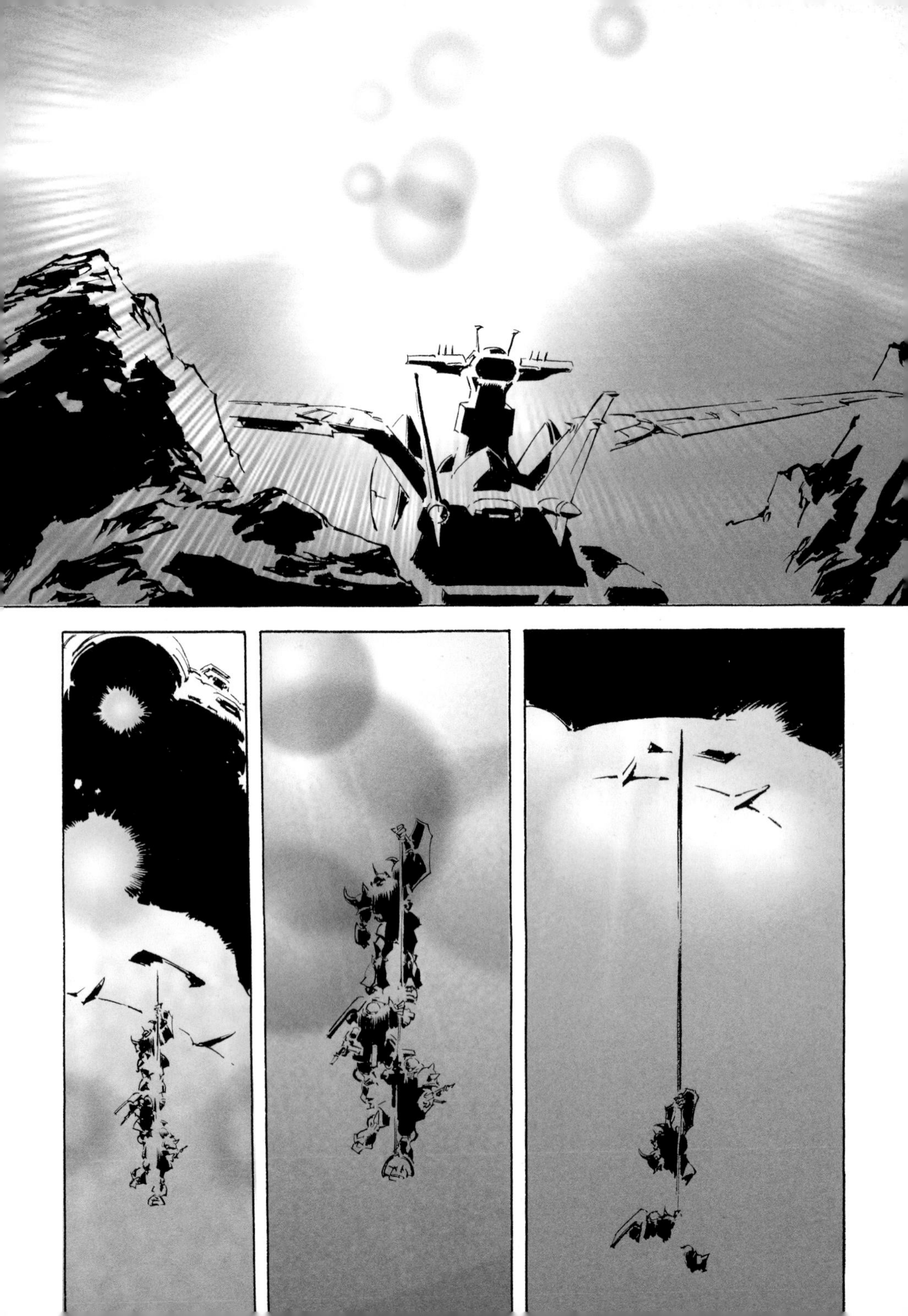

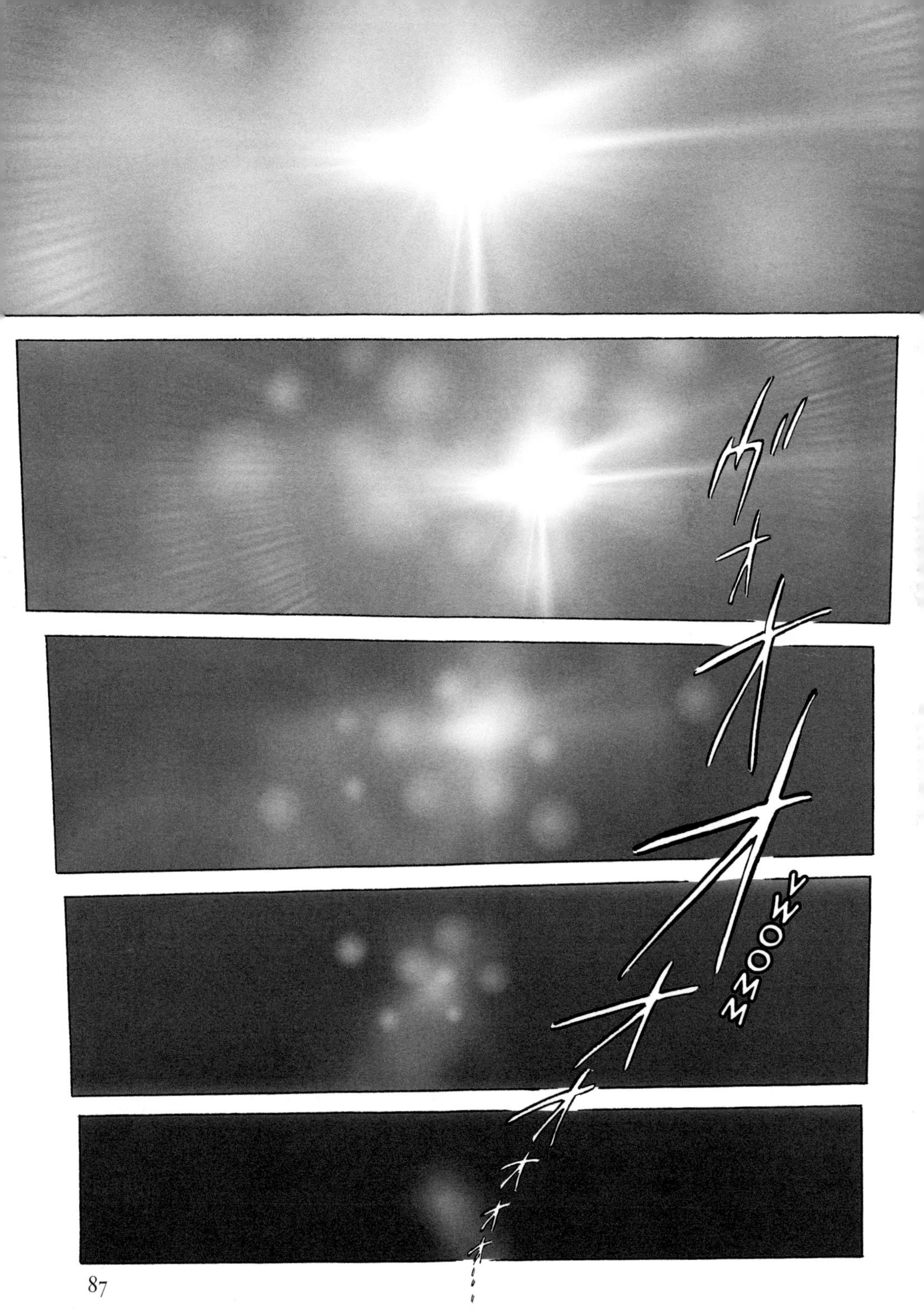
ヴォオオオオオォォォ…
VWOOMM

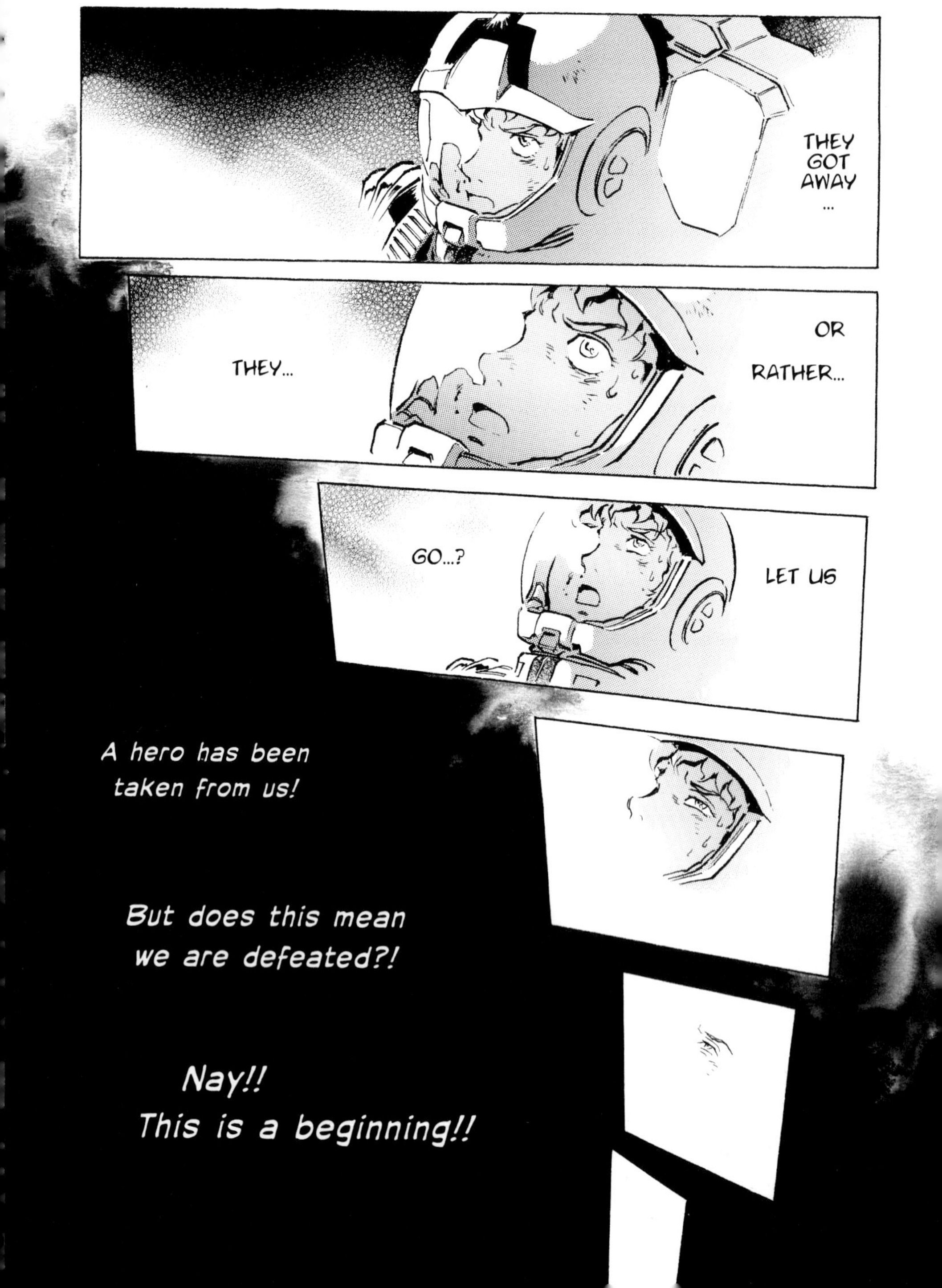
THEY GOT AWAY ...
OR RATHER...
THEY...
LET US
GO...?
A hero has been taken from us!
But does this mean we are defeated?!
Nay!! This is a beginning!!

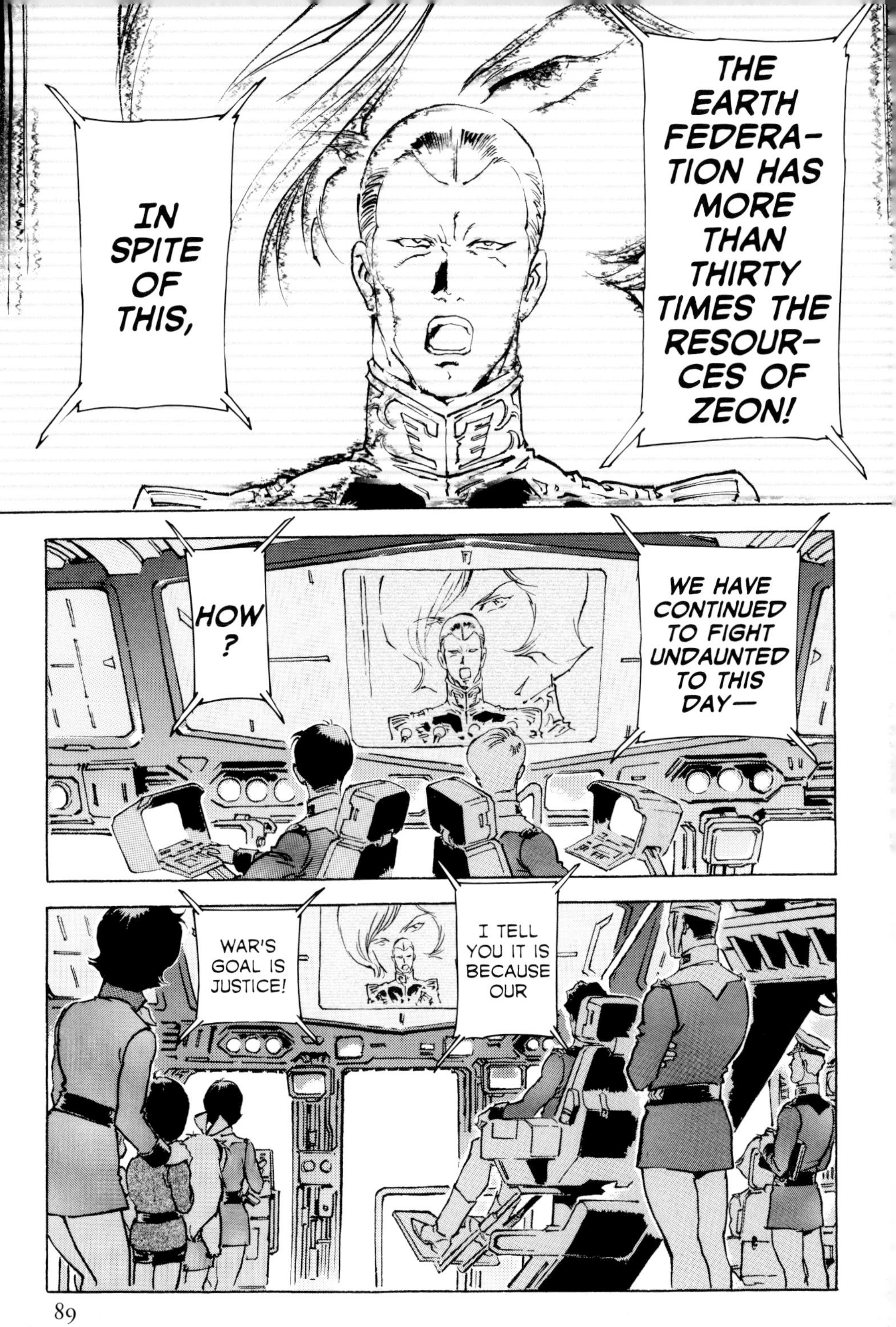
THE EARTH FEDERATION HAS MORE THAN THIRTY TIMES THE RESOURCES OF ZEON!
IN SPITE OF THIS,
WE HAVE CONTINUED TO FIGHT UNDAUNTED TO THIS DAY—
HOW?
I TELL YOU IT IS BECAUSE OUR
WAR'S GOAL IS JUSTICE!

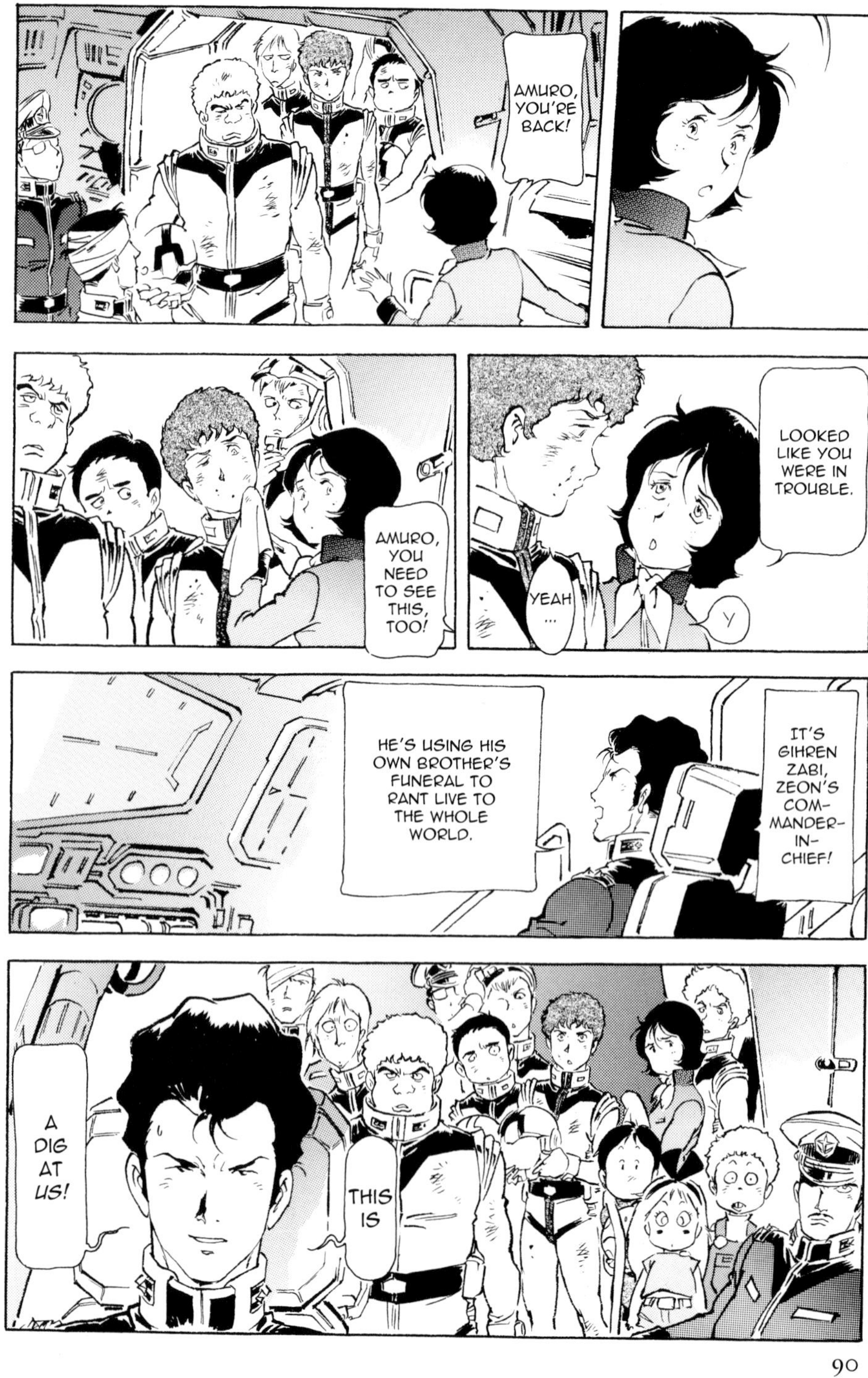
AMURO, YOU'RE BACK!
LOOKED LIKE YOU WERE IN TROUBLE.
Y
YEAH ...
AMURO, YOU NEED TO SEE THIS, TOO!
IT'S GIHREN ZABI, ZEON'S COM-MANDER-IN-CHIEF!
HE'S USING HIS OWN BROTHER'S FUNERAL TO RANT LIVE TO THE WHOLE WORLD.
THIS IS
A DIG AT US!

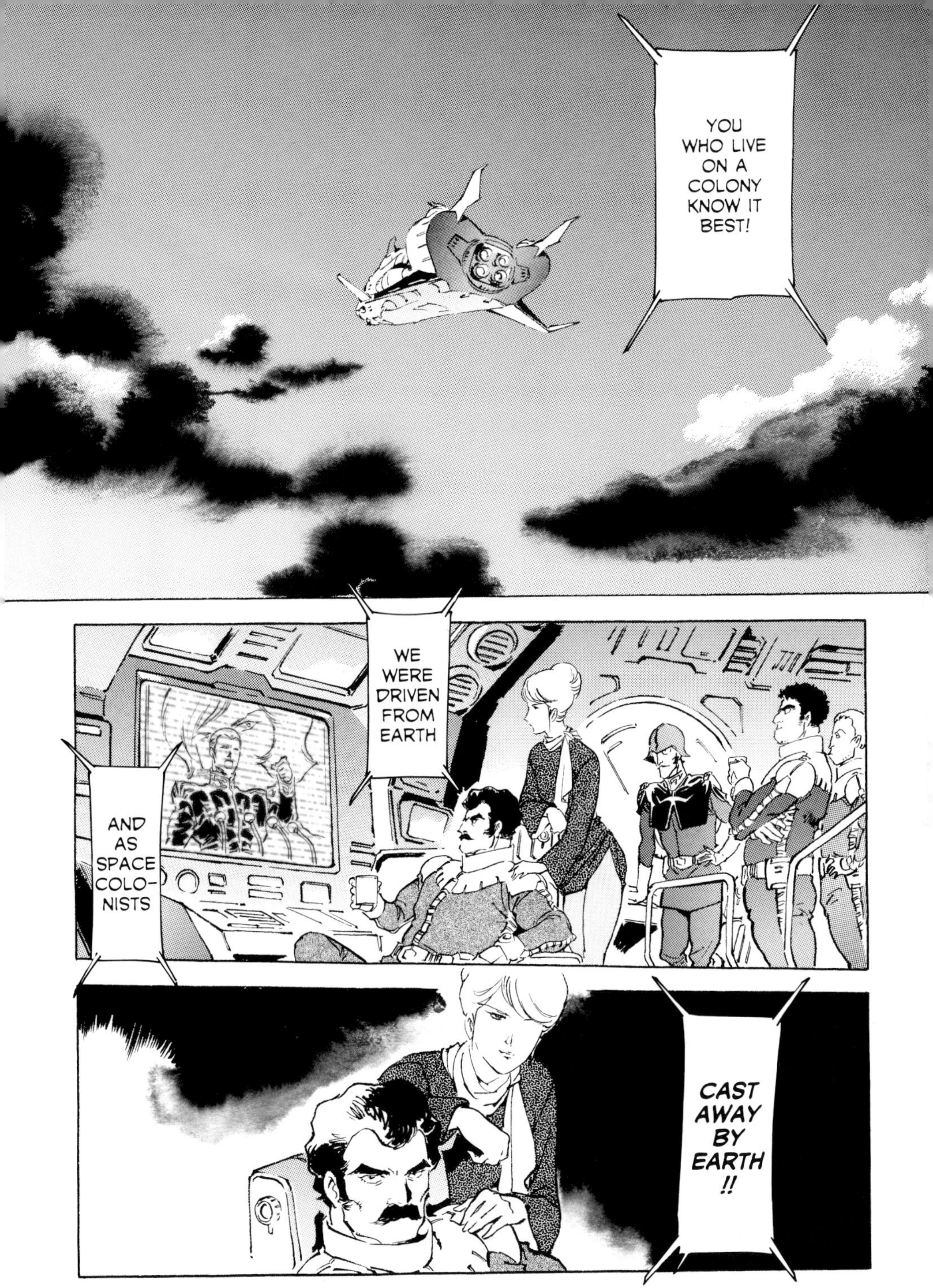
YOU WHO LIVE ON A COLONY KNOW IT BEST!
WE WERE DRIVEN FROM EARTH
AND AS SPACE COLONISTS
CAST AWAY BY EARTH !!

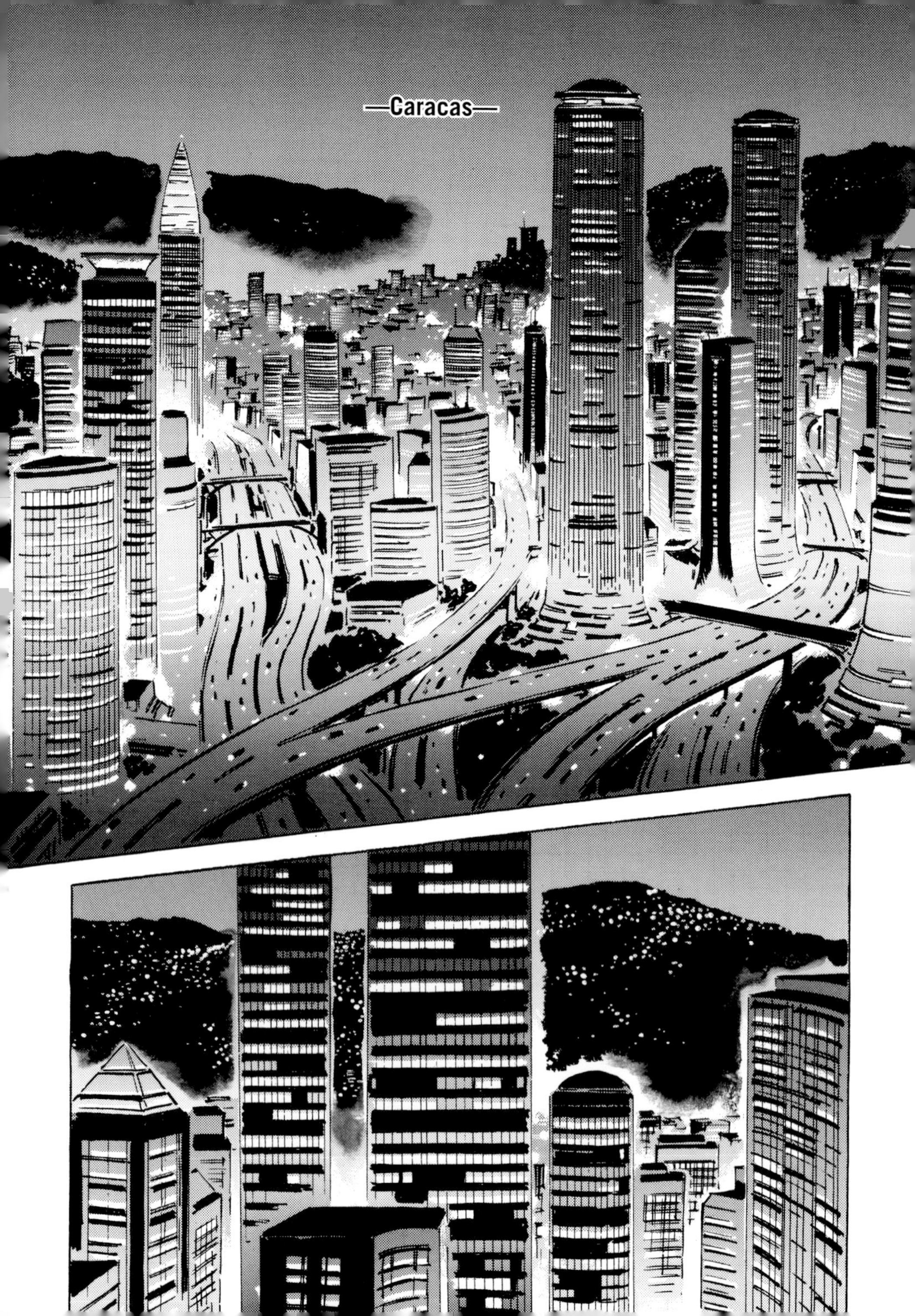
—Caracas—

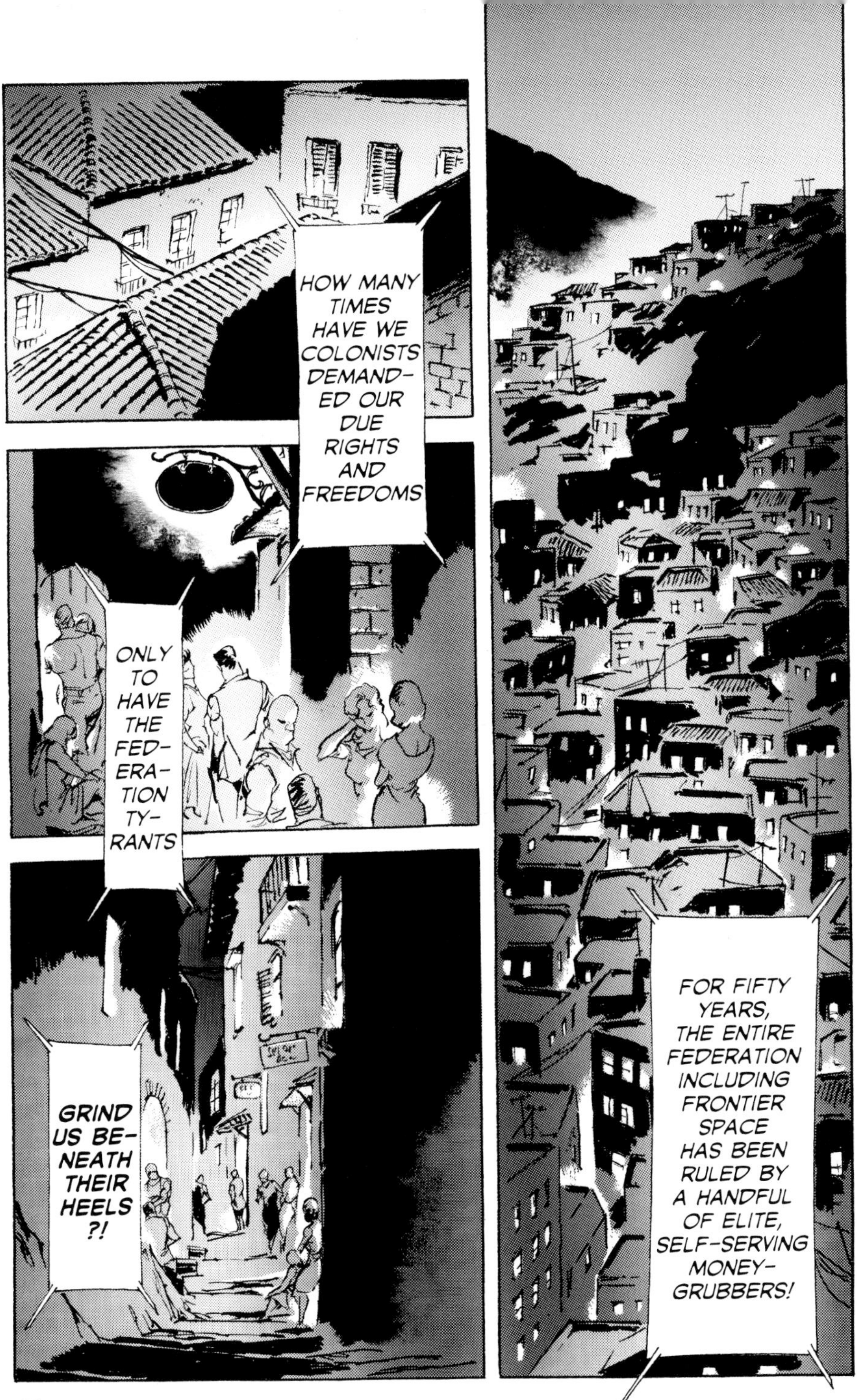
FOR FIFTY YEARS, THE ENTIRE FEDERATION INCLUDING FRONTIER SPACE HAS BEEN RULED BY A HANDFUL OF ELITE, SELF-SERVING MONEY-GRUBBERS!
HOW MANY TIMES HAVE WE COLONISTS DEMANDED OUR DUE RIGHTS AND FREEDOMS
ONLY TO HAVE THE FEDERATION TYRANTS
GRIND US BENEATH THEIR HEELS?!

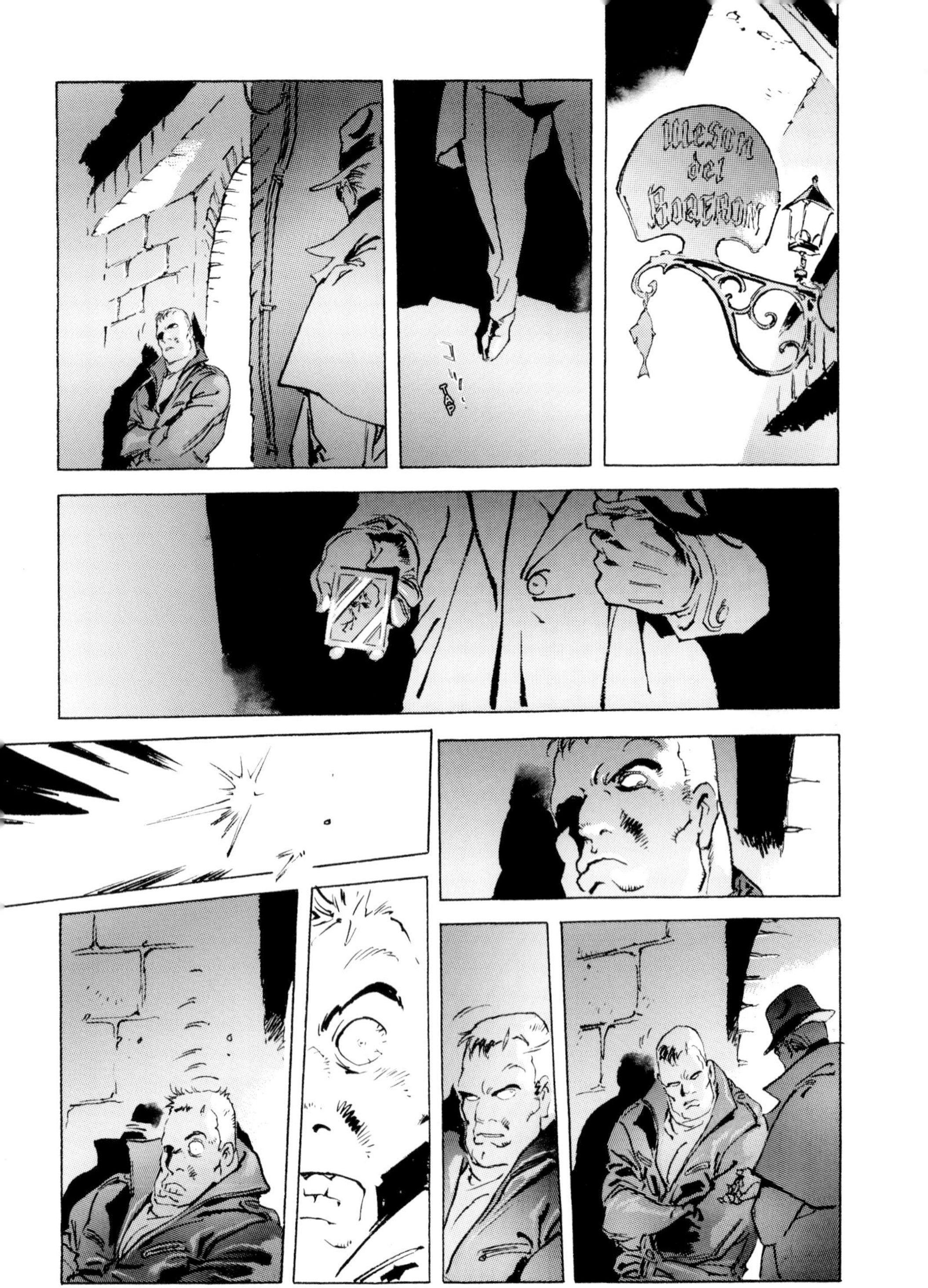
Meson del Boqeron
TAP

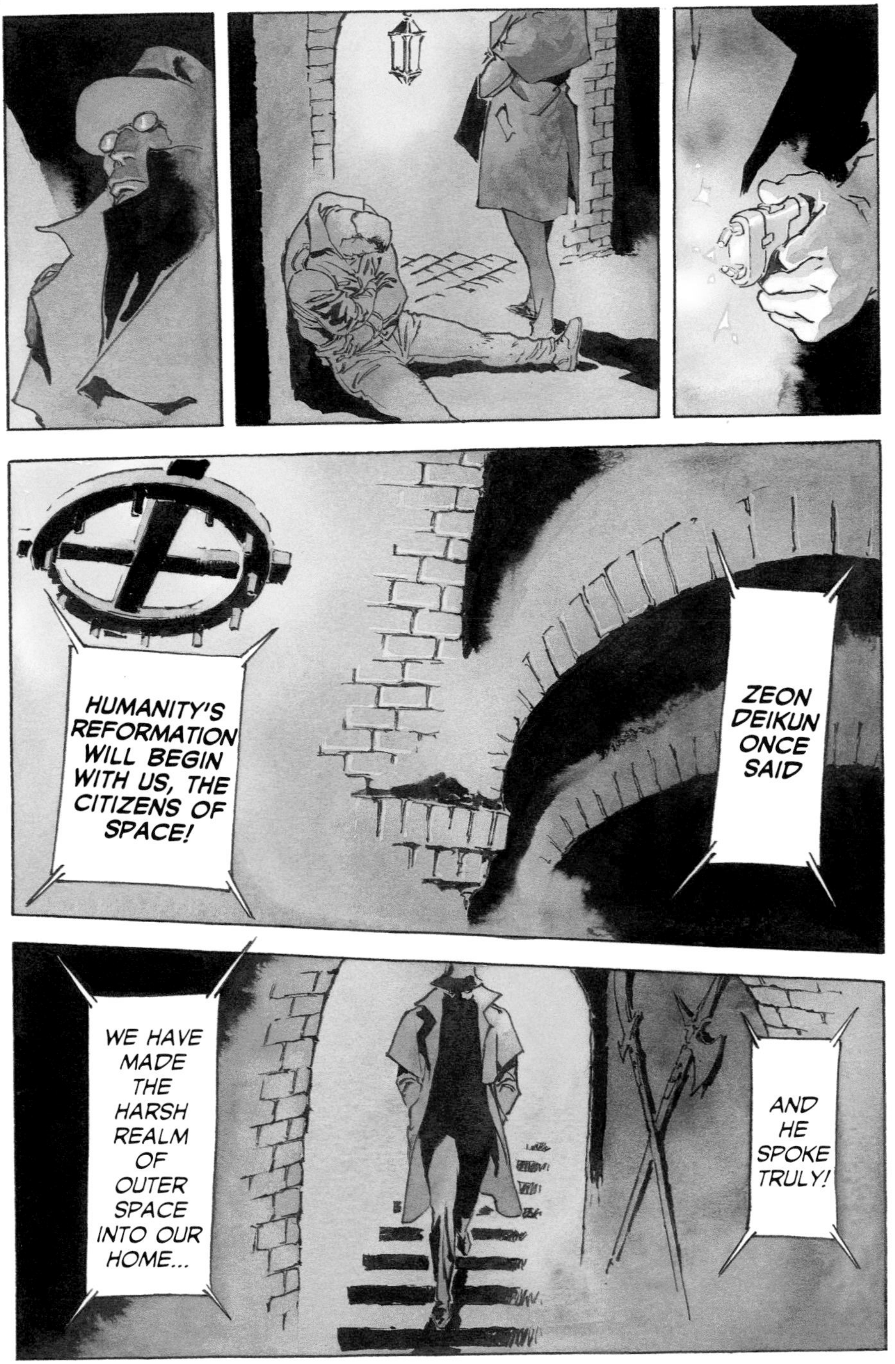
ZEON DEIKUN ONCE SAID
HUMANITY'S REFORMATION WILL BEGIN WITH US, THE CITIZENS OF SPACE!
WE HAVE MADE THE HARSH REALM OF OUTER SPACE INTO OUR HOME...
AND HE SPOKE TRULY!

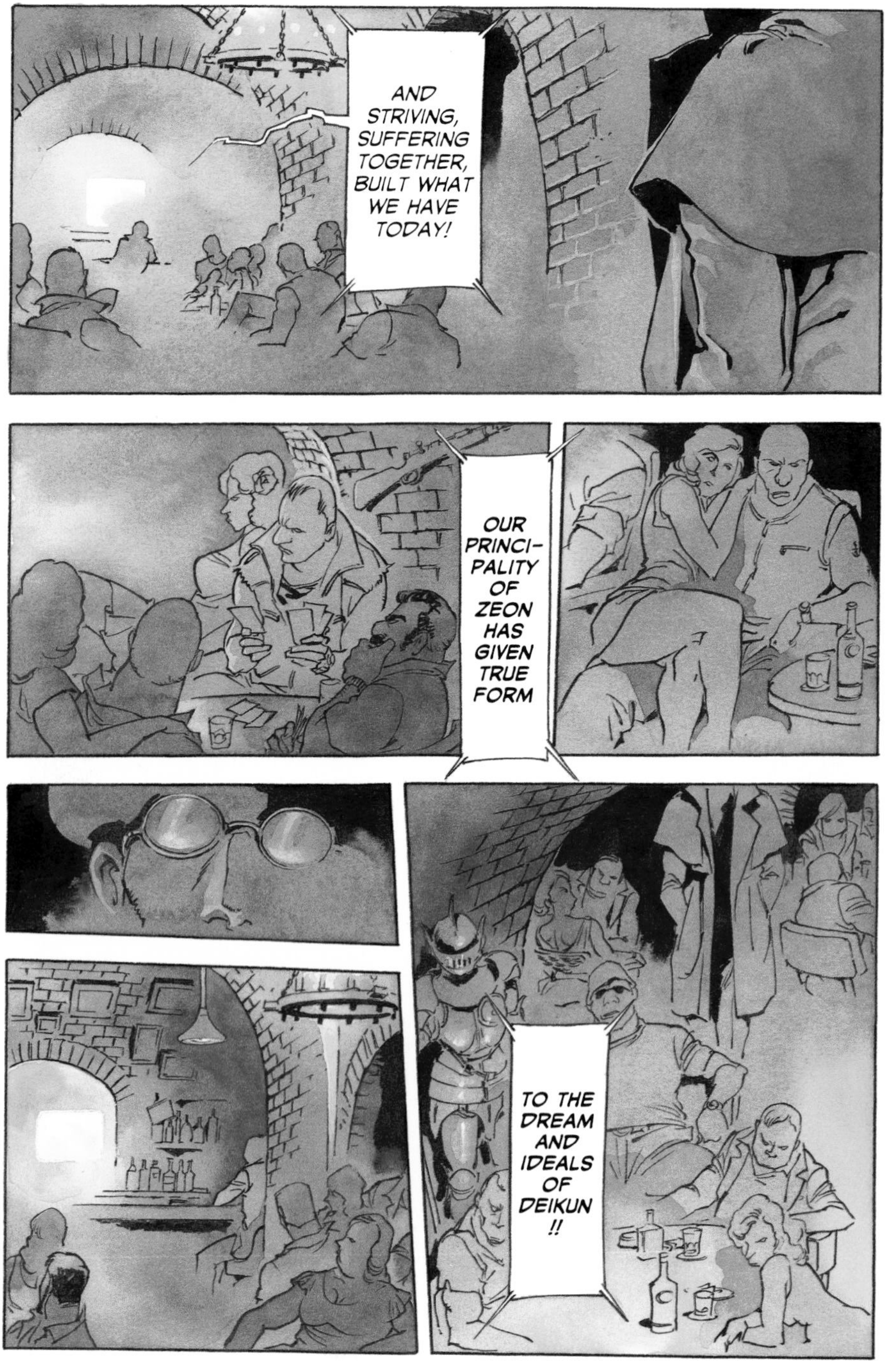
AND STRIVING, SUFFERING TOGETHER, BUILT WHAT WE HAVE TODAY!
OUR PRINCI- PALITY OF ZEON HAS GIVEN TRUE FORM
TO THE DREAM AND IDEALS OF DEIKUN !!

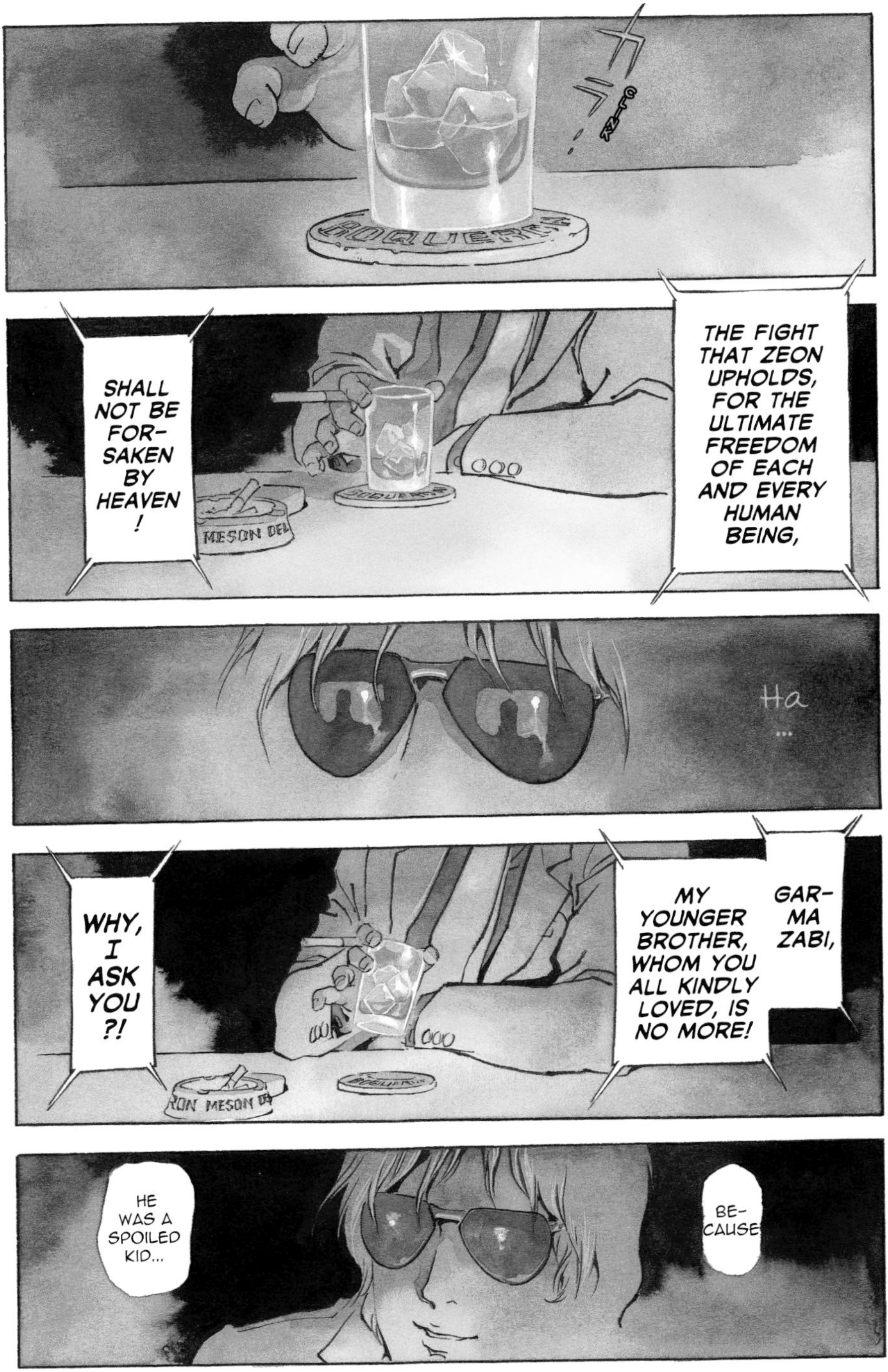
THE FIGHT THAT ZEON UPHOLDS, FOR THE ULTIMATE FREEDOM OF EACH AND EVERY HUMAN BEING,
SHALL NOT BE FOR-SAKEN BY HEAVEN!
Ha...
GAR-MA ZABI,
MY YOUNGER BROTHER, WHOM YOU ALL KINDLY LOVED, IS NO MORE!
WHY, I ASK YOU?!
BE-CAUSE
HE WAS A SPOILED KID...

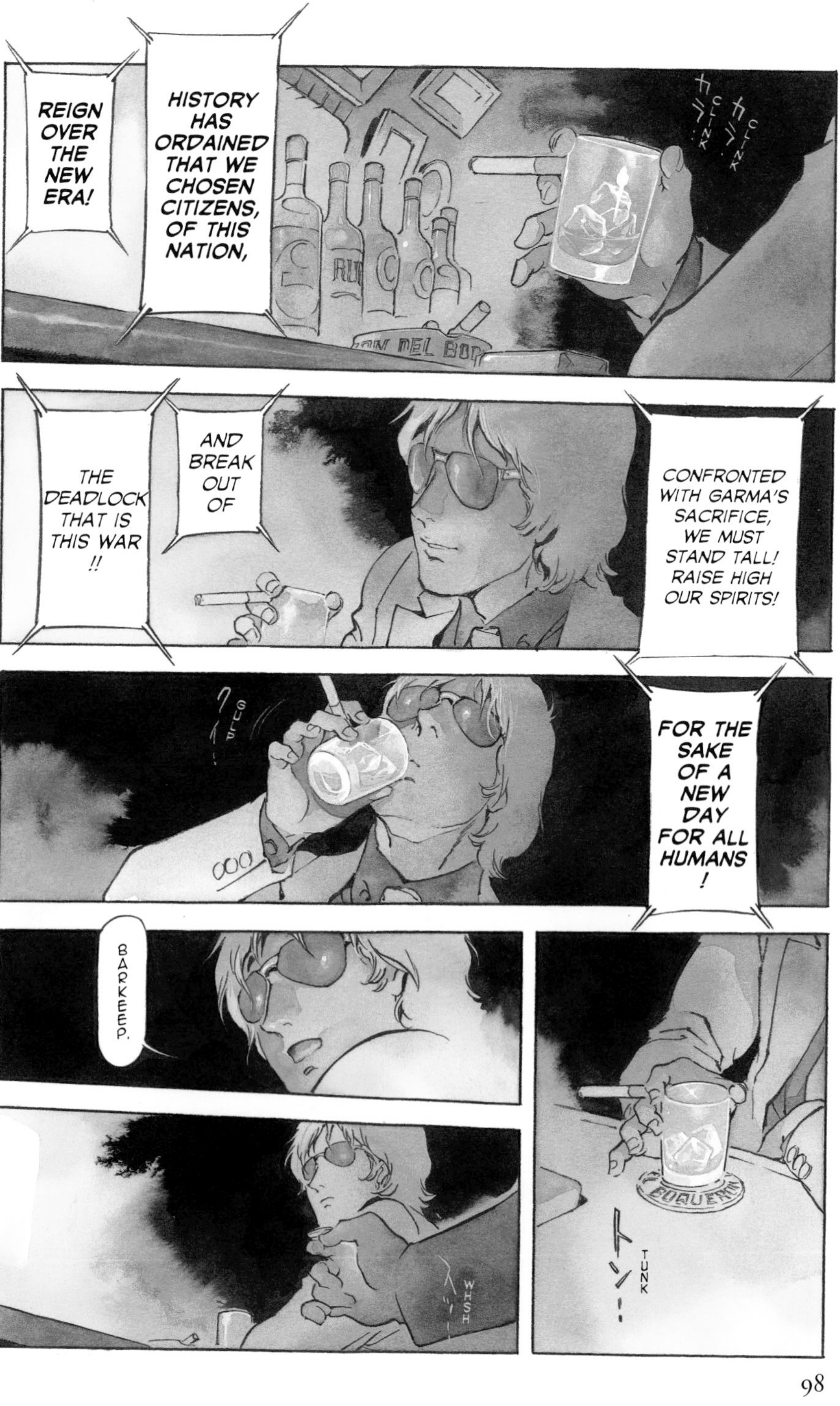
HISTORY HAS ORDAINED THAT WE CHOSEN CITIZENS, OF THIS NATION,
REIGN OVER THE NEW ERA!
CLINK
CLINK
CONFRONTED WITH GARMA'S SACRIFICE, WE MUST STAND TALL! RAISE HIGH OUR SPIRITS!
AND BREAK OUT OF
THE DEADLOCK THAT IS THIS WAR !!
FOR THE SAKE OF A NEW DAY FOR ALL HUMANS !
GULP
BOQUERON
TUNK
BARKEEP.
WHSH

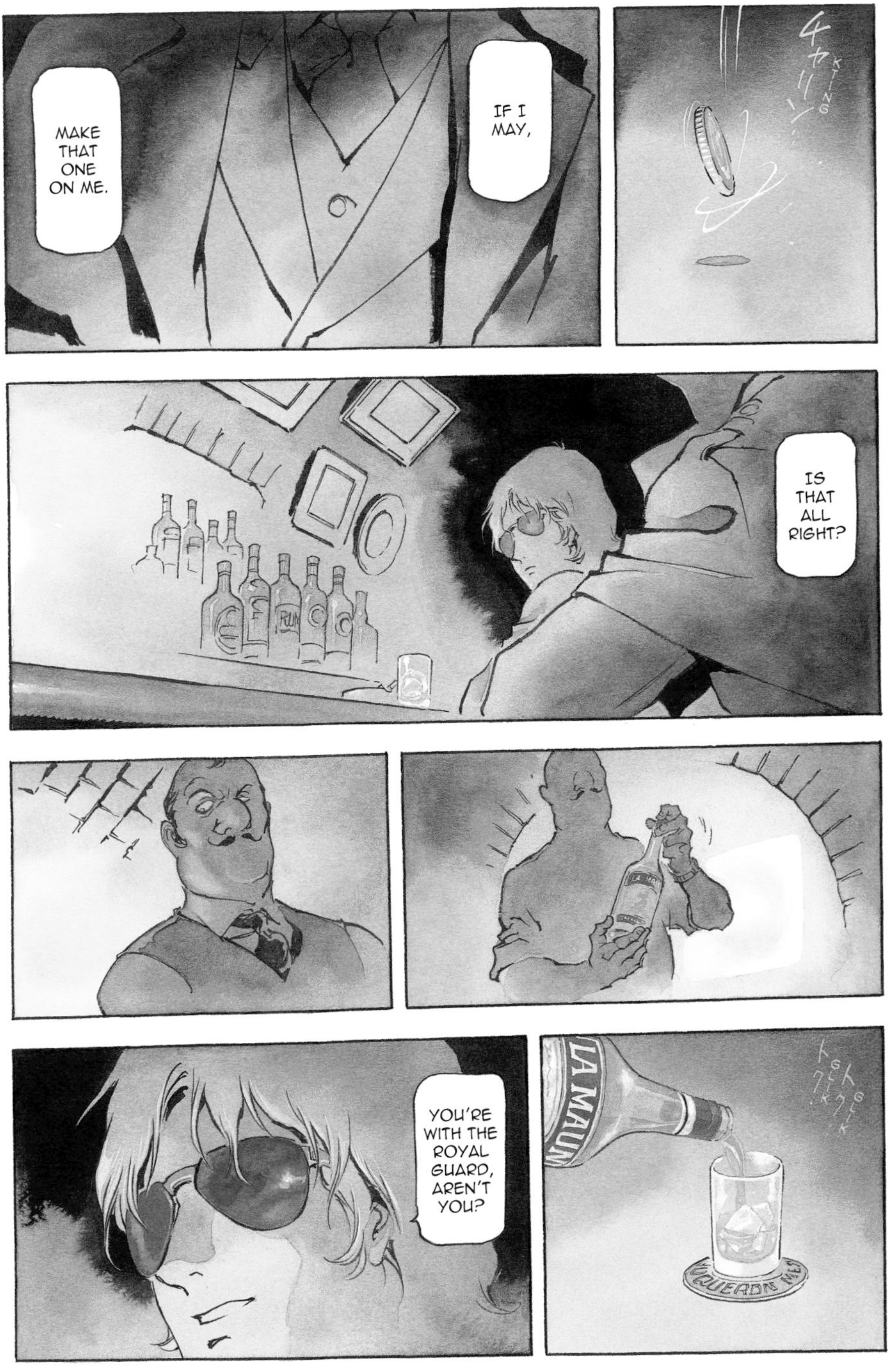
KTING
IF I MAY,
MAKE THAT ONE ON ME.
IS THAT ALL RIGHT?
GLIK GLIK
YOU'RE WITH THE ROYAL GUARD, AREN'T YOU?

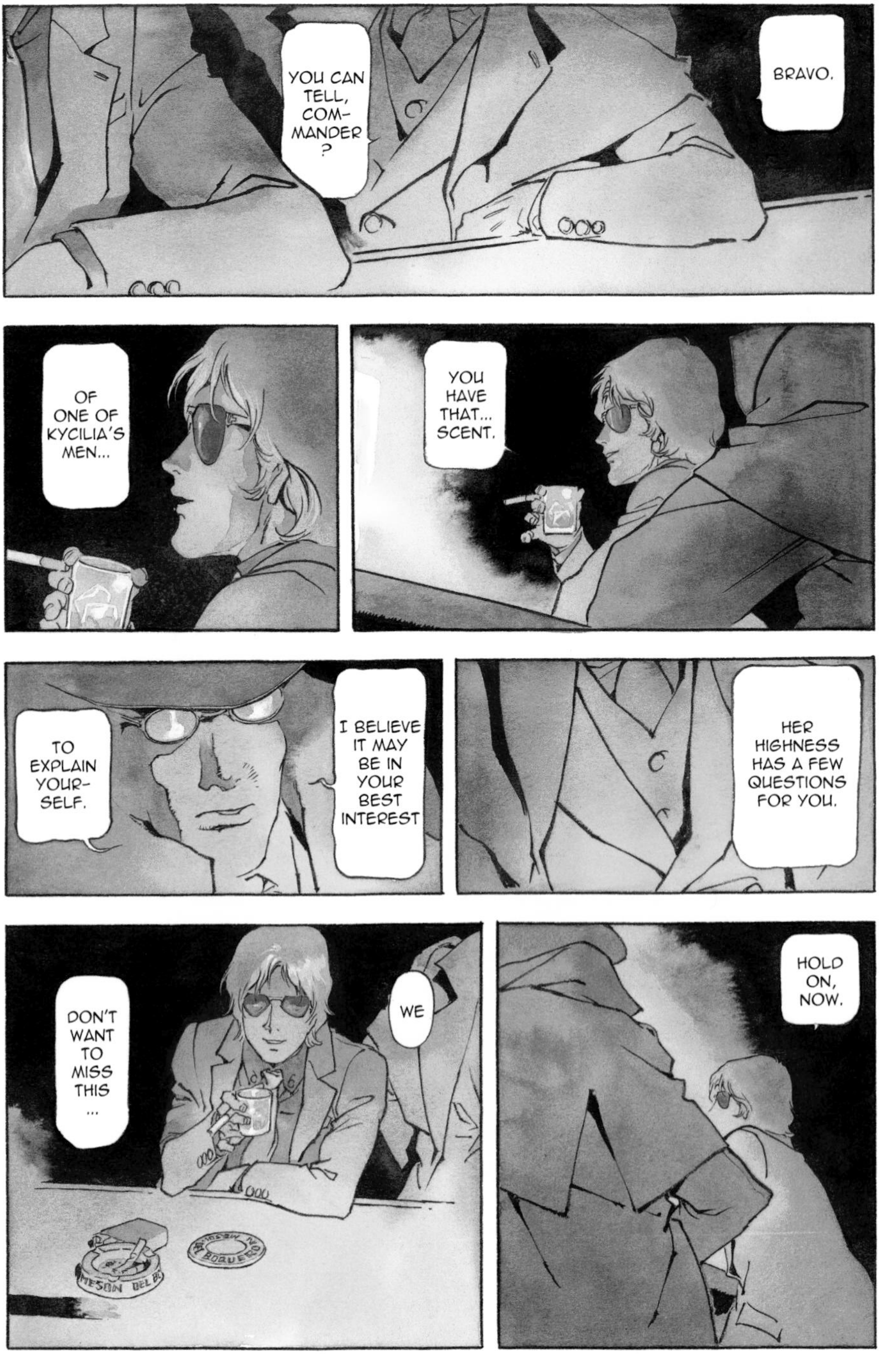
BRAVO.
YOU CAN TELL, COM-MANDER ?
YOU HAVE THAT... SCENT.
OF ONE OF KYCILIA'S MEN...
HER HIGHNESS HAS A FEW QUESTIONS FOR YOU.
I BELIEVE IT MAY BE IN YOUR BEST INTEREST
TO EXPLAIN YOUR-SELF.
HOLD ON, NOW.
WE
DON'T WANT TO MISS THIS ...

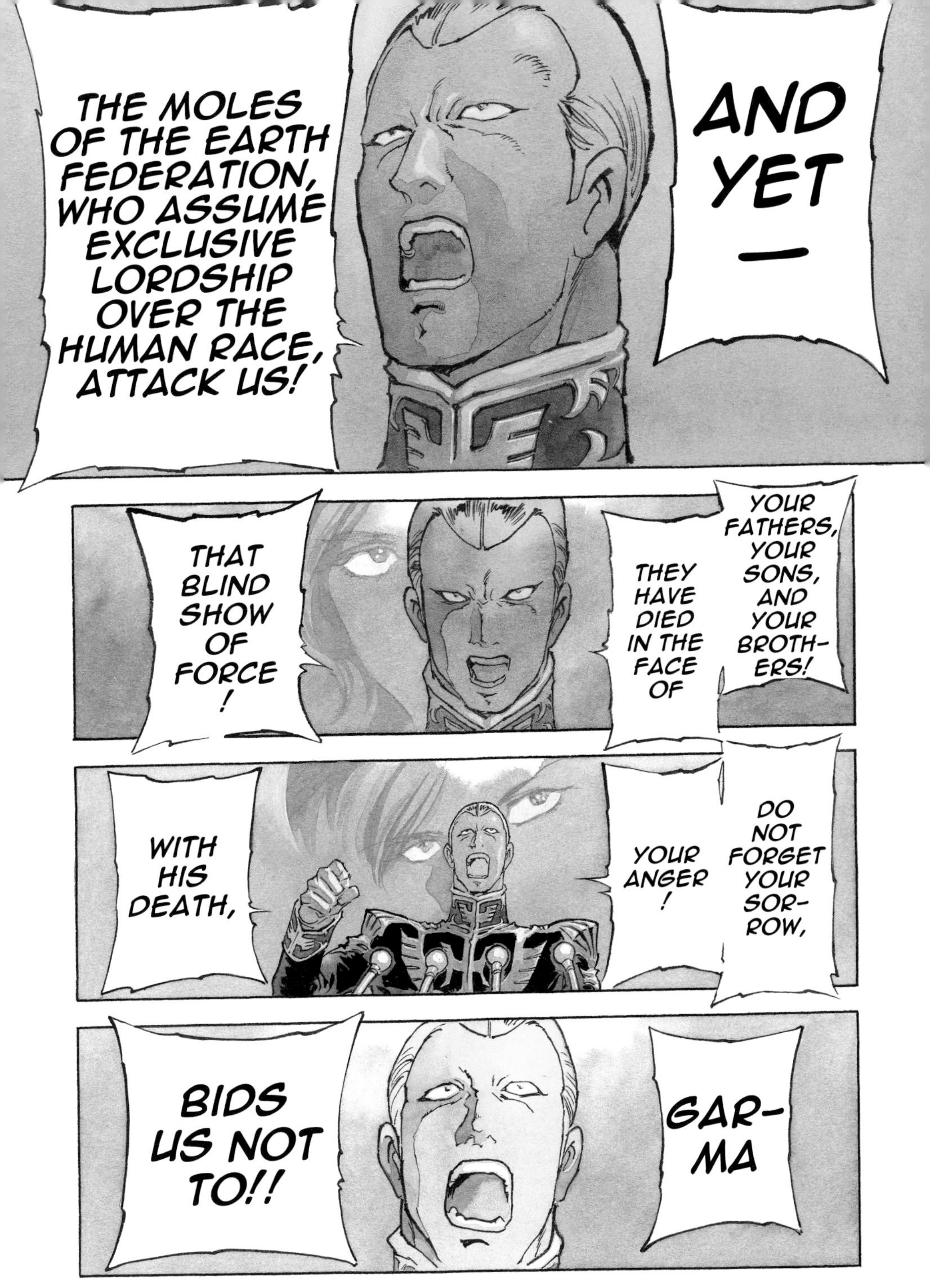
AND YET —
THE MOLES OF THE EARTH FEDERATION, WHO ASSUME EXCLUSIVE LORDSHIP OVER THE HUMAN RACE, ATTACK US!
YOUR FATHERS, YOUR SONS, AND YOUR BROTHERS!
THEY HAVE DIED IN THE FACE OF
THAT BLIND SHOW OF FORCE!
DO NOT FORGET YOUR SORROW,
YOUR ANGER!
WITH HIS DEATH,
GAR-MA
BIDS US NOT TO!!

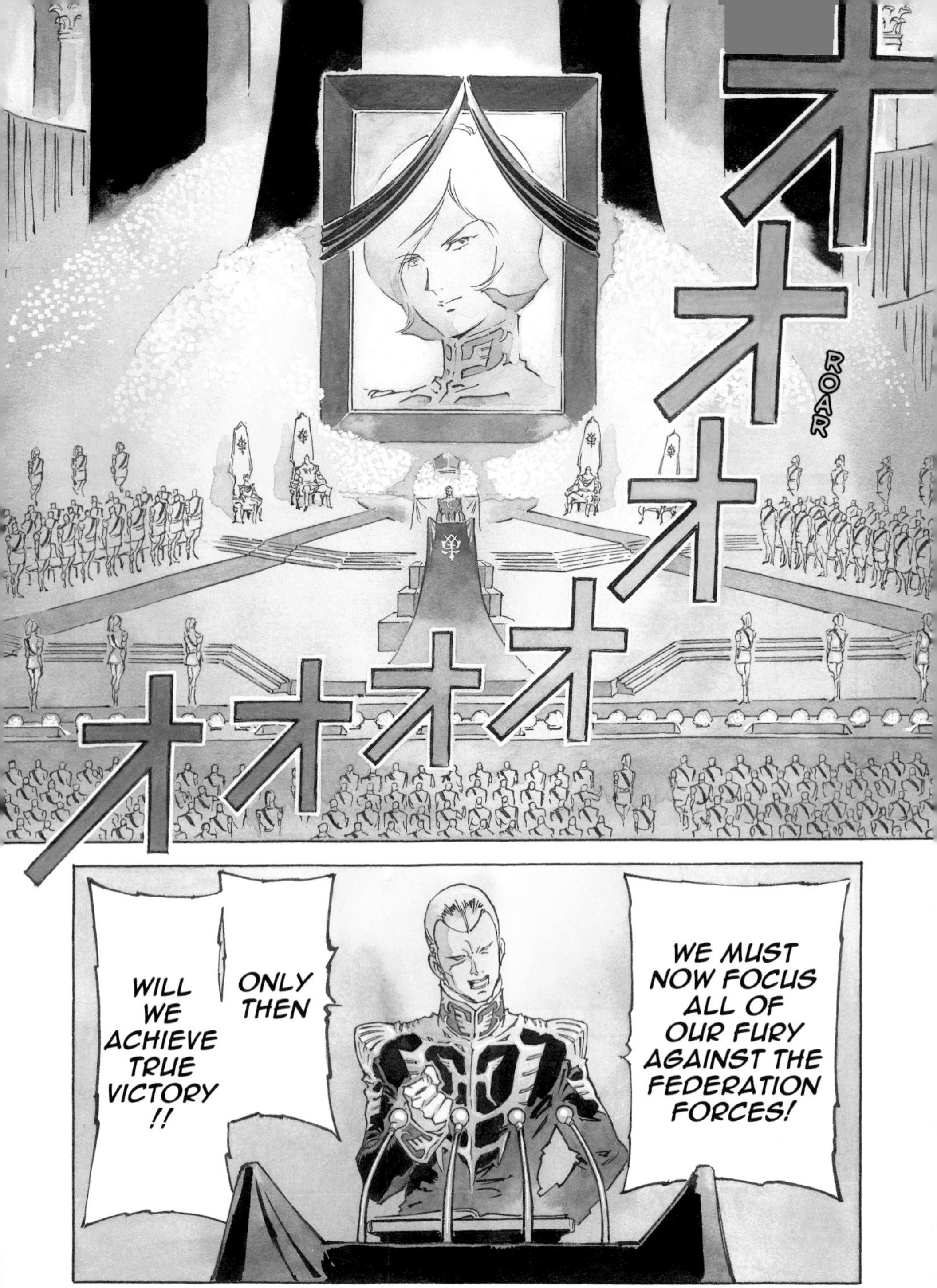
オオオオオオオオ
ROAR
WE MUST NOW FOCUS ALL OF OUR FURY AGAINST THE FEDERATION FORCES!
ONLY THEN
WILL WE ACHIEVE TRUE VICTORY!!

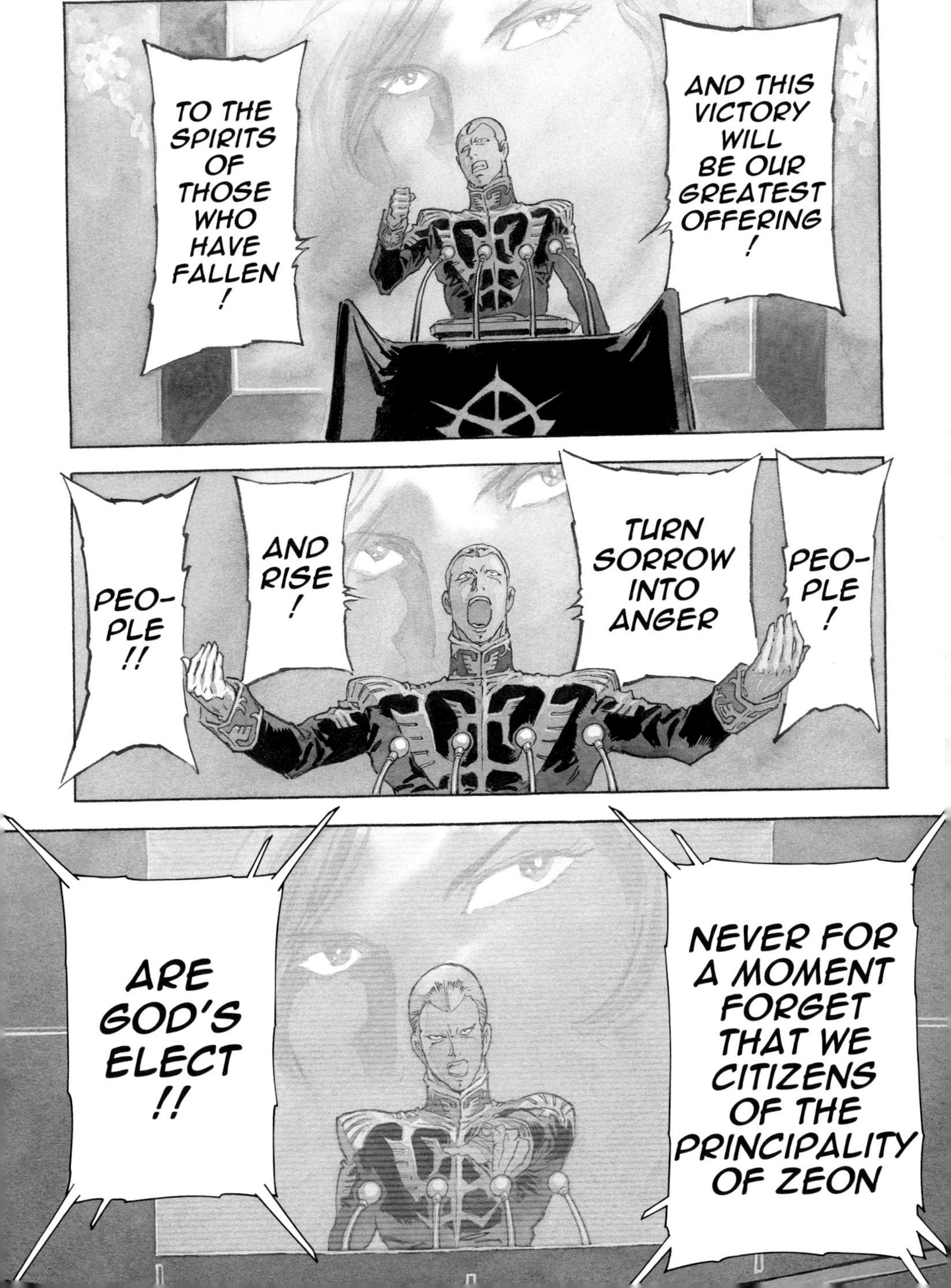
AND THIS VICTORY WILL BE OUR GREATEST OFFERING!
TO THE SPIRITS OF THOSE WHO HAVE FALLEN!
PEO-PLE!
TURN SORROW INTO ANGER
AND RISE!
PEO-PLE!!
NEVER FOR A MOMENT FORGET THAT WE CITIZENS OF THE PRINCIPALITY OF ZEON
ARE GOD'S ELECT!!

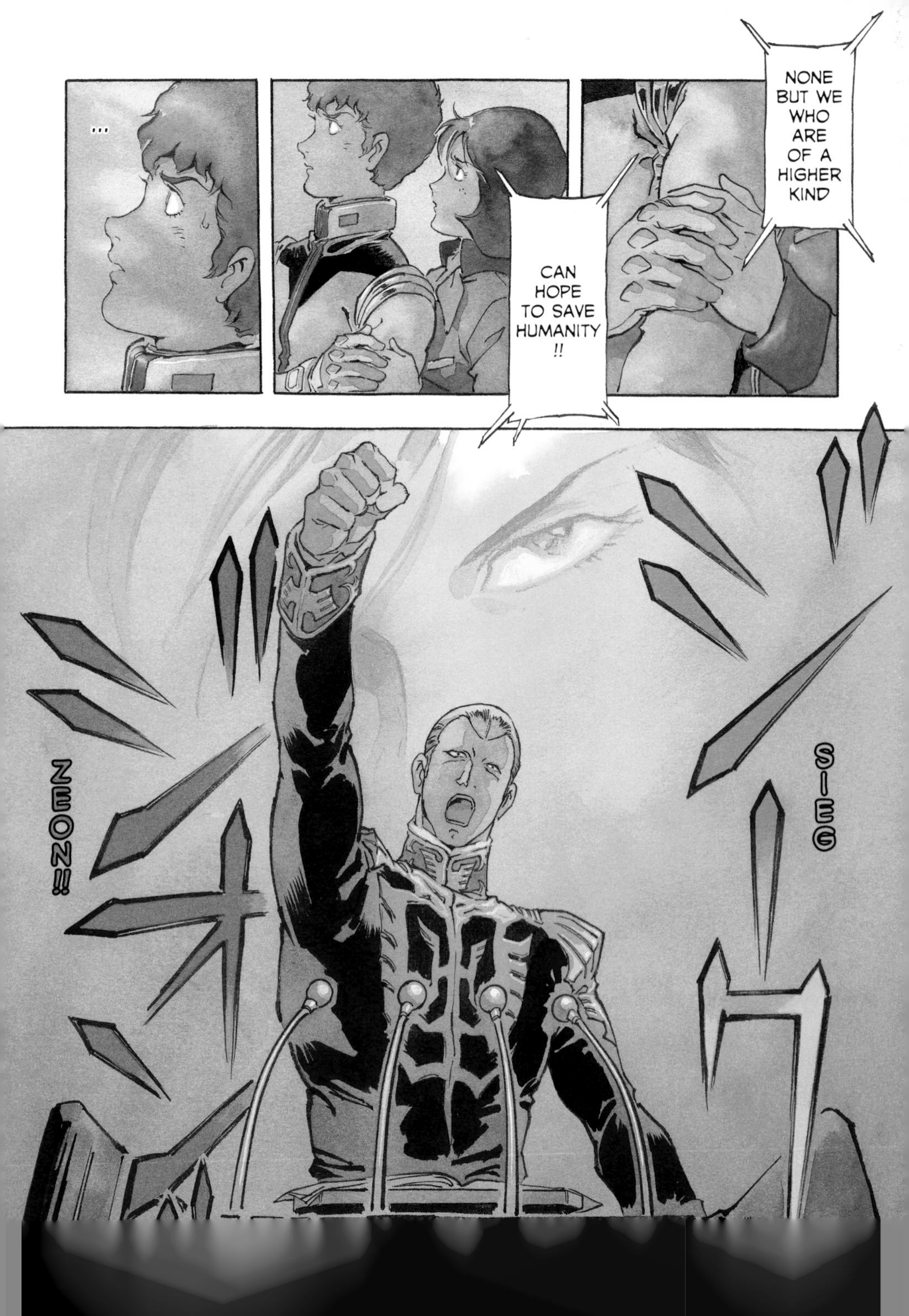
NONE BUT WE WHO ARE OF A HIGHER KIND
CAN HOPE TO SAVE HUMANITY !!
...
SIEG
ZEON!!

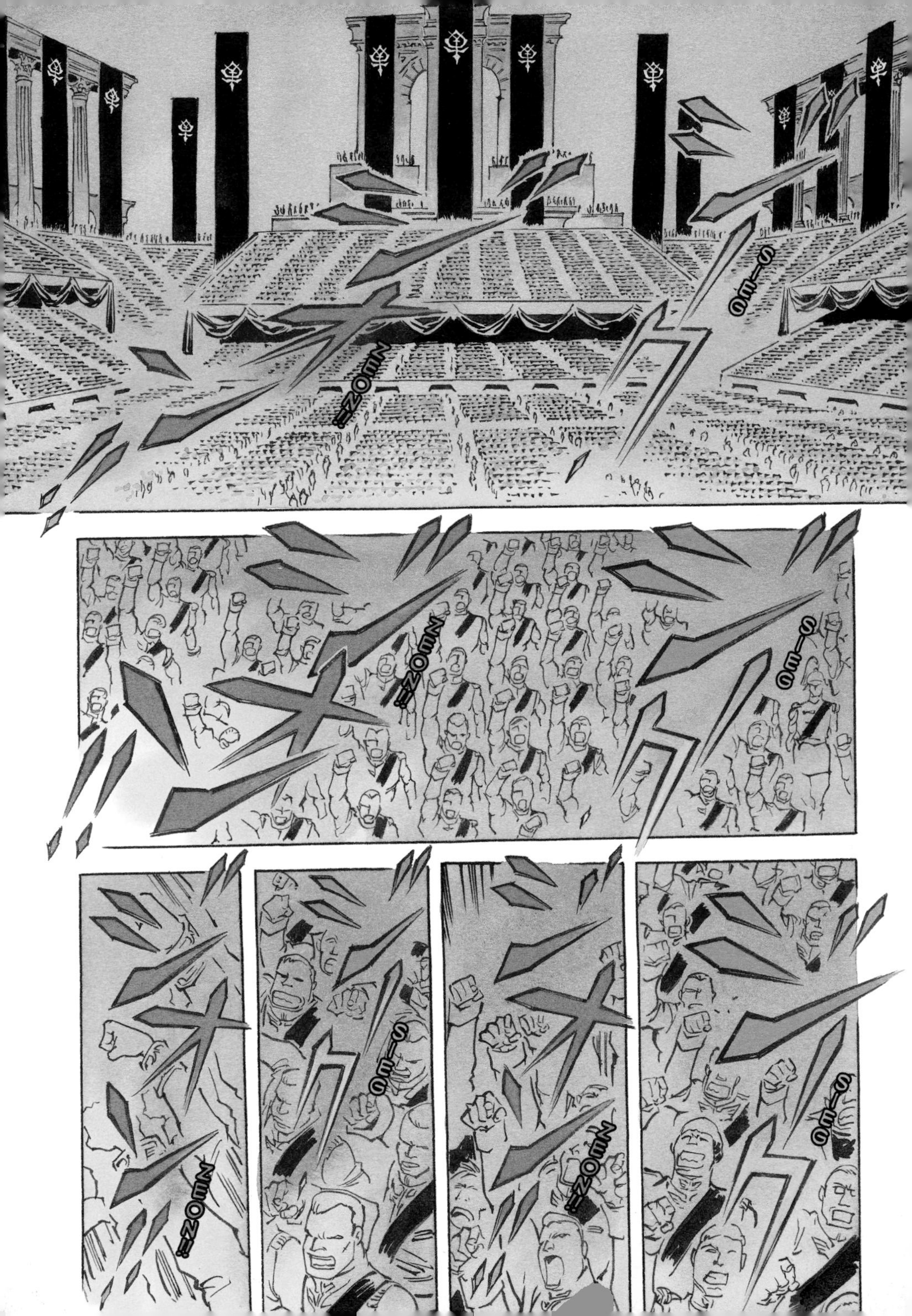
SIEG
ZEON!!
SIEG
ZEON!!
SIEG
ZEON!!
SIEG
ZEON!!

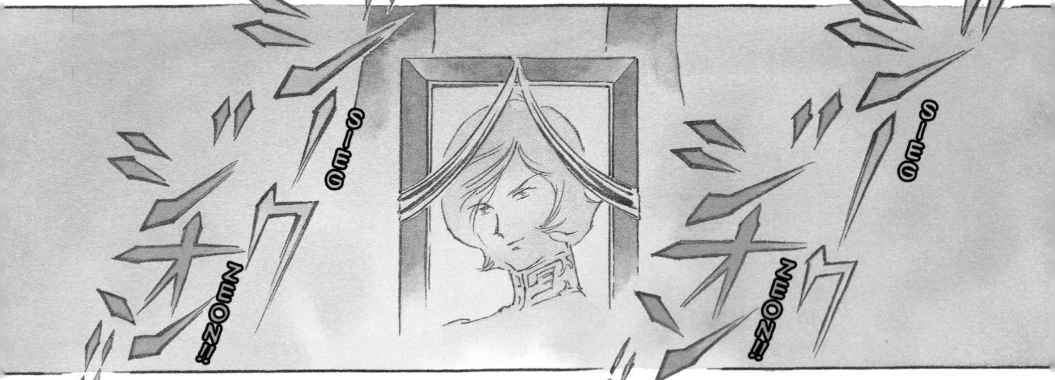
ジーク
SIEG
ジオン
ZEON!!
ジーク
SIEG
ジオン
ZEON!!
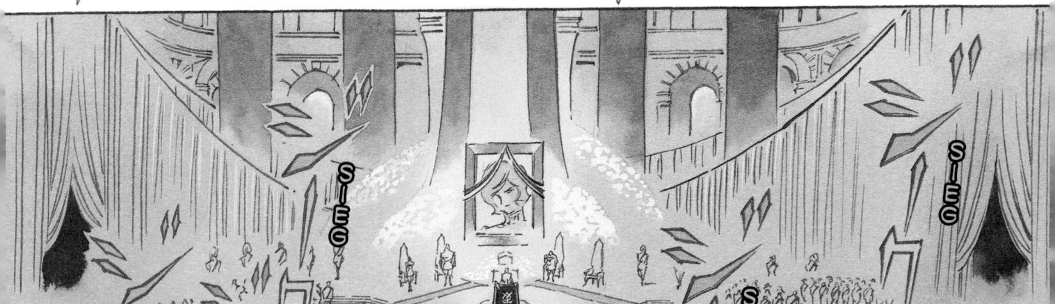
ジーク
SIEG
ジオン
ZEON!!
SIEG
ジオン
ZEON!!
ジーク
SIEG
ジオン
ZEON!!
SIEG
ジオン
ZEON!!
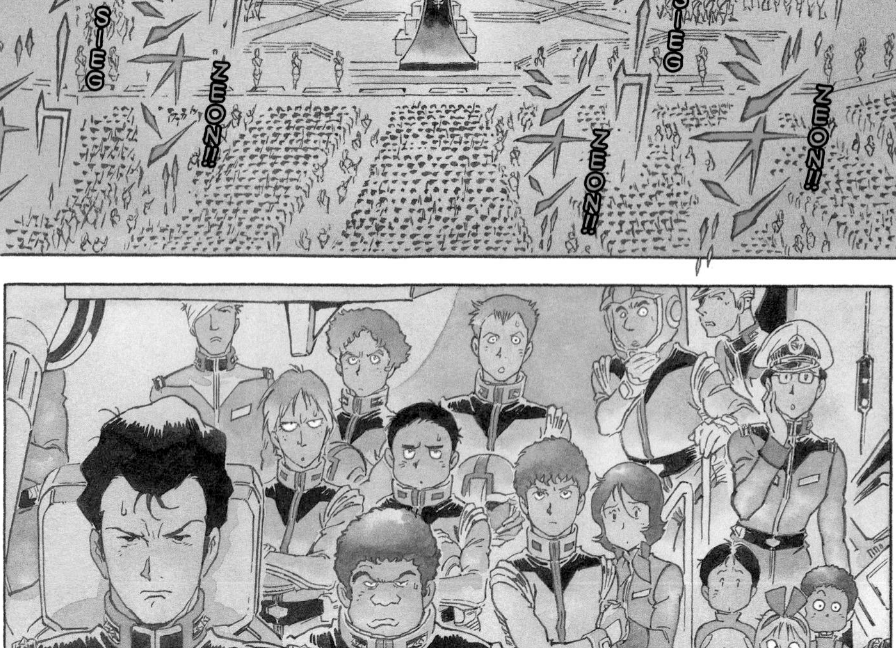

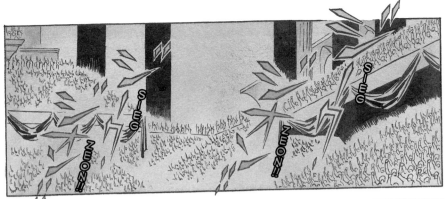

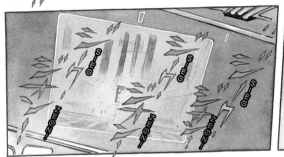

HOW
DARE
HE?!

OURS
...

THE
EN-
EMY
...

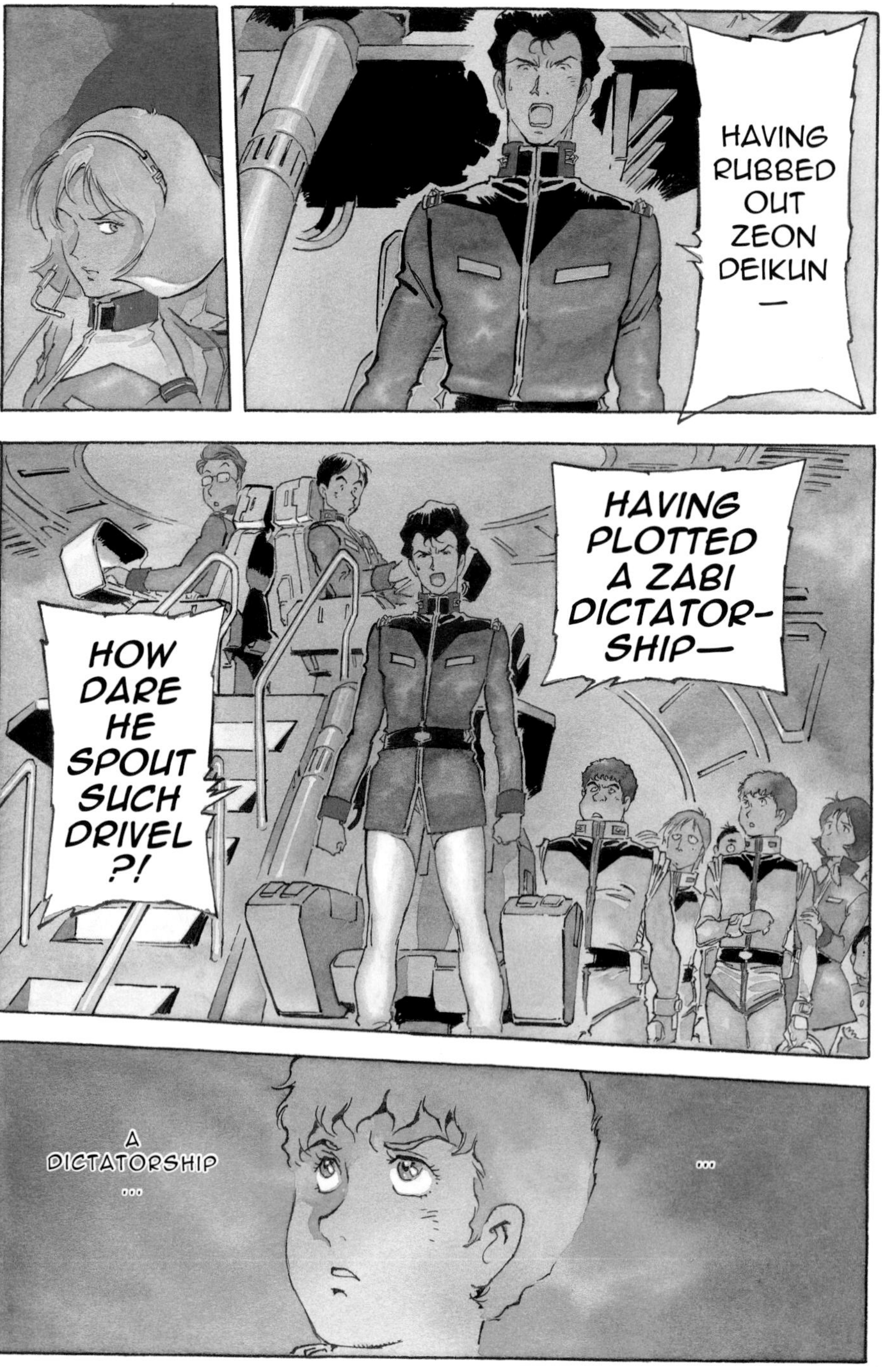
HAVING RUBBED OUT ZEON DEIKUN —
HAVING PLOTTED A ZABI DICTATOR-SHIP—
HOW DARE HE SPOUT SUCH DRIVEL?!
A DICTATORSHIP ...
...

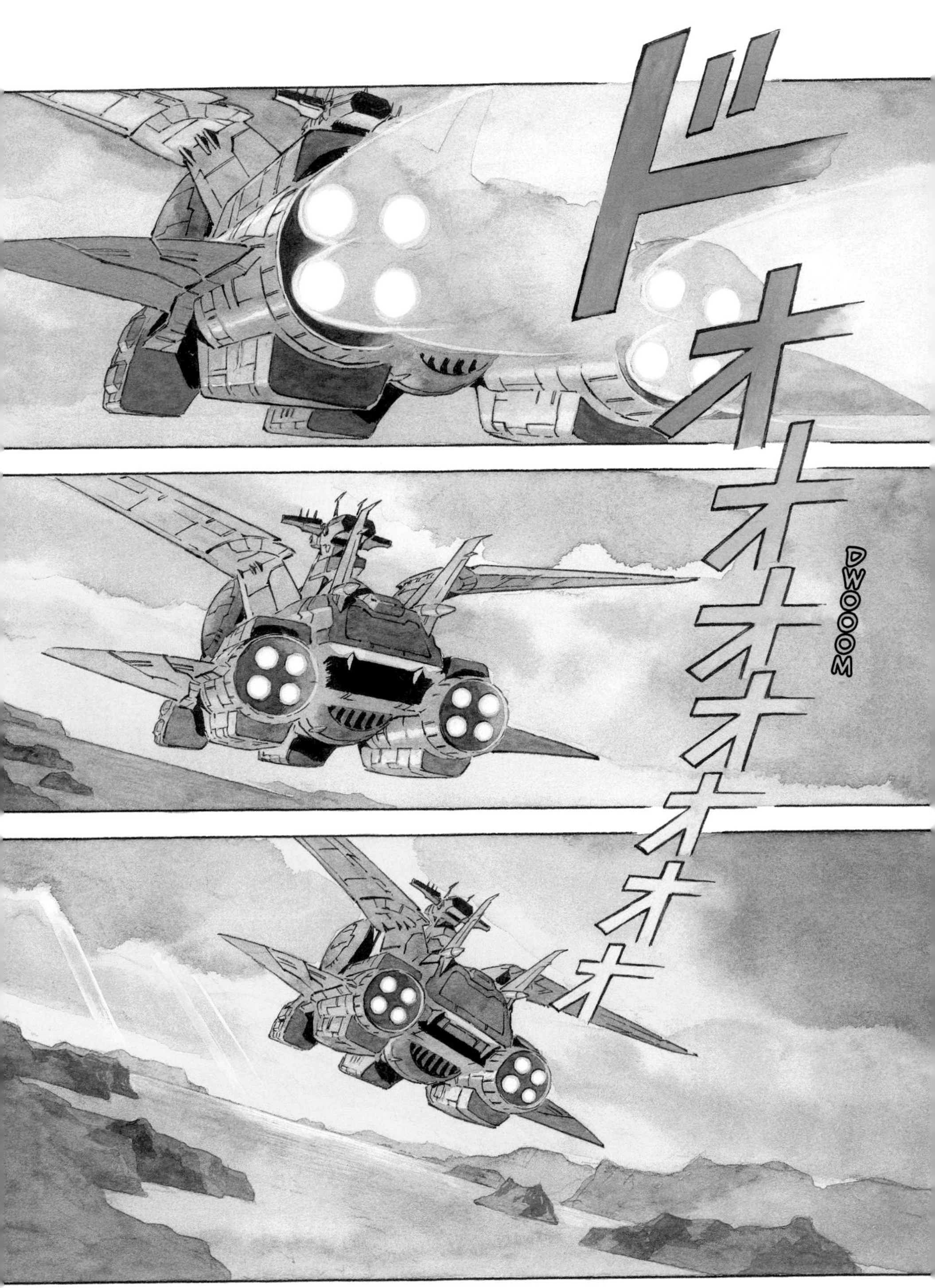
ドオオオオオオ
DWOOOOM

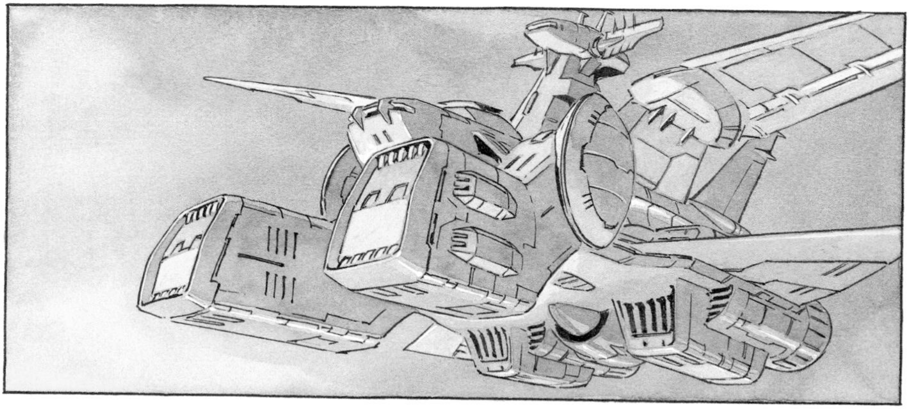
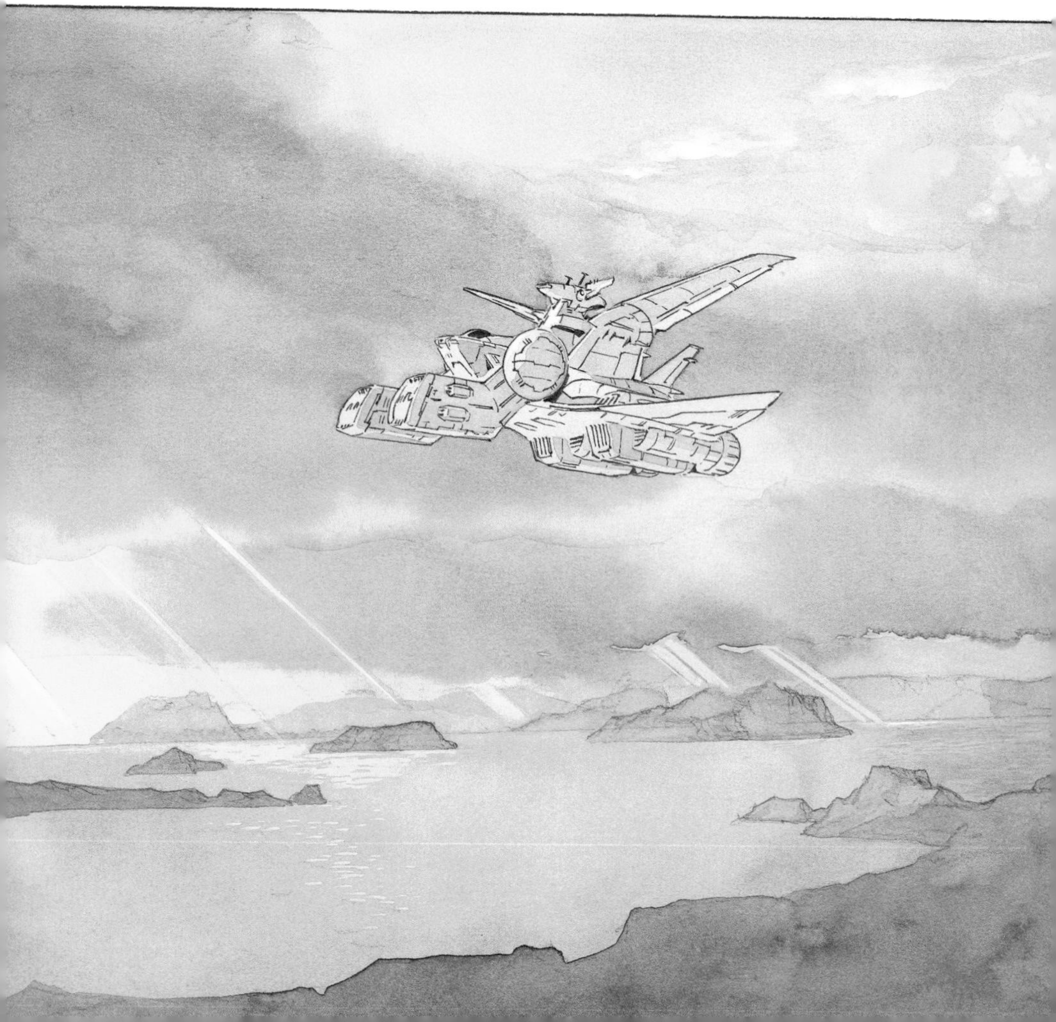

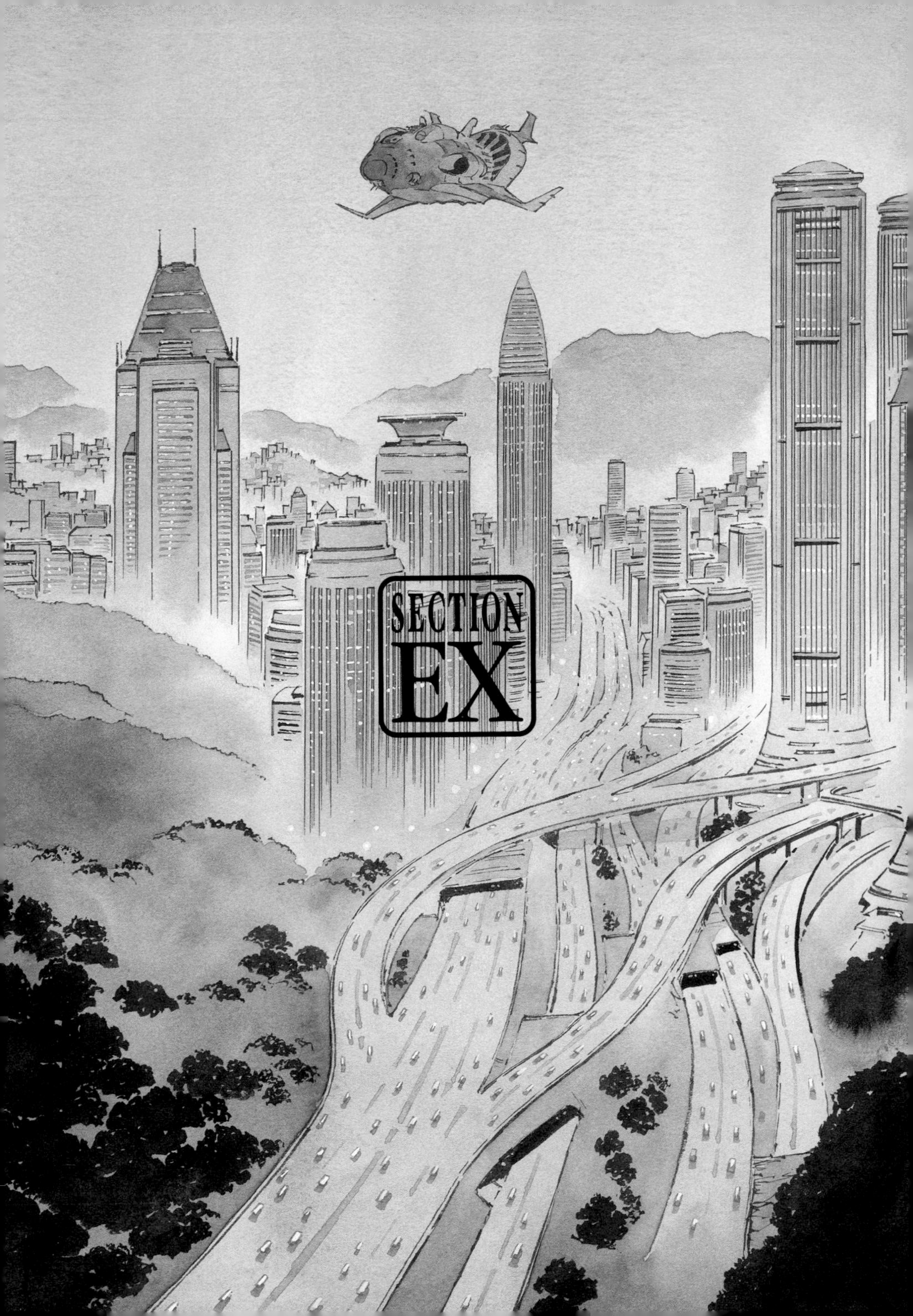
SECTION
EX

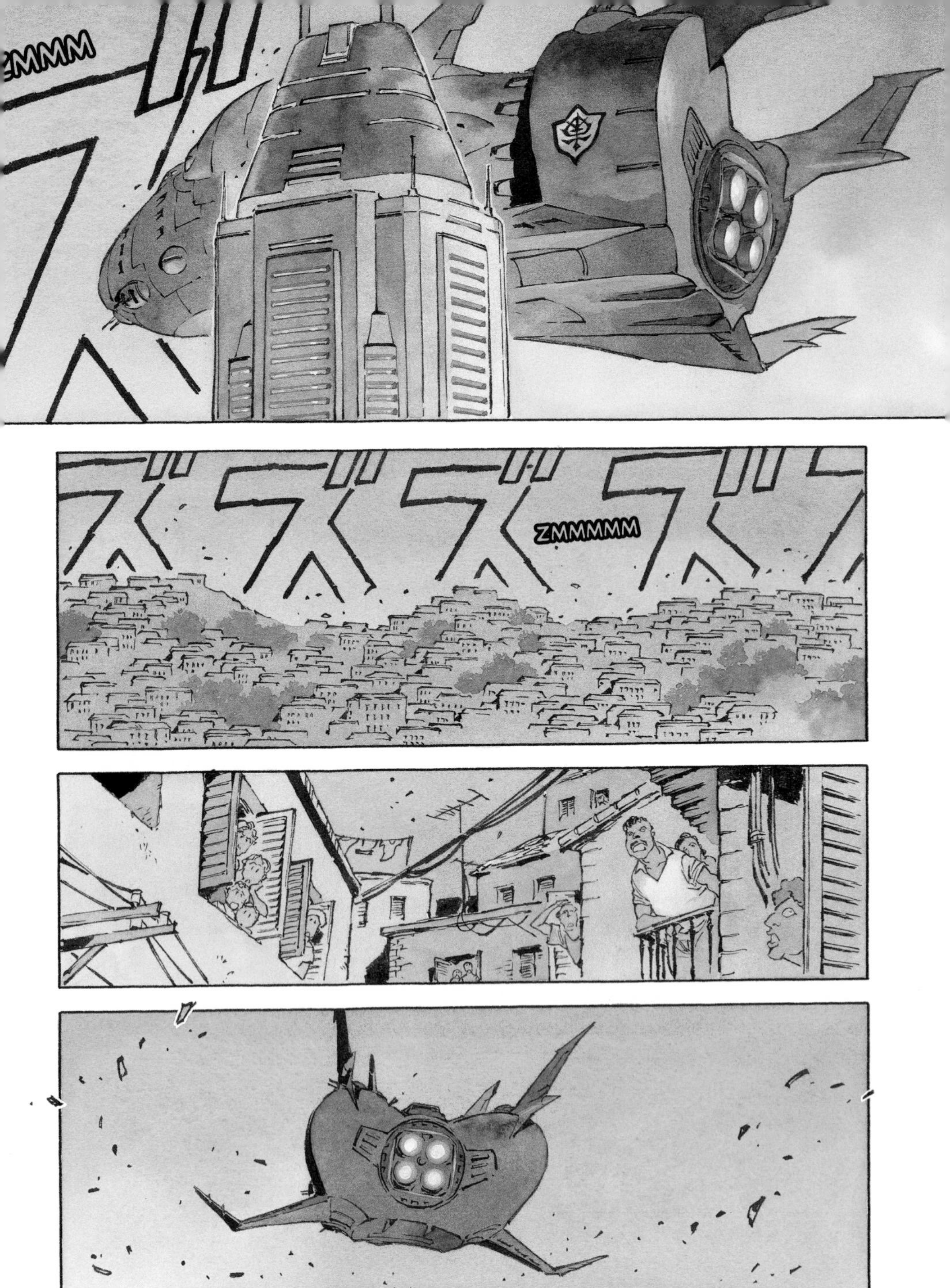
ZMMMM
ズズズズ
ZMMMMM

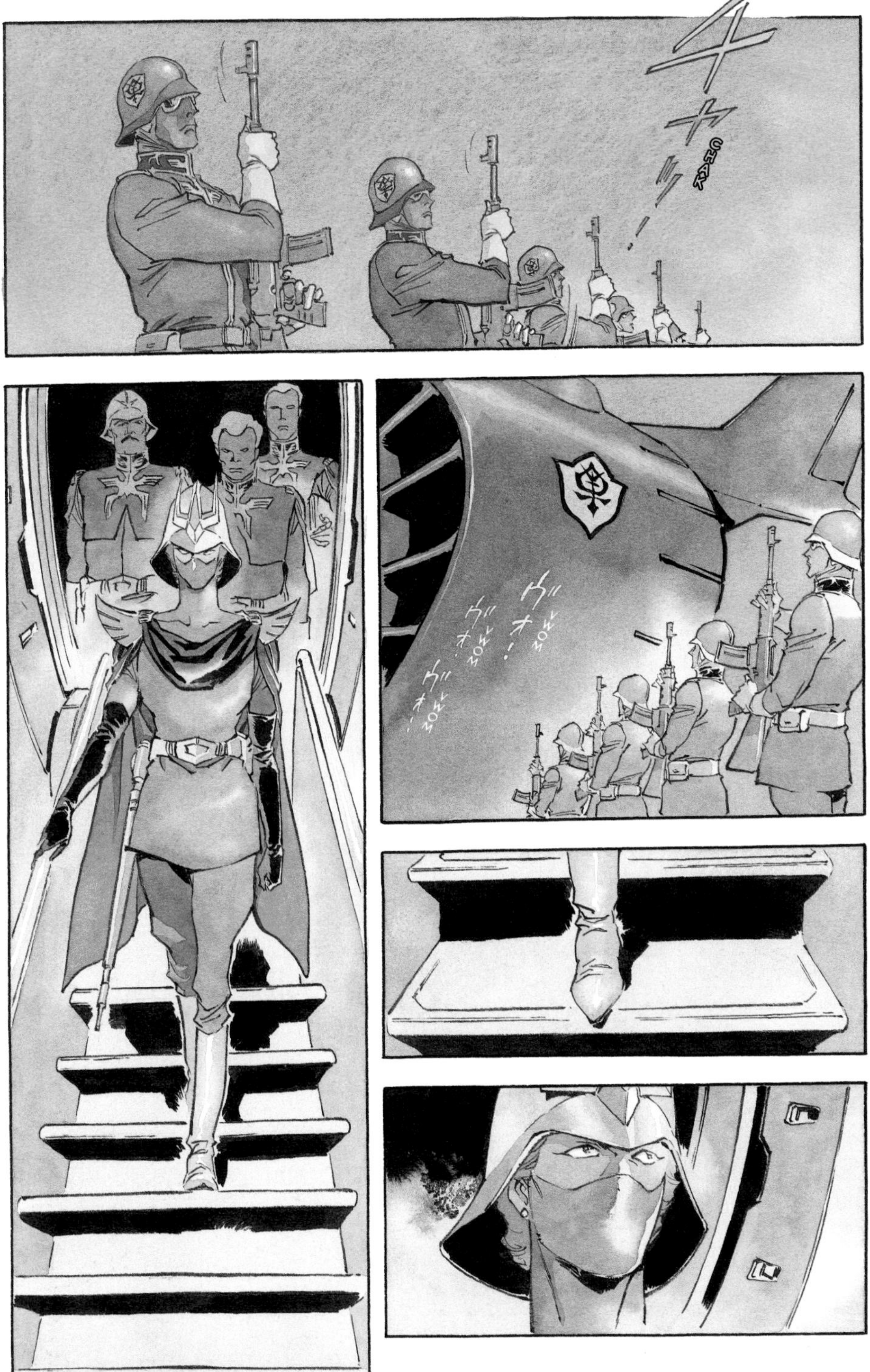
CHAK
ヴォ!
VWOM
ヴォ!
VWOM
ヴォ!
VWOM

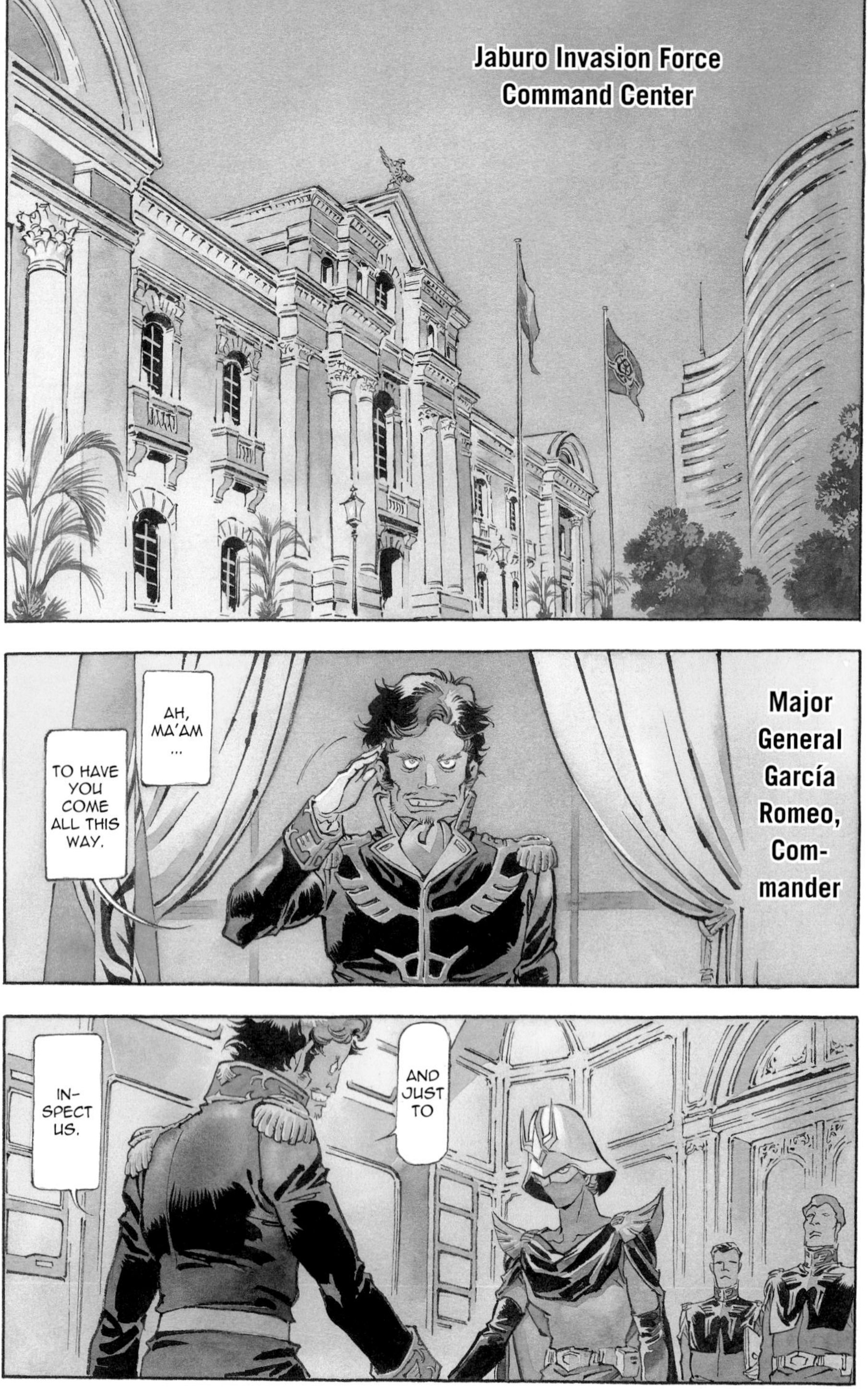
Jaburo Invasion Force Command Center
Major General García Romeo, Commander
AH, MA'AM ...
TO HAVE YOU COME ALL THIS WAY.
AND JUST TO
IN-SPECT US.

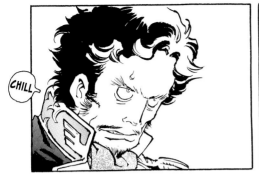

CHILL
NOT EVEN AN ANT COULD ESCAPE FROM JABURO.
AS YOU CAN SEE, MA'AM, OUR FORCES HAVE THE ENEMY UNDER HEAVY SIEGE.
CARACAS
R.ORINOCO
MANAUS
R.AMAZON
SO, WE BELIEVE THE CORE OF JABURO IS IN THE PACARAIMA MOUNTAINS IN THE MIDDLE OF THE HIGHLANDS.
OUR MAIN FORCE SITS IN MANAUS. FROM THERE,
AT THE PROPER TIME, WE WILL STRIKE IN A FLASH
AND PUT AN END TO IT.

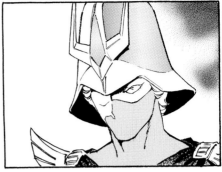

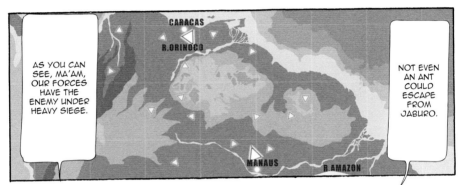

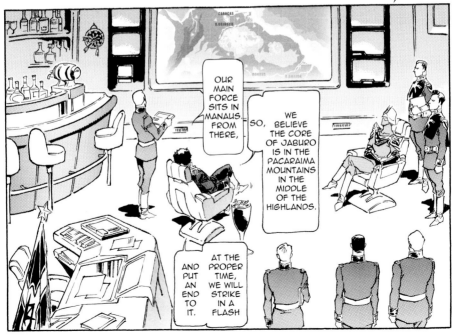

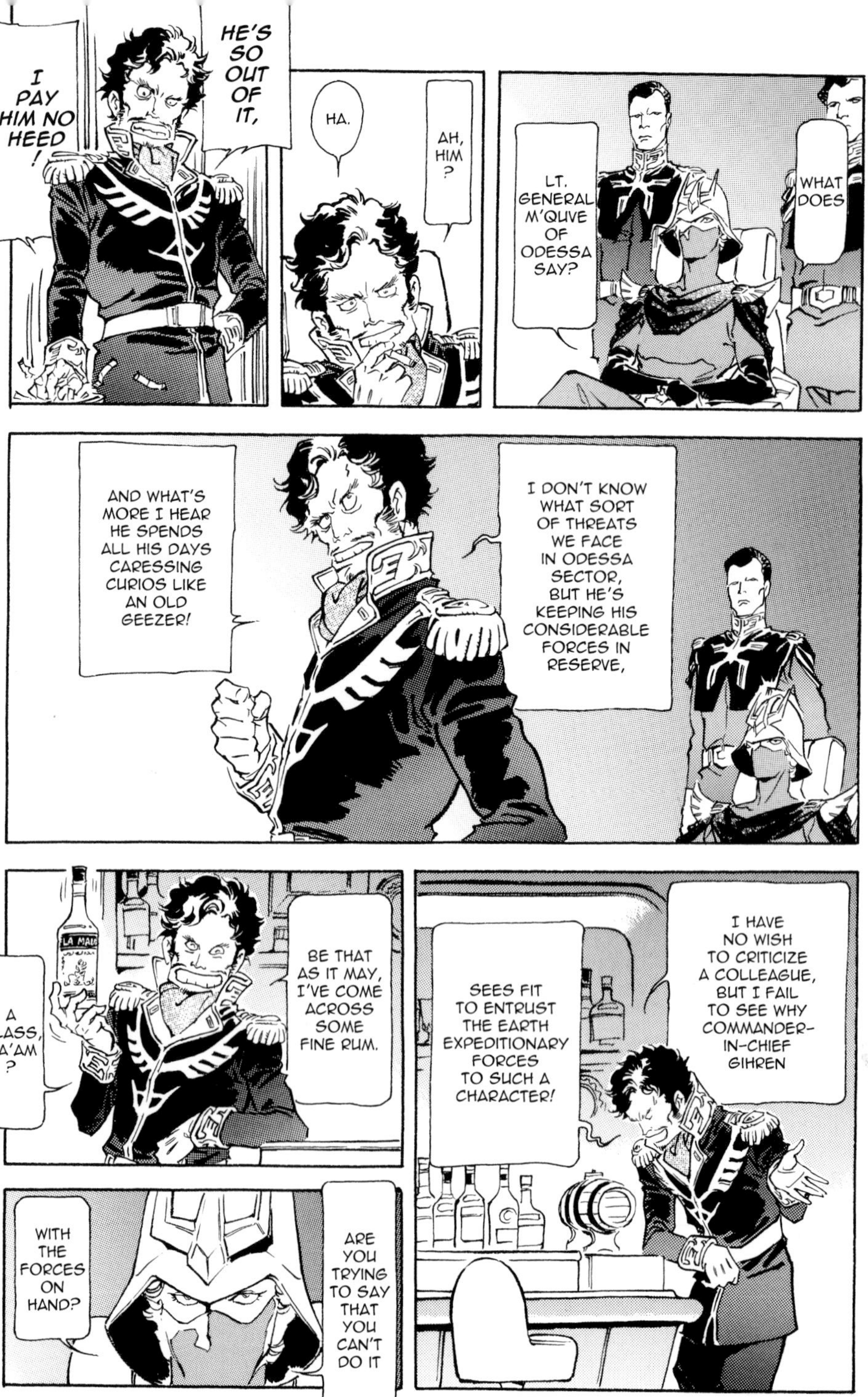
WHAT DOES
LT. GENERAL M'QUVE OF ODESSA SAY?
AH, HIM?
HA.
HE'S SO OUT OF IT,
I PAY HIM NO HEED!
I DON'T KNOW WHAT SORT OF THREATS WE FACE IN ODESSA SECTOR, BUT HE'S KEEPING HIS CONSIDERABLE FORCES IN RESERVE,
AND WHAT'S MORE I HEAR HE SPENDS ALL HIS DAYS CARESSING CURIOS LIKE AN OLD GEEZER!
I HAVE NO WISH TO CRITICIZE A COLLEAGUE, BUT I FAIL TO SEE WHY COMMANDER-IN-CHIEF GIHREN
SEES FIT TO ENTRUST THE EARTH EXPEDITIONARY FORCES TO SUCH A CHARACTER!
BE THAT AS IT MAY, I'VE COME ACROSS SOME FINE RUM.
A GLASS, MA'AM?
ARE YOU TRYING TO SAY THAT YOU CAN'T DO IT
WITH THE FORCES ON HAND?

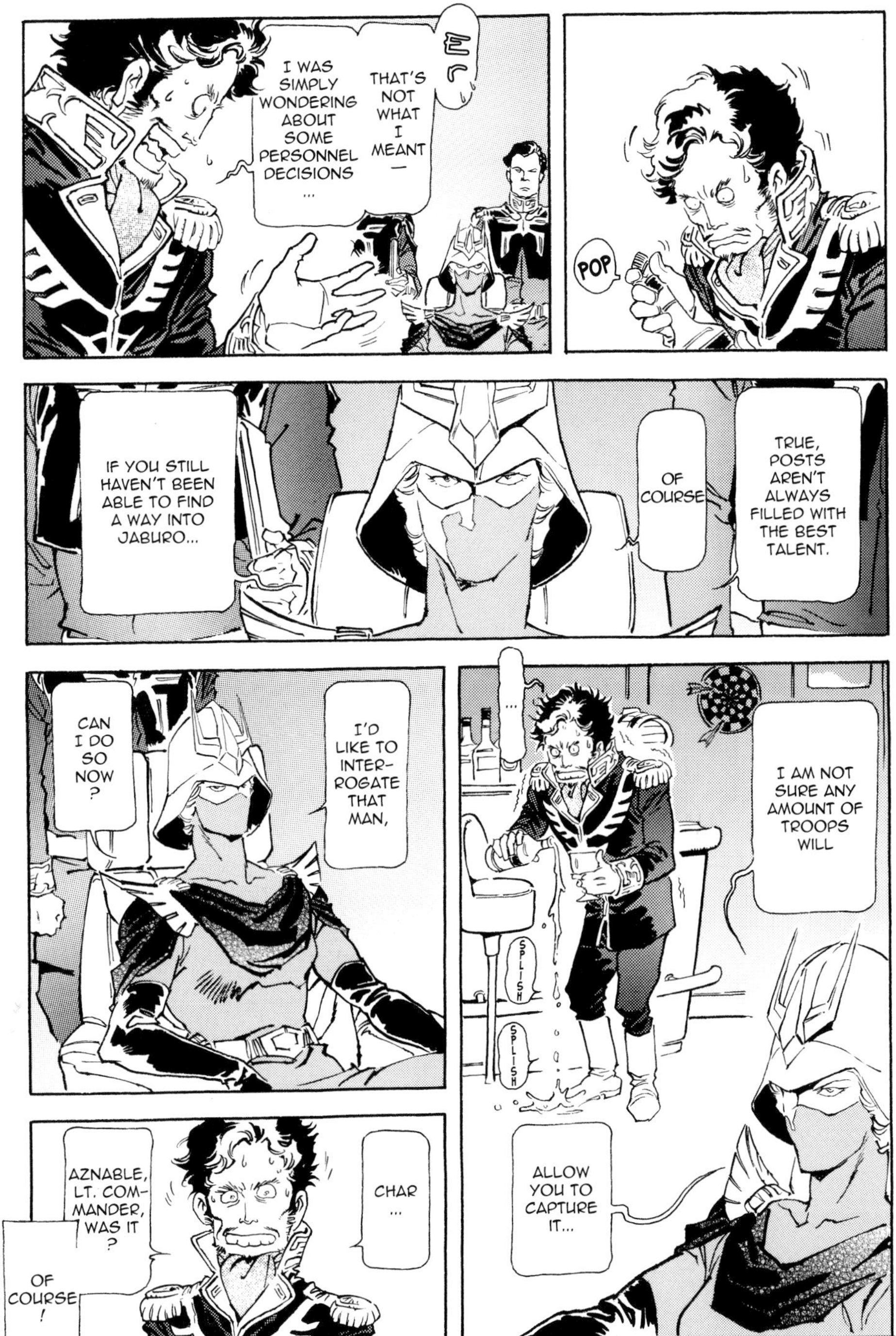
POP
Er
THAT'S NOT WHAT I MEANT—
I WAS SIMPLY WONDERING ABOUT SOME PERSONNEL DECISIONS...
TRUE, POSTS AREN'T ALWAYS FILLED WITH THE BEST TALENT.
OF COURSE
IF YOU STILL HAVEN'T BEEN ABLE TO FIND A WAY INTO JABURO...
...
I AM NOT SURE ANY AMOUNT OF TROOPS WILL
SPLISH
SPLISH
ALLOW YOU TO CAPTURE IT...
I'D LIKE TO INTERROGATE THAT MAN,
CAN I DO SO NOW?
CHAR...
AZNABLE, LT. COMMANDER, WAS IT?
OF COURSE!

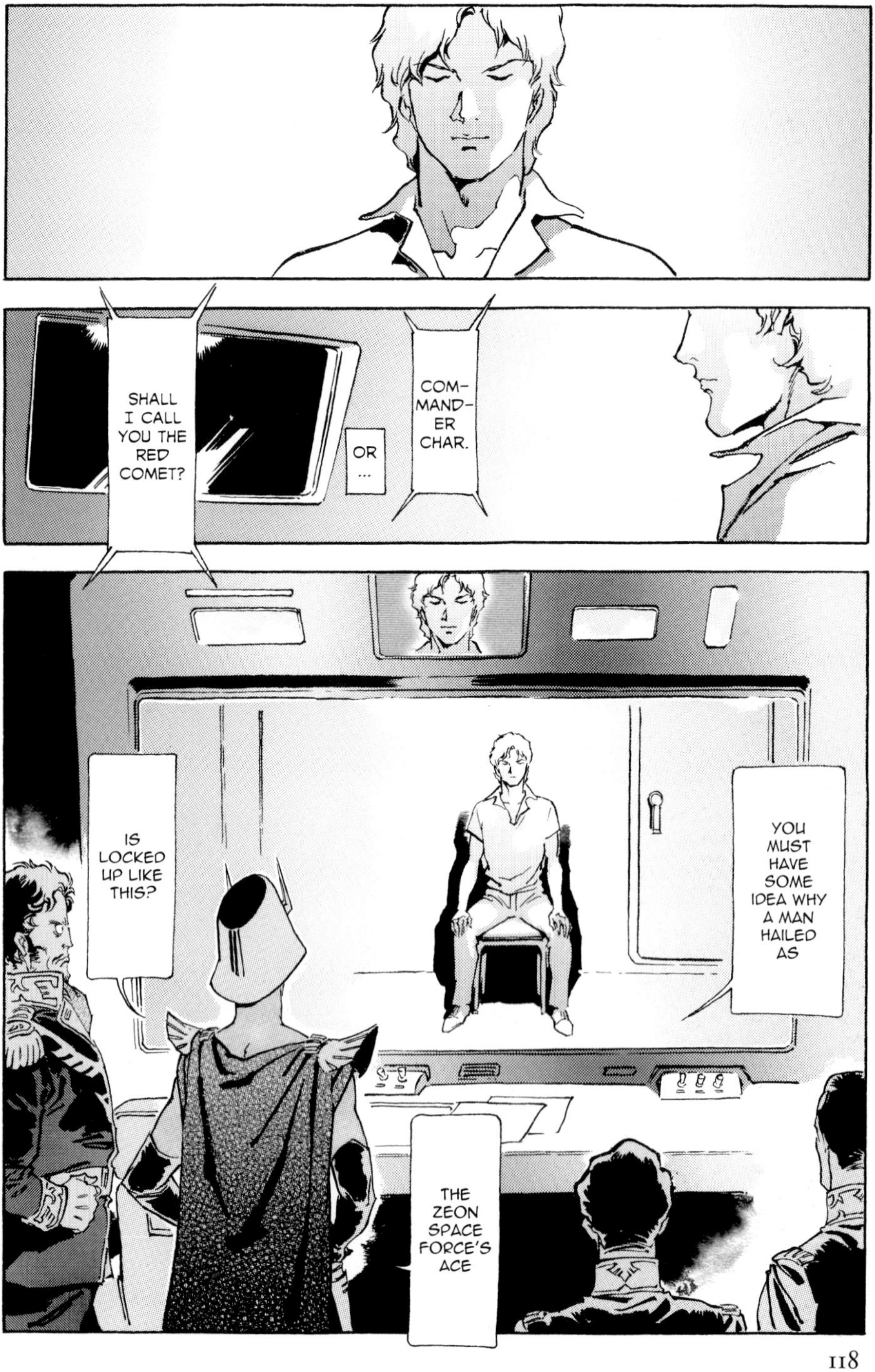
COM-MANDER CHAR.
OR ...
SHALL I CALL YOU THE RED COMET?
YOU MUST HAVE SOME IDEA WHY A MAN HAILED AS
THE ZEON SPACE FORCE'S ACE
IS LOCKED UP LIKE THIS?

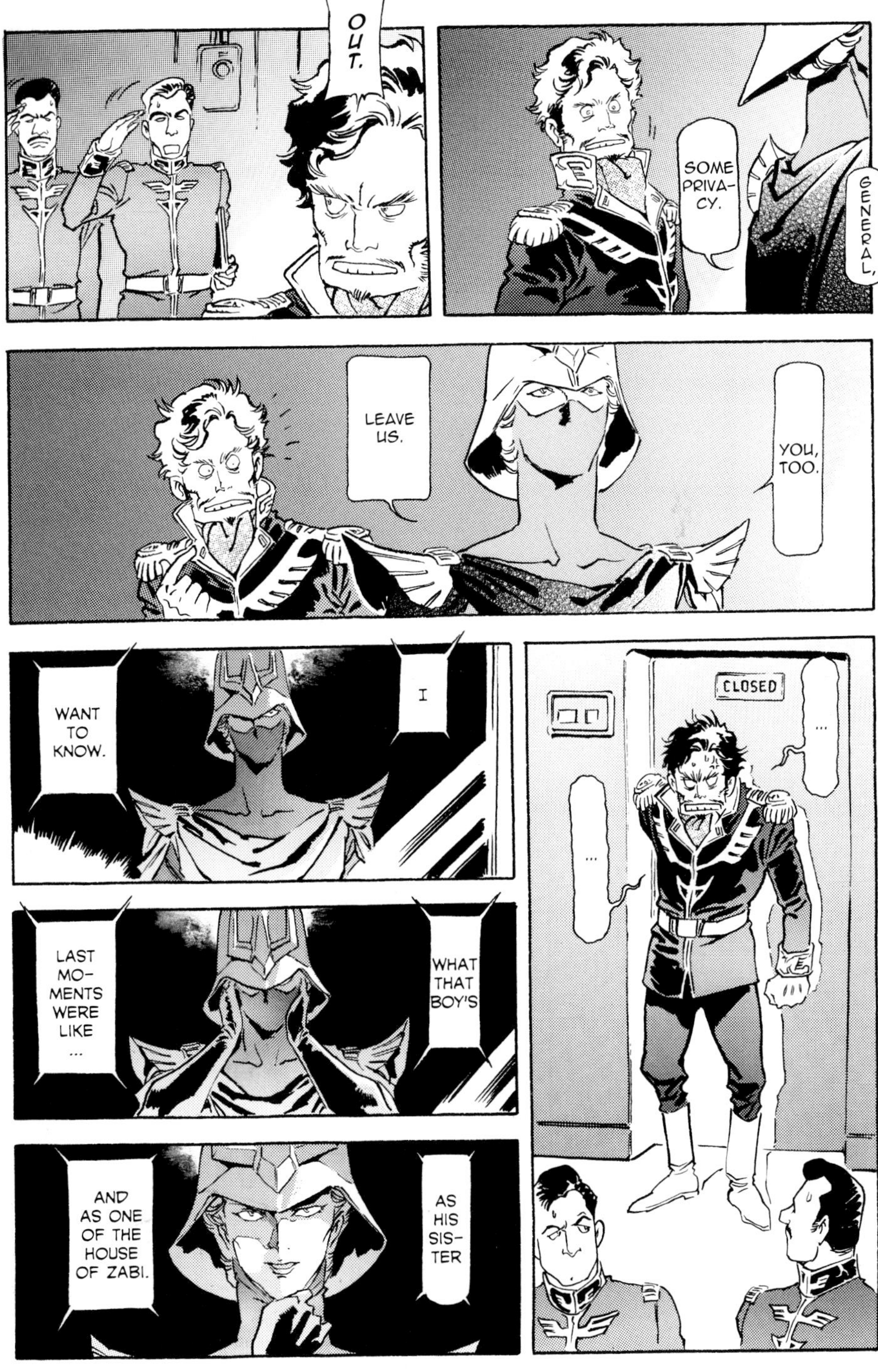
GENERAL,
SOME PRIVA-CY.
OUT.
YOU, TOO.
LEAVE US.
...
...
I
WANT TO KNOW.
WHAT THAT BOY'S
LAST MO-MENTS WERE LIKE ...
AS HIS SIS-TER
AND AS ONE OF THE HOUSE OF ZABI.

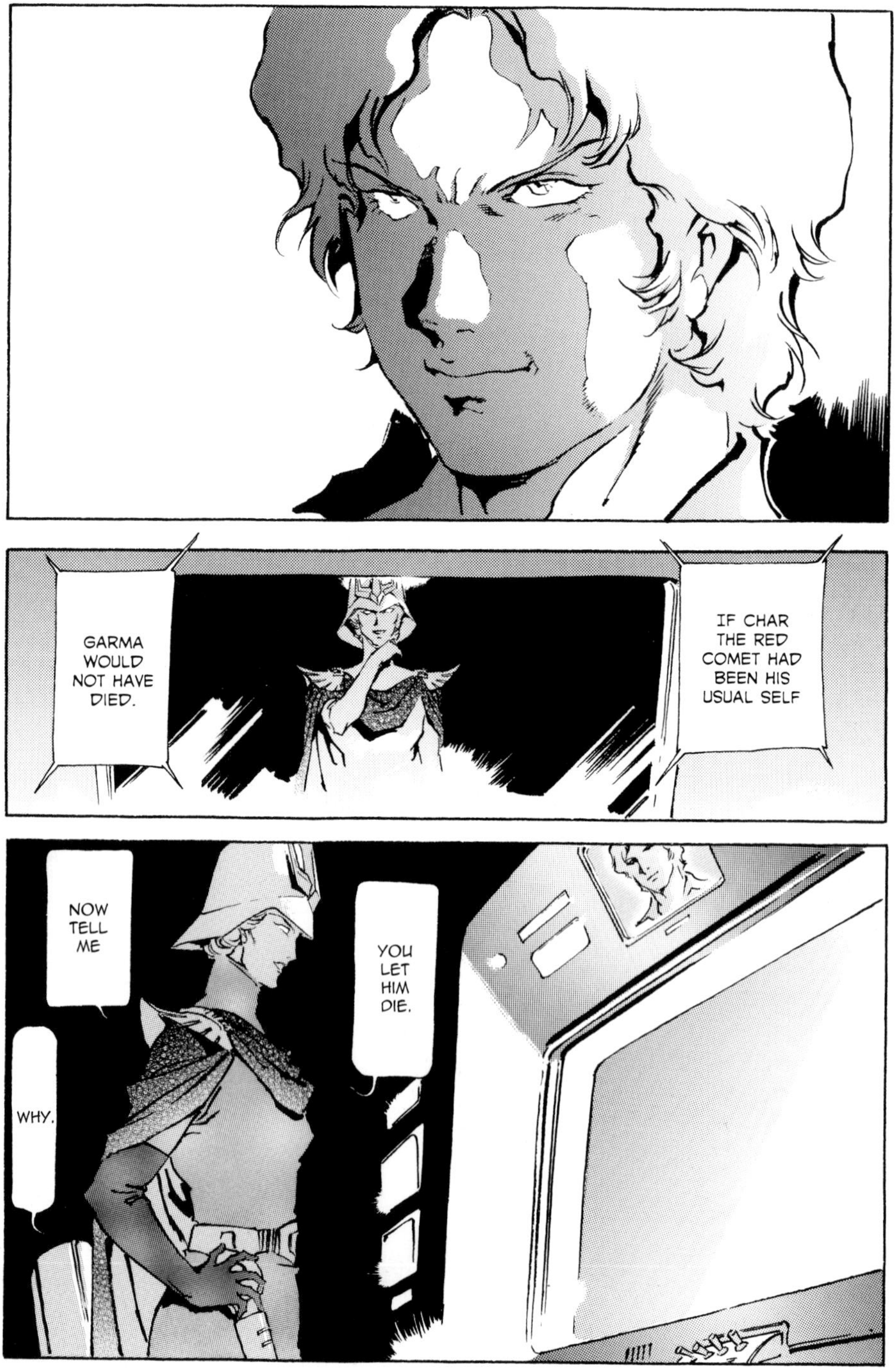
IF CHAR THE RED COMET HAD BEEN HIS USUAL SELF
GARMA WOULD NOT HAVE DIED.
YOU LET HIM DIE.
NOW TELL ME
WHY.

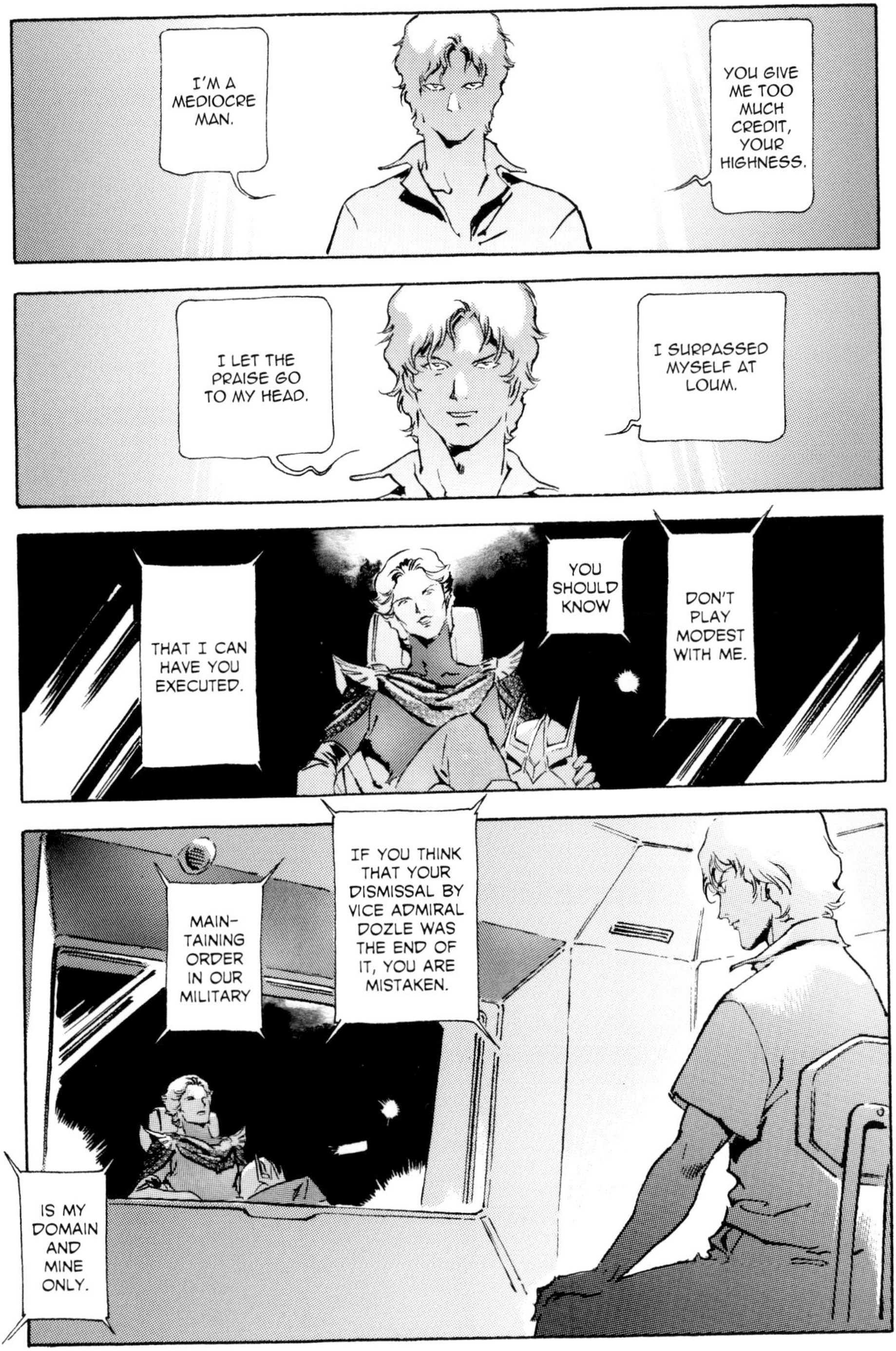
YOU GIVE ME TOO MUCH CREDIT, YOUR HIGHNESS.
I'M A MEDIOCRE MAN.
I SURPASSED MYSELF AT LOUM.
I LET THE PRAISE GO TO MY HEAD.
DON'T PLAY MODEST WITH ME.
YOU SHOULD KNOW
THAT I CAN HAVE YOU EXECUTED.
IF YOU THINK THAT YOUR DISMISSAL BY VICE ADMIRAL DOZLE WAS THE END OF IT, YOU ARE MISTAKEN.
MAIN-TAINING ORDER IN OUR MILITARY
IS MY DOMAIN AND MINE ONLY.

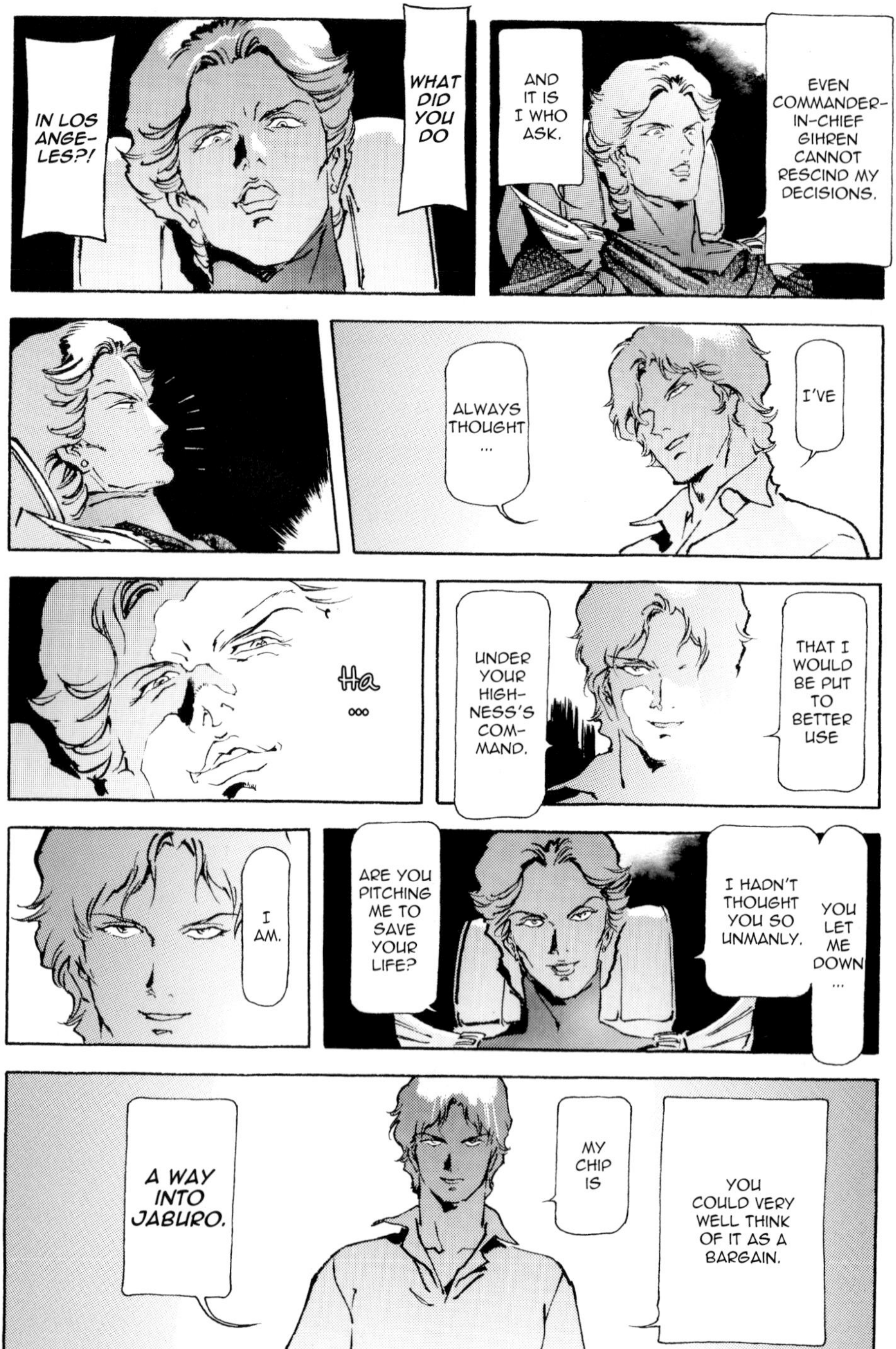
EVEN COMMANDER-IN-CHIEF GIHREN CANNOT RESCIND MY DECISIONS.
AND IT IS I WHO ASK.
WHAT DID YOU DO
IN LOS ANGE-LES?!
I'VE
ALWAYS THOUGHT ...
THAT I WOULD BE PUT TO BETTER USE
UNDER YOUR HIGH-NESS'S COM-MAND.
Ha ...
YOU LET ME DOWN ...
I HADN'T THOUGHT YOU SO UNMANLY.
ARE YOU PITCHING ME TO SAVE YOUR LIFE?
I AM.
YOU COULD VERY WELL THINK OF IT AS A BARGAIN.
MY CHIP IS
A WAY INTO JABURO.

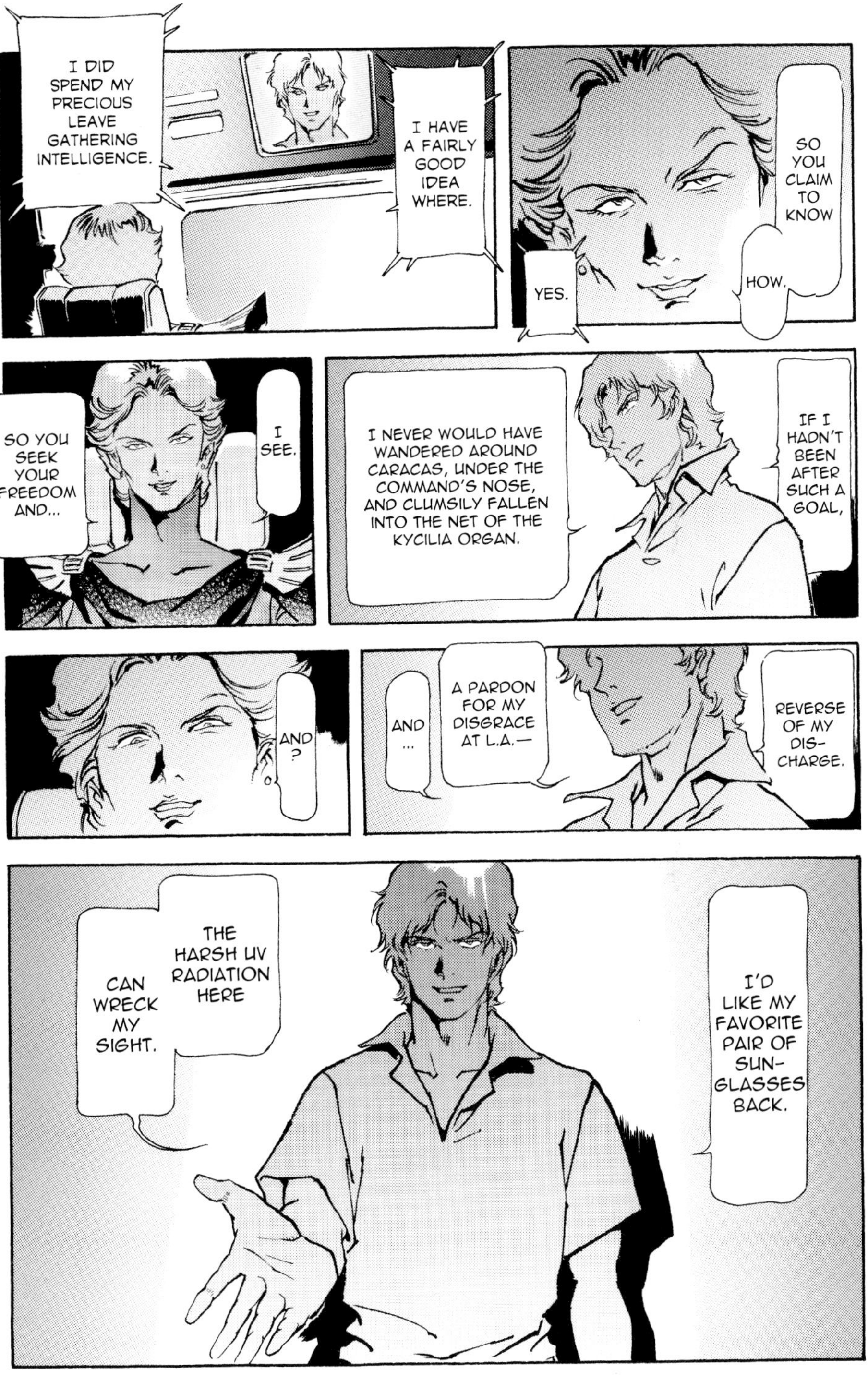
SO YOU CLAIM TO KNOW
HOW.
YES.
I HAVE A FAIRLY GOOD IDEA WHERE.
I DID SPEND MY PRECIOUS LEAVE GATHERING INTELLIGENCE.
IF I HADN'T BEEN AFTER SUCH A GOAL,
I NEVER WOULD HAVE WANDERED AROUND CARACAS, UNDER THE COMMAND'S NOSE, AND CLUMSILY FALLEN INTO THE NET OF THE KYCILIA ORGAN.
I SEE.
SO YOU SEEK YOUR FREEDOM AND...
REVERSE OF MY DIS-CHARGE.
A PARDON FOR MY DISGRACE AT L.A.—
AND ...
AND ?
I'D LIKE MY FAVORITE PAIR OF SUN-GLASSES BACK.
THE HARSH UV RADIATION HERE
CAN WRECK MY SIGHT.

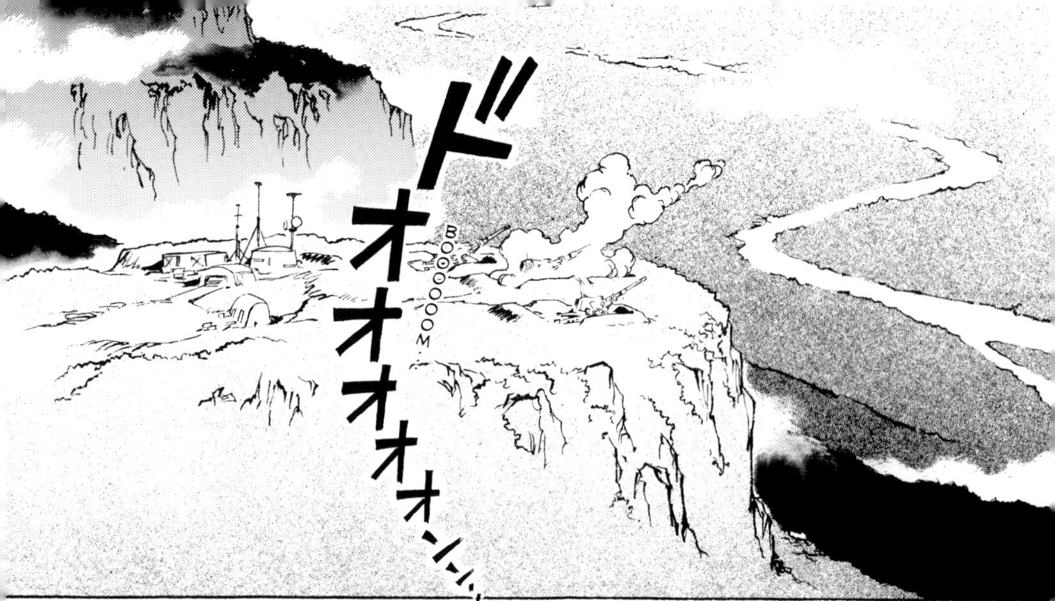
ドオオオオーン…
BOOOOOOM..
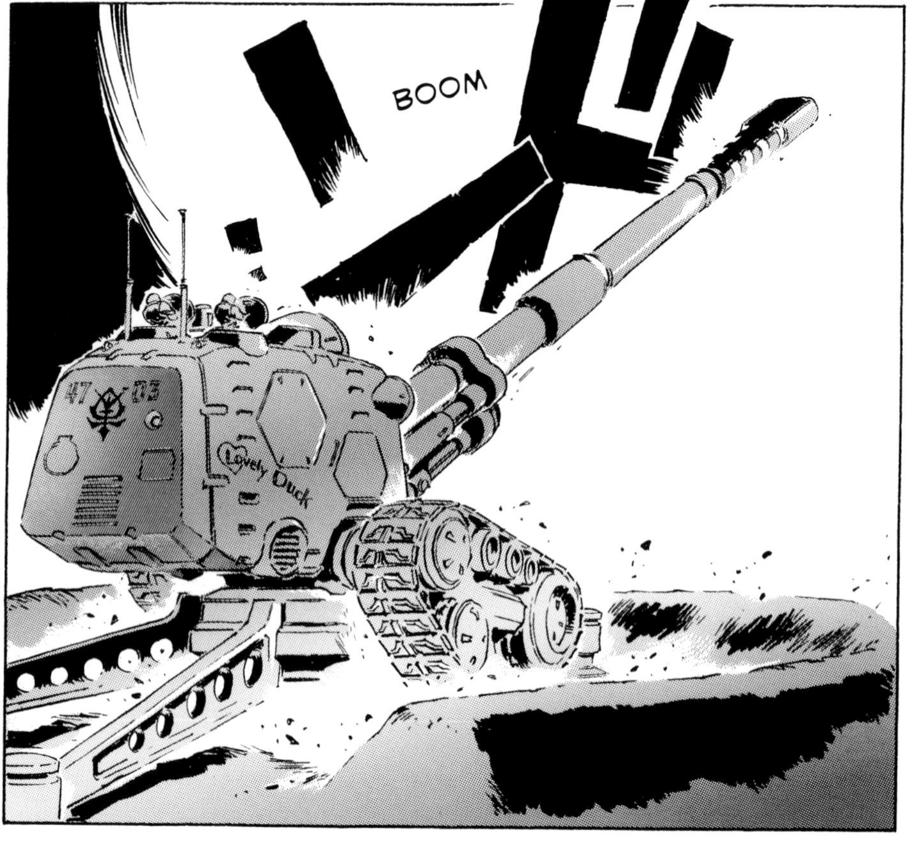
BOOM

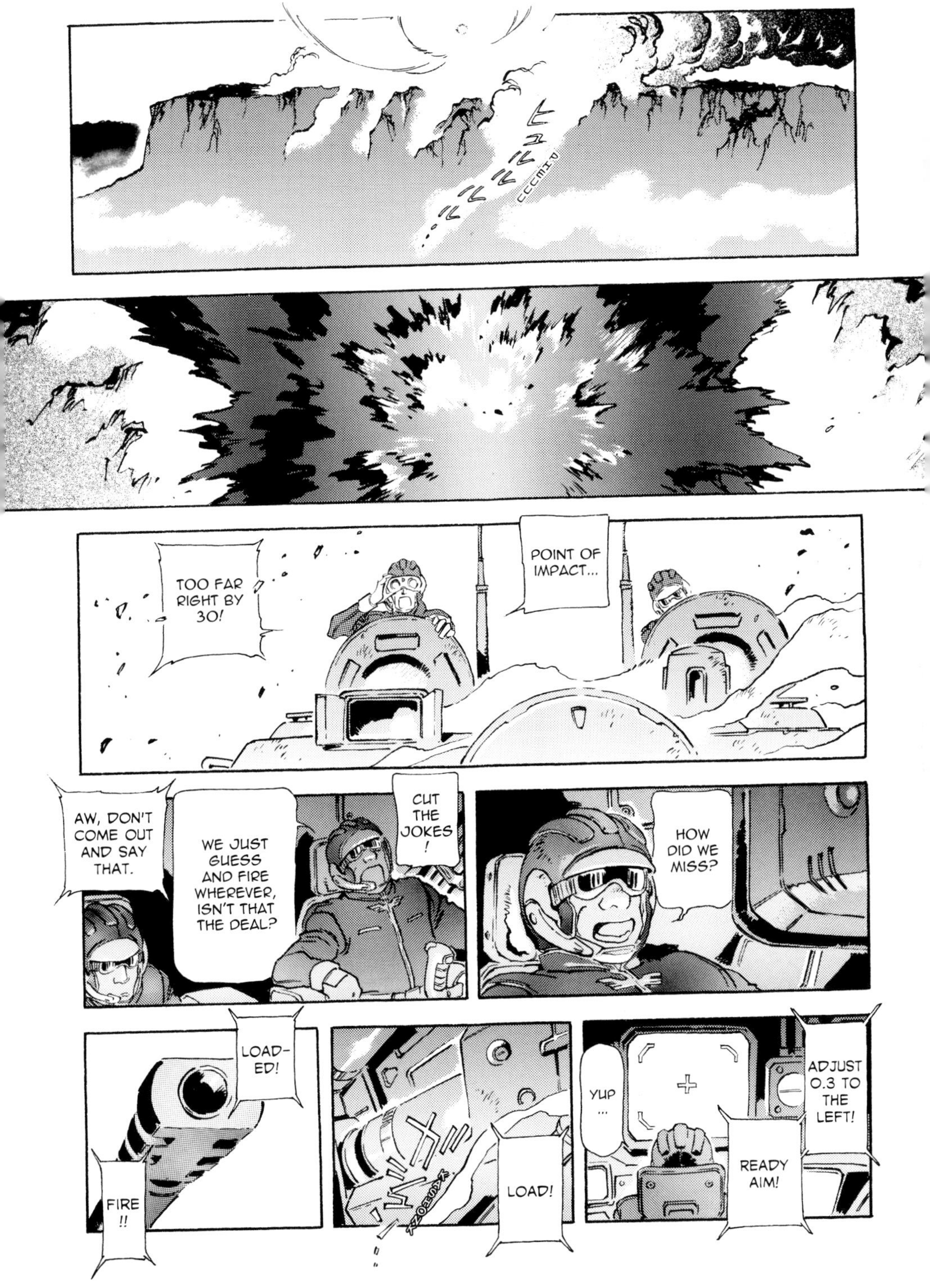
ヒュルルル
POINT OF IMPACT...
TOO FAR RIGHT BY 30!
HOW DID WE MISS?
CUT THE JOKES!
WE JUST GUESS AND FIRE WHEREVER, ISN'T THAT THE DEAL?
AW, DON'T COME OUT AND SAY THAT.
ADJUST 0.3 TO THE LEFT!
READY AIM!
YUP...
LOAD!
LOADED!
FIRE!!

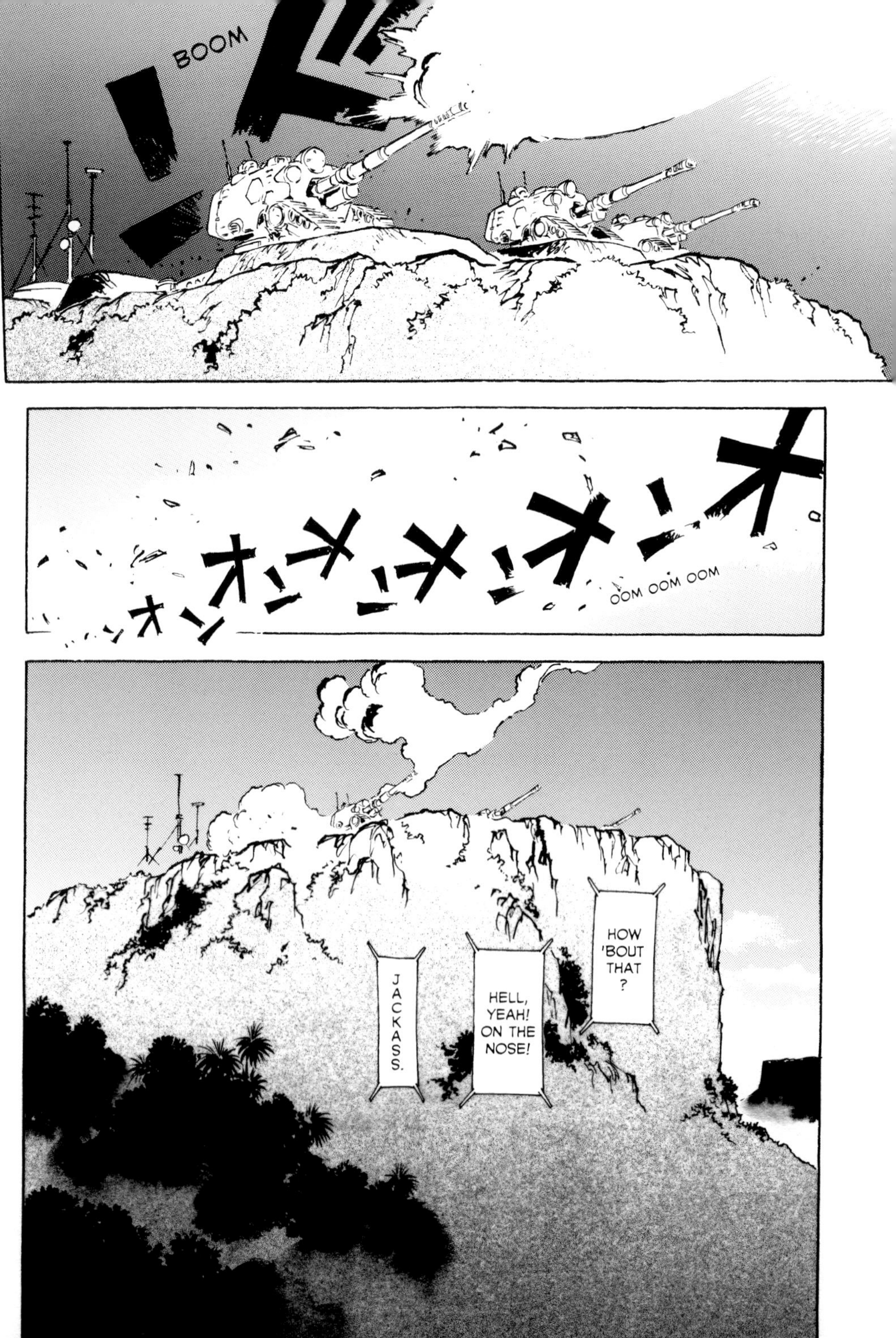
BOOM
OOM OOM OOM
HOW 'BOUT THAT?
HELL, YEAH! ON THE NOSE!
JACKASS.

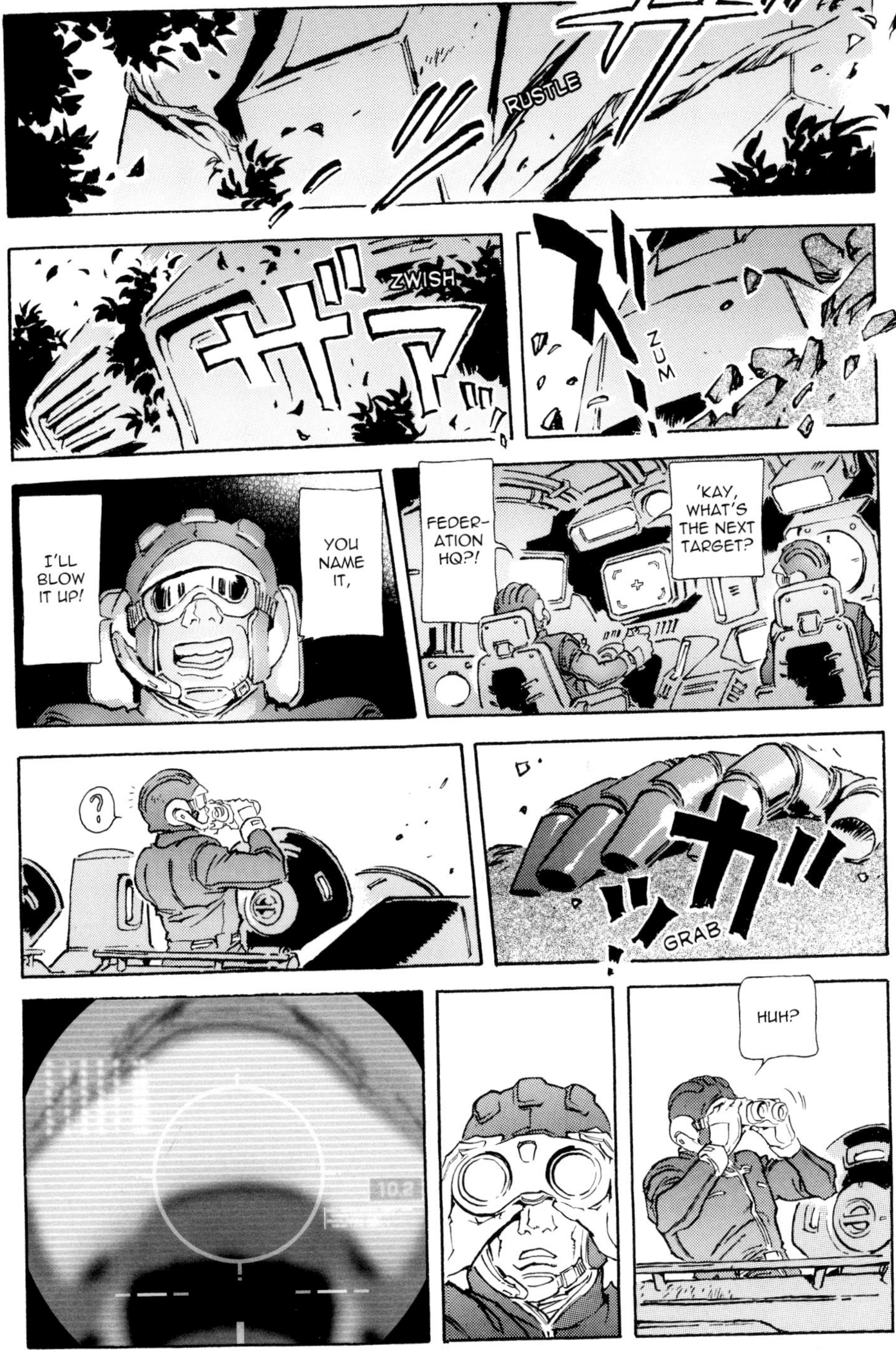
RUSTLE
ZUM
ZWISH
'KAY, WHAT'S THE NEXT TARGET?
FEDER-ATION HQ?!
YOU NAME IT,
I'LL BLOW IT UP!
GRAB
?
HUH?

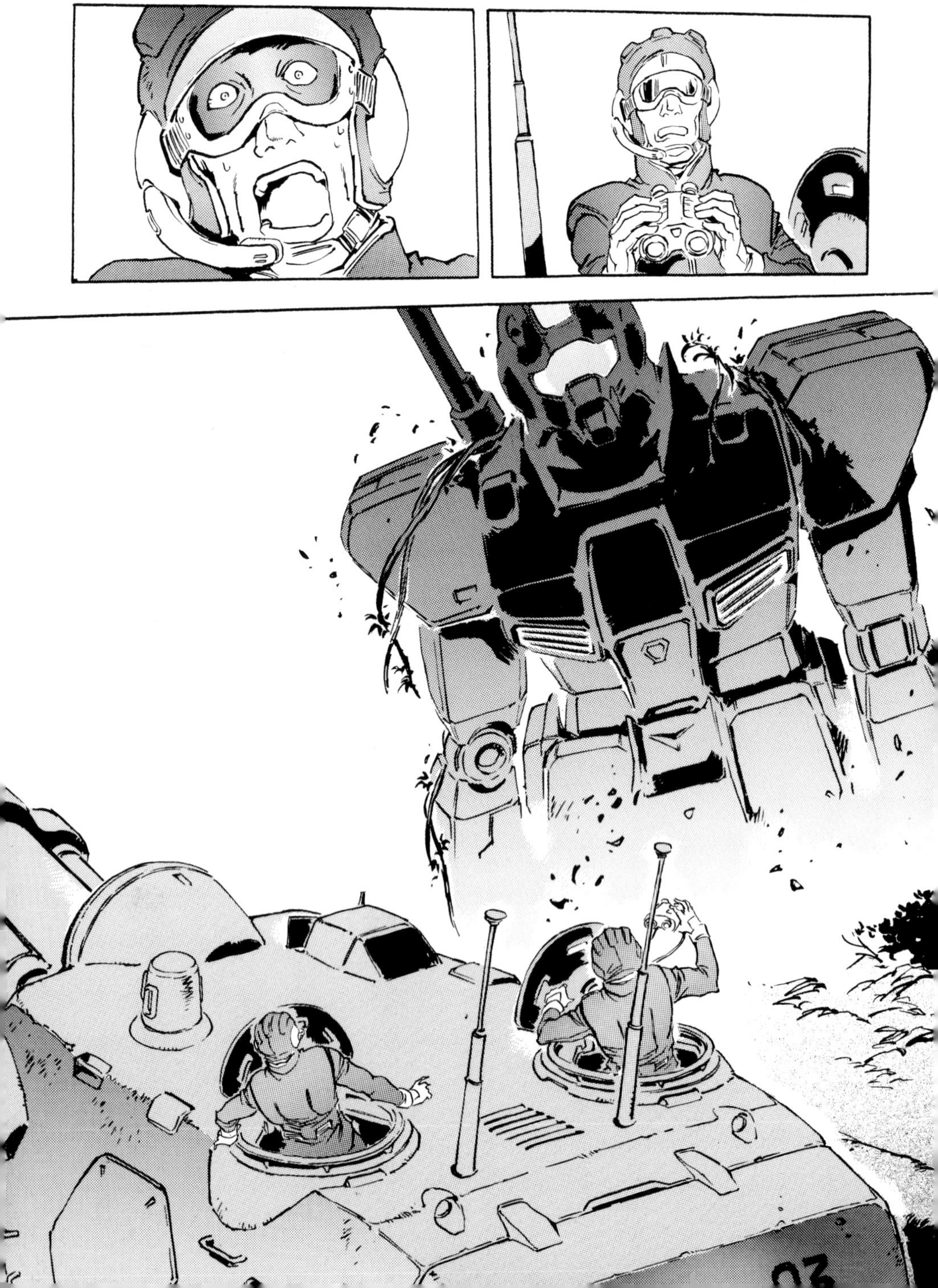

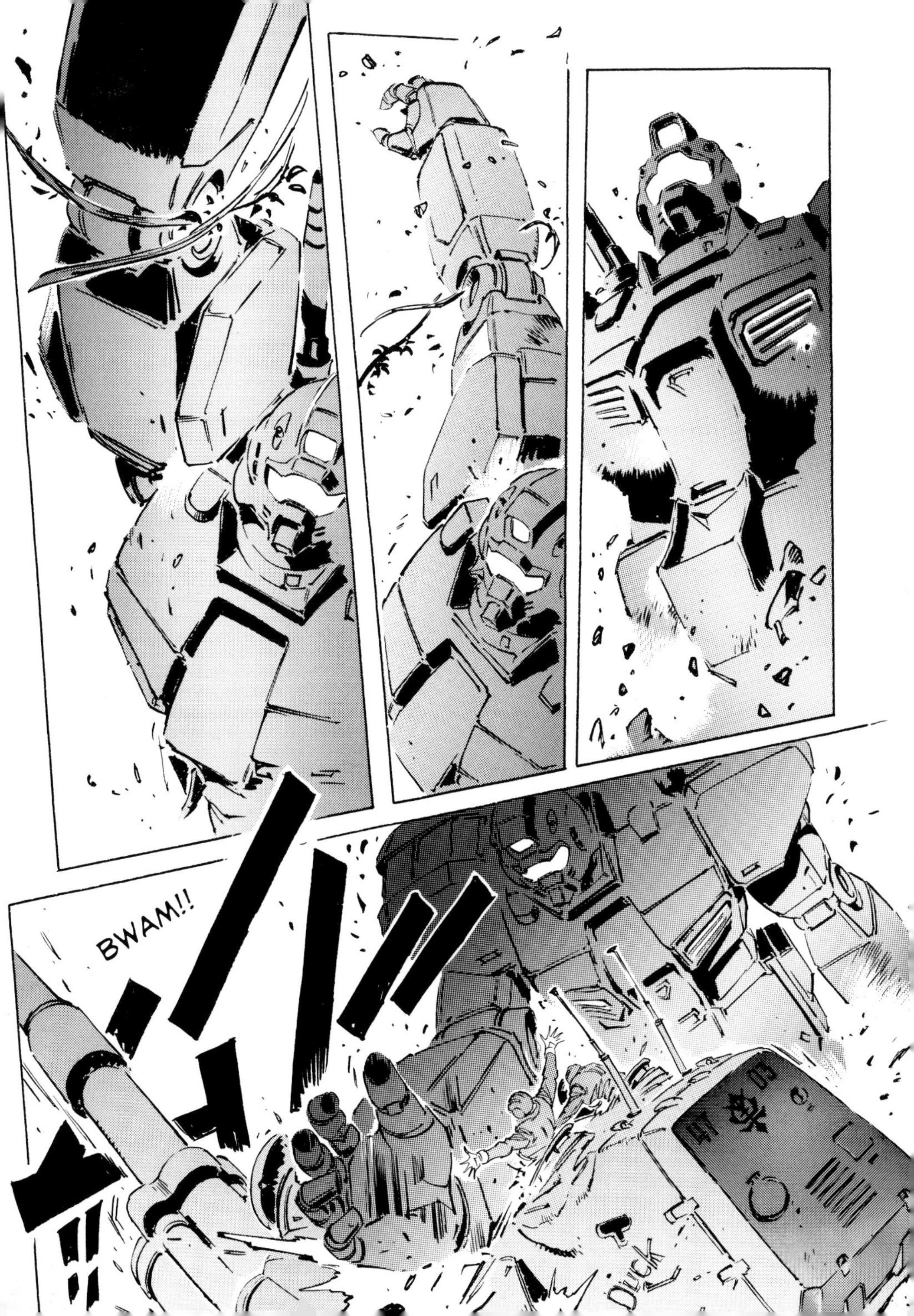
BWAM!!
DUCK

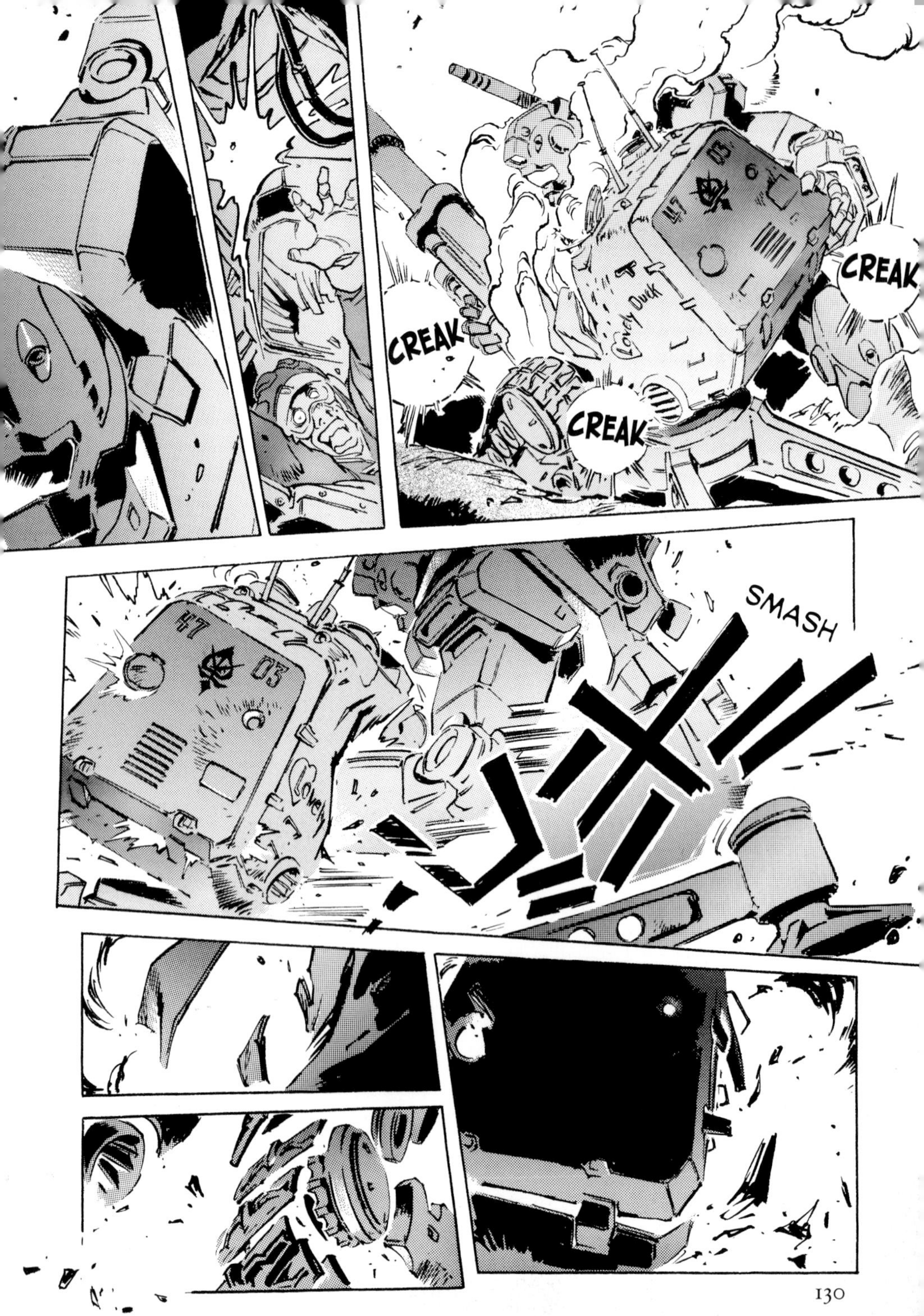
CREAK
CREAK
CREAK
SMASH

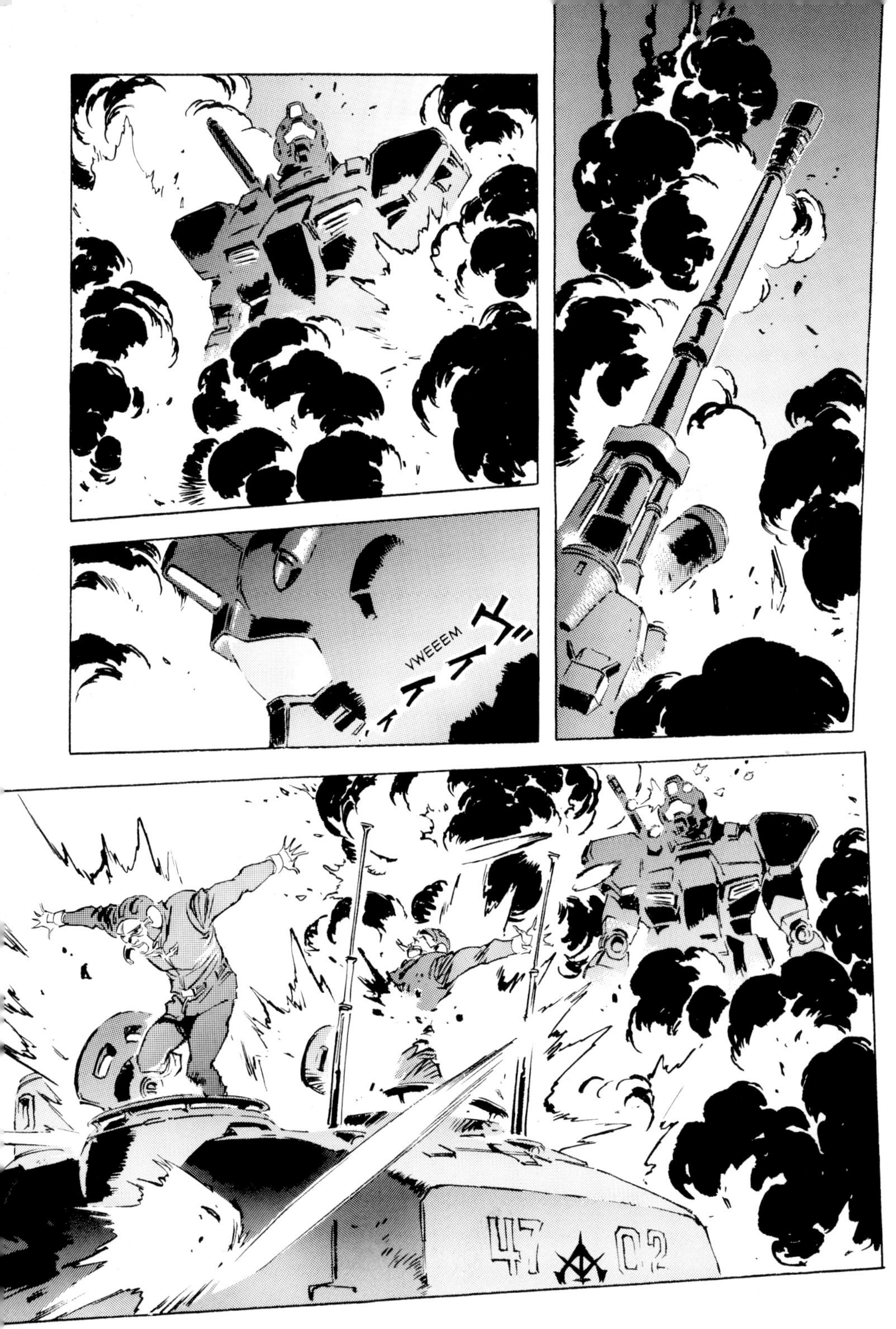
VWEEEM

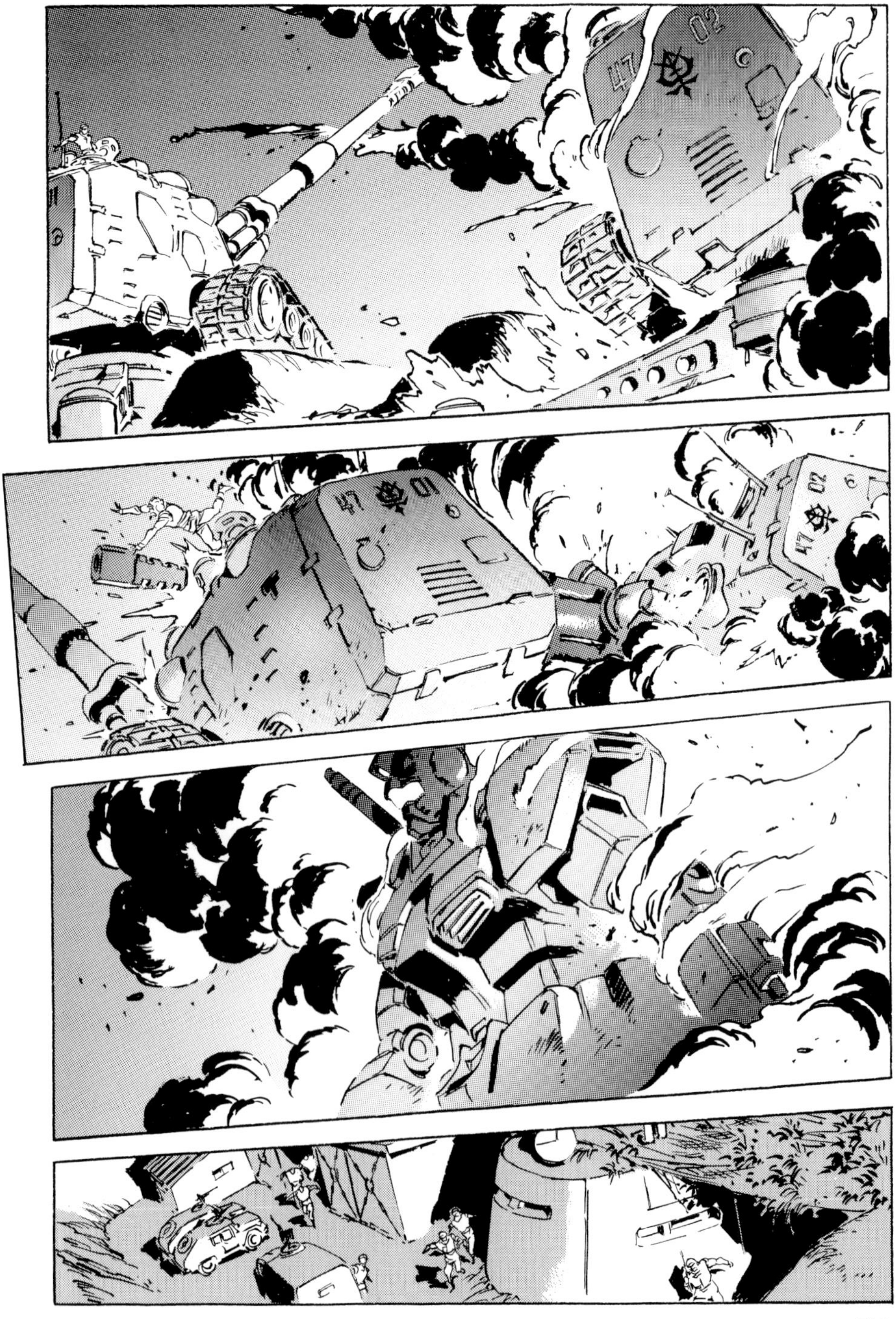

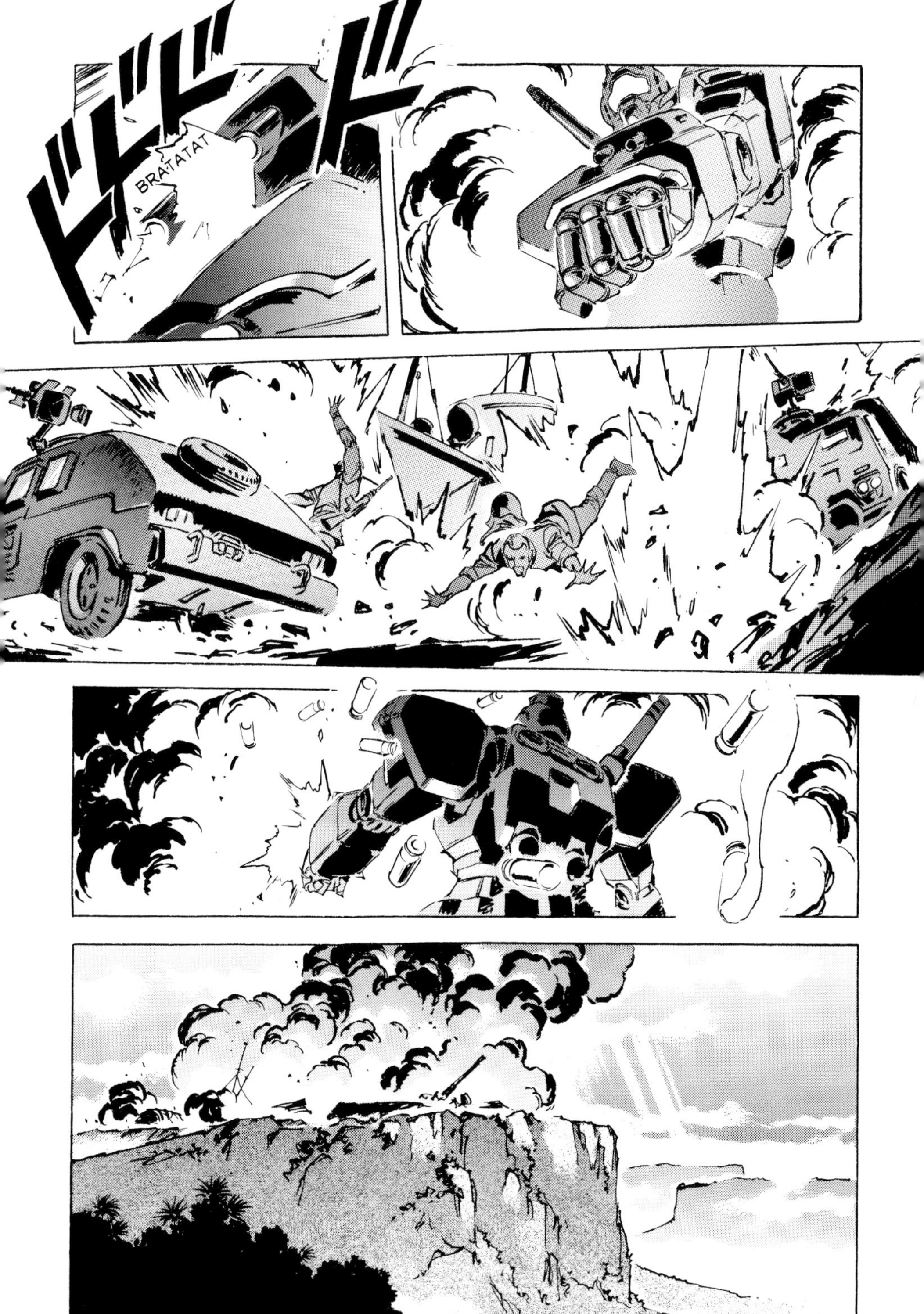
ドドドド
BRA-TATAT

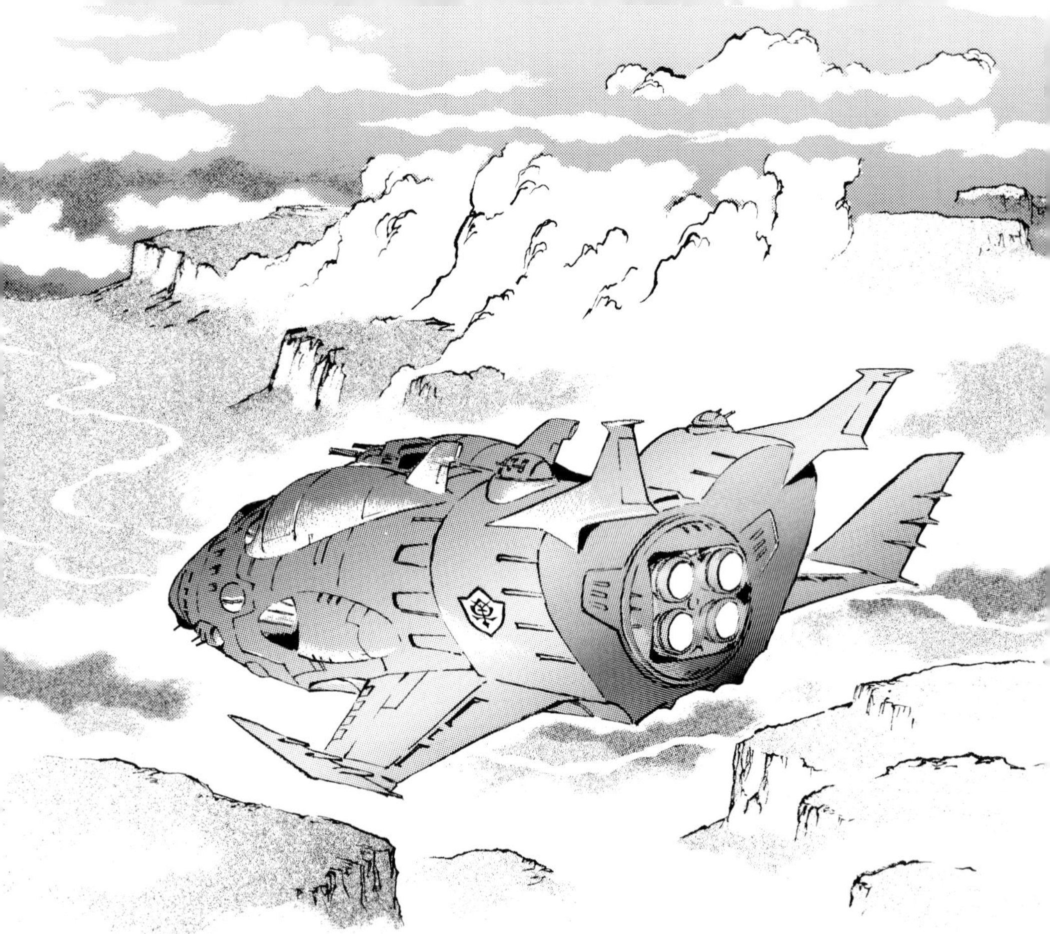
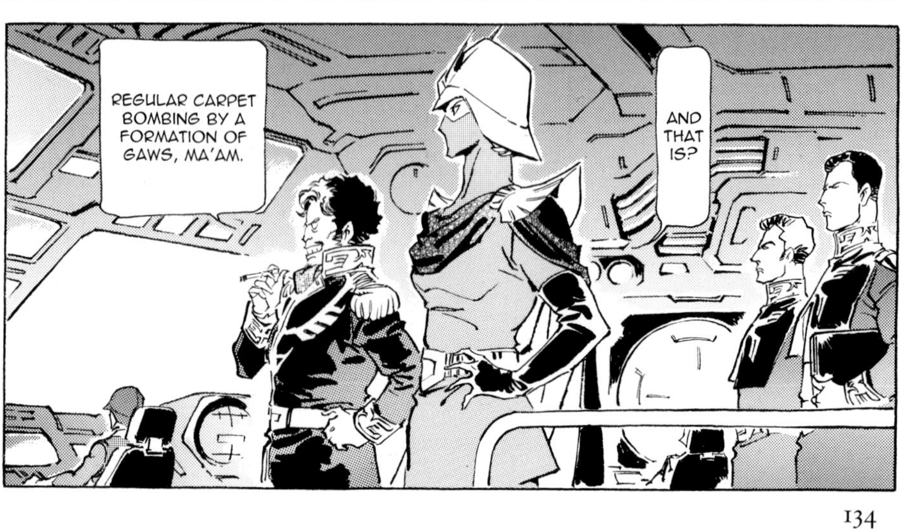
AND THAT IS?
REGULAR CARPET BOMBING BY A FORMATION OF GAWS, MA'AM.

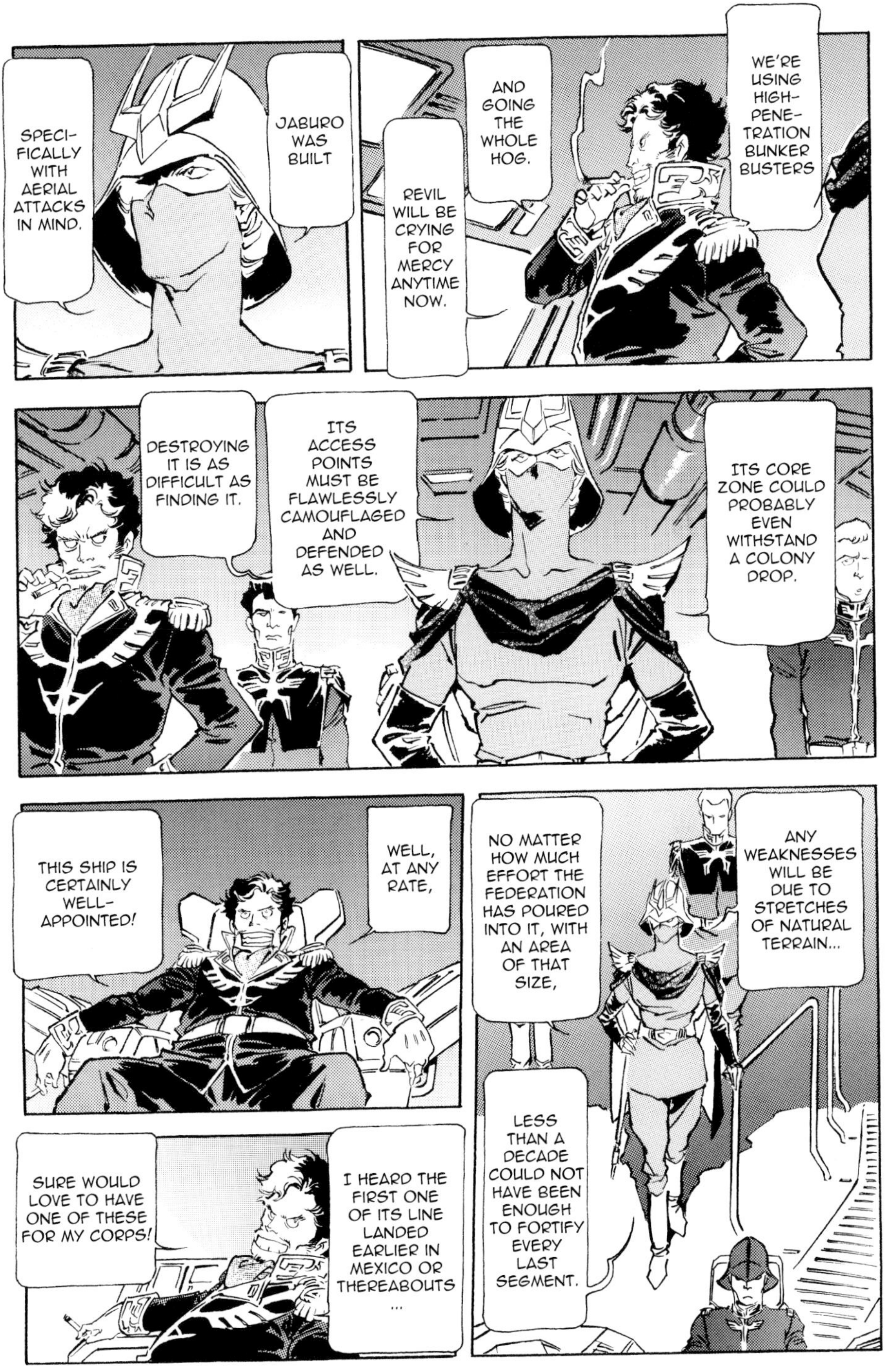
WE'RE USING HIGH-PENETRATION BUNKER BUSTERS
AND GOING THE WHOLE HOG.
REVIL WILL BE CRYING FOR MERCY ANYTIME NOW.
JABURO WAS BUILT
SPECIFICALLY WITH AERIAL ATTACKS IN MIND.
ITS CORE ZONE COULD PROBABLY EVEN WITHSTAND A COLONY DROP.
ITS ACCESS POINTS MUST BE FLAWLESSLY CAMOUFLAGED AND DEFENDED AS WELL.
DESTROYING IT IS AS DIFFICULT AS FINDING IT.
ANY WEAKNESSES WILL BE DUE TO STRETCHES OF NATURAL TERRAIN...
NO MATTER HOW MUCH EFFORT THE FEDERATION HAS POURED INTO IT, WITH AN AREA OF THAT SIZE,
LESS THAN A DECADE COULD NOT HAVE BEEN ENOUGH TO FORTIFY EVERY LAST SEGMENT.
WELL, AT ANY RATE,
THIS SHIP IS CERTAINLY WELL-APPOINTED!
I HEARD THE FIRST ONE OF ITS LINE LANDED EARLIER IN MEXICO OR THEREABOUTS...
SURE WOULD LOVE TO HAVE ONE OF THESE FOR MY CORPS!

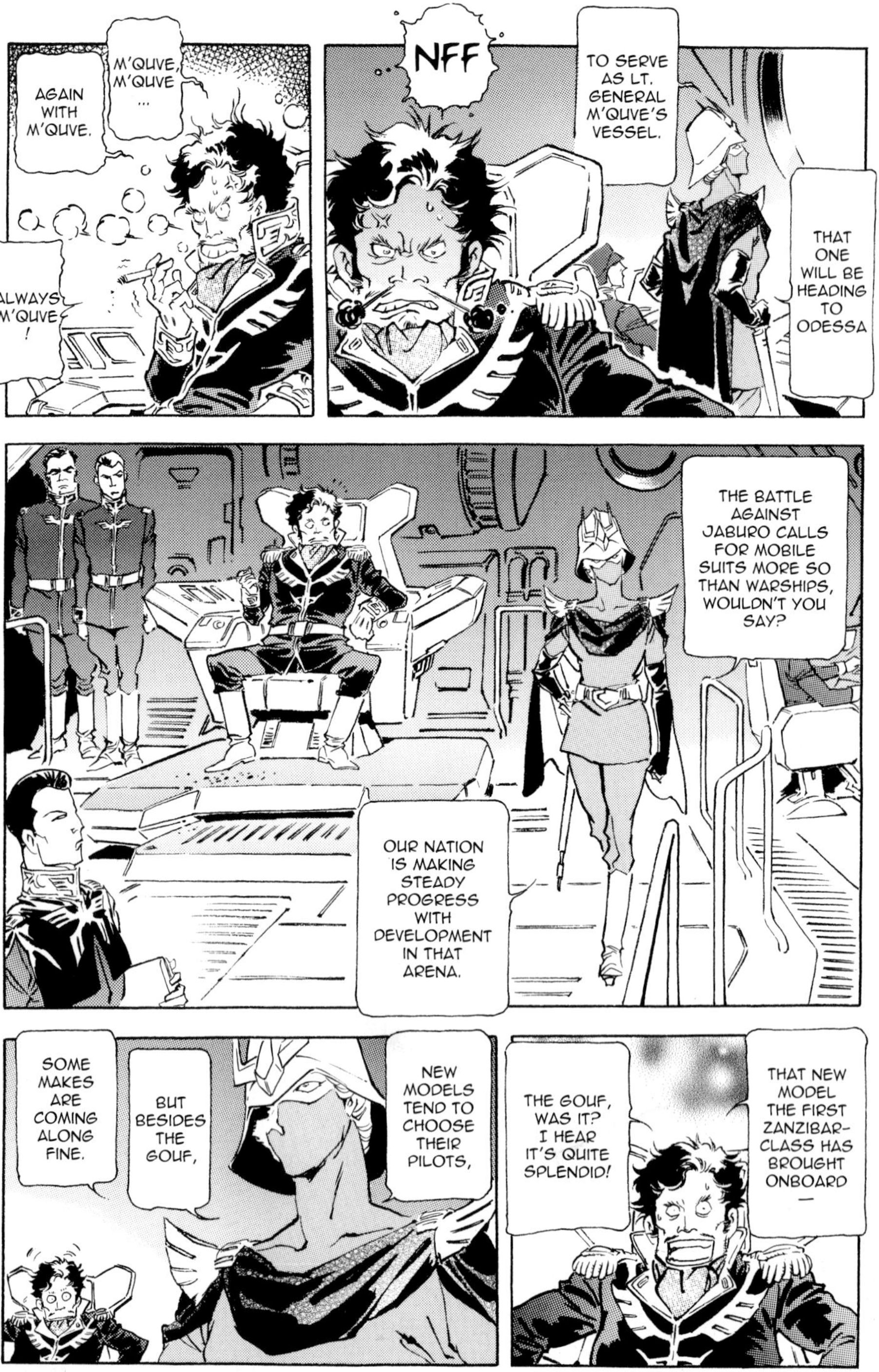
THAT ONE WILL BE HEADING TO ODESSA
TO SERVE AS LT. GENERAL M'QUVE'S VESSEL.
NFF
M'QUVE, M'QUVE ...
AGAIN WITH M'QUVE.
ALWAYS M'QUVE!
THE BATTLE AGAINST JABURO CALLS FOR MOBILE SUITS MORE SO THAN WARSHIPS, WOULDN'T YOU SAY?
OUR NATION IS MAKING STEADY PROGRESS WITH DEVELOPMENT IN THAT ARENA.
THAT NEW MODEL THE FIRST ZANZIBAR-CLASS HAS BROUGHT ONBOARD —
THE GOUF, WAS IT? I HEAR IT'S QUITE SPLENDID!
NEW MODELS TEND TO CHOOSE THEIR PILOTS,
BUT BESIDES THE GOUF,
SOME MAKES ARE COMING ALONG FINE.

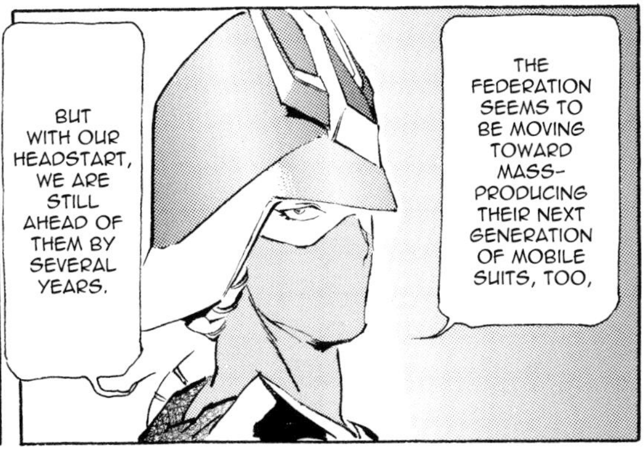
THE FEDERATION SEEMS TO BE MOVING TOWARD MASS-PRODUCING THEIR NEXT GENERATION OF MOBILE SUITS, TOO,
BUT WITH OUR HEADSTART, WE ARE STILL AHEAD OF THEM BY SEVERAL YEARS.

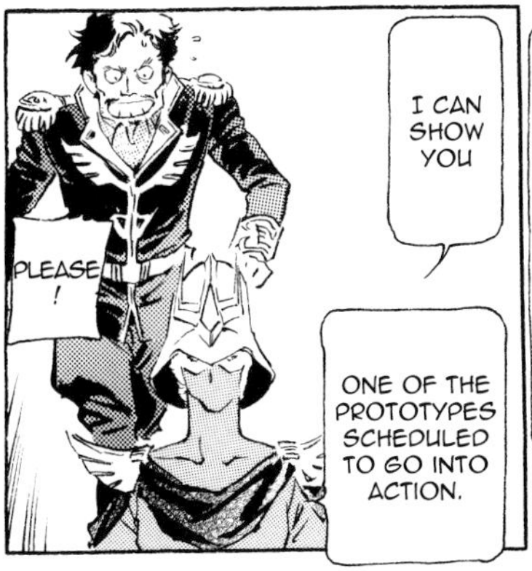
I CAN SHOW YOU
ONE OF THE PROTOTYPES SCHEDULED TO GO INTO ACTION.
PLEASE!

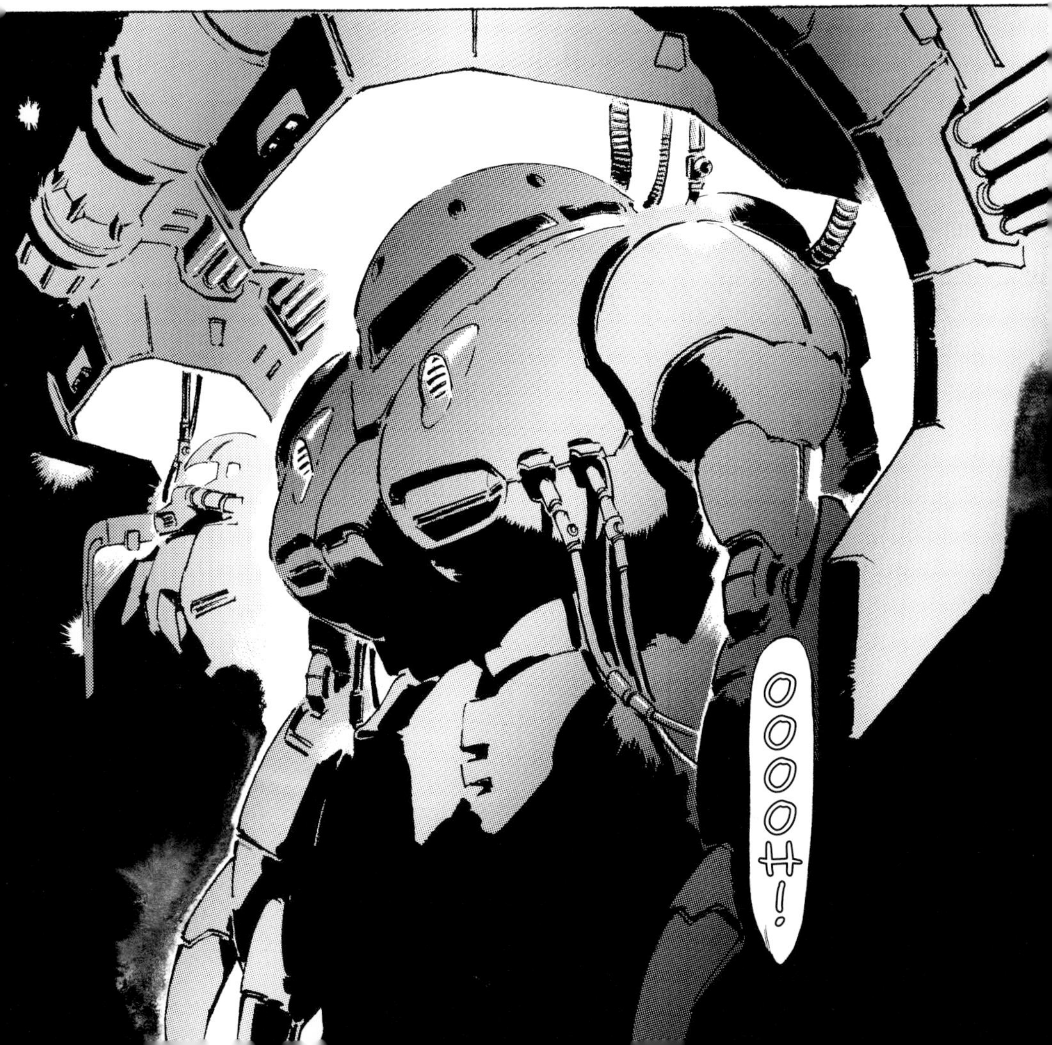
OOOOOH!

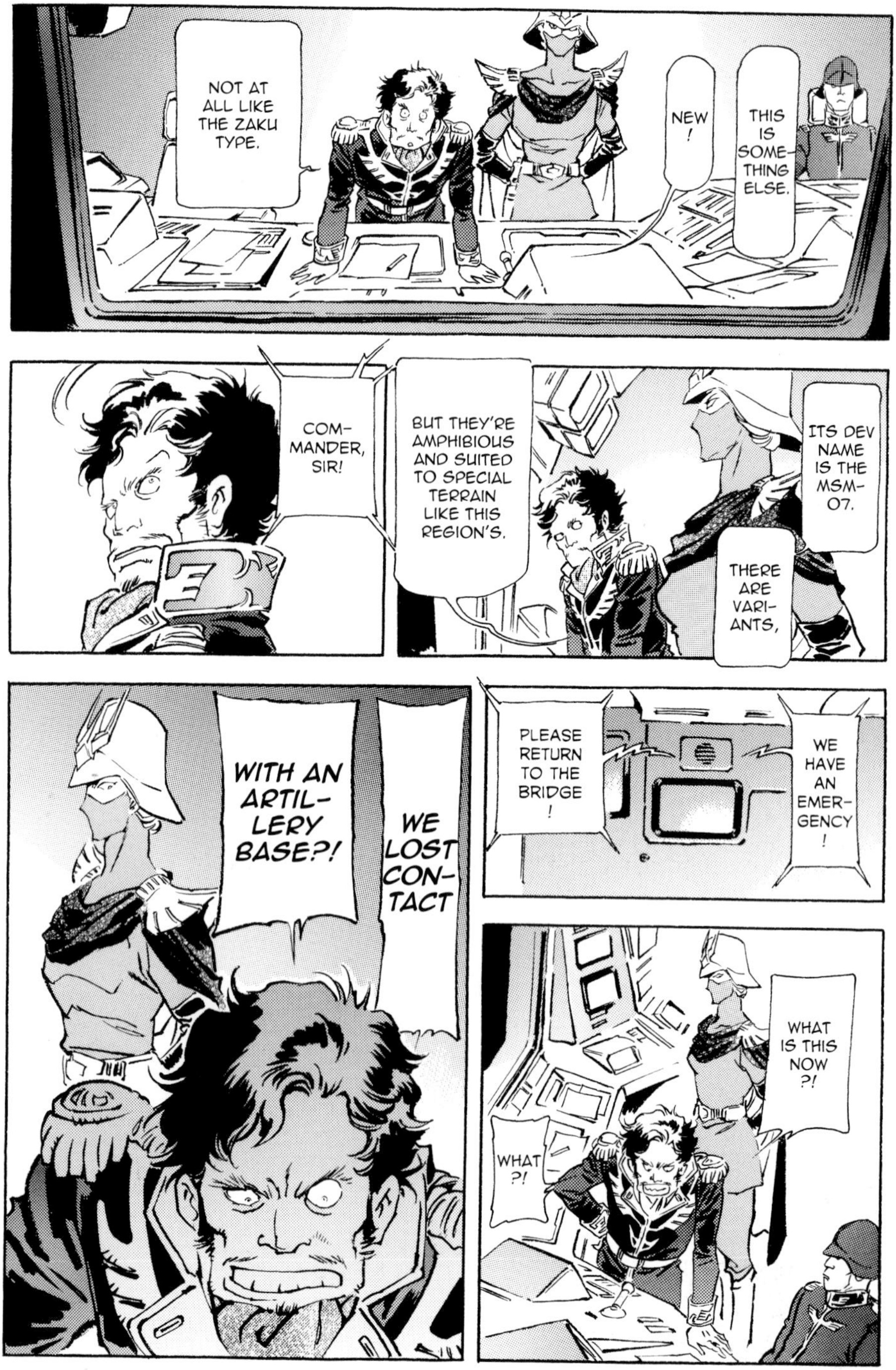

THIS IS SOMETHING ELSE.
NEW!
NOT AT ALL LIKE THE ZAKU TYPE.
ITS DEV NAME IS THE MSM-07.
THERE ARE VARIANTS,
BUT THEY'RE AMPHIBIOUS AND SUITED TO SPECIAL TERRAIN LIKE THIS REGION'S.
COMMANDER, SIR!
WE HAVE AN EMERGENCY!
PLEASE RETURN TO THE BRIDGE!
WHAT IS THIS NOW?!
WHAT?!
WE LOST CONTACT
WITH AN ARTILLERY BASE?!

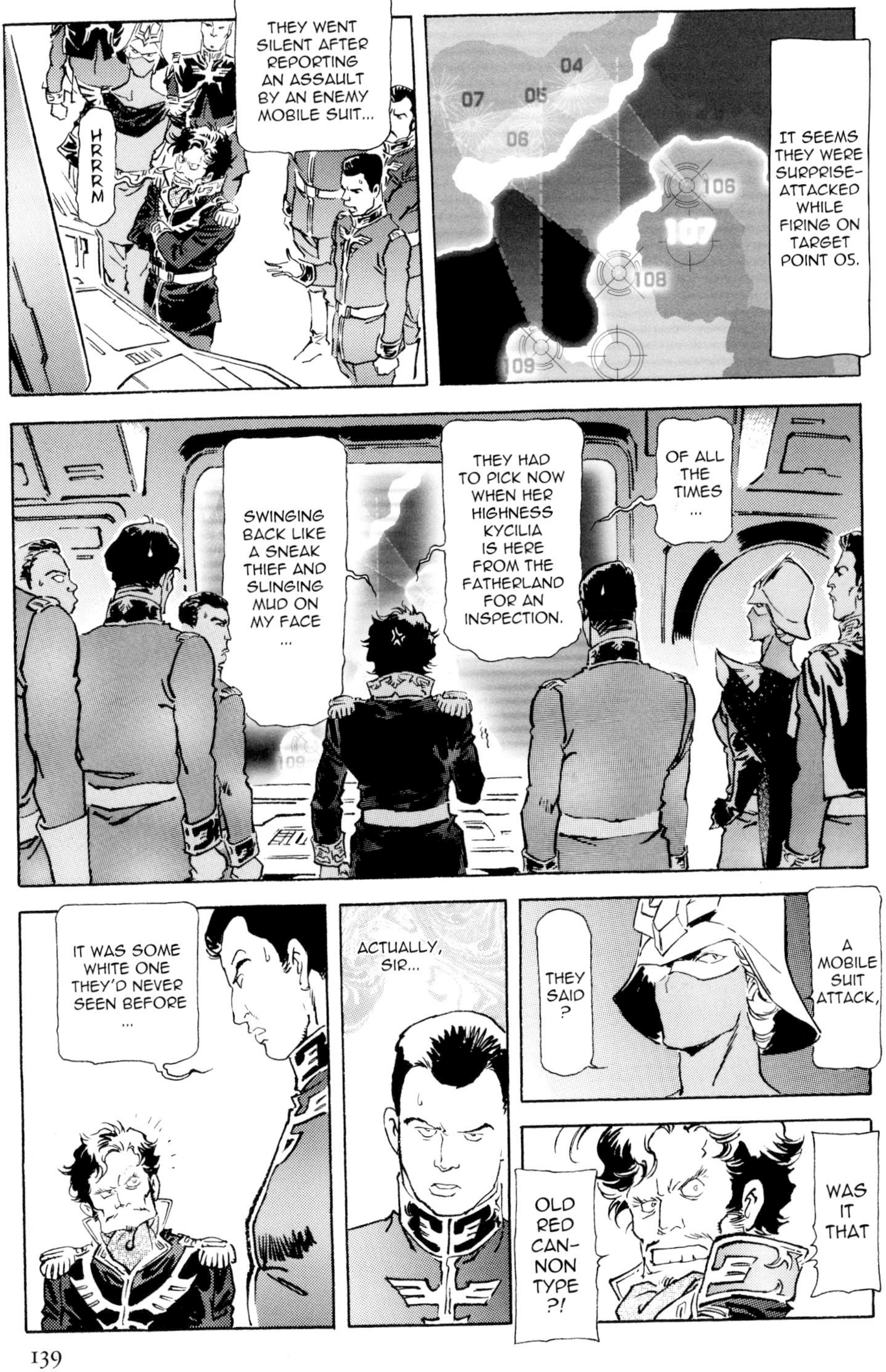
IT SEEMS THEY WERE SURPRISE-ATTACKED WHILE FIRING ON TARGET POINT 05.
04
07
05
06
106
107
108
109
THEY WENT SILENT AFTER REPORTING AN ASSAULT BY AN ENEMY MOBILE SUIT...
HRRRM
OF ALL THE TIMES ...
THEY HAD TO PICK NOW WHEN HER HIGHNESS KYCILIA IS HERE FROM THE FATHERLAND FOR AN INSPECTION.
SWINGING BACK LIKE A SNEAK THIEF AND SLINGING MUD ON MY FACE ...
A MOBILE SUIT ATTACK,
THEY SAID?
WAS IT THAT
OLD RED CAN-NON TYPE?!
ACTUALLY, SIR...
IT WAS SOME WHITE ONE THEY'D NEVER SEEN BEFORE ...

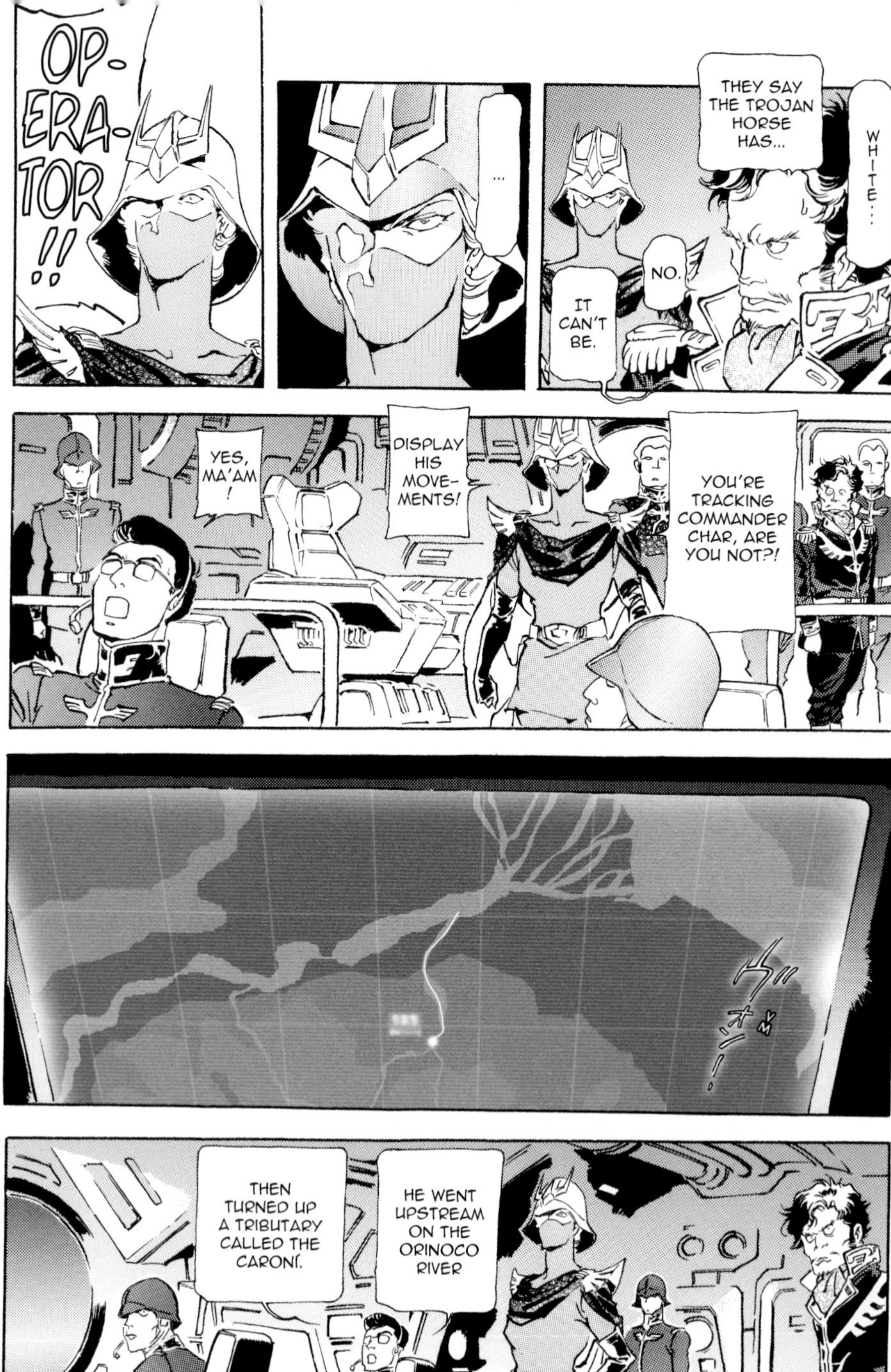
THEY SAY THE TROJAN HORSE HAS...
WHITE...
NO.
IT CAN'T BE.
...
OPERATOR!!
YOU'RE TRACKING COMMANDER CHAR, ARE YOU NOT?!
DISPLAY HIS MOVEMENTS!
YES, MA'AM!
HE WENT UPSTREAM ON THE ORINOCO RIVER
THEN TURNED UP A TRIBUTARY CALLED THE CARONÍ.

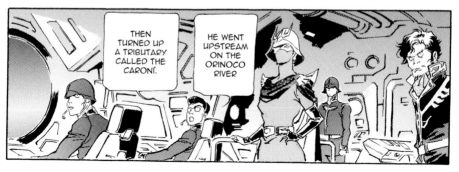

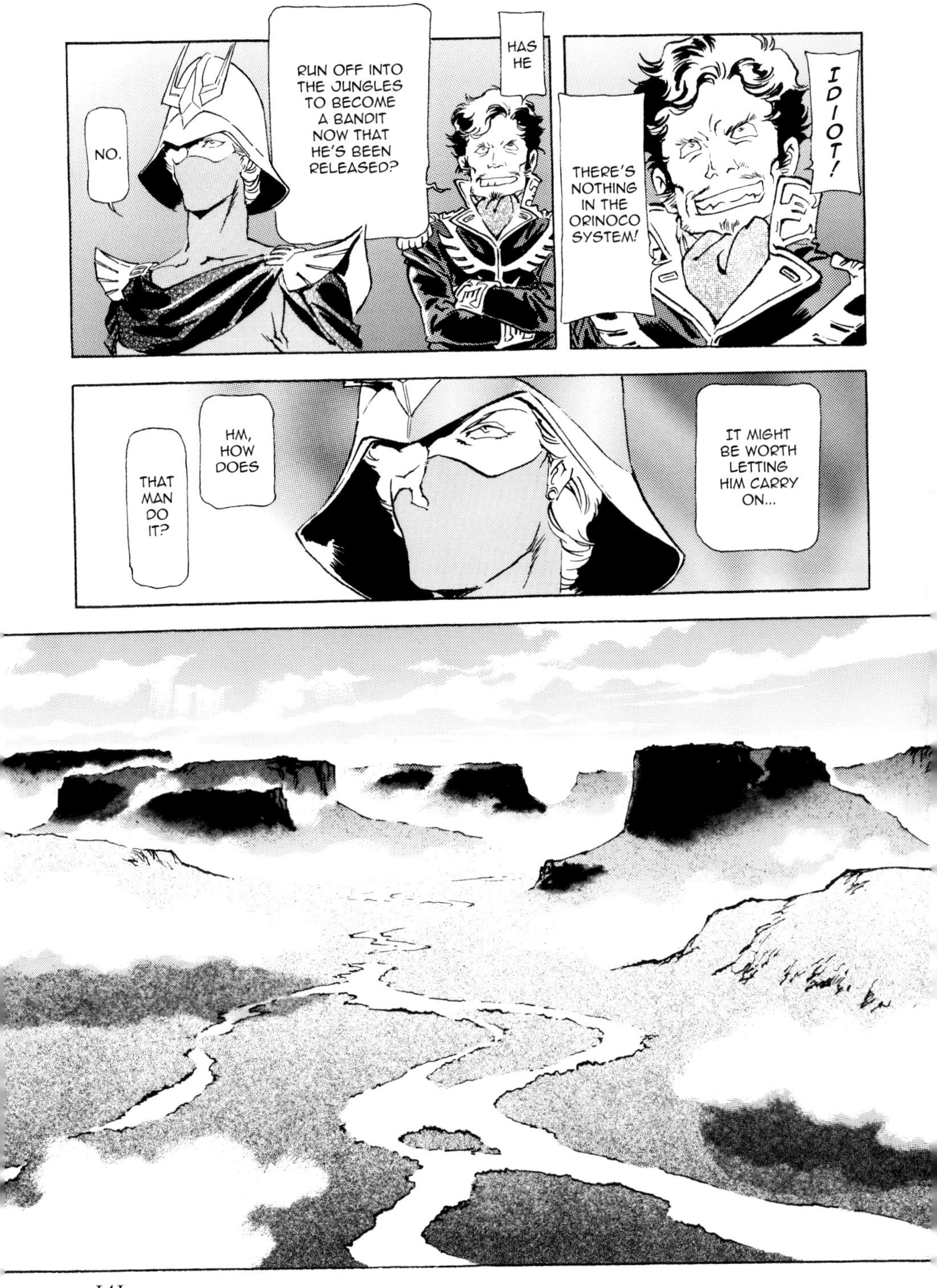
IDIOT!
THERE'S NOTHING IN THE ORINOCO SYSTEM!
HAS HE
RUN OFF INTO THE JUNGLES TO BECOME A BANDIT NOW THAT HE'S BEEN RELEASED?
NO.
IT MIGHT BE WORTH LETTING HIM CARRY ON...
HM, HOW DOES
THAT MAN DO IT?

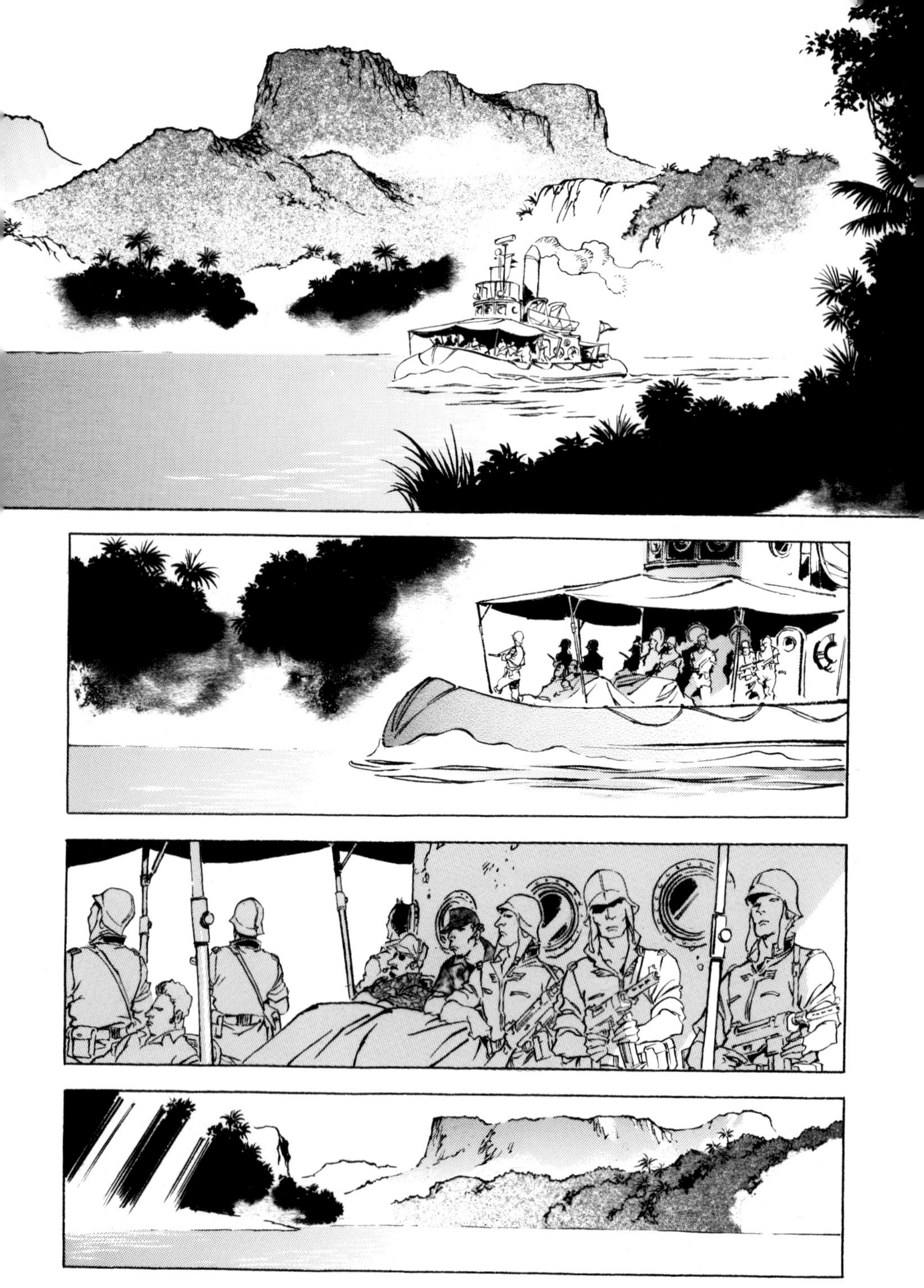

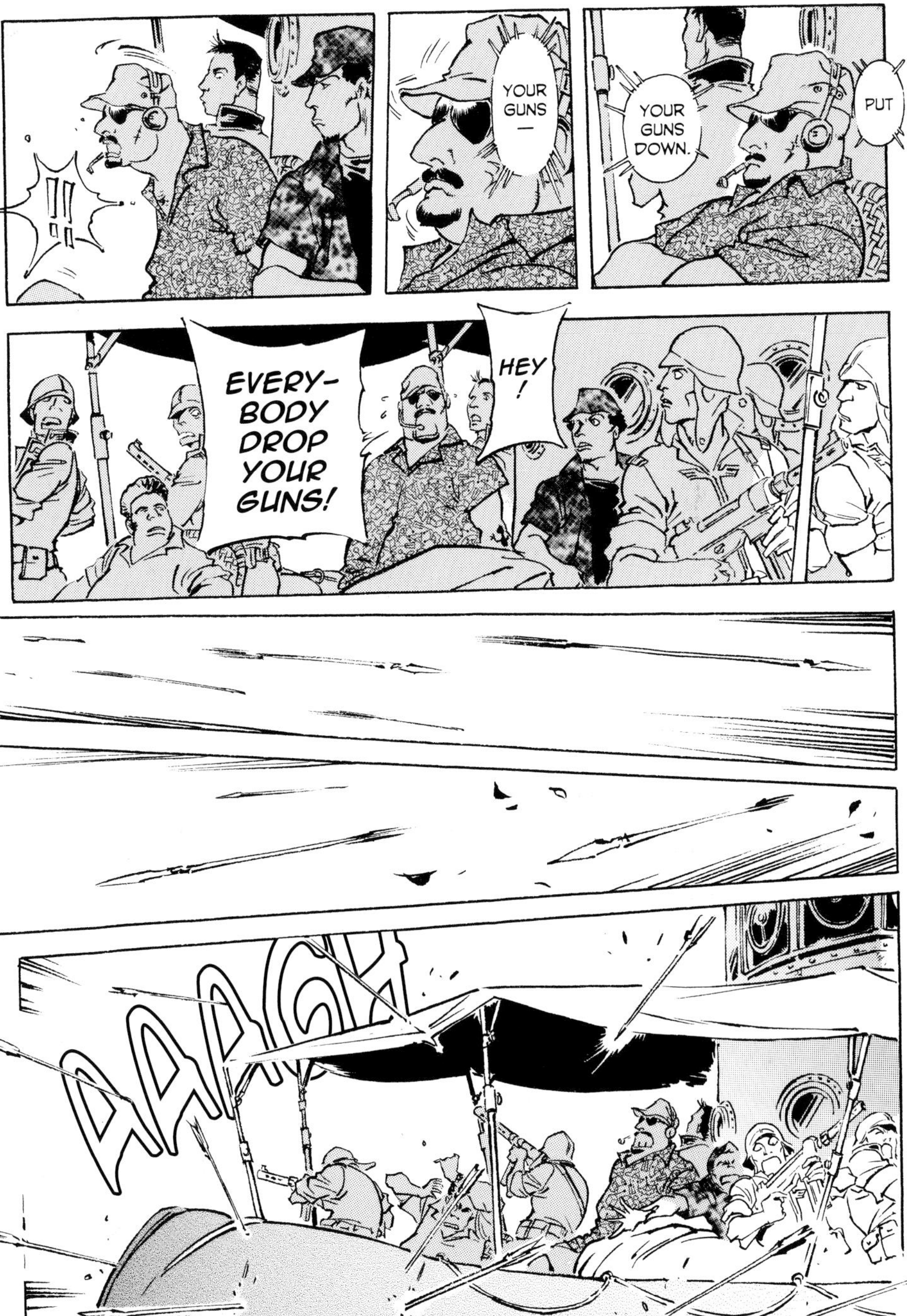
PUT
YOUR GUNS DOWN.
YOUR GUNS —
!!
!!
HEY!
EVERY-BODY DROP YOUR GUNS!
AAAGH

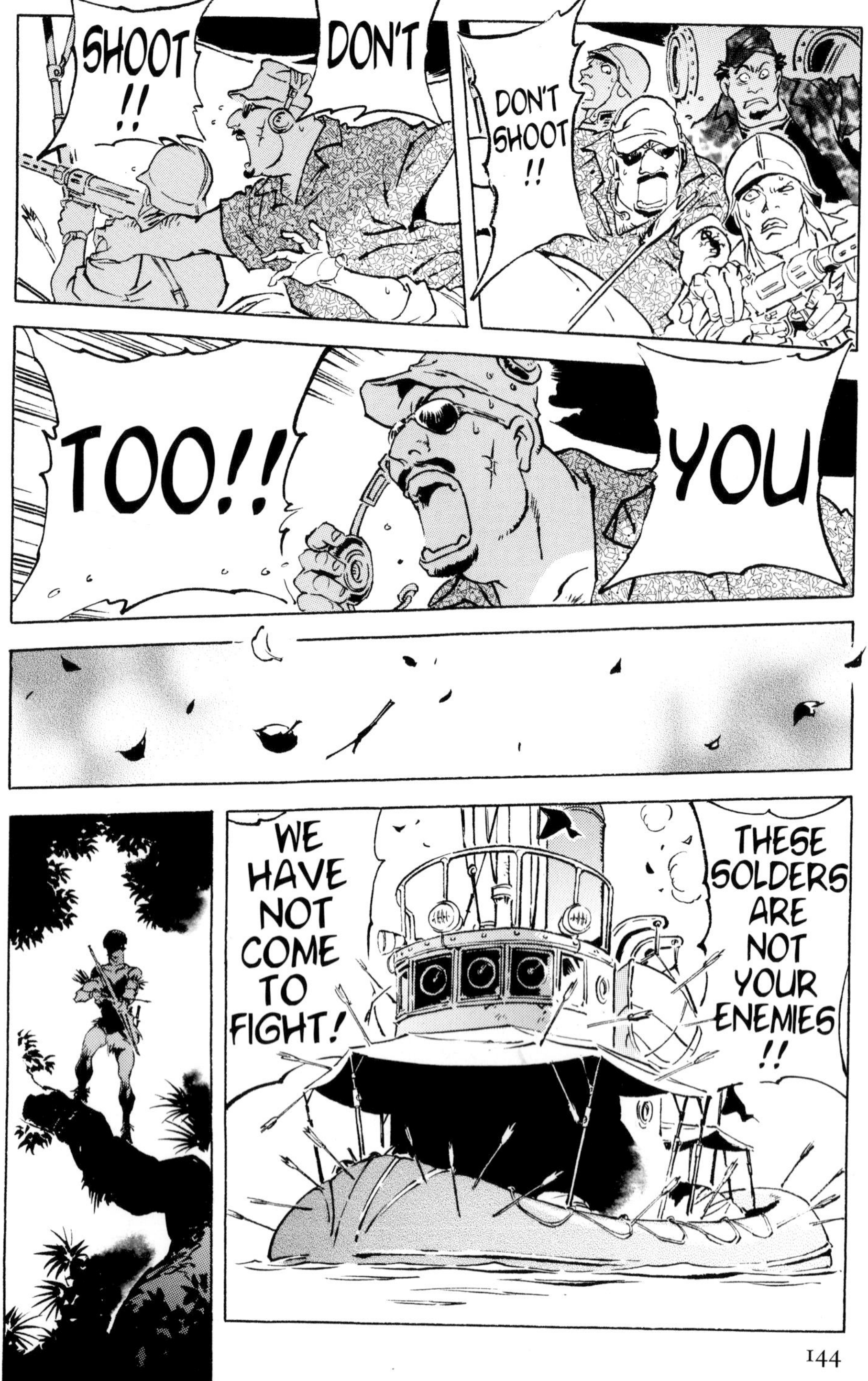

DON'T SHOOT!!
DON'T
SHOOT!!
YOU
TOO!!
THESE SOLDERS ARE NOT YOUR ENEMIES!!
WE HAVE NOT COME TO FIGHT!

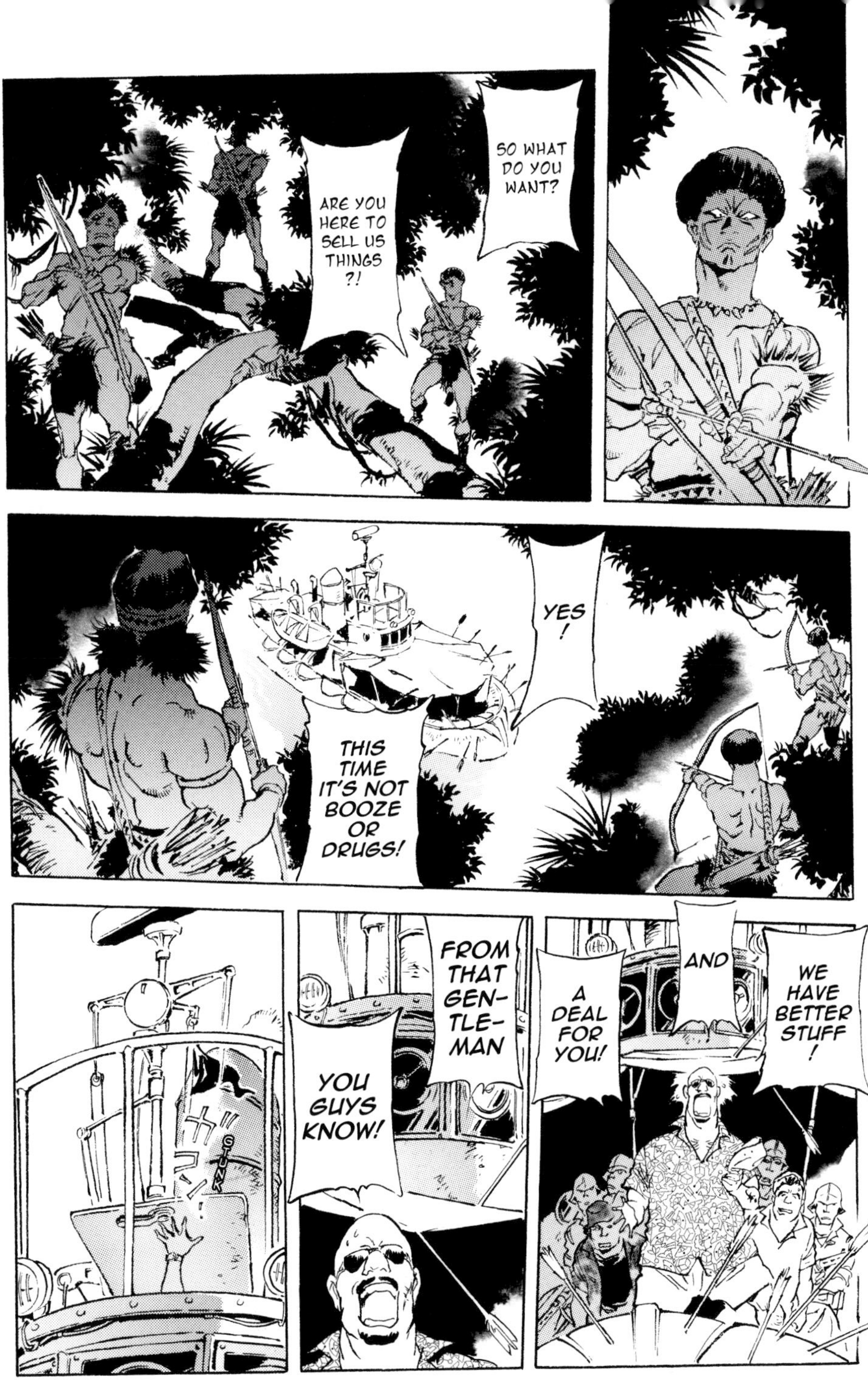
SO WHAT DO YOU WANT?
ARE YOU HERE TO SELL US THINGS ?!
YES!
THIS TIME IT'S NOT BOOZE OR DRUGS!
WE HAVE BETTER STUFF!
AND
A DEAL FOR YOU!
FROM THAT GENTLEMAN
YOU GUYS KNOW!
ガコン!
GUNK

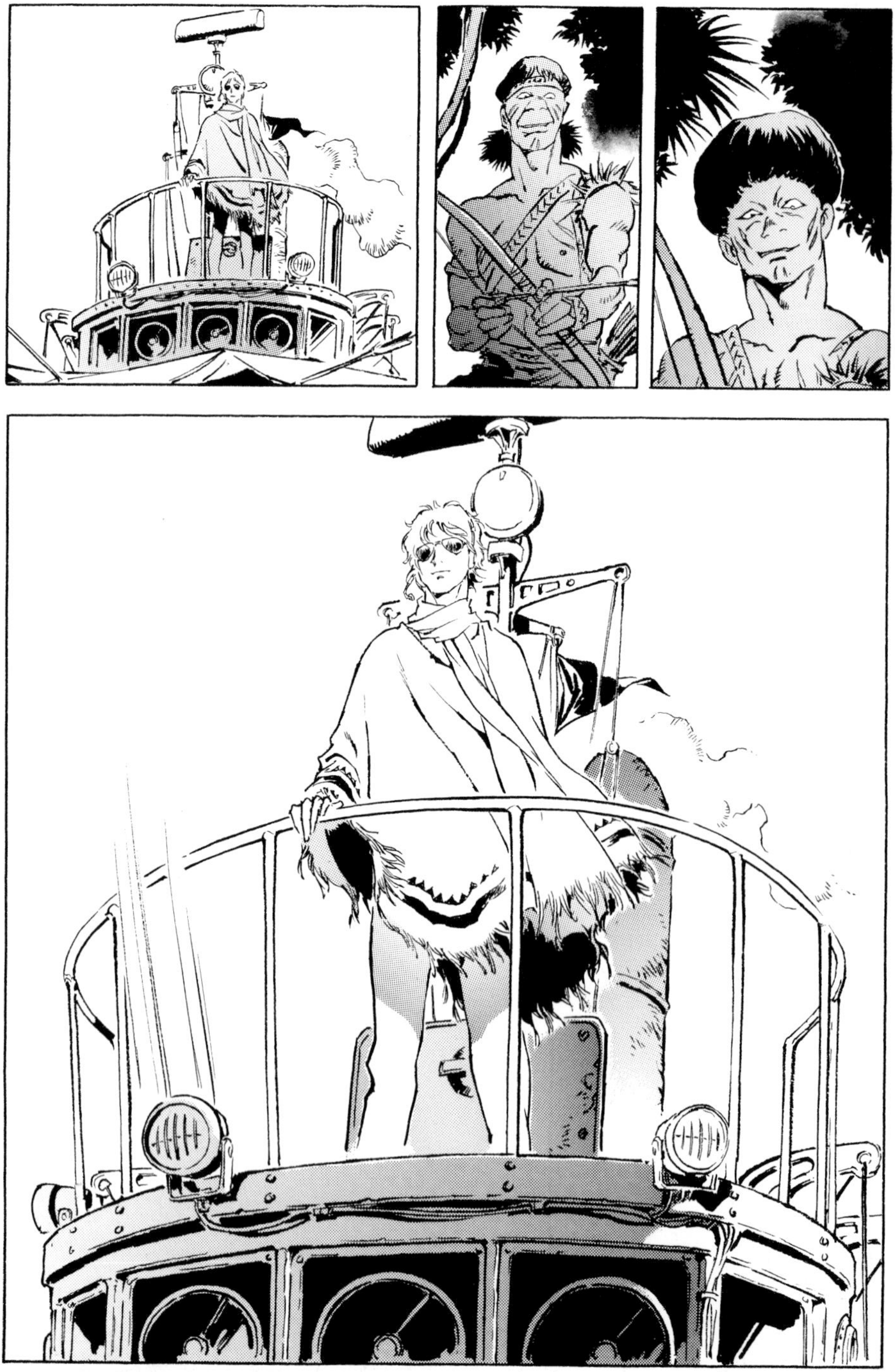

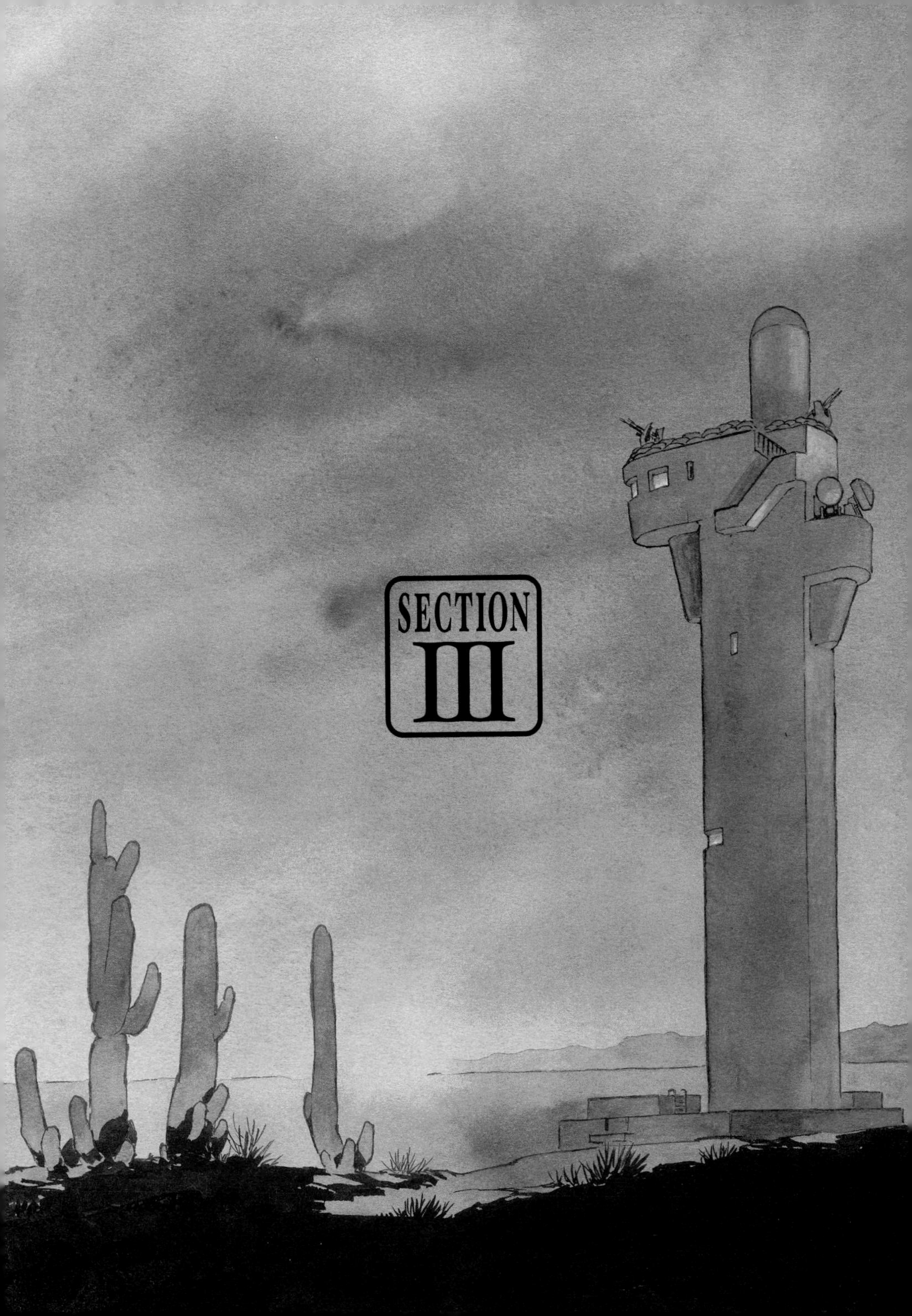
SECTION
III

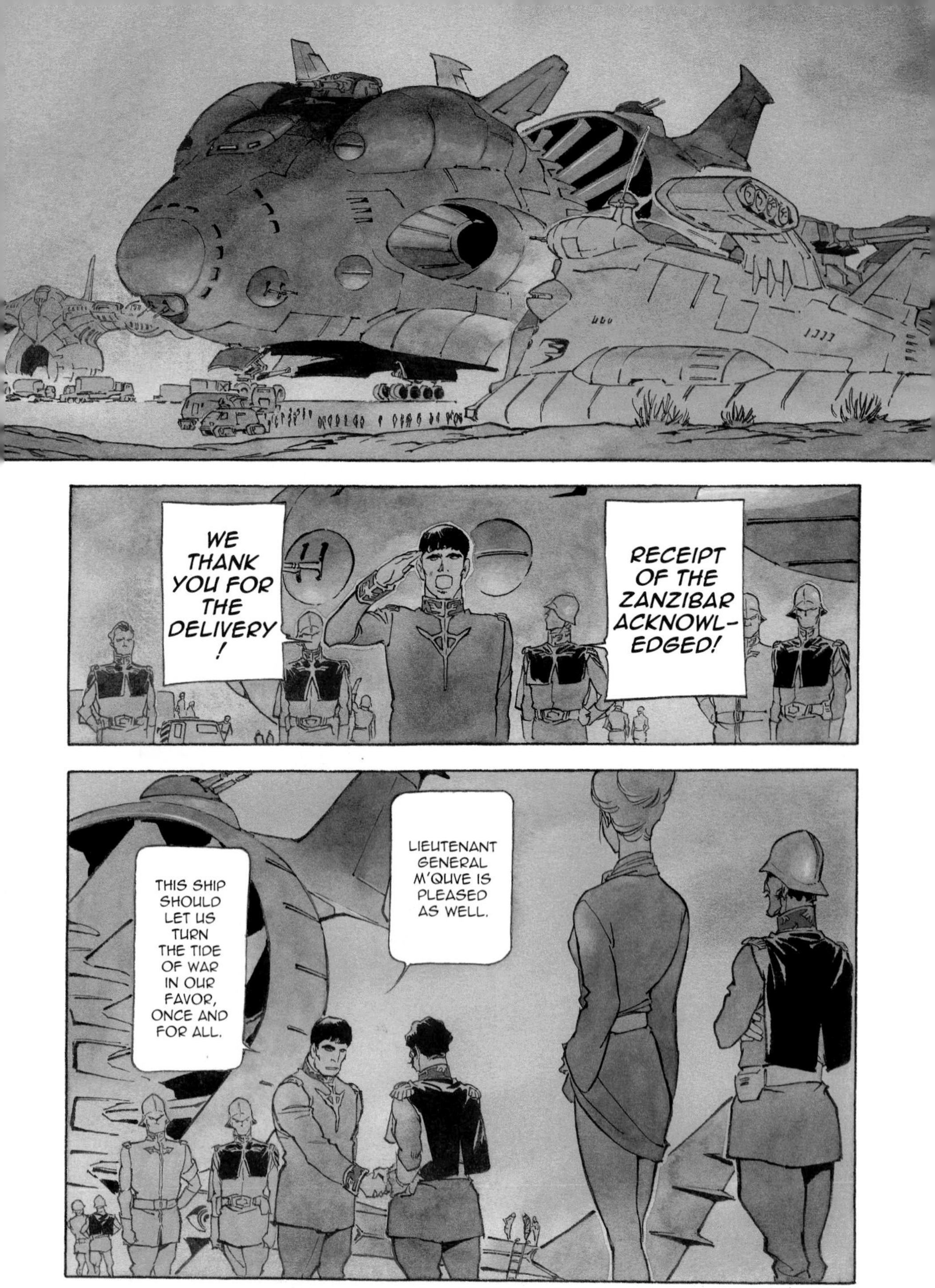
RECEIPT OF THE ZANZIBAR ACKNOWL-EDGED!
WE THANK YOU FOR THE DELIVERY!
LIEUTENANT GENERAL M'QUVE IS PLEASED AS WELL.
THIS SHIP SHOULD LET US TURN THE TIDE OF WAR IN OUR FAVOR, ONCE AND FOR ALL.

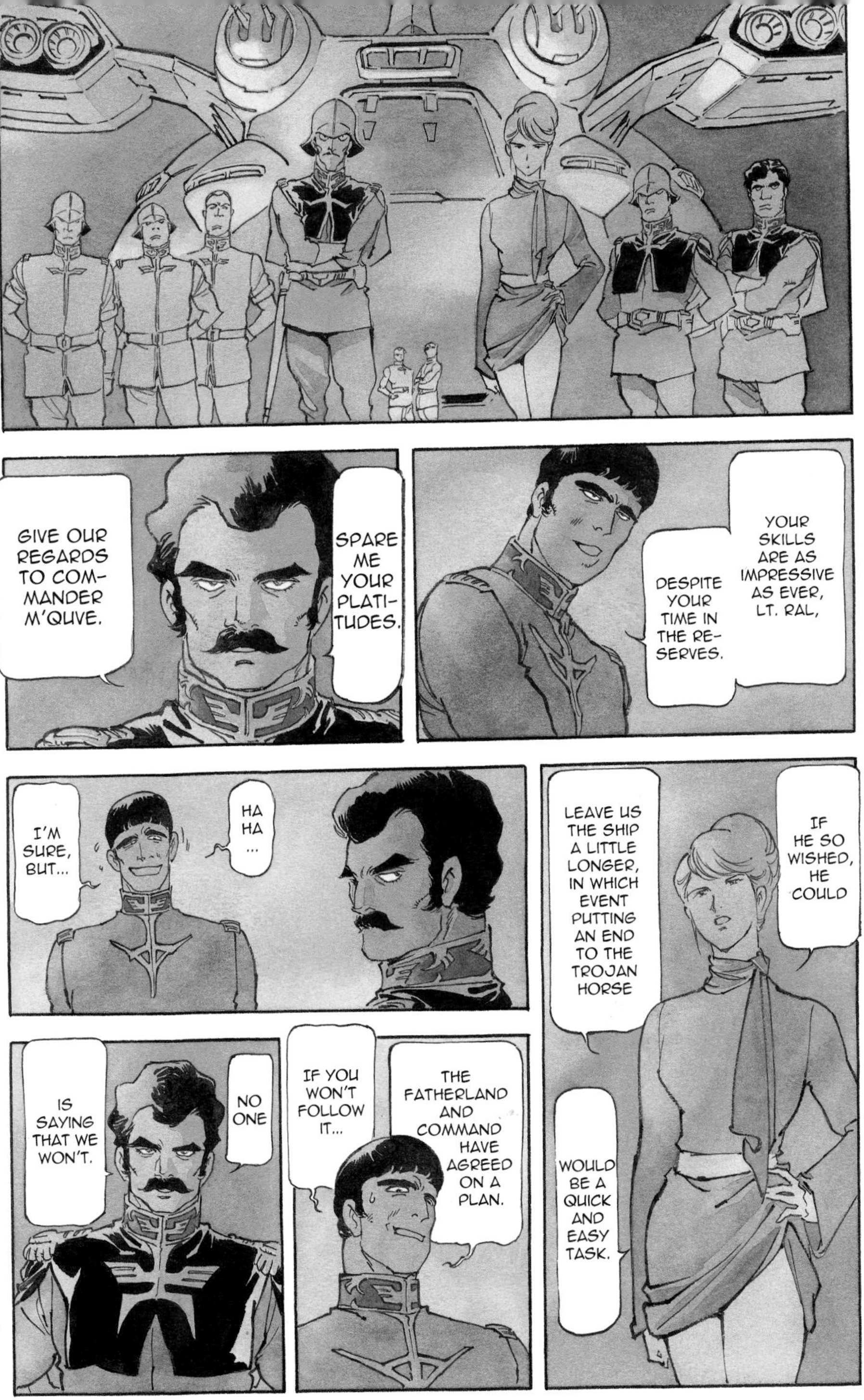
YOUR SKILLS ARE AS IMPRESSIVE AS EVER, LT. RAL,
DESPITE YOUR TIME IN THE RE-SERVES.
SPARE ME YOUR PLATI-TUDES.
GIVE OUR REGARDS TO COM-MANDER M'QUVE.
IF HE SO WISHED, HE COULD
LEAVE US THE SHIP A LITTLE LONGER, IN WHICH EVENT PUTTING AN END TO THE TROJAN HORSE
WOULD BE A QUICK AND EASY TASK.
HA HA ...
I'M SURE, BUT...
THE FATHERLAND AND COMMAND HAVE AGREED ON A PLAN.
IF YOU WON'T FOLLOW IT...
NO ONE
IS SAYING THAT WE WON'T.

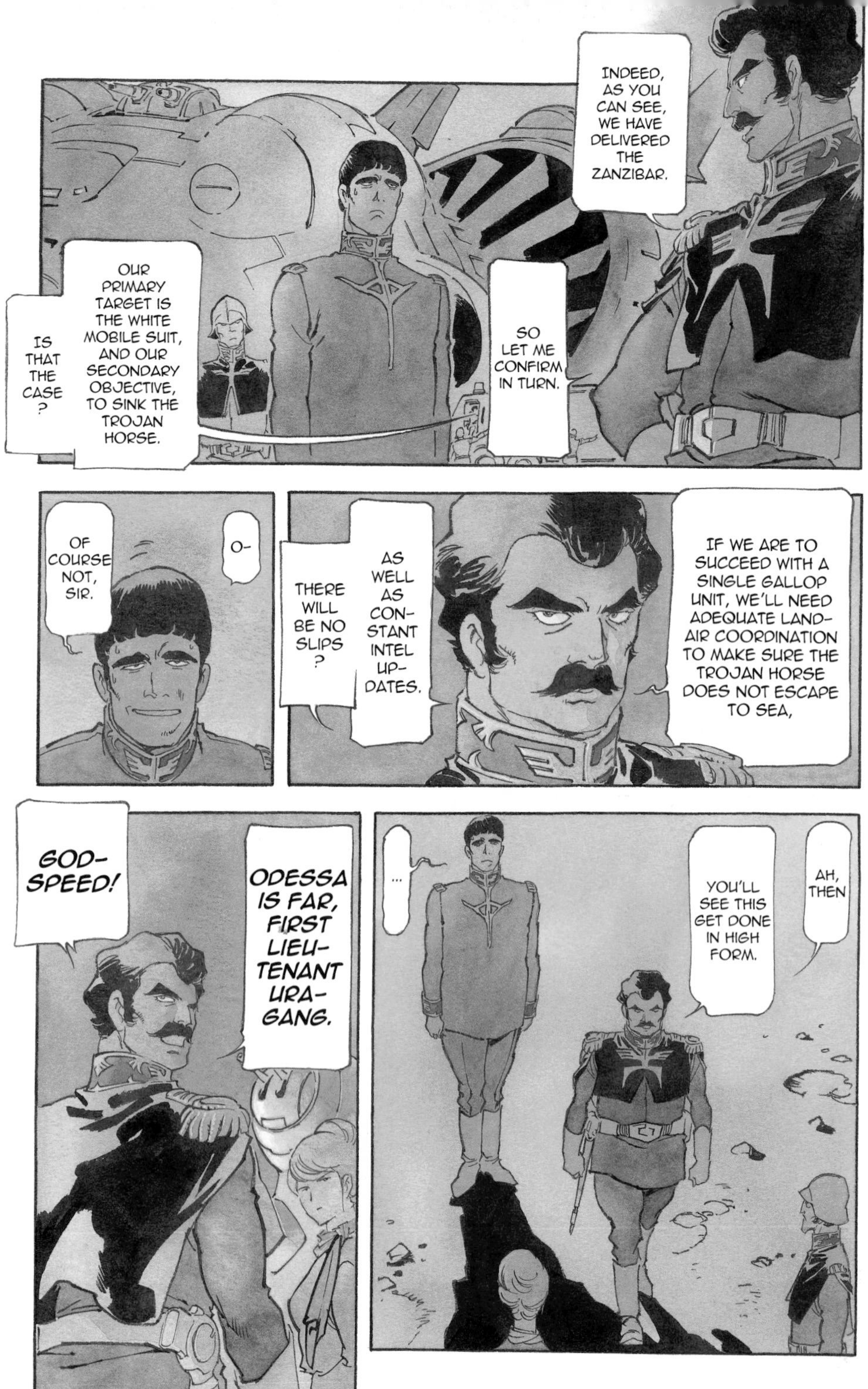

INDEED, AS YOU CAN SEE, WE HAVE DELIVERED THE ZANZIBAR.
SO LET ME CONFIRM IN TURN.
OUR PRIMARY TARGET IS THE WHITE MOBILE SUIT, AND OUR SECONDARY OBJECTIVE, TO SINK THE TROJAN HORSE.
IS THAT THE CASE?
IF WE ARE TO SUCCEED WITH A SINGLE GALLOP UNIT, WE'LL NEED ADEQUATE LAND-AIR COORDINATION TO MAKE SURE THE TROJAN HORSE DOES NOT ESCAPE TO SEA,
AS WELL AS CONSTANT INTEL UPDATES.
THERE WILL BE NO SLIPS?
O-
OF COURSE NOT, SIR.
AH, THEN
YOU'LL SEE THIS GET DONE IN HIGH FORM.
...
ODESSA IS FAR, FIRST LIEUTENANT URAGANG.
GODSPEED!

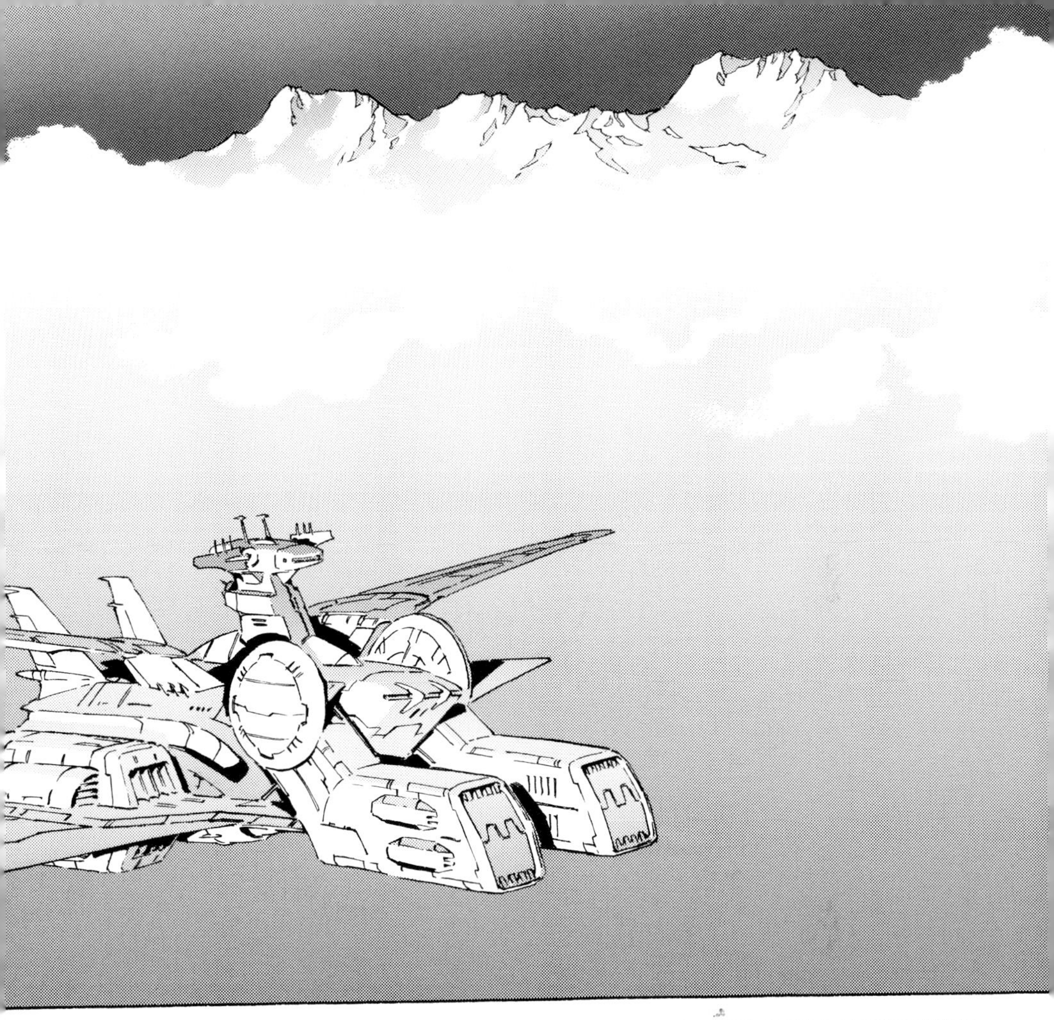

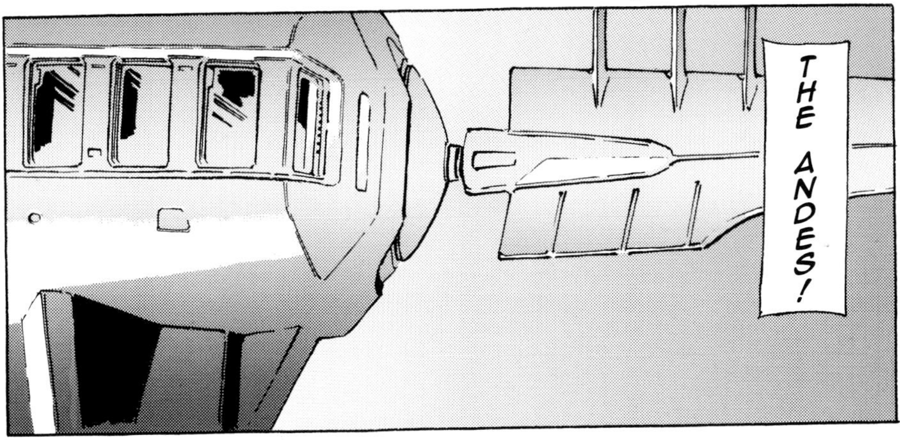
THE ANDES!

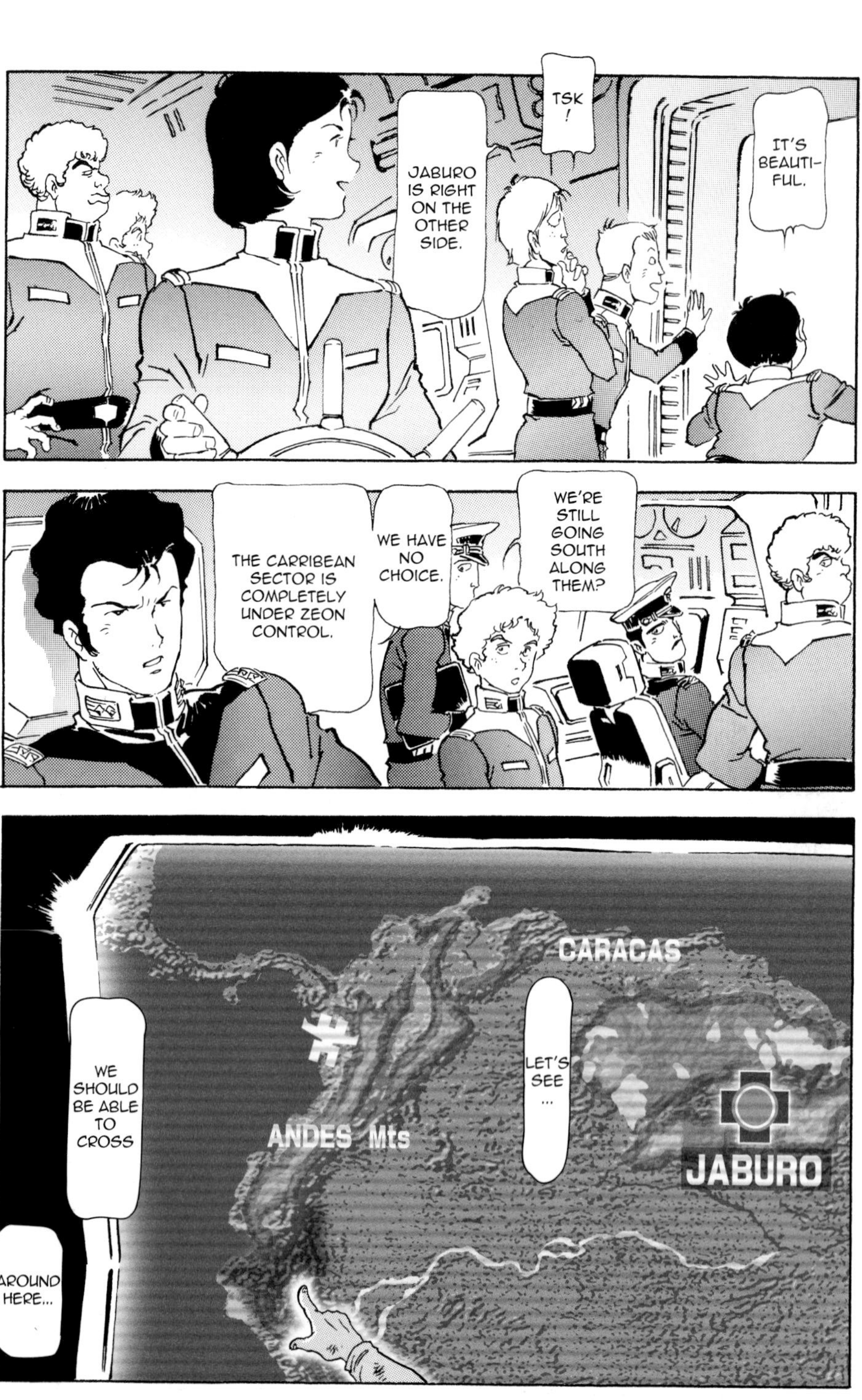
IT'S BEAUTI-FUL.
TSK!
JABURO IS RIGHT ON THE OTHER SIDE.
WE'RE STILL GOING SOUTH ALONG THEM?
WE HAVE NO CHOICE.
THE CARRIBEAN SECTOR IS COMPLETELY UNDER ZEON CONTROL.
CARACAS
LET'S SEE ...
JABURO
WE SHOULD BE ABLE TO CROSS
ANDES Mts
AROUND HERE...

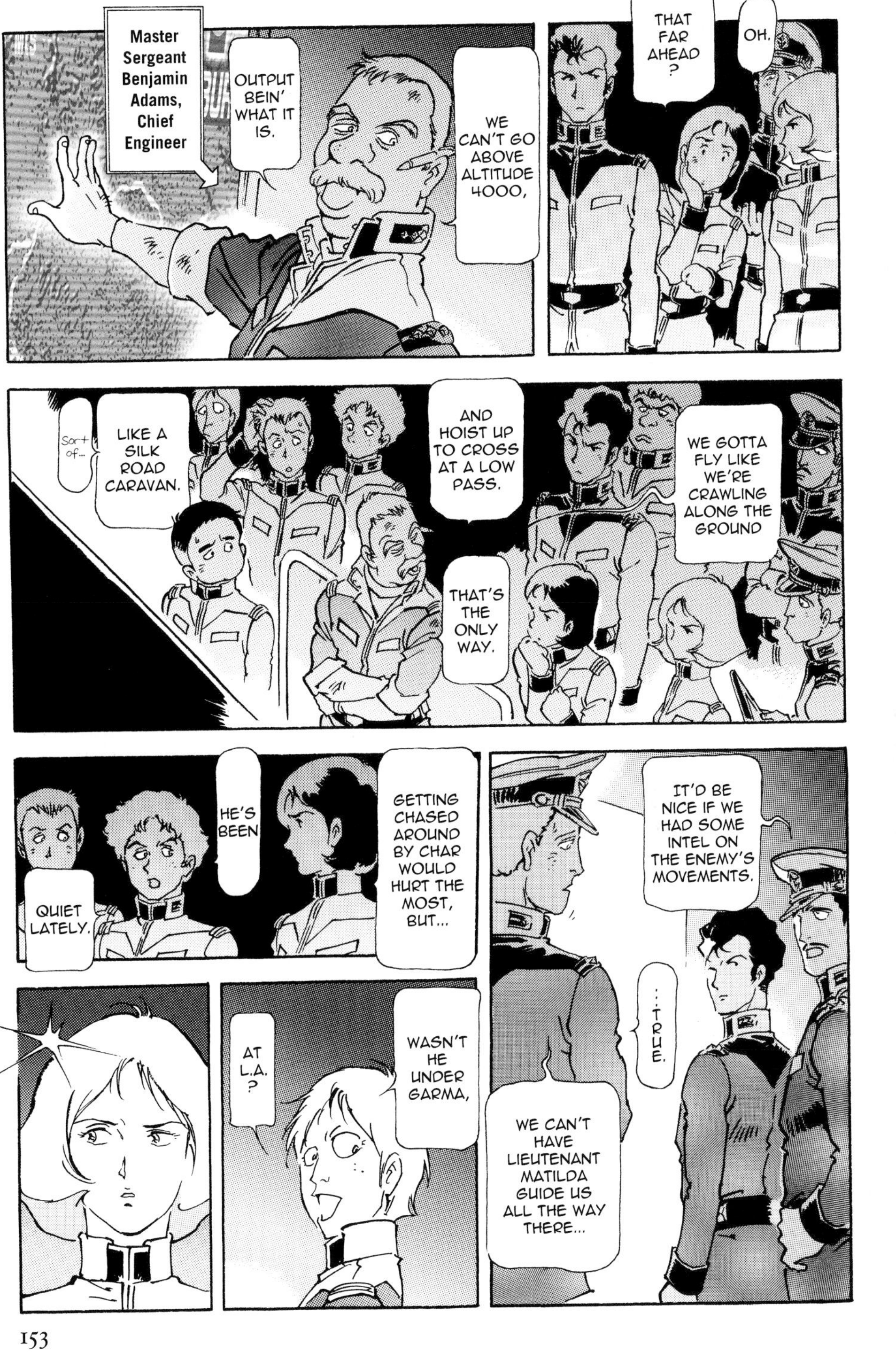
OH.
THAT FAR AHEAD?
WE CAN'T GO ABOVE ALTITUDE 4000,
OUTPUT BEIN' WHAT IT IS.
Master Sergeant Benjamin Adams, Chief Engineer
WE GOTTA FLY LIKE WE'RE CRAWLING ALONG THE GROUND
AND HOIST UP TO CROSS AT A LOW PASS.
THAT'S THE ONLY WAY.
LIKE A SILK ROAD CARAVAN.
Sort of...
IT'D BE NICE IF WE HAD SOME INTEL ON THE ENEMY'S MOVEMENTS.
...TRUE.
WE CAN'T HAVE LIEUTENANT MATILDA GUIDE US ALL THE WAY THERE...
GETTING CHASED AROUND BY CHAR WOULD HURT THE MOST, BUT...
HE'S BEEN
QUIET LATELY.
WASN'T HE UNDER GARMA,
AT L.A.?

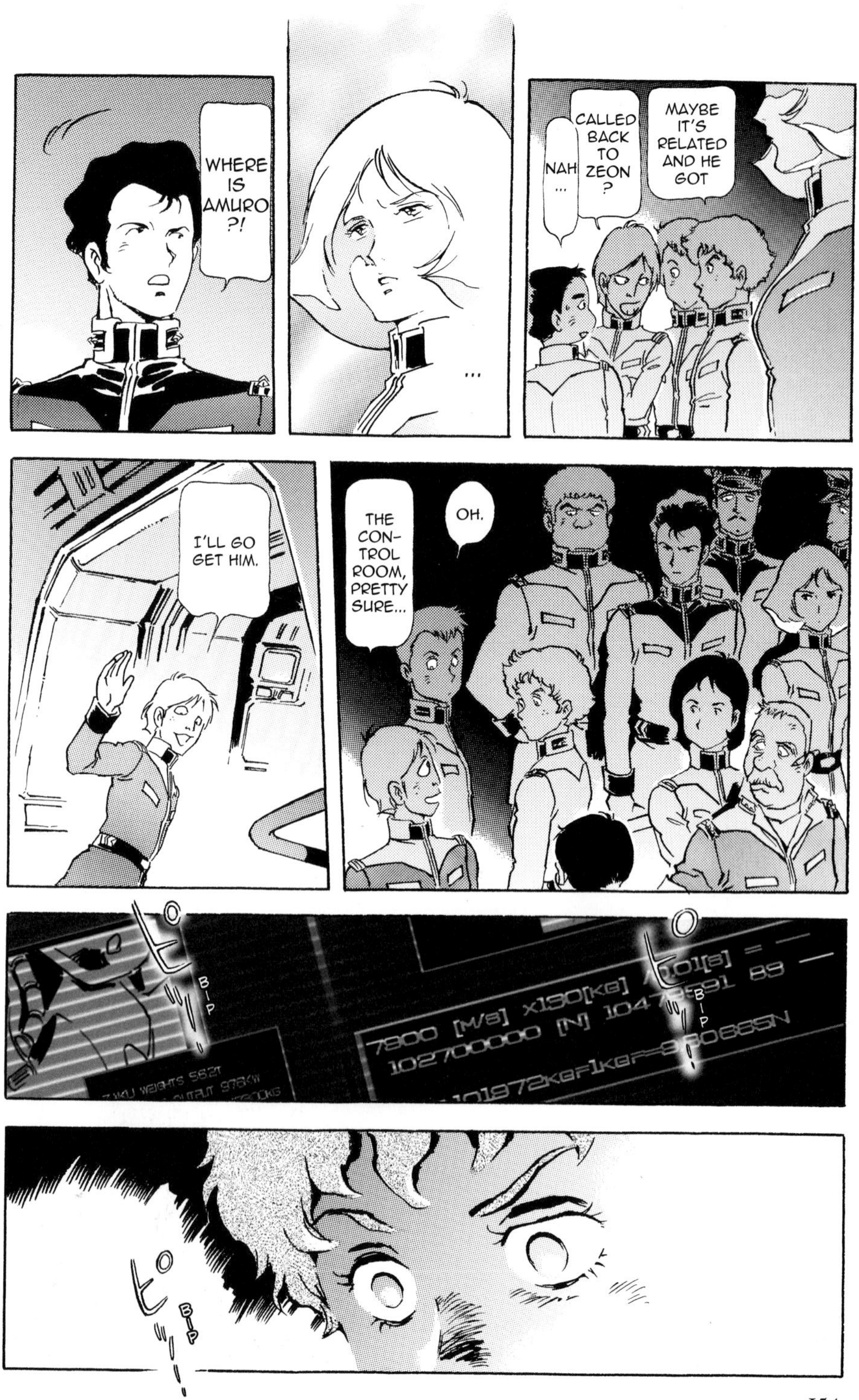
MAYBE IT'S RELATED AND HE GOT
CALLED BACK TO ZEON?
NAH...
...
WHERE IS AMURO?!
OH.
THE CON-TROL ROOM, PRETTY SURE...
I'LL GO GET HIM.
BIP
BIP
BIP

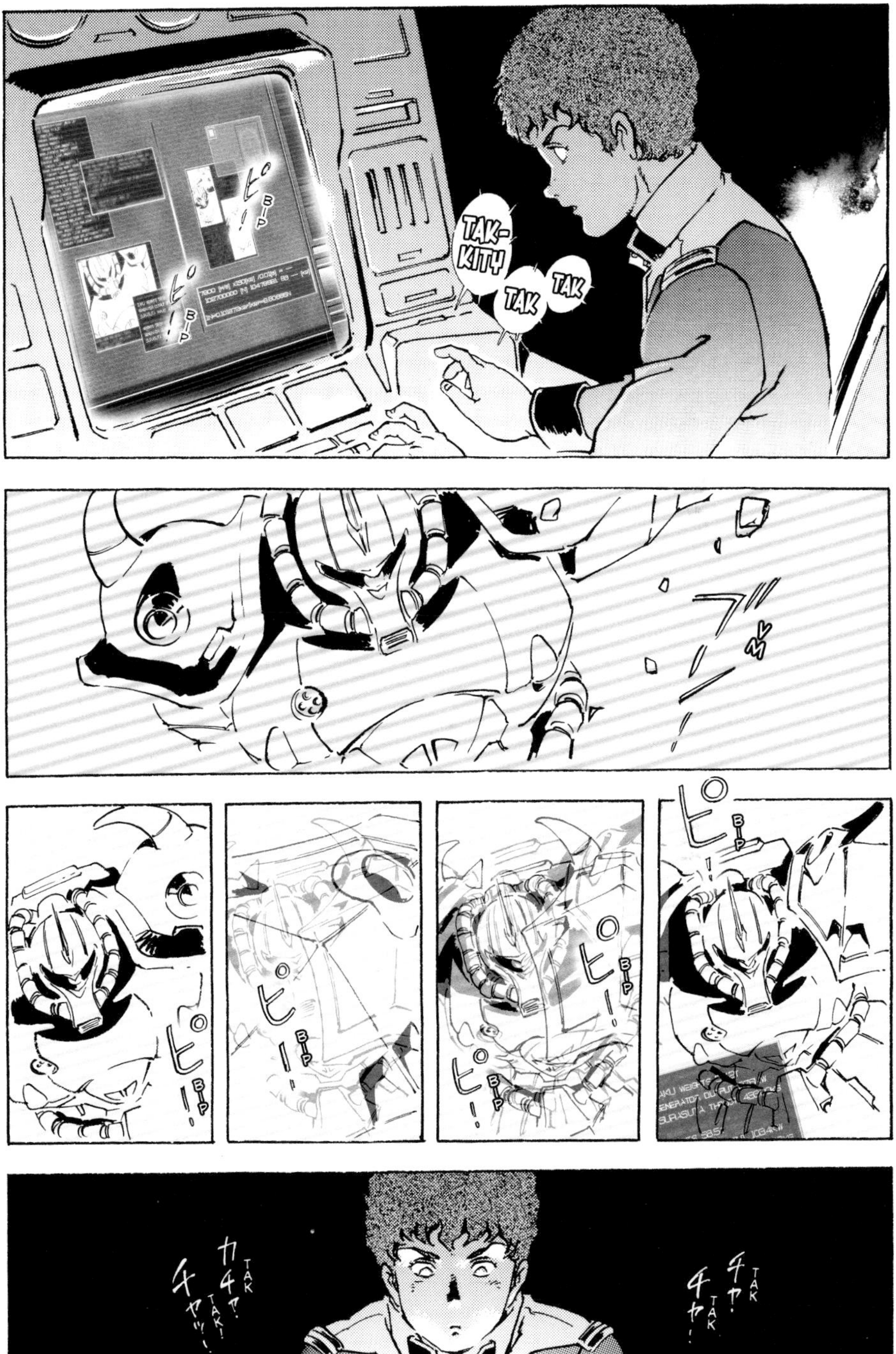
ピ BIP
ピ BIP
TAK
TAK
TAK-KITY
ブーン VM
ピ BIP
ピ BIP
ピ BIP
ピ BIP
ピ BIP
ピ BIP
チャ TAK
チャ TAK
カチャ TAK
チャッ TAK!

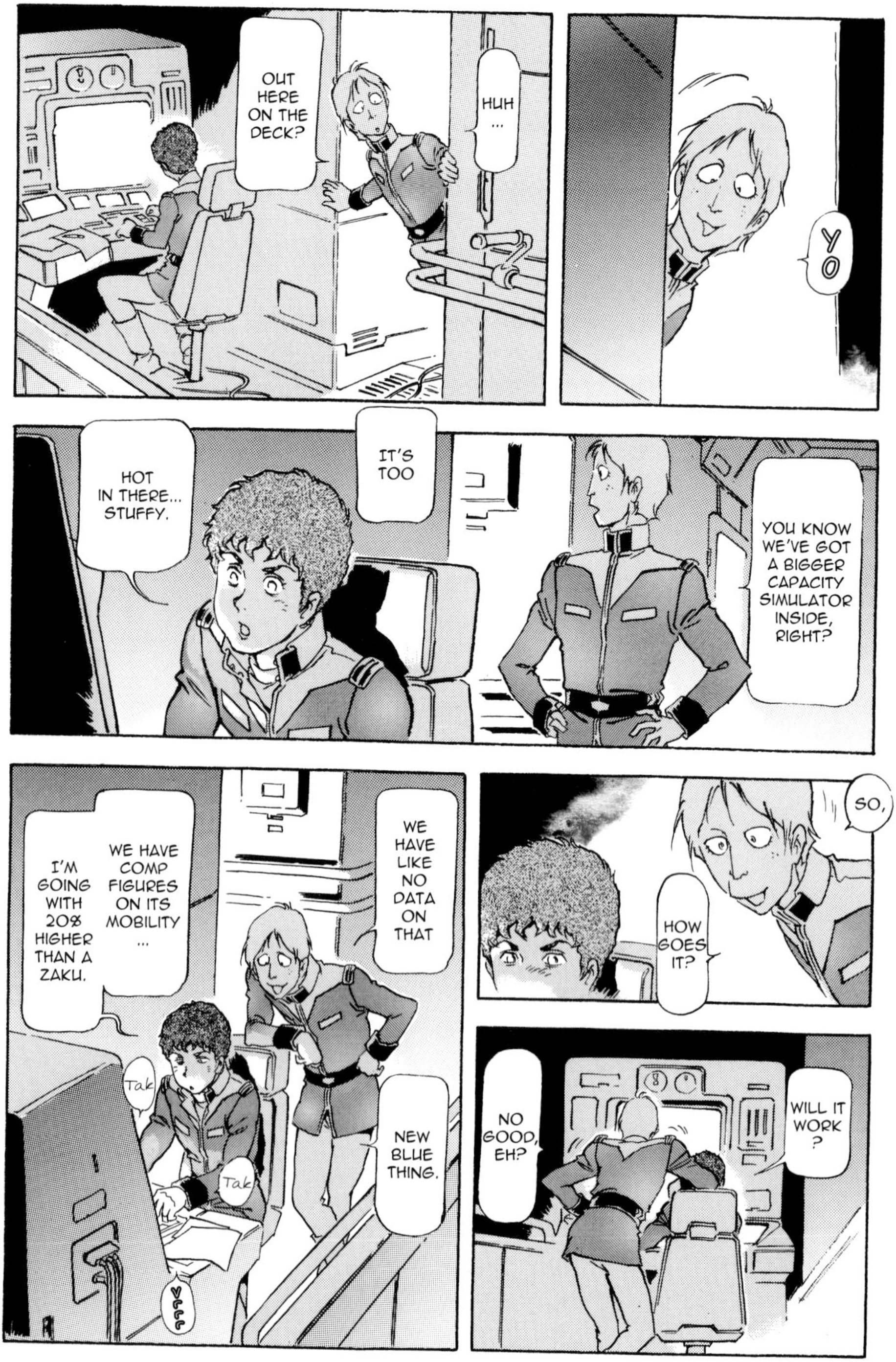
YO
HUH ...
OUT HERE ON THE DECK?
YOU KNOW WE'VE GOT A BIGGER CAPACITY SIMULATOR INSIDE, RIGHT?
IT'S TOO
HOT IN THERE... STUFFY.
SO,
HOW GOES IT?
WILL IT WORK ?
NO GOOD, EH?
WE HAVE LIKE NO DATA ON THAT
NEW BLUE THING.
WE HAVE COMP FIGURES ON ITS MOBILITY ...
I'M GOING WITH 20% HIGHER THAN A ZAKU.
Tak
Tak
VFFF

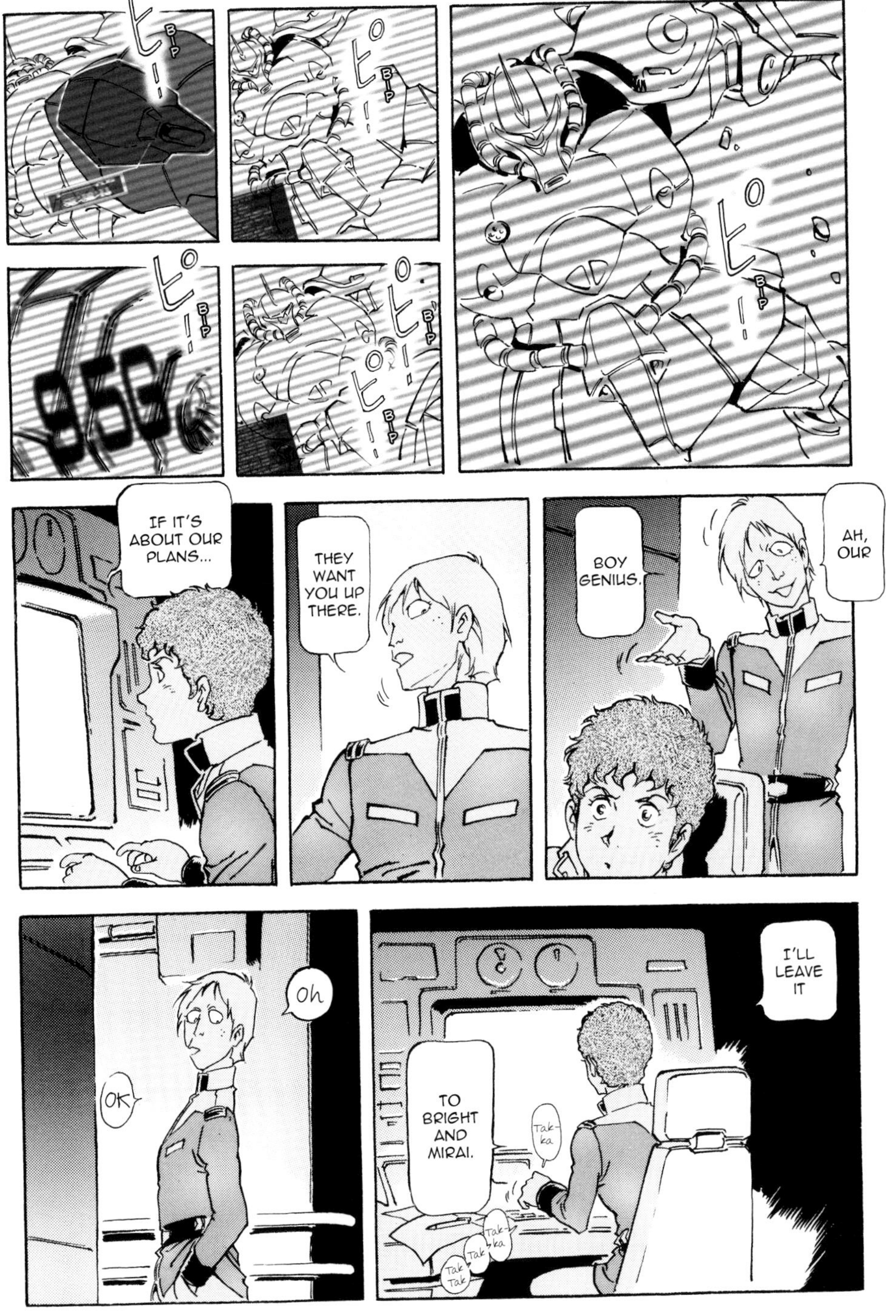
ピ! BIP
ピ! BIP
ピ! BIP
ピ! BIP
ピ! BIP
ピ! BIP
AH, OUR
BOY GENIUS.
THEY WANT YOU UP THERE.
IF IT'S ABOUT OUR PLANS...
I'LL LEAVE IT
TO BRIGHT AND MIRAI.
Tak-ka
Tak-ka
Tak
Tak Tak
Oh
OK

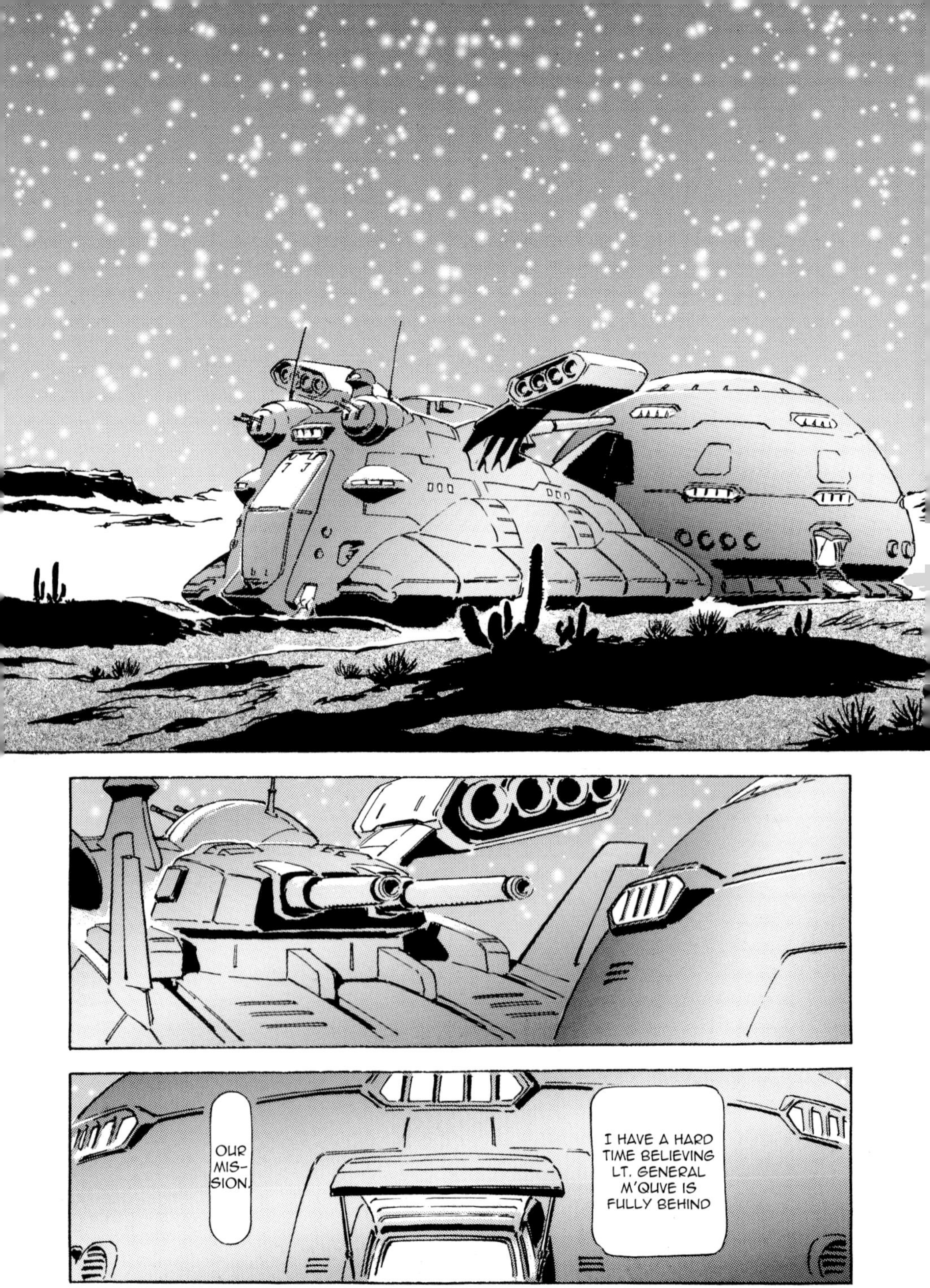
I HAVE A HARD TIME BELIEVING LT. GENERAL M'QUVE IS FULLY BEHIND
OUR MIS-SION.

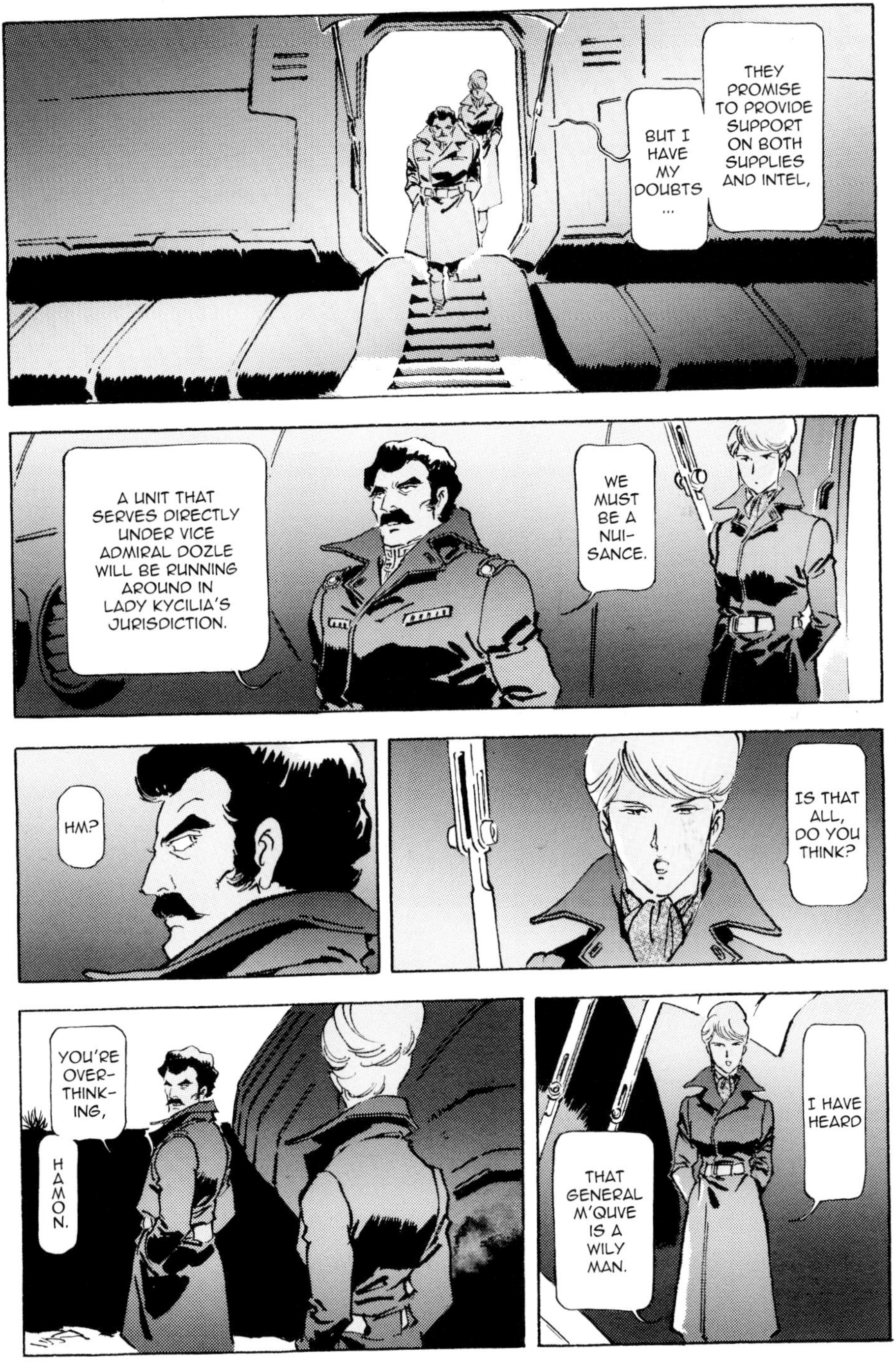
THEY PROMISE TO PROVIDE SUPPORT ON BOTH SUPPLIES AND INTEL,
BUT I HAVE MY DOUBTS ...
WE MUST BE A NUISANCE.
A UNIT THAT SERVES DIRECTLY UNDER VICE ADMIRAL DOZLE WILL BE RUNNING AROUND IN LADY KYCILIA'S JURISDICTION.
IS THAT ALL, DO YOU THINK?
HM?
I HAVE HEARD
THAT GENERAL M'QUVE IS A WILY MAN.
YOU'RE OVER-THINKING,
HAMON.

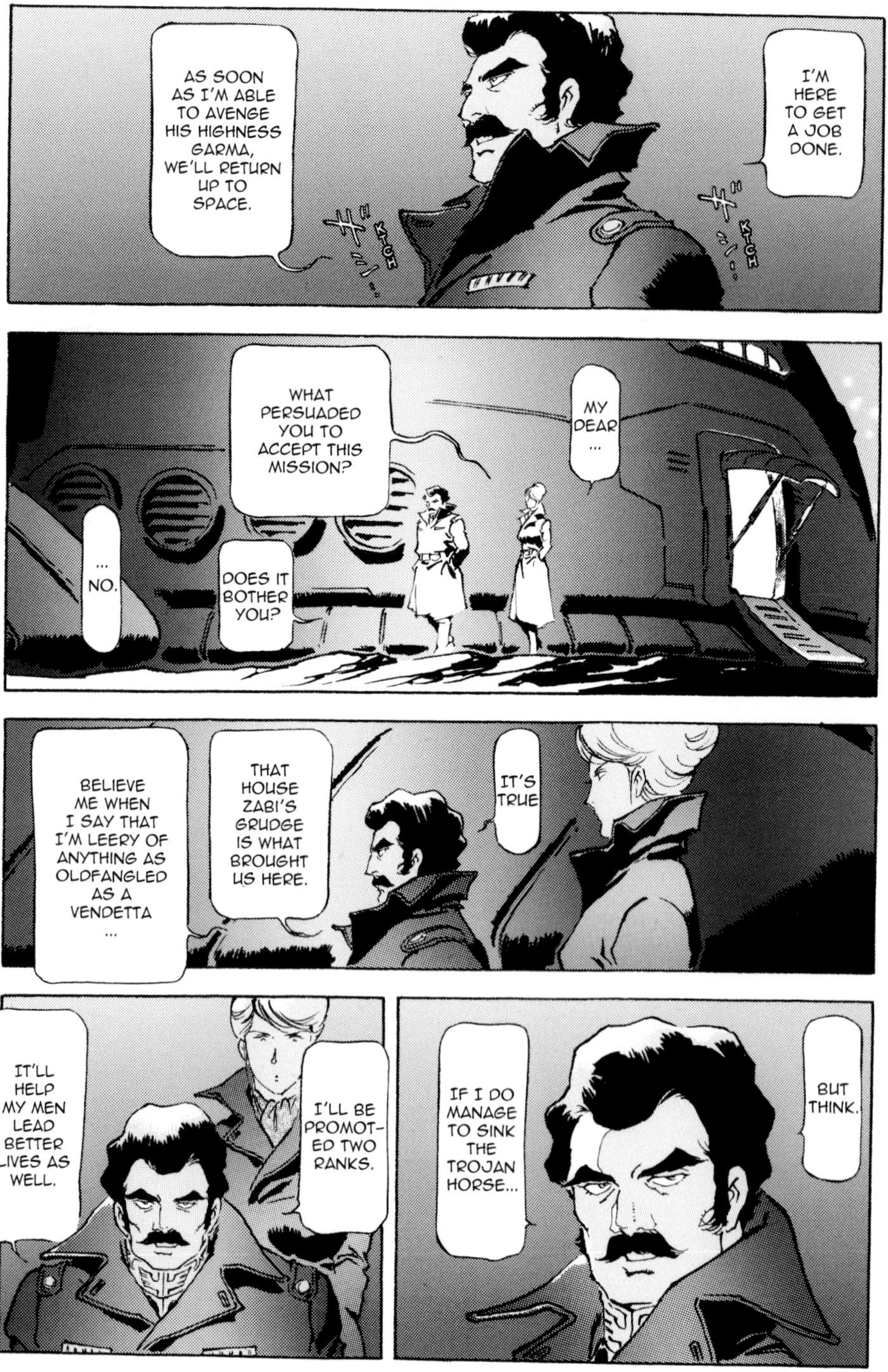
I'M HERE TO GET A JOB DONE.
KTCH
KTCH
AS SOON AS I'M ABLE TO AVENGE HIS HIGHNESS GARMA, WE'LL RETURN UP TO SPACE.
MY DEAR ...
WHAT PERSUADED YOU TO ACCEPT THIS MISSION?
DOES IT BOTHER YOU?
... NO.
IT'S TRUE
THAT HOUSE ZABI'S GRUDGE IS WHAT BROUGHT US HERE.
BELIEVE ME WHEN I SAY THAT I'M LEERY OF ANYTHING AS OLDFANGLED AS A VENDETTA ...
BUT THINK.
IF I DO MANAGE TO SINK THE TROJAN HORSE...
I'LL BE PROMOT-ED TWO RANKS.
IT'LL HELP MY MEN LEAD BETTER LIVES AS WELL.

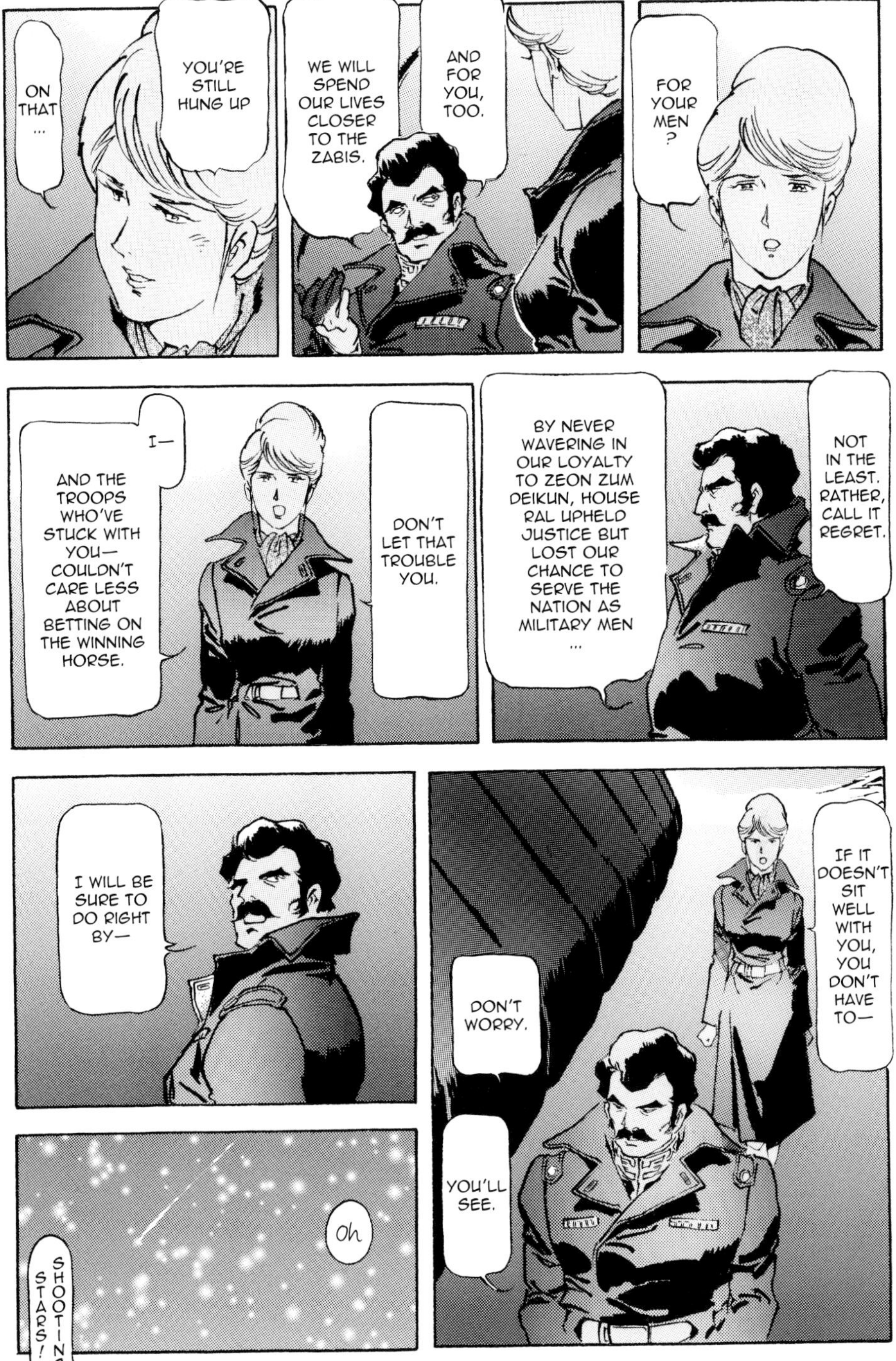
FOR YOUR MEN?
AND FOR YOU, TOO.
WE WILL SPEND OUR LIVES CLOSER TO THE ZABIS.
YOU'RE STILL HUNG UP
ON THAT...
NOT IN THE LEAST. RATHER, CALL IT REGRET.
BY NEVER WAVERING IN OUR LOYALTY TO ZEON ZUM DEIKUN, HOUSE RAL UPHELD JUSTICE BUT LOST OUR CHANCE TO SERVE THE NATION AS MILITARY MEN...
DON'T LET THAT TROUBLE YOU.
I— AND THE TROOPS WHO'VE STUCK WITH YOU— COULDN'T CARE LESS ABOUT BETTING ON THE WINNING HORSE.
IF IT DOESN'T SIT WELL WITH YOU, YOU DON'T HAVE TO—
DON'T WORRY.
YOU'LL SEE.
I WILL BE SURE TO DO RIGHT BY—
Oh
SHOOTING STARS!

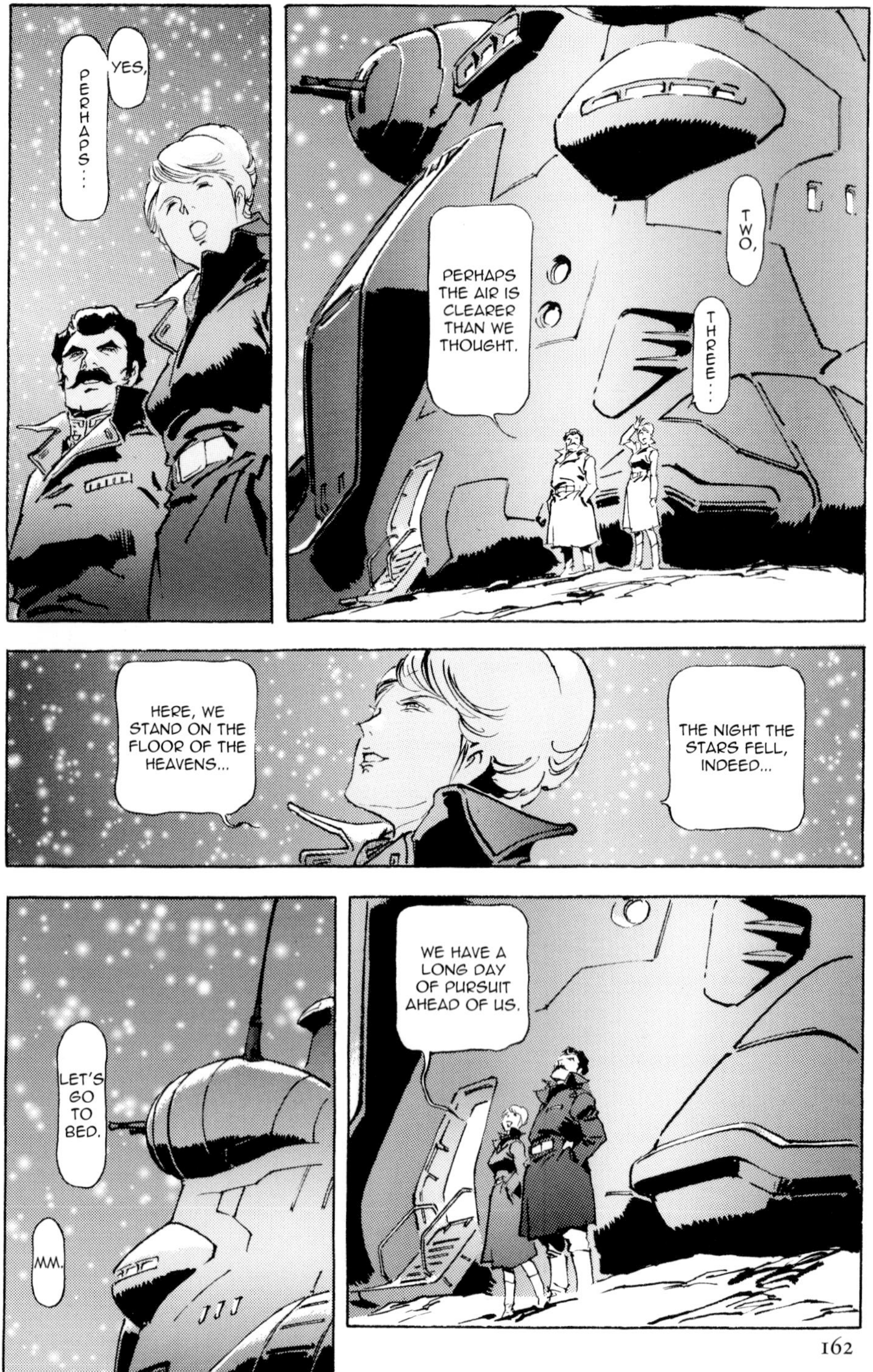
TWO,
THREE...
PERHAPS THE AIR IS CLEARER THAN WE THOUGHT.
YES,
PERHAPS...
THE NIGHT THE STARS FELL, INDEED...
HERE, WE STAND ON THE FLOOR OF THE HEAVENS...
WE HAVE A LONG DAY OF PURSUIT AHEAD OF US.
LET'S GO TO BED.
MM.

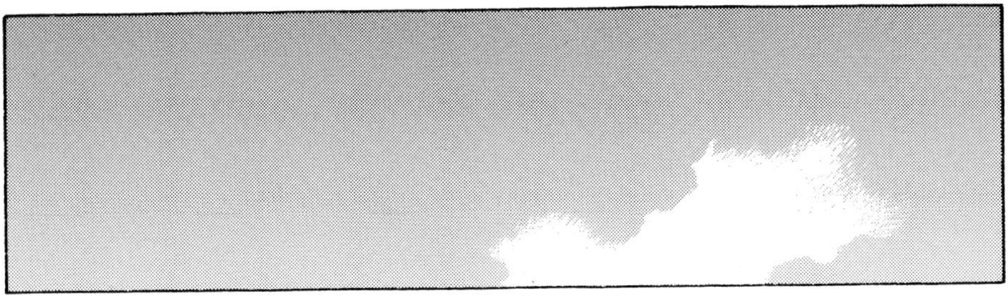

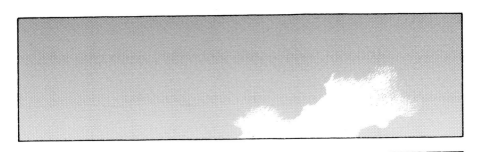

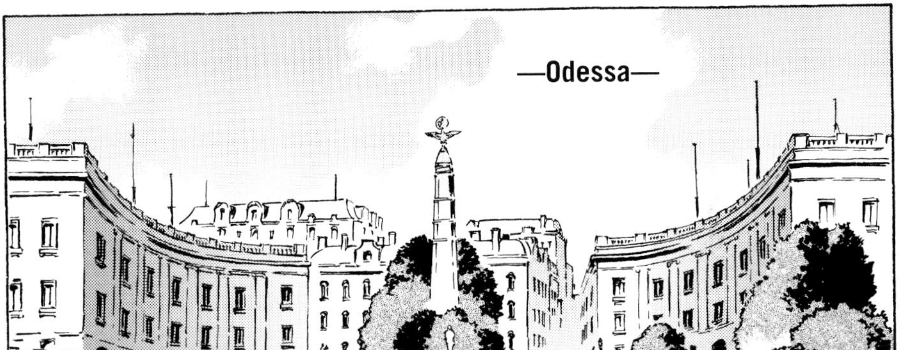
—Odessa—

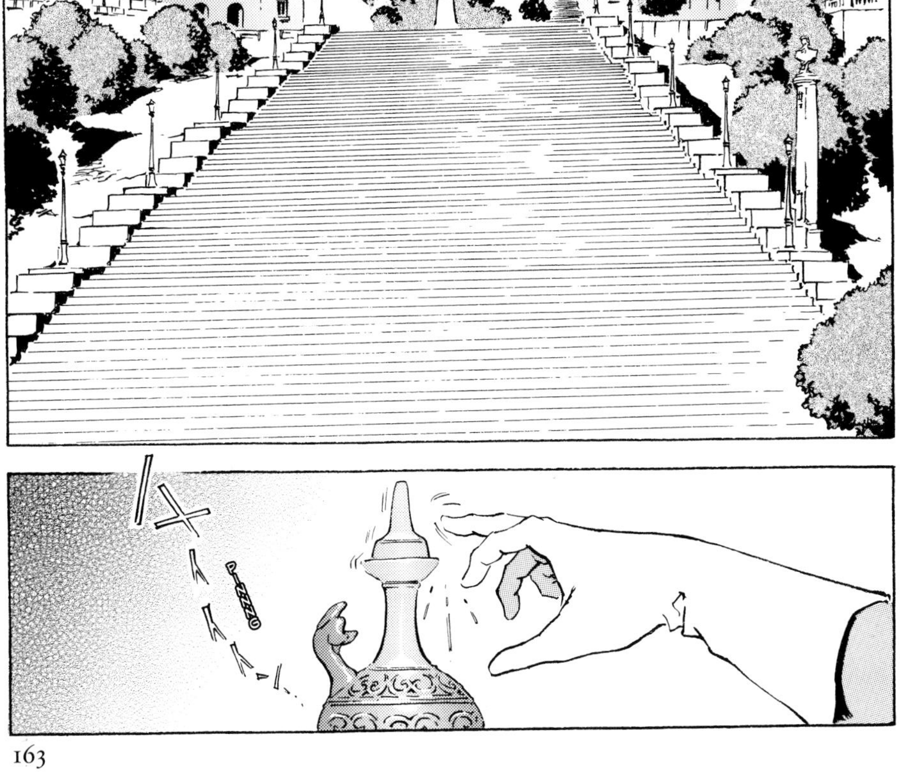

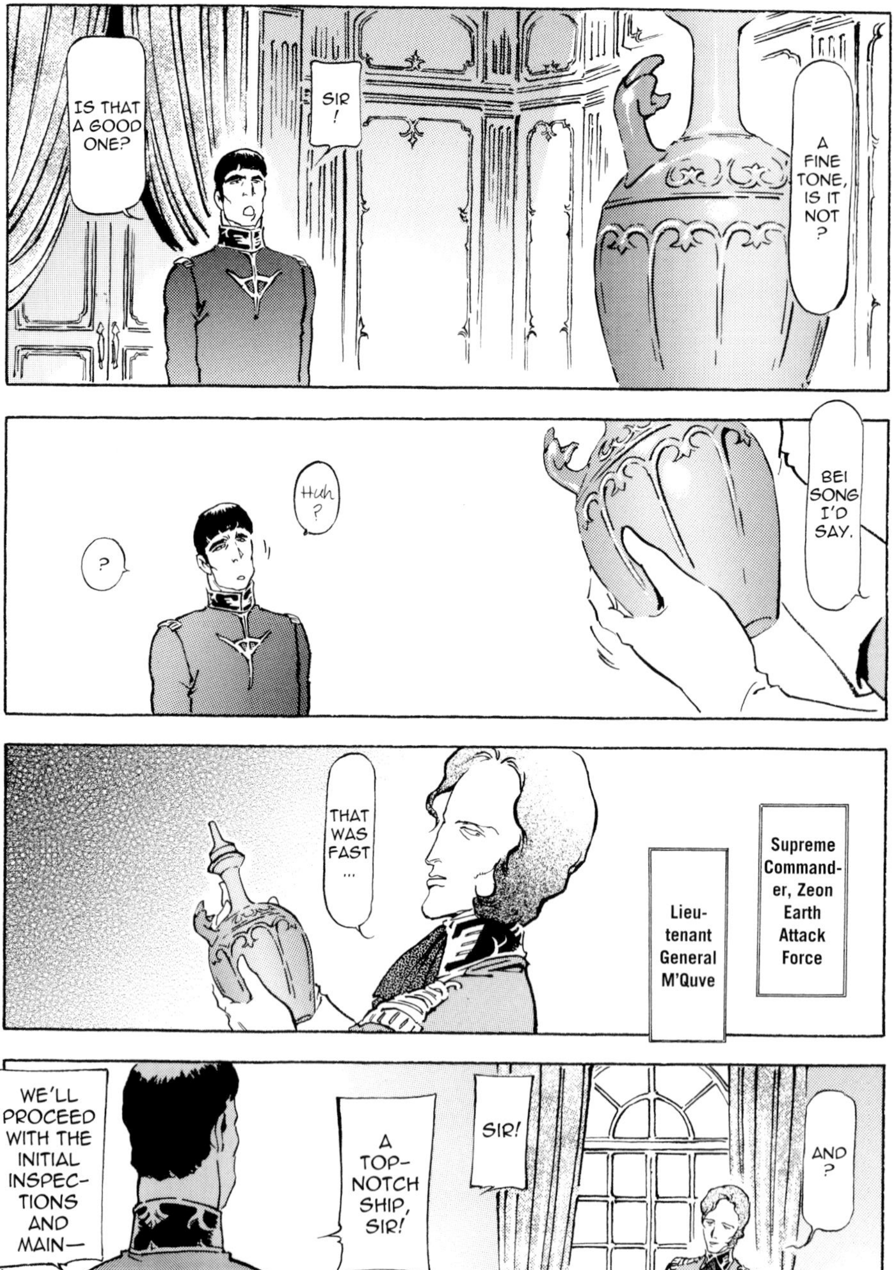
A FINE TONE, IS IT NOT?
SIR!
IS THAT A GOOD ONE?
BEI SONG I'D SAY.
Huh?
?
Supreme Command-er, Zeon Earth Attack Force
Lieu-tenant General M'Quve
THAT WAS FAST...
AND?
SIR!
A TOP-NOTCH SHIP, SIR!
WE'LL PROCEED WITH THE INITIAL INSPEC-TIONS AND MAIN—

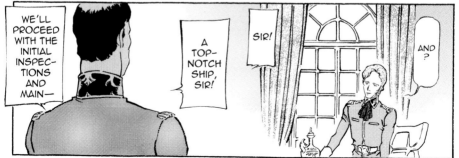

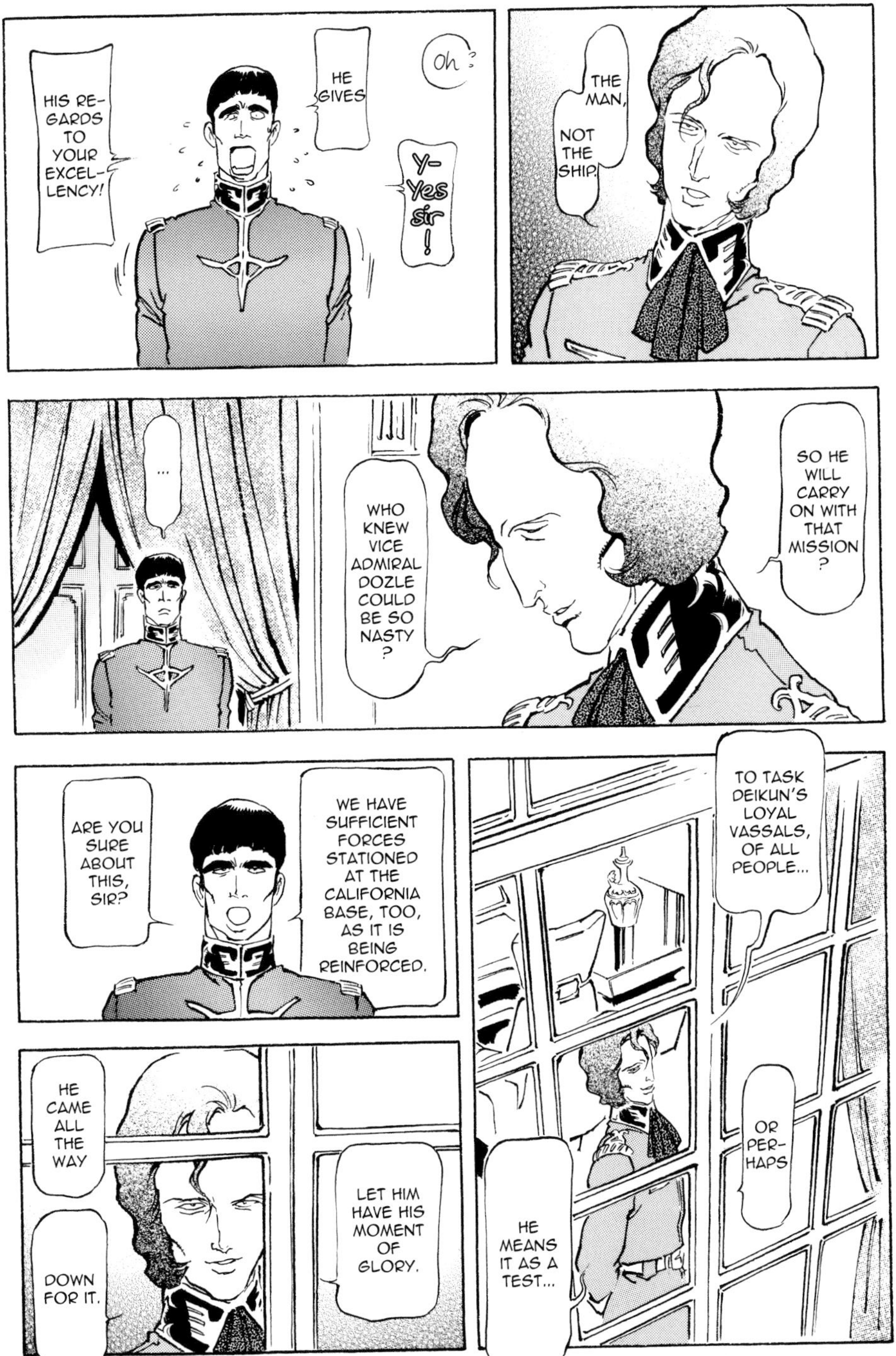
THE MAN, NOT THE SHIP.
Oh?
Y-Yes sir!
HE GIVES
HIS REGARDS TO YOUR EXCELLENCY!
SO HE WILL CARRY ON WITH THAT MISSION?
WHO KNEW VICE ADMIRAL DOZLE COULD BE SO NASTY?
...
TO TASK DEIKUN'S LOYAL VASSALS, OF ALL PEOPLE...
OR PERHAPS
HE MEANS IT AS A TEST...
WE HAVE SUFFICIENT FORCES STATIONED AT THE CALIFORNIA BASE, TOO, AS IT IS BEING REINFORCED.
ARE YOU SURE ABOUT THIS, SIR?
HE CAME ALL THE WAY
DOWN FOR IT.
LET HIM HAVE HIS MOMENT OF GLORY.

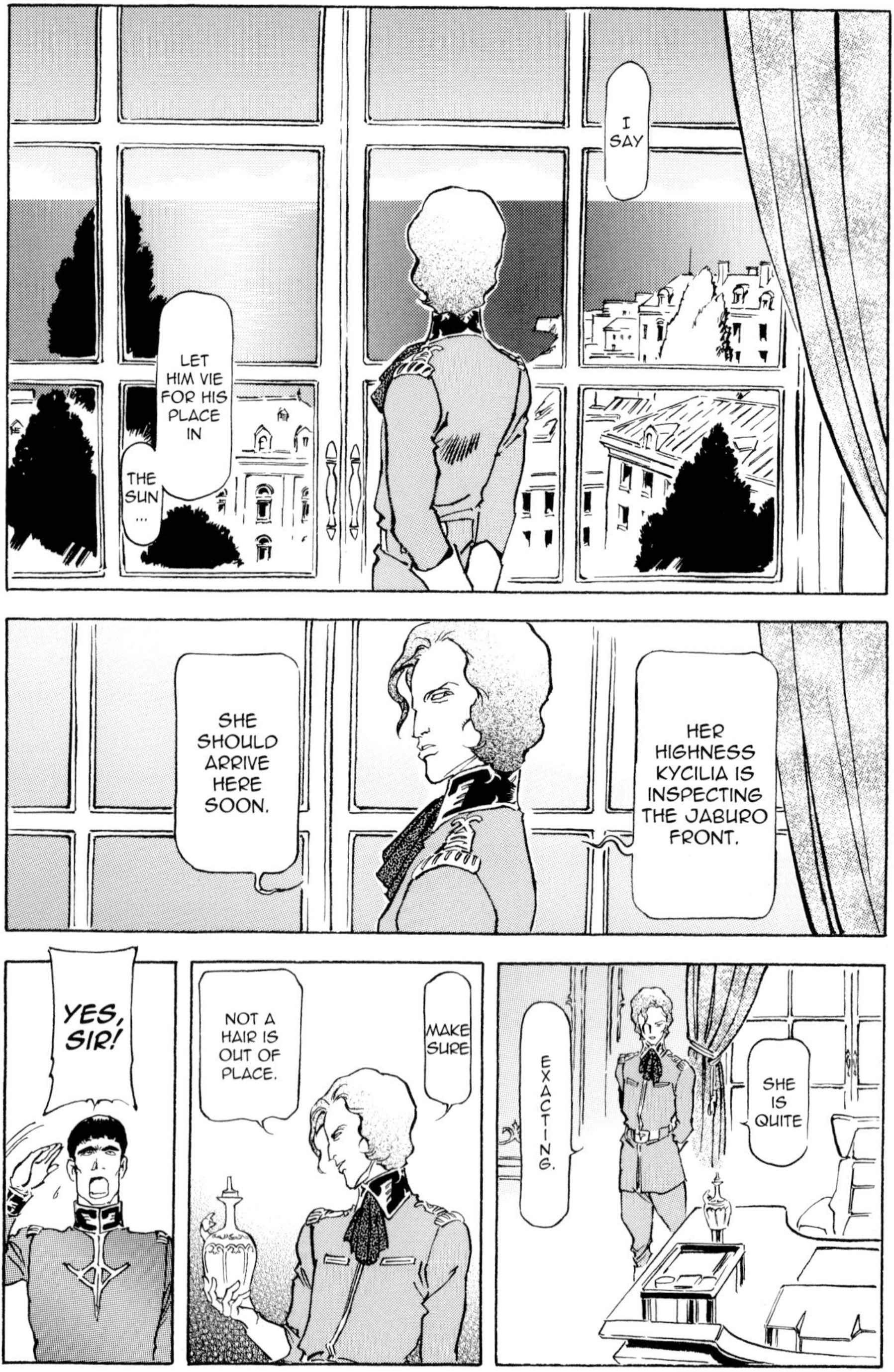
I SAY
LET HIM VIE FOR HIS PLACE IN
THE SUN ...
HER HIGHNESS KYCILIA IS INSPECTING THE JABURO FRONT.
SHE SHOULD ARRIVE HERE SOON.
SHE IS QUITE
EXACTING.
MAKE SURE
NOT A HAIR IS OUT OF PLACE.
YES, SIR!

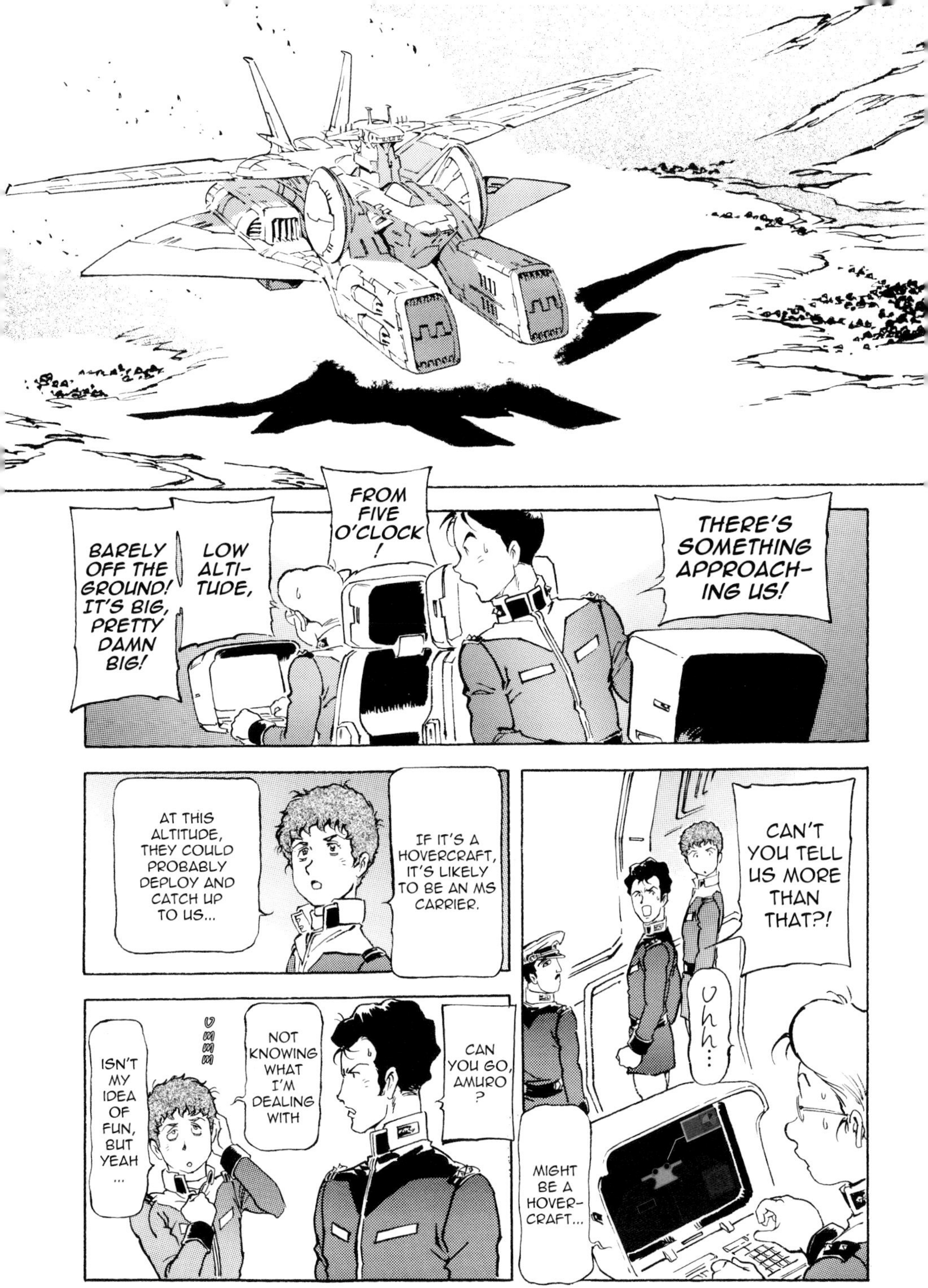
THERE'S SOMETHING APPROACHING US!
FROM FIVE O'CLOCK!
LOW ALTITUDE,
BARELY OFF THE GROUND! IT'S BIG, PRETTY DAMN BIG!
CAN'T YOU TELL US MORE THAN THAT?!
Uhh...
MIGHT BE A HOVERCRAFT...
IF IT'S A HOVERCRAFT, IT'S LIKELY TO BE AN MS CARRIER.
AT THIS ALTITUDE, THEY COULD PROBABLY DEPLOY AND CATCH UP TO US...
CAN YOU GO, AMURO?
NOT KNOWING WHAT I'M DEALING WITH
Ummm
ISN'T MY IDEA OF FUN, BUT YEAH...

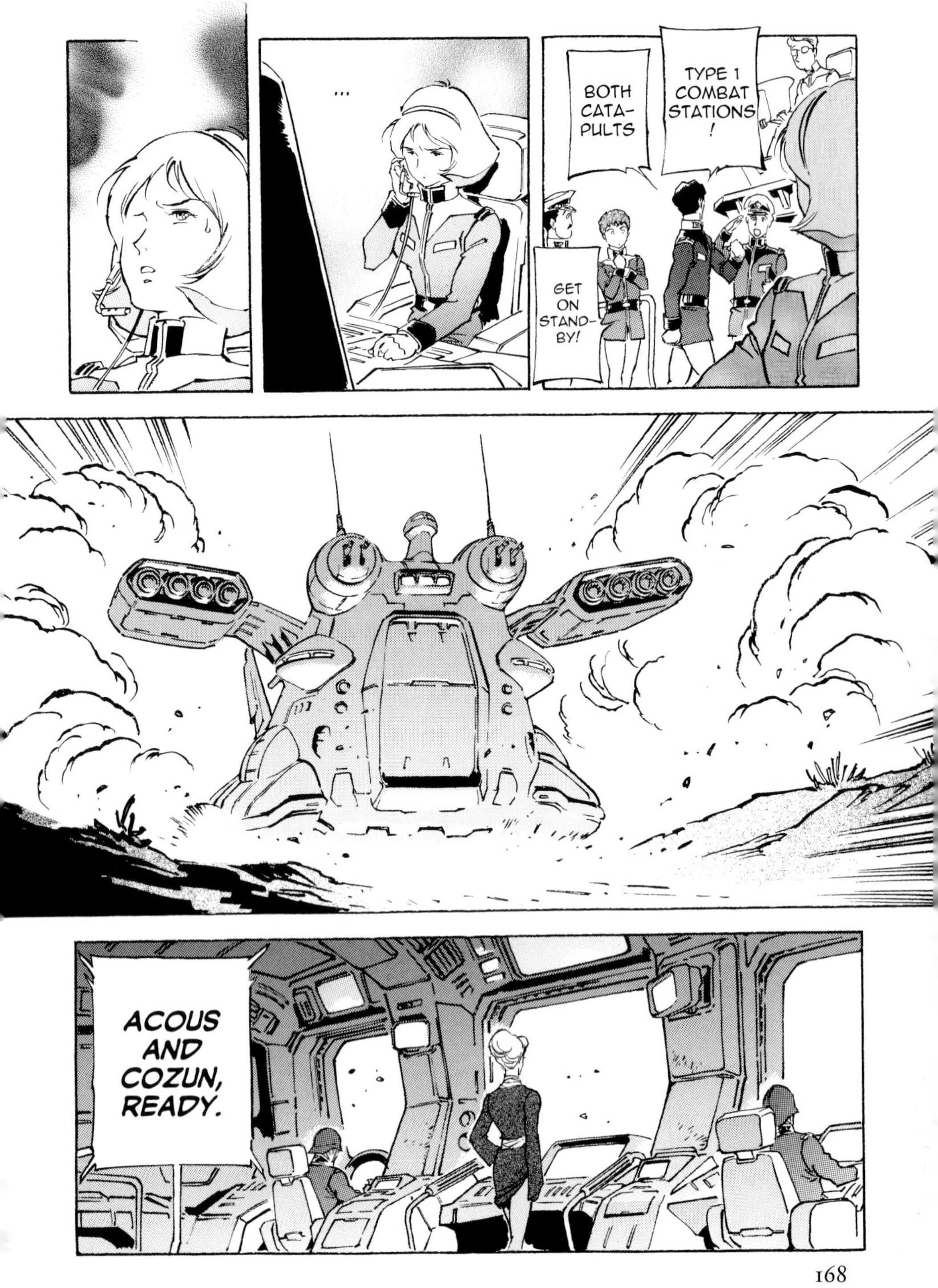
TYPE 1 COMBAT STATIONS!
BOTH CATA-PULTS
GET ON STAND-BY!
...
ACOUS AND COZUN, READY.

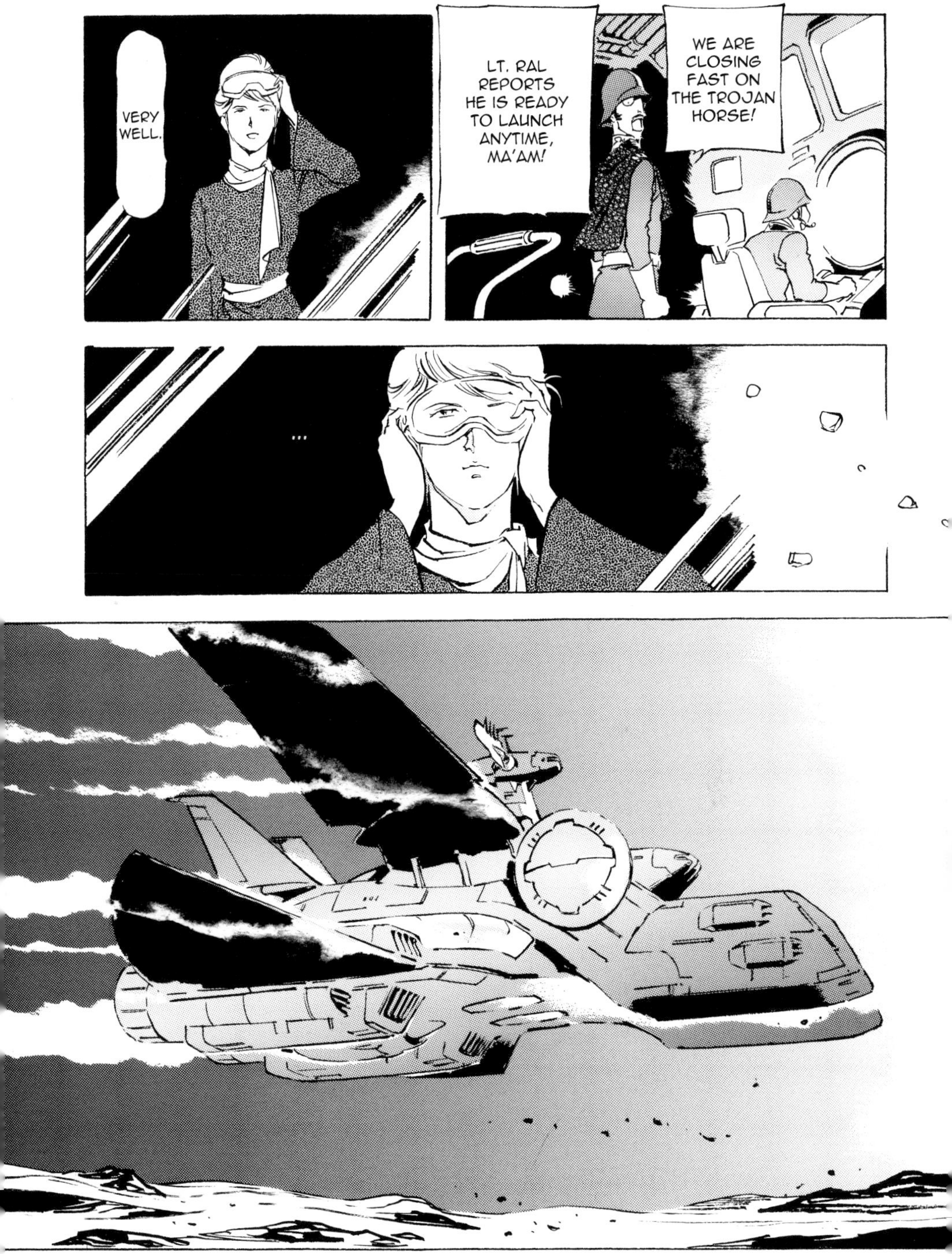
WE ARE CLOSING FAST ON THE TROJAN HORSE!
LT. RAL REPORTS HE IS READY TO LAUNCH ANYTIME, MA'AM!
VERY WELL.
...

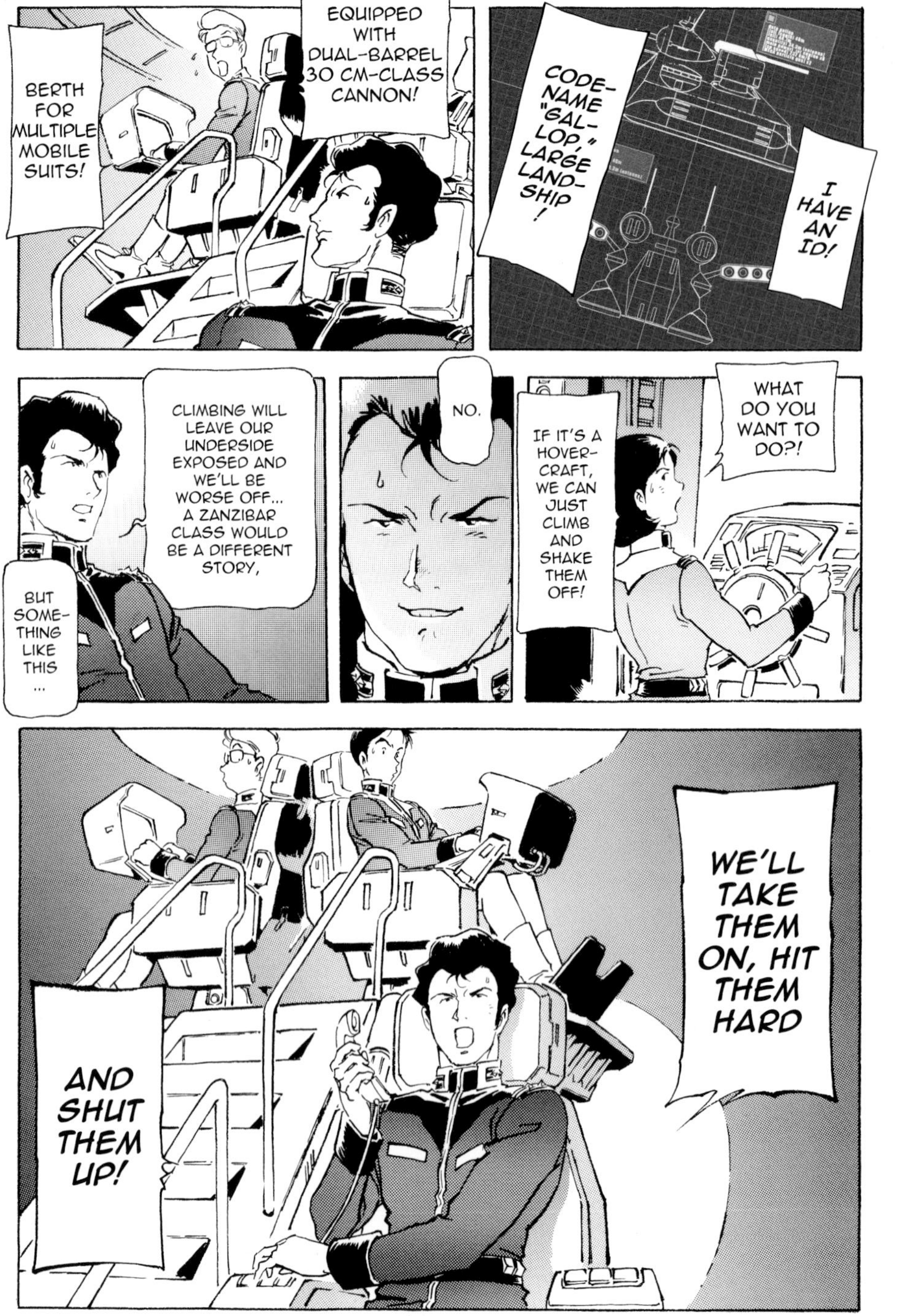
I HAVE AN ID!
CODE-NAME "GALLOP," LARGE LANDSHIP!
EQUIPPED WITH DUAL-BARREL 30 CM-CLASS CANNON!
BERTH FOR MULTIPLE MOBILE SUITS!
WHAT DO YOU WANT TO DO?!
IF IT'S A HOVERCRAFT, WE CAN JUST CLIMB AND SHAKE THEM OFF!
NO.
CLIMBING WILL LEAVE OUR UNDERSIDE EXPOSED AND WE'LL BE WORSE OFF... A ZANZIBAR CLASS WOULD BE A DIFFERENT STORY,
BUT SOMETHING LIKE THIS ...
WE'LL TAKE THEM ON, HIT THEM HARD
AND SHUT THEM UP!

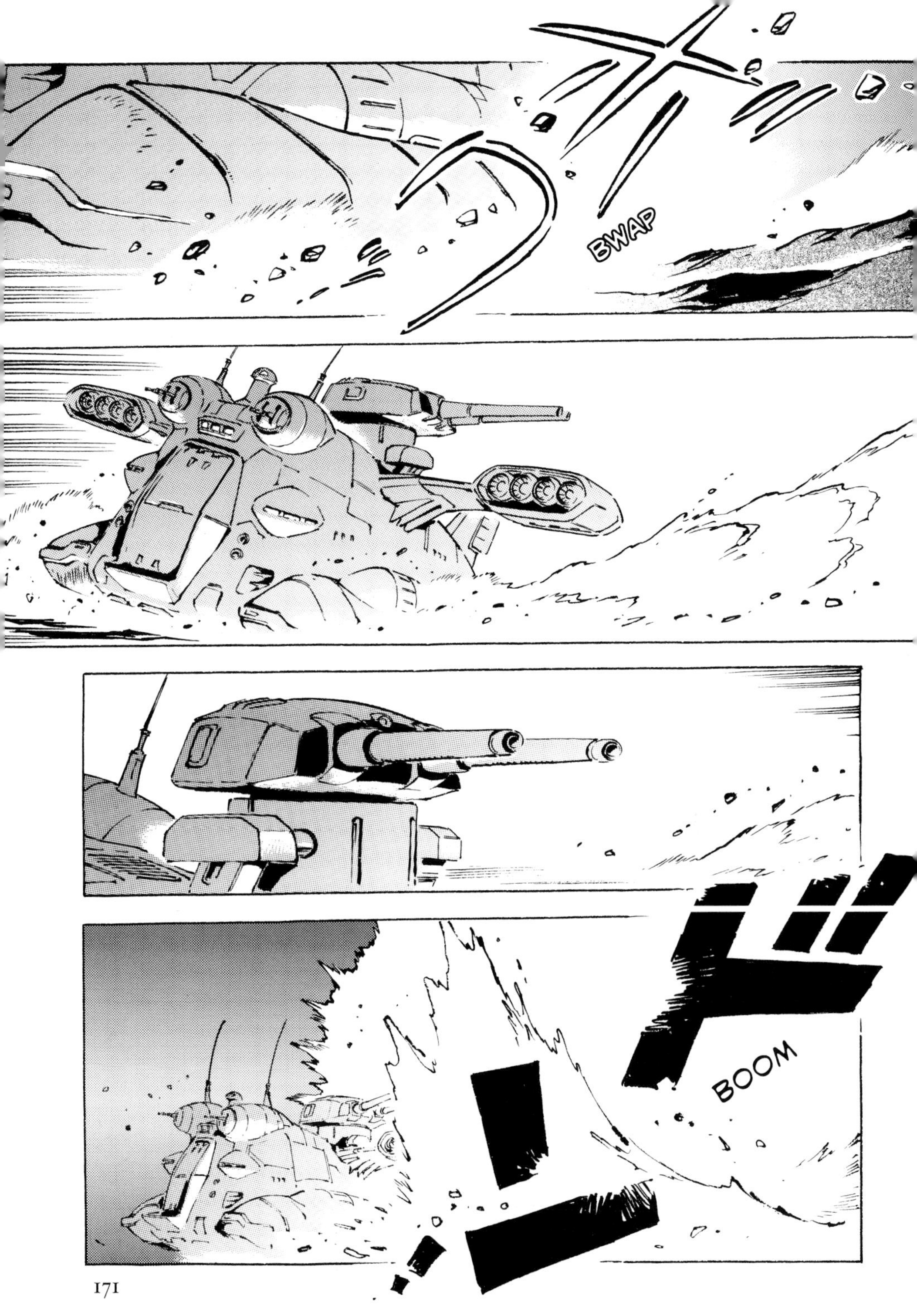
BWAP
BOOM

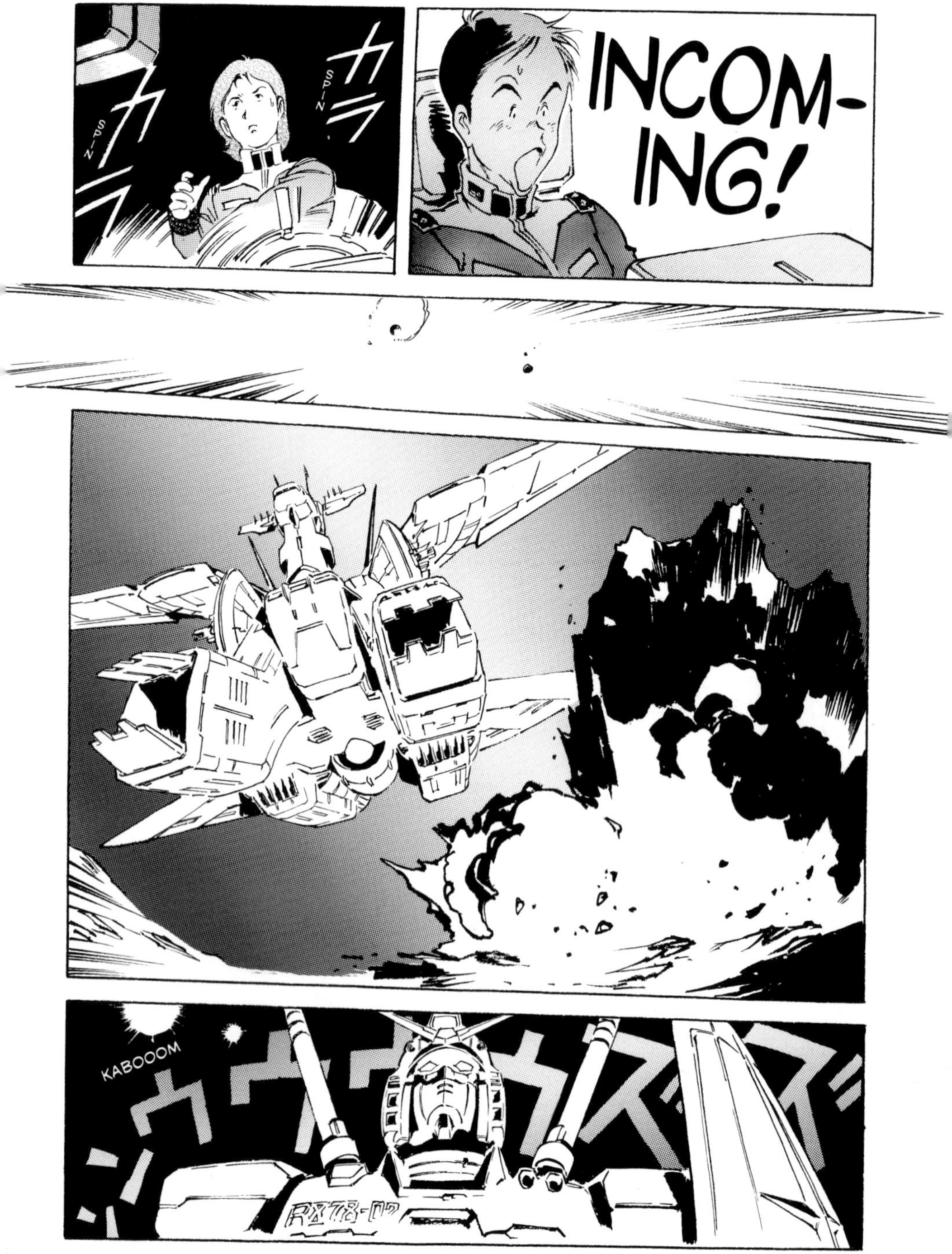
INCOM-
ING!
SPIN
SPIN
KABOOOM

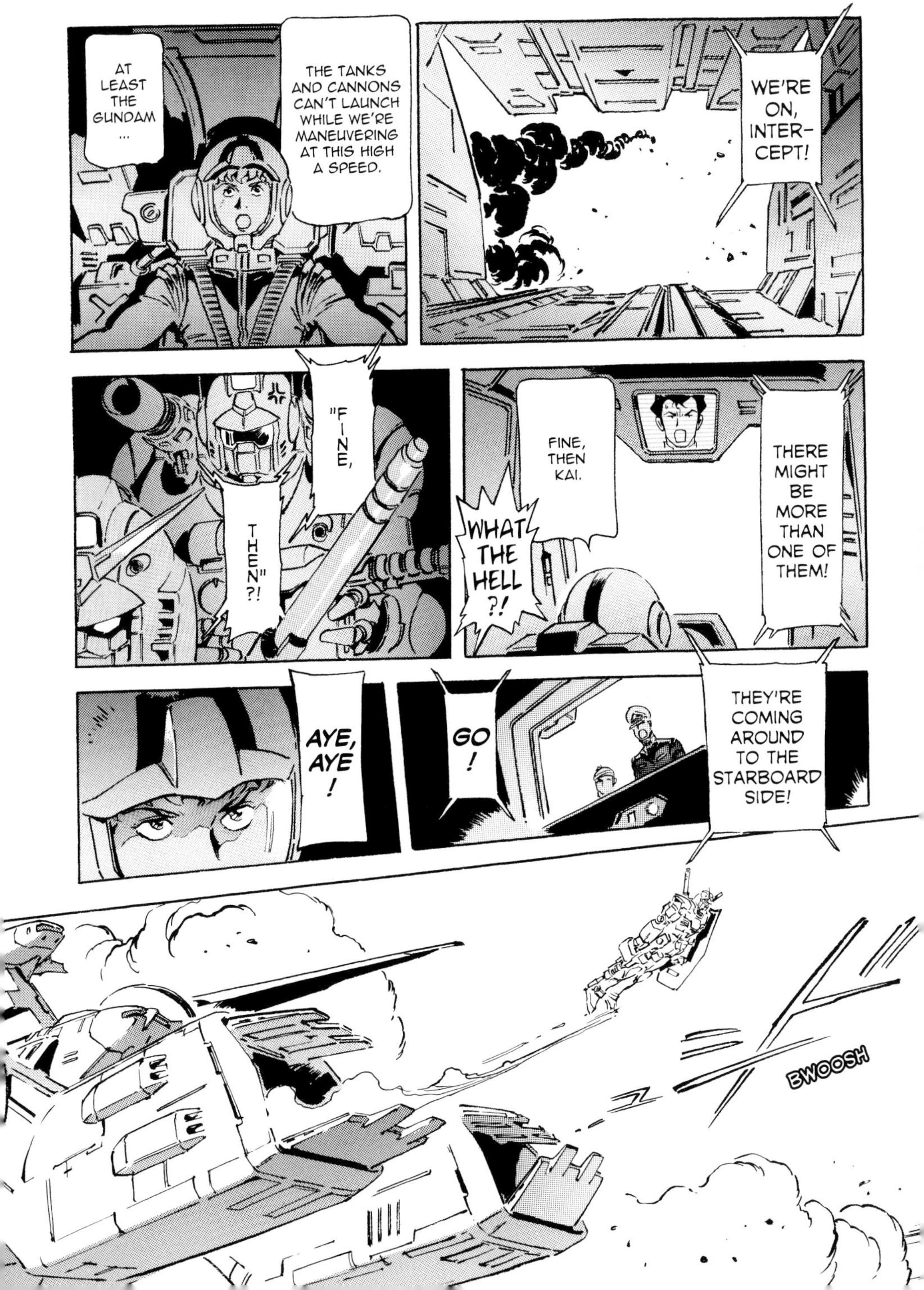
WE'RE ON, INTERCEPT!
THE TANKS AND CANNONS CAN'T LAUNCH WHILE WE'RE MANEUVERING AT THIS HIGH A SPEED.
AT LEAST THE GUNDAM ...
THERE MIGHT BE MORE THAN ONE OF THEM!
FINE, THEN KAI.
WHAT THE HELL ?!
"FINE, THEN"?!
THEY'RE COMING AROUND TO THE STARBOARD SIDE!
GO!
AYE, AYE!
BWOOSH

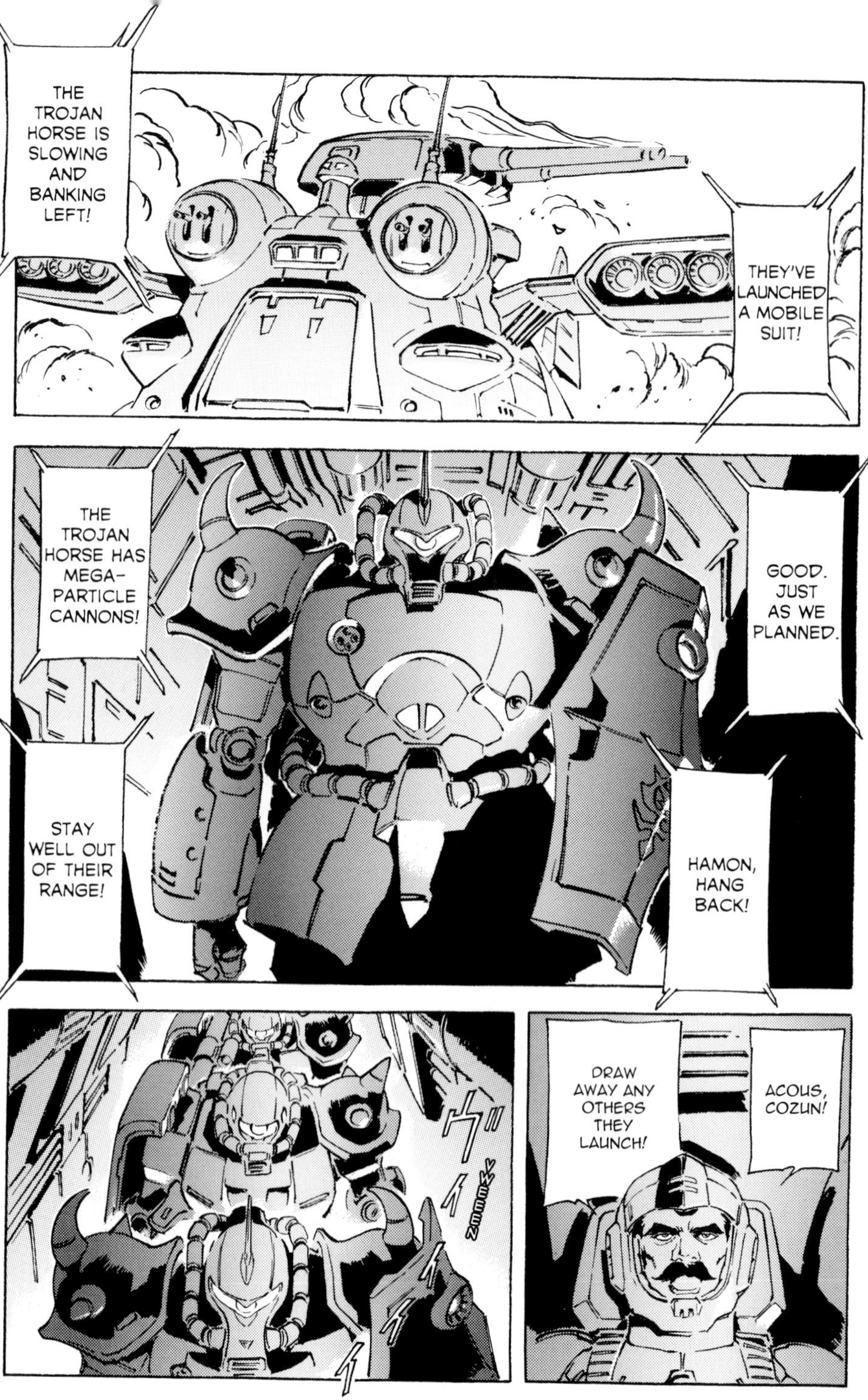
THE TROJAN HORSE IS SLOWING AND BANKING LEFT!
THEY'VE LAUNCHED A MOBILE SUIT!
THE TROJAN HORSE HAS MEGA-PARTICLE CANNONS!
GOOD. JUST AS WE PLANNED.
HAMON, HANG BACK!
STAY WELL OUT OF THEIR RANGE!
ACOUS, COZUN!
DRAW AWAY ANY OTHERS THEY LAUNCH!
VWEEEN

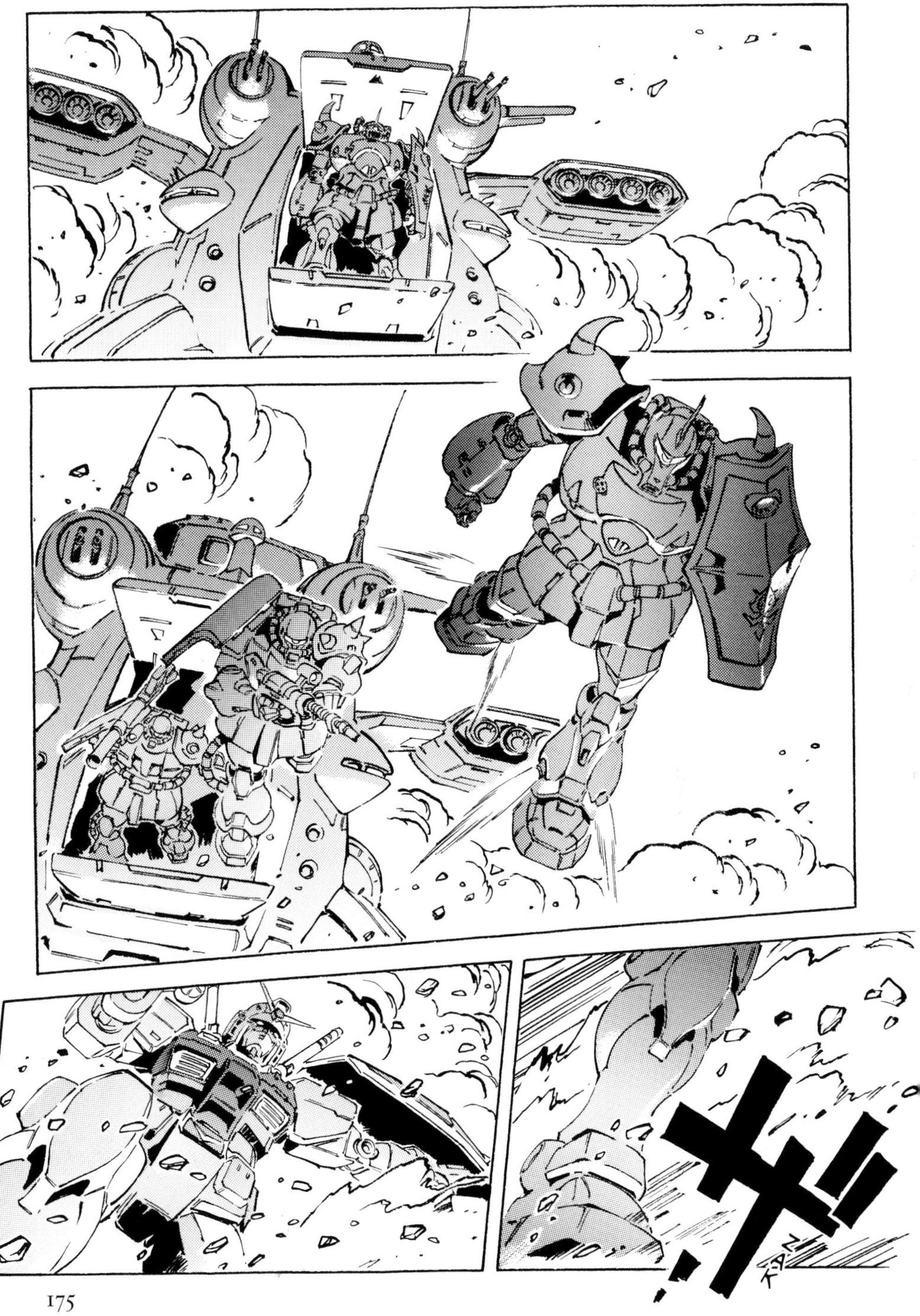

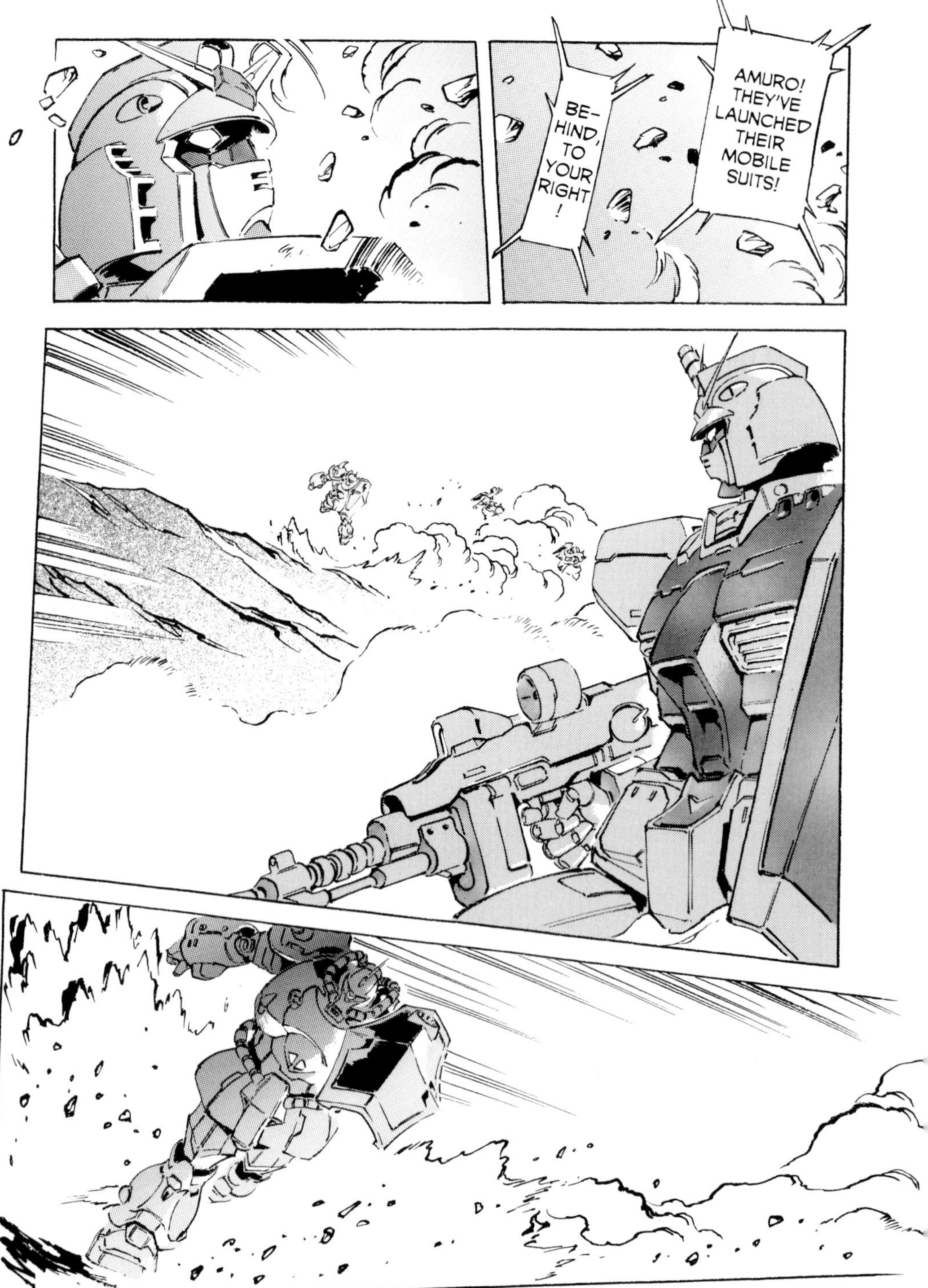
AMURO! THEY'VE LAUNCHED THEIR MOBILE SUITS!
BE-HIND, TO YOUR RIGHT!

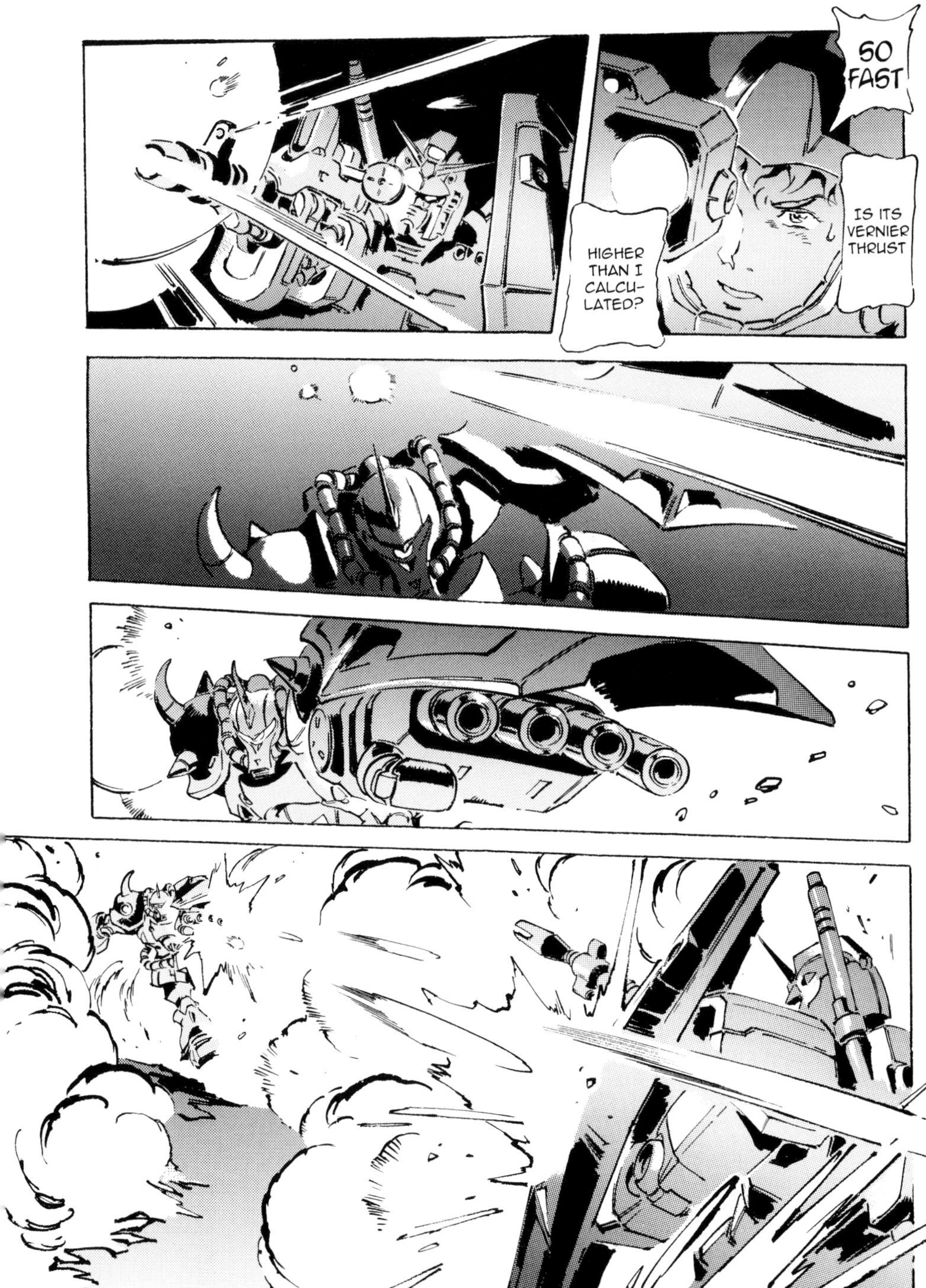
SO FAST
IS ITS VERNIER THRUST
HIGHER THAN I CALCULATED?

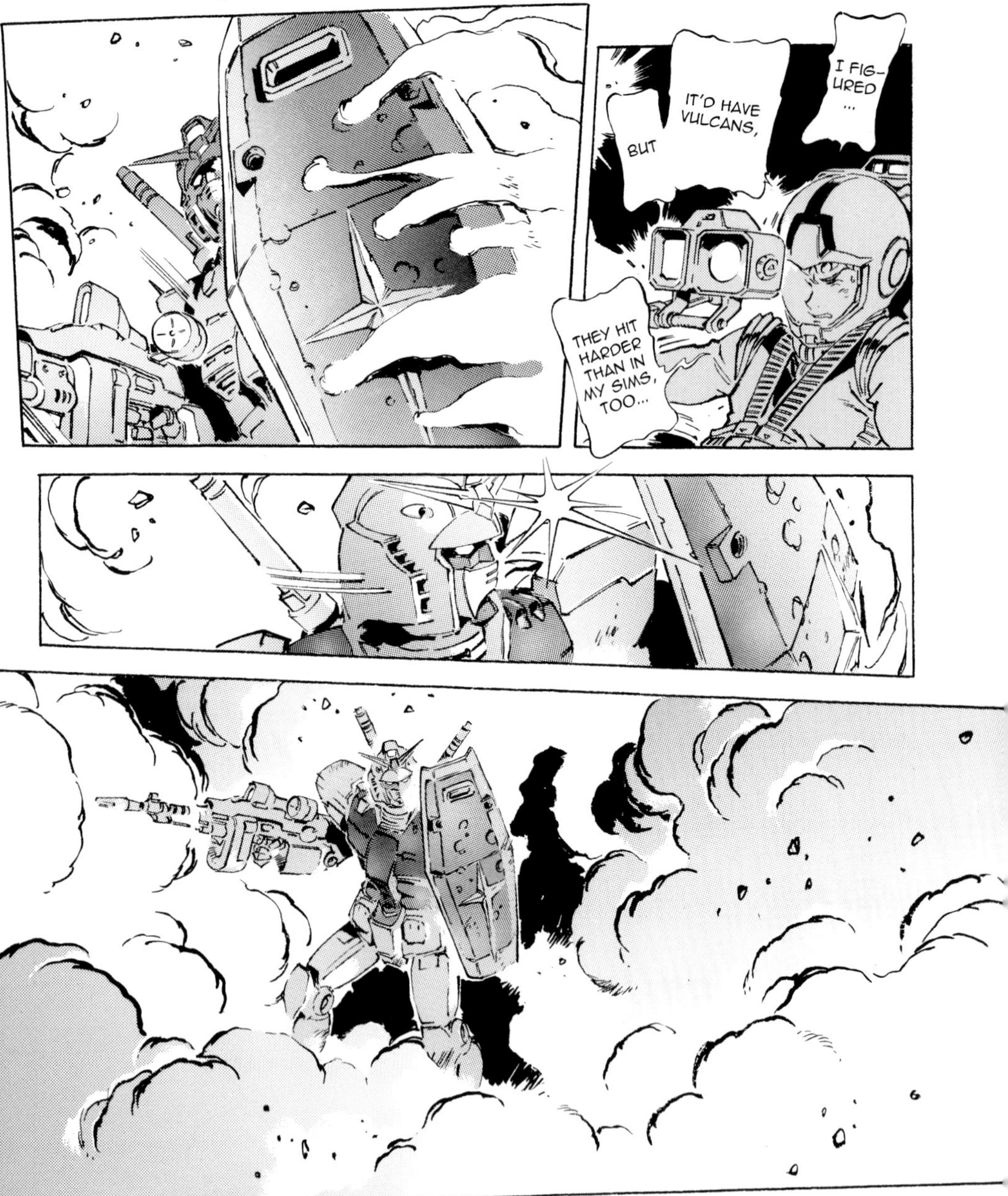
I FIG-URED ...
IT'D HAVE VULCANS,
BUT
THEY HIT HARDER THAN IN MY SIMS, TOO...
LIKE A SMOKE-SCREEN
WOULD WORK!

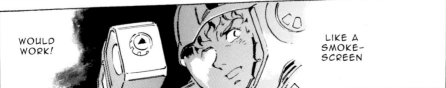

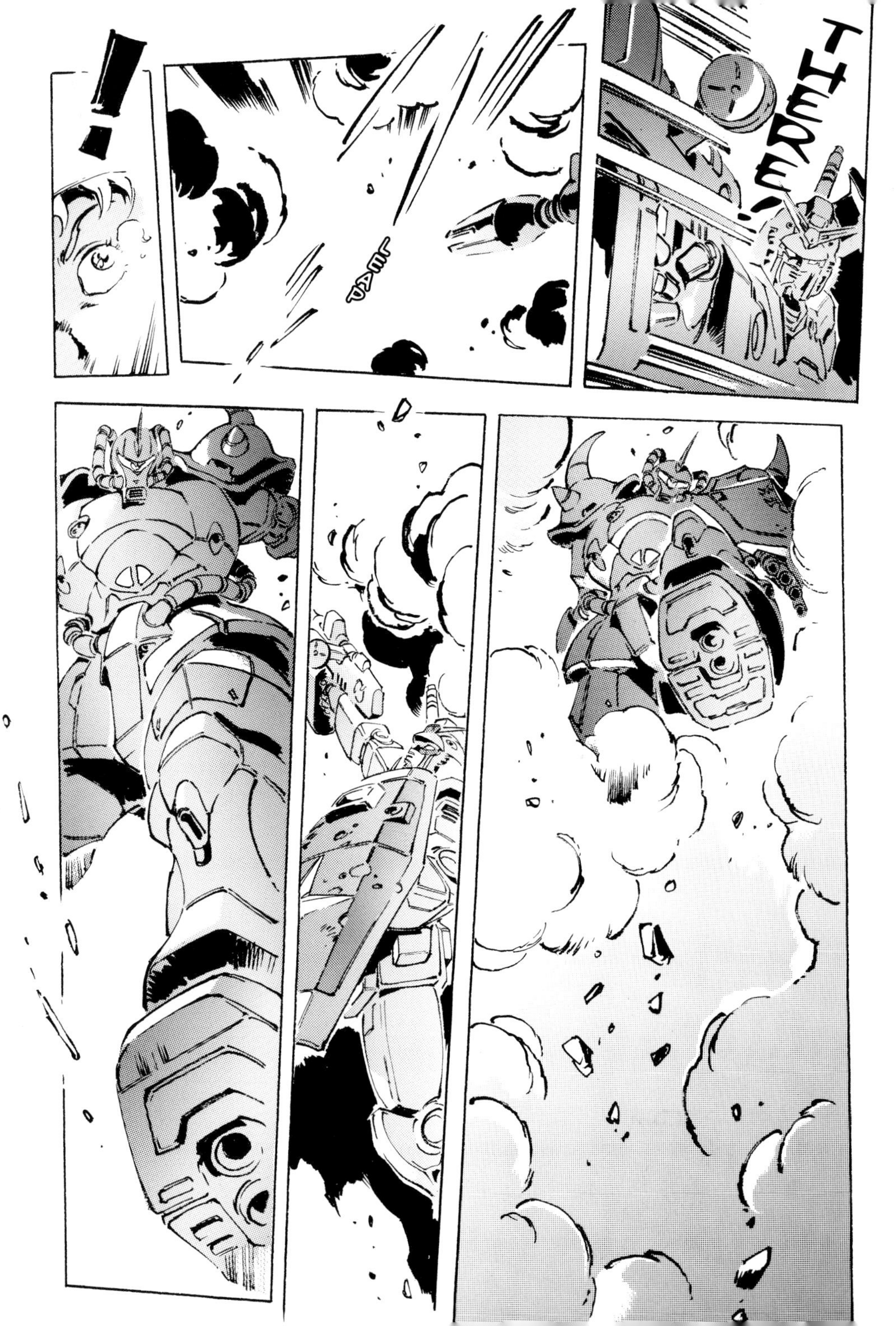
THERE!
LEAP
!

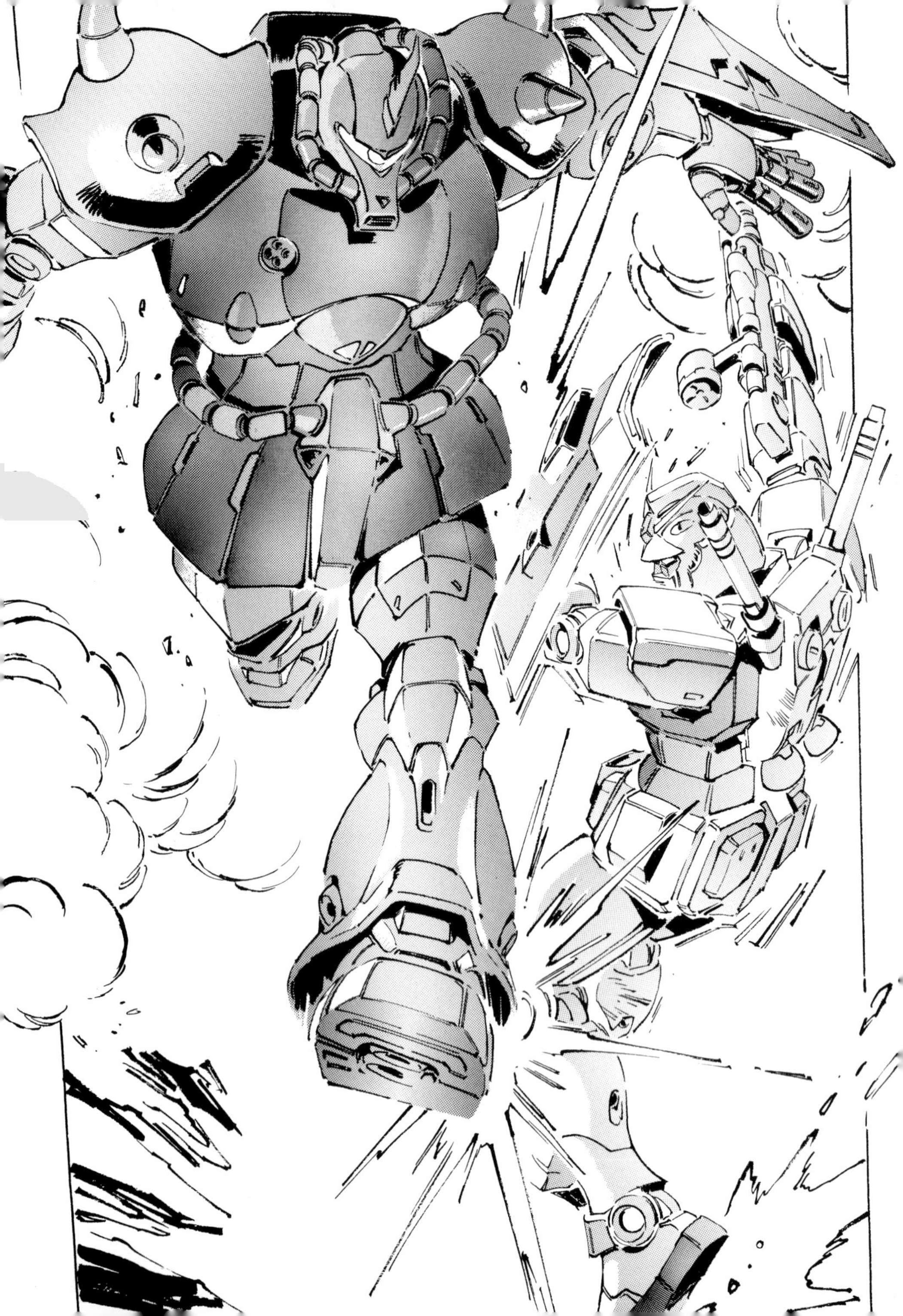

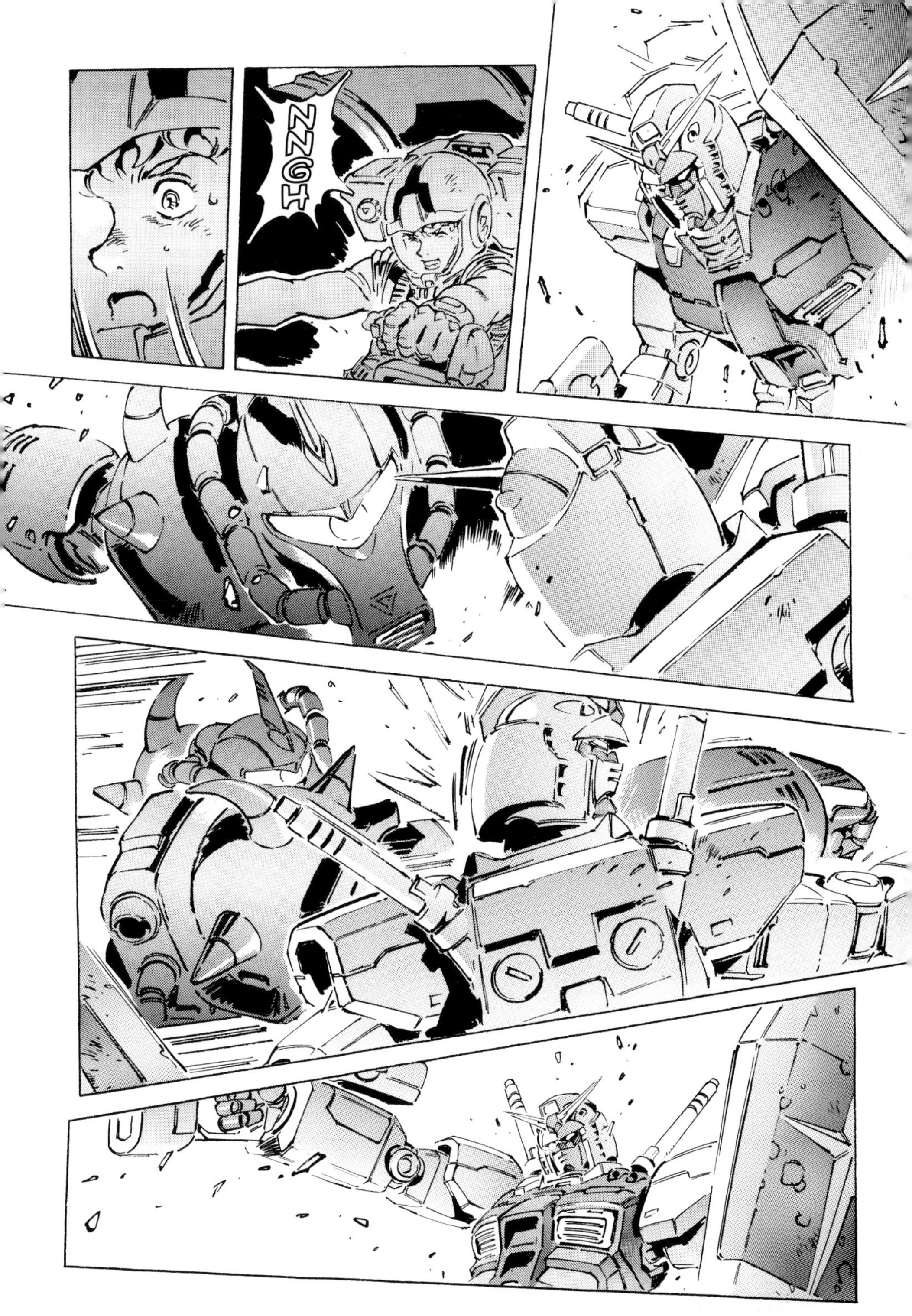
NNGH

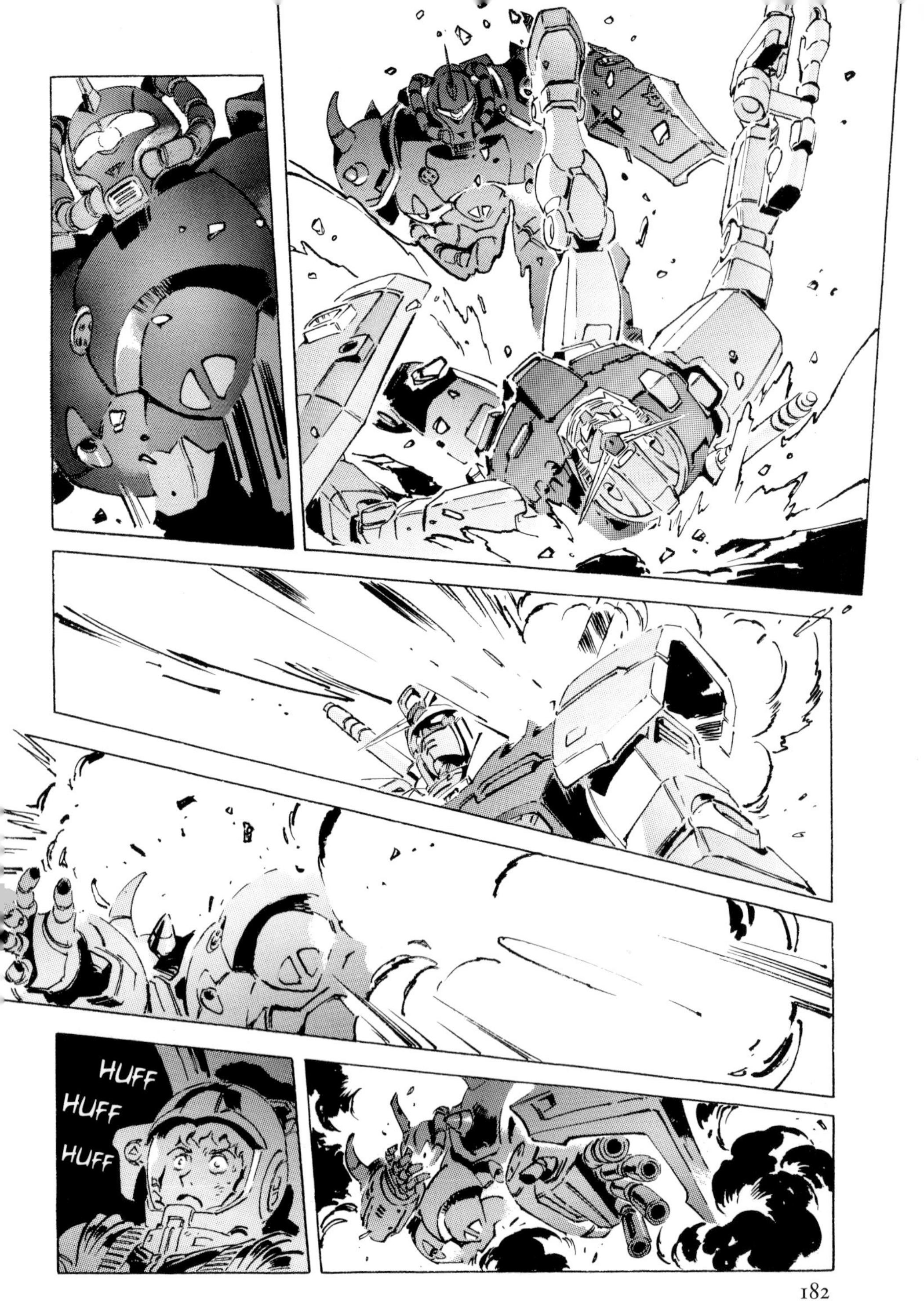
HUFF
HUFF
HUFF

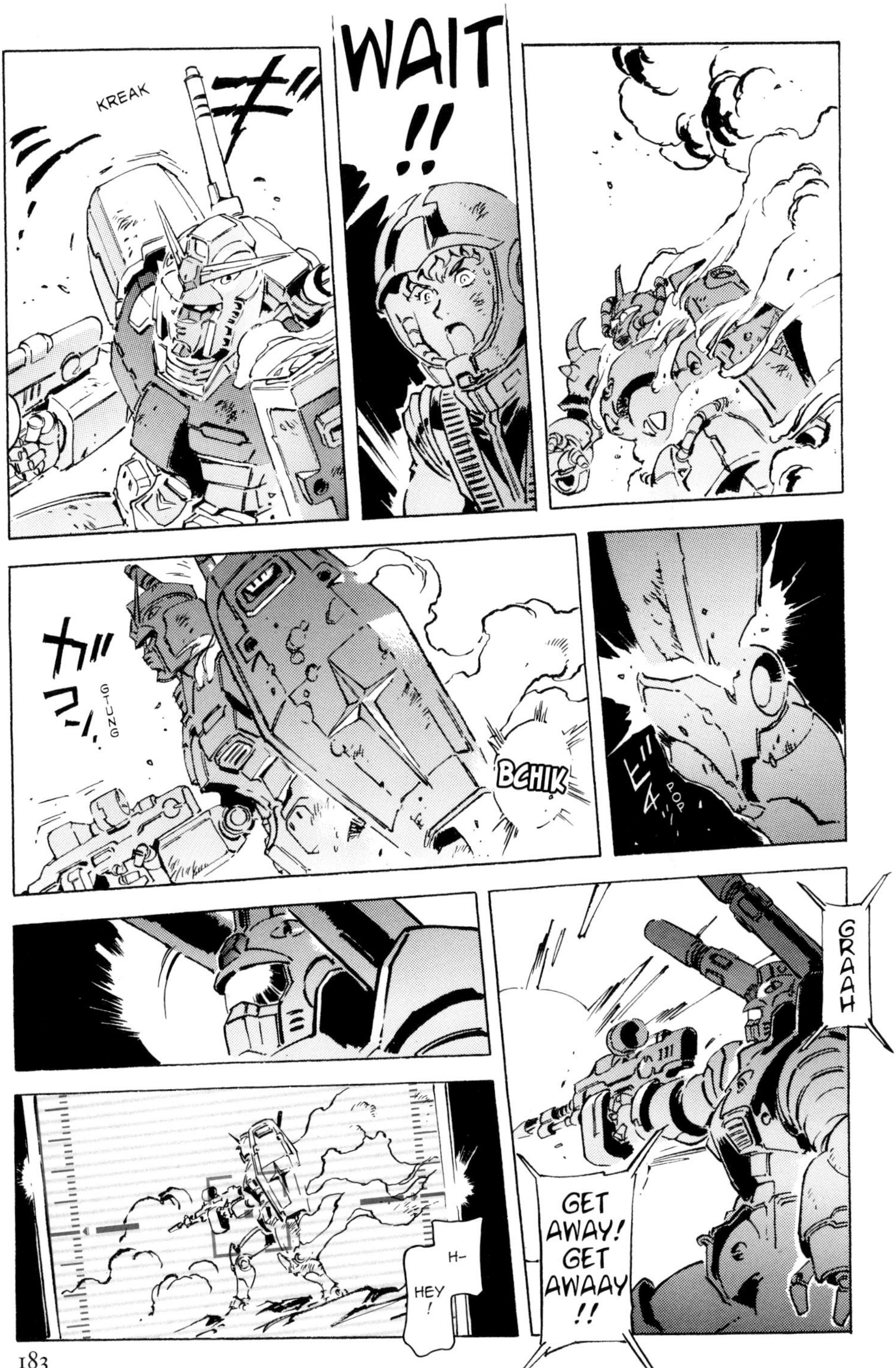
WAIT !!
KREAK
POP
BCHIK
GTUNG
GRAAH
GET AWAY! GET AWAAY !!
H- HEY !

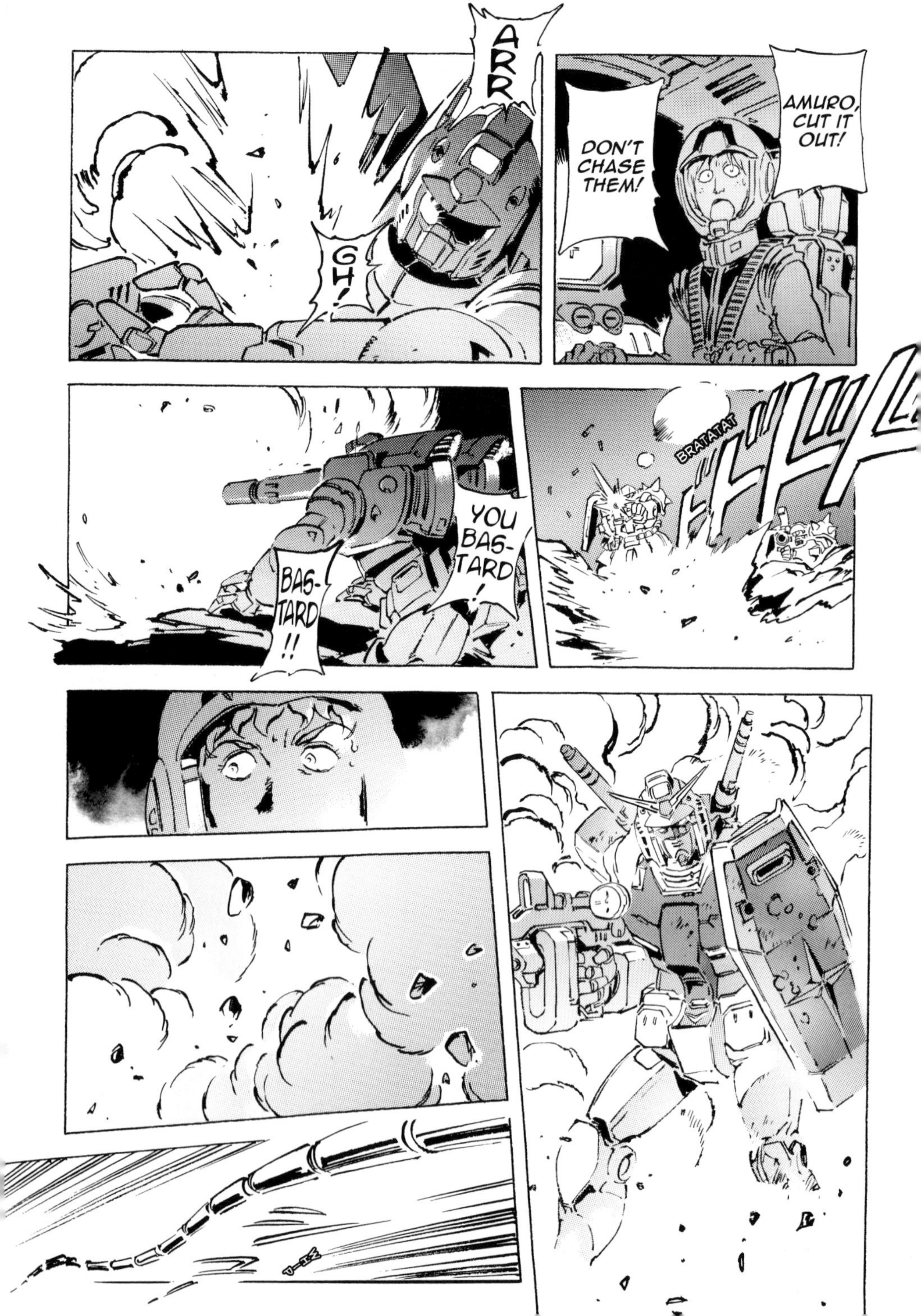
AMURO, CUT IT OUT!
DON'T CHASE THEM!
ARR
GH!
BRATATAT
YOU BASTARD!
BASTARD!!

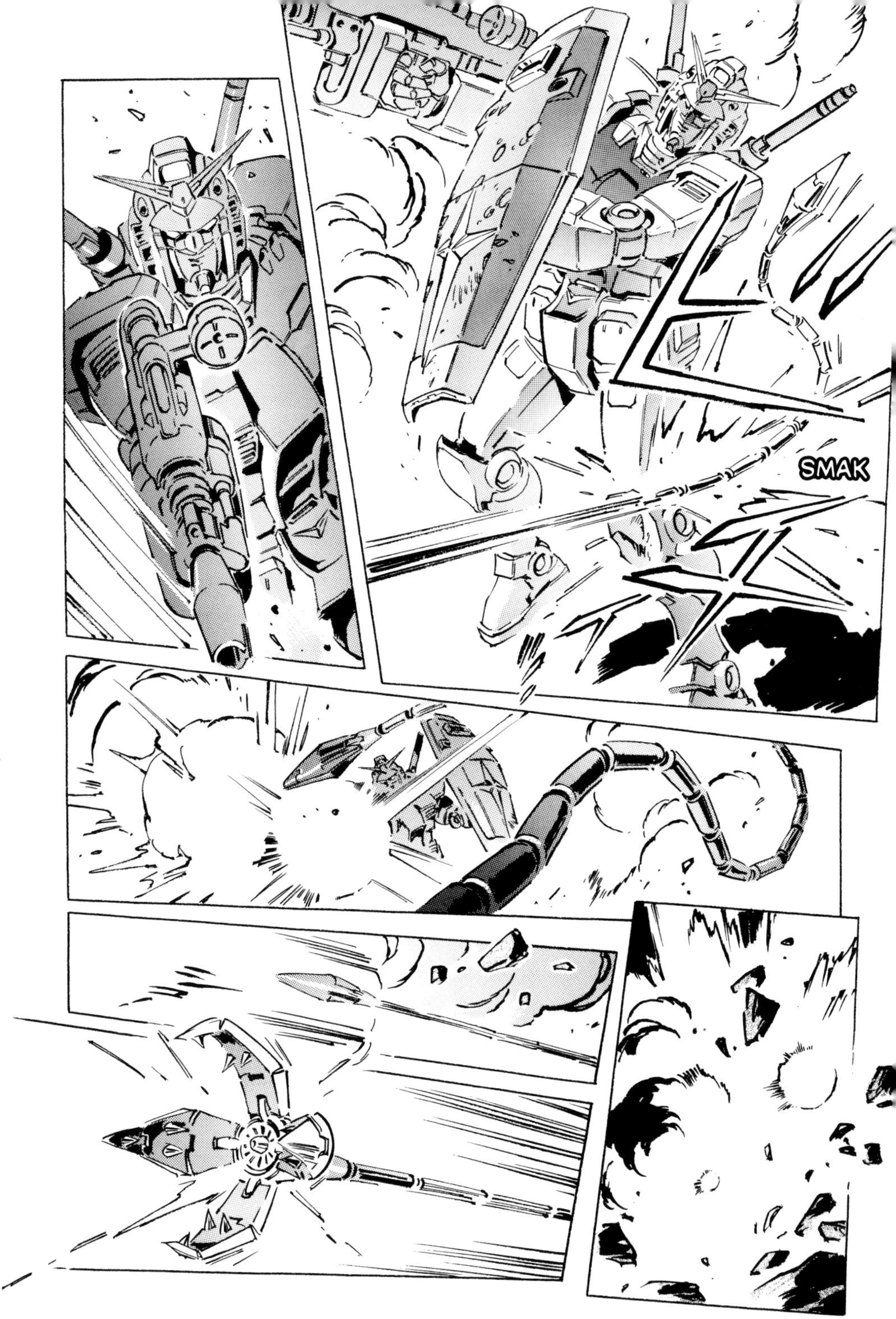
SMAK

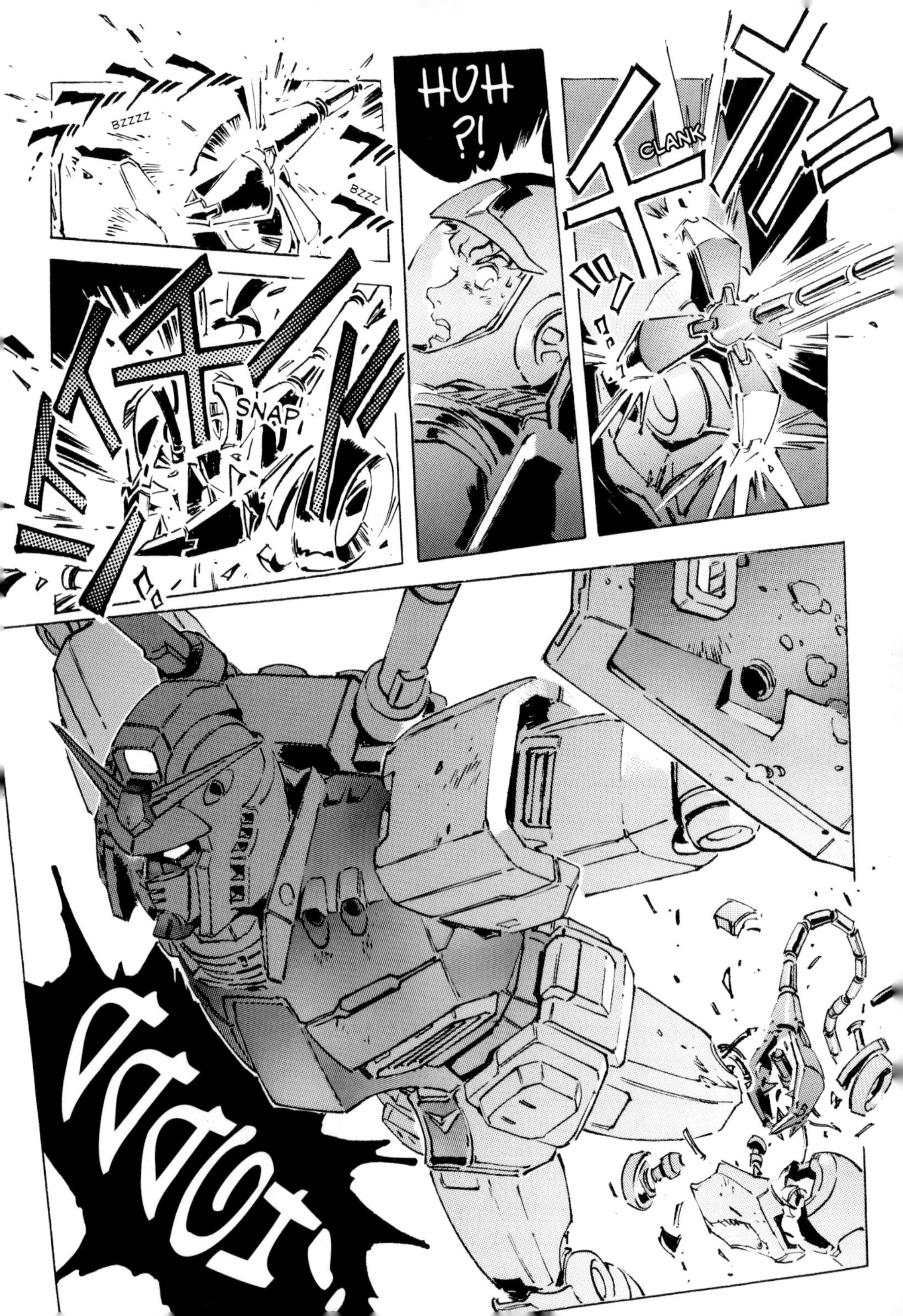
CLANK
HUH ?!
BZZZZ
BZZZ
SNAP

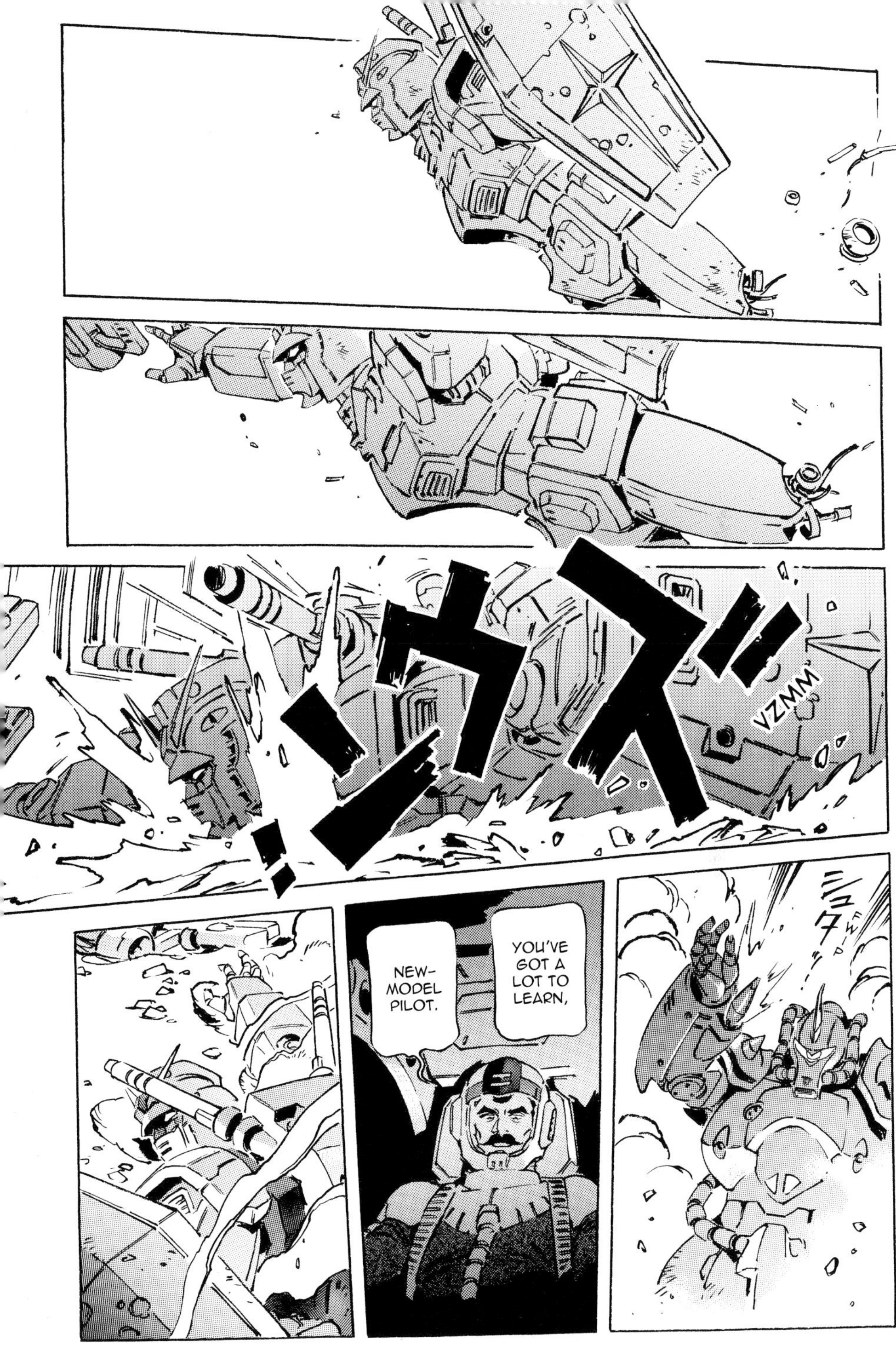
VZMM
FWIP
YOU'VE GOT A LOT TO LEARN,
NEW-MODEL PILOT.

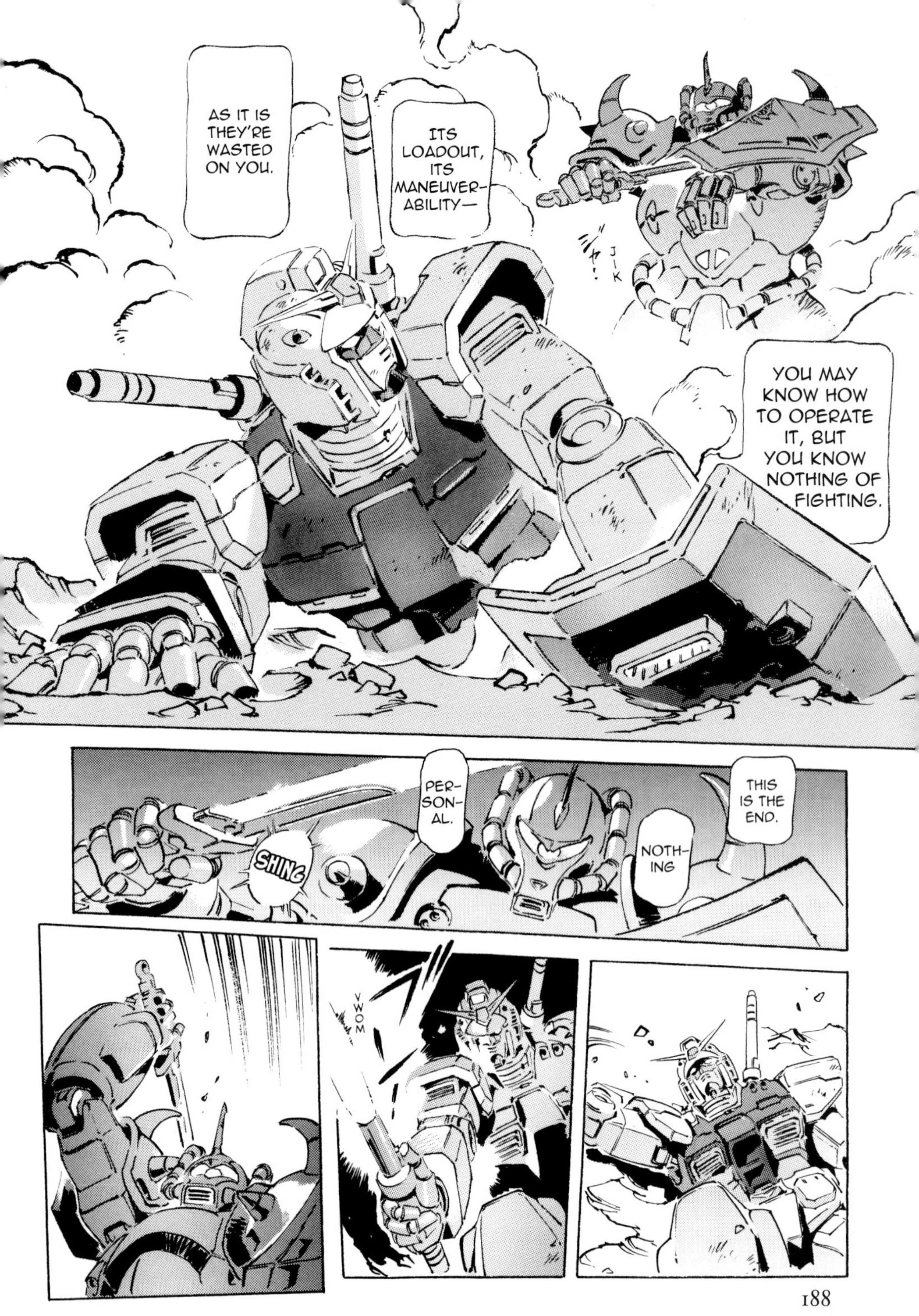
ITS LOADOUT, ITS MANEUVER-ABILITY—
AS IT IS THEY'RE WASTED ON YOU.
JIK
YOU MAY KNOW HOW TO OPERATE IT, BUT YOU KNOW NOTHING OF FIGHTING.
THIS IS THE END.
NOTH-ING
PER-SON-AL.
SHING
VWOM

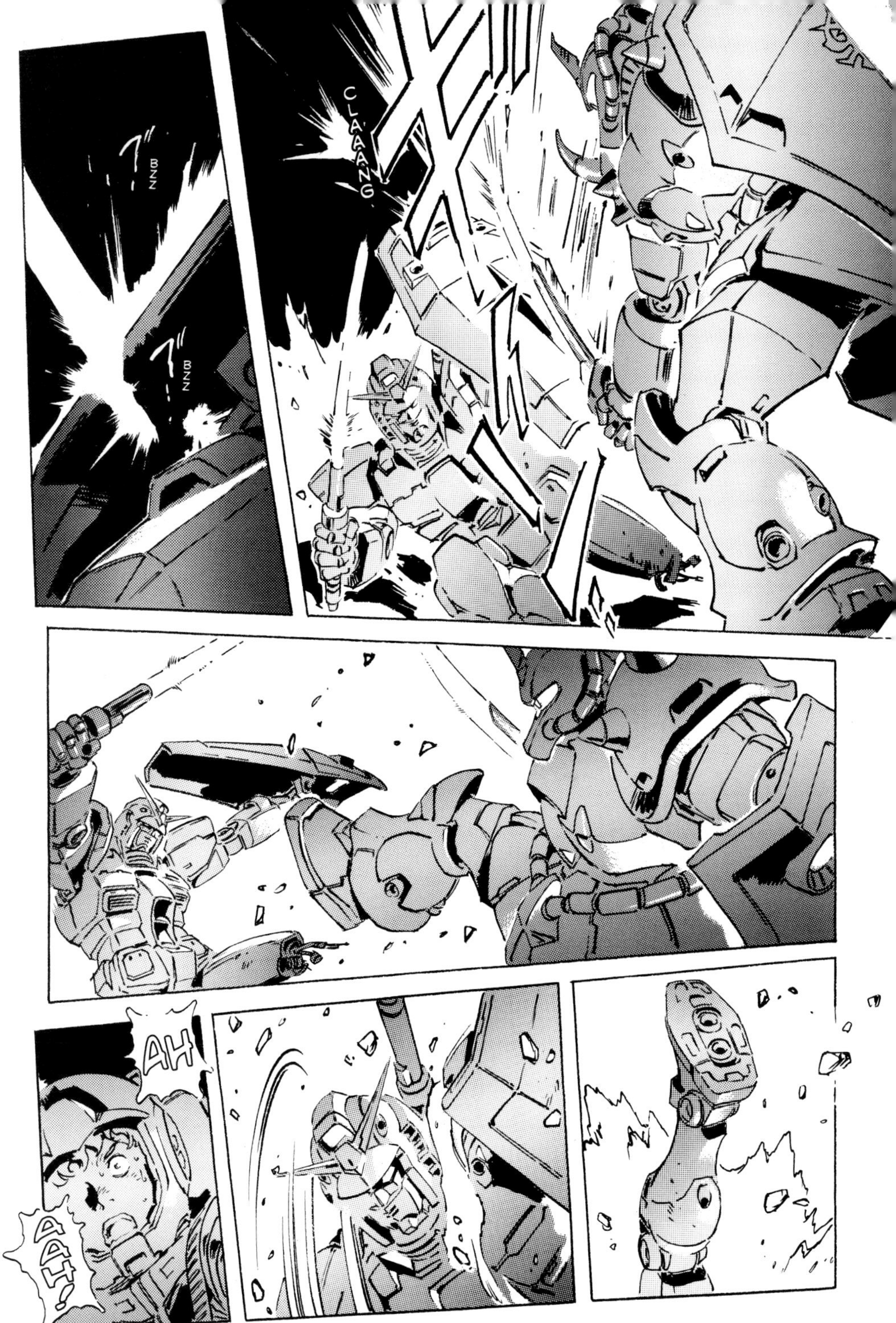
CLAAANG
BZZ
BZZ
AH
AAH!

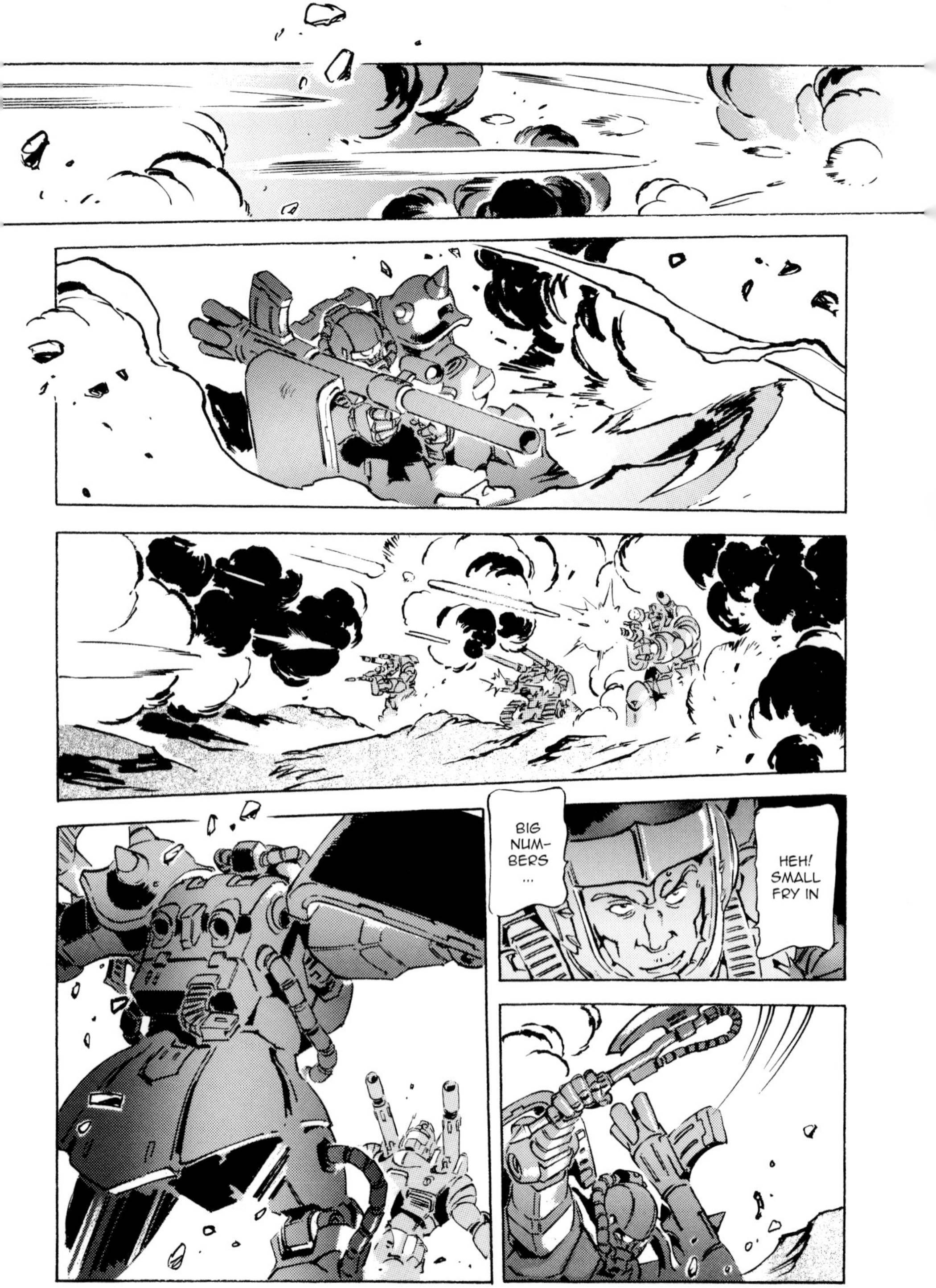
HEH! SMALL FRY IN
BIG NUM-BERS ...

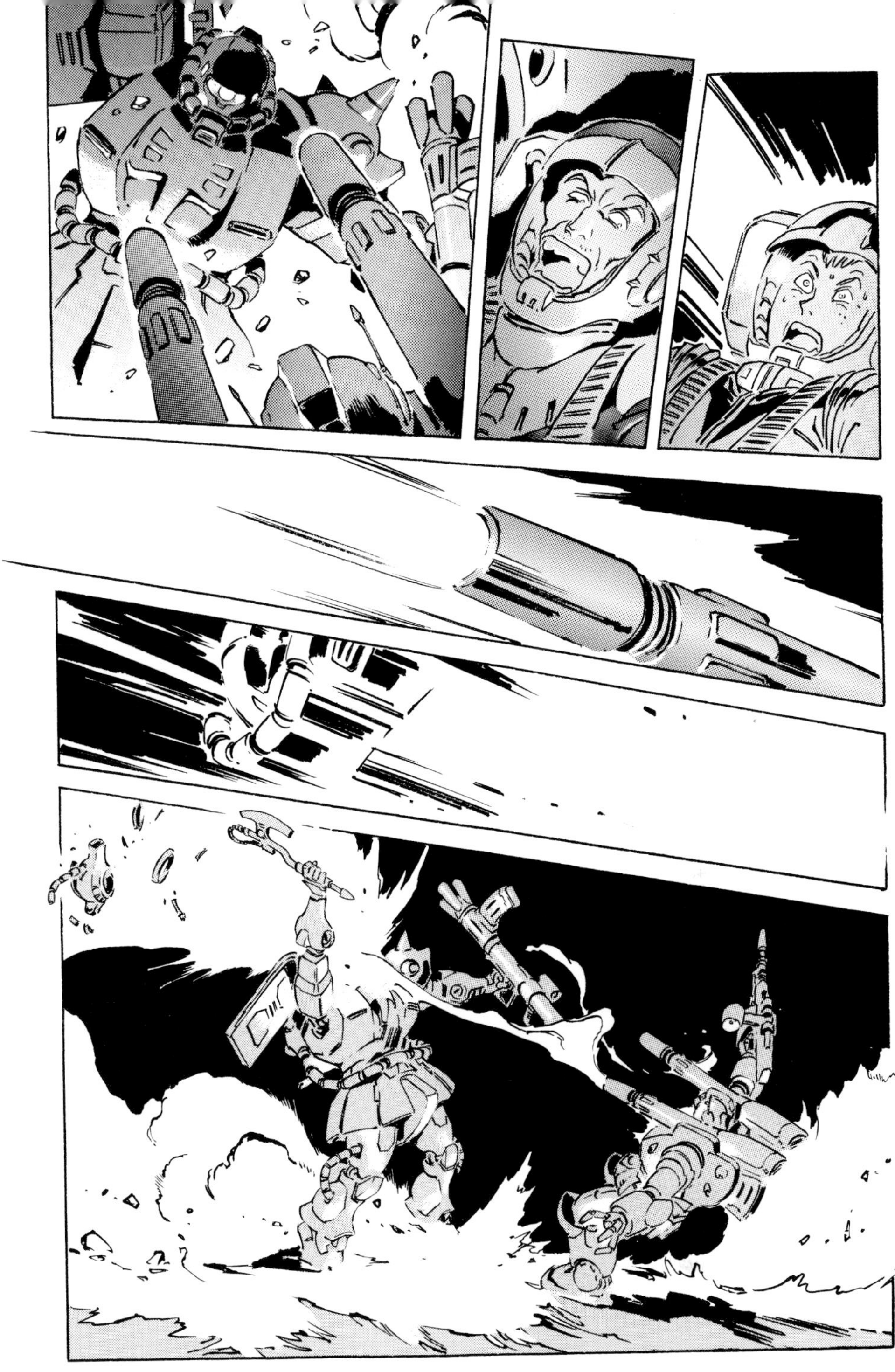

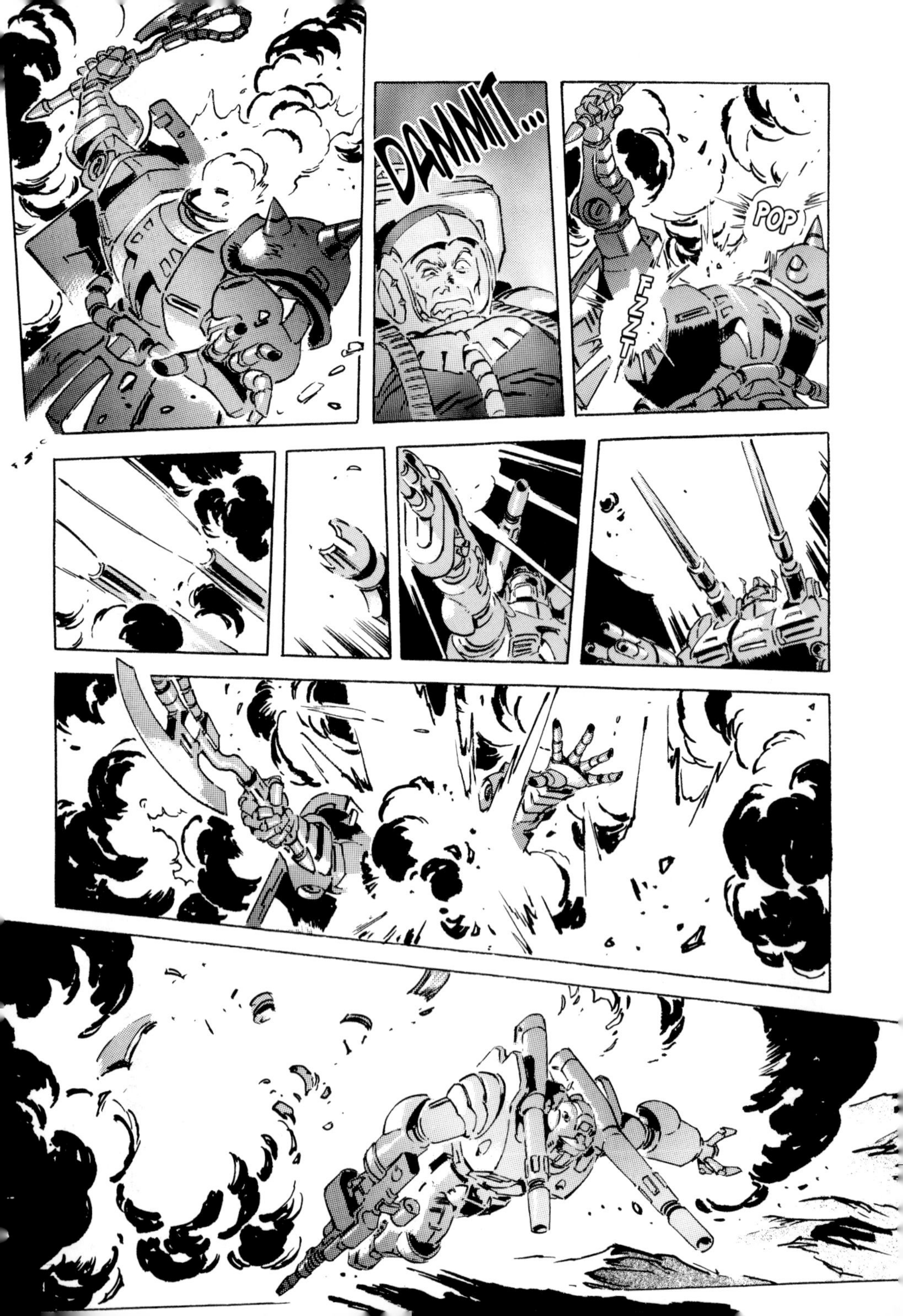
POP
FZZNT
DAMMIT...

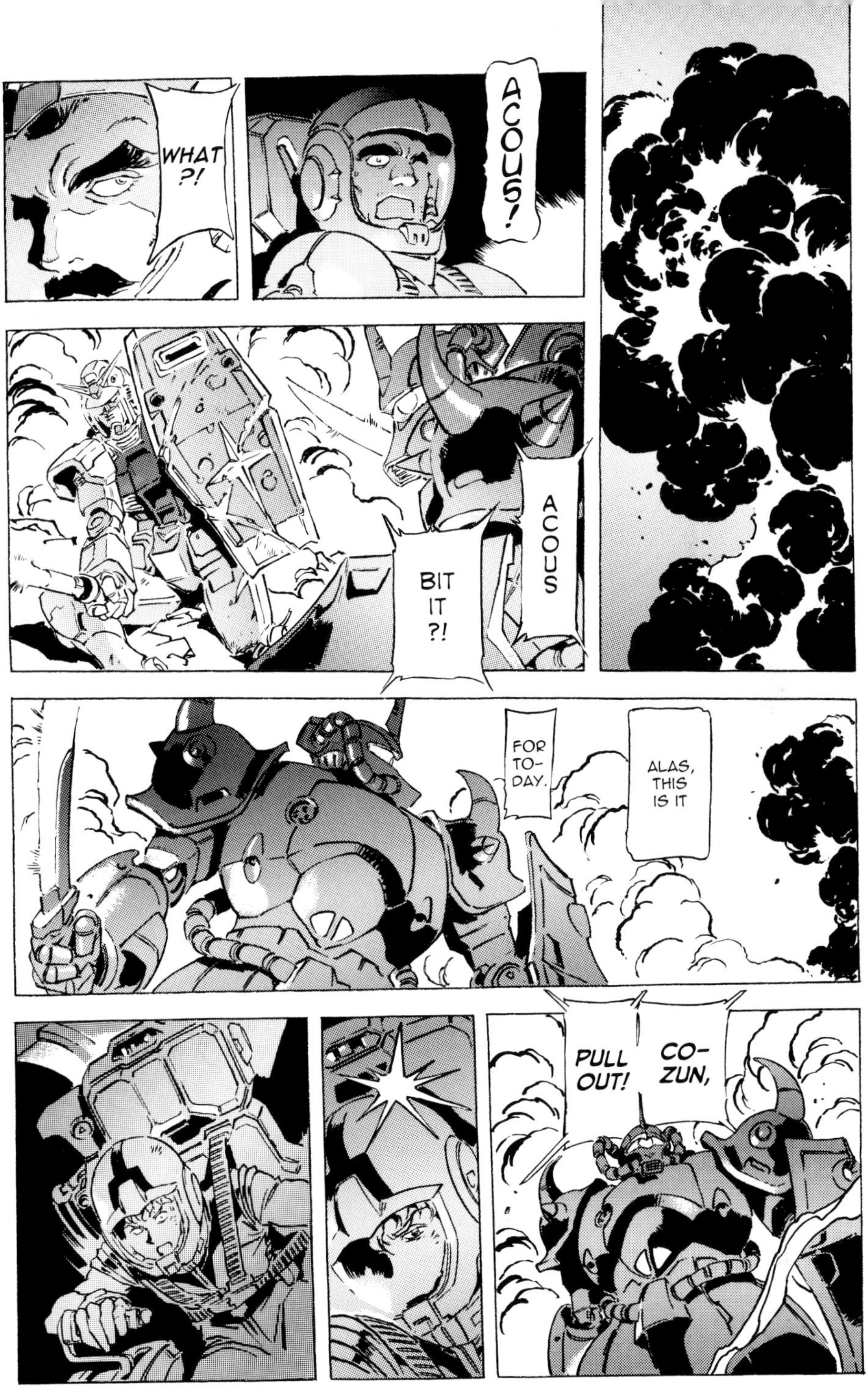
ACOUS!
WHAT?!
ACOUS
BIT IT?!
ALAS, THIS IS IT
FOR TODAY.
CO-ZUN,
PULL OUT!

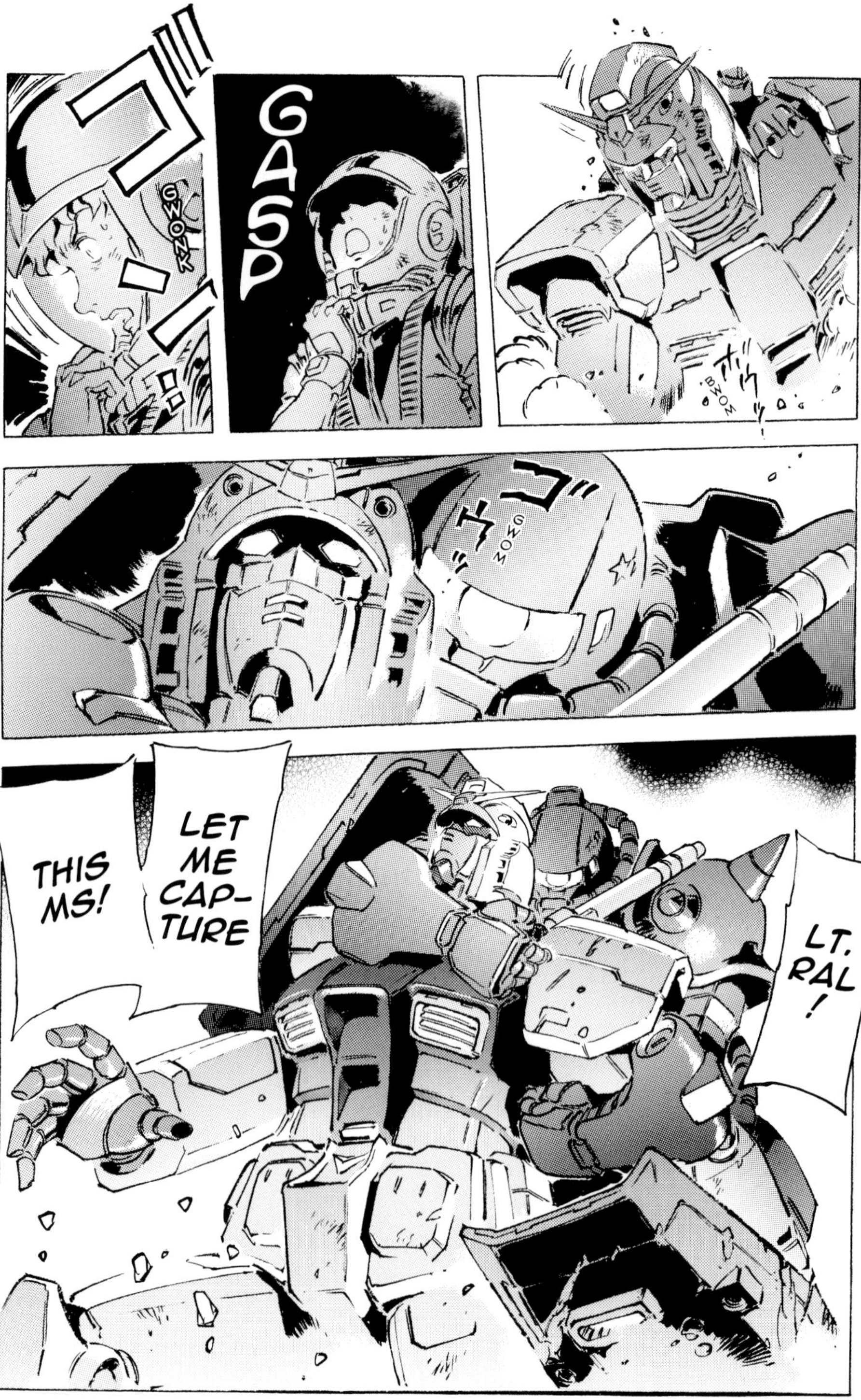
BWOM
GASP
GWONK
GWOM
LT. RAL!
LET ME CAPTURE
THIS MS!

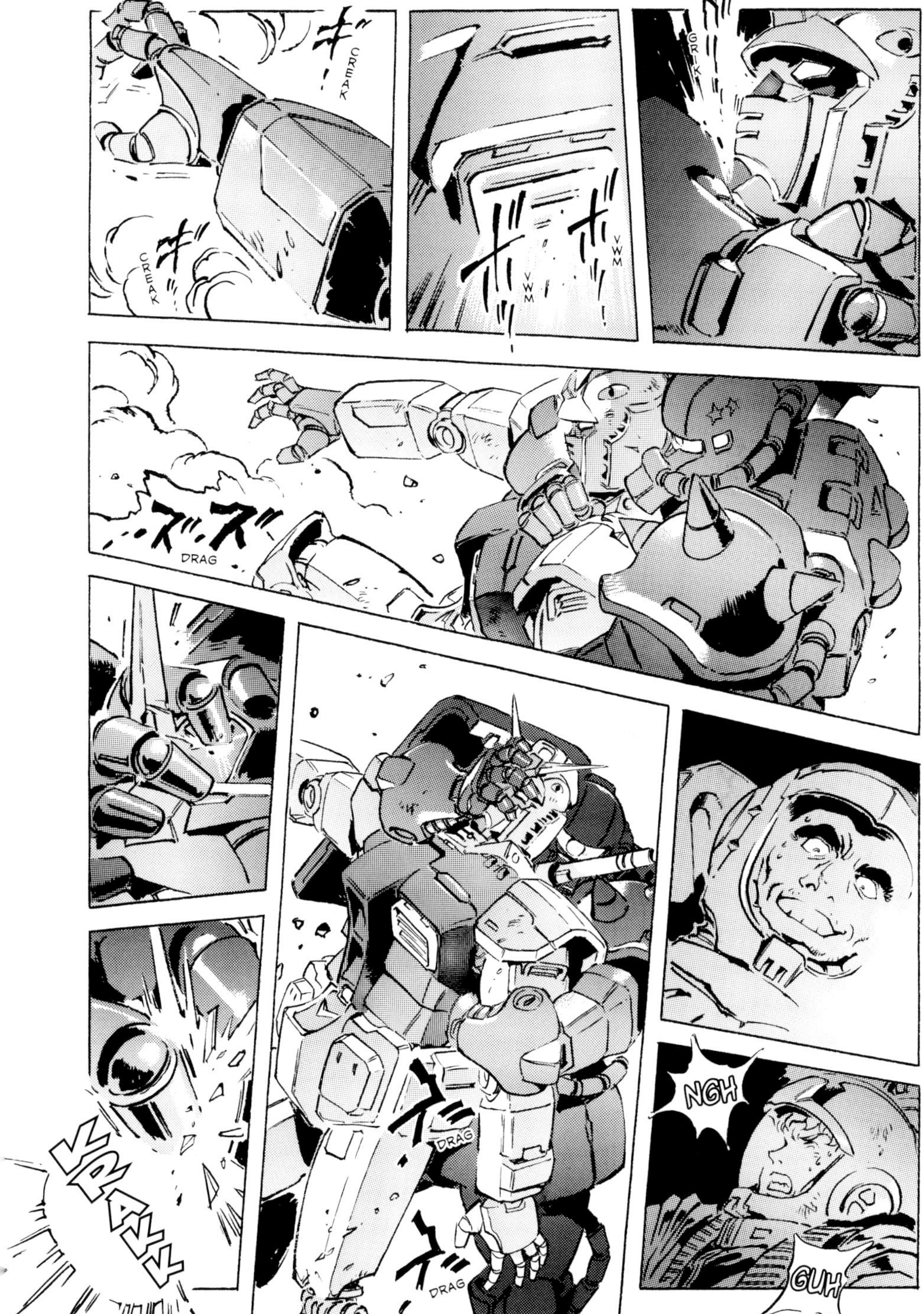
GRIK
VWM
VWM
CREAK
CREAK
DRAG
NGH
GUH
DRAG
DRAG
KRAKK

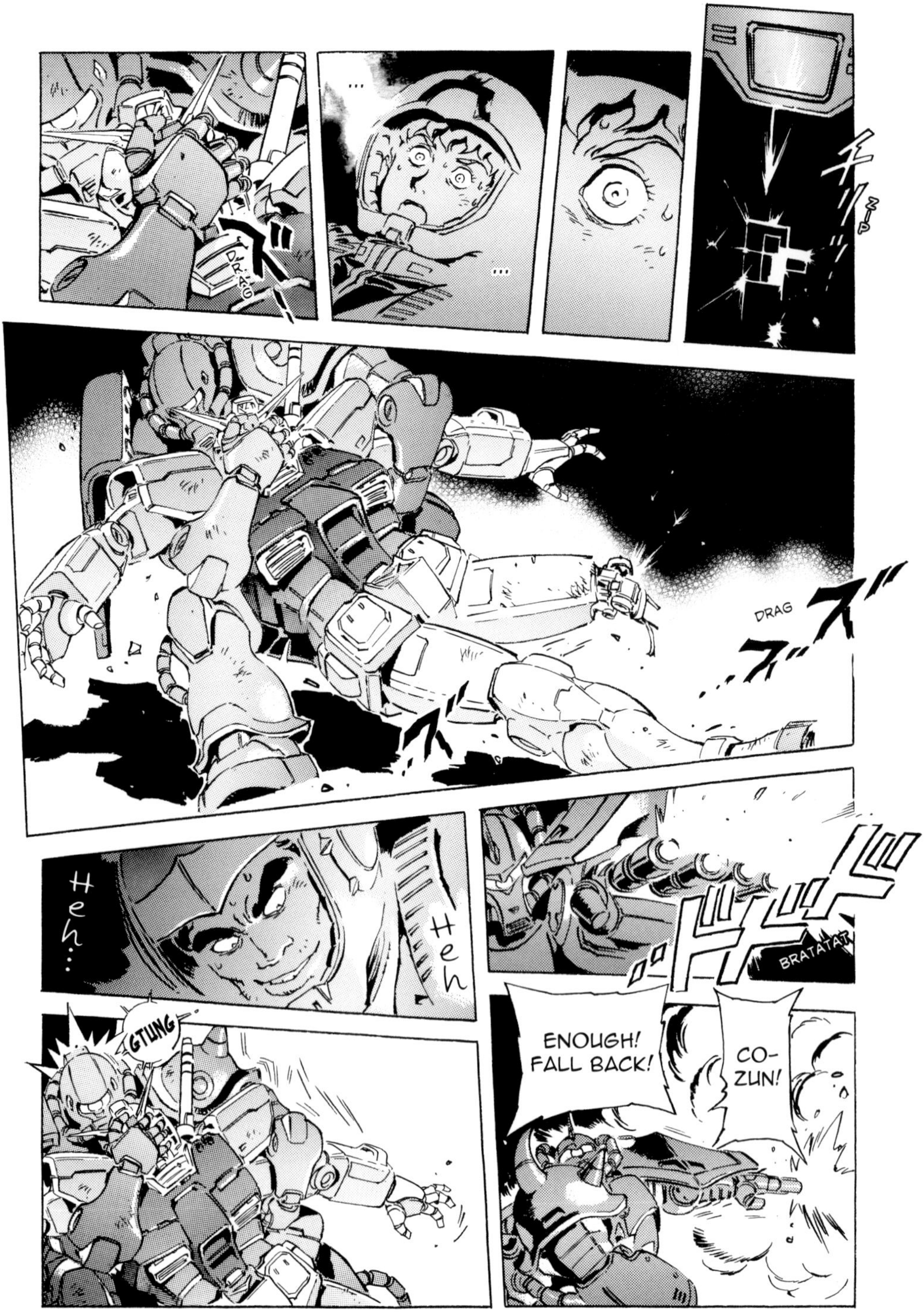

ZIP
...
...
DRAG
DRAG
BRATATAT
Heh...
Heh
ENOUGH! FALL BACK!
CO-ZUN!
GTUNG

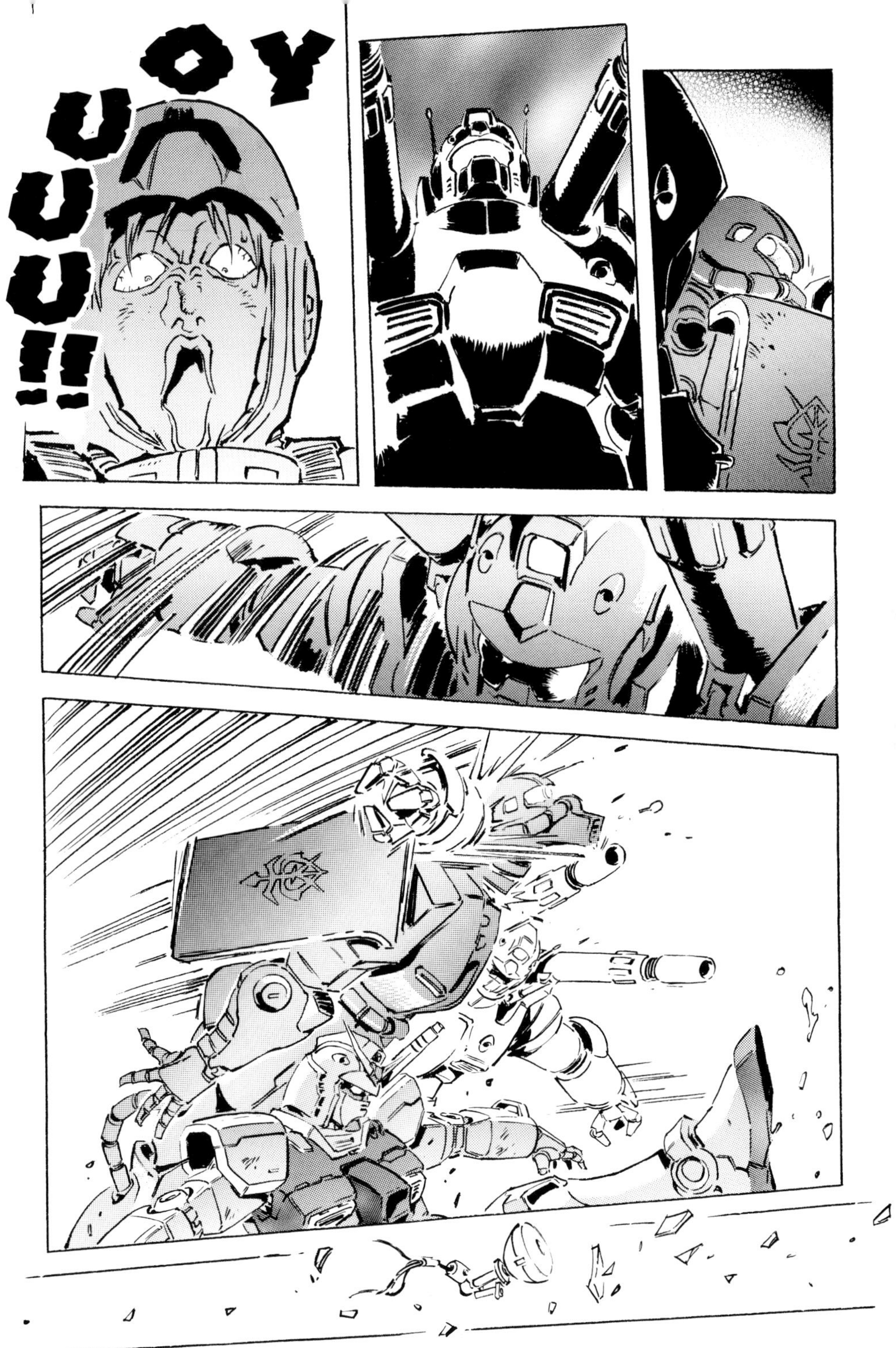
YOUUU!!

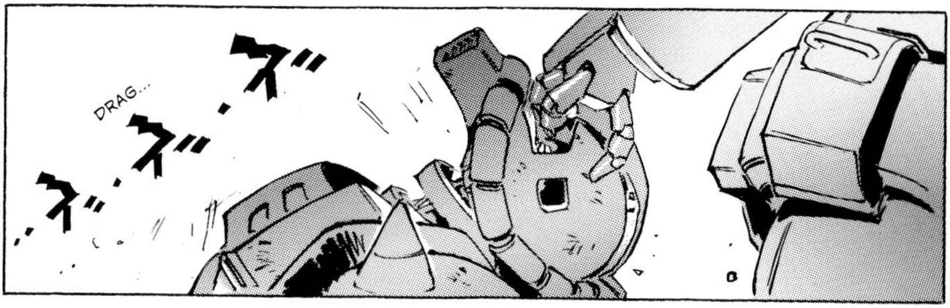
DRAG...
ズ・ズ・ズ

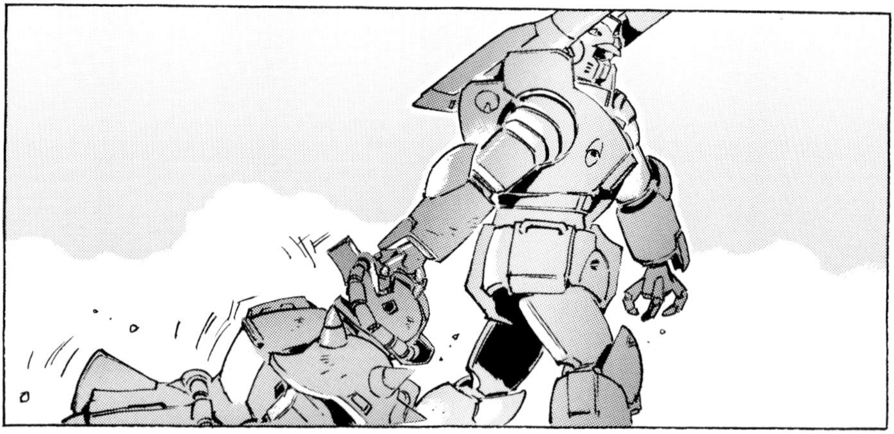

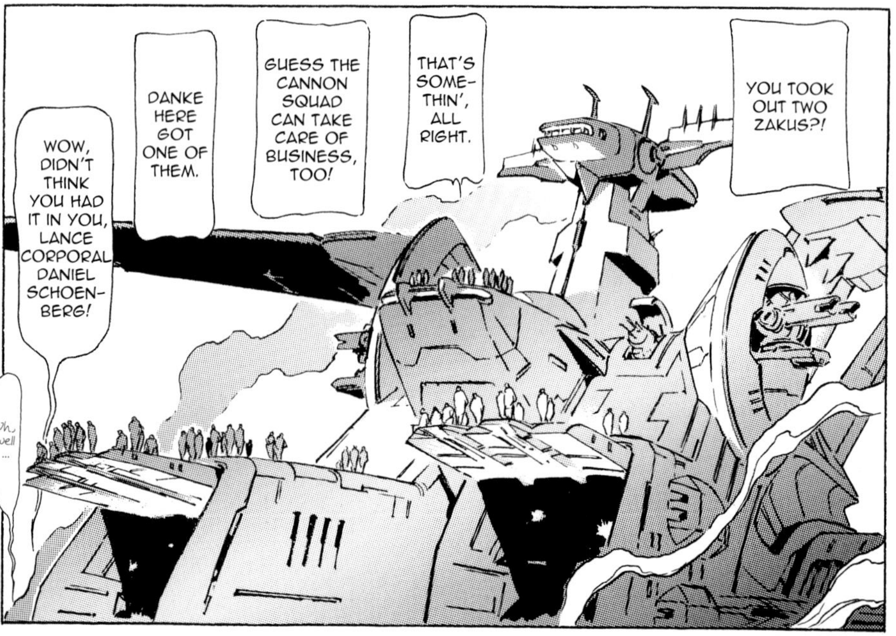
YOU TOOK OUT TWO ZAKUS?!
THAT'S SOME-THIN', ALL RIGHT.
GUESS THE CANNON SQUAD CAN TAKE CARE OF BUSINESS, TOO!
DANKE HERE GOT ONE OF THEM.
WOW, DIDN'T THINK YOU HAD IT IN YOU, LANCE CORPORAL DANIEL SCHOENBERG!
Uh, well...

HANDLE YOUR CAPTIVES IN LINE WITH THE ANTARCTIC TREATY, Y'HEAR ME?

I'M AN OFFICER. SHOW SOME RESPECT.

AND DON'T TRY ANYTHING!!

COME OUT WITH YOUR HANDS UP!

RRRM

...

...

OUR GUNDAM WARRIOR GALLANTLY RETURNS!

AH

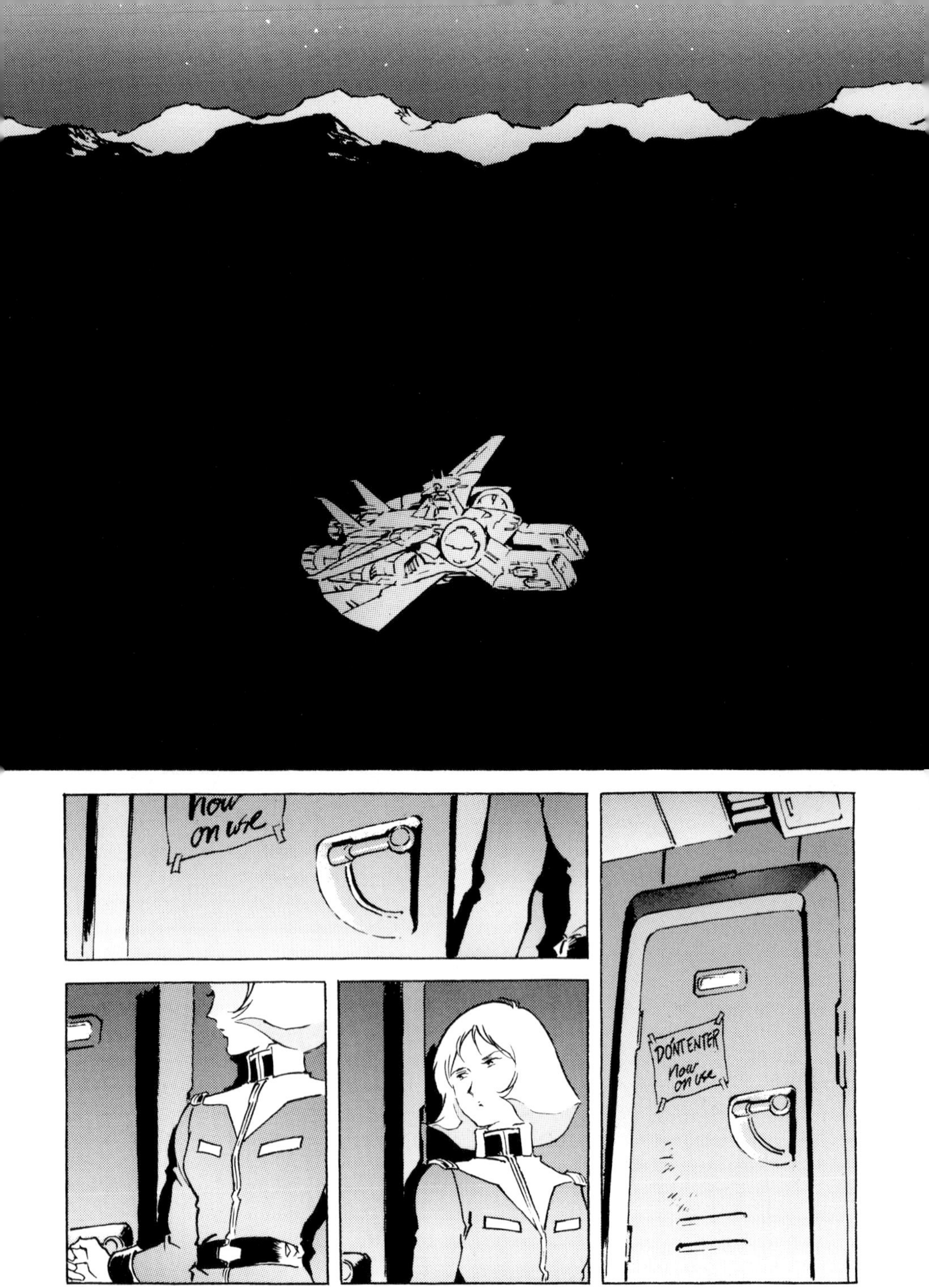
DON'T ENTER
now on use
now on use

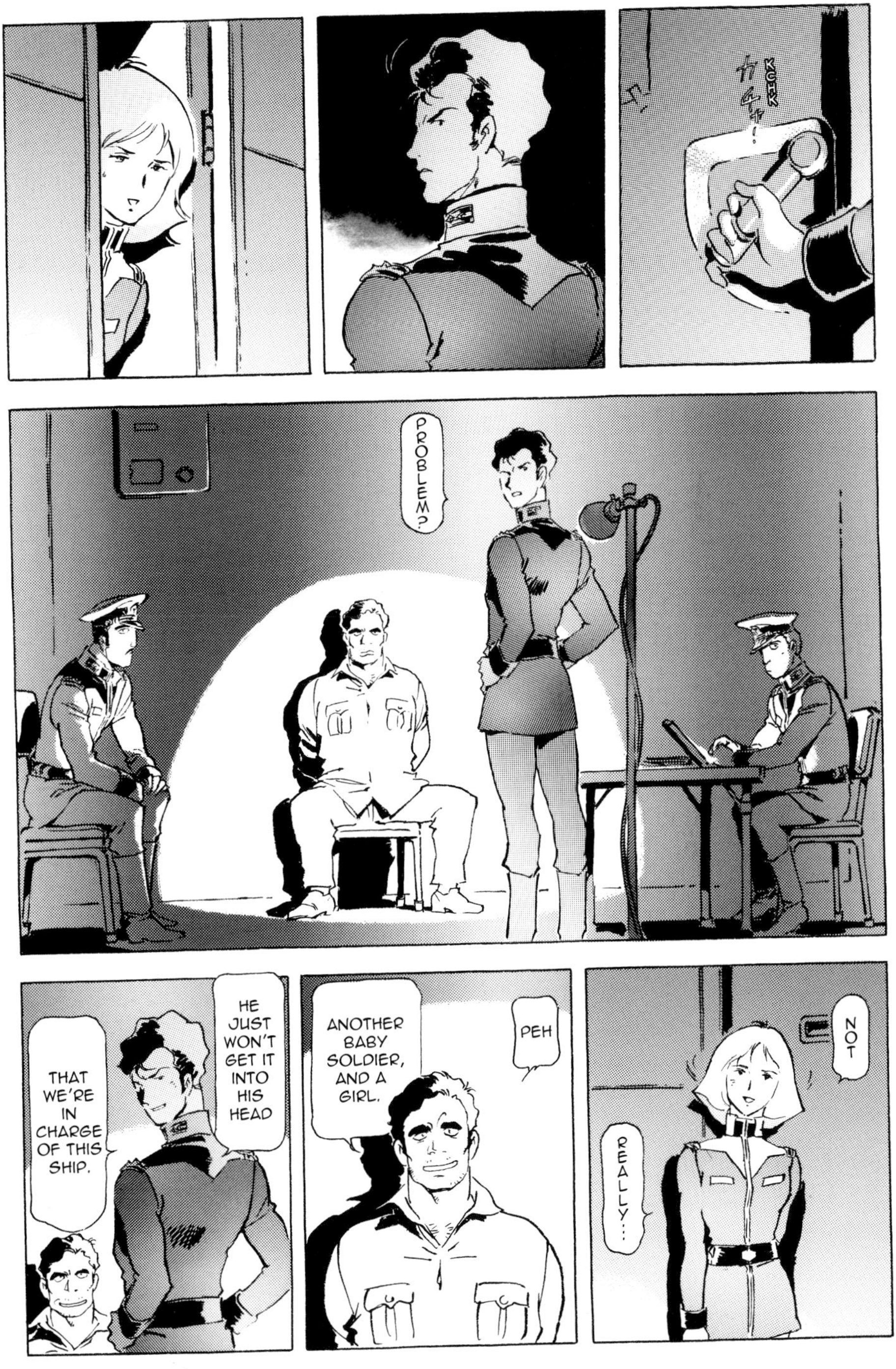
KCHK
PROBLEM?
NOT REALLY...
PEH
ANOTHER BABY SOLDIER, AND A GIRL.
HE JUST WON'T GET IT INTO HIS HEAD
THAT WE'RE IN CHARGE OF THIS SHIP.

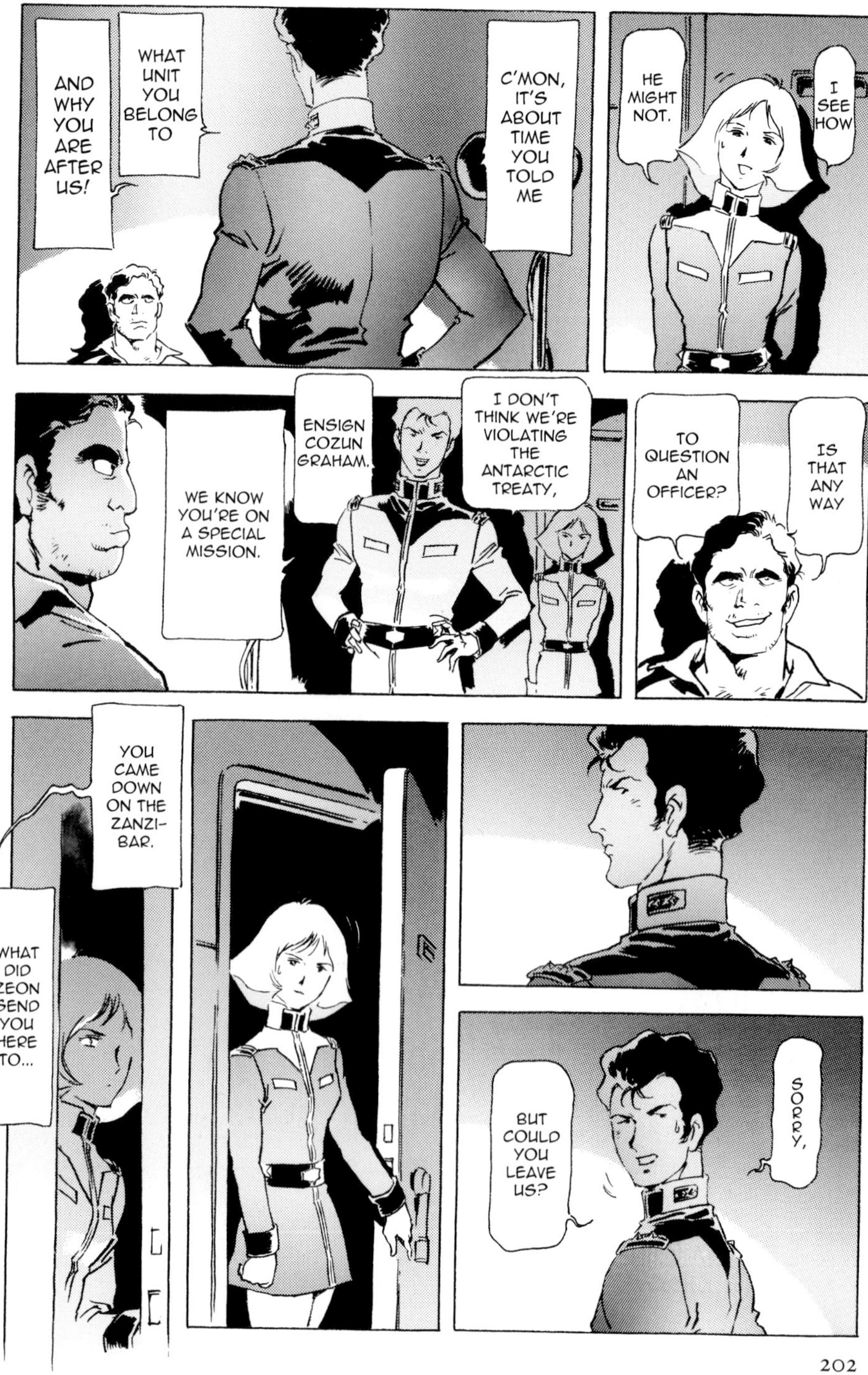
I SEE HOW
HE MIGHT NOT.
C'MON, IT'S ABOUT TIME YOU TOLD ME
WHAT UNIT YOU BELONG TO
AND WHY YOU ARE AFTER US!
IS THAT ANY WAY
TO QUESTION AN OFFICER?
I DON'T THINK WE'RE VIOLATING THE ANTARCTIC TREATY,
ENSIGN COZUN GRAHAM.
WE KNOW YOU'RE ON A SPECIAL MISSION.
SORRY,
BUT COULD YOU LEAVE US?
YOU CAME DOWN ON THE ZANZI-BAR.
WHAT DID ZEON SEND YOU HERE TO...

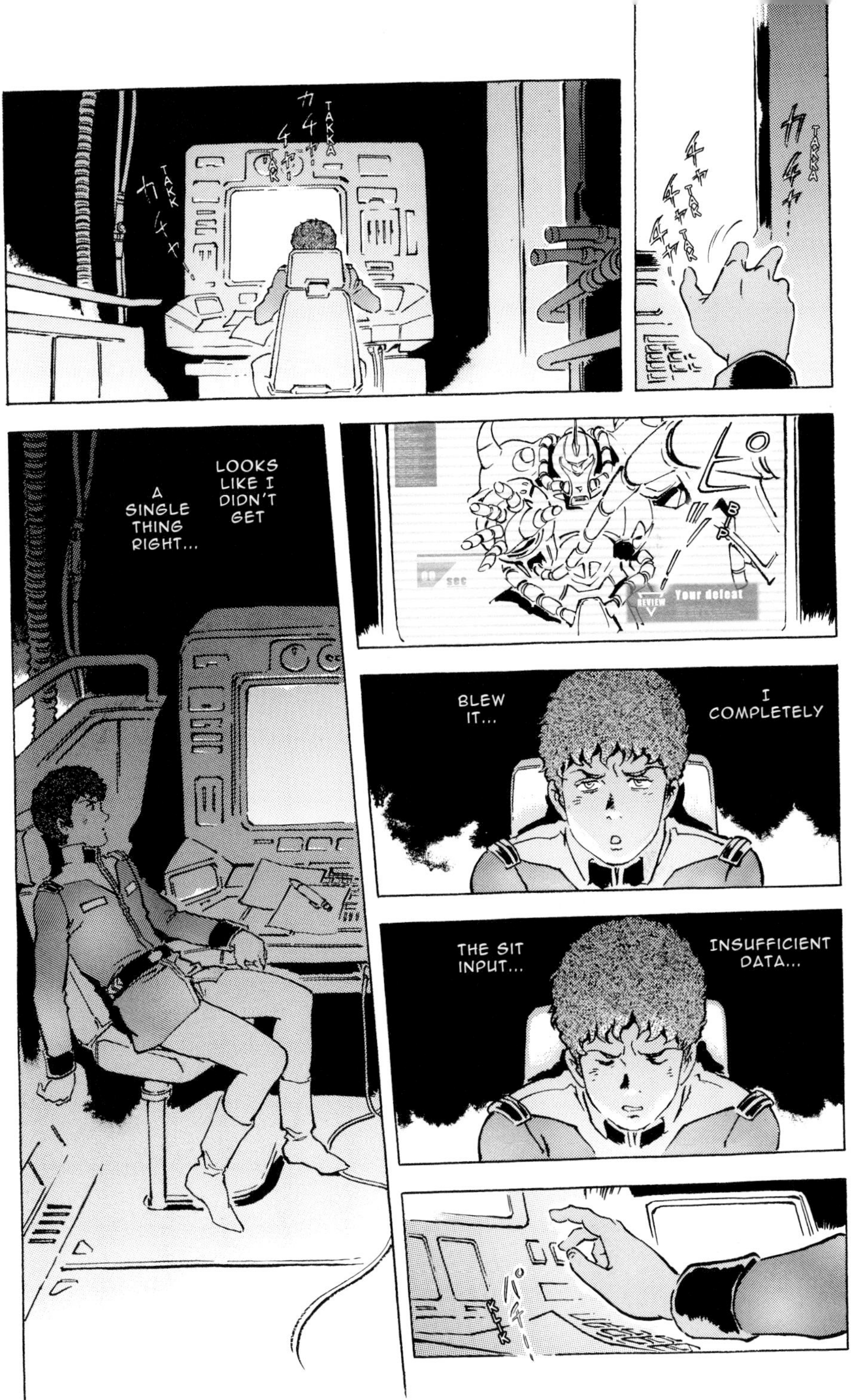
TAKKA
TAR
TAR
TAR
TAKKA
TAR
TAKK
BIP
sec
REVIEW
Your defeat
I COMPLETELY BLEW IT...
INSUFFICIENT DATA...
THE SIT INPUT...
KLIK
LOOKS LIKE I DIDN'T GET
A SINGLE THING RIGHT...

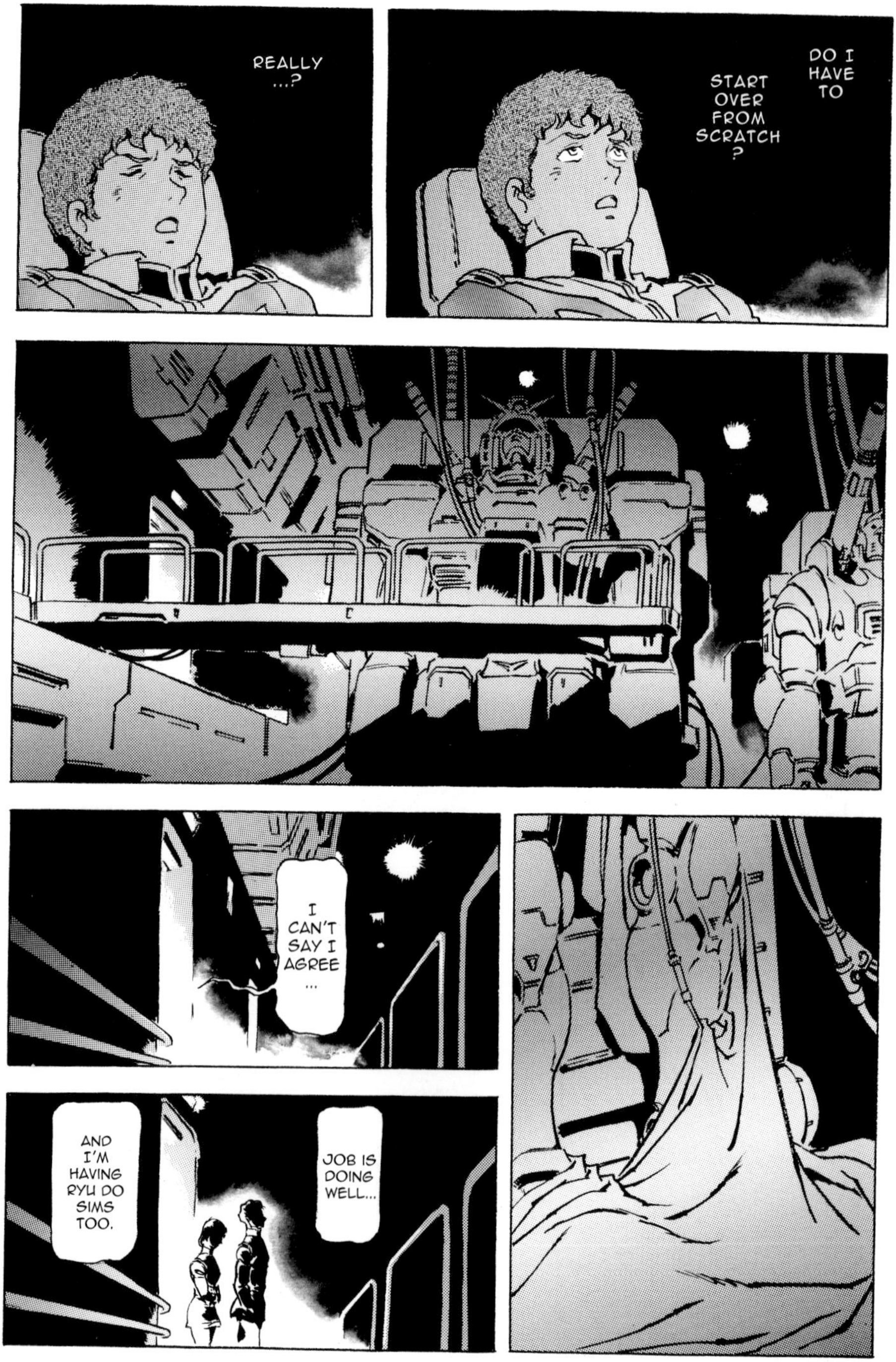
DO I HAVE TO
START OVER FROM SCRATCH ?
REALLY ...?
I CAN'T SAY I AGREE ...
JOB IS DOING WELL...
AND I'M HAVING RYU DO SIMS TOO.

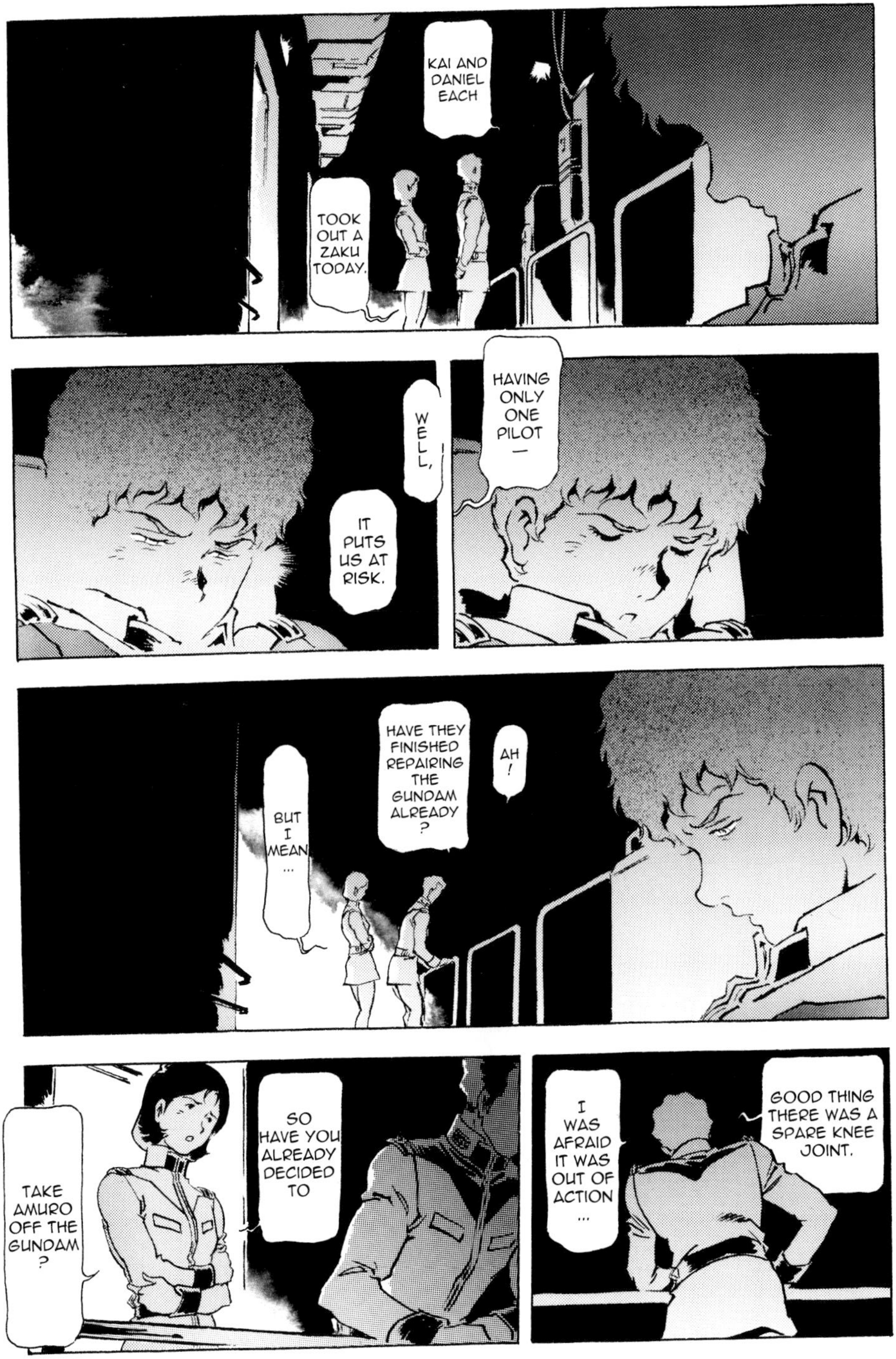
KAI AND DANIEL EACH
TOOK OUT A ZAKU TODAY.
HAVING ONLY ONE PILOT —
WELL,
IT PUTS US AT RISK.
AH!
HAVE THEY FINISHED REPAIRING THE GUNDAM ALREADY?
BUT I MEAN ...
GOOD THING THERE WAS A SPARE KNEE JOINT.
I WAS AFRAID IT WAS OUT OF ACTION ...
SO HAVE YOU ALREADY DECIDED TO
TAKE AMURO OFF THE GUNDAM?

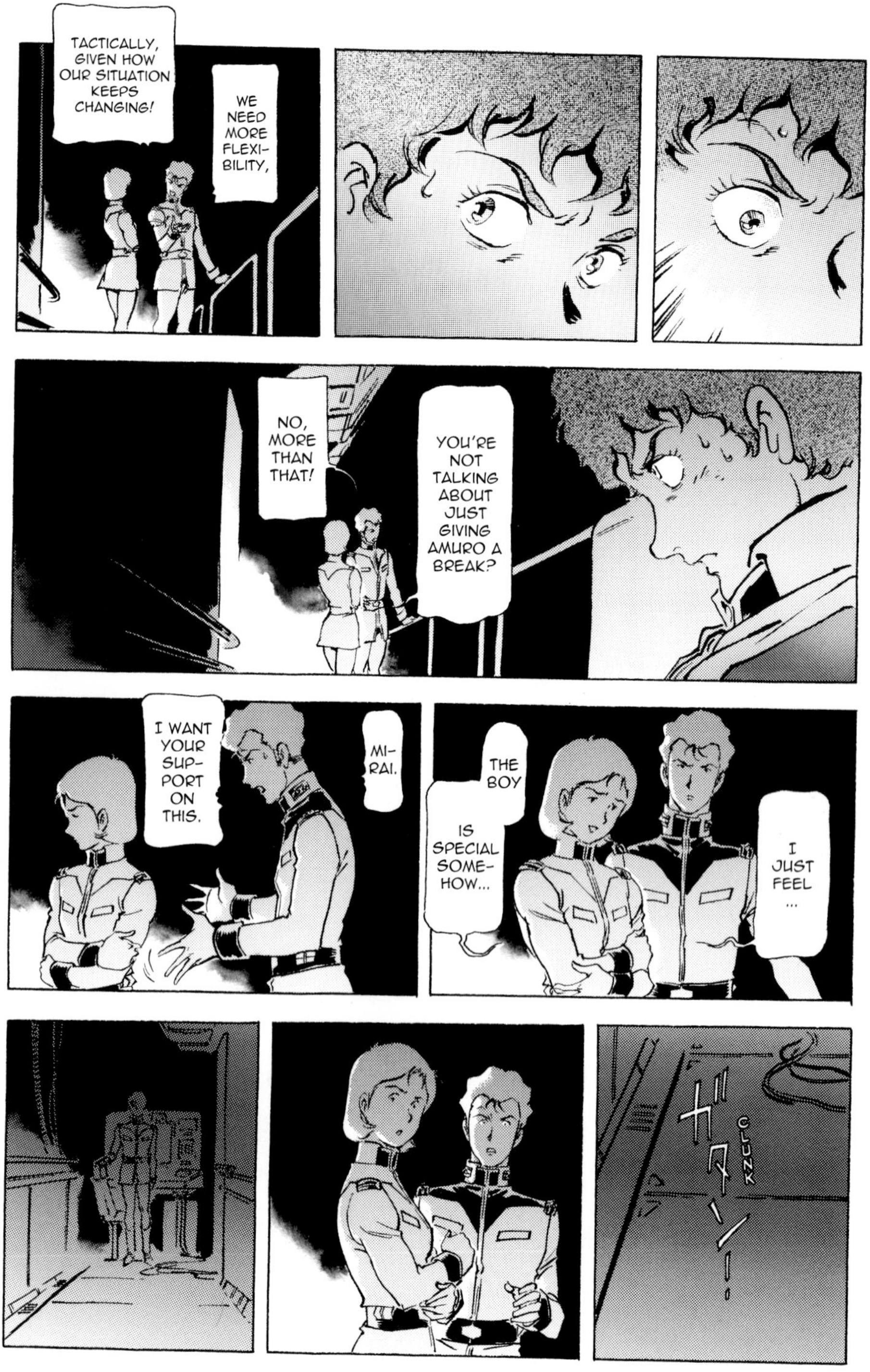
WE NEED MORE FLEXIBILITY,
TACTICALLY, GIVEN HOW OUR SITUATION KEEPS CHANGING!
YOU'RE NOT TALKING ABOUT JUST GIVING AMURO A BREAK?
NO, MORE THAN THAT!
I JUST FEEL ...
THE BOY
IS SPECIAL SOMEHOW...
MI-RAI.
I WANT YOUR SUPPORT ON THIS.
ガタン
CLUNK

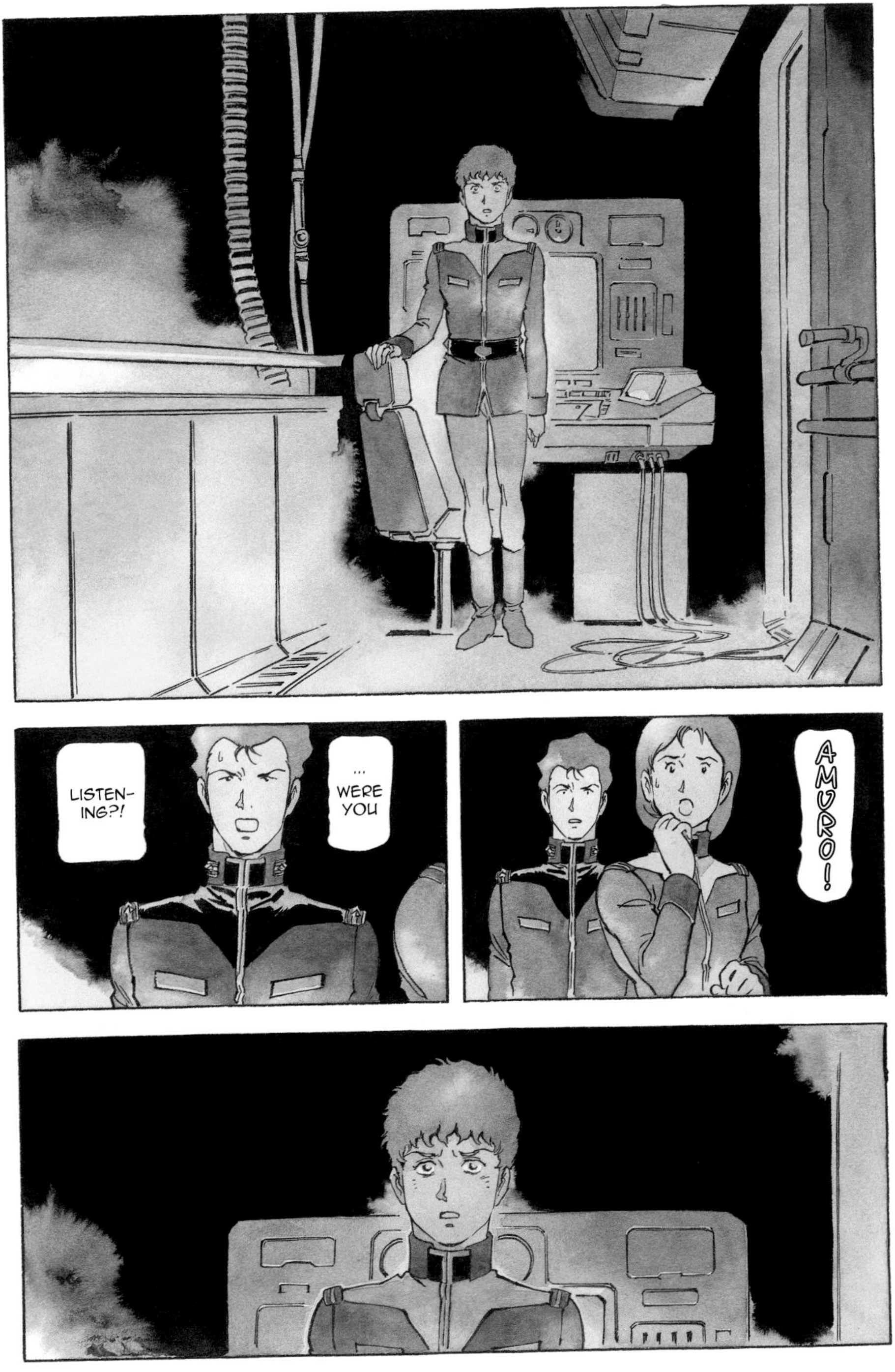
AMURO!
... WERE YOU
LISTEN-ING?!

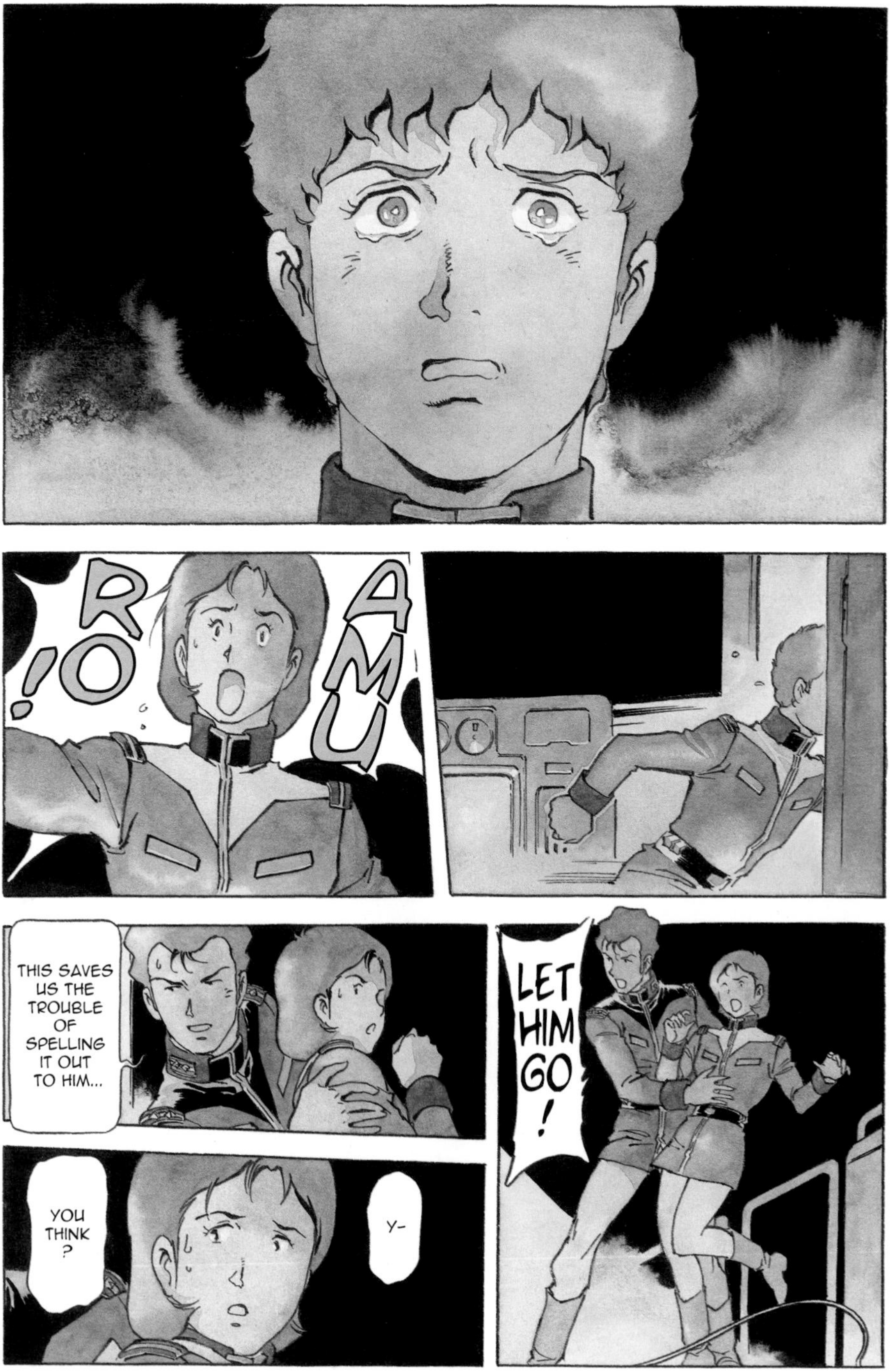
AMURO!
LET HIM GO!
THIS SAVES US THE TROUBLE OF SPELLING IT OUT TO HIM...
Y-
YOU THINK?

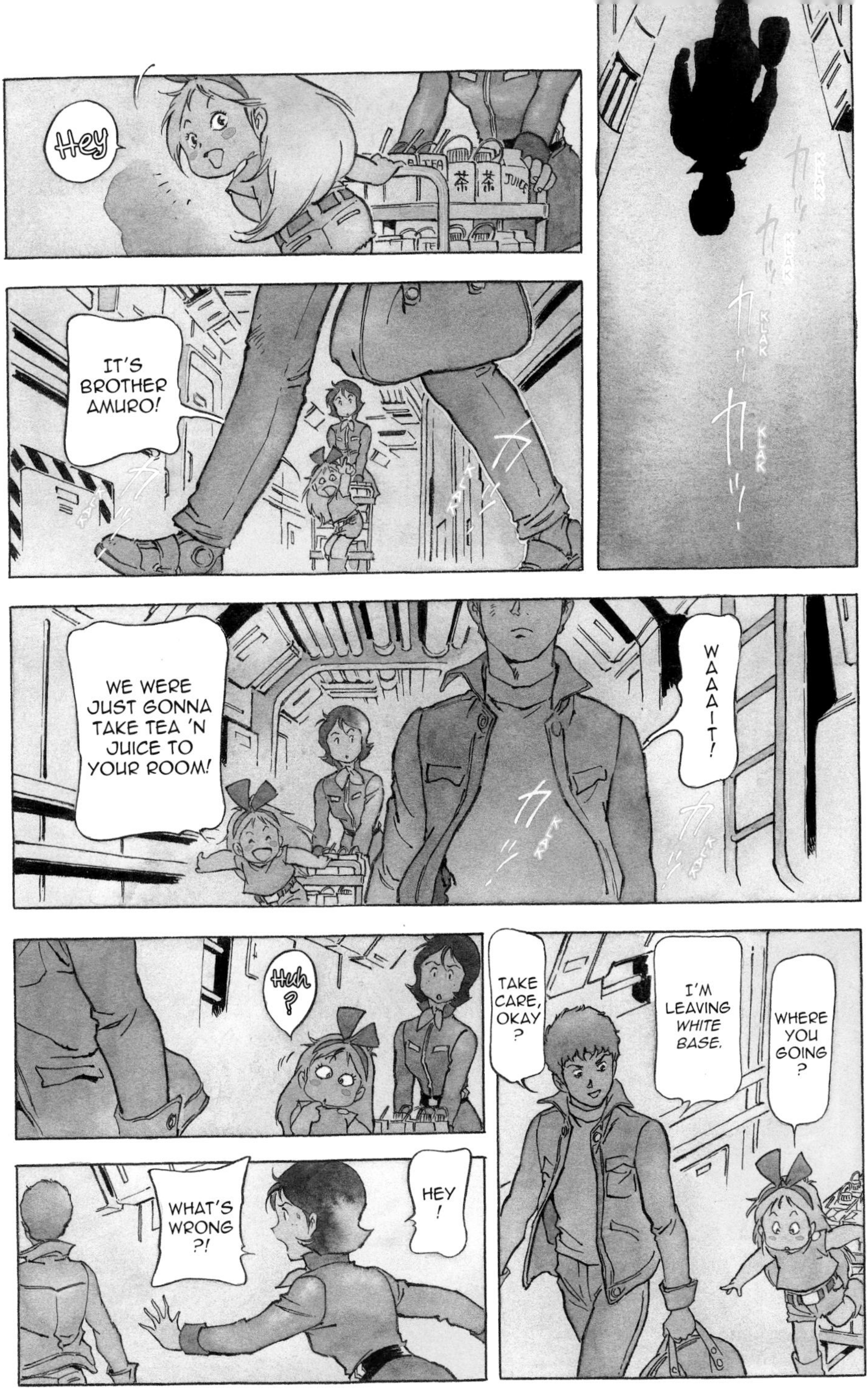
KLAK
KLAK
KLAK
KLAK
Hey
IT'S BROTHER AMURO!
KLAK
KLAK
WAAAAIT!
WE WERE JUST GONNA TAKE TEA 'N JUICE TO YOUR ROOM!
KLAK
KLAK
WHERE YOU GOING ?
I'M LEAVING WHITE BASE.
TAKE CARE, OKAY ?
Huh ?
HEY !
WHAT'S WRONG ?!

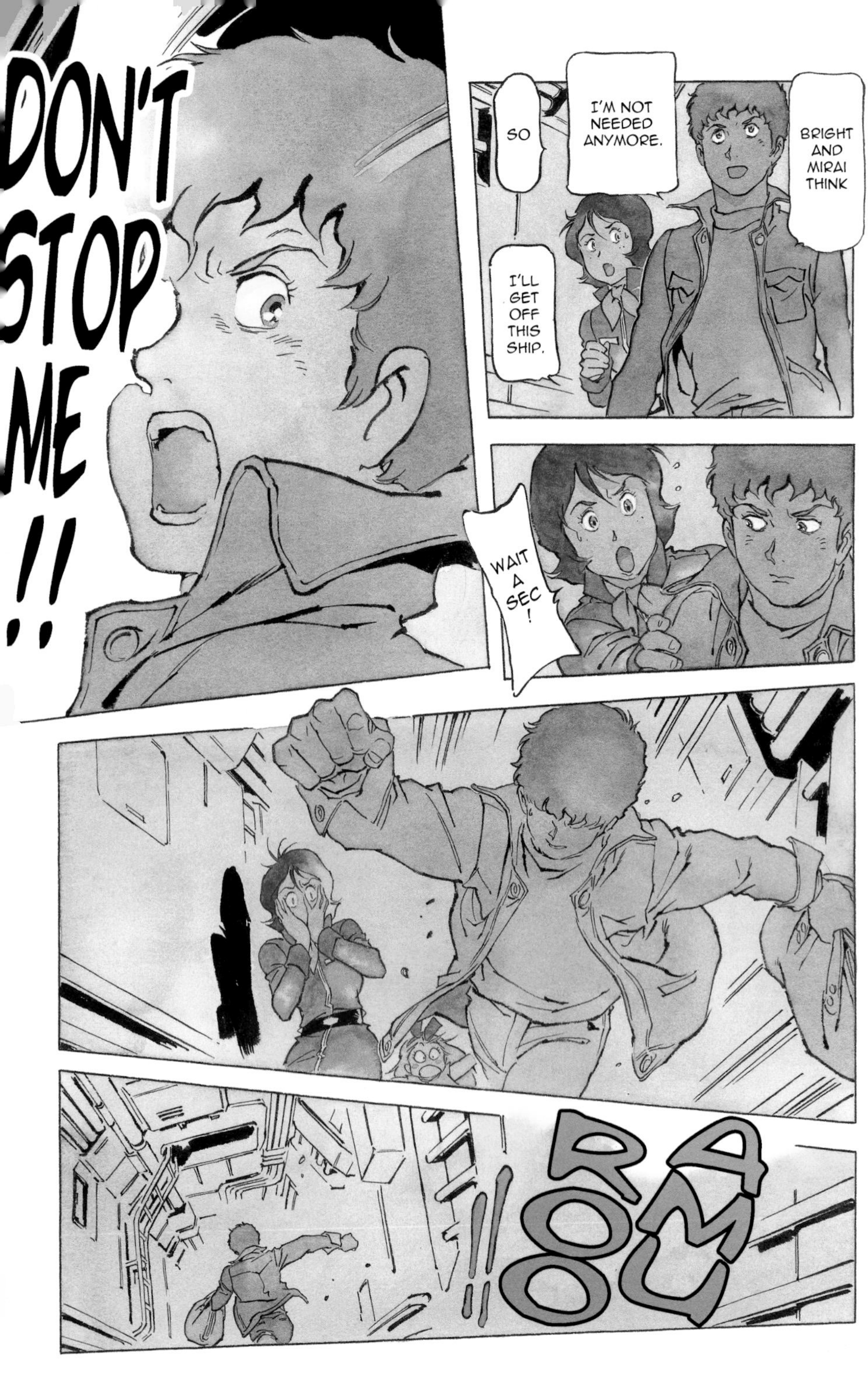
BRIGHT AND MIRAI THINK
I'M NOT NEEDED ANYMORE.
SO
I'LL GET OFF THIS SHIP.
WAIT A SEC!
DON'T STOP ME!!

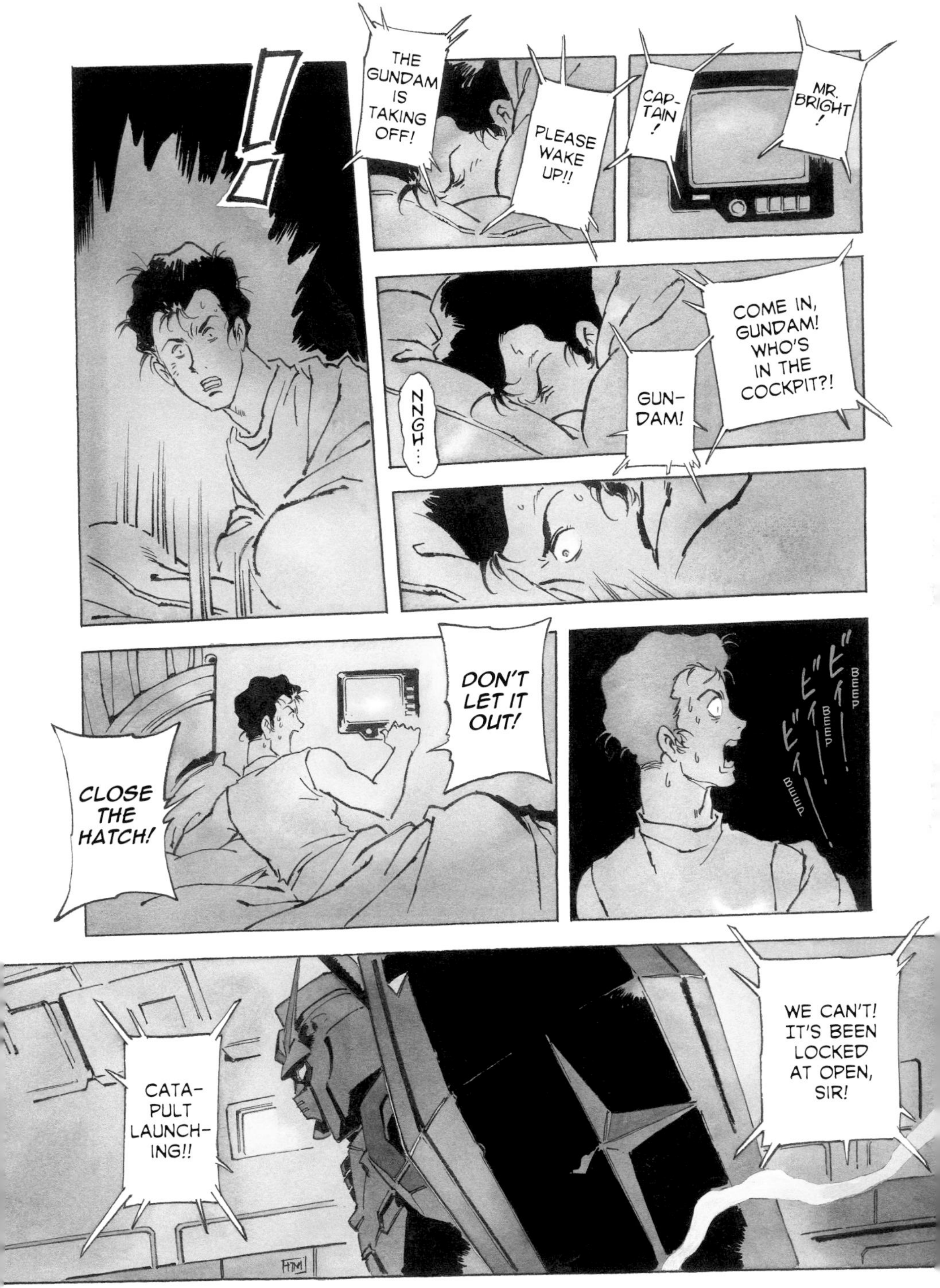
MR. BRIGHT!
CAP-TAIN!
PLEASE WAKE UP!!
THE GUNDAM IS TAKING OFF!
COME IN, GUNDAM! WHO'S IN THE COCKPIT?!
GUN-DAM!
NNGH...
!
BEEP
BEEP
BEEP
DON'T LET IT OUT!
CLOSE THE HATCH!
WE CAN'T! IT'S BEEN LOCKED AT OPEN, SIR!
CATA-PULT LAUNCH-ING!!

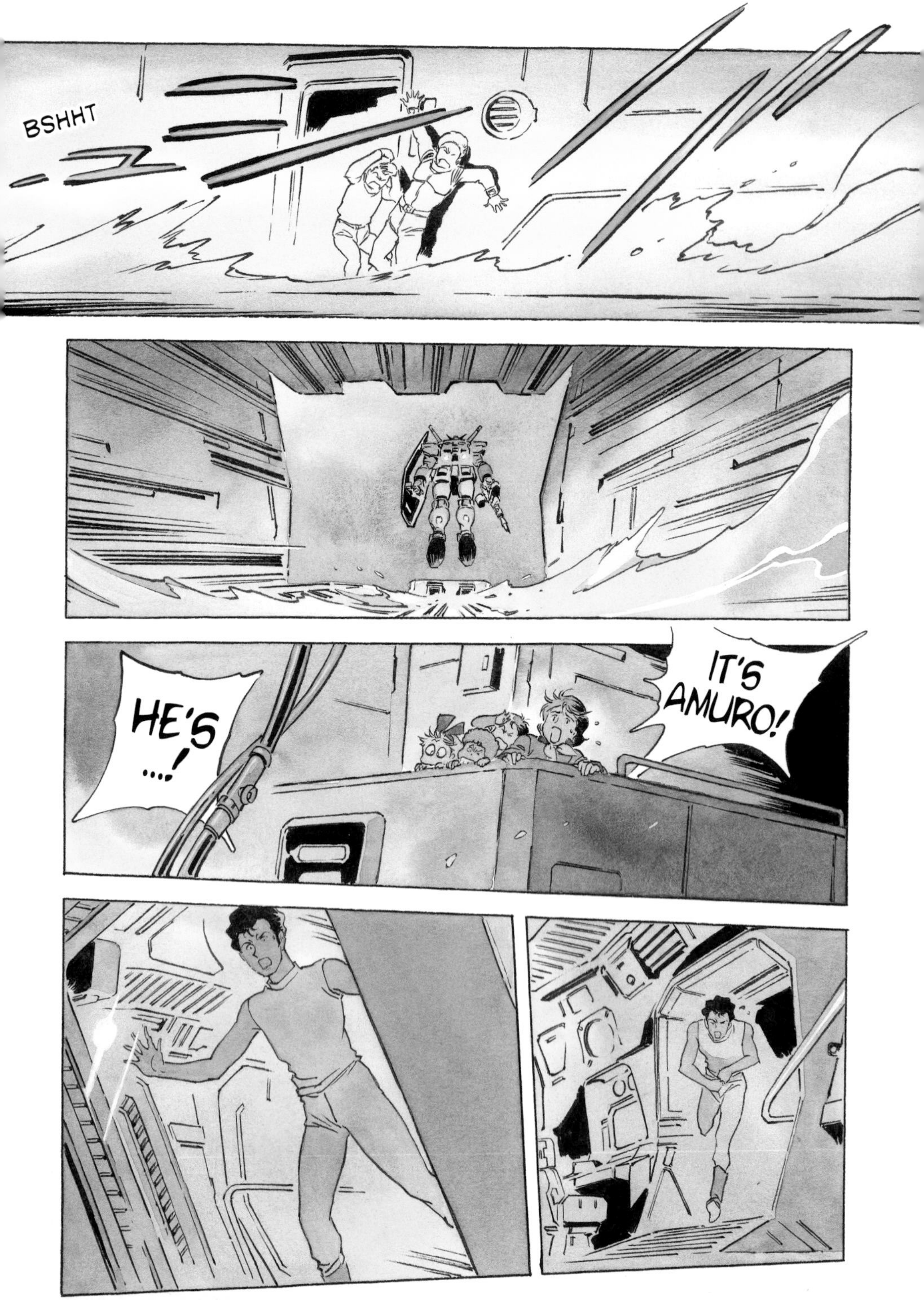
BSHHT
IT'S AMURO!
HE'S ...!

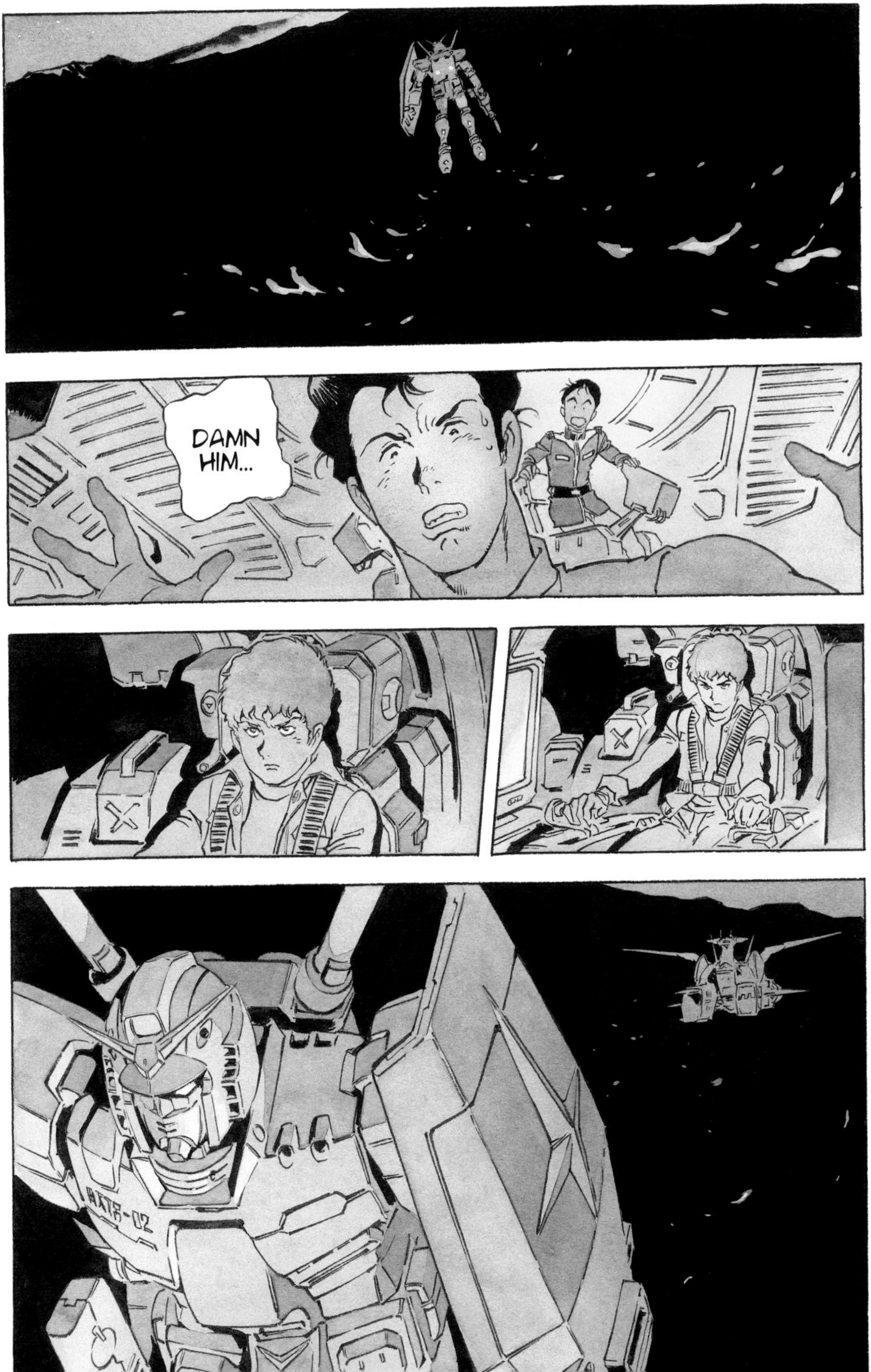
DAMN HIM...
RX78-02

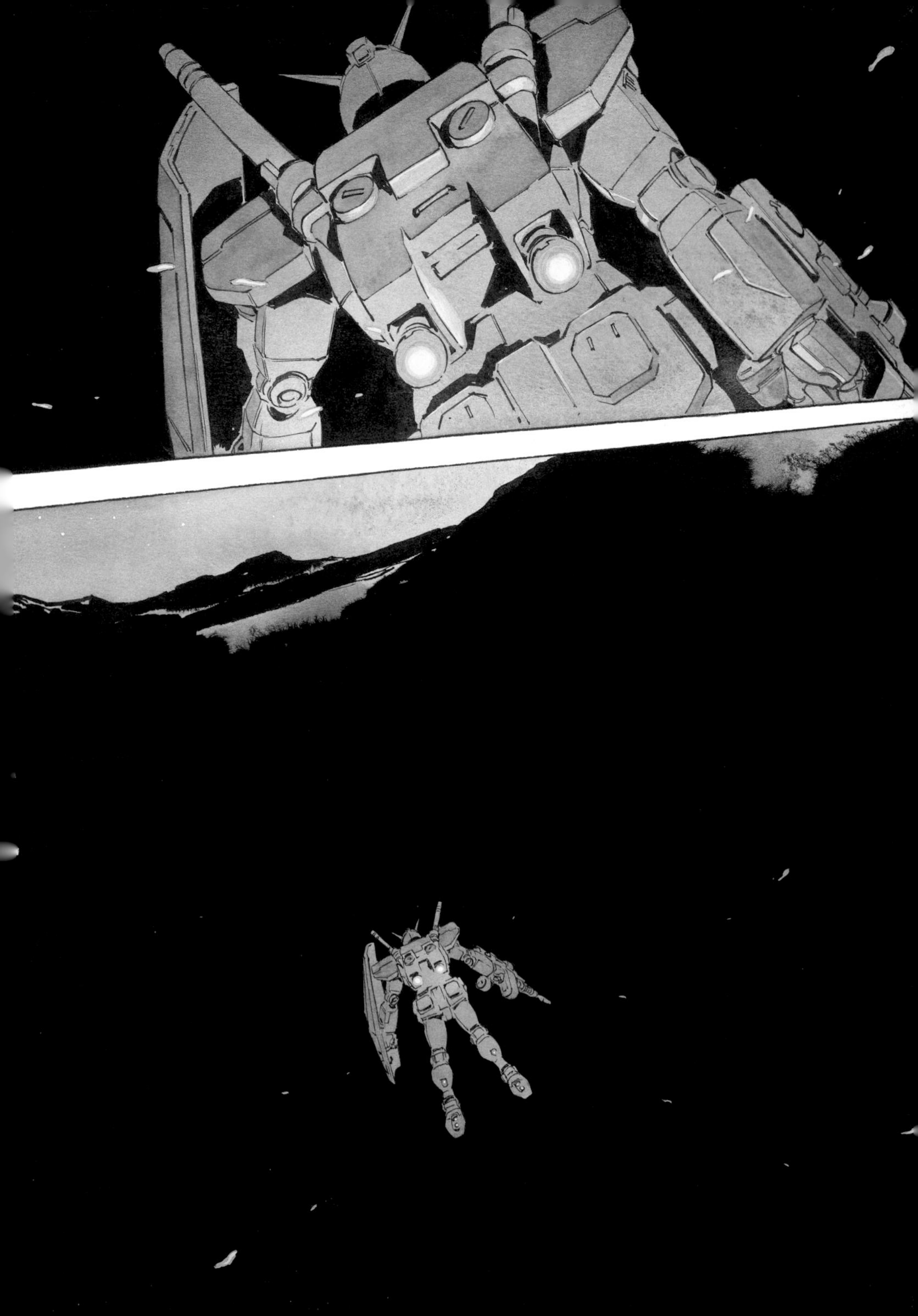

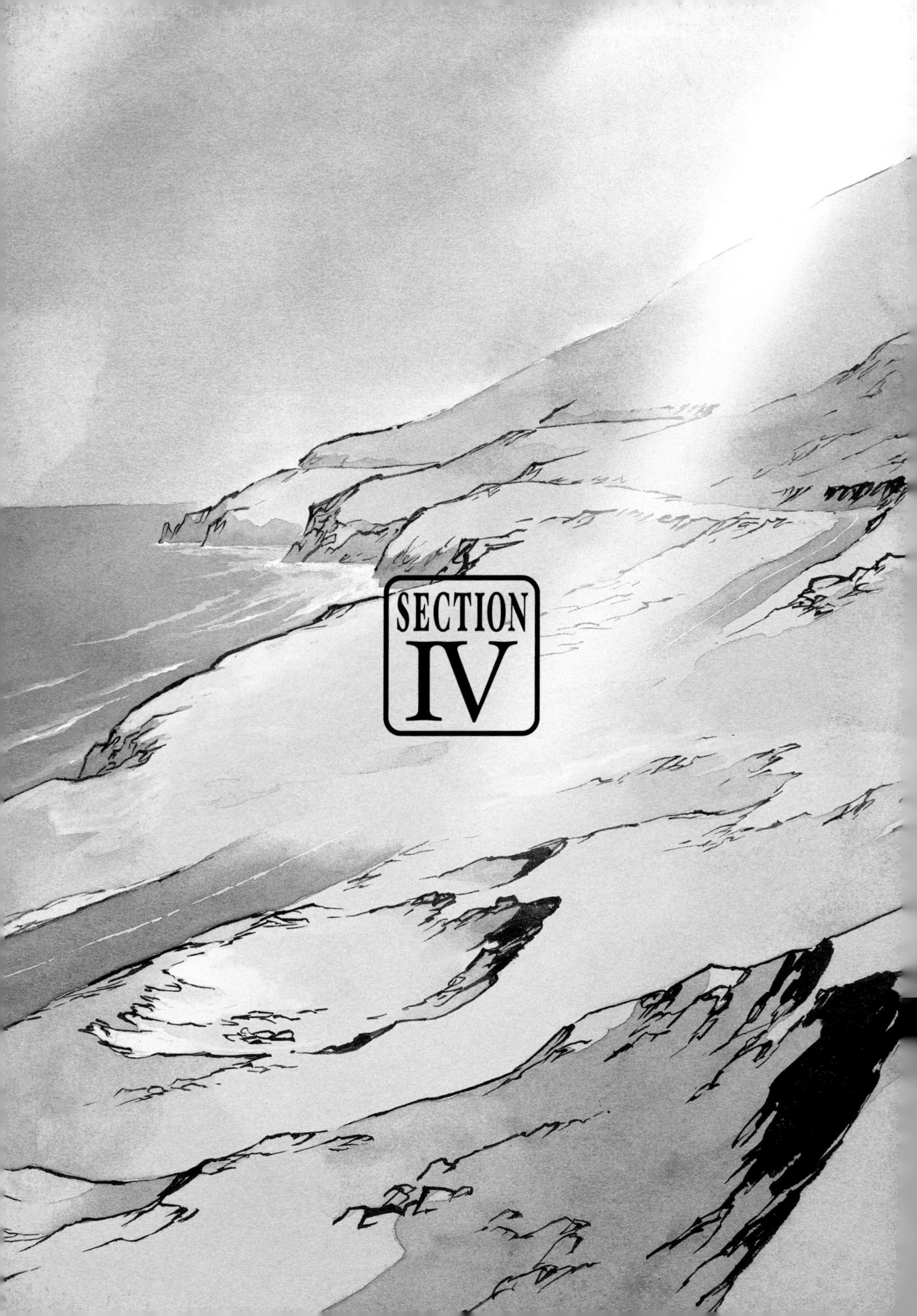
SECTION
IV

ZST
ズ
ズ
ザ
ZSHK
ザ
ZSHK
ザ
ZSHK
ザク
GROAN...

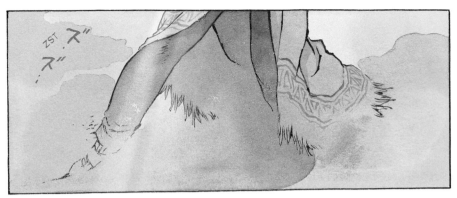

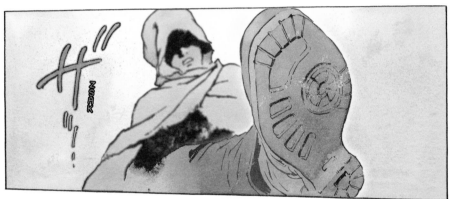

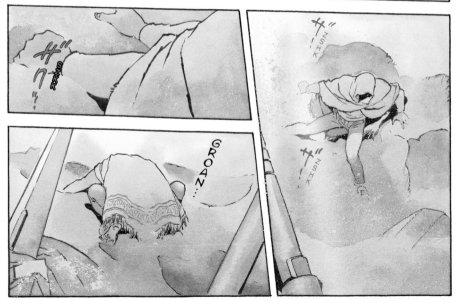

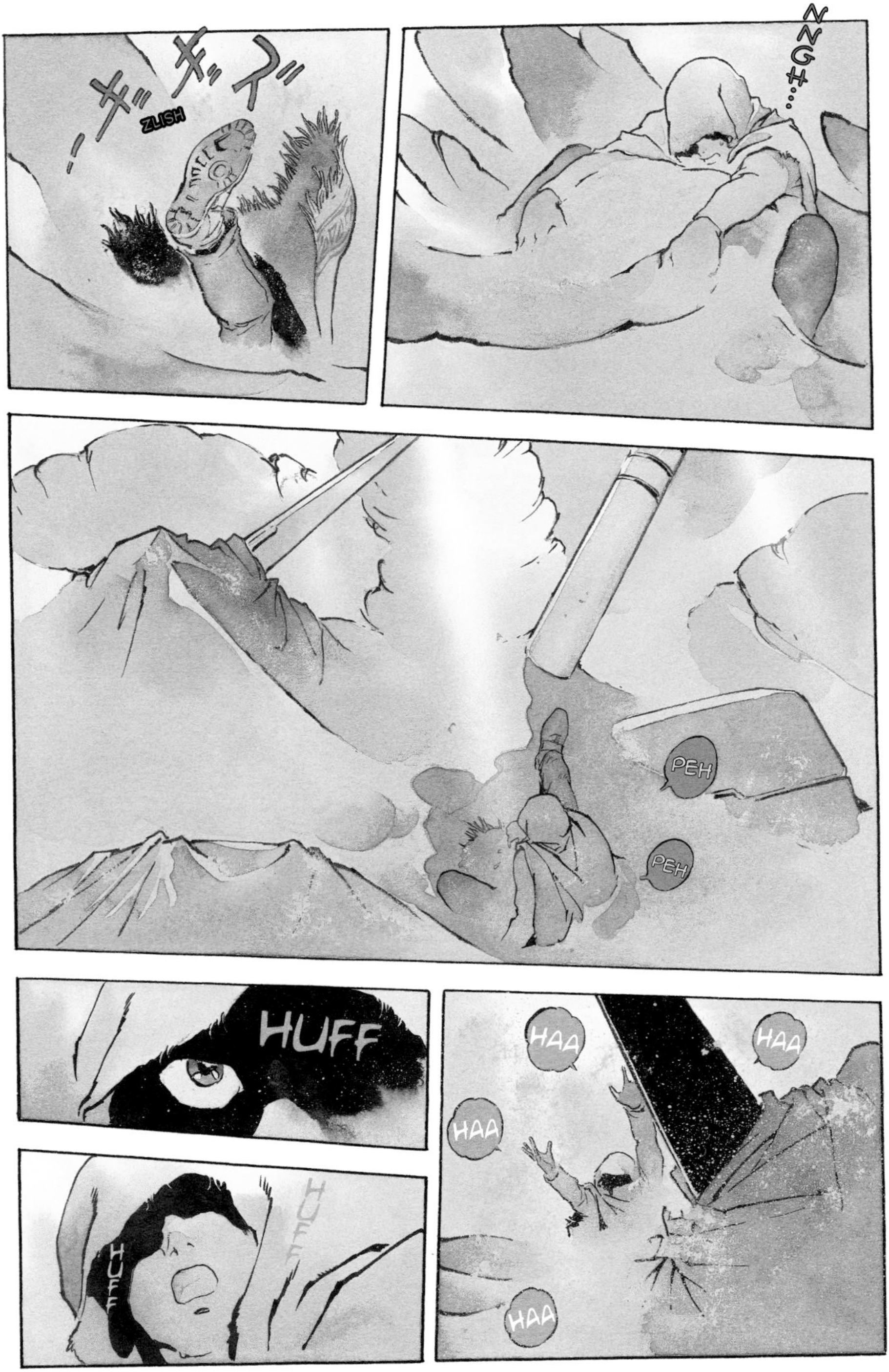
NNGH...
ギギッイ゛
ZLISH
PEH
PEH
HAA
HAA
HAA
HAA
HUFF
HUFF
HUFF

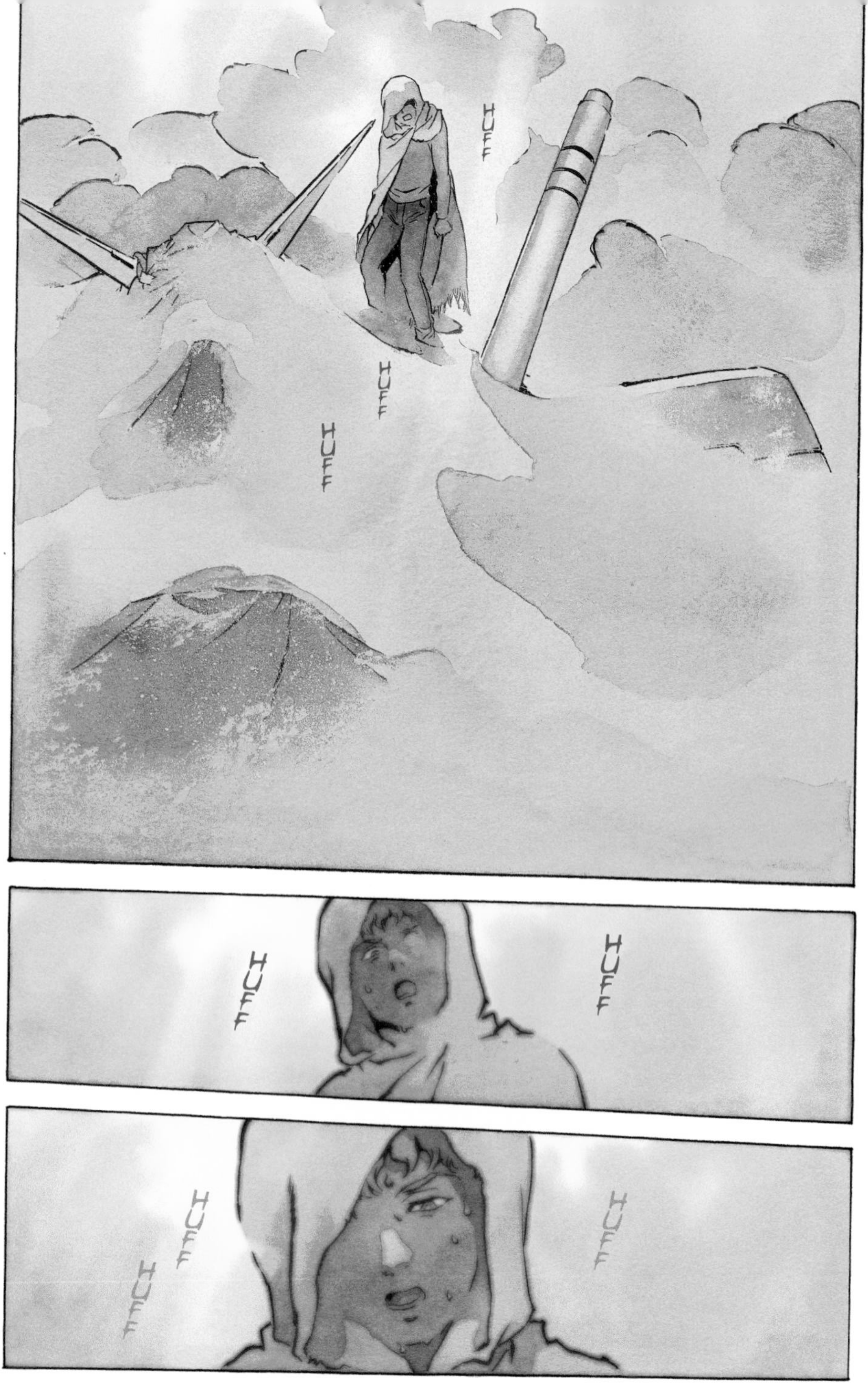
HUFF
HUFF
HUFF
HUFF
HUFF
HUFF
HUFF
HUFF

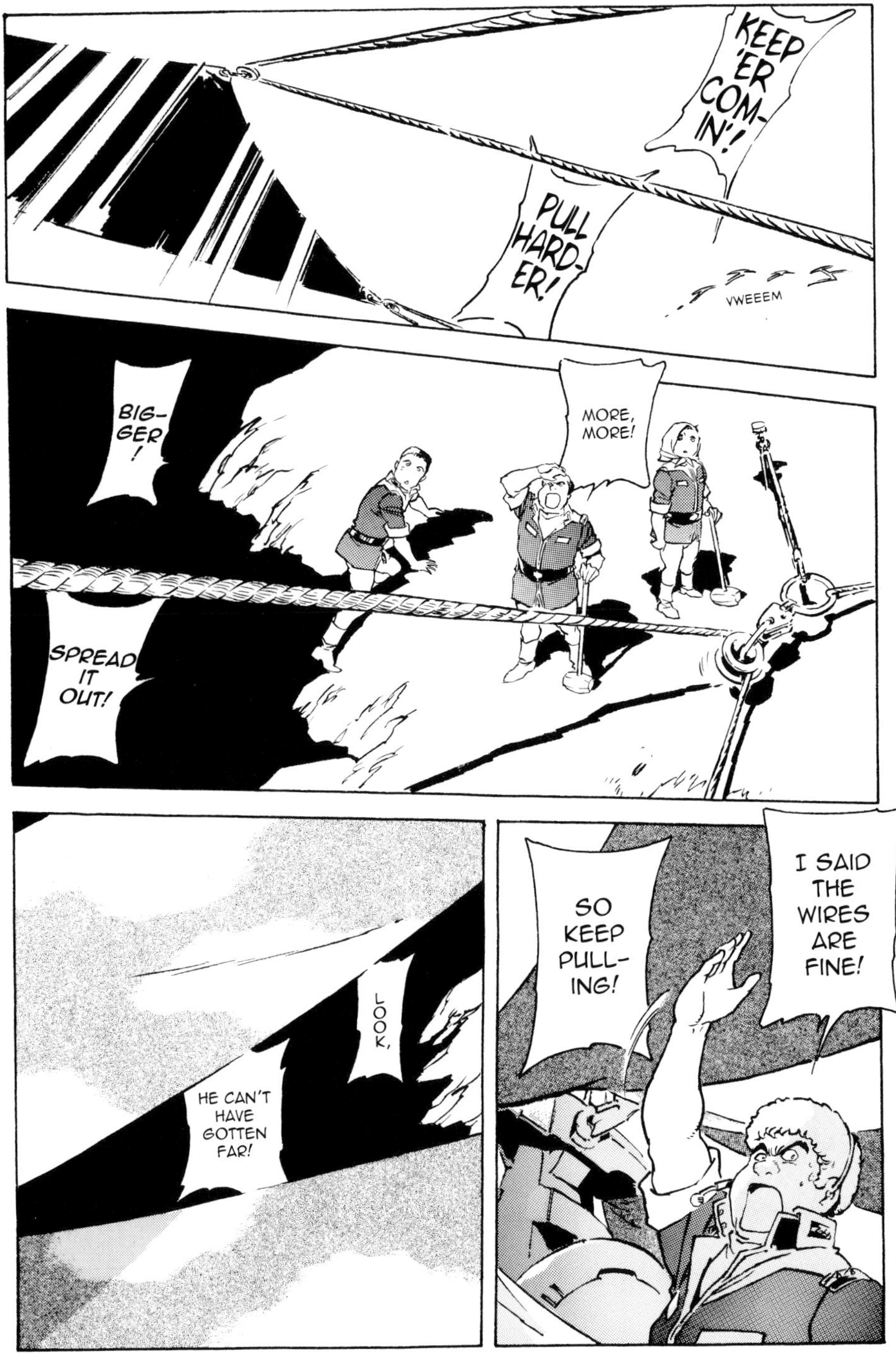
KEEP 'ER COMIN'!
PULL HARDER!
VWEEEM
MORE, MORE!
BIGGER!
SPREAD IT OUT!
I SAID THE WIRES ARE FINE!
SO KEEP PULLING!
LOOK,
HE CAN'T HAVE GOTTEN FAR!

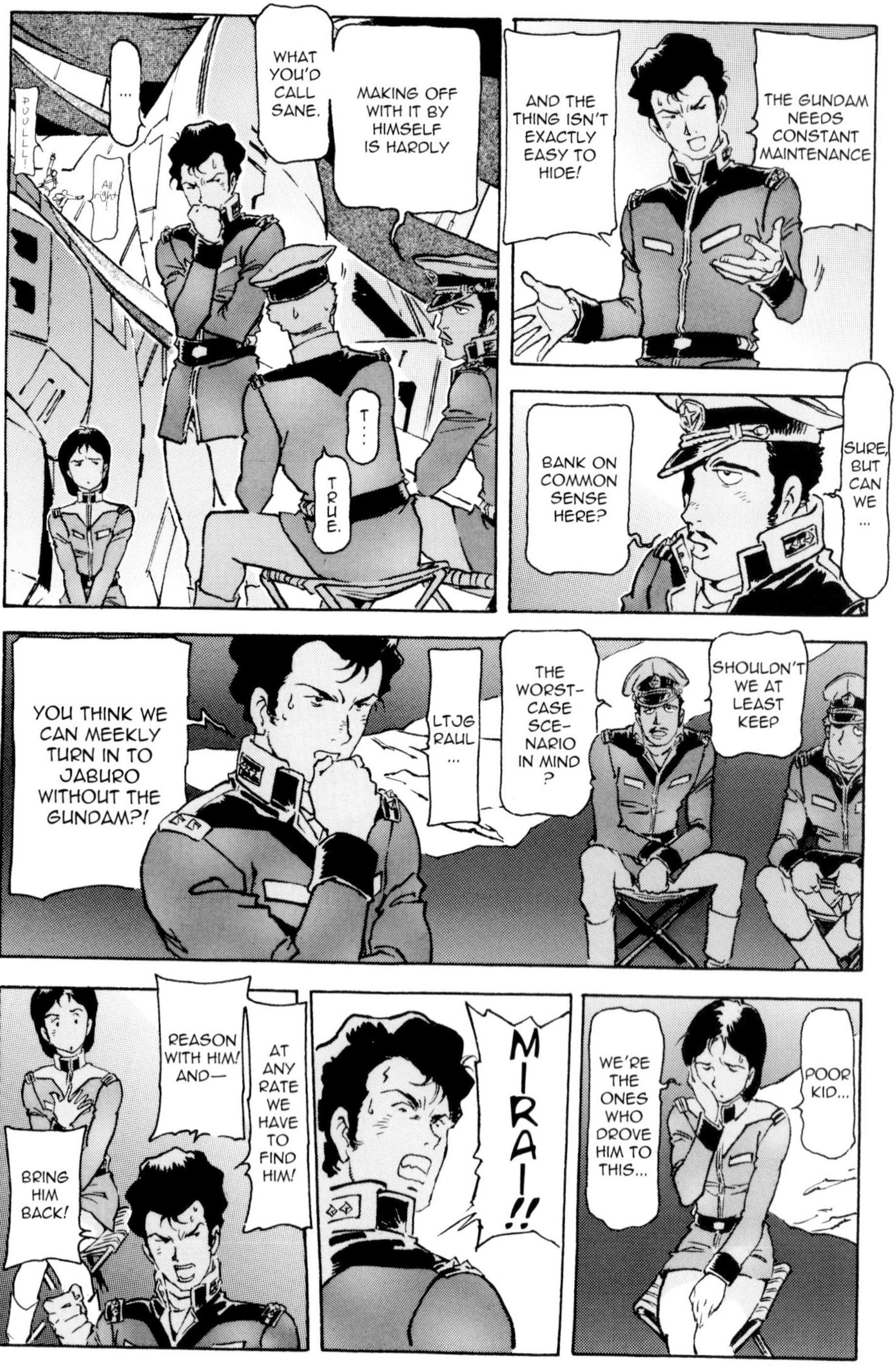
THE GUNDAM NEEDS CONSTANT MAINTENANCE
AND THE THING ISN'T EXACTLY EASY TO HIDE!
SURE, BUT CAN WE ...
BANK ON COMMON SENSE HERE?
MAKING OFF WITH IT BY HIMSELF IS HARDLY
WHAT YOU'D CALL SANE.
...
PUULLL!
All right!
T... TRUE.
SHOULDN'T WE AT LEAST KEEP
THE WORST-CASE SCENARIO IN MIND?
LTJG RAUL...
YOU THINK WE CAN MEEKLY TURN IN TO JABURO WITHOUT THE GUNDAM?!
POOR KID...
WE'RE THE ONES WHO DROVE HIM TO THIS...
MIRAI!!
AT ANY RATE WE HAVE TO FIND HIM!
REASON WITH HIM! AND—
BRING HIM BACK!

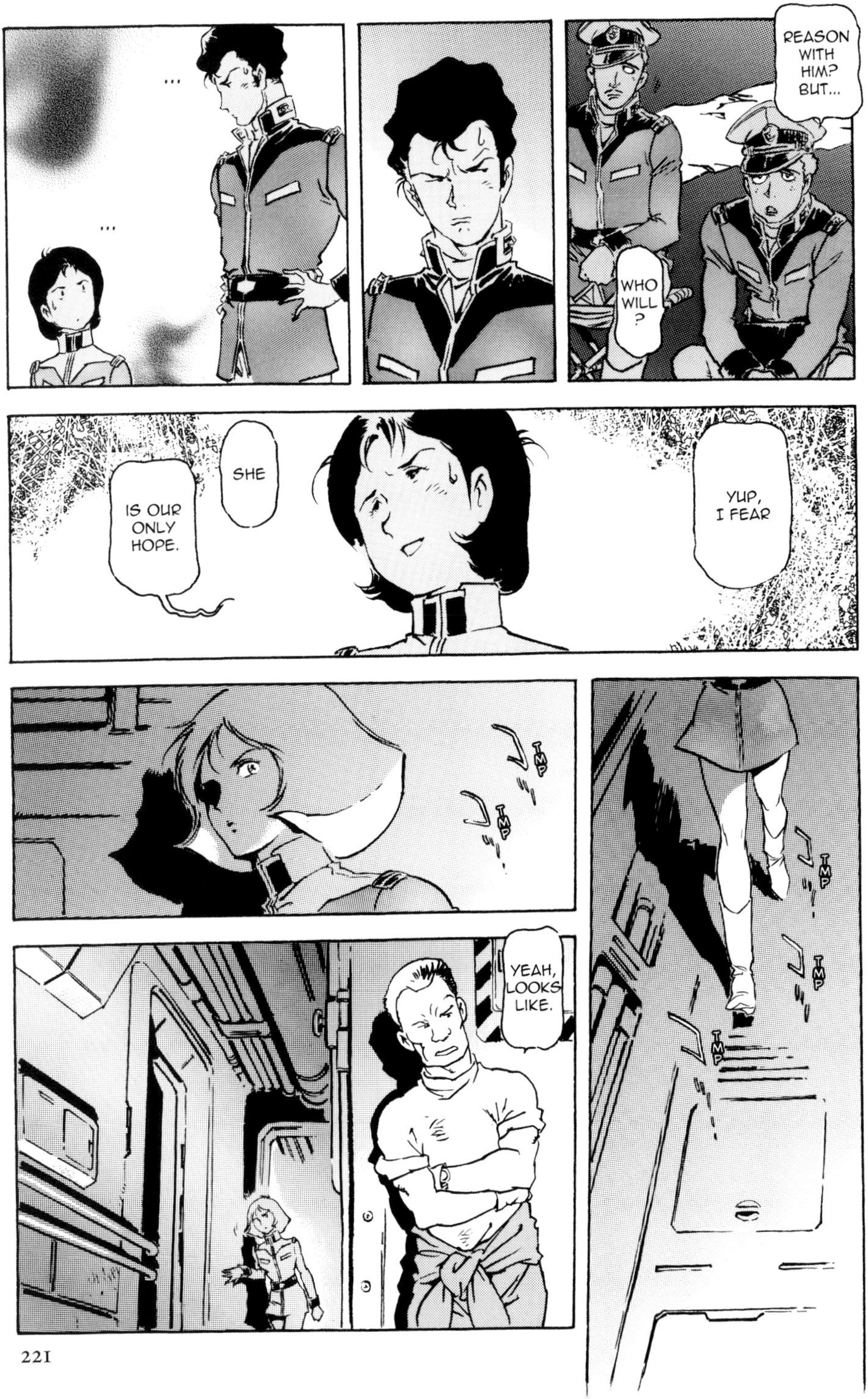
REASON WITH HIM? BUT...
WHO WILL?
...
...
YUP, I FEAR
SHE
IS OUR ONLY HOPE.
TMP
TMP
TMP
TMP
TMP
YEAH, LOOKS LIKE.

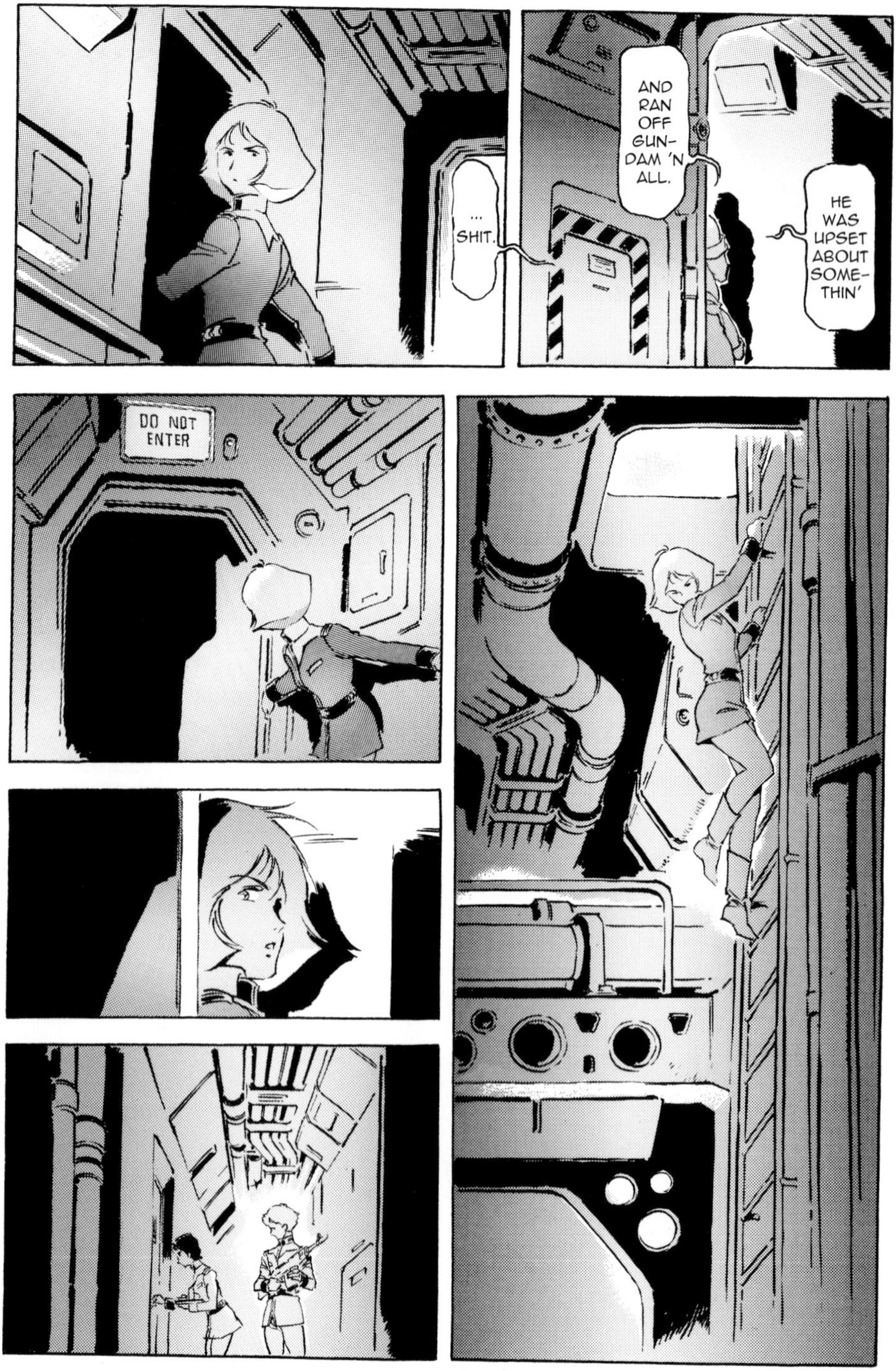
HE WAS UPSET ABOUT SOMETHIN'
AND RAN OFF GUN-DAM 'N ALL.
... SHIT.
DO NOT ENTER

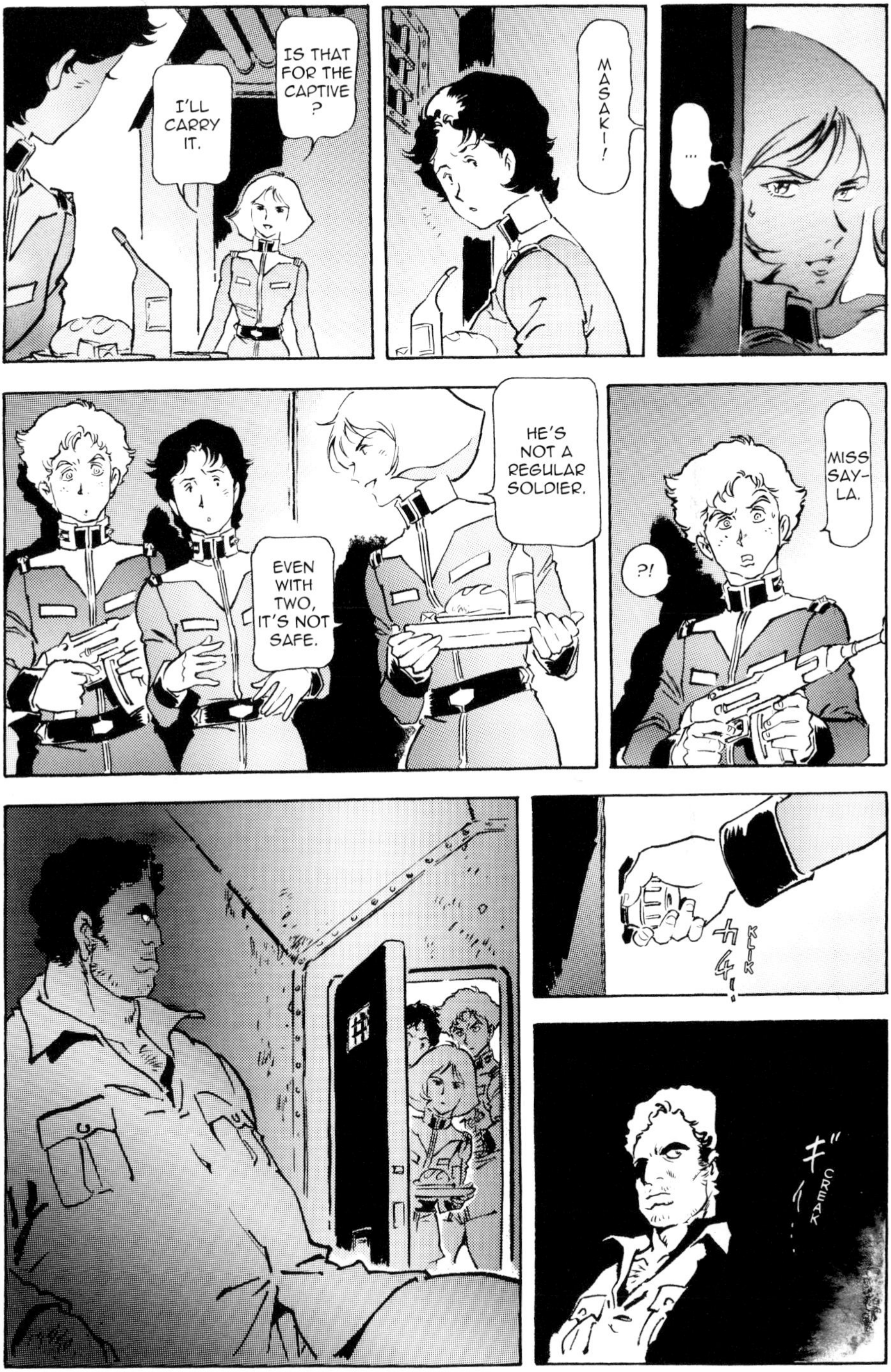
...
MASAKI!
IS THAT FOR THE CAPTIVE?
I'LL CARRY IT.
MISS SAY-LA.
?!
HE'S NOT A REGULAR SOLDIER.
EVEN WITH TWO, IT'S NOT SAFE.
KLIK
CREAK

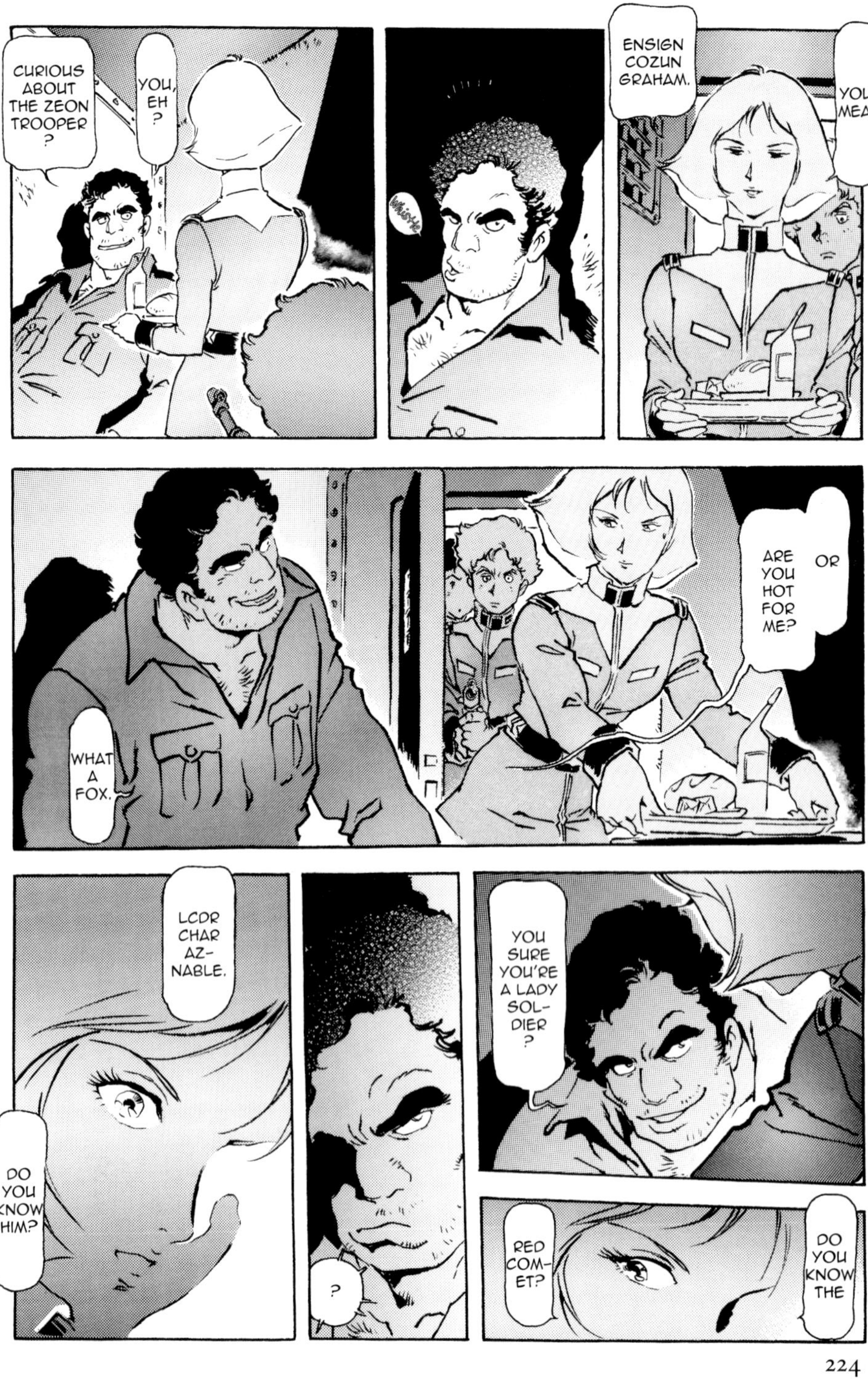
YOUR MEAL,
ENSIGN COZUN GRAHAM.
Whistle
YOU, EH?
CURIOUS ABOUT THE ZEON TROOPER?
OR
ARE YOU HOT FOR ME?
WHAT A FOX.
YOU SURE YOU'RE A LADY SOL-DIER?
DO YOU KNOW THE
RED COM-ET?
?
LCDR CHAR AZ-NABLE.
DO YOU KNOW HIM?

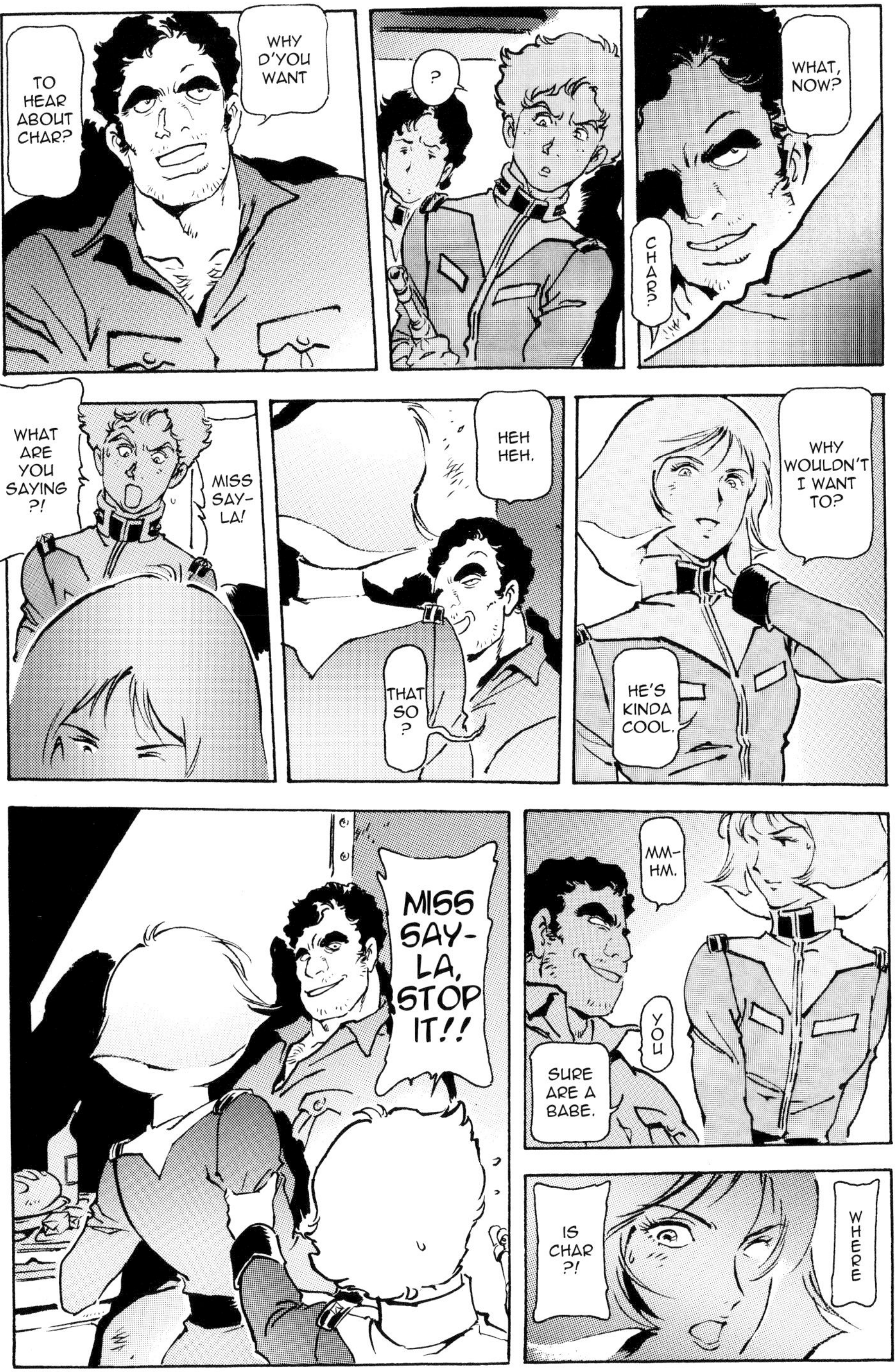
WHAT, NOW?
CHAR?
?
WHY D'YOU WANT
TO HEAR ABOUT CHAR?
WHY WOULDN'T I WANT TO?
HE'S KINDA COOL.
HEH HEH.
THAT SO?
MISS SAY-LA!
WHAT ARE YOU SAYING?!
MM-HM.
YOU
SURE ARE A BABE.
WHERE
IS CHAR?!
MISS SAY-LA, STOP IT!!

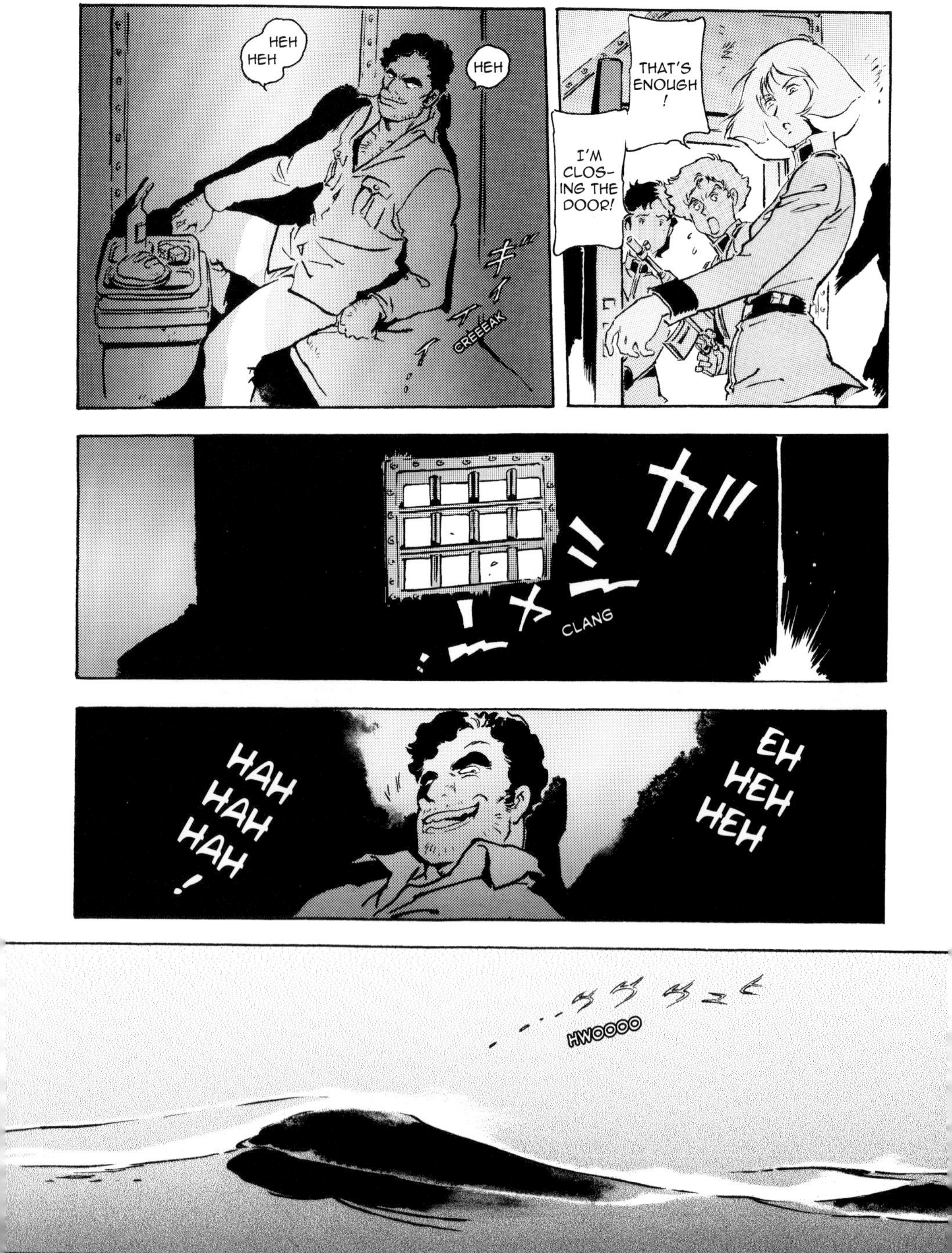
THAT'S ENOUGH!
I'M CLOSING THE DOOR!
HEH HEH
HEH
CREEEAK
CLANG
EH HEH HEH
HAH HAH HAH!
HWOOOO

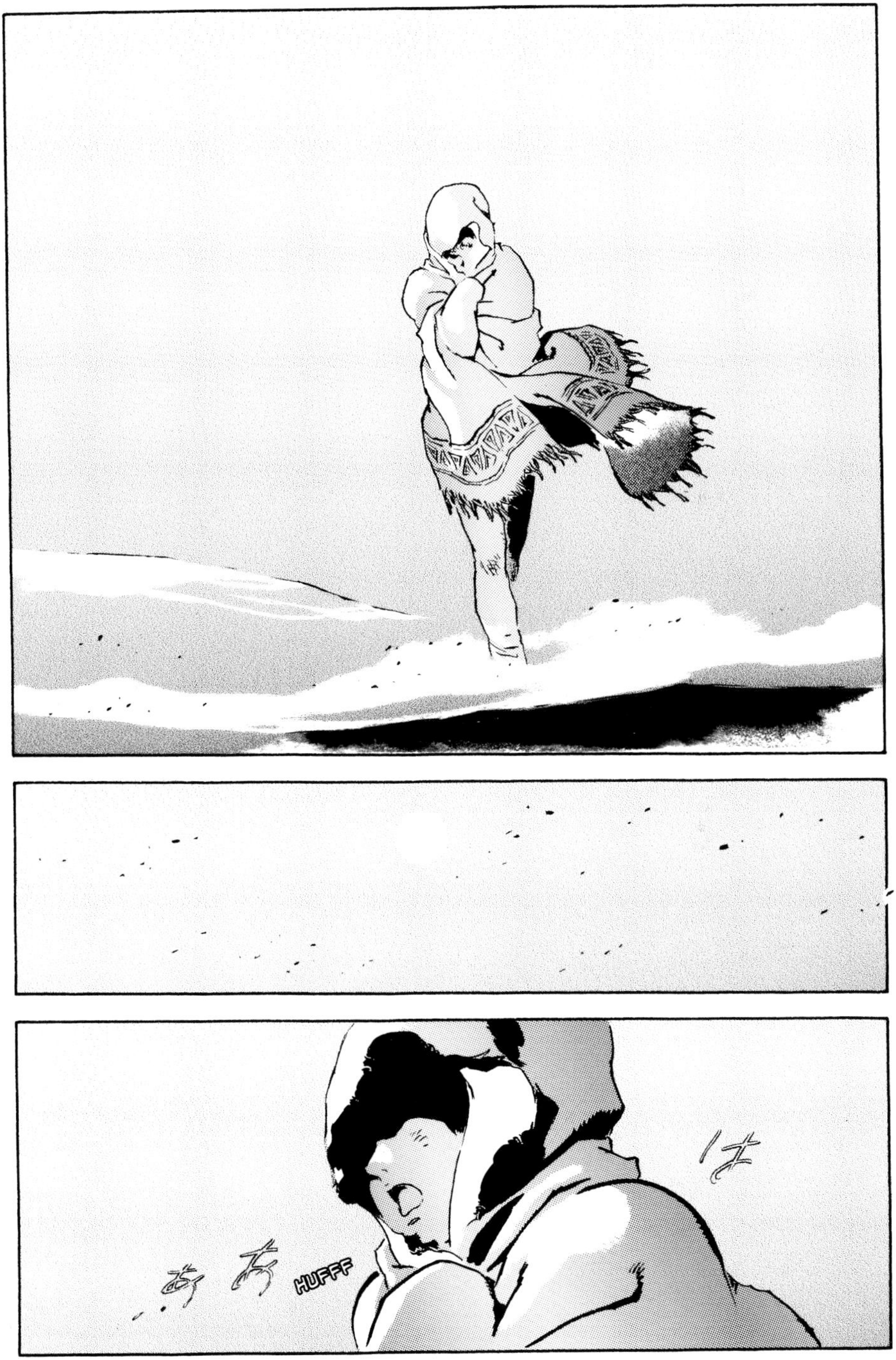
は
あ あ
HUFFF

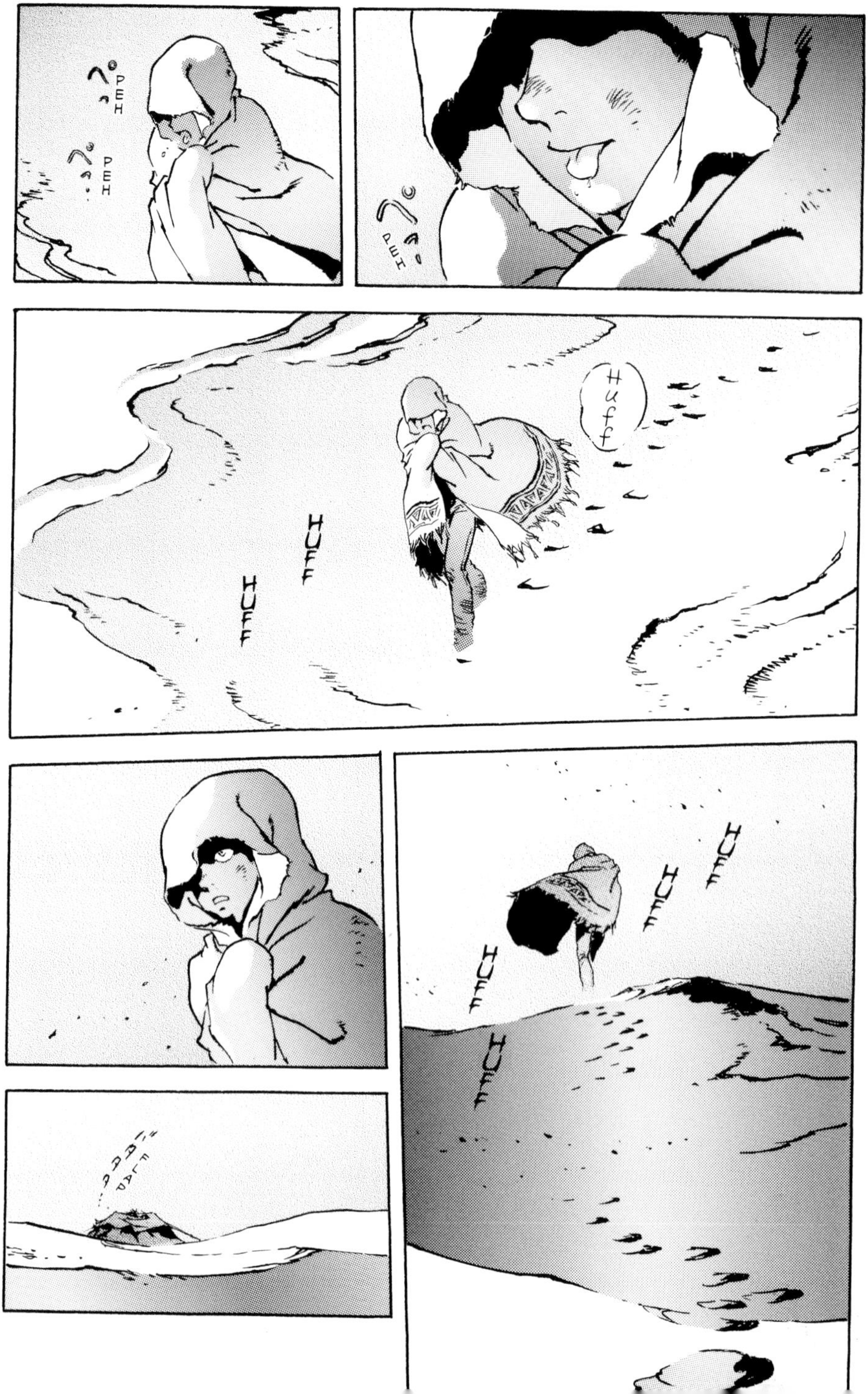
PEH
PEH
PEH
Huff
HUFF
HUFF
HUFF
HUFF
HUFF
HUFF
FLAP

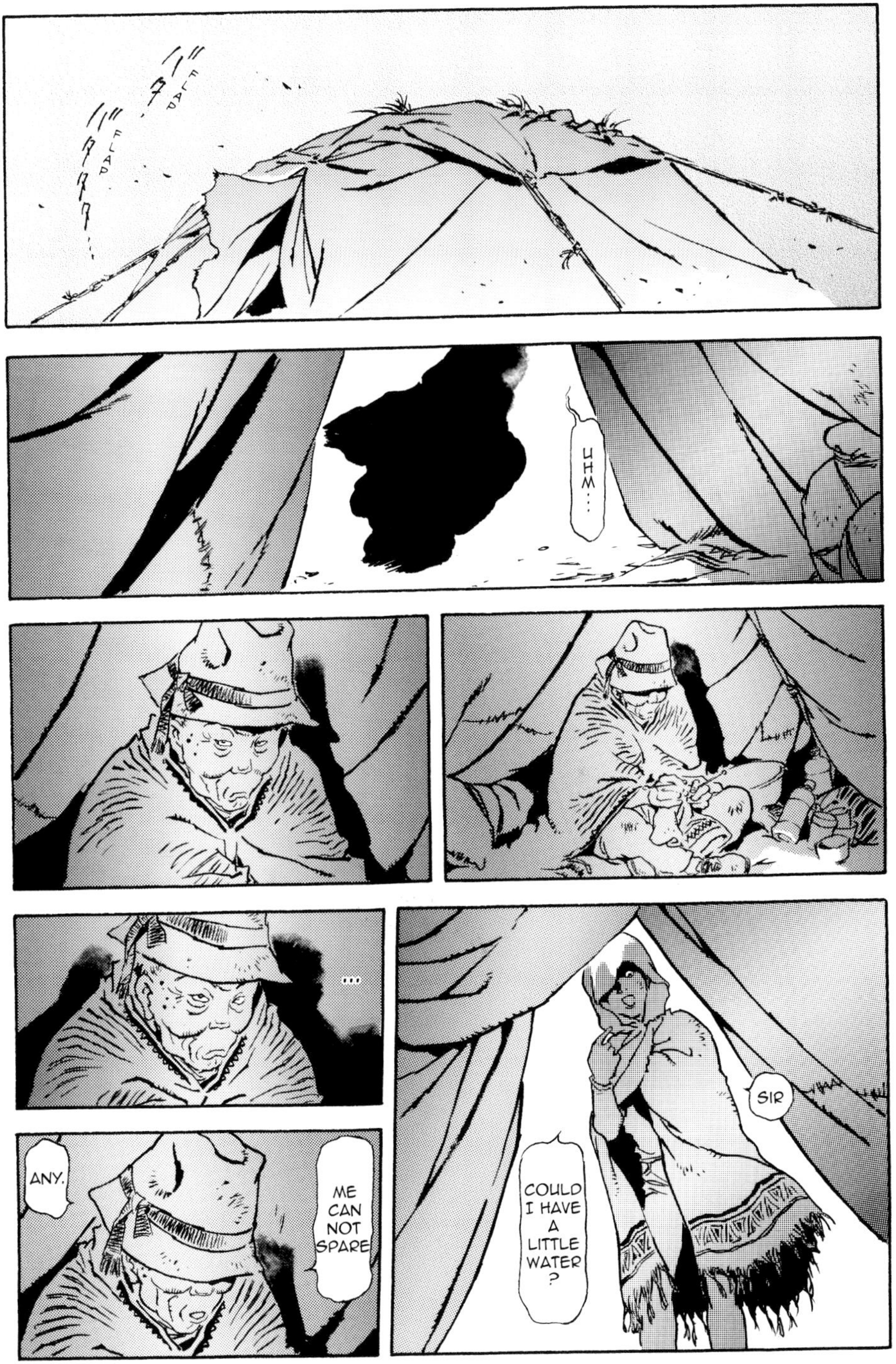

バタ
FLAP
バタタタ…
FLAP
UHM...
SIR
COULD I HAVE A LITTLE WATER?
...
ME CAN NOT SPARE
ANY.

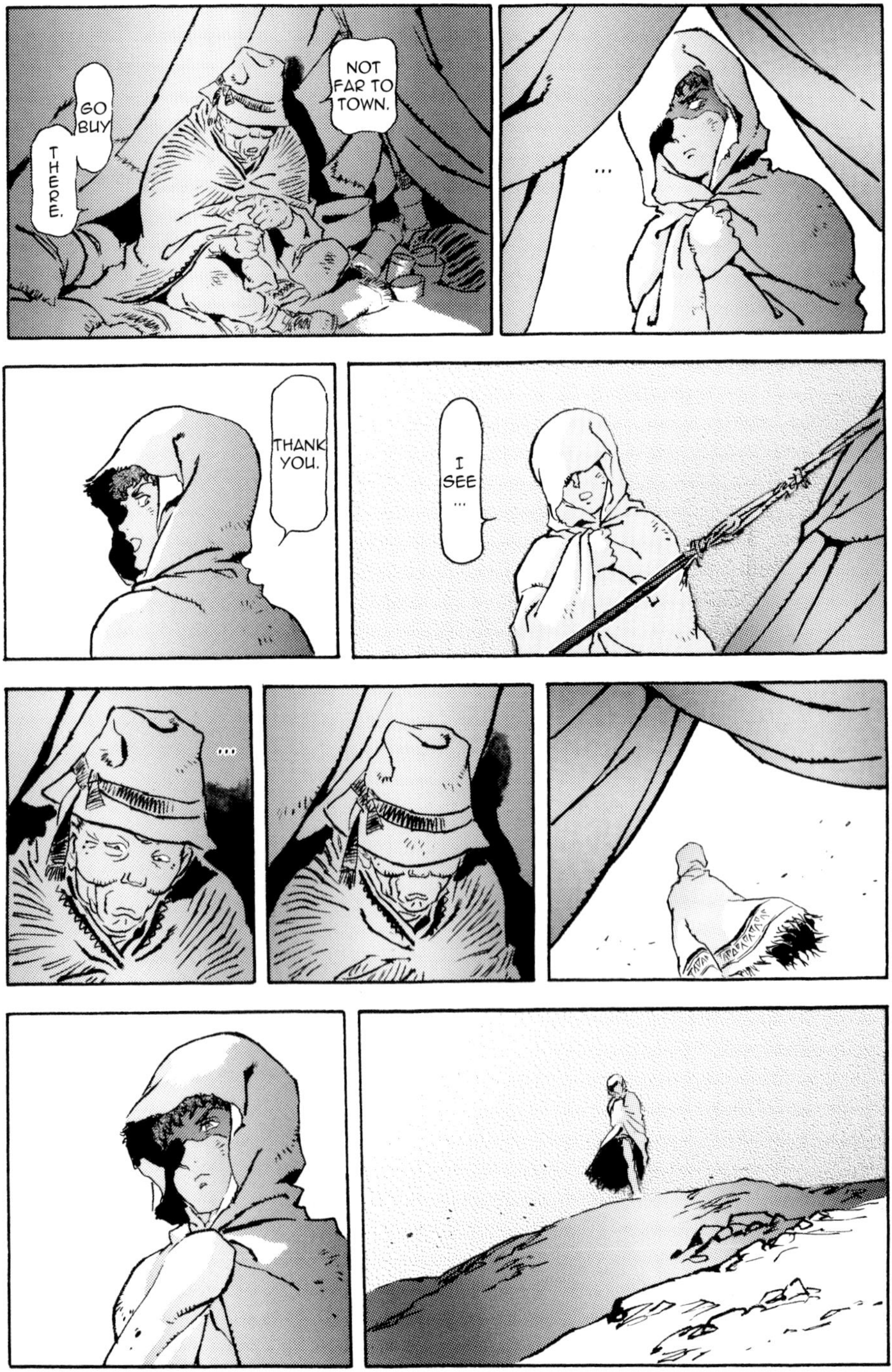
...
NOT FAR TO TOWN.
GO BUY THERE.
I SEE ...
THANK YOU.
...

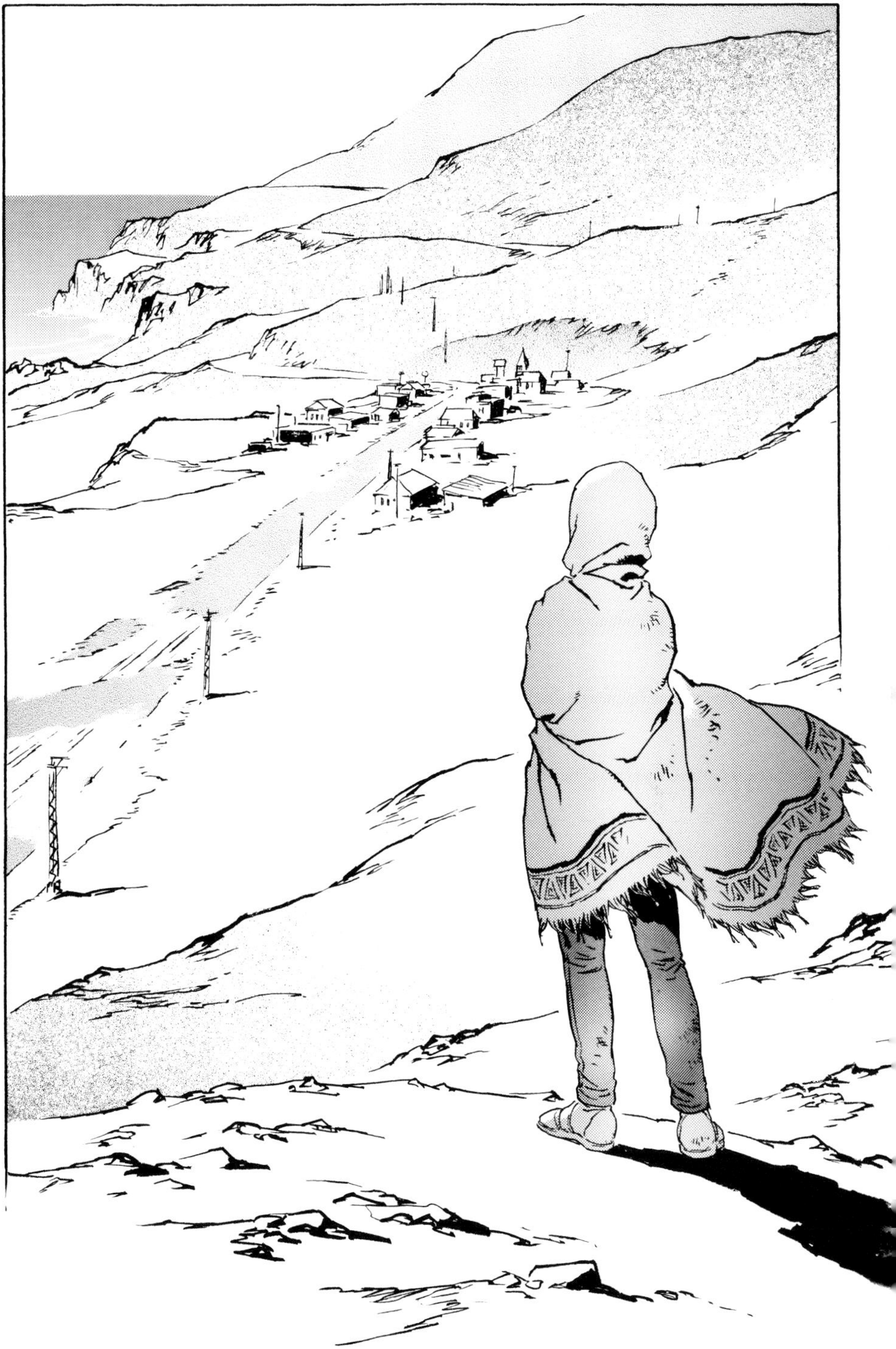

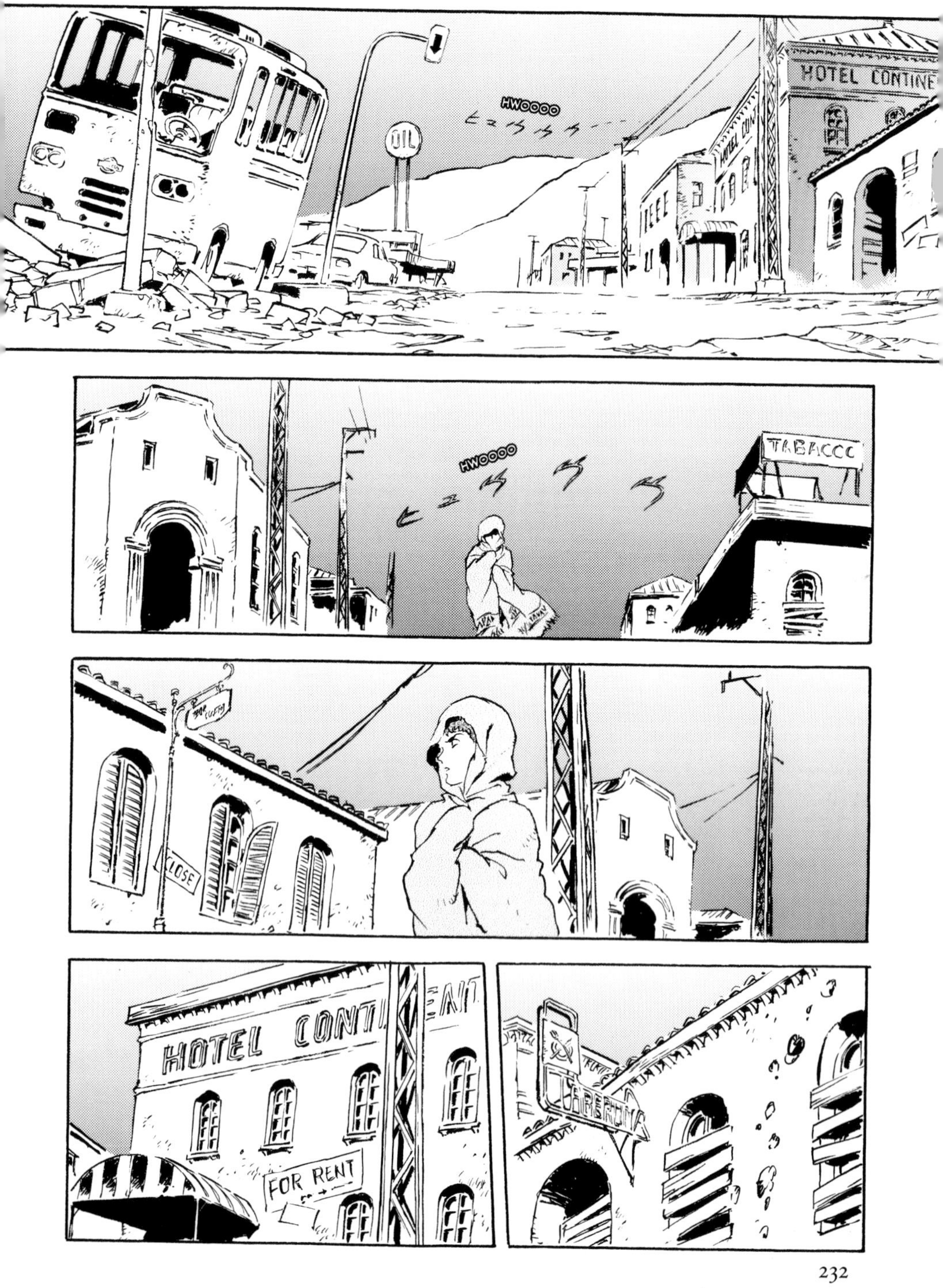
HOTEL CONTINE
HWOOOO
OIL
TABACCC
HWOOOO
CLOSE
HOTEL CONTI
FOR RENT

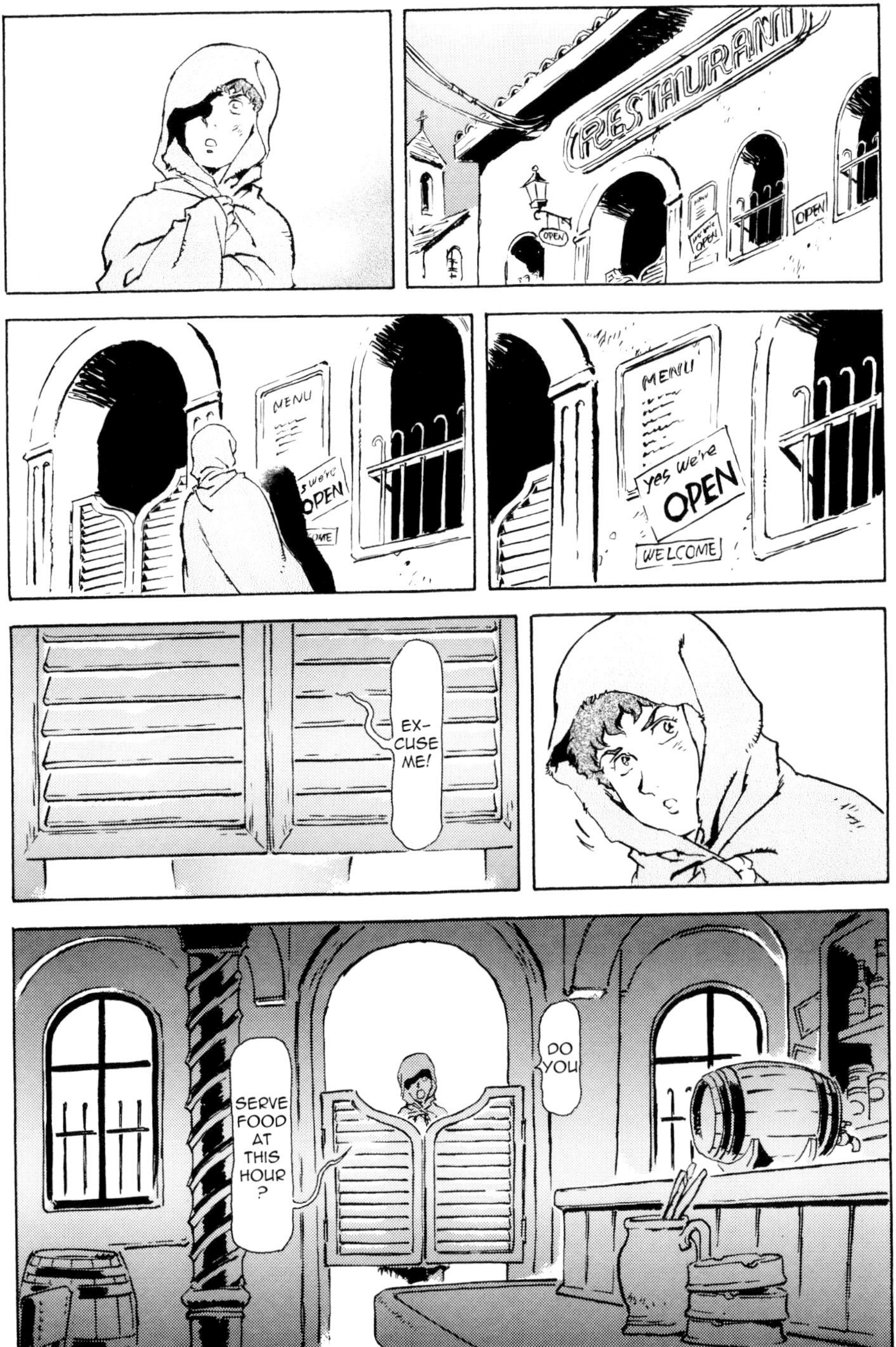
RESTAURANT
OPEN
OPEN
MENU
Yes We're
OPEN
WELCOME
MENU
EX-CUSE ME!
DO YOU
SERVE FOOD AT THIS HOUR?

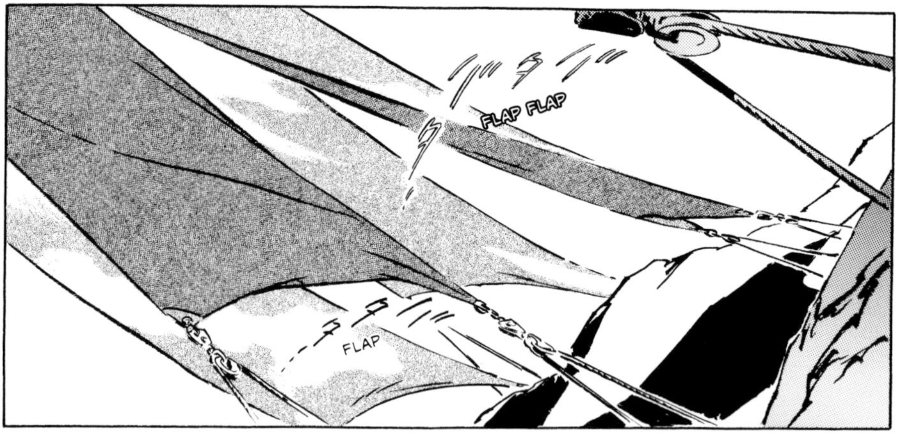
FLAP FLAP
FLAP

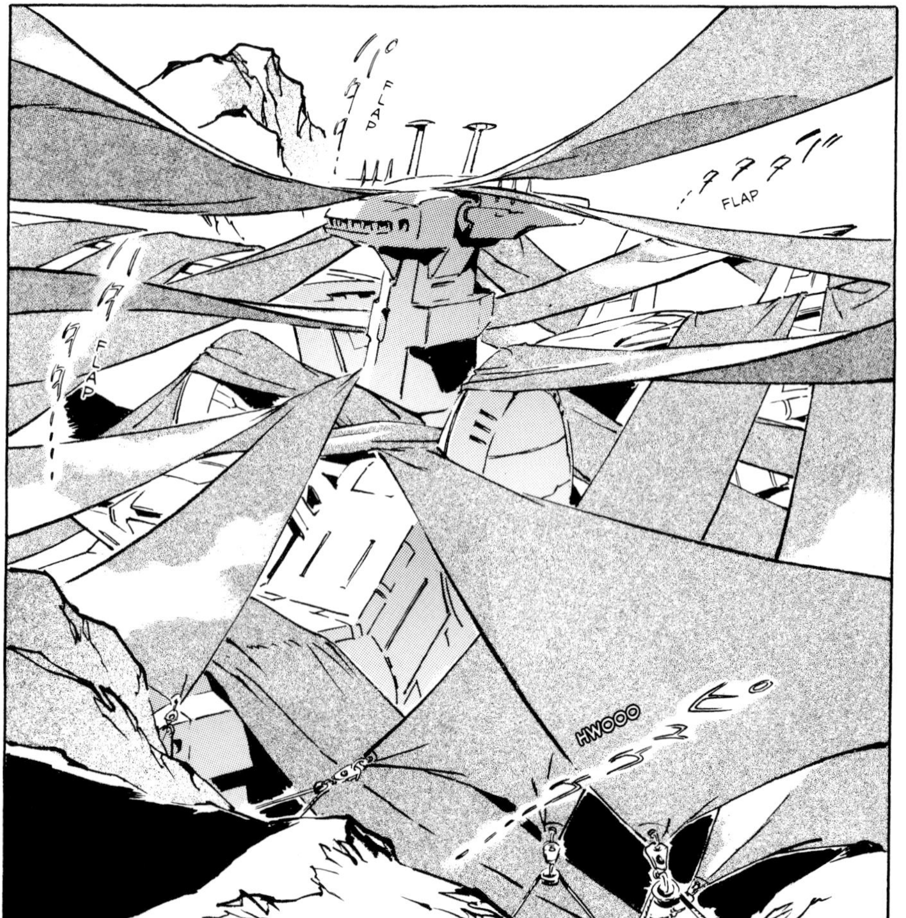
FLAP
FLAP
FLAP
HWOOO

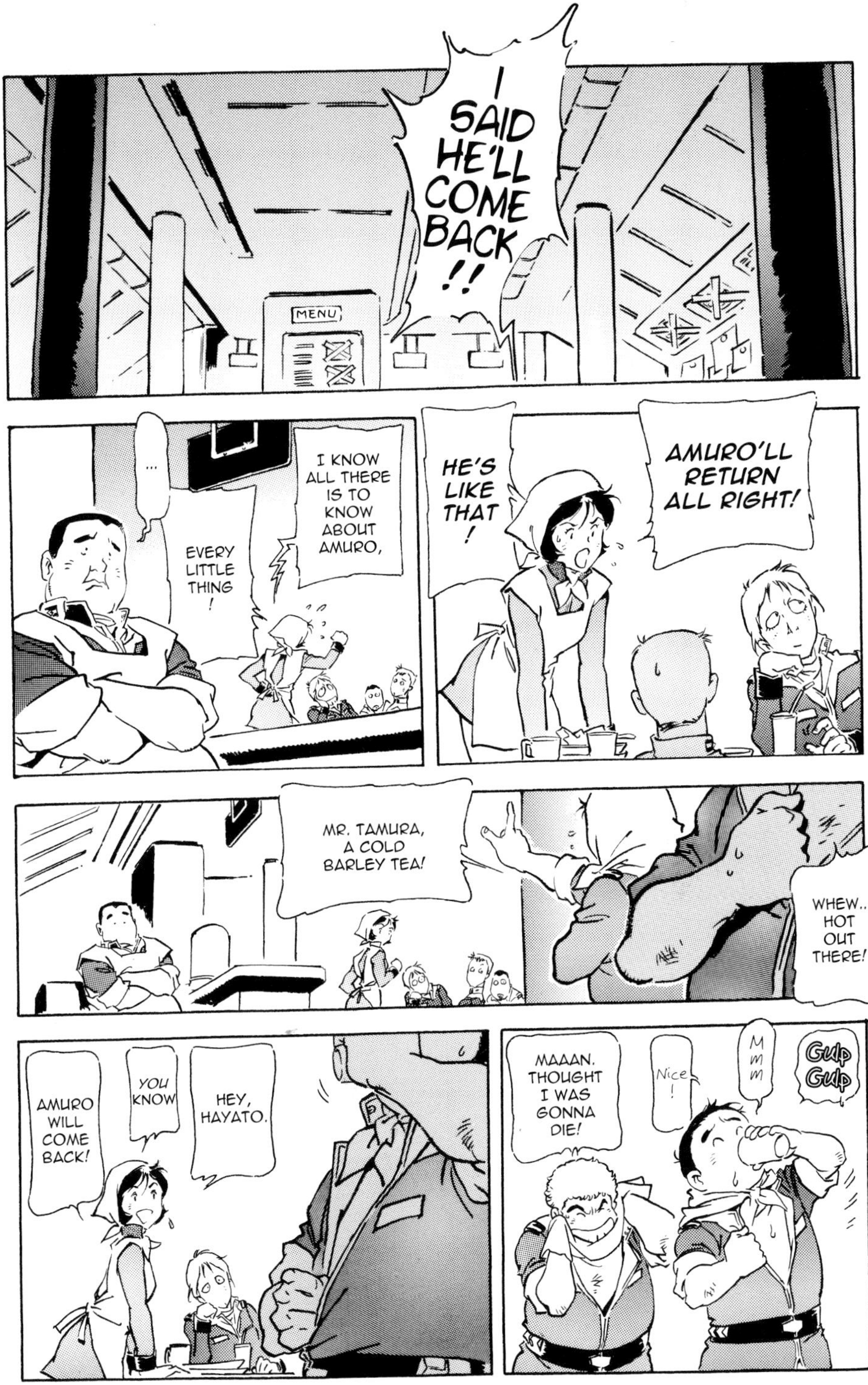
I SAID HE'LL COME BACK!!
MENU
AMURO'LL RETURN ALL RIGHT!
HE'S LIKE THAT!
I KNOW ALL THERE IS TO KNOW ABOUT AMURO,
EVERY LITTLE THING!
...
WHEW... HOT OUT THERE!
MR. TAMURA, A COLD BARLEY TEA!
Gulp Gulp
MMM
Nice!
MAAAN. THOUGHT I WAS GONNA DIE!
HEY, HAYATO.
YOU KNOW
AMURO WILL COME BACK!

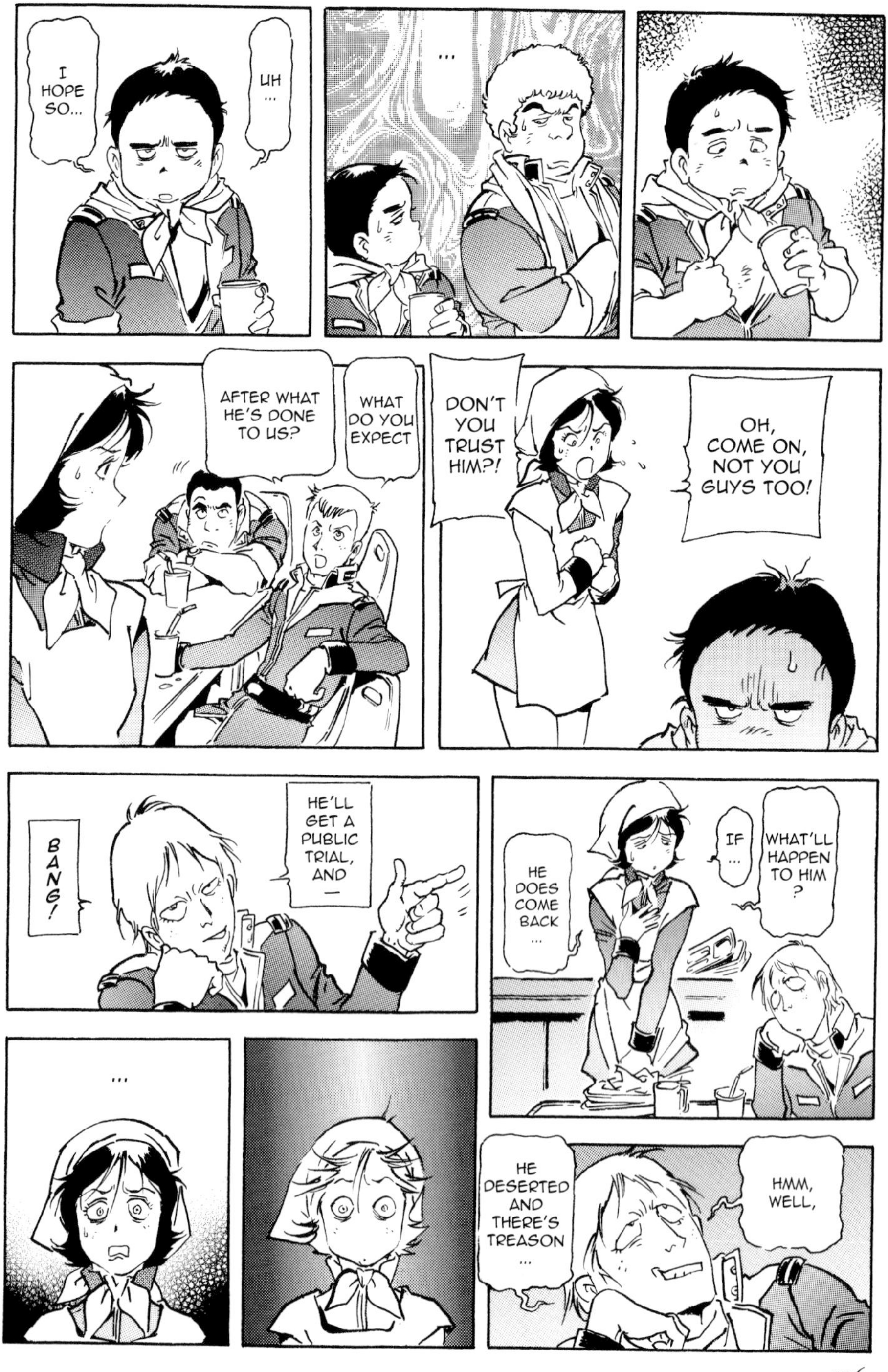
...
UH ...
I HOPE SO...
OH, COME ON, NOT YOU GUYS TOO!
DON'T YOU TRUST HIM?!
WHAT DO YOU EXPECT
AFTER WHAT HE'S DONE TO US?
WHAT'LL HAPPEN TO HIM ?
IF ...
HE DOES COME BACK ...
HE'LL GET A PUBLIC TRIAL, AND —
BANG!
HMM, WELL,
HE DESERTED AND THERE'S TREASON ...
...

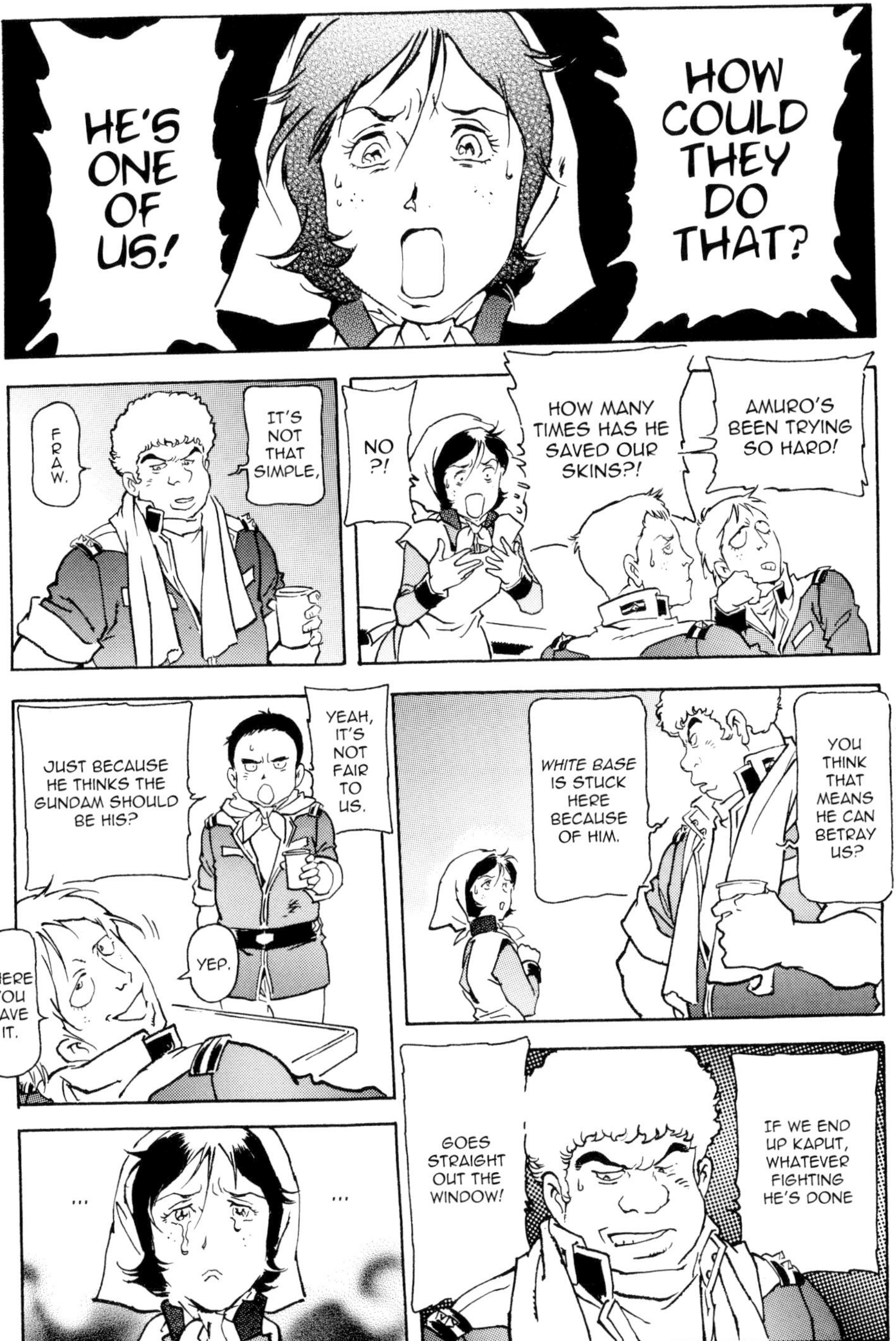
HOW COULD THEY DO THAT?
HE'S ONE OF US!
AMURO'S BEEN TRYING SO HARD!
HOW MANY TIMES HAS HE SAVED OUR SKINS?!
NO ?!
IT'S NOT THAT SIMPLE,
FRAW.
YOU THINK THAT MEANS HE CAN BETRAY US?
WHITE BASE IS STUCK HERE BECAUSE OF HIM.
YEAH, IT'S NOT FAIR TO US.
JUST BECAUSE HE THINKS THE GUNDAM SHOULD BE HIS?
YEP.
THERE YOU HAVE IT.
IF WE END UP KAPUT, WHATEVER FIGHTING HE'S DONE
GOES STRAIGHT OUT THE WINDOW!
...
...

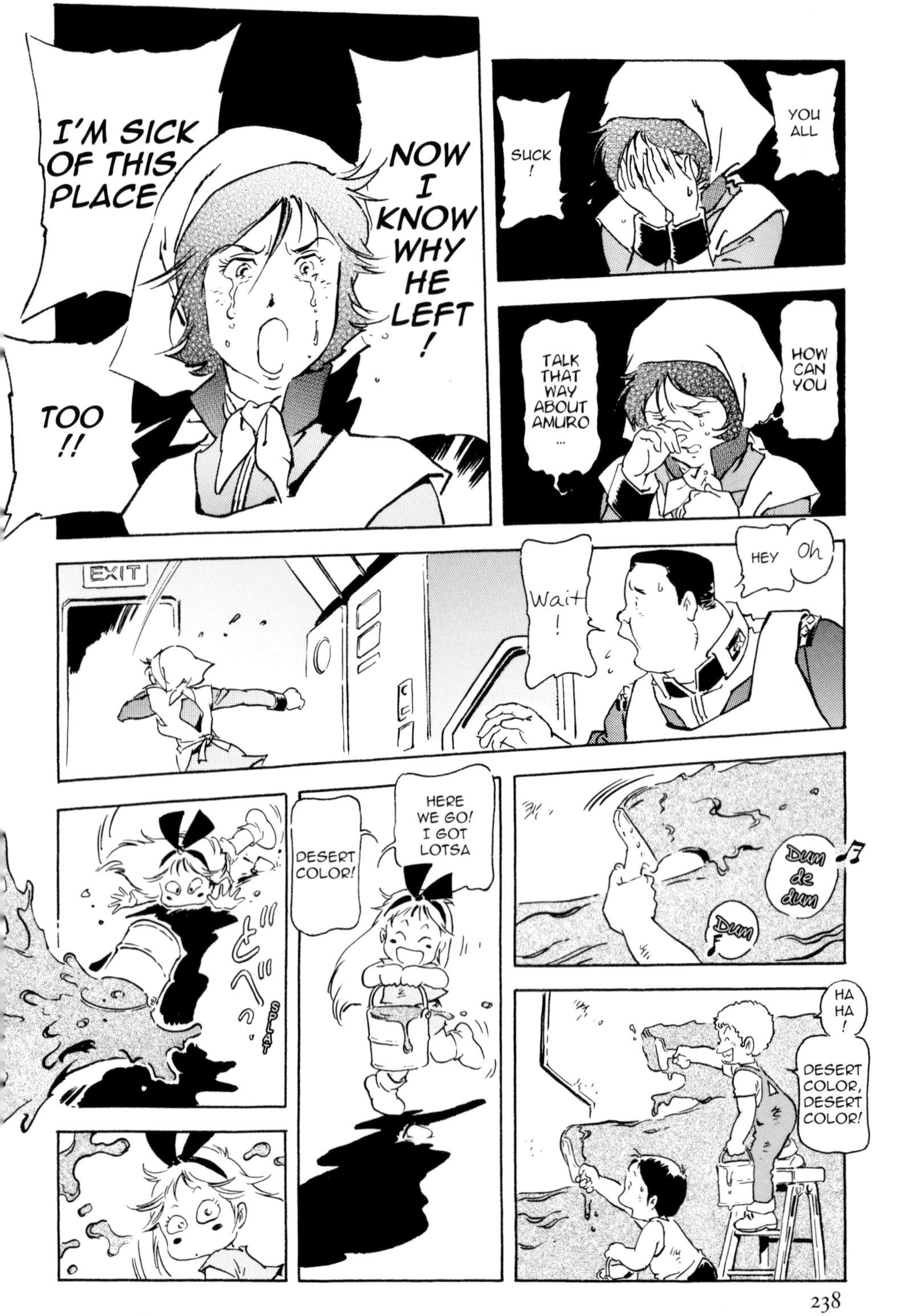
YOU ALL
SUCK!
HOW CAN YOU
TALK THAT WAY ABOUT AMURO ...
NOW I KNOW WHY HE LEFT!
I'M SICK OF THIS PLACE
TOO!!
HEY
Oh
Wait!
Dum de dum
Dum
HA HA!
DESERT COLOR, DESERT COLOR!
HERE WE GO! I GOT LOTSA
DESERT COLOR!
SPLAT

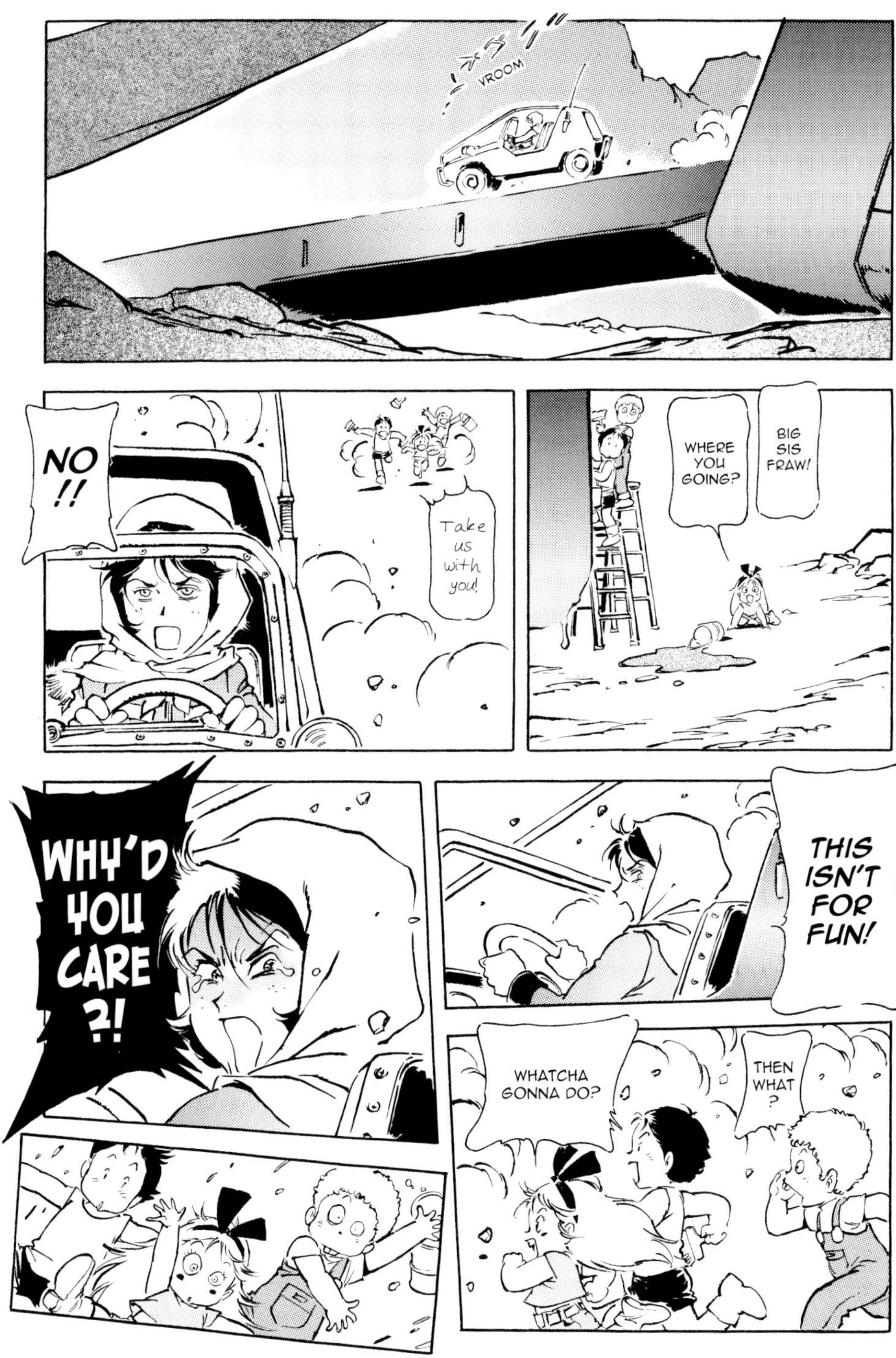
VROOM
BIG SIS FRAW!
WHERE YOU GOING?
Take us with you!
NO!!
THIS ISN'T FOR FUN!
WHY'D YOU CARE?!
THEN WHAT?
WHATCHA GONNA DO?

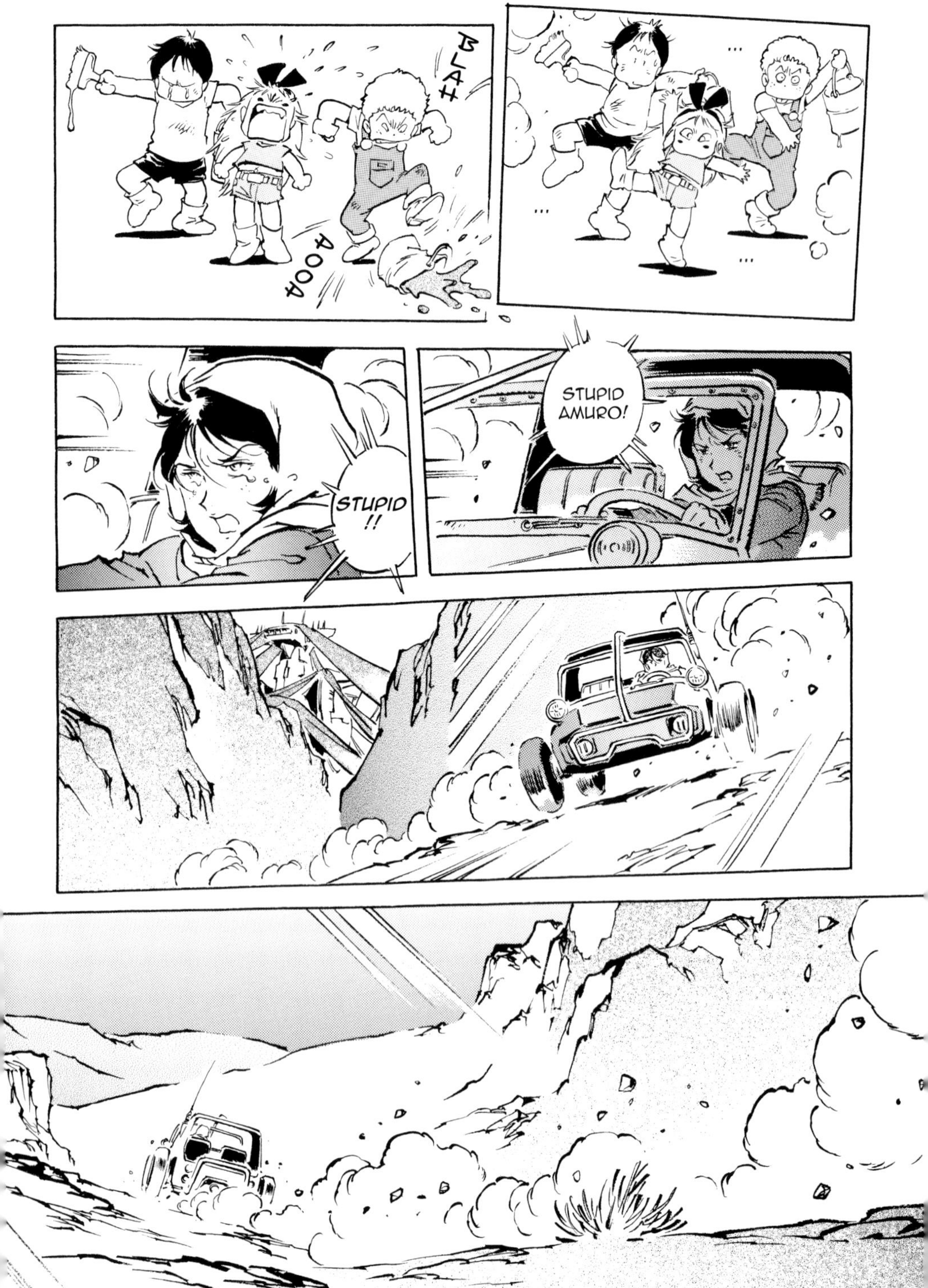
...
...
...
BLAH
STUPID AMURO!
STUPID !!

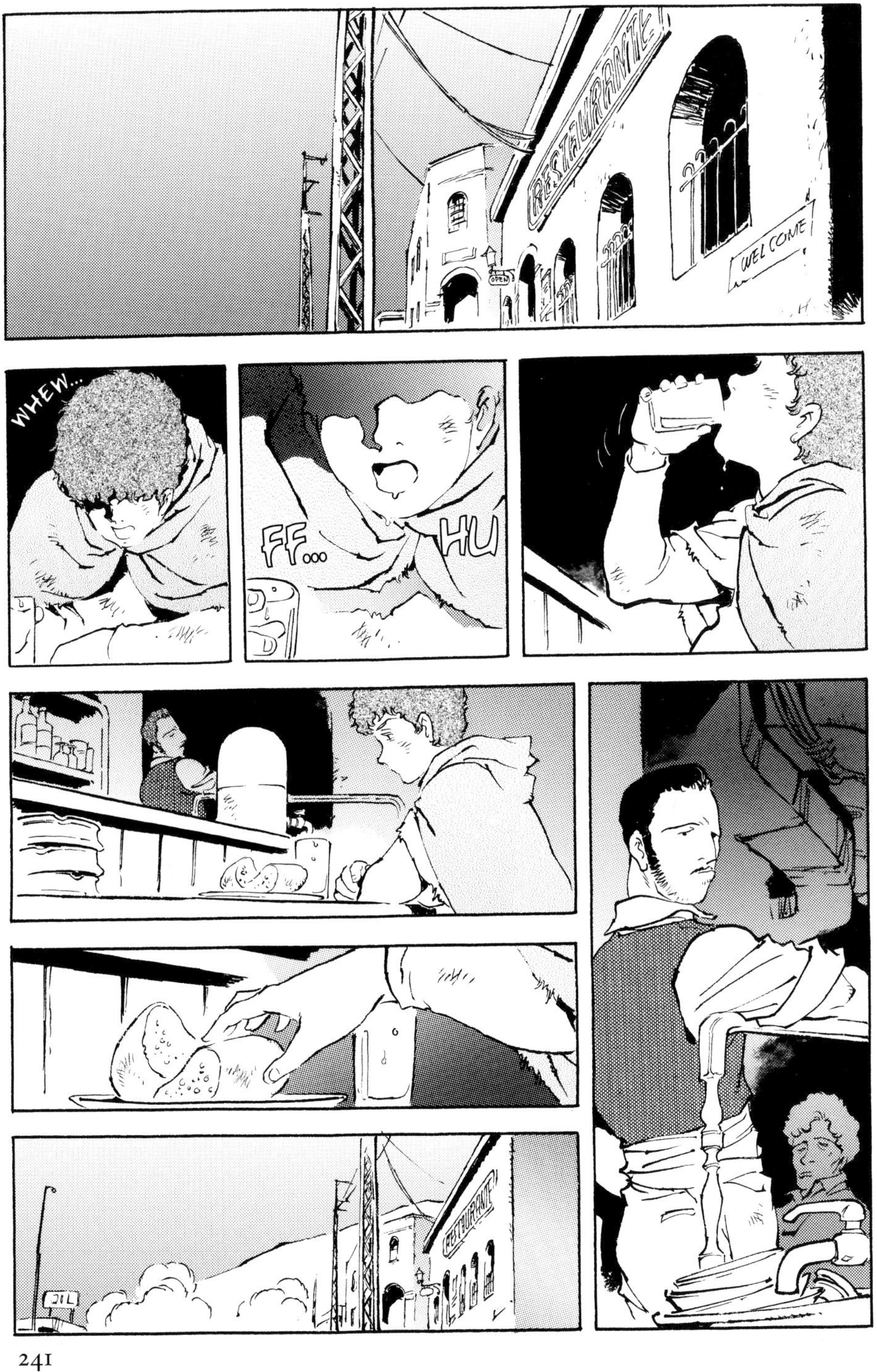
RESTAURANTE
WELCOME
OPEN
FF... HU
WHEW...
RESTAURANTE

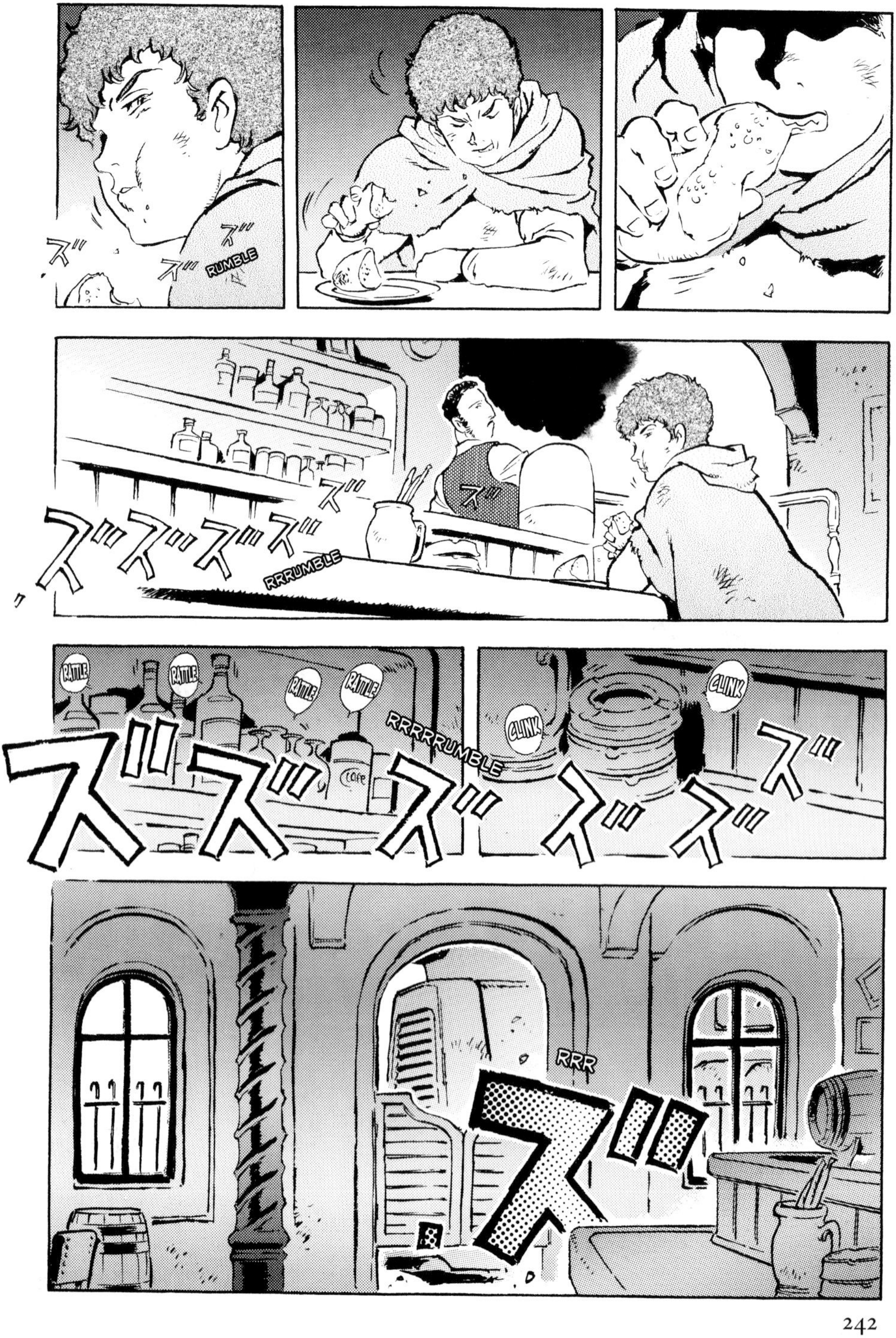
ズ
ズ
ズ
RUMBLE
ズ
ズ
ズズズズ
RRRUMBLE
CLINK
CLINK
ズズズズ
RATTLE
RATTLE
RATTLE
RATTLE
RRRRRUMBLE
ズズ
RRR
ズ

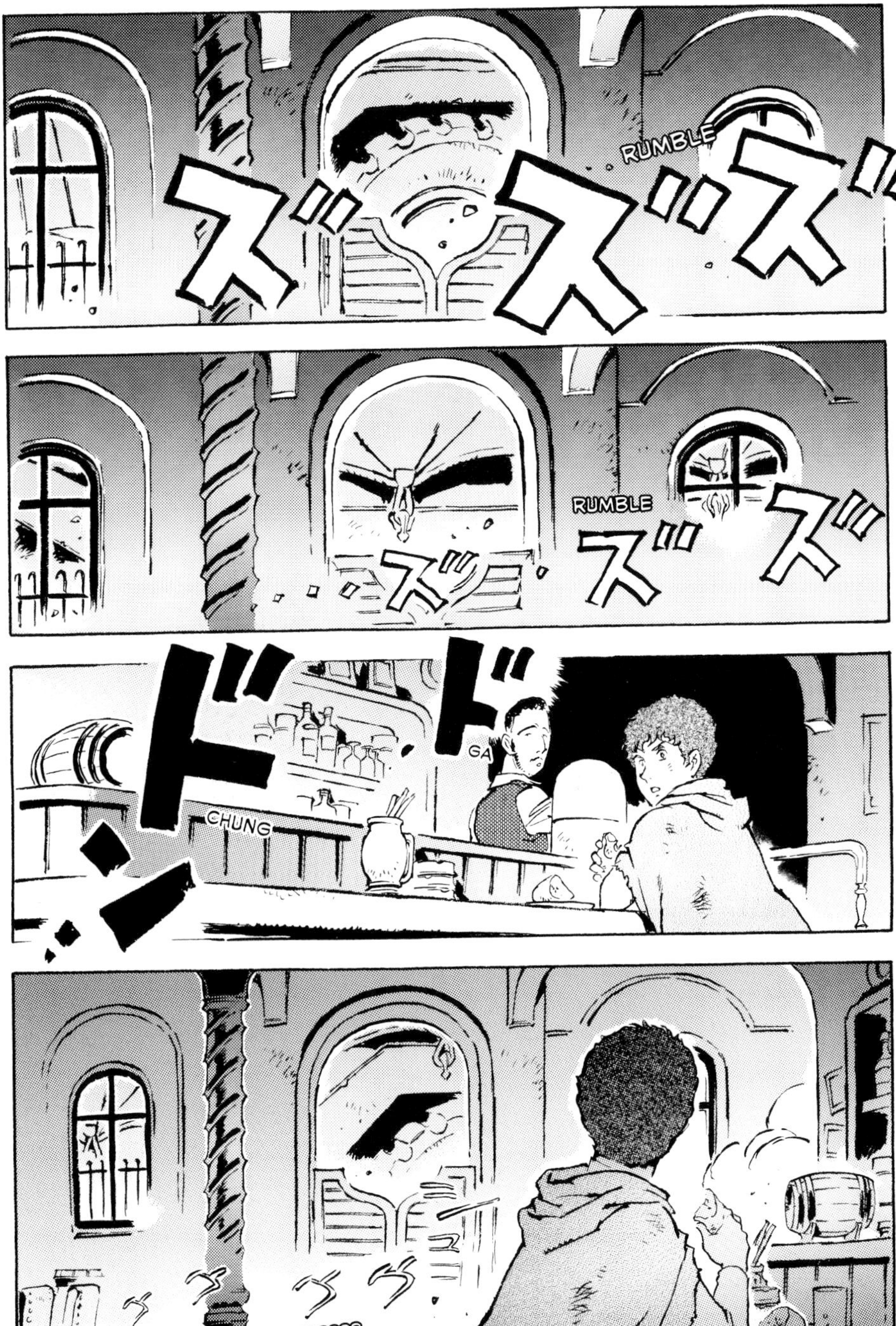
RUMBLE
RUMBLE
GA
CHUNG
HISSSSSS

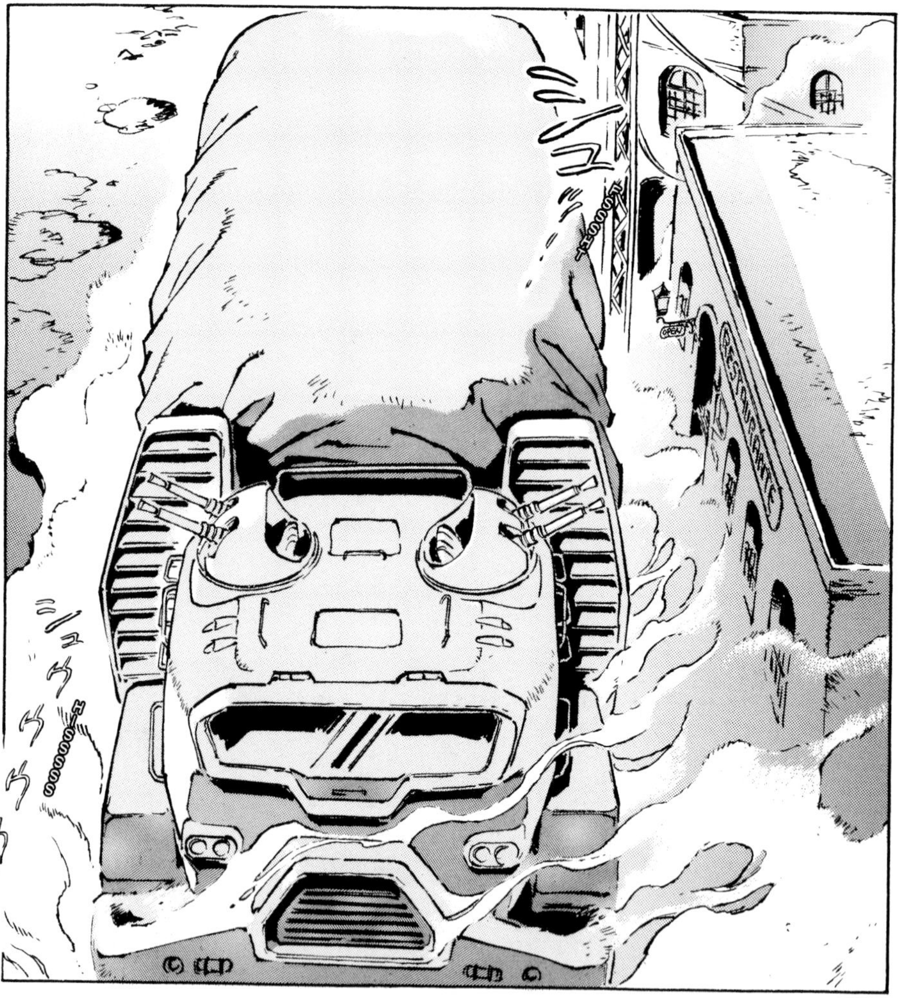
SSSSH!
OPEN
RESTAURANT
SSSSSSSH

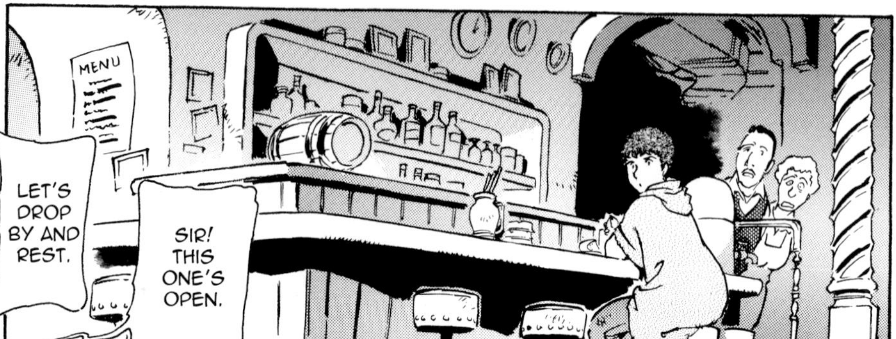
MENU
SIR! THIS ONE'S OPEN.
LET'S DROP BY AND REST.

WE'RE HERE TO CHILL SOME.

OLD MAN.

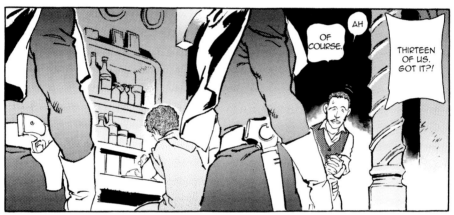

AH

OF COURSE.

THIRTEEN OF US. GOT IT?!

HOOO, FINALLY SOME SHADE.

I FEEL ALIVE AGAIN.

OVER HERE, LADY HA-MON!

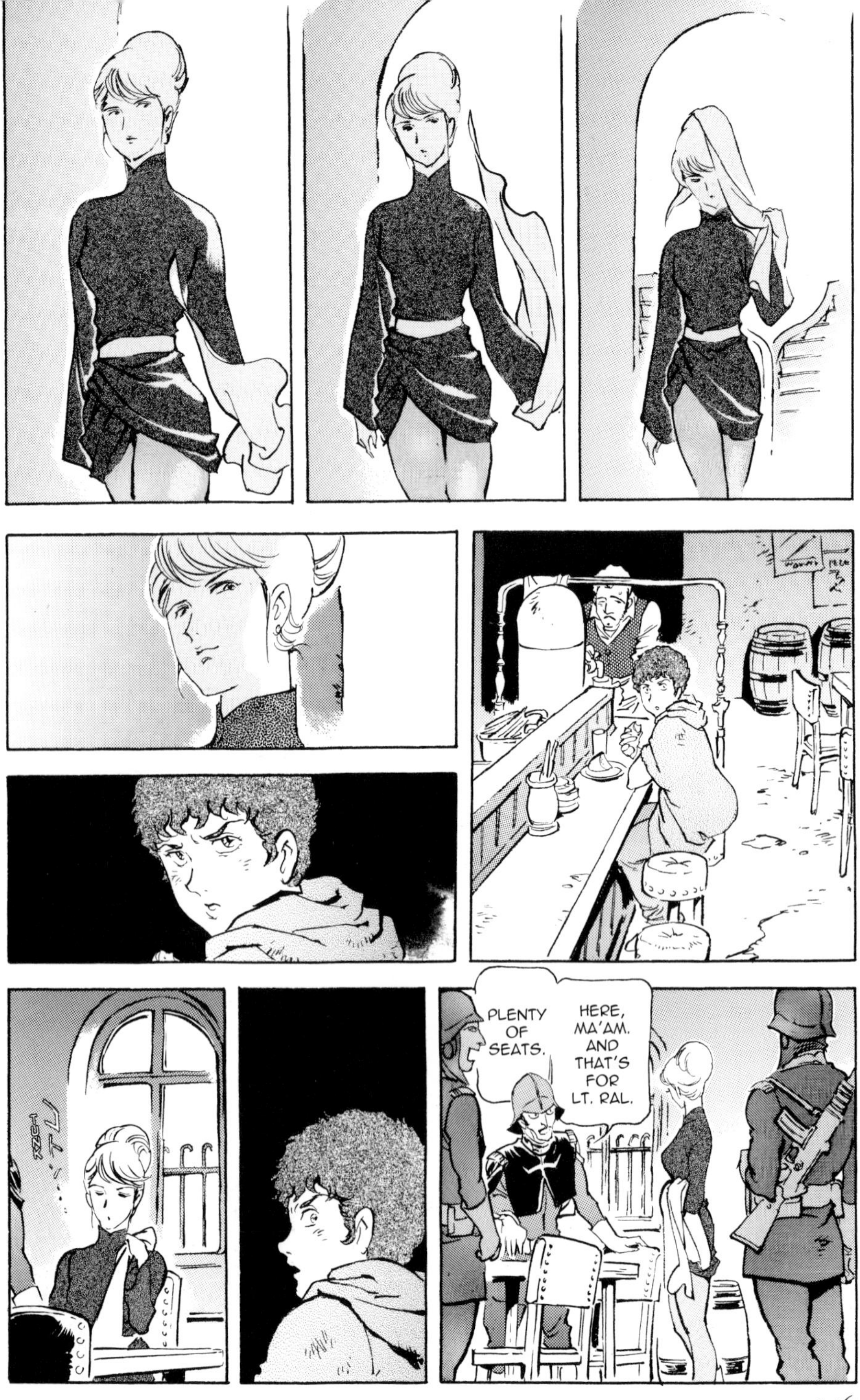
PLENTY OF SEATS.
HERE, MA'AM. AND THAT'S FOR LT. RAL.
TUNK

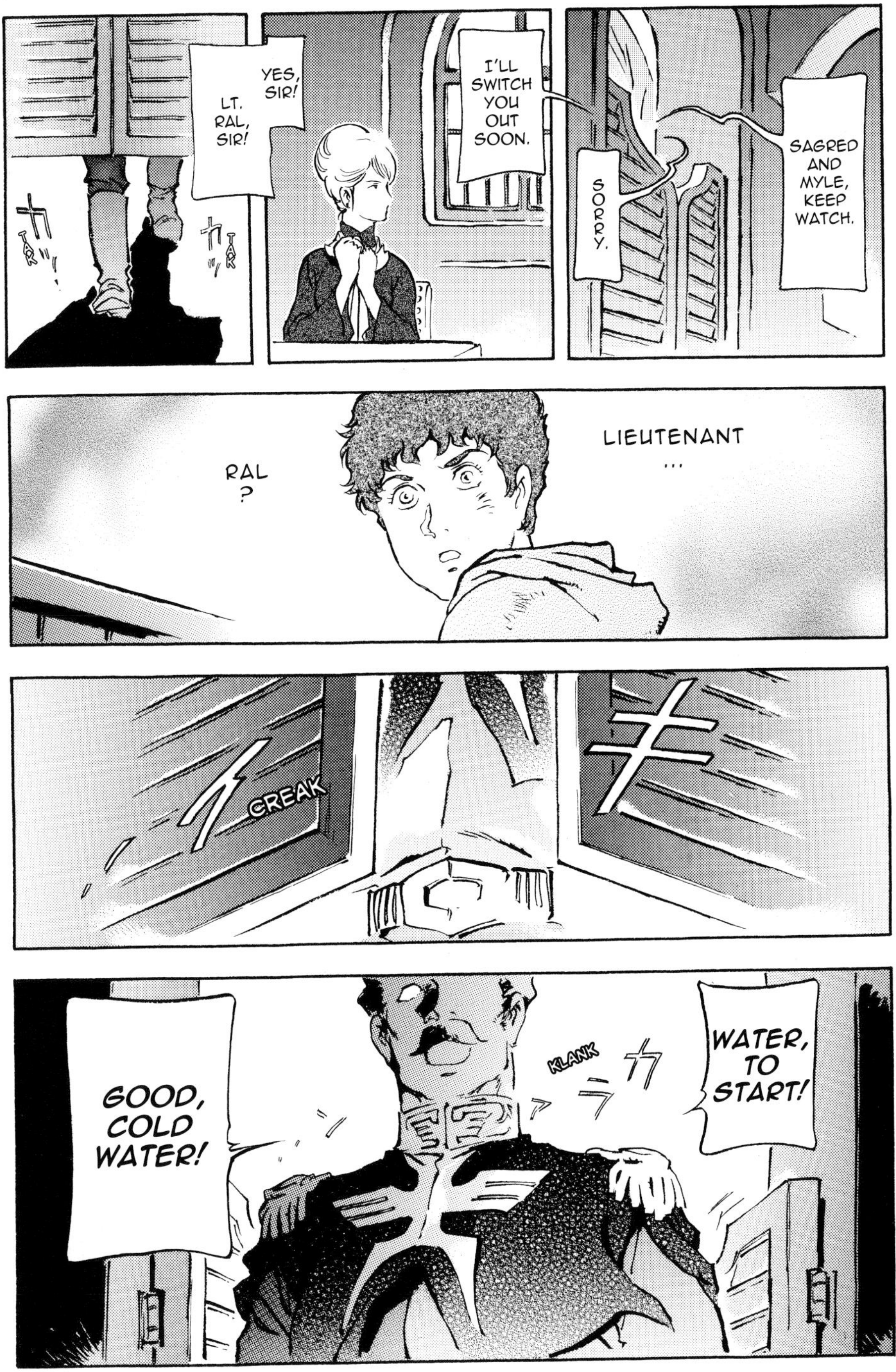

SAGRED AND MYLE, KEEP WATCH.
SORRY.
I'LL SWITCH YOU OUT SOON.
YES, SIR!
LT. RAL, SIR!
TAR
TAR
LIEUTENANT ...
RAL ?
CREAK
WATER, TO START!
KLANK
GOOD, COLD WATER!

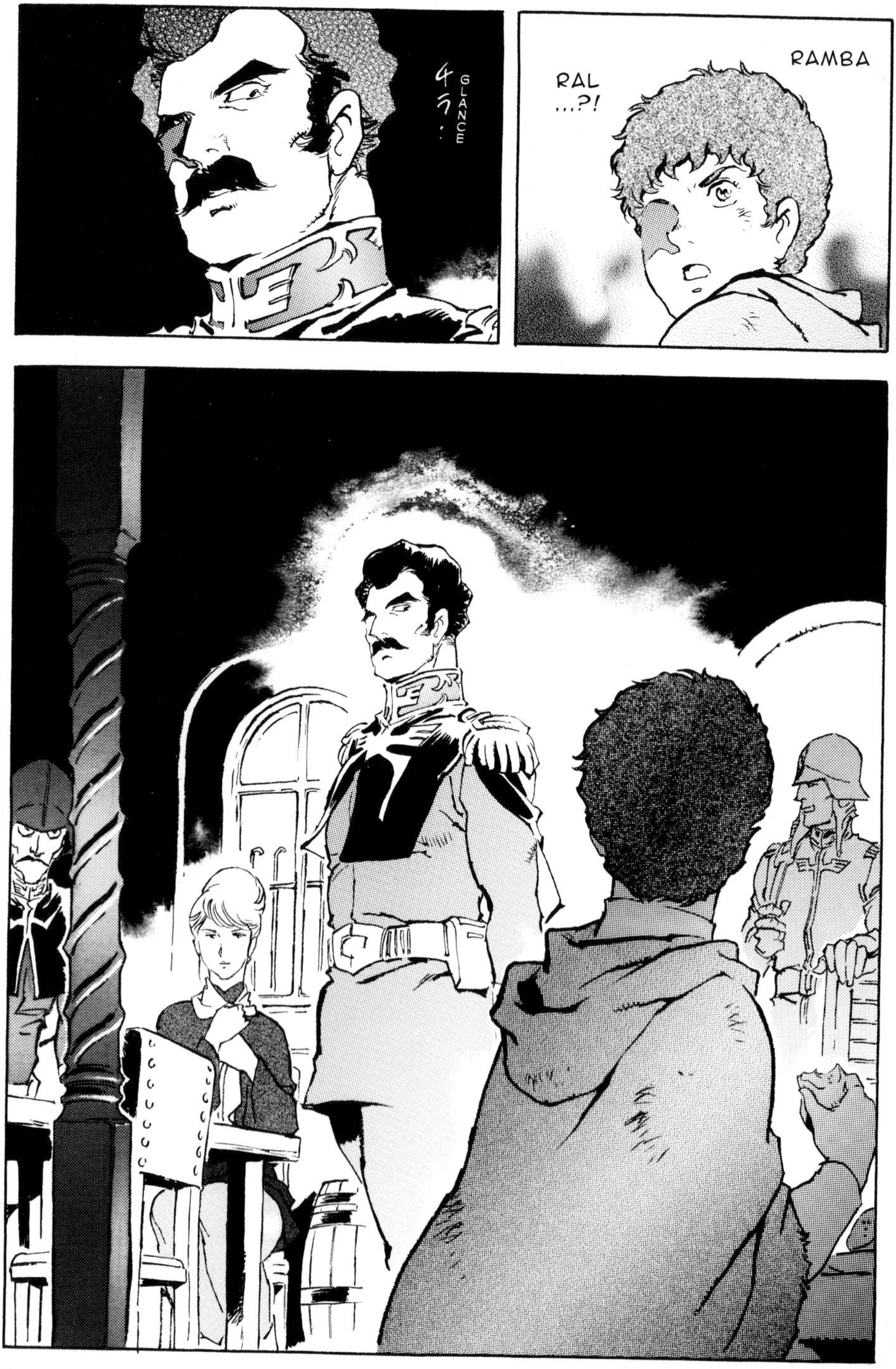
RAMBA
RAL ...?!
チラ・
GLANCE

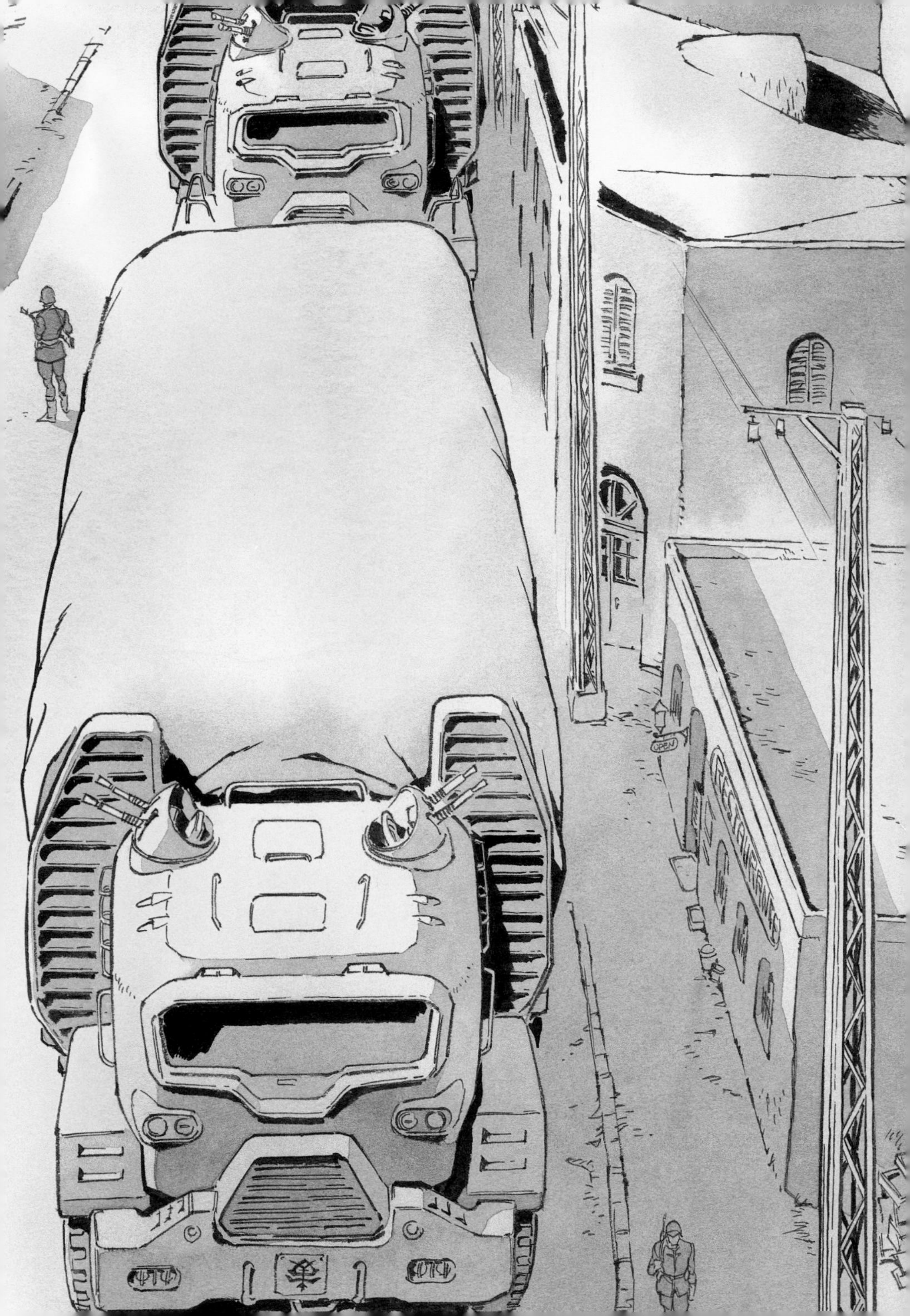
OPEN

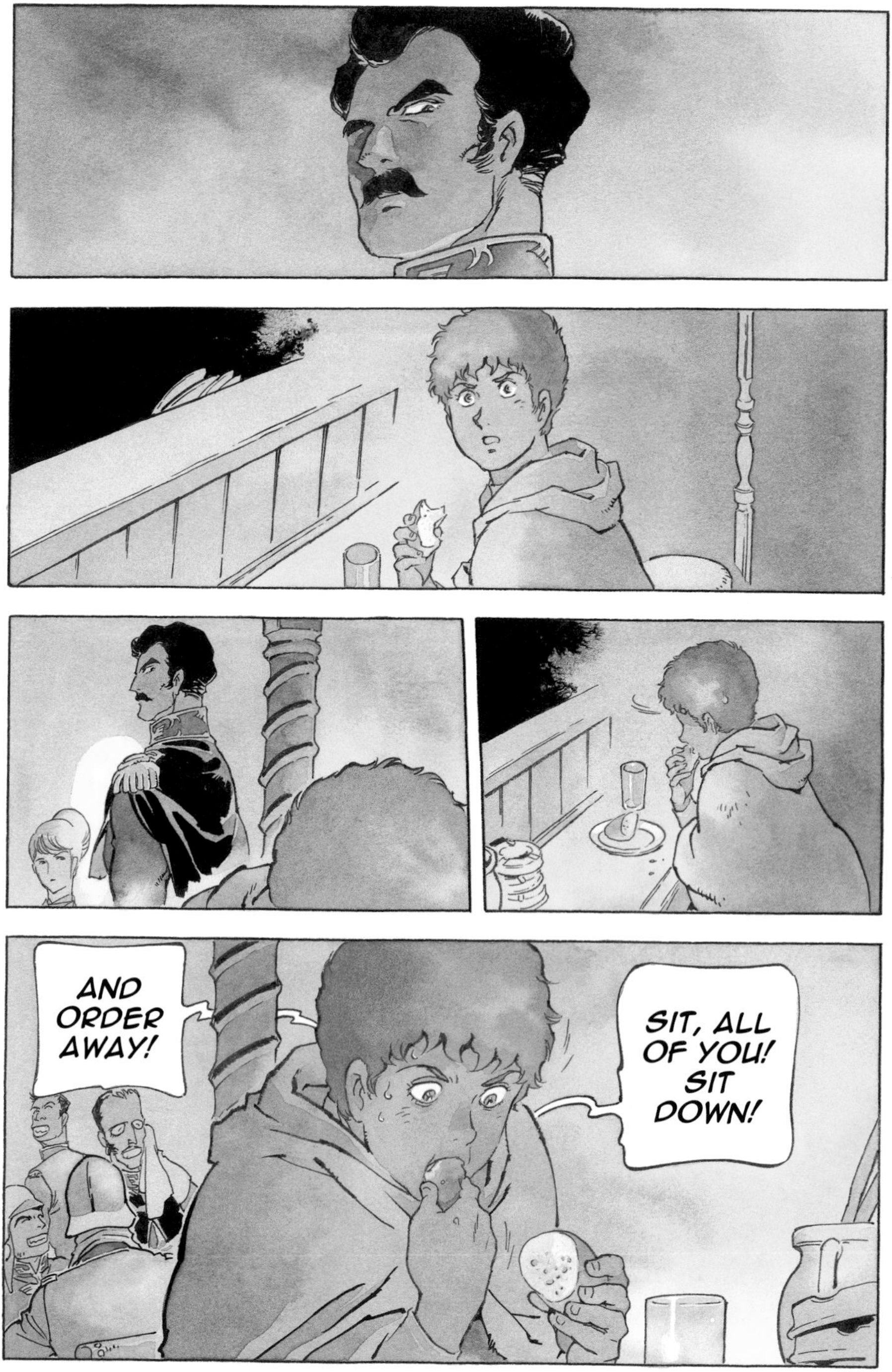
SIT, ALL OF YOU! SIT DOWN!
AND ORDER AWAY!

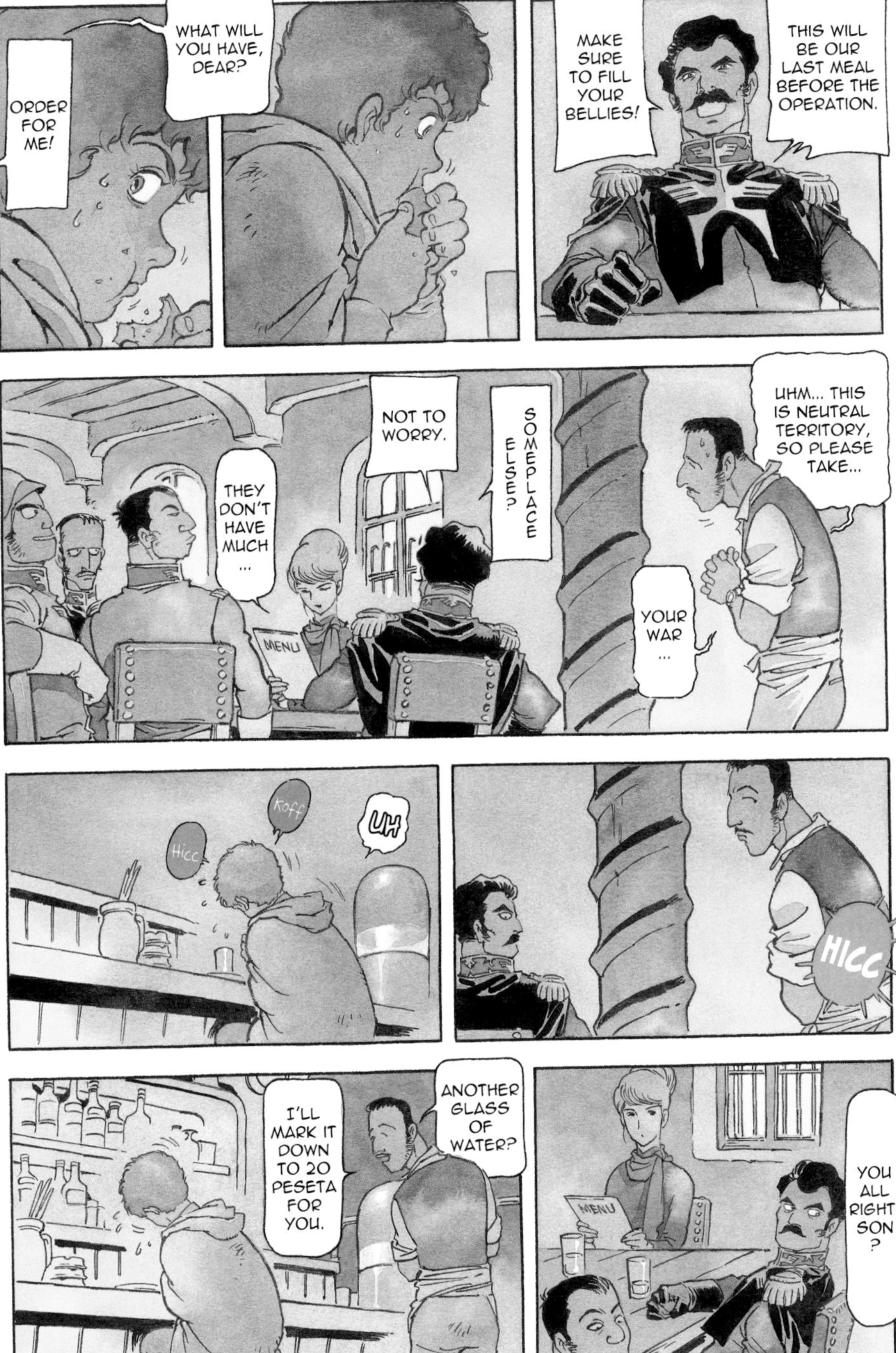
THIS WILL BE OUR LAST MEAL BEFORE THE OPERATION.
MAKE SURE TO FILL YOUR BELLIES!
WHAT WILL YOU HAVE, DEAR?
ORDER FOR ME!
UHM... THIS IS NEUTRAL TERRITORY, SO PLEASE TAKE...
YOUR WAR ...
SOMEPLACE ELSE?
NOT TO WORRY.
THEY DON'T HAVE MUCH ...
MENU
HICC
UH
Koff
Hicc
YOU ALL RIGHT, SON ?
MENU
ANOTHER GLASS OF WATER?
I'LL MARK IT DOWN TO 20 PESETA FOR YOU.

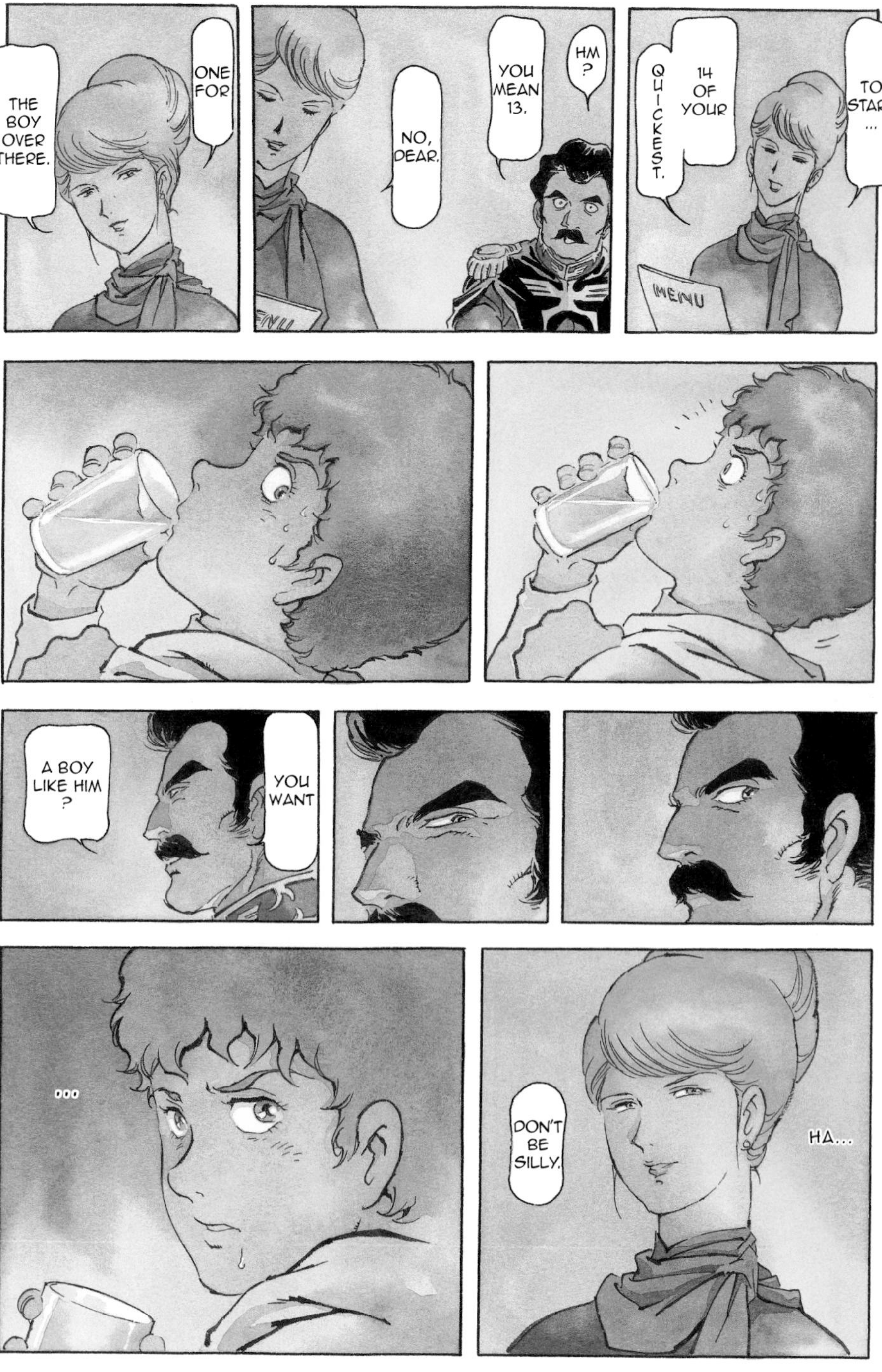

TO START ...
14 OF YOUR QUICKEST.
HM?
YOU MEAN 13.
NO, DEAR.
ONE FOR
THE BOY OVER THERE.
YOU WANT
A BOY LIKE HIM?
HA...
DON'T BE SILLY.
...

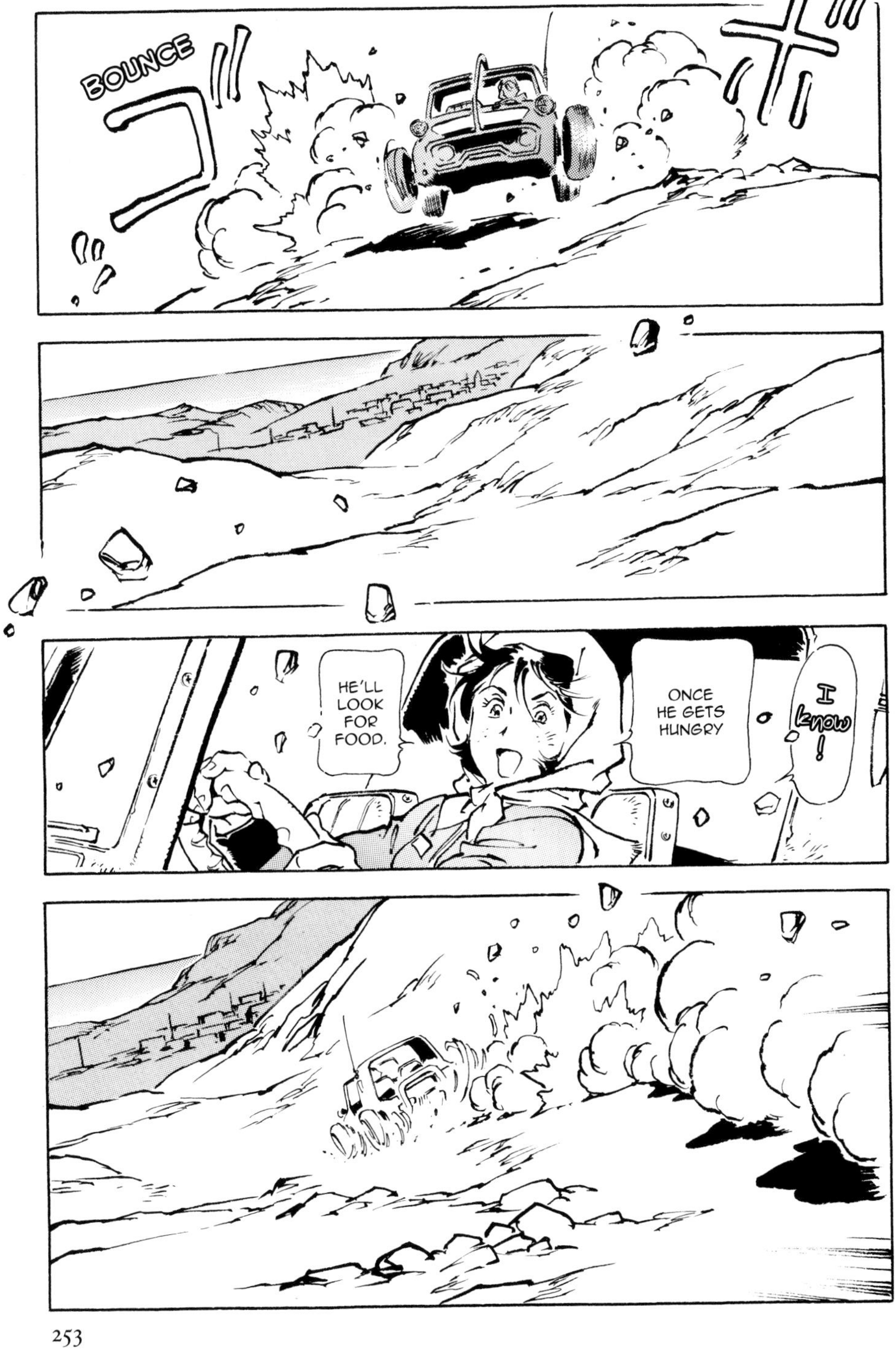
BOUNCE
I know!
ONCE HE GETS HUNGRY
HE'LL LOOK FOR FOOD.

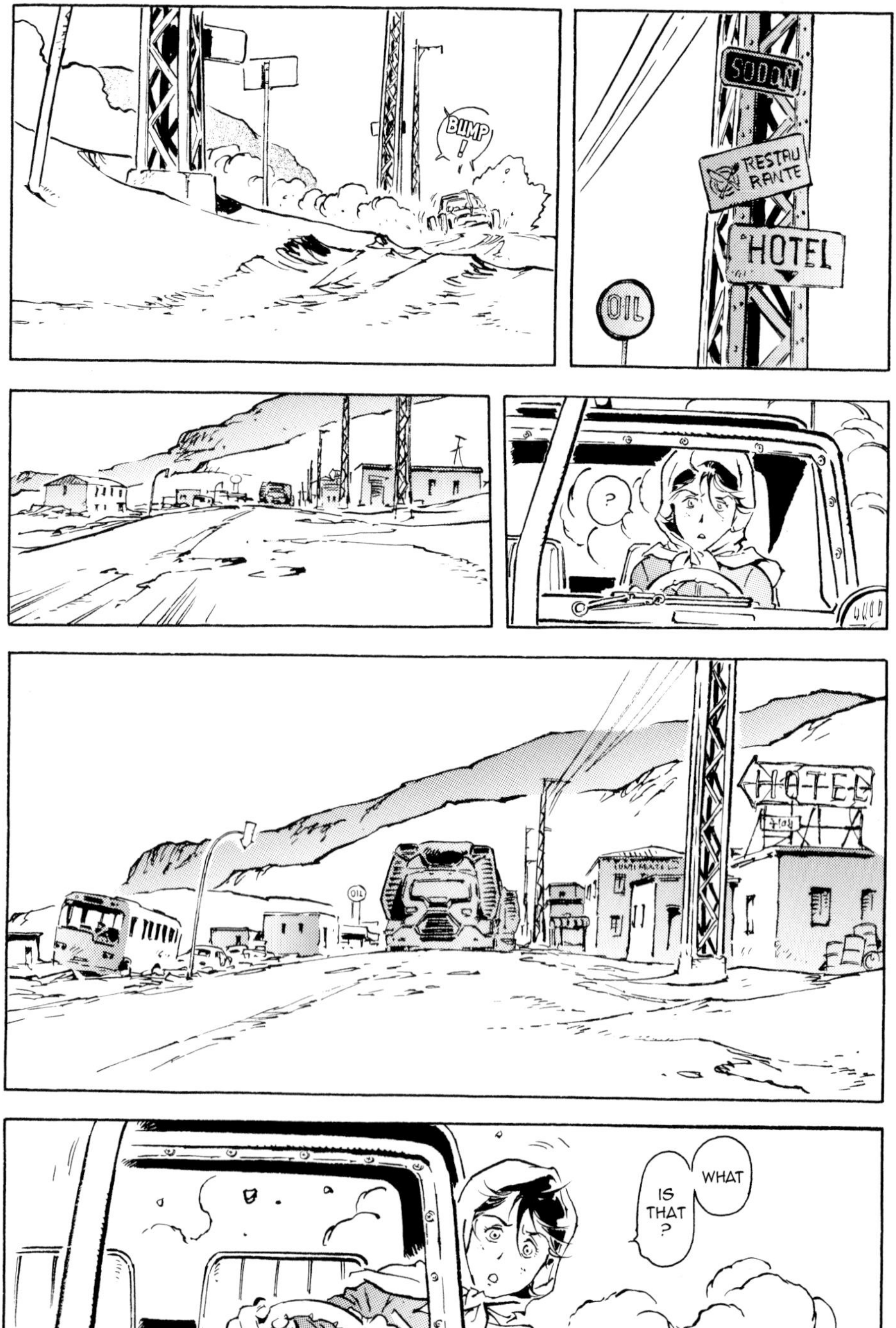
SODON
RESTAU RANTE
HOTEL
OIL
BUMP !
?
HOTEL
OIL
WHAT IS THAT ?

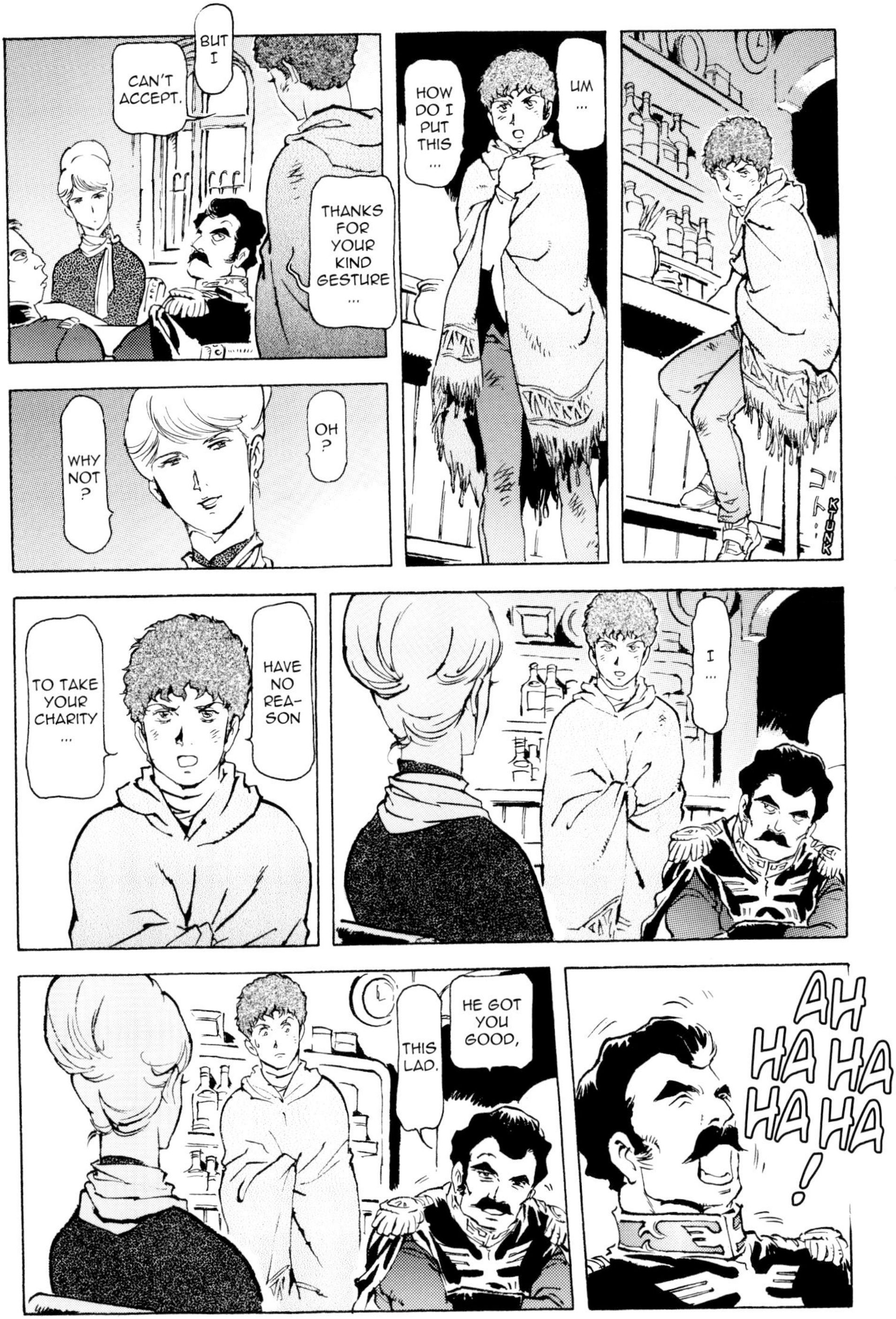
KLUNK
UM ...
HOW DO I PUT THIS ...
THANKS FOR YOUR KIND GESTURE ...
BUT I
CAN'T ACCEPT.
OH?
WHY NOT?
I ...
HAVE NO REA-SON
TO TAKE YOUR CHARITY ...
AH HA HA HA HA HA!
HE GOT YOU GOOD,
THIS LAD.

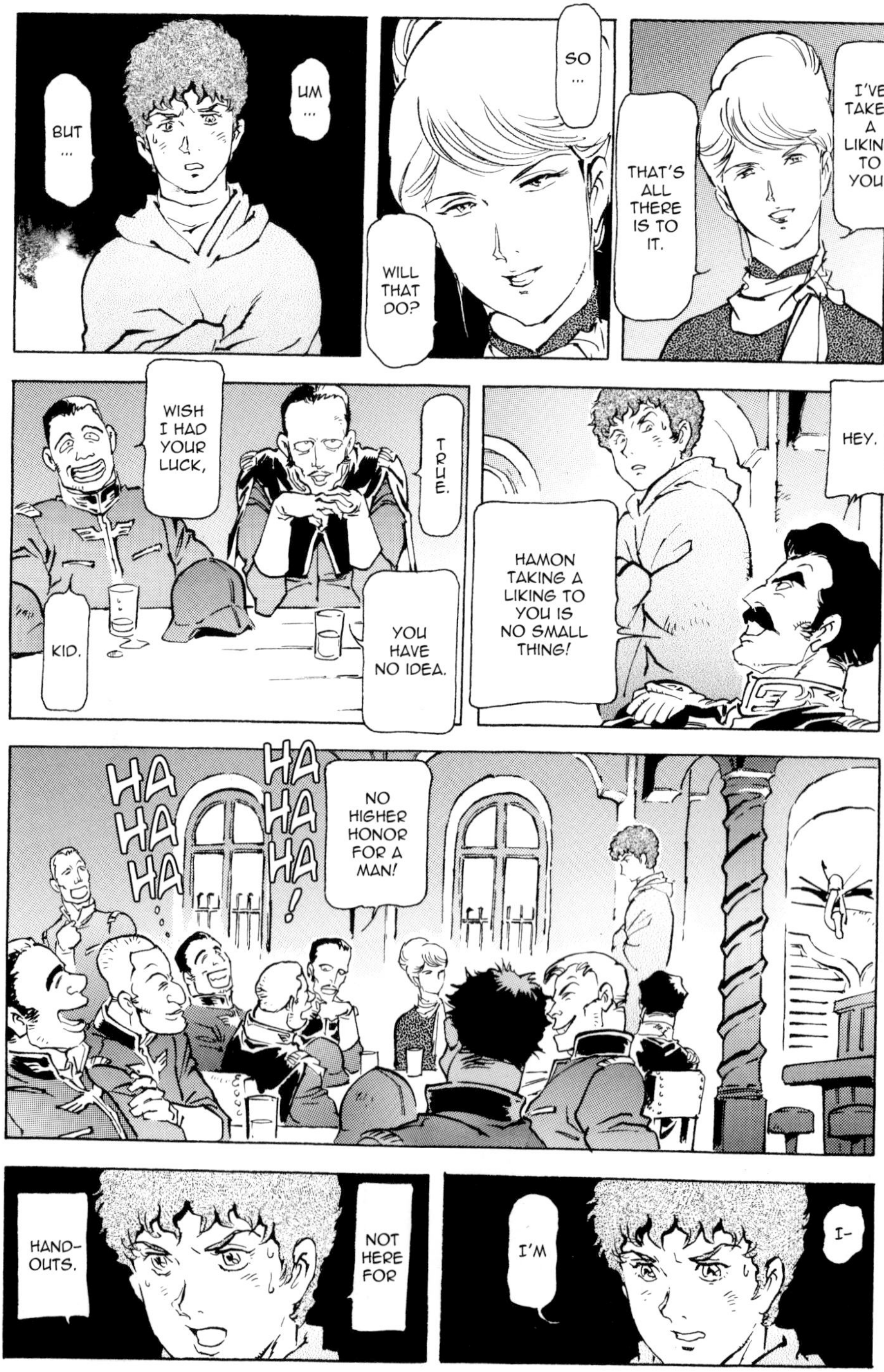
I'VE TAKEN A LIKING TO YOU.
THAT'S ALL THERE IS TO IT.
SO ...
WILL THAT DO?
UM ...
BUT ...
HEY.
HAMON TAKING A LIKING TO YOU IS NO SMALL THING!
TRUE.
WISH I HAD YOUR LUCK,
YOU HAVE NO IDEA.
KID.
NO HIGHER HONOR FOR A MAN!
HA HA HA HA!
HA HA HA HA
I-
I'M
NOT HERE FOR
HAND-OUTS.

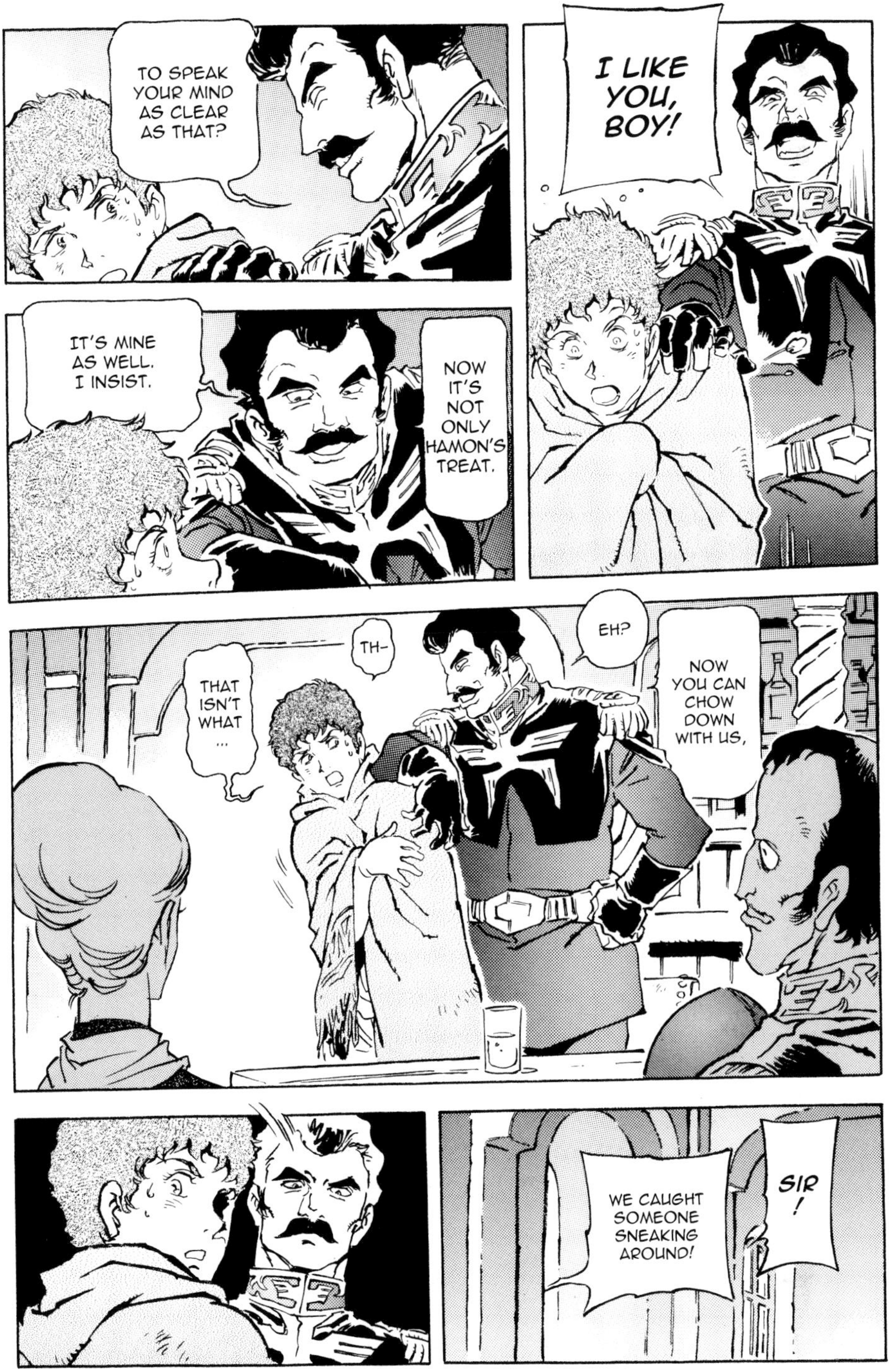
I LIKE YOU, BOY!
TO SPEAK YOUR MIND AS CLEAR AS THAT?
NOW IT'S NOT ONLY HAMON'S TREAT.
IT'S MINE AS WELL. I INSIST.
NOW YOU CAN CHOW DOWN WITH US,
EH?
TH-
THAT ISN'T WHAT ...
SIR!
WE CAUGHT SOMEONE SNEAKING AROUND!

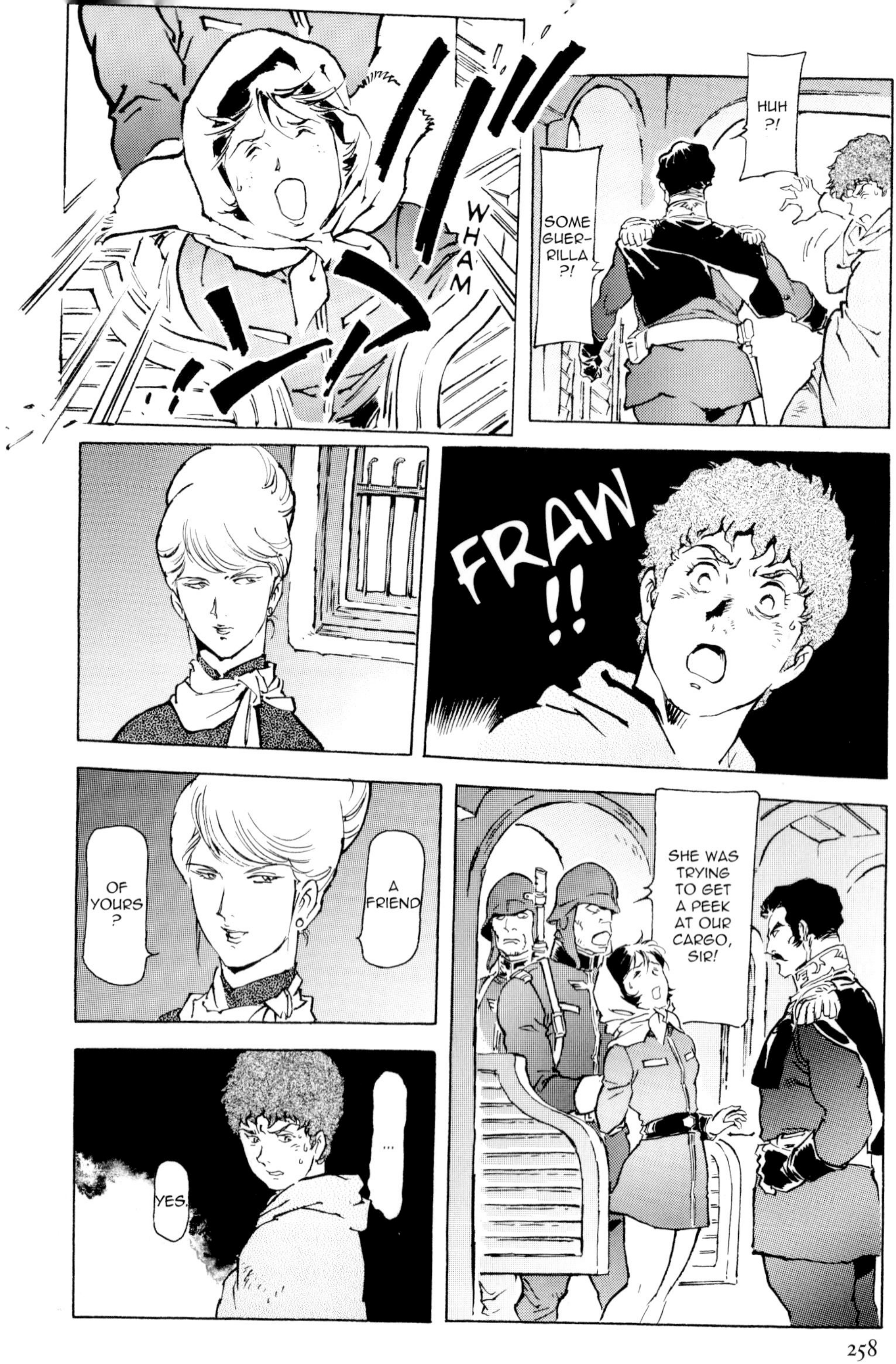
HUH ?!
SOME GUERRILLA ?!
WHAM
FRAW !!
SHE WAS TRYING TO GET A PEEK AT OUR CARGO, SIR!
A FRIEND
OF YOURS ?
...
YES.

SOMETHING'S OFF.

ARE YOU SURE?

NO MISTAKE, SIR!

AH

MENU

SHE'S JUST A CHILD.

BUT, SIR, SHE'S WEARING A FEDERATION MILITARY UNIFORM!

SHE'S HIS GIRLFRIEND.

AND IT SEEMS

IT DOES APPEAR TO BE THEIRS.

HAMON?

WHAT SAY YOU,

AMURO!!

OHO

MENU

...

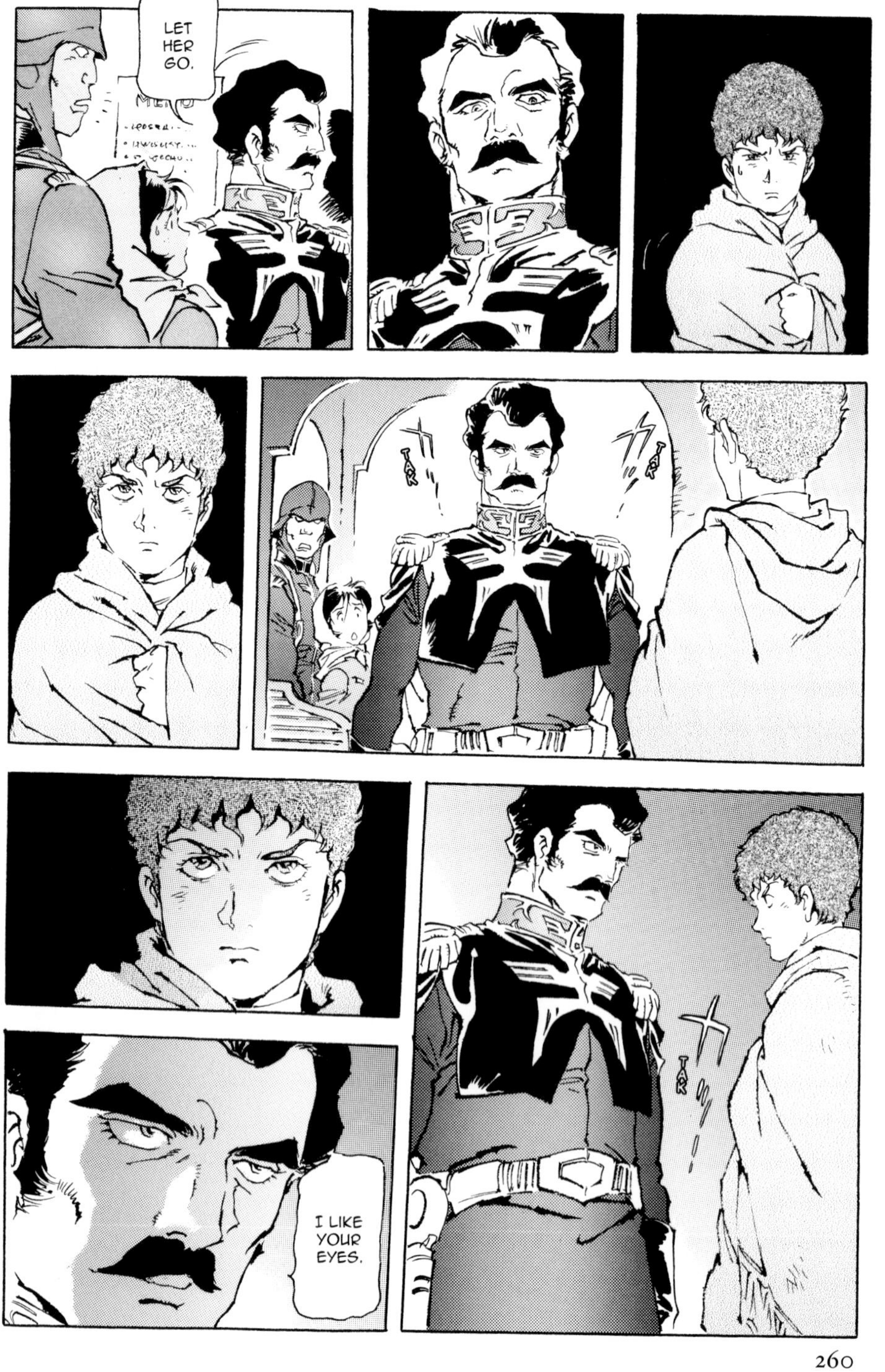
LET HER GO.
TAK
TAK
TAK
I LIKE YOUR EYES.

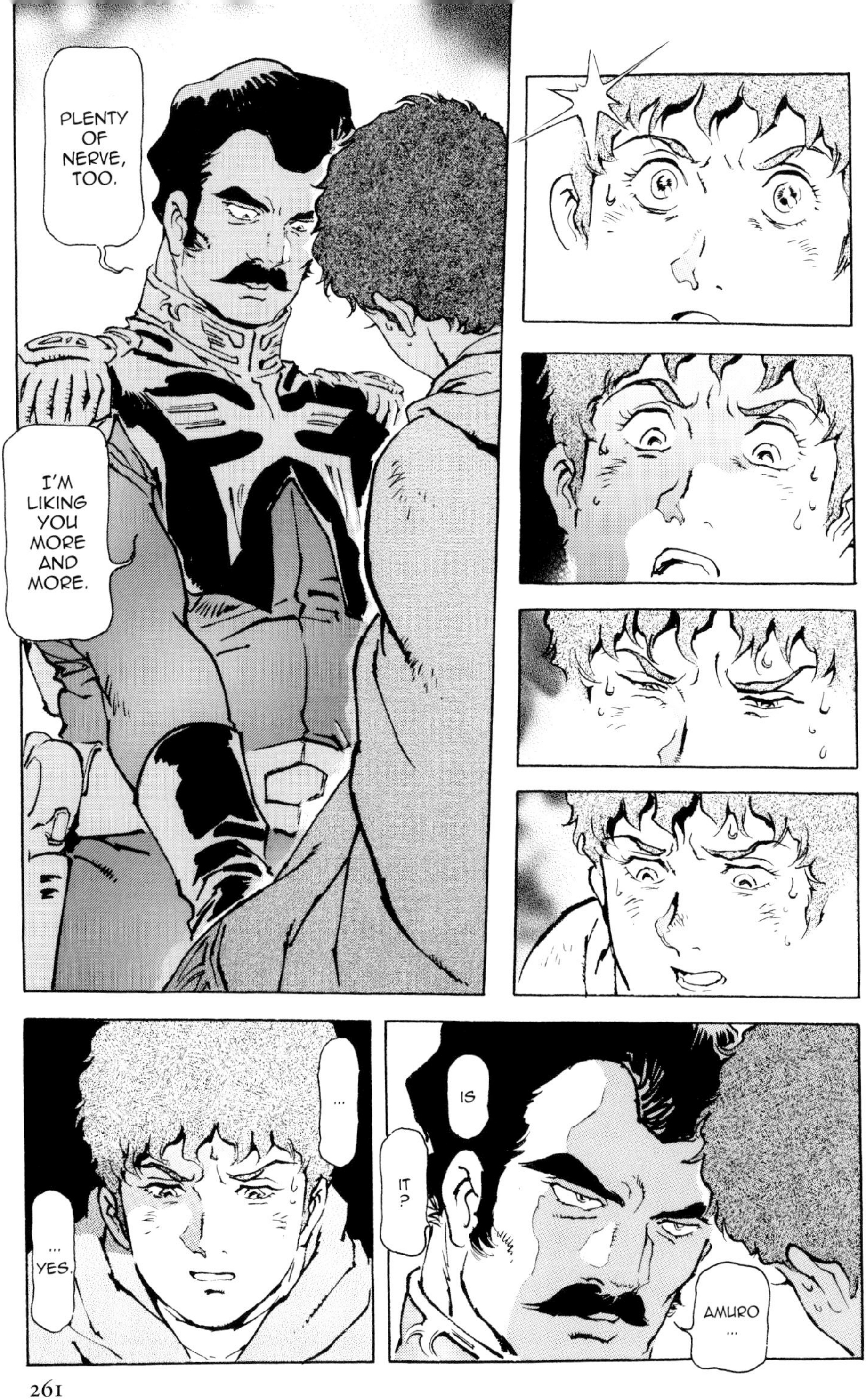
PLENTY OF NERVE, TOO.
I'M LIKING YOU MORE AND MORE.
IS
IT?
AMURO ...
...
... YES.

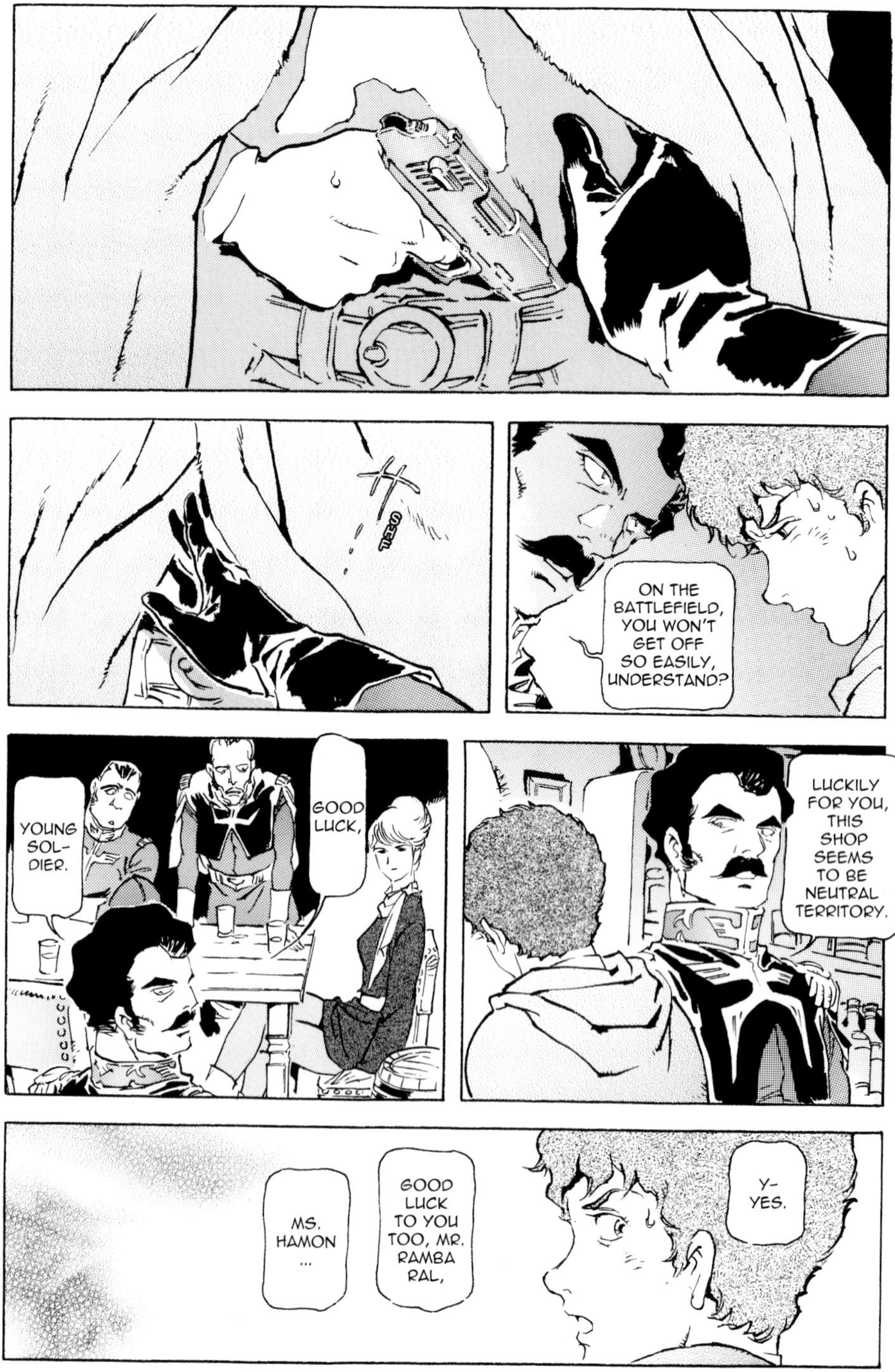
ON THE BATTLEFIELD, YOU WON'T GET OFF SO EASILY, UNDERSTAND?
LUCKILY FOR YOU, THIS SHOP SEEMS TO BE NEUTRAL TERRITORY.
GOOD LUCK,
YOUNG SOL-DIER.
Y-YES.
GOOD LUCK TO YOU TOO, MR. RAMBA RAL,
MS. HAMON ...

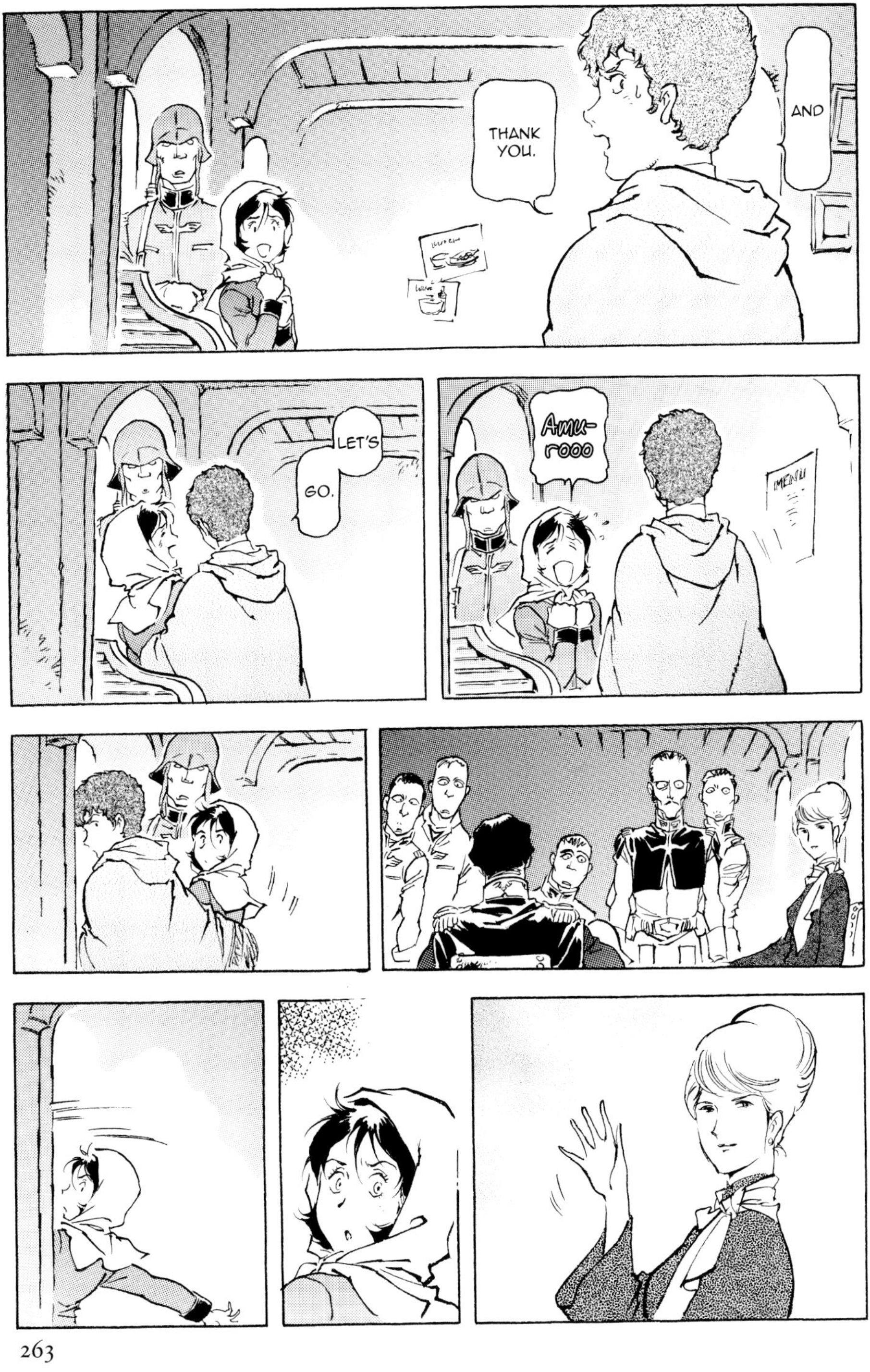
AND
THANK YOU.
Amu-rooo
LET'S GO.

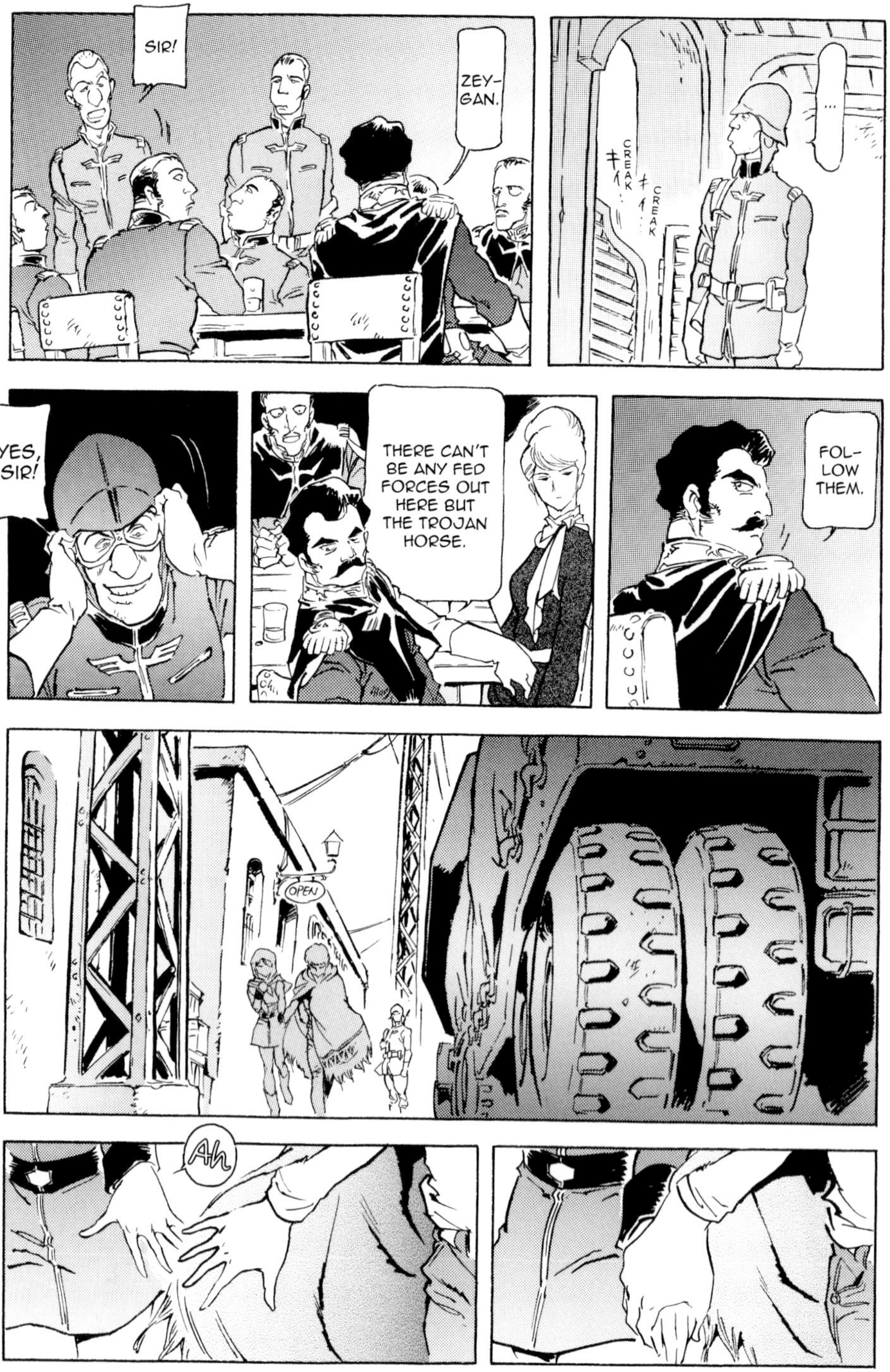
...
キィ…
CREAK
キィ…
CREAK
ZEY-GAN.
SIR!
FOL-LOW THEM.
THERE CAN'T BE ANY FED FORCES OUT HERE BUT THE TROJAN HORSE.
YES, SIR!
OPEN
Ah

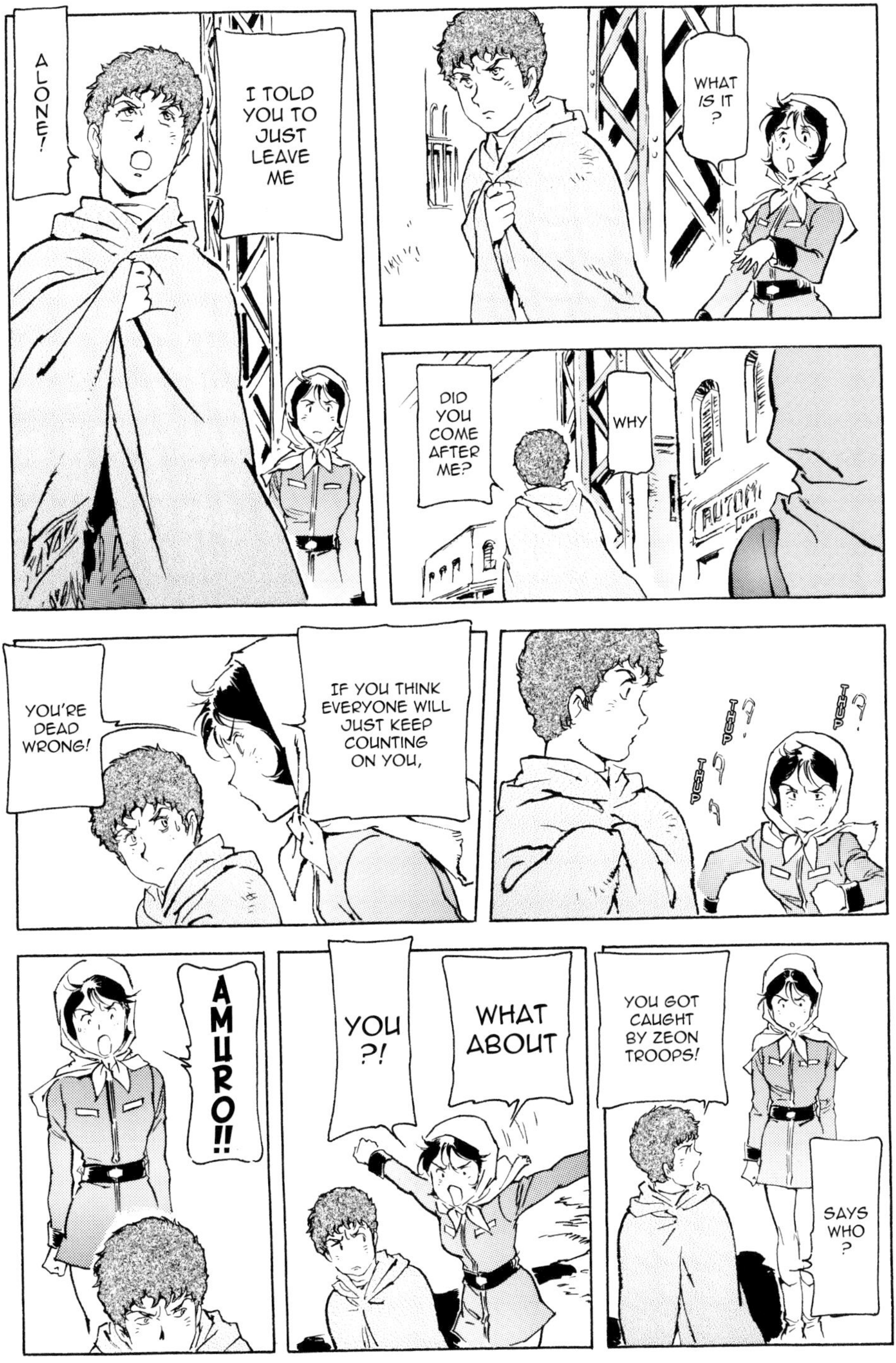
WHAT IS IT?
WHY
DID YOU COME AFTER ME?
I TOLD YOU TO JUST LEAVE ME
ALONE!
THUP
THUP
THUP
IF YOU THINK EVERYONE WILL JUST KEEP COUNTING ON YOU,
YOU'RE DEAD WRONG!
YOU GOT CAUGHT BY ZEON TROOPS!
SAYS WHO?
WHAT ABOUT
YOU?!
AMURO!!

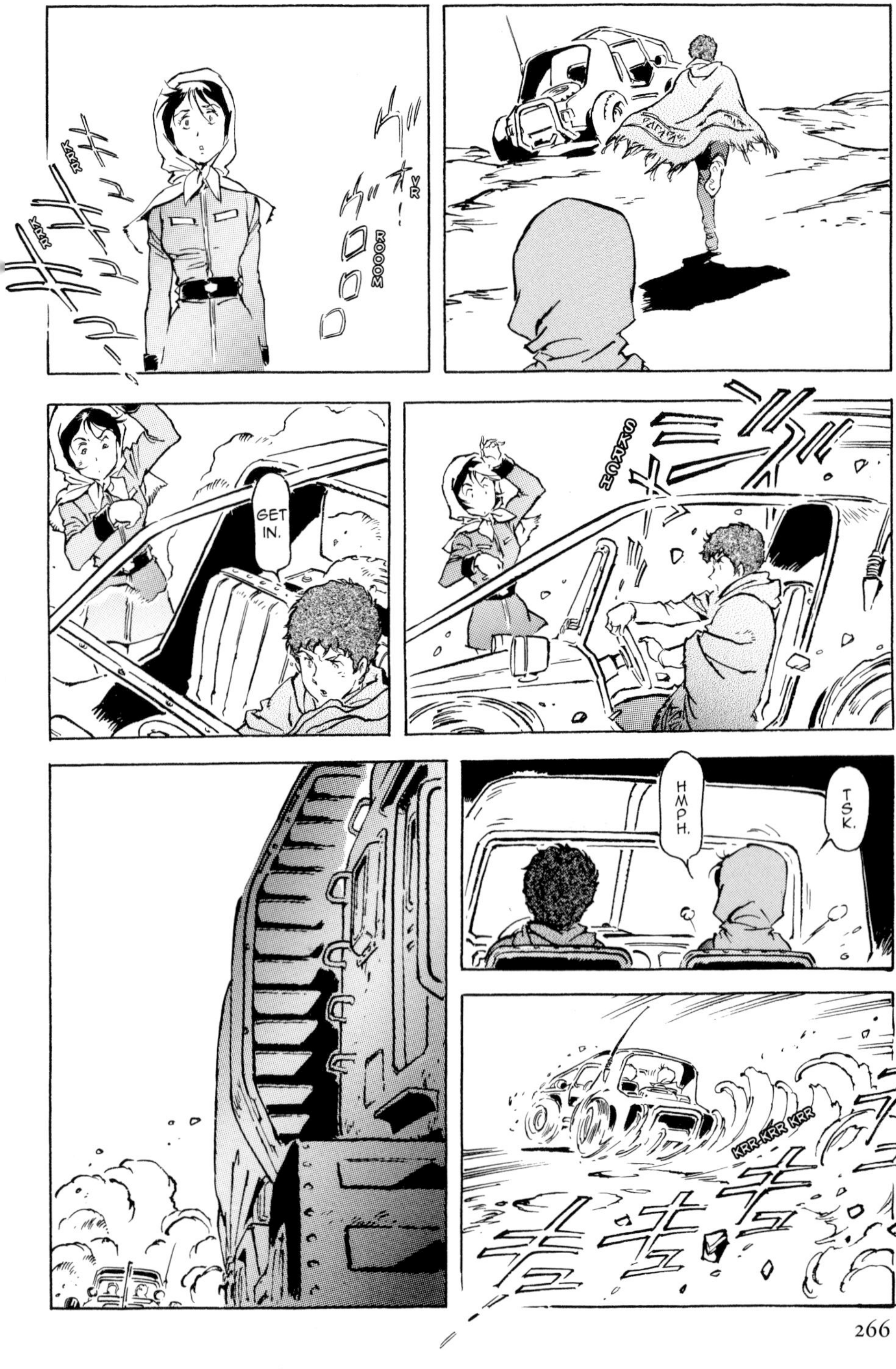
VR
ROOOM
KRRK
KRRK
SKRCH
GET IN.
TSK.
HMPH.
KRR-KRR KRR

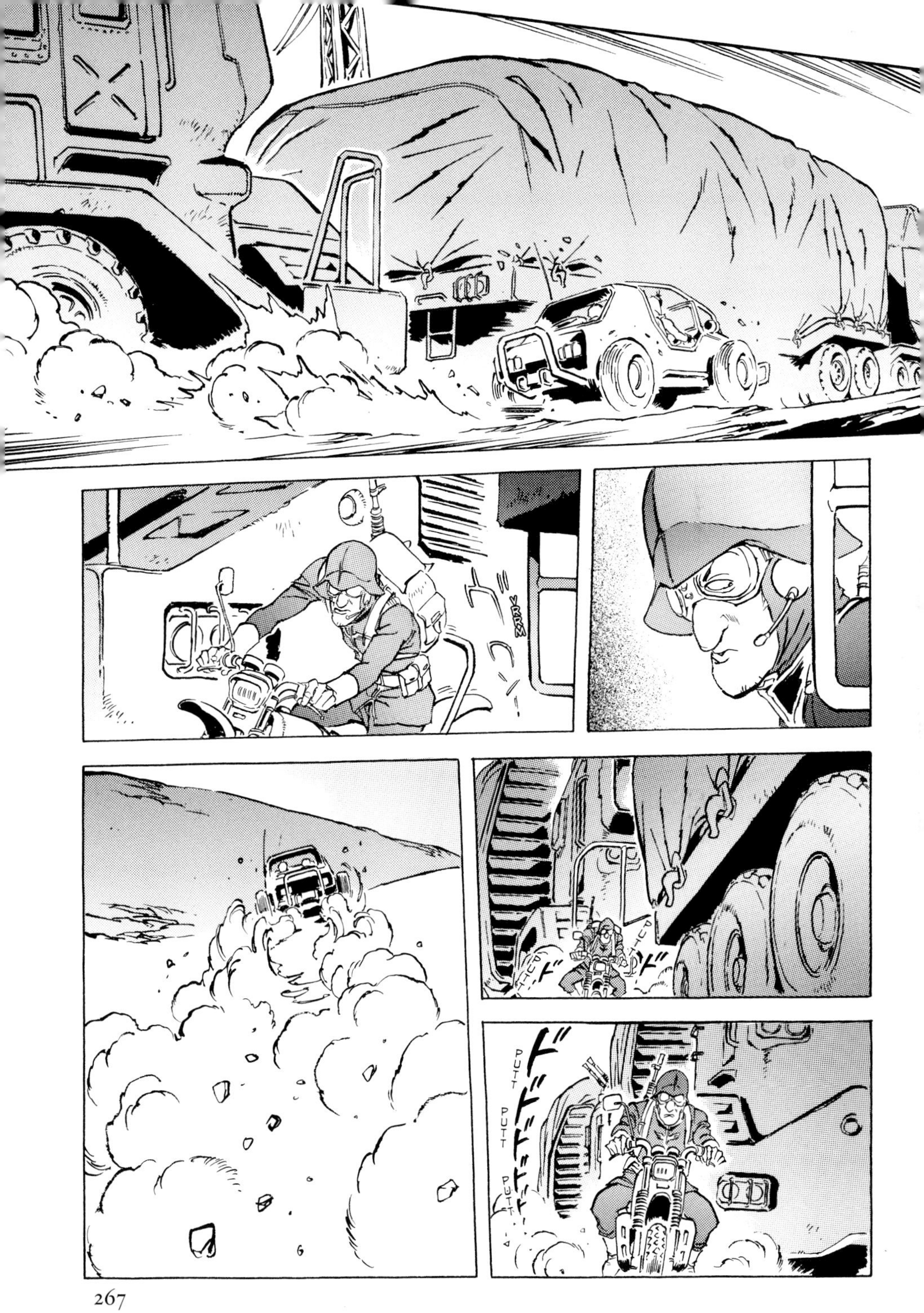
VRRM
PUTT
PUTT
ド
ド
PUTT
PUTT
PUTT
ドドドドド

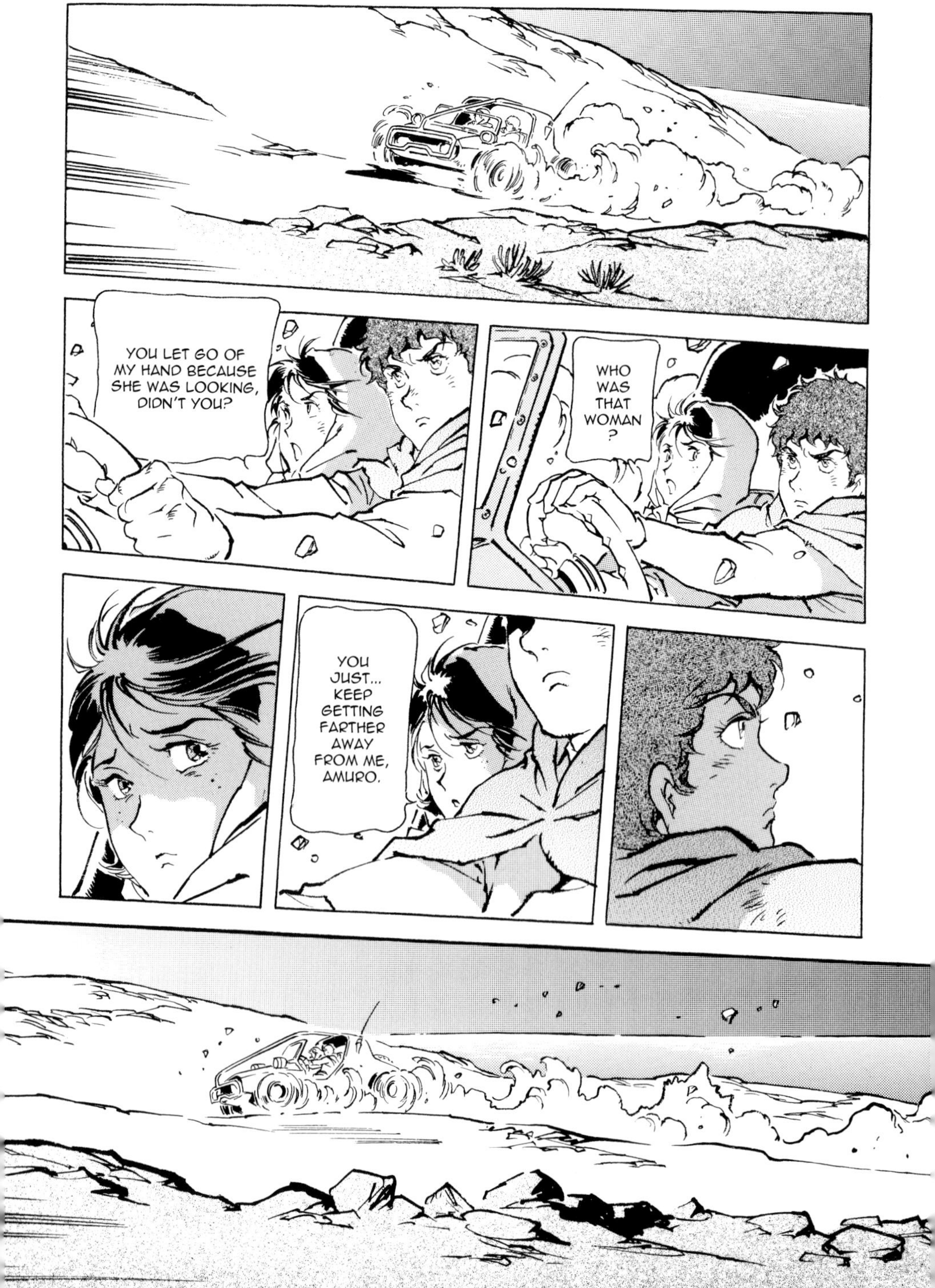
WHO WAS THAT WOMAN?
YOU LET GO OF MY HAND BECAUSE SHE WAS LOOKING, DIDN'T YOU?
YOU JUST... KEEP GETTING FARTHER AWAY FROM ME, AMURO.

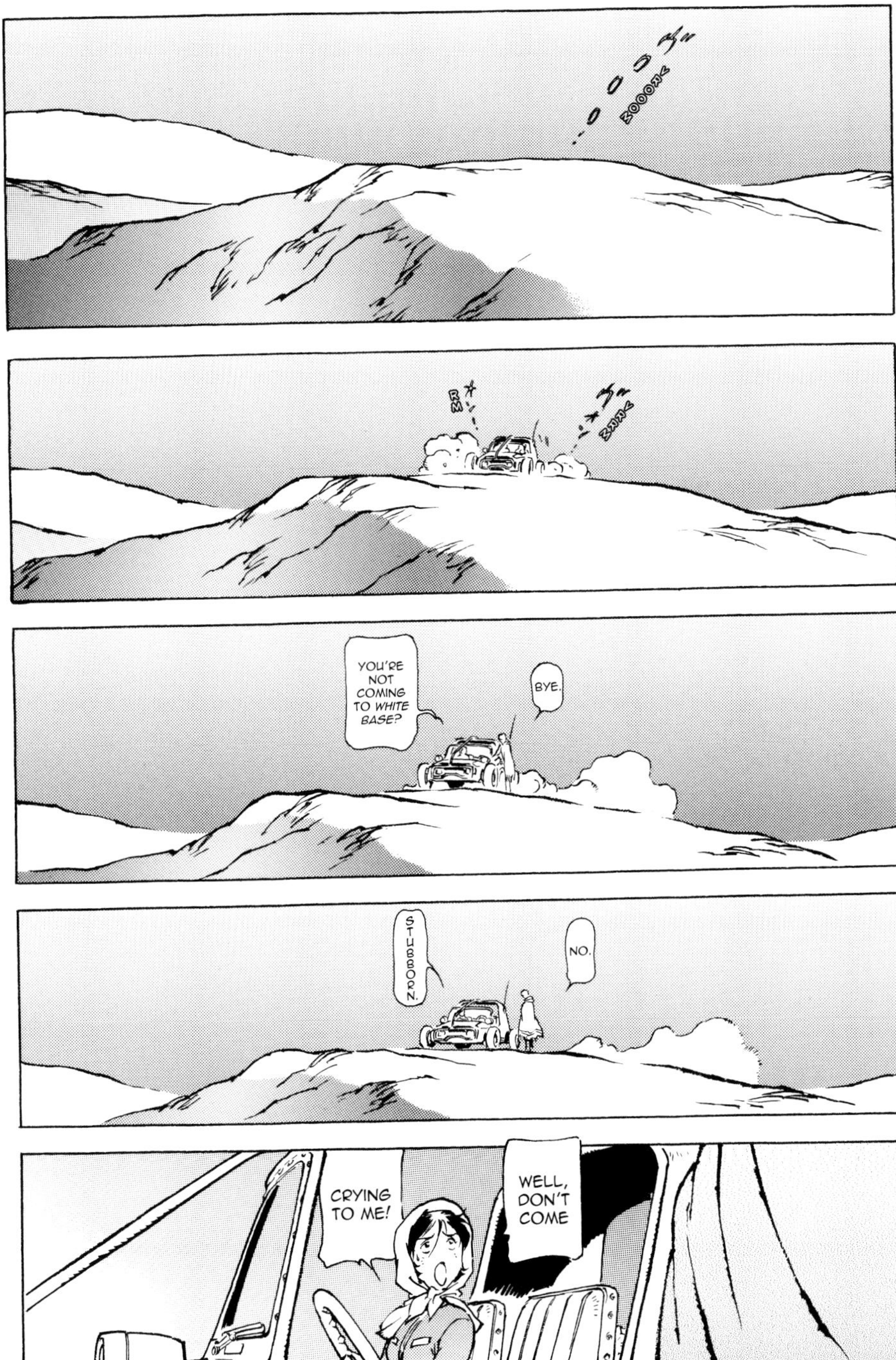
RM
BYE.
YOU'RE NOT COMING TO WHITE BASE?
NO.
STUBBORN.
WELL, DON'T COME
CRYING TO ME!

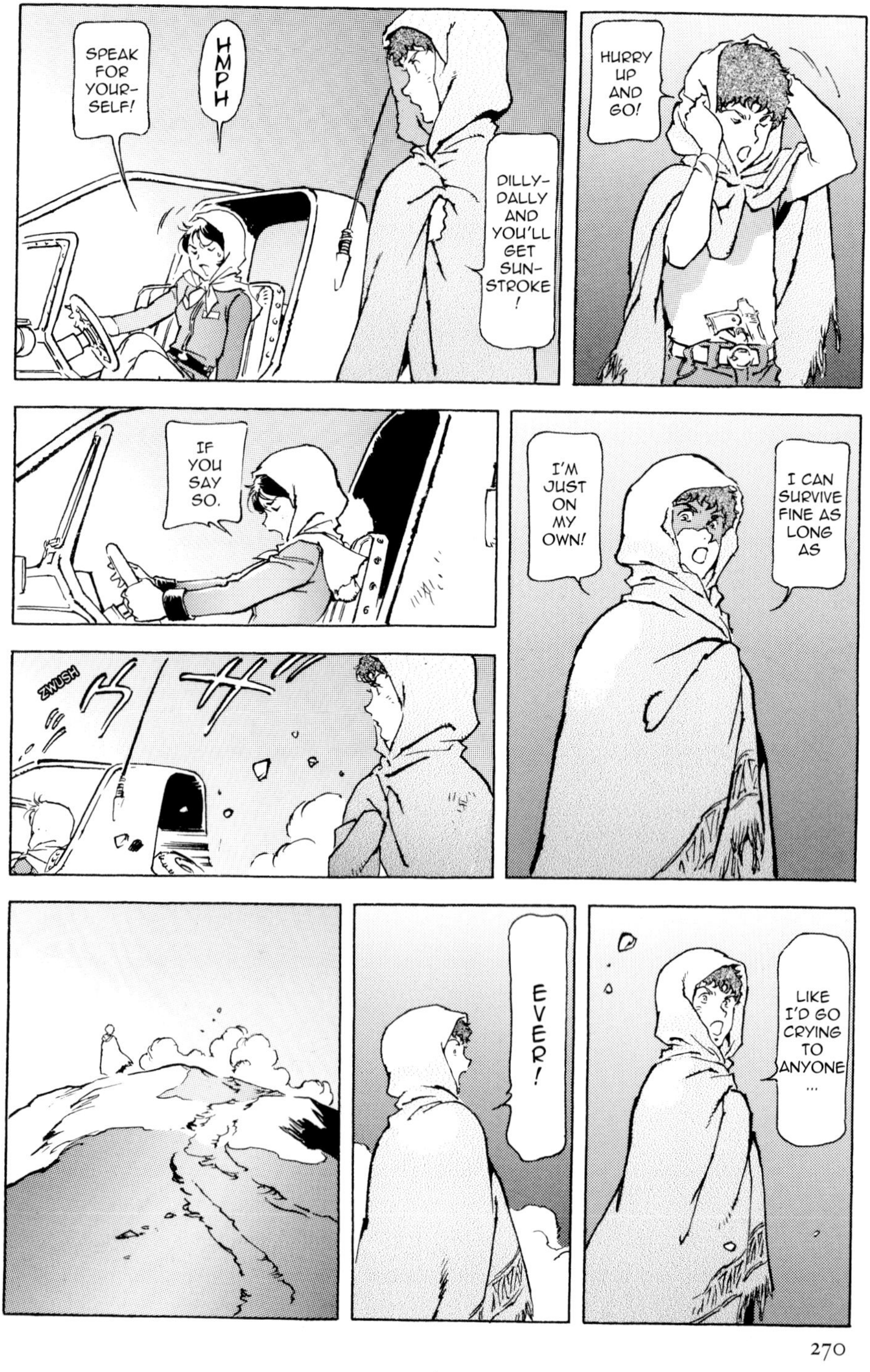
HURRY UP AND GO!
DILLY-DALLY AND YOU'LL GET SUN-STROKE!
HMPH
SPEAK FOR YOUR-SELF!
I CAN SURVIVE FINE AS LONG AS
I'M JUST ON MY OWN!
IF YOU SAY SO.
ZWUSH
LIKE I'D GO CRYING TO ANYONE...
EVER!

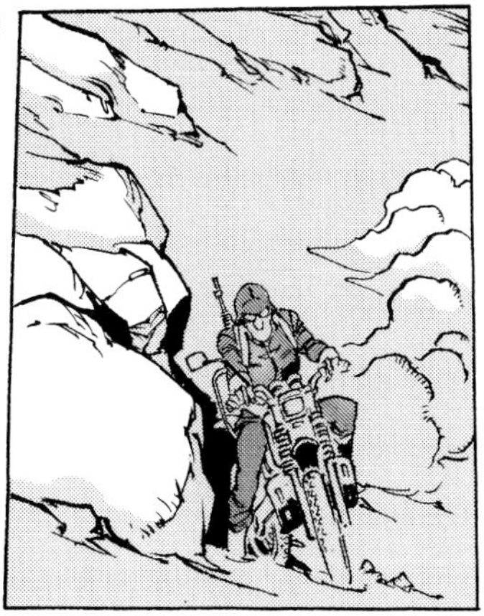

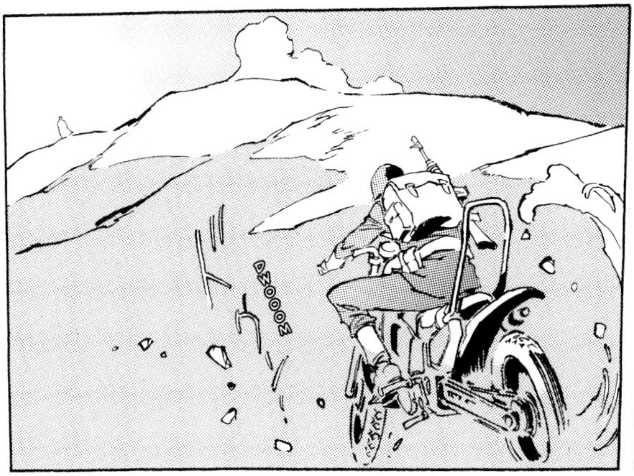
ドウン
DWOOOM

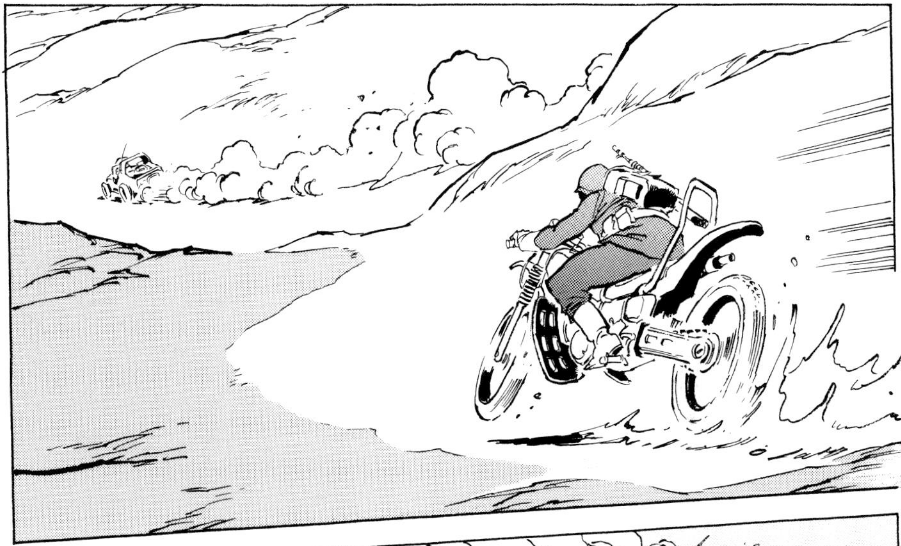

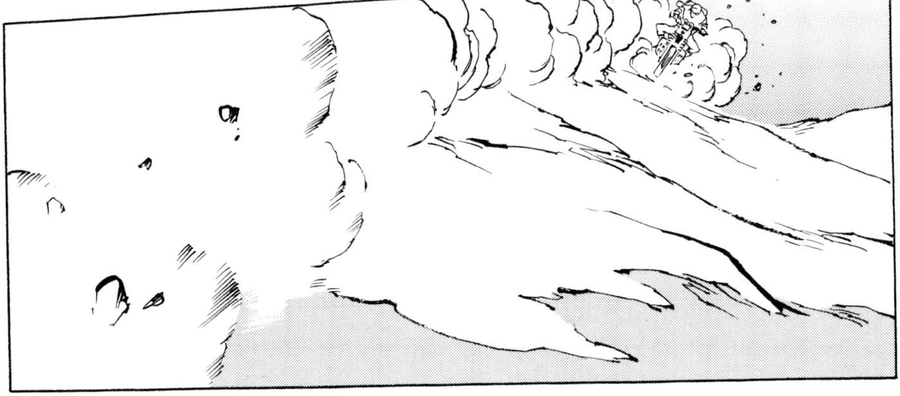

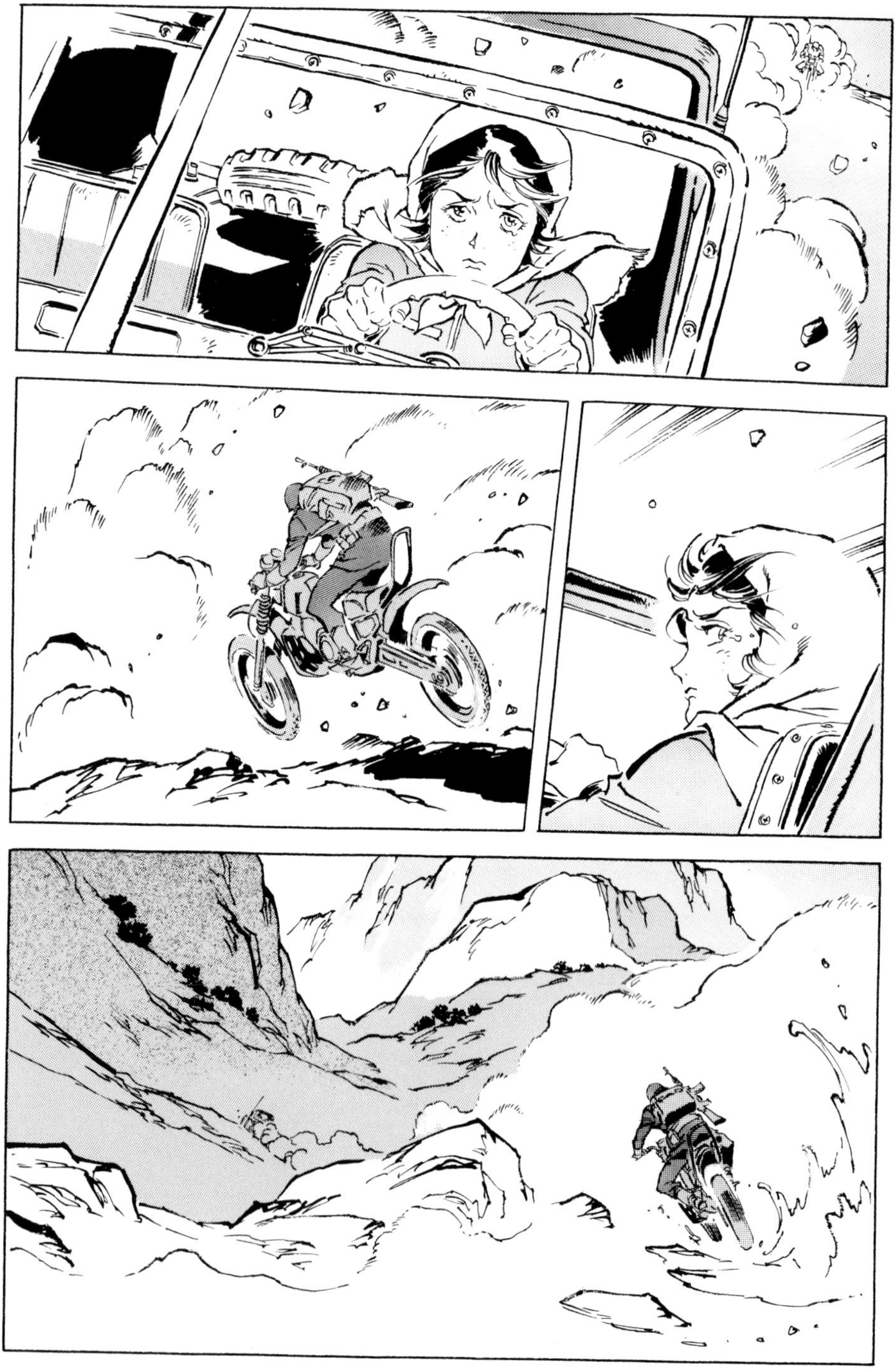

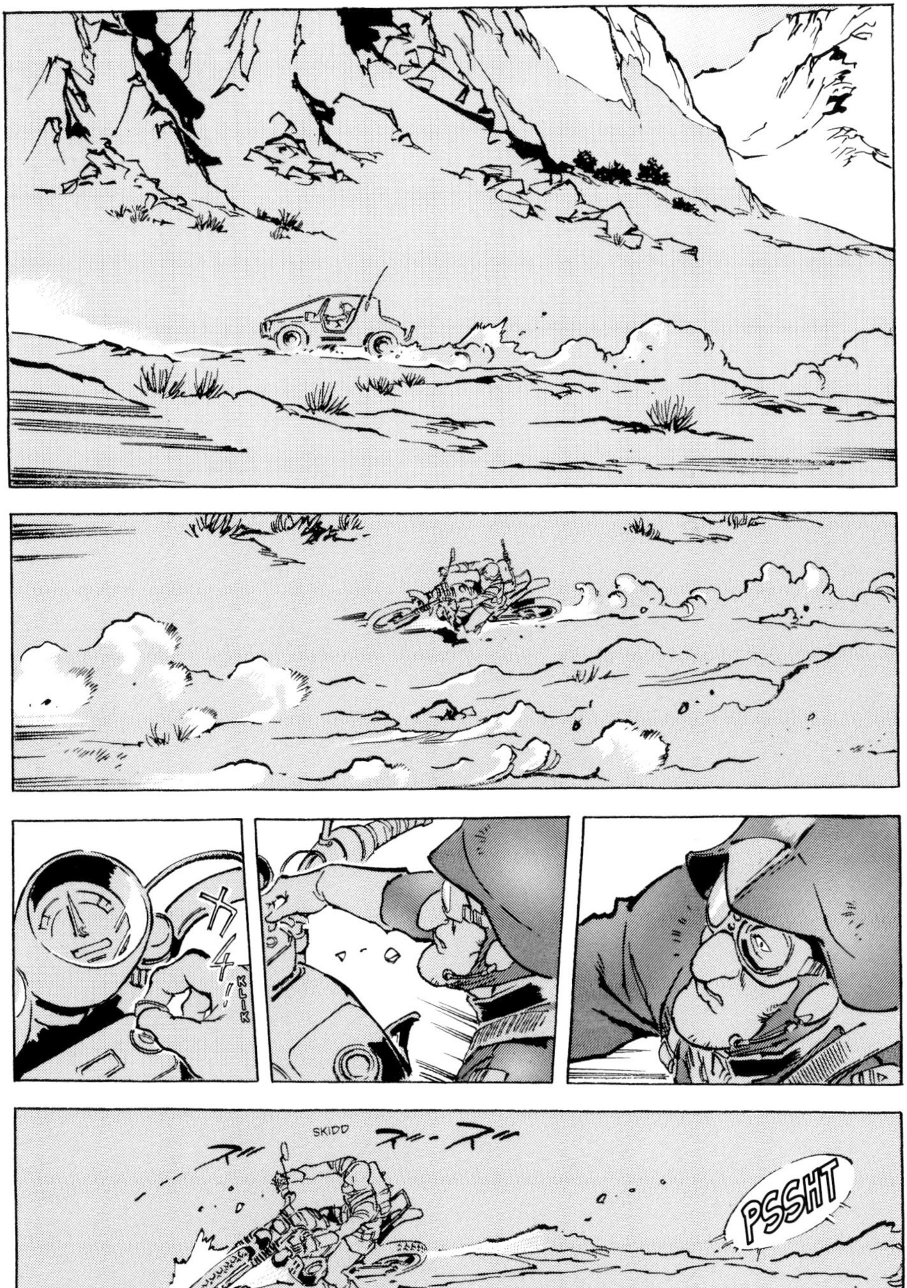
KLIK
SKIDD
PSSHT

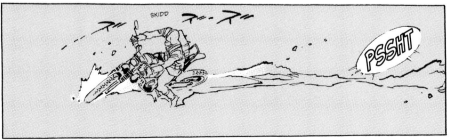

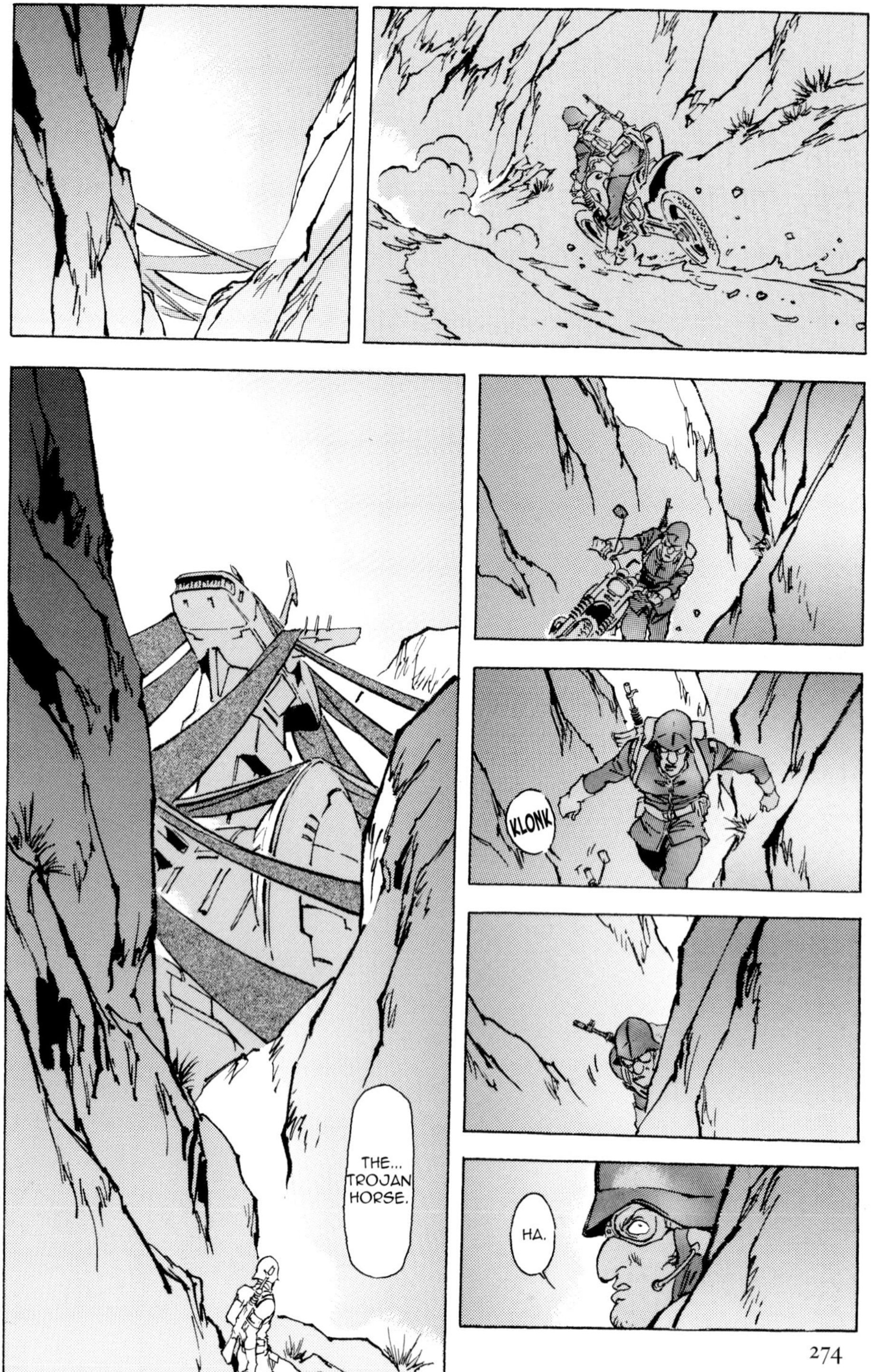
KLONK
HA.
THE... TROJAN HORSE.

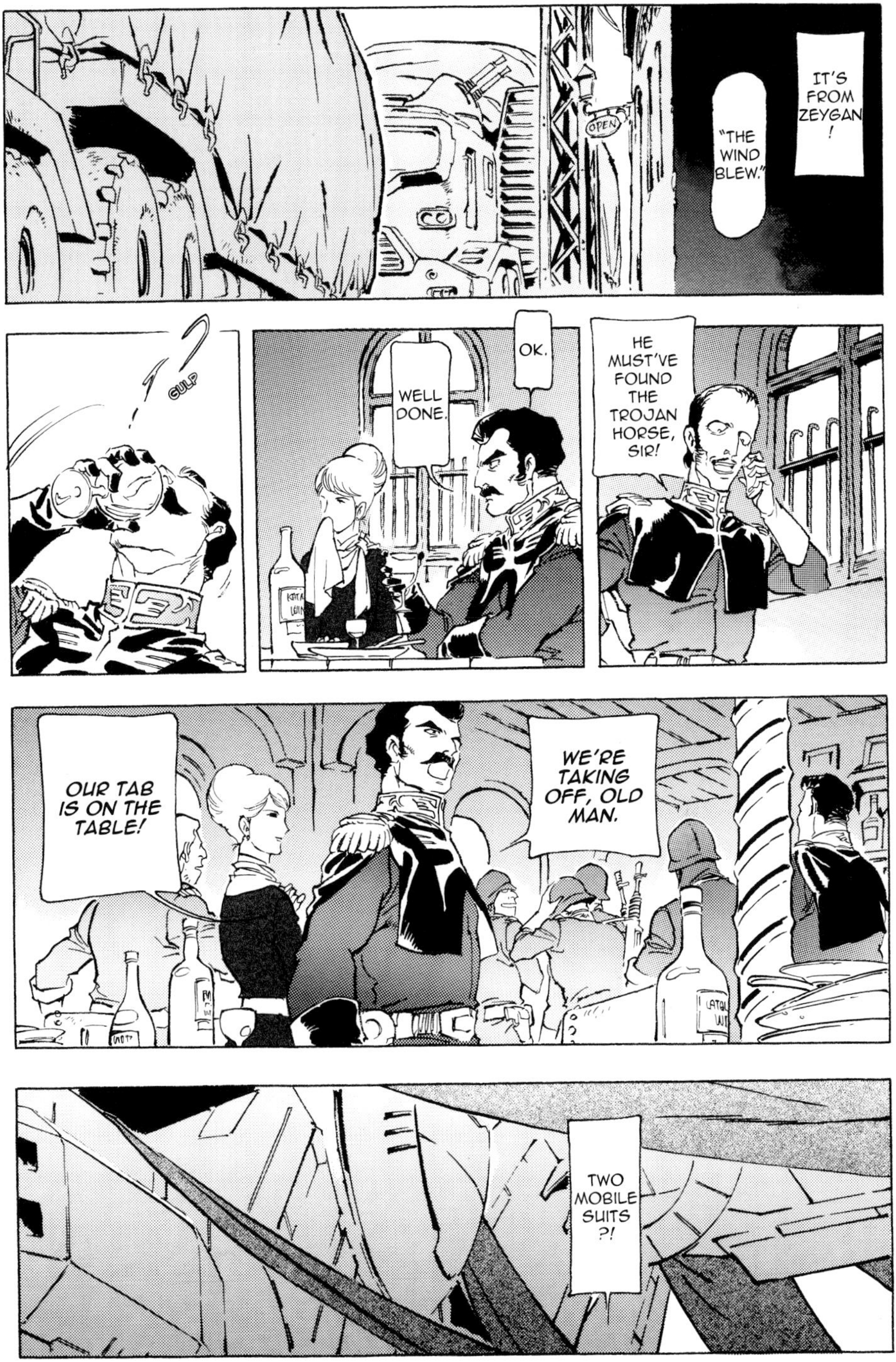
IT'S FROM ZEYGAN!
"THE WIND BLEW."
HE MUST'VE FOUND THE TROJAN HORSE, SIR!
OK.
WELL DONE.
GULP
WE'RE TAKING OFF, OLD MAN.
OUR TAB IS ON THE TABLE!
TWO MOBILE SUITS ?!

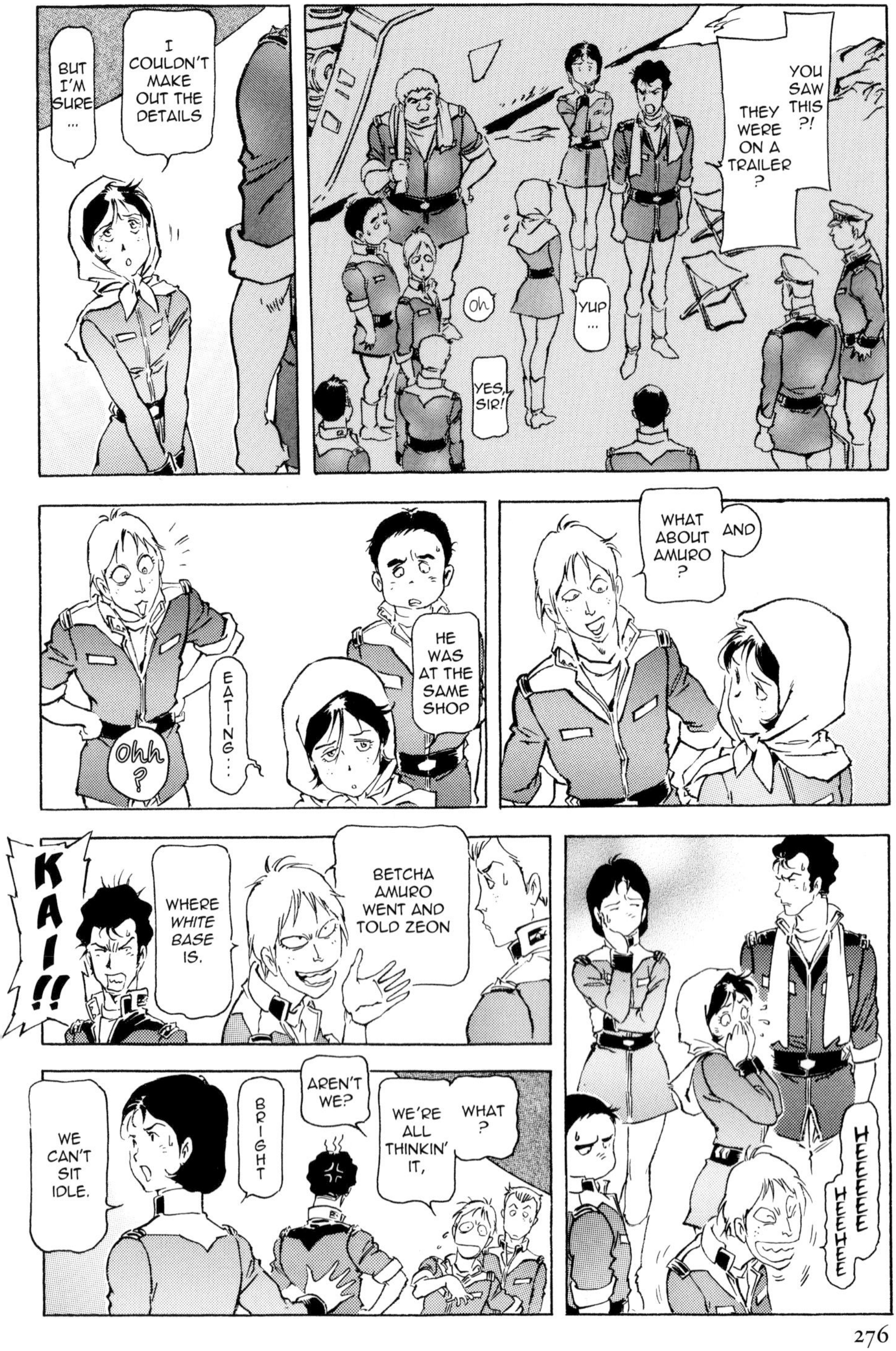
YOU SAW THIS?!
THEY WERE ON A TRAILER?
YUP...
Oh
YES, SIR!
I COULDN'T MAKE OUT THE DETAILS
BUT I'M SURE...
AND
WHAT ABOUT AMURO?
HE WAS AT THE SAME SHOP
EATING...
Ohh?
HEEEEEE HEEHEE
BETCHA AMURO WENT AND TOLD ZEON
WHERE WHITE BASE IS.
KAI!!
WHAT?
WE'RE ALL THINKIN' IT,
AREN'T WE?
BRIGHT
WE CAN'T SIT IDLE.

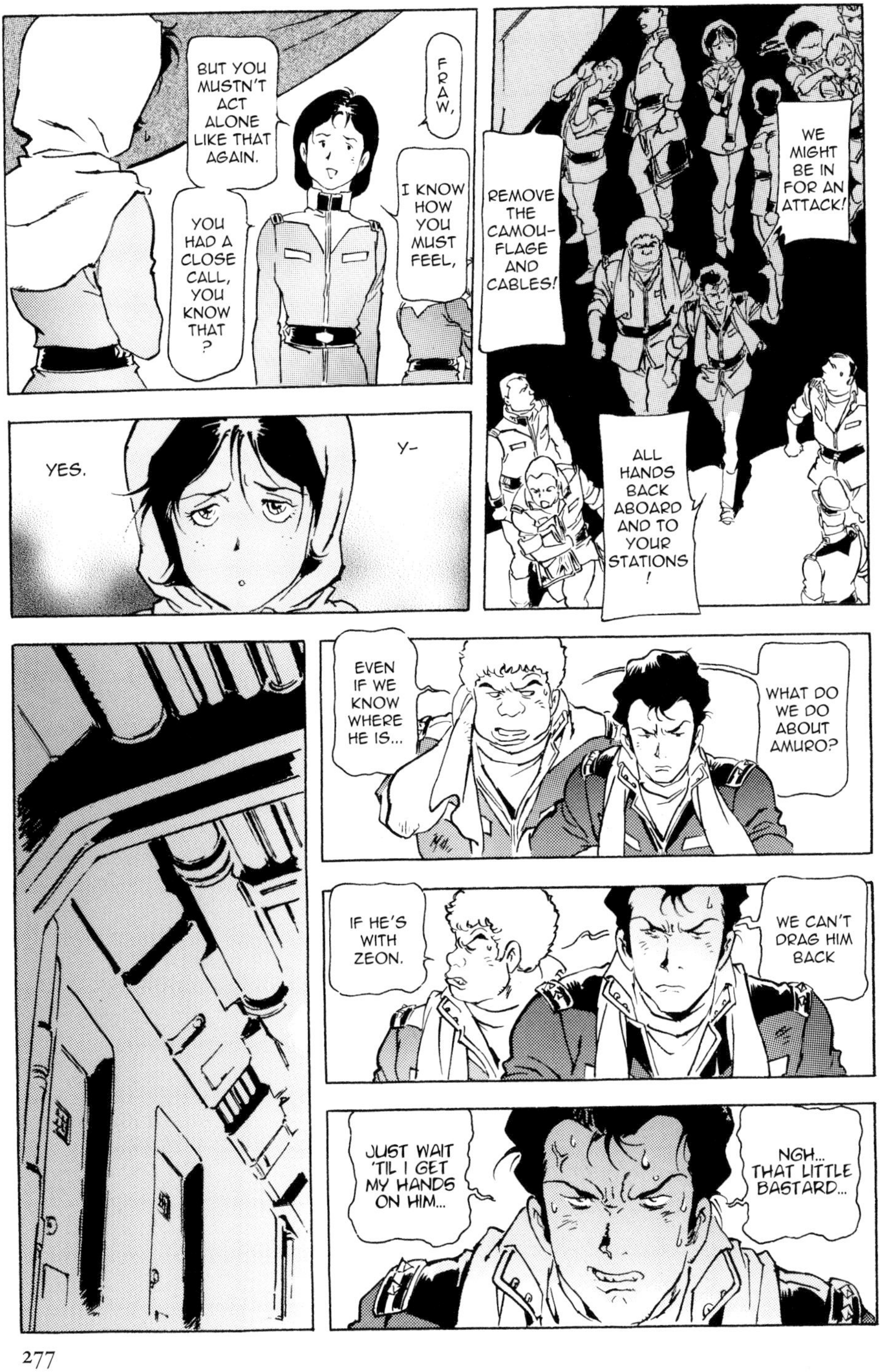
WE MIGHT BE IN FOR AN ATTACK!
REMOVE THE CAMOUFLAGE AND CABLES!
ALL HANDS BACK ABOARD AND TO YOUR STATIONS!
FRAW,
I KNOW HOW YOU MUST FEEL,
BUT YOU MUSTN'T ACT ALONE LIKE THAT AGAIN.
YOU HAD A CLOSE CALL, YOU KNOW THAT?
Y-
YES.
WHAT DO WE DO ABOUT AMURO?
EVEN IF WE KNOW WHERE HE IS...
WE CAN'T DRAG HIM BACK
IF HE'S WITH ZEON.
NGH... THAT LITTLE BASTARD...
JUST WAIT 'TIL I GET MY HANDS ON HIM...

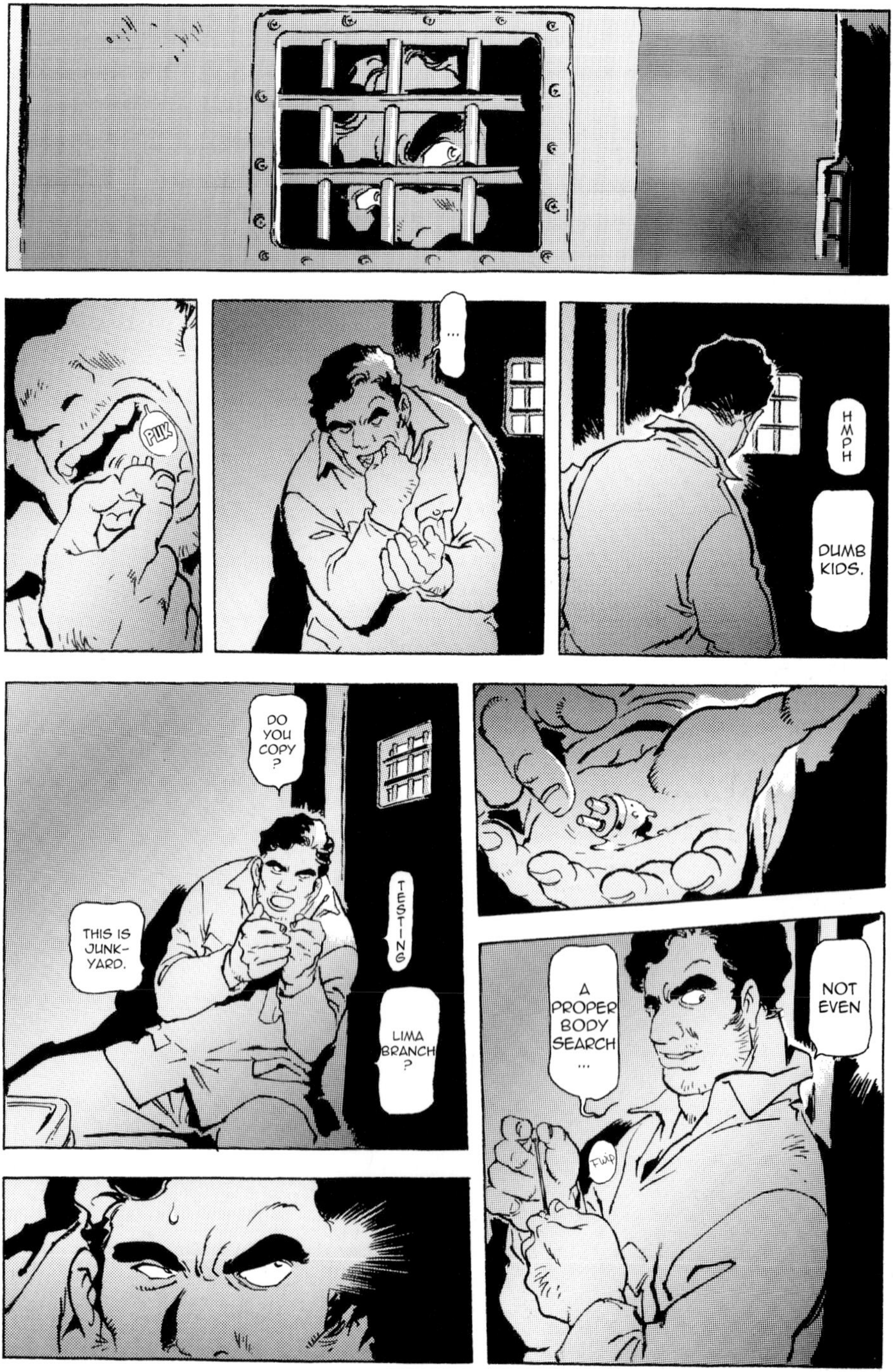
HMPH
DUMB KIDS.
...
PUK
THIS IS JUNK-YARD.
TESTING
LIMA BRANCH?
DO YOU COPY?
NOT EVEN
A PROPER BODY SEARCH...
Fwip

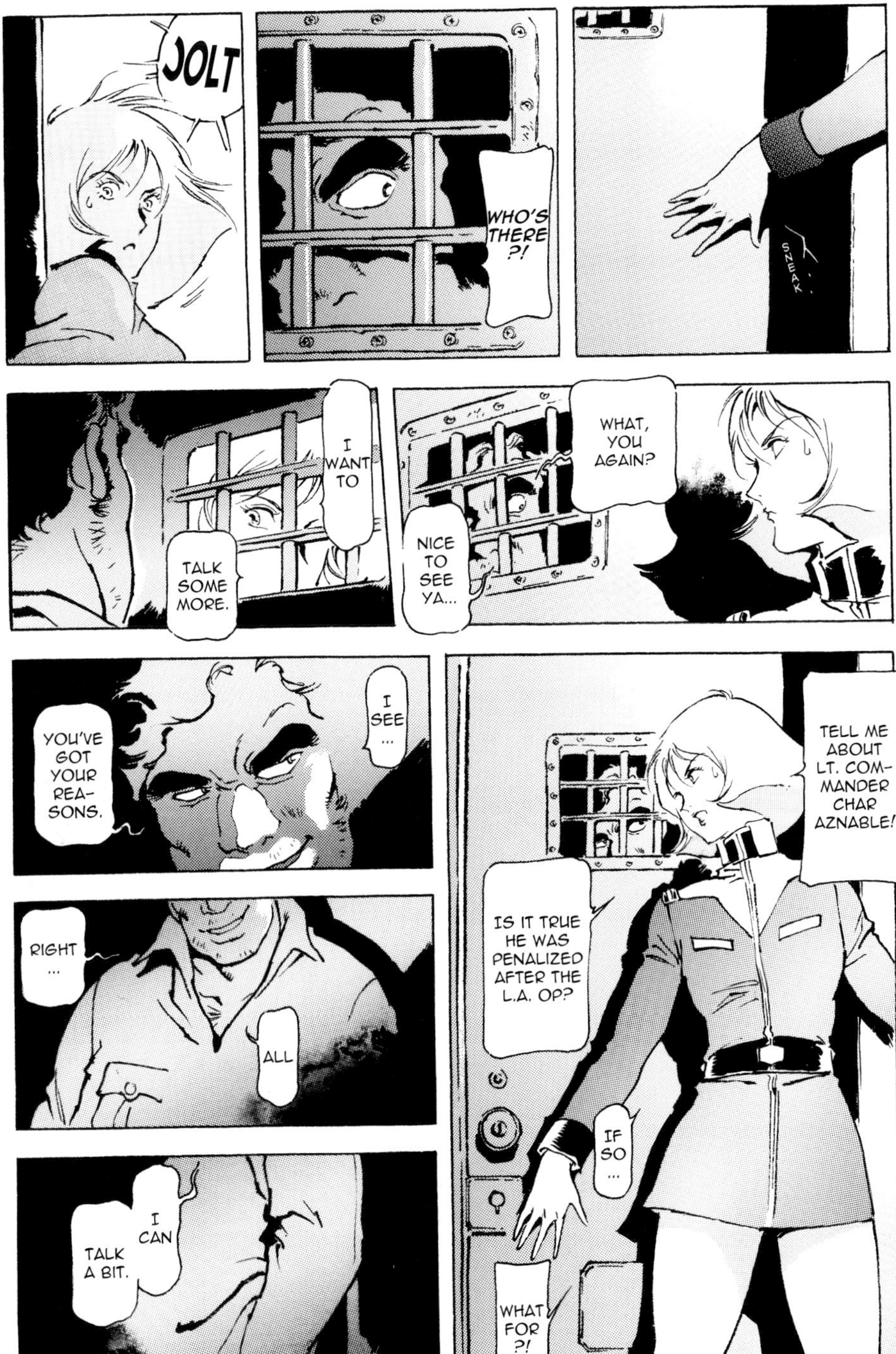
SNEAK
WHO'S THERE ?!
JOLT
WHAT, YOU AGAIN?
NICE TO SEE YA...
I WANT TO
TALK SOME MORE.
TELL ME ABOUT LT. COMMANDER CHAR AZNABLE!
IS IT TRUE HE WAS PENALIZED AFTER THE L.A. OP?
IF SO ...
WHAT FOR ?!
I SEE ...
YOU'VE GOT YOUR REASONS.
ALL
RIGHT ...
I CAN
TALK A BIT.

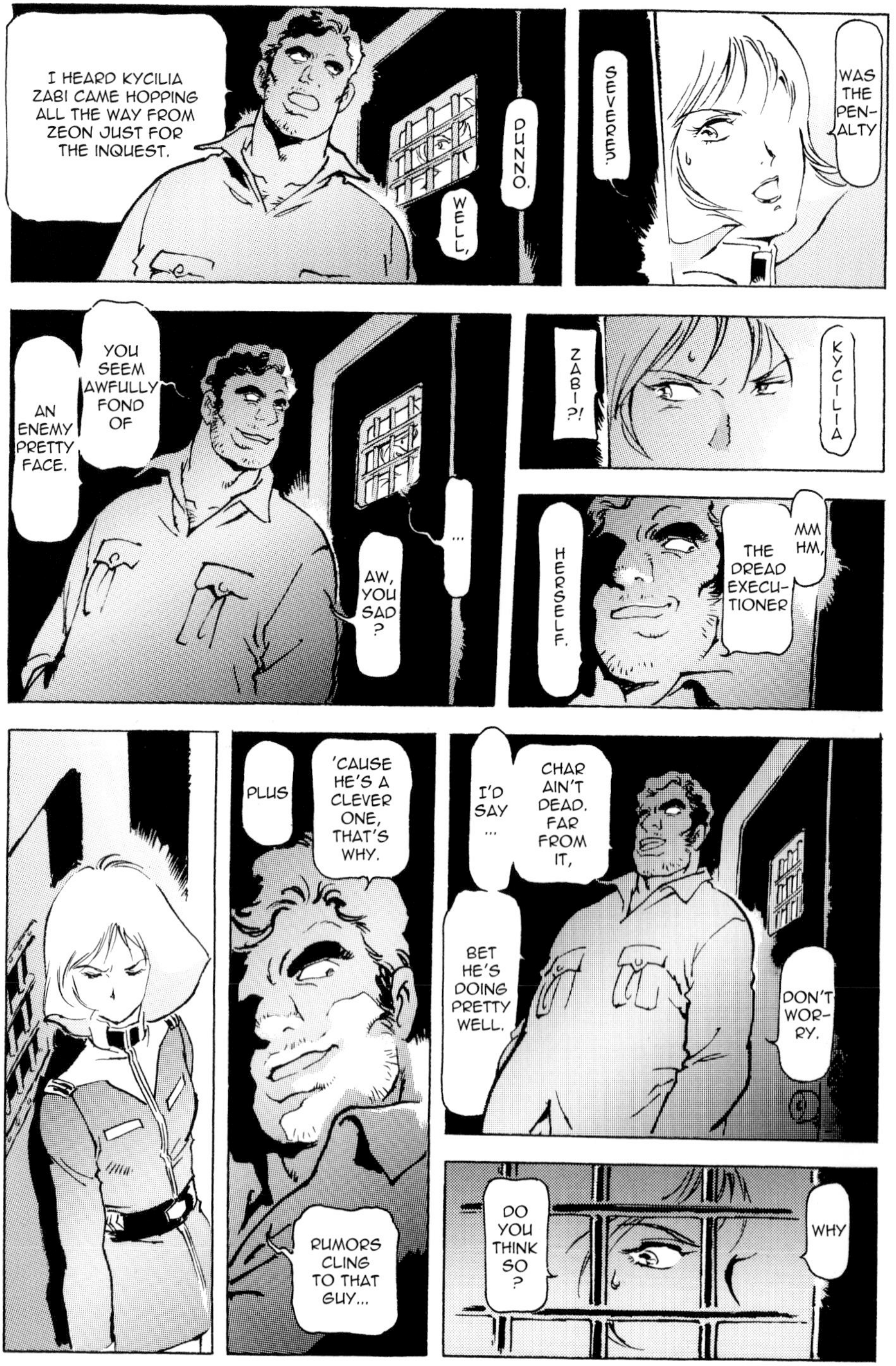
WAS THE PEN-ALTY
SEVERE?
WELL,
DUNNO.
I HEARD KYCILIA ZABI CAME HOPPING ALL THE WAY FROM ZEON JUST FOR THE INQUEST.
KYCILIA
ZABI?!
MM HM, THE DREAD EXECUTIONER
HERSELF.
...
AW, YOU SAD?
YOU SEEM AWFULLY FOND OF
AN ENEMY PRETTY FACE.
DON'T WOR-RY.
CHAR AIN'T DEAD. FAR FROM IT,
I'D SAY ...
BET HE'S DOING PRETTY WELL.
WHY
DO YOU THINK SO?
'CAUSE HE'S A CLEVER ONE, THAT'S WHY.
PLUS
RUMORS CLING TO THAT GUY...

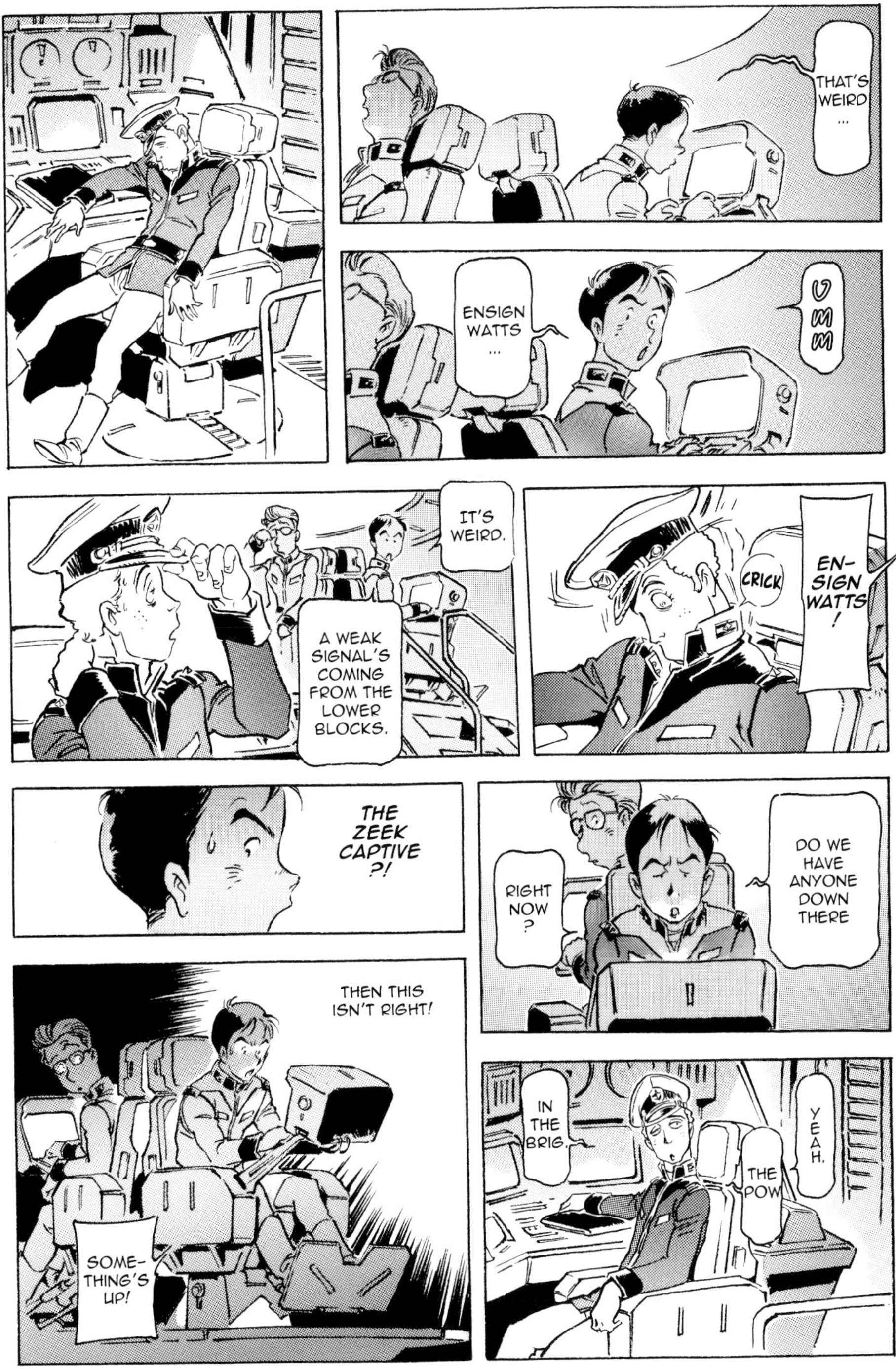
THAT'S WEIRD ...
UMM
ENSIGN WATTS ...
EN-SIGN WATTS!
CRICK
IT'S WEIRD.
A WEAK SIGNAL'S COMING FROM THE LOWER BLOCKS.
DO WE HAVE ANYONE DOWN THERE
RIGHT NOW ?
THE ZEEK CAPTIVE ?!
YEAH.
THE POW
IN THE BRIG.
THEN THIS ISN'T RIGHT!
SOME-THING'S UP!

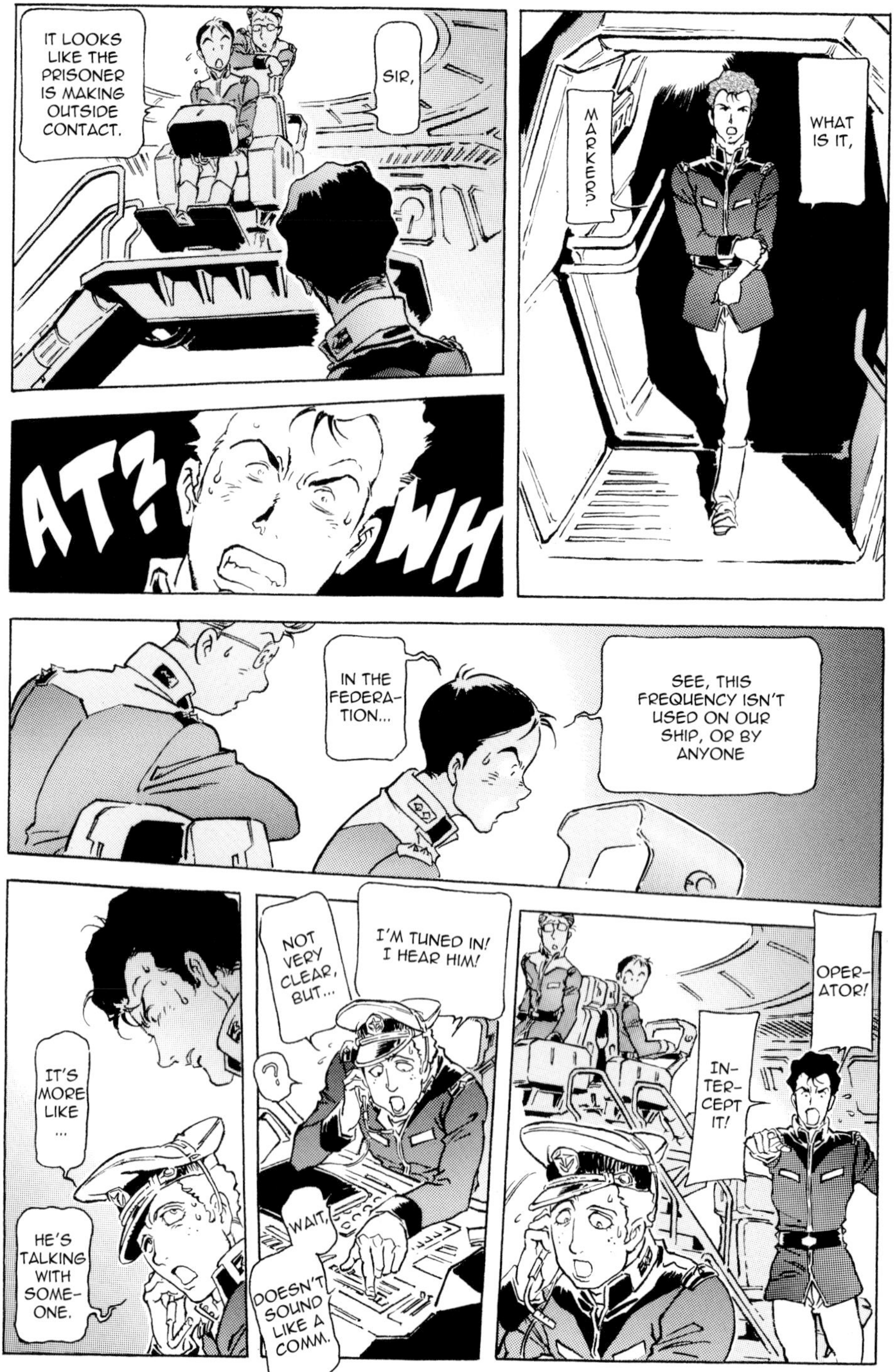
WHAT IS IT,
MARKER?
SIR,
IT LOOKS LIKE THE PRISONER IS MAKING OUTSIDE CONTACT.
WHAT?
SEE, THIS FREQUENCY ISN'T USED ON OUR SHIP, OR BY ANYONE
IN THE FEDERATION...
OPERATOR!
INTERCEPT IT!
I'M TUNED IN! I HEAR HIM!
NOT VERY CLEAR, BUT...
?
WAIT,
DOESN'T SOUND LIKE A COMM.
IT'S MORE LIKE ...
HE'S TALKING WITH SOMEONE.

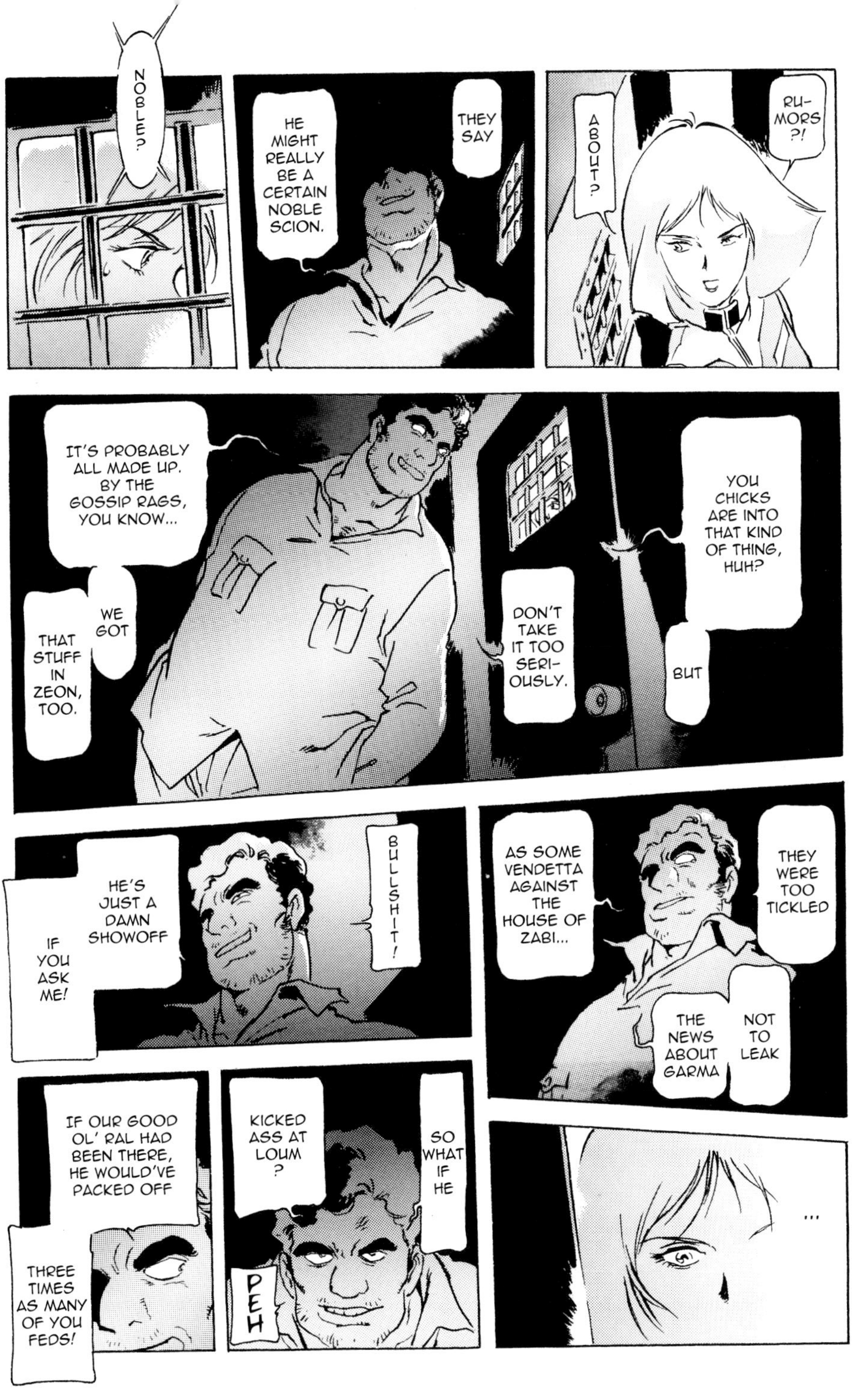
RU-MORS?!
ABOUT?
THEY SAY
HE MIGHT REALLY BE A CERTAIN NOBLE SCION.
NOBLE?
YOU CHICKS ARE INTO THAT KIND OF THING, HUH?
BUT
DON'T TAKE IT TOO SERI-OUSLY.
IT'S PROBABLY ALL MADE UP. BY THE GOSSIP RAGS, YOU KNOW...
WE GOT
THAT STUFF IN ZEON, TOO.
THEY WERE TOO TICKLED
NOT TO LEAK
THE NEWS ABOUT GARMA
AS SOME VENDETTA AGAINST THE HOUSE OF ZABI...
BULLSHIT!
HE'S JUST A DAMN SHOWOFF
IF YOU ASK ME!
...
SO WHAT IF HE
KICKED ASS AT LOUM?
PEH
IF OUR GOOD OL' RAL HAD BEEN THERE, HE WOULD'VE PACKED OFF
THREE TIMES AS MANY OF YOU FEDS!

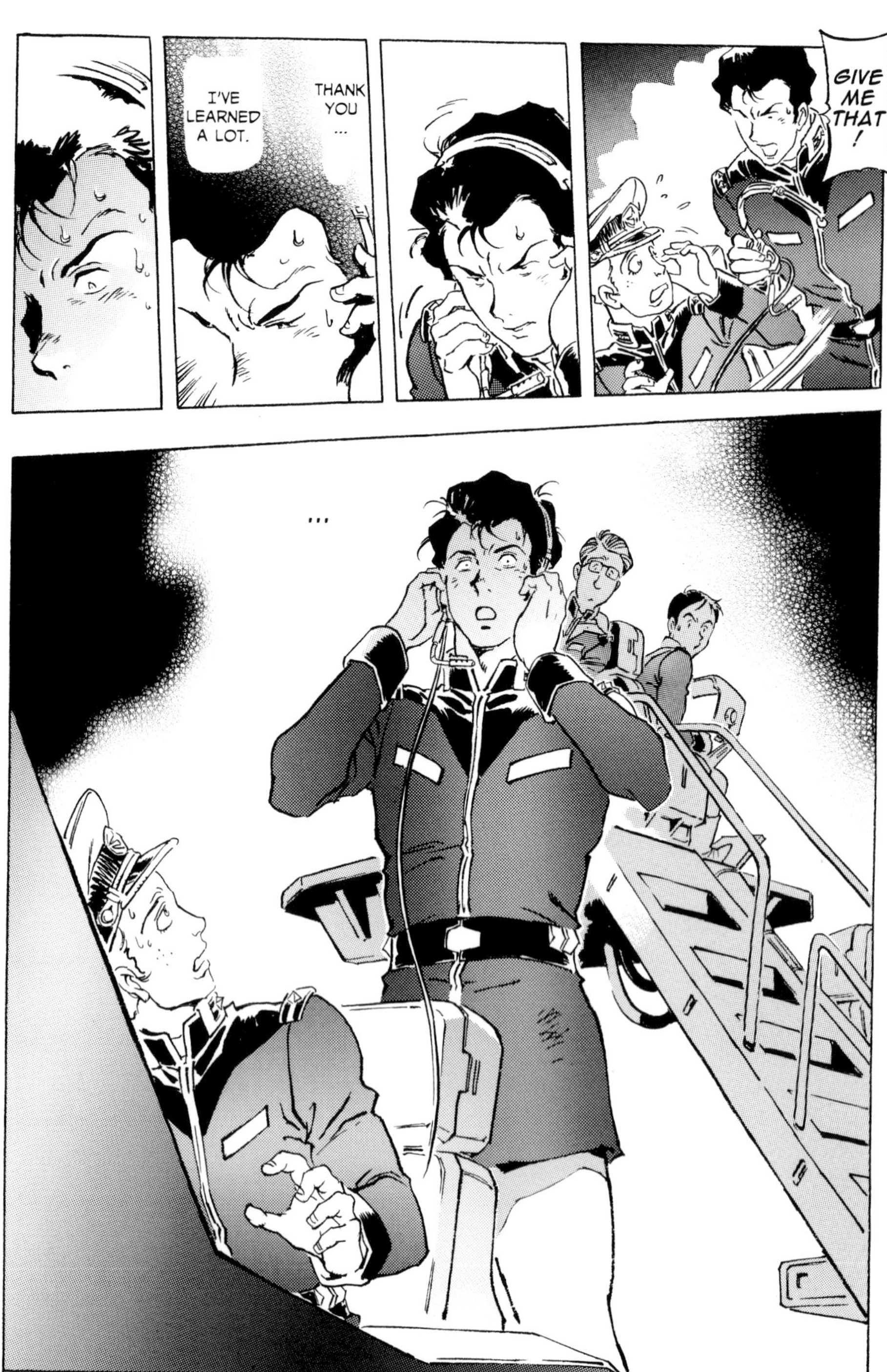
GIVE ME THAT!
THANK YOU ...
I'VE LEARNED A LOT.
...

SECTION V

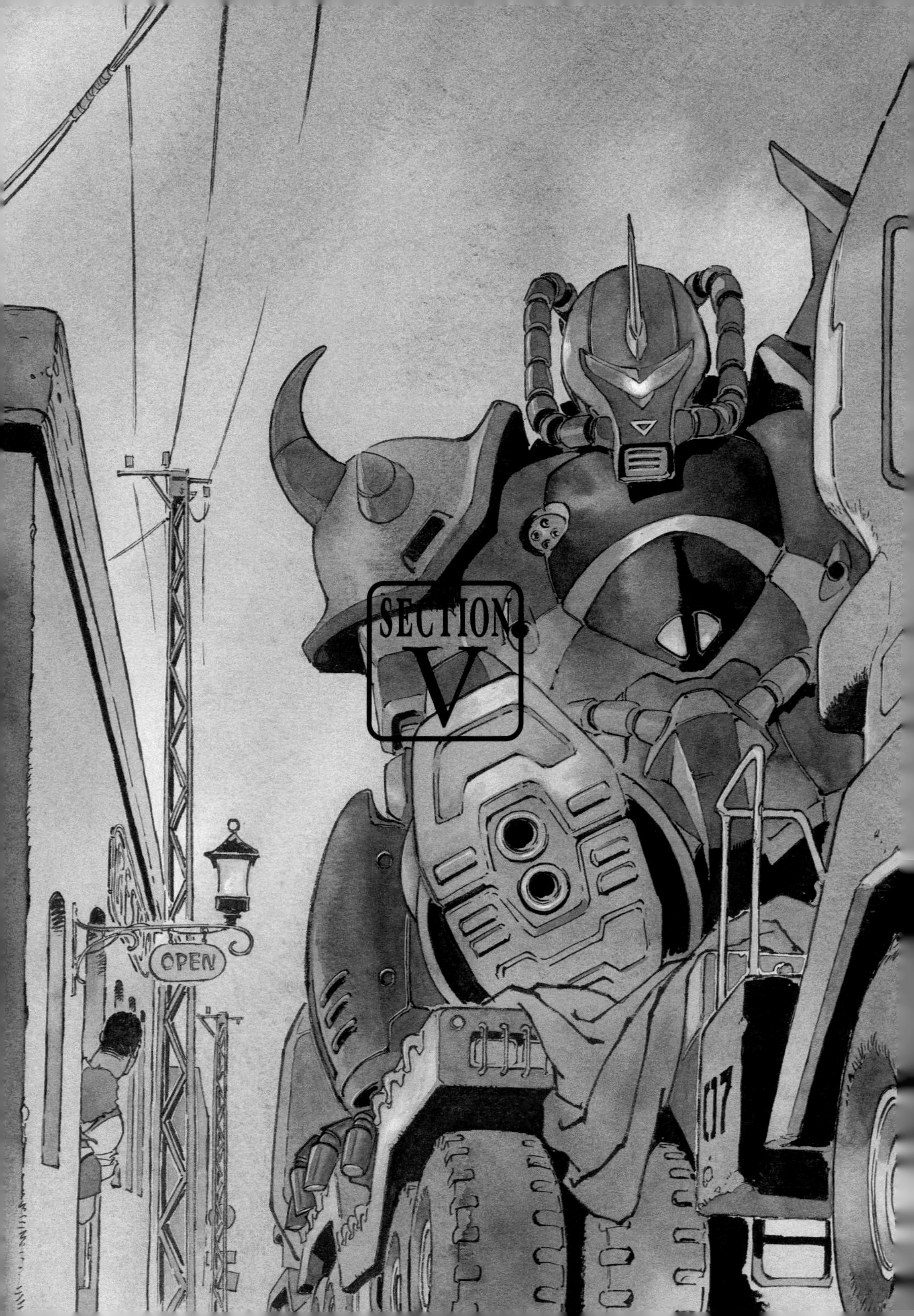
OPEN
07

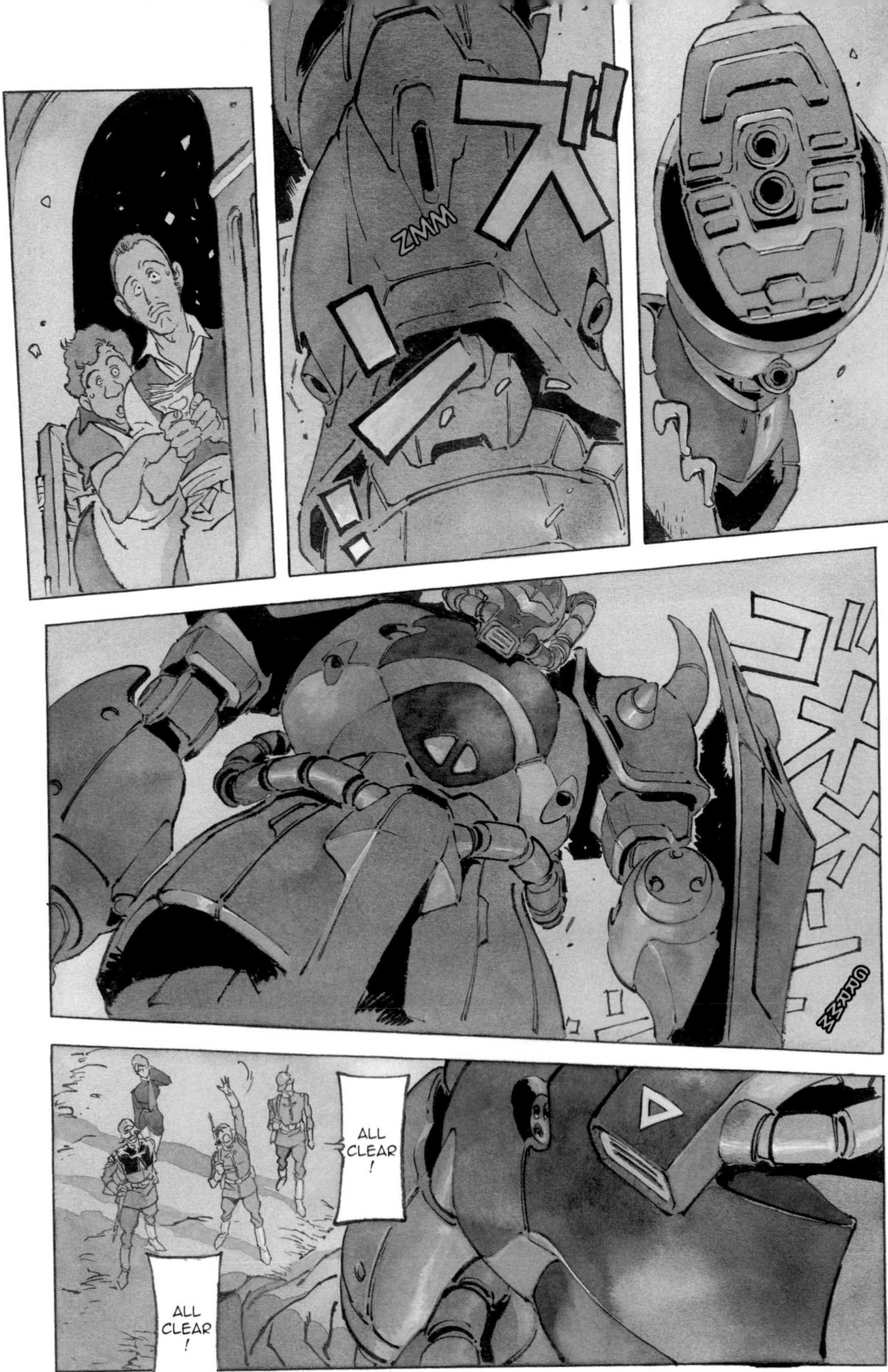
ズ
ZMM
GRRZZ
ALL CLEAR!
ALL CLEAR!

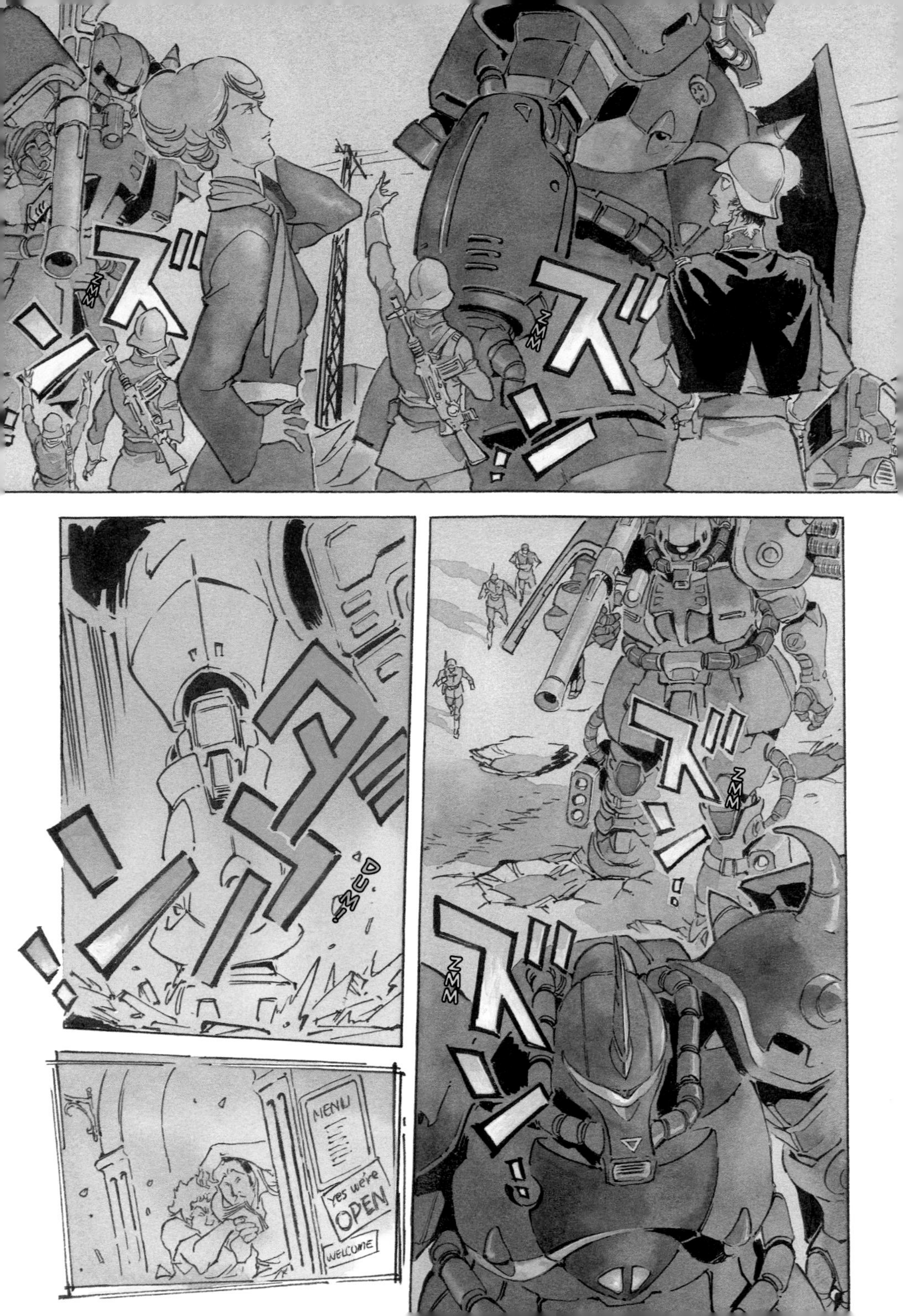
ZMM
ZMM
ZMM
ZMM
DUM!
MENU
Yes we're OPEN
WELCOME

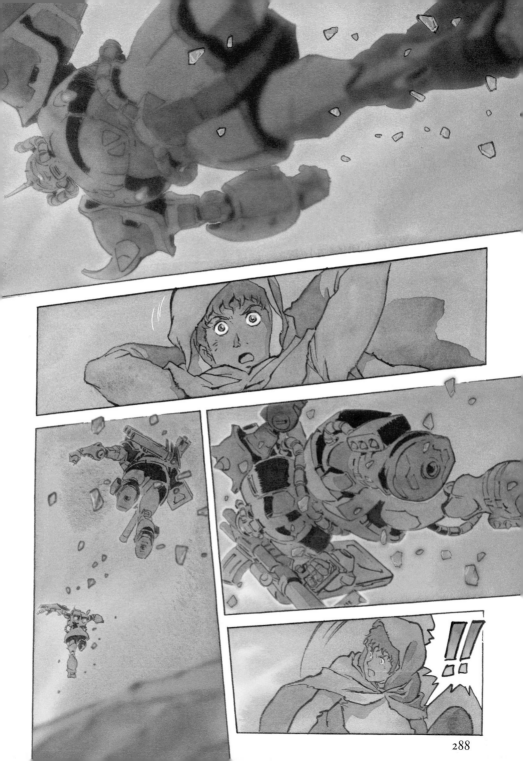

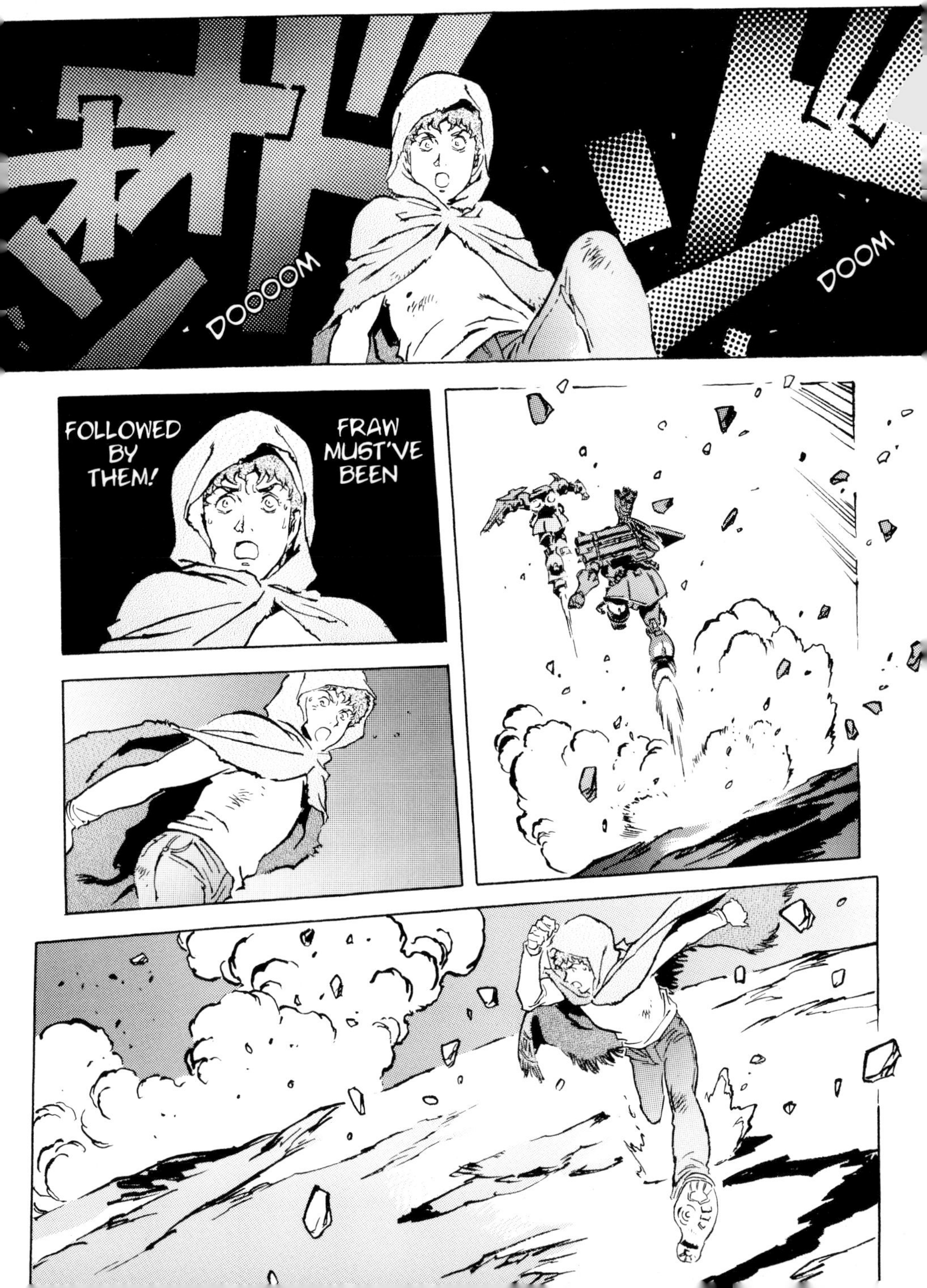
DOOM
DOOOOOM
FRAW MUST'VE BEEN
FOLLOWED BY THEM!

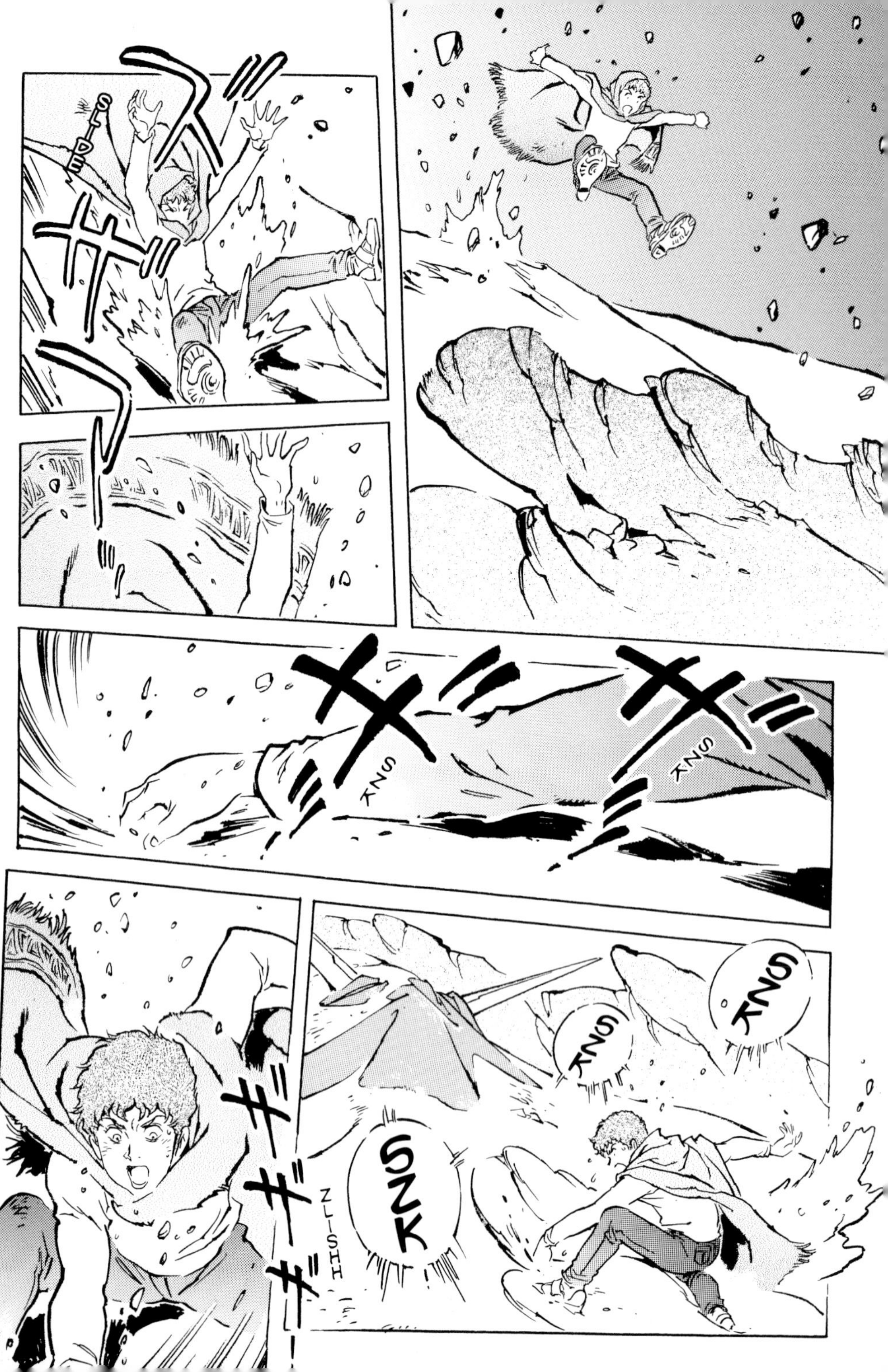
SLIDE
SNK
SNK
SNK
SNK
SZK
ZLISHH

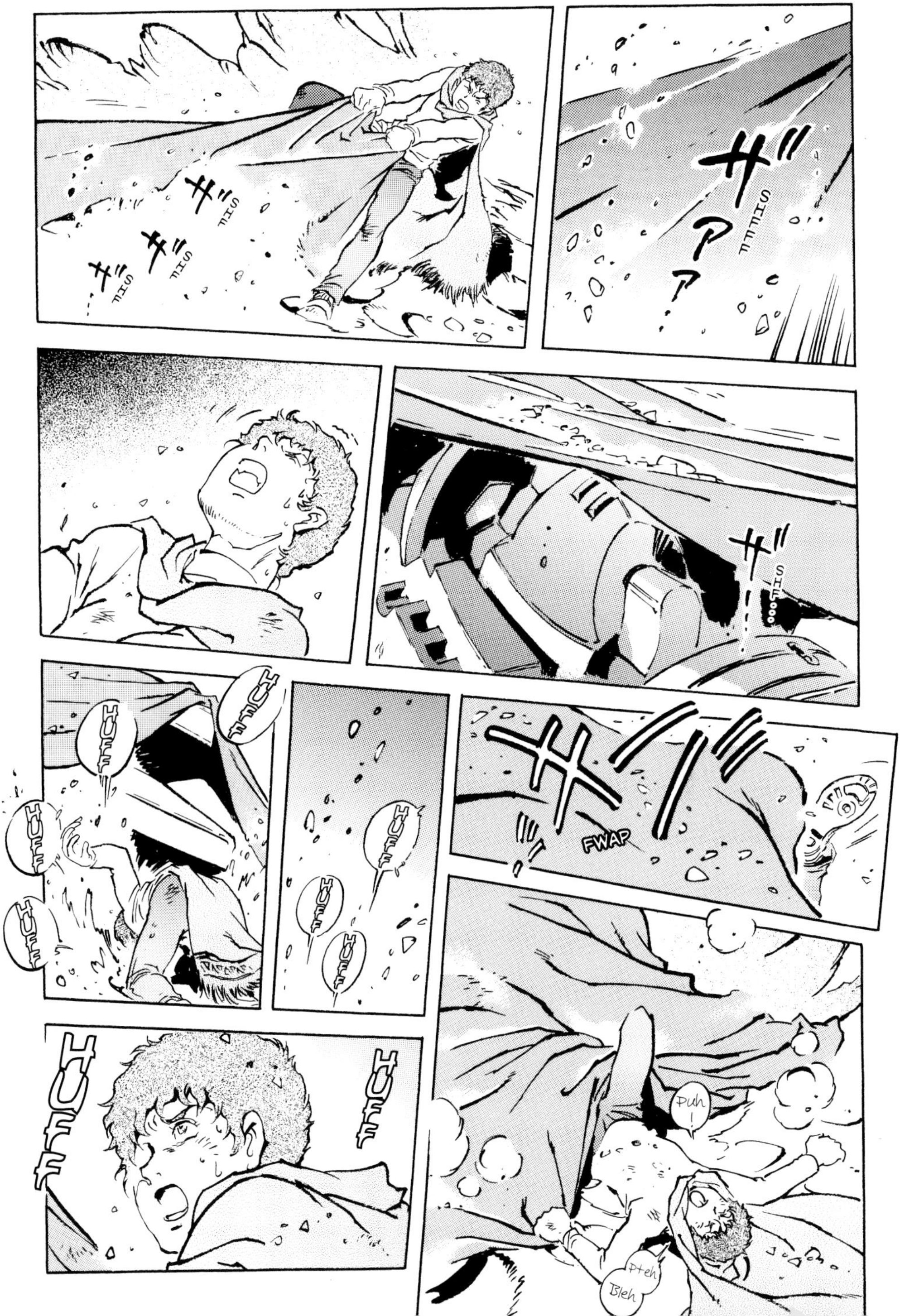

SHFFF
SHF
SHF
SHF
SHFooo
FWAP
HUFF
HUFF
HUFF
HUFF
HUFF
HUFF
HUFF
Puh!
Pteh
Bleh
HUFF
HUFF

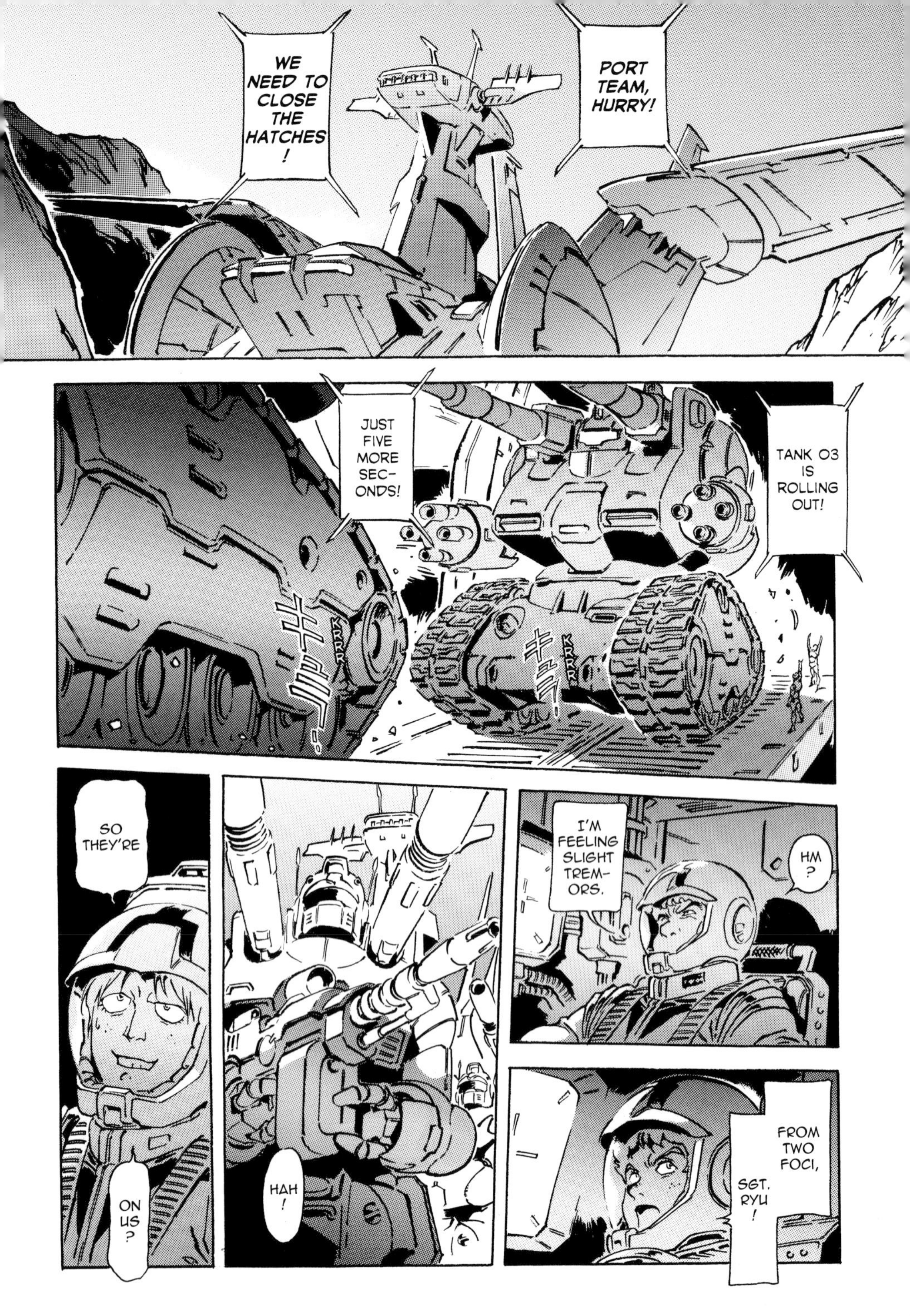
PORT TEAM, HURRY!
WE NEED TO CLOSE THE HATCHES!
TANK 03 IS ROLLING OUT!
JUST FIVE MORE SEC-ONDS!
KRRR
KRRR
HM?
I'M FEELING SLIGHT TREMORS.
FROM TWO FOCI,
SGT. RYU!
HAH!
SO THEY'RE
ON US?

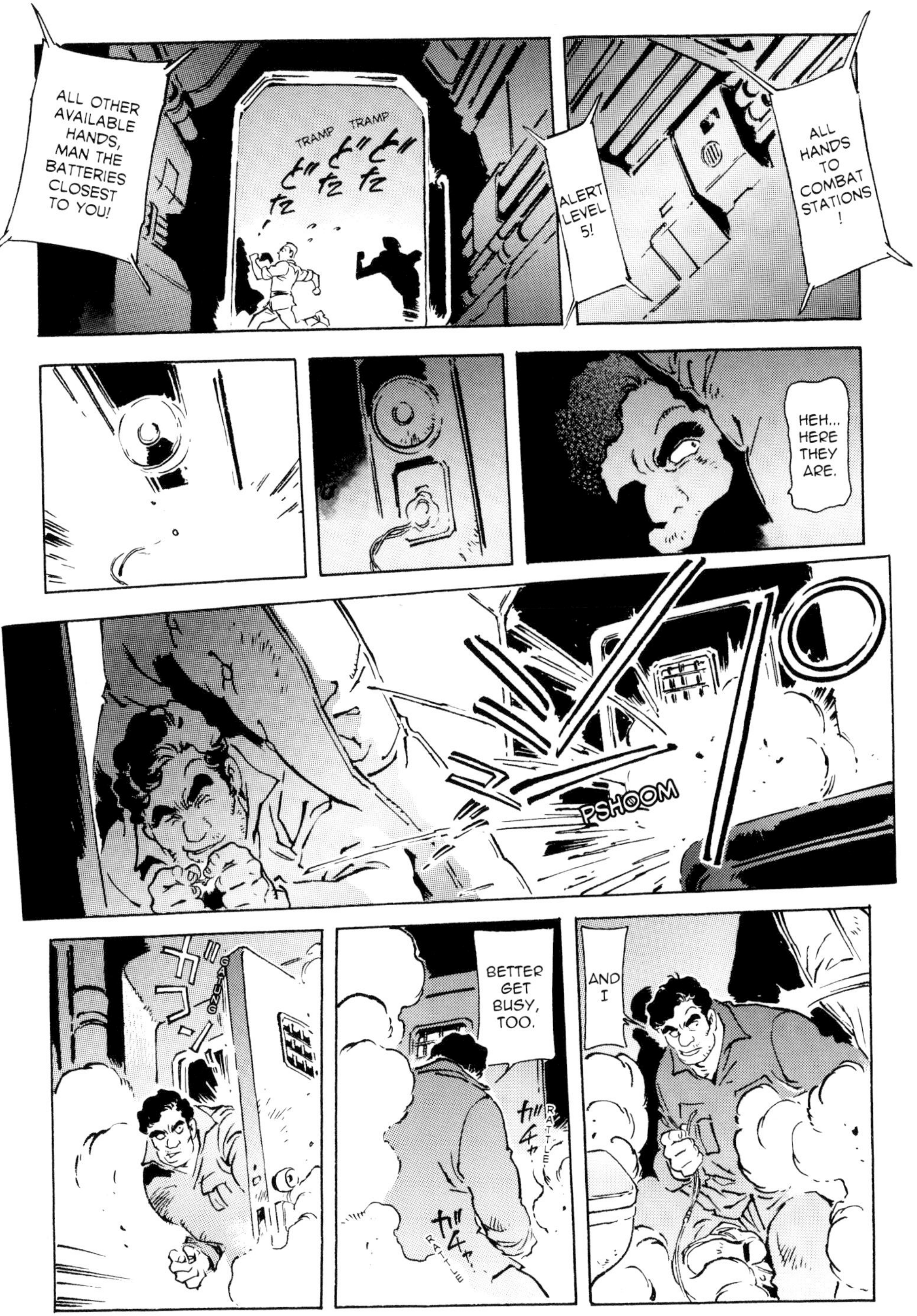
ALL HANDS TO COMBAT STATIONS!
ALERT LEVEL 5!
ALL OTHER AVAILABLE HANDS, MAN THE BATTERIES CLOSEST TO YOU!
TRAMP TRAMP
HEH... HERE THEY ARE.
PSHOOM
AND I
BETTER GET BUSY, TOO.
RATTLE
RATTLE
GATUNG

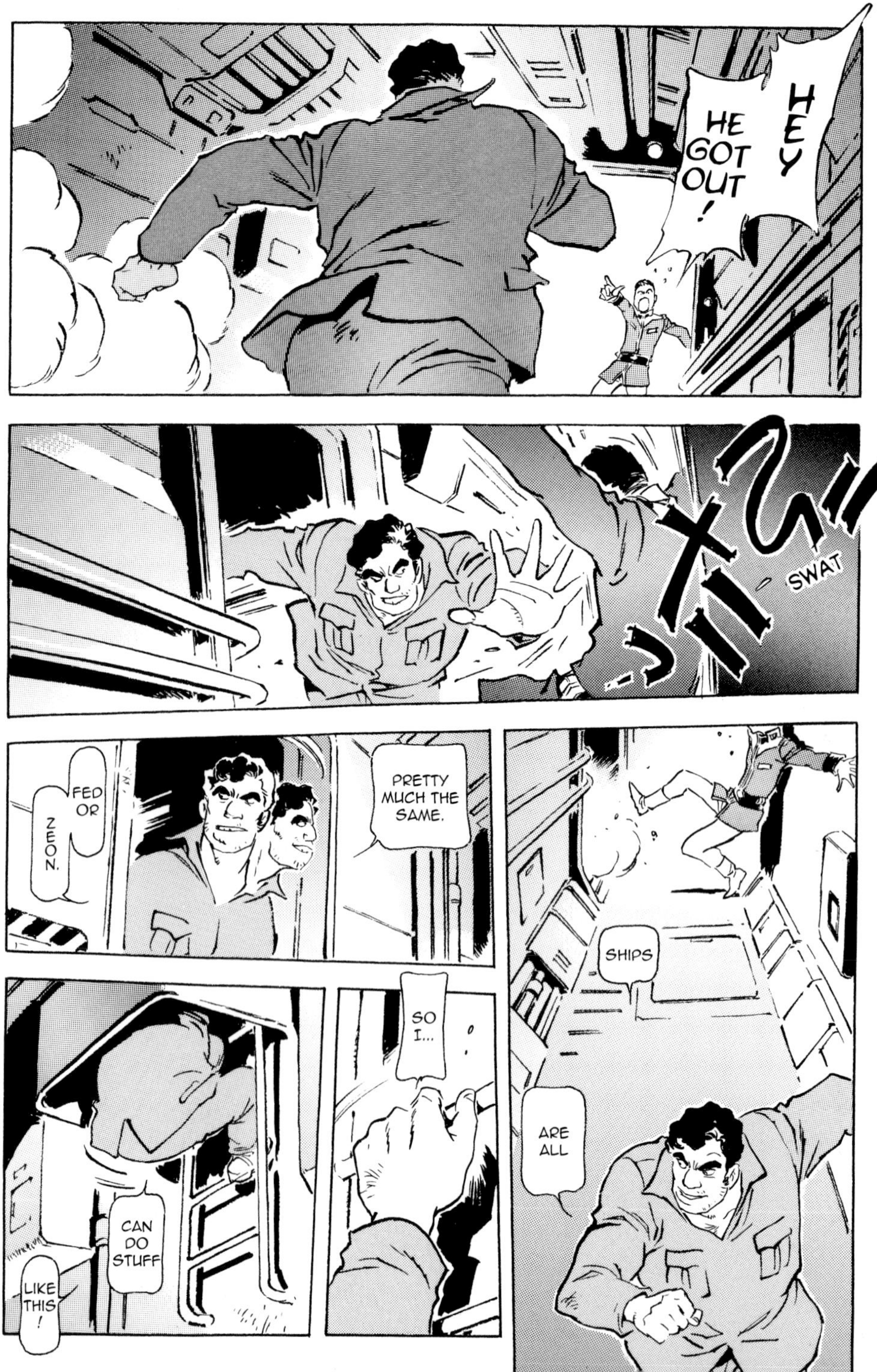
HEY
HE GOT OUT!
SWAT
SHIPS
ARE ALL
PRETTY MUCH THE SAME.
FED OR
ZEON.
SO I...
CAN DO STUFF
LIKE THIS!

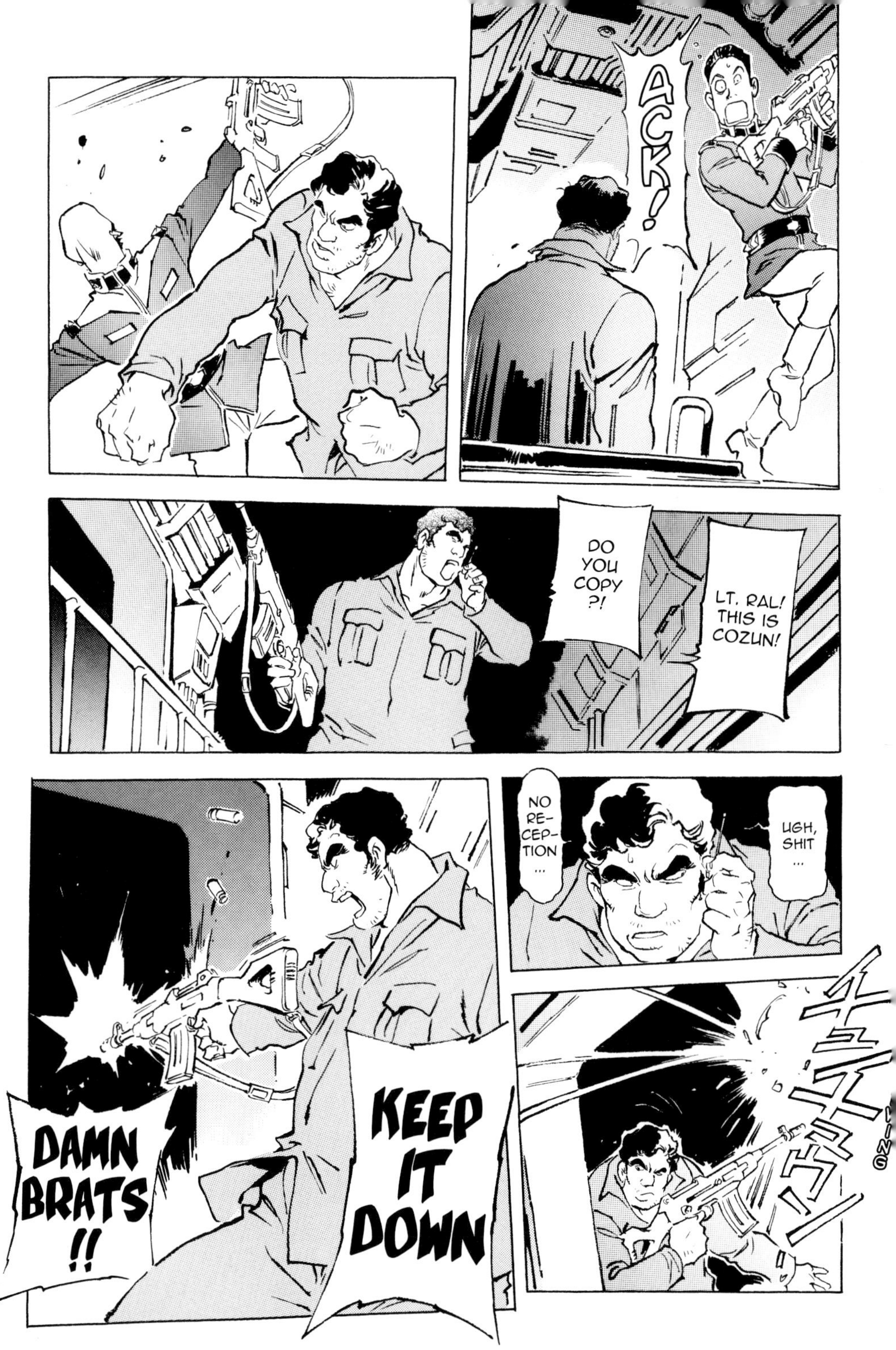
ACK!
LT. RAL! THIS IS COZUN!
DO YOU COPY?!
UGH, SHIT...
NO RECEPTION...
KEEP IT DOWN
DAMN BRATS!!

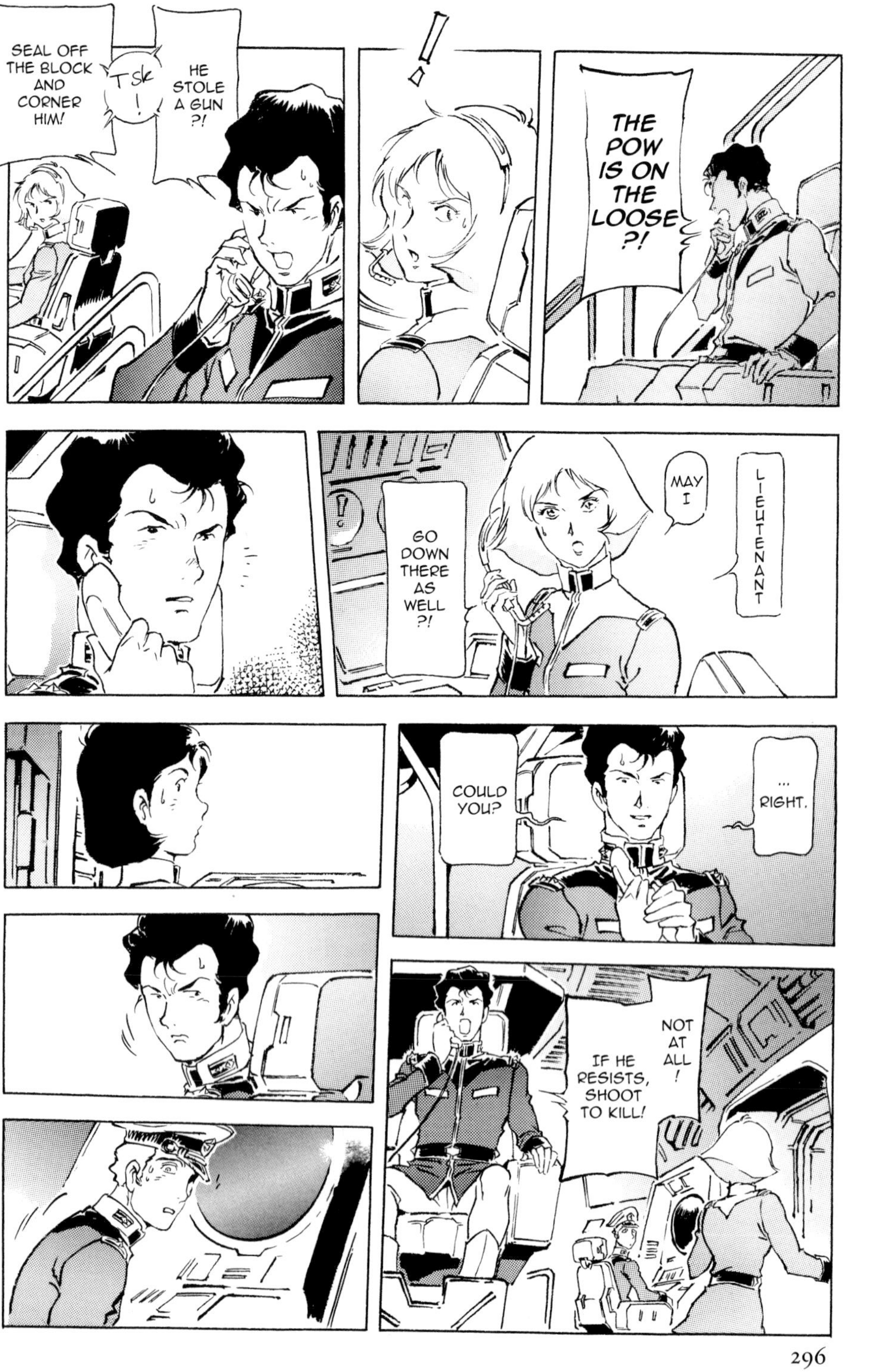
THE POW IS ON THE LOOSE ?!
!
HE STOLE A GUN ?!
TSK !
SEAL OFF THE BLOCK AND CORNER HIM!
LIEUTENANT
MAY I
GO DOWN THERE AS WELL ?!
... RIGHT.
COULD YOU?
NOT AT ALL !
IF HE RESISTS, SHOOT TO KILL!

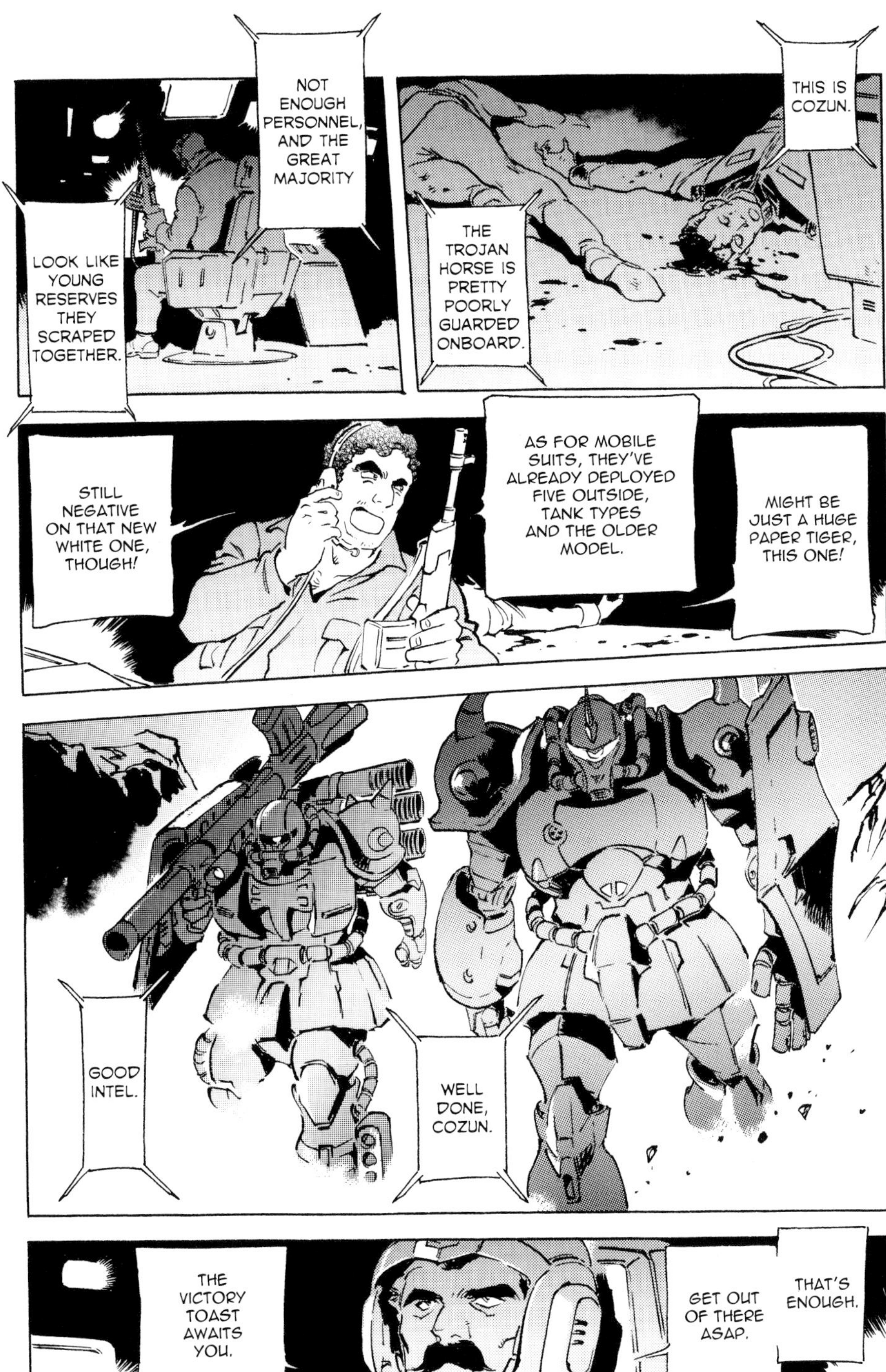
THIS IS COZUN.
THE TROJAN HORSE IS PRETTY POORLY GUARDED ONBOARD.
NOT ENOUGH PERSONNEL, AND THE GREAT MAJORITY
LOOK LIKE YOUNG RESERVES THEY SCRAPED TOGETHER.
AS FOR MOBILE SUITS, THEY'VE ALREADY DEPLOYED FIVE OUTSIDE, TANK TYPES AND THE OLDER MODEL.
MIGHT BE JUST A HUGE PAPER TIGER, THIS ONE!
STILL NEGATIVE ON THAT NEW WHITE ONE, THOUGH!
WELL DONE, COZUN.
GOOD INTEL.
THAT'S ENOUGH.
GET OUT OF THERE ASAP.
THE VICTORY TOAST AWAITS YOU.

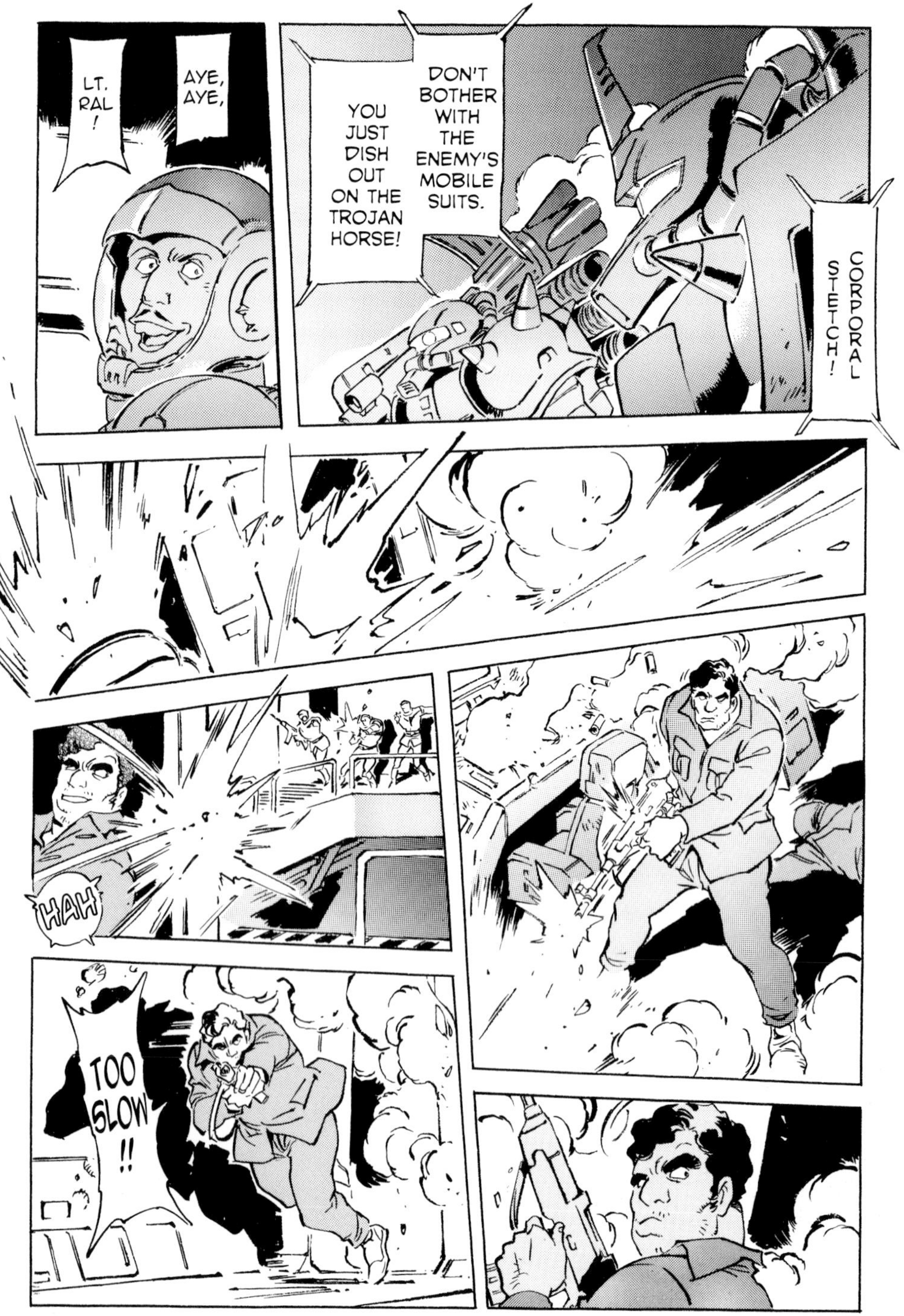
CORPORAL STETCH!
DON'T BOTHER WITH THE ENEMY'S MOBILE SUITS.
YOU JUST DISH OUT ON THE TROJAN HORSE!
AYE, AYE,
LT. RAL!
HAH
TOO SLOW !!

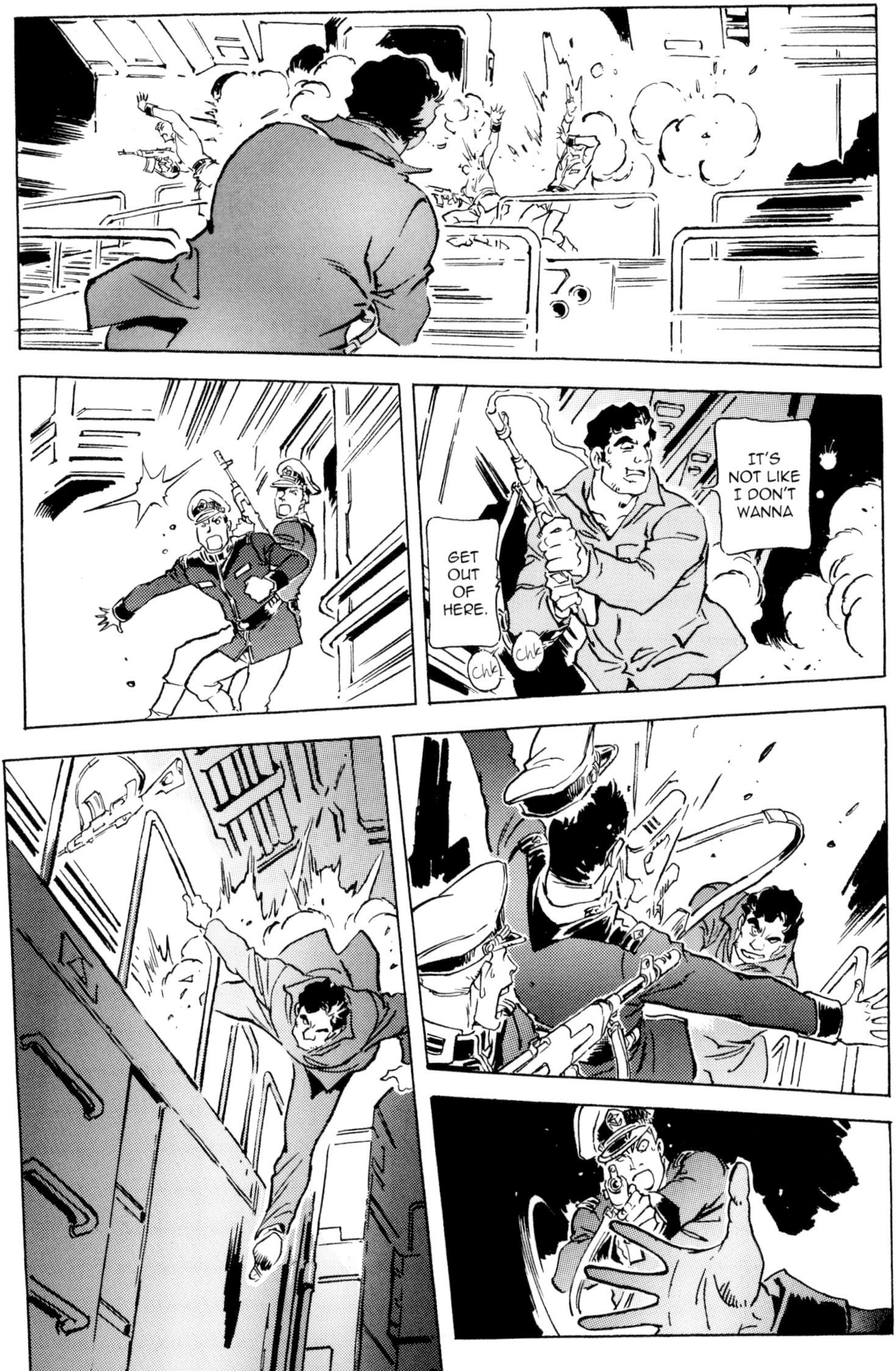
IT'S NOT LIKE I DON'T WANNA
GET OUT OF HERE.
Chk
Chk

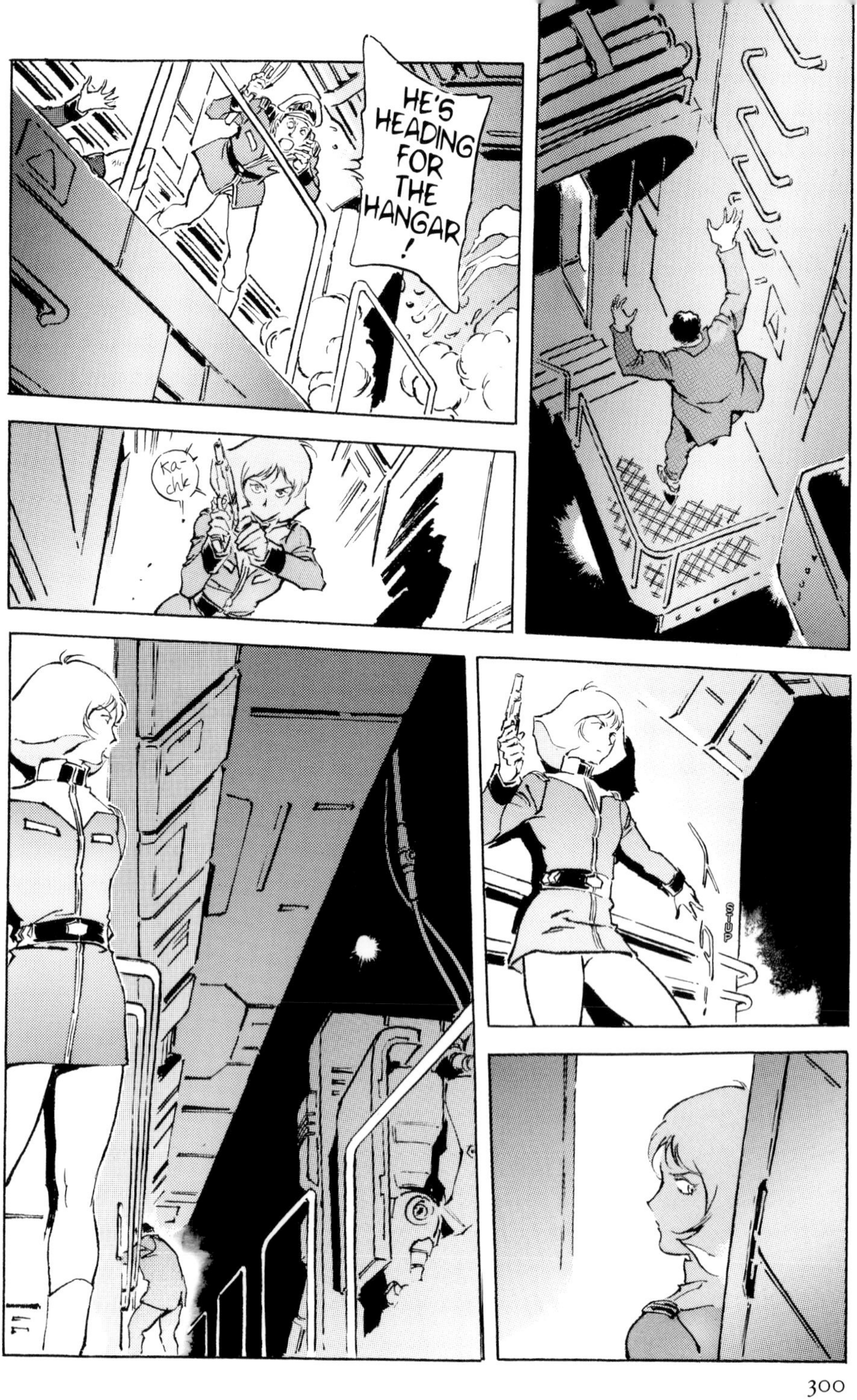
HE'S HEADING FOR THE HANGAR!
Ka-chk!
STUP

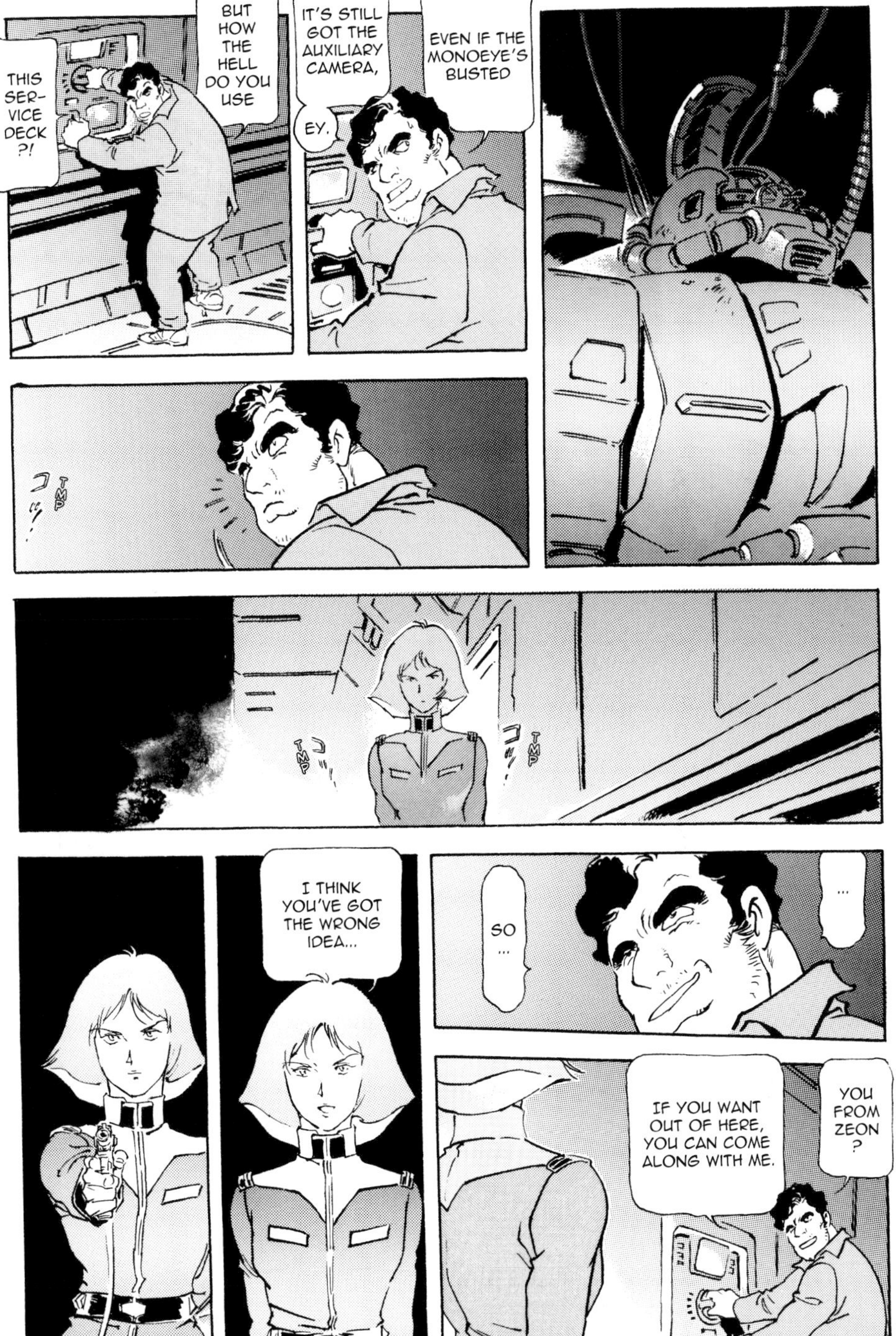
EVEN IF THE MONOEYE'S BUSTED
IT'S STILL GOT THE AUXILIARY CAMERA,
EY.
BUT HOW THE HELL DO YOU USE
THIS SER-VICE DECK ?!
TMP
TMP
TMP
...
SO ...
YOU FROM ZEON ?
IF YOU WANT OUT OF HERE, YOU CAN COME ALONG WITH ME.
I THINK YOU'VE GOT THE WRONG IDEA...

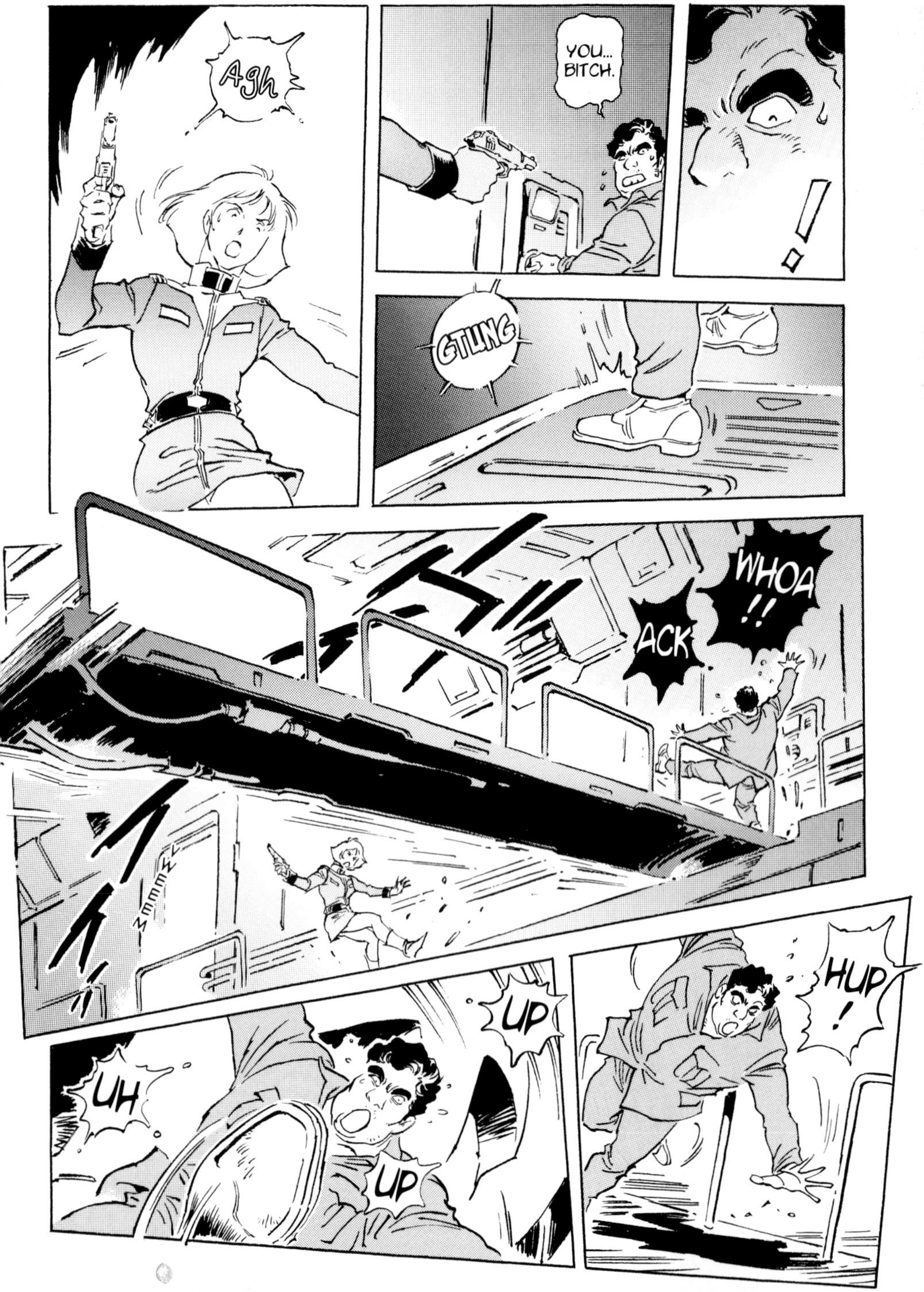
!
YOU... BITCH.
GTUNG
Agh
WHOA !!
ACK
HUP !
UP
UH
UP

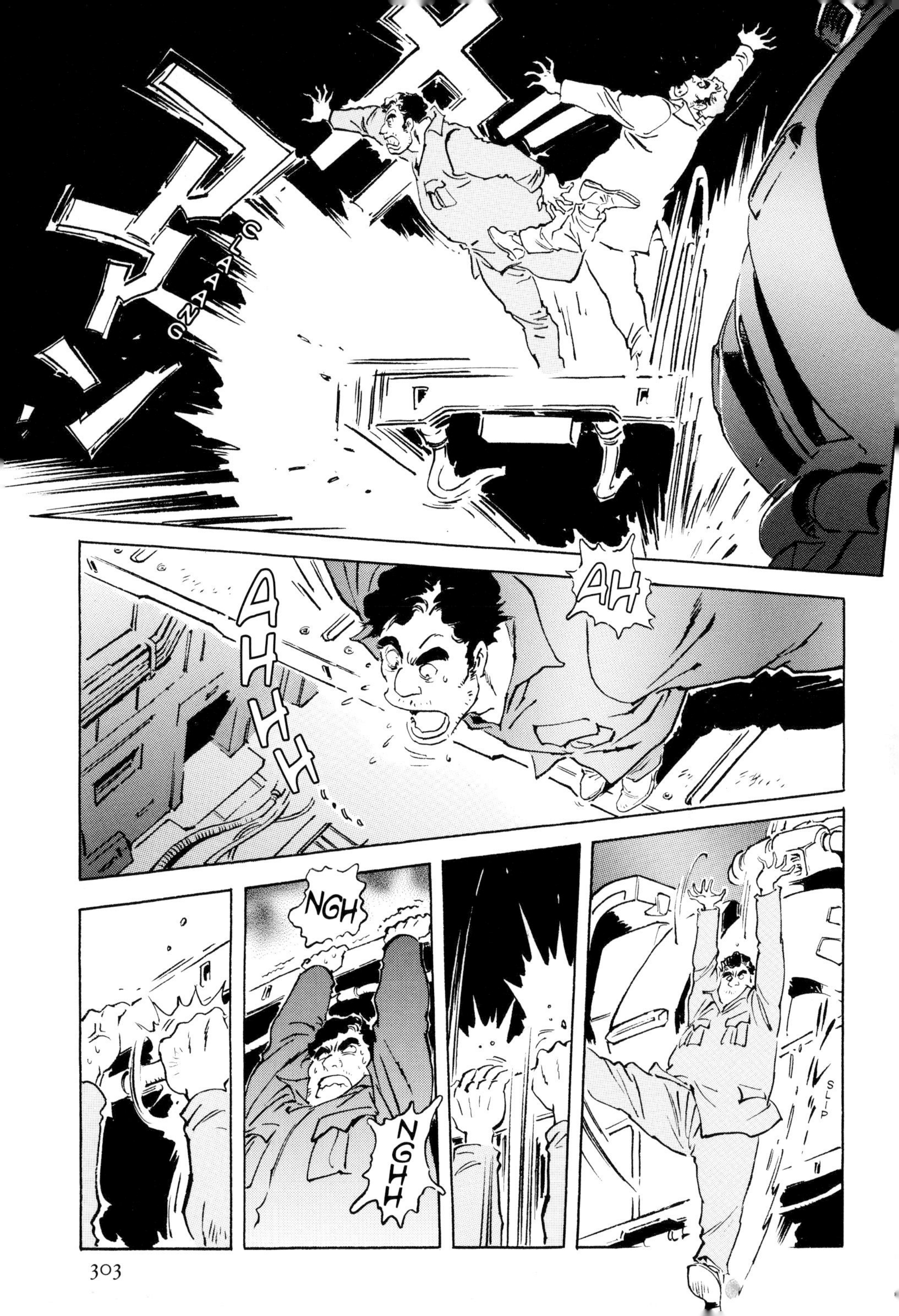
CLAAANG
AH
AHHH...
SLIP
NGH
NGHH

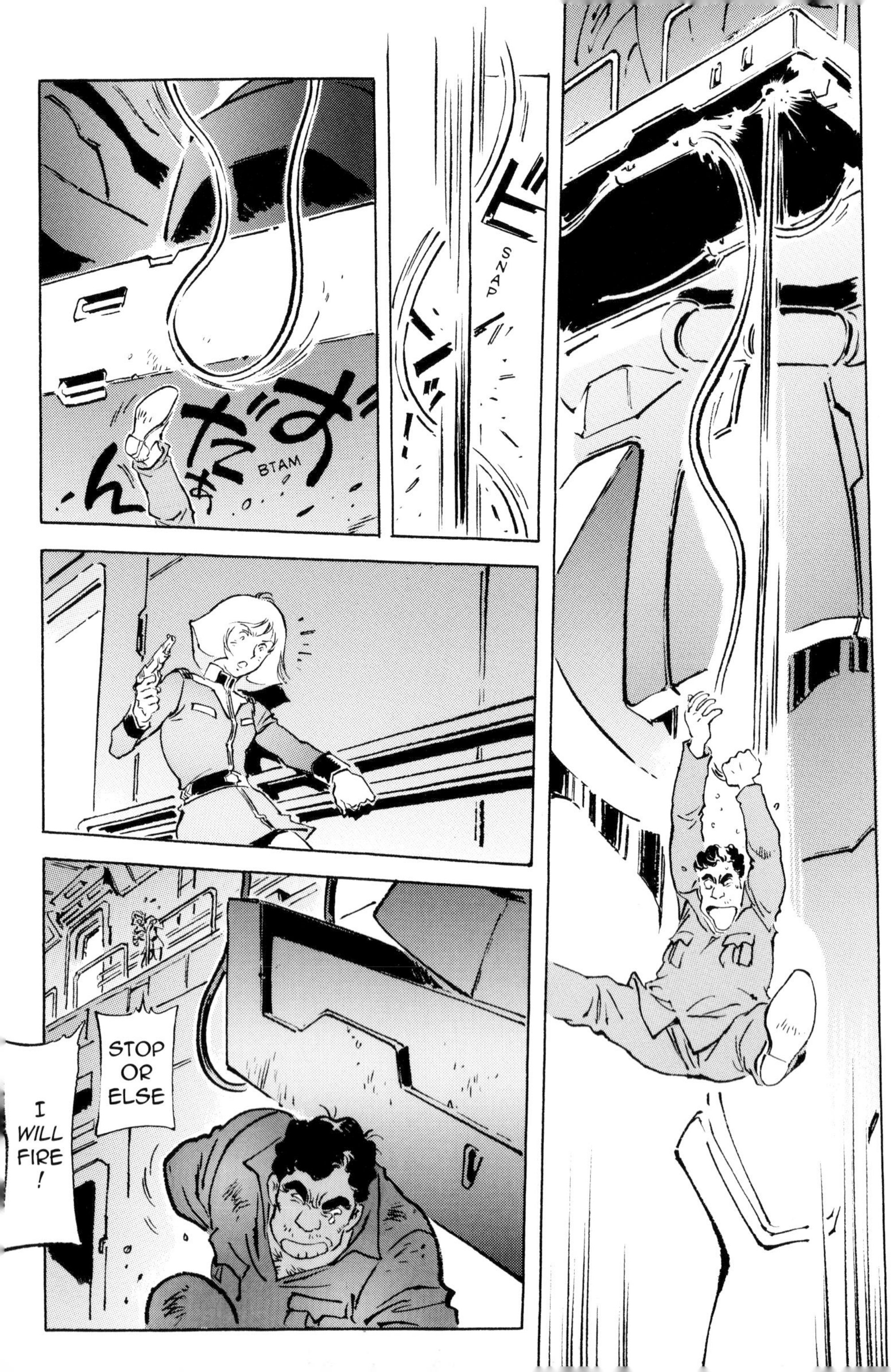
SNAP
BTAM
STOP OR ELSE
I WILL FIRE !

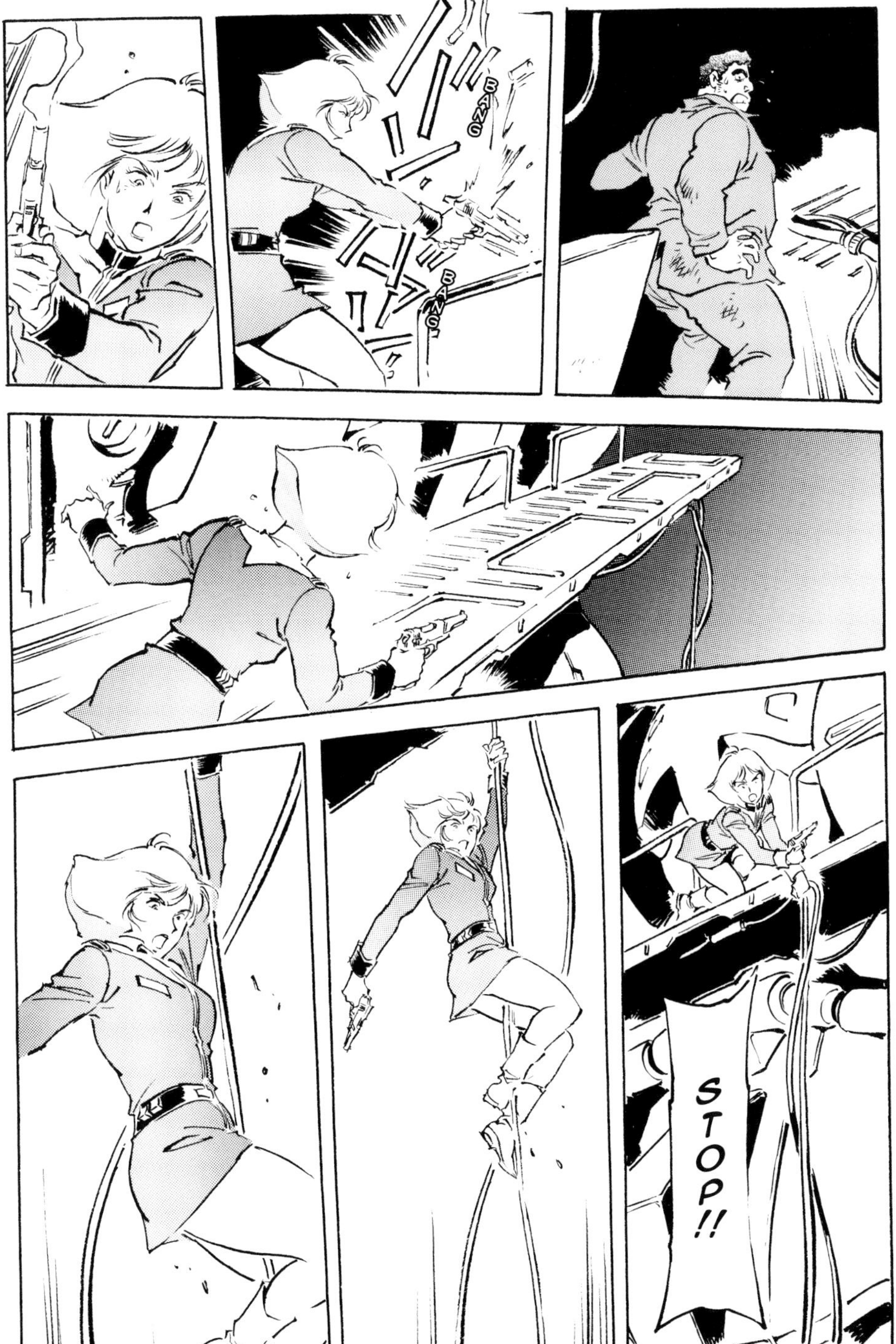
BANG
BANG
STOP!!

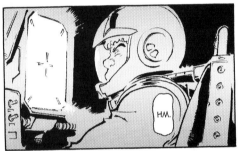

HM.

RYU
...

IT'S
TOO
QUIET,

SNORRRE

MAYBE THEY
GAVE UP AND
TURNED BACK
AFTER SEEIN'
OUR TIGHT
DEFENSES...

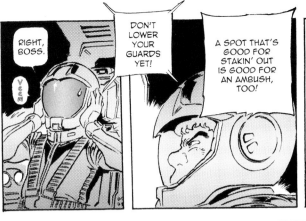

WAKE UP, KAI!
A SPOT THAT'S GOOD FOR STAKIN' OUT IS GOOD FOR AN AMBUSH, TOO!
DON'T LOWER YOUR GUARDS YET!
RIGHT, BOSS.
Veem
JOB!
DANIEL TOO, EVERYTHING OKAY?!
YANG! N'XAU!
HOW'S IT LOOK ON YOUR SIDE?!
ALL CLEAR TO THE REAR TOO, SIR!
VISIBILITY OPTIMAL!
THE STARS ARE OUT, SARGE.
PRETTY...
ズン
ZUM

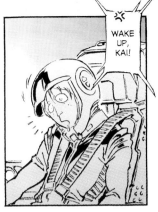

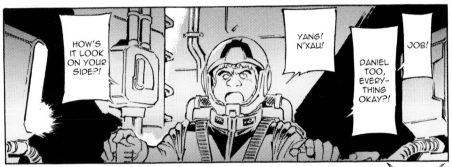

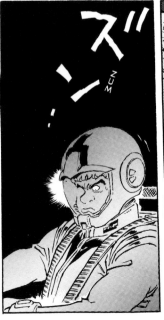

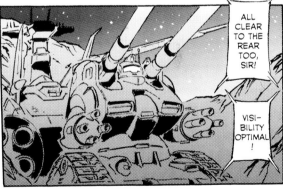

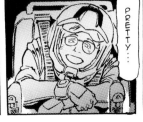

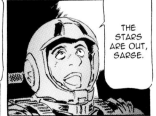

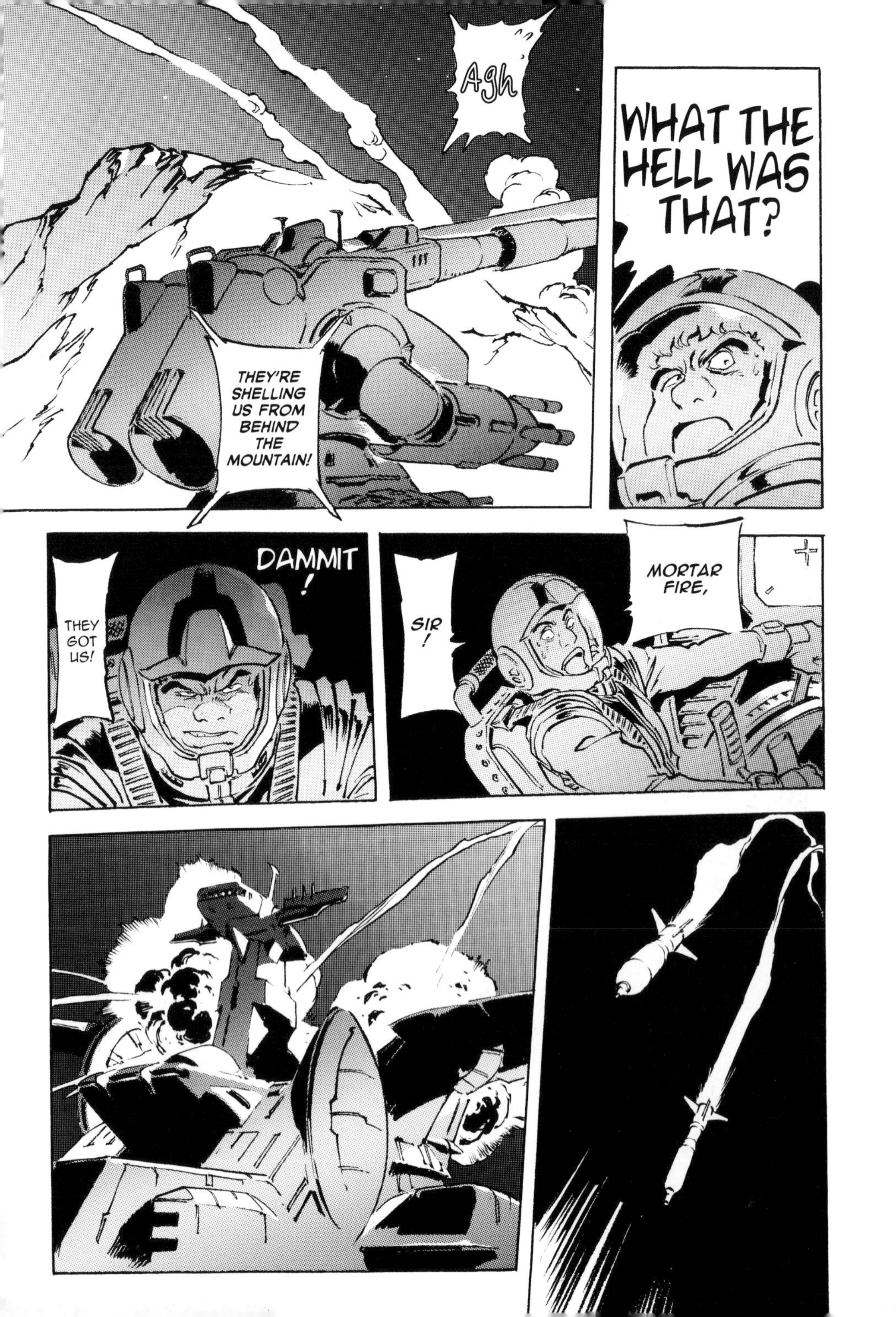
WHAT THE HELL WAS THAT?
Agh
THEY'RE SHELLING US FROM BEHIND THE MOUNTAIN!
MORTAR FIRE,
SIR!
DAMMIT!
THEY GOT US!

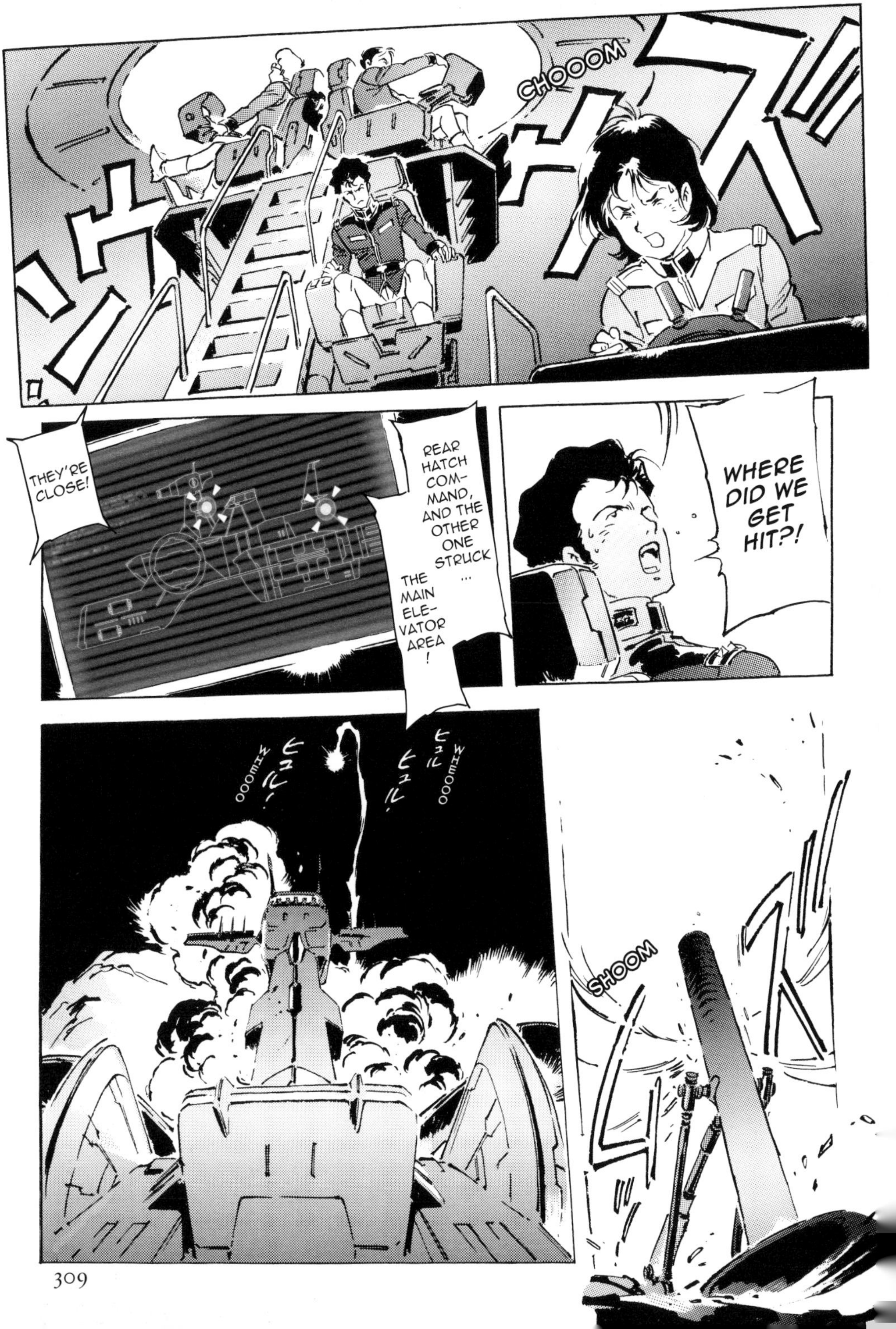
CHOOOM
WHERE DID WE GET HIT?!
REAR HATCH COMMAND, AND THE OTHER ONE STRUCK...
THE MAIN ELEVATOR AREA!
THEY'RE CLOSE!
SHOOM
ヒュル ヒュル!
WHEOOO
ヒュル ヒュル!
WHEOOO

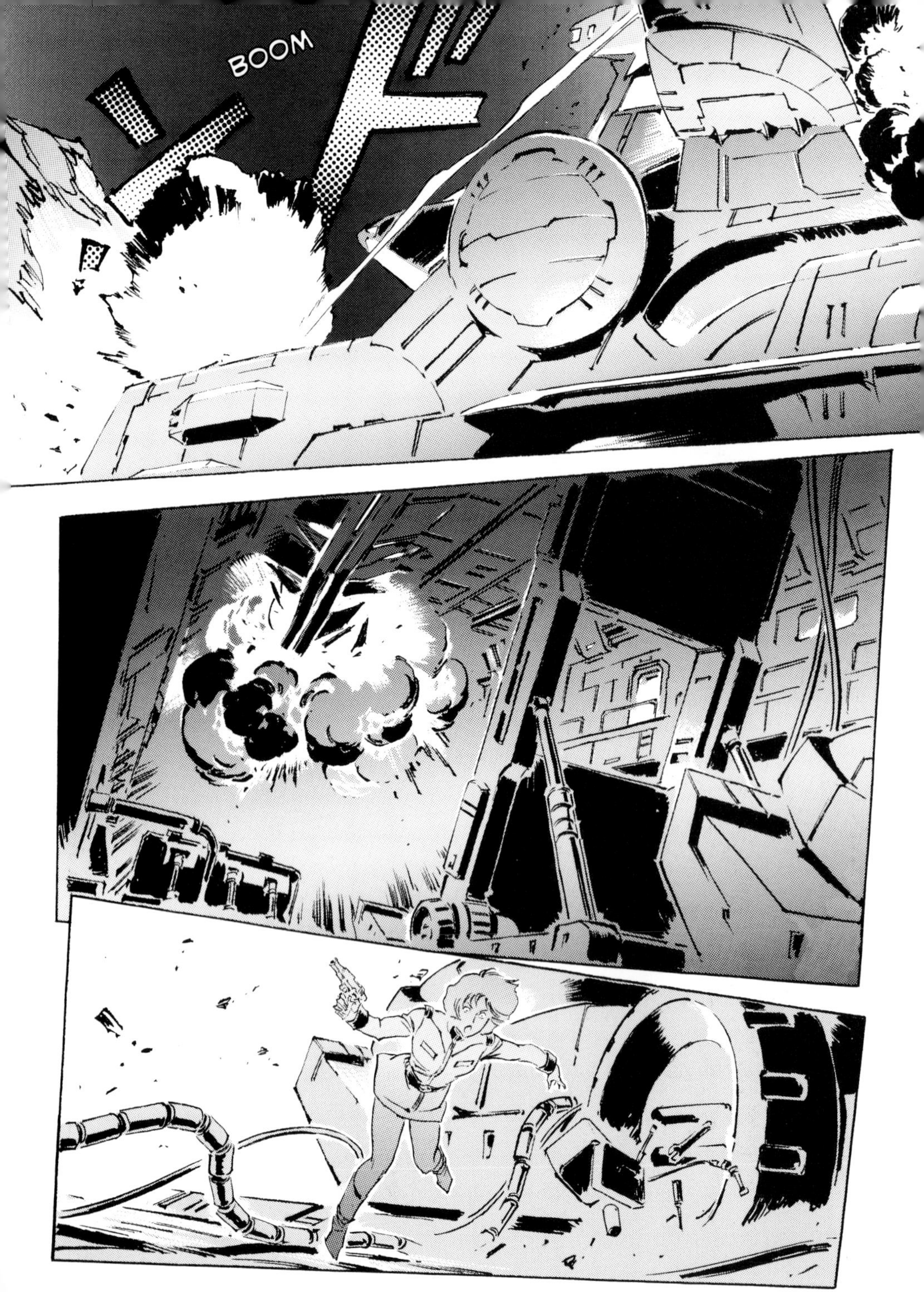
BOOM

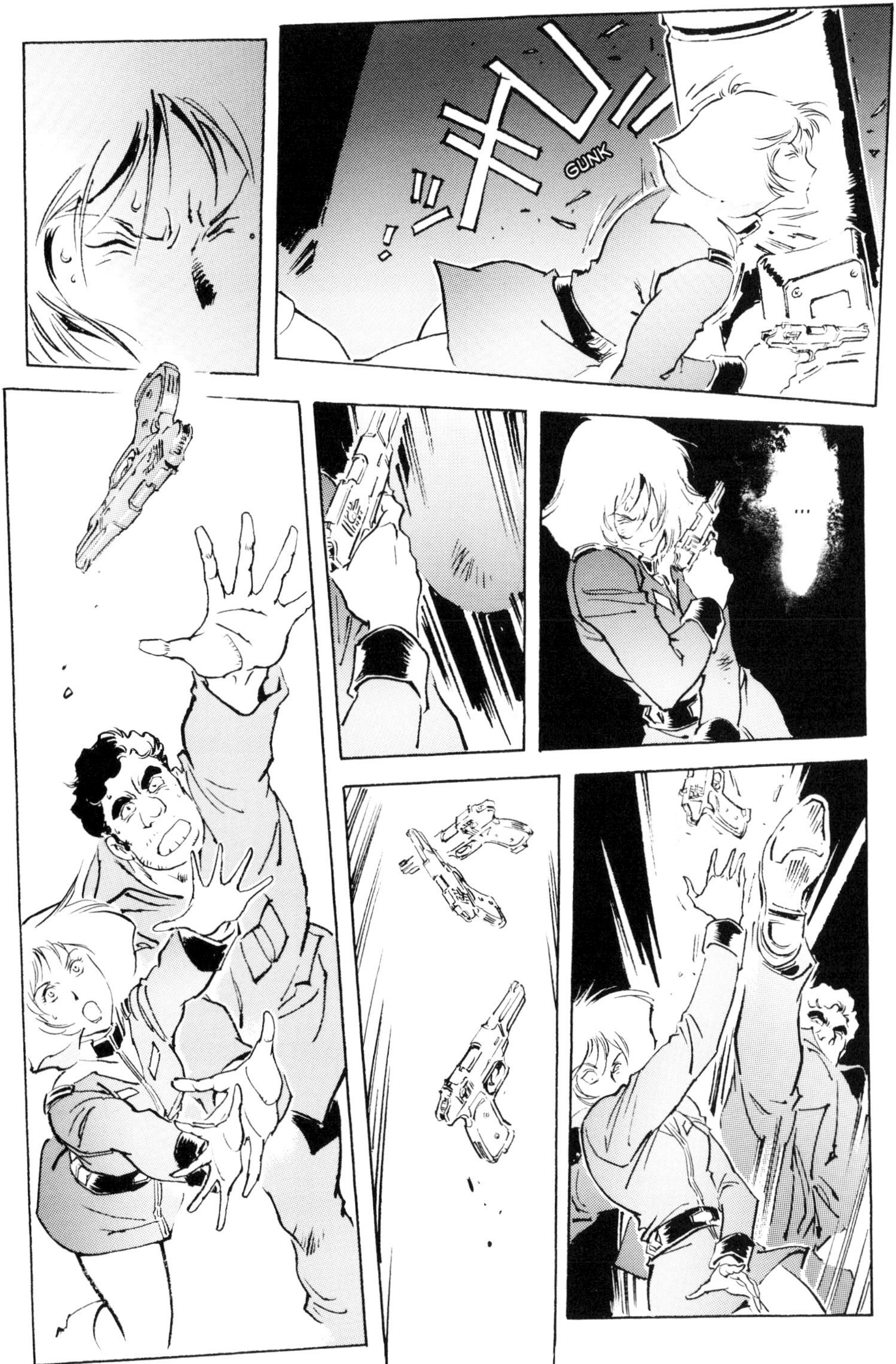
GUNK
...

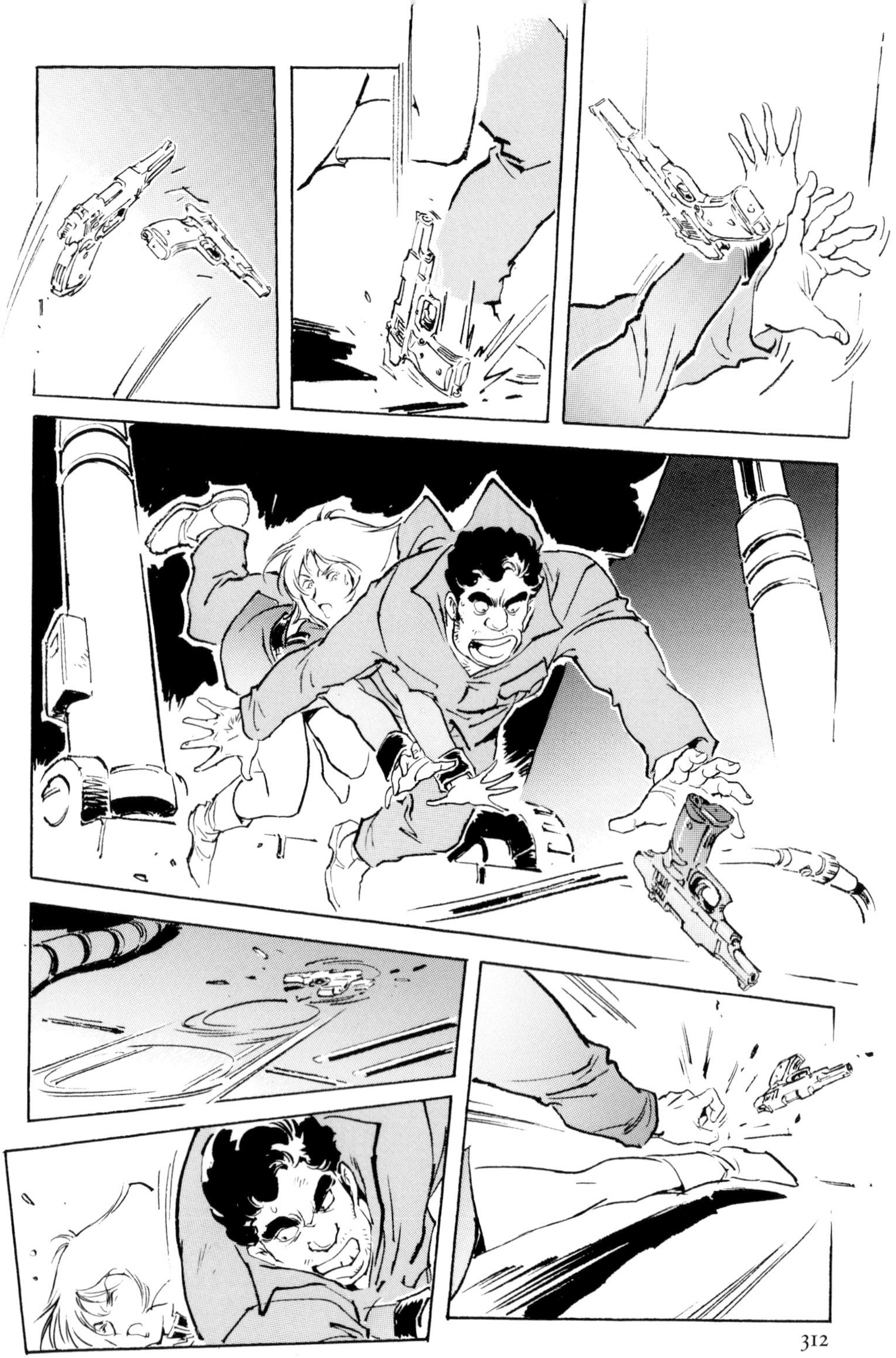

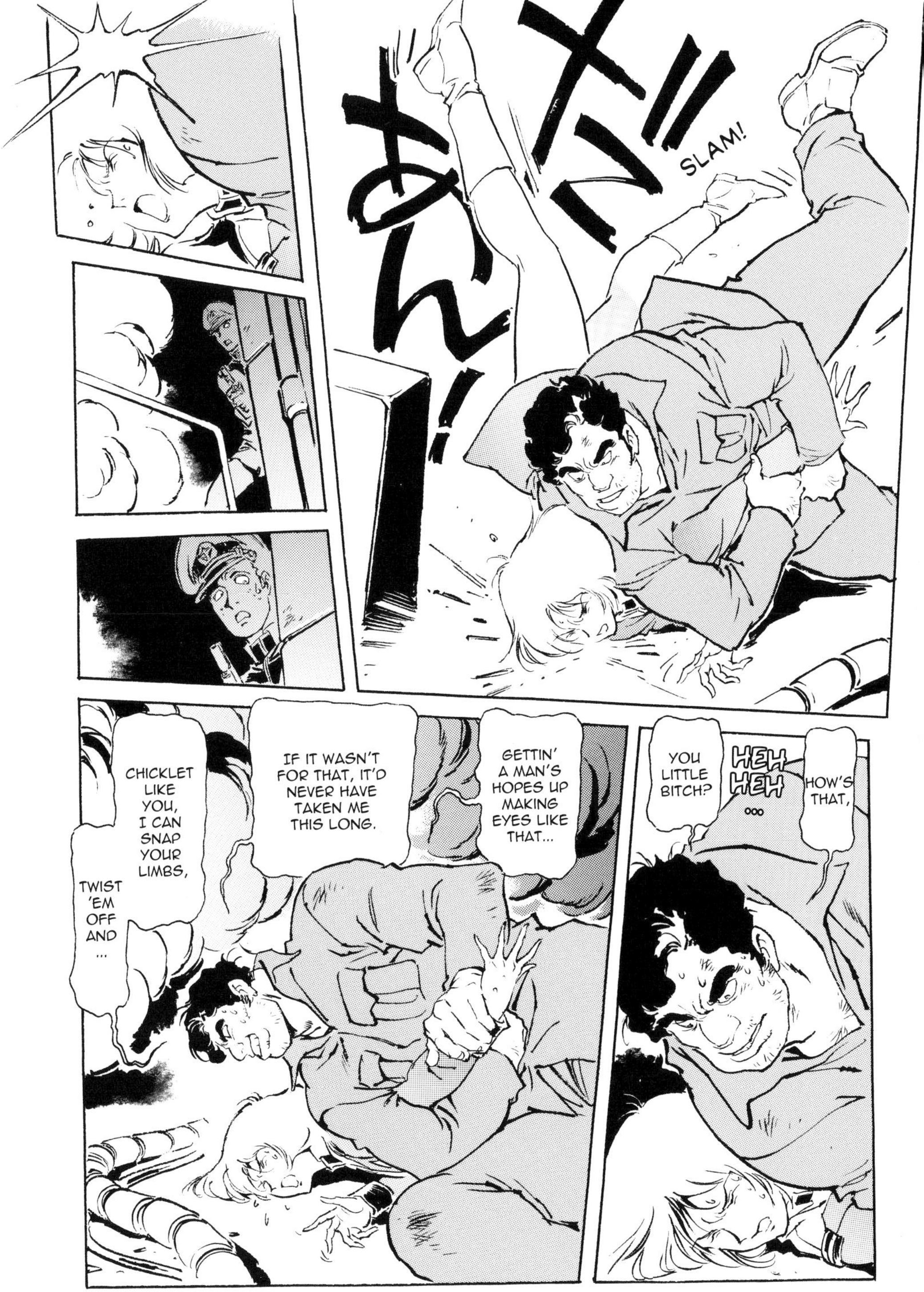
だあん!!
SLAM!
HOW'S THAT,
HEH HEH ...
YOU LITTLE BITCH?
GETTIN' A MAN'S HOPES UP MAKING EYES LIKE THAT...
IF IT WASN'T FOR THAT, IT'D NEVER HAVE TAKEN ME THIS LONG.
CHICKLET LIKE YOU, I CAN SNAP YOUR LIMBS,
TWIST 'EM OFF AND ...

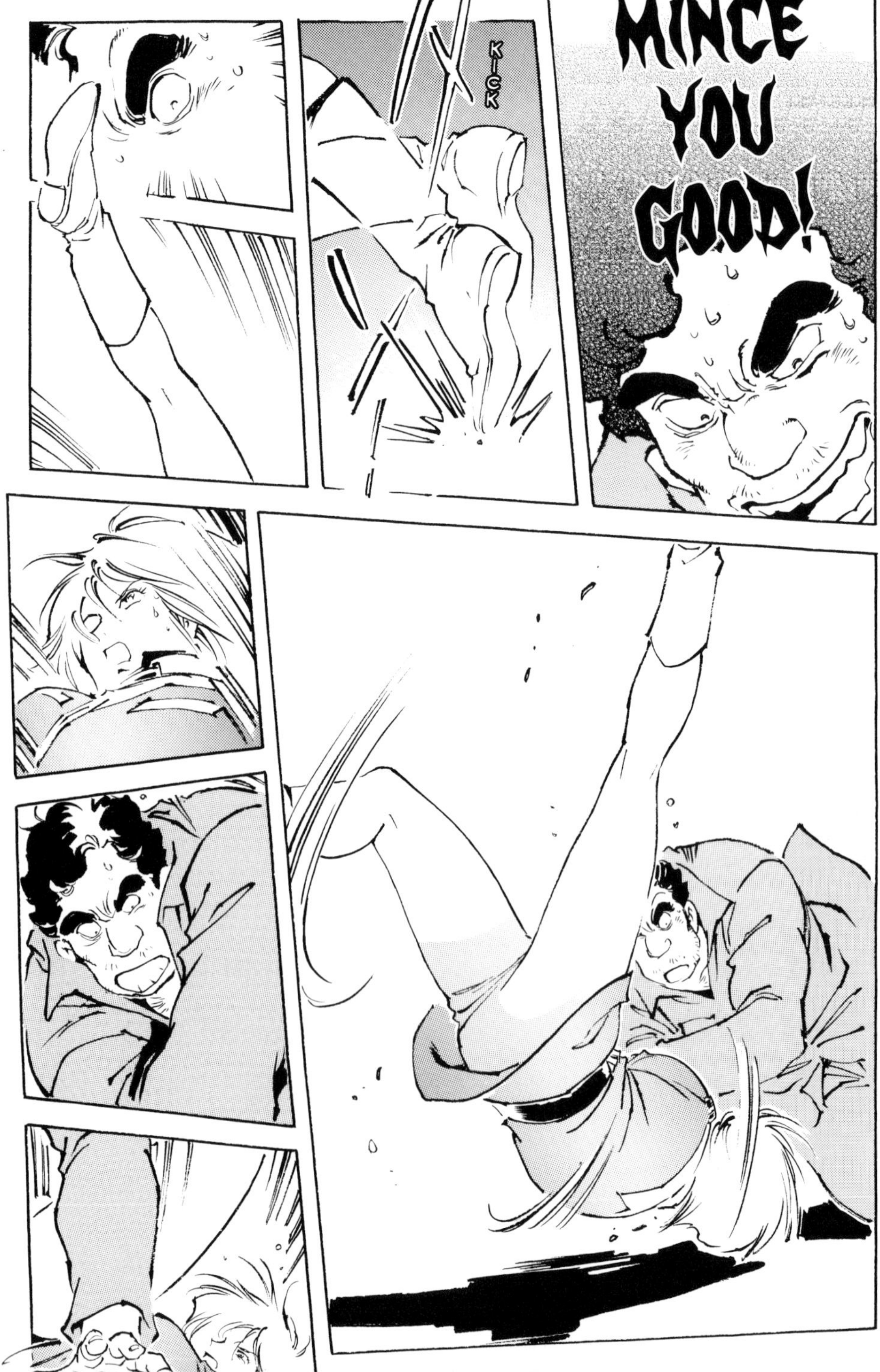
MINCE YOU GOOD!
KICK

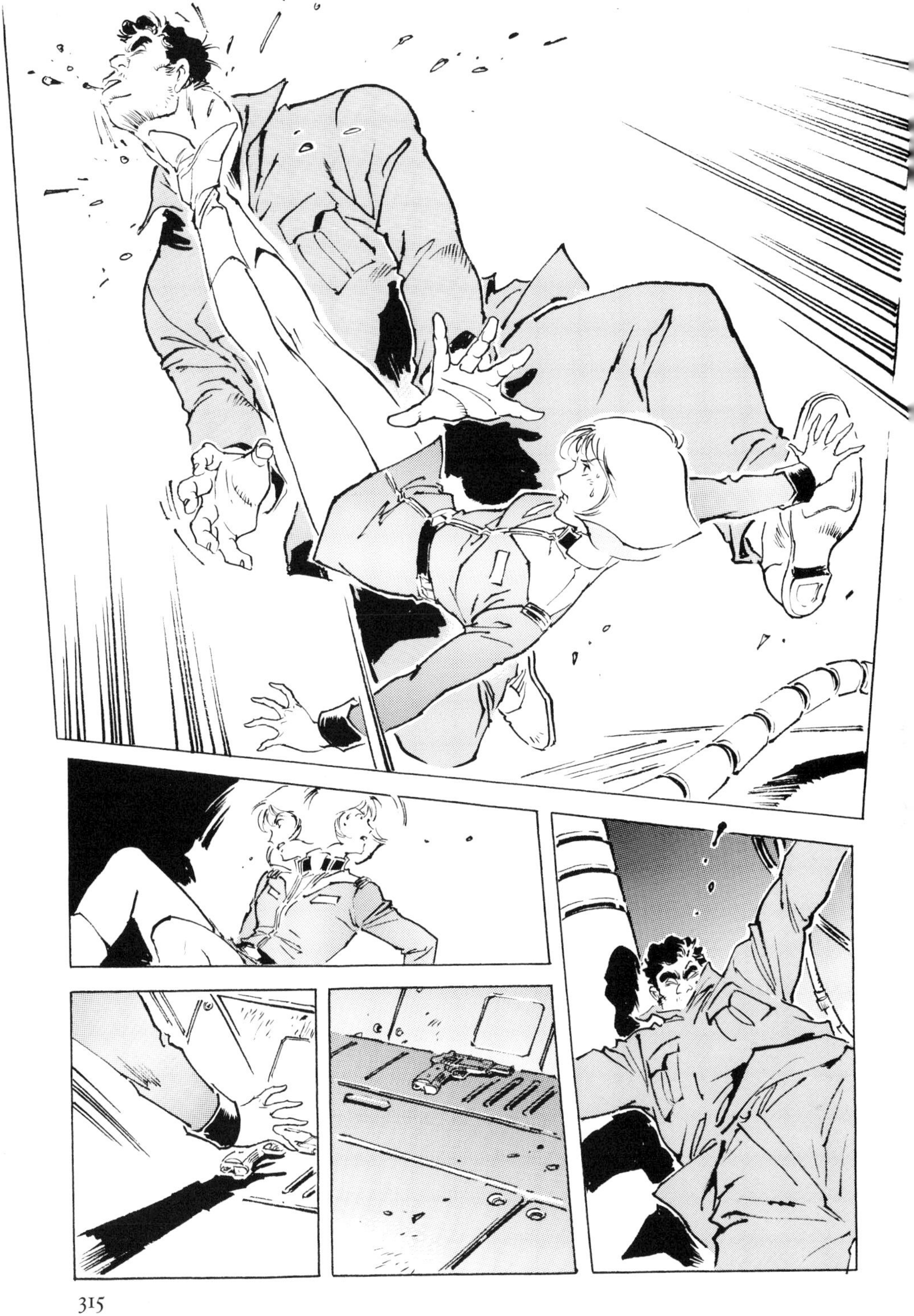

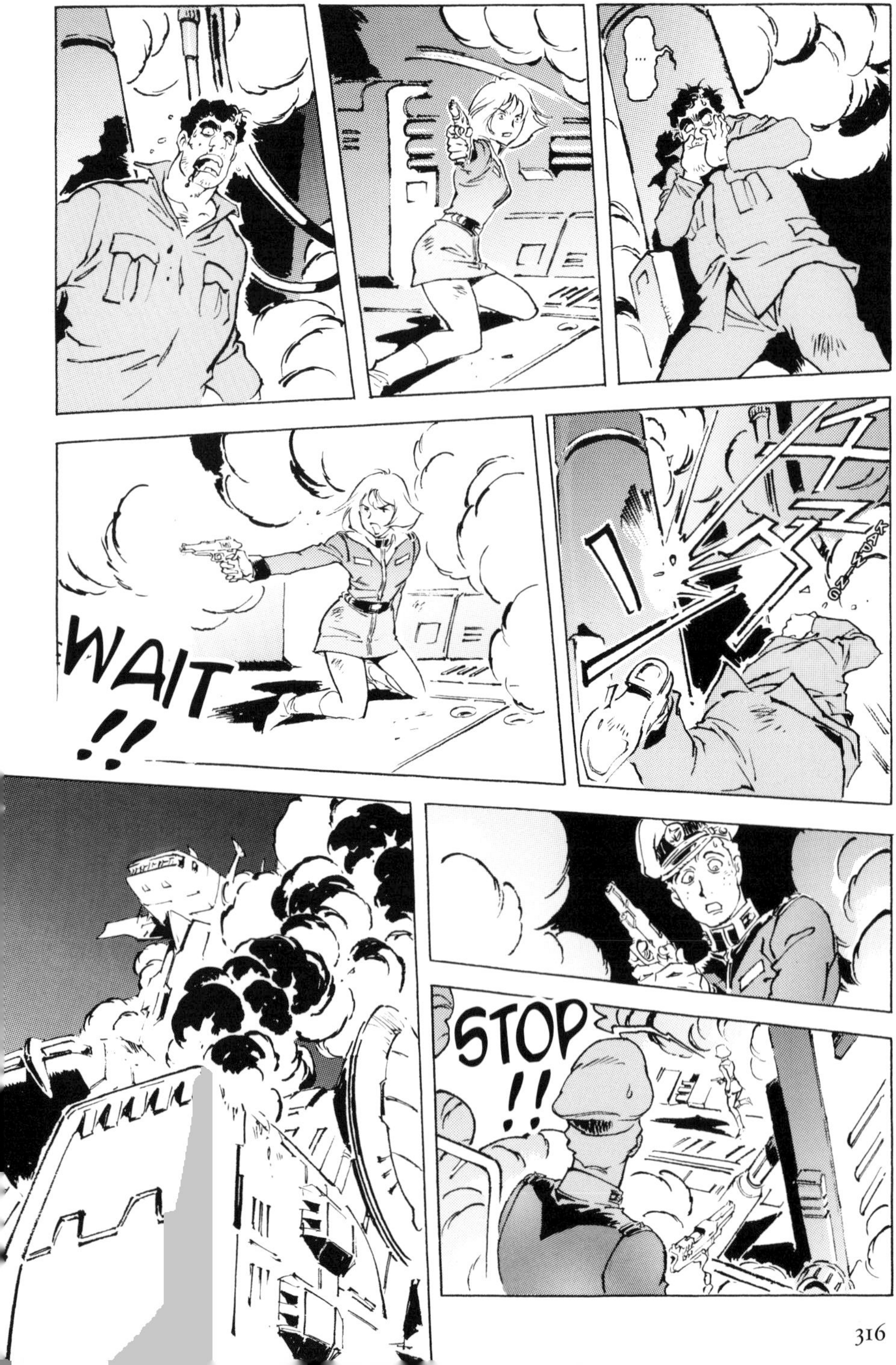
...
WAIT !!
STOP !!

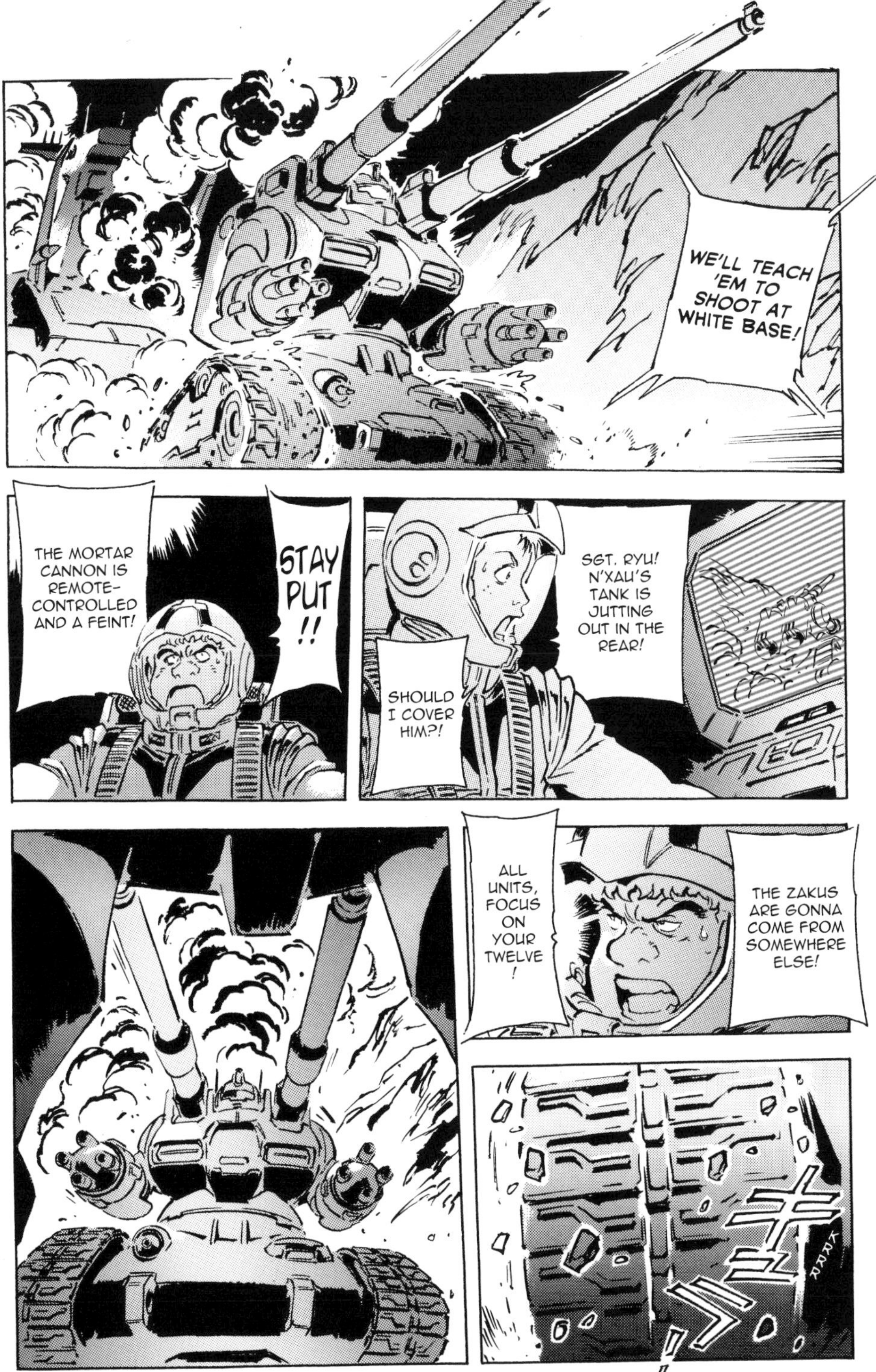

WE'LL TEACH 'EM TO SHOOT AT WHITE BASE!
SGT. RYU! N'XAU'S TANK IS JUTTING OUT IN THE REAR!
SHOULD I COVER HIM?!
STAY PUT!!
THE MORTAR CANNON IS REMOTE-CONTROLLED AND A FEINT!
THE ZAKUS ARE GONNA COME FROM SOMEWHERE ELSE!
ALL UNITS, FOCUS ON YOUR TWELVE!

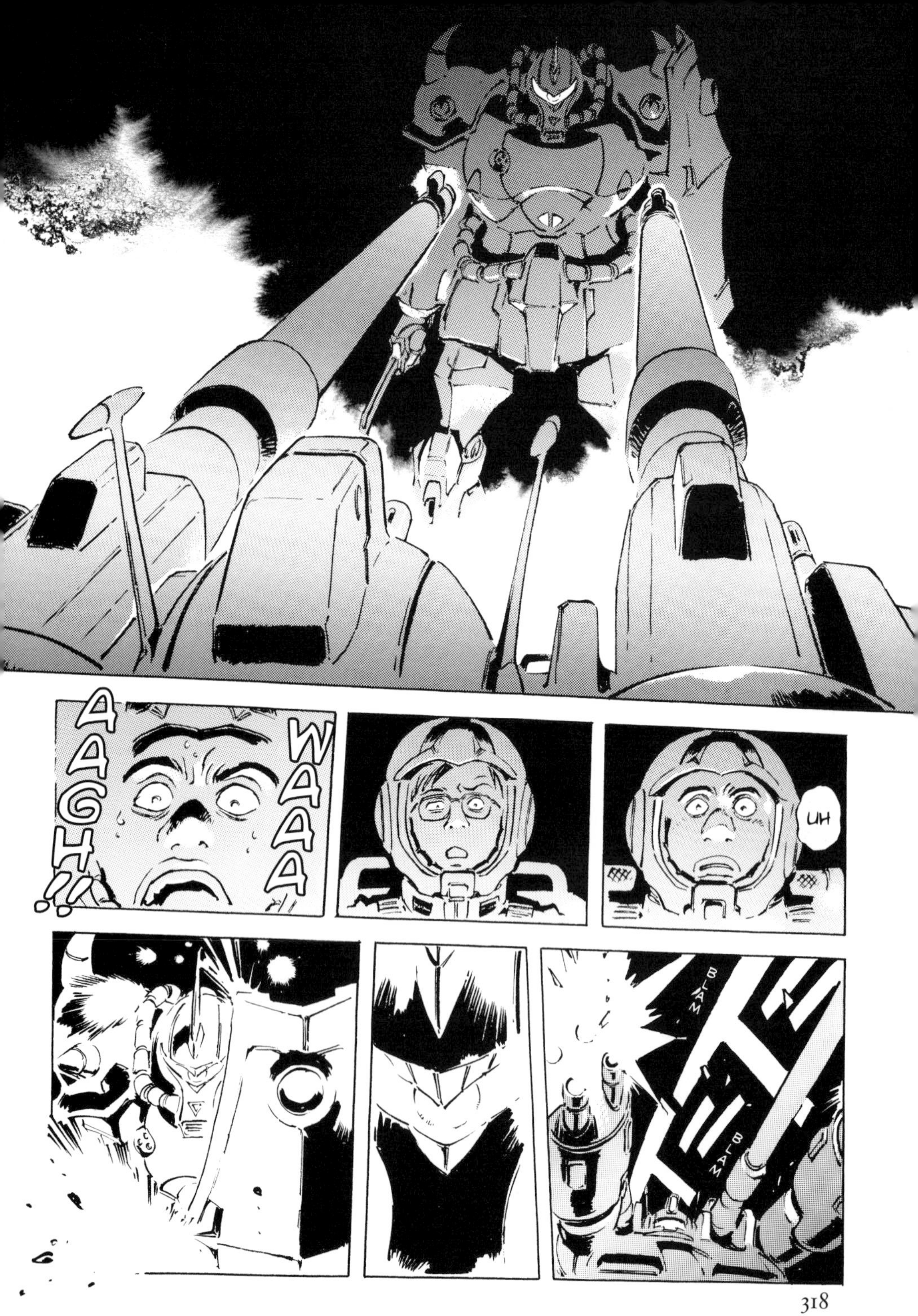
UH
WAAAA
AAGH!!
BLAM
BLAM

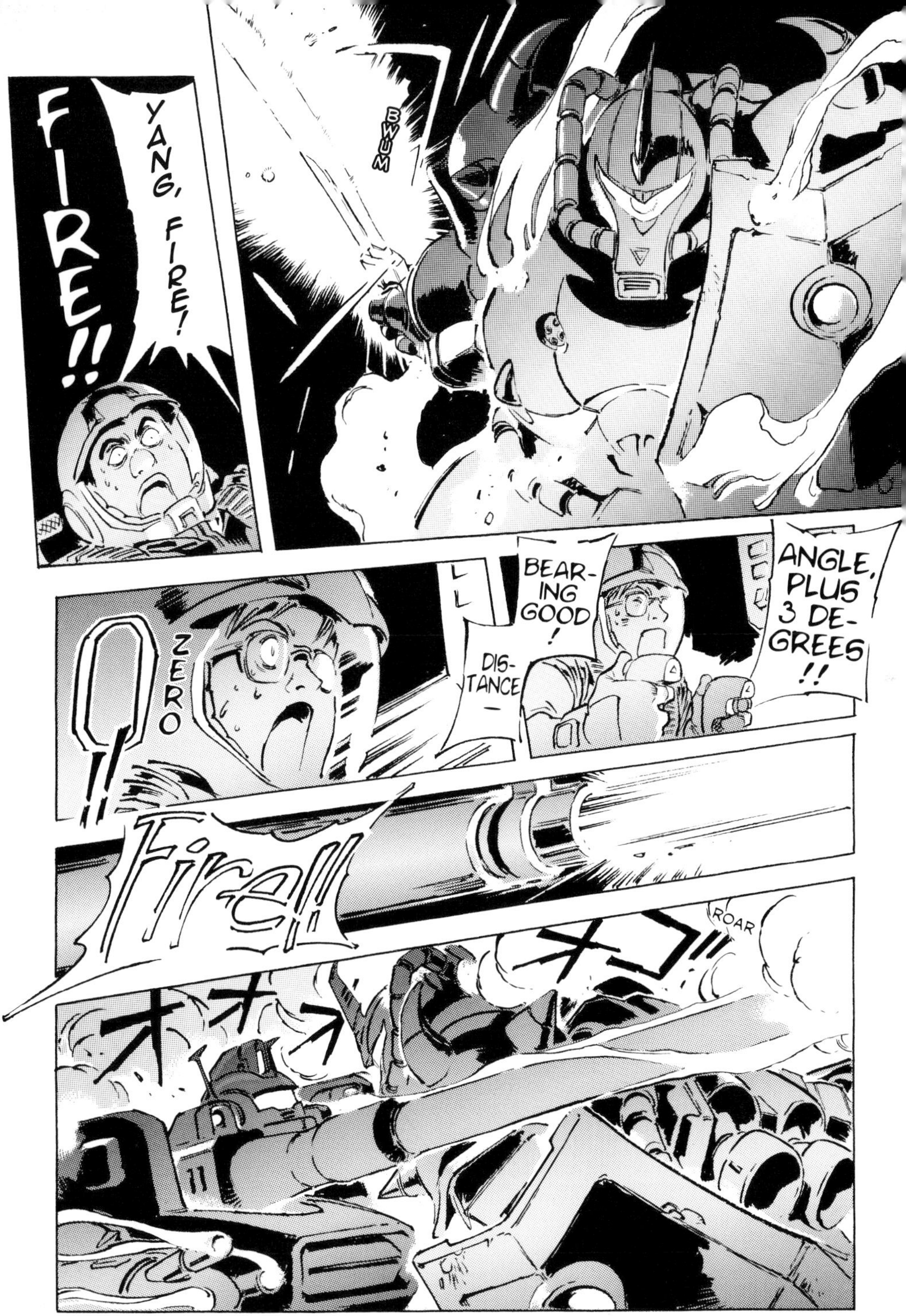

BWUM
YANG, FIRE!
FIRE!!
ANGLE, PLUS 3 DEGREES!!
BEARING GOOD!
DISTANCE—
ZERO
0!!
Fire!!
ROAR

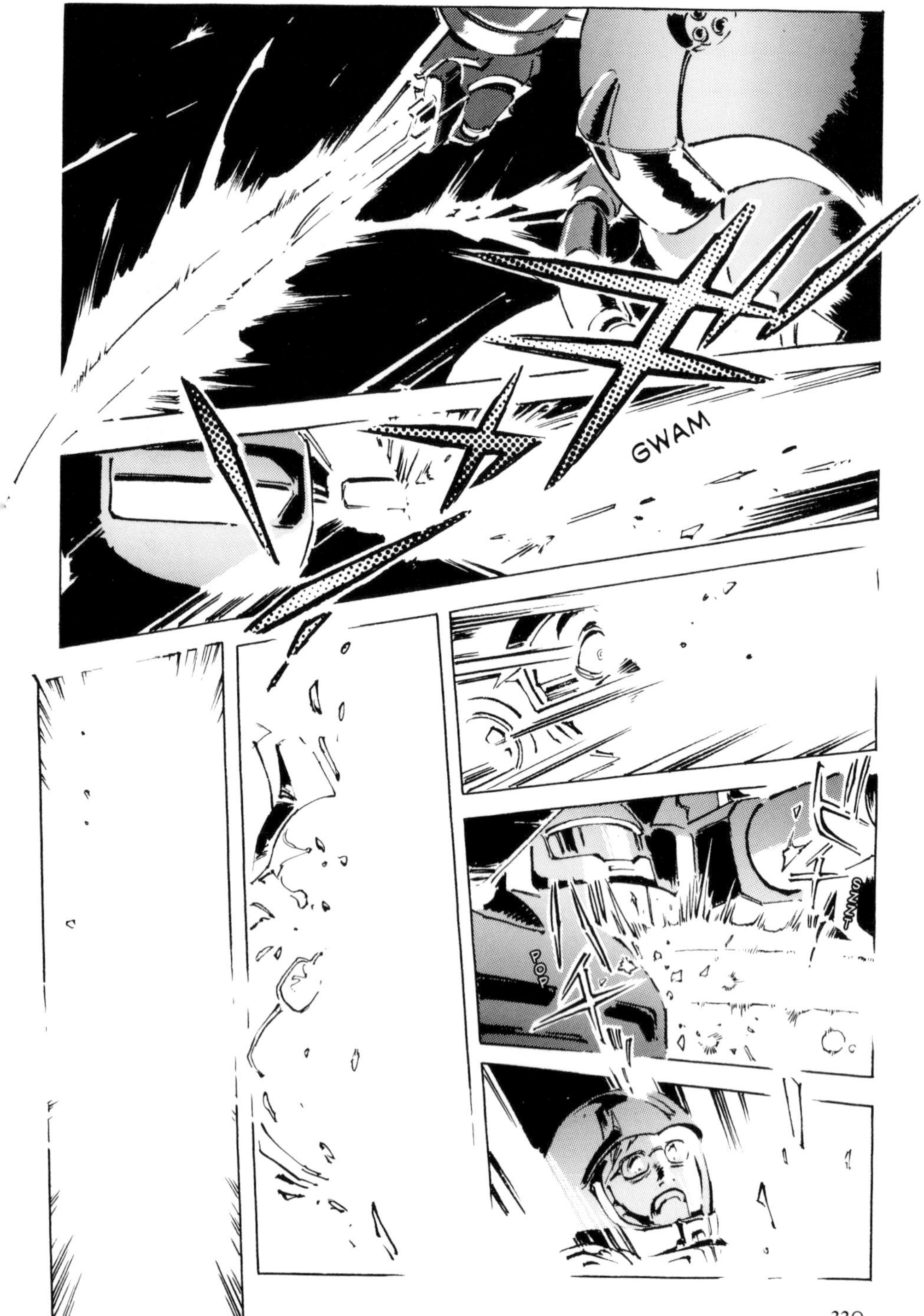
GWAM
SNNN-
POP

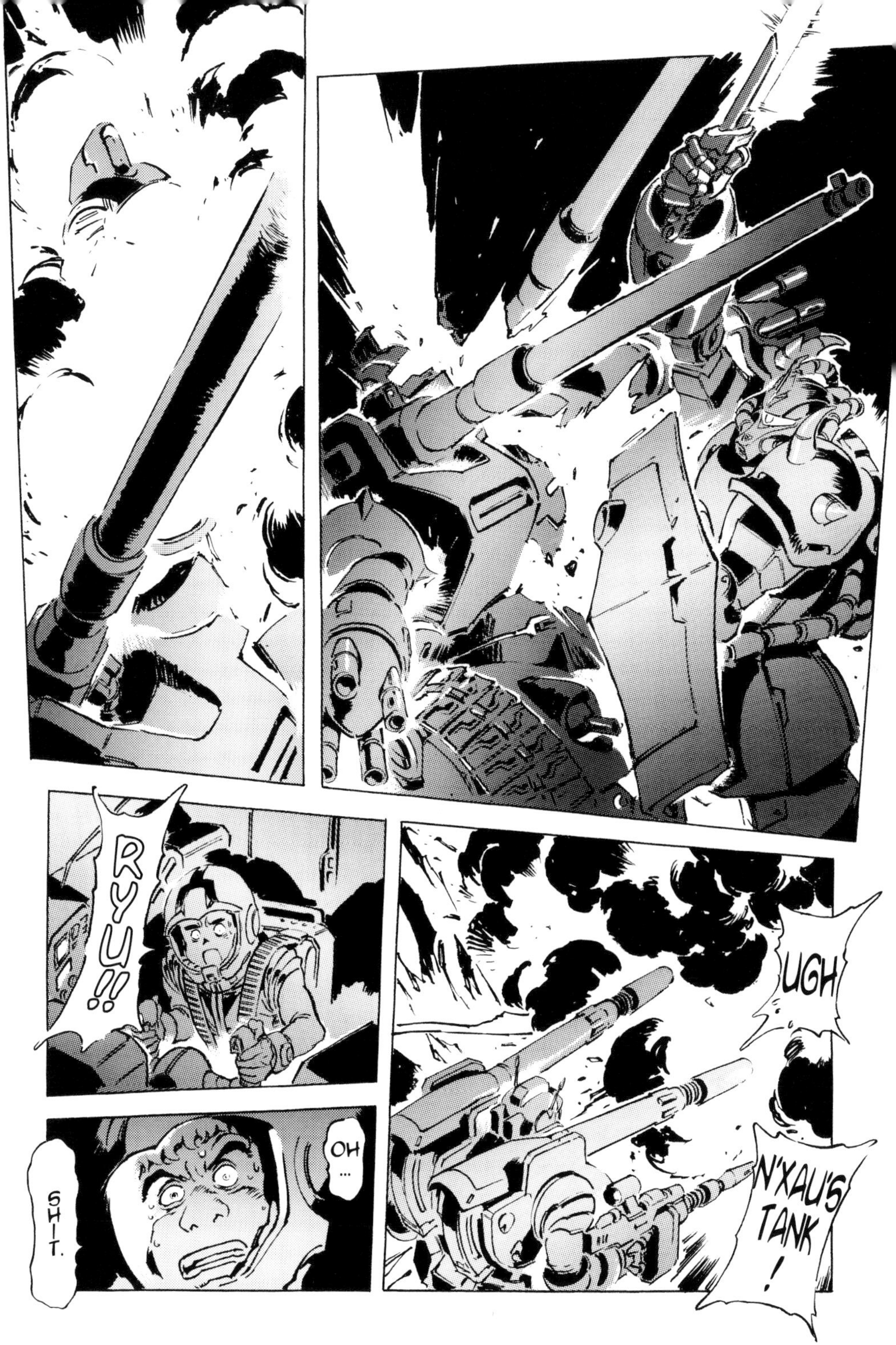
UGH
N'XAU'S TANK!
RYUU!!
OH... SHIT.

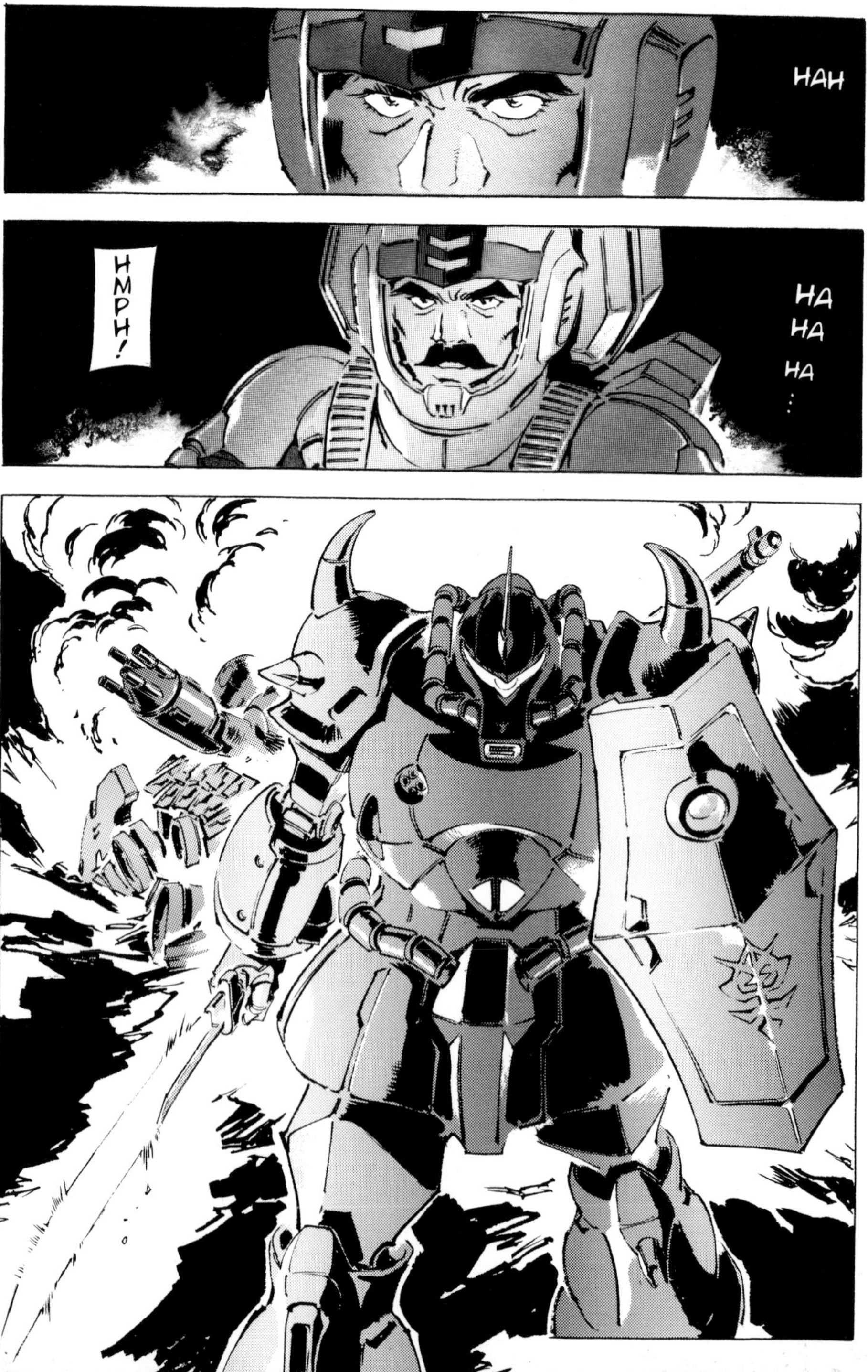
HAH
HA HA HA...
HMPH!

SECTION VI

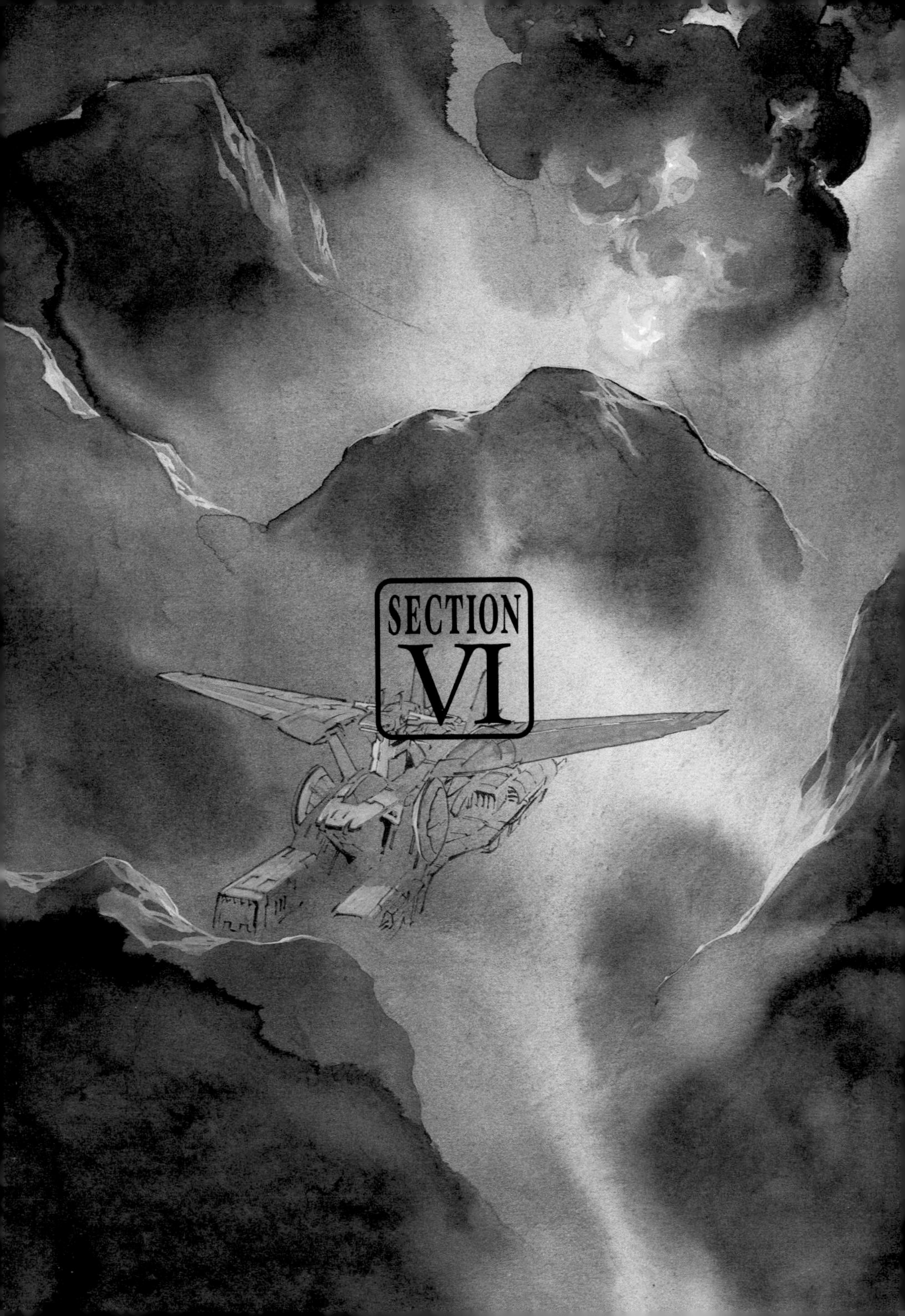

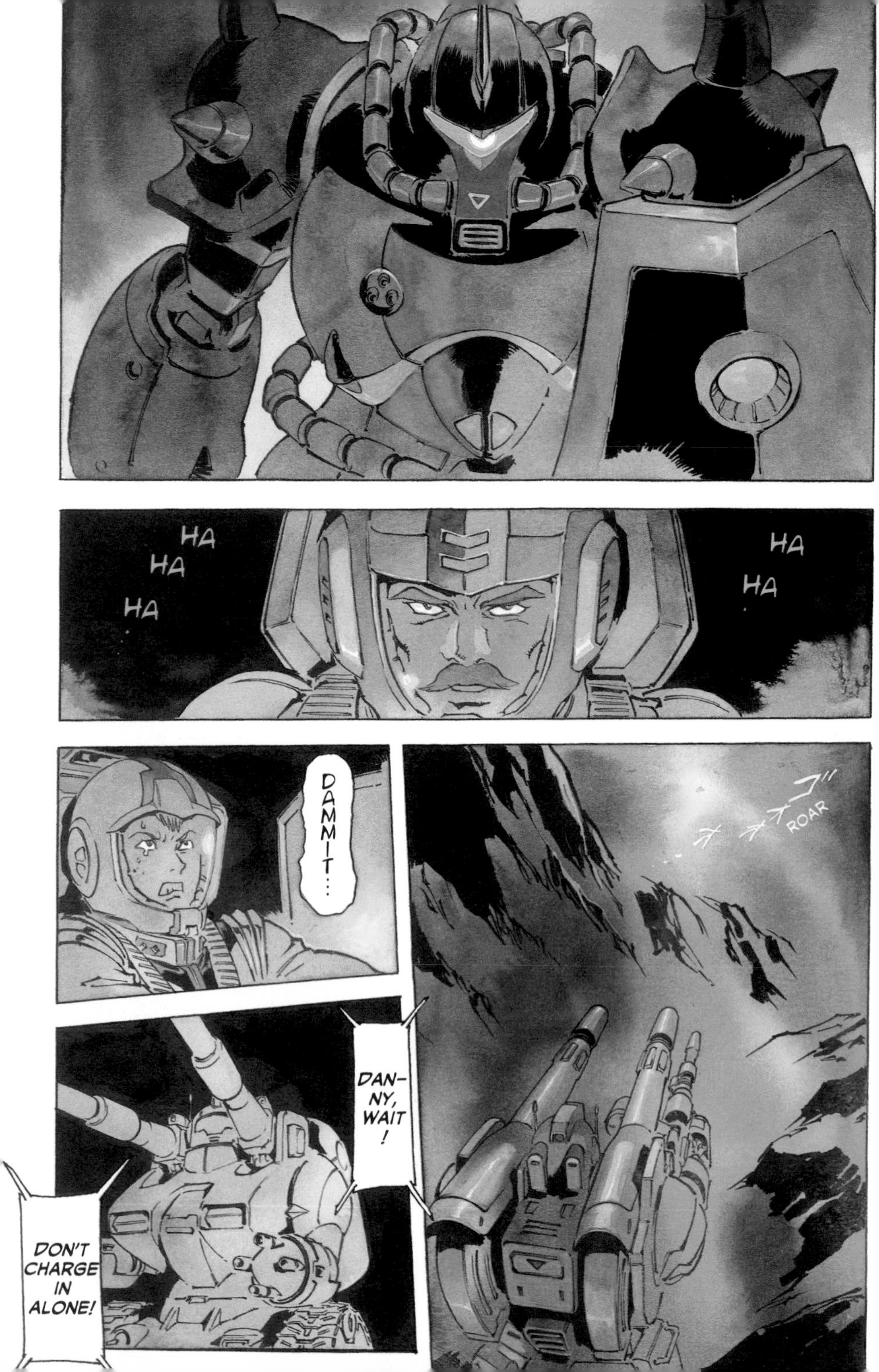
HA
HA
HA
HA
HA
ROAR
DAMMIT...
DANNY, WAIT!
DON'T CHARGE IN ALONE!

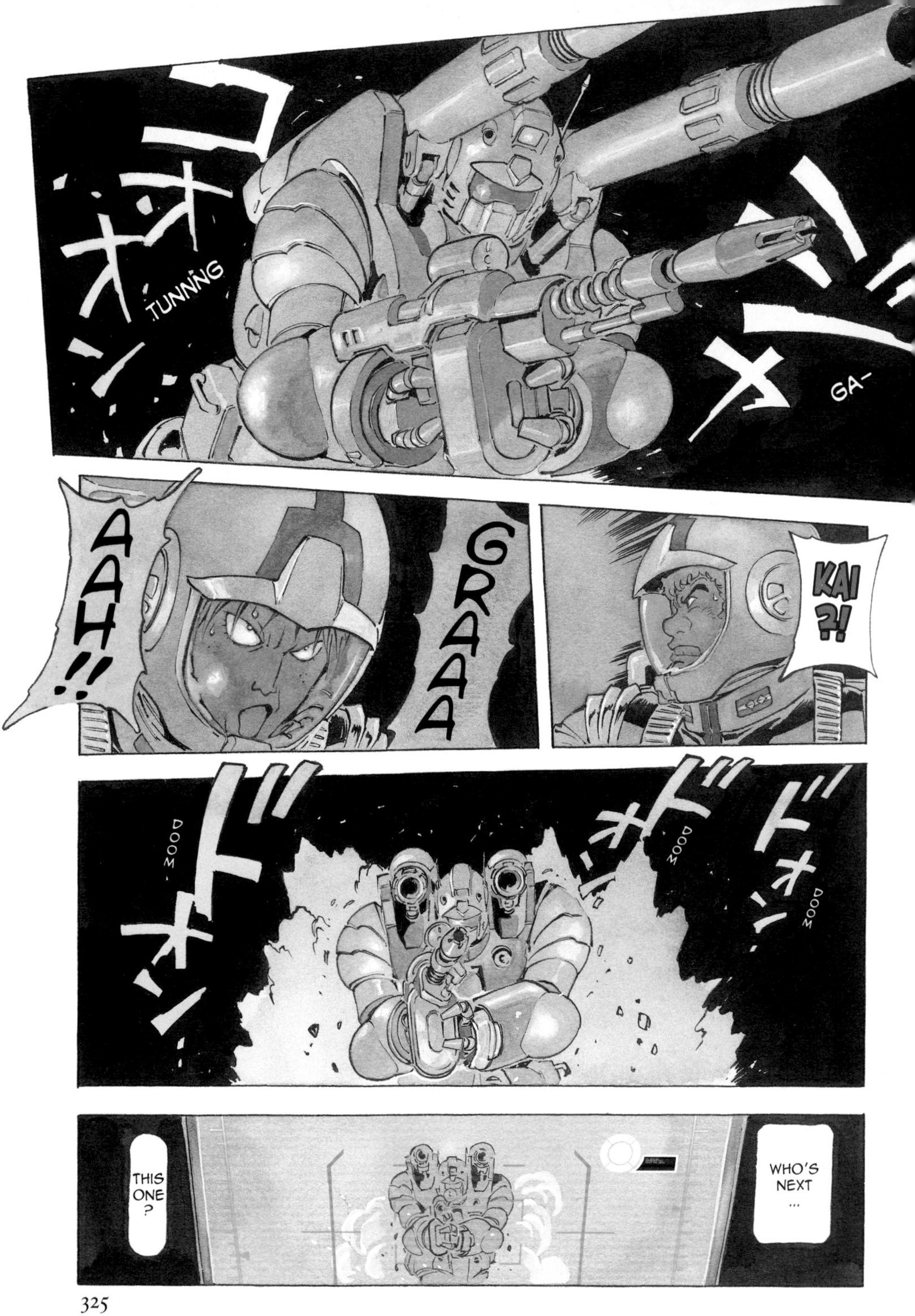
GA-
TUNNING
KAI ?!
GRAAAA
AAH!!
DOOM
DOOM
DOOM
WHO'S NEXT ...
THIS ONE ?

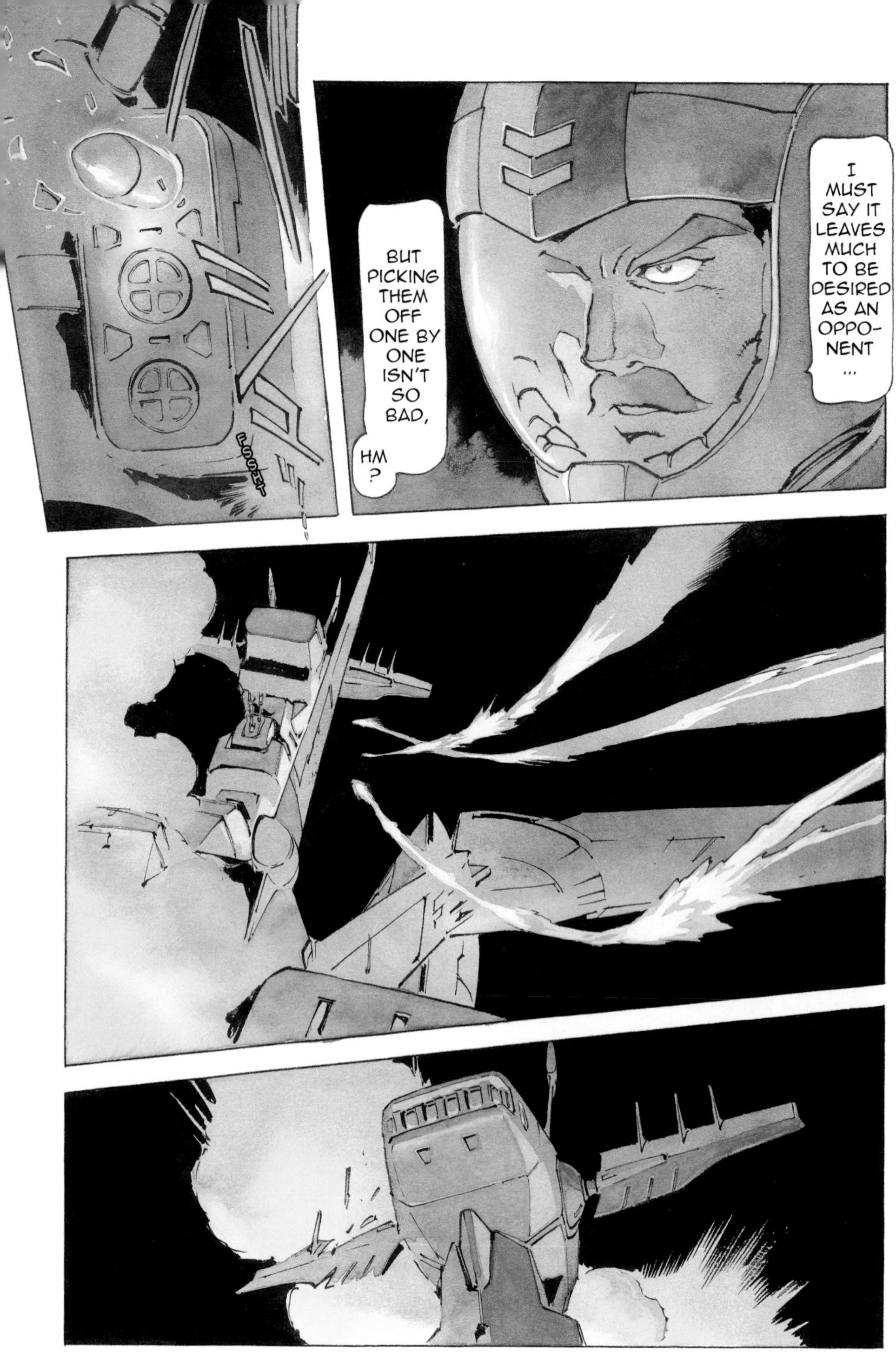
I MUST SAY IT LEAVES MUCH TO BE DESIRED AS AN OPPO-NENT ...
BUT PICKING THEM OFF ONE BY ONE ISN'T SO BAD,
HM ?
FSSHT

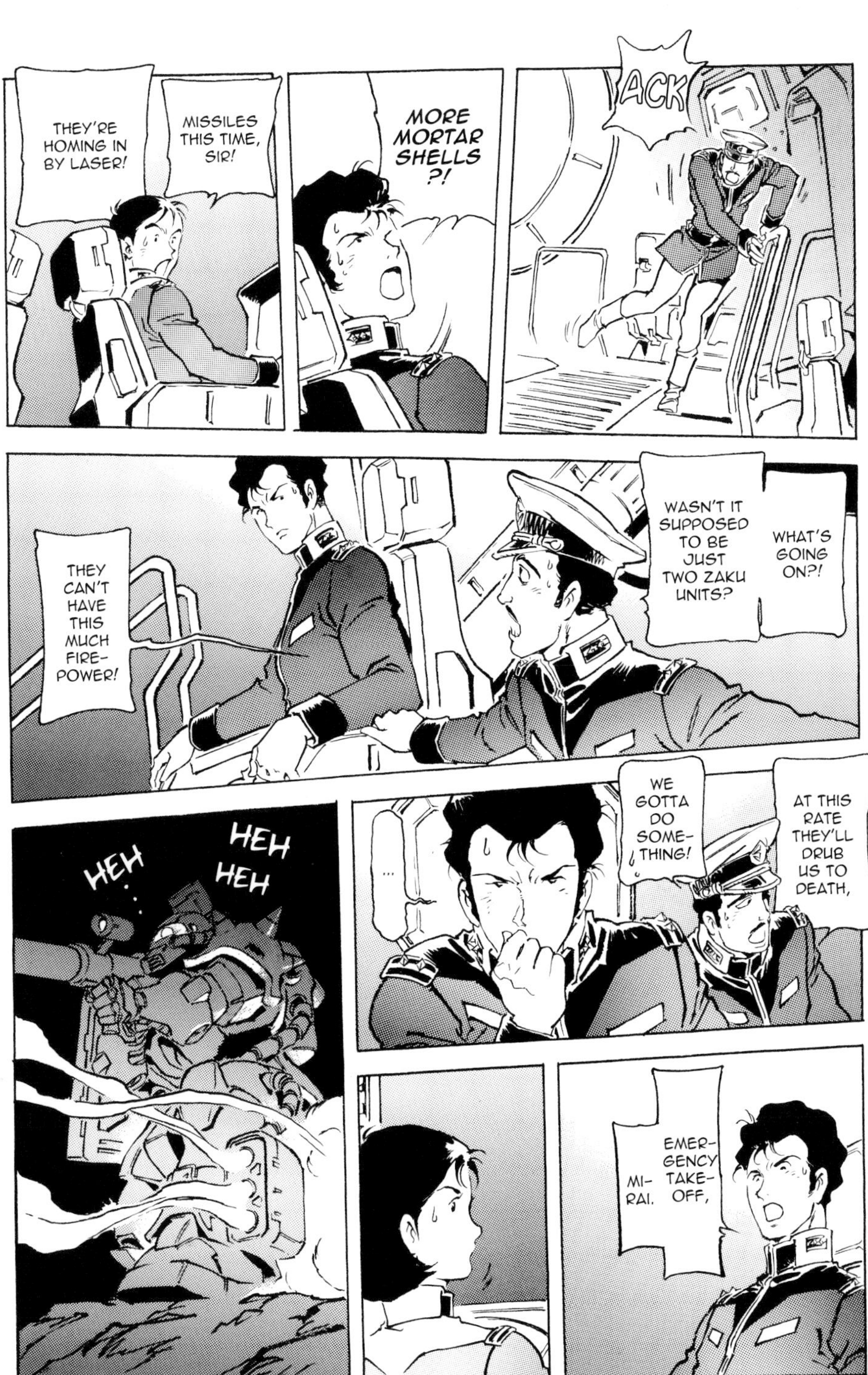
ACK
MORE MORTAR SHELLS ?!
MISSILES THIS TIME, SIR!
THEY'RE HOMING IN BY LASER!
WHAT'S GOING ON?!
WASN'T IT SUPPOSED TO BE JUST TWO ZAKU UNITS?
THEY CAN'T HAVE THIS MUCH FIRE-POWER!
AT THIS RATE THEY'LL DRUB US TO DEATH,
WE GOTTA DO SOME-THING!
...
HEH HEH
HEH
EMERGENCY TAKE-OFF,
MI-RAI.

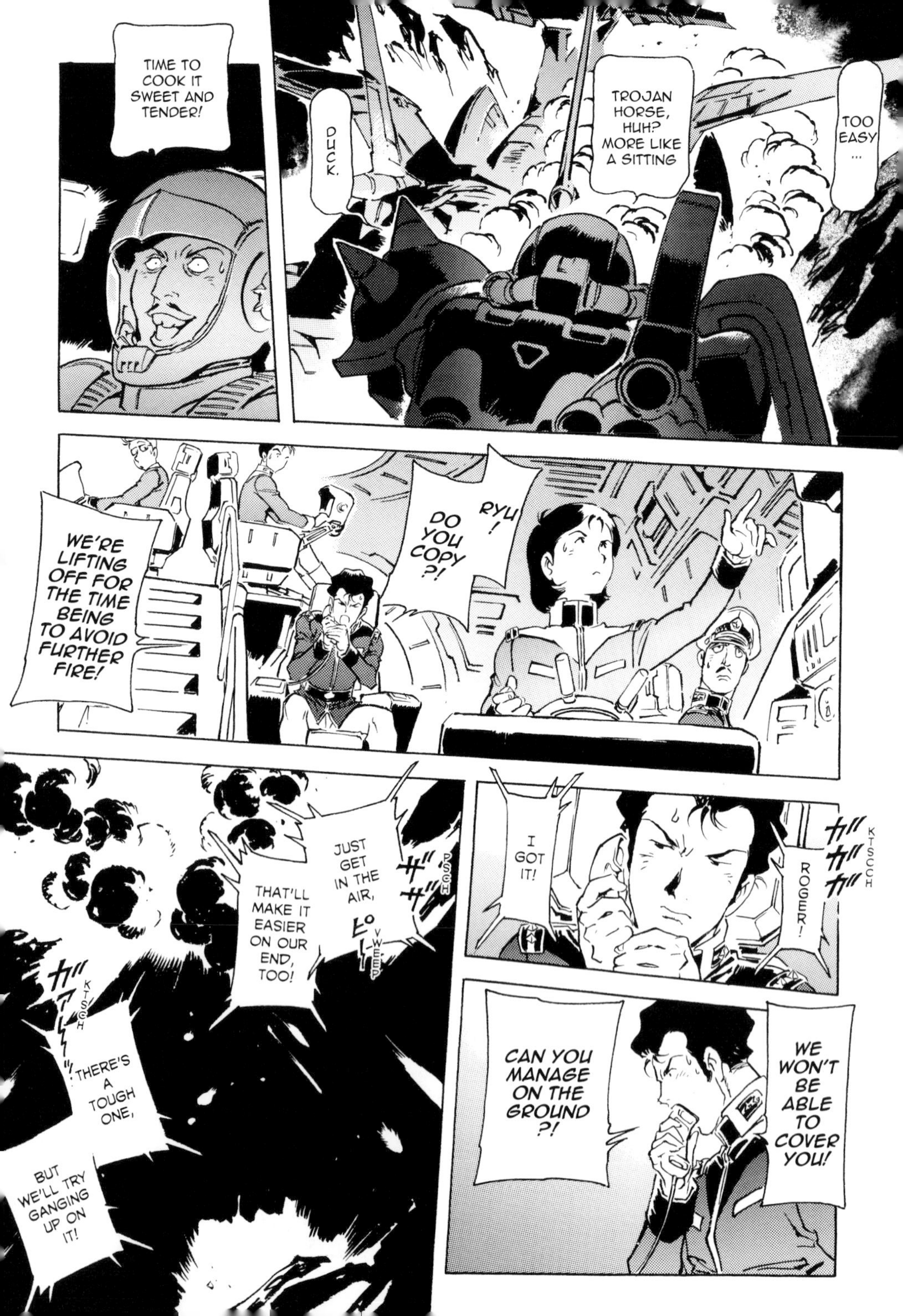

TOO EASY ...
TROJAN HORSE, HUH? MORE LIKE A SITTING
DUCK.
TIME TO COOK IT SWEET AND TENDER!
RYU!
DO YOU COPY?!
WE'RE LIFTING OFF FOR THE TIME BEING TO AVOID FURTHER FIRE!
KTSCCH
ROGER!
I GOT IT!
WE WON'T BE ABLE TO COVER YOU!
CAN YOU MANAGE ON THE GROUND?!
PSSCH
JUST GET IN THE AIR,
THAT'LL MAKE IT EASIER ON OUR END, TOO!
VWEEP
KTSCH
THERE'S A TOUGH ONE,
BUT WE'LL TRY GANGING UP ON IT!

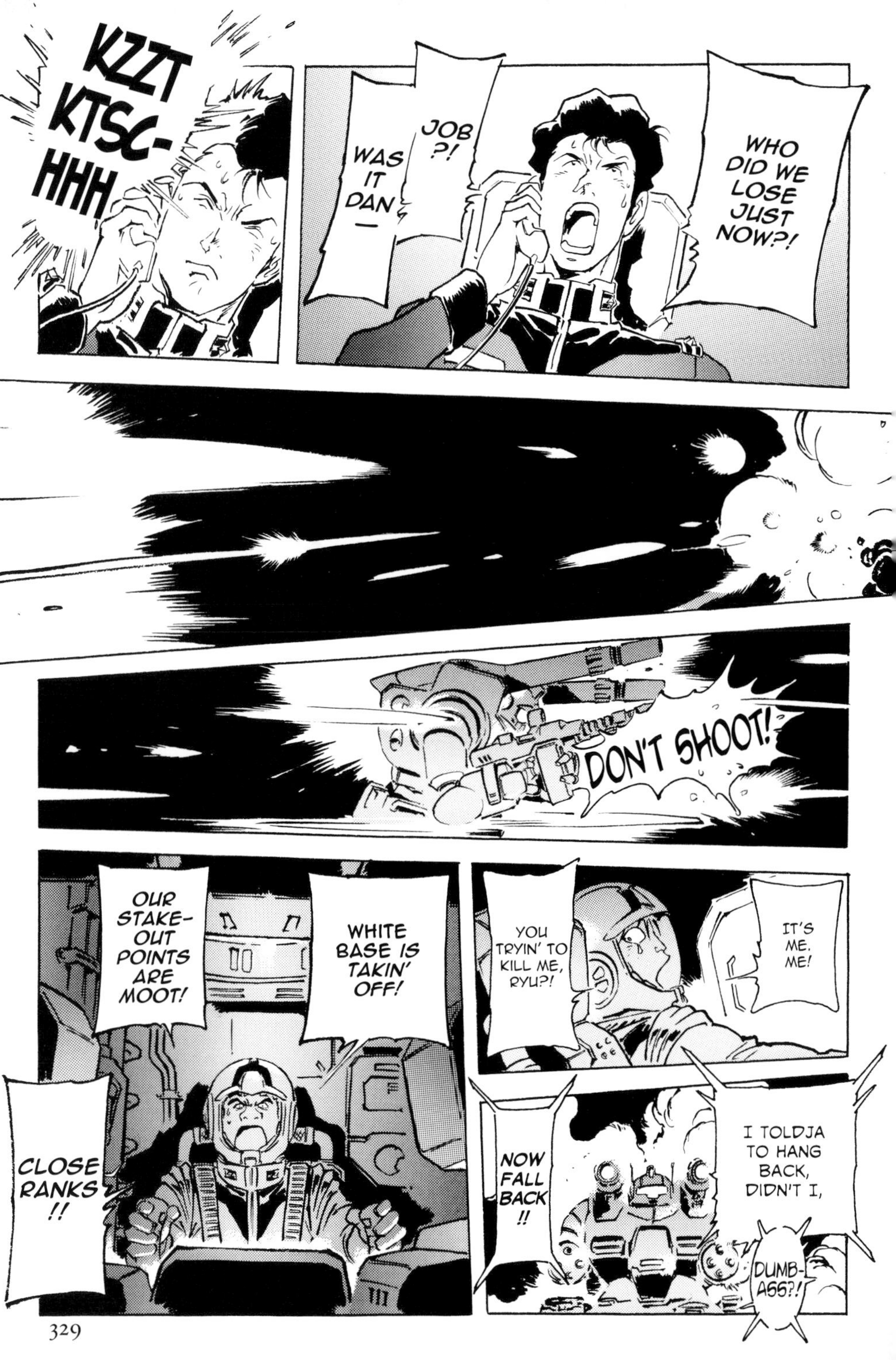
WHO DID WE LOSE JUST NOW?!
JOB?!
WAS IT DAN —
KZZT KTSC-HHH
DON'T SHOOT!
IT'S ME. ME!
YOU TRYIN' TO KILL ME, RYU?!
I TOLDJA TO HANG BACK, DIDN'T I,
DUMB-ASS?!
NOW FALL BACK!!
WHITE BASE IS TAKIN' OFF!
OUR STAKE-OUT POINTS ARE MOOT!
CLOSE RANKS!!

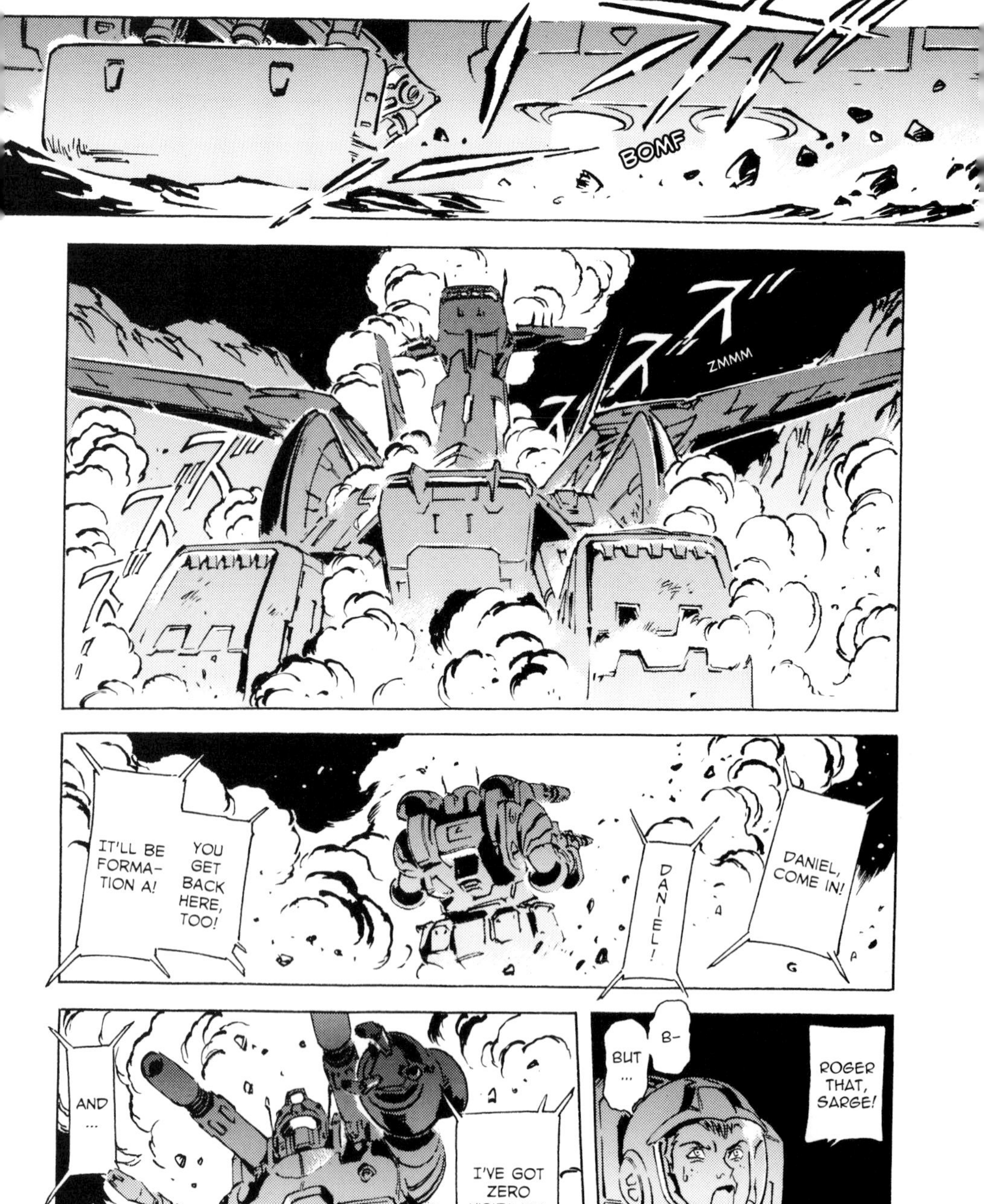
BOMF
ZMMM
DANIEL, COME IN!
DANIEL!
YOU GET BACK HERE, TOO!
IT'LL BE FORMATION A!
ROGER THAT, SARGE!
B- BUT ...
I'VE GOT ZERO VISIBILITY.
AND ...

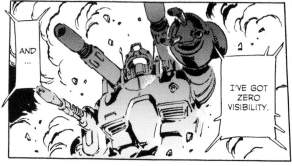

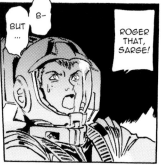

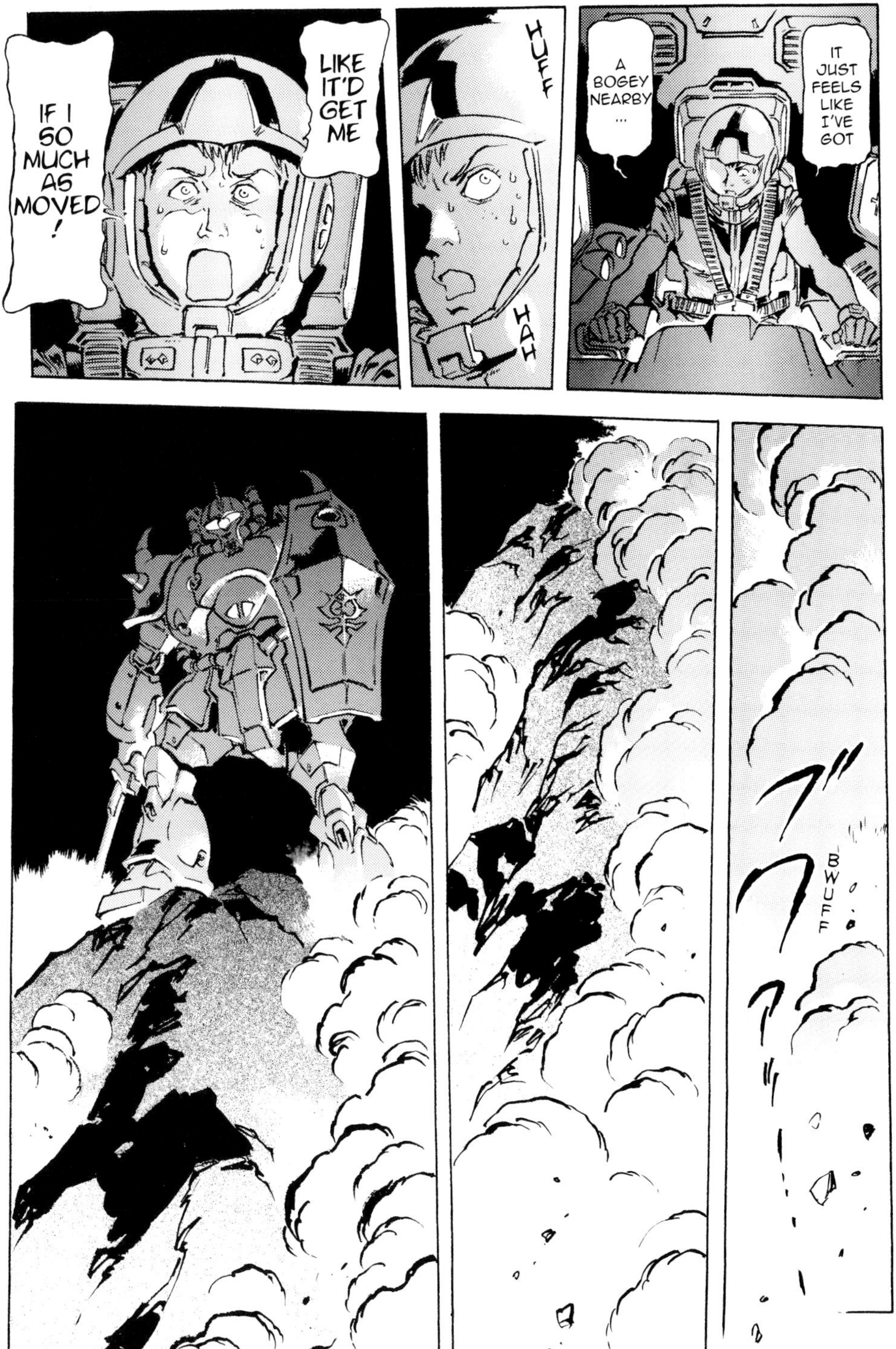
IT JUST FEELS LIKE I'VE GOT
A BOGEY NEARBY ...
HUFF
HAH
LIKE IT'D GET ME
IF I SO MUCH AS MOVED!
BWUFF

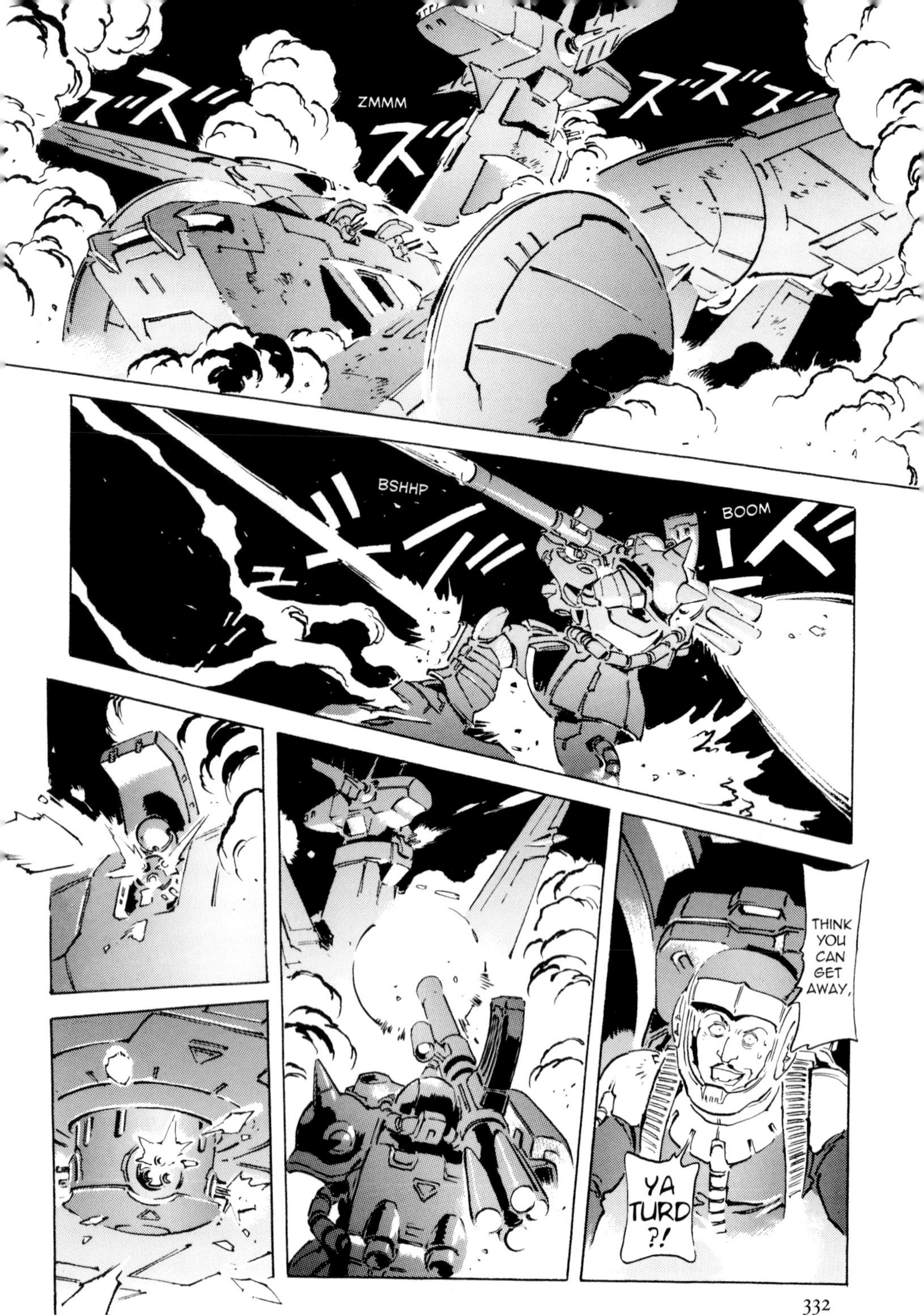
ZMMM
BOOM
BSHHP
THINK YOU CAN GET AWAY,
YA TURD ?!

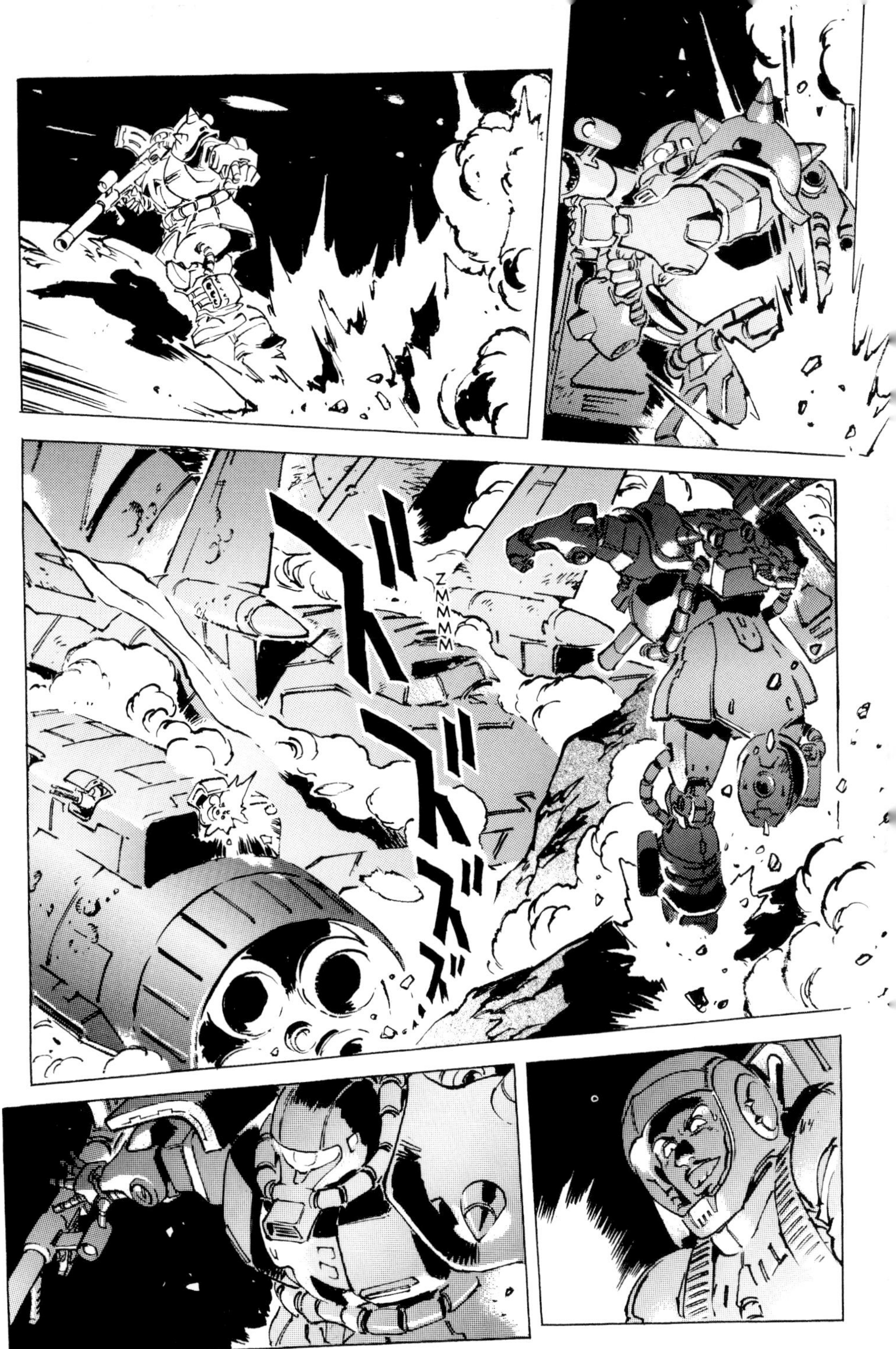
ズズズズ
ZMMMM

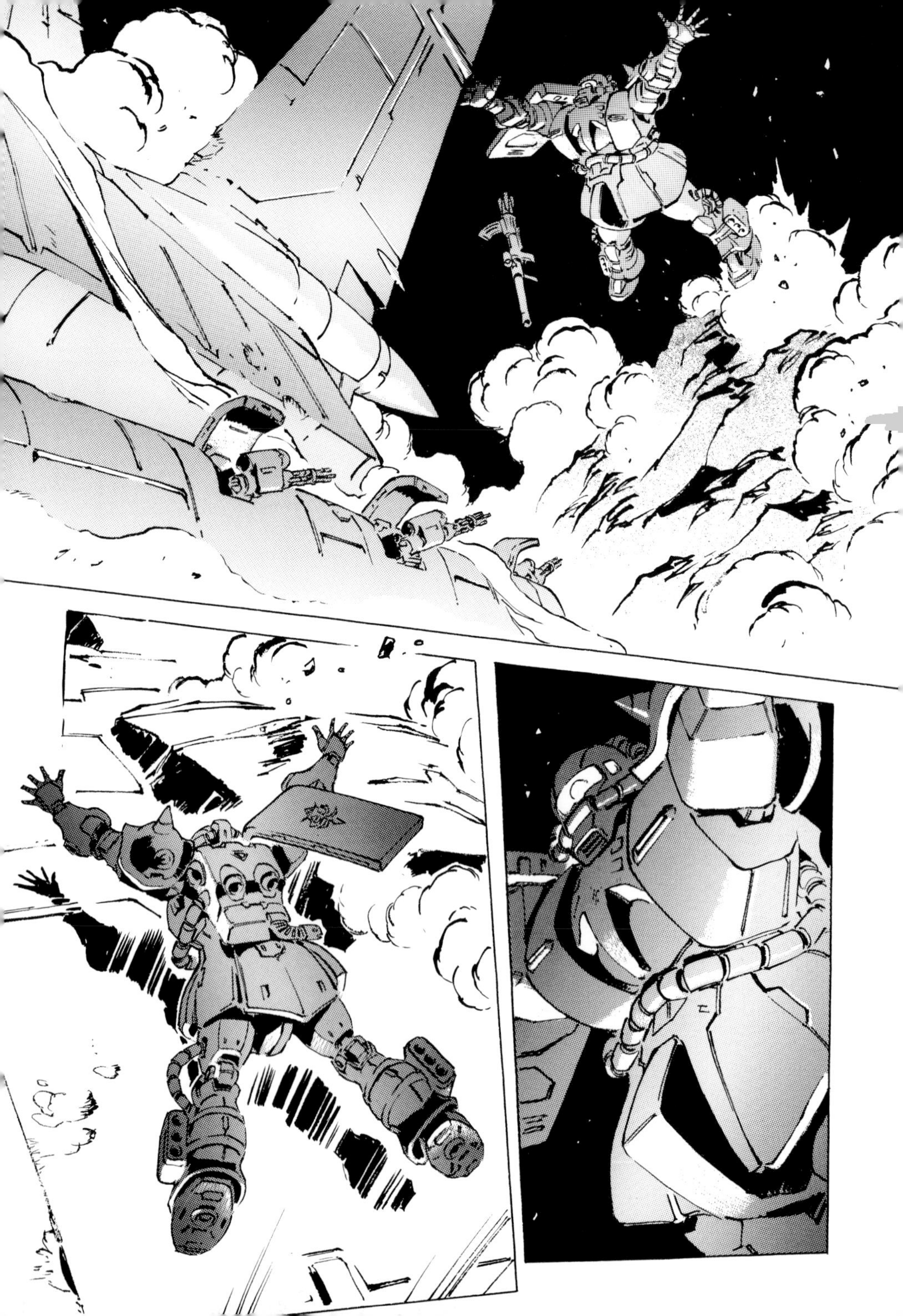

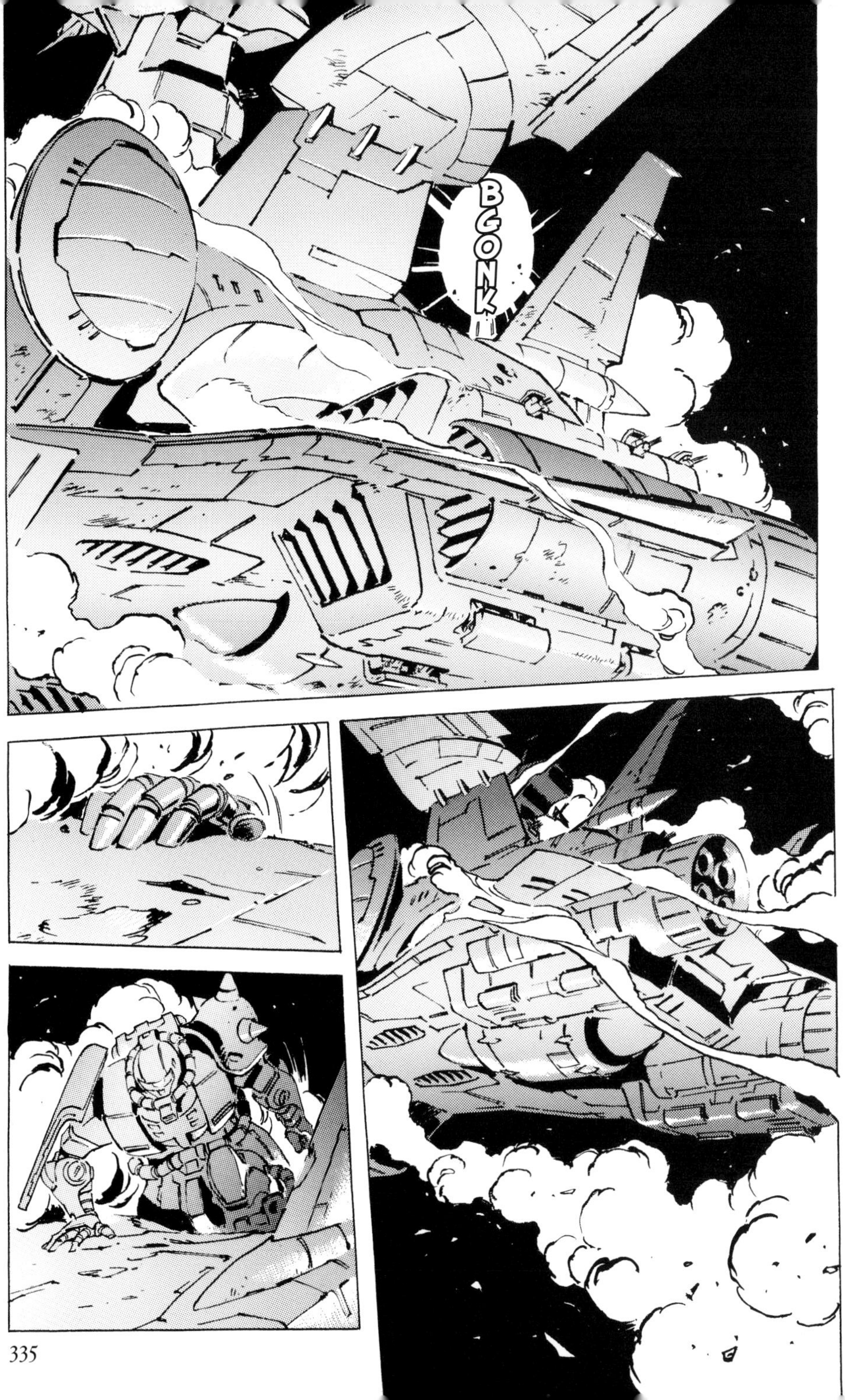
BGONK

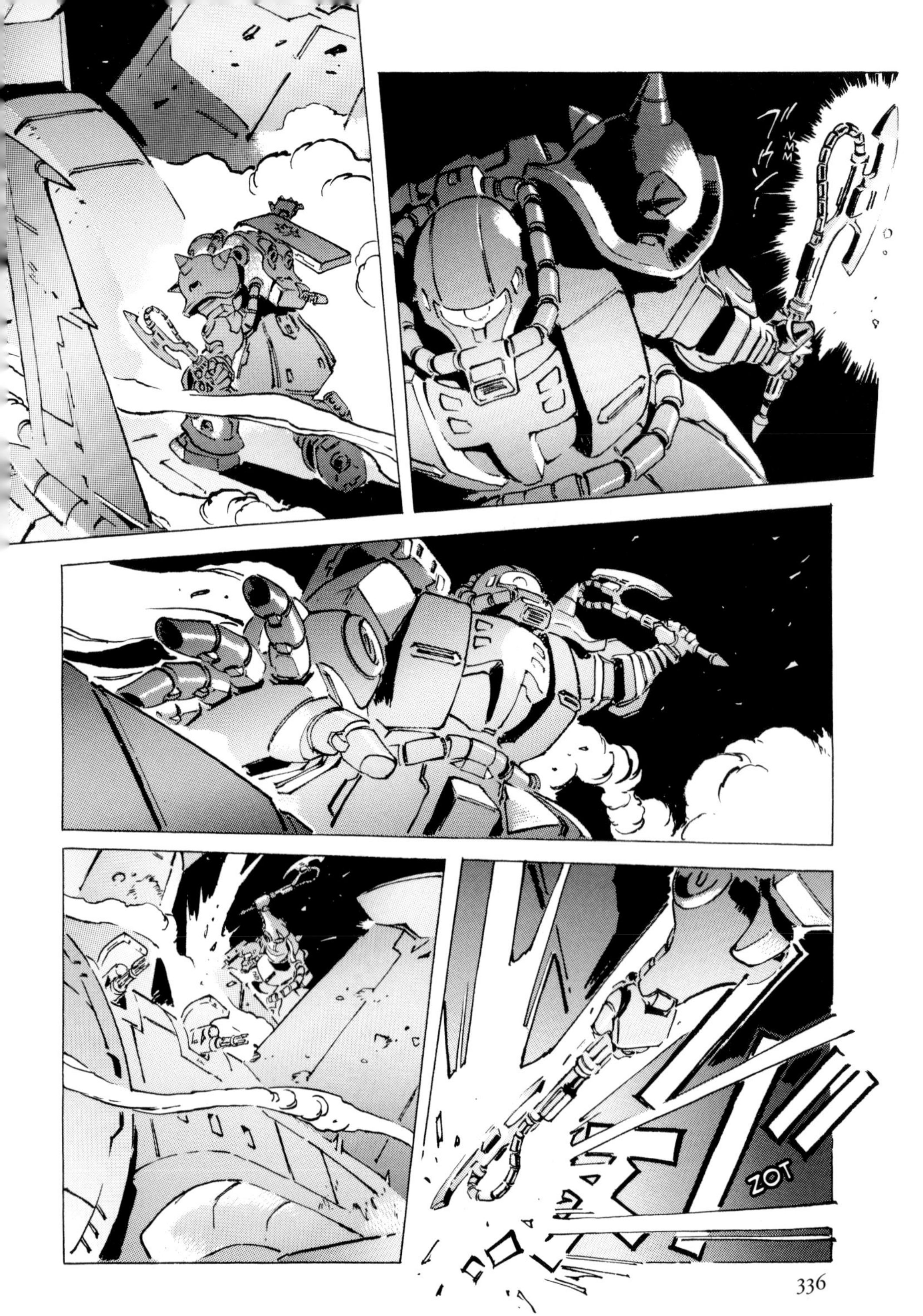
ブゥン!
VMM
ZOT

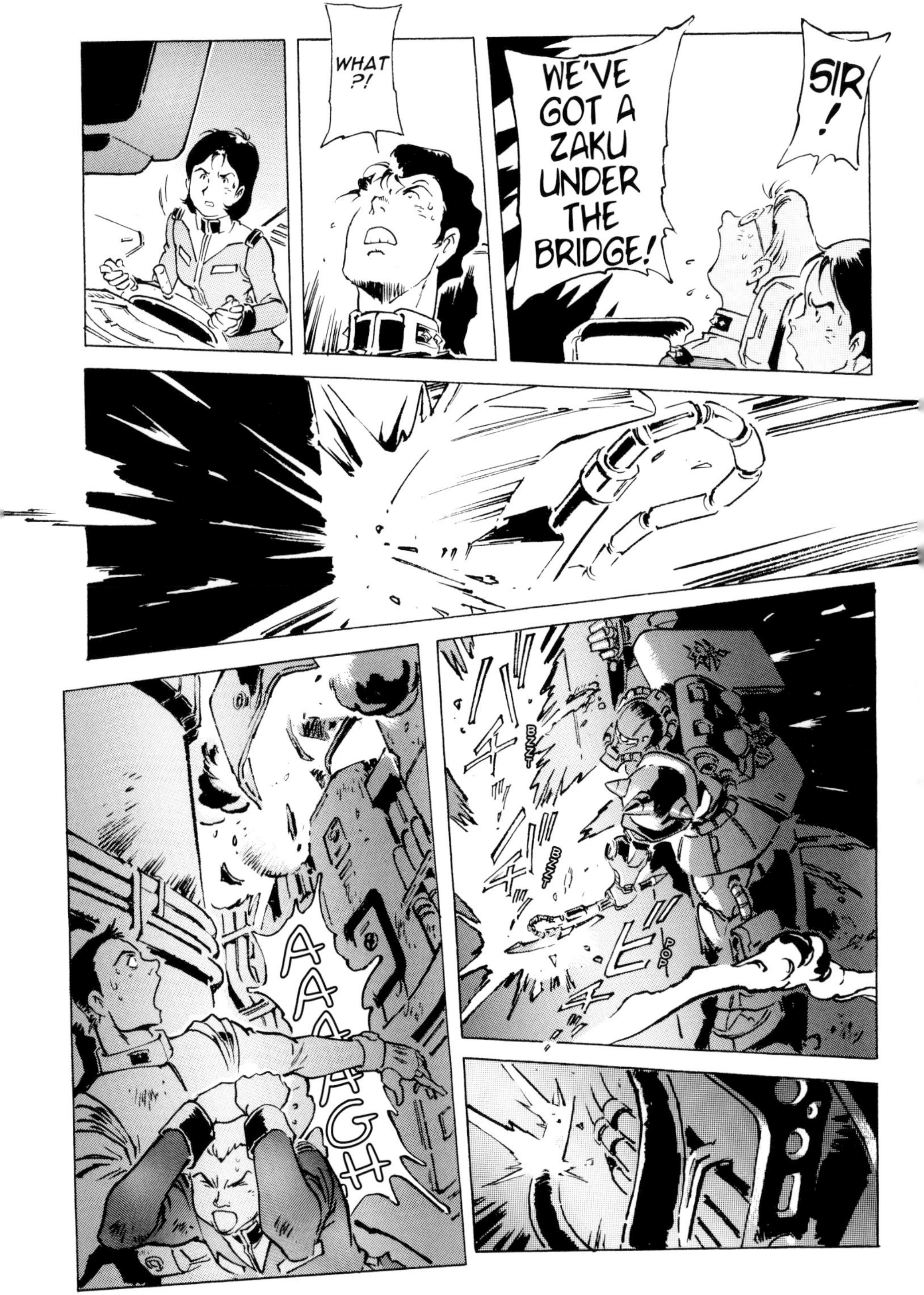
SIR!
WE'VE GOT A ZAKU UNDER THE BRIDGE!
WHAT?!
BZZT
BZZZT
POP
AAAAAGH

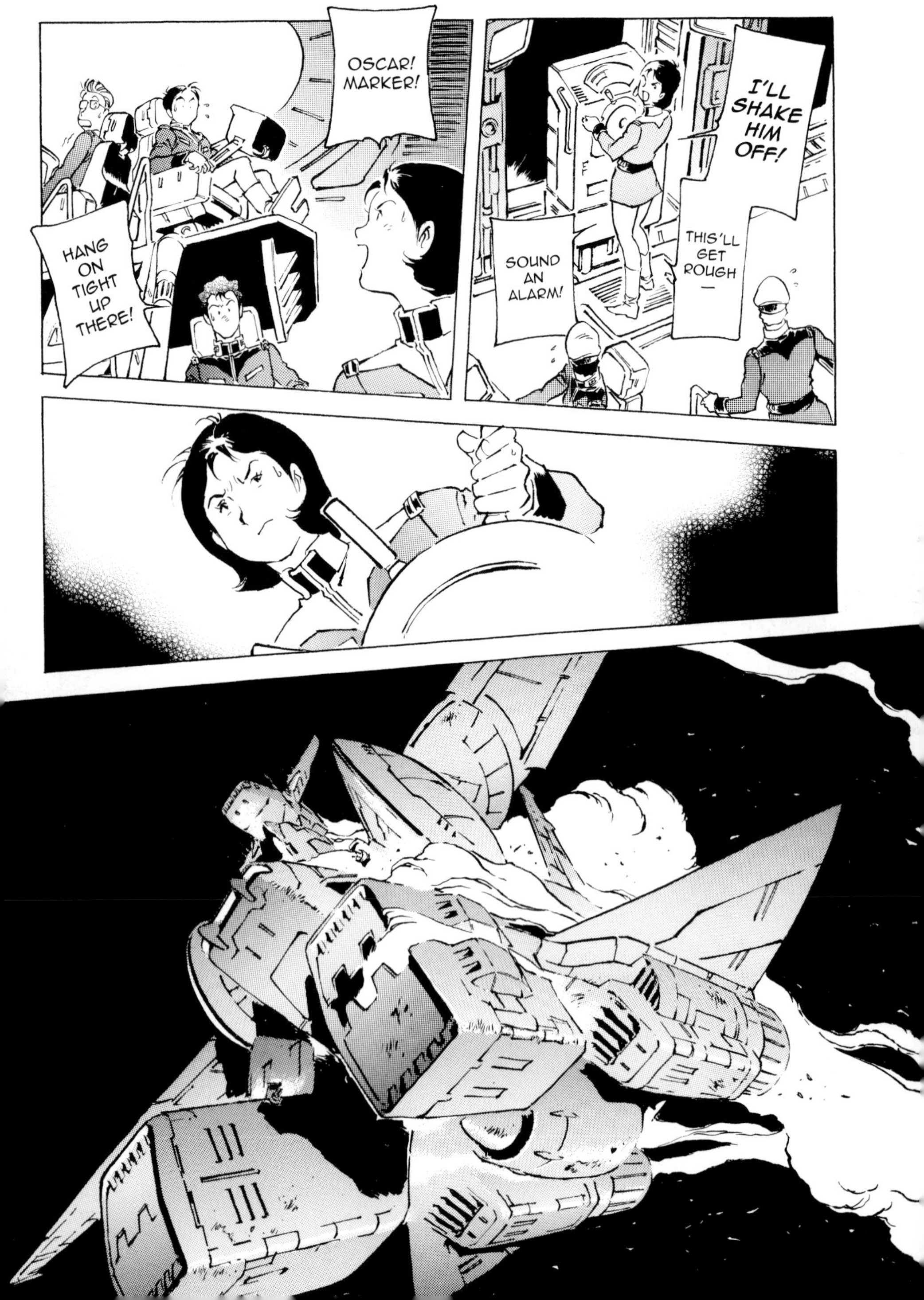
I'LL SHAKE HIM OFF!
THIS'LL GET ROUGH —
SOUND AN ALARM!
OSCAR! MARKER!
HANG ON TIGHT UP THERE!

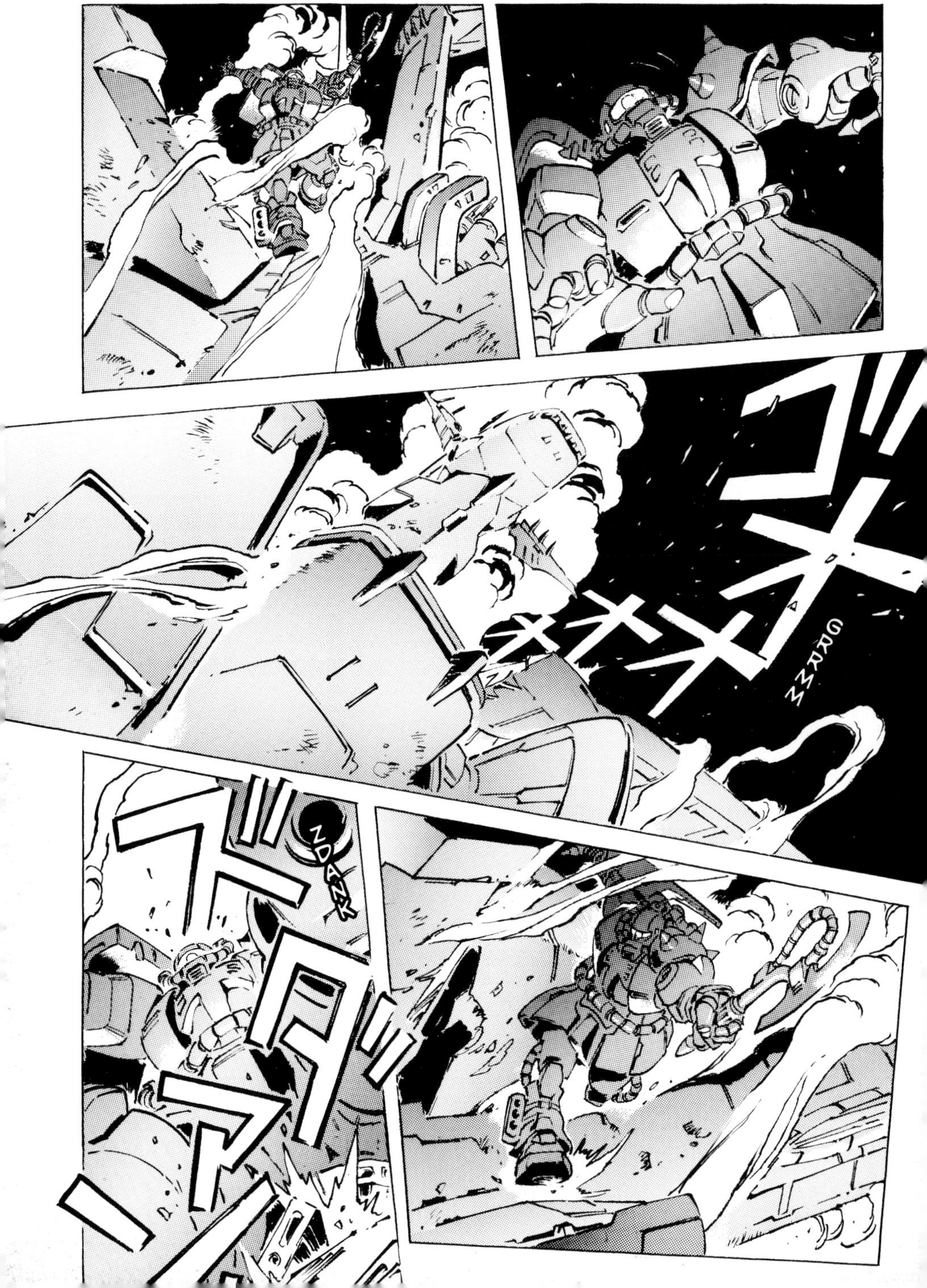
ゴオオオ
GRRMM
ズドドーン
ZDANK

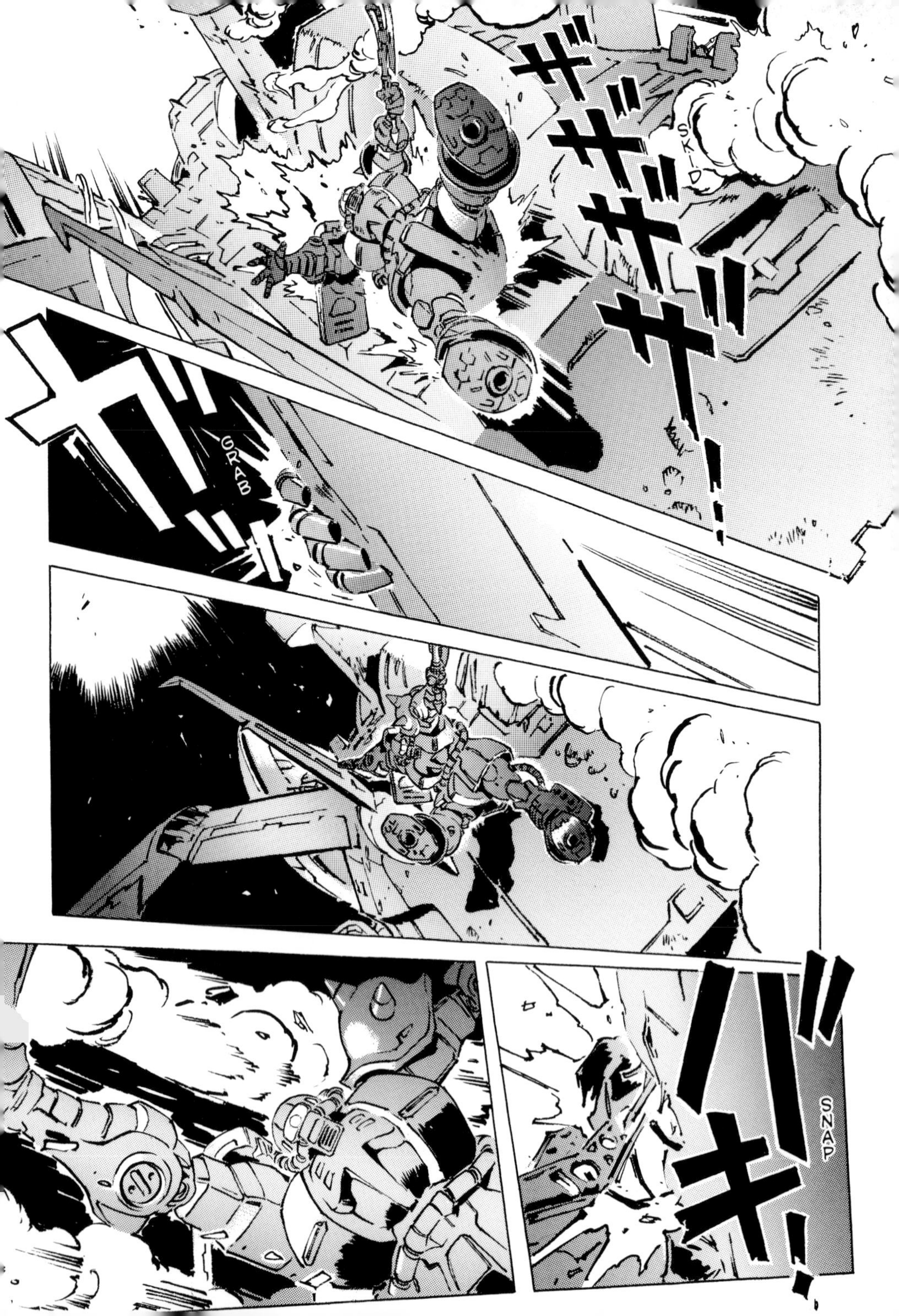
SKID
GRAB
SNAP

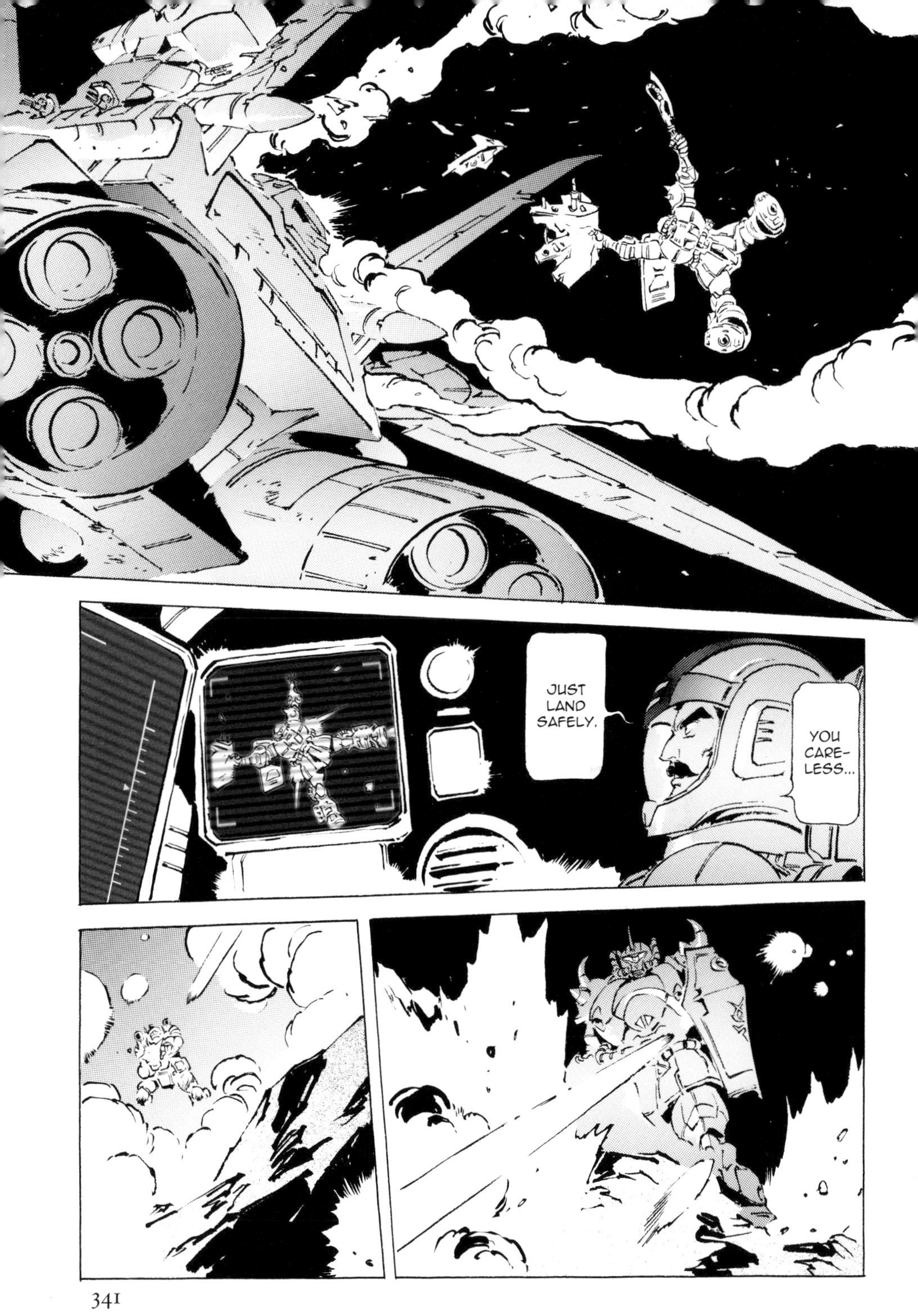
YOU CARE-LESS...
JUST LAND SAFELY.

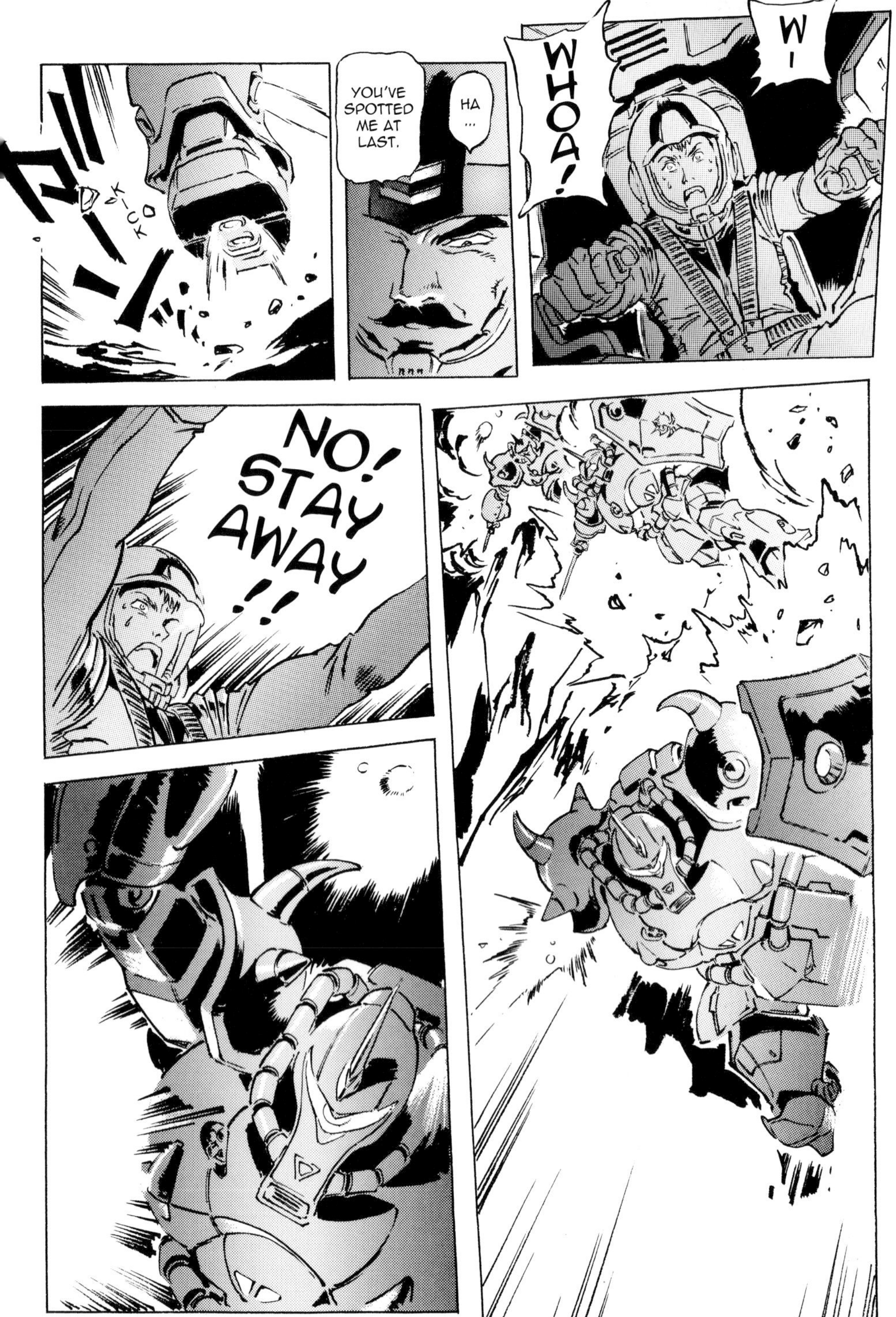

WI
WHOA!
HA...
YOU'VE SPOTTED ME AT LAST.
KICK
NO! STAY AWAY!!!

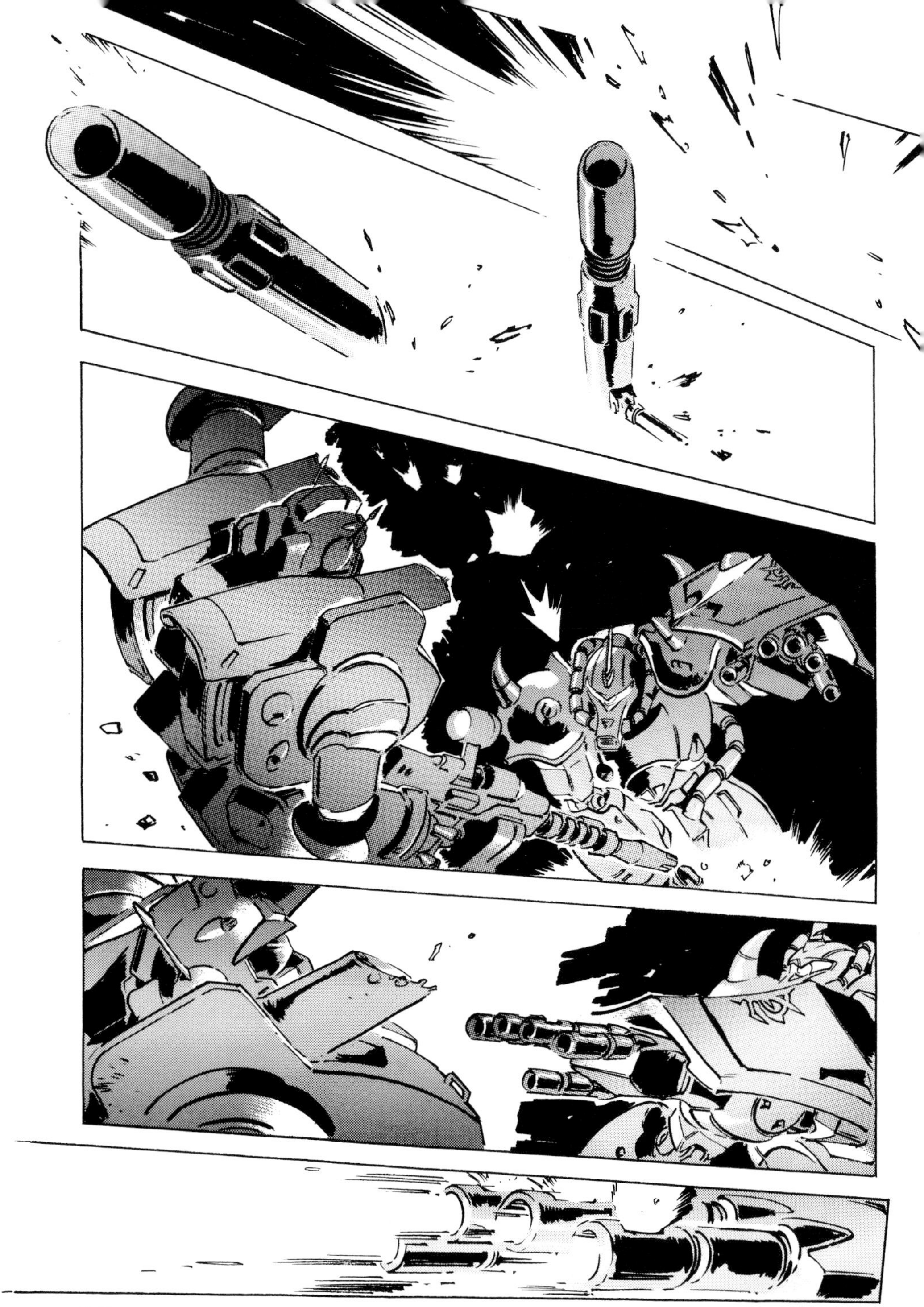

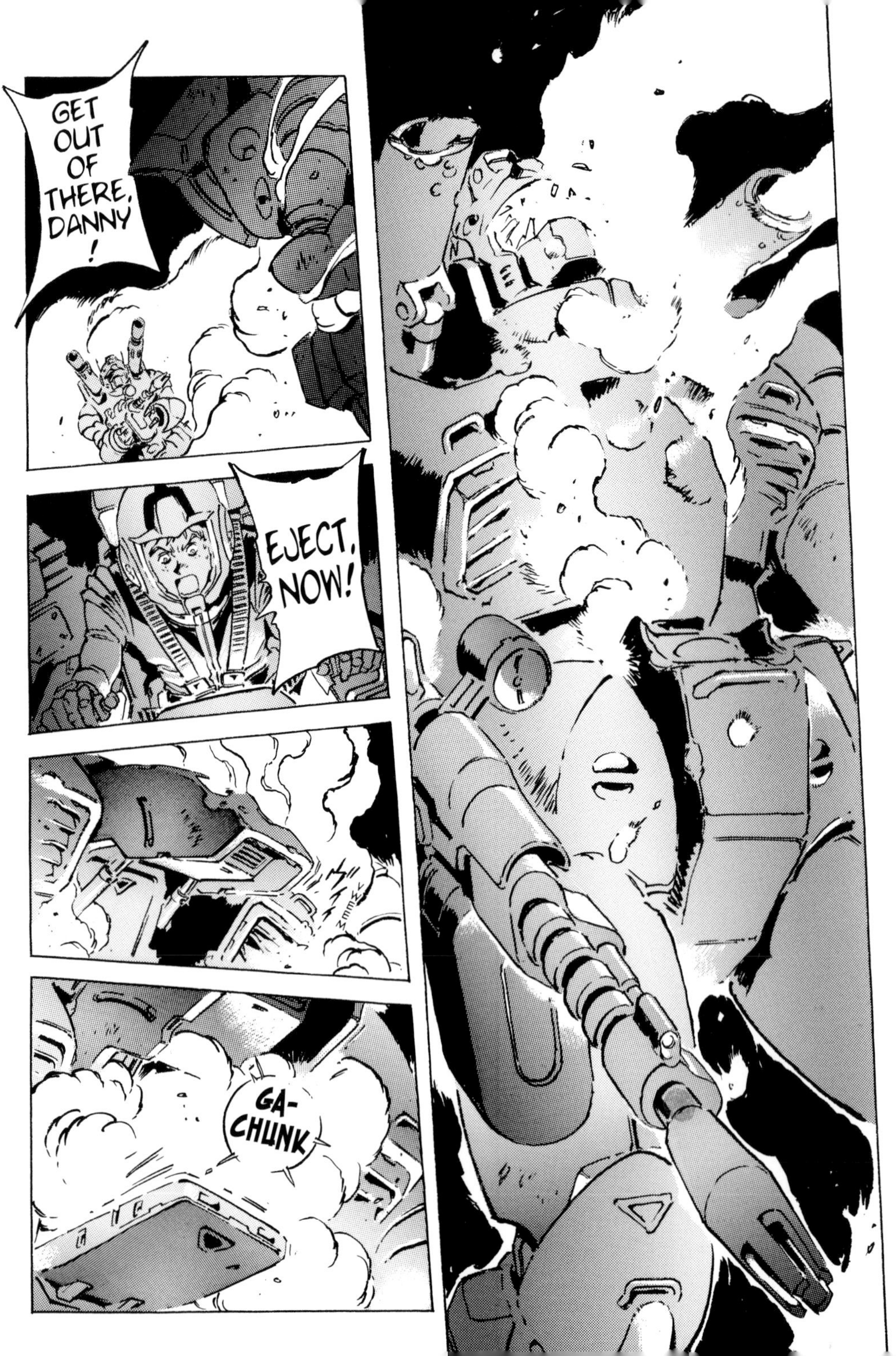
GET OUT OF THERE, DANNY!
EJECT, NOW!
GA-CHUNK

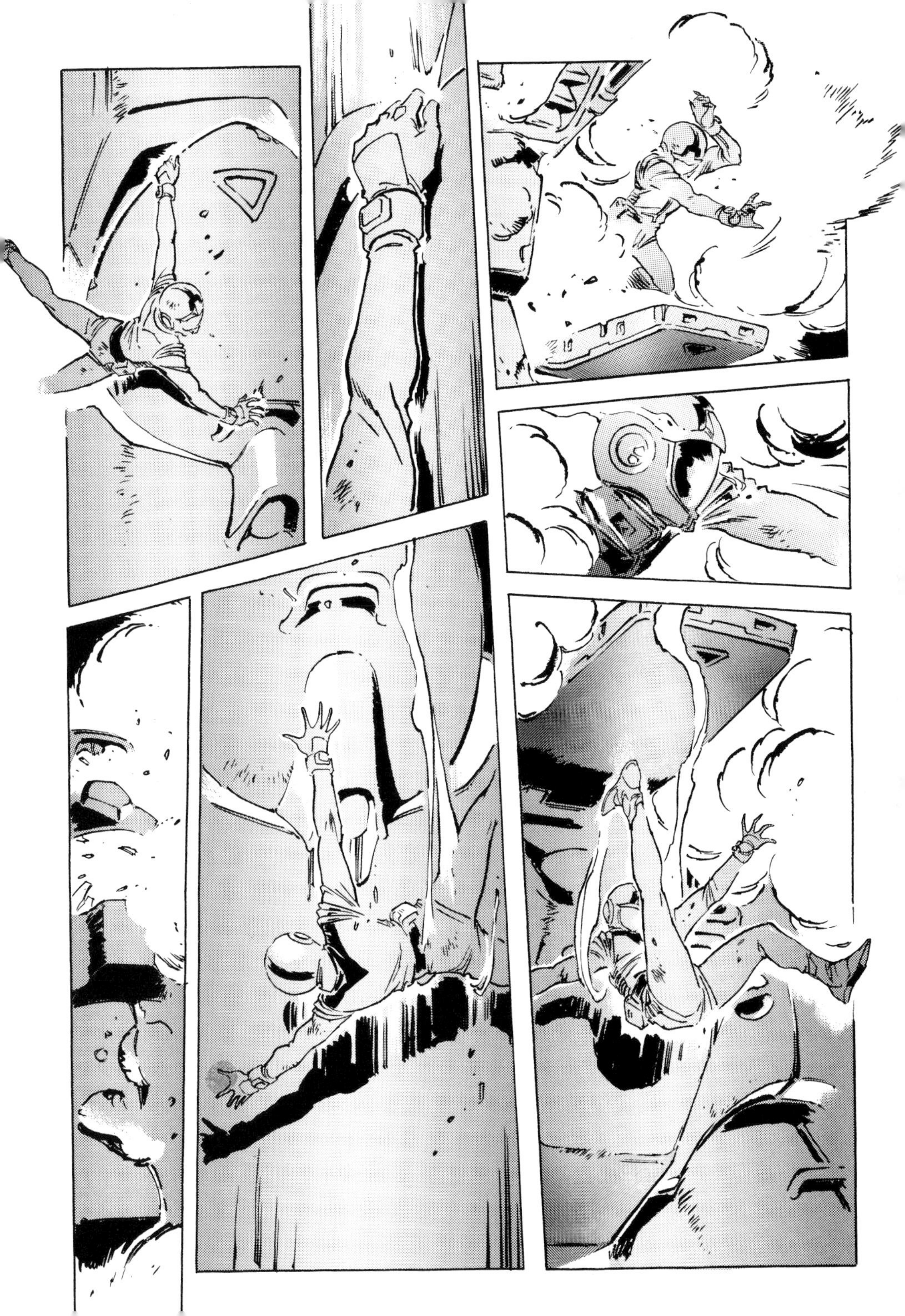

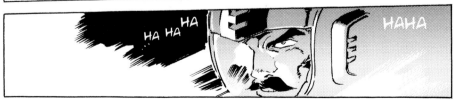

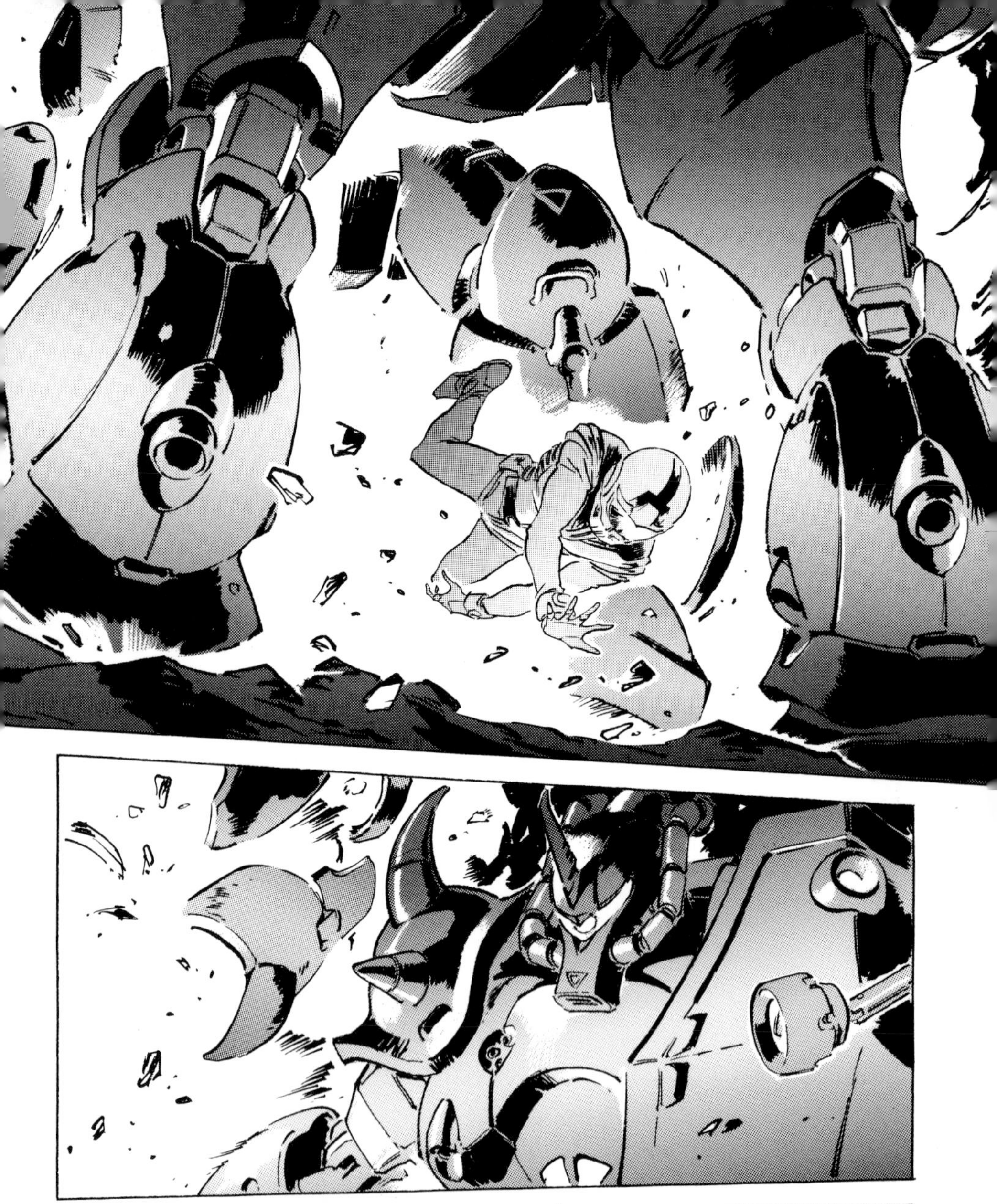
HAHA
HA HA HA

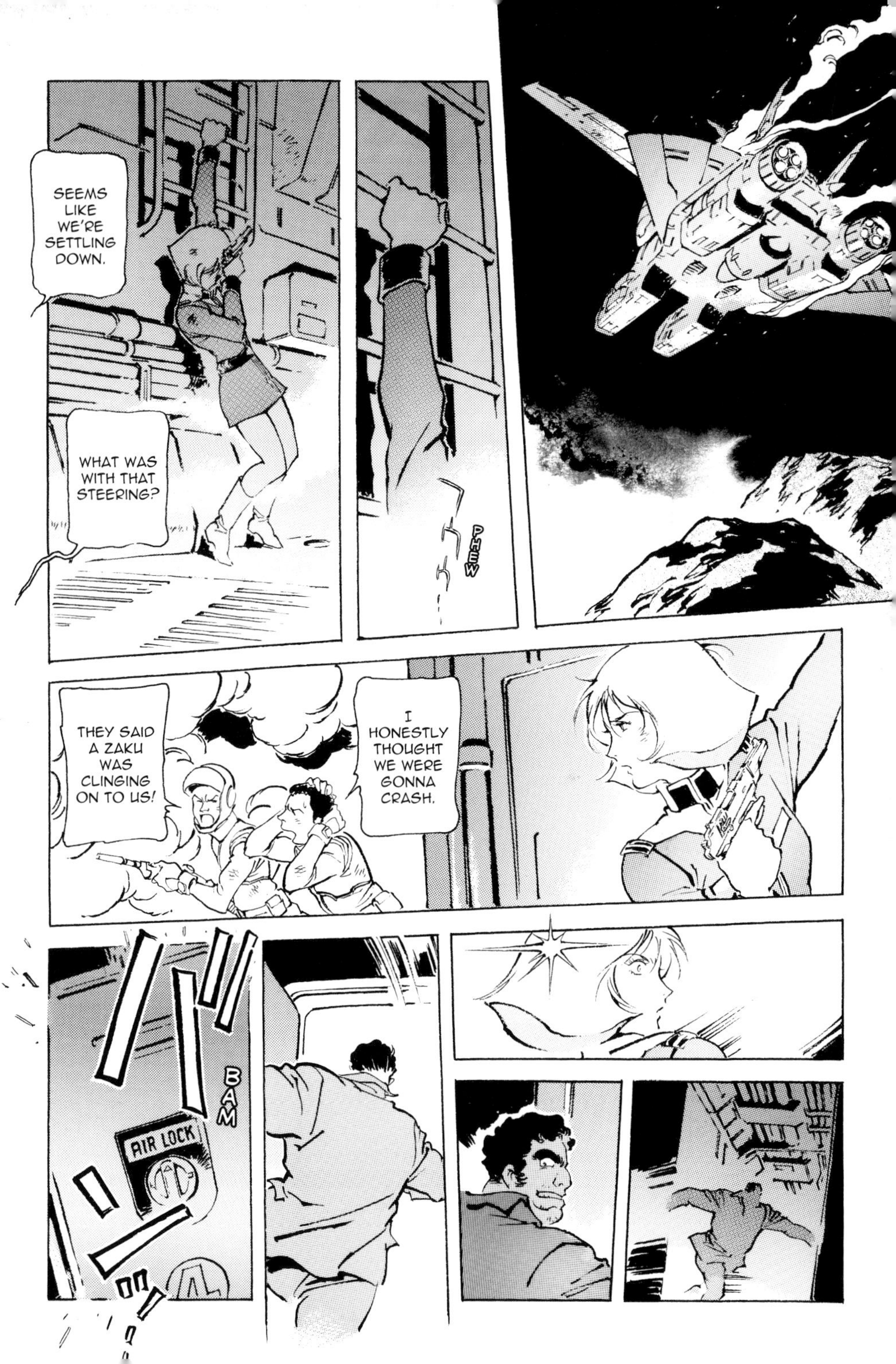
PHEW
SEEMS LIKE WE'RE SETTLING DOWN.
WHAT WAS WITH THAT STEERING?
I HONESTLY THOUGHT WE WERE GONNA CRASH.
THEY SAID A ZAKU WAS CLINGING ON TO US!
BAM
AIR LOCK

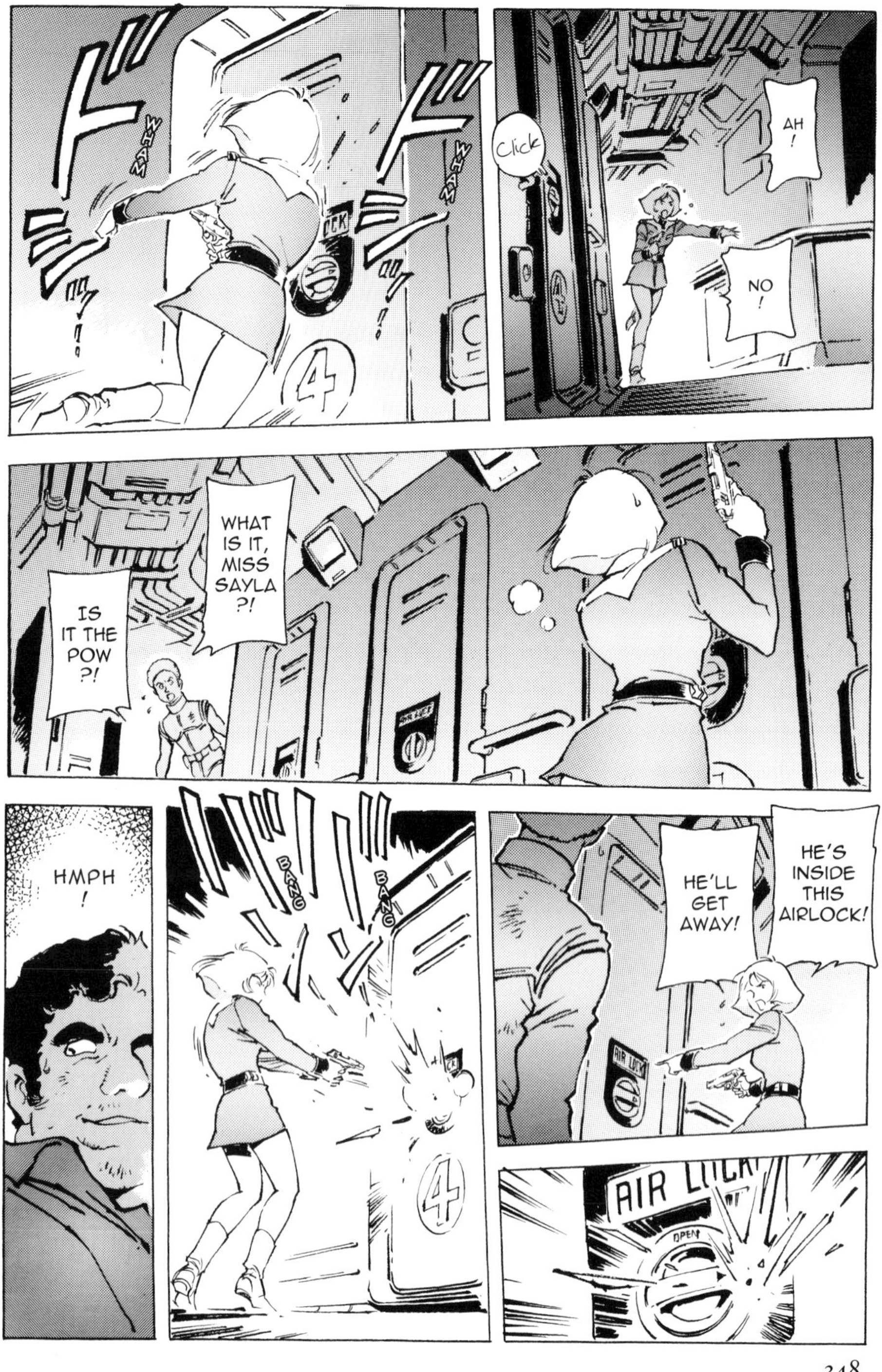
AH!
Click
NO!
ド
WHAM
ド
WHAM
WHAT IS IT, MISS SAYLA?!
IS IT THE POW?!
HE'S INSIDE THIS AIRLOCK!
HE'LL GET AWAY!
BANG
BANG
HMPH!

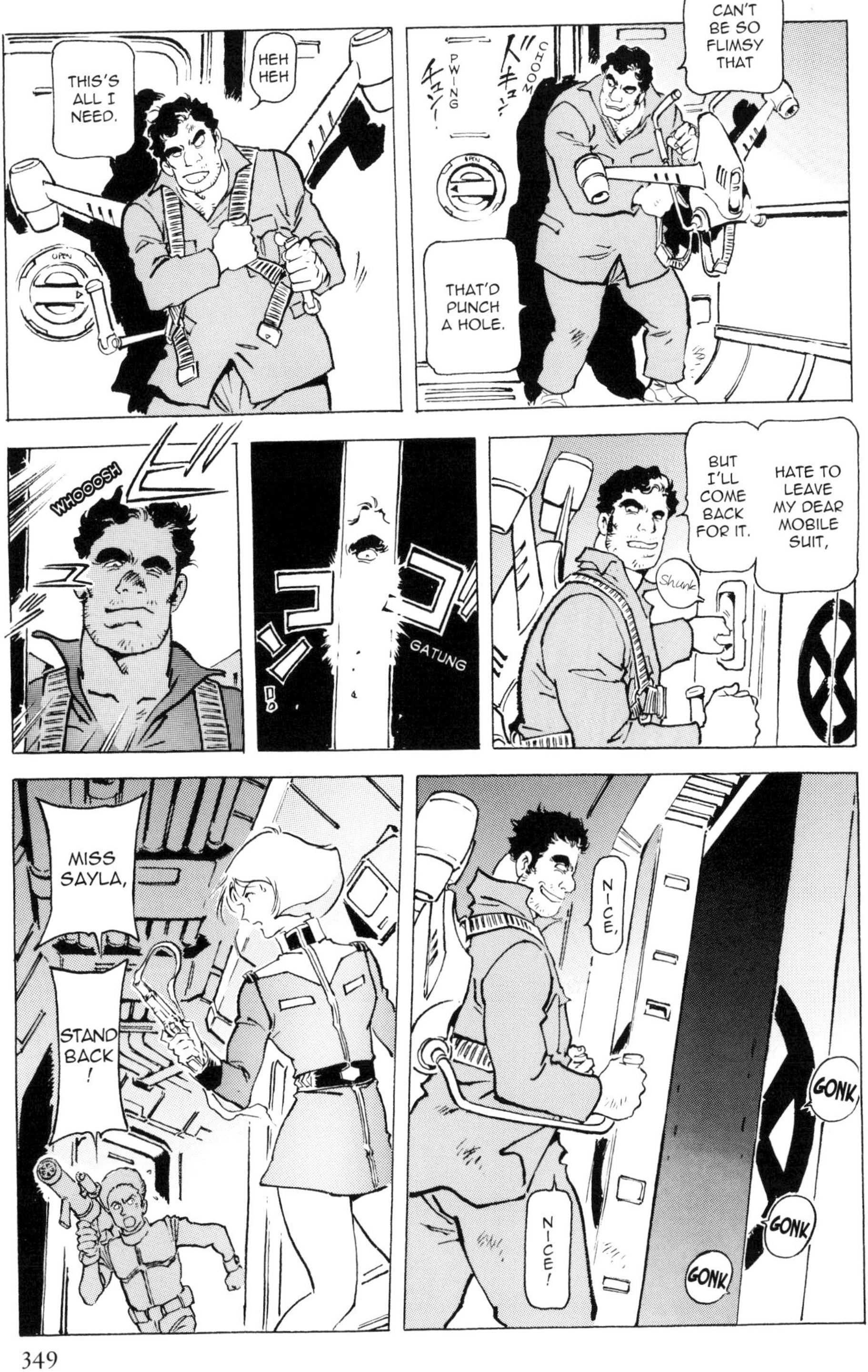
CAN'T BE SO FLIMSY THAT
CHOOM
PWING
THAT'D PUNCH A HOLE.
HEH HEH
THIS'S ALL I NEED.
HATE TO LEAVE MY DEAR MOBILE SUIT,
BUT I'LL COME BACK FOR IT.
Shunk
GATUNG
WHOOOSH
NICE,
NICE!
GONK
GONK
GONK
MISS SAYLA,
STAND BACK!

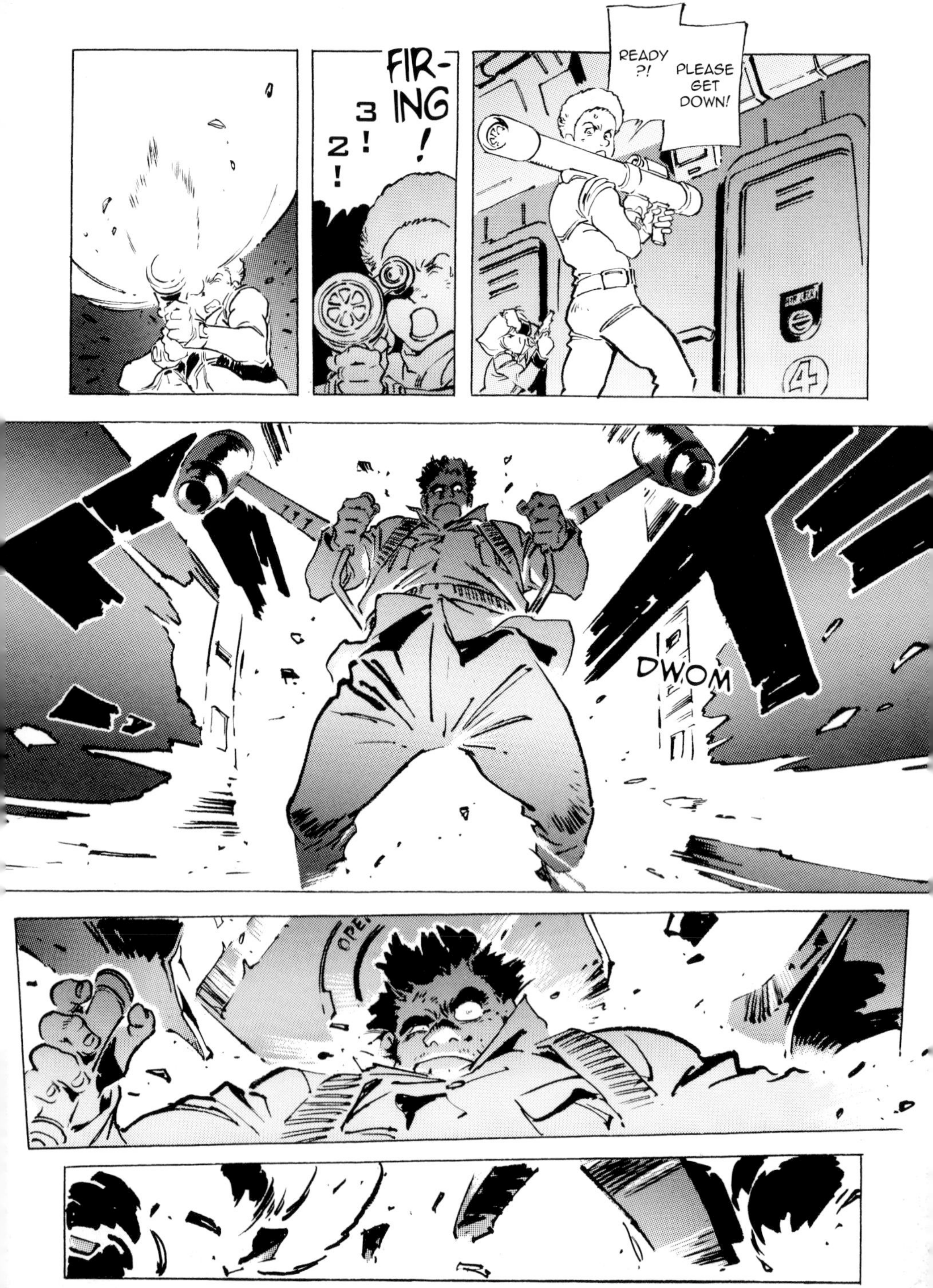
PLEASE GET DOWN!
READY ?!
FIR-ING!
3!
2!
DWOM

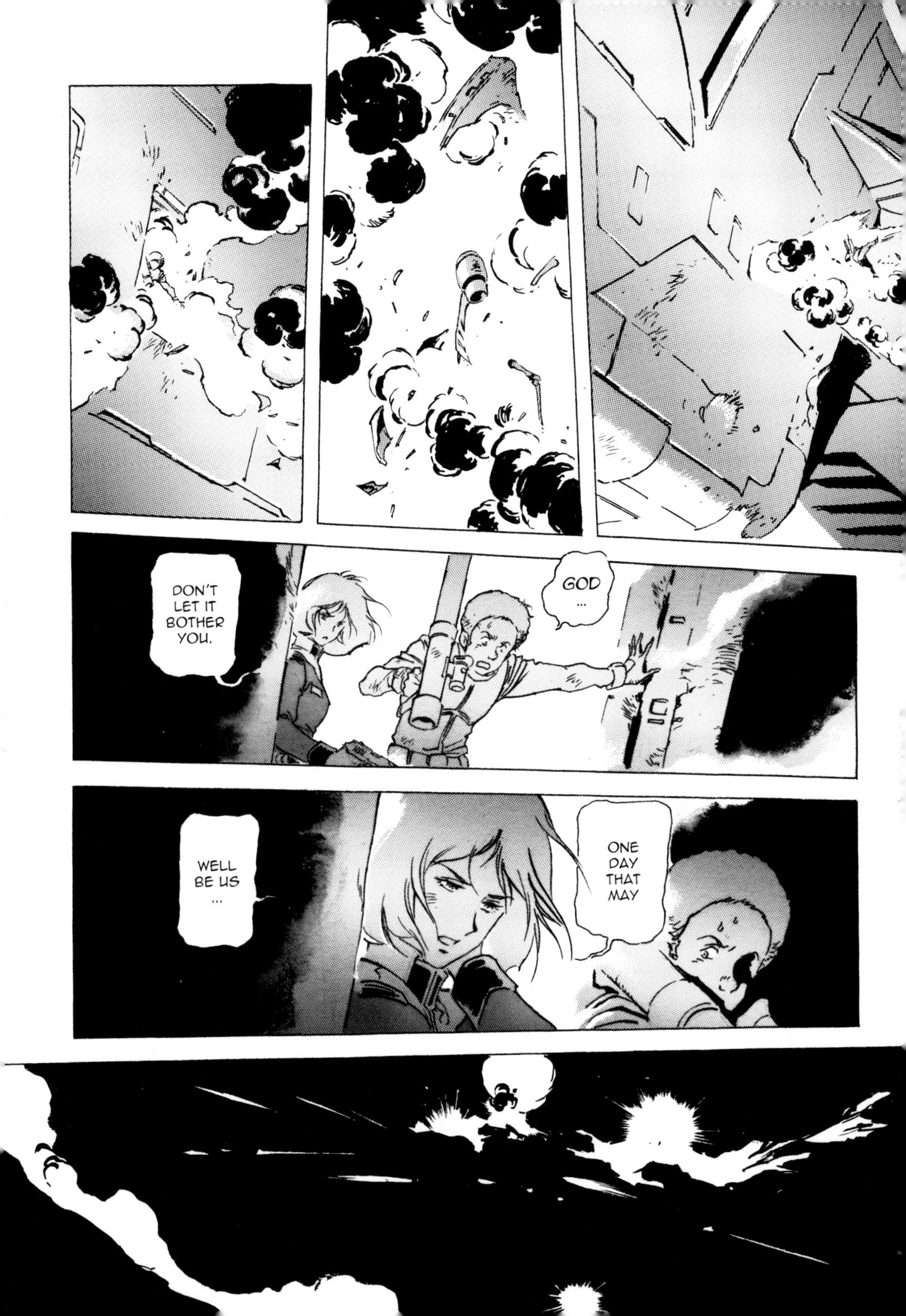
GOD ...
DON'T LET IT BOTHER YOU.
ONE DAY THAT MAY
WELL BE US ...

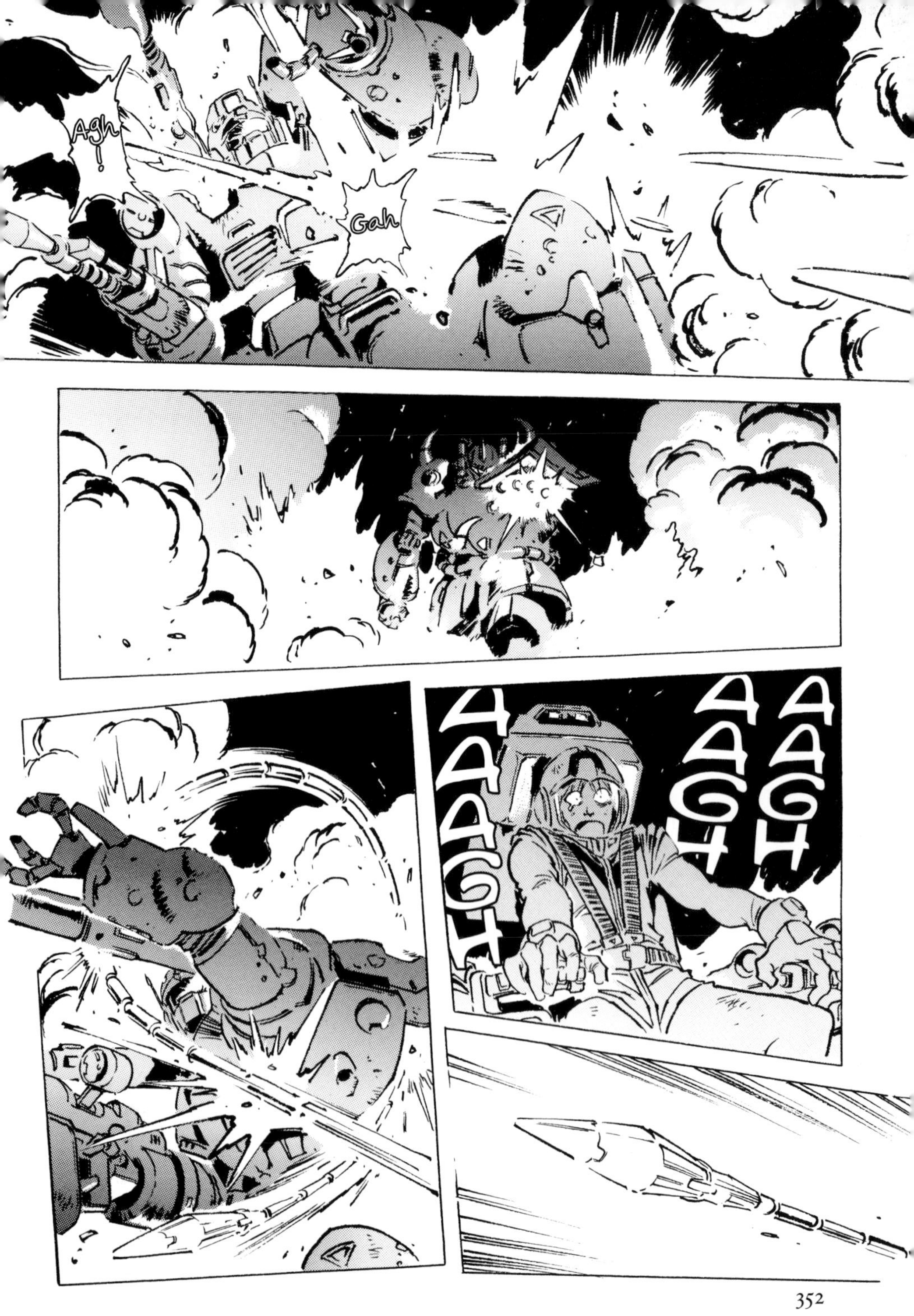
Gah
Agh!
AAAAGH
AAGH
AAGH

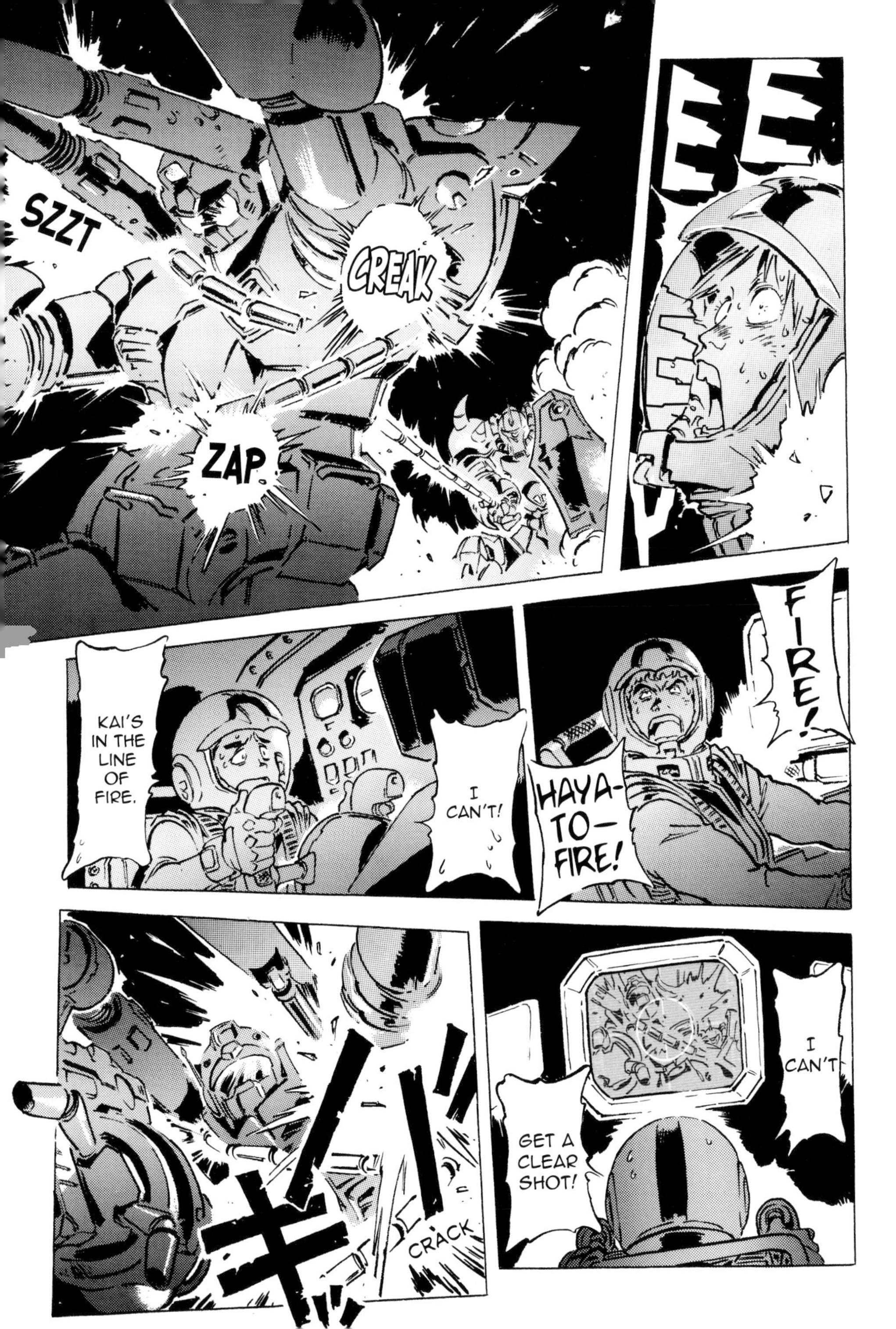
EE
CREAK
SZZT
ZAP
FIRE!
HAYA-TO— FIRE!
I CAN'T!
KAI'S IN THE LINE OF FIRE.
I CAN'T
GET A CLEAR SHOT!
CRACK

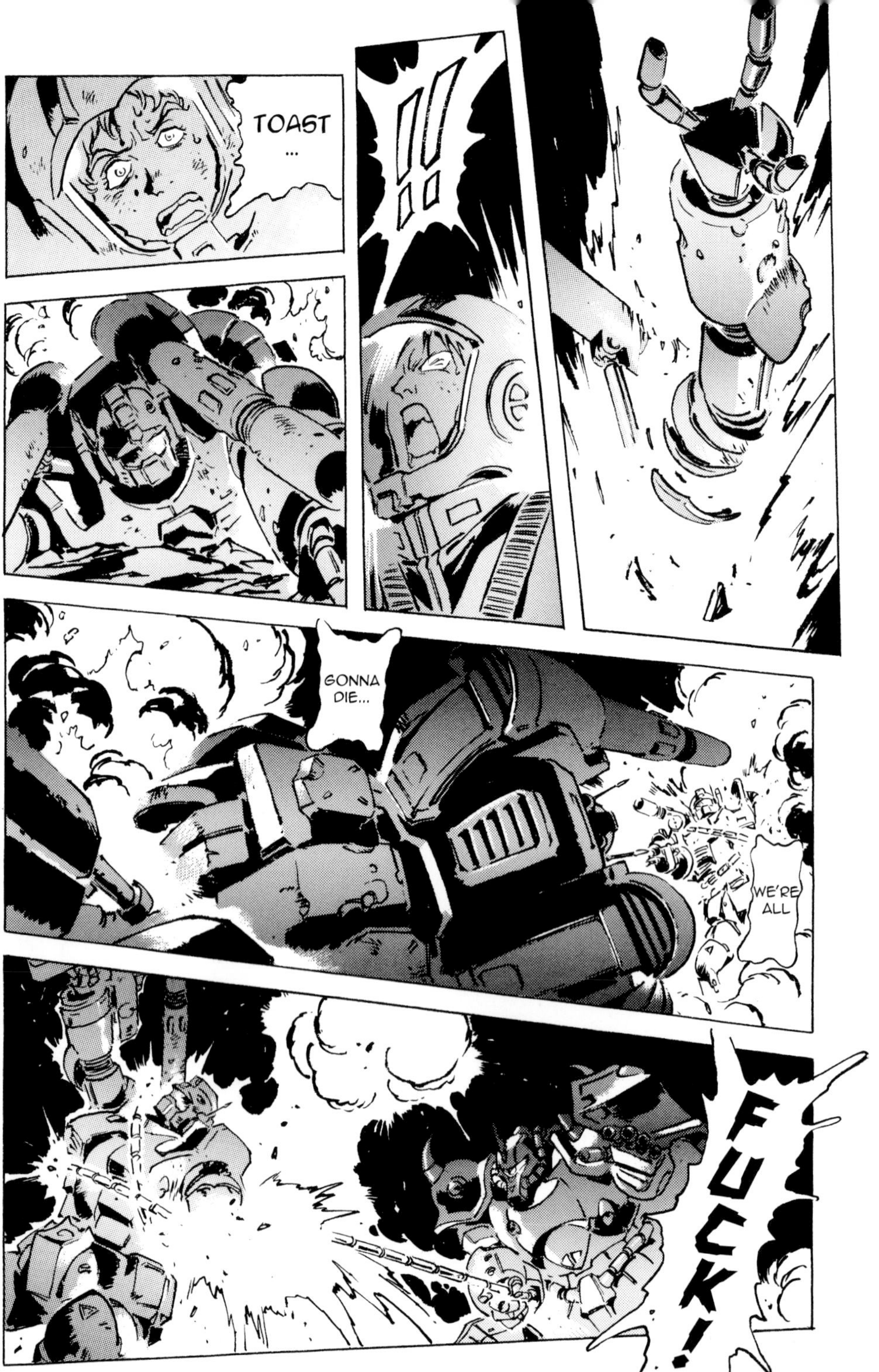
!!
TOAST ...
WE'RE ALL
GONNA DIE...
FUCK!

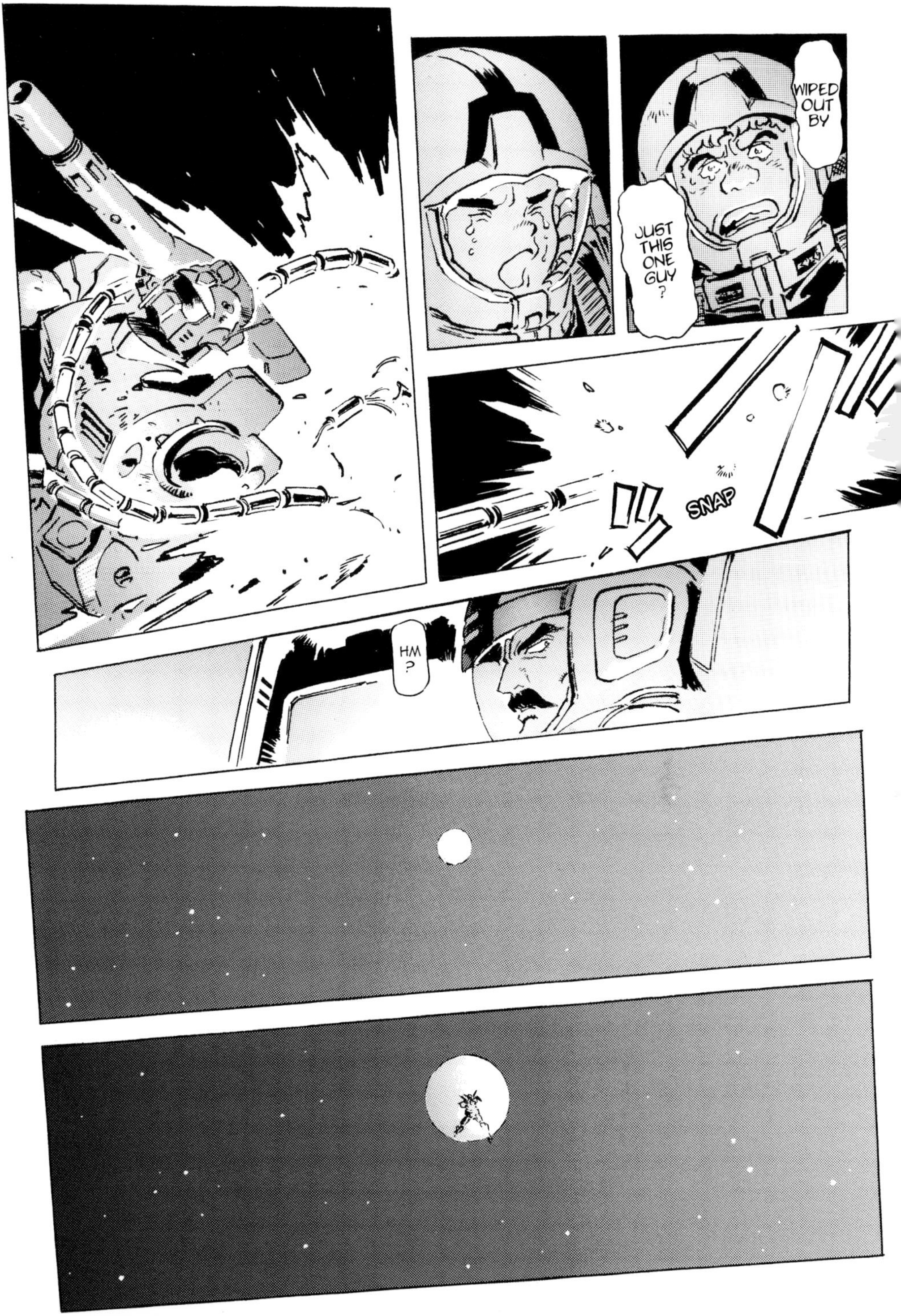
WIPED OUT BY
JUST THIS ONE GUY?
SNAP
HM?

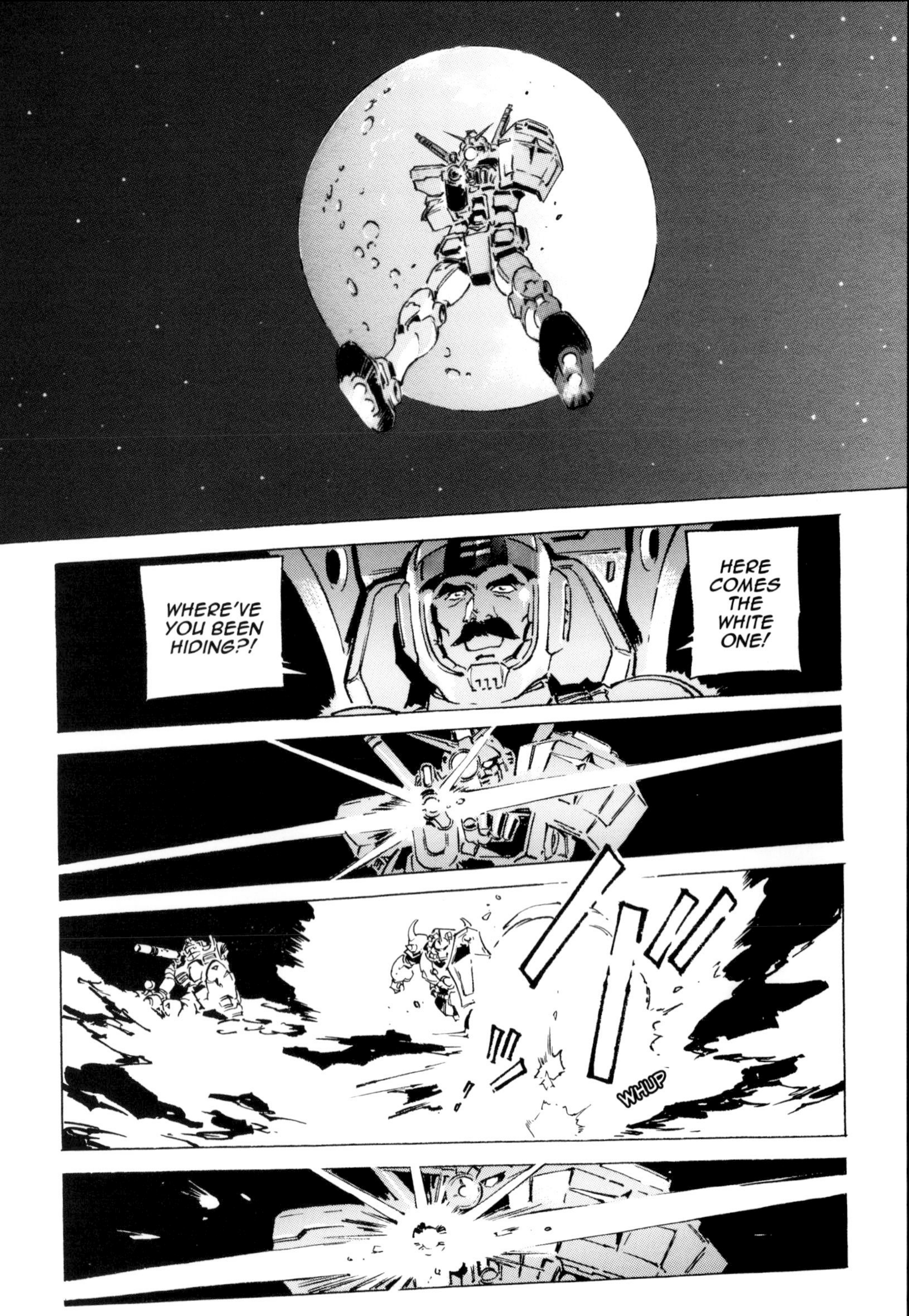
HERE COMES THE WHITE ONE!
WHERE'VE YOU BEEN HIDING?!
WHUP

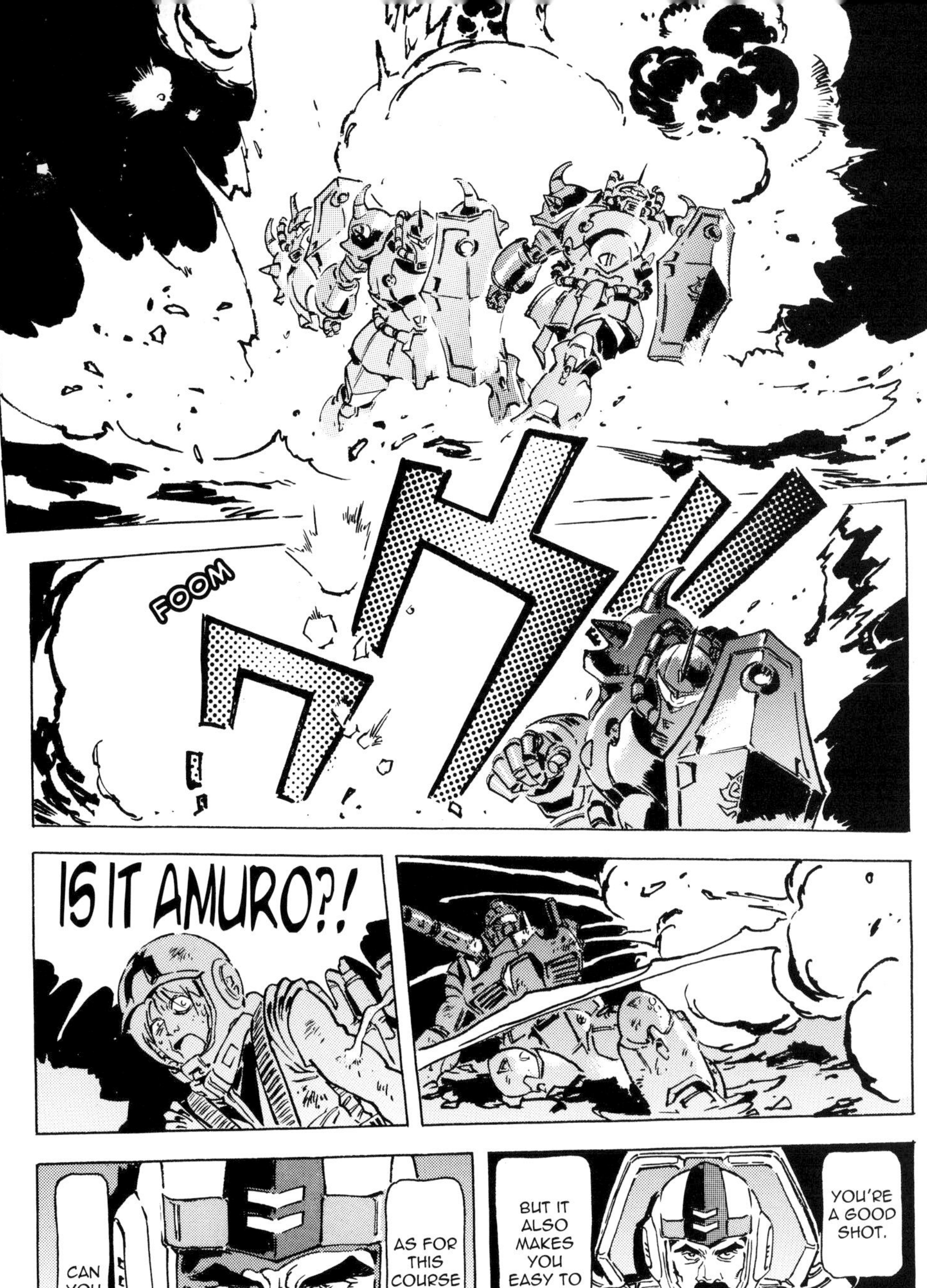
FOOM
IS IT AMURO?!
YOU'RE A GOOD SHOT.
BUT IT ALSO MAKES YOU EASY TO READ.
NOW—
AS FOR THIS COURSE OF DE-SCENT OF YOURS.
CAN YOU JOG IT?

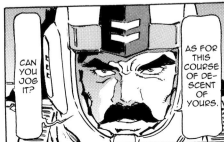

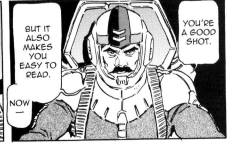

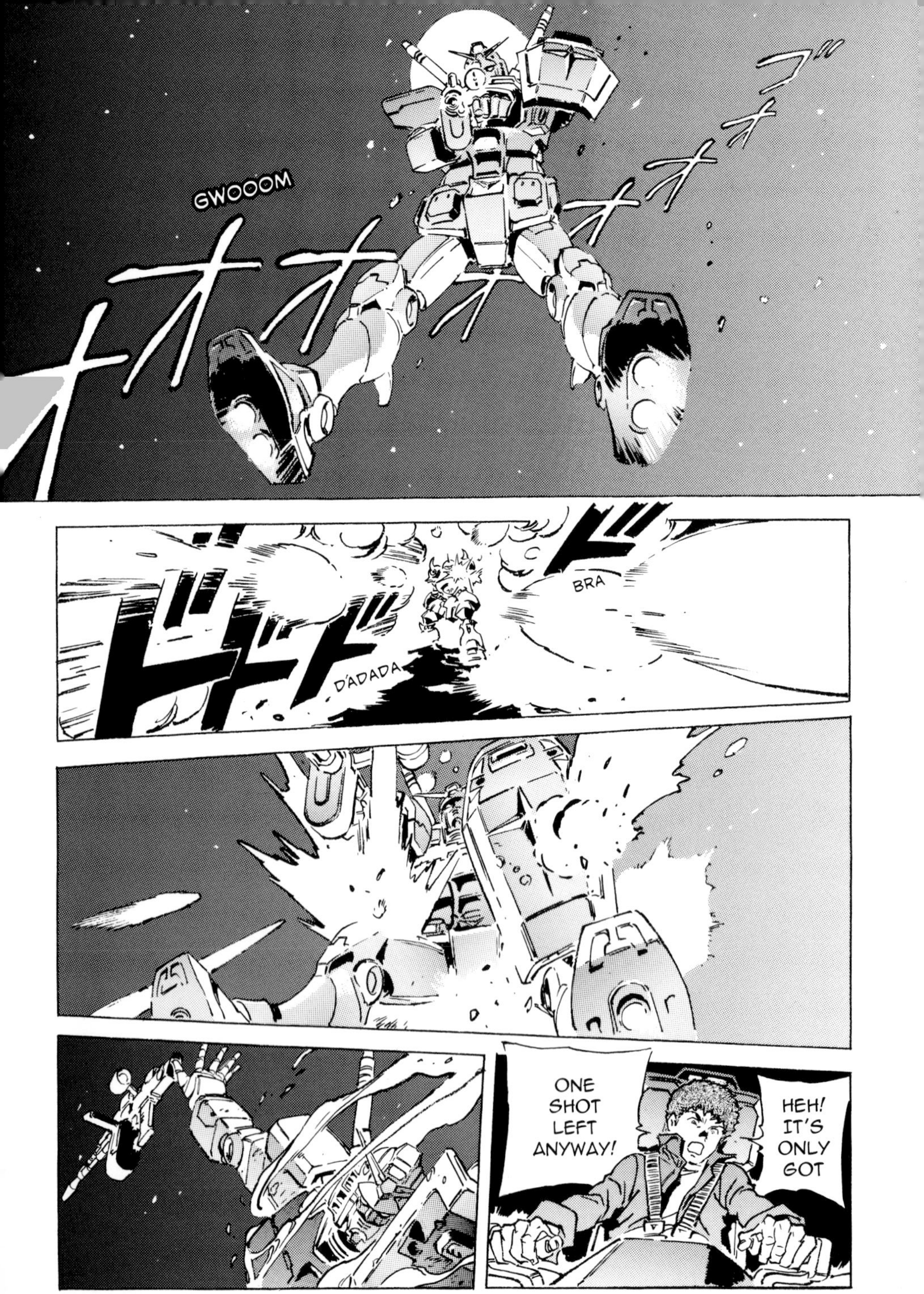
GWOOOM
BRA
D'ADADA
HEH! IT'S ONLY GOT
ONE SHOT LEFT ANYWAY!

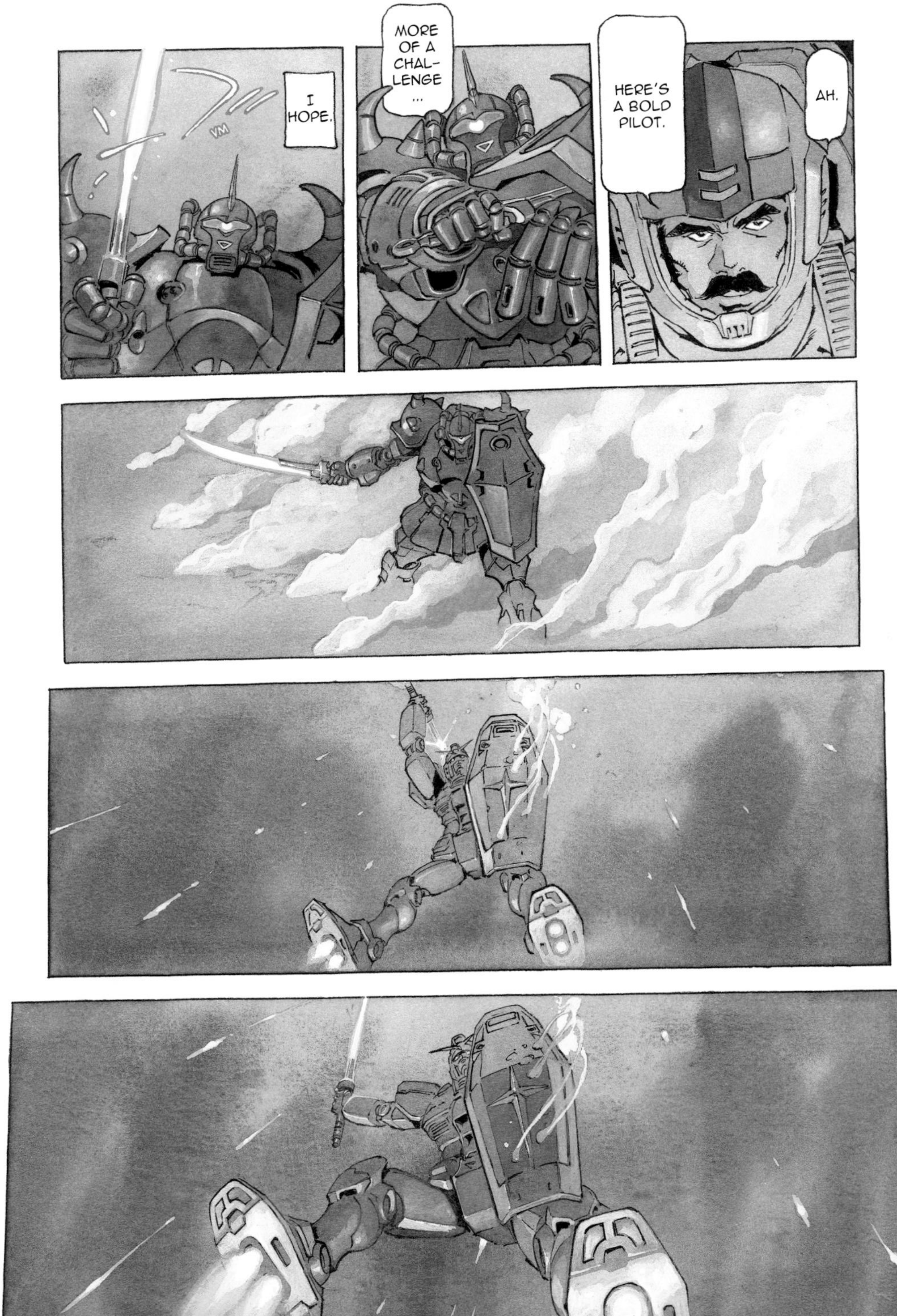
AH.
HERE'S A BOLD PILOT.
MORE OF A CHAL-LENGE ...
I HOPE.
VM

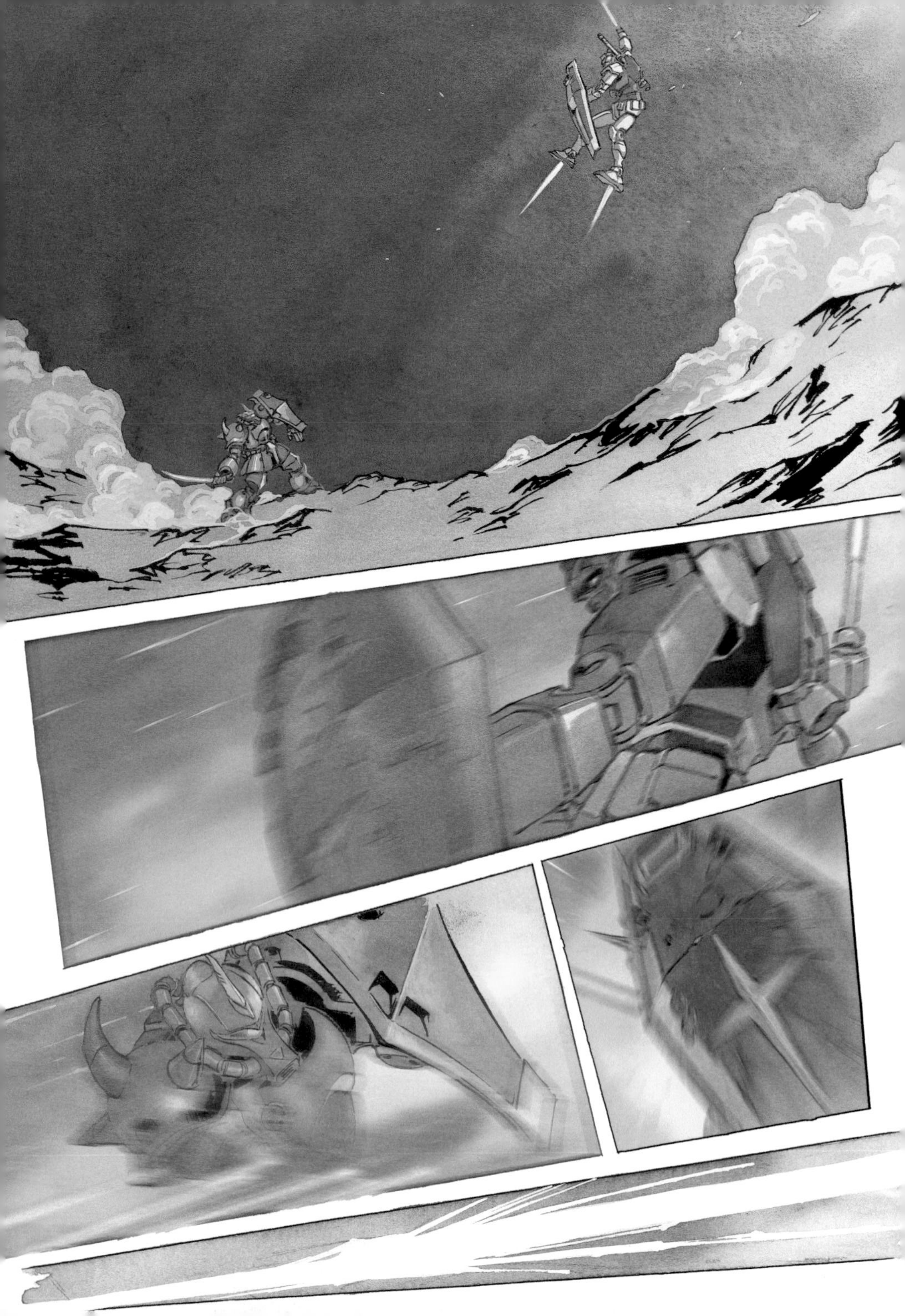

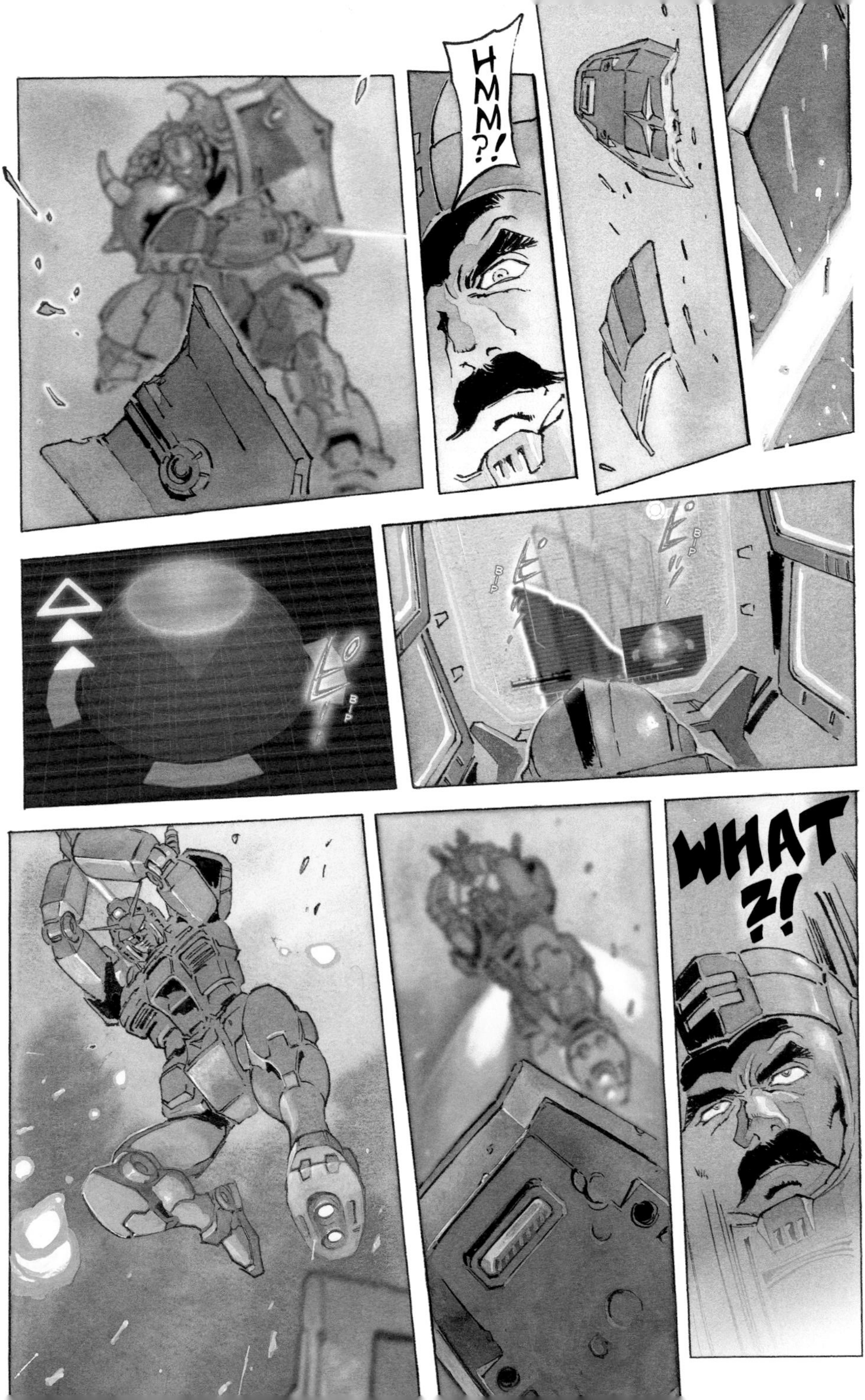
HMM?!
BIP
BIP
BIP
WHAT?!

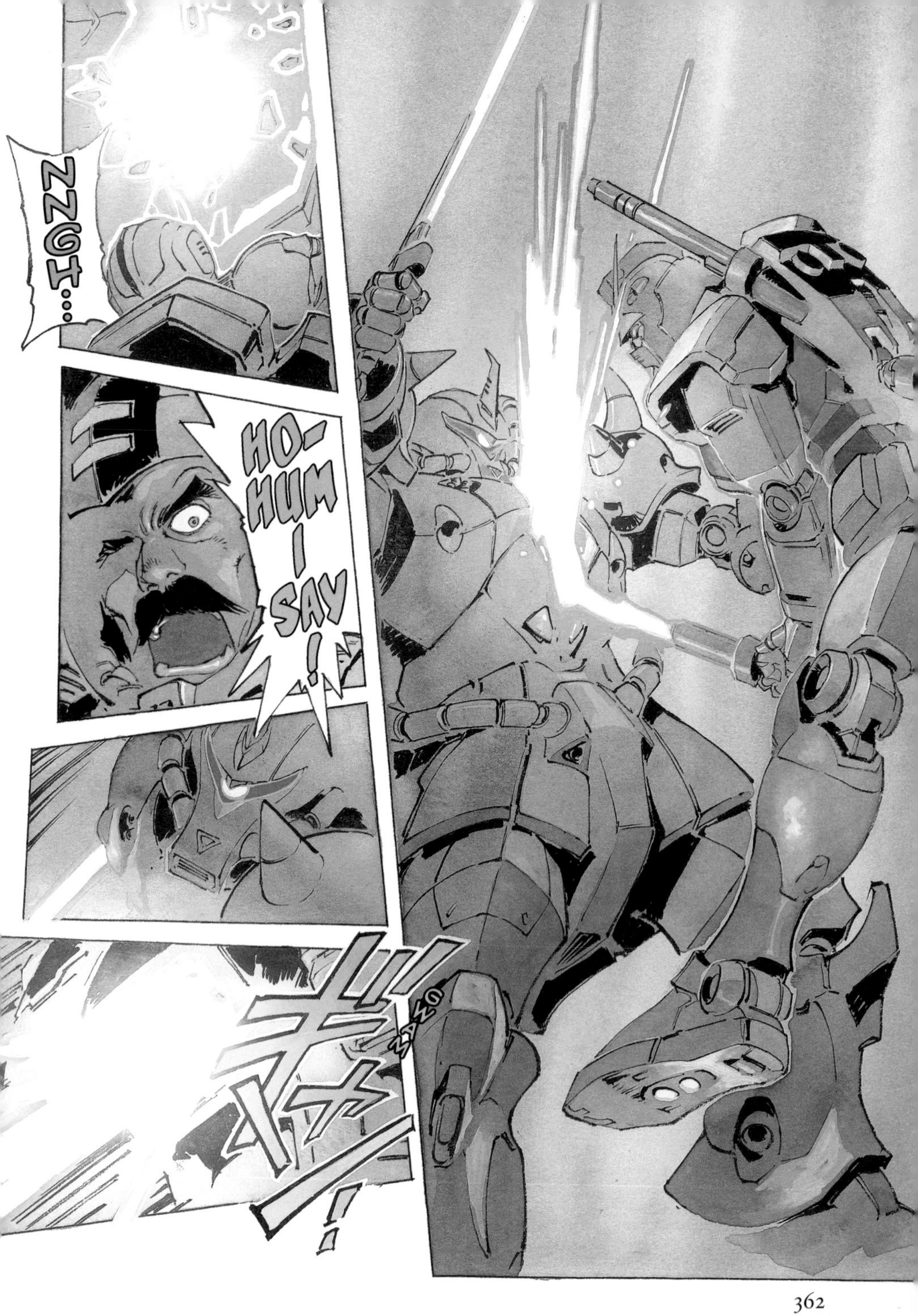
NNGH...
HO-HUM I SAY!
GNAW

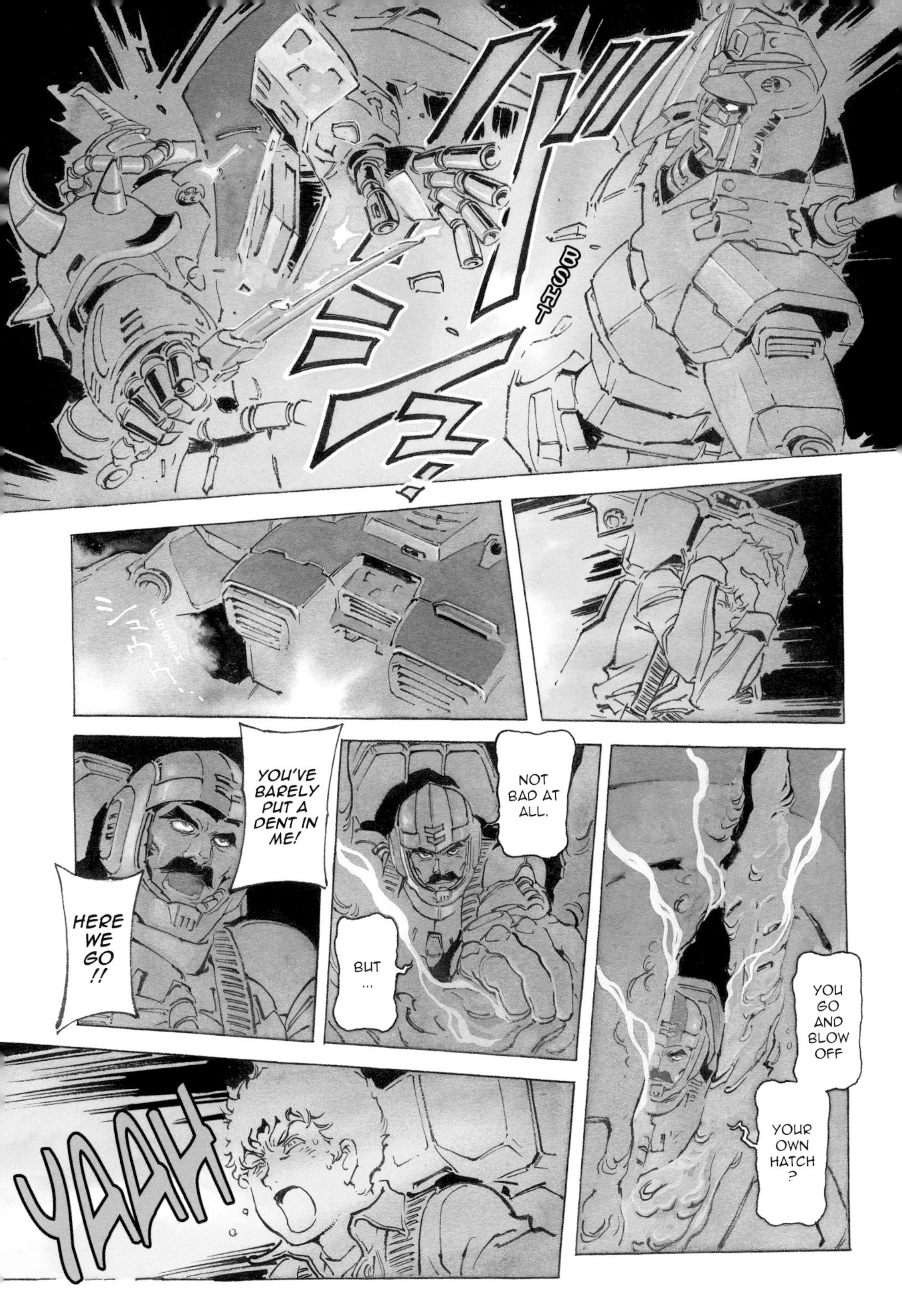
WOSH—
FSSSH
YOU GO AND BLOW OFF
YOUR OWN HATCH?
NOT BAD AT ALL.
BUT ...
YOU'VE BARELY PUT A DENT IN ME!
HERE WE GO!!
YAAAH

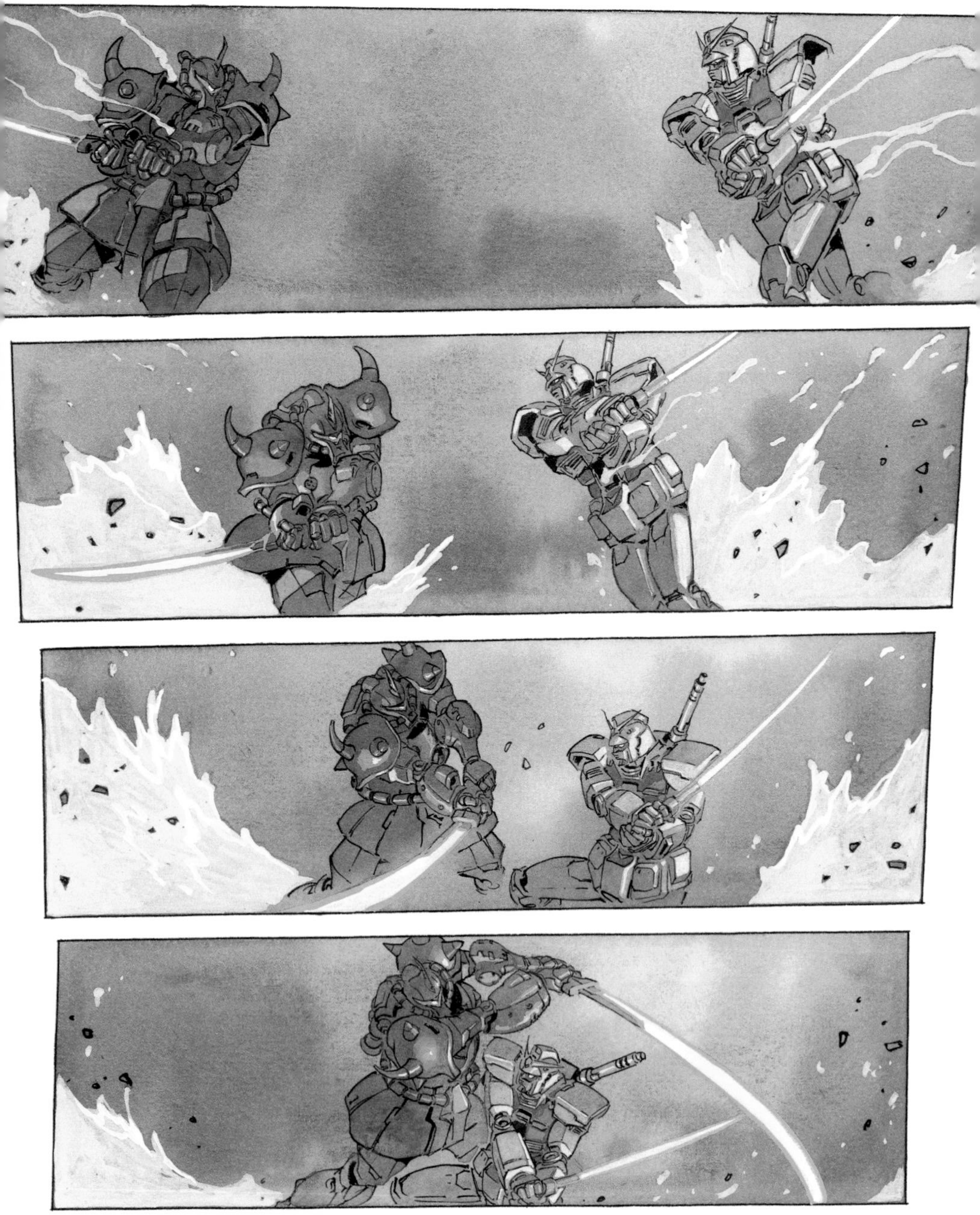

NNG

CLAN

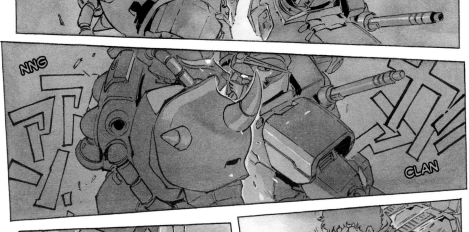

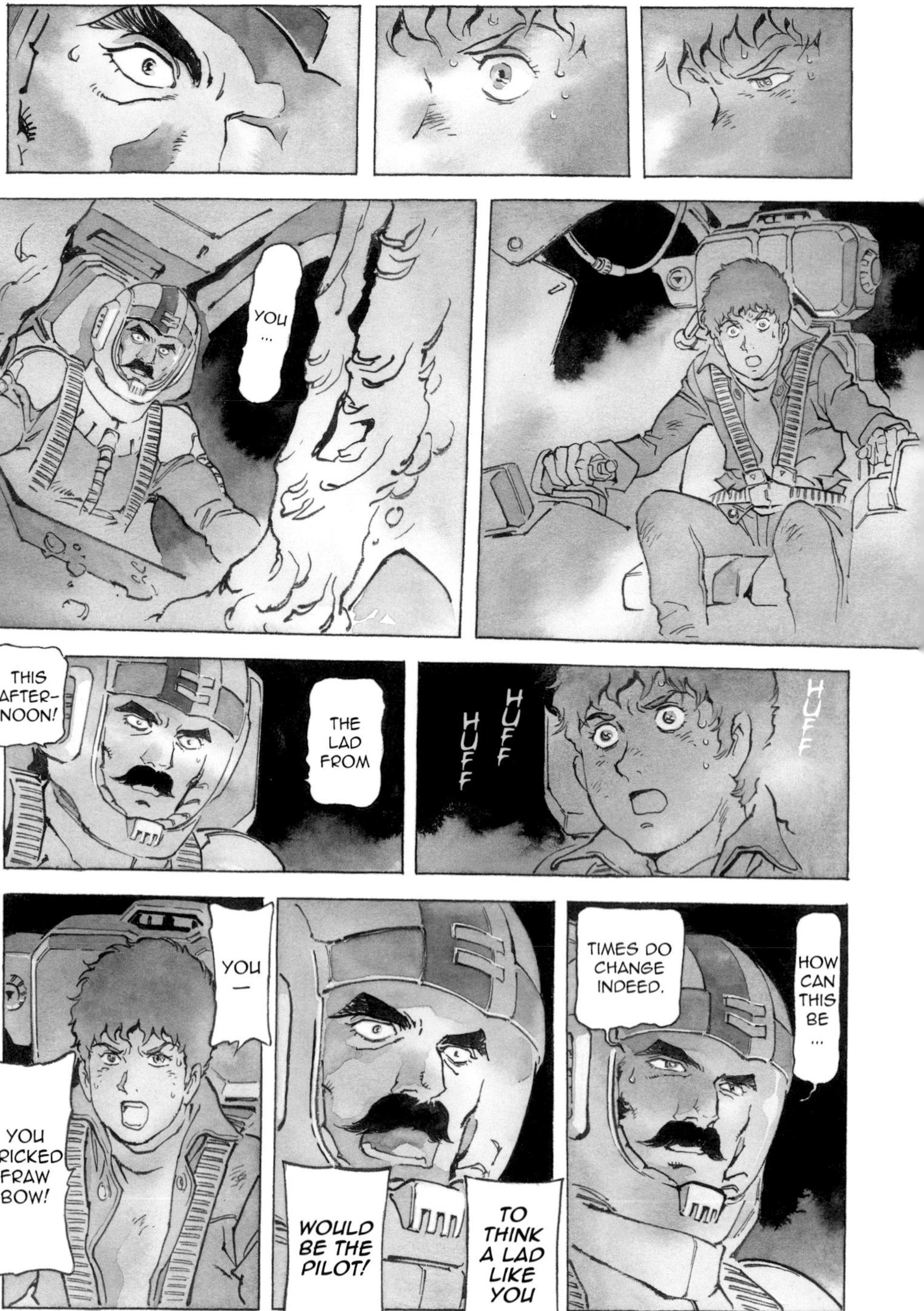
YOU ...
HUFF
HUFF
HUFF
THE LAD FROM
THIS AFTERNOON!
HOW CAN THIS BE ...
TIMES DO CHANGE INDEED.
TO THINK A LAD LIKE YOU
WOULD BE THE PILOT!
YOU—
YOU TRICKED FRAW BOW!

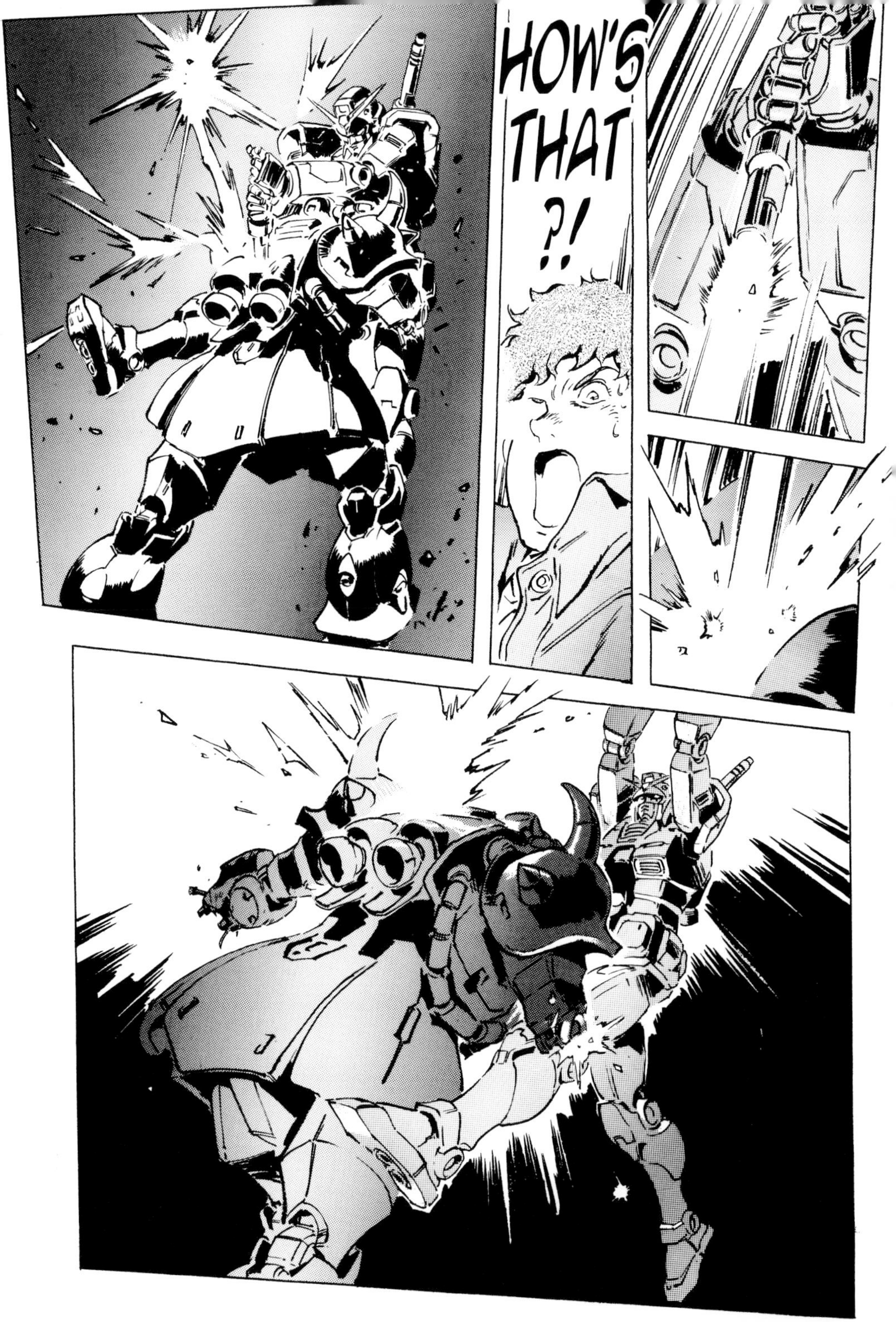
HOW'S THAT ?!

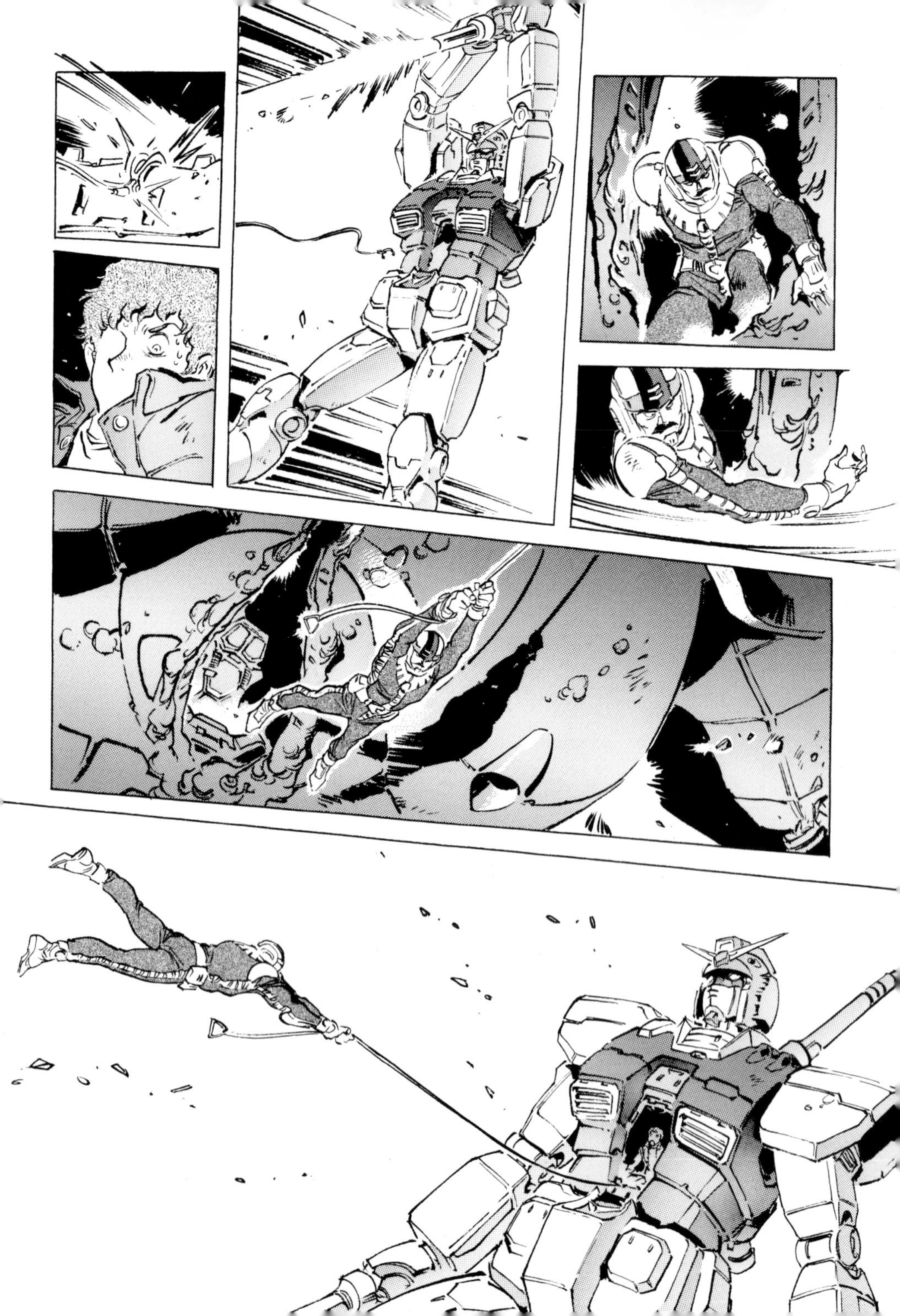

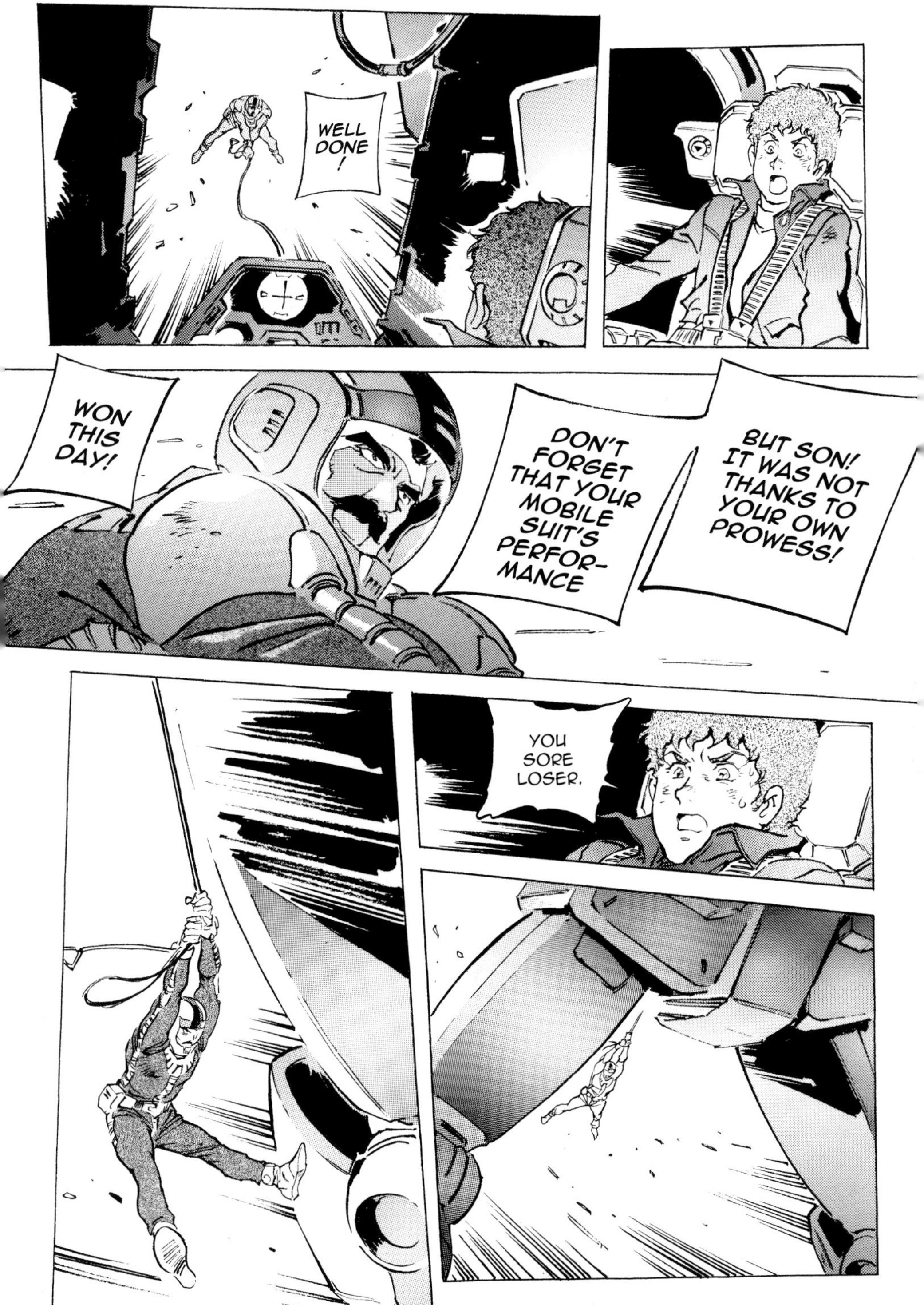
WELL DONE!
BUT SON! IT WAS NOT THANKS TO YOUR OWN PROWESS!
DON'T FORGET THAT YOUR MOBILE SUIT'S PERFOR-MANCE
WON THIS DAY!
YOU SORE LOSER.

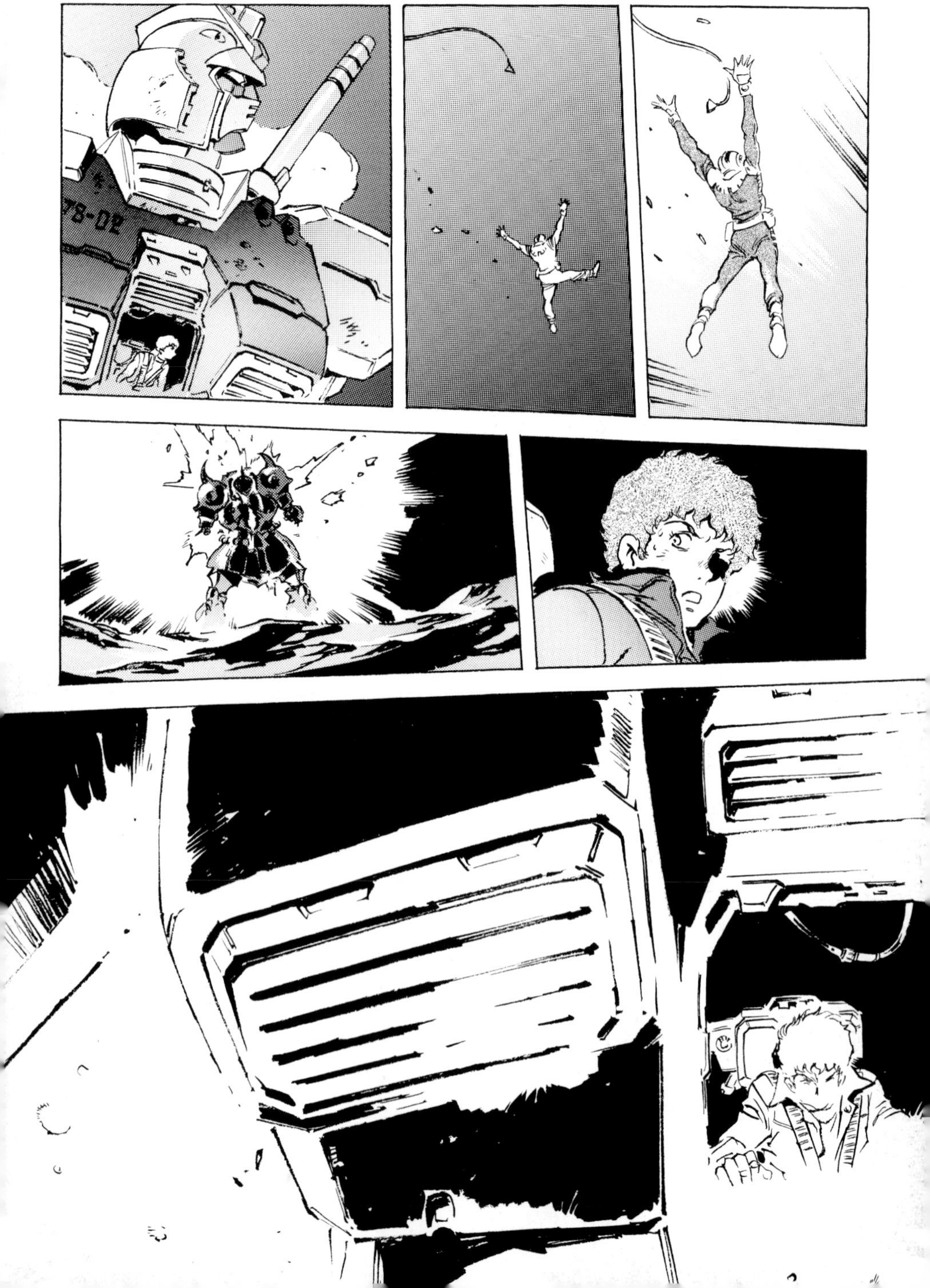
78-02

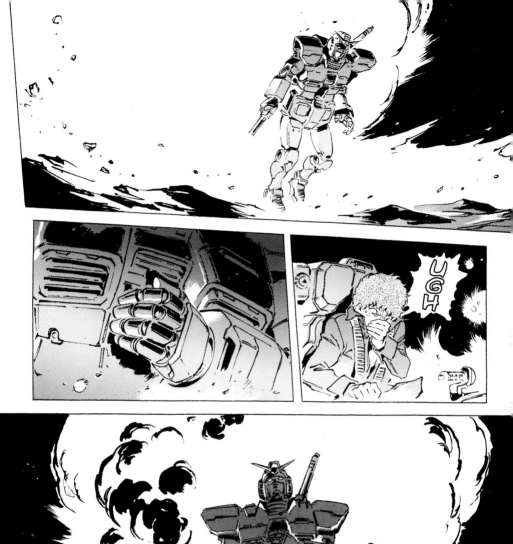

UGH

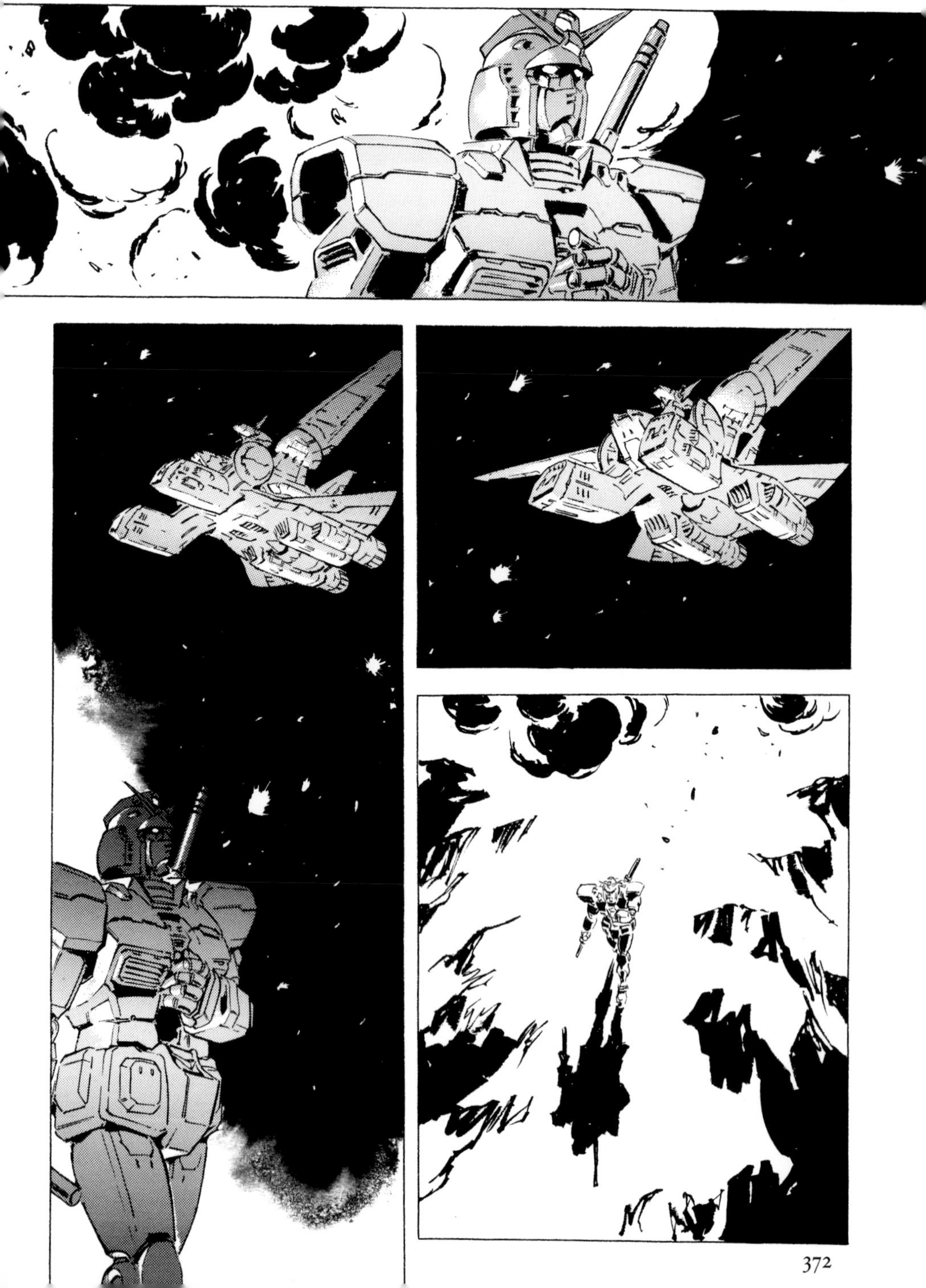

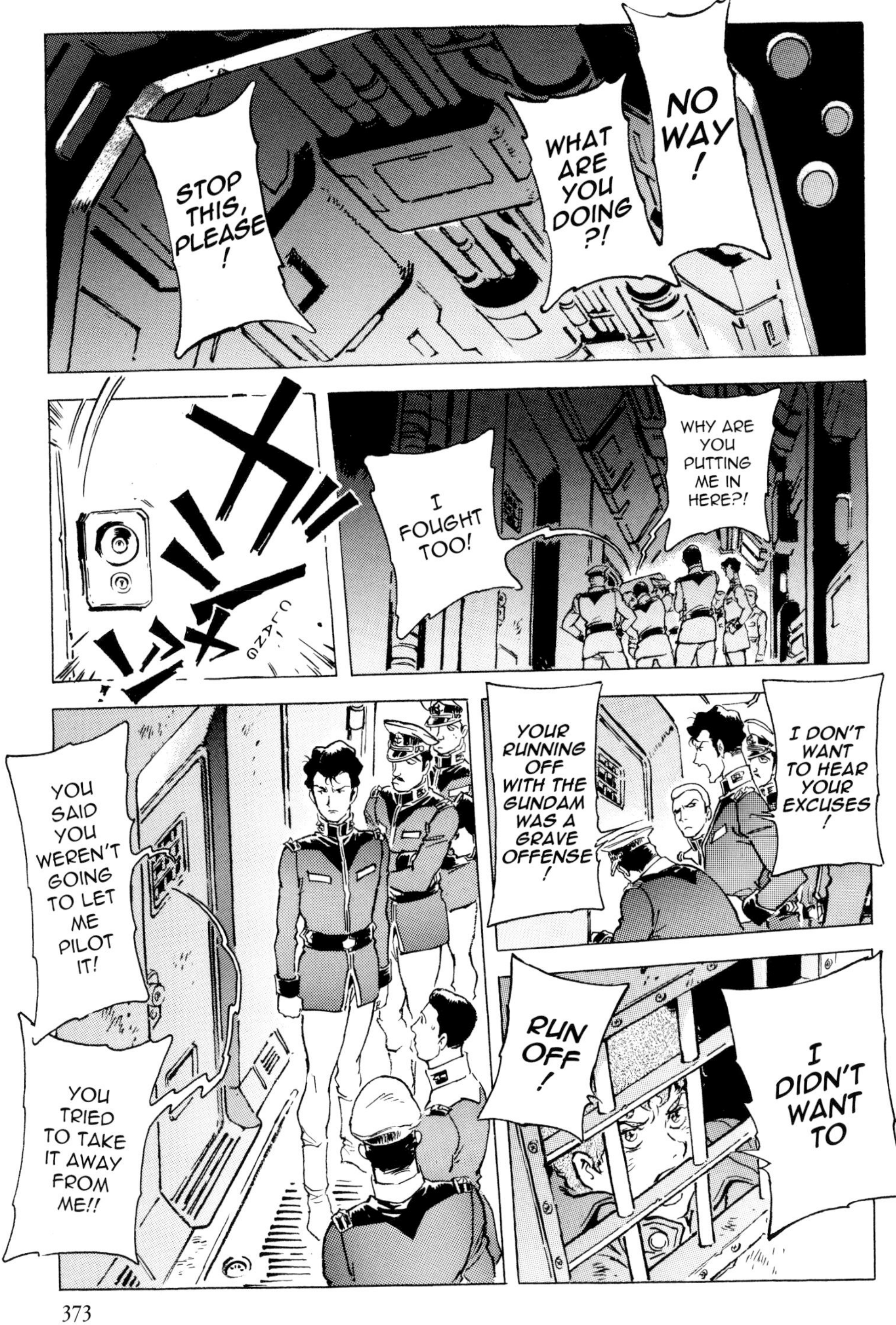
NO WAY!
WHAT ARE YOU DOING?!
STOP THIS, PLEASE!
WHY ARE YOU PUTTING ME IN HERE?!
I FOUGHT TOO!
I DON'T WANT TO HEAR YOUR EXCUSES!
YOUR RUNNING OFF WITH THE GUNDAM WAS A GRAVE OFFENSE!
I DIDN'T WANT TO
RUN OFF!
YOU SAID YOU WEREN'T GOING TO LET ME PILOT IT!
YOU TRIED TO TAKE IT AWAY FROM ME!!

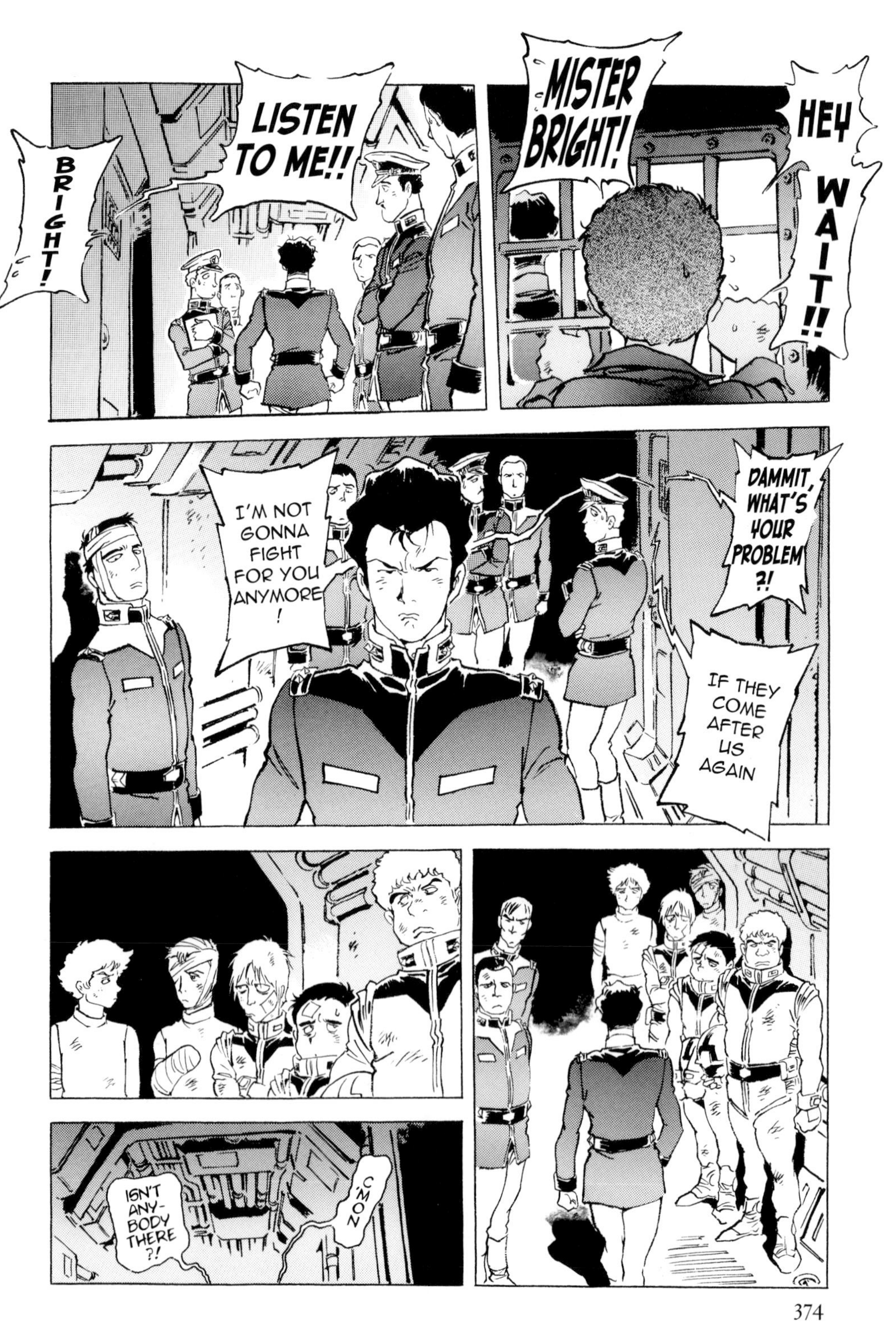
HEY WAIT!!
MISTER BRIGHT!
LISTEN TO ME!!
BRIGHT!
DAMMIT, WHAT'S YOUR PROBLEM?!
IF THEY COME AFTER US AGAIN
I'M NOT GONNA FIGHT FOR YOU ANYMORE!
C'MON
ISN'T ANYBODY THERE?!

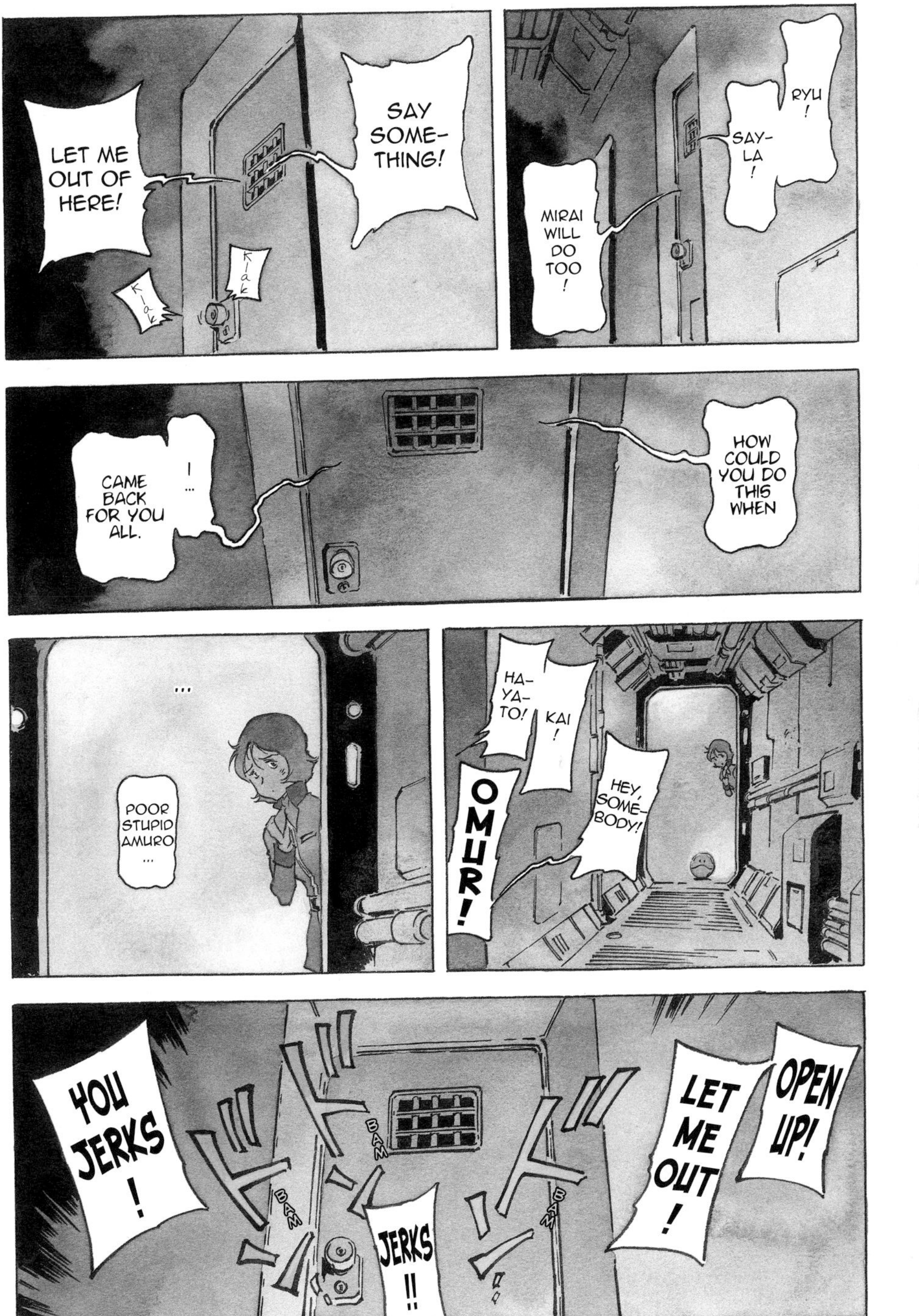
RYU!
SAY-LA!
MIRAI WILL DO TOO!
SAY SOME-THING!
LET ME OUT OF HERE!
Klak
Klak
HOW COULD YOU DO THIS WHEN
I ... CAME BACK FOR YOU ALL.
KAI!
HA-YA-TO!
HEY, SOME-BODY!
OMURI!
...
POOR STUPID AMURO ...
OPEN UP!
LET ME OUT!
BAM
BAM
JERKS!!
BAM
YOU JERKS!

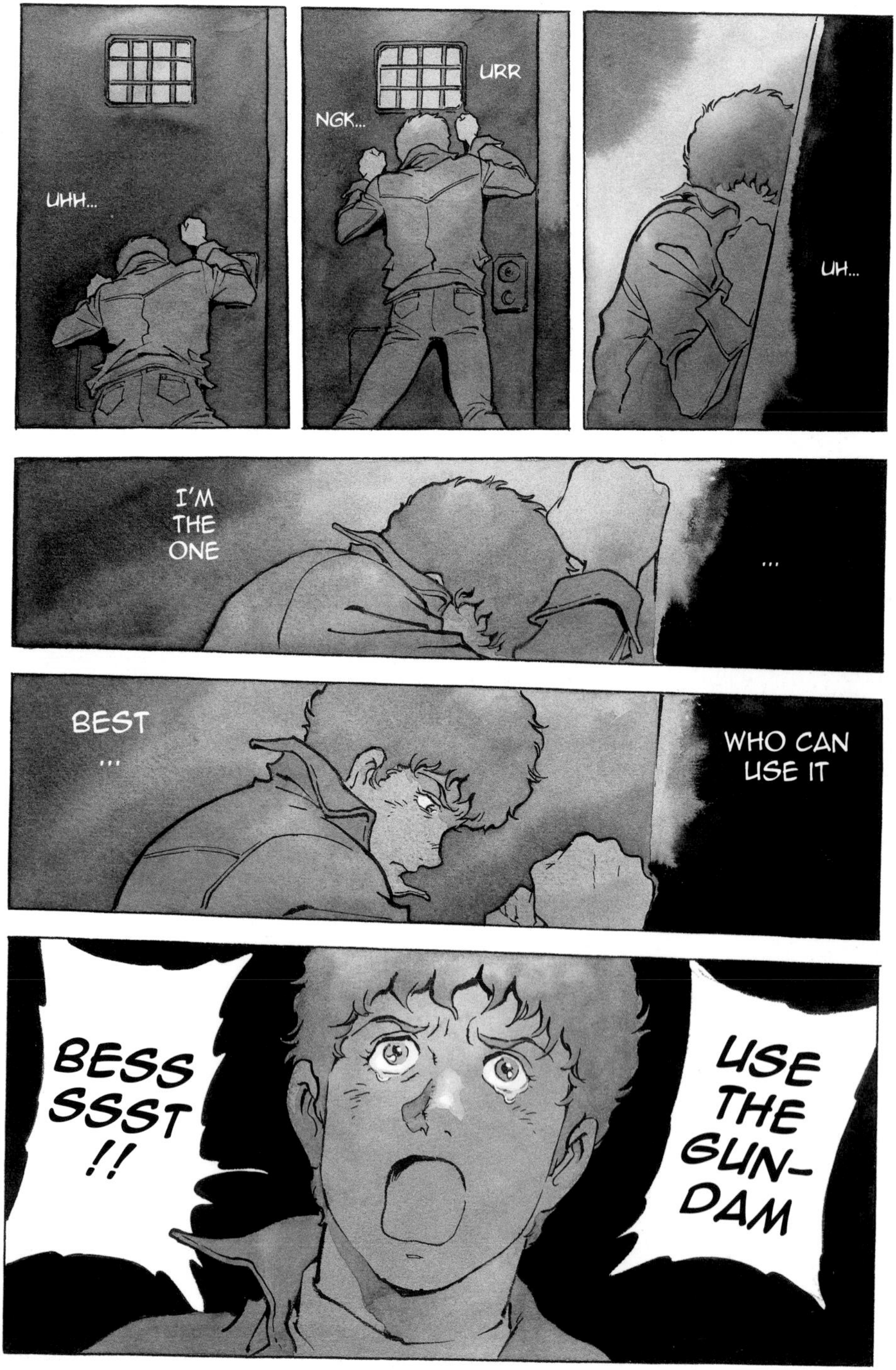
UH...
URR
NGK...
UHH...
...
I'M THE ONE
WHO CAN USE IT
BEST ...
USE THE GUN-DAM
BESS SSST !!

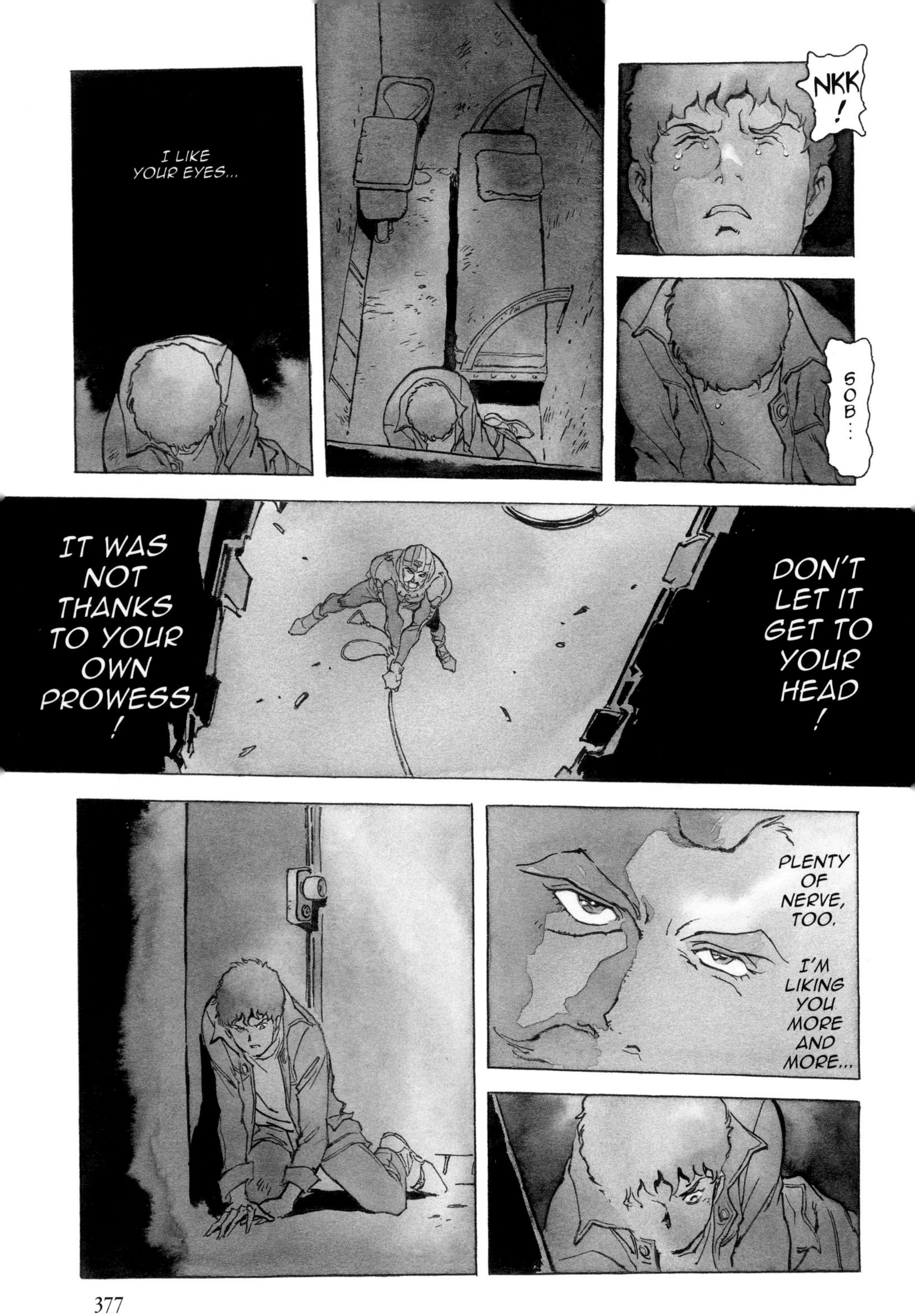
NKK!
SOB...
I LIKE YOUR EYES...
DON'T LET IT GET TO YOUR HEAD!
IT WAS NOT THANKS TO YOUR OWN PROWESS!
PLENTY OF NERVE, TOO.
I'M LIKING YOU MORE AND MORE...

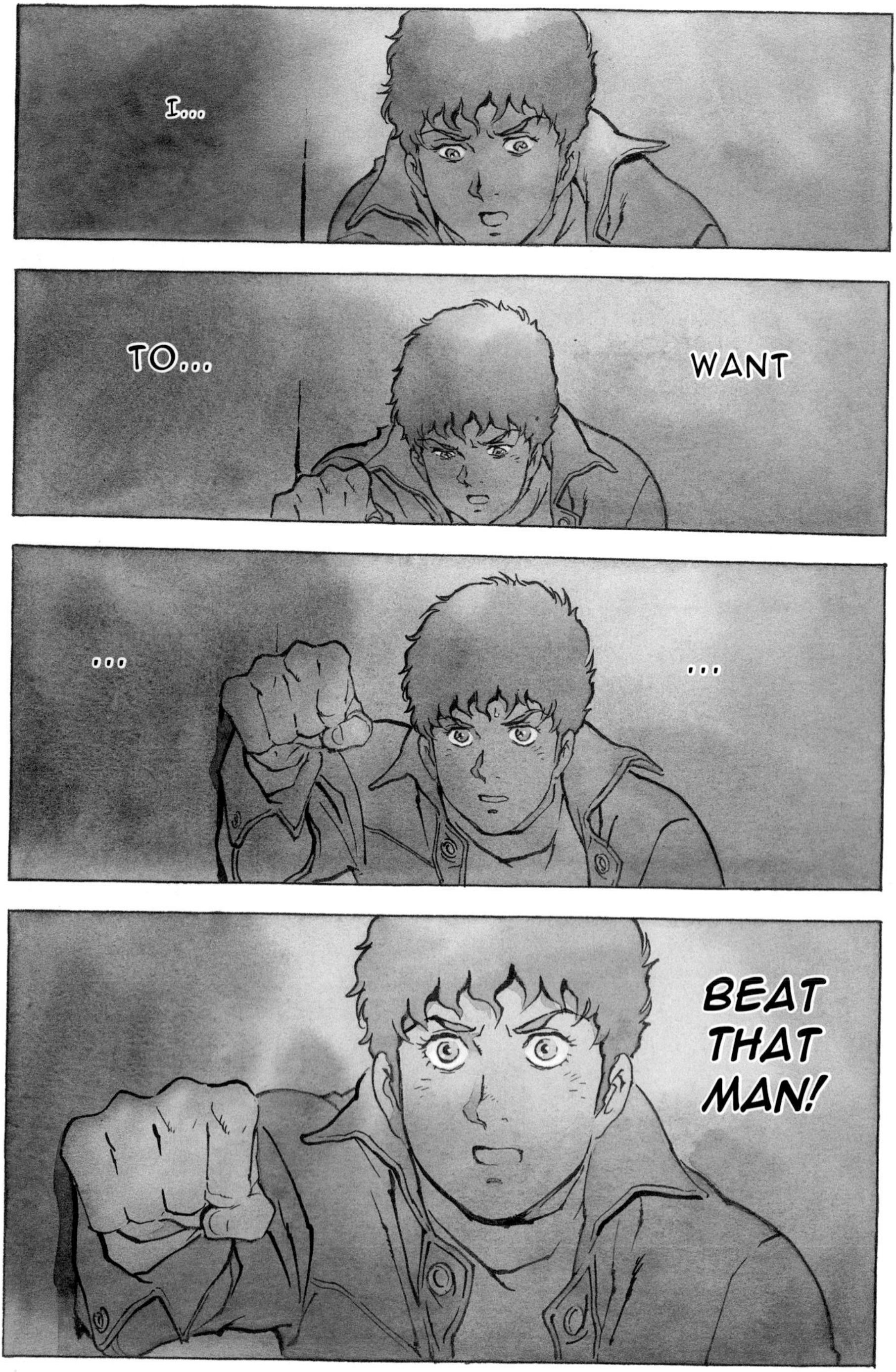
I...
WANT
TO...
...
...
BEAT THAT MAN!

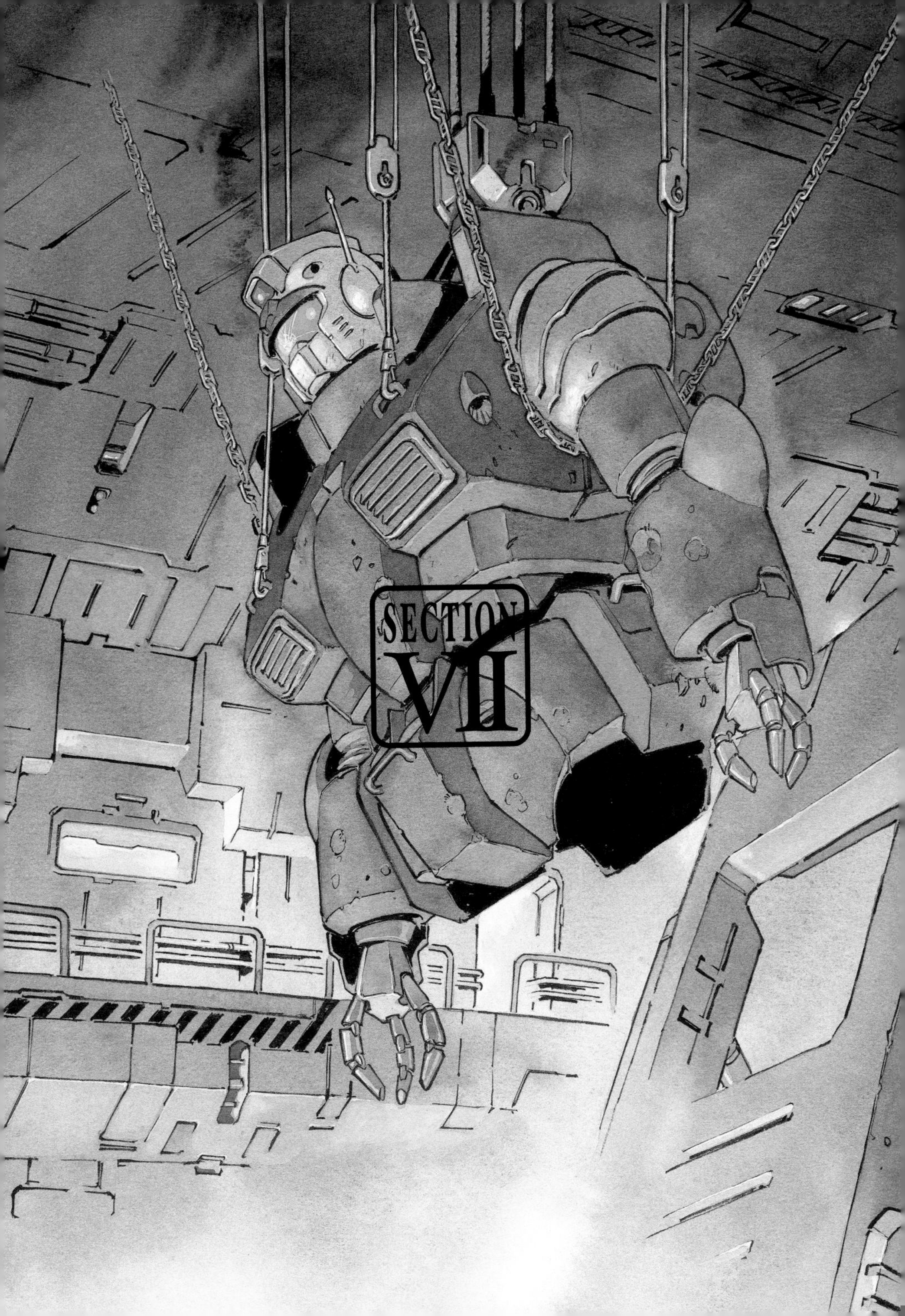
SECTION
VII

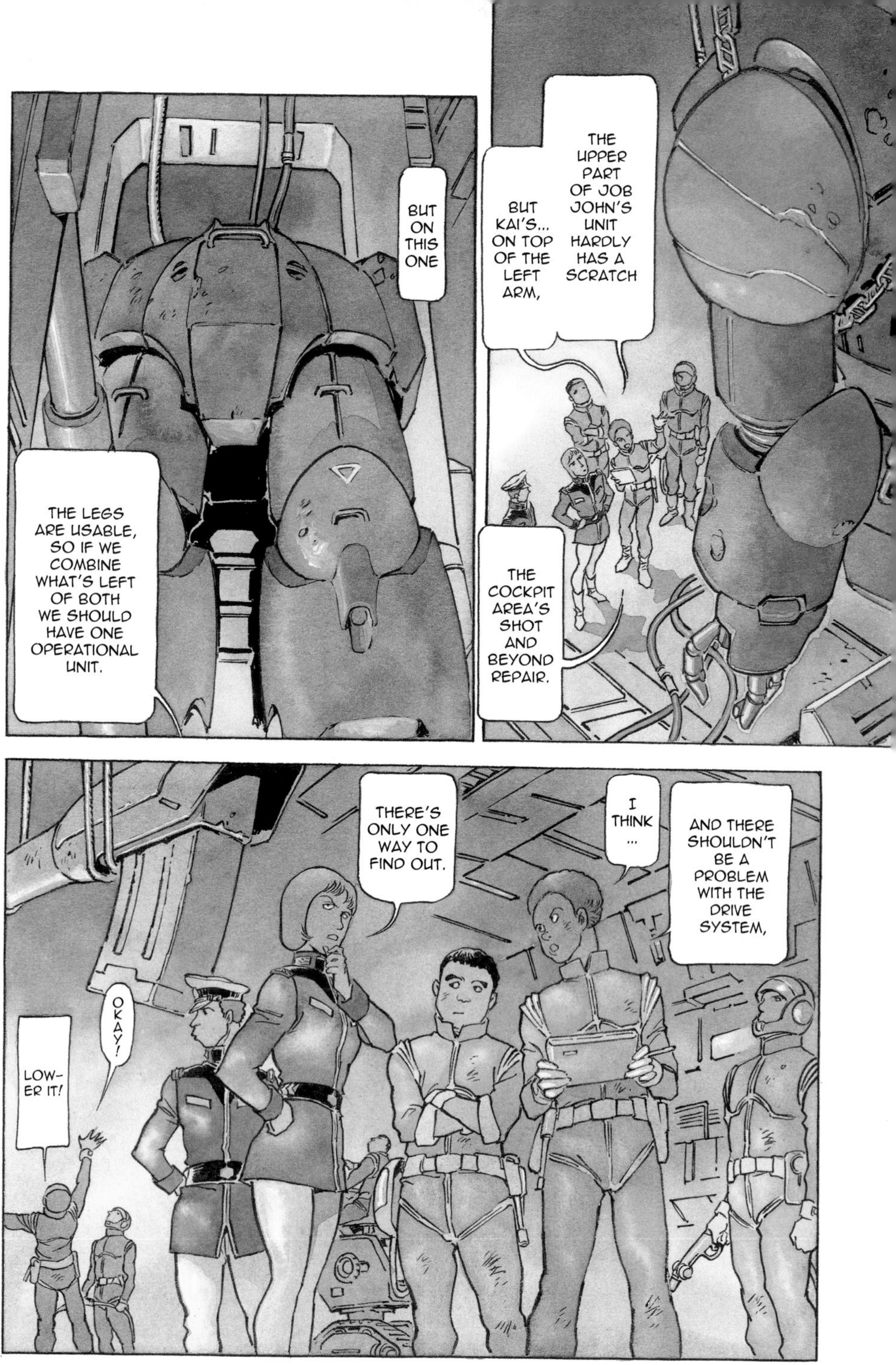
THE UPPER PART OF JOB JOHN'S UNIT HARDLY HAS A SCRATCH
BUT KAI'S... ON TOP OF THE LEFT ARM,
THE COCKPIT AREA'S SHOT AND BEYOND REPAIR.
BUT ON THIS ONE
THE LEGS ARE USABLE, SO IF WE COMBINE WHAT'S LEFT OF BOTH WE SHOULD HAVE ONE OPERATIONAL UNIT.
AND THERE SHOULDN'T BE A PROBLEM WITH THE DRIVE SYSTEM,
I THINK ...
THERE'S ONLY ONE WAY TO FIND OUT.
OKAY!
LOWER IT!

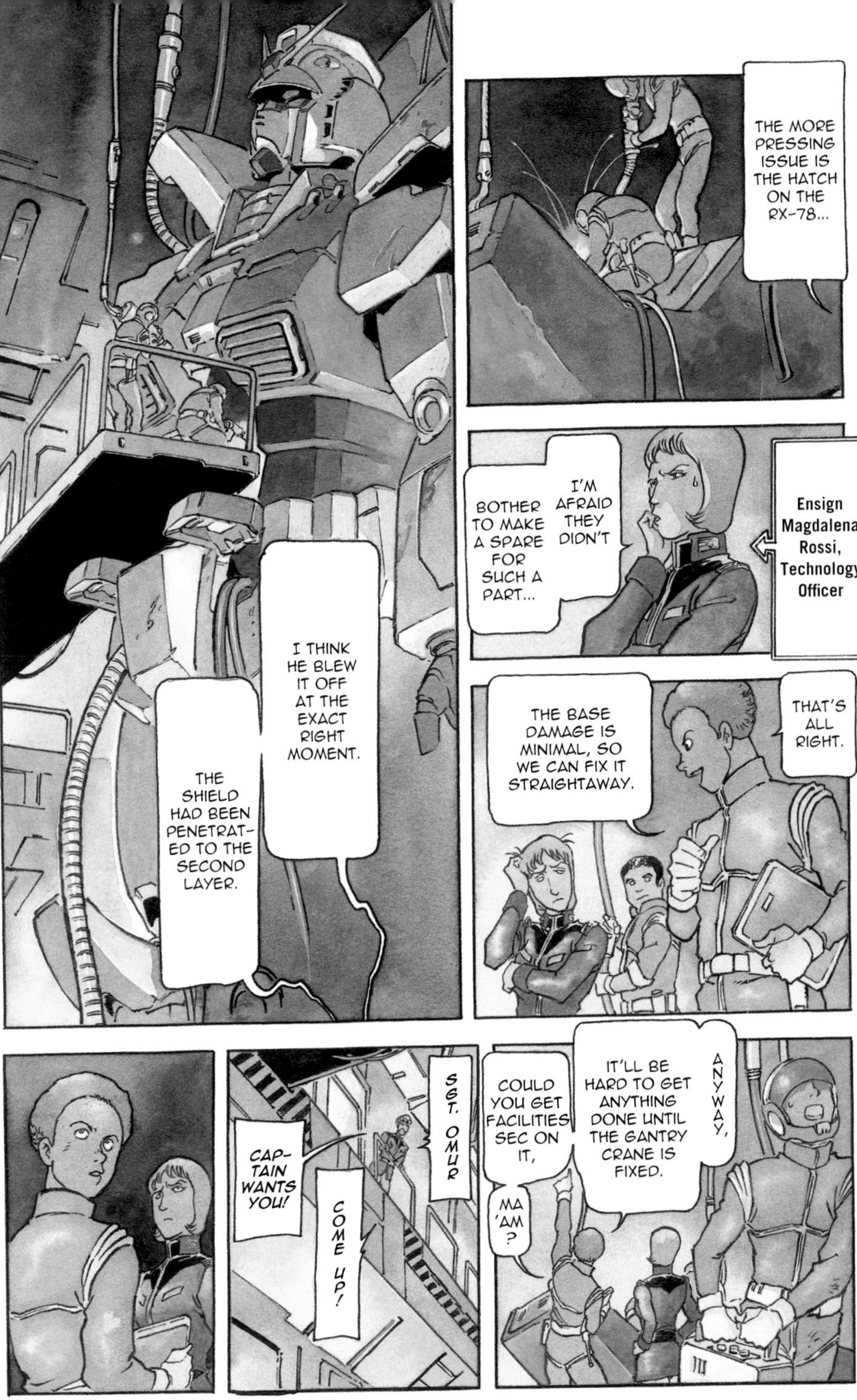
THE MORE PRESSING ISSUE IS THE HATCH ON THE RX-78...
I'M AFRAID THEY DIDN'T BOTHER TO MAKE A SPARE FOR SUCH A PART...
Ensign Magdalena Rossi, Technology Officer
THAT'S ALL RIGHT.
THE BASE DAMAGE IS MINIMAL, SO WE CAN FIX IT STRAIGHTAWAY.
I THINK HE BLEW IT OFF AT THE EXACT RIGHT MOMENT.
THE SHIELD HAD BEEN PENETRATED TO THE SECOND LAYER.
ANYWAY,
IT'LL BE HARD TO GET ANYTHING DONE UNTIL THE GANTRY CRANE IS FIXED.
COULD YOU GET FACILITIES SEC ON IT,
MA'AM?
SGT. OMUR
CAPTAIN WANTS YOU!
COME UP!

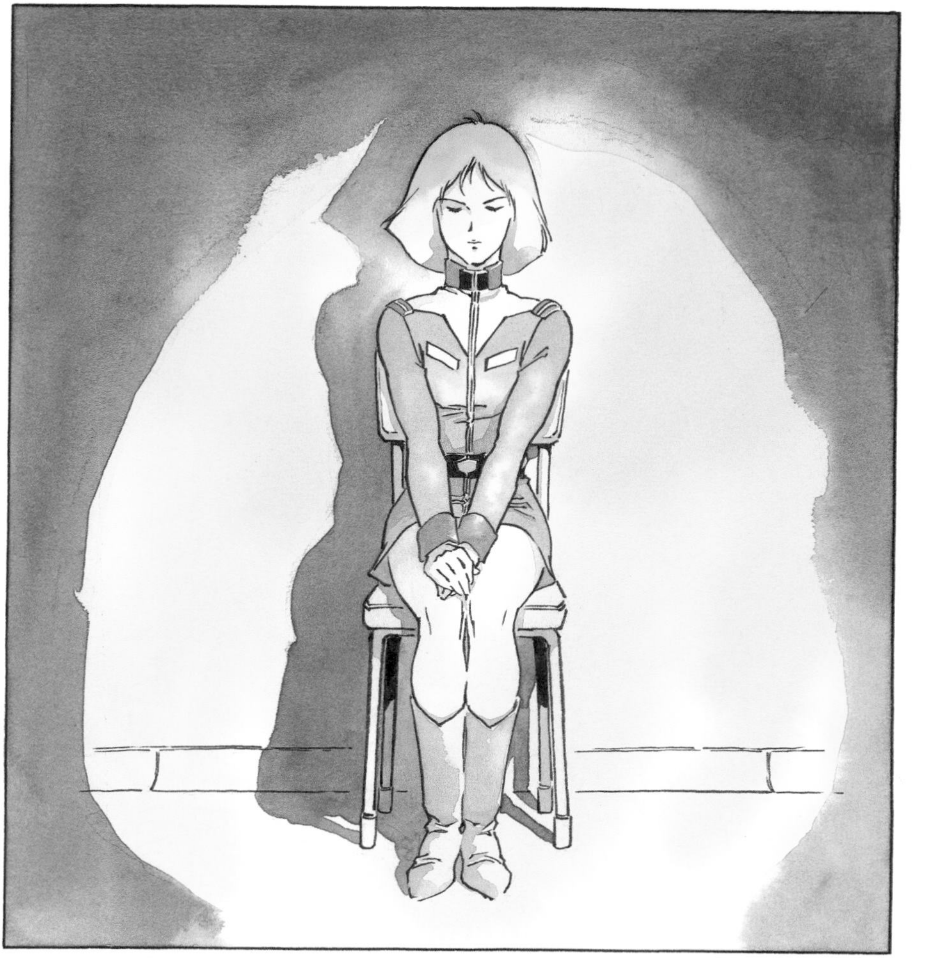

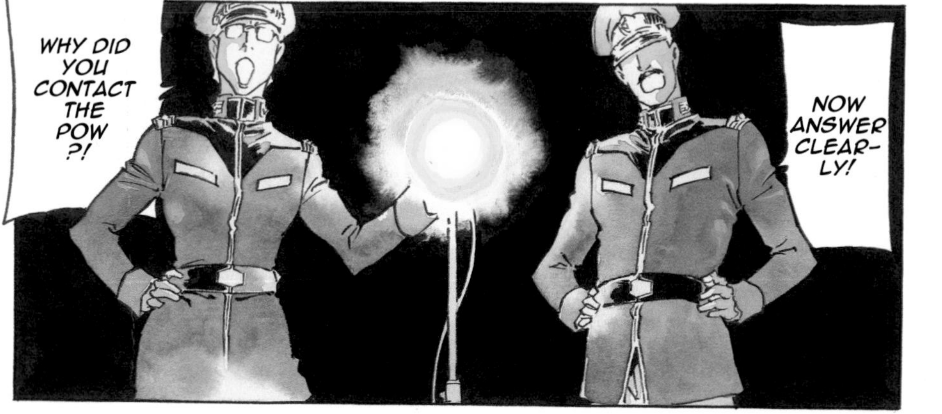
NOW ANSWER CLEAR-LY!
WHY DID YOU CONTACT THE POW ?!

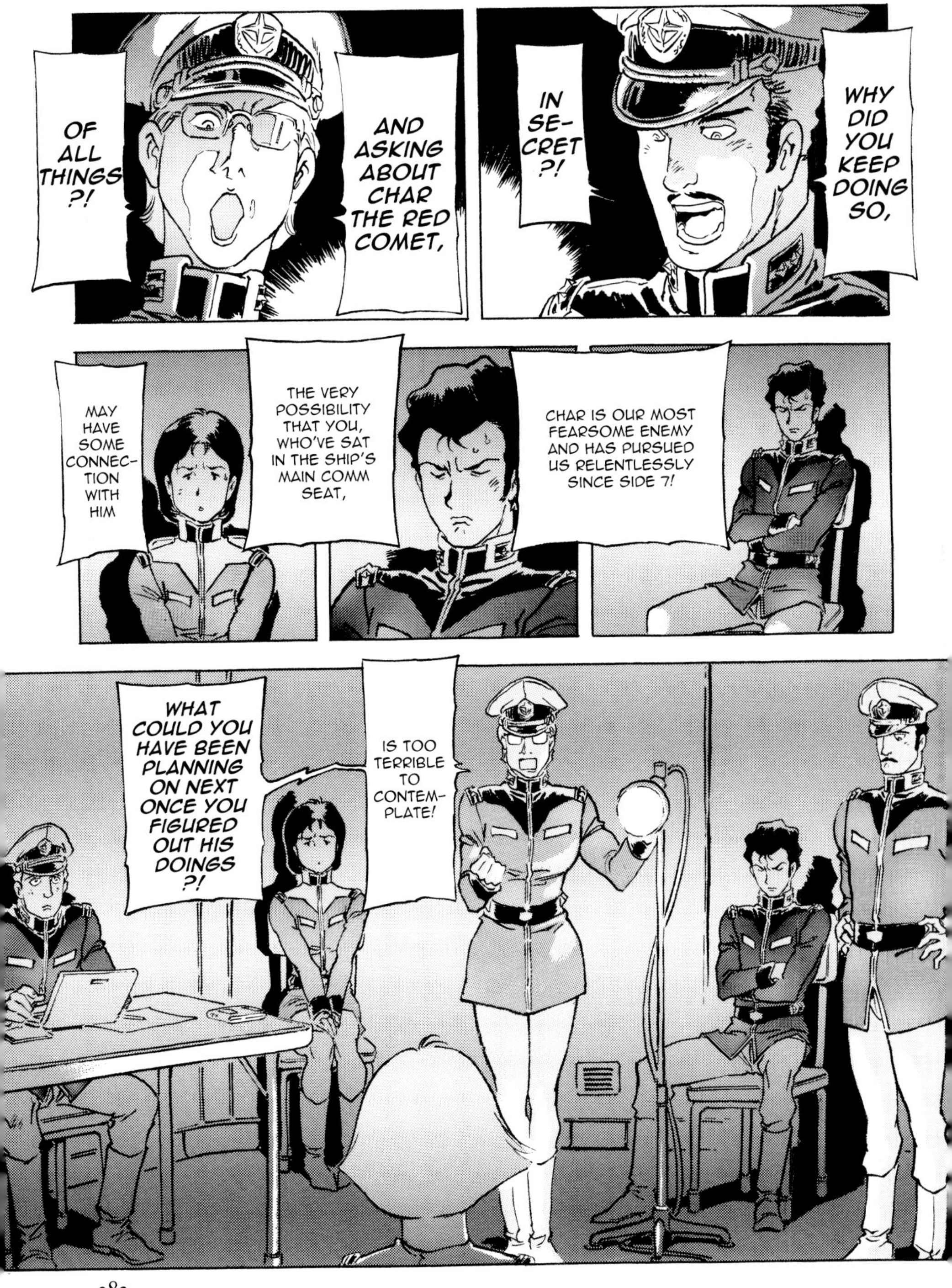
WHY DID YOU KEEP DOING SO,
IN SE-CRET?!
AND ASKING ABOUT CHAR THE RED COMET,
OF ALL THINGS?!
CHAR IS OUR MOST FEARSOME ENEMY AND HAS PURSUED US RELENTLESSLY SINCE SIDE 7!
THE VERY POSSIBILITY THAT YOU, WHO'VE SAT IN THE SHIP'S MAIN COMM SEAT,
MAY HAVE SOME CONNEC-TION WITH HIM
IS TOO TERRIBLE TO CONTEM-PLATE!
WHAT COULD YOU HAVE BEEN PLANNING ON NEXT ONCE YOU FIGURED OUT HIS DOINGS?!

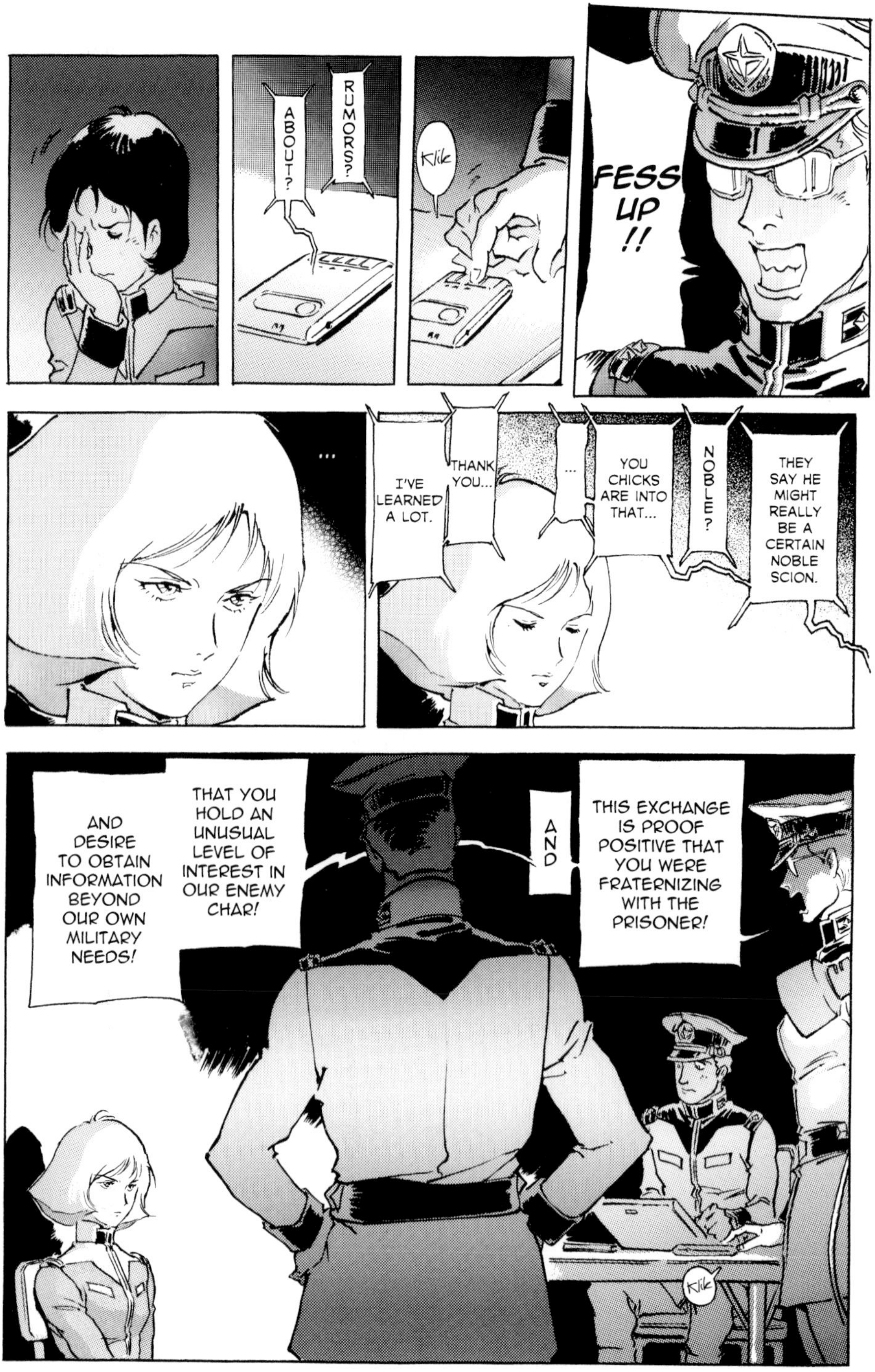
FESS UP!!
Klik
RUMORS?
ABOUT?
THEY SAY HE MIGHT REALLY BE A CERTAIN NOBLE SCION.
NOBLE?
YOU CHICKS ARE INTO THAT...
...
THANK YOU...
I'VE LEARNED A LOT.
...
THIS EXCHANGE IS PROOF POSITIVE THAT YOU WERE FRATERNIZING WITH THE PRISONER!
AND
THAT YOU HOLD AN UNUSUAL LEVEL OF INTEREST IN OUR ENEMY CHAR!
AND DESIRE TO OBTAIN INFORMATION BEYOND OUR OWN MILITARY NEEDS!
Klik

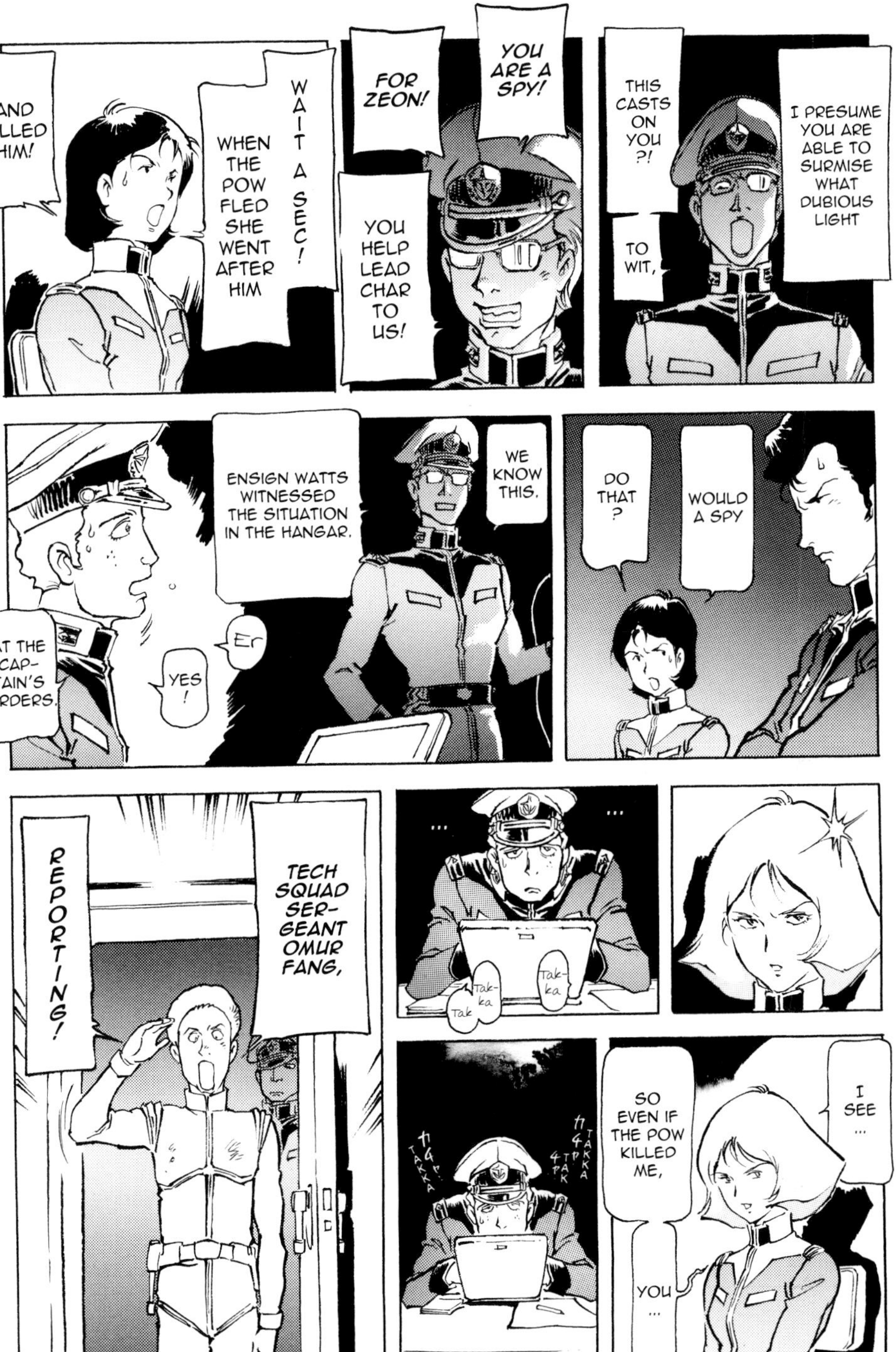
I PRESUME YOU ARE ABLE TO SURMISE WHAT DUBIOUS LIGHT
THIS CASTS ON YOU ?!
TO WIT,
YOU ARE A SPY!
FOR ZEON!
YOU HELP LEAD CHAR TO US!
WAIT A SEC!
WHEN THE POW FLED SHE WENT AFTER HIM
AND KILLED HIM!
WOULD A SPY
DO THAT ?
WE KNOW THIS.
ENSIGN WATTS WITNESSED THE SITUATION IN THE HANGAR.
Er
YES!
AT THE CAPTAIN'S ORDERS.
...
...
Tak-ka
Tak-ka
Tak
I SEE ...
SO EVEN IF THE POW KILLED ME,
YOU ...
TAKKA
TAKKA
TAK
TECH SQUAD SERGEANT OMUR FANG,
REPORTING!

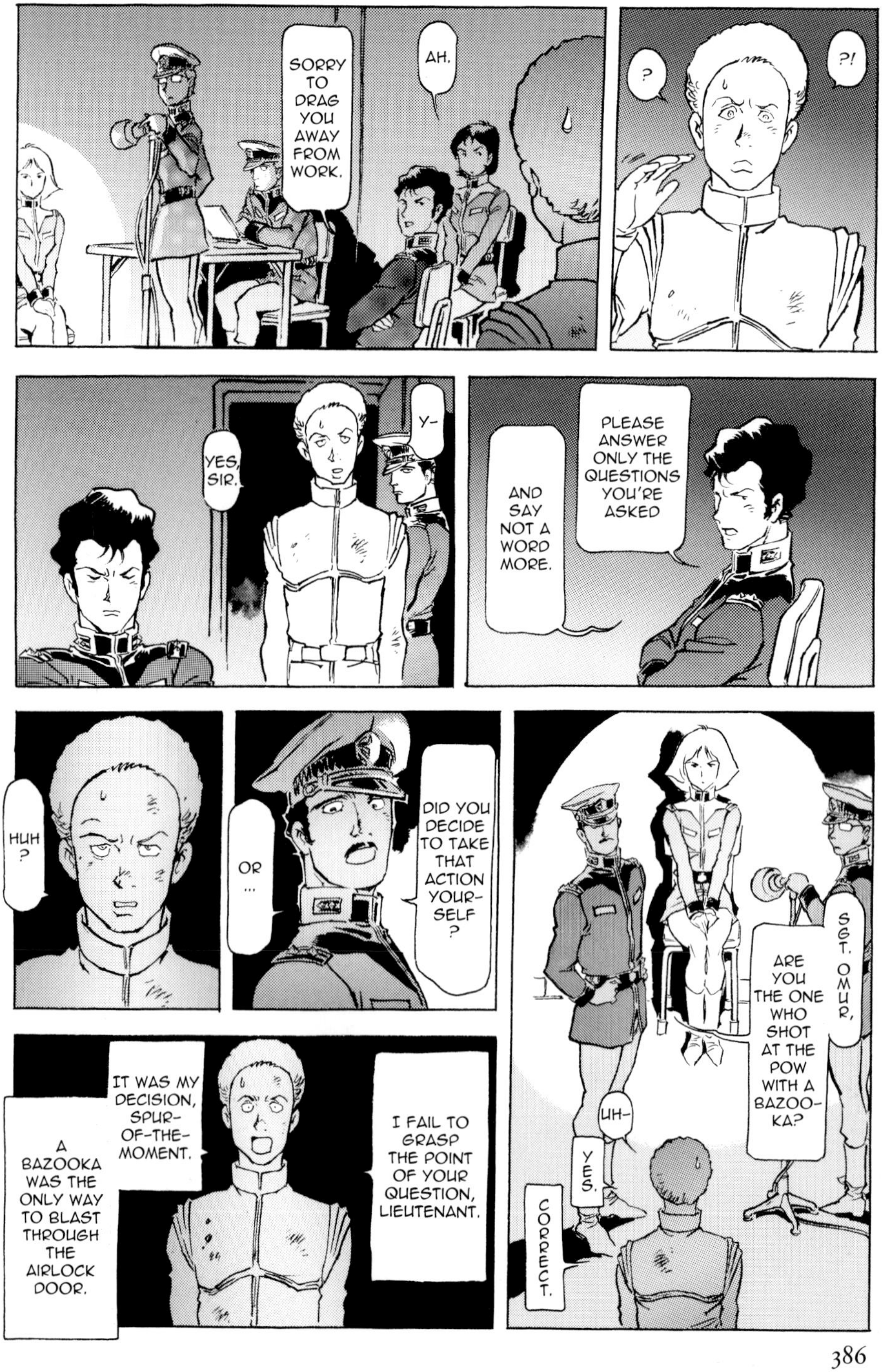
?!
?
SORRY TO DRAG YOU AWAY FROM WORK.
AH.
PLEASE ANSWER ONLY THE QUESTIONS YOU'RE ASKED
AND SAY NOT A WORD MORE.
Y-
YES, SIR.
SGT. OMUR,
ARE YOU THE ONE WHO SHOT AT THE POW WITH A BAZOOKA?
UH-
YES.
CORRECT.
DID YOU DECIDE TO TAKE THAT ACTION YOURSELF?
OR ...
HUH?
I FAIL TO GRASP THE POINT OF YOUR QUESTION, LIEUTENANT.
IT WAS MY DECISION, SPUR-OF-THE-MOMENT.
A BAZOOKA WAS THE ONLY WAY TO BLAST THROUGH THE AIRLOCK DOOR.

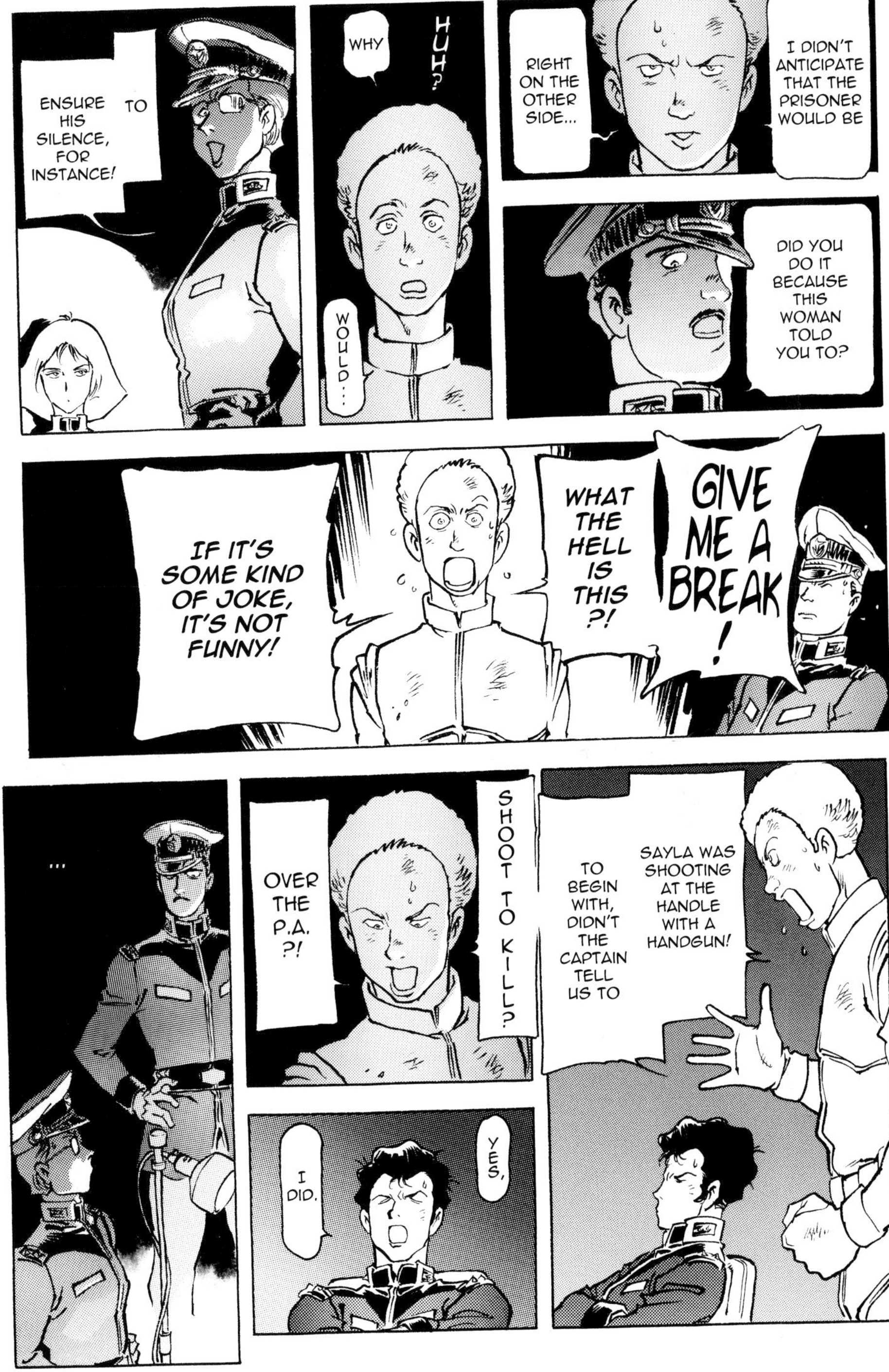

I DIDN'T ANTICIPATE THAT THE PRISONER WOULD BE
RIGHT ON THE OTHER SIDE...
DID YOU DO IT BECAUSE THIS WOMAN TOLD YOU TO?
HUH?
WHY
WOULD...
TO ENSURE HIS SILENCE, FOR INSTANCE!
GIVE ME A BREAK!
WHAT THE HELL IS THIS?!
IF IT'S SOME KIND OF JOKE, IT'S NOT FUNNY!
SAYLA WAS SHOOTING AT THE HANDLE WITH A HANDGUN!
TO BEGIN WITH, DIDN'T THE CAPTAIN TELL US TO
SHOOT TO KILL?
OVER THE P.A.?!
YES,
I DID.
...

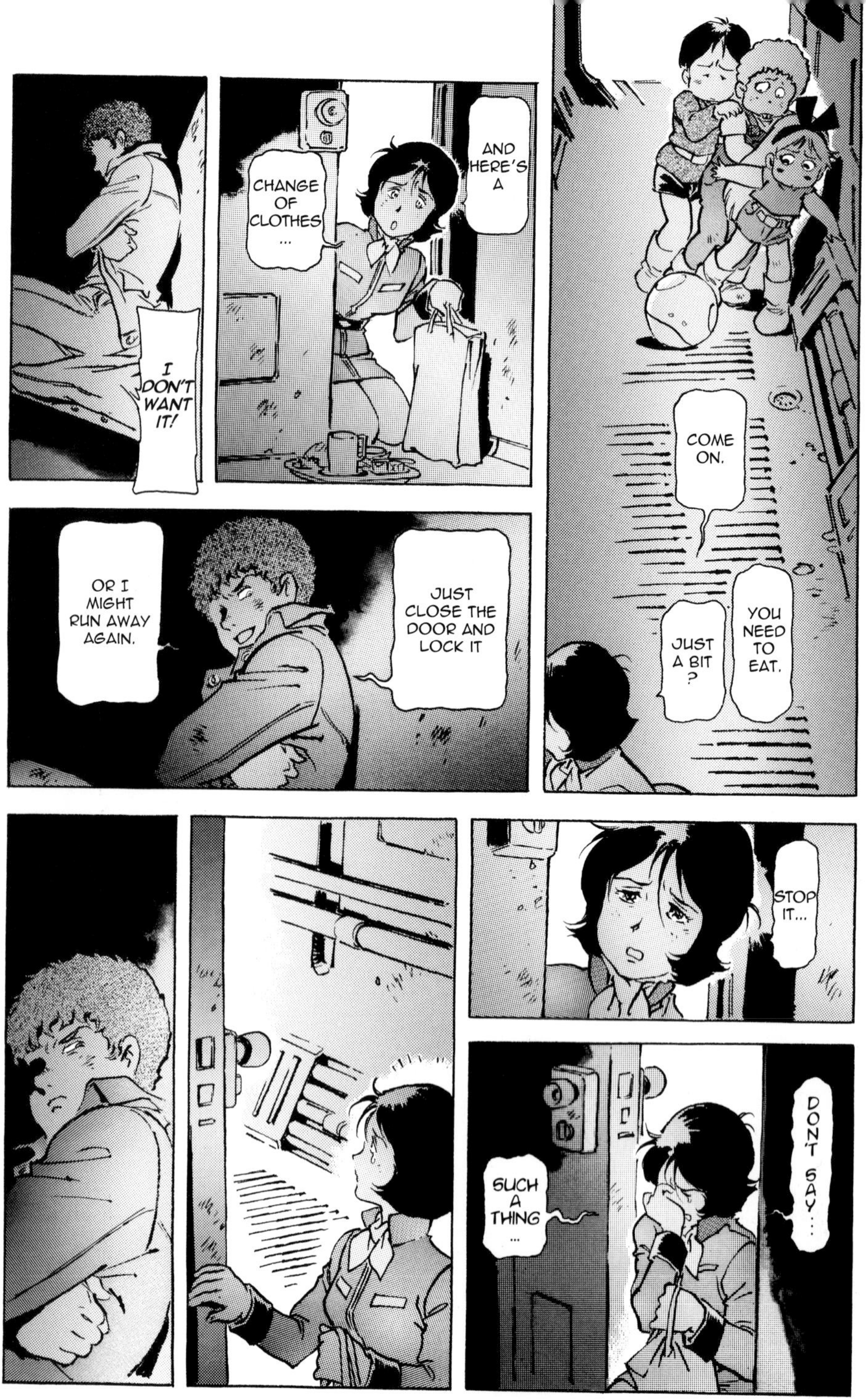
COME ON.
YOU NEED TO EAT.
JUST A BIT?
AND HERE'S A
CHANGE OF CLOTHES...
I DON'T WANT IT!
JUST CLOSE THE DOOR AND LOCK IT
OR I MIGHT RUN AWAY AGAIN.
STOP IT...
DON'T SAY...
SUCH A THING...

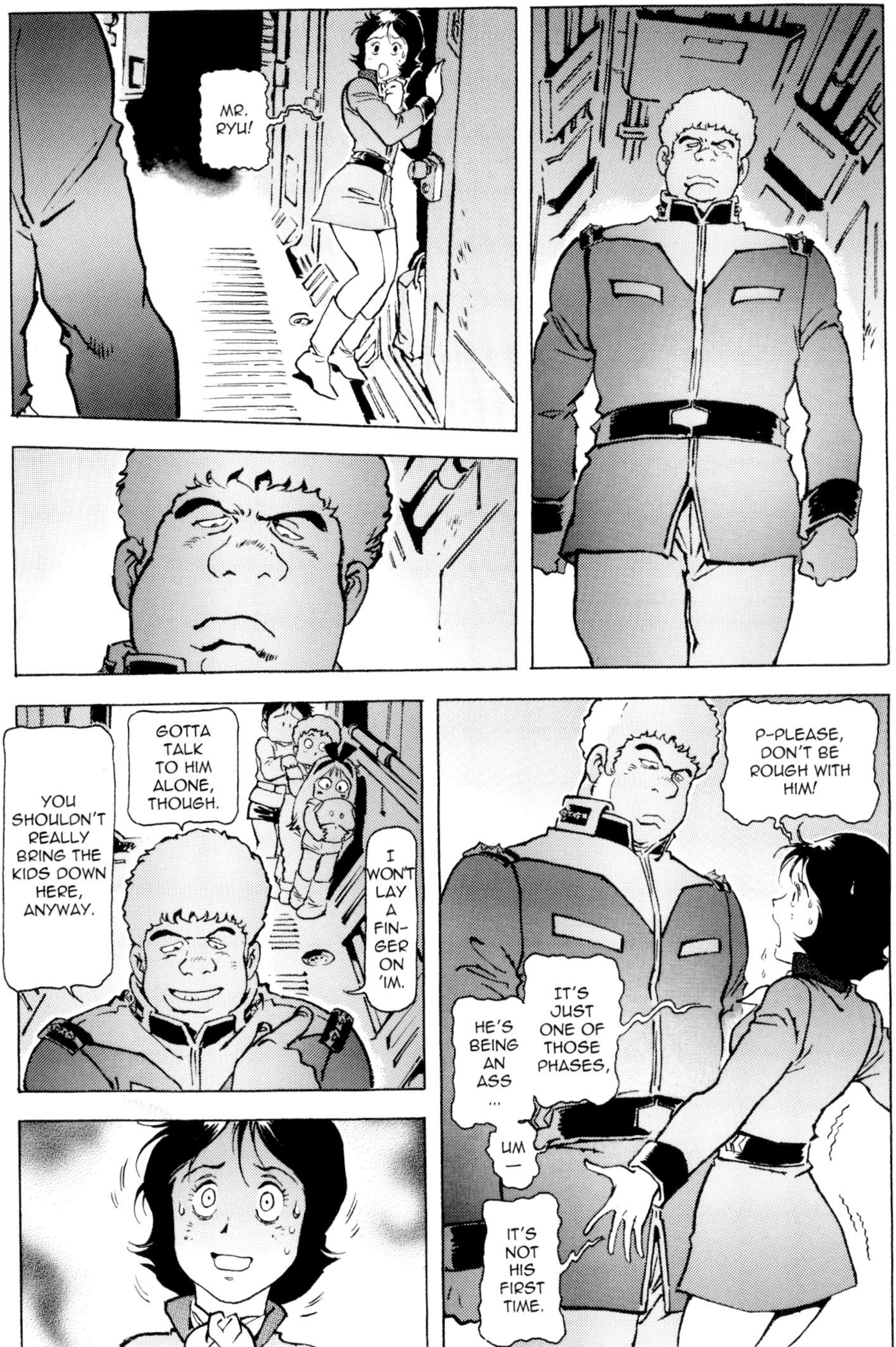
MR. RYU!
P-PLEASE, DON'T BE ROUGH WITH HIM!
IT'S JUST ONE OF THOSE PHASES,
HE'S BEING AN ASS ...
UM—
IT'S NOT HIS FIRST TIME.
GOTTA TALK TO HIM ALONE, THOUGH.
YOU SHOULDN'T REALLY BRING THE KIDS DOWN HERE, ANYWAY.
I WON'T LAY A FINGER ON 'IM.

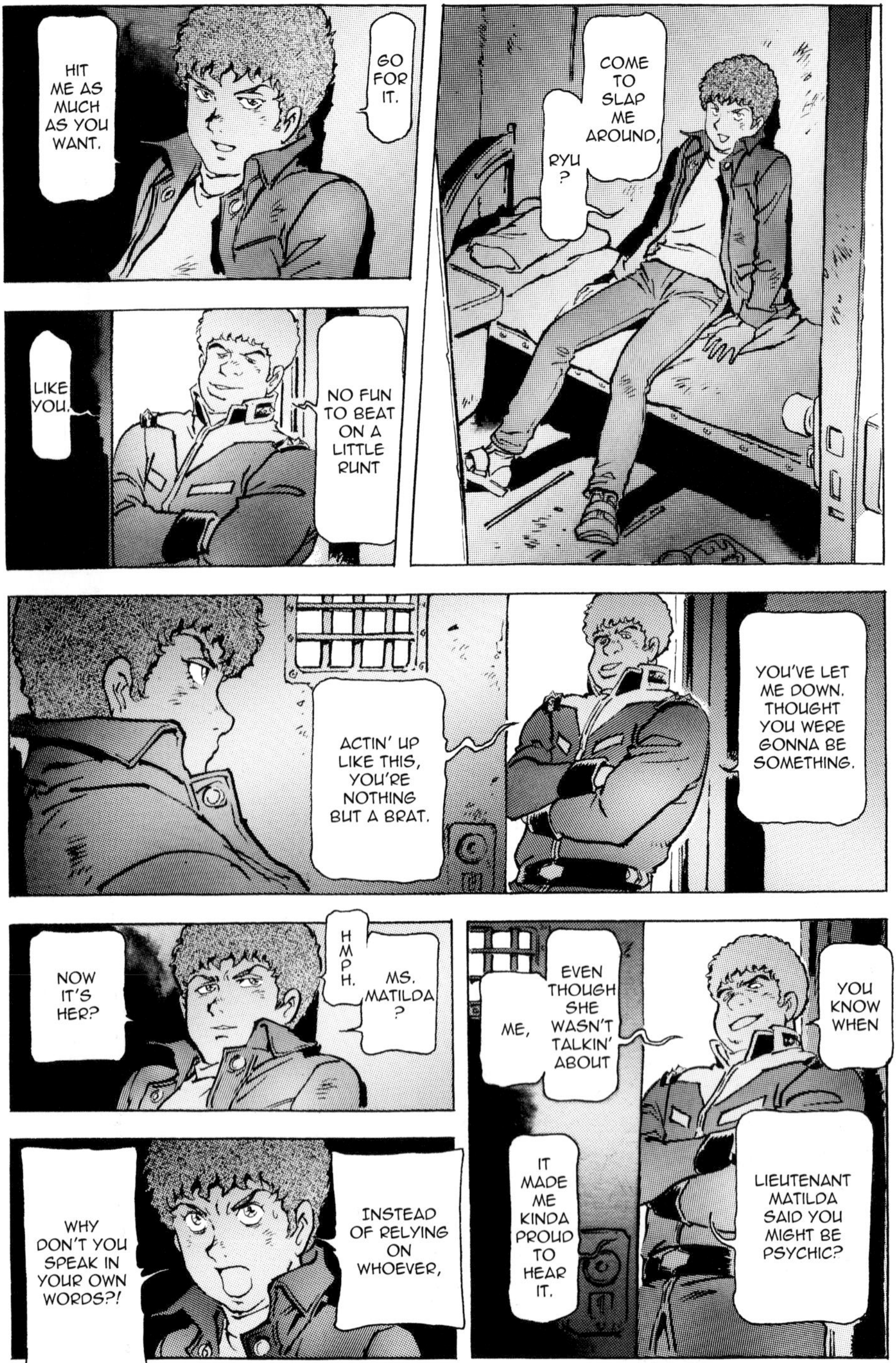
COME TO SLAP ME AROUND,
RYU?
GO FOR IT.
HIT ME AS MUCH AS YOU WANT.
NO FUN TO BEAT ON A LITTLE RUNT
LIKE YOU.
YOU'VE LET ME DOWN. THOUGHT YOU WERE GONNA BE SOMETHING.
ACTIN' UP LIKE THIS, YOU'RE NOTHING BUT A BRAT.
YOU KNOW WHEN
EVEN THOUGH SHE WASN'T TALKIN' ABOUT
ME,
LIEUTENANT MATILDA SAID YOU MIGHT BE PSYCHIC?
IT MADE ME KINDA PROUD TO HEAR IT.
MS. MATILDA?
HMPH.
NOW IT'S HER?
INSTEAD OF RELYING ON WHOEVER,
WHY DON'T YOU SPEAK IN YOUR OWN WORDS?!

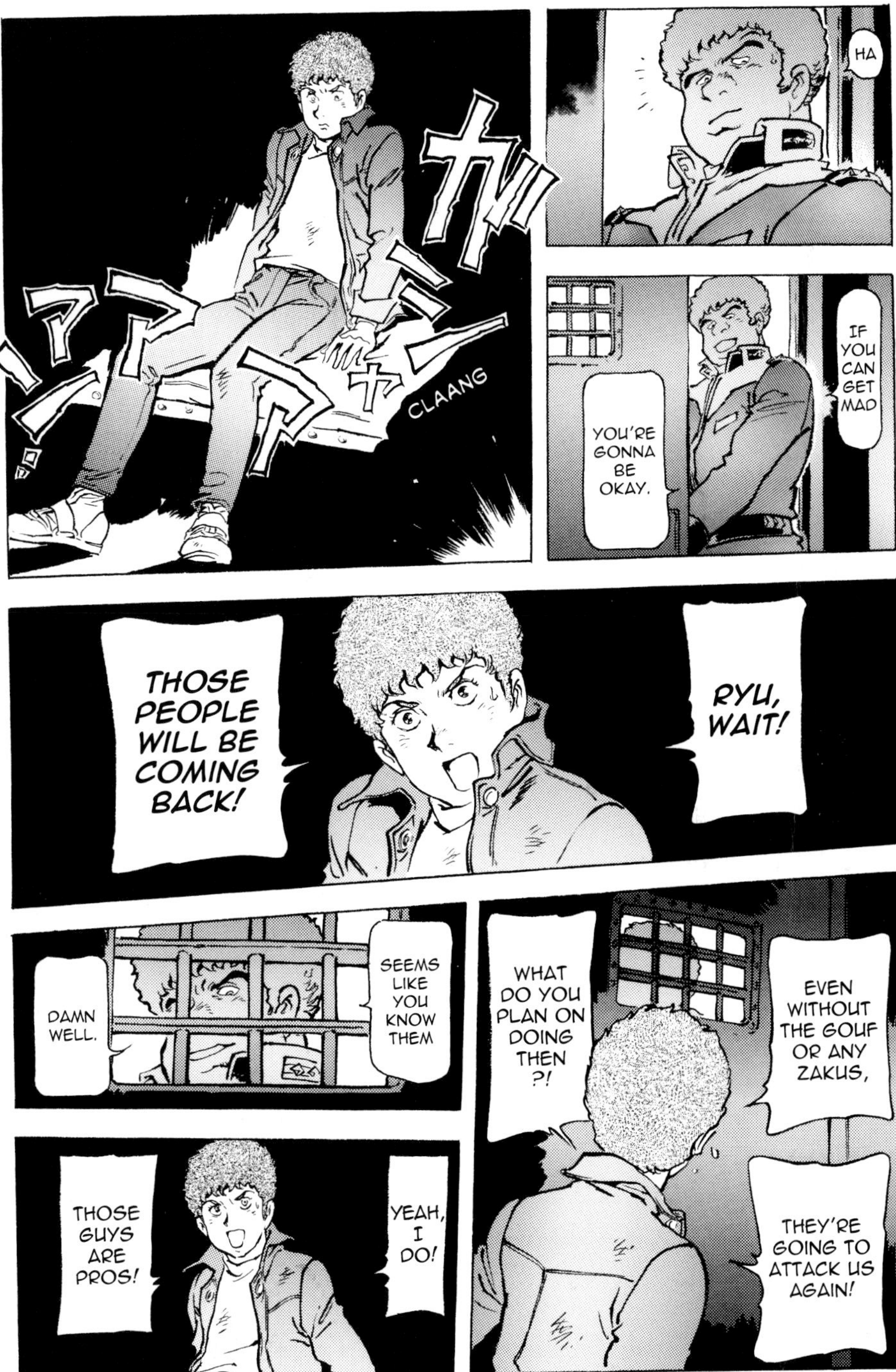
HA
IF YOU CAN GET MAD
YOU'RE GONNA BE OKAY.
CLAANG
RYU, WAIT!
THOSE PEOPLE WILL BE COMING BACK!
EVEN WITHOUT THE GOUF OR ANY ZAKUS,
THEY'RE GOING TO ATTACK US AGAIN!
WHAT DO YOU PLAN ON DOING THEN ?!
SEEMS LIKE YOU KNOW THEM
DAMN WELL.
YEAH, I DO!
THOSE GUYS ARE PROS!

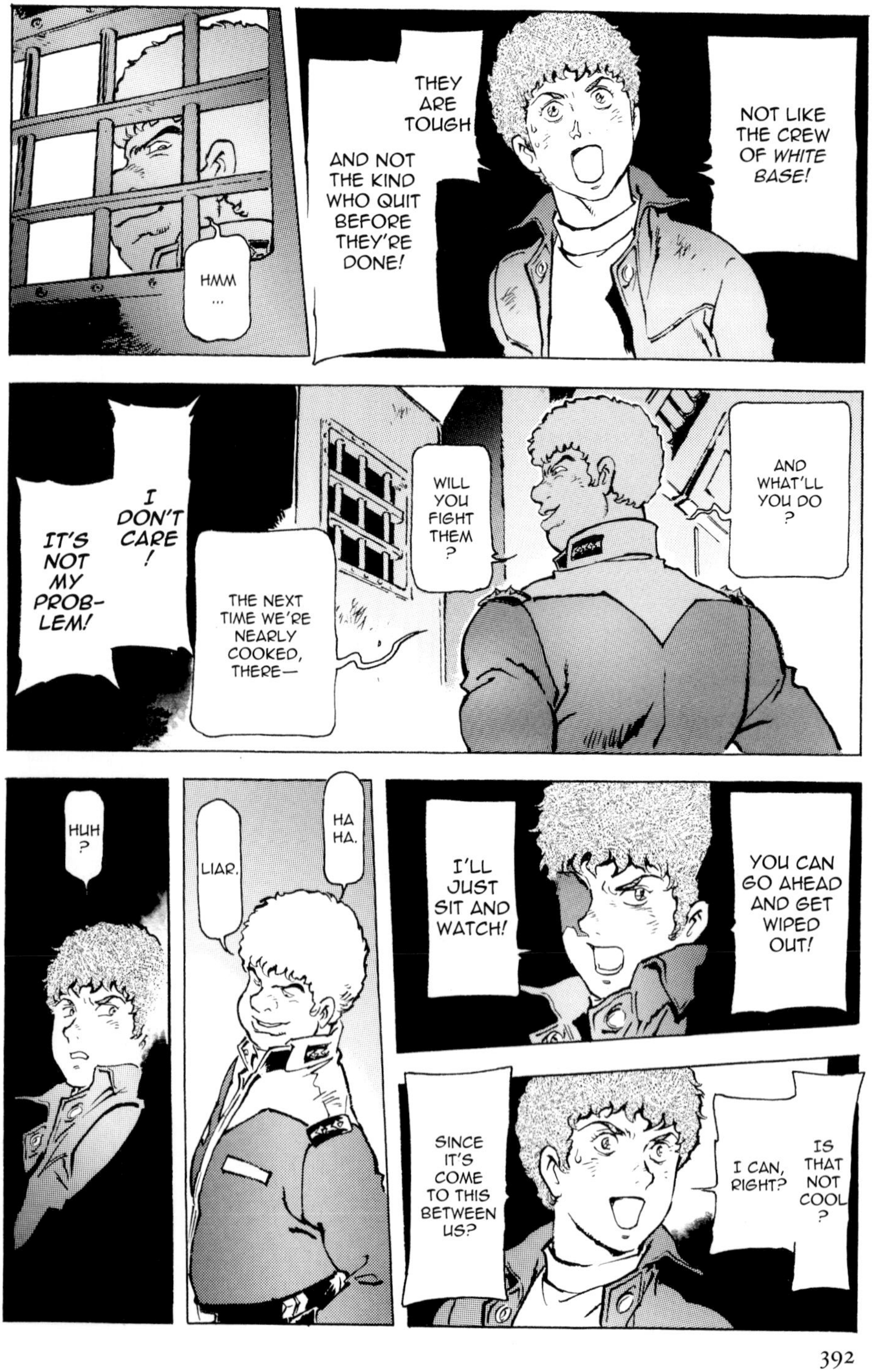
NOT LIKE THE CREW OF *WHITE BASE!*
THEY ARE TOUGH
AND NOT THE KIND WHO QUIT BEFORE THEY'RE DONE!
HMM ...
AND WHAT'LL YOU DO?
WILL YOU FIGHT THEM?
THE NEXT TIME WE'RE NEARLY COOKED, THERE—
I DON'T CARE!
IT'S NOT MY PROB-LEM!
YOU CAN GO AHEAD AND GET WIPED OUT!
I'LL JUST SIT AND WATCH!
IS THAT NOT COOL?
I CAN, RIGHT?
SINCE IT'S COME TO THIS BETWEEN US?
HA HA.
LIAR.
HUH?

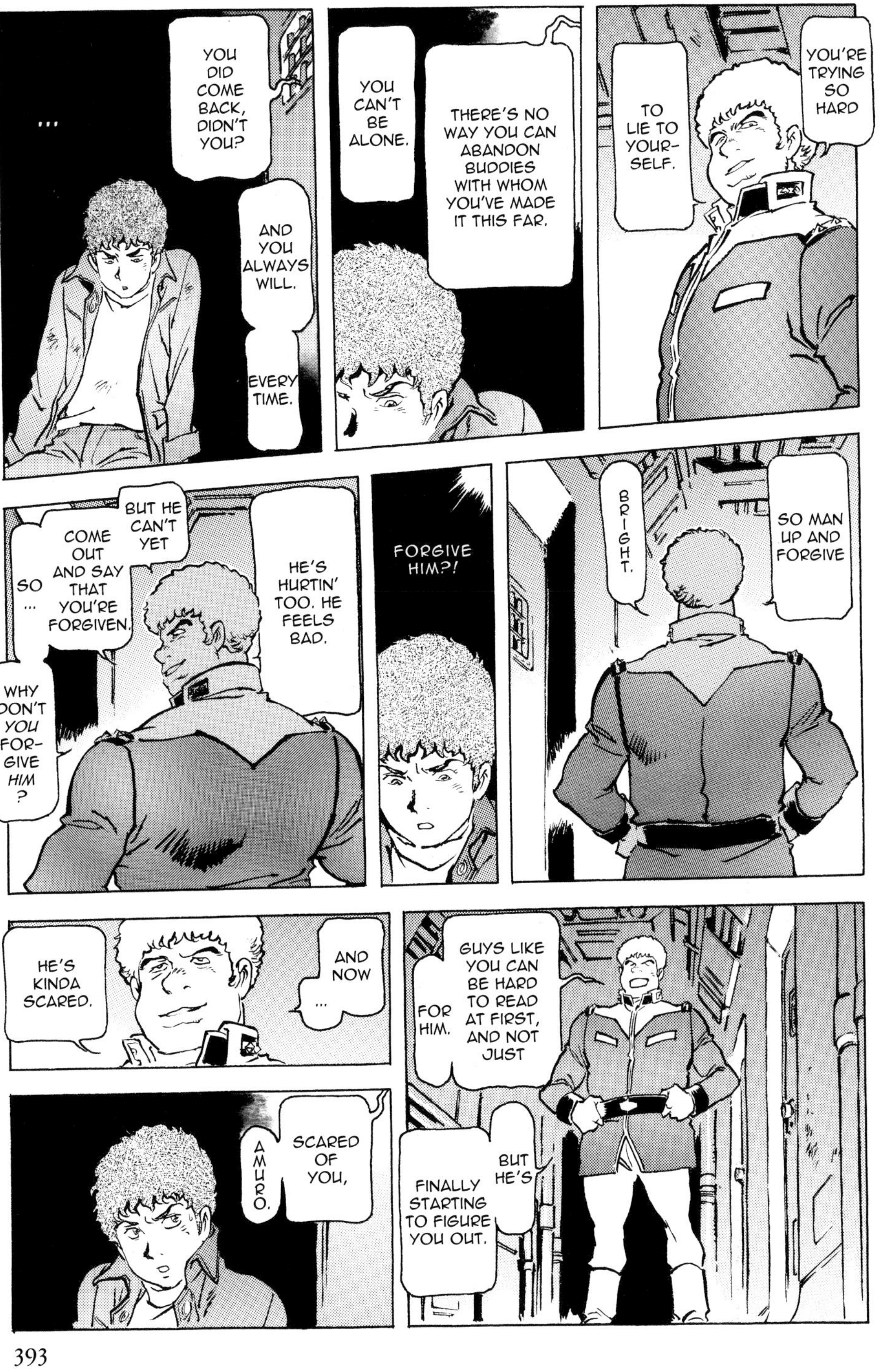
YOU'RE TRYING SO HARD
TO LIE TO YOURSELF.
THERE'S NO WAY YOU CAN ABANDON BUDDIES WITH WHOM YOU'VE MADE IT THIS FAR.
YOU CAN'T BE ALONE.
YOU DID COME BACK, DIDN'T YOU?
AND YOU ALWAYS WILL.
EVERY TIME.
...
SO MAN UP AND FORGIVE
BRIGHT.
FORGIVE HIM?!
HE'S HURTIN' TOO. HE FEELS BAD.
BUT HE CAN'T YET
COME OUT AND SAY THAT YOU'RE FORGIVEN.
SO ...
WHY DON'T *YOU* FORGIVE *HIM*?
GUYS LIKE YOU CAN BE HARD TO READ AT FIRST, AND NOT JUST
FOR HIM.
BUT HE'S
FINALLY STARTING TO FIGURE YOU OUT.
AND NOW ...
HE'S KINDA SCARED.
SCARED OF YOU,
AMURO.

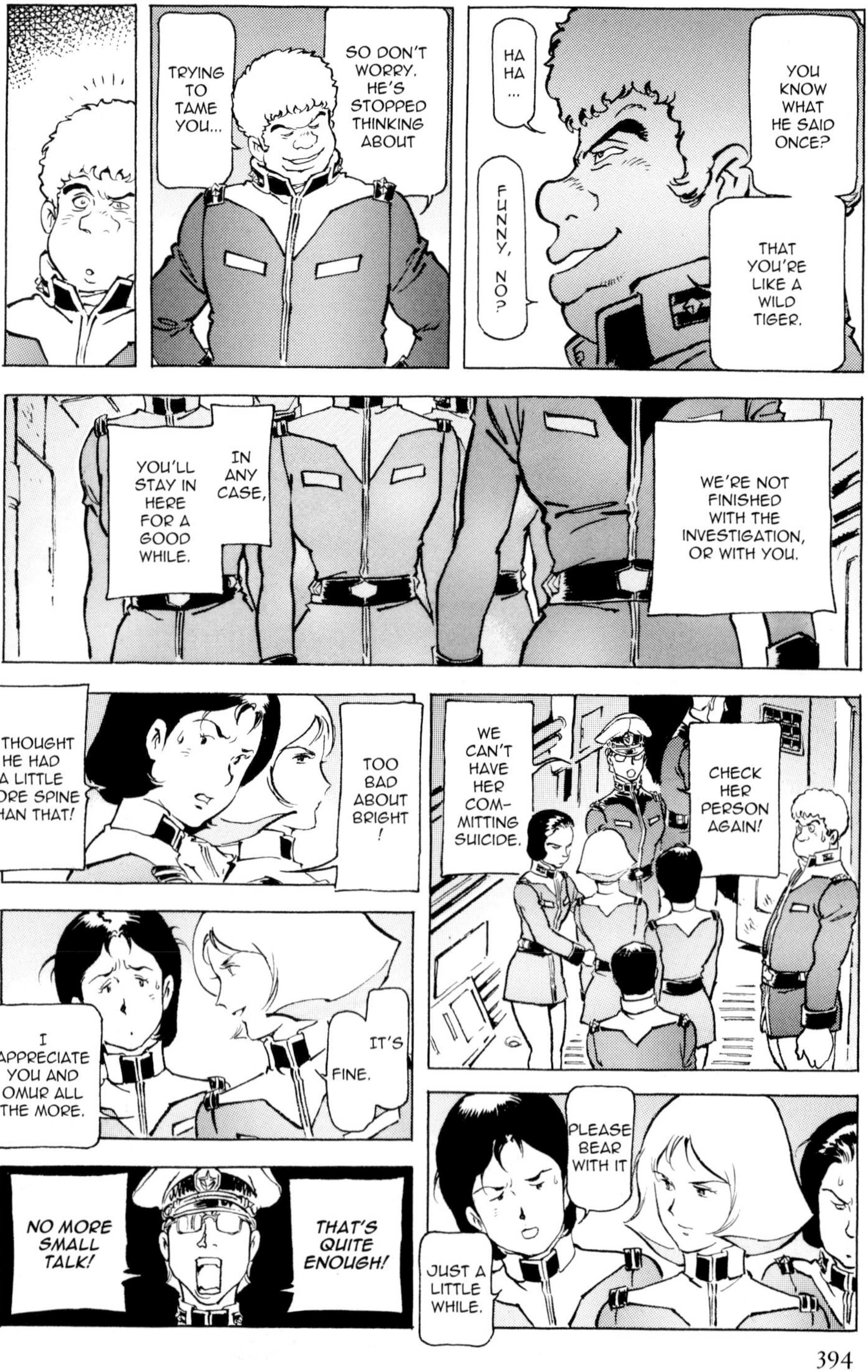
YOU KNOW WHAT HE SAID ONCE?
THAT YOU'RE LIKE A WILD TIGER.
HA HA ...
FUNNY, NO?
SO DON'T WORRY. HE'S STOPPED THINKING ABOUT
TRYING TO TAME YOU...
WE'RE NOT FINISHED WITH THE INVESTIGATION, OR WITH YOU.
IN ANY CASE,
YOU'LL STAY IN HERE FOR A GOOD WHILE.
CHECK HER PERSON AGAIN!
WE CAN'T HAVE HER COM-MITTING SUICIDE.
TOO BAD ABOUT BRIGHT!
I THOUGHT HE HAD A LITTLE MORE SPINE THAN THAT!
IT'S FINE.
I APPRECIATE YOU AND OMUR ALL THE MORE.
PLEASE BEAR WITH IT
JUST A LITTLE WHILE.
THAT'S QUITE ENOUGH!
NO MORE SMALL TALK!

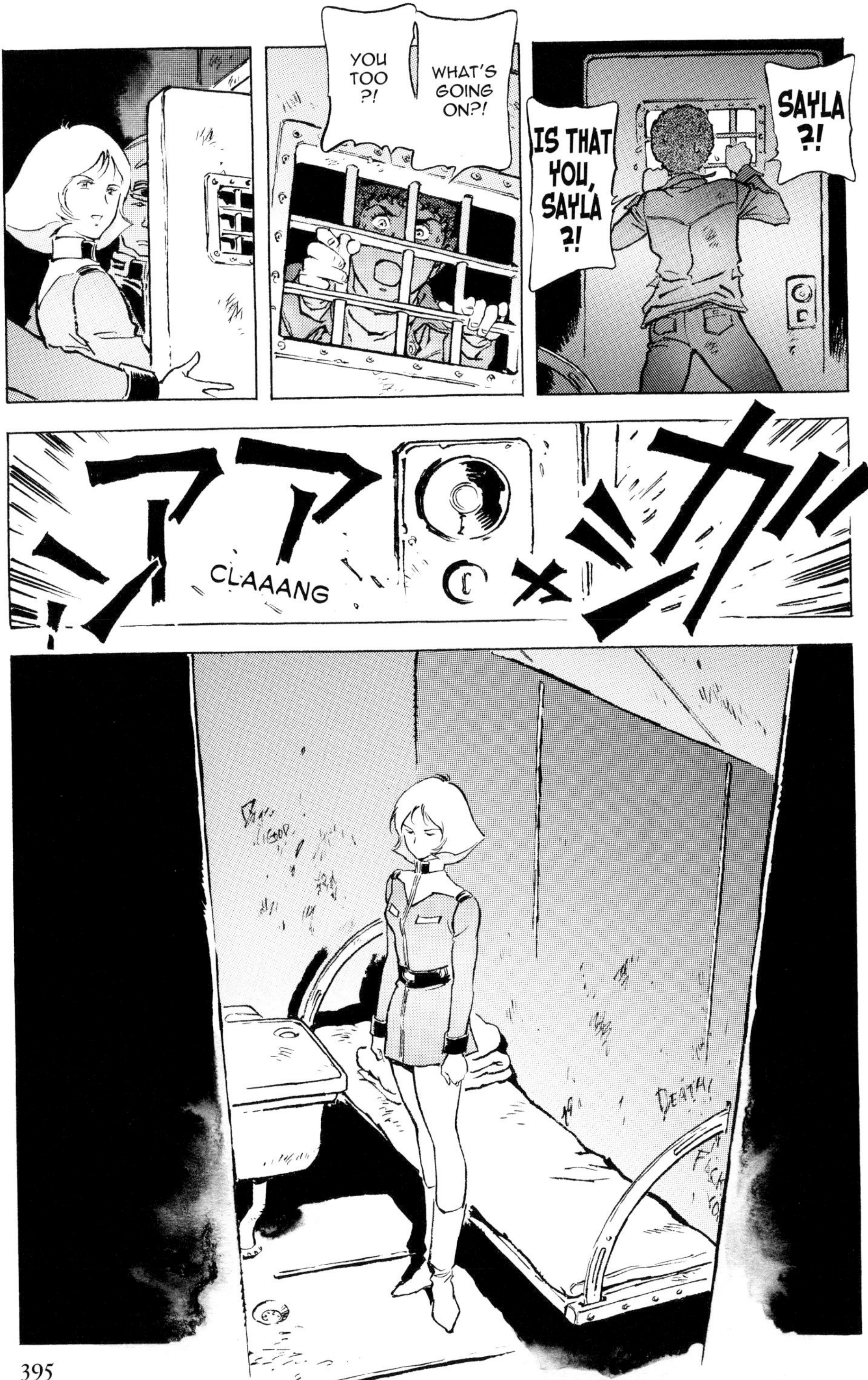
SAYLA ?!
IS THAT YOU, SAYLA ?!
WHAT'S GOING ON?!
YOU TOO ?!
CLAAANG
DEATH!

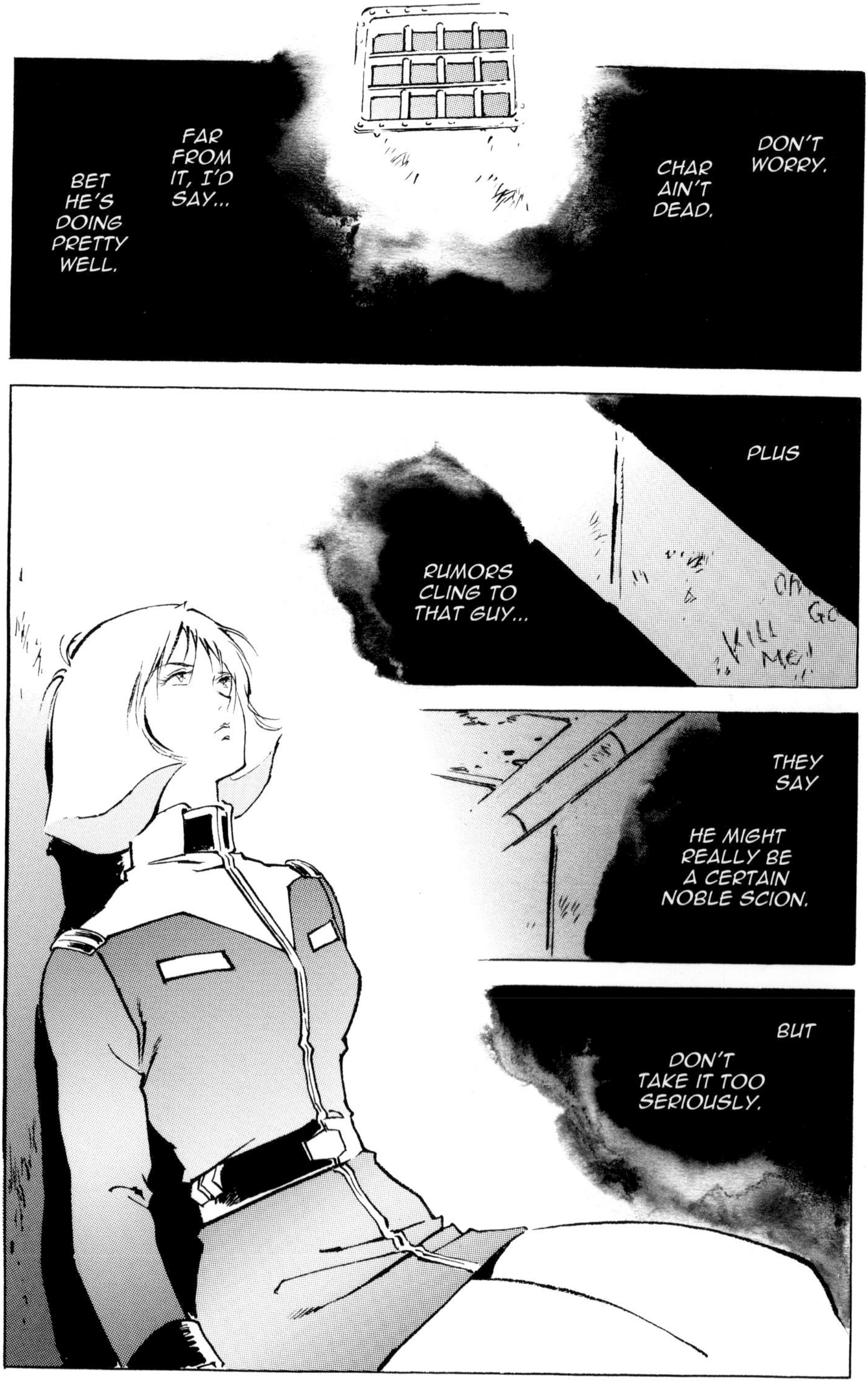
DON'T WORRY.
CHAR AIN'T DEAD.
FAR FROM IT, I'D SAY...
BET HE'S DOING PRETTY WELL.
PLUS
RUMORS CLING TO THAT GUY...
THEY SAY
HE MIGHT REALLY BE A CERTAIN NOBLE SCION.
BUT
DON'T TAKE IT TOO SERIOUSLY.

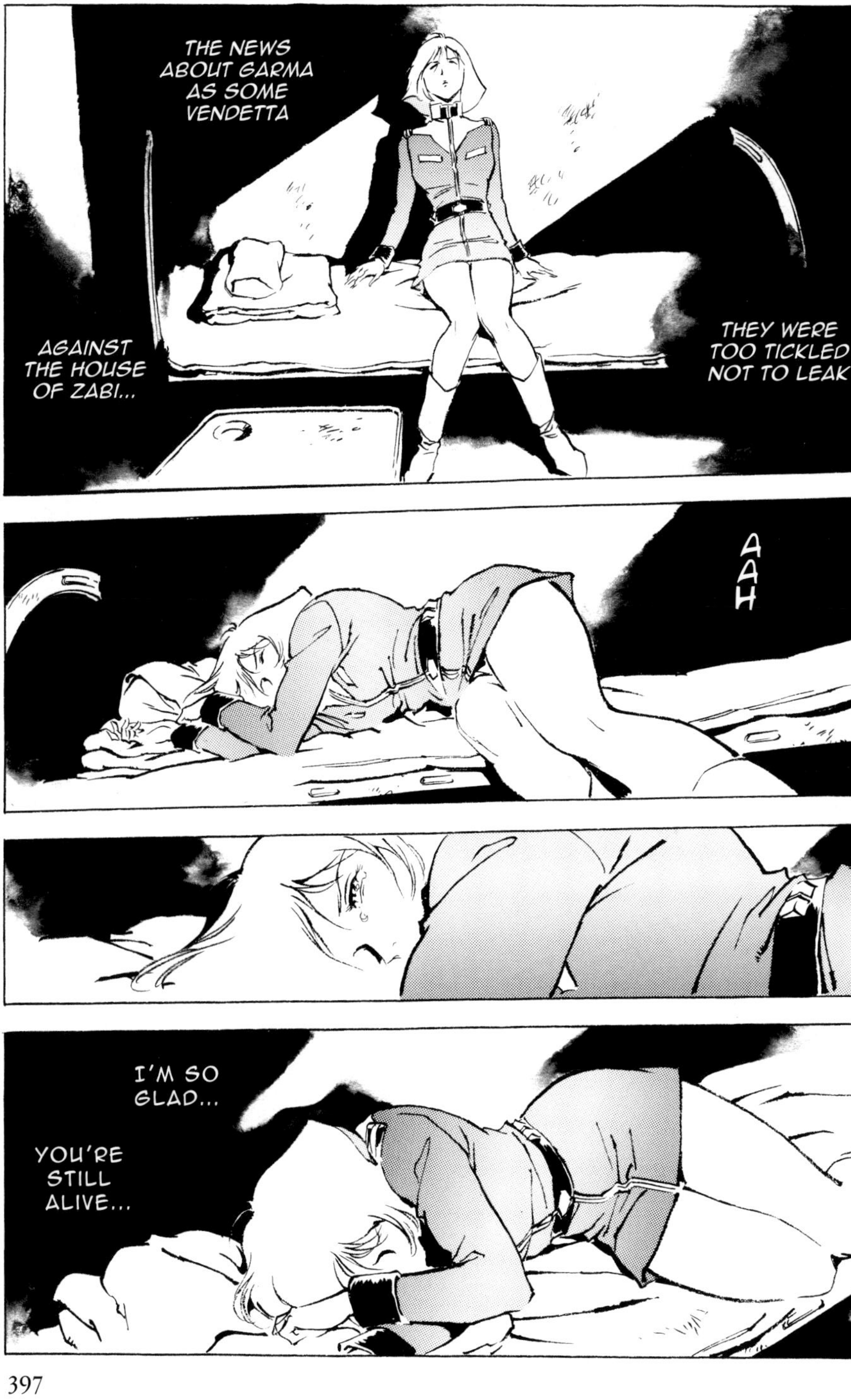
THE NEWS ABOUT GARMA AS SOME VENDETTA
AGAINST THE HOUSE OF ZABI...
THEY WERE TOO TICKLED NOT TO LEAK
AAH
I'M SO GLAD...
YOU'RE STILL ALIVE...

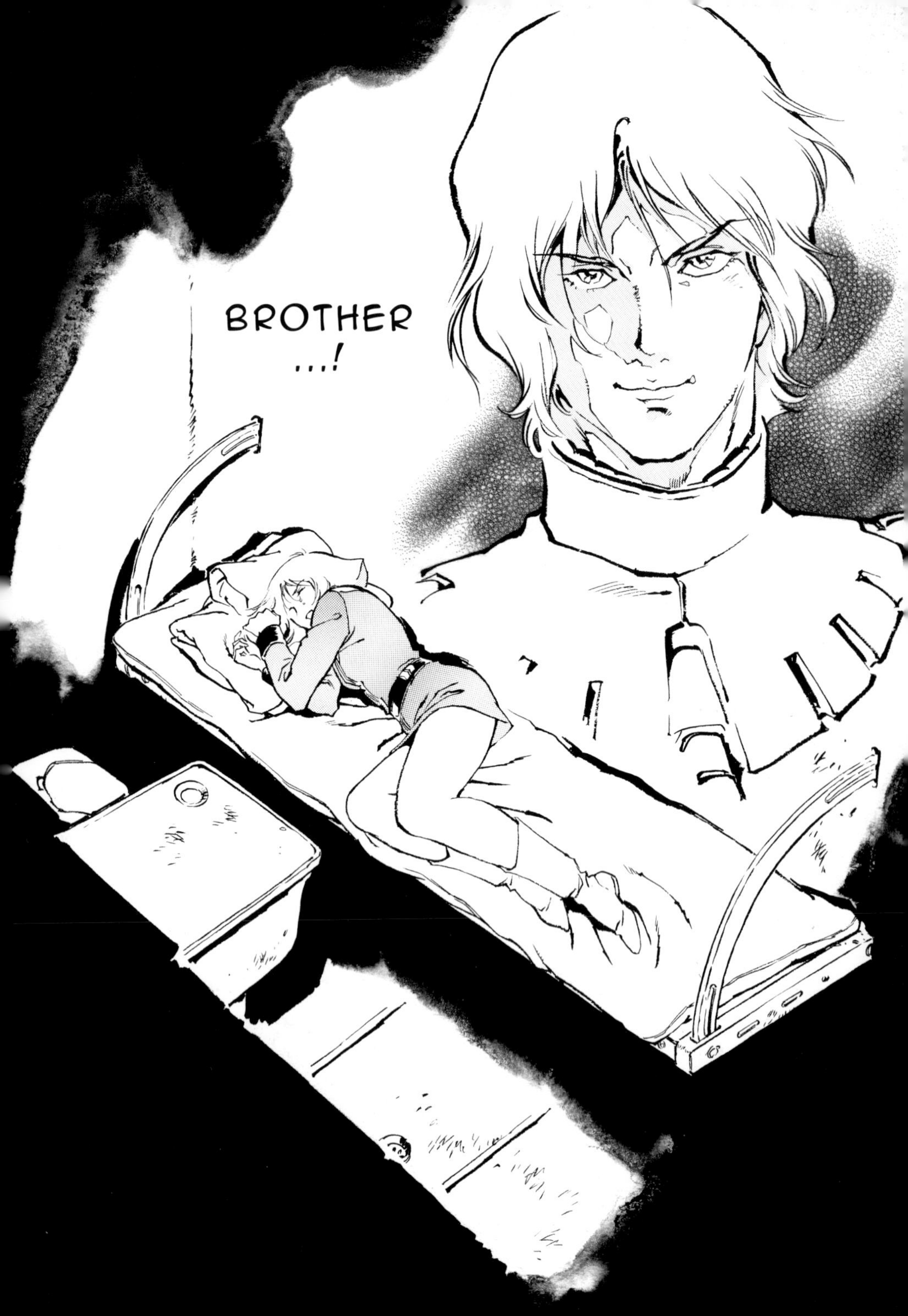
BROTHER
...!

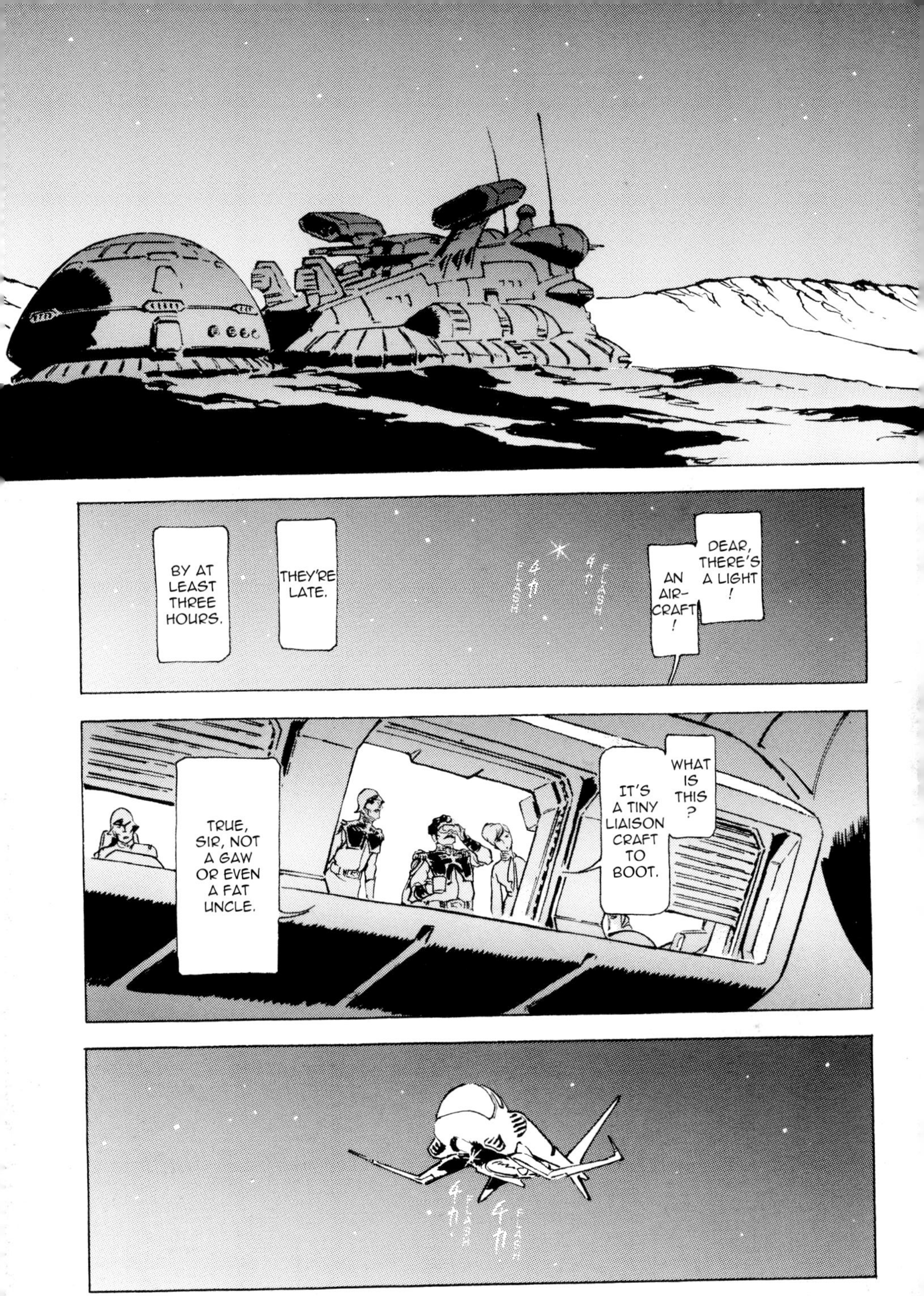
DEAR, THERE'S A LIGHT!
AN AIR-CRAFT!
FLASH
FLASH
THEY'RE LATE.
BY AT LEAST THREE HOURS.
WHAT IS THIS?
IT'S A TINY LIAISON CRAFT TO BOOT.
TRUE, SIR, NOT A GAW OR EVEN A FAT UNCLE.
FLASH
FLASH

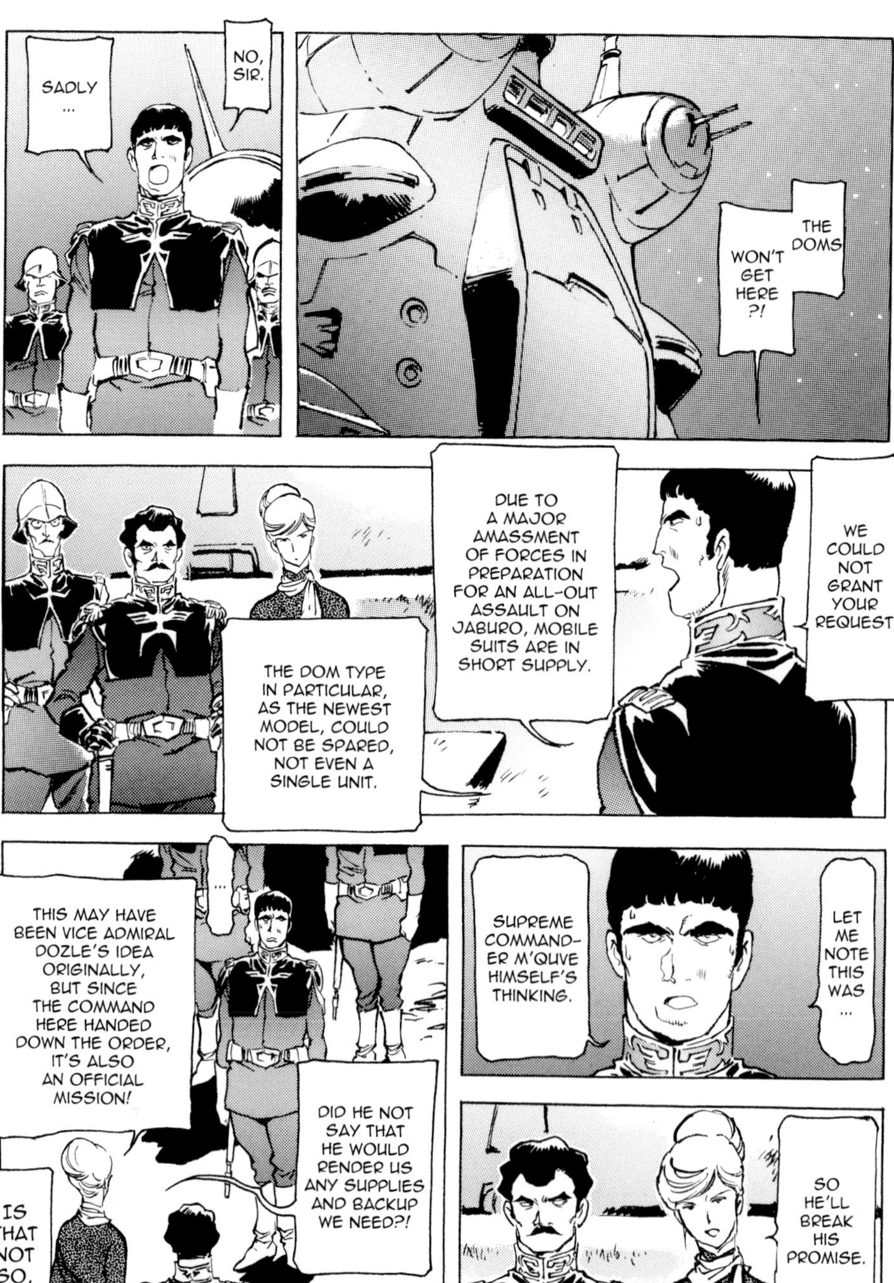
THE DOMS WON'T GET HERE?!
NO, SIR.
SADLY ...
WE COULD NOT GRANT YOUR REQUEST.
DUE TO A MAJOR AMASSMENT OF FORCES IN PREPARATION FOR AN ALL-OUT ASSAULT ON JABURO, MOBILE SUITS ARE IN SHORT SUPPLY.
THE DOM TYPE IN PARTICULAR, AS THE NEWEST MODEL, COULD NOT BE SPARED, NOT EVEN A SINGLE UNIT.
LET ME NOTE THIS WAS ...
SUPREME COMMANDER M'QUVE HIMSELF'S THINKING.
SO HE'LL BREAK HIS PROMISE.
...
THIS MAY HAVE BEEN VICE ADMIRAL DOZLE'S IDEA ORIGINALLY, BUT SINCE THE COMMAND HERE HANDED DOWN THE ORDER, IT'S ALSO AN OFFICIAL MISSION!
DID HE NOT SAY THAT HE WOULD RENDER US ANY SUPPLIES AND BACKUP WE NEED?!
IS THAT NOT SO, LT. URAGANG?!

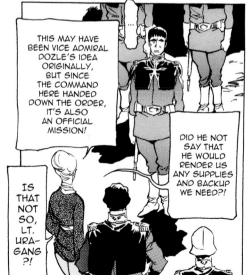

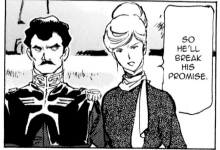

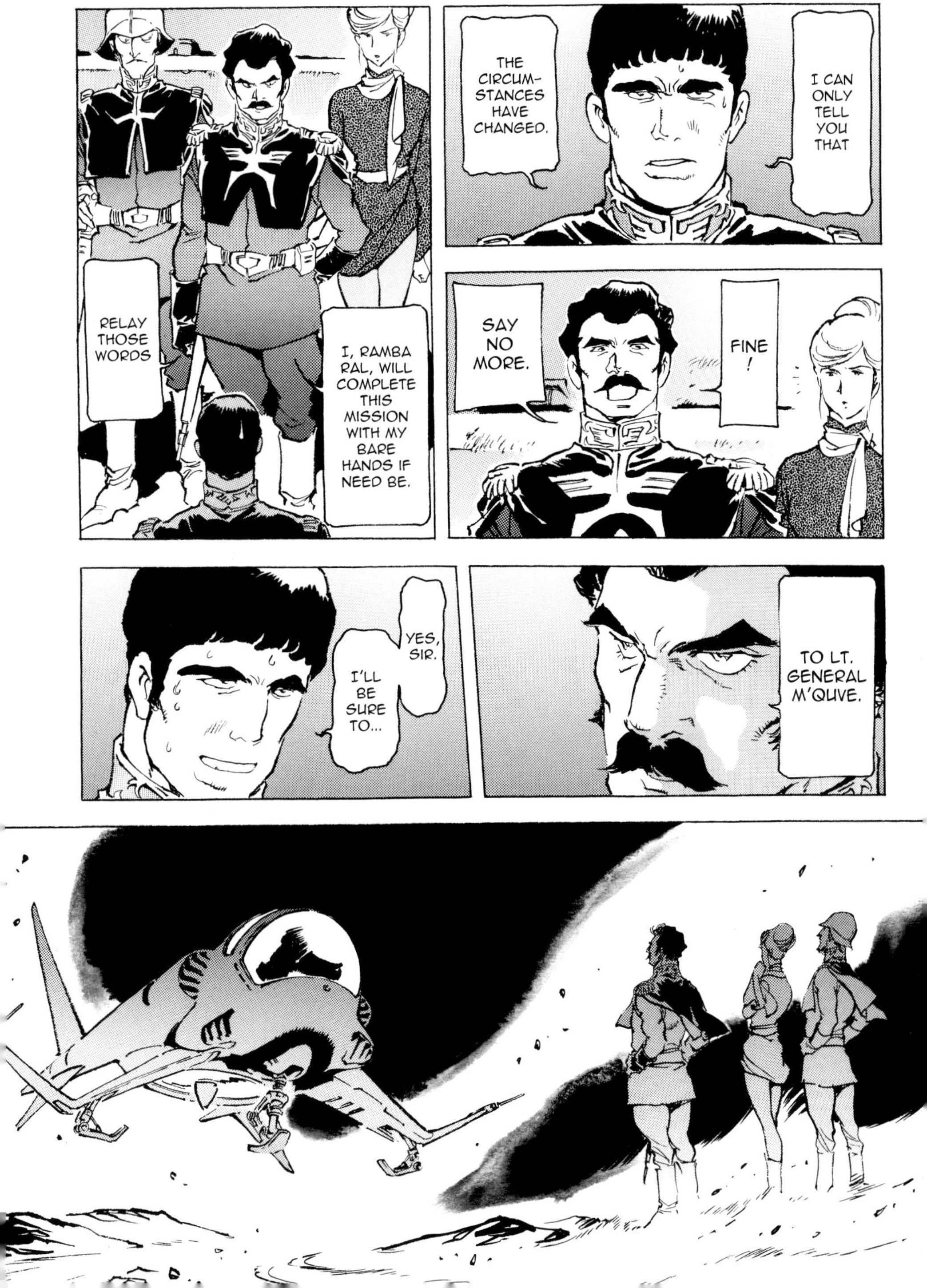
I CAN ONLY TELL YOU THAT
THE CIRCUM-STANCES HAVE CHANGED.
FINE!
SAY NO MORE.
I, RAMBA RAL, WILL COMPLETE THIS MISSION WITH MY BARE HANDS IF NEED BE.
RELAY THOSE WORDS
TO LT. GENERAL M'QUVE.
YES, SIR.
I'LL BE SURE TO...

IT'S TURNED OUT JUST AS YOU FEARED, HAMON.

WHAT I DO BEST.

WHAT WILL YOU DO?

SO

WILL PREFER IT THAT WAY, SIR!

THE MEN

CLAMP?

WELL,

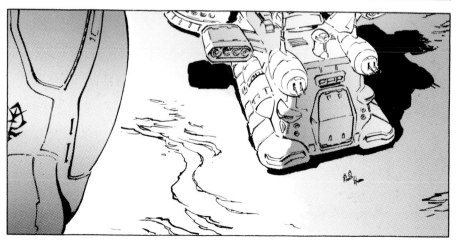

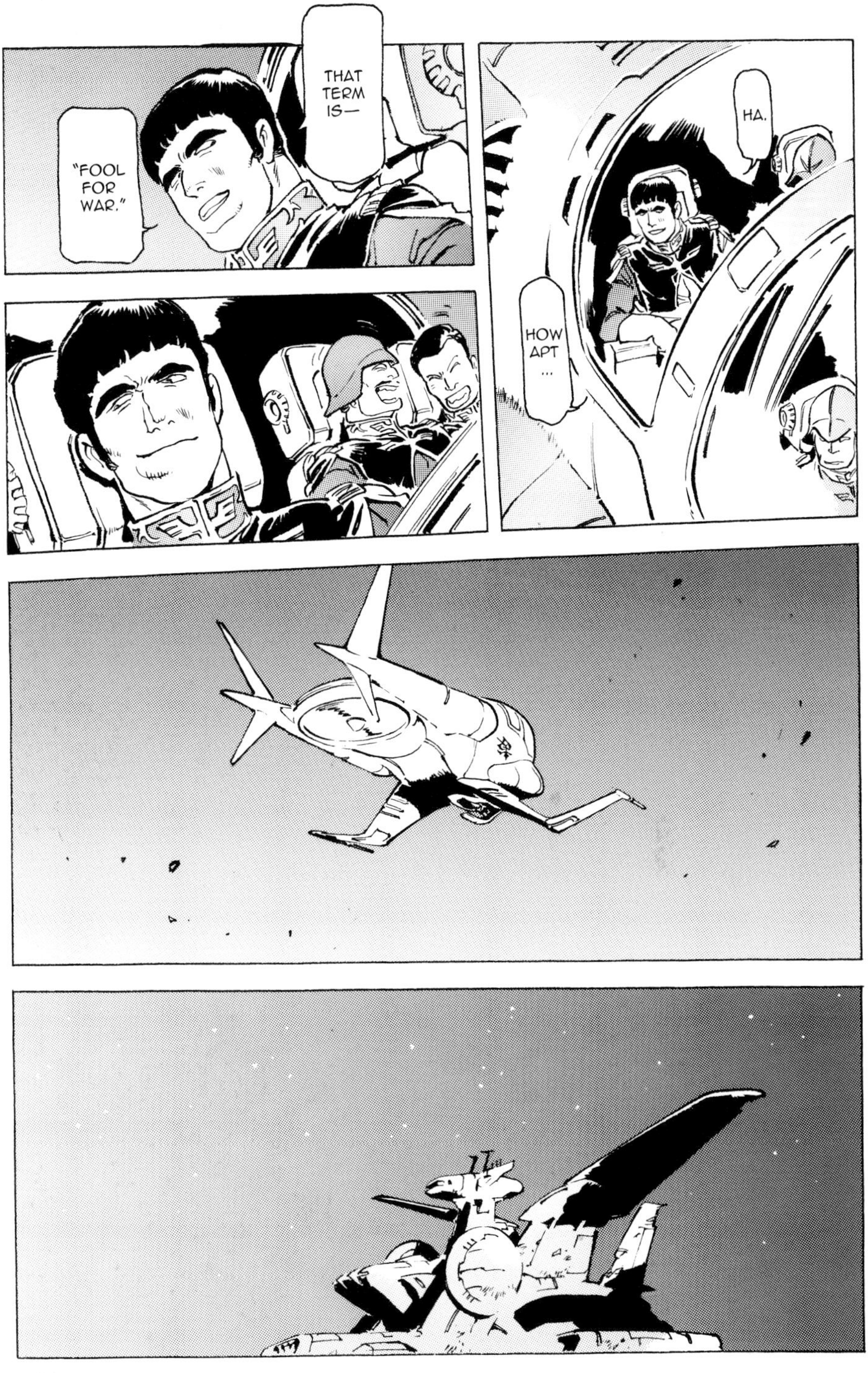
HA.
HOW APT ...
THAT TERM IS—
"FOOL FOR WAR."

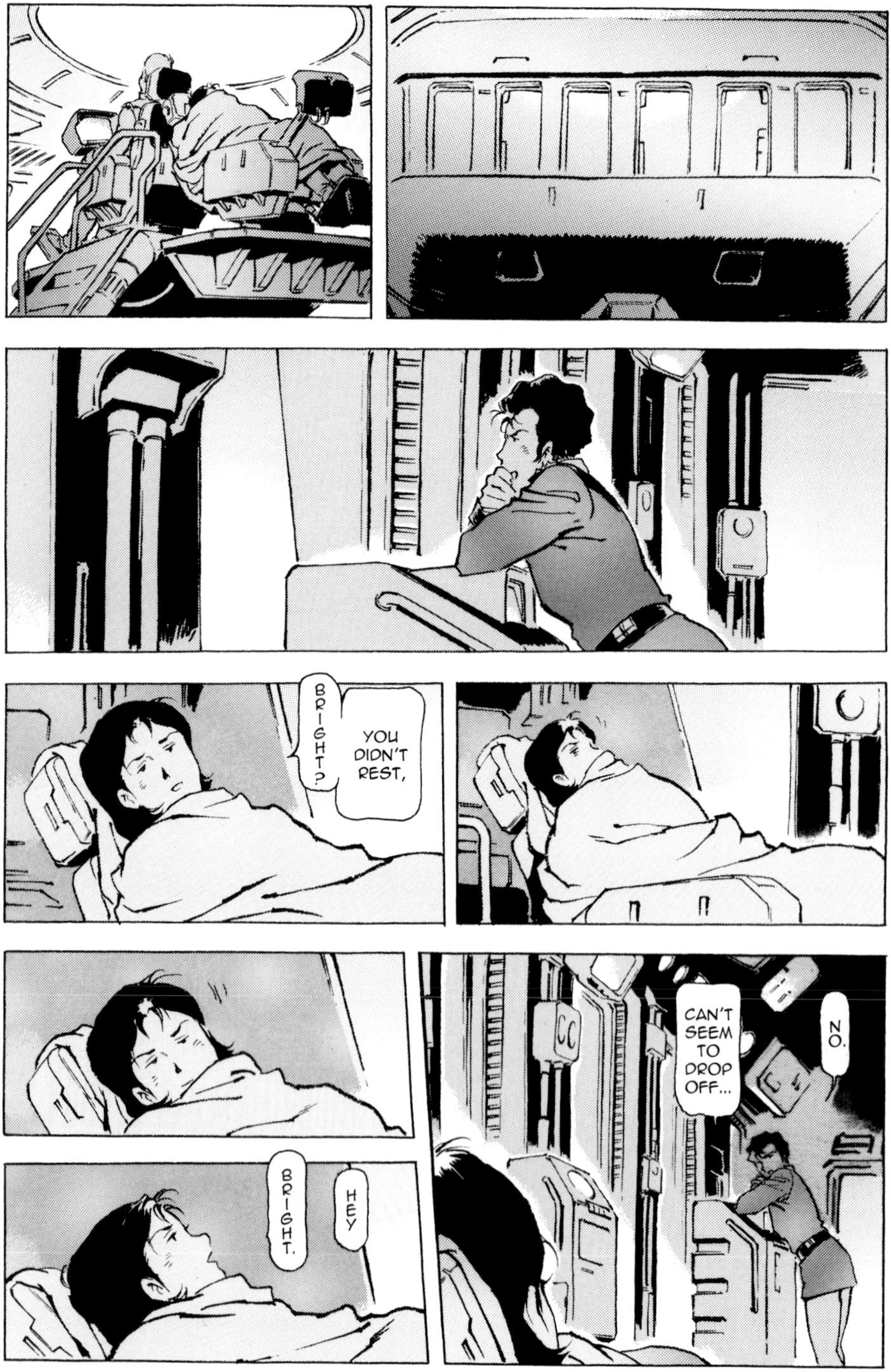
YOU DIDN'T REST,
BRIGHT?
NO.
CAN'T SEEM TO DROP OFF...
HEY
BRIGHT.

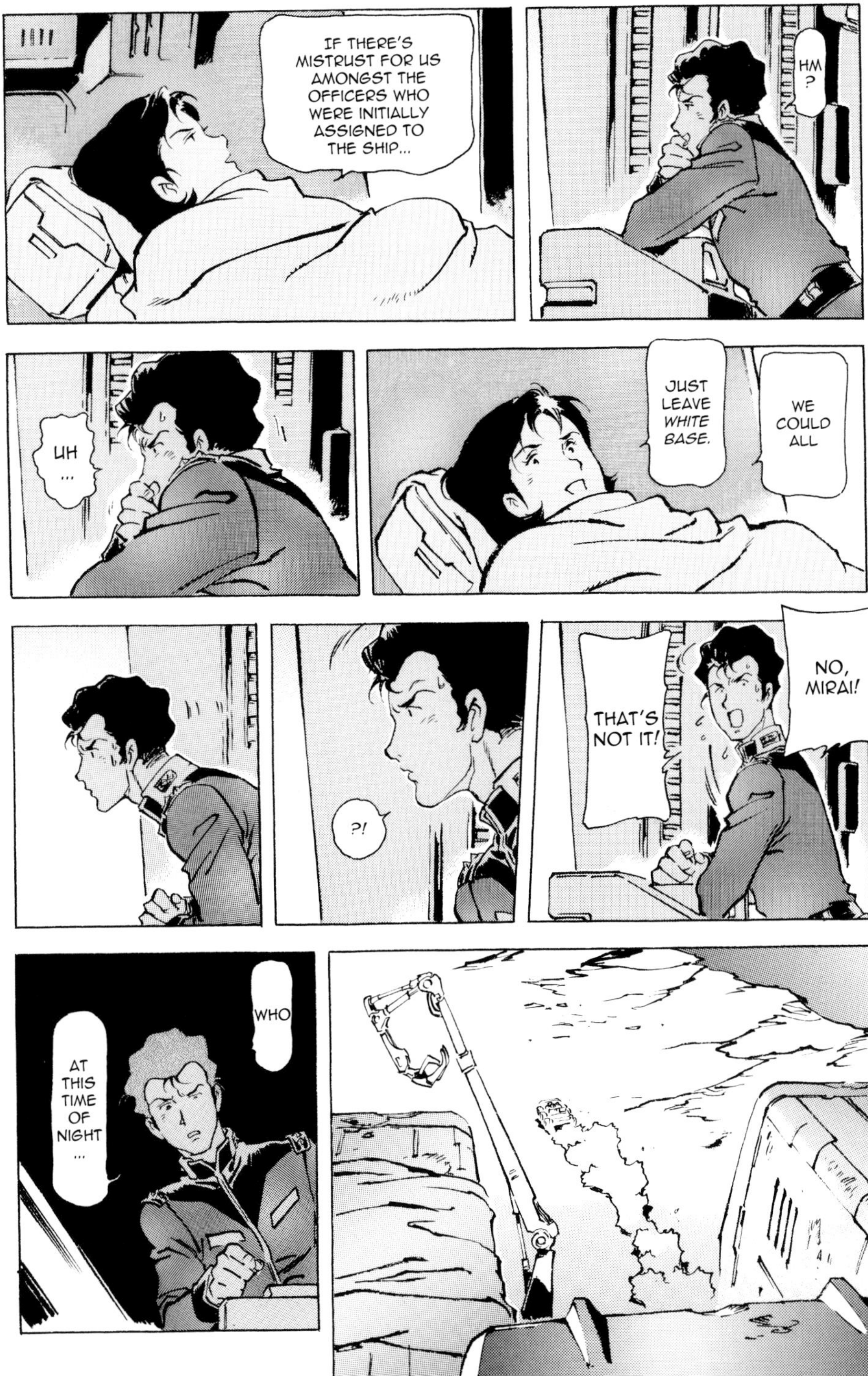
HM?
IF THERE'S MISTRUST FOR US AMONGST THE OFFICERS WHO WERE INITIALLY ASSIGNED TO THE SHIP...
WE COULD ALL
JUST LEAVE WHITE BASE.
UH ...
NO, MIRAI!
THAT'S NOT IT!
?!
WHO
AT THIS TIME OF NIGHT ...

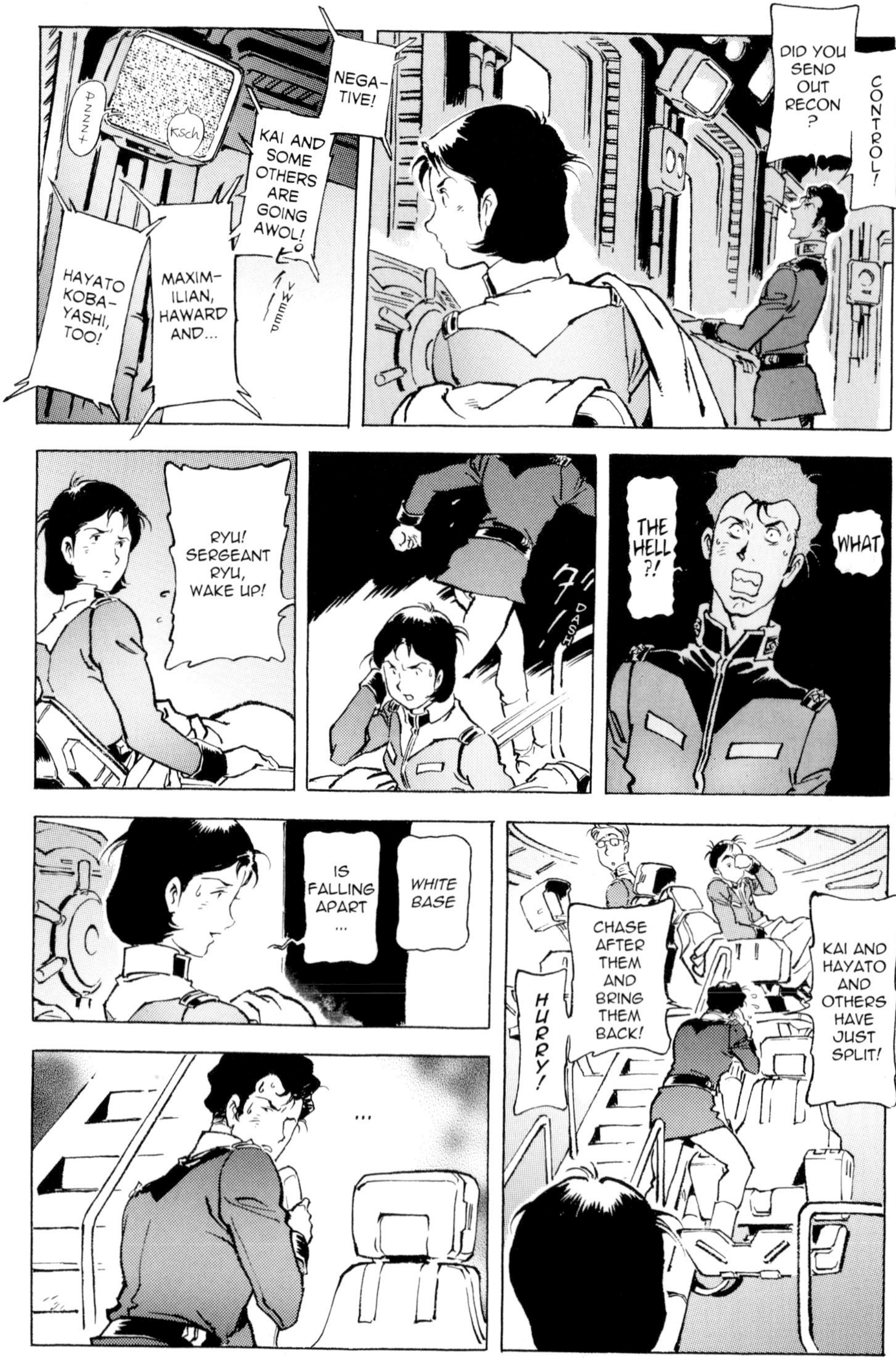
CONTROL!
DID YOU SEND OUT RECON?
NEGA-TIVE!
Pzzzt
Ksch
KAI AND SOME OTHERS ARE GOING AWOL!
VWEEP
MAXIM-ILIAN, HAWARD AND...
HAYATO KOBA-YASHI, TOO!
WHAT
THE HELL?!
DASH
RYU! SERGEANT RYU, WAKE UP!
KAI AND HAYATO AND OTHERS HAVE JUST SPLIT!
CHASE AFTER THEM AND BRING THEM BACK!
HURRY!
WHITE BASE
IS FALLING APART...
...

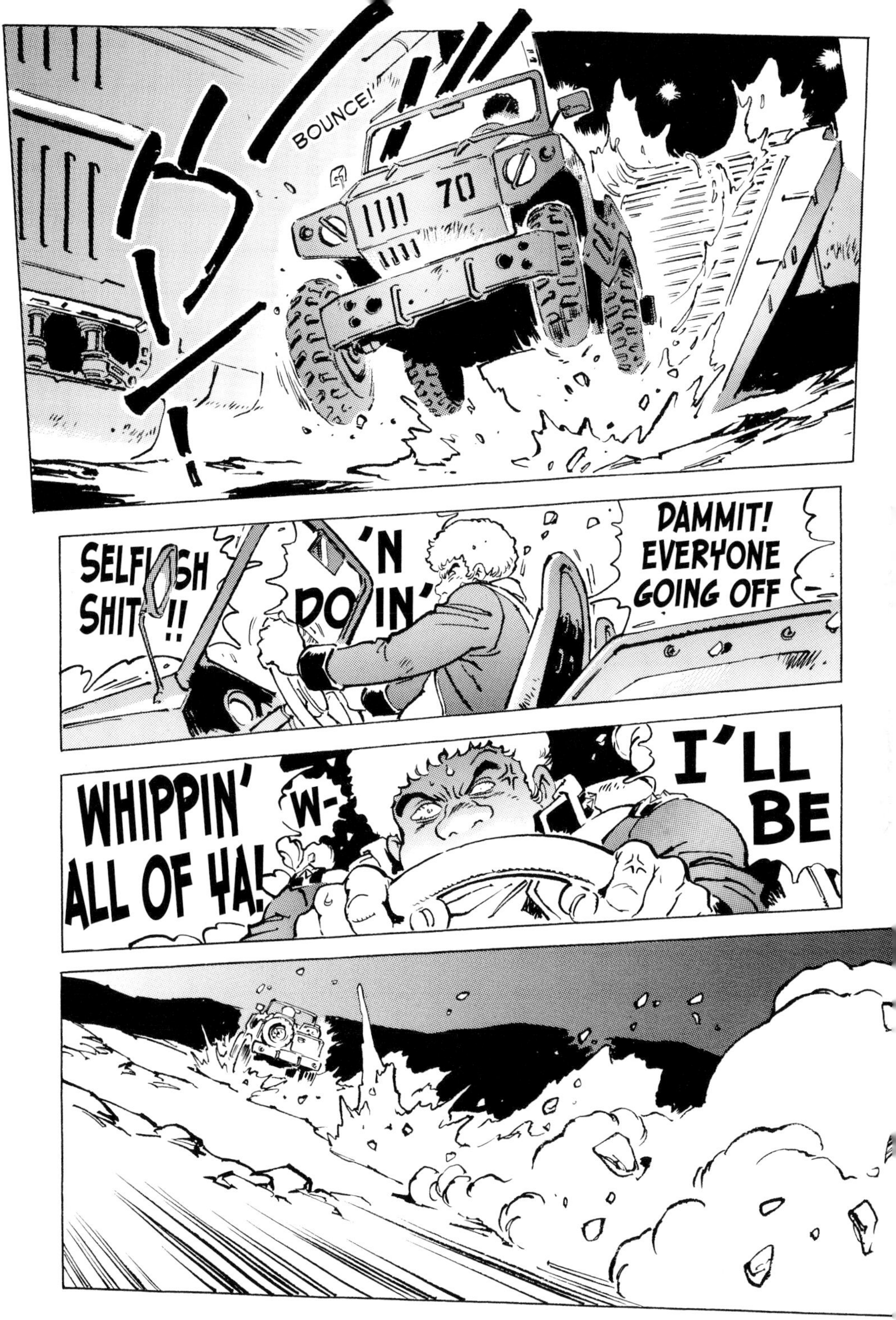
BOUNCE!
DAMMIT! EVERYONE GOING OFF
'N DOIN'
SELFISH SHIT!!
I'LL BE
W-
WHIPPIN' ALL OF YA!

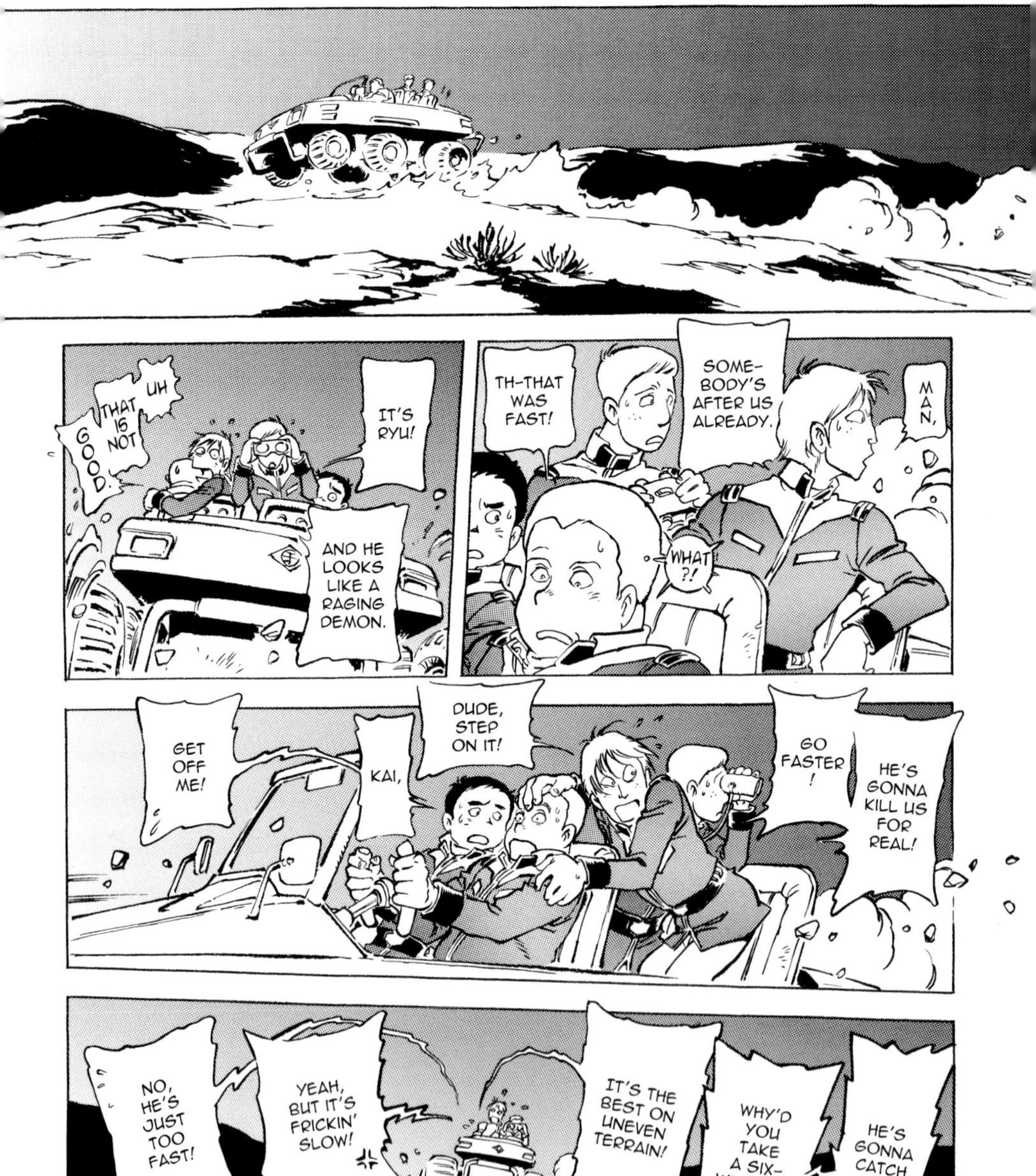
MAN,
SOME-BODY'S AFTER US ALREADY.
TH-THAT WAS FAST!
WHAT ?!
IT'S RYU!
AND HE LOOKS LIKE A RAGING DEMON.
UH
THAT IS NOT GOOD.
HE'S GONNA KILL US FOR REAL!
GO FASTER!
KAI,
DUDE, STEP ON IT!
GET OFF ME!
HE'S GONNA CATCH US!
WHY'D YOU TAKE A SIX-WHEELER BUGGY ANYWAY ?!
IT'S THE BEST ON UNEVEN TERRAIN!
YEAH, BUT IT'S FRICKIN' SLOW!
NO, HE'S JUST TOO FAST!

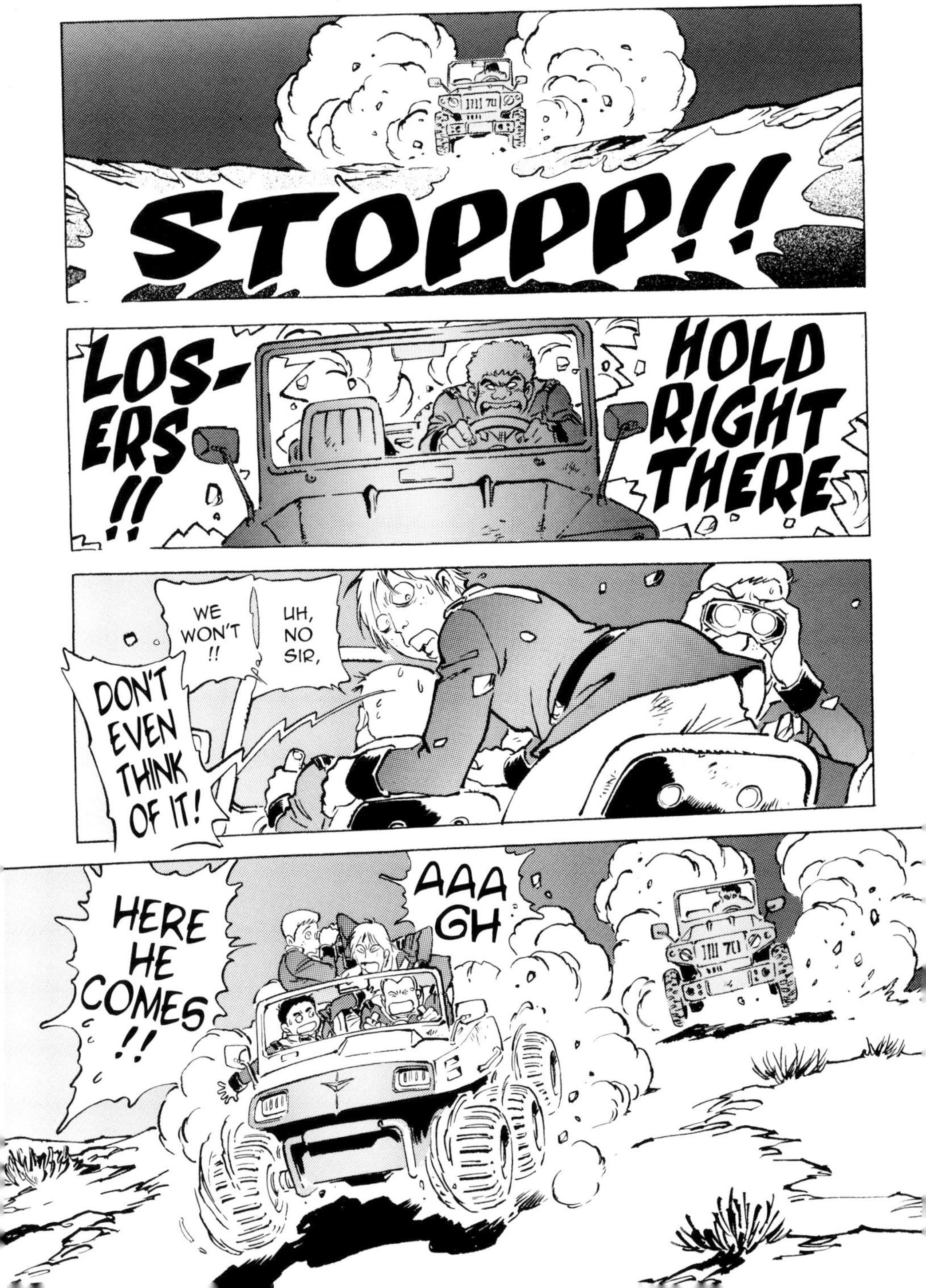
STOPPP!!
HOLD RIGHT THERE
LOS-ERS!!
UH, NO SIR,
WE WON'T!!
DON'T EVEN THINK OF IT!
AAAGH
HERE HE COMES!!

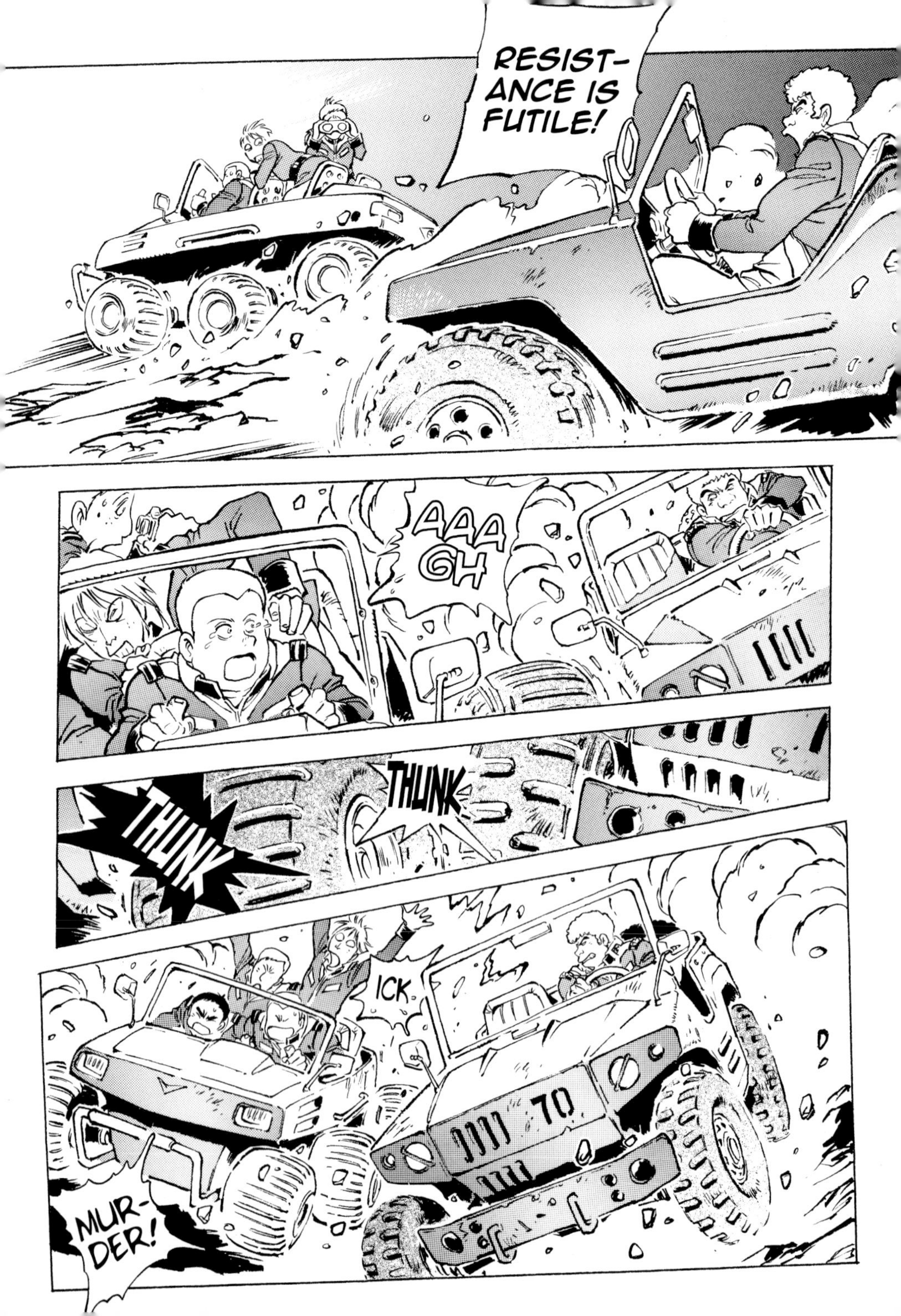
RESIST-
ANCE IS
FUTILE!
AAA
GH
THUNK
THUNK
ICK
MUR-
DER!

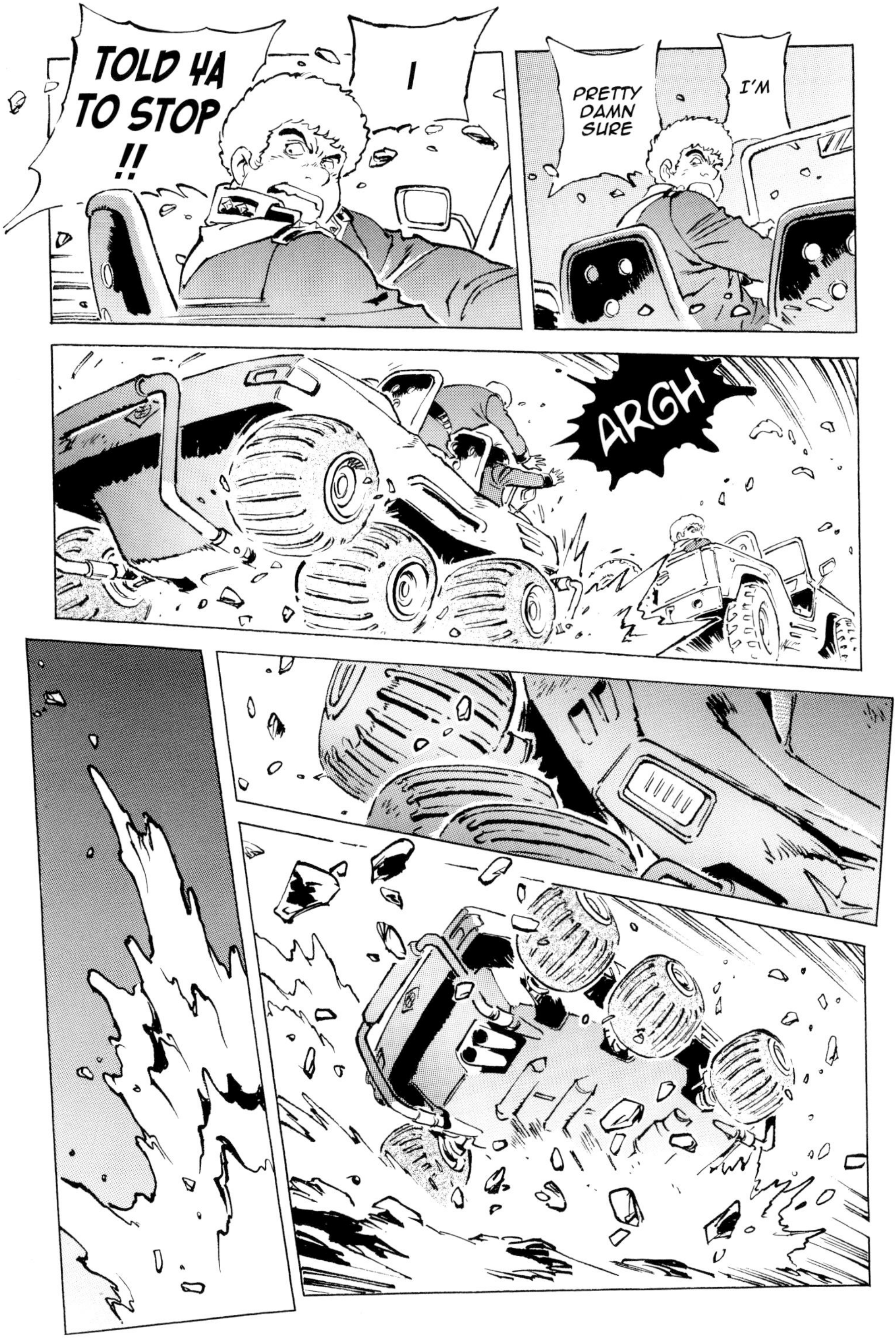
I'M
PRETTY DAMN SURE
I
TOLD YA TO STOP !!
ARGH

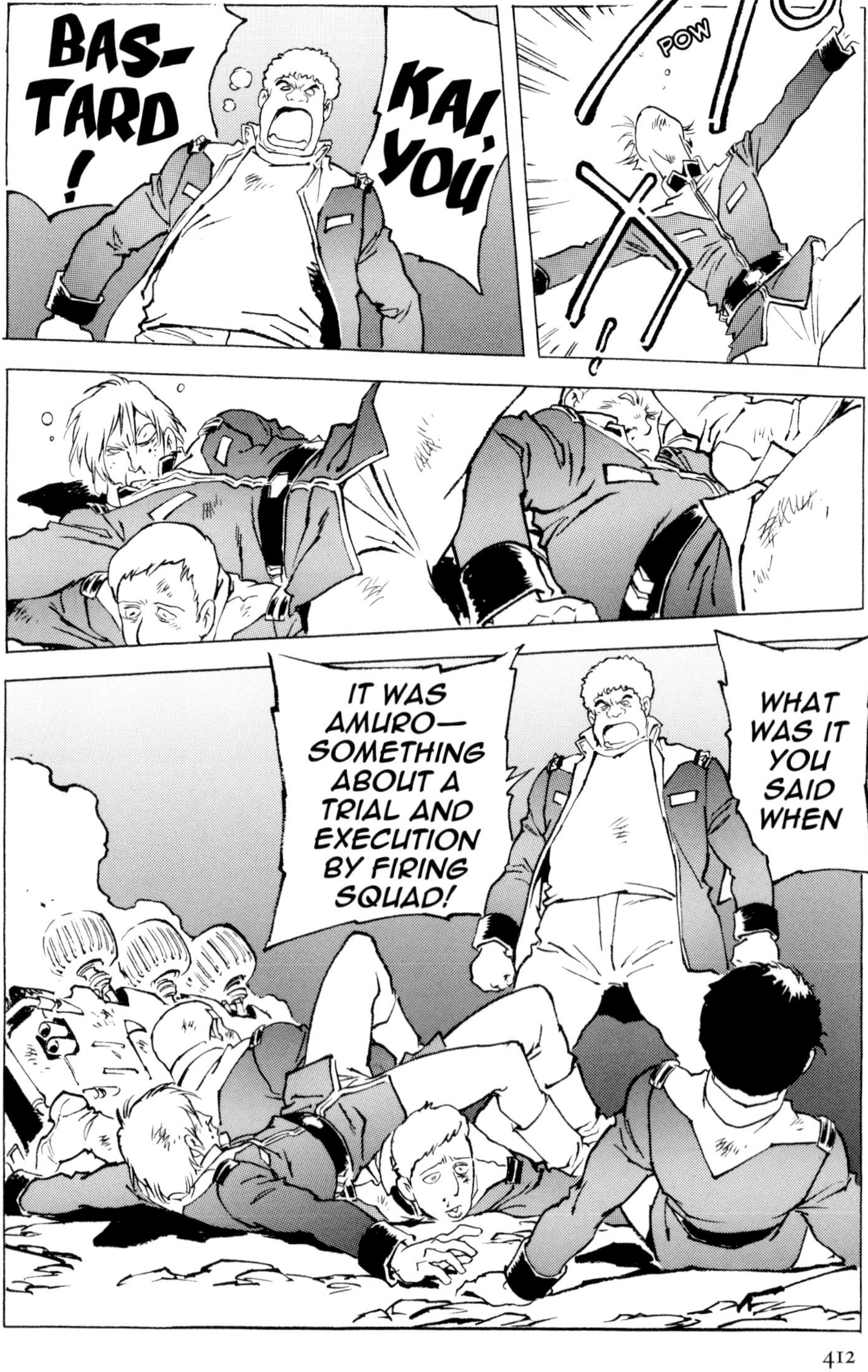
POW
KAI, YOU
BAS-TARD!
WHAT WAS IT YOU SAID WHEN
IT WAS AMURO—SOMETHING ABOUT A TRIAL AND EXECUTION BY FIRING SQUAD!

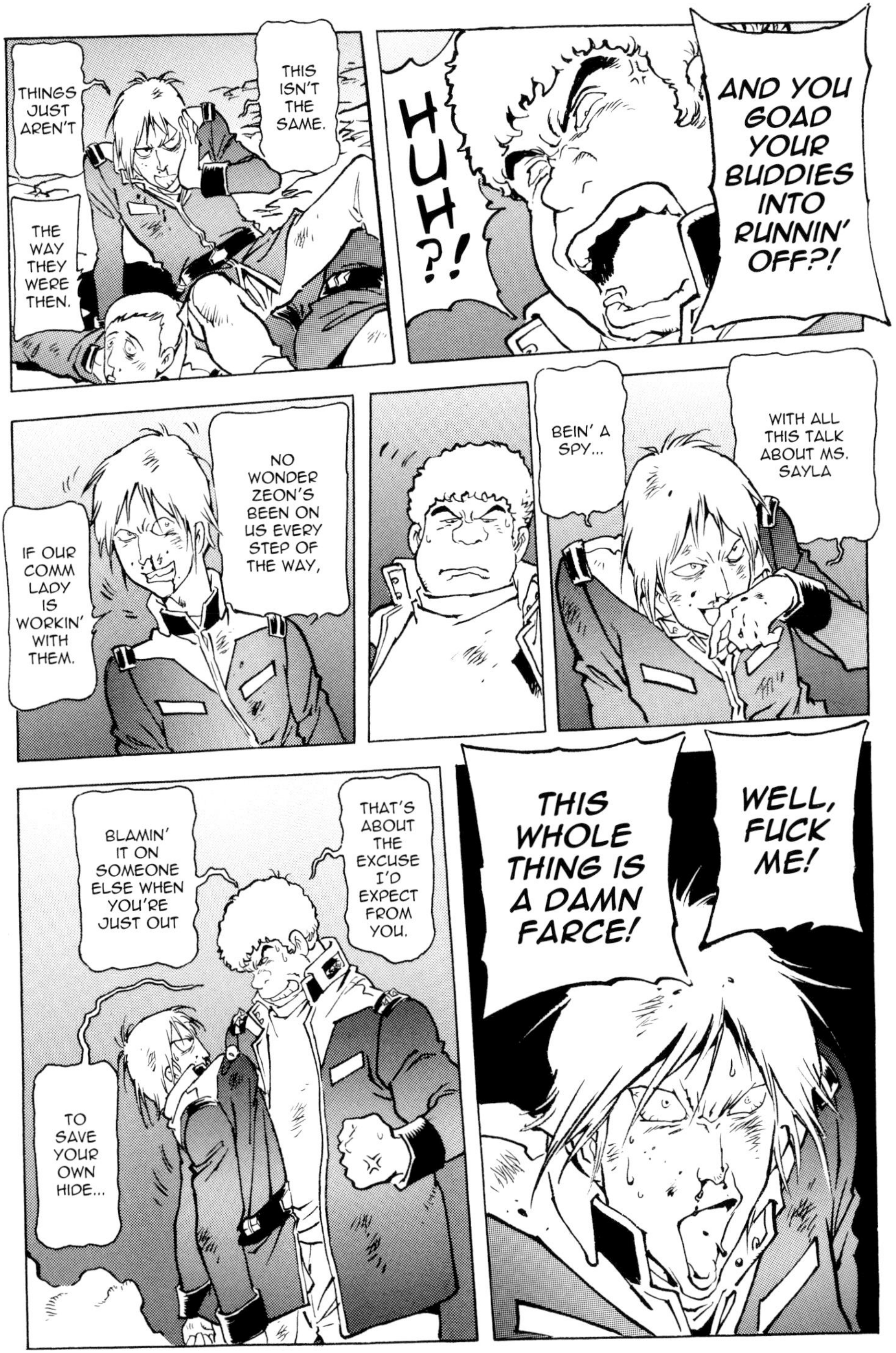
AND YOU GOAD YOUR BUDDIES INTO RUNNIN' OFF?!
HUH?!
THIS ISN'T THE SAME.
THINGS JUST AREN'T
THE WAY THEY WERE THEN.
WITH ALL THIS TALK ABOUT MS. SAYLA
BEIN' A SPY...
NO WONDER ZEON'S BEEN ON US EVERY STEP OF THE WAY,
IF OUR COMM LADY IS WORKIN' WITH THEM.
WELL, FUCK ME!
THIS WHOLE THING IS A DAMN FARCE!
THAT'S ABOUT THE EXCUSE I'D EXPECT FROM YOU.
BLAMIN' IT ON SOMEONE ELSE WHEN YOU'RE JUST OUT
TO SAVE YOUR OWN HIDE...

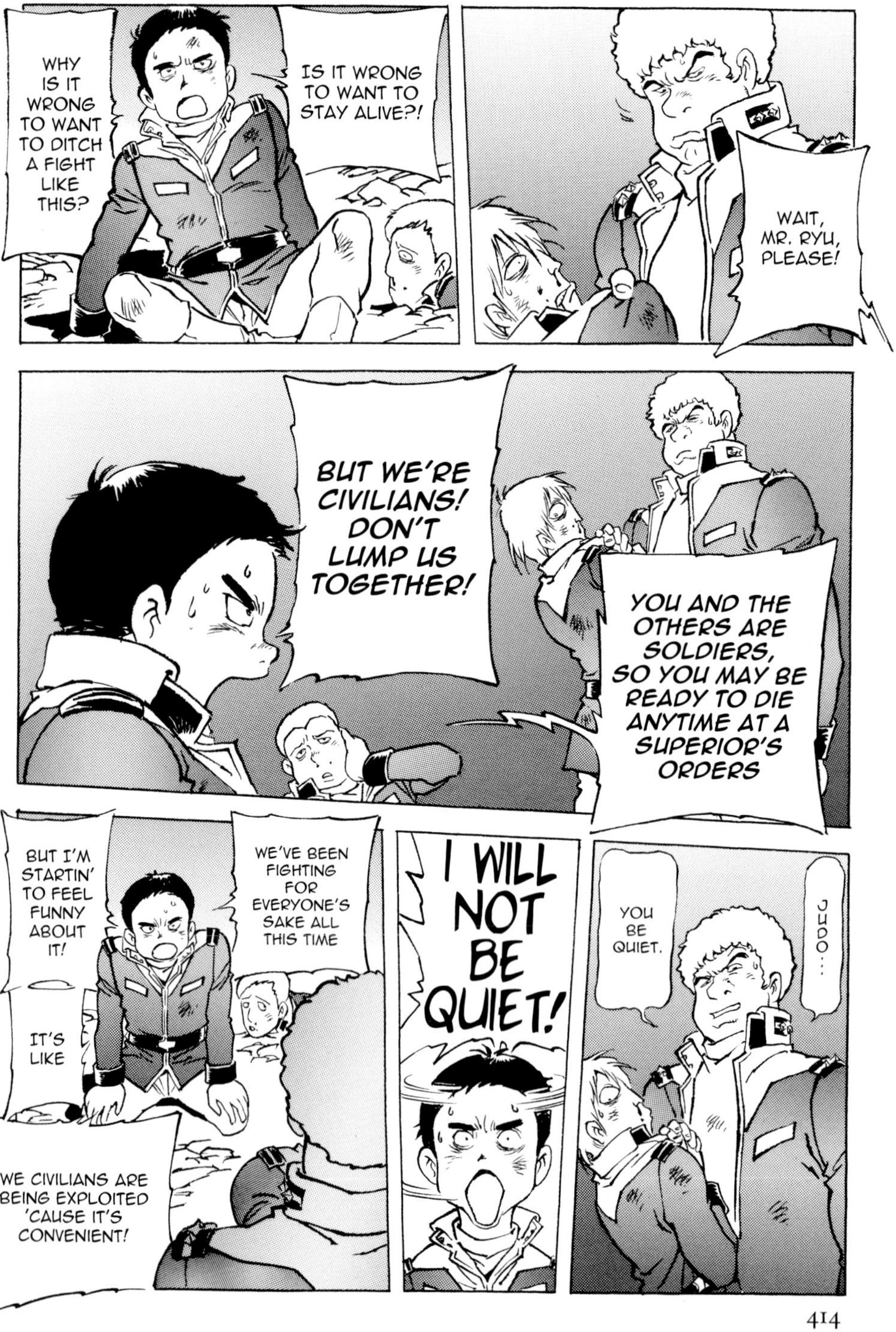
WAIT, MR. RYU, PLEASE!
IS IT WRONG TO WANT TO STAY ALIVE?!
WHY IS IT WRONG TO WANT TO DITCH A FIGHT LIKE THIS?
YOU AND THE OTHERS ARE SOLDIERS, SO YOU MAY BE READY TO DIE ANYTIME AT A SUPERIOR'S ORDERS
BUT WE'RE CIVILIANS! DON'T LUMP US TOGETHER!
JUDO...
YOU BE QUIET.
I WILL NOT BE QUIET!
WE'VE BEEN FIGHTING FOR EVERYONE'S SAKE ALL THIS TIME
BUT I'M STARTIN' TO FEEL FUNNY ABOUT IT!
IT'S LIKE
WE CIVILIANS ARE BEING EXPLOITED 'CAUSE IT'S CONVENIENT!

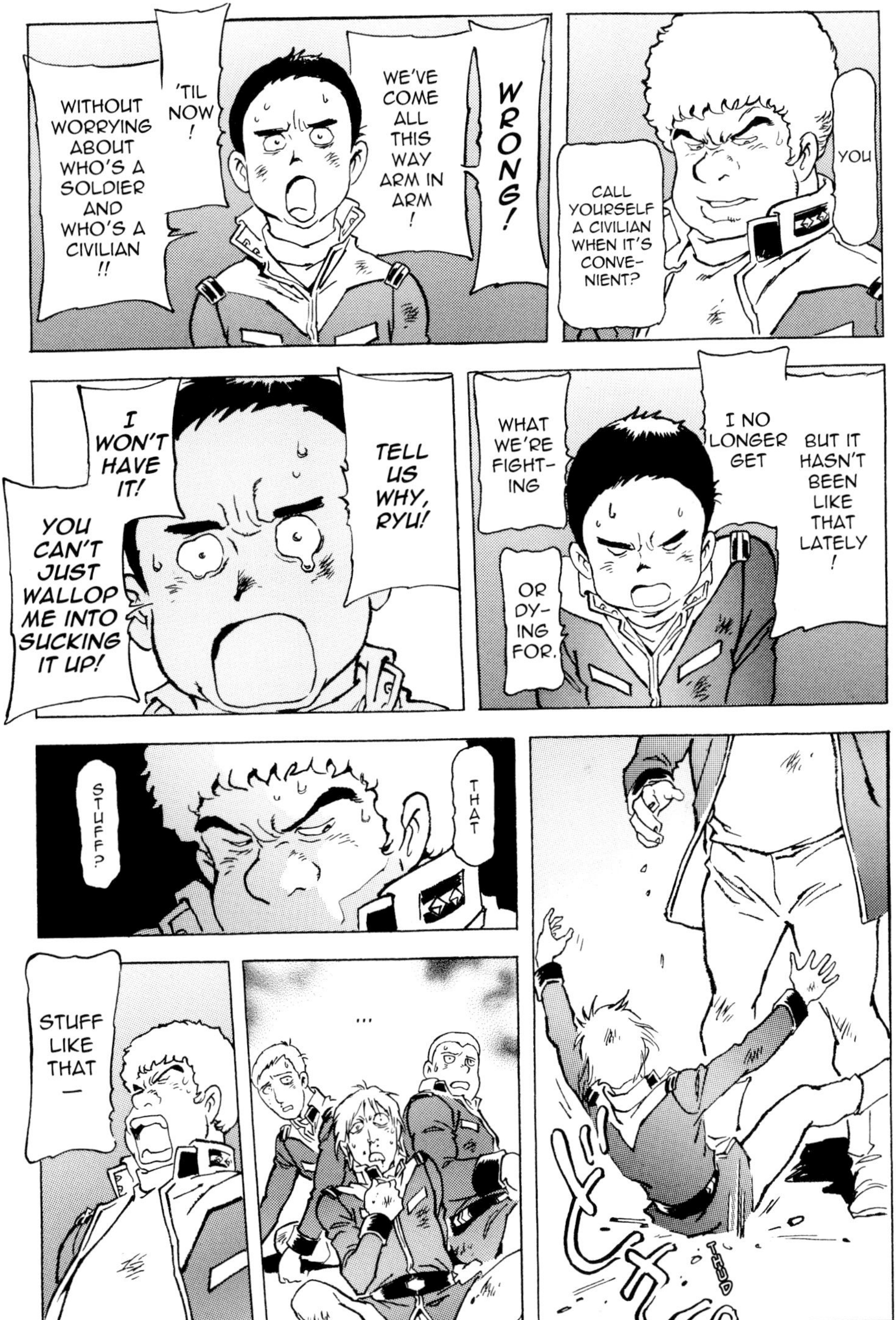
YOU
CALL YOURSELF A CIVILIAN WHEN IT'S CONVENIENT?
WRONG!
WE'VE COME ALL THIS WAY ARM IN ARM!
'TIL NOW!
WITHOUT WORRYING ABOUT WHO'S A SOLDIER AND WHO'S A CIVILIAN!!
BUT IT HASN'T BEEN LIKE THAT LATELY!
I NO LONGER GET
WHAT WE'RE FIGHTING
OR DYING FOR.
TELL US WHY, RYU!
I WON'T HAVE IT!
YOU CAN'T JUST WALLOP ME INTO SUCKING IT UP!
THUD
THAT
STUFF?
...
STUFF LIKE THAT—

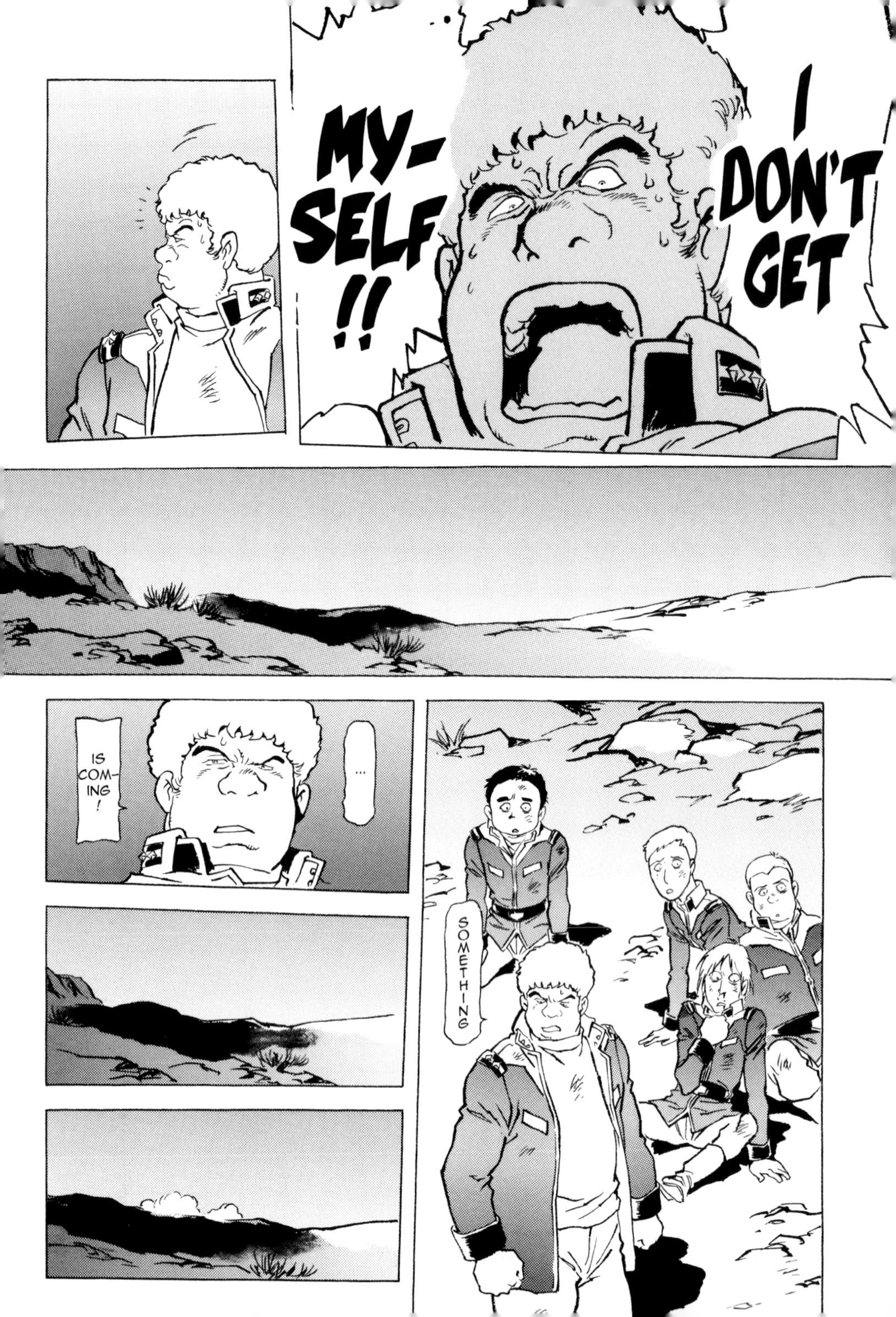
I DON'T GET
MY-SELF!!
SOMETHING
...
IS COM-ING!

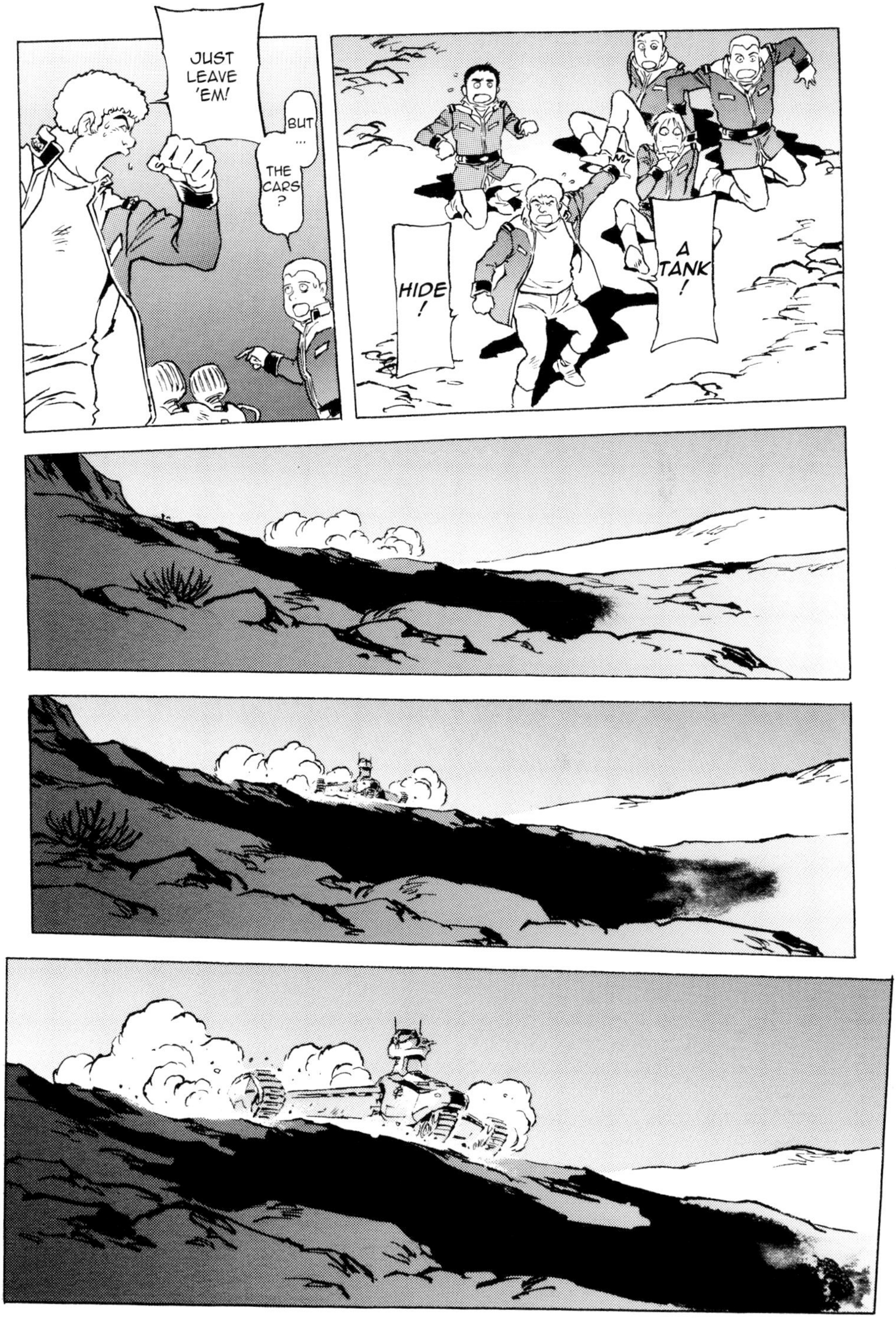
A TANK!
HIDE!
BUT... THE CARS?
JUST LEAVE 'EM!

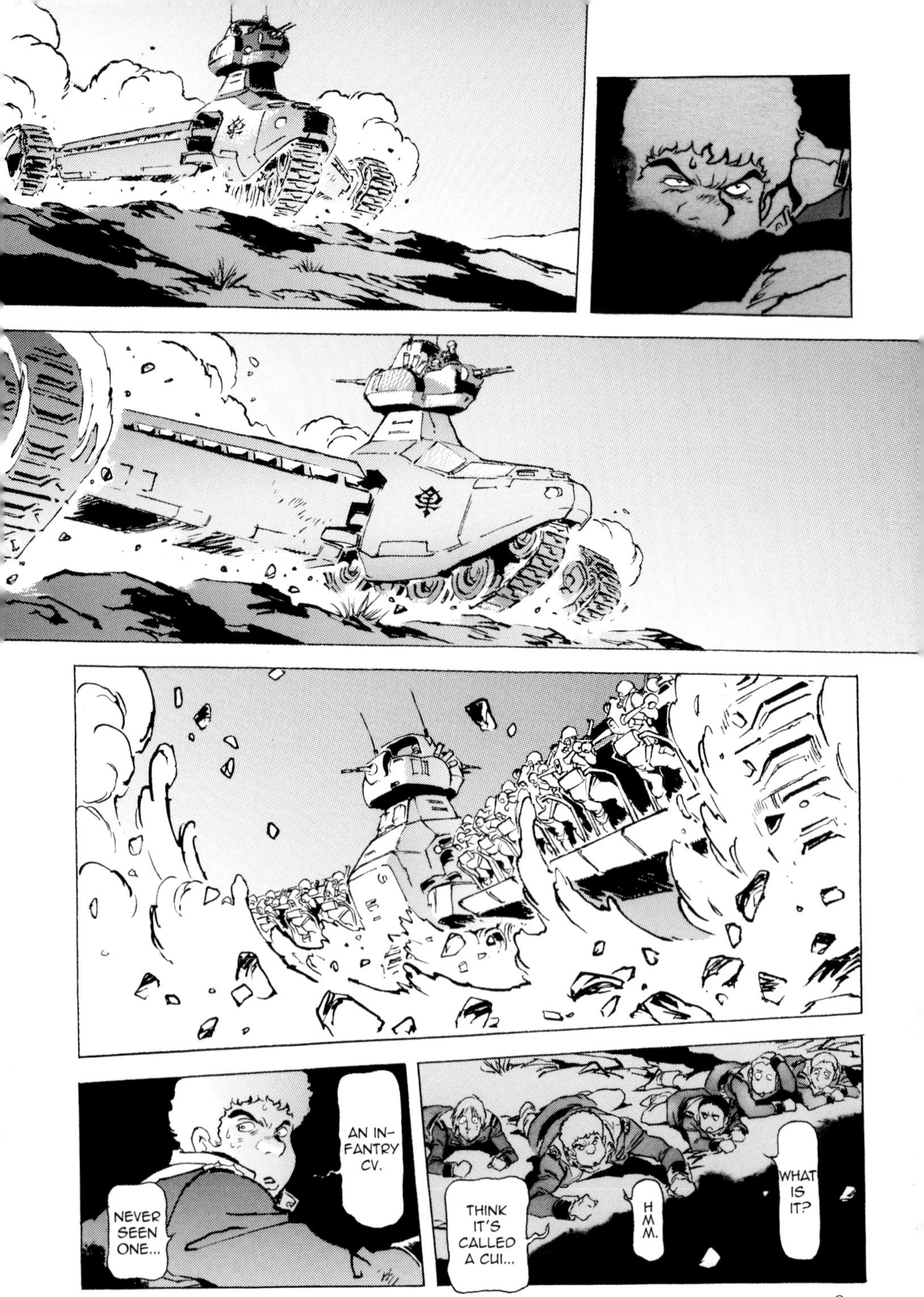

WHAT IS IT?
HMM.
THINK IT'S CALLED A CUI...
AN IN-FANTRY CV.
NEVER SEEN ONE...

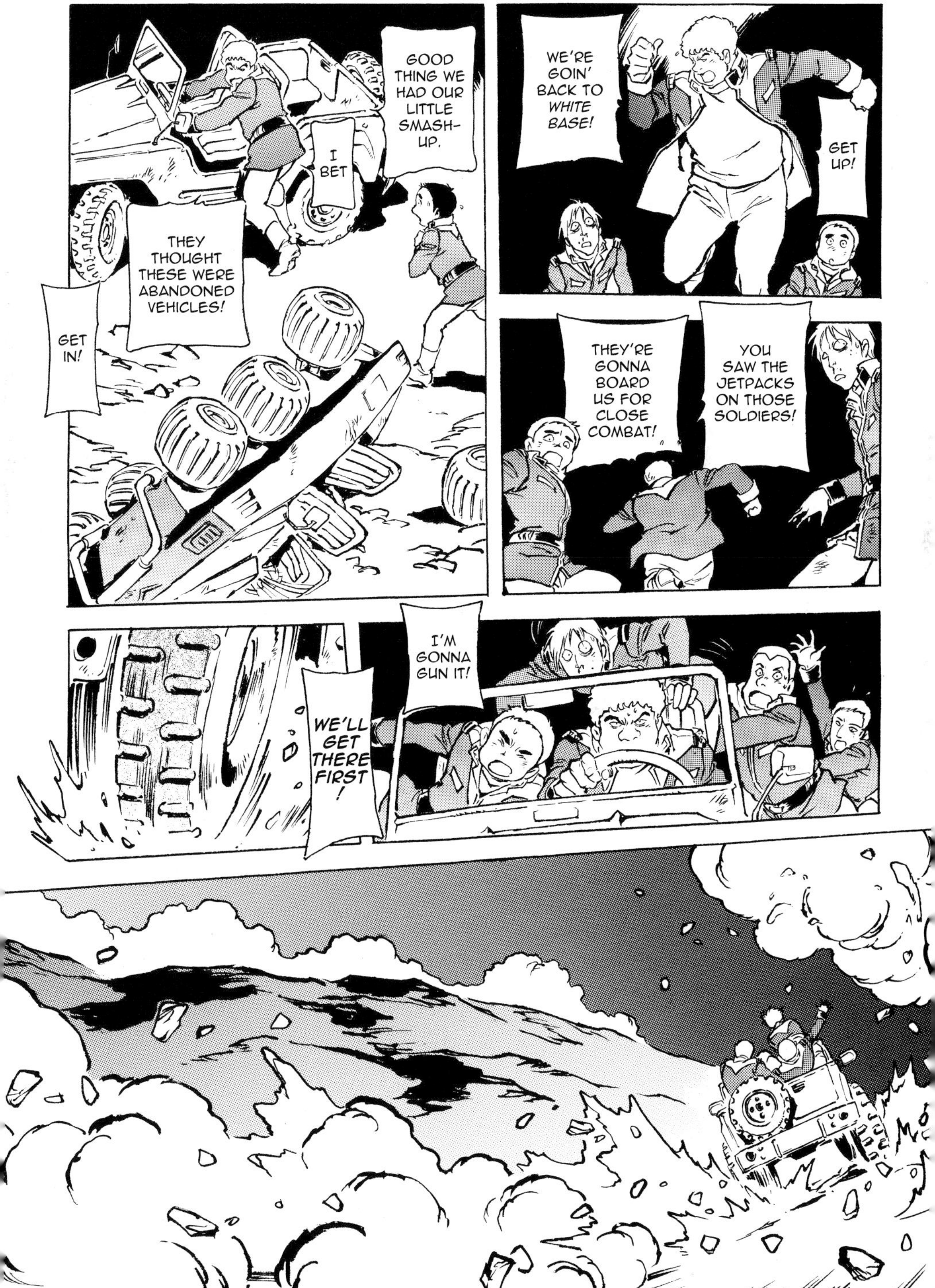
WE'RE GOIN' BACK TO WHITE BASE!
GET UP!
YOU SAW THE JETPACKS ON THOSE SOLDIERS!
THEY'RE GONNA BOARD US FOR CLOSE COMBAT!
GOOD THING WE HAD OUR LITTLE SMASH-UP.
I BET
THEY THOUGHT THESE WERE ABANDONED VEHICLES!
GET IN!
I'M GONNA GUN IT!
WE'LL GET THERE FIRST!

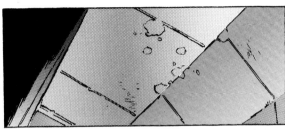

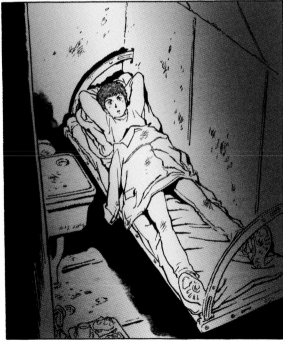

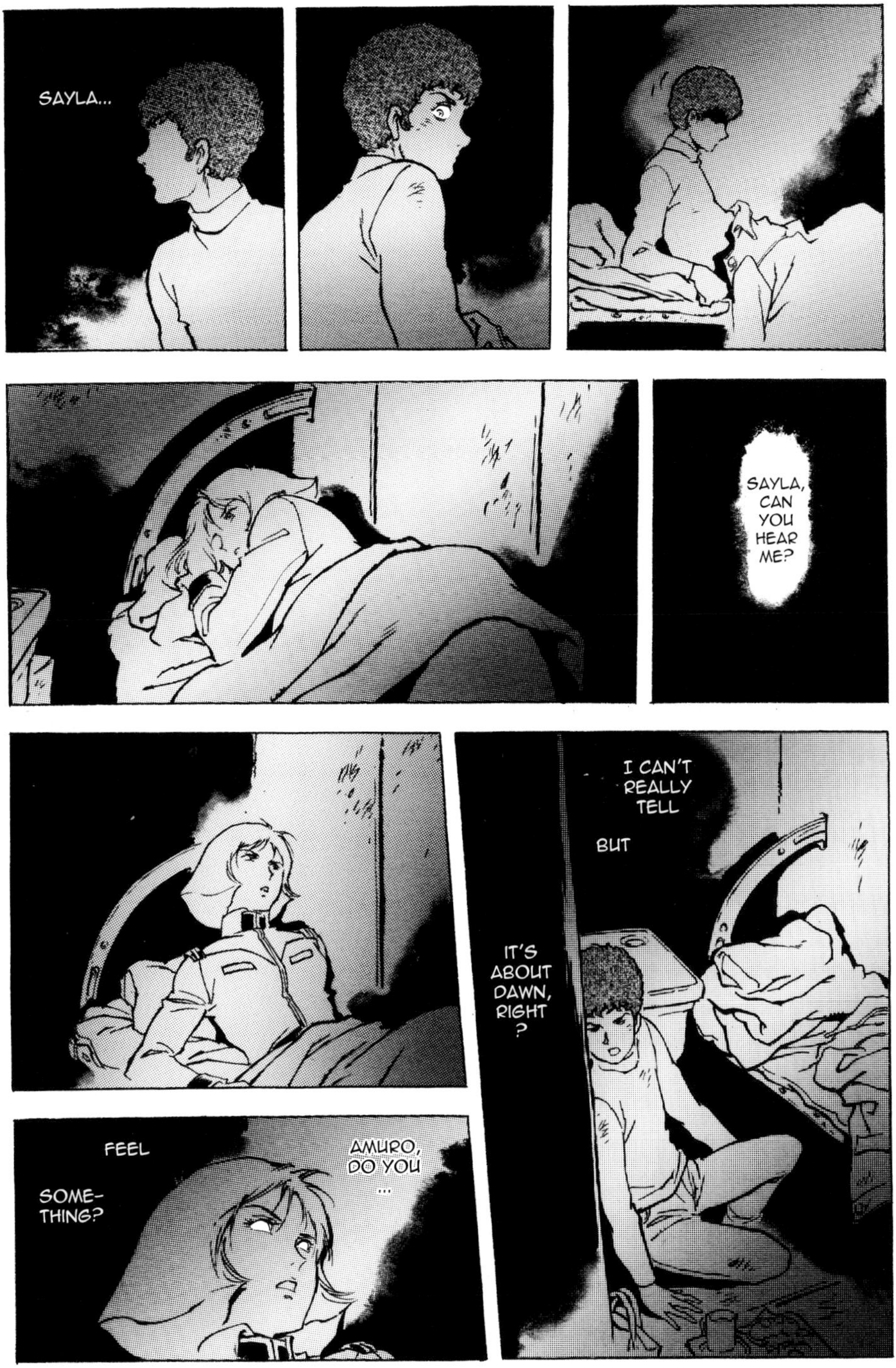
SAYLA...
SAYLA, CAN YOU HEAR ME?
I CAN'T REALLY TELL
BUT
IT'S ABOUT DAWN, RIGHT?
AMURO, DO YOU ...
FEEL
SOMETHING?

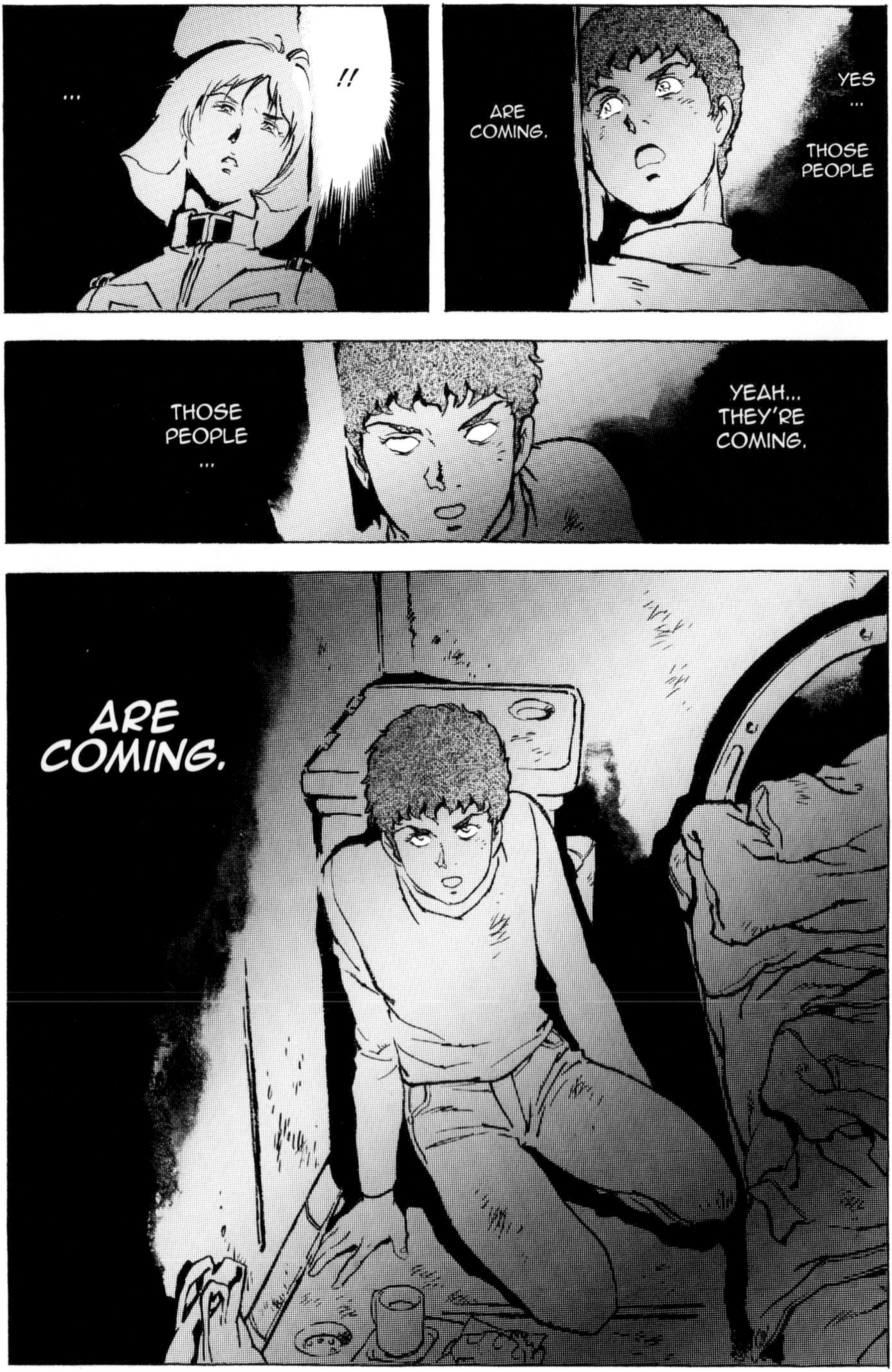
YES ... THOSE PEOPLE
ARE COMING.
!!
...
YEAH... THEY'RE COMING.
THOSE PEOPLE ...
ARE COMING.

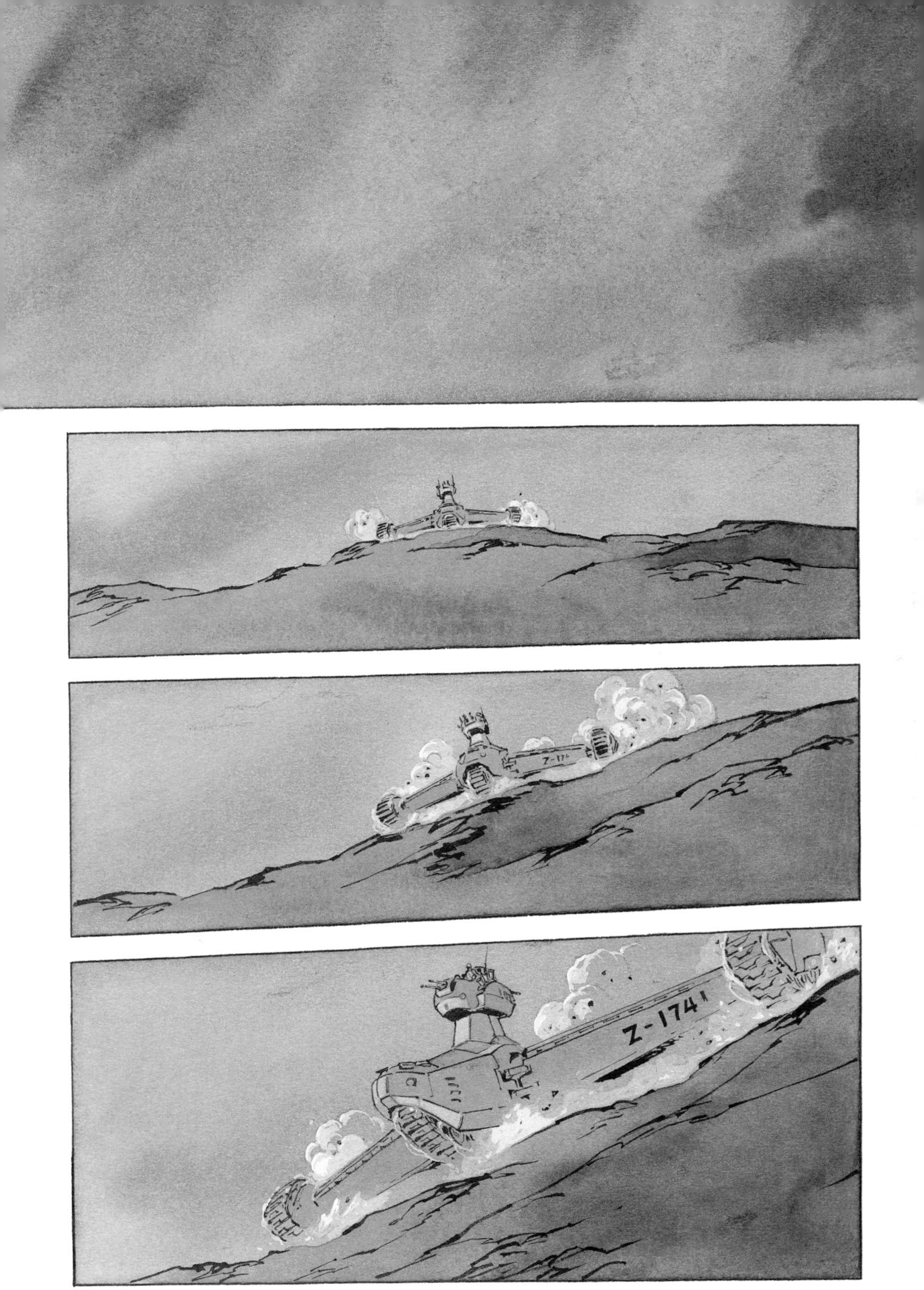
Z-174
Z-174

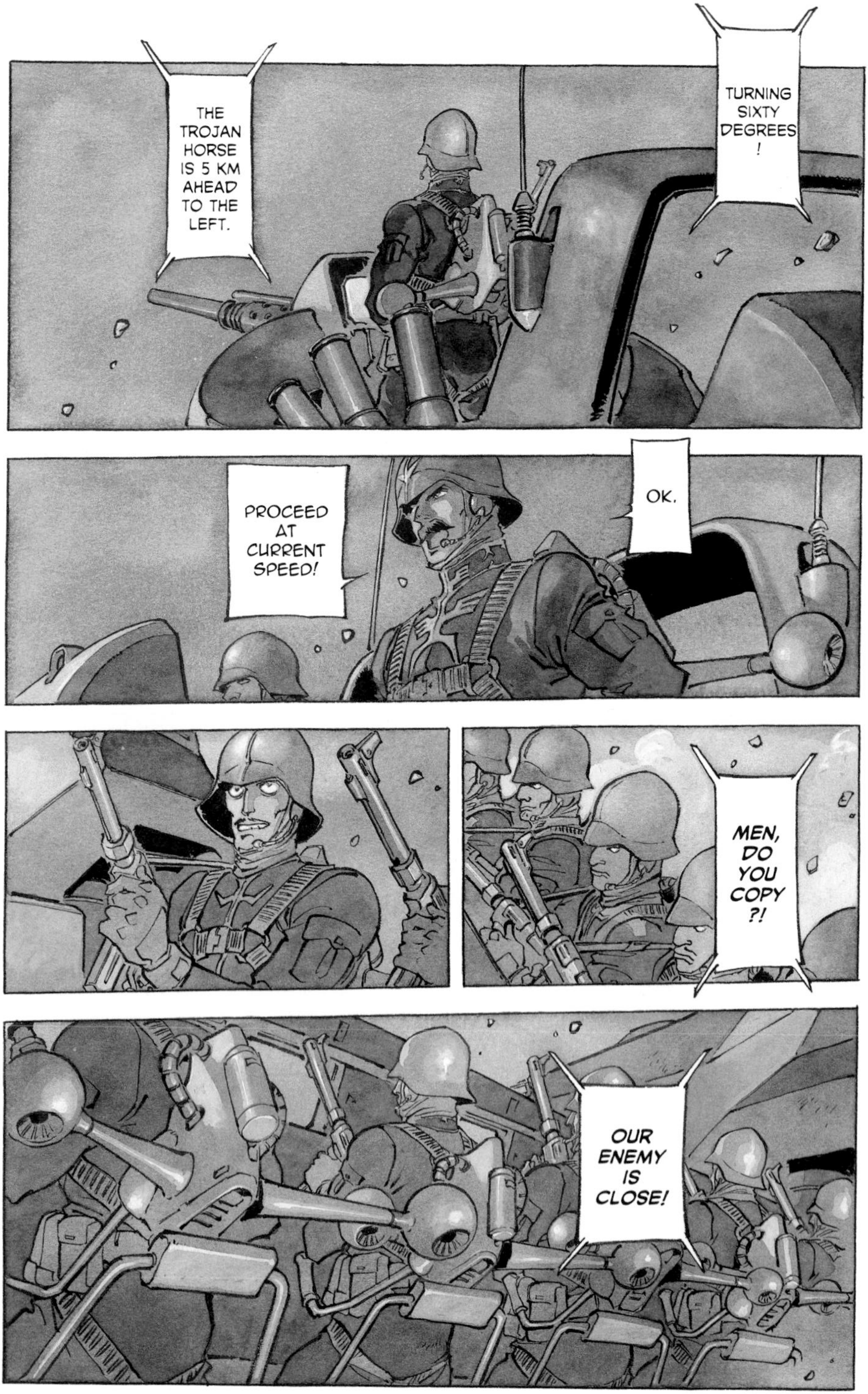
TURNING SIXTY DEGREES!
THE TROJAN HORSE IS 5 KM AHEAD TO THE LEFT.
OK.
PROCEED AT CURRENT SPEED!
MEN, DO YOU COPY?!
OUR ENEMY IS CLOSE!

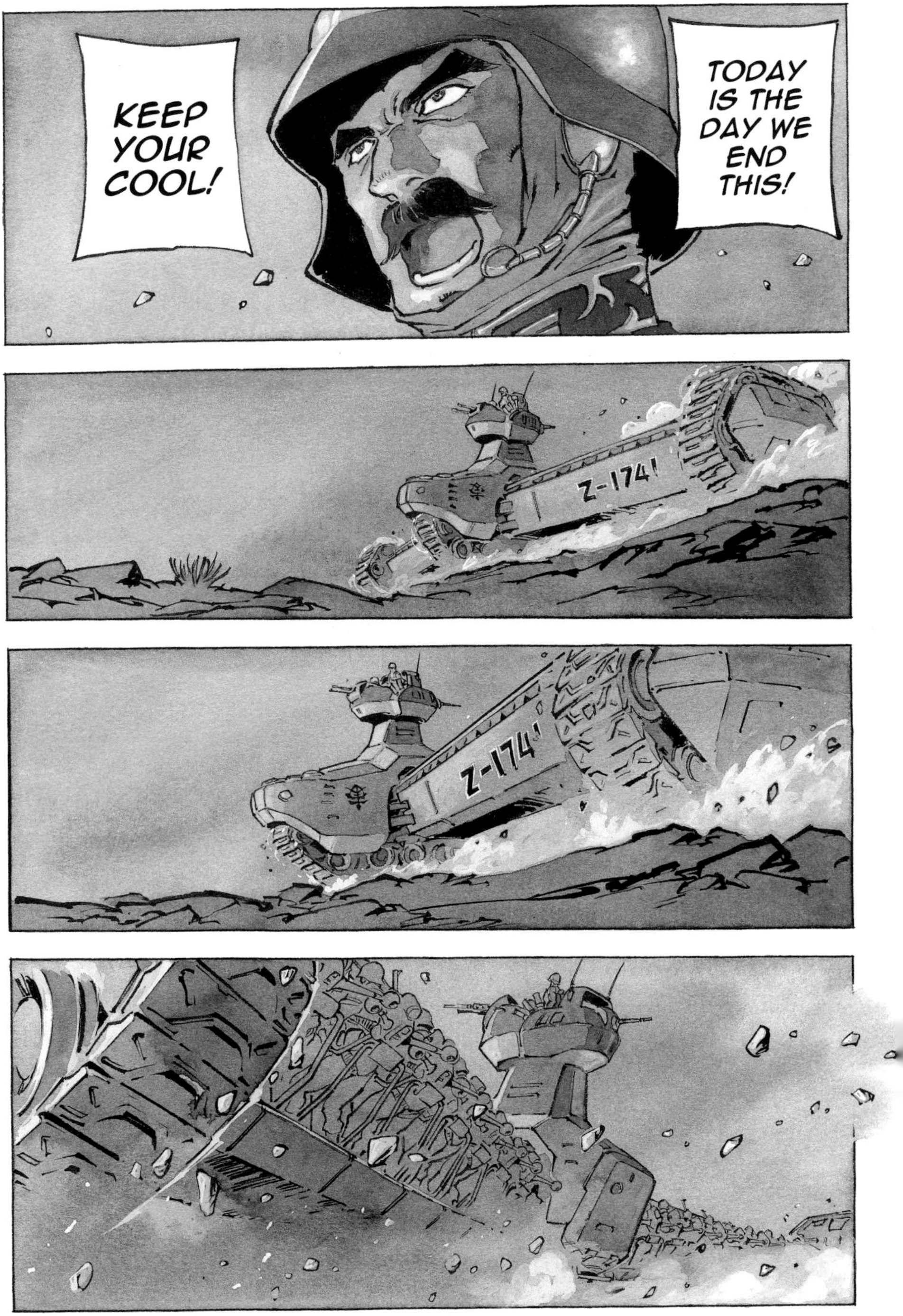
TODAY IS THE DAY WE END THIS!
KEEP YOUR COOL!
Z-174
Z-174

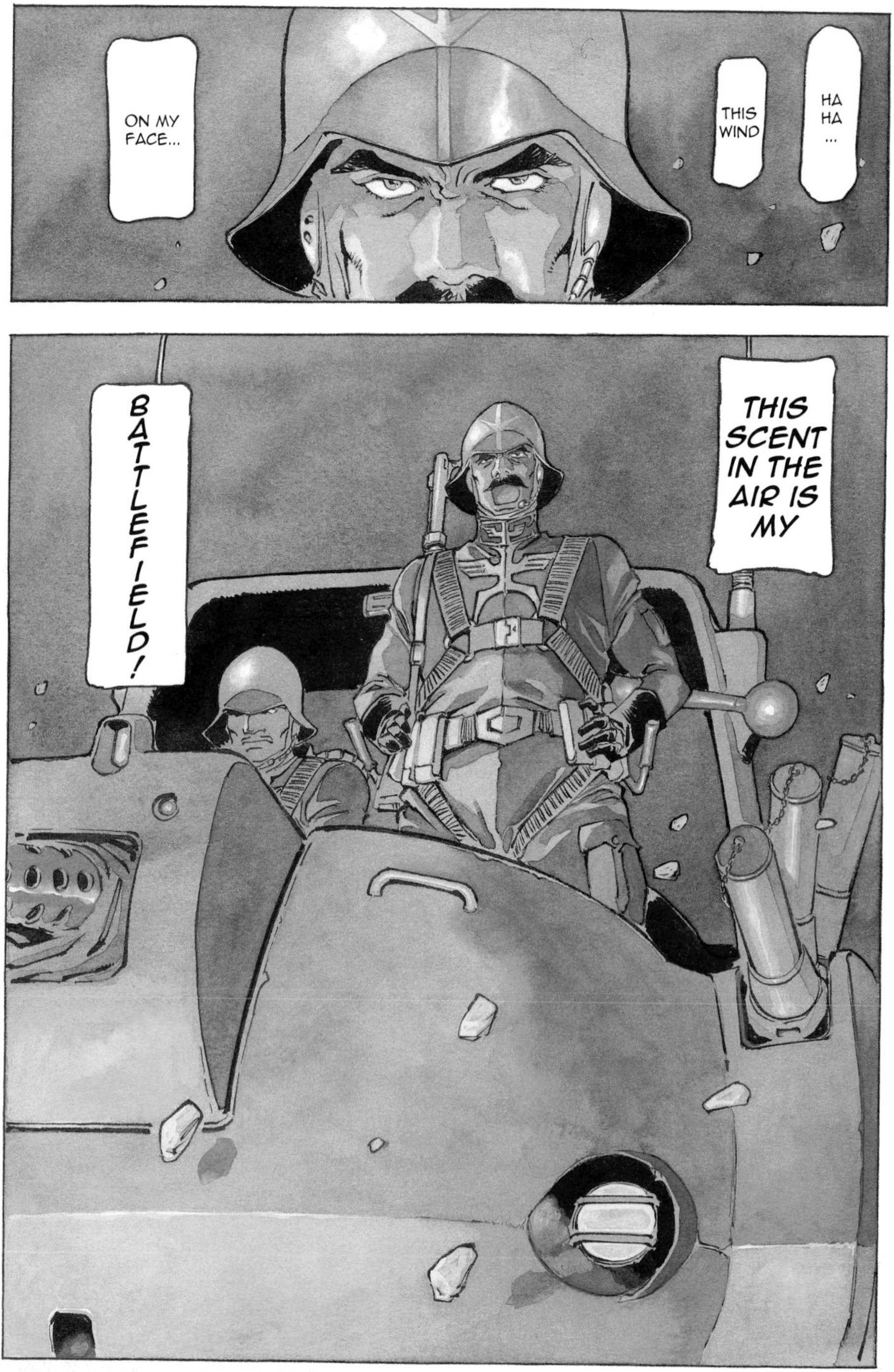
HA HA ...
THIS WIND
ON MY FACE...
THIS SCENT IN THE AIR IS MY
BATTLEFIELD!

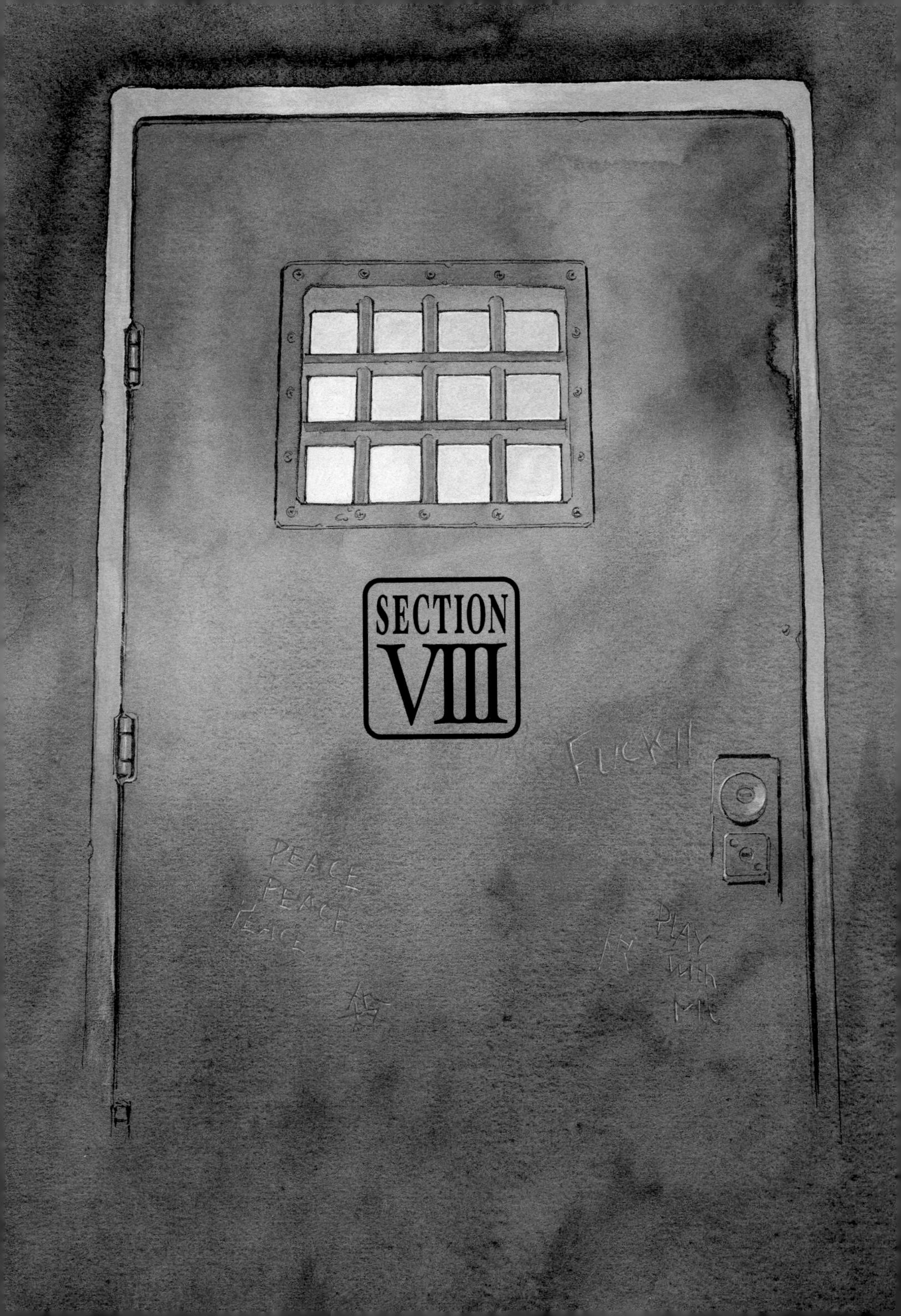
SECTION
VIII
FUCK!!
PEACE
PEACE
PEACE
PLAY
with
me

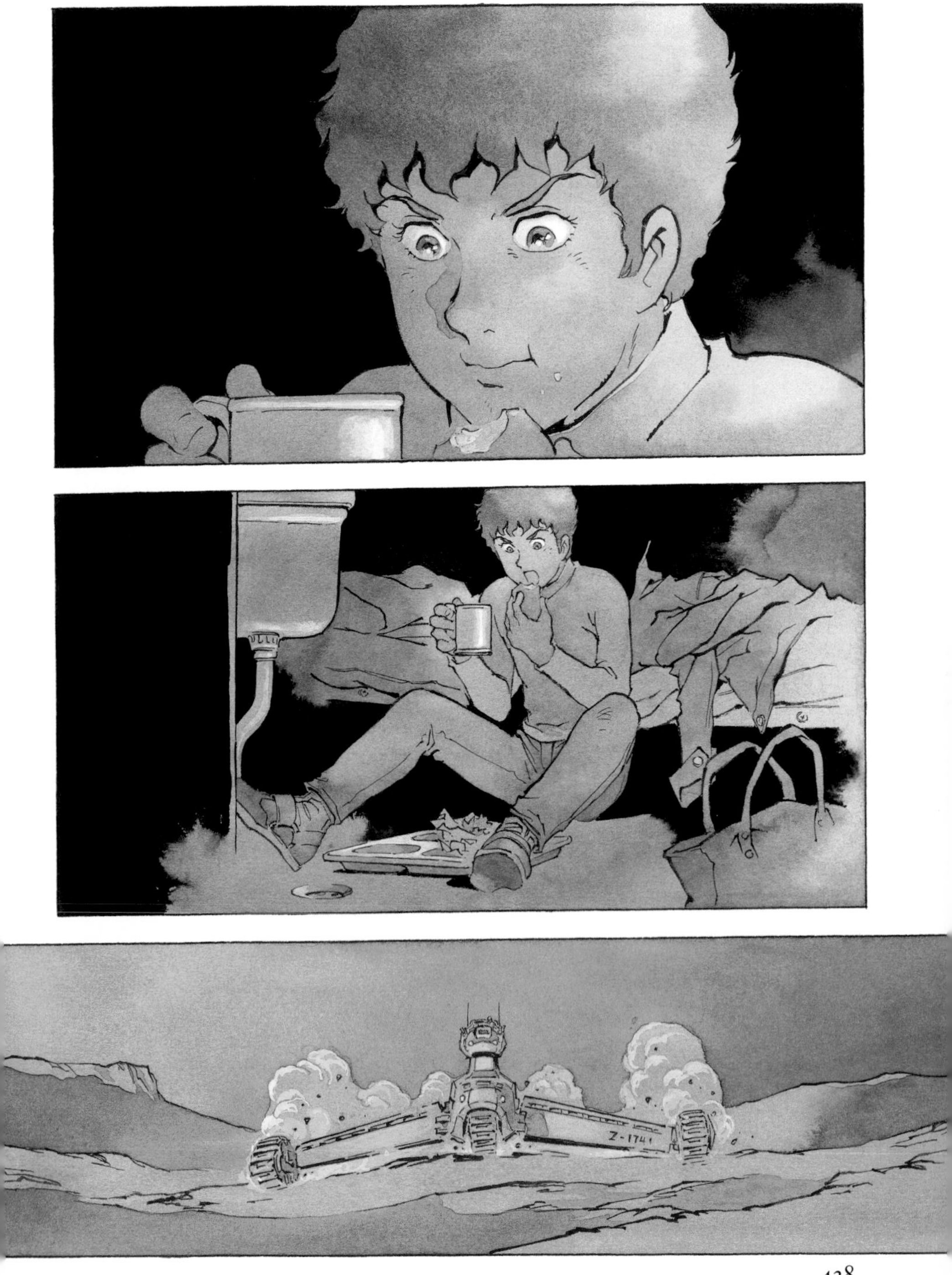
Z-1741

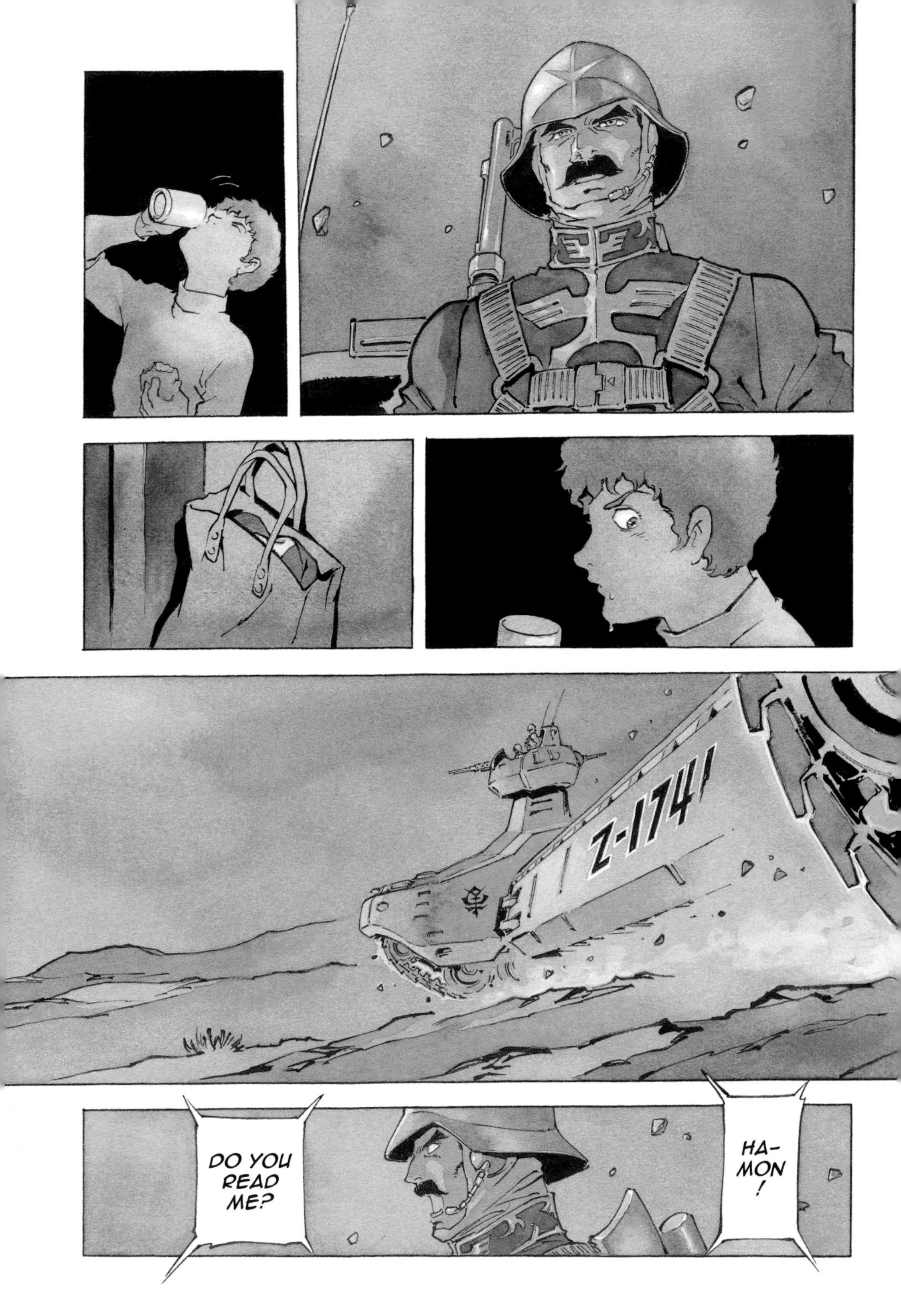
Z-174
HA-MON!
DO YOU READ ME?

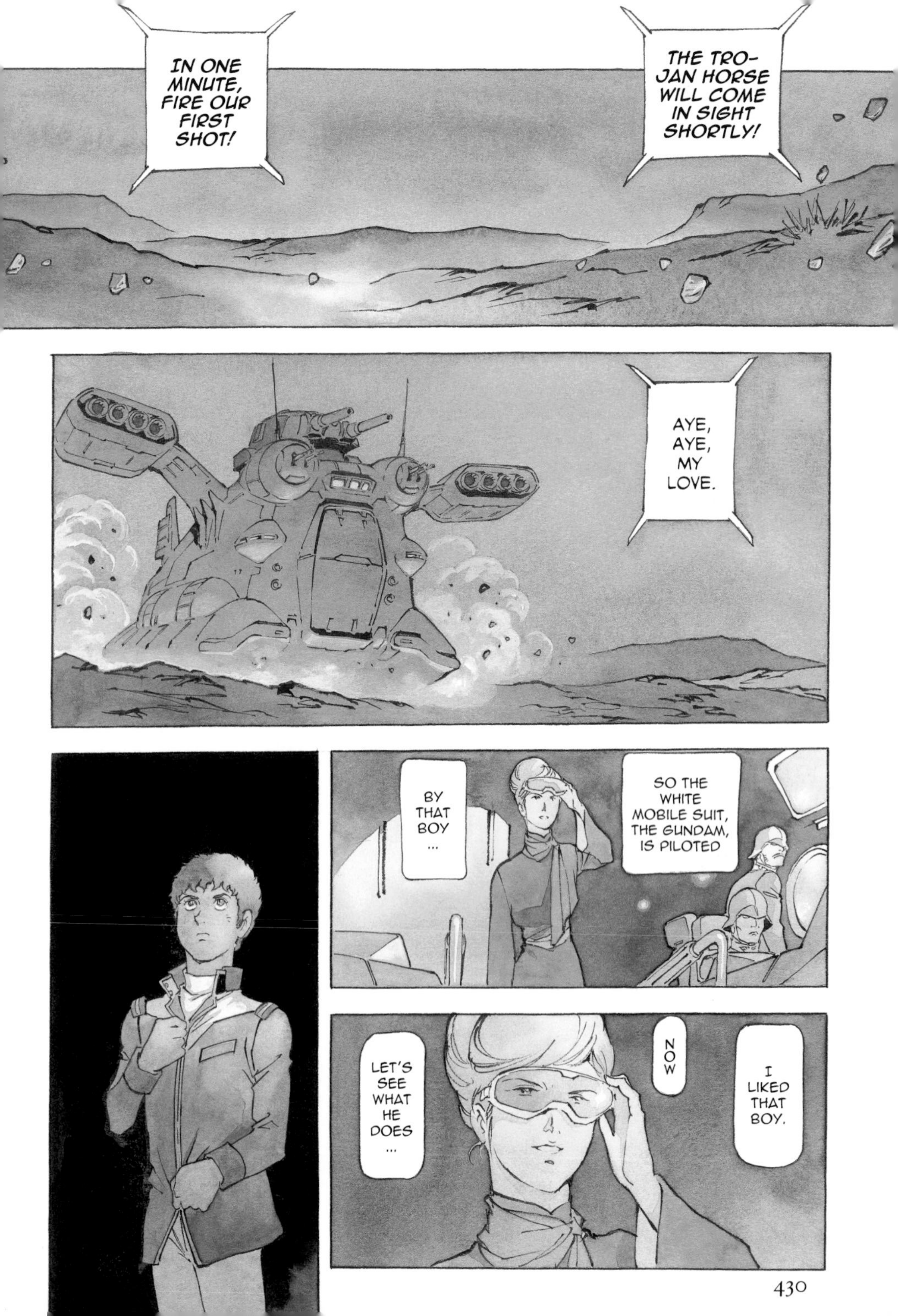
THE TROJAN HORSE WILL COME IN SIGHT SHORTLY!
IN ONE MINUTE, FIRE OUR FIRST SHOT!
AYE, AYE, MY LOVE.
SO THE WHITE MOBILE SUIT, THE GUNDAM, IS PILOTED
BY THAT BOY ...
I LIKED THAT BOY.
NOW
LET'S SEE WHAT HE DOES ...

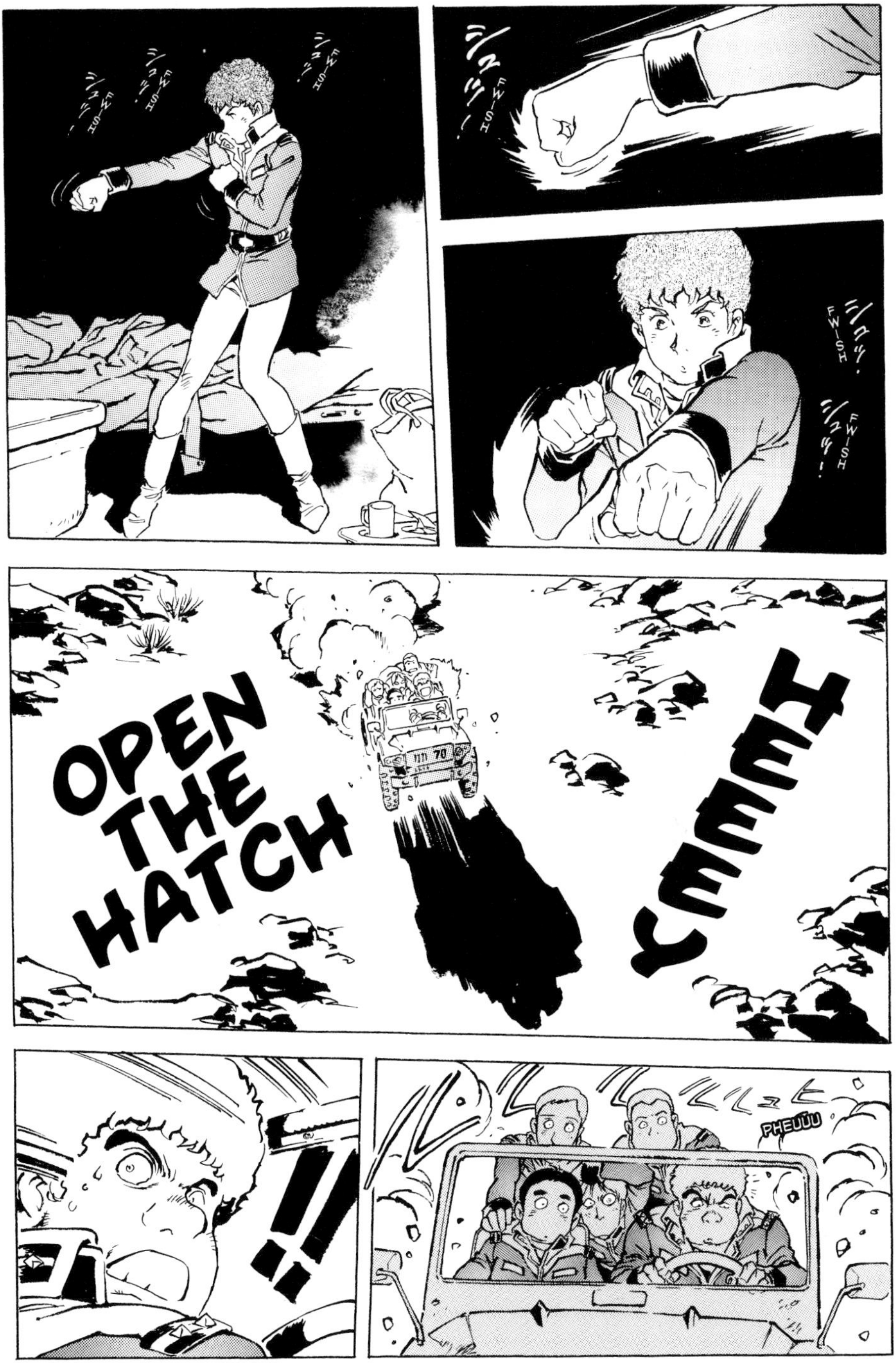
シュッ!
FWISH
シュッ!
FWISH
シュッ!
FWISH
シュッ!
FWISH
シュッ!
FWISH
シュッ!
FWISH
HEEEEY
OPEN THE HATCH
ルルュヒー
PHEUŬU
!!

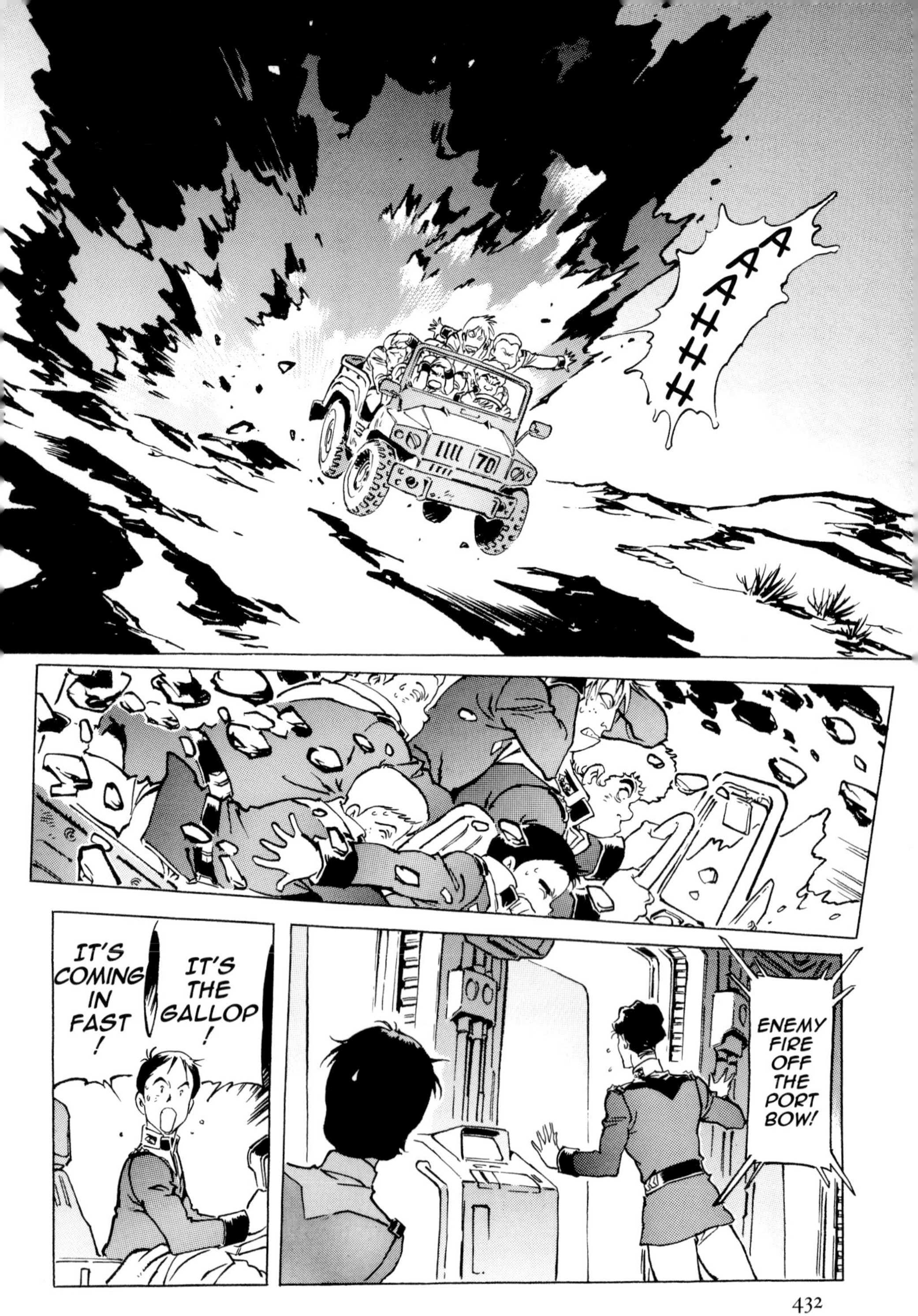
AAAHHHH
ENEMY FIRE OFF THE PORT BOW!
IT'S THE GALLOP!
IT'S COMING IN FAST!

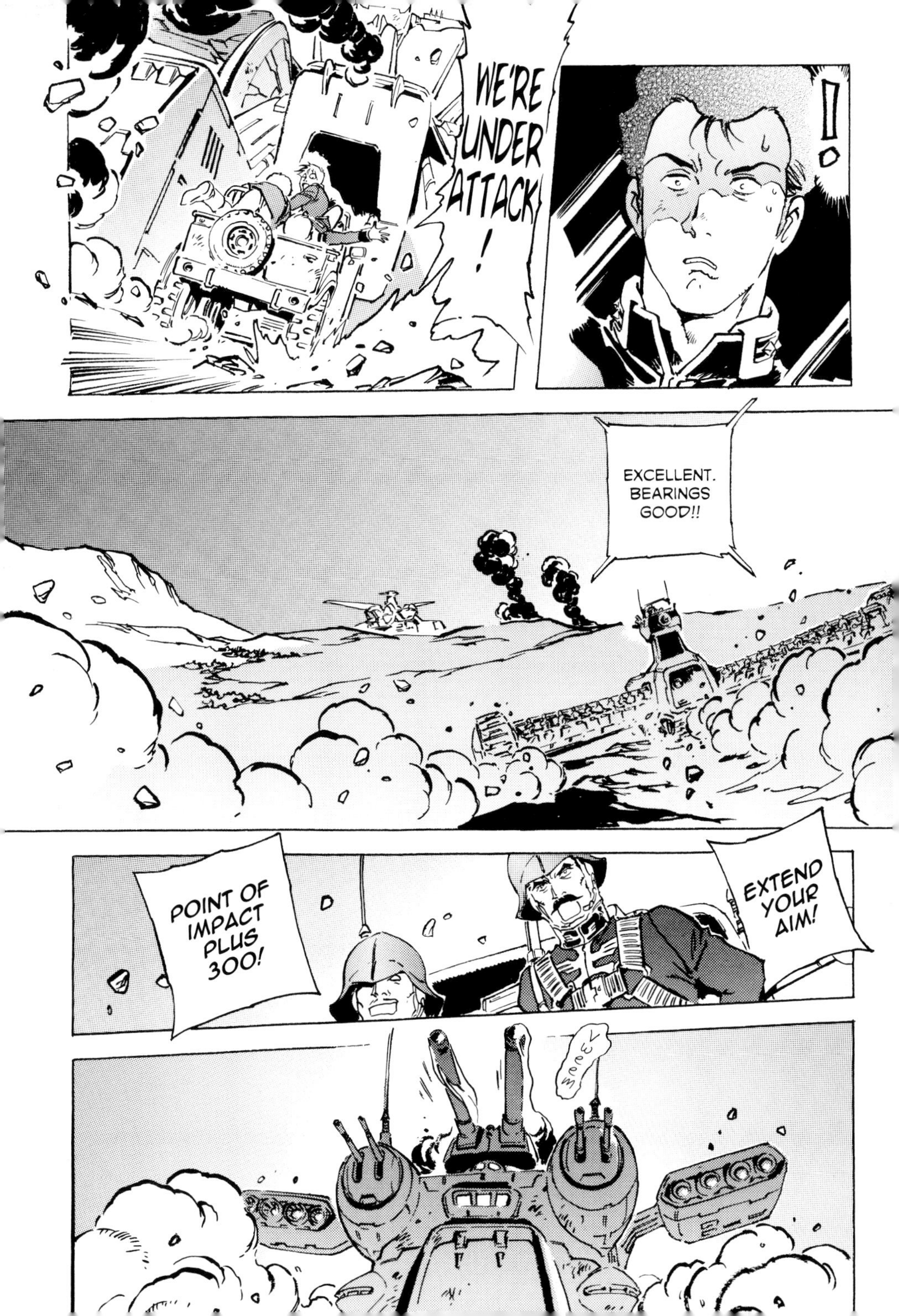
!
WE'RE UNDER ATTACK! !
EXCELLENT. BEARINGS GOOD!!
EXTEND YOUR AIM!
POINT OF IMPACT PLUS 300!
Vweem

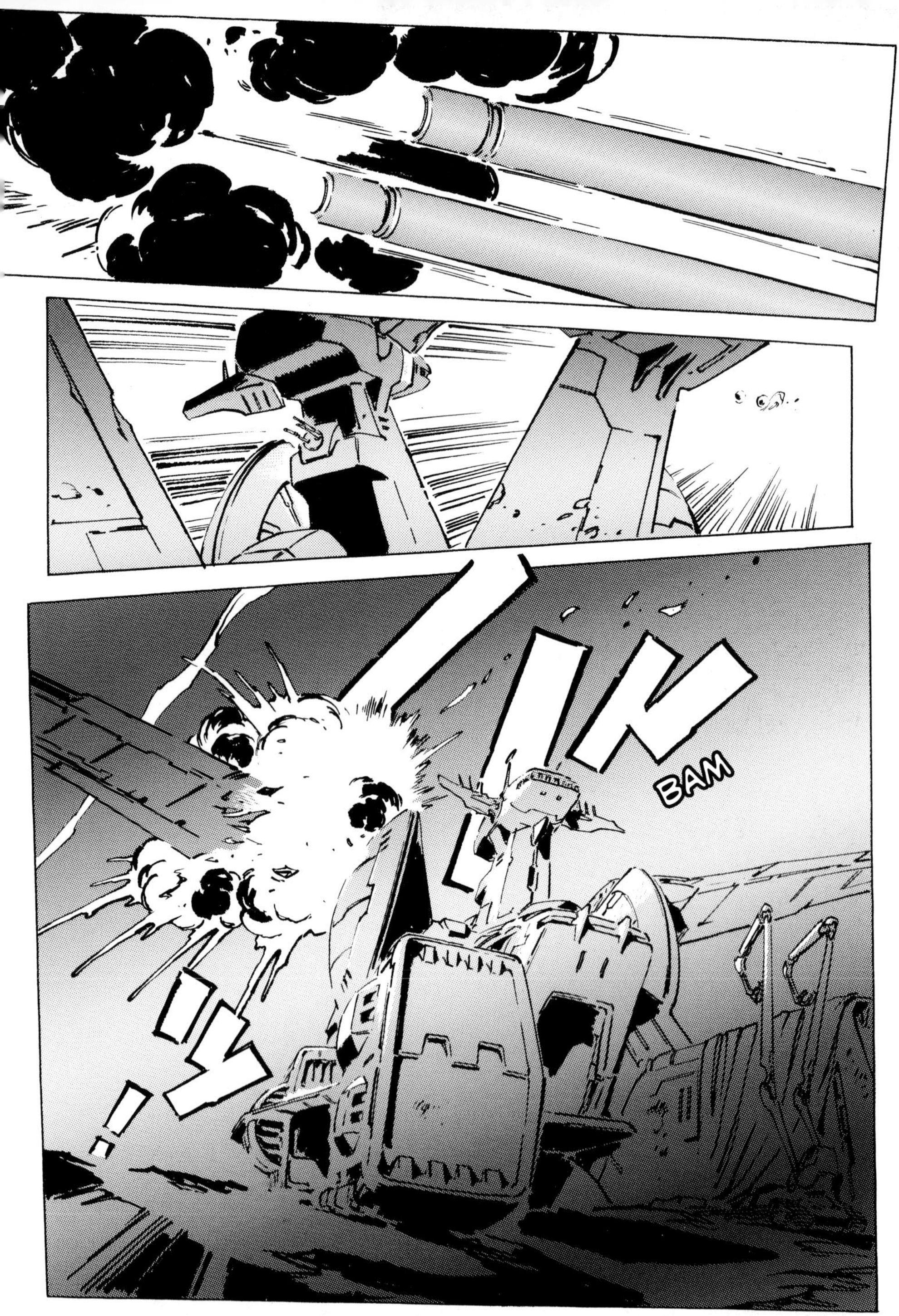
BAM

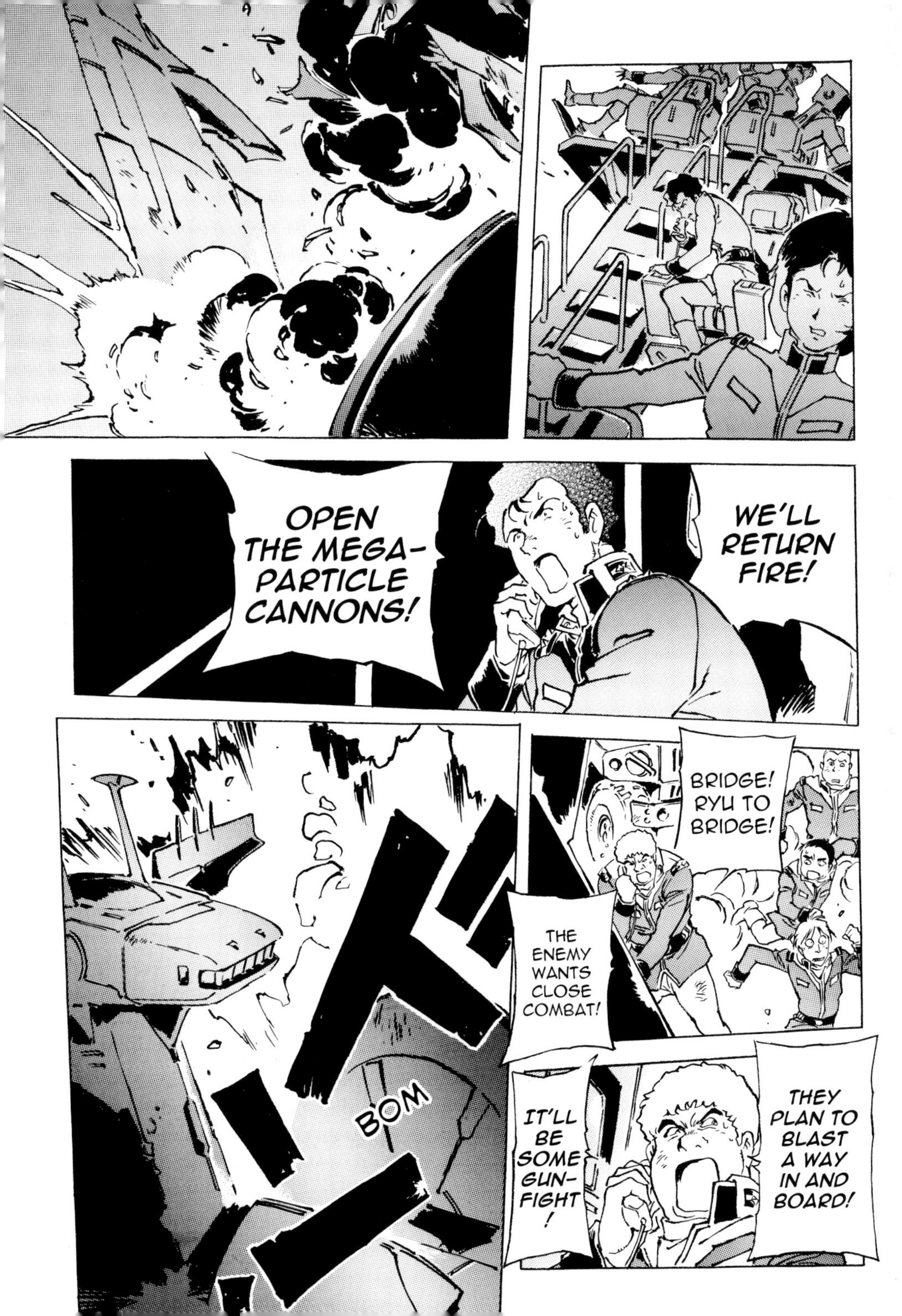
WE'LL RETURN FIRE!
OPEN THE MEGA-PARTICLE CANNONS!
BRIDGE! RYU TO BRIDGE!
THE ENEMY WANTS CLOSE COMBAT!
THEY PLAN TO BLAST A WAY IN AND BOARD!
IT'LL BE SOME GUN-FIGHT!
BOM

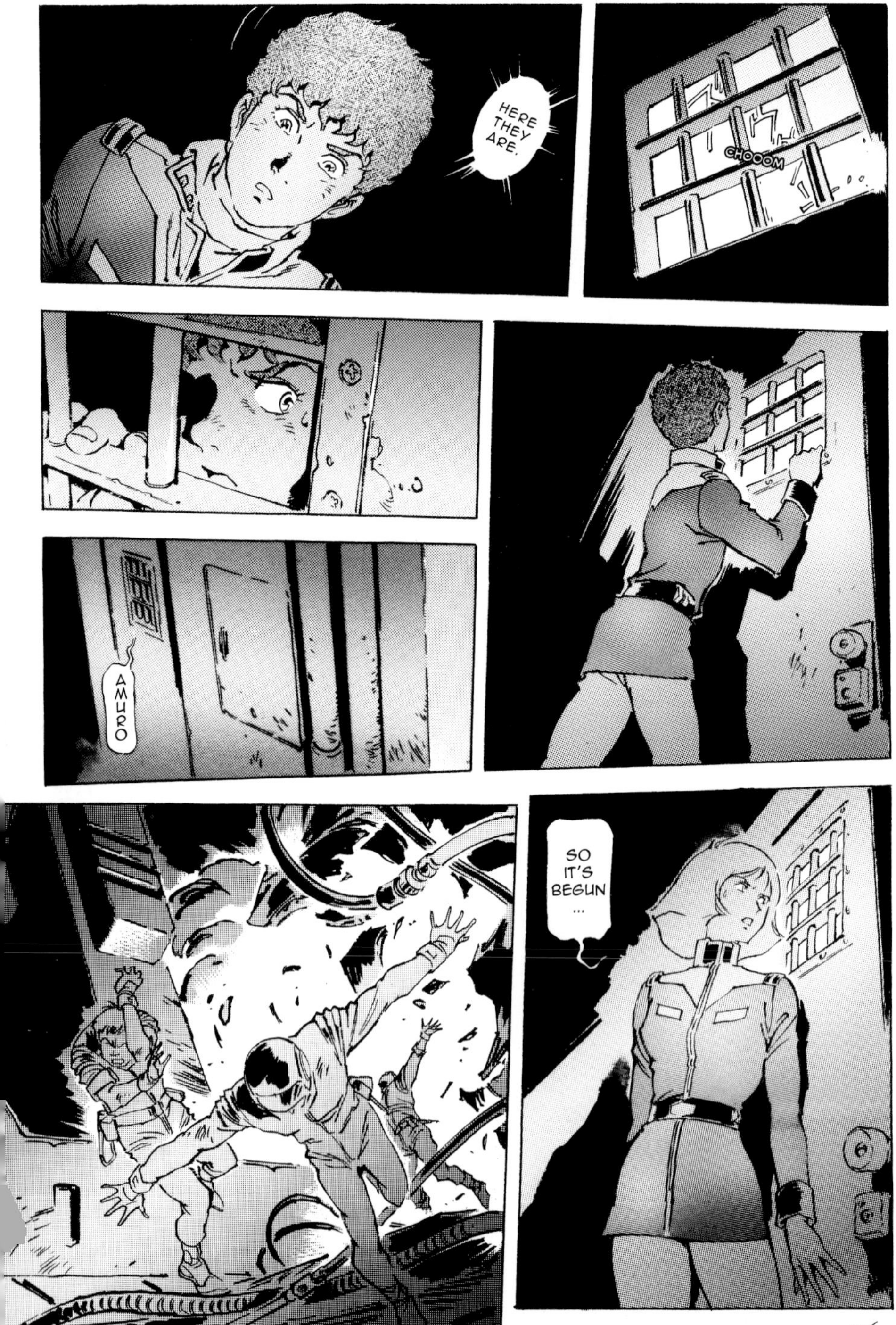
CHOOOM
HERE THEY ARE.
AMURO
SO IT'S BEGUN ...

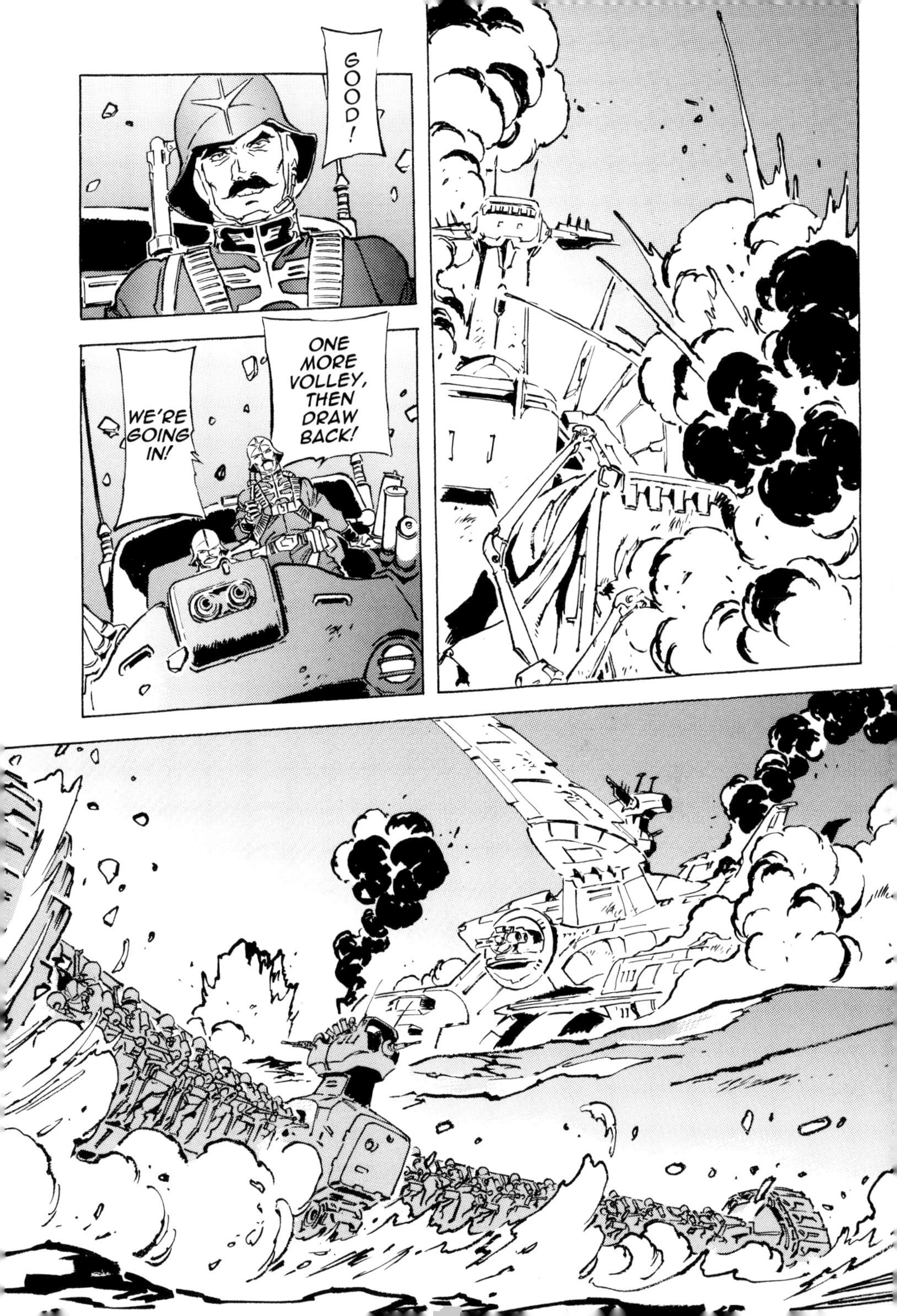
GOOD!
ONE MORE VOLLEY, THEN DRAW BACK!
WE'RE GOING IN!

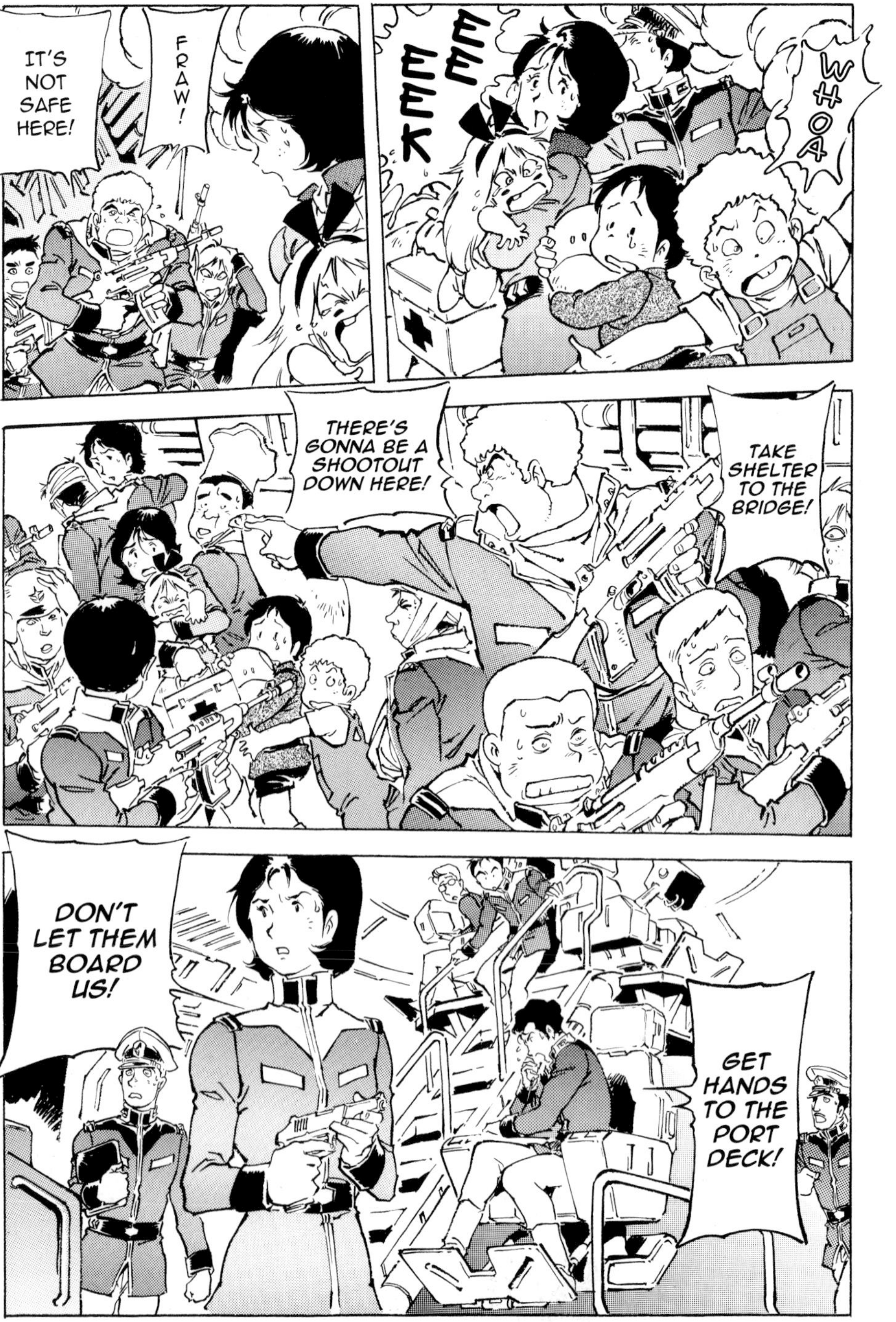
WHOA
EEEEK
FRAW!
IT'S NOT SAFE HERE!
TAKE SHELTER TO THE BRIDGE!
THERE'S GONNA BE A SHOOTOUT DOWN HERE!
GET HANDS TO THE PORT DECK!
DON'T LET THEM BOARD US!

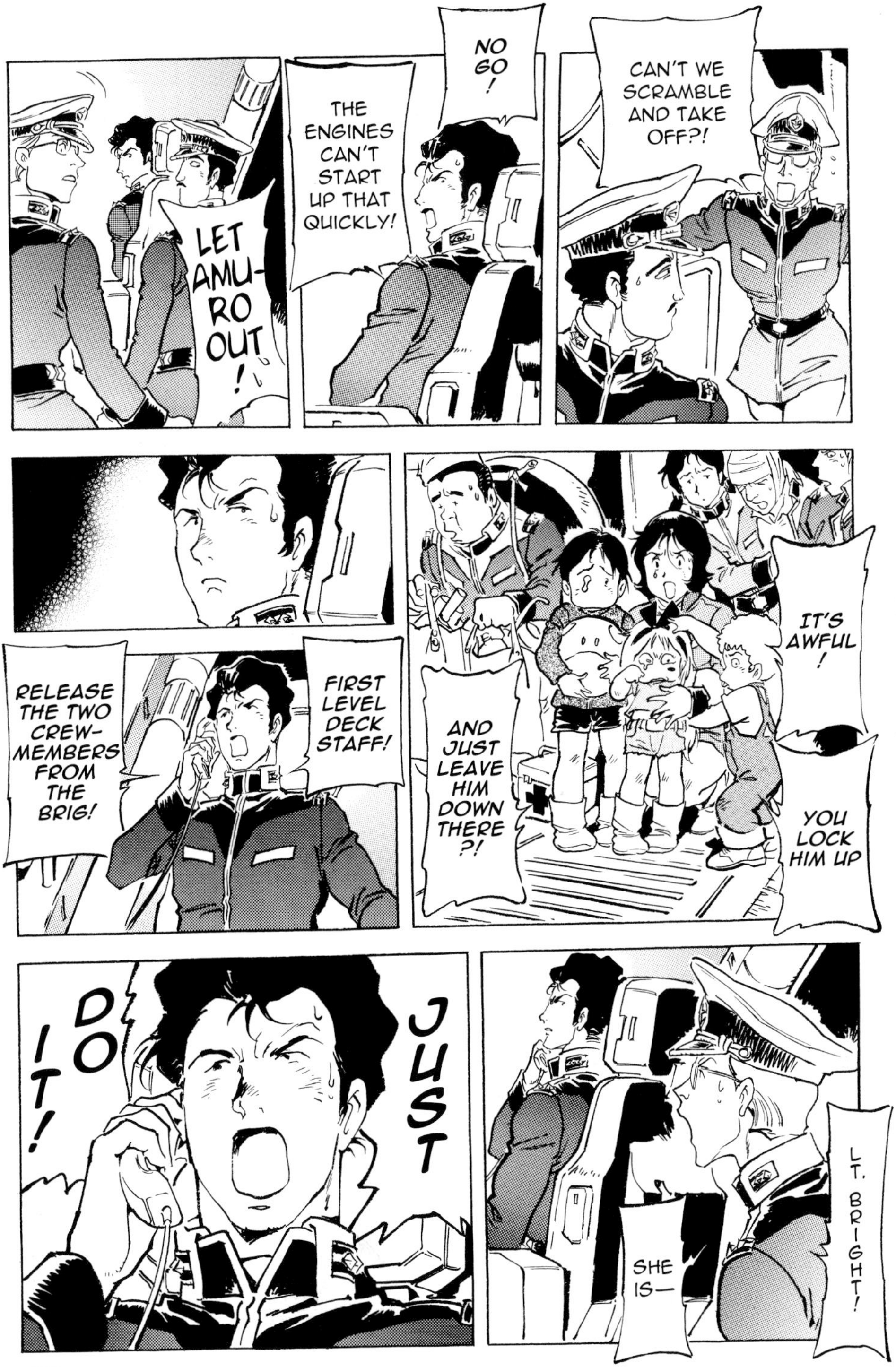
CAN'T WE SCRAMBLE AND TAKE OFF?!
NO GO!
THE ENGINES CAN'T START UP THAT QUICKLY!
LET AMURO OUT!
IT'S AWFUL!
YOU LOCK HIM UP
AND JUST LEAVE HIM DOWN THERE?!
FIRST LEVEL DECK STAFF!
RELEASE THE TWO CREWMEMBERS FROM THE BRIG!
LT. BRIGHT!
SHE IS—
JUST DO IT!

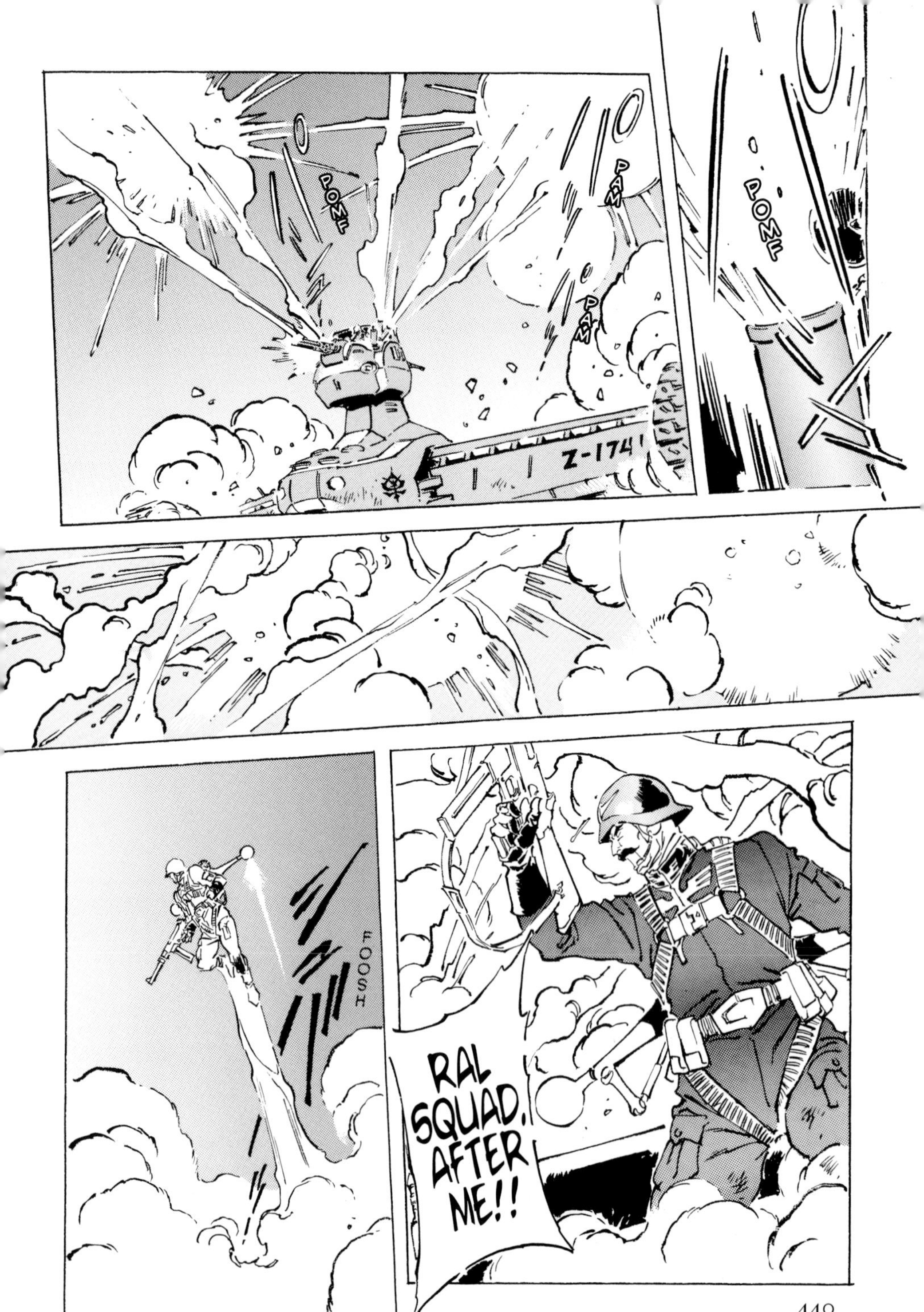
POMF
POMF
PAM
PAM
Z-174
RAL SQUAD, AFTER ME!!
FOOSH

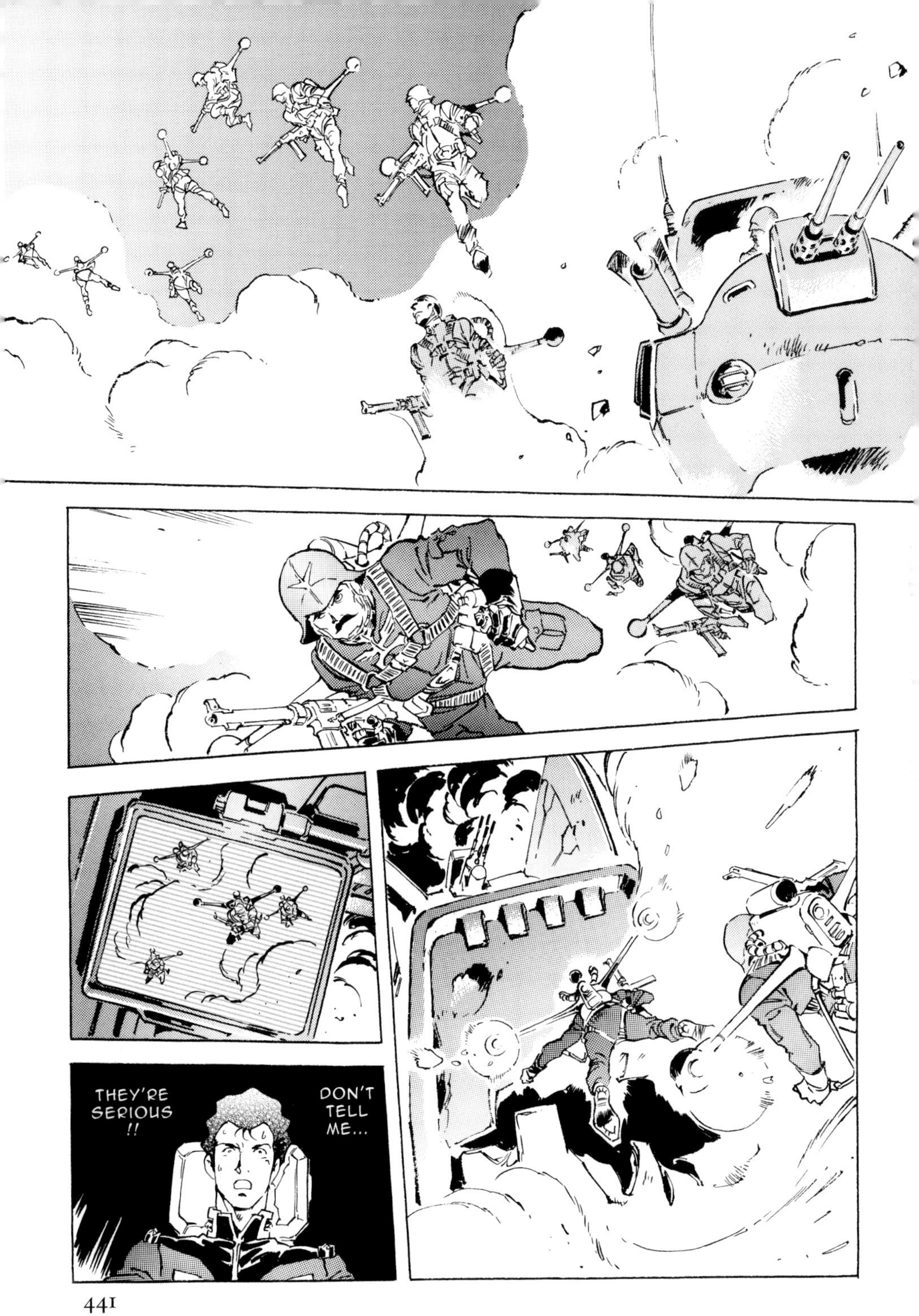
DON'T TELL ME...
THEY'RE SERIOUS !!

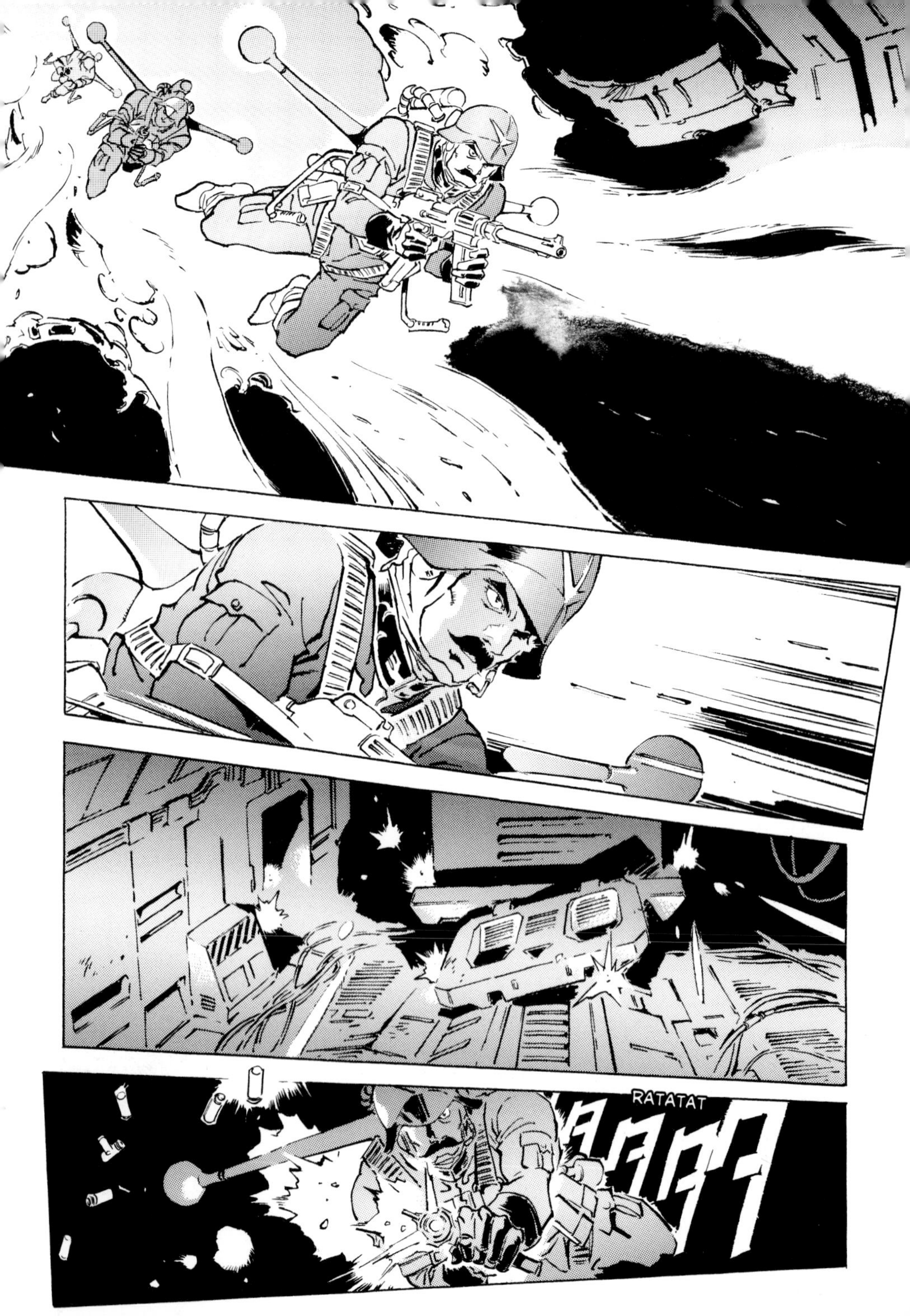
RATATAT

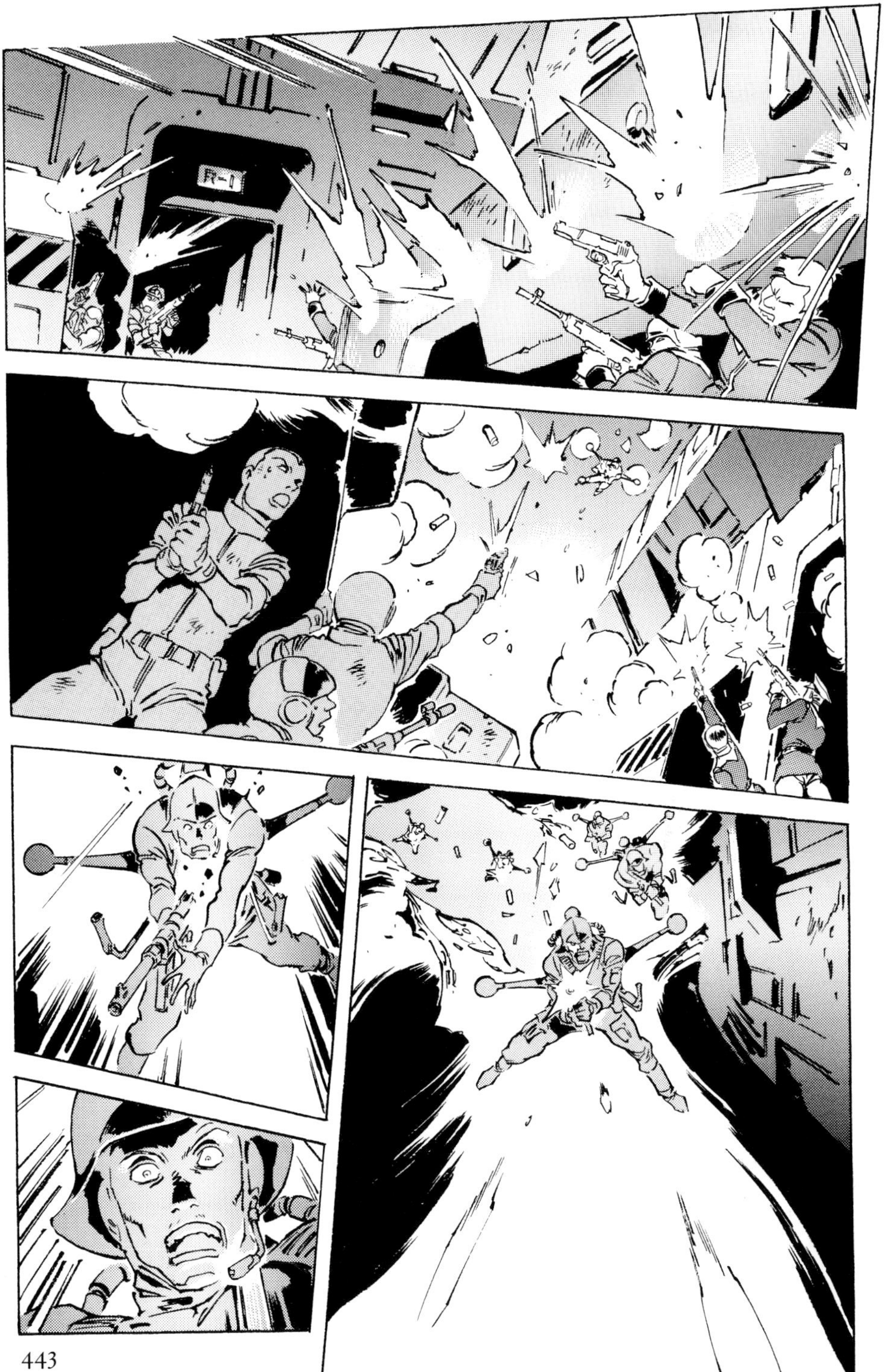
R-1

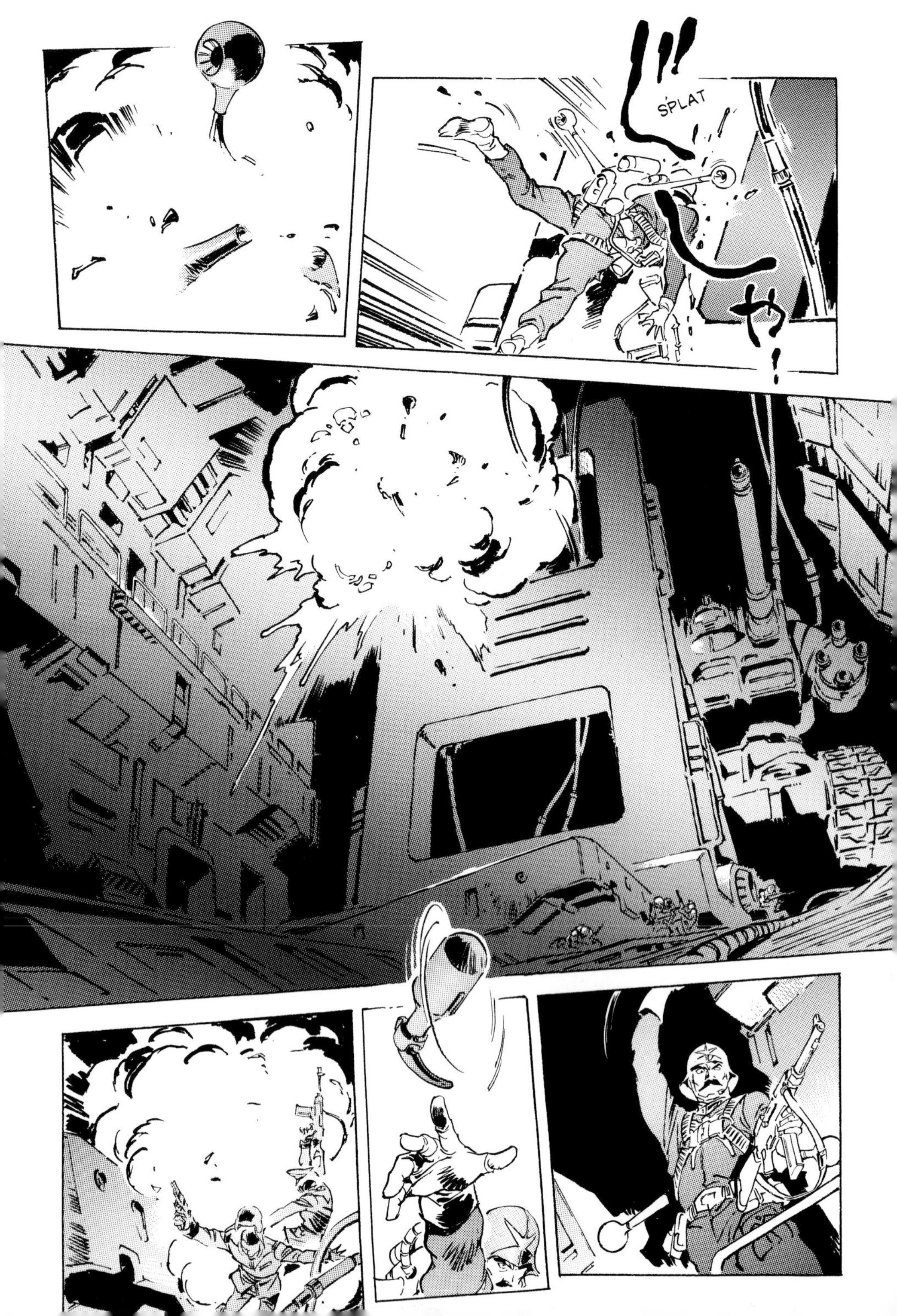
SPLAT

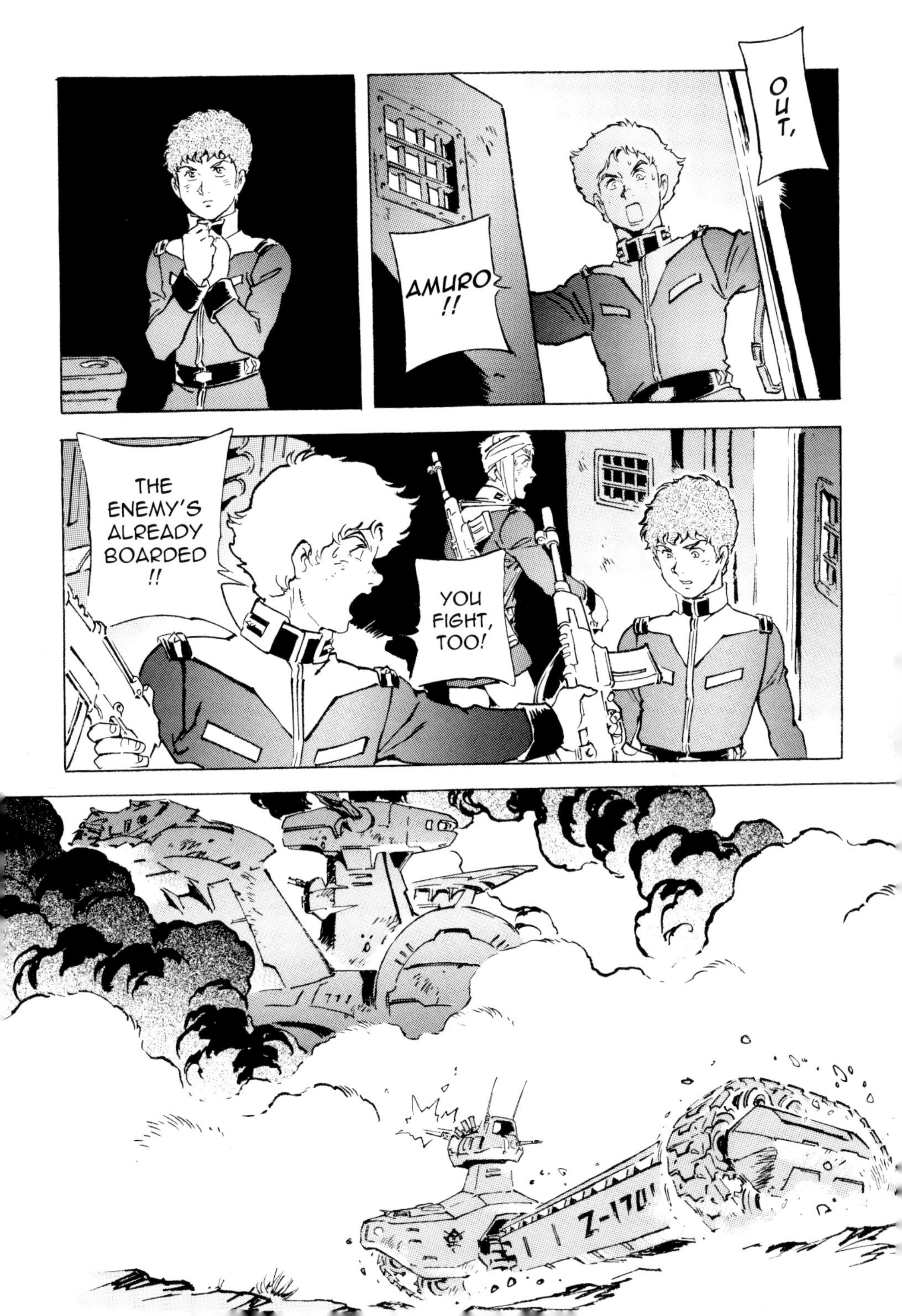
OUT,
AMURO!!
THE ENEMY'S ALREADY BOARDED!!
YOU FIGHT, TOO!
Z-170'

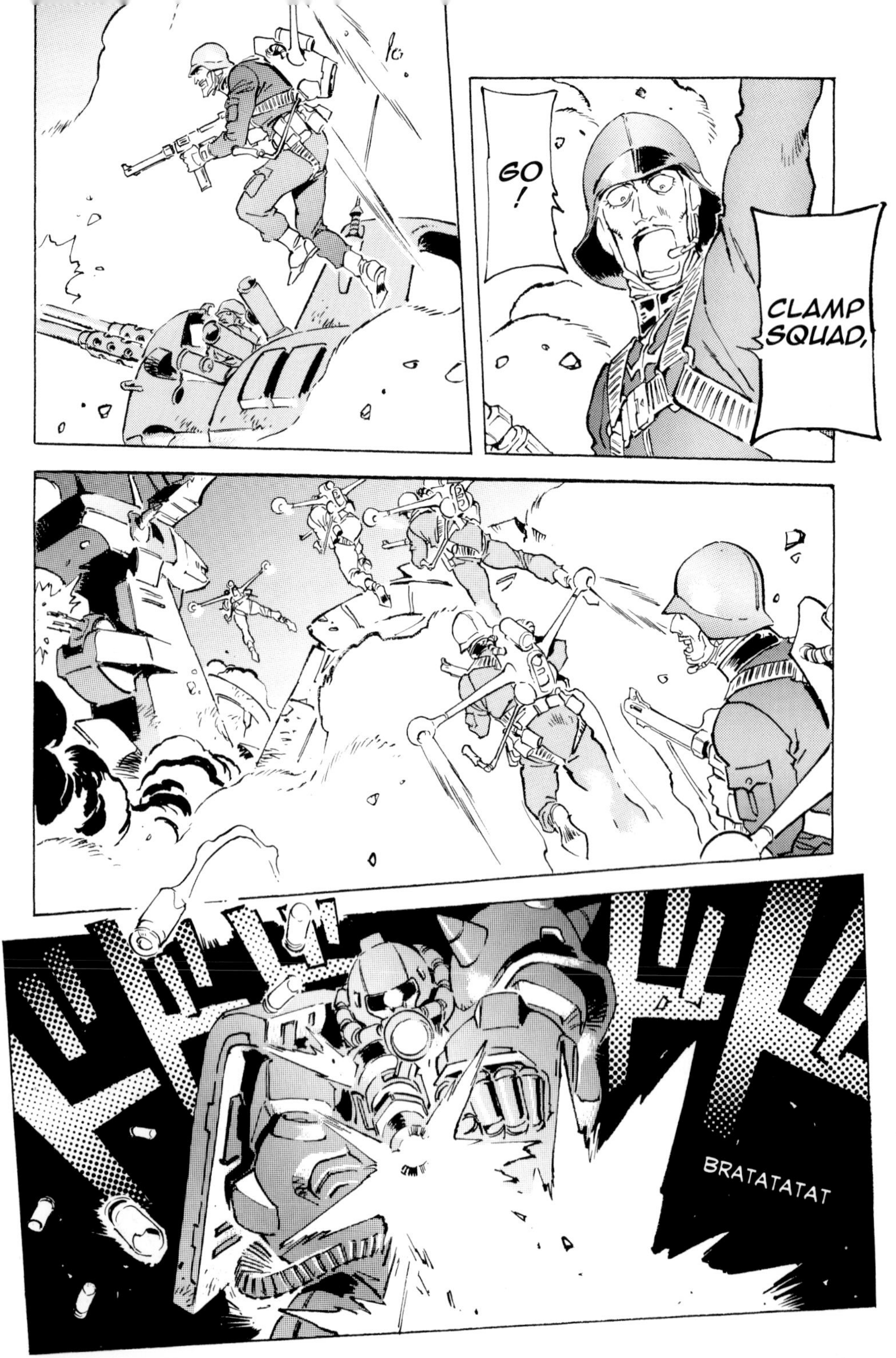
CLAMP SQUAD,
GO!
BRATATATAT

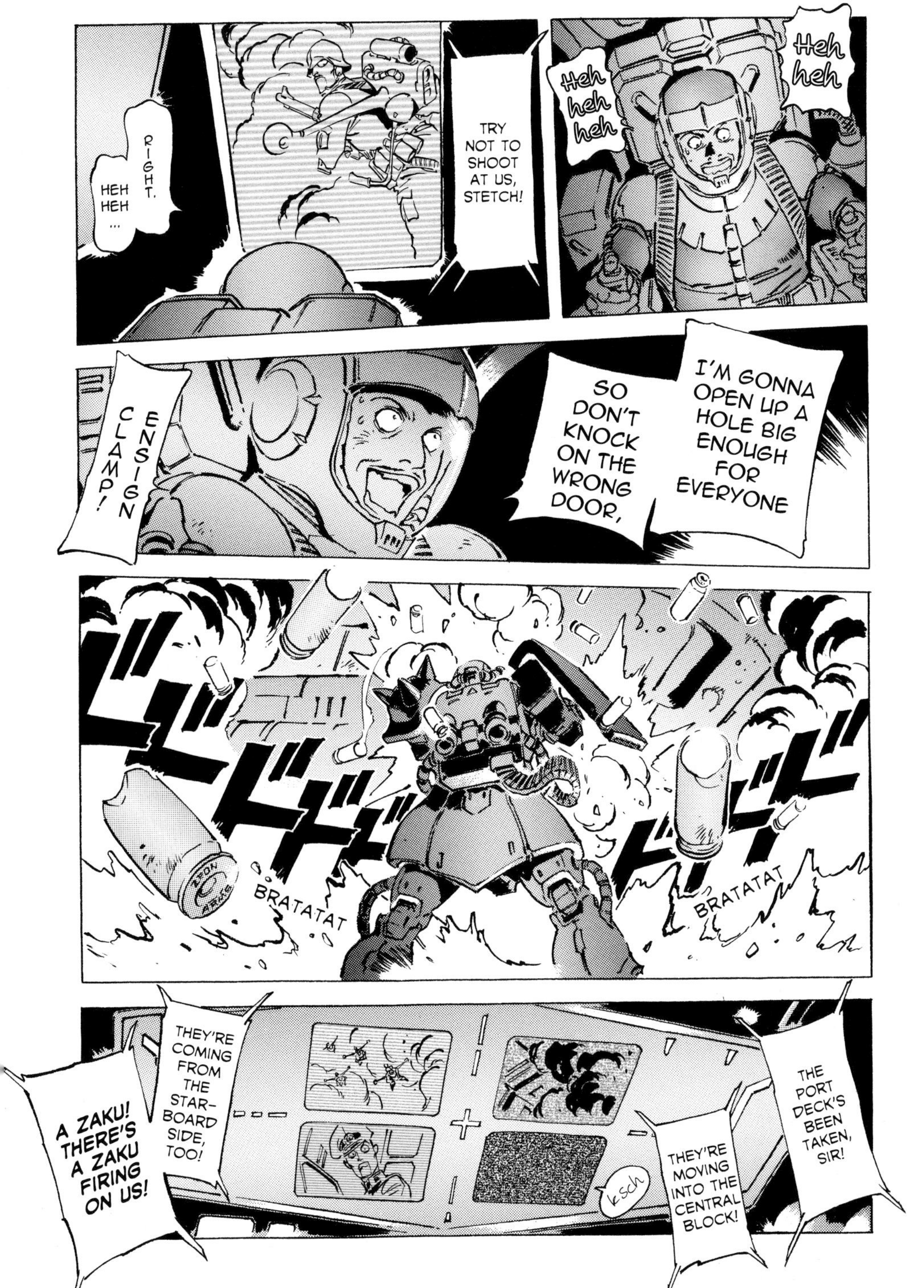
Heh heh
Heh heh heh
TRY NOT TO SHOOT AT US, STETCH!
RIGHT.
HEH HEH ...
I'M GONNA OPEN UP A HOLE BIG ENOUGH FOR EVERYONE
SO DON'T KNOCK ON THE WRONG DOOR,
ENSIGN CLAMP!
BRATATAT
BRATATAT
THE PORT DECK'S BEEN TAKEN, SIR!
THEY'RE MOVING INTO THE CENTRAL BLOCK!
ksch
THEY'RE COMING FROM THE STAR-BOARD SIDE, TOO!
A ZAKU! THERE'S A ZAKU FIRING ON US!

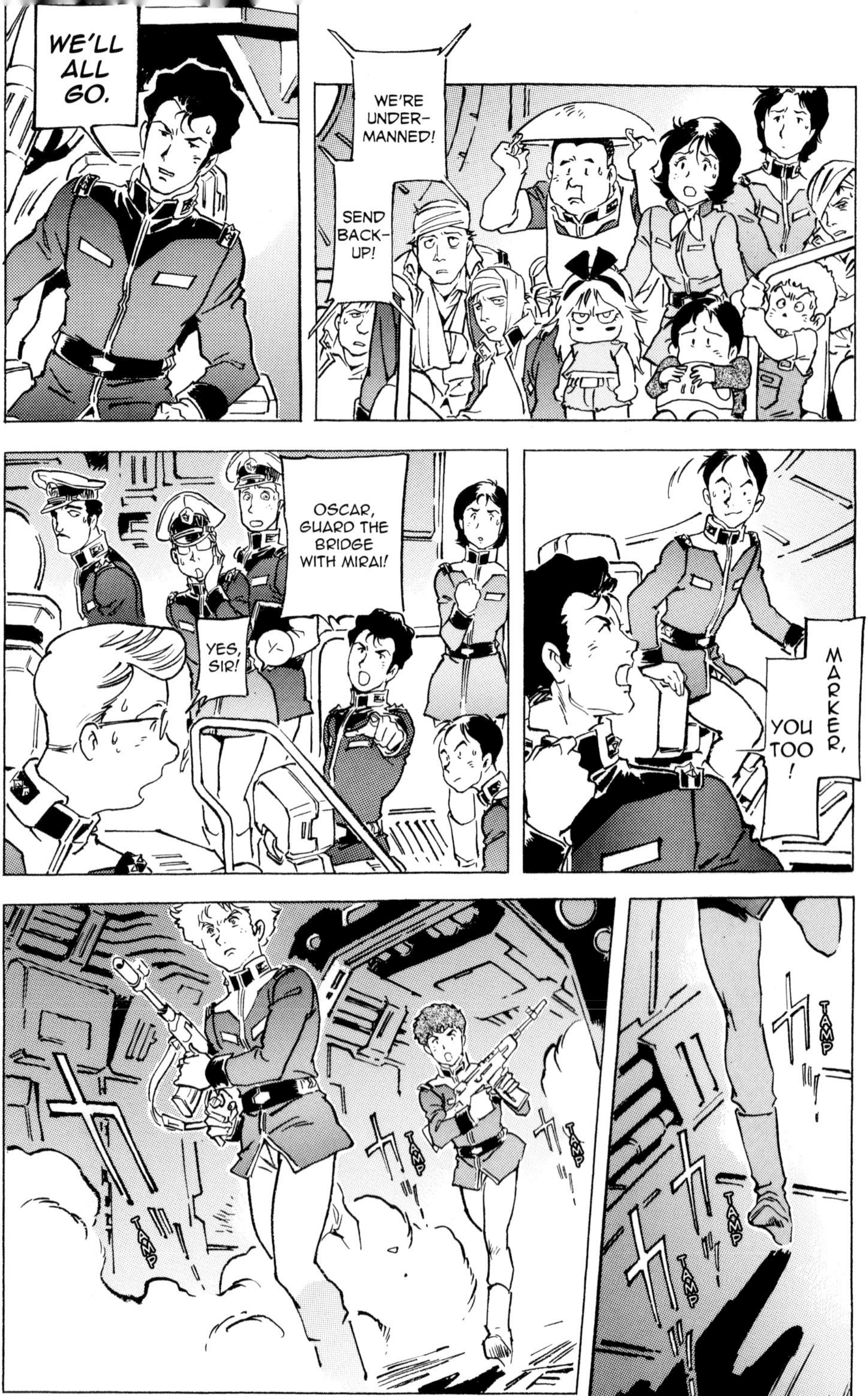
WE'RE UNDER-MANNED!
SEND BACK-UP!
WE'LL ALL GO.
MARKER, YOU TOO!
OSCAR, GUARD THE BRIDGE WITH MIRAI!
YES, SIR!
TAMP
TAMP
TAMP
TAMP
TAMP
TAMP

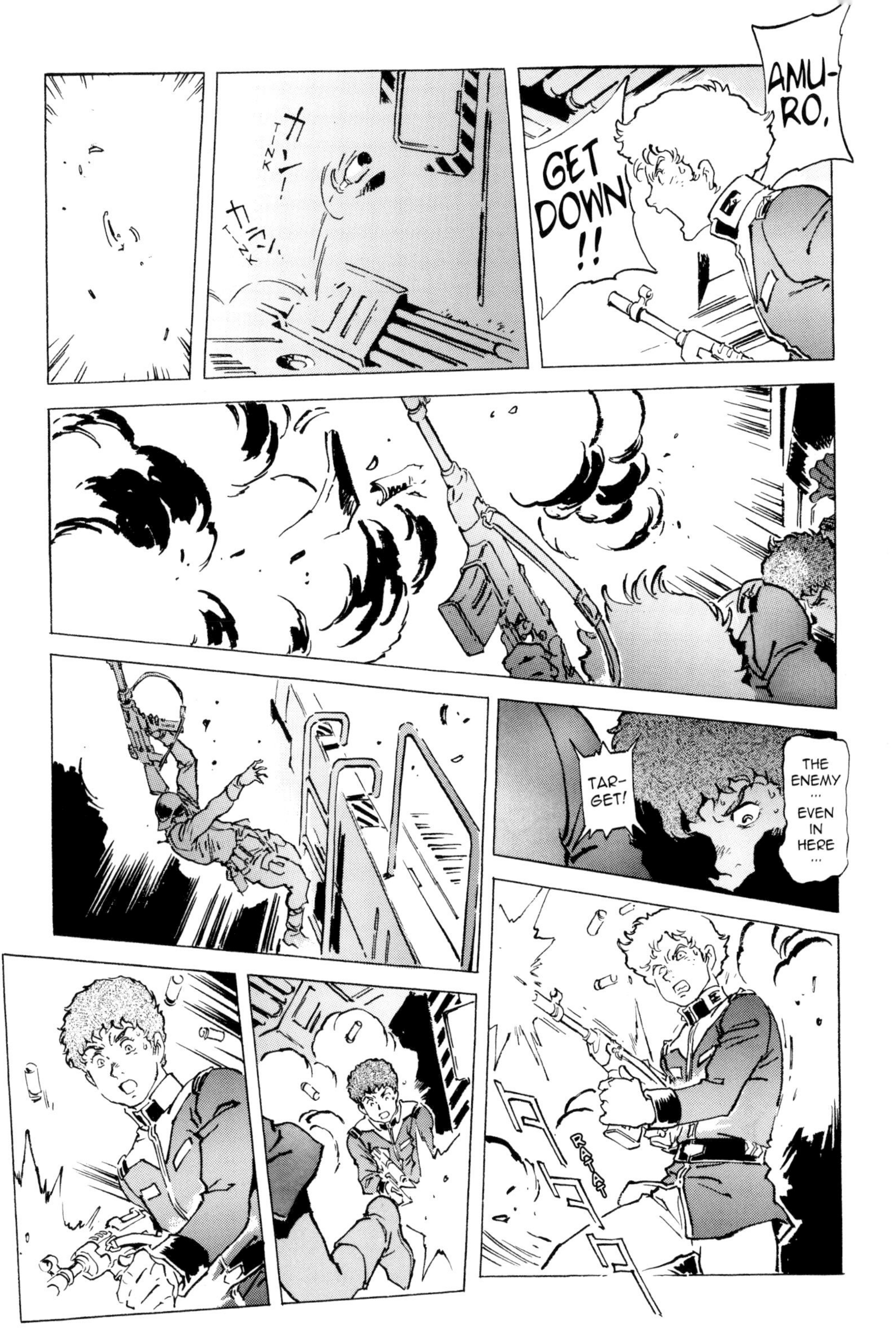
AMU-RO,
GET DOWN!!
TINK
TINK
THE ENEMY ... EVEN IN HERE ...
TAR-GET!
RA-TA-TAT

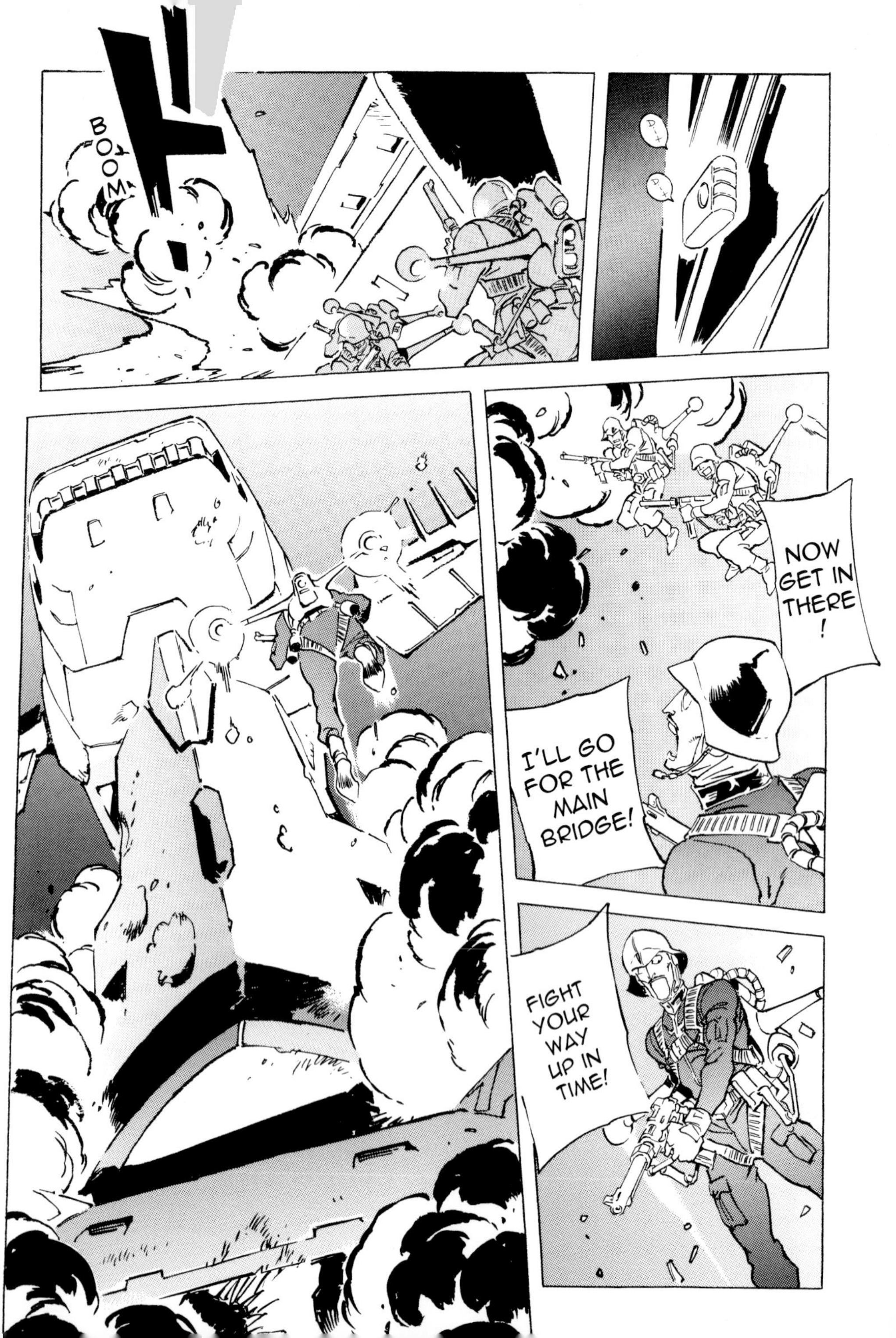
ド
BOOM
NOW GET IN THERE!
I'LL GO FOR THE MAIN BRIDGE!
FIGHT YOUR WAY UP IN TIME!

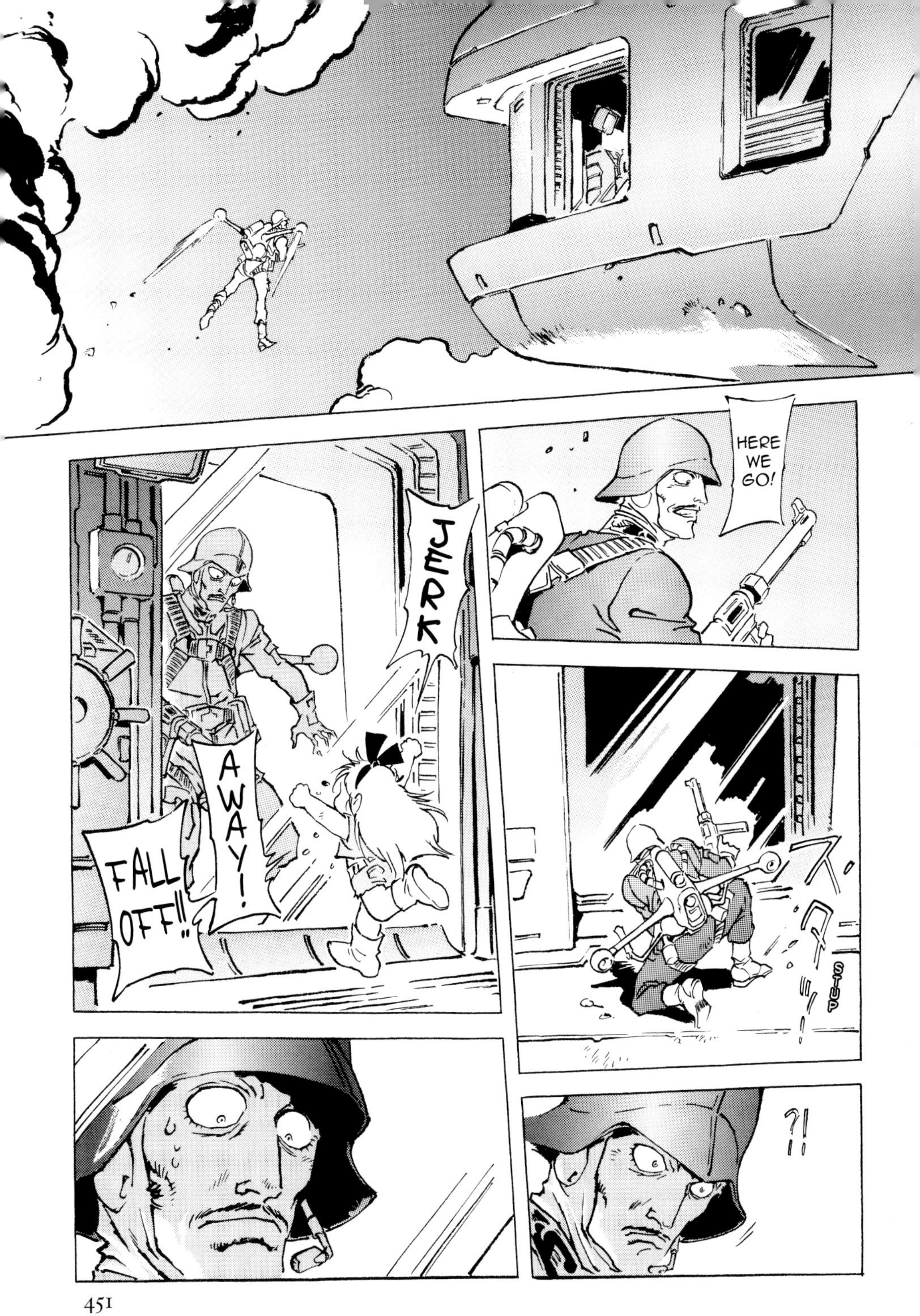

HERE WE GO!
SLIP
JERK
AWAY!
FALL OFF!!
?!

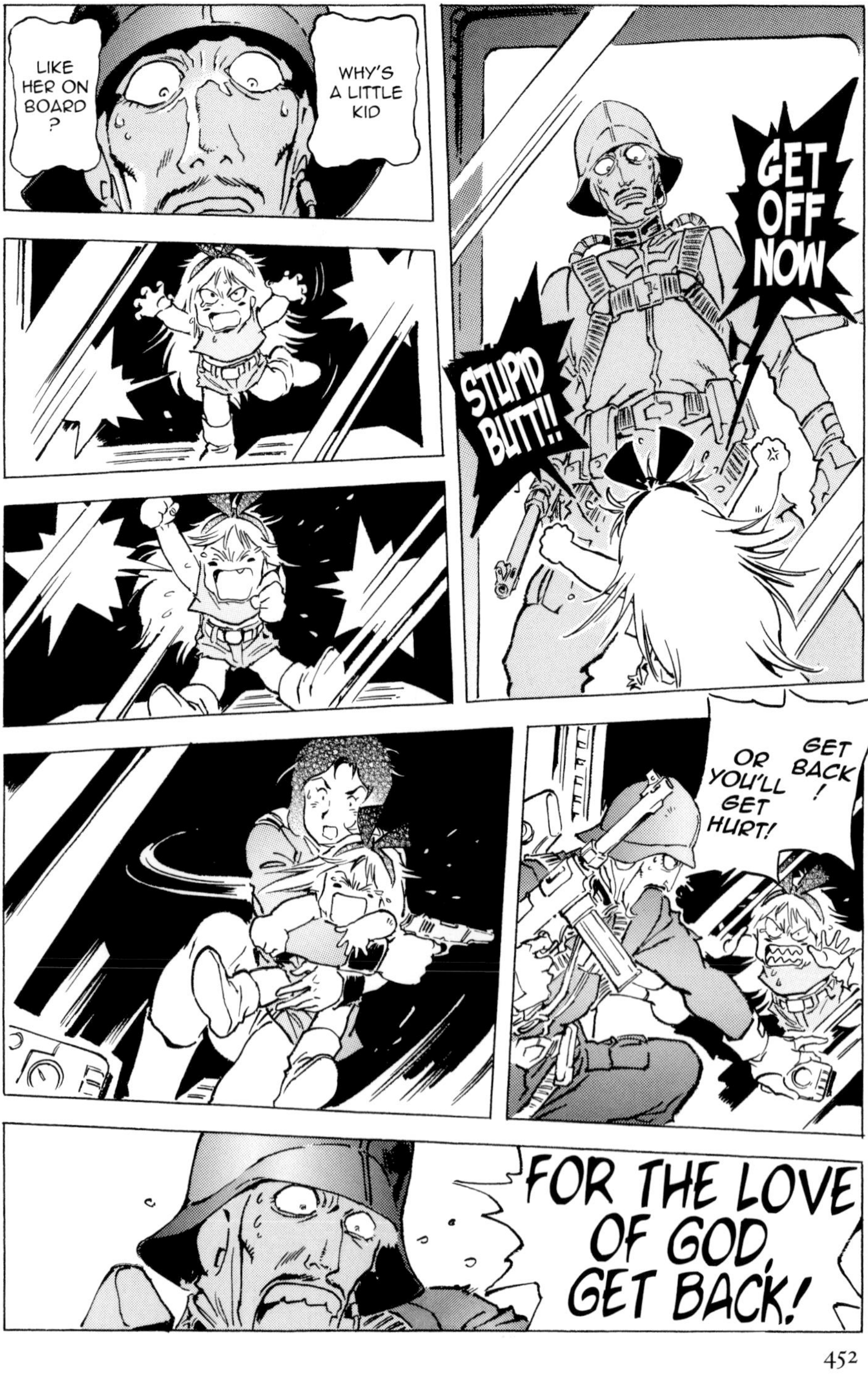
GET OFF NOW
STUPID BUTT!!
WHY'S A LITTLE KID
LIKE HER ON BOARD ?
GET BACK !
OR YOU'LL GET HURT!
FOR THE LOVE OF GOD, GET BACK!

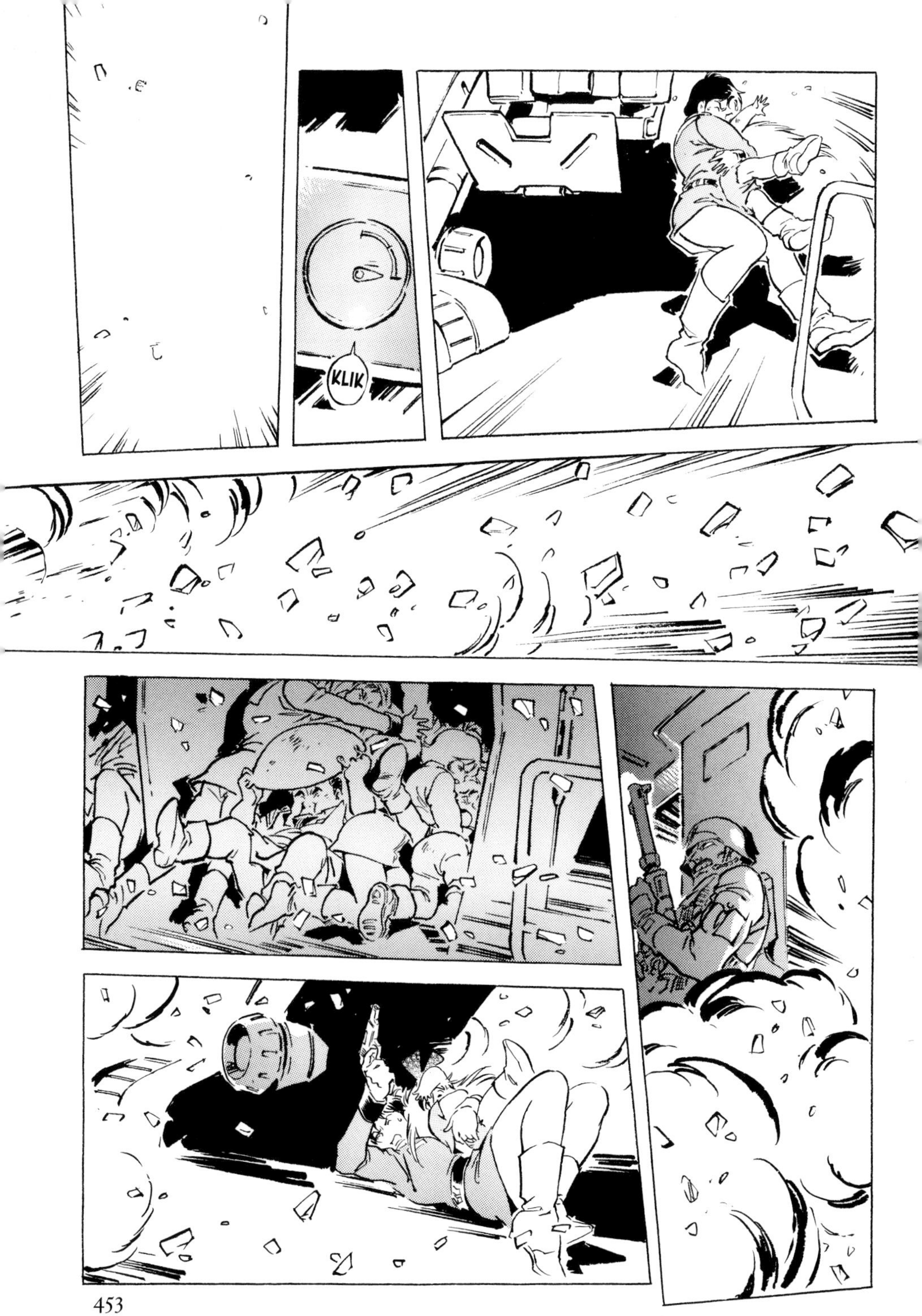
KLIK

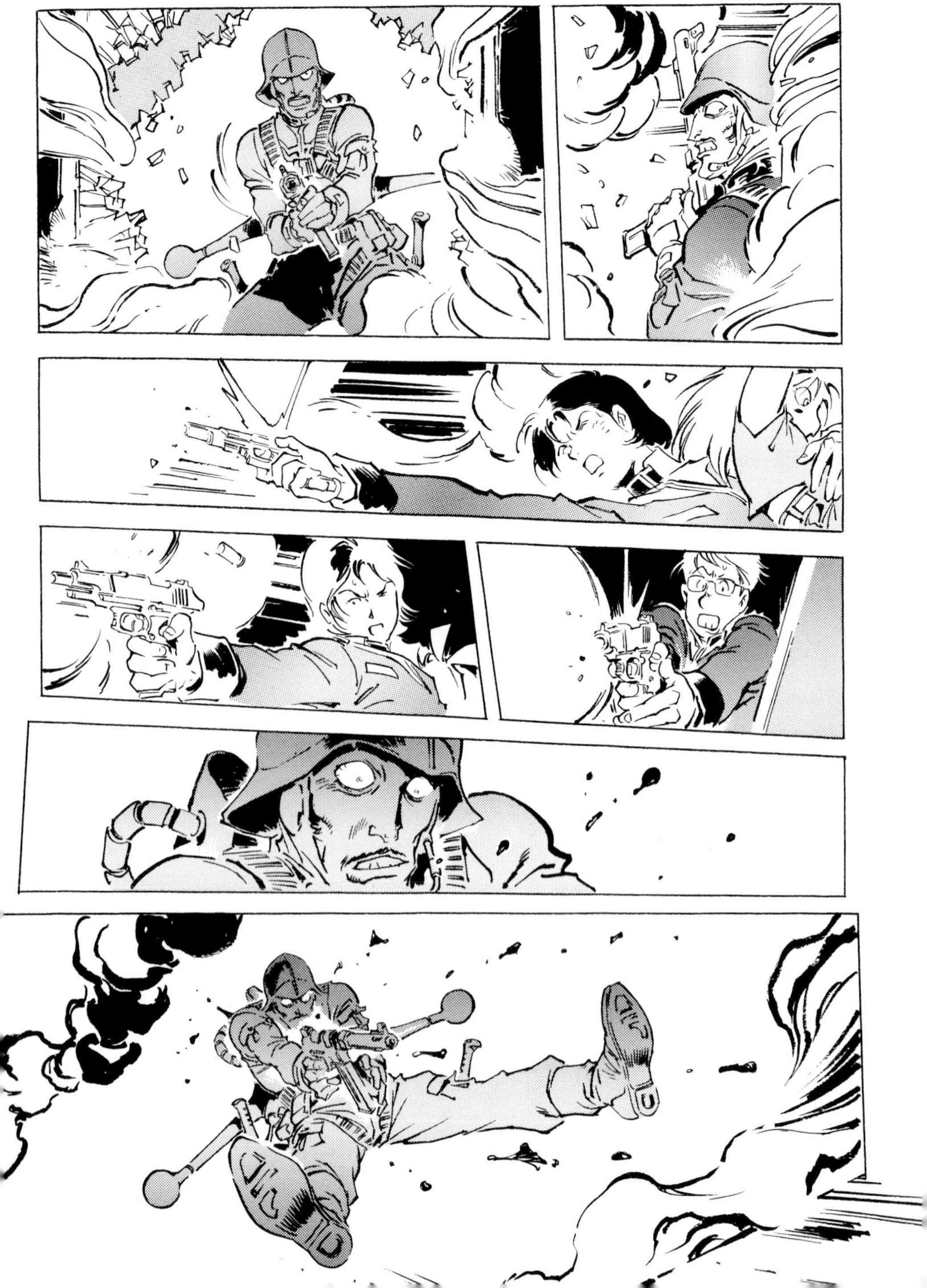

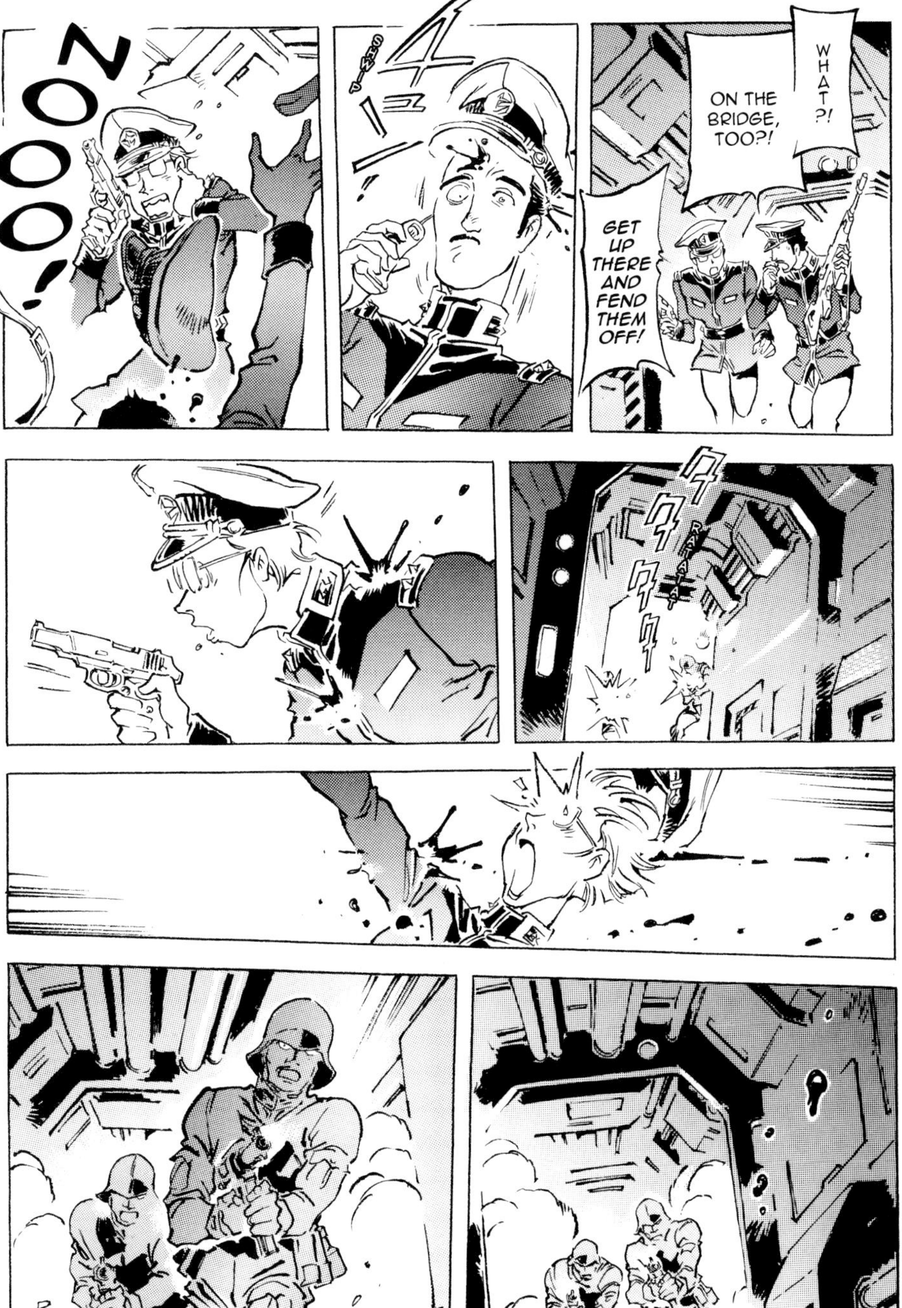
WHAT?!
ON THE BRIDGE, TOO?!
GET UP THERE AND FEND THEM OFF!
SHWIP
NOOOO!
RATATAT

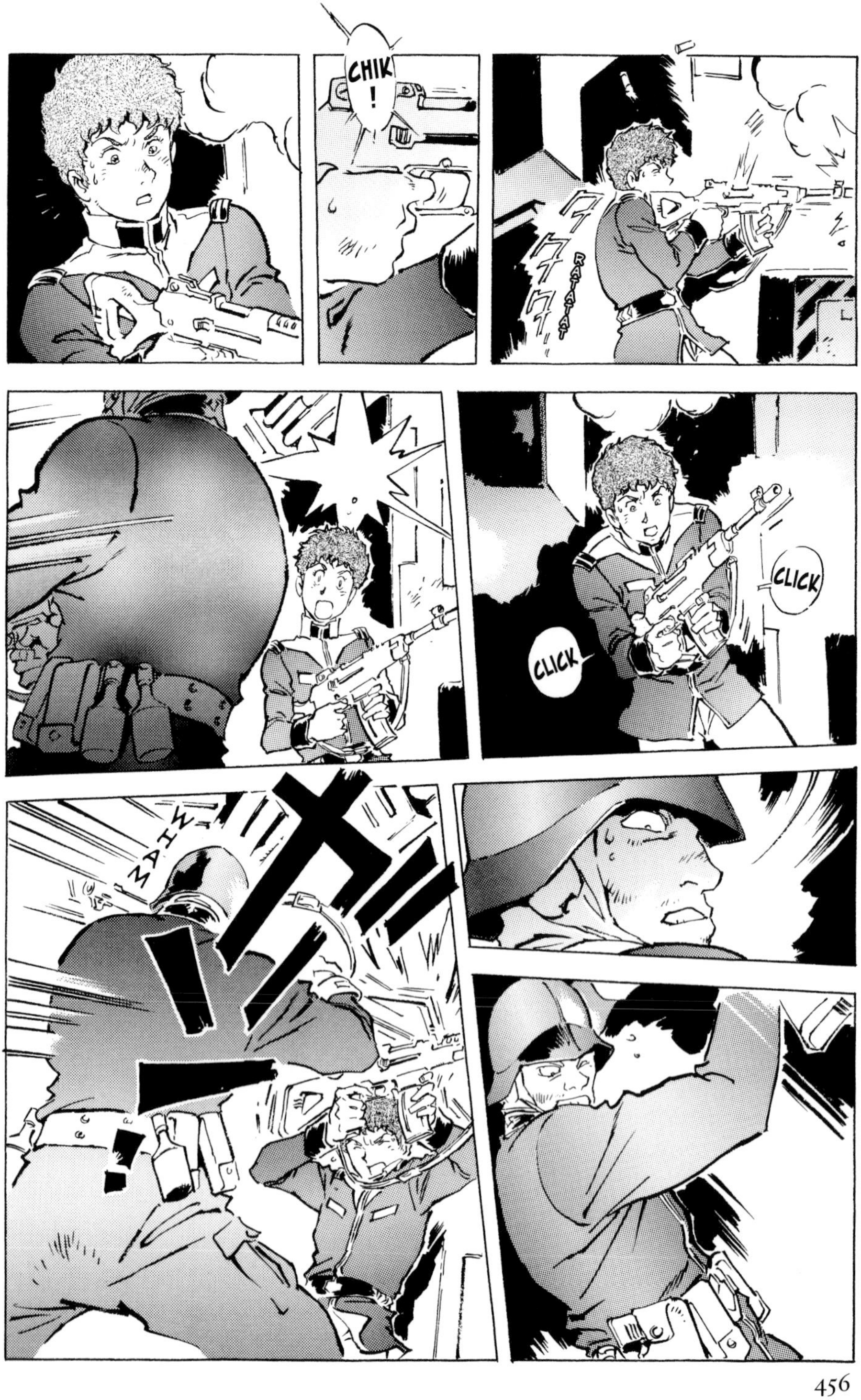
RATATATAT
CHIK
!
CLICK
CLICK
WHAM

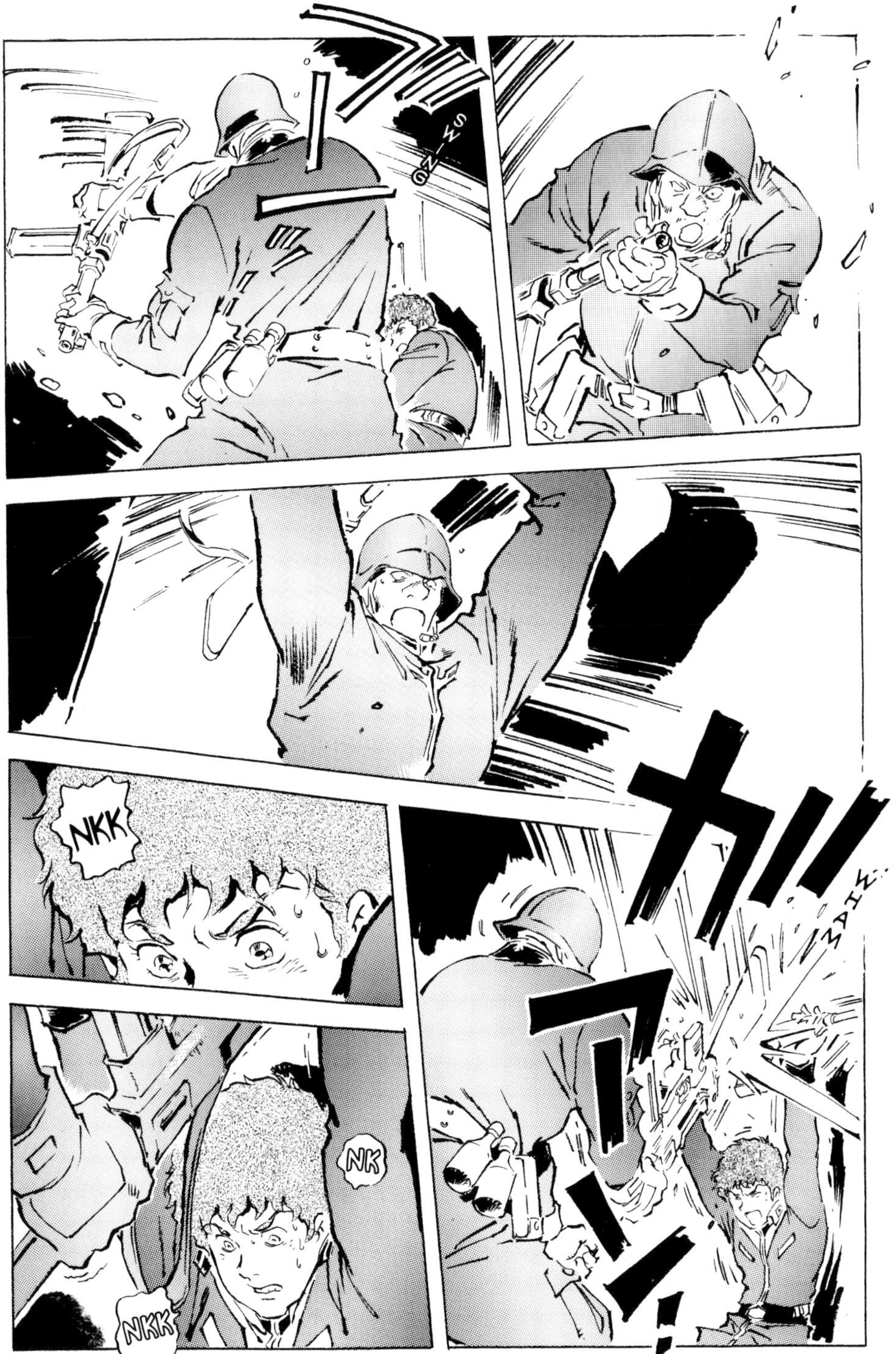
SWING
ガァン!
WHAM
NKK
NK
NKK

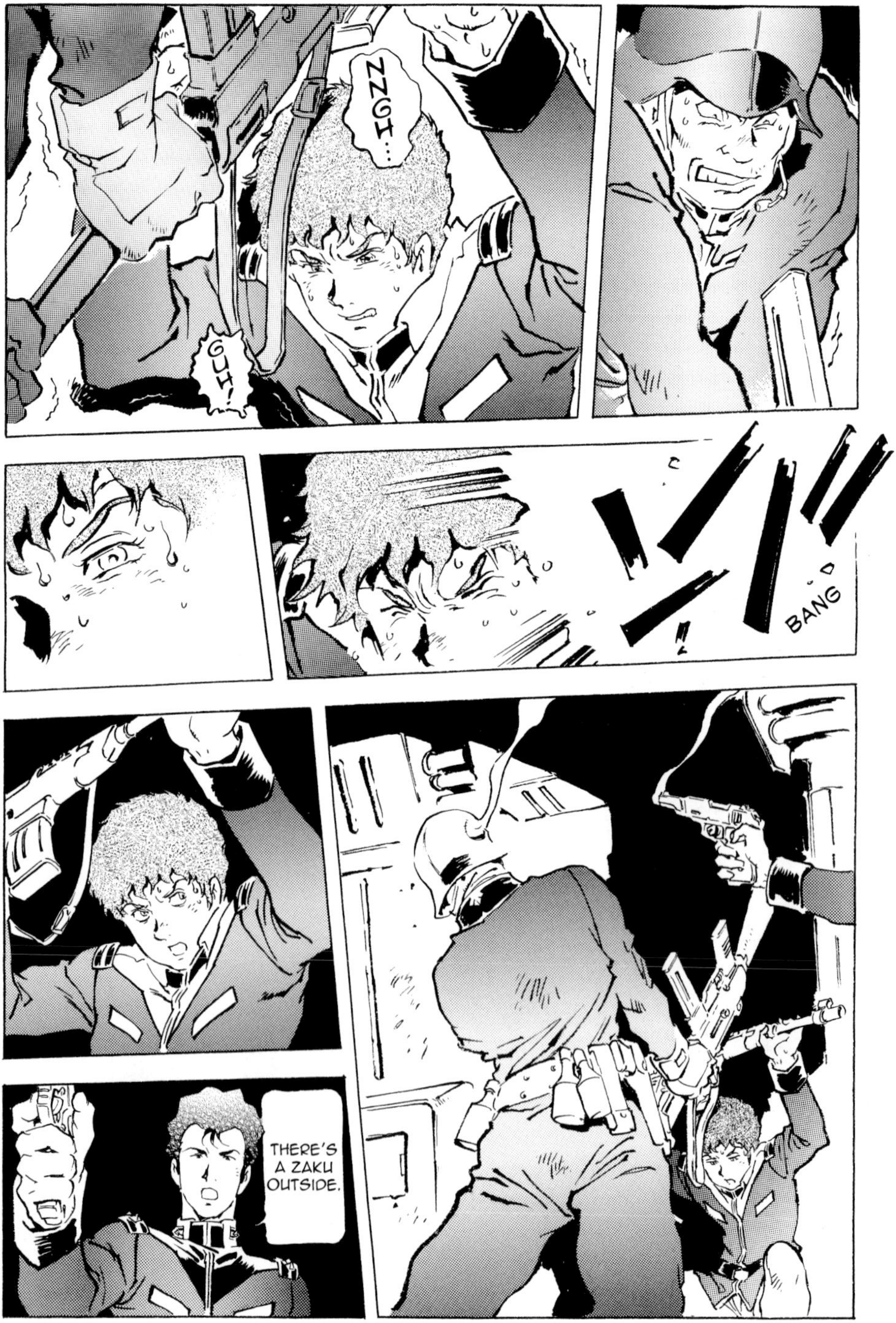
NNGH...
GUH!
BANG
THERE'S A ZAKU OUTSIDE.

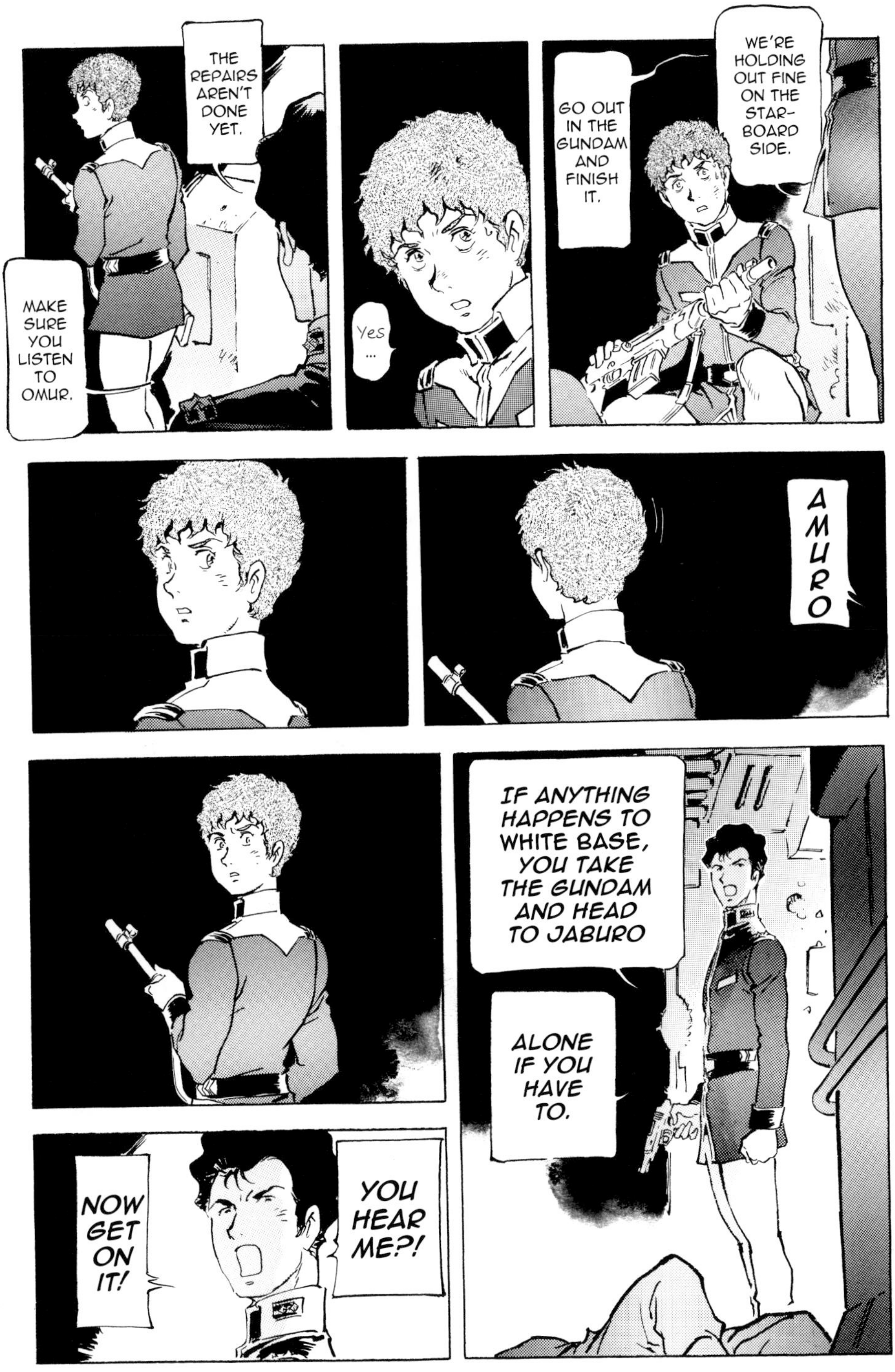
WE'RE HOLDING OUT FINE ON THE STAR-BOARD SIDE.
GO OUT IN THE GUNDAM AND FINISH IT.
Yes ...
THE REPAIRS AREN'T DONE YET.
MAKE SURE YOU LISTEN TO OMUR.
AMURO
IF ANYTHING HAPPENS TO WHITE BASE, YOU TAKE THE GUNDAM AND HEAD TO JABURO
ALONE IF YOU HAVE TO.
YOU HEAR ME?!
NOW GET ON IT!

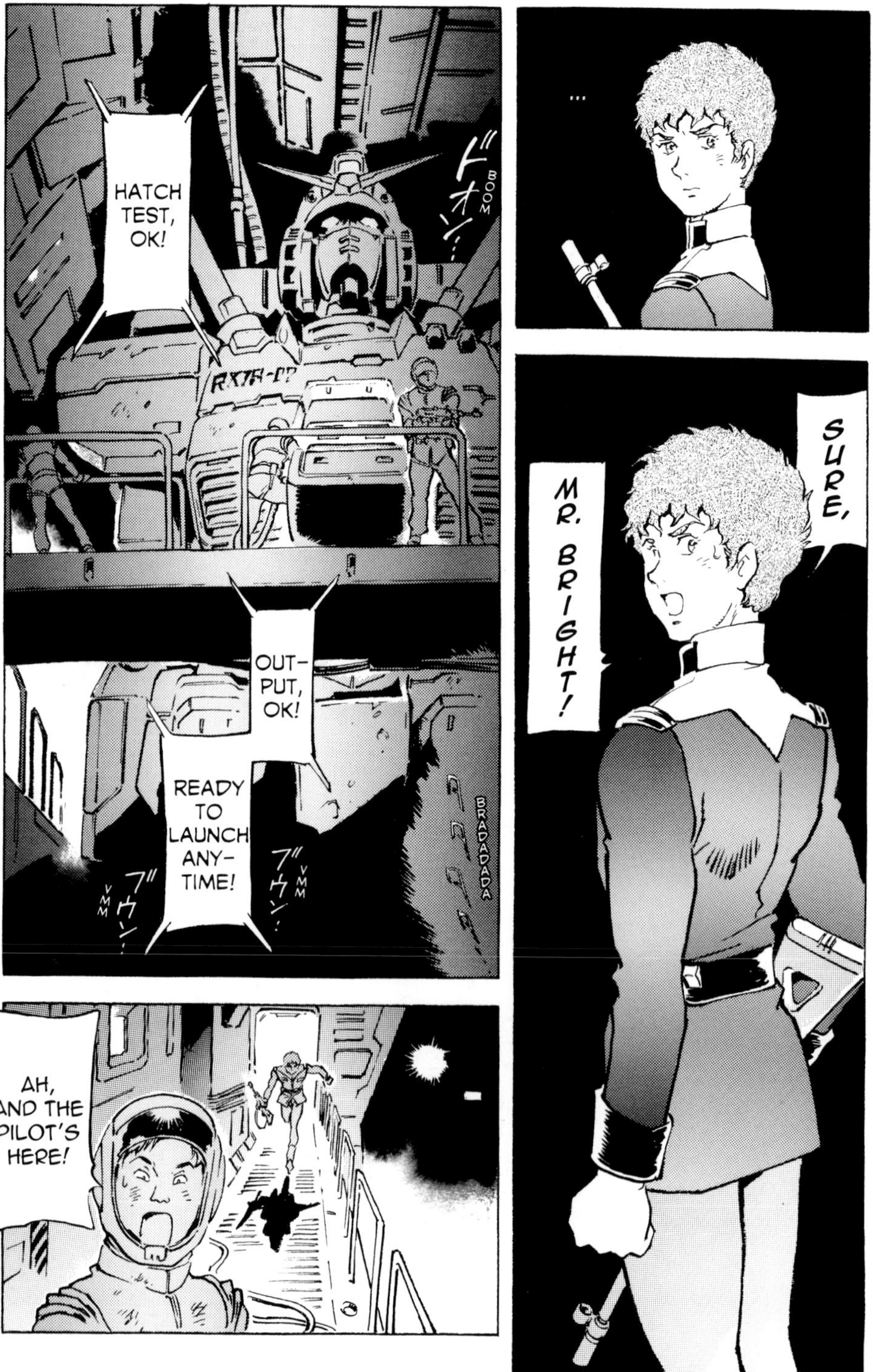
...
SURE, MR. BRIGHT!
HATCH TEST, OK!
ドオン…
BOOM
OUT-PUT, OK!
READY TO LAUNCH ANY-TIME!
BRADADADA
ブウン…
VMM
ブウン…
VMM
AH, AND THE PILOT'S HERE!

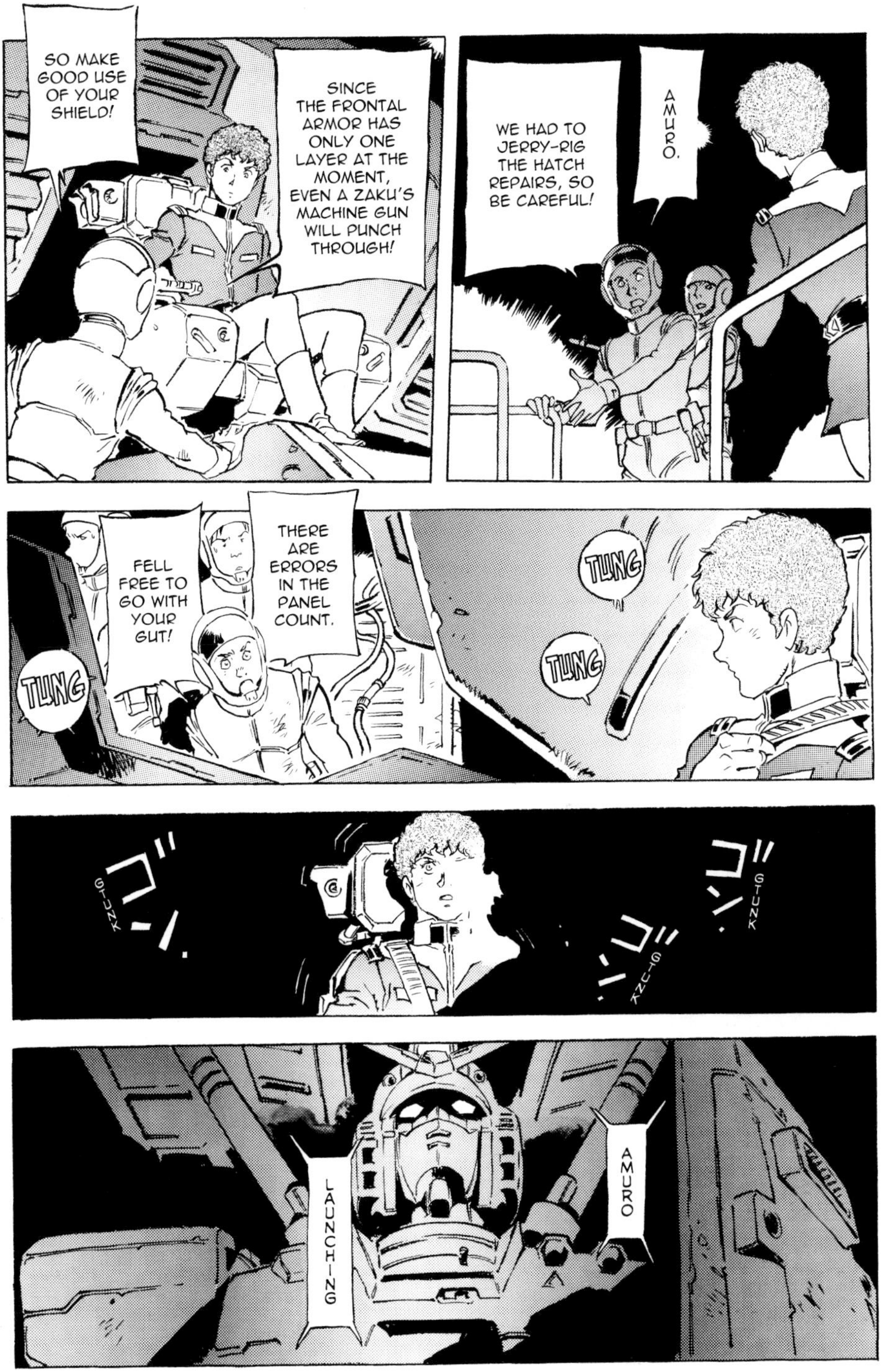
AMURO.
WE HAD TO JERRY-RIG THE HATCH REPAIRS, SO BE CAREFUL!
SINCE THE FRONTAL ARMOR HAS ONLY ONE LAYER AT THE MOMENT, EVEN A ZAKU'S MACHINE GUN WILL PUNCH THROUGH!
SO MAKE GOOD USE OF YOUR SHIELD!
TUNG
TUNG
THERE ARE ERRORS IN THE PANEL COUNT.
FELL FREE TO GO WITH YOUR GUT!
TUNG
ゴン.
GTUNK
ゴン.
GTUNK
ゴン.
GTUNK
AMURO
LAUNCHING

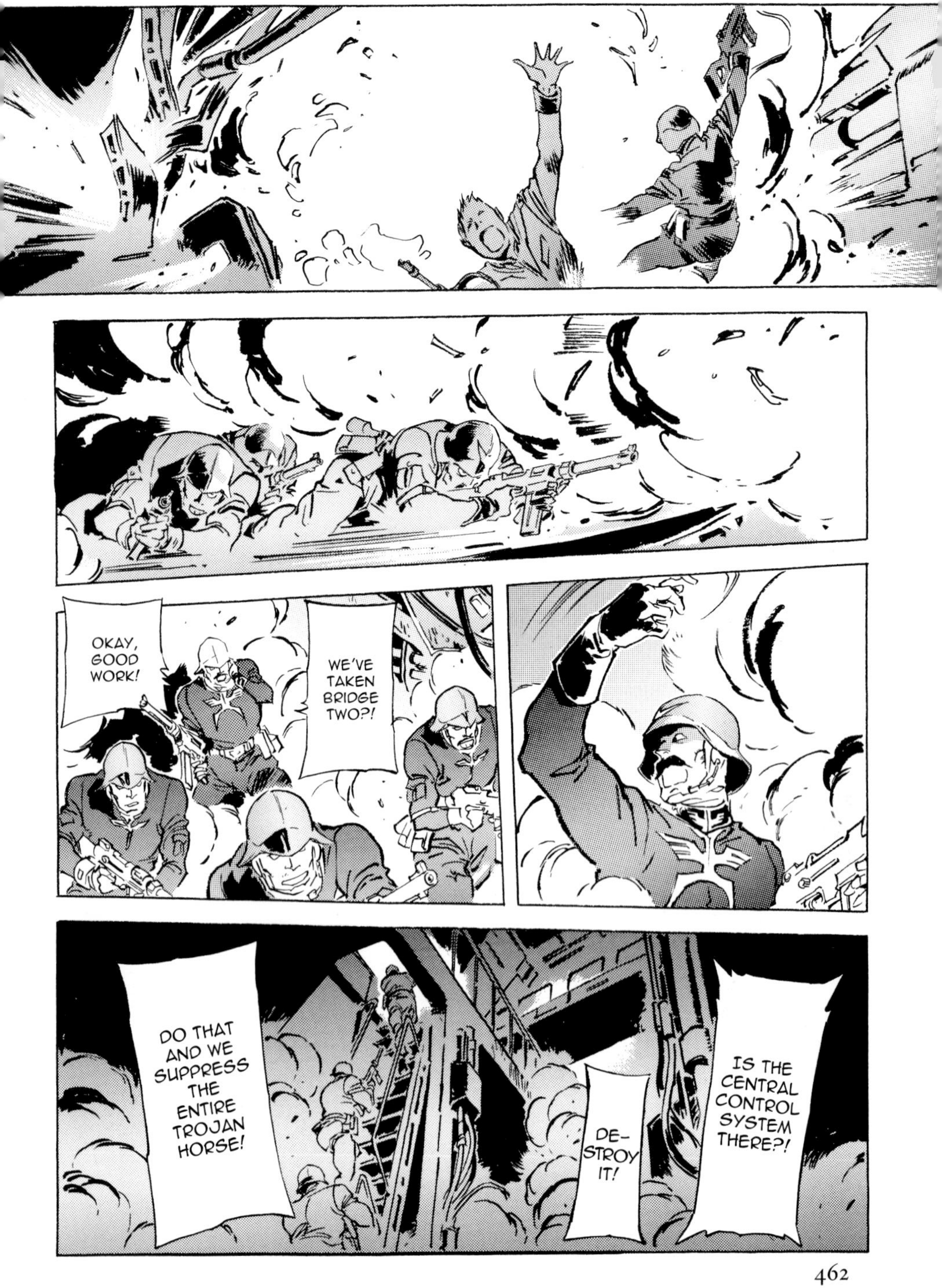
WE'VE TAKEN BRIDGE TWO?!
OKAY, GOOD WORK!
IS THE CENTRAL CONTROL SYSTEM THERE?!
DE-STROY IT!
DO THAT AND WE SUPPRESS THE ENTIRE TROJAN HORSE!

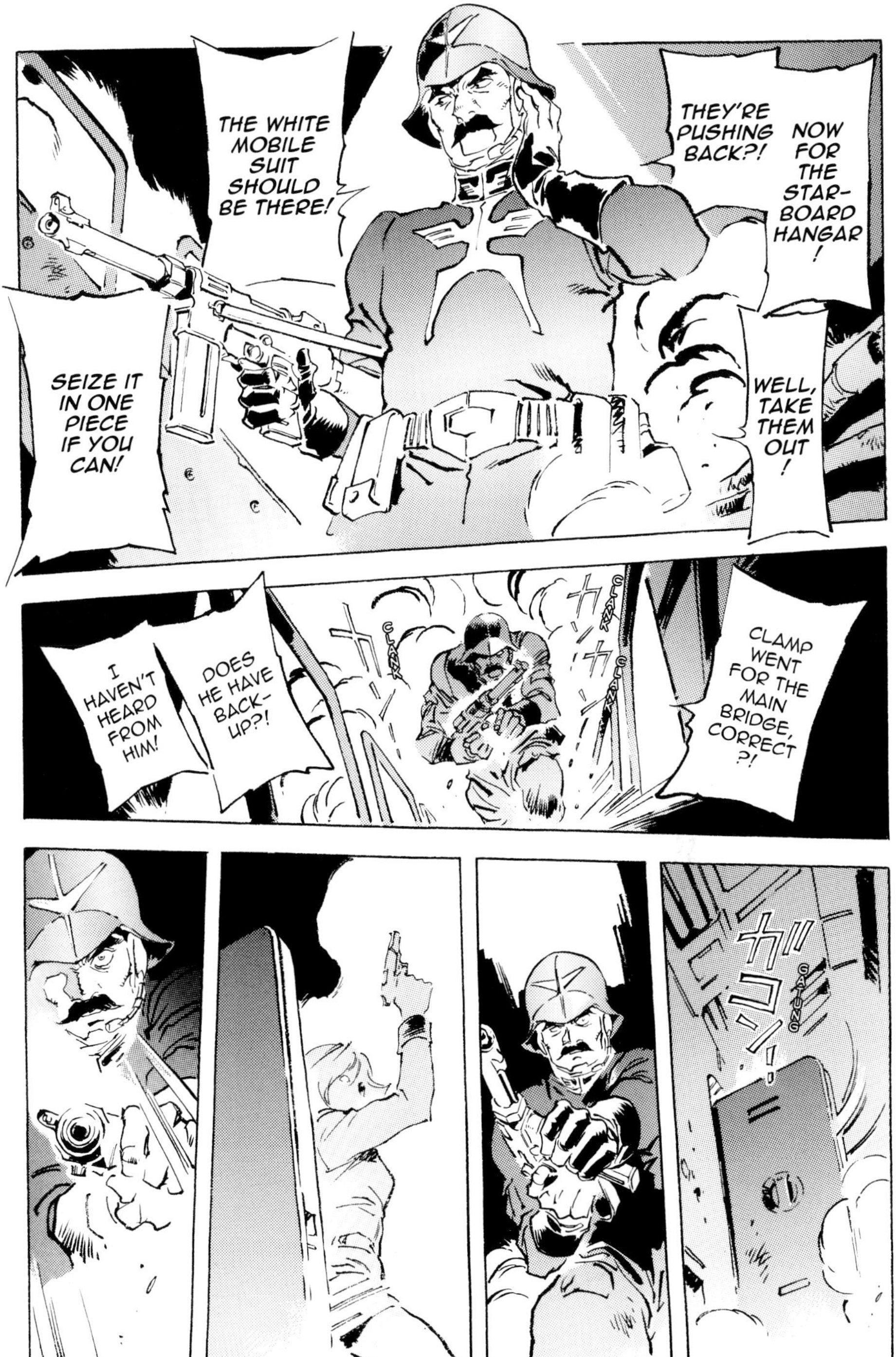
THEY'RE PUSHING BACK?!
NOW FOR THE STAR-BOARD HANGAR!
THE WHITE MOBILE SUIT SHOULD BE THERE!
WELL, TAKE THEM OUT!
SEIZE IT IN ONE PIECE IF YOU CAN!
CLAMP WENT FOR THE MAIN BRIDGE, CORRECT?!
CLANK
CLANK
CLANK
DOES HE HAVE BACK-UP?!
I HAVEN'T HEARD FROM HIM!
ガコン!!
GA-UNG

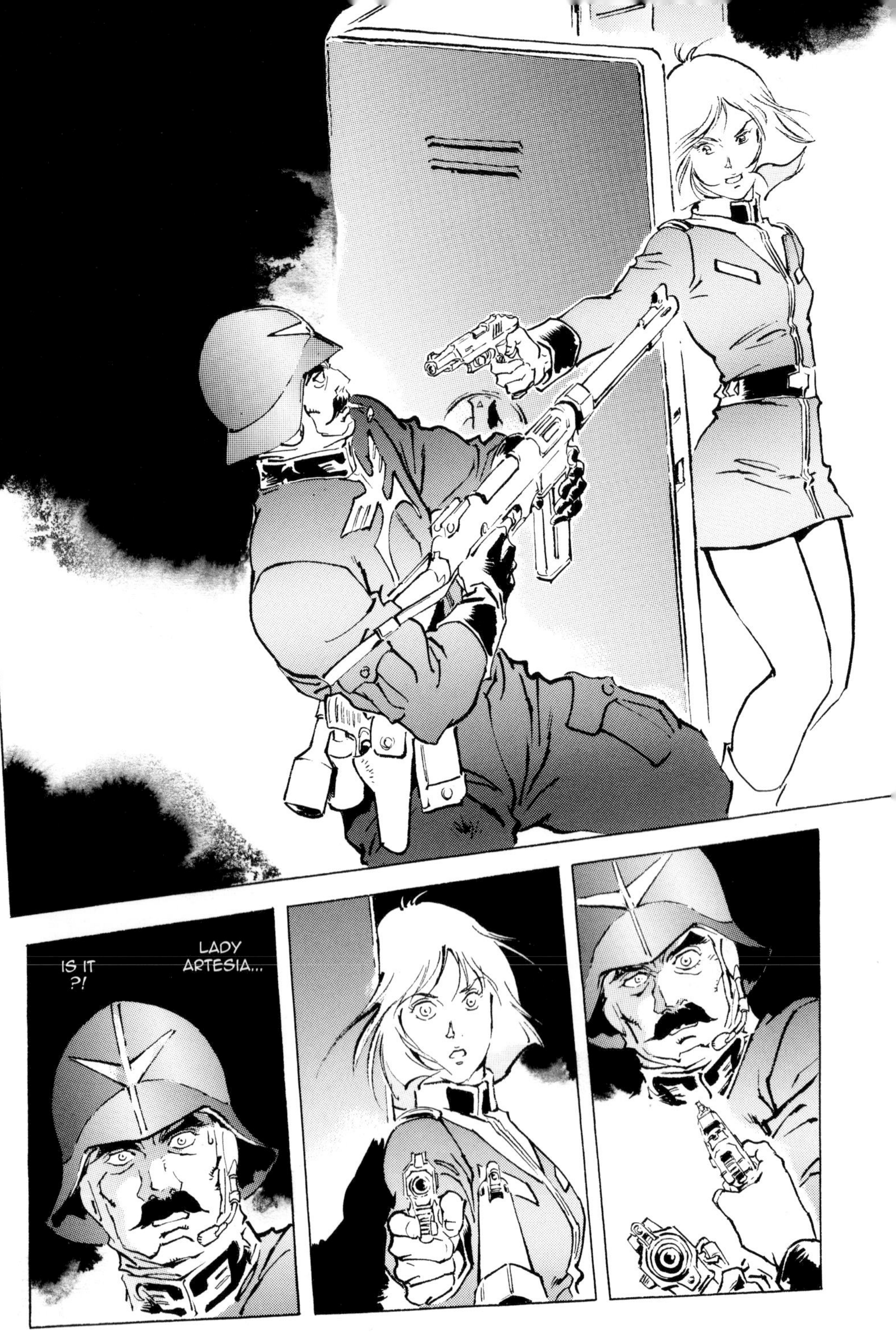
LADY ARTESIA...
IS IT ?!

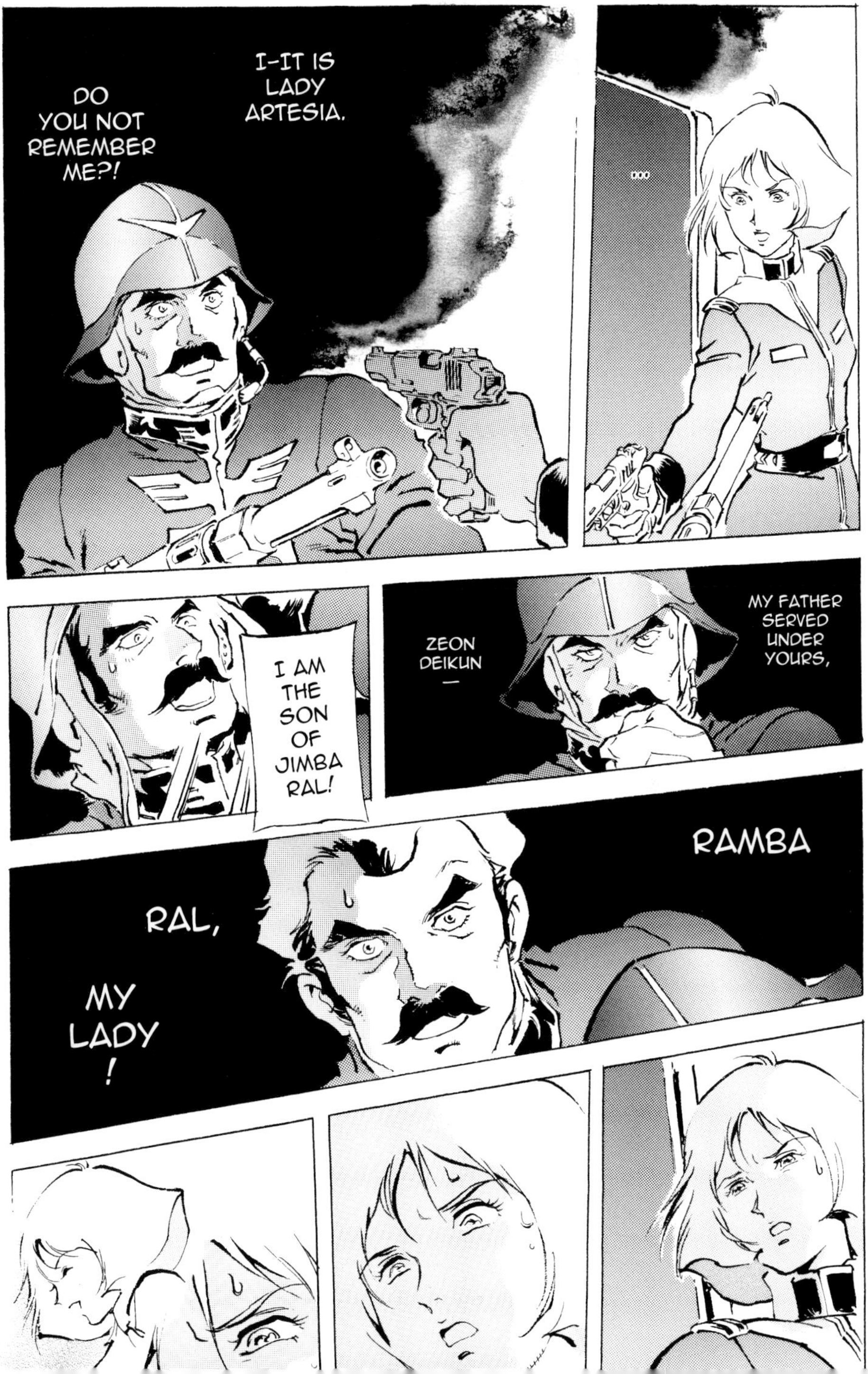
...
I-IT IS LADY ARTESIA.
DO YOU NOT REMEMBER ME?!
MY FATHER SERVED UNDER YOURS,
ZEON DEIKUN —
I AM THE SON OF JIMBA RAL!
RAMBA
RAL,
MY LADY !

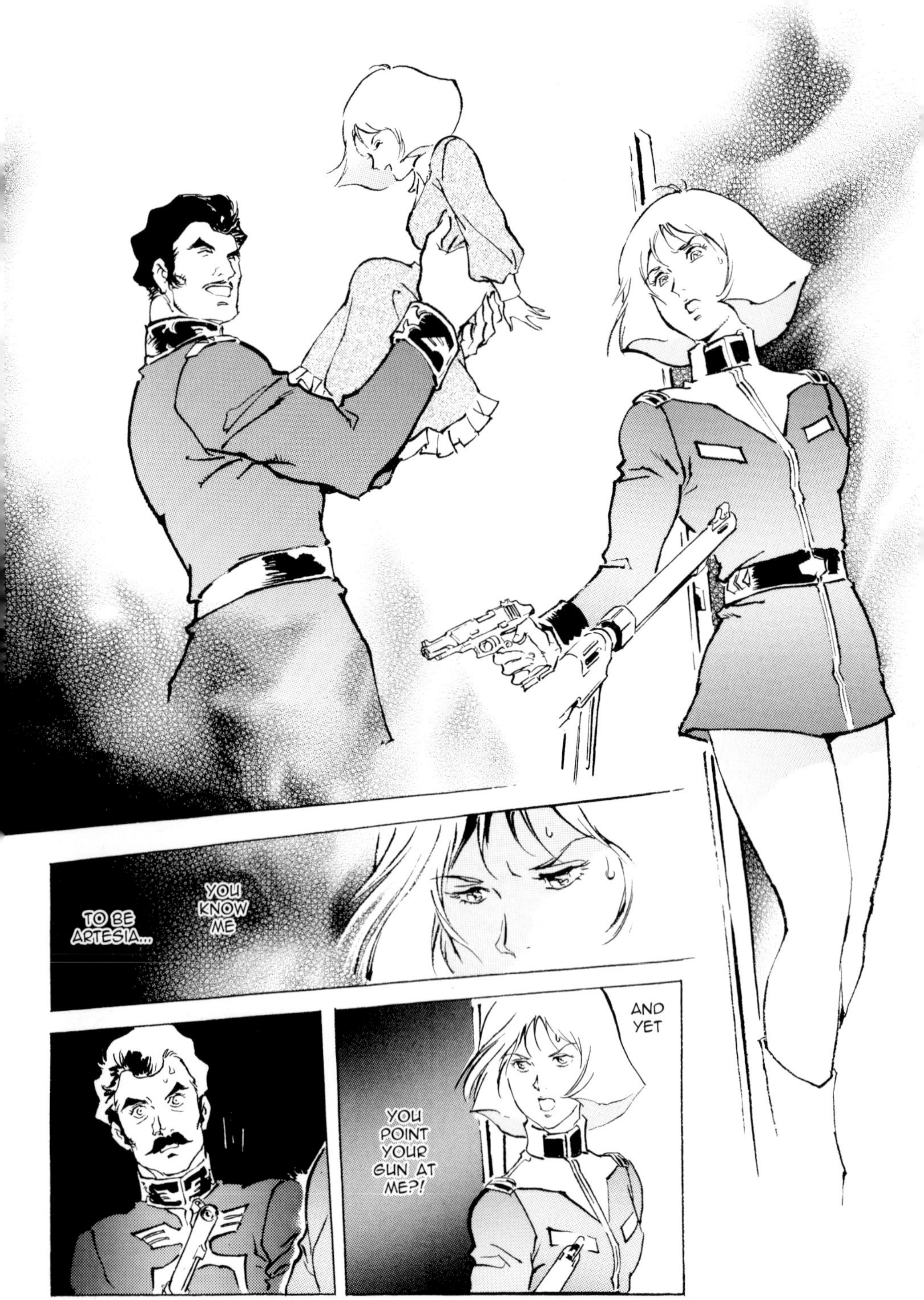
YOU KNOW ME
TO BE ARTESIA...
AND YET
YOU POINT YOUR GUN AT ME?!

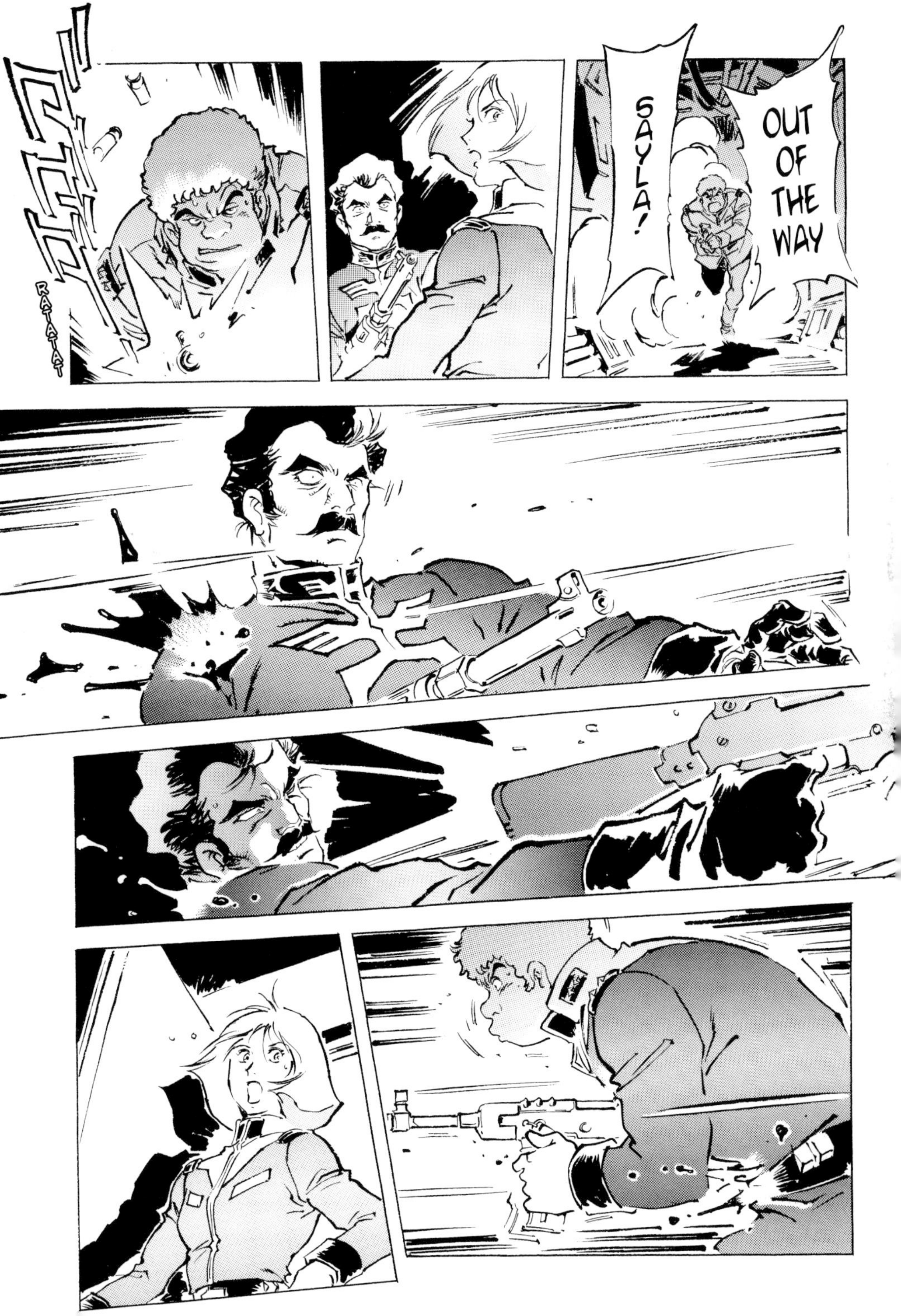
OUT OF THE WAY
SAYLA!
RATATAT

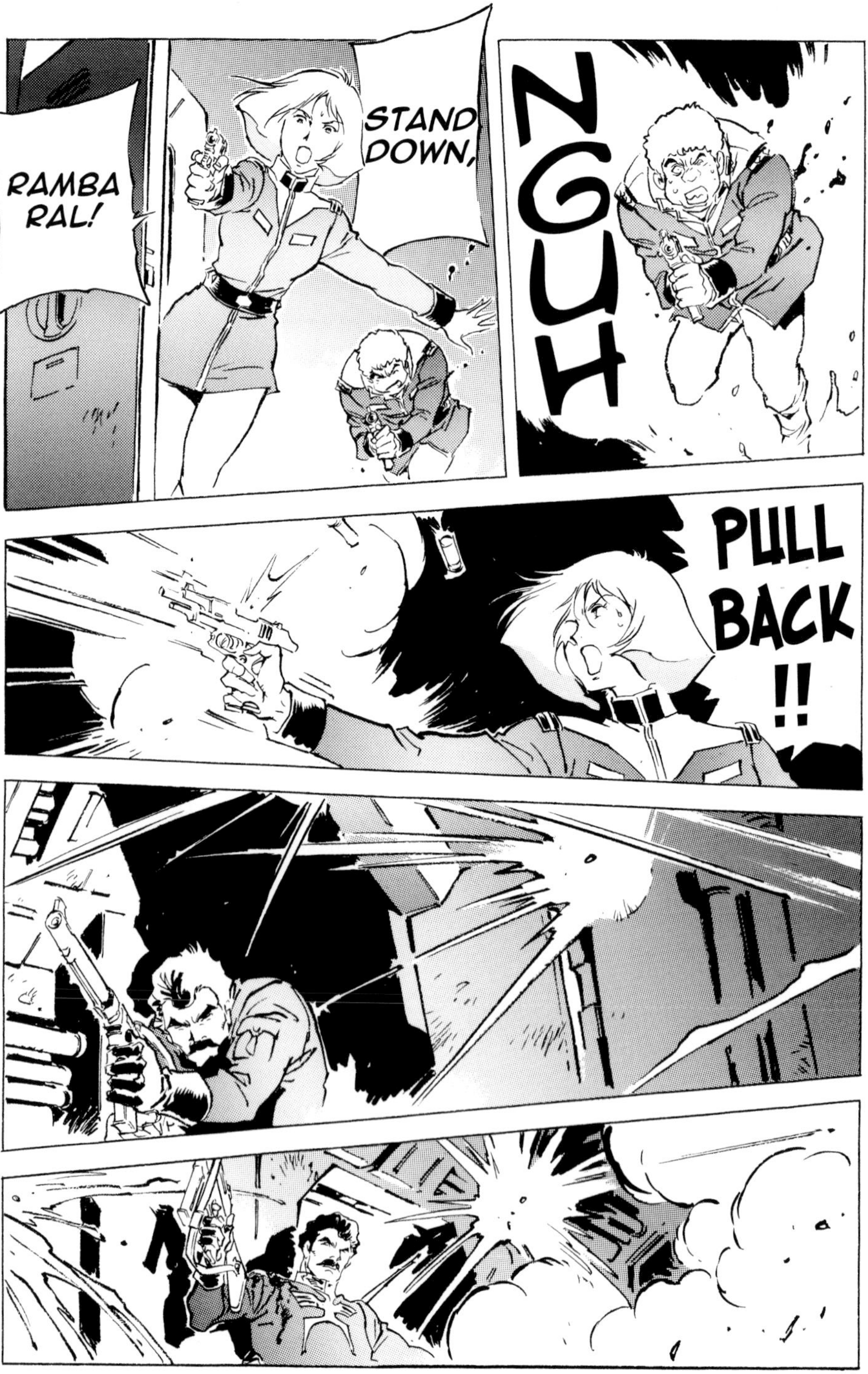
NGUH
STAND DOWN,
RAMBA RAL!
PULL BACK !!

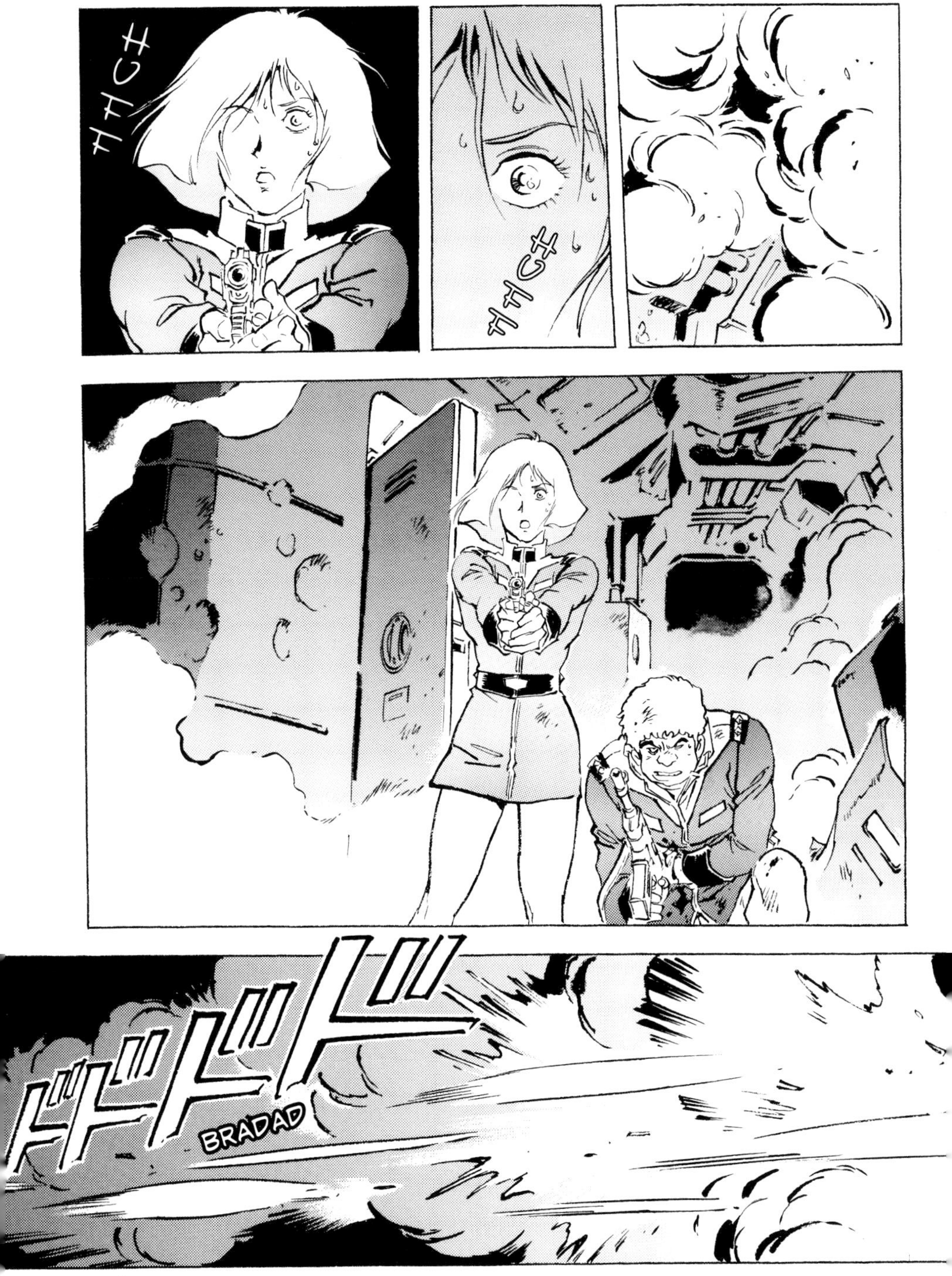
HAGH
HAGH
BRADAD

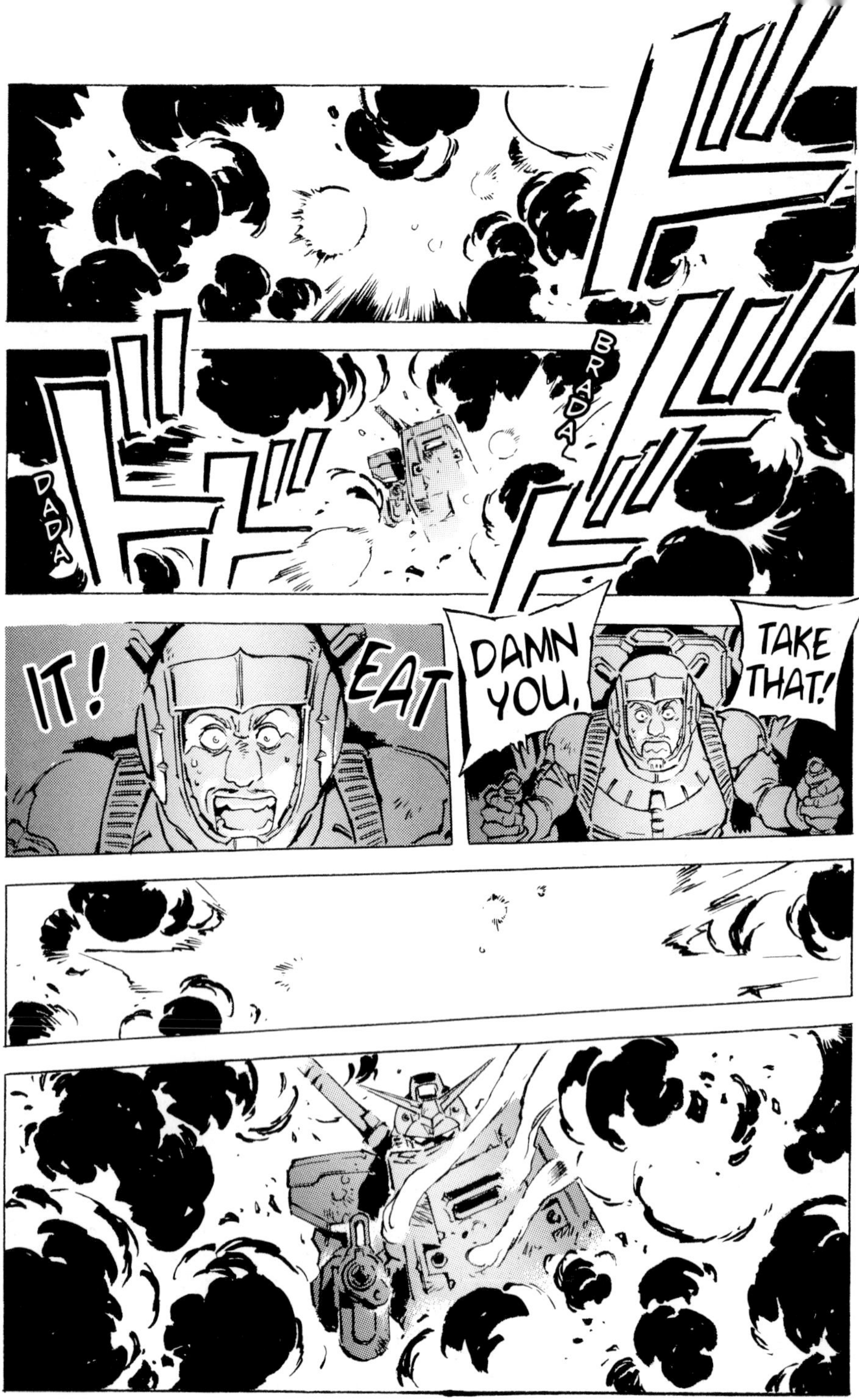
BRADA
DADA
TAKE THAT!
DAMN YOU,
EAT IT!

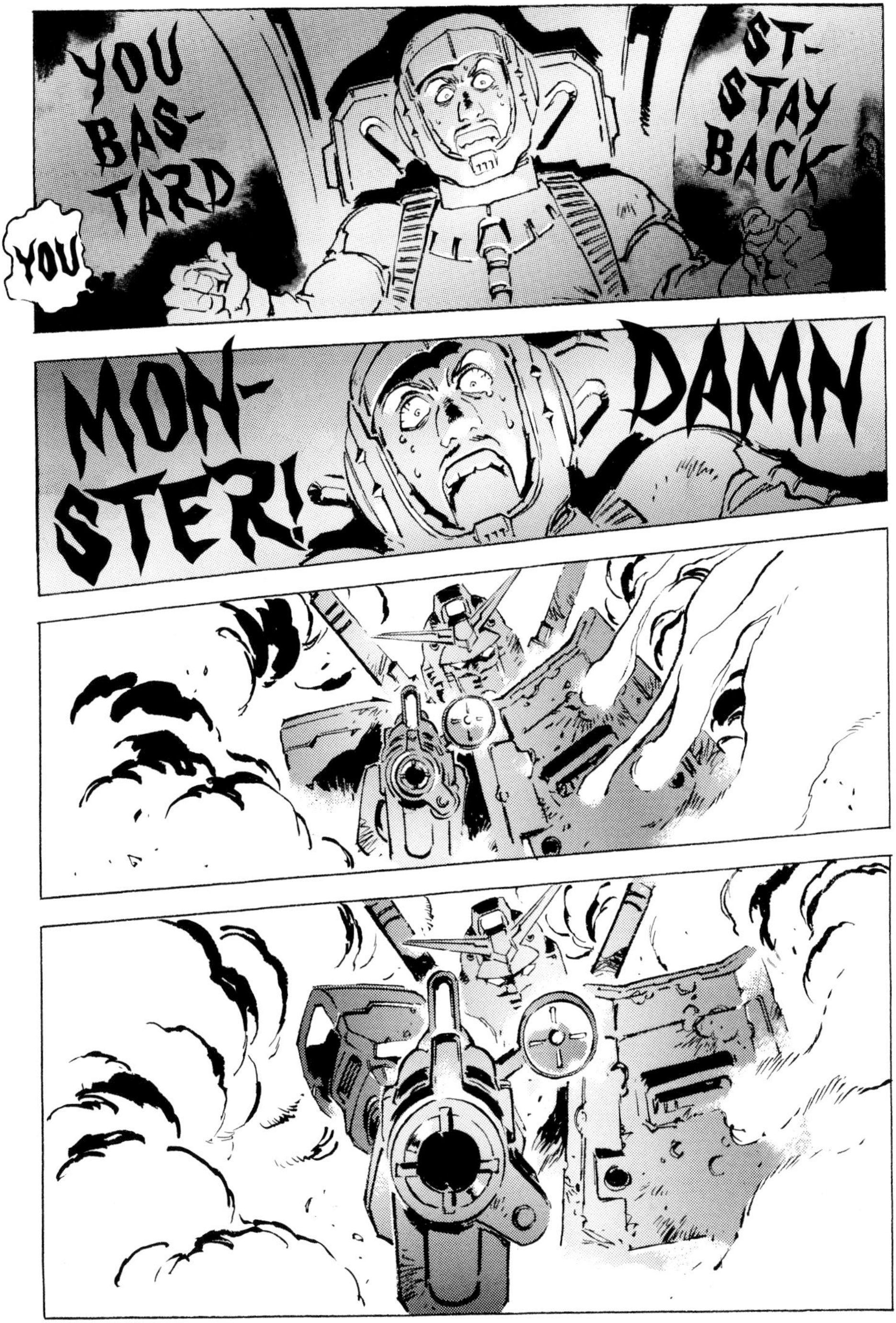
ST-STAY BACK
YOU BASTARD
YOU
DAMN
MONSTER!

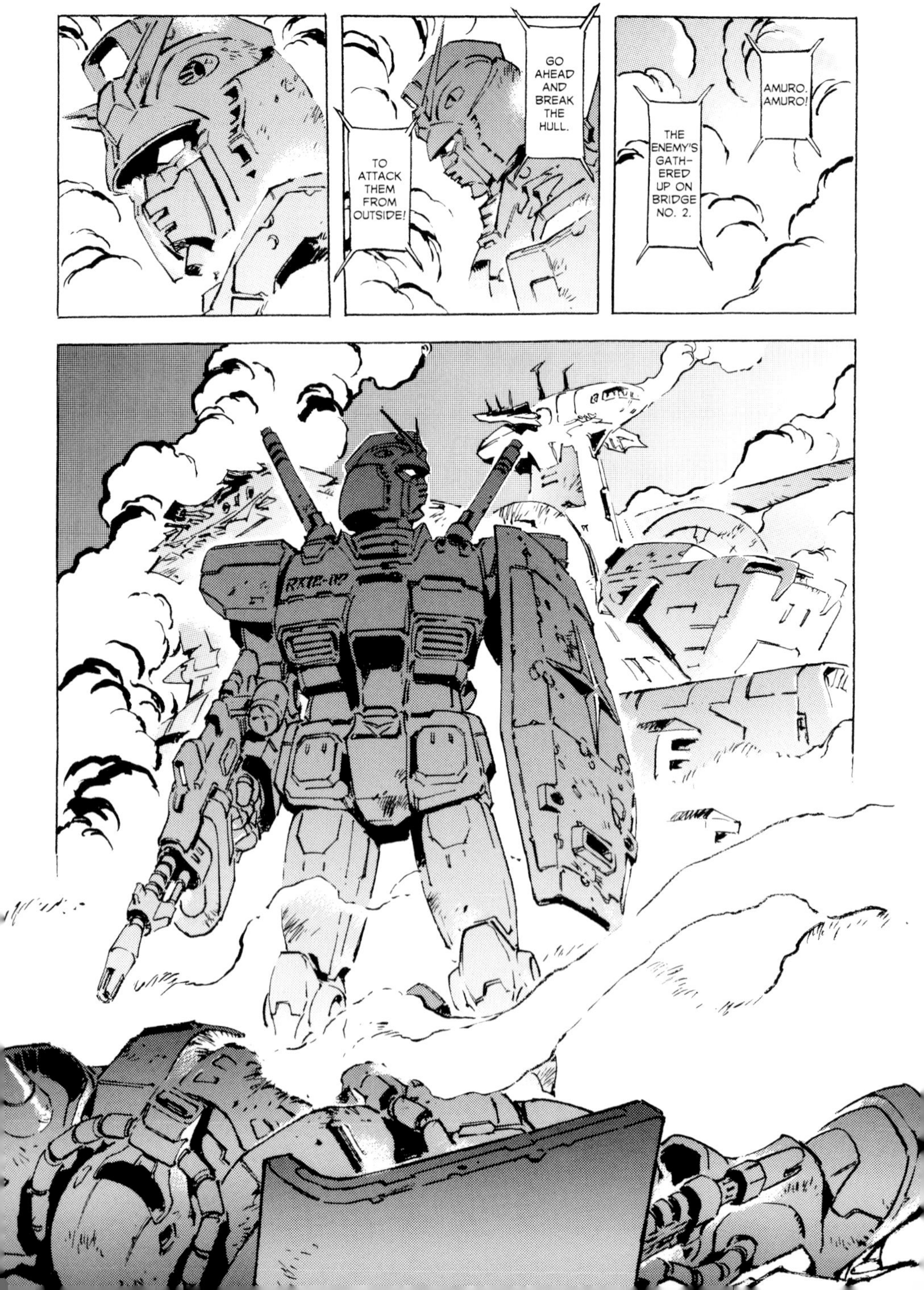
AMURO. AMURO!
THE ENEMY'S GATH-ERED UP ON BRIDGE NO. 2.
GO AHEAD AND BREAK THE HULL.
TO ATTACK THEM FROM OUTSIDE!

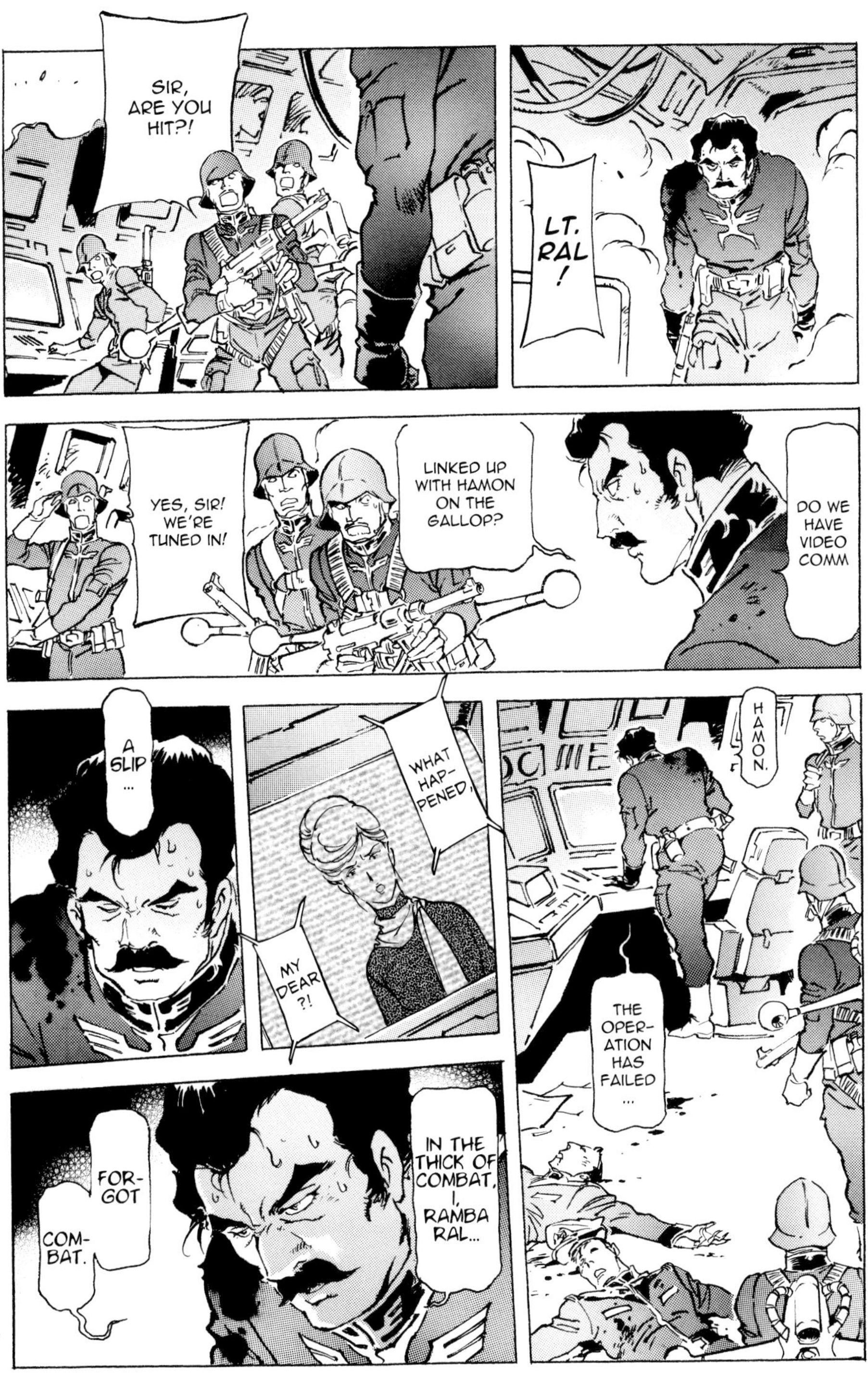
LT. RAL!
SIR, ARE YOU HIT?!
DO WE HAVE VIDEO COMM
LINKED UP WITH HAMON ON THE GALLOP?
YES, SIR! WE'RE TUNED IN!
HAMON.
THE OPERATION HAS FAILED ...
WHAT HAP-PENED,
MY DEAR?!
A SLIP ...
IN THE THICK OF COMBAT, I, RAMBA RAL...
FOR-GOT COM-BAT.

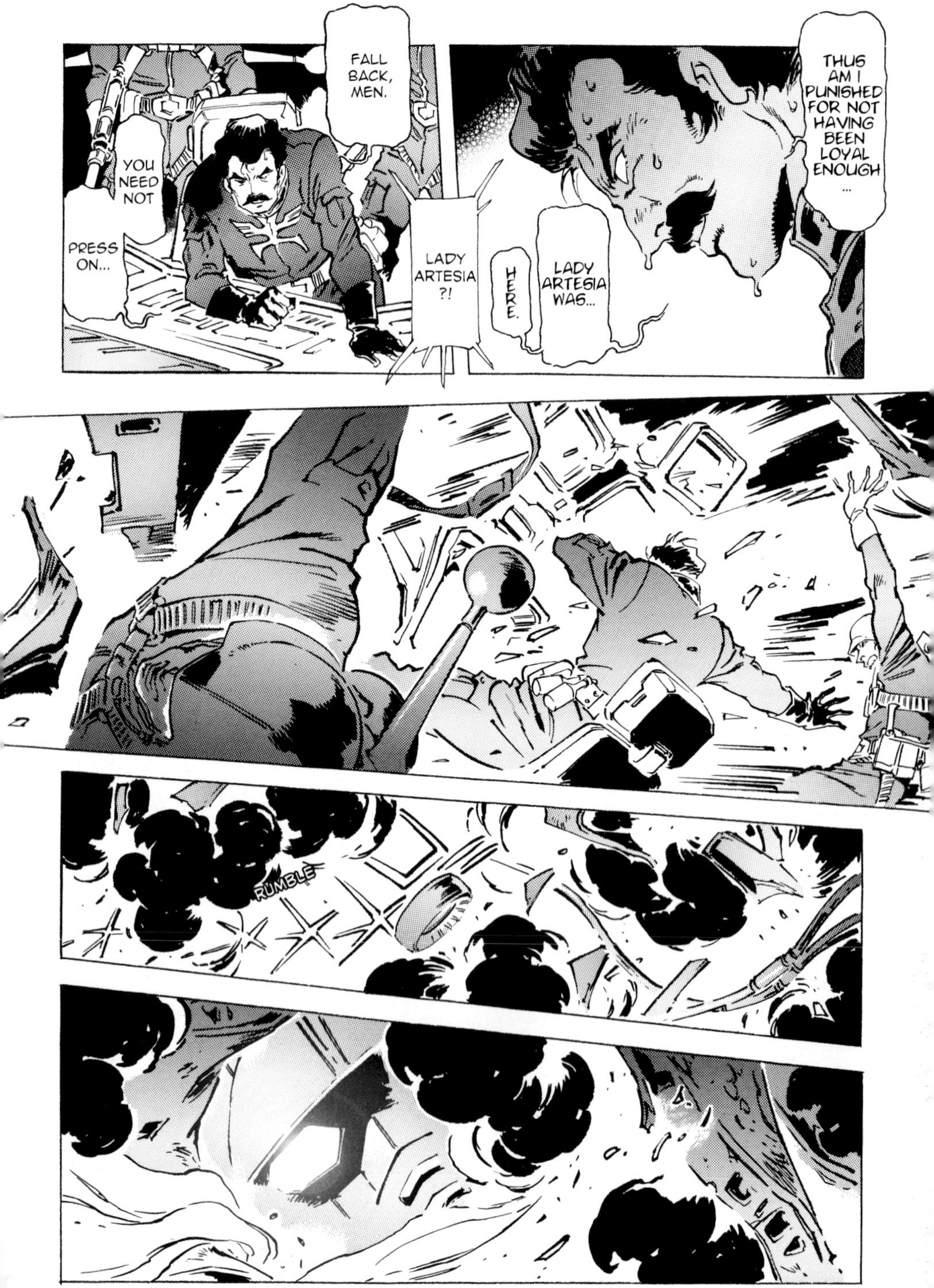
THUS AM I PUNISHED FOR NOT HAVING BEEN LOYAL ENOUGH ...
LADY ARTESIA WAS...
HERE.
LADY ARTESIA ?!
FALL BACK, MEN.
YOU NEED NOT
PRESS ON...
RUMBLE

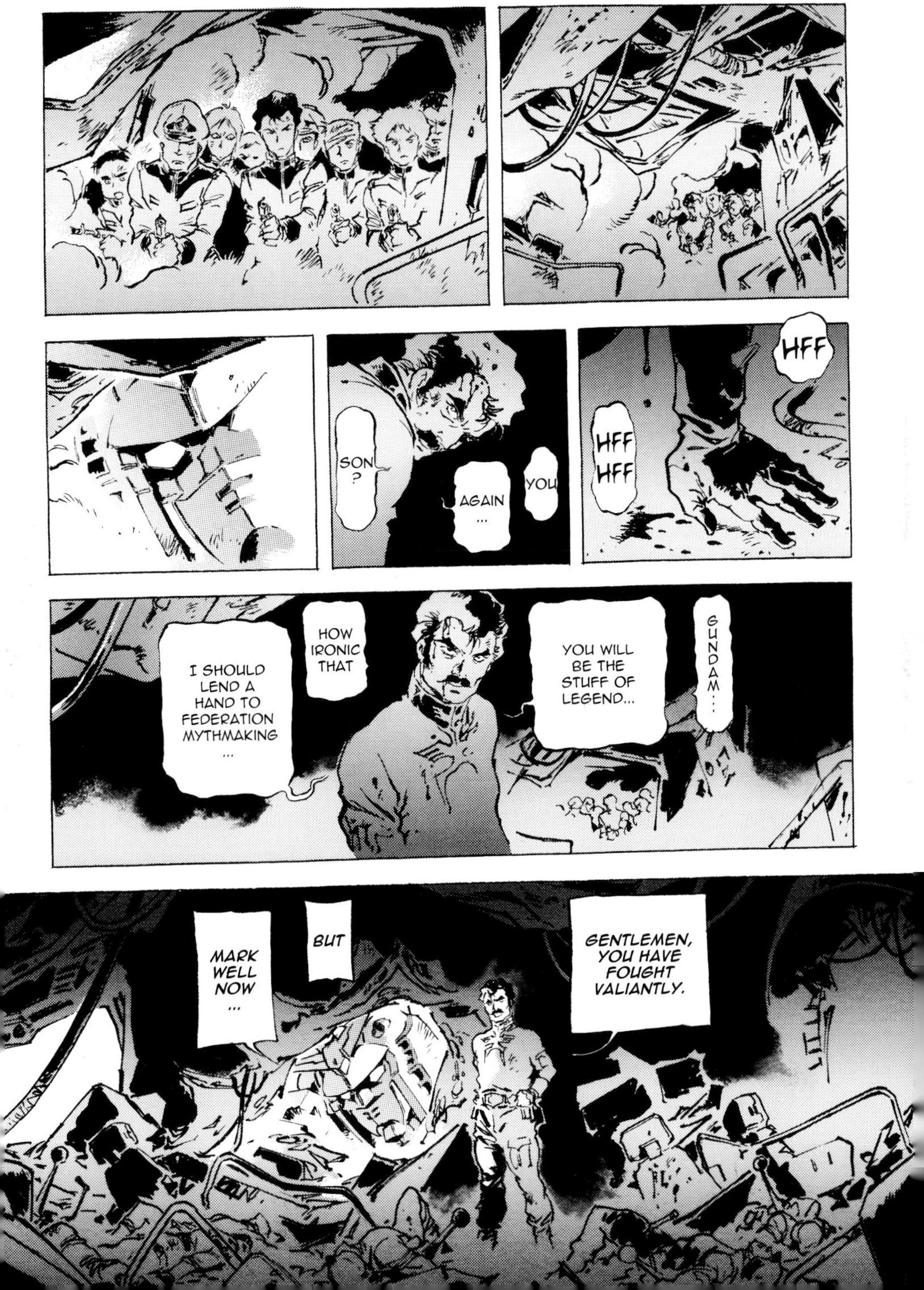
HFF
HFF HFF
YOU
AGAIN ...
SON ?
GUNDAM...
YOU WILL BE THE STUFF OF LEGEND...
HOW IRONIC THAT
I SHOULD LEND A HAND TO FEDERATION MYTHMAKING ...
GENTLEMEN, YOU HAVE FOUGHT VALIANTLY.
BUT
MARK WELL NOW ...

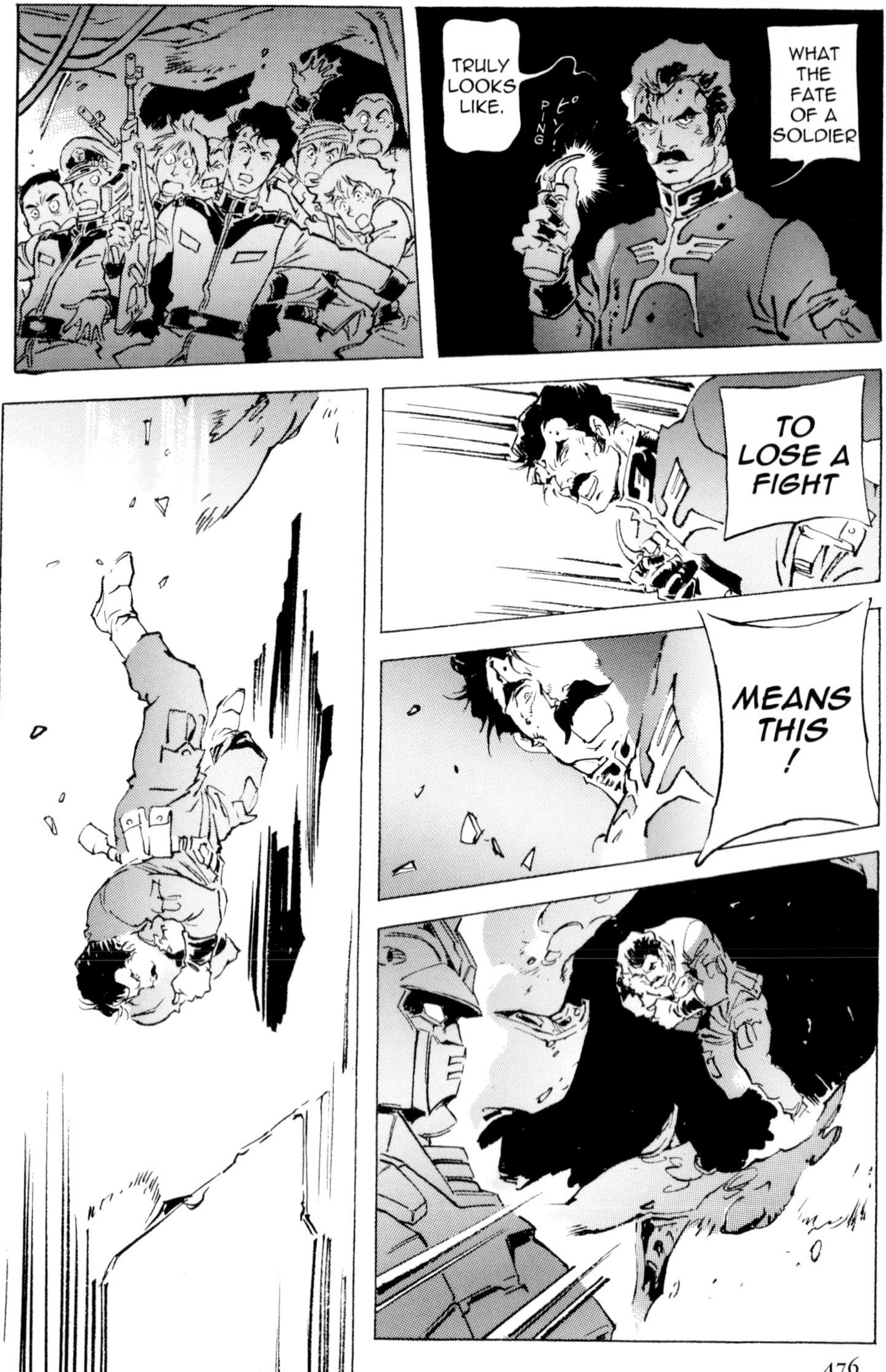

WHAT THE FATE OF A SOLDIER
TRULY LOOKS LIKE.
PING
TO LOSE A FIGHT
MEANS THIS!

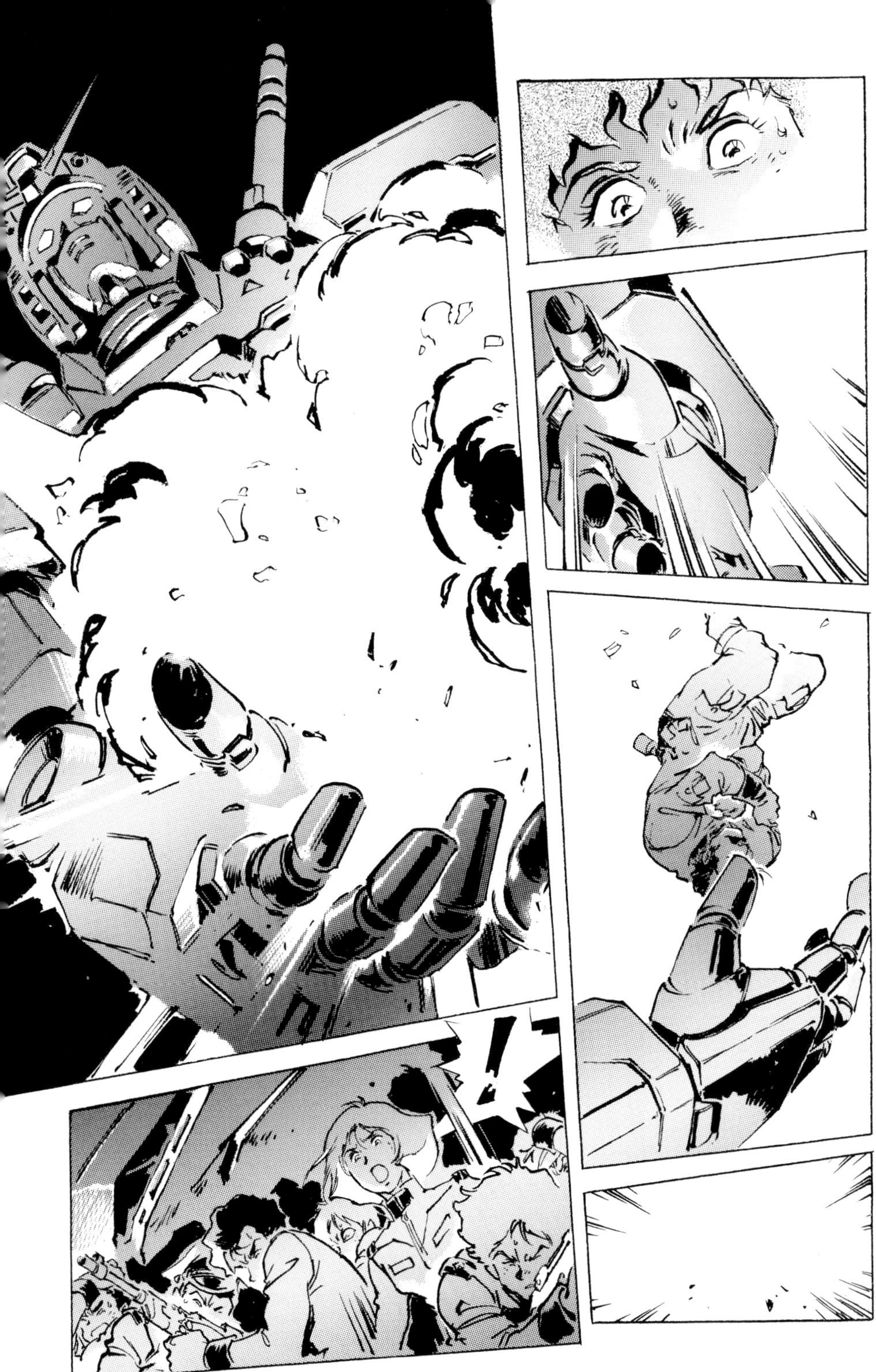
!

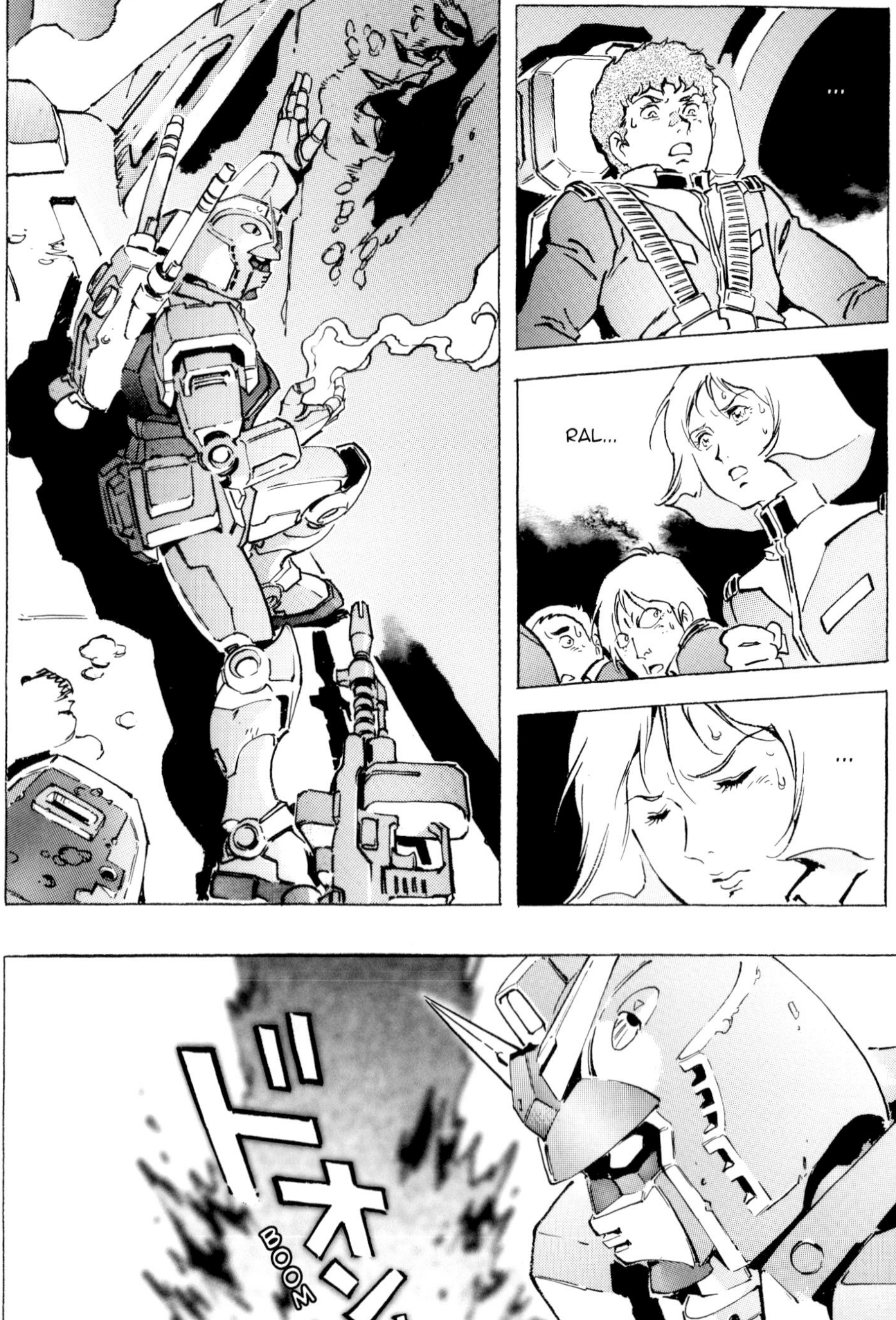
...
RAL...
...
BOOM

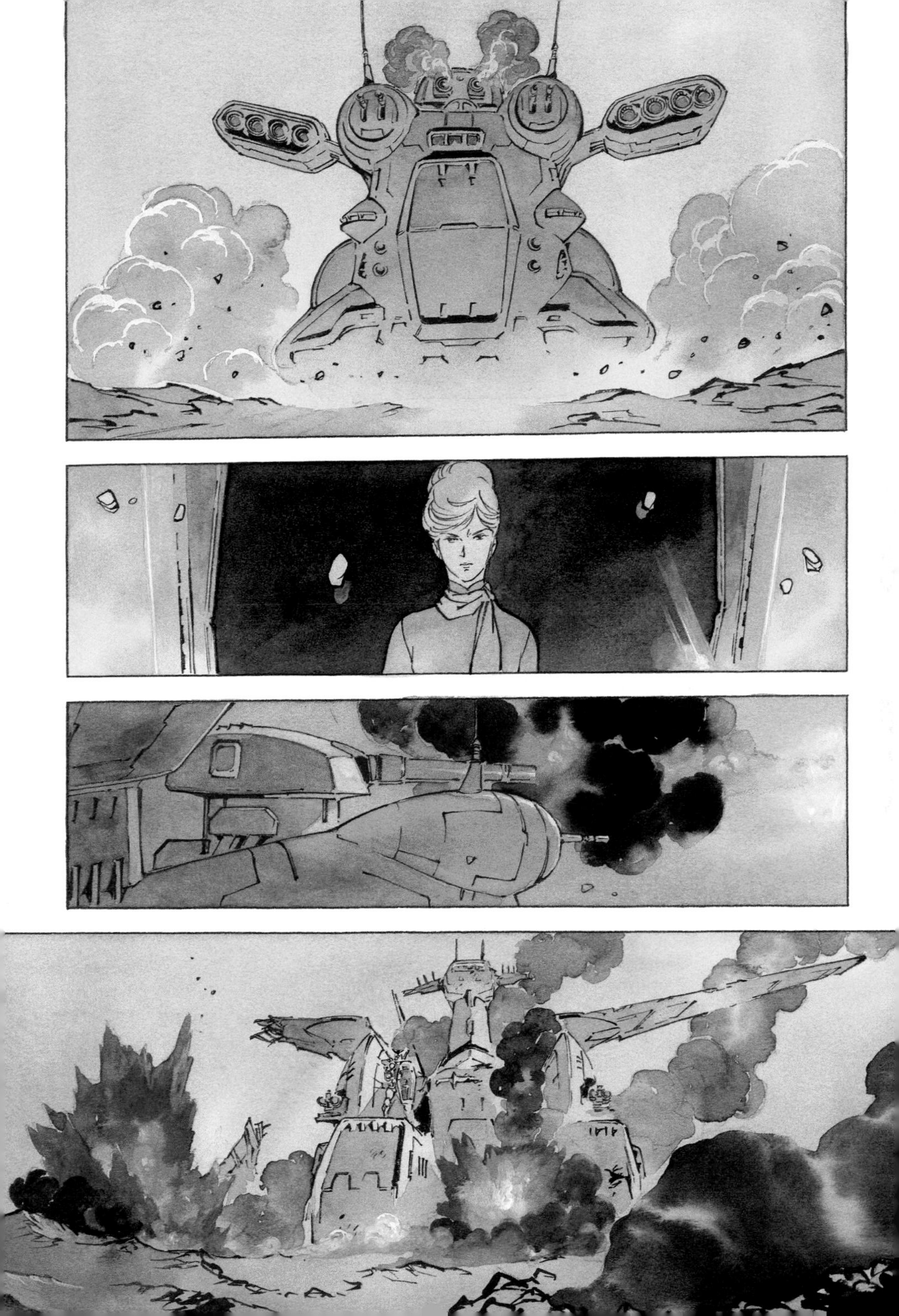

RAMBA RAL IS DEAD, OKAY?!

MS. HA- MON !

STOP !!

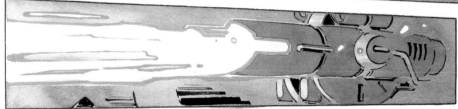

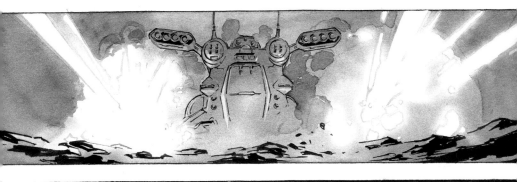

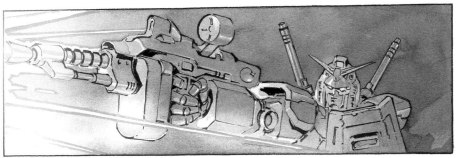

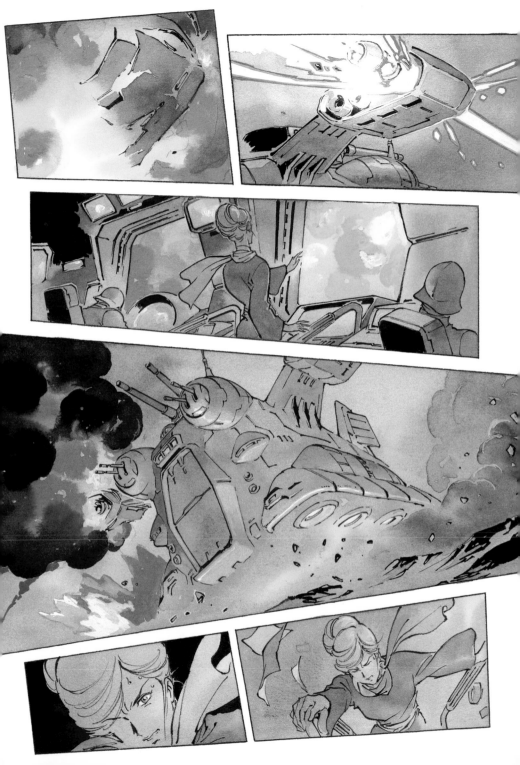

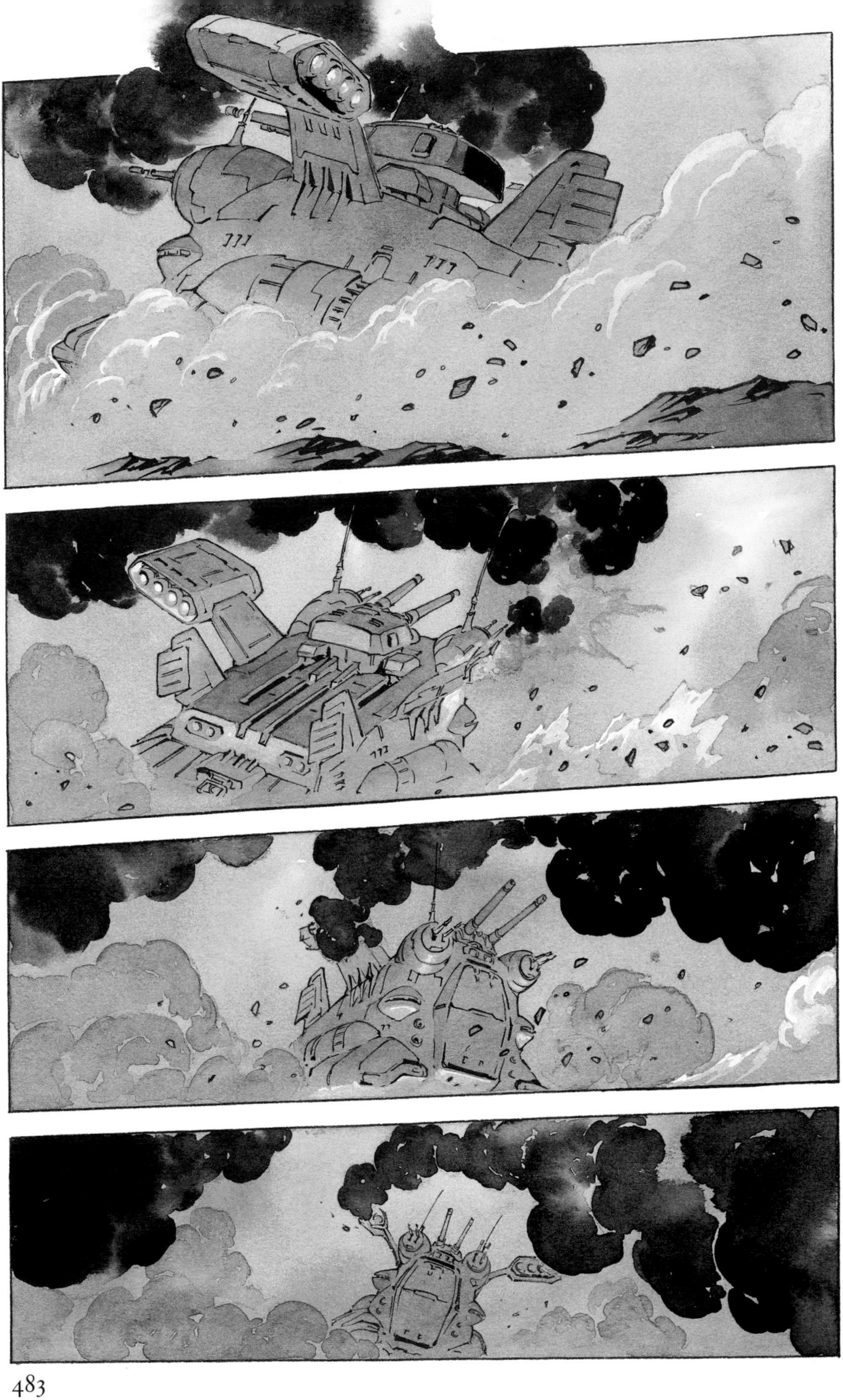

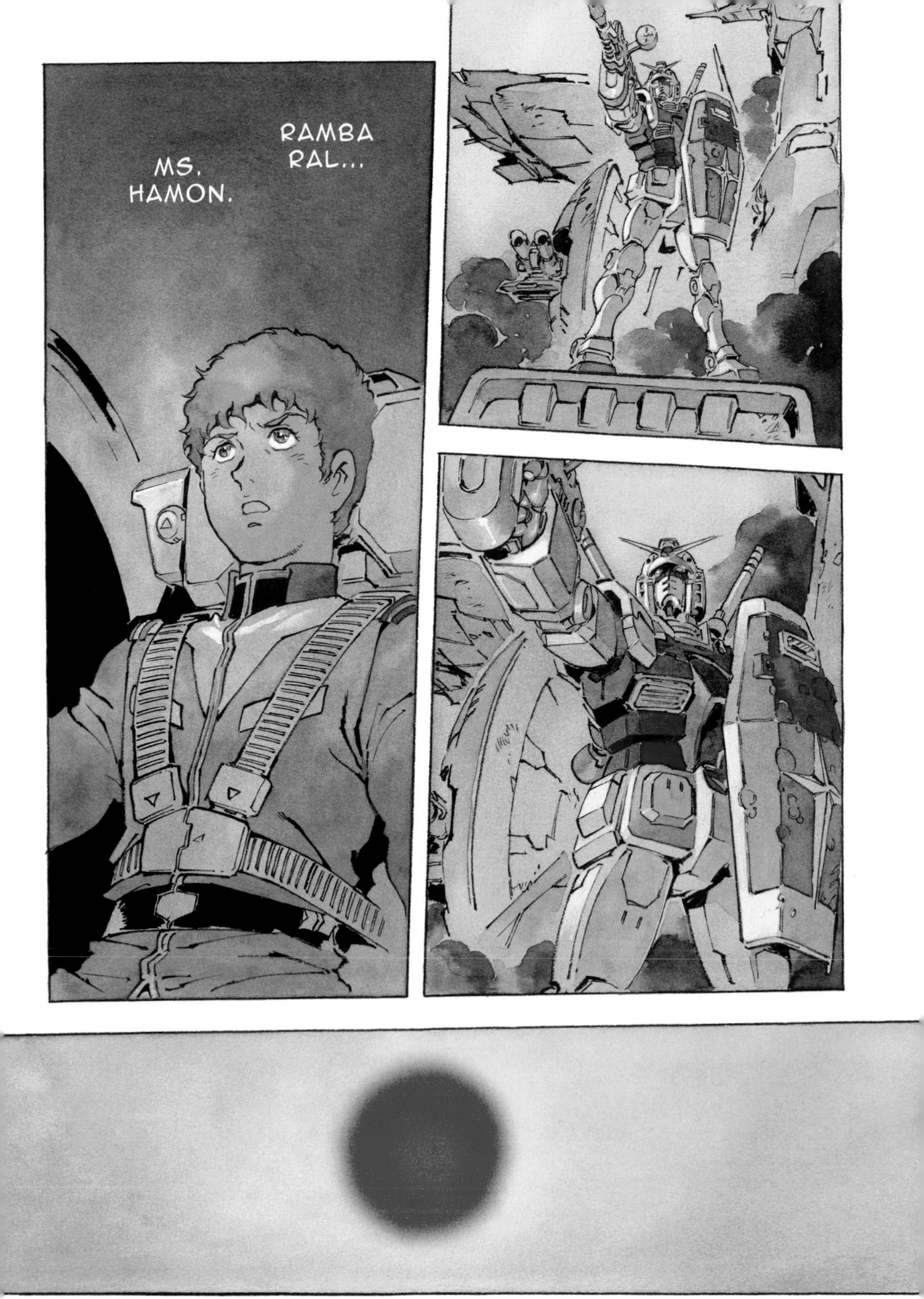
RAMBA RAL...
MS. HAMON.

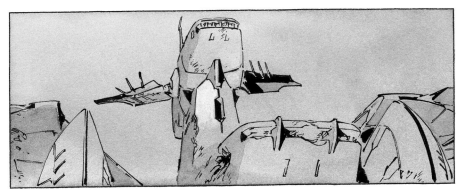

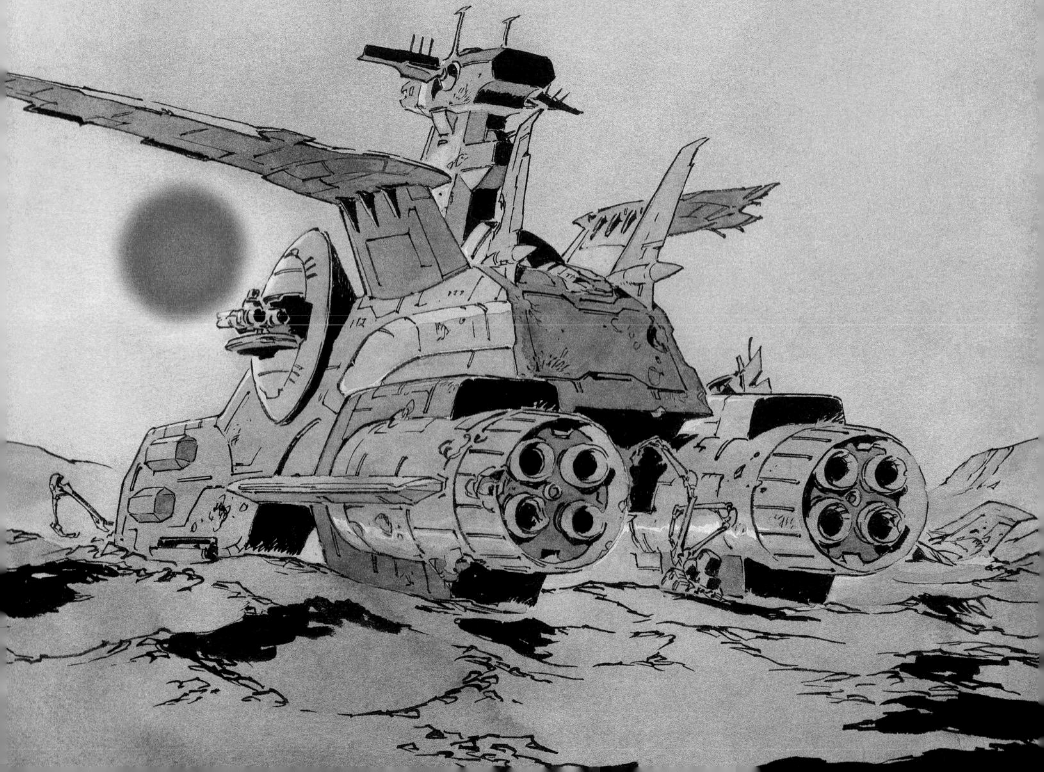

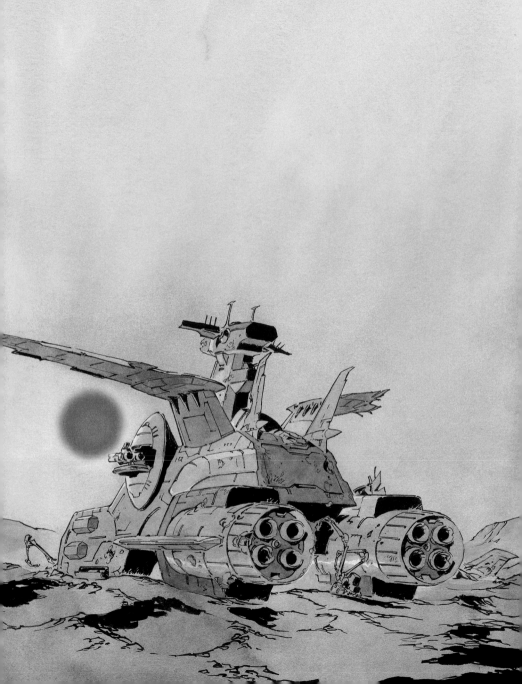

to be continued...

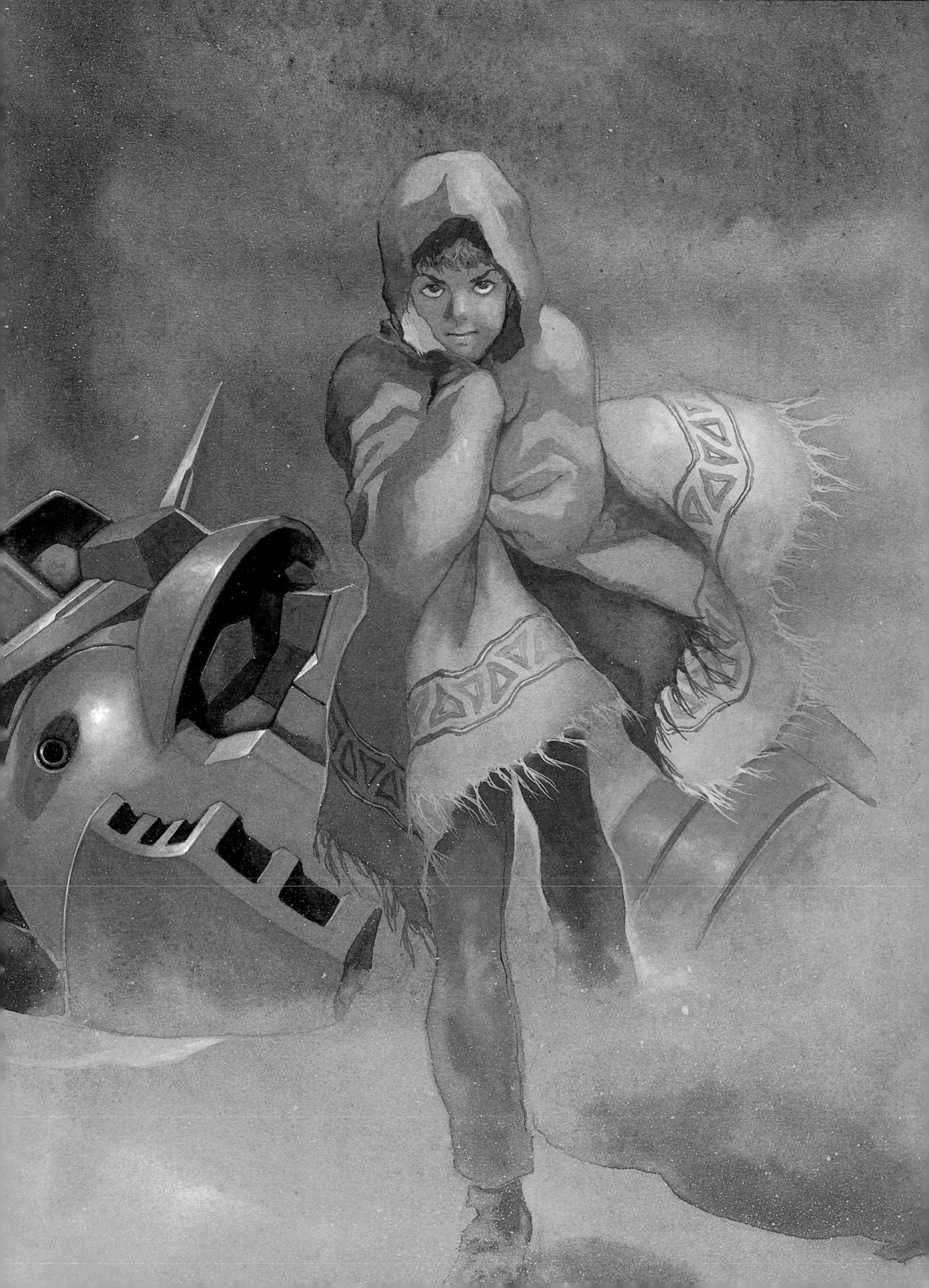

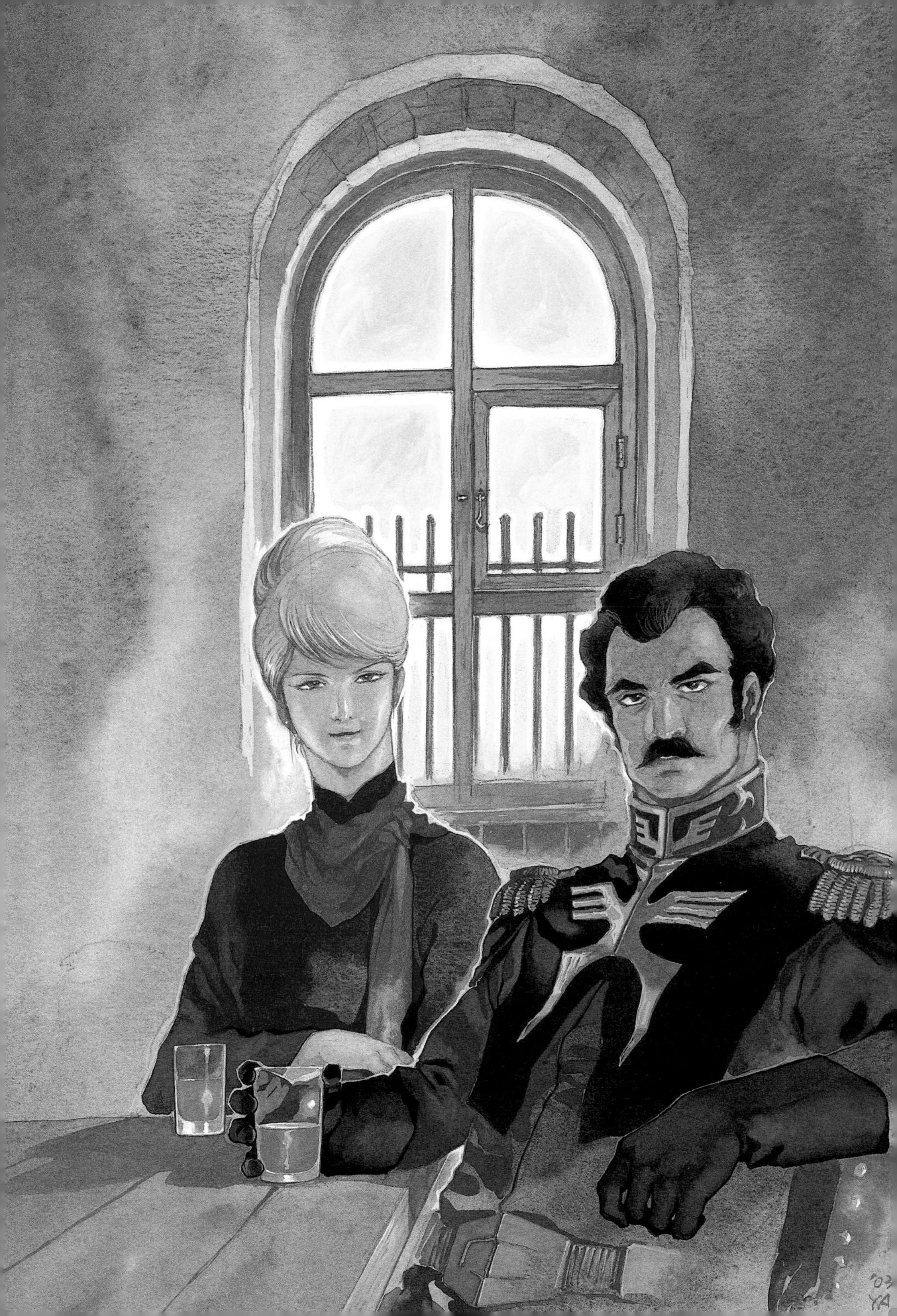

ecial Contribution from

imoku Kio

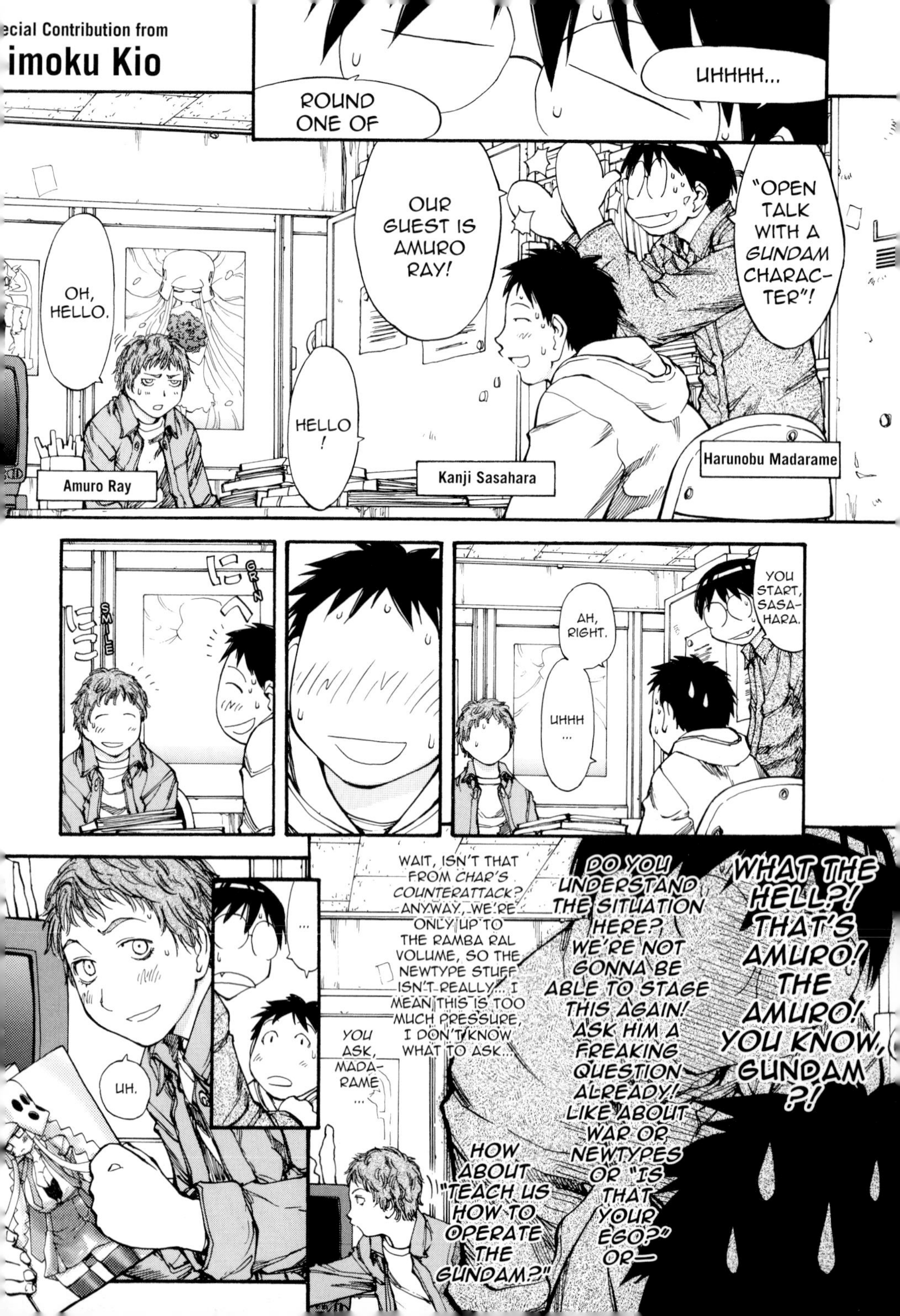

UHHHH...
ROUND ONE OF
"OPEN TALK WITH A GUNDAM CHARAC-TER"!
OUR GUEST IS AMURO RAY!
HELLO !
OH, HELLO.
Harunobu Madarame
Kanji Sasahara
Amuro Ray
YOU START, SASA-HARA.
AH, RIGHT.
UHHH ...
GRIN
SMILE
WHAT THE HELL?! THAT'S AMURO! THE AMURO! YOU KNOW, GUNDAM ?!
DO YOU UNDERSTAND THE SITUATION HERE? WE'RE NOT GONNA BE ABLE TO STAGE THIS AGAIN! ASK HIM A FREAKING QUESTION ALREADY! LIKE ABOUT WAR OR NEWTYPES OR "IS THAT YOUR EGO?" OR—
WAIT, ISN'T THAT FROM CHAR'S COUNTERATTACK? ANYWAY, WE'RE ONLY UP TO THE RAMBA RAL VOLUME, SO THE NEWTYPE STUFF ISN'T REALLY... I MEAN THIS IS TOO MUCH PRESSURE, I DON'T KNOW WHAT TO ASK...
YOU ASK, MADA-RAME ...
HOW ABOUT "TEACH US HOW TO OPERATE THE GUNDAM?"
...
UH.

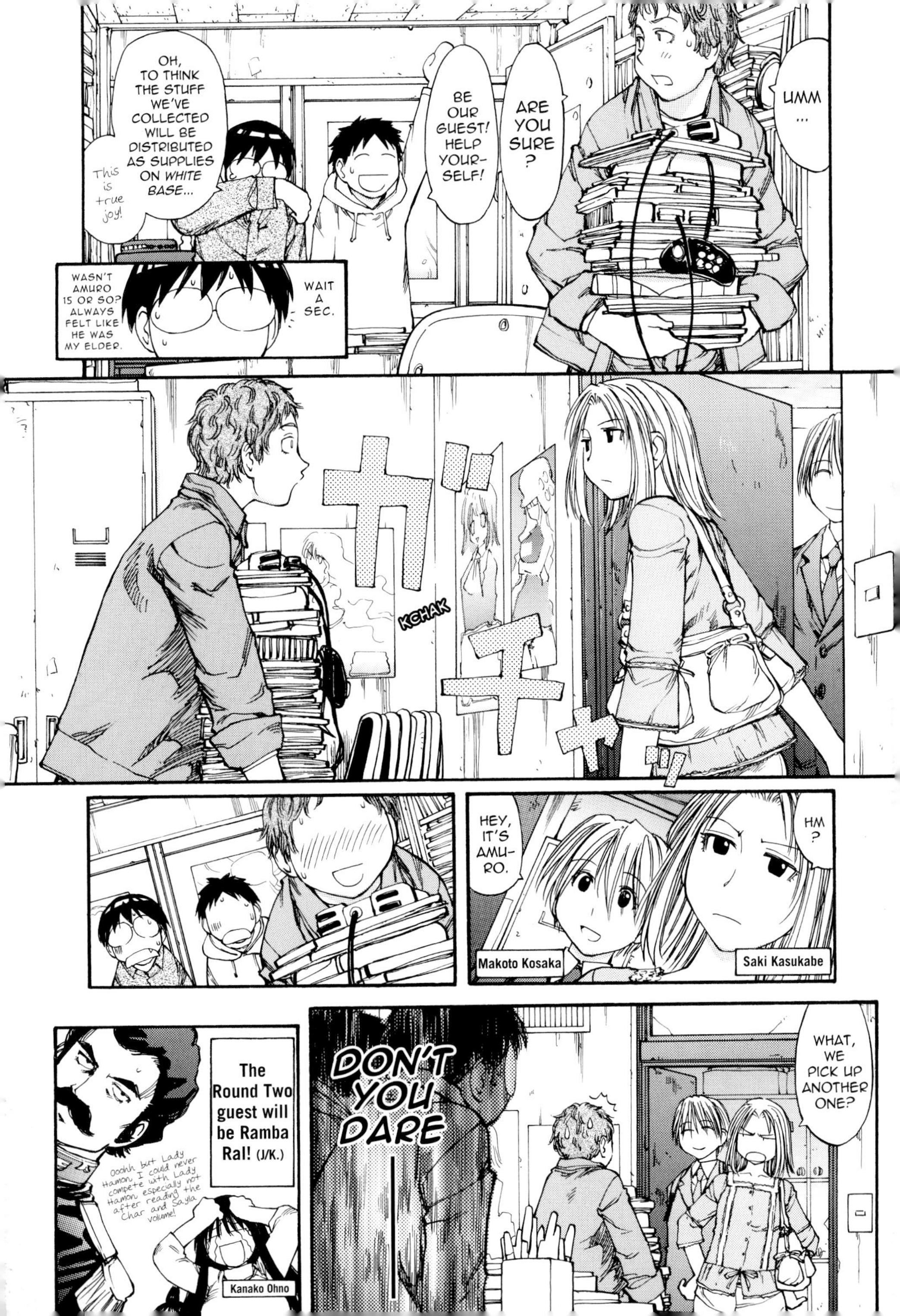
UMM ...
ARE YOU SURE?
BE OUR GUEST! HELP YOURSELF!
OH, TO THINK THE STUFF WE'VE COLLECTED WILL BE DISTRIBUTED AS SUPPLIES ON WHITE BASE...
This is true joy!
WAIT A SEC.
WASN'T AMURO 15 OR SO? ALWAYS FELT LIKE HE WAS MY ELDER.
KCHAK
HM?
HEY, IT'S AMURO.
Saki Kasukabe
Makoto Kosaka
WHAT, WE PICK UP ANOTHER ONE?
DON'T YOU DARE
The Round Two guest will be Ramba Ral! (J/K.)
Ooohh but Lady Hamon, I could never compete with Lady Hamon especially not after reading the Char and Sayla volume!
Kanako Ohno

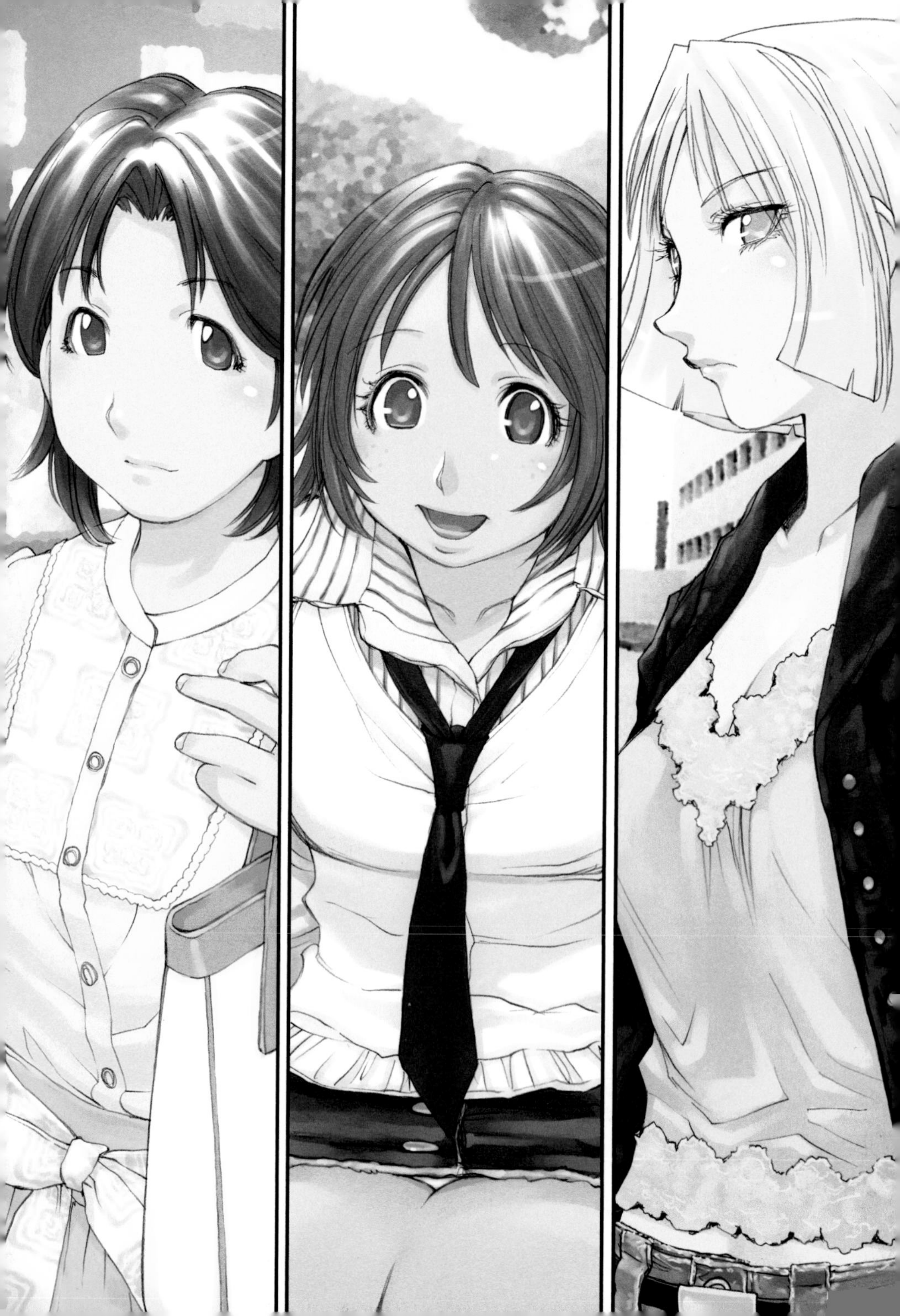

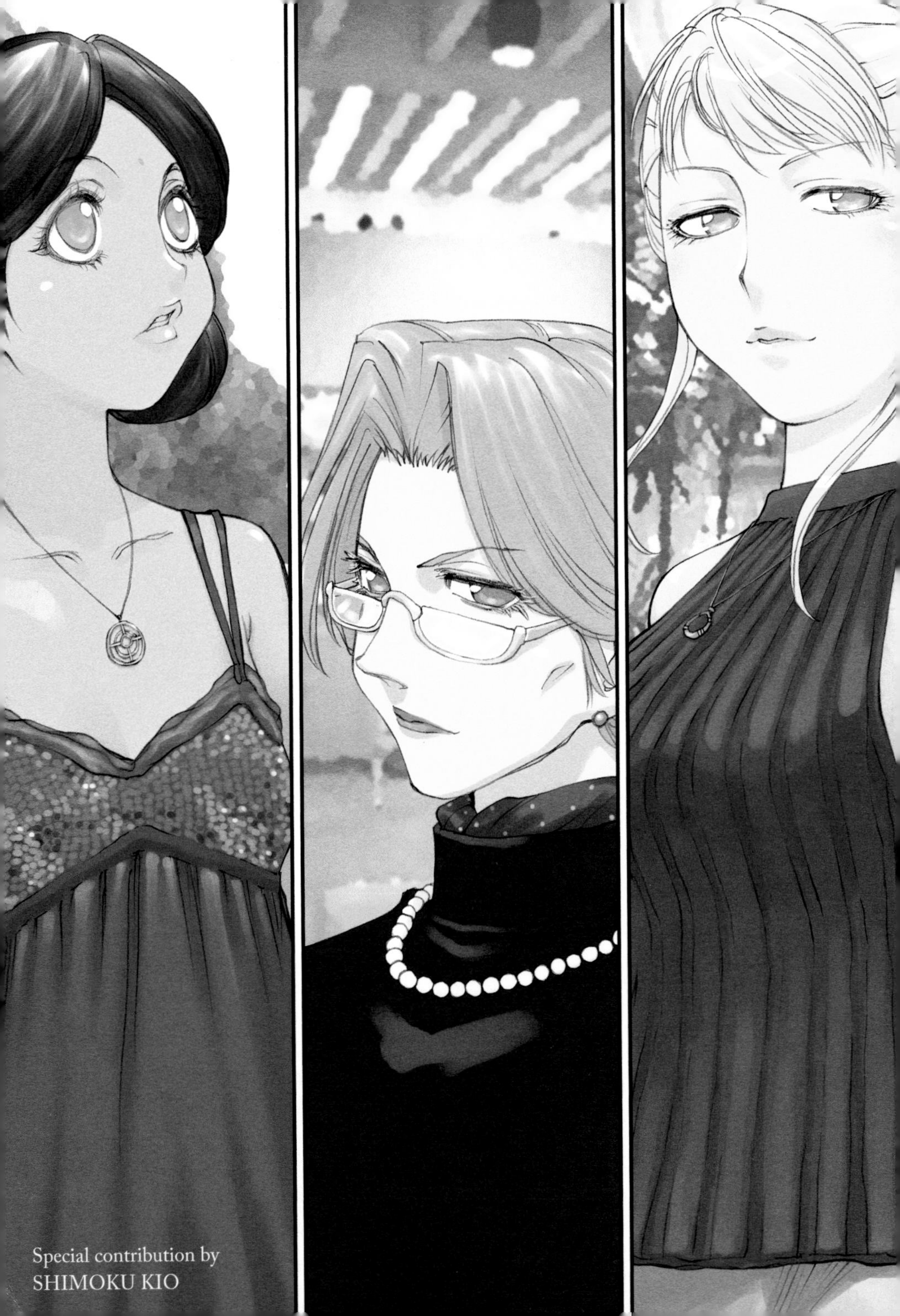
Special contribution by
SHIMOKU KIO

that too. I picture someone struggling desperately in the dark to elude pursuit. *Man, a kid wouldn't get this,* I think as I read it. The rich characterization of each member of the Zabi family, the way the Federation forces are steeped in bureaucracy—all the little things like that add up to a ridiculously enjoyable story. And I guess the fact that I can enjoy those parts now means that I may have grown up... Although I'm definitely not gonna tell you that *Gundam* made a man out of me, ha ha!

I mean, obviously, you can pretty much tell from this essay, I'm still completely a kid. When I think about it, though, when I was younger I went for Fraw Bow as a matter of course, but now I prefer Lady Hamon and Lady Kycilia and so on. So there's growth for you. And having said that, I think I'll close. To Mr. Yasuhiko, and to all the intermediaries who ran around to make this happen, thank you for such an amazing opportunity. I'll push myself harder so that my name might someday be worthy of its place in this volume.

Shimoku Kio
April 10, 2007

Shimoku Kio
Born in 1974, Mr. Kio made his manga debut at the age of twenty in Kodansha's *Monthly Afternoon* magazine. His major works are *Fourth Year*, *Fifth Year*, and *Genshiken*. At the time of this contribution, he was the storyboard manager for *Kujibiki Unbalance* (drawn by Keito Koume), which was originally a work within a work in *Genshiken*.

I'm so sorry! To think a greenhorn like me has contributed a silly piece that will enter the annals of history, in this lovely Collector's Edition... When I was asked to do this, I just went into deer-in-the-headlights mode, thinking, "What? *Why?!*" and I was going to decline. But then Mr. Yasuhiko said to me, "Think of it as partaking in the festivities. Just have fun," and I felt like I had no choice but to do it. Writing commentary is *totally* beyond me, though... I mean, I was in kindergarten when *Gundam* was first on TV! I got into it with the theater release and Gunpla models, and then with *Arion* and *Venus Wars* I was all like "Wouldn't it be cool if Yasuhiko made *Gundam* into a manga too, hurr hurr!" What can an irresponsible kid like that say about it now? "Don't feed the otaku, especially the 30+ demographic"? I mean, all I can do is draw manga! And so I took the liberty of drawing the same kind of stuff I always do...

Um, okay, so I'll try a little commentary. I do a manga called *Genshiken* (I'm talking about my own work?!) about a college otaku club. Basically they just hang out in the club room and do nothing but talk about otaku stuff... For some reason Mr. Yasuhiko likes it, and that's why I was asked to do this. I wish I could tell my elementary school self: "In the future, you'll get to know Yoshika-zu Yasuhiko!" ...LOL, no way I would have believed that. Besides, in retrospect, I wonder how much of *Gundam* I really understood back then.

Every time I pick up a volume of *The Origin*, I go "Was it such a grown-up story?!" With Amuro and the supporting cast of young characters, it has the essence of a coming-of-age story, but who knew it went so deep... The parts that are original to the manga, in "Char and Sayla" and "Starting a War" and "Loum," are just amazing. The darkness of history is depicted there with luscious depth, the sort that comes through in other Yasuhiko œuvres such as *A Revolutionary Dog* and *Rainbow Trotsky*. Actually all of his other works are like

AIZOUBAN MOBILE SUIT GUNDAM THE ORIGIN vol. 3

Translation: Melissa Tanaka

Production: Grace Lu
Hiroko Mizuno
Anthony Quintessenza

© Yoshikazu YASUHIKO 2006

© SOTSU • SUNRISE

First published in Japan in 2007 by Kadokawa Shoten, Co., Ltd., Tokyo

English translation rights arranged with Kadokawa Shoten, Co., Ltd.
through Tuttle-Mori Agency, Inc., Tokyo

Translation copyright © 2013 Vertical, Inc.

Published by Vertical, Inc., New York

Originally published in Japanese as *Kidou Senshi Gundam THE ORIGIN*
volumes 5 and 6 in 2002, 2003 and re-issued in hardcover as *Aizouban Kidou Senshi Gundam
THE ORIGIN III -Ranba Raru-* in 2006, by Kadokawa Shoten, Co., Ltd.

Kidou Senshi Gundam THE ORIGIN first serialized in *Gundam Ace,*
Kadokawa Shoten, Co., Ltd., 2001-2011

ISBN: 978-1-935654-97-1

Manufactured in the United States of America

First Edition

Vertical, Inc.
451 Park Avenue South
7th Floor
New York, NY 10016
www.vertical-inc.com